Fodor's

ESSENTIAL AUSTRALIA

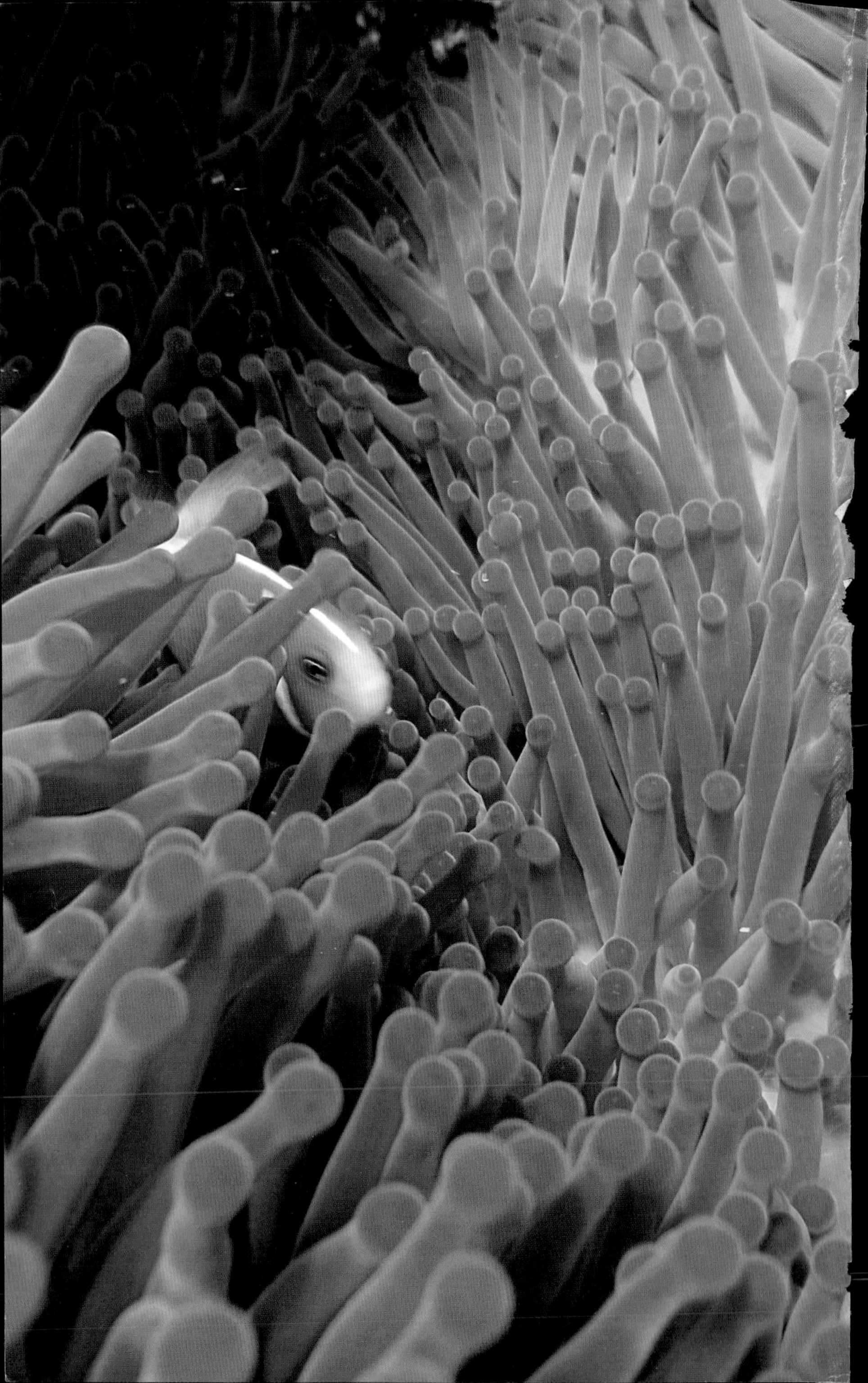

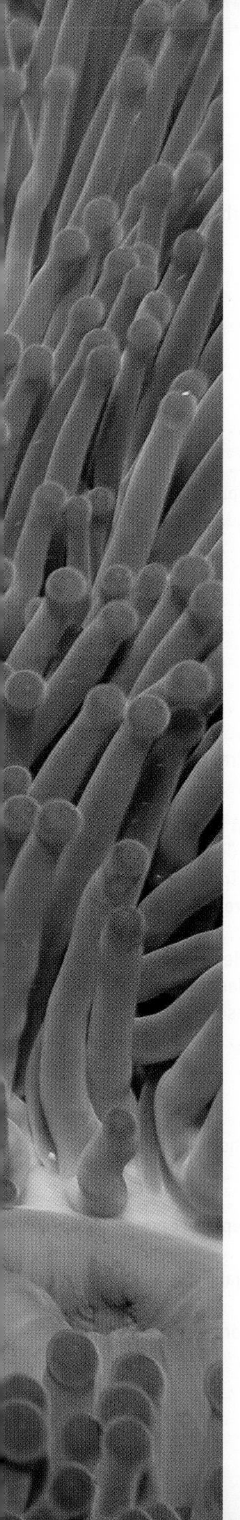

Welcome to Australia

A vast island continent, Australia teems with natural and cultural treasures. Relax on gorgeous beaches along the sprawling coastline, or plunge below the water in Queensland to explore the Great Barrier Reef. Nature enthusiasts revel in exciting adventures in the interior, from trekking around majestic Uluru to spotting wildlife in tropical rain forests. But there's more to life Down Under than outdoor activities. Cosmopolitan cities like Sydney and Melbourne entice with thriving dining and arts scenes, while world-class vineyards abound.

TOP REASONS TO GO

★ **Cool Cities:** Vibrant Sydney, artsy Melbourne, laid-back Brisbane, far-flung Perth.

★ **Beaches:** From Bondi to the Gold Coast, stylish strands cater to all tastes.

★ **Food and Wine:** Mod Oz cuisine, top-notch whites and reds, and, of course, the barbie.

★ **Untamed Nature:** Adventures await in the Great Barrier Reef, the Outback, and Tasmania.

★ **Aboriginal Culture:** A rich heritage of music, art, and stories continues to thrive.

★ **Unique Wildlife:** From kangaroos to koalas, the wildlife here is sure to delight.

Contents

Fodor's Features

MAPS

Chapter 1

EXPERIENCE AUSTRALIA

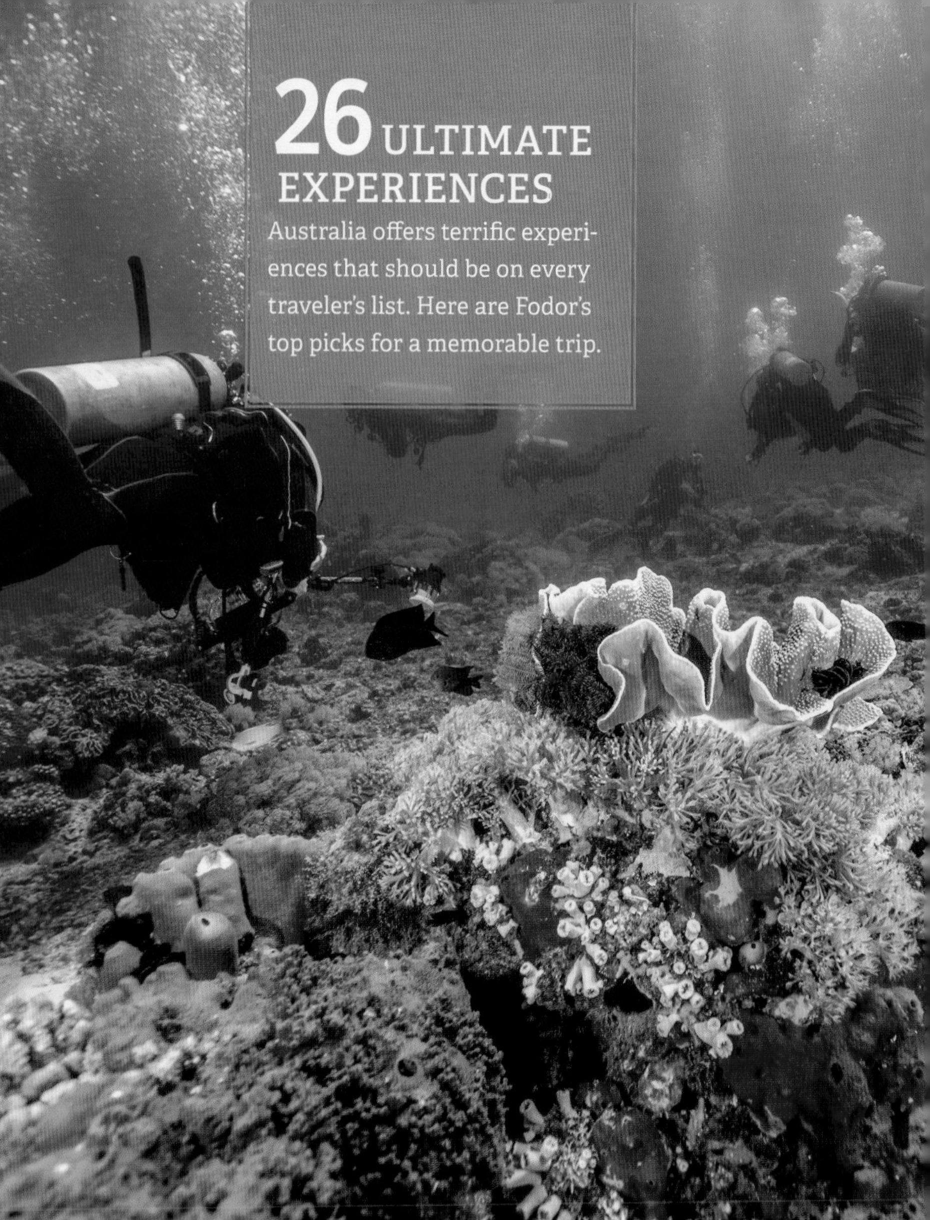

26 ULTIMATE EXPERIENCES

Australia offers terrific experiences that should be on every traveler's list. Here are Fodor's top picks for a memorable trip.

1 Dive the Great Barrier Reef

The world's largest coral reef and one of the world's most spectacular natural attractions, the Great Barrier Reef can be explored on a day tour from Cairns or Port Douglas but is best experienced over a few days. Maybe even charter your own yacht. (Ch. 9)

2 Shop For Aboriginal Art

Symbolic dot paintings and landscapes make beautiful souvenirs, and reputable galleries and cooperatives now offer ethical shopping opportunities.

3 Marvel at the Big Banana

An Australian penchant for giant food has resulted in novelty structures across the country. The Big Banana is a popular New South Wales attraction. (Ch. 4)

4 Float in an Ocean Pool

Bermagui's Blue Pool is a natural ocean pool at the base of a cliff that is constantly refreshed with clear ocean water. Great for views and an invigorating swim. (Ch. 4)

5 Catch Footy Fever

Fast-paced Aussie Rules Football or Footy is the most popular sport in Australia. Go to a match (March to October), eat meat pies and sauce, and bond with locals. (Ch. 5)

6 Take an Epic Train Trip

Travel by train across Australia, through the majestic Blue Mountains and spectacular Nullarbor Plains, stopping at some of Australia's greatest sights along the way. (Ch. 3)

7 Indigenous Culture

From rock art at Kakadu, Nourlangie Rock, and Ubirr to Aboriginal artists at work at Uluru, to understand Australia you need to visit its red heart. (Ch. 11)

8 Bungle Bungles

Hike this striking landscape of sandstone domes, through the towering walls of the narrow Echidna Chasm and to the amphitheater of Cathedral Gorge. (Ch. 11)

9 Climb the Sydney Harbour Bridge

An iconic must-do, the 3½-hour climb of the world's largest steel bridge rewards climbers with unbeatable 360-degree views of Sydney. (Ch. 3)

10 The Three Capes Track

This four-day bushwalk through rain forest, grasslands, and along steep bluffs takes you to the edge of the world, but with cabins and yoga mats along the way. (Ch. 7)

11 Kangaroo Island

One of the best places in Australia to see native wildlife up close, Kangaroo Island offers kangaroos aplenty as well as wild koalas, rare birds and seals, and black swans, too. (Ch. 10)

12 Parkes Observatory

Known for receiving the first images of the Apollo 11 moon landing, Parkes Observatory still offers some of the clearest skies and best star-spotting in Australia. (Ch. 4)

13 Feel the MONA Effect

Hobart's eclectic Museum of Old and New Art presents playful and provocative art in a subterranean, multitier labyrinth cut into sandstone cliffs. (Ch. 7)

14 Hyams Beach

Located on the southern shores of Jervis Bay, Hyams Beach has clear, turquoise waters and pristine, bleached-white sands that have been recognized as the whitest sands in the world. (Ch. 4)

15 Sip Local Wine

The acclaimed Barossa wine region is home to prestigious winemakers, including Penfolds and Henschke Cellars, as well as the popular labels Wolf Blass and Jacob's Creek. (Ch. 10)

16 Penguin Watch on Phillip Island

Watch the world's smallest species of penguins return home to their sandy burrows and see fur seals and koalas in their natural habits at this haven for wildlife. (Ch. 6)

17 Great Ocean Road Trip

Enjoy expansive views of the Southern Ocean, pretty coastal towns, and temperate rain forests on an epic coastline drive from Melbourne to the Twelve Apostles and beyond. (Ch. 6)

18 Sunset at Uluru

Walk Uluru's base trail before relaxing at a sunset viewing area to see this iconic sandstone monolith shift from ocher to orange to dark red. (Ch. 11)

19 Go Glamping

Secluded, luxurious safari tents with private decks and fire pits in the stunning setting of Ikara-Flinders Ranges National Park bring you close to nature in style. (Ch. 10)

20 Surf School

Just north of Sydney, Newcastle boasts two world-class surfing beaches and multiple local surf schools. Beginner surf lessons usually run over three days. (Ch. 3)

21 Sail the Whitsundays

Bareboat through the waters of the idyllic Whitsunday islands and let the wind take you where it will, stopping only to swim, snorkel, or snooze. (Ch. 9)

22 Experience Café Culture

Melbourne is the epicenter of the nation's coffee obsession, and you'll find a bewildering variety of caffeinated beverages in cute cafés tucked into its alleyways. (Ch. 5)

23 Coober Pedy

A "cool" stop halfway between Adelaide and Alice Springs, this small opal-mining town avoids desert heat with its unique subterranean residences, museum, bar, and hotel. (Ch. 10)

24 Turtle-Hatching

Ranger-led Turtle Encounters take place November to March at Mon Repos Conservation Park where thousands of baby turtles make a nightly dash from sandy nests to warm waters. (Ch. 8)

25 Litchfield National Park

A day trip from Darwin, this park offers some of the best, and prettiest, swimming holes in the Top End, including Buley Rockholes and Wangi and Florence Falls. (Ch. 11)

26 Fall in Love with a Quokka

Rottnest Island off the coast of Perth is home to a cat-size marsupial (and social media star) with a cuddly appearance and a tendency to smile. (Ch. 12)

WHAT'S WHERE

1 Sydney. One of the most naturally beautiful cities in the world, Sydney blends beachside cool with multiculturalism and Victorian-era colonial architecture. Arts, tourism, and business thrive around Sydney Harbour.

2 New South Wales. Southeastern Australia displays most of the continent's rural and coastal variations: historic towns, mountains, dramatic beaches, and world-class vineyards.

3 Melbourne. Melbourne is Australia's most European city and a cultural melting pot; you can see that in its fantastic food and café scene.

4 Victoria. Rugged coastline, historic towns, wineries, fairy penguins, and national parks are reason enough to explore the Victorian countryside.

5 Tasmania. From Freycinet Peninsula to wild South West National Park, Tasmania's natural beauty testifies to Australia's topographic diversity. Don't miss the relics of the island's volatile days as a penal colony.

6 South East Queensland. Name your pleasure and

you'll find it in South East Queensland: a cosmopolitan, soon-to-be Olympic city, beaches, lush rain forests, great restaurants, and easy access to family-friendly parks.

7 The Great Barrier Reef. Queensland's crown jewel is the 2,600-km-long (1,616-mile-long) Great Barrier Reef. More than 3,000 reefs and 900 islands make up this aquatic universe.

8 Adelaide and South Australia. Well-planned and picturesque Adelaide has many charms, including its festival of the arts. Be sure to take a tour of the region's renowned wine country, and then unwind on a Murray River cruise.

9 The Outback. This region stuns with its diversity. In the country's vast, central desert region are Uluru and Kata Tjuta, monoliths of deep significance to the local Aboriginal people. Darwin is the gateway to World Heritage wetlands, monster cattle ranches, and rock art.

10 Perth and Western Australia. This is a remote, awe-inspiring region and the producer of much of Australia's mineral wealth. It includes the country's sunniest capital, Perth, and top-notch wine valleys.

Ultimate Sydney

CLIMB THE HARBOUR BRIDGE

Climb the arches of one of the most famous bridges in the world for breathtaking views of one of the most iconic harbors in the world. The climb can be done by day or night and takes about three hours. Alternately, walk the bridge free of charge via the stairs on Cumberland Street.

CATCH THE MANLY FERRY

Sydneysiders use the iconic Manly Ferry to commute to and from the city center. For visitors it offers glorious views of the harbor and an escape to Manly Beach where you can wander the Corso's pedestrian strip before cooling off at one of Sydney's famed surf beaches.

THE ROYAL BOTANIC GARDEN

With over 70 acres of lawns and planted gardens, rare native and exotic plants, and a romantic rose garden, the Botanic Garden is an oasis of green in the heart of the city. Catch changing plant-theme exhibitions at the Calyx, and The Art Gallery of NSW is in the garden, too.

EAT AUSTRALIAN–CHINESE FOOD

Chinese food is the most popular cuisine in Australia, so if you want to eat like a local in Sydney, you'll want to visit Sydney's lively Chinatown, Australia's largest Chinatown. The area is especially alive on weekend mornings with the Cantonese tradition of *yum cha*, where diners are served from dozens of roaming trolleys bearing delights such as dim sum, roast duck, Singapore noodles, and steamed pork buns. Locals flock to Nine Dragons for all-day service.

TASTE AUTHENTIC SICILIAN GELATO

Founded in Darlinghurst in 2002, Gelato Messina has gained a cult following across Australia for its out-of-this-world flavors (like baklava and matcha) that change weekly. Made with milk from the Palumbo brothers' own dairy farm, Gelato Messina takes its name from their parents' hometown in Italy and continues the tradition with a modern twist.

SWIM IN SYDNEY HARBOUR

Balmoral Beach, tucked away in the northern side of the harbor, is sandy and protected from the waves that crash on the rest of the coastline. There are also some shady trees behind the beach, making it the perfect spot for a family day out. While here, stop by the trendy Bathers' Pavilion for a coffee and grab a fish-and-chips from Bottom of the Harbour.

Bondi to Coogee coastal walk

BONDI TO COOGEE COASTAL WALK

Bondi Beach, while beautiful, is often extremely crowded during the summer months. Fortunately, local favorites Tamarama, Bronte, and Coogee are all easily accessible via a 4-mile cliff-top walk that winds along the coast and offers stunning views, parks, bays, rock pools, and beaches on the way.

STROLL BARANGAROO

Sydney's coolest new neighborhood is an ongoing urban renewal project that runs along Sydney Harbour, offering a promenade open for walking and cycling, and trendy boutiques, cafés, and restaurants, most notably the three-level architectural gem, Barangaroo House.

SEE A SHOW AT THE OPERA HOUSE

Tucked under the unique sail design of this iconic sight are multiple venues that host everything from rap to musical theater. The Australian Ballet, the Sydney Dance Company, and the Australian Opera Company are all regulars, with over 40 shows a week performed in total.

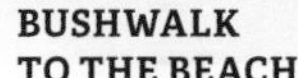

BUSHWALK TO THE BEACH

Ku–ring–gai Chase National Park is only 15 miles north of the Sydney city center but feels a world away with rain forests, cliffs, mangroves, and hidden beaches. The Resolute Beach track is a classic 2-mile trail that takes in Red Hands Cave, which contains Aboriginal art made over 2,000 years ago as well as engravings made by the Guringai people. The destination, Resolute Beach, is a secluded, sandy stretch with views of Barrenjoey Headland and Pittwater. A permit system is in effect between October and May so book early if your dates are limited.

Australia's Top Natural Wonders

LAKE HILLIER
This bubblegum-pink lake off the coast of Western Australia is not fully understood by scientists: the unique color is likely caused by high salinity combined with a specific bacteria, but unlike other pink lakes, Lake Hillier's waters remain bright all year round, even when bottled.

CRADLE MOUNTAIN
Part of the Tasmanian Wilderness World Heritage Area, the majestic Cradle Mountain looms over grasslands, rain forest, pines and beech trees, as well as gorgeous alpine lakes. To reach the summit is a full-day hike, and you might just encounter Tasmanian devils and echidnas along the way.

KAKADU NATIONAL PARK
Australia's largest national park is home to some of Australia's most significant Aboriginal rock art sites (Ubirr and Nourlangie); the rock pool made famous by the Crocodile Dundee movie; thousands of plant species and wildlife; and over 30 established bushwalk trails.

BLUE MOUNTAINS
This World Heritage area offers stunning scenery and dramatic valleys, canyons, and cliff faces carved by wind and water over millennia; Aboriginal engravings; excellent bushwalks; and some of the country's most diverse flora and fauna. Sunlight refracting off the fine oil mist from the world's most ecologically diverse tract of eucalypt forests gives the mountains their famous hue.

LORD HOWE ISLAND
In the Tasman Sea, between Australia and New Zealand, this secluded natural paradise is packed full of outdoor activities, thanks to a sheltered lagoon on one side and a pumping surf beach on the other. Almost half the island's native plants are endemic, including a cloud forest on the island's highest point, Mt. Gower. Only 400 tourists are permitted to stay on the island at a time.

THE PINNACLES
Dutch explorers first thought these pillars were the remains of an ancient city (if you look closely, you might be able to make out humanlike figures among the ghostly limestone pillars), while others compare this bizarre Western Australian landscape to the surface of Mars.

GREAT BARRIER REEF
This 2,600-km-long (1,616-mile-long) fragile natural wonder is the world's largest collection of reefs, and the delicate and complex ecosystem it supports just off the coast of Queensland contains 300 types of coral and 1,500 fish species of every size and color.

LAKE EYRE
About every eight years, Lake Eyre fills and blooms with wildflowers and waterbirds, but Australia's largest lake is usually dry, salty, and unbelievably vast. If you're not lucky enough to catch it full, the salt flats are impressive in themselves, as land and sky are difficult to separate.

DAINTREE RAIN FOREST
The oldest tropical rain forest in the world, World Heritage—listed Daintree Rain Forest is so beautiful that it served as the inspiration for the alien landscapes of Pandora in *Avatar* and so special that Sir David Attenborough declared it "the most extraordinary place on earth." Trek through lush jungles and discover ancient ferns and rare animals like tree-kangaroos and spotted quolls.

FLINDERS RANGES
With deep craters, rocky gorges, and weathered peaks, the 800-million-year-old rugged Flinders Ranges in South Australia's Outback form some of the most dramatic landscapes in the country. Favorite hiking trails include Mount Remarkable (with, yes, remarkable views) and the huge natural amphitheater of Wilpena Pound. Look for the endangered Yellow-footed Rock Wallaby.

Australia's Outdoor Adventures and Wildlife

SAIL THE WHITSUNDAYS (QLD)
Charter your own boat to skip the tourist spots and discover the Whitsundays at your own pace. Spend your days snorkeling crystal clear waters and your nights stargazing from the deck. If you don't feel confident bareboating, guided trips are also available.

SHUCK OYSTERS IN COFFIN BAY (SA)
Wade offshore to a semi-submerged pontoon on top of a working oyster farm in South Australia's Coffin Bay, where you will learn how oysters grow and are farmed. Learn to properly shuck, and eat, Pacific and Angasi oysters while sipping a chilled glass of white wine.

BIKE DOWN SAND DUNES IN LORD HOWE ISLAND (NSW)
Feel the wind on your face as you race down the paperwhite sand dunes of Lord Howe Island on a 400cc quad bike. Bike 164-foot-high sand dunes—the largest moving dunes in the southern hemisphere—then head inland to explore the bushland.

HOT-AIR BALLOON OVER YARRA VALLEY (VIC)
Sip a glass of wine on a sunrise tour over Victoria's breathtaking Yarra Valley, one of Australia's most important and picturesque wine regions, and watch the sweeping valley transform into a spectacle of color, as the corridors of grapevines are bathed in pink light.

SURF AT BELLS BEACH (VIC)
Famous on the international surfing scene for its clean waves and consistent right-hander, this Victoria beach is home to the world's longest-running surf competition—the Rip Curl Pro Bells Beach—and the final scene of *Point Break* was also filmed here. If you're just a beginner, don't worry, the beach is suitable for all surfing levels.

CAVE DIVE ON THE LIMESTONE COAST (SA)
You'll feel like you're on another planet as you explore the mysterious landscape of South Australia's Limestone Coast, a region known for its water-filled caves and magical sinkholes. Popular spots include Kilsby Sinkhole, a shimmering crystal clear chamber located in the middle of a sheep paddock and Piccaninnie Ponds in Mount Gambier.

CAMP WITH KANGAROOS AT PEBBLY BEACH (NSW)
Seeing a kangaroo is at the top of most people's agendas when they come to Australia. At Pebbly Beach in Murramarang National Park, you can go one better and camp alongside the

Discover the Red Centre experience

beloved animal. This picturesque beach is surrounded by thousands of acres of natural bushland, which have begun to regenerate after being devastated by the 2019 bushfires. The beach is famous for its swimming kangaroos. You'll see them sunbathing on the beach, grazing on the grass, and welcoming guests at the national park campsite.

DISCOVER THE RED CENTRE (NT)

Immerse yourself in the rich culture of the Yankunytjatjara and Pitjantjatjara people with a trip to the Red Centre in the Northern Territory. This extraordinary landscape of sweeping deserts, rocky gorges, and burnt-orange plains will pull you in with its magic and mystery. Listen to Dreamtime stories by a fire on a visit to Uluru, one of the most sacred Aboriginal sites. Be awed by the immense scope of the red-tinged Kings Canyon in Watarrka National Park. At the end of the day, cool off in still, secluded waterholes surrounded by soaring rocks and eucalyptus trees.

CANOE KATHERINE GORGE (NT)

Paddle slowly along a maze of sandstone waterways and take in rocky riverbanks teeming with native flora and fauna, rock art, waterfalls, and swimming holes. An overnight canoe tour allows you to travel farther upstream and reach the more remote, and stunning, gorges.

HIKE THE OVERLAND TRACK (TAS)

Considered one of the country's most famous trails, this track leads through the World Heritage-listed Cradle Mountain to Lake St. Claire, the deepest lake in Australia. You'll pass through eucalyptus forests, waterfalls, swimming holes, and breathtaking views of the mountain ranges. You might even come across an echidna, quoll, or wombat.

Australia's Best Beaches

TURQUOISE BAY
One of the best snorkeling spots in Western Australia, these turquoise waters are home to a marine wonderland. Prime snorkeling is at the northern end, near the seagrass area. At the south end of the beach you can try drift snorkeling, letting the current carry you along the reef.

WHITEHAVEN BEACH
Located on Whitsunday Island in the Great Barrier Reef, this beach is a 7-km (4-mile) stretch of unspoiled, tropical paradise alongside turquoise waters. Because the sand is made almost entirely of silica—which gives it its milk-white color—it doesn't retain heat, meaning you can stroll barefoot.

MONKEY BEACH
Nestled on Great Keppel Island in the Great Barrier Reef, this secluded beach is a great way to explore the reef without the hustle and bustle of tourists. Think soft white sand, aquamarine water, and chirping tropical birds. Look out for kookaburras and the colorful rainbow lorikeets.

BONDI BEACH
No list of Australian beaches would be complete without Bondi, the beach that most defines Aussie beach culture. This sweeping 1-km (½-mile) stretch of white sand never fails to impress. Take in the view from one of the coastal heads or enjoy the sight from Bondi Icebergs, a saltwater swimming pool that's been a local landmark for a century.

BRONTE BEACH
This Sydney beach is the ideal spot to surf, swim, and grab a quality cup of coffee. Bronte Beach has a more relaxed feel than its iconic neighbor Bondi and is great for all swimming levels. Young kids can play in the section of the beach protected by rocks, affectionately known as the Bogey Hole, surfers can enjoy the swell and, for those who like to do laps, there is a 30-meter seawater pool nestled into the coast. The beach also has lots of green space for picnics and barbecues and, if you walk farther back, you'll even find a small waterfall.

HYAMS BEACH
Drive three hours south of Sydney to the world's whitest sands. Located on the southern shores of Jervis Bay, you can snorkel in the clear, turquoise waters, spot whales and dolphins on the horizon, follow walking trails through Booderee National Park, and glamp at Paperbark Camp.

Hyam's beach in Jervis Bay, NSW

LUCKY BAY
One of Australia's best-kept secrets, beautiful Lucky Bay is located in Cape Le Grande National Park near Esperance in Western Australia and offers shimmering turquoise seas, blinding-white sands, and sunbathing kangaroos. Its remote location means you may be lucky enough to have it to yourself—well, you and the kangaroos.

NOOSA MAIN BEACH
Surrounded by tropical rain forest, Noosa is one of the few beach spots to offer the tranquility of a natural paradise with the perks of a cosmopolitan hub. You can eat organic ice cream while wading through the rippling blue waters, sip on a cocktail while watching the sun set, and sunbathe as colorful birds fly overhead.

PORT NOARLUNGA BEACH
Located south of Adelaide, this family-friendly beach has golden sand, calm waters, and a marine reserve that is home to more than 200 marine plant species and 60 fish species. Jump off the jetty right into a school of fish (or pop into the village for some fish-and-chips).

PEBBLY BEACH
Say hi to cheerful kangaroos at this idyllic little beach in the Murramarang National Park in New South Wales. At Pebbly Beach you share the relaxing, golden sands with kangaroos, sea eagles, and the odd goanna (an Australian monitor lizard). Take a stroll in the surrounding bushland and you'll likely find even more curious creatures.

WINEGLASS BAY
With its snow-white sand, deep blue waters, soaring green mountains, and near perfect crescent shape, Wineglass Bay is a popular destination to pop the question, but it is also a great place to enjoy sailing, fishing, and sea kayaking. You'll probably meet a kangaroo or two on the beach.

Australia's Top Indigenous Experiences

LORD'S KAKADU AND ARNHEMLAND SAFARIS
Stay in a private camp in the middle of Kakadu where you are immersed in Aboriginal culture and stunning scenery. Learn about bush tucker and playing the didgeridoo, and visit Nourlangie Rock and pristine billabongs and waterfalls.

K'GARI
K'Gari, pronounced "gurri" and meaning "paradise" to the Butchulla people, is the traditional name of Fraser Island. Visitors can follow traditional pathways like the Fraser Island Great Walk, or take a 4WD tour of the island with Nomads Fraser Island to learn about Butchulla culture.

YIRIBANA GALLERY
At the heart of the Art Gallery of New South Wales, the Yiribana Gallery is devoted to Aboriginal and Torres Strait Islander art. The gallery showcases selections from a broad collection of works including key contemporary artists like Ian Abdulla and Bidjigal artist Esme Timbery.

MBANTUA GALLERY
This gallery with outposts in Darwin and Alice Springs, specializes in exhibiting and selling the works of Aboriginal artists. In addition to an extensive collection of paintings, both old and new, you'll find bowls, spears, shields, and hair belts.

KOOMAL DREAMING TOUR
This three-hour tour in Wadandi and Bibbulman country (Margaret River) offers a guided walk to forage for native foods and medicines, a lunch featuring native ingredients, and a telling of Dreamtime—the period when Ancestral Spirits walked the earth and created life—in the depths of Ngilgi Cave.

BUSH TUCKER CUISINE
"Bush tucker," a wide assortment of native-derived ingredients that has been integral to the diet of the continent's Indigenous peoples for tens of thousands of years, is slowly making its way onto mainstream menus as Australians embrace the locavore concept. Look for ingredients such as lemon myrtle, quandong, lilli pillies, bush tomatoes, and native meats such as emu, wallaby, kangaroo, and crocodile. You can find bush tucker at restaurants, including The Kungkas Can Cook café in Alice Springs, The Tin Humpy in Sydney, and the Tali Wiru and Bush Tucker Journey experiences at Ayers Rock Resort at Uluru.

Uluru-Kata Tjuta National Park

ULURU-KATA TJUTA NATIONAL PARK

Yankunytjatjara and Pitjantjatjara people believe this landscape was created at the beginning of time by ancestral beings and it remains a sacred place for the Anangu. It's a UNESCO World Heritage site with a museum, both ancient rock art and contemporary Indigenous art, and walking trails.

WUKALINA WALK

The *wukalina* walk is a three-night, four-day Palawa-owned and -operated guided walk based in the stunning natural landscape of the Bay of Fires in Tasmania/lutruwita. Guests walk with Palawa guides, encounter native wildlife, and learn about the area's history, and then stay in Palawa-inspired domed huts and a lighthouse-keepers cottage. Traditional dinners include muttonbird, wallaby, and doughboys.

BUNGLE BUNGLE TOUR

Bungle Bungle Guided Tours employs Aboriginal guides who share the cultural significance of the mountain range and the Aboriginal connection to the land. Learn about bush tucker, Aboriginal customs, and why Purnululu is World Heritage listed on guided day or overnight tours.

INGAN TOURS, QUEENSLAND

Aboriginal-owned and -operated Ingan Tours brings travelers into the rain forest of the northern reaches of Queensland, home to the Jirrbal rainforest people. Tour operator Dr. Ernie Grant, an Elder of the Jirrbal, possesses knowledge of topics like mythology and ethnobotany, which has helped to make Ingan's tours particularly precious. Take a kayak tour of Tully Gorge National Park to explore how the Jirribal people knew and used the natural creeks and rivers.

10 Things to Buy in Australia

ICONIC DESIGNERS
Some renowned high-end Australian designers to look for include Zimmermann, Alice McCall, Akira Isogawa, Ginger and Smart, and Camilla and Marc. High-street labels include Spell & The Gypsy Collective, Réalisation Par, Aje, and Nobody Denim.

AKUBRA HAT
A quintessential symbol of Australian working life, fourth-generation family-owned Akubra has been making its fur felt hats in NSW since 1874. While the brand carries more urban styles such as the trilby and fedora, it's the classic Bushman or Cattleman hats that you'll want to take home.

SWIMMERS
Known for its beautiful beaches and beach culture, it makes sense that Australia is home to some of the best swimwear brands. Labels to look for include Seafolly, Matteau, Baku, Palm, and Zulu & Zephyr. The Bronte Surf Life Saving Club in Sydney sells swimwear along the promenade.

UGGS
PSA: the UGG brand is a U.S.-based company run by an Australian. "Ugg" is actually a generic term for sheepskin boots that have been made and worn Down Under since the 1930s. Avoid boots that pretend to be Aussie and are made in China and look for the Emu brand: their boots are made in Australia from local sheepskin.

VEGEMITE
Leaving Australia without a jar of Vegemite is like leaving Spain without olive oil or Switzerland without chocolate. Vegemite may not be to everyone's taste, but few things are more iconically Australian—it is found in 90% of Aussie homes. Best enjoyed on toast (the staple Australian breakfast).

BEGA CHEESE
The friend in every Australian fridge, Bega cheese is based in Bega in NSW, but its bitey cheddar cheese is found in supermarkets across the country. This is not a fancy impress-your-guests cheese—for that, buy Unicorn cheese from Nowra Farmhouse—but it's a real taste of Australia.

INDIGENOUS ART
If you are visiting the Red Centre, allow time to stop at an Aboriginal art center. There are three important ones in the Kimberleys—Warmun, Waringarri, and Mowanjum—and more scattered across Arnhem Land. If you're not heading inland you can find great works at the Aboriginal-run gallery Boomalli in Sydney

Kakadu National Park Indigenous design

and Koolie Heritage Trust in Melbourne. The Ayers Rock Resort near Uluru has a number of galleries and artist programs, including live-in residencies, which allow visitors to have a personal connection with the art and artist. The Kaiela Arts Centre, in Shepparton, Victoria on Yorta Yorta country, empowers artists and designers to share their traditions through art.

KANGAROO JERKY

Kangaroo is a uniquely Australian meat that is a lean meat, and high in protein, iron, and zinc. It's 100% free-range, making it one of the most sustainable meats available. Kangaroo jerky is also a great souvenir for your human and canine friends. Kangaroo jerky is easily available in grocery stores, supermarkets, online, and at Duty Free.

WINE

Whether it's a Shiraz from one of the top producers in the Barossa Valley, a Yarra Valley chardonnay, a Hunter Valley semillon, or a discovery from a lesser-known Margaret River label, you will want to bring wine home. Pack wine skins or have the winery ship for you.

BEAUTY PRODUCTS

With one of the harshest but also botanically diverse environments in the world it's no wonder Aussie beauty brands are some of the most innovative. Look for Sukin and Aesop skin care, which are readily available at pharmacies throughout Australia. Bondi Sands tanning products will give you that Bondi glow without the risk of skin cancer. Miranda Kerr's Kora Organics, and Kevin Murphy hair care, are other Australian beauty brands to look out for. Melbourne-based Frank Body coffee scrubs and skin-care kits have a cult following. Also, hit up the supermarket or pharmacy for emu oil moisturizer, macadamia oil, and avocado oil.

What to Eat and Drink in Australia

QUANDONG

Also known as the "native peach" or "wild peach," quandongs have long been a staple in Indigenous diets and mythology in the central desert and southern regions of Australia. These sweet, tart fruits are highly nutritious.

MORETON BAY BUGS

Also known as Bay lobster, Moreton Bay Bugs (named after the bay near Brisbane) are a sweet, lobsterlike crustacean consumed on Australia's east coast à la blue crabs in Maryland or crawfish in New Orleans. Look for "Bugs" in seafood restaurants.

LEMON-LIME AND BITTERS

Tangy, tasty, refreshing, and with a low alcohol content, few drinks quench a desert thirst like a cold glass of lemon-lime and bitters. Made with soda water, lime cordial, and Angostura bitters, it is consumed on a grand scale Down Under, be it bottled, canned, or homemade.

KANGAROO

Australia is perhaps the only country that eats its national icon. You'll find this lean meat in restaurants across Australia and in many supermarkets: look for kanga bangas (kangaroo sausages), steaks, and jerky. Aussies are encouraged to eat kangaroo meat to control a ballooning roo population.

AVO-TOAST

America has its pancakes, France has its croissants, and Australia has its avocado toast. Every self-respecting café has smashed avocado on toasted sourdough bread, often served with almond butter and citrus curd or crumbled feta. Yes, it's overpriced, but it's not just toast, it's tradition!

TIM TAMS

With sales of about 35 million packs a year, Australia's national biscuit is made up of two layers of chocolate-malted biscuit, separated by a light chocolate filling and coated in melted chocolate. Tim Tam Slam: bite off opposite corners of cookie and use as a straw to drink hot chocolate.

THE FLAT WHITE

The origins of this less-foamy cappuccinoesque drink, made with two shots of a sweet, concentrated espresso and heated, full-fat milk, is a touchy subject in Aussie-Kiwi relations, but it is agreed to be an essential way to start the day, especially in Sydney or Melbourne.

Kangaroo

HUNTER VALLEY SEMILLON

Like the Coonawarra region in South Australia or the Yarra Valley in Victoria, the Hunter Valley in New South Wales produces some of the country's most iconic labels. The climate is ideally suited to the semillon grape and it's rare to find semillon unblended outside Australia. Semillon can be paired with seafood, including shellfish, pork, veal, chicken, and blue cheese. Look for producers like Tyrell's, Rothbury Estate, Pokolbin Estate, and McWilliams Mount Pleasant.

FERAL BREWING CO. BEER

While Australia is better known for its wine, it also has a burgeoning craft beer scene, so maybe skip the cheesy Foster's and go indie. One of the most notable is Feral Brewing Co., a Western Australian independent brewery behind the pale ale Hop Hog and IBA Karma Citra.

MEAT PIES

Have you even been to Australia if you didn't eat a meat pie? A flaky pastry package filled with diced or minced meat and gravy, and often cheese, mushrooms, and onions, too, the humble meat pie is known as Australia's national dish. Typically enjoyed smothered in ketchup at a footy game.

WYNN'S BLACK LABEL CABERNET SAUVIGNON

Wynn's Coonawarra Estate began making wine in South Australia in the 1890s. The Black Label Cabernet Sauvignon is made from the top 20% of fruit grown in Wynn's terra rossa vineyards. It's an icon of Australian wine and known as an affordable, excellent "must."

BARRAMUNDI

Barramundi is the Aboriginal name for a type of sea bass that is native to Australia and the Indo-Pacific. It literally translates as "large-scaled silver fish." It's lean, packed with protein and Omega-3s.

What to Watch and Read

MOVIE: *TRACKS*

This scenic and touching story follows one woman's near-impossible 2,000-mile walk from Alice Springs in the Northern Territory, to the coast of the Indian Ocean. The movie treks across the Gibson desert, past Ayers Rock, and through sacred Indigenous grounds, with beautiful footage of wild Australia.

BOOK: *THE SONGLINES* BY BRUCE CHATWIN

The Songlines catalogs Chatwin's travels to Alice Springs, in the Central Australian desert, where he studied Aboriginal life past and present. While sometimes criticized for its colonialist-skewed observations, Chatwin's earnestness to understand the nature of man and man in nature shines through, and provides insight into the Australian landscape and the history of nomadic life.

BOOK: *THE SWAN BOOK* BY ALEXIS WRIGHT

Full of folkloric, surreal beauty and heartbreak, Indigenous author and land activist Alexis Wright paints a vivid picture of Aboriginal people and landscape in the Gulf of Carpentaria. With a fantastical story of a young girl's experience in an imagined future Australia, Wright predicts the outcome of the long-standing, destructive treatment of Indigenous people. The novel won literary acclaim and was short-listed for Australia's Miles Franklin Award.

BOOK: *DARK EMU* BY BRUCE PASCOE

Debunking the pervasive colonial myth that Australia's first peoples were hunter-gatherers, Bruce Pascoe's *Dark Emu* is essential reading. In the book, Pascoe draws extensively from the diaries of early explorers, detailing the ways in which Aboriginal systems of food production and land management were previously understated or ignored.

BOOK: *JOHNNO* BY DAVID MALOUF

The first novel of prolific Australian author David Malouf, *Johnno* is a loosely autobiographical story about childhood, friendship, and memories, with the coastal city of Brisbane and its upper-class culture as a backdrop. It's a tender coming-of-age novel and a fair portrait of life in Brisbane and Queensland's Gold Coast.

BOOK: *PICNIC AT HANGING ROCK* BY JOAN LINDSAY

Lindsay's dramatic literary feat (recently turned into an Amazon Prime miniseries starring Natalie Dormer from *Game of Thrones*) is the haunting tale of a group of schoolgirls who mysteriously vanish while on a Valentine's Day picnic. The novel and its fictional premise have turned Hanging Rock (a geological formation northwest of Melbourne, with a real history as a sacred Indigenous site) into a folkloric destination popular with tourists and local fans.

BOOK: *BIG LITTLE LIES* BY LIANE MORIARTY

Moriarty's gripping and emotionally charged novel is about female friendship, social politics, and the secrets and shame in the wealthy beach towns and private-school worlds of Australia's coast. Moriarty's depiction of the drama of elite suburban life inspired Nicole Kidman and Reese Witherspoon to star in (and executive produce) an HBO miniseries of the same name—though the setting for the show was moved to Monterey, California.

MOVIE: *THE SAPPHIRES*

Irish actor Chris O'Dowd leads a girl band of Aboriginal Australians in the late '60s and and early '70s, as they travel to Vietnam to entertain the troops. The musical film is feel-good and funny, but touches on real issues of race, war, and human rights on both the Australian and world stage.

BOOK: *THE RABBIT-PROOF FENCE* BY DORIS PILKINGTON

In 1931, three young Aboriginal girls walked more than 1,600 km (1,000 miles) from the Moore River Native Settlement on the Western Coast, where they had been forced to live separated from their families, back home to the Jigalong community of Western Australia.

TV SERIES: *HOME AND AWAY*

Alan Bateman's long-running soap opera, filled with plenty of sex, drugs, and Australian beach drama, is widely popular throughout Australia and the United Kingdom. Filmed mostly in Sydney's Northern Beaches, the show is set in a fictional beach town in New South Wales.

MOVIE: *A CRY IN THE DARK* (*EVIL ANGELS* IN AUSTRALIA)

To familiarize yourself with the long, press-ridden murder trial of Lindy Chamberlain (played here by Meryl Streep) is to understand a critical piece of Australian popular culture throughout the last few decades. In a sweep of popularity and controversy similar to the OJ Simpson trial in the states, Chamberlain's story captured Australian minds and television screens after her two-month-old daughter went missing while the family was camping in Uluru, Central Australia. Lindy was convicted of murder, acquitted only after years spent appealing her case, swearing all along that she saw a wild dingo leave the tent where her little girl had been sleeping.

MOVIE: *PRISCILLA QUEEN OF THE DESERT*

In a wild road trip full of performance, personality, and diverse Australian walks of life, this comedic drama follows two drag queens and a transgender woman as they travel across the Australian Outback in a tour bus named Priscilla. The 1994 film was a huge hit, and is celebrated for bringing a positive portrayal of LGBTQ people to mainstream Australian (and international) audiences.

MOVIE: *EMILY IN JAPAN: THE MAKING OF AN EXHIBITION*

This documentary follows Aboriginal artist Emily Kame Kngwarreye (a native of Utopia, Central Australia), whose humble start to painting in her late seventies led to her becoming one of Australia's most prolific and highly regarded artists.

MOVIE: *ROGUE*

Worried there was a lack of giant killer crocodiles on this list? In this amped-up, *JAWS*-like horror-thriller, Australia's scariest predator is larger than life and hungry for humans. Between the animatronic, jaw-clamping thrills, big splashes, and narrow escapes, there are beautiful shots of Australia's Kakadu National Park.

MOVIE: *MURIEL'S WEDDING*

In PJ Hogan's 1994 romantic comedy, an ABBA-loving, wedding-crazed Toni Collette (nominated for a Golden Globe in her role as the adorable and bumbling Muriel Heslop) leaves life in her oppressive, cliquey beach town to find herself (and maybe love) in big-city Sydney. A story more about friendship and self-discovery than marriage, the movie is warm and quirky in a delightfully Australian way.

MOVIES: *MAD MAX* SERIES

George Miller's adventure franchise (*Mad Max*, *Mad Max 2*, *Mad Max Beyond Thunderdome*, and *Mad Max: Fury Road*) takes viewers on frenzied chases through a postapocalyptic Australian wasteland. The first three, starring a shockingly young Mel Gibson, were filmed in the 1980s in and around Melbourne. Scenes in 2015's *Mad Max: Fury Road* are actually of the Namib Desert, in Namibia and South Africa.

ABORIGIN PAST

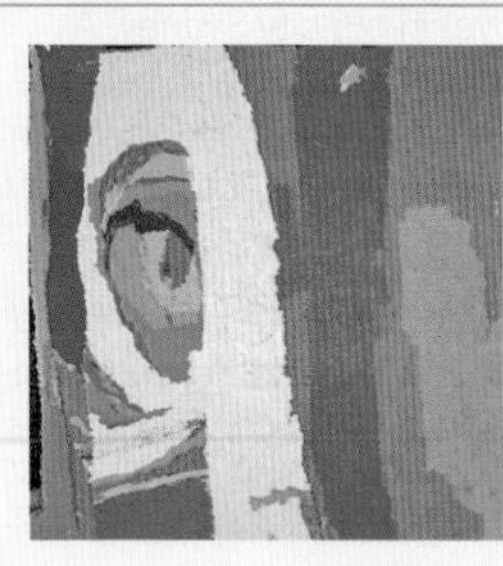

Today's Australian Aboriginals are guardians of the world's oldest living culture. Most experts agree that it was about 50,000 years ago (possibly as many as 80,000) when the continent's first inhabitants migrated south across a landmass that once connected Australia to Indonesia and Malaysia. These first Australians brought with them a wealth of stories, songs, tribal customs, and ceremonies—many of which are still practiced today.

AL ART, AND PRESENT

All Aboriginal ideology is based upon the creation period known as The Dreaming. During this primordial time, totemic ancestors (who were associated with particular animals, plants, and natural phenomena) lived on and journeyed across the earth. The legends of these ancestors—what they did, where they traveled, who they fought and loved—are considered sacred, and have been passed down among Aboriginal tribes for thousands of years. Though these stories are largely shared in secret rituals, they have also been documented through the creation of unique, highly symbolic artworks.

This is why Aboriginal art, despite traditional beginnings as rock carvings and ochre paintings on bark, now hang in some of the world's finest museums. These works aren't just beautiful; they're also profound cultural artifacts—and a window into humanity's oldest surviving civilization.

(top right) Nourlangie Rock, Kakadu;
(top left) Art by Emily Kame Kngwarreye;
(bottom left) Work from Papunya Tula;

EARLY ABORIGINAL ART

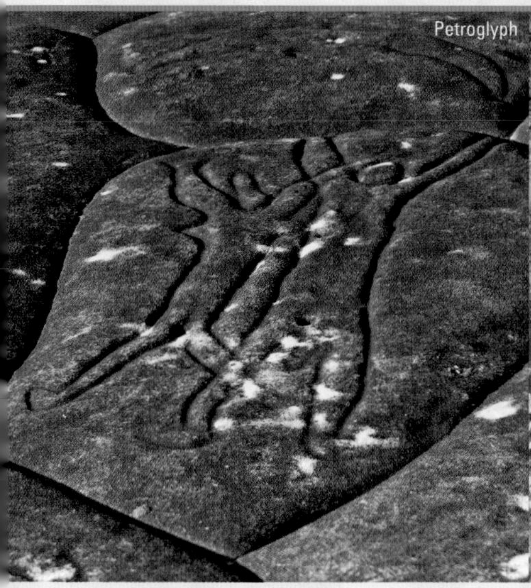

Petroglyph

"X-ray" style pictograph

Aboriginal and Torres Strait Islander people are the traditional custodians of the Australian continent and adjacent islands, and guardians of the world's oldest living culture. More than 60,000 years ago the continent's first inhabitants migrated south across a landmass that once connected Australia to Indonesia and Malaysia. They brought with them a wealth of stories, songs, customs, and ceremonies—many of which are still practiced today.

PETROGLYPHS

The earliest Aboriginal artworks were petroglyphs—engravings carved into flat rock surfaces or faces of cliffs (most likely using pointed stones or shards of shell). Some surviving etchings show lines and circles similar to those in modern-day paintings; others depict animals, fish, birds, and human or spirit figures. The oldest known engravings on the continent, at Pilbara

PROTECTING ROCK-ART SITES

Given the centuries of weathering they've endured, it's remarkable that so many ancient rock art sites remain intact. In many places, the longevity of the artworks can be attributed to local Aboriginal tribes, who consider it a sacred responsibility to preserve and repaint fading images. Help preservation efforts by staying on marked paths, not touching the artwork, and taking a tour of the site with an indigenous guide.

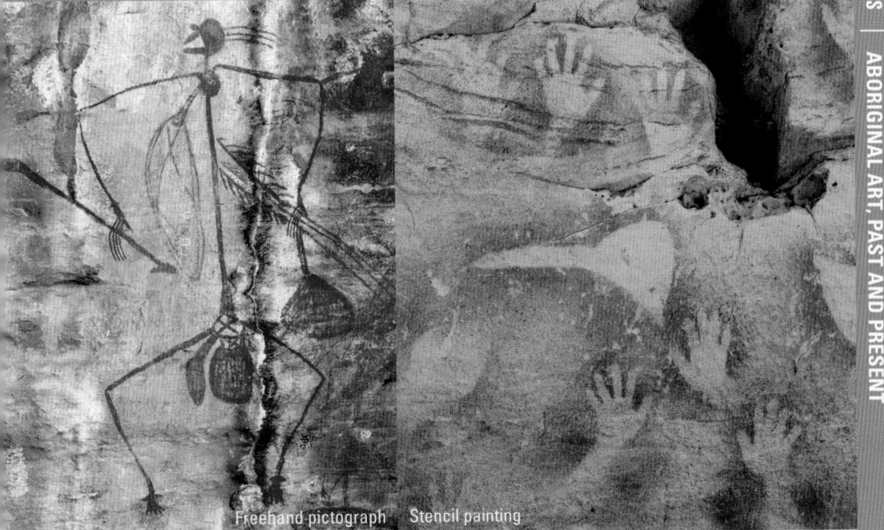

Freehand pictograph Stencil painting

in Western Australia and Olary in South Australia, are estimated to be 40,000 years old. Perhaps the most visited, though, are those in Ku-rin-gai Chase National Park, less than an hour's drive north of Sydney.

PICTOGRAPHS

Other early Aboriginal artists chose to paint images rather than etch them. Using ochres and mineral pigments, and employing sticks, feathers, and their own fingers as brushes, these ancient painters chose sheltered spots—like the insides of caves and canyons—for their mural-like images. Protection from the elements allowed many of these ancient rock paintings to survive; today they're still found all over Australia.

REGIONAL STYLES

The styles of painting varied by region. In the Northern Territory, in Arnhem Land and what is now Kakadu National Park, early Aboriginals painted "X-ray" portraits of humans and animals with their skeletons and internal organs clearly displayed. The Kimberley and Burrup Peninsula in Western Australia are rich repositories of elegant freehand paintings portraying human, animal, and ancestral Dreaming figures. And Queensland, especially the area that is now Carnarvon National Park, is known for its stencil paintings, in which the artists sprayed paint from their mouths.

EARTH TONES (LITERALLY)

Early Aboriginal artists used the earth to make pigments. Red, yellow, and brown were made from mineral-rich clays. Black was created with charcoal or charred tree bark; white from crushed gypsum rock; and grey from ashes left over from cooking fires. Modern artists may mix their pigments with oil or acrylic, but the traditional palette remains the same.

DECIPHERING "DOT PAINTINGS"

Ancient symbols and intricate dot motifs combine to create powerful works of art.

To a visitor wandering through a gallery, Aboriginal artwork can seem deceptively simple. Many traditional paintings feature basic designs—wavy lines, concentric circles—comprised of myriad tiny dots. They look as though they were created with the end of a paint-covered stick (and indeed, most were).

But the swirling motifs in these "dot paintings" aren't just abstractions—they're visual representations of ancestral legends.

According to Aboriginal beliefs, as the ancestors lived their lives during the Dreaming, they also gave shape to the landscape. In each spot where the ancestor shot an arrow, danced, or gave birth, an enduring mark was left on the topography: a hill, a ravine, a rock spire. As they conjured these geographical features, they sang out their names—composing singing maps of the territory they covered. Each is known as a "songline," and they crisscross the entire continent.

Now thousands of years old, these songs are still memorized and sung by many of today's Aboriginal peoples. Songlines are the basis of all indigenous traditions and tribal laws; learning and teaching the songs are considered sacred—and very secret—duties. Over many centuries, however, artists have revealed parts of the songlines through the symbology of dot paintings.

The symbols may seem cryptic, but many are recurring and give clues to the ancestral stories they depict. Shapes punctuating dot paintings usually correspond to landmarks: bodies of water, rock formations, campsites, or resting places. The lines that surround the shapes and connect them represent the tracks of the ancestors as they moved from place to place. Each dot painting is, in effect, a sacred walking map that plots an ancestor's journey.

COMMON SYMBOLS IN ABORIGINAL ART

woman

emu tracks

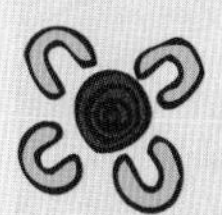
four women sitting around a campfire

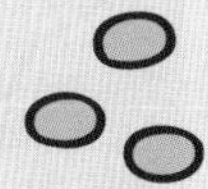
ants, fruits, flowers, or eggs

well or main campsite

water, fire, smoke, lightning, or bushfire

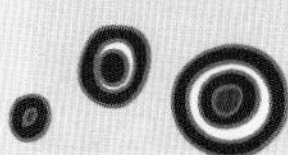
holes, clouds, or nests

Honey ant

Coolamon (wooden dish)

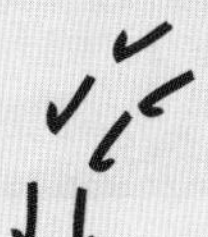
kangaroo tracks

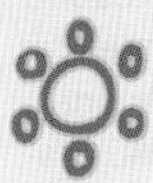
star

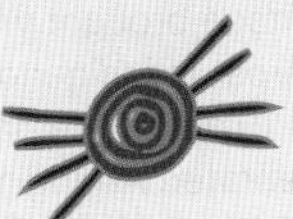
meeting place

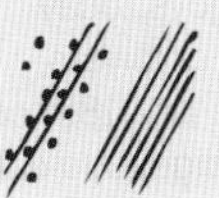
traveling paths or heavy rain

running water connecting two waterholes

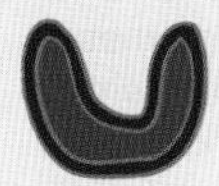
man

Witchetty grub

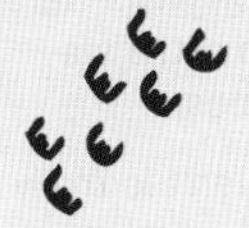
possum tracks

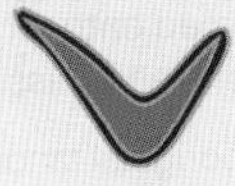
boomerang

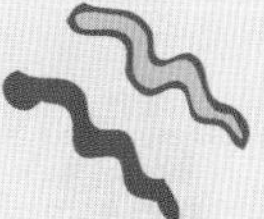
snake

spear

cloud, rainbow, sandhill, or cliff

people sitting

THE DAWNING OF ABORIGINAL ART APPRECIATION

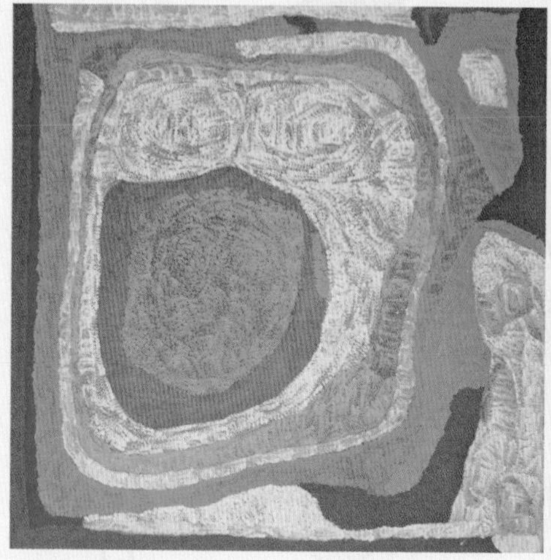

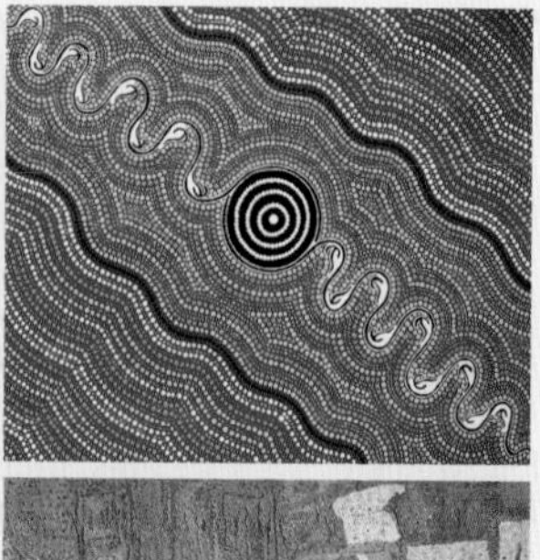

(left) Contemporary painting done in earth tones by a member of the Papunya Tula Artists collective; (top right) artwork from the Warlukurlangu Artists Aboriginal Corporation; (bottom right) Papunya Tula artwork.

IN THE BEGINNING . . .

It took a long time for Aboriginal art to gain the recognition it enjoys today. Australia's first European colonists, who began arriving in the late 18th century, saw the complex indigenous cultures it encountered as primitive, and believed that, as "nomads," Aboriginals had no claim to the land. Consequently, expansion into tribal lands went unchecked; during the 19th and early 20th centuries, most Aboriginals were forced onto white-owned cattle stations and missionary outposts.

Aboriginal land rights weren't formally acknowledged until 1976, when the first legislation was passed granting claim of title to natives with "traditional association" to the land. This watershed decision (called the Aboriginal Land Rights Act) allowed for the establishment of tribal land councils, which—in partnership with the Australian government—today manage many of the country's national parks and sacred ancient sites.

BREAKING GROUND

The growing awareness of Aboriginal heritage brought with it an increased interest in indigenous art. Before the 1970s, there had been only one celebrated Aboriginal artist in Australia—Albert Namatjira, who grew up on a Lutheran mission in Hermannsburg (in what is now the Northern Territory). In the 1930s, Namatjira studied under a white Australian artist and learned to paint sophisticated watercolor landscapes. Though these had almost nothing in common with traditional indigenous artworks, they won Namatjira enormous fame (by the 1950s, he was listed in *Who's Who*) which reinforced an idea that was

Curators often provide relevant historical context.

already burgeoning in the country: that Aboriginal creativity should receive the same attention and scholarship as non-Aboriginal forms of art.

Renowned artist David Malangi, Central Arnhem Land.

ABORIGINAL ART CENTERS

Perhaps the single most significant event in modern Aboriginal art history occurred in 1973, with the formation of the Aboriginal Arts Board. The advent of this agency, as part of the government-funded Australia Council for the Arts, heralded a new level of respect for indigenous art. Its aim was to establish a standardized support system for Aboriginal artists through grant money.

But early board members (who came from both European and Aboriginal backgrounds) found this to be another challenge. Aboriginal artists were scattered all over the continent, many of them in isolated, far-flung camps surrounded by vast desert or impenetrable rainforests. How was the organization to find these artists, decide which of them deserved funds, and then dispense those funds in an organized way?

The solution was to set up art centers at specific Aboriginal communities around the country—helmed by art-industry specialists who could both cultivate connections with local artists and manage their nuts-and-bolts requirements (like arranging for deliveries of art supplies, and for transport of finished artworks to exhibitors and buyers).

The plan worked, and is still working. There are some 50 Aboriginal art centers in Australia today (most in the Northern Territory and Western Australia), and they collectively represent more than a thousand artists. These centers are the conduit by which most modern Aboriginal works get to art dealers—and then on to galleries, museums, auction houses, and private collectors.

PAPUNYA TULA

Brenda Nungarrayi Lynch, well-known Western Desert artist.

The founding members of the Aboriginal Arts Board were inspired by the example of a particular Northern Territory desert settlement, Papunya Tula. Here, with the help of a white Australian art teacher, residents had begun to create and then sell "Dreaming paintings" (what are known today as dot paintings) to nearby galleries. By 1972, the community had established its own thriving and successful art collective, Papunya Tula Artists.

Today Papunya Tula Artists (which has never been government-subsidized) is the most famous Aboriginal art center in the country. The highly acclaimed dot paintings of its artists have hung in New York's Metropolitan Museum of Art and Paris's Musée du Quai Branly; their annual dollar sales are in the millions.

ABORIGINAL ART TODAY

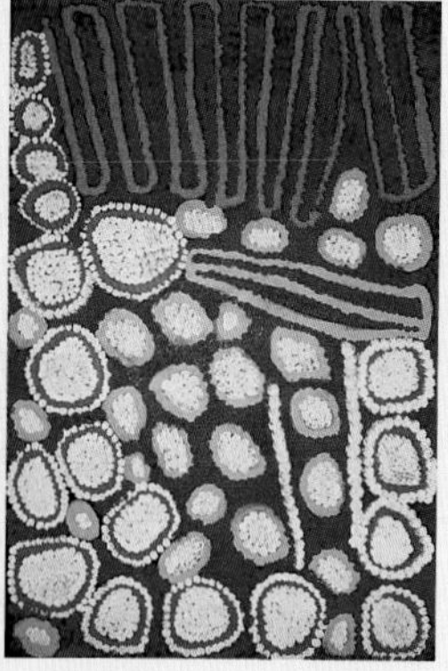

(left) Art by Emily Kame Kngwarreye, Utopia Central Australia; (right) Papunya Tula.

Over the past 30 years, the art world's regard for Aboriginal works has skyrocketed—not just in Australia, but all over the world. Ancient etchings and modern dot paintings now hang in museums from London's British to the Chicago Art Institute; gallerists and art dealers vie to represent rising Aboriginal art stars; and many artists who got their start at art centers in the 1980s (such as Dorothy Napangardi, Michael Nelson Tjakamarra, and Paddy Stewart Tjapaljarri) are near-celebrities today. A few of these pioneers of the modern Aboriginal art movement (like Rover Thomas and David Malangi) were in their seventies and eighties by the time their canvases began decorating exhibit halls and commanding six-figure auction bids.

Some of Australia's most celebrated Aboriginal artists, though, never got to see just how popular their work became. Clifford "Possum" Tjapaltjarri, for example, whose painting *Warlugulong* sold at a Sotheby's auction in 2007 for $2.4 million—the highest price ever paid for a piece of Aboriginal art—died five years beforehand. And Emily Kame Kngwarreye died in 1996, a dozen years before the National Museum of Australia mounted a huge solo exhibition of her work.

The new generation of Aboriginal artists faces its own set of obstacles. The appetite among art dealers for a steady supply of works to sell has led some of them to cut exploitative deals directly with artists (rather than working through the relative safety net of art centers). Other opportunists have mass-produced paintings and then sold them as "authentic"—thus tainting the integrity of the real Aboriginal art market.

But even these problems, unsavory though they are, can be seen from a certain angle as signs of positive change. It was only decades ago, after all, that the phrase "Aboriginal artist" seemed oxymoronic for many Australians. Today, those "primitive" assemblages of lines, circles, and dots account for almost 75 percent of the country's art sales. They have, in effect, helped put Australia on the map.

Today, symbols might be just half the story: colors can range from calm and subdued to bright and vibrant.

TIPS FOR WHERE AND HOW TO BUY ART

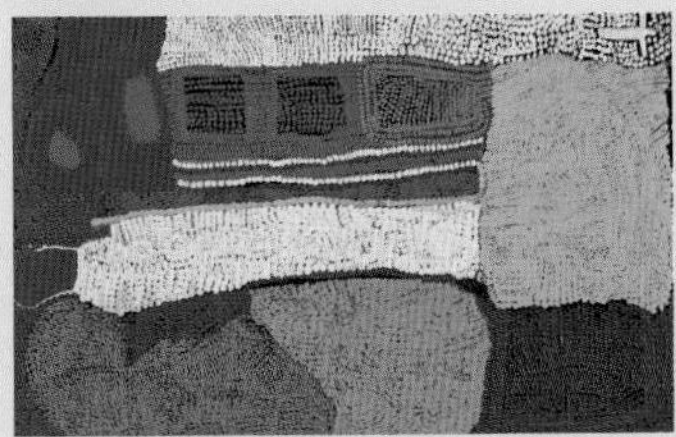

The most easily accessible sources for buying Aboriginal art are galleries. When considering a purchase, ascertain the art's authenticity and ethicality. The Australian Indigenous Art Trade Association recommends asking:

- Is the artwork documented with a certificate of authenticity from a reputable source, or by photos of the artist with the art?
- How did the artwork get to the gallery? Is the artist represented by a recognized art center, cooperative, or respected dealer?
- Is it clear that the artist was treated fairly and paid a fair price for putting the artwork on the market?

MUSEUM AND GALLERY COLLECTIONS

Australia has hundreds of galleries and museums at least partially devoted to Aboriginal artworks. Here are some of the best:

PERMANENT COLLECTIONS

The Australian Museum, Sydney
australianmuseum.net.au

The National Gallery of Australia, Canberra
nga.gov.au

Queensland Art Gallery, Brisbane
www.qagoma.qld.gov.au

National Gallery of Victoria, Melbourne
www.ngv.vic.gov.au

ROTATING EXHIBITIONS

Aboriginal Fine Arts Gallery, Darwin
www.aaia.com.au

Gallery Gabrielle Pizzi, Melbourne

www.gabriellepizzi.com.au

Australia Today

GOVERNMENT

Australia is a constitutional monarchy, and the Queen of England is Australia's queen as well. Her only role under the constitution, however, is to appoint her representative in Australia, the governor-general, which she does on advice from Australia's prime minister. In 1975 the governor-general caused a political crisis when he sacked the prime minister and his government and installed the opposition minority as caretaker until new elections could be held. The governor-general retains that power, but his or her duties are primarily ceremonial. Australia's government is elected for three-year terms, with no limit on how many terms a prime minister can serve. Controversially, Australia has had six prime ministers between 2010 and 2018. Voting is compulsory for all citizens 18 years and older, and failure to vote can result in a fine.

ECONOMY

Australia is a major exporter of wheat and wool, iron ore and gold, liquefied natural gas and coal. The major industries are mining, industrial and transport equipment, energy and utilities, agriculture, finance, and health care. The service sector dominates the domestic economy.

Abundant natural assets and massive government spending initially softened the impact of the global financial crisis that started in 2008. Demand for Australia's commodities from China and India has dipped, and mining has slowed. These developments have led to a slowdown in the country's economic growth.

TOURISM

On- and offshore wonders, unique wildlife, beach culture, Indigenous history, and multicultural cuisines help maintain Australia's multibillion-dollar tourism industry. The major challenges are keeping Australia on travelers' radars as other countries gain popularity, and protecting the most fragile attractions. Climate change has already affected the Great Barrier Reef, a World Heritage site on most visitors' must-see lists, and programs are in place to try to minimize the impact of rising sea temperatures and nearby mining sites. Contentious logging of old-growth forests for pulp, particularly in Tasmania, continues, and the opening of new mines rarely fits comfortably with conservation and cultural issues.

RELIGION

Australia's first settlers were predominantly English, Irish, and Scottish Christians. Now, almost two-thirds of Australians call themselves Christians (52%), with Islam a distant second (2.6%), and Buddhism third (2.4%); however, almost a third of the population (30%) ticked "no religion" on the 2016 census. Active church worship has declined over recent decades, and many religions struggle to attract members.

LITERATURE

Life Down Under has bred contemporary writers who speak with distinctly Australian voices. Tim Winton's book *Breath* brilliantly evokes the power of surfing and the angst of adolescence, while Kate Grenville's acclaimed *The Secret River* explores Australia's brutal colonial past and its effect on Indigenous people. Look out for award-winning authors Alexis Wright, Kim Scott, Tara June Winch, Michelle de Kretser, Christos Tsiolkas, David Malouf, and Helen Garner, among others. Morris Gleitzman and Andy Griffiths write (mostly) laugh-out-loud books for children and the young at heart.

Chapter 2

TRAVEL SMART

Updated by
Melissa Fagan

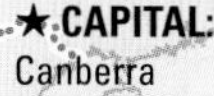

★ CAPITAL:
Canberra

POPULATION:
24.6 million

LANGUAGE:
English; multiple Indigenous languages

$ CURRENCY:
Australian dollar

COUNTRY CODE:
61

⚠ EMERGENCIES:
000

DRIVING:
On the left

ELECTRICITY:
240 volts, 50 cycles alternating current (AC). Wall outlets take slanted three-prong plugs and plugs with two flat prongs set in a V.

TIME:
15 hours ahead of New York

WEB RESOURCES:
www.australia.com,
www.australiangeographic.com,
www.traveller.com.au

INDONESIA

AUSTRALIA

Canberra

NEW ZEALAND

Know Before You Go

AUSTRALIA IS BIGGER THAN YOU THINK

Australia is about the same size in terms of land mass as the continental United States. However, the population density is around nine people per square mile compared to 94 people per square mile in the States, so you can drive for hours without seeing even a gas station. For first-time visitors, it usually makes the most sense to travel the east coast (via Brisbane, Sydney, and Melbourne) first and then venture into the interior, or fly north or west.

YOU NEED A VISA

Visitors to Australia need an Electronic Travel Authority (ETA), a type of electronic visa, to enter the country for short-term tourism or business stays. Citizens of the United States and Canada can apply online (*www.eta.homeaffairs.gov.au/ETAS3/etas)*; visas cost $15 USD and the average processing time is less than one day.

TIP→ **Be sure your visa details match your passport exactly or you may be refused entry upon arrival.**

CUSTOMS IS STRICT

Gruff manners. Unfriendly faces. Nothing says "Welcome to Australia" like sniffing dogs and rude customs agents. While the Border Force Officials represent the Australian government, they do not represent the Australian people who are generally warm, friendly, and generous in spirit. With that in mind, just follow the instructions, fill out the forms, and don't try to sneak anything in: if the dogs don't sniff out your guilty conscience, the agents will.

WITH THAT IN MIND, PACK MINDFULLY!

Australian customs officials are tasked with an important job: making sure no unexpected plants or animals get into the country that could upset the delicate ecosystem. The insects, spiders, and micro-organisms that might have snuck into your backpack, hidden in the dirt on your hiking boots cozied into those bamboo place mats you bought in Bali, are all unwanted critters in Australia.

If your visit to Australia is part of a larger international itinerary (lucky you), consider all purchases on the way. Check the Border Force's website for a list of what must be declared or avoided entirely. Also, be sure to carefully clean hiking or camping equipment before you travel.

ALWAYS WAS, ALWAYS WILL BE

In Australia, you are on the unceded lands of Aboriginal and Torres Strait Islander people who have lived here for 60,000 years. The continent's first peoples come from many groups with rich and diverse cultures, with more than 250 distinct languages spoken. Wherever you go, get to know whose country you're on; pay your respects, and tread lightly.

THE OUTBACK IS NOT A REAL PLACE

If you tell an Australian you're going to the Outback, they'll likely ask you to be a bit more specific. Alongside "the bush," which connotes more substantial vegetation, the phrase "the Outback" is used by some city slickers to refer to basically the whole interior of the continent.

You could be visiting Uluru in the Red Centre (which, by the way, is almost 300 miles from Alice Springs). You could be exploring the rugged Top End stretching south from Darwin. Or, you could be driving across one of Australia's many deserts or the arid Nullarbor Plain. Whichever Outback destination you choose, it's bound to be an unforgettable adventure (just make sure to take a good look at the map before you decide).

HIRE A CAR

Due to Australia's low population density, public transportation outside of capital cities is woeful. If you want to travel independently anywhere other than the east coast, a rental car is almost essential as buses can be indirect and infrequent and intercity trains are expensive and often slow. Domestic flights are often a good option, but Australia's vastness lends itself to road trips, and a car is the best way to discover natural beauty off the beaten track.

YOU DON'T NEED TO TIP

Thanks to a relatively high minimum wage (around US$15 for an unskilled worker), tipping is completely optional in Australia and usually reserved for exceptional service. Australians rarely tip in cafés or casual restaurants, and at fine-dining restaurants it is common to leave a 10% tip or simply round up the bill for a big group.

THE CAPITAL CITY ISN'T SYDNEY OR MELBOURNE

When the separate colonies became the federation of Australia in 1901, the newly created nation needed a capital. After strong competition between Sydney and Melbourne, a site roughly in between the two was chosen in 1908. Though often referred to as a big country town, over the past decade Canberra has evolved into a creative, green city with a high standard of living.

THE SUN IS DANGEROUS

Australia has one of the highest rates of melanoma in the world, so it is essential to "Slip, Slop, Slap" (wear a shirt and hat, put on sunscreen) whenever you're in the sun. Seeking shade in the hottest part of the day is a great idea, too! For eco-friendly sunscreens, look for those that are mineral-based with zinc oxide and/or titanium dioxide and avoid formulas with oxybenzone and octinoxate.

AUSTRALIA HAS RAIN FORESTS AND MOUNTAINS AS WELL AS DESERTS AND BEACHES

Such a large geographic area across changing climatic zones means there's a bunch of different ecosystems to explore in Australia. Ever heard of the Daintree Rainforest? Well, it's the oldest continuously surviving tropical rain forest in the world. At the other extreme, the picturesque Mt. Feathertop is part of the Australian Alps and is covered in snow for half the year. All this and more coexist Down Under.

AUSTRALIA IS FOODIE HEAVEN

The Australian food scene has come a long way since the 1980s, when Paul Hogan enticed travelers with a shrimp on the barbie. Meat pies, Vegemite, and fairy bread (white bread and butter covered in sprinkles) are still popular, but experimental and international dining options are now de rigueur, even outside the major cities. Bush tucker featuring native ingredients like kangaroo, lemon myrtle, wattleseed, and finger lime are increasingly available; look for offerings from First Nations–run businesses.

BONDI IS FAR FROM AUSTRALIA'S BEST BEACH

Bondi may be an icon, and beautiful in its own way, but it's far from Australia's best beach. And it's crowded! On weekends and in summer, it is almost impossible to find a patch of sand not occupied by a sunburned backpacker. Thankfully, Sydney alone has over 100 beaches, stretching from Cronulla in the south to Palm Beach in the north. And if you head north or south along the coastline, you'll find thousands of pristine sandy beaches, many protected in national parks, and not a tacky souvenir shop in sight.

Getting Here and Around

Australia is divided into six states and two territories—Northern Territory (NT) and Australian Capital Territory (ACT)—similar to the District of Columbia. Tasmania, the smallest state, is an island off mainland Australia's southeast point.

Air

Qantas is Australia's flagship carrier. It operates direct flights to Sydney from New York, Dallas, San Francisco, and Los Angeles, and from Los Angeles to Melbourne and Brisbane. Because Pacific-route flights from the United States to Australia cross the international date line, you lose a day, but regain it on the journey home. Flight time is usually around 20 hours.

Australia's large distances mean that flying is often the locals' favorite way of getting from one city to another. On routes between popular destinations like Sydney, Melbourne, and Brisbane there are often several flights each hour, although you usually need to book well in advance to obtain the cheapest fares.

Boat

Organized boat tours from the Queensland mainland are the only way to visit the Great Barrier Reef. The Great Barrier Reef Marine Park Authority website has helpful advice on how to choose a tour operator and lists which companies are ecotourism-certified.

The daily ferries *Spirit of Tasmania I* and *II* take 10 hours to connect Melbourne with Devonport on Tasmania's north coast. Make reservations as early as possible, particularly during the busy December and January school holidays.

Bus

Bus travel in Australia is comfortable and well organized. Australia's national bus network is run by Greyhound Australia (no connection to Greyhound in the United States), which serves far more destinations than any plane or train services. Murrays Coaches is another affordable option for travel between Canberra and the east coast. However, Australia is a vast continent, and bus travel requires plenty of time.

Car

Driving is generally easy in Australia, once you adjust to traveling on the left side of the road and the prevalence of roundabouts. When you're preparing a driving itinerary, it's vital to bear in mind the huge distances involved and calculate travel time and stopovers accordingly.

Australia's cities have good public transport, so there's not much point in renting a car if you're staying in an urban area, but outside city limits a car is practically a necessity. However, remote roads through the country's interior can pose problems for inexperienced travelers, with few gas stations and plenty of opportunities for a flat tire.

Most rental companies in Australia accept driving licenses from other countries, including the United States, provided that the information on the license is clear and in English. Otherwise, an International Driver's Permit is required (but they'll still want to see your regular license, too). Rental companies have varying policies and charges for unusual trips, such as lengthy cross-state expeditions around the Top End and Western Australia. Ask about additional mileage, fuel, and insurance charges if you're planning to cover a lot of ground.

Another popular way to see Australia is to rent a camper van (motor home). For road trips longer than a couple of months, rental costs add up, so buying a car or van (and selling it at the end of your trip) might be more economical.

Gas is known in Australia as "petrol." Self-service petrol stations are plentiful near major cities and in rural towns. In really out-of-the-way places, carrying a spare petrol can is a good idea, as smaller petrol stations often close at night and on Sunday, though in major cities and on main highways there are plenty of stations open round the clock.

Intercity highways are usually in good condition, but more remote roads can often be unpaved or full of potholes and are better suited to a 4WD. Animals—kangaroos and livestock, primarily—are common causes of road accidents in rural Australia, especially at dusk and dawn, so make sure to keep an eye out.

Always carry plenty of water with you and don't count on your cell phone working in the middle of nowhere. The Australian Automobile Association has a branch in each state and it's affiliated with AAA worldwide, with reciprocal services to American members, including emergency road service.

From	To	Distance	Main Highway Names
Sydney	Melbourne	873 km (542 miles)/1,043 km (648 miles)	Hume/Princes
Sydney	Brisbane	982 km (610 miles)	Pacific
Brisbane	Cairns	1,699 km (1,056 miles)	Bruce
Melbourne	Adelaide	732 km (455 miles) /912 km (567 miles)	Dukes/Pacific
Adelaide	Perth	2,716 km (1,688 miles)	Eyre and Great Eastern
Adelaide	Alice Springs	1,544 km (959 miles)	Stuart
Alice Springs	Darwin	1,503 km (934 miles)	Stuart
Darwin	Cairns	2,885 km (1,793 miles)	Bruce, Flinders, Barkley, and Stuart

Cruise

Cruises along the Great Barrier Reef and between the Whitsunday Islands are popular, as well as across the Top End and between Brisbane and Sydney. Other routes connect Australia's east coast with New Zealand and the Pacific.

Pacific Dawn, Australia's biggest cruise liner, sails various one- and two-week Pacific and New Zealand cruises out of Brisbane, while *Pacific Jewel* runs "Island Hopper" tours and a short Brisbane to Sydney cruise. The *Pacific Pearl* also cruises the Pacific, leaving from Sydney. All three are owned by P&O, known in the rest of the world as Princess Cruises.

Princess Cruises' huge *Sapphire Princess* sails between New Zealand and Australia at the end of its 33-day cruise from Seattle, Washington. The smaller *Dawn Princess* travels between the Australian east coast, New Zealand, and the South Pacific, departing Sydney and Brisbane.

Regent Seven Seas' *Seven Seas Voyager* docks at several points on Australia's east and north coasts, including Sydney, Brisbane, and Darwin, on cruises to Indonesia, Singapore, and Papua New Guinea. Crystal Cruises' Australia and New Zealand tours take in a range of popular destinations on the east coast and Top End, including Melbourne, Sydney, Brisbane, the Great Barrier Reef, Cairns, and Darwin. Some cruises even encompass the beautiful coastlines of Western Australia and Tasmania. Silversea's *Silver Whisper* follows a similar route plan and also encompasses Hong Kong.

Cunard's *Queen Elizabeth* sails from New York and San Francisco to Sydney, and calls at Australian ports on round-the-world cruises, too. So do its *Queen Mary 2* and *Queen Victoria*.

Taxi

Taxis are available in cities and major towns throughout Australia, especially outside airports, bus stations, and train stations. In other areas hailing a taxi on the street is practically unheard of, so call ahead to avoid long wait times.

Train

Australia has a network of long-distance trains providing first- and economy-class service along the east and south coasts, across the south of the country from Sydney to Perth, and through the middle of the country between Adelaide and Darwin. Most long-distance trains are operated by various state-government-owned enterprises.

Essentials

Customs and Duties

Australian customs regulations are notoriously strict. Australia is free from many pests and diseases endemic in other places, and it wants to stay that way. Customs procedures are very thorough, and it can take up to an hour to clear them.

All animals are subject to quarantine and many foodstuffs and natural products are forbidden. If in doubt, declare something—the worst-case scenario is that it will be taken from you, without a fine.

Airport sniffer dogs patrol arrivals areas, and even an innocent dried flower forgotten between the pages of a book could cause problems.

Otherwise, nonresidents over 18 may bring in 25 cigarettes (or 25 grams of cigars or tobacco) and 2¼ liters of alcohol. Adults can bring in other taxable goods (that is, luxury items like perfume and jewelry) to the value of A$900.

Dining

Fresh ingredients, friendly service, innovative flavor combinations, and great value for your money mean that eating out Down Under is usually a pleasant experience. Australia's British heritage is evident in the hearty food served in pubs, roadhouses, and country hotels. On the other hand, proximity to Asia and multicultural influences brings delicious and authentic cuisine from all over the world, especially in the cities. Native ingredients, and a focus on local produce, are featuring on more and more menus.

PAYING

At most restaurants you ask for the bill at the end of the meal. At sandwich bars, burger joints, takeout spots, and some cafés, you pay up front. Visa and MasterCard are widely accepted in all but the simplest eateries, but American Express cards may not be accepted or may incur an additional fee.

RESERVATIONS AND DRESS

It's a good idea to make a reservation if you can. In some places (Sydney, for example) it's expected, though be prepared to be allocated only a two-hour window. Book as far ahead as you can (often 30 days), and reconfirm as soon as you arrive. (Large parties should always call ahead to check the reservations policy.) Many popular restaurants may not take reservations at all, so be prepare to arrive early and wait. For popular restaurants, formal dress codes are rare, although at fine-dining establishments in Sydney and Melbourne a jacket and tie are expected.

Health and Safety

COVID-19

COVID-19 brought travel to a virtual standstill for most of 2020 and into 2021, but vaccinations have made travel possible and safe again. However, each destination (and each business within that destination) may have its own requirements and regulations. Travelers may expect to continue to wear a mask in public and obey any other rules (and nonvaccinated travelers may face certain restrictions). Given how abruptly travel was curtailed at the onset of the pandemic, it is wise to consider protecting yourself by purchasing a travel insurance policy that will reimburse you for cancellation costs related to COVID-19. Not all travel insurance policies protect against pandemic- related cancellations, so always read the fine print.

Essentials

OTHER CONCERNS

Sunburn and sunstroke are the greatest health hazards when visiting Australia. Stay out of the sun in the middle of the day (the hottest hours are generally 11 am–2 pm) and, regardless of whether you normally burn, follow the locals' example and slather on the sunscreen. Dehydration is another concern, especially in the Outback. It's easy to avoid: carry plenty of water and drink it often.

Some of the world's deadliest creatures call Australia home. The chances of running into one are low, particularly in urban areas, but wherever you go, pay close heed to any warnings given by hotel staff, tour operators, lifeguards, or locals in general. The best advice is to always be cautious, and double-check the situation at each stop with the appropriate authority.

Australian coastal waters are also home to strong currents known as "rips." Pay close attention to the flags raised on beaches, and only swim in areas patrolled by lifeguards. If you get caught in a rip, the standard advice is never to swim against it, as you rapidly become exhausted. Instead, try to relax and float parallel to the shore: eventually the current will subside and you will be able to swim back to the shore, albeit farther down the coast.

Immunizations

There are no immunizations required to enter Australia. However, all travelers should confirm they are up-to-date with routine vaccinations. Cases of dengue fever have occurred in Far North Queensland, so you should speak to your doctor if you are planning to visit that area.

Lodging

Australia operates a rating system of one to five stars. Five-star hotels include on-site dining options, concierge and valet services, a business center, and, of course, very luxurious rooms. Four stars denote an exceptional property that just doesn't have all the extras needed for five. Three stars means quality fittings and service.

Judging from the huge number of short-term rental properties in Australia, many locals prefer doing their own thing to being in a hotel and it's easy for you to do likewise. Serviced apartments and peer-to-peer accommodation options are plentiful in Australia for those who'd rather avoid the big hotel chains. Homestays in rural and regional areas are another great way to experience the real Australia.

Airbnb has also emerged as a popular type of accommodation in Australia. Here you'll find houses and apartments as well as properties off the beaten track, including farm stays, rain-forest retreats, and houseboats, often with a much more intimate feel and at significantly lower prices than traditional establishments.

Packing

A light sweater or jacket will keep you comfy in autumn, but winter in the southern states demands a heavier coat—ideally a raincoat with a zip-out lining. On the other hand, summer can be sweltering, so light shirts and breezy pants are in order. Sydney is famously temperate, whereas Melbourne is known to experience four seasons in one day.

Wherever you are, your accessories of choice are high-quality sunglasses and a hat with a brim—the sun is strong and dangerous.

Carry insect repellent and avoid lotions or perfume in the tropics, as they attract mosquitoes and other insects. Flies are a consistent annoyance in rural and regional areas.

You should pack sturdy walking boots if you're planning any bushwalking, otherwise sneakers or flats are fine for sightseeing. Flip-flops are confusingly referred to as thongs Down Under, and are popular in casual settings.

Whether you're hitting the beach, a river, a waterhole or simply the hotel pool, cooling off is Australia's favorite pastime. Variously referred to as togs, bathers, or swimmers around the country, a swimsuit is essential all year round.

 Passports and Visas

All U.S. citizens require a valid passport to enter Australia for stays of any length, plus the relevant visa. Your passport should be valid for at least three months after your planned departure from Australia and must have at least two empty pages for arrival and departure stamps.

For tourist stays of 90 days or less, U.S. citizens can apply for an Electronic Travel Authority (ETA). The ETA is valid for one year and permits the visa holder to enter Australia for multiple stays of three months or less each time. You can apply online via the Department of Home Affairs website and the cost is US$15. If all your details are correct, the visa should be granted within 24 hours.

 Tours

ABORIGINAL CULTURE

Adventure Tours Australia

This company runs a host of both long and short trips, working in close partnership with Aboriginal communities to curate experiences like the three-day Uluru Adventure and four-day Kakadu, Katherine, and Kakadu Adventure. ☎ *07/5401–5555* 🌐 *www.adventuretours.com.au* 🎫 *From A$110.*

Diverse Travel Australia

This agency specializes in experiences that capture the essence of Australia, including tours focused on Aboriginal art and cultural experiences. ☎ *08/8234–8324* 🌐 *www.diversetravel.com.au* 🎫 *From A$69.*

BIKING

AllTrails

Discover Australia's hidden gems and untouched terrain with AllTrails' small-group and self-guided cycling tours throughout the country. ☎ *03/9645–3355* 🌐 *www.alltrails.com.au* 🎫 *From A$450.*

BIRD-WATCHING

Birdwatch Australia

Led by expert birders, this company tailors individual and small-group guided bird-watching and nature tours throughout Australia. ☎ *02/4422–0616* 🌐 *www.australianaturallytravel.com.au* 🎫 *From A$125.*

Kimberley Birdwatching

Join leading Australian ornithologists for intimate bird-watching tours in the Kimberley and northern Australia, with camping, boating, and farm-stay options. ✉ *Broome* ☎ *08/9192–1246, 0429/706–800 mobile* 🌐 *www.kimberleybirdwatching.com.au* 🎫 *From A$90.*

CULTURE

National Geographic Expeditions

Local experts lead National Geographic's extensive Australia expeditions, which take in the Great Barrier Reef and Uluru, including exclusive expeditions by private jet. ☎ *888/966–8687 in U.S.* 🌐 *www.nationalgeographicexpeditions.com* 🎫 *From $5099.*

Essentials

SEIT Outback Australia
Join SEIT to experience small-group tours and workshops in Central Australia, working in partnership with Aboriginal communities and operators. ☎ *08/8956–3156* 🌐 *www.seitoutbackaustralia.com.au* 🎫 *From A$73.*

Smithsonian Journeys
Learning is the focus of Smithsonian Journeys' small-group tours, led by university professors. Their 22-day Splendors of Australia and New Zealand tour covers the best of Australia—and much of New Zealand, too. ☎ *855/338–8687* 🌐 *www.smithsonianjourneys.org* 🎫 *From $10,184.*

DIVING

Daintree Air Services
Local flightseeing company Daintree Air Services' Ultimate Dive package includes 18 dives in nine days. The Great Barrier Reef, Coral Sea, and a wreck dive are included. ☎ *1800/246–206 in Australia, 07/4034–9300 outside Australia* 🌐 *www.daintreeair.com.au* 🎫 *From A$160.*

Diversion Dive Travel
Working with dive operators around Australia, Diversion connects you with Australia's diving hot spots including the Great Barrier Reef, Christmas Island, and the south and west Australian coasts. ☎ *1800/607–913 within Australia, 07/4039–0200 outside Australia* 🌐 *www.diversiondivetravel.com.au* 🎫 *From A$630.*

ECOTOURS AND SAFARIS

Northern Experience Eco Tours
Experience the beauty of North Queensland's World Heritage-listed Wet Tropics rain forests and the Atherton Tablelands with this family-owned, ecotour operator. Trips include swimming in waterfalls, a lake cruise, visiting national parks, Aboriginal Dreamtime education and stories, as well as plentiful encounters with local flora and fauna. ☎ *07/4058–0268* 🌐 *www.northernexperience.com.au* 🎫 *From A$389.*

Sacred Earth Safaris
This family-operated tour company specializes in 4WD tours through remote and Top End Australia, including the Kakadu and Kimberley frontiers, the Nullabor Plain, the Flinders Ranges, Kangaroo Island, and Pilbara. ☎ *0415/692–855, 08/8536–2234* 🌐 *www.sacredearthsafaris.com.au* 🎫 *From A$1635.*

Tread Lightly Eco Tours
This Advanced Ecotourism–certified operator runs guided bushwalking, 4WD, astronomy, and glowworm tours, among others, through the Blue Mountains National Park, west of Sydney. ☎ *0414/976–752* 🌐 *www.treadlightly.com.au* 🎫 *From A$83.*

Wayoutback Australian Safaris
This tour company employs certified ecotour operators who run camping and accommodated safaris, as well as desert walks, throughout Australia, with a strong focus on Aboriginal culture. 🌐 *www.wayoutback.com.au* 🎫 *From A$239.*

FOOD AND WINE

Adelaide's Top Food and Wine Tours
Eat and drink your way around the famous vineyards and purveyors of the Barossa Valley, McLaren Vale, Clare Valley, and Adelaide Hills on these personalized, small-group tours. ☎ *08/8386–0888* 🌐 *www.topfoodandwinetours.com.au* 🎫 *From A$85.*

Artisans of Leisure
This company's indulgent nine-day Food and Wine Australia tour divides time between vineyards, markets, and luxurious hotels. ☎ *800/214–8144 in U.S.* 🌐 *www.artisansofleisure.com* 🎫 *From US$13,100.*

Two Fat Blokes
Experience full- and half-day tours showcasing local wines and gourmet produce in the Hunter Valley region. ☎ *0414/316–859 in Australia, 2/4998–6699 outside Australia* 🌐 *www.twofatblokes.com.au* *From A$89.*

HIKING

Australian Walking Holidays
Mix hiking with other adventure activities with one of Australian Walking Holidays' guided or self-guided trips. ☎ *1300/767–381 in Australia, 02/8270–8400 international* 🌐 *www.australianwalkingholidays.com.au* *From A$125.*

Auswalk
This company has a huge range of hiking expeditions all over Australia. There are group departures and customized self-guided tours, with accommodation and sightseeing included. ☎ *03/9597–9767 outside Australia, 1300/777–878 in Australia* 🌐 *www.auswalk.com.au* *From A$895.*

US Embassy/Consulate

There are U.S. consulates in Melbourne, Perth, and Sydney and the U.S. Embassy in Canberra. The embassy and consulates can offer a variety of services to U.S. citizens, including legal and medical assistance, passport and citizenship services, voting, emergency financial assistance, and emergency services in the unlikely event of arrest, death, serious injury, or crime.

Enroll in STEP (Smart Traveler Enrollment Program) before your departure for easy access to information and so you can be contacted in an emergency. Consulates can be reached by phone, mail, or email; find the relevant details online.

When to Go

Australia's climate can be broadly divided into north and south. Most travelers choose to avoid the south's winters (July to August) and the north's summers (December to February).

The east coast can be visited all year round, with high season over summer (especially school holidays in December and January) and low season over winter. Spring and fall are ideal times to visit. However, the tropical north (including Darwin and the Great Barrier Reef) experiences a heavy rainy season in summer which both slows the flow of tourists and often means lower prices.

Much of Western Australia, South Australia, the Northern Territory, and interior New South Wales can be uncomfortably hot during summer, especially if you're planning on making the most of the great outdoors. Of course, nights in the Outback can also get very chilly. Again, fall and spring are the perfect compromise.

"Stinger season," when there is a high risk of jellyfish in northern Queensland, runs from October to May, when beaches will often be signposted with the risk level. More than 30 popular beaches north of Banny Point are protected by a visible enclosure to keep out the majority of stingers. Wet suits or other protective clothing are also recommended during this time of year.

Great Itineraries

First Timer's Itinerary: Sydney, the Great Barrier Reef, Uluru

This classic 10-day journey takes in three of Australia's most natural treasures, including the Blue Mountains, the Great Barrier Reef, and Uluru.

DAYS 1–2: EXPLORING SYDNEY

On your first day in Australia's largest city, visit the world-renowned **Sydney Opera House,** stopping for lunch at the Opera Bar with its sweeping views of the cityscape and Harbour Bridge. In the afternoon, take a guided walking tour through the historic **Rocks** area beyond **Circular Quay.** After some much-needed rest, start the second day with a harbor cruise. You can enjoy the best vantage points for seeing this spectacular city and its magnificent waterfront setting. In the afternoon, head over to **Sydney Harbour Bridge,** where a trek up the stairs of the South East Pylon rewards you with an unbeatable harbor panorama.

DAY 3: DAY TRIP TO THE BLUE MOUNTAINS

Leave Sydney in the morning on a day trip to the Blue Mountains, approximately one hour away by car or bus. Head for **Katoomba** at the peak of the Blue Mountains National Park, where the **Three Sisters** await, an unusual rock formation representing three sisters who were turned to stone according to Aboriginal legend. Head to neighboring **Scenic World** and choose the scenic skyway, walkway, railway, or cableway to experience the majesty of the Jamison Valley. On your way back, make a small detour in the pretty garden village of **Leura,** with its many fine coffee shops, restaurants, and galleries. Return to Sydney for dinner and stay the night there.

DAY 4: WINE TOUR OF THE HUNTER VALLEY

Take an organized day trip from Sydney to the **Hunter Valley Wine Region,** 150 km (93 miles) north of Sydney, and spend the day experiencing a selection of more than 150 wineries and cellar doors. Discover the region's finest Shiraz or Chardonnay and taste some of the freshest produce and best cheeses that Australia has to offer. Return to Sydney at night for dinner.

DAY 5: FLIGHT TO CAIRNS

Fly to Cairns, a tropical city nestled in North Queensland and the gateway to the Great Barrier Reef. Relax after your three-hour flight from Sydney with a visit to the **Cairns Tropical Zoo** to cuddle a koala. At night, take in the atmosphere by strolling along the **Esplanade,** or beat the heat by taking a dip in the pristine **Cairns Lagoon.**

DAY 6: KURANDA VILLAGE AND TJAPUKAI ABORIGINAL CULTURAL PARK

Take a full-day tour of nearby **Kuranda** village and the surrounding rain forest. Experience one of Australia's most scenic rail journeys, the **Skyrail Rainforest Cableway,** for a bird's-eye view over the forest. After lunch, head to the **Tjapukai Aboriginal Cultural Park** to watch traditional Aboriginal dances and listen to music and informational talks—perhaps even try your hand at throwing a boomerang or playing the didgeridoo!

DAY 7: CRUISE TO THE GREAT BARRIER REEF

Book a full-day cruise from Cairns to the **Great Barrier Reef** and get up close and personal with the abundant sea life of the world's largest coral reef system. With some of the best snorkeling and diving on the planet, nothing beats getting in the water and swimming with groupers, clown fish, and rays. Then revel in the

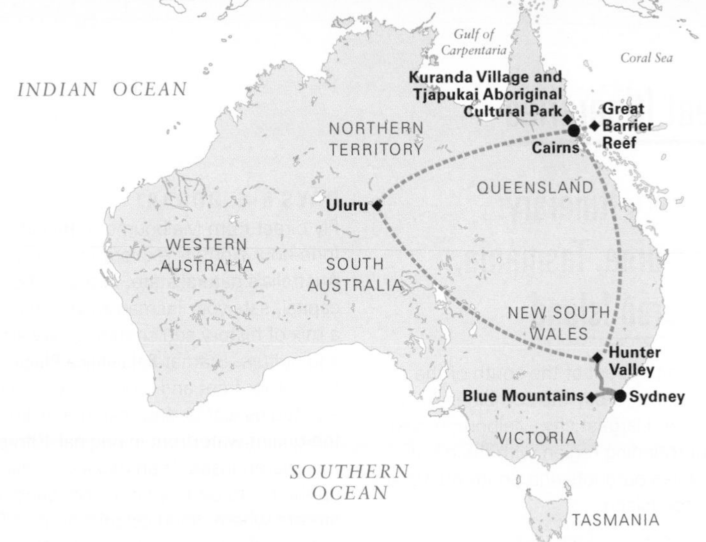

fact you're experiencing one of the seven wonders of the natural world firsthand.

DAYS 8–9: TWO DAYS IN ULURU

Rise and shine early to catch the three-hour flight inland to the physical and spiritual heart of Australia: World Heritage–listed **Uluru,** the iconic symbol of the Australian Outback. Once you arrive and check in at Ayers Rock Resort, book a seat at the **Sounds of Silence** dinner, where you can feast on a barbecue buffet of kangaroo, crocodile, and barramundi and marvel at the immense desert sky.

Wake up before dawn the next morning to catch the majestic sunrise over Uluru (Ayers Rock). See the magnificence of Uluru as its surface changes color with the rising sun, from pink to blood-red to mauve throughout the day. Afterward, walk around Uluru's base with a guide and learn about how this sacred site was created by spirit ancestors in the Dreamtime. In the afternoon, sign up for a tour of **Kata Tjuta** (the Olgas), the nearby rock domes over which you can watch the sun set.

DAY 10: BACK TO SYDNEY

Once you return to Sydney, take the short ferry ride to **Taronga Zoo** and stroll around the zoo's harborside location, spying kangaroos, koalas, and other animal natives.

Tips

- If driving around Sydney, avoid traveling at peak times. Either leave early or head off later, once the commuter traffic has died down.
- Cairns has a wide range of hotels and resorts to suit any budget—a romantic getaway, weekend escape, or family vacation. It's worth booking ahead and finding somewhere central to the city.
- When visiting the Great Barrier Reef for a dive or snorkel experience, the best time of year is in the winter months when marine stingers aren't present in the water and there is less need for a protective wet suit.

If you have time, a short bus or train ride to the world-famous Bondi Beach is in order for a taste of Sydney's much heralded beach life. Spend early evening at the Bondi Icebergs club, where you can enjoy a glass of Australian wine while gazing out over the picturesque southern end of the beach.

Great Itineraries

Southern Itinerary: Melbourne, Tasmania, Kangaroo Island

Taking in the best of the south of the country, this 11-day trip combines Australia's second-largest city, Melbourne, and the surrounding region with the great Tasmanian outdoors and South Australia's Kangaroo Island.

DAYS 1–2: MELBOURNE

Start off in Australia's cultural capital, **Melbourne,** with its world-class shopping and thriving arts scene. No visit to Melbourne is complete without a freshly made espresso. Some of the best are on **Degraves Street,** directly off Flinders. Sit down at an outdoor table and enjoy delicious eggs Benedict with your coffee. Jump on the free city circle tram to get an overview of the city. It offers good hop-on, hop-off transportation for visitors and locals alike.

DAY 3: YARRA VALLEY WINE REGION

Leave the sights and sounds of Melbourne for a day of wine tasting at the **Yarra Valley.** It's within easy driving distance of the city, but your best bet is to go with a winery tour, which often provide transfers from the CBD. These generally include visits to four or five wineries and lunch. Return to Melbourne for dinner.

DAY 4: MELBOURNE AND PHILLIP ISLAND

Explore the farther reaches of the city by visiting the trendy suburbs of **Richmond, St Kilda, Fitzroy,** or **Prahran.** All offer great café and shopping strips with a more laid-back feel than in downtown Melbourne. Take an evening tour to nearby **Phillip Island** to see the **Little Penguin Parade,** when the world's smallest penguins come ashore after a day's fishing.

DAYS 5–6: HOBART

Fly direct from Melbourne to **Hobart** (one-hour flight) to explore Tasmania, Australia's natural state. In the harbor capital, sate your Tasmanian appetite with a mix of history and contemporary art and culture. Start at **Salamanca Place** on the harbor front and browse the galleries, art studios, cafés, and restaurants lining the quaint waterfront in original 19th-century warehouses. Then make your way up the hill to Battery Point and wander streets where grand colonial houses face out over the Derwent River. The **Museum of Old and New Art (MONA)** is a must-see for art lovers and visitors alike, and is only a 15-minute drive (or 25-minute ferry ride) from the center of Hobart.

DAY 7: PORT ARTHUR

Hire a car and make the 90-minute drive to **Port Arthur** on the Tasman Peninsula or join the cruise from Hobart to Port Arthur aboard the MV *Marana,* which takes approximately 2½ hours. Experience Australia's most intact convict site with more than 30 buildings, ruins, and restored homes. Hop on board a short cruise to the **Isle of the Dead** to join a guided tour of the settlement's island burial ground and learn about the lives of the people who lived in Port Arthur. On your return to Hobart, grab a bite to eat at Salamanca Place and enjoy some art, crafts, music, and theater at the Salamanca Arts Centre.

DAY 8: BACK TO MELBOURNE

Fly back to Melbourne in the morning, and then it's time for shopping. A great place to start is at the **Queen Victoria Market** on Elizabeth Street, a shopping institution that showcases a wide range of quality food, clothing, jewelry, new-age products, and souvenirs. For more upmarket items, head to **Emporium Melbourne, QV Retail,** or **Melbourne GPO.** If you're feeling shopped out, take a trip to the **Eureka Skydeck 88** for impressive and expansive views of the city from the southern hemisphere's highest viewing platform.

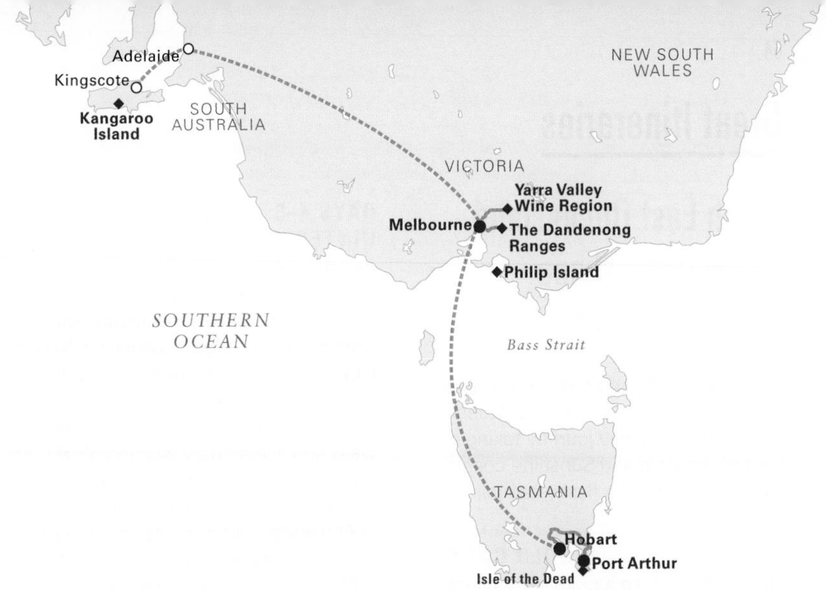

DAY 9: THE DANDENONG RANGES

You've tried the Yarra Valley but haven't yet explored the Dandenong Ranges, a tranquil region of towering rain forests and quaint mountain villages, just a short half-hour drive or one-hour train ride from Melbourne city (disembark at Hurstbridge, Lilydale, or Belgrave station, where you'll find connecting buses). You can hike through the **Dandenong Ranges National Park** and enjoy incredible views of Melbourne's skyline from the Skyhigh, perched on top of Mt. Dandenong. Afterward, explore your creative interests among the shops, galleries, and tearooms of nearby Olinda, Belgrave, and Sassafras. Overnight at one of the many quaint B&Bs nestled in the mountains, or make the brief journey back to Melbourne.

DAYS 10–11: KANGAROO ISLAND

Visiting the southern tip of Australia wouldn't be complete without a trip to **Kangaroo Island,** Australia's third-largest island. The island is a pristine wilderness located southwest of Adelaide and home to some of the largest untouched populations of native Australian animals. Take the short flight to **Adelaide** from Melbourne and then a further flight or ferry ride across to the island. **Sealink Ferries** offers a range of single- and multi-day tours and accommodation packages, showcasing the best of the region's wildlife, coastline, and specialty food and wine.

If adventure is your thing, Kangaroo Helicopters offers a Heli Experience and Scenic Flight or, for wildlife enthusiasts, options include guided tours within the Seal Bay or Kelly Hill Conservation Parks. Fly via Adelaide back to Melbourne or on to the next stage of your journey.

Great Itineraries

South East Queensland Itinerary: Brisbane and the Gold Coast

Discover the thriving coastline and verdant hinterlands of South East Queensland with this 12-day journey taking in the best of the Gold and Sunshine coasts, including the state's flashy capital, Brisbane.

DAY 1: SYDNEY TO GOLD COAST

From Sydney, take a quick, 80-minute flight to Gold Coast Airport at Coolangatta. Pick up a rental car or board a shuttle bus for the coastal hubs of **Surfers Paradise, Broadbeach,** or **Main Beach,** and check into your hotel for the next three nights. After a leisurely café lunch, spend the afternoon exploring the area's beaches or get cultural with a visit to HOTA (Home of the Arts). The Gold Coast's light rail system, **G:Link,** will ferry you between different hot spots with ease.

DAYS 2–3: GOLD COAST

Experience the Gold Coast like the locals do by signing up for a surf lesson with **Get Wet Surf School** at Main Beach. During your two-hour class you're likely to stand up at least once on the board, and get the photos to prove it. Refuel with lunch at Southport's glitzy **Marina Mirage** and then relax on the beach for the rest of the day.

The following day, make your way over to the Gold Coast's famous theme parks. Drive or catch a shuttle north to Oxenford for **Movie World** and **Wet'n'Wild,** or travel another 10 minutes farther up the highway to Coomera for the area's top park, **Dreamworld.**

DAYS 4–5: GOLD COAST HINTERLAND

Pack up the car or board a bus for the scenic 90-minute drive via Mount Tamborine to **O'Reilly's Rainforest Retreat.** Nestled on the edge of **Lamington National Park,** O'Reilly's is the perfect base for a range of wilderness experiences, including hiking, bird-watching, a treetop walk, and a legendary evening glowworm tour through the creeks and caves of the hinterland. Spend the night in one of O'Reilly's luxurious villas or under the stars in the adjacent campground, before rising early to complete the two-hour circuit to Python Rock and Moran's Falls, taking in the spectacular views and abundant birdlife along the way. After lunch and bird feeding at O'Reilly's, jump back in the car or reboard your coach and head north for two hours to **Brisbane,** the region's capital and host of the 2032 Olympics.

DAYS 6–8: BRISBANE

Spend a day getting to know Queensland's river city. Start with breakfast at one of the many alfresco cafés in the South Bank and West End, before getting your cultural fix at the **Queensland Cultural Centre.** Treat yourself to sweeping views onboard the **Wheel of Brisbane,** or join **River City Cruises** for a sightseeing tour of the area's most famous landmarks. The city's best shopping, dining, and cultural precincts are almost all within walking distance of the CBD, but if the heat gets the better of you, the hop-on, hop-off **Brisbane Explorer** bus runs a regular service between the inner-city's top attractions.

No visit to Brisbane is complete without a trip to **Lone Pine Koala Sanctuary** to cuddle this famous marsupial. Make a day of it by catching the **MV *Miramar*** cruise from Brisbane Cultural Centre to Lone Pine, which departs at 10 am.

Hand-feed kangaroos and emus, take in the sheepdog show, and get your photo with a koala. Upon your return, catch a green cab (rickshaw) or CityCat ferry from South Bank to New Farm, where you can relax with a sunset drink at the **Brisbane Powerhouse.**

Rise early the following morning to join a day tour from Brisbane to **Moreton Island.** An easy 75-minute cruise from the Port of Brisbane, you can spend the day snorkeling, kayaking, or sailing in the island's azure waters. Most tours include transfers, lunch, and activities packages, and will have you back at your hotel in Brisbane by nightfall.

DAYS 9–12: SUNSHINE COAST

The next morning, drive north on the Bruce Highway for roughly 90 minutes to the Sunshine Coast. This region is less densely populated than its southern counterpart, with larger distances between towns and beaches, so a rental car is your best bet for the final leg of your journey.

Check into a hotel overlooking one of the region's top beaches at **Caloundra, Mooloolaba, Coolum, Maroochydoore,** or **Noosa** for the next two nights. After you've settled in, join a tour to the **Teewah Coloured Sands,** an area of spectacular multicolor dunes outside Noosa. You could also book a river cruise or canoe trip with **Everglades Ecosafaris.** In May to November, migrating whales pass through this area; try spotting them from the headland, or treat yourself to an unforgettable whale-watching cruise.

The next morning, make the short journey west to Beerwah, home of Steve Irwin's **Australia Zoo.** Here you can spend the day getting to know a wide range of Australian animals, including the park's most famous residents: crocodiles. Once you've finished at the park, travel south another 15 minutes to **The Glasshouse Mountains Lookout,** a place of natural mystique and Aboriginal legend.

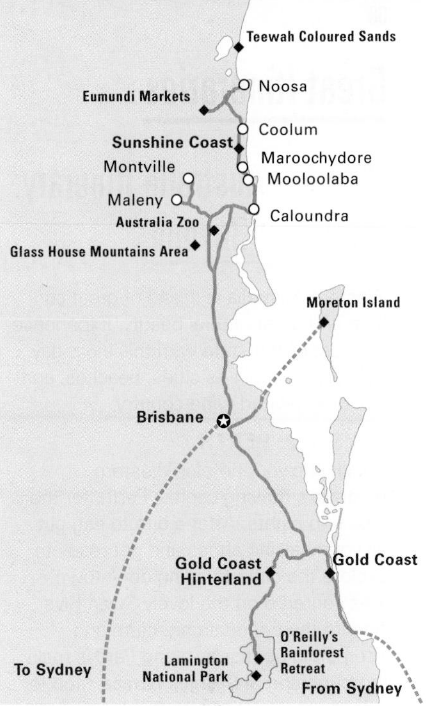

Head inland to its Sunshine Coast's tranquil hinterland on the final day. Browse the area's famous **Eumundi Markets** (open only on Wednesday and Saturday). The best of the region's B&Bs and retreats are clustered around **Maleny** and **Montville**: picturesque mountain villages full of charming cottage gardens, eclectic shops and cafés, and sweeping views to the coast.

Drive back to Brisbane the following morning and catch a plane back to Sydney.

Great Itineraries

Western Australia Itinerary: Perth and Beyond

Western Australia is a land of great contrast and great natural beauty. Experience the best of the state with this eight-day itinerary taking in its cities, beaches, and world-renowned wine country.

DAYS 1–2: PERTH

Check into your hotel in Western Australia's thriving capital, Perth, for the next two nights. After a bite to eat, put on your walking shoes and get ready to explore the city's bustling downtown area centered on the lovely Swan River. Admire the period architecture and interesting boutiques along Perth's main thoroughfare, **St Georges Terrace,** stop for a photo at quaint **London Court,** a replica of a Tudor England, and then continue on to leafy **King's Park**—1,000 acres of greenery in the city. Here, you can admire the native wildflowers, take a treetop walk, join a guided tour, learn about the city's history, and enjoy stunning panoramic views of the CBD below. Afterward, head back to the city center for a leisurely dinner at one of the many alfresco restaurants along the banks of the Swan River.

Rise early to make the most of your second day in Perth. Sate your appetite with breakfast at trendy Northbridge, before a morning of cultural learning the **Art Gallery of Western Australia.** After lunch, slap on the sunscreen and board a train to **Cottesloe,** Perth's most popular beach. Take a dip, book in for a surf lesson, or simply stroll the esplanade, taking in the view as the day dissolves over the ocean.

DAYS 3–4: FREMANTLE AND ROTTNEST ISLAND

No trip to Western Australia is complete without a visit to **Fremantle,** a cosmopolitan port city, brimming with heritage architecture and natural beauty. While "Freo," as the locals call it, is only a 40-minute train ride from the Perth CBD, this port city is best accessed the traditional way: by boat. Departing Barrack Street Jetty, **Captain Cook Cruises** escorts you along the Swan River to Fremantle. Upgrade your ticket to include a **Fremantle Tram Tour** upon arrival, and you'll be ready to conquer your choice of attractions: **The Fremantle Market, Fremantle Prison, Western Australian Maritime Museum,** the **Round House,** and **Kings Square.** As night falls, treat yourself to dinner at one of Freo's many impressive seafood restaurants, or feast alfresco with takeout from iconic harborside fish-and-chippery **Cicerello's.**

The following day, make your way to the crown jewel of the region: beautiful **Rottnest Island.** This former penal colony has been reborn as a prized holiday destination, enticing visitors with its warm, clear waters, laid-back vibe, and stunning array of tropical fish, coral, and marine life. Whether by helicopter, air taxi, or ferry, the island is an easy jaunt from downtown Fremantle. Join a chartered cruise for dolphin, whale, and seal spotting, as well as snorkeling and diving tours. Visit **Rottnest Mueum** and the **Wadjemup Lighthouse,** take the scenic **Oliver Hill Train,** or simply float the day away at **Little Salmon Bay,** a snorkeling haven full of colorful fish and coral reefs. Overnight at one of the hotels or villas on island, or return to Fremantle for a well-earned rest.

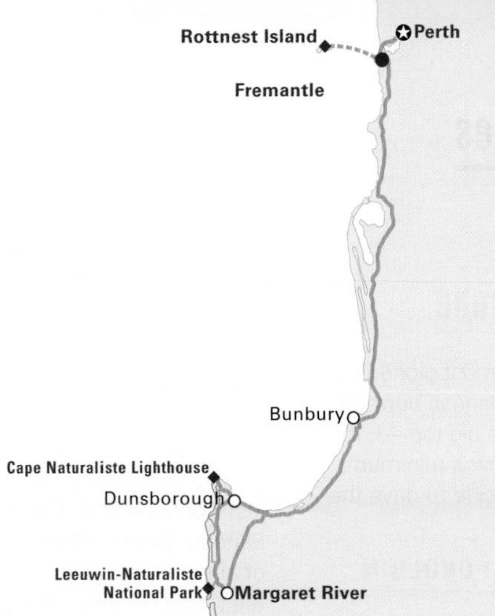

DAYS 5–8: MARGARET RIVER

After all that beach time, it's time for something completely different: wine tourism in the South West Wine Region, Western Australia's most popular tourist destination. It's best either to go with a guided tour or to rent a car to make the final leg of your journey a breeze. Drive two hours south to **Bunbury,** where you can spend the afternoon swimming with dolphins or relaxing on a whale-watching cruise (in season). Afterward, travel south another 70 minutes to the picturesque coastal town of **Margaret River,** your base for the next three nights.

While the beaches of Margaret River entice with their sparkling waters and dramatic headlands, it's the surrounding wine country that really tempts travelers. Though many top wineries are only a short drive away, your best bet is to put safety first and let someone else take care of the driving for you. A range of winery tours departs Margaret River daily, letting travelers taste their way through the best of the region's vineyards, microbreweries, and providores.

Alternately, those with a taste for adventure will find plenty to do in and around Margaret River itself, including surfing, horse riding, rock climbing, whale-watching, and hiking. Some of the region's best trails run through the nearby **Leeuwin-Naturaliste National Park,** where rugged coastline, ancient caves, and dense bushland all meet to reward hikers with stunning biodiversity and breathtaking views.

Bid Margaret River adieu by venturing 50 minutes north to the quaint **Cape Naturaliste Lighthouse,** where a short 1½-km (1-mile) walk rewards you with uninterrupted ocean views and the chance to spot migrating whales. Top off the afternoon by indulging your sweet tooth at the iconic **Simmo's Ice Creamery** in downtown **Dunsborough,** just a 15-minute drive away, before making the three-hour journey back to Perth.

Great Itineraries

Road Trip: From Sydney to Brisbane

Drive along one of the most glorious and seductive stretches of land in northern New South Wales. It's a big trip—1,100 km (687 miles)—so allow a minimum of seven days if you decide to drive the entire route.

DAY 1: SYDNEY TO POKOLBIN, 175 KM (109 MILES)

Start the journey heading north out of Sydney, with the famed Harbour Bridge in your rearview mirror. Take the Sydney–Newcastle (F3) Freeway about 75 km (47 miles) north to the Peats Ridge Road exit, and wind through the forested hills to Wollombi, a delightful town founded in 1820. Browse the antiques shops, sandstone courthouse, and museum. Next, head northeast to Cessnock and Pokolbin, the hub of the Lower Hunter, and spend the day tasting—and buying—fine wines and artisanal cheeses. Know that Australia has a strict 0.5 blood alcohol limit when driving. Be sure to choose a designated driver or, better yet, take one of our recommended wine-tasting tours.

DAY 2: POKOLBIN TO PORT MACQUARIE, 271 KM (168 MILES)

Get up early with the birds and drive east via Cessnock to the Pacific Highway. Turn north for the long drive to Port Macquarie, Australia's third-oldest settlement. Have a well-earned lunch break in the café at Sea Acres Rainforest Centre and then stroll the elevated boardwalk—or take a guided tour—through centuries-old cabbage tree palms. Make a quick visit to the Koala Hospital in Port Macquarie for feeding time (3 pm), and then head into town for a lazy afternoon on a beach. The most pressing question is: Which of the 13 regional beaches should you laze on?

DAY 3: PORT MACQUARIE TO COFFS, 260 KM (162½ MILES)

After a rest and an alfresco breakfast, resume driving up the Pacific Highway. Leave the highway 140 km (88 miles) north at the exit to Bellingen, one of the prettiest towns on the New South Wales north coast. It's a nice place to stop for lunch and a quick peek into a few galleries. Continue inland up onto the Dorrigo Plateau. Dorrigo National Park is one of about 50 reserves and parks within the World Heritage–listed Gondwana Rainforests of Australia. Stopping into the Dorrigo Rainforest Centre to learn about the area is gratifying, as is the forest canopy Skywalk. Back in your car, drive on to Dorrigo town and turn right onto the winding, partly unpaved, but scenic road to Corumba and Coffs Harbour. Now you've earned a two-night stay in Coffs.

DAY 4: COFFS, NO DRIVING

Scuba dive on the Solitary Isles? White-water raft the Nymboida River? Or kick back on a beach? However you spend your day, don't miss an evening stroll to Muttonbird Island from Coffs Harbour marina. From September to April you can watch muttonbirds (or shearwaters) returning to their burrows. When the whales are about, it's also a good humpback viewing spot.

DAY 5: COFFS TO BYRON BAY, 247 KM (154 MILES)

Drive north again, past Coffs Harbour's landmark Big Banana and up the coast to Byron Bay.

There is just too much to do in Byron: kayak with dolphins; dive with gray nurse sharks; go beachcombing and swimming; tread the Cape Byron Walking Track; or tour the lighthouse atop Cape Byron, which is mainland Australia's easternmost point. It's best to decide over lunch at open-air Beach Byron Bay Café, a local legend. When the sun sets, wash off the salt and head out for some great seafood and then overnight in Byron Bay—there's everything from hostels to high-end villas.

DAY 6: BYRON BAY TO MURWILLUMBAH, 53 KM (33 MILES)

Catch up on the Byron Bay you missed yesterday before driving north to Murwillumbah and its remarkable natural landmark. Wollumbin (Mt. Warning) is the 3,800-foot magma chamber of an extinct shield volcano. Drive to the Pinnacle Walk and Lookout, not far from the arty village of Uki. From here, on a clear day, there is a 360-degree view of one of the world's largest calderas, with mountainous rims on three sides and the Tweed River running through its eroded east rim. Afterward, reward yourself with a night at the EcOasis Resort (bookings essential).

DAY 7: MURWILLUMBAH TO BRISBANE, 50 KM (31 MILES)

Relaxed and reinvigorated, you should make your way over the New South Wales border to Queensland and Australia's most developed stretch of coastline. With Brisbane just 90 minutes' drive farther north, you can spend as much or as little time as you want on the Gold Coast. Visit theme parks; toss dice at the casino; ride waves in gorgeous sunshine. Don't miss feeding the lorikeets at Currumbin Wildlife Sanctuary before Brisbane beckons.

Tips

- Unleaded petrol, diesel, and LPG are available at gas stations along most of this route.
- Motel rooms are easy to find, except during school holidays and long weekends. To avoid driving around after a day at the wheel, book ahead. The staff at your previous night's accommodation should be able to help you arrange the next night.
- If hiring a car for the trip, check that it contains a GPS. In case of technological failures, pick up a good road map or touring atlas before heading out of Sydney.
- Mobile speed radars are used throughout Australia, and fines are high. Stick to the speed limits.

Great Itineraries

Road Trip: Great Ocean Road

Arguably one of the country's most spectacular drives, the iconic Great Ocean Road hugs the windswept, rugged coastline just west of Melbourne. Allow six days for this 900-km (562-mile) road trip and be prepared to enjoy some of Victoria's best.

DAY 1: MELBOURNE TO APOLLO BAY, 187 KM (117 MILES)

Having escaped Melbourne, drive down the Princes Freeway for about 75 km (47 miles) to the Torquay/Great Ocean Road turnoff. A quarter-hour more at the wheel brings you to Torquay, Australia's premier surfing and windsurfing resort town. On your way out of town, detour to Bell's Beach, the setting for Australia's principal surfing competition each Easter. The renowned Great Ocean Road officially starts 30 km (19 miles) beyond Bell's Beach, but the dramatic splendor of Victoria's southwest coast reveals itself sooner.

Stop in Lorne, at the foot of the lush Otway Ranges, for lunch. Once you're back on the road, slow down and enjoy it. The winding Great Ocean Road is narrow; don't pass unless you can see far ahead. There are designated pull-over areas where you can safely enjoy the vista.

Drive the 45 km (28 miles) to Apollo Bay for dinner and the night.

DAY 2: APOLLO BAY TO PORT FAIRY, 234 KM (146 MILES)

The 91-km (57-mile) Great Ocean Walk starts just west of Apollo Bay in Marengo. Here the Great Ocean Road heads inland. Stay on the main road to Lavers Hill; then detour about 17 km (11 miles) east to the Otway Fly. This 1,969-foot-long elevated treetop walk takes you up into the rain-forest canopy for a bird's-eye view of giant myrtle beech, blackwood, and mighty mountain ash. Backtrack to Lavers Hill and the Great Ocean Road. The road's most famous landmarks lie along a 32-km (20-mile) stretch of coast within Port Campbell National Park.

First stop is the Twelve Apostles. Take a helicopter flight for a jaw-dropping view of the coast. Next stop is Loch Ard Gorge, a natural gallery of sea sculpture. Don't stay in your car if the sun doesn't show, though. Only when a howling wind is roughing up the Southern Ocean will you fully appreciate why this is called the Shipwreck Coast. Leaving the Great Ocean Road now, drive to the maritime village of Port Fairy for the night. In whale season (June–November), divert to Logan's Beach, in Warrnambool, where southern right cows and calves often loll just off the beach.

DAY 3: PORT FAIRY TO HALLS GAP, 146 KM (91 MILES)

Take a leisurely postbreakfast promenade around Port Fairy, Victoria's second-oldest town and widely considered to be its prettiest. Then backtrack 7 km (4½ miles) to the Penshurst/Dunkeld Road and drive 74 km (46 miles) north to Dunkeld, on the edge of the Grampians National Park. Stop for lunch before undertaking the 60-km (37-mile) drive to Halls Gap. Be sure to slow down and enjoy one of the most picturesque drives in the Grampians; pull in at the Brambuk Cultural Centre, just before Halls Gap, and learn about the park's rich Aboriginal history. Check into your Halls Gap accommodation for two nights.

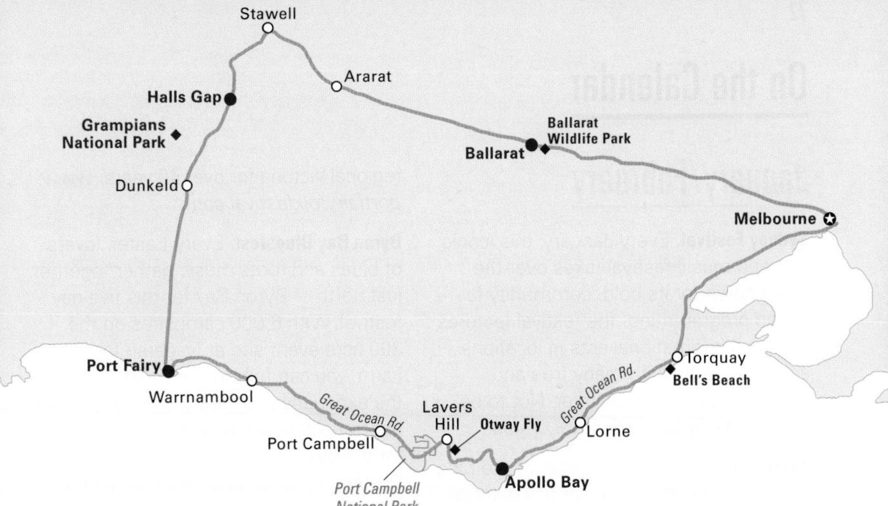

DAY 4: GRAMPIANS NATIONAL PARK, NO DRIVING

Spend a day exploring on foot. Walks of varied grades showcase the Grampians' extraordinary geology; don't miss the Pinnacle Walk, just out of Halls Gap, the valley and ranges view from Chatauqua Peak, and Hollow Mountain in the park's north.

DAY 5: HALLS GAP TO BALLARAT, 140 KM (88 MILES)

Drive out of Halls Gap to Ararat, on the Western Highway, and follow the highway east to the famous gold town of Ballarat. Spend the rest of the morning among the gold-rush-era Victorian architecture on Sturt and Lydiard Streets. Visit the Ballarat Fine Art Gallery, if only to see the tattered remains of the Southern Cross flag that the rebels flew during the 1854 Eureka uprising over mine license fees. Spend the afternoon at Sovereign Hill, where you can pan for gold, ride a horse-drawn stagecoach, and stick your teeth together with old-fashioned candy.

DAY 6: BALLARAT TO MELBOURNE, 111 KM (69 MILES)

Have encounters with saltwater crocodiles, snakes, wombats, kangaroos, and other Australian fauna at Ballarat Wildlife Park. After that, continue your journey or head back to Melbourne.

Tips

- Unleaded petrol, diesel, and LPG are available at gas stations in major centers; however, LPG is rare in small country towns.
- There is a petrol price cycle in Victoria; try to fill up on Tuesday and Wednesday, and avoid buying fuel on Friday.
- Choosing accommodation as you go gives you flexibility in when and where you stop. For peace of mind, though, you might prefer to prebook.
- Fixed speed radars are used on Victoria's major freeways, and fines are high. Stick to the speed limits.
- Watch for animals straying onto the road, especially on rural roads near sunset and sunrise.

On the Calendar

January/February

Sydney Festival. Every January, this iconic arts and music festival takes over the city. Known for its bold, community-focused programming, the festival features local and international acts in locations across the city, with many free and child-friendly events on offer. Not to be missed. *www.sydneyfestival.org.au.*

Parkes Elvis Festival. For lovers of the King and kitsch, head to this five-day extravaganza dedicated to all things Elvis in rural New South Wales. *www.parkeselvisfestival.com.au.*

Australian Open. The first of four annual grand-slam tennis events is held in Melbourne every January. For tennis fans and sports lovers alike. *ausopen.com.*

Sydney Gay and Lesbian Mardi Gras. One of the world's longest-standing, iconic celebrations of LGBTQI pride takes place each February in Sydney. Book early, and prepare to dance and be bedazzled. *www.mardigras.org.au.*

Adelaide Fringe. Head to Adelaide in February for the southern hemisphere's biggest arts festival. Featuring theater, music, cabaret, visual arts, and more in venues across Adelaide and South Australia, this monthlong festival is the ideal way to toast the end of summer. *www.adelaidefringe.com.au.*

March/April

Port Fairy Folk Music Festival. In March, head to Port Fairy on Victoria's south coast for four days of music, arts, and culture. Featuring local and international acts, this world-famous festival has been bringing arts, culture, and folk music to regional Victoria for over 40 years. *www.portfairyfolkfestival.com.*

Byron Bay Bluesfest. Every Easter, lovers of blues and roots music gather together just north of Byron Bay for this five-day festival. With 6,000 campsites on the 300-acre event site at Tyagarah Tea Tree Farm, you can fully immerse yourself in the experience, or take a break from your beach holiday and head to the festival for the day. The Boomerang Festival features First Nations performances and workshops as part of the Bluesfest lineup. *www.bluesfest.com.au.*

Melbourne International Comedy Festival. For a few weeks in March and April, comedy takes over central Melbourne. One of the three largest comedy festivals in the world, the festival brings together comic acts from around Australia and the world, with a focus on irreverence, creativity, and innovation. *www.comedyfestival.com.au.*

May/June

Vivid Sydney–Light, Music and Ideas. This annual festival lights up Sydney's harborside precinct and city streets, including iconic structures like the Harbour Bridge and Opera House, with innovative art displays and 3–D light projections. The festival also features a lineup of curated musical events and thought-provoking talks. *www.vividsydney.com.*

Uluru Camel Cup. Head to Uluru in the heart of the Northern Territory for a weekend of Outback fun. There's plenty to see and do on and off the racetrack, with whip-cracking displays, helicopter rides, and a starlit ball all on offer. *www.ulurucamelracingclub.com.*

Hunter Valley Food & Wine Festival. With events happening across the month of June, head to the renowned wine region north of Sydney. Amid warm autumn days and crisp nights, enjoy long lunches, wine tasting, and fireside conversation. *www.winecountry.com.au/events/wine-and-food-festival.*

Blues on Broadbeach. Draws a range of international and Australian acts to perform across Broadbeach on the Gold Coast, and best of all it's all free! Takes place across four days in May, when the air and sea are still balmy; the ideal time for a visit to the Gold Coast. *www.bluesonbroadbeach.com.*

July/August

Laura Quinkan Dance Festival. Showcasing stories enacted through dance, celebrating culture and recognizing history, the Laura Quinkan Dance Festival takes place in Laura, Cape York, in July. *www.lauraquinkanfestival.com.au.*

Huon Valley Midwinter Festival. Head to the apple orchards of Tasmania for a celebration of the region's apple-harvest history. *www.huonvalleymidwinterfest.com.au.*

Darwin Festival. Head to the Top End in August, when the days are warm and dry, the nights are cool, and the Darwin Festival takes over town. *www.darwin-festival.org.au.*

September/October

Brisbane Festival. Evolving from the Warana Festival, which started in 1961 with the theme "entertainment for the people, by the people," this citywide event takes place each September. *www.brisbanefestival.com.au.*

Birdsville Races. One of Australia's most iconic annual events, this horse-race meet in far-flung Birdsville, a frontier town on the edge of the Simpson Desert, is well worth the pilgrimage. The program also includes bush cricket and boxing displays. *www.birdsvilleraces.com.*

Floriade. Australia's biggest springtime celebration takes place every September in the nation's capital, Canberra. Each year, Canberra's Commonwealth Park is filled with more than 1 million blooms. The monthlong flower festival also features an array of music and cultural events. *www.floriadeaustralia.com.*

Sculpture by the Sea. The world's largest free outdoor public art exhibition takes place every year along the coastline between Bondi and Coogee in Sydney. *www.sculpturebythesea.com.*

November/December

Western Australia Gourmet Escape. Western Australia is justifiably world famous for its food and wine, and there is no better time to experience the region's culinary delights than at the Gourmet Escape in November. Many of the world's culinary superstars rub shoulders with local talent, showcasing premium produce and wine in Perth, Rottnest Island, Swan Valley, and the Margaret River Region. *www.gourmetescape.com.au.*

Sydney New Year's Eve. One of the world's great New Year's Eve parties and fireworks displays and a truly once-in-a-lifetime experience. Join the crowds at Circular Quay, book in to a harborside hotel, or spend the night on a chartered yacht for a memorable start to the new year. *www.sydney.com/destinations/sydney/sydney-city/new-years-eve-sydney.*

Contacts

Air

AIRPORTS Brisbane Airport. *07/3406–3000* *www.bne.com.au.* **Melbourne Airport.** *03/9297–1600* *www.melbourneairport.com.au.* **Sydney Airport.** *02/9667–9111* *www.sydneyairport.com.au.*

AIRLINES Qantas. *1800/227–4500 in U.S., 131–313 in Australia* *www.qantas.com.au.*

Boat and Ferry

Great Barrier Reef Marine Park Authority. *07/4750–0700* *www.gbrmpa.gov.au.* **Spirit of Tasmania.** *1800/634–906* *www.spiritoftasmania.com.au.* **Sealink Ferries.** *131–301* *www.sealink.com.au.*

Bus

Greyhound Australia. *1300/473–946* *www.greyhound.com.au.* **Murrays Coaches.** *132–251* *www.murrays.com.au.* **Public Transport Victoria.** *03/9662–2505* *www.ptv.vic.gov.au.* **Transport NSW.** *02/4907–7501* *transportnsw.info.*

Car and Taxi

Australian Automobile Association. *02/6247–7311* *www.aaa.asn.au.* **Taxis Combined (Victoria, NSW and South Australia).** *132–227* *www.taxiscombined.com.au.*

Embassy

CANBERRA U.S. Embassy. *Moonah Pl., Yarralumla, Canberra* *02/6214–5600* *au.usembassy.gov/embassy-consulates/canberra.*

PERTH U.S. Consulate. *16 St. George's Tce., Perth* *08/6144–5100* *au.usembassy.gov/embassy-consulates/perth.*

SYDNEY U.S. Consulate. *MLC Centre, 19–29 Martin Pl., Level 10, Sydney* *300/139–399* *au.usembassy.gov/embassy-consulates/sydney.*

Train

Public Transport Victoria. *03/9662–2505* *www.ptv.vic.gov.au.* **Rail Australia.** *1800/872–467 in Australia, 07/3235–1122 outside Australia* *www.railaustralia.com.au.* **Transport NSW.** *02/4907–7501* *transportnsw.info.*

Visitor Information

CANBERRA *02/6205–0044* *visitcanberra.com.au*

NATIONAL PARKS *1800/803–772* *www.environment.gov.au*

NEW SOUTH WALES *1800/067–676* *www.visitnsw.com*

NORTHERN TERRITORY *1300/138–886* *northernterritory.com*

QUEENSLAND *07/3535–3535* *teq.queensland.com*

SOUTH AUSTRALIA *1300/588–140* *southaustralia.com*

TASMANIA *03/6238–4222* *www.discovertasmania.com.au*

VICTORIA *03/9658–9658* *www.visitvictoria.com*

WESTERN AUSTRALIA *08/9483–1111* *www.westernaustralia.com*

Chapter 3

SYDNEY

Updated by
Amy Nelmes Bissett

Sights	Restaurants	Hotels	Shopping	Nightlife
★★★★☆	★★★★★	★★★★★	★★★☆☆	★★★☆☆

WELCOME TO SYDNEY

TOP REASONS TO GO

★ **A Harbor Sail:** Take a ferry, sail a yacht, or paddle a kayak, but make sure you get out into Sydney Harbour. It's a glorious sight. Check out the Sydney Harbour section for tours of the harbor by boat.

★ **A Night at the Opera:** From rock to rap, theater to tap dancing, there's always something interesting happening at the world's most famous playhouse.

★ **Exquisite Dining:** Sydney restaurants are among the finest eateries in the world. Don't miss out on the fresh seafood and top-notch Mod Oz and Asian cuisines.

★ **Glorious Beaches:** Sydneysiders are besotted by the beach, and you'll be, too. With 100 to choose from, you can watch surfers ride the waves or paddle around the calmer waters of a sheltered harbor beach.

★ **National Parks and Wildlife:** Sydney's untamed beauty is close at hand. See native birds and colorful wildflowers just a few miles from the city.

Sydney is built around its huge harbor. The city center and main attractions are on the south shore. Harbour Bridge connects The Rocks on the south side with Milsons Point on the north side. Greater Sydney is vast, some 80 km (50 miles) from north to south and 70 km (43 miles) from east to west; however, the city center is relatively small. From the Opera House and Circular Quay the city stretches south for about 3 km (2 miles), and east to west for about 2 km (1 mile). Beyond the harbor, the city center is essentially a business and shopping precinct, with colonial and modern buildings. The restaurant and nightlife suburbs of Darlinghurst, Surry Hills, and Potts Point flank the city's eastern and southern edges.

1 Sydney Harbour. This spectacular waterway has a 240-km (149-mile) shoreline of bays, headlands, and quiet beaches. It's the city's jewel.

2 The Rocks. Sydney's oldest area, The Rocks, is full of restored 19th-century warehouses and pubs with great views of the famous bridge.

3 Domain and Macquarie Street. This stately quarter of town contains Parliament House, formal gardens, and the Domain, where concerts are staged.

4 The Opera House and the Royal Botanic Gardens. The white "sails" of the Opera House dominate the harbor; the neighboring Royal Botanic Gardens are an oasis on the harbor's edge.

5 Darling Harbour and Barangaroo. A former goods yard on the city's western edge, Darling Harbour now houses museums, the aquarium, restaurants, and hotels while neighboring Barangaroo is a newly opened precinct with waterfront restaurants, bars, and stores.

6 Sydney City Center. Dominated by 880-foot Sydney Tower, the city center is packed with historic and modern shopping arcades.

7 Inner City and the Eastern Suburbs. A few miles east of the city you'll find palatial harborside homes, beaches, and café-culture, bohemian-chic enclaves.

8 Greater Sydney. National parks, beautiful beaches, and relics of Sydney's colonial past can all be explored within an hour of the city center.

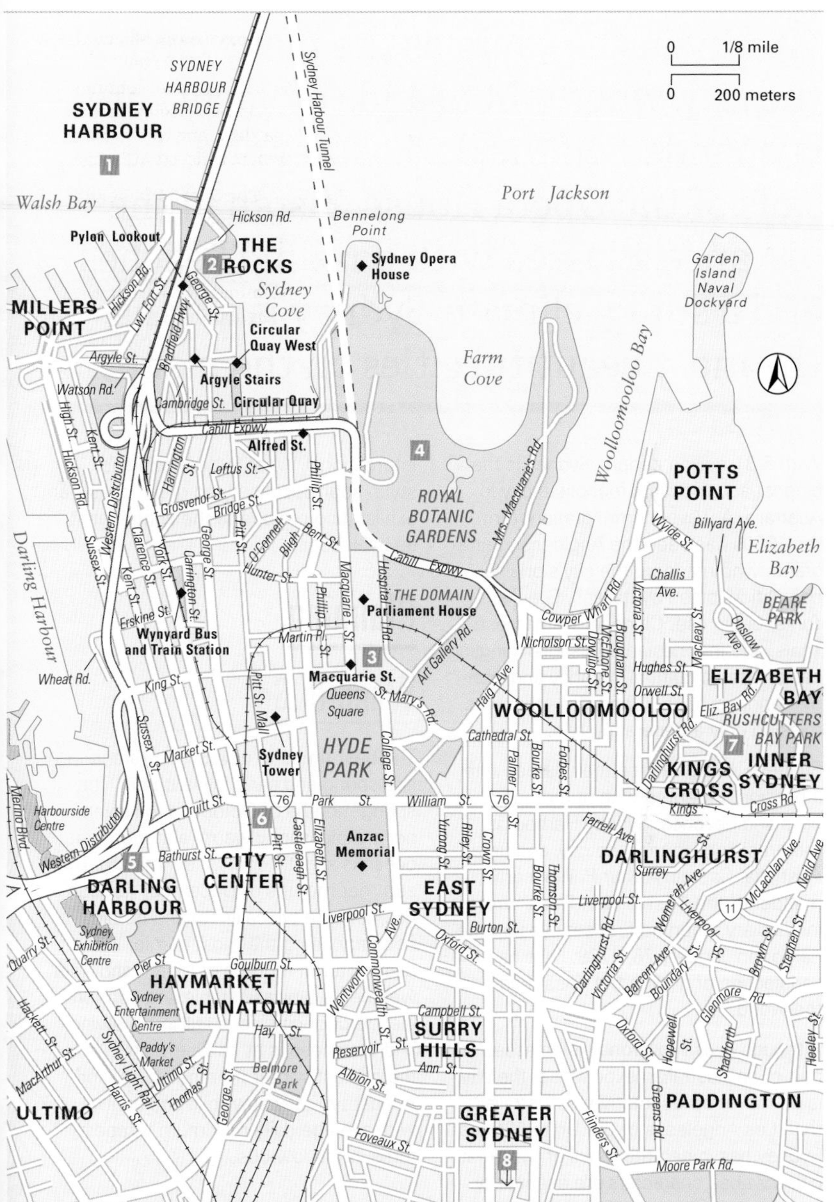
SYDNEY HARBOUR BRIDGE
SYDNEY HARBOUR
Walsh Bay
Pylon Lookout
THE ROCKS
MILLERS POINT
Sydney Cove
Circular Quay West
Argyle Stairs
Circular Quay
Alfred St.
Bennelong Point
Sydney Opera House
Port Jackson
Farm Cove
ROYAL BOTANIC GARDENS
THE DOMAIN
Parliament House
Macquarie St.
Queens Square
HYDE PARK
Sydney Tower
Wynyard Bus and Train Station
Darling Harbour
Harbourside Centre
DARLING HARBOUR
CITY CENTER
Anzac Memorial
EAST SYDNEY
WOOLLOOMOOLOO
Woolloomooloo Bay
Garden Island Naval Dockyard
POTTS POINT
Elizabeth Bay
BEARE PARK
ELIZABETH BAY
RUSHCUTTERS BAY PARK
KINGS CROSS
INNER SYDNEY
DARLINGHURST
Sydney Exhibition Centre
HAYMARKET
CHINATOWN
Sydney Entertainment Centre
Paddy's Market
Belmore Park
ULTIMO
SURRY HILLS
GREATER SYDNEY
PADDINGTON
0 1/8 mile
0 200 meters

Sydney belongs to the exclusive club of cities that generate excitement. At the end of a marathon flight there's renewed vitality in the cabin as the plane circles the city, where thousands of yachts are suspended on the dark water and the sails of the Opera House glisten in the distance. Blessed with dazzling beaches and a sunny climate, Sydney is among the most beautiful cities on the planet.

With 5.31 million people, Sydney is the biggest and most cosmopolitan city in Australia. A wave of immigration from the 1950s has seen the Anglo-Irish immigrants who made up the city's original population joined by Italians, Greeks, Turks, Lebanese, Chinese, Vietnamese, Thais, and Indonesians. This intermingling has created a cultural vibrancy and energy—and a culinary repertoire—that was missing only a generation ago.

Sydneysiders embrace their harbor with a passion. Indented with numerous bays and beaches, Sydney Harbour is the presiding icon for the city, and urban Australia. Captain Arthur Phillip, commander of the 11-ship First Fleet, wrote in his diary when he first set eyes on the harbor on January 26, 1788: "We had the satisfaction of finding the finest harbor in the world."

Although a visit to Sydney is an essential part of an Australian experience, the city is no more representative of Australia than Los Angeles is of the United States. Sydney has joined the ranks of the great cities whose characters are essentially international. What Sydney offers is style, sophistication, and great looks—an exhilarating prelude to the continent at its back door.

Planning

When to Go

The best times to visit Sydney are in late spring and early fall (autumn). The spring months of October and November are pleasantly warm, although the ocean is slightly cool for swimming. The summer months of December through February are typically hot and humid, February being the most humid. In the early autumn months of March and April weather is typically stable and comfortable, outdoor city life is still in full swing, and the ocean is at its warmest. Even the coolest winter months of July and August typically stay mild and sunny, with average daily maximum temperatures in the low 60s.

Planning Your Time

You really need three days in Sydney to see the essential city center, while six days would give you time to explore the beaches and inner suburbs.

Start with an afternoon **Harbour Express Cruise** for some of the best views of the city. Follow with a tour of **The Rocks,** the nation's birthplace, and take a sunset walk up onto the **Sydney Harbour Bridge.** The following day, take a tour of the famous **Sydney Opera House** and a stroll through the **Royal Botanic Gardens** to visit **Mrs. Macquarie's Chair** for a wonderful view of the harbor icons. Spend some time exploring the city center and another spectacular panorama from the top of **Sydney Tower.** Include a walk around Macquarie Street, a living reminder of Sydney's colonial history, and, if you have time, the contrasting experience of futuristic Darling Harbour, with its museums and aquarium, and colorful, aromatic **Chinatown.** Barangaroo, the city's trendy new multimillion-dollar harbor-front development is a must visit. You'll find a range of restaurants, lots of activity and people-watching, and plenty of shopping options.

On your third day make your way to **Bondi,** Australia's most famous beach, and if the weather is kind follow the cliff-top walking path to Coogee Beach. The next day catch the ferry to **Manly** to visit its beach and the historic Quarantine Station. From here, take an afternoon bus tour to the northern beaches, or return to the city to shop or visit museums and galleries. Options for the last day include a trip to the **Blue Mountains** west of the city or a wildlife park such as **WILD LIFE Sydney Zoo** at Darling Harbour or **Taronga Zoo,** on the north side of the harbor.

Getting Here and Around

AIR

Sydney's main airport is Kingsford–Smith International, 8 km (5 miles) south of the city. Kingsford–Smith's international (T1) and domestic terminals (T2 and T3) are 3 km (2 miles) apart. To get from one to the other, take a taxi for about A$22, use the complimentary Airport Shuttle Bus (called the TBus; it takes 10 minutes), or take the Airport Link train, A$13.80, which takes two minutes. Destination New South Wales has two information counters in the arrivals level of the international terminal. One provides free maps and brochures and handles general inquiries. The other books accommodations and tours, and sells travel insurance. Both counters are open daily from approximately 6 am to 11 pm. You can convert your money to Australian currency at the Travelex offices in both the arrival and departure areas.

AIRPORT TRANSFERS

Airport Link rail travels to the city center in 15 minutes. A one-way fare is A$13.80. Taxis are available outside the terminal buildings. Fares are about A$45 to A$55 to city and Kings Cross hotels. There are a couple of shuttle-bus services from the airport that drop passenger at hotels in the city center, Kings Cross, and Darling Harbour for around A$15 to A$17 one-way and A$28 round-trip.

TIP→ Passengers with only a little luggage can save money by taking the state government–run bus No. 400, to Bondi Junction. The fare is a mere A$5 for the hour-long bus ride, and is ideal for those staying at nearby Bondi Beach.

BUS

Bus travel in Sydney is slow due to congested streets and the undulating terrain. Fares are calculated in sections; the minimum section fare (A$3.80) applies to trips in the inner-city area, such as between Circular Quay and Kings Cross, or from Bondi Junction railway station to Bondi Beach. Bus information can be found at www.transportnsw.info.

CAR

With the assistance of a good road map you shouldn't have too many problems driving in and out of Sydney, thanks to the decent freeway system. However, driving a car around Sydney is not recommended because of congestion and lack of parking space. If you decide to drive a rental car, it costs between A$75 and A$85 per day. Local operator Bayswater Car Rental has cars from as little as A$31 per day (on a seven-day rental plan) for a one-year-old vehicle. Camper vans that sleep two people can be hired from operator Jucy Rentals for A$39 a day and A$130 in the January peak season.

CRUISE

There are two cruise ship terminals in Sydney. The Overseas Passenger Terminal (OPT) is on the western side of Circular Quay in the heart of The Rocks; White Bay Cruise Terminal is in Rozelle, 6 km (4 miles) west of the city center. There is a taxi stand near the White Bay terminal, and it's the best way to get into the city center for sightseeing, as the nearest public bus stop is around 3 km (2 miles) away—a taxi ride to the city costs around A$20, A$50 to the airport.

TAXI

Taxis charge A$2.19 per km (½ mile), plus a flag fall (hiring charge) of A$3.60. Extra charges apply to baggage weighing more than 55 pounds, telephone bookings, and Harbour Bridge and tunnel tolls. Fares are 20% higher between 10 pm and 6 am, when the numeral "2" will be displayed in the tariff indicator on the meter, plus an additional A$2.50 flag fall surcharge.

■ TIP→ Uber isn't allowed into Sydney's airport for pickups but can be used for drop-offs.

TRAM AND TRAIN

The Sydney Light Rail is an efficient link between Central Station, Darling Harbour, the Star City casino/entertainment complex, Sydney fish markets, and two inner Western Suburbs. The modern trams operate at 10- to 30-minute intervals 24 hours a day. One-way tickets are A$3.20. The main terminal for long-distance, intercity, and Sydney suburban trains is Central Station. There are a number of good-value train passes including the Discovery Pass, which at A$275 (for one month) allows unlimited travel between Sydney, Canberra, Melbourne, and Brisbane. Sydney's suburban train network, City Rail, links the city with dozens of suburbs as well as Blue Mountains and South Coast towns. Tickets start from A$4 one-way and are sold at all City Rail stations. Off-peak day return tickets are the best option.

Discounts and Deals

To save money on admissions into attractions, the best option is **The Sydney Pass** (*www.gocity.com/sydney*), which gets you into 40 Sydney sights and attractions, including the Opera House, Sydney Aquarium, and harbor cruises. Several different cards are available, including four-, five-, and seven-attraction choices. Prices start at A$80 for a pass with entry to three attractions.

NSW Transport operates all of the Sydney trains, buses, and ferries and the best way to travel on these is with an Opal card (it's similar to Oyster in London or Octopus in Hong Kong). Buses in Sydney no longer sell individual tickets so you will need an Opal card to travel. Opal cards can be bought at the airport or from most newsagents throughout the city for free. To top up, there are machines at newsagents, train stations, wharves, and light-rail stops. You can also refill your card online at *www.opal.com.au*. **■ TIP→ Tap your Opal card on the reader when getting on but be sure to tap off, too, or you will be charged for the full route.**

Restaurants

Sydney is blessed with excellent dining. Its 4,500-plus restaurants range from ultrahip and expensive celebrity chef venues overlooking the harbor to übercool eateries in the fringe suburbs of Darlinghurst and Surry Hills to neighborhood Italian and Asian joints loved by locals.

Hotels

The Sydney hotel sector is the strongest in Australia with consistent occupancy levels in the mid to high 80% range and average rates growing sharply. In recent years, the city has seen an influx of new hotels, including the much-anticipated $A2 billion Crown Hotel in Barangaroo, as well as a variety of unique boutique properties in heritage buildings in the city suburbs of Surry Hills, Darlinghurst, and Kings Cross/Potts Point.

Restaurant and hotel reviews have been shortened. For full information, visit Fodors.com.

What It Costs in Australian Dollars

$	$$	$$$	$$$$
RESTAURANTS			
under A$36	A$36–A$45	A$46–A$65	over A$65
HOTELS			
under A$201	A$201–A$300	A$301–A$450	over A$450

Tours

SIGHTSEEING TOURS

Big Bus Tours

This fleet of brightly colored double-decker buses (with open tops) follows two routes: the Sydney route has 25 stops, and the Bondi and Bays has 10 stops. Both trips take 90 minutes. Sydney trips depart Circular Quay at 8:30 am daily (last bus departs at 7:30 pm); the Bondi bus departs Eddy Avenue, Central Station at 9 am daily (last bus at 7:30 pm). ✉ *157 George St., Sydney* ☎ *02/9567–8400* 🌐 *www.bigbustours.com* 🎫 *From A$56.*

Mount 'n Beach Safaris

This operator runs tours to the Blue Mountains and minicoaches around Sydney and the Hunter Valley, from A$257. The company's most popular tour, The Blue Mountains Hike The World Heritage, provides the opportunity to see koalas and kangaroos, have morning tea in the bush, and explore the highlights of the Blue Mountains. ✉ *68 Whiting St., Artarmon, Sydney* ☎ *02/9972–0899* 🌐 *www.mountnbeachsafaris.com.au* 🎫 *From A$257.*

Oz Jet Boating

These bright red boats are the most distinctive of the jet boats operating on Sydney Harbour. The bow is painted with huge white teeth to resemble a shark. The 30-minute rides, at 75 kph (47 mph), zip past the Opera House, Harbour Bridge, and Clark and Shark islands, and perform 270-degree spins. Despite passengers being issued hooded raincoats, they always get wet. At least two trips run every day (at noon and 3) and more on the weekends and in summertime. Rides are A$68, and occasional discounts (for Internet bookings) are offered in the winter and spring. ✉ *Sydney Harbour, Circular Quay, Eastern Pontoon, Sydney Harbour* ☎ *02/9808–3700* 🌐 *www.ozjetboating.com.au* 🎫 *From A$68.*

SPECIAL-INTEREST TOURS

Aboriginal Heritage Tour

The Aboriginal Heritage Tour (A$42) is a tour of the Royal Botanic Gardens' display of plants that were growing before Europeans arrived on Sydney's shores in 1788. The tour, which operates Wednesday, Friday, and Saturday at 10 am (1½ hours duration), is led by an Aboriginal guide who explains the plants and their uses and bush foods. ✉ *Royal Botanic Gardens, Mrs. Macquaries Rd., Circular*

Quay ✣ Tours depart from info booth outside Garden Shop at Palm Grove Centre ☎ 02/9231–8111 🌐 www.rbgsyd.nsw.gov.au 🎫 From A$42.

Bonza Bike Tours
Bonza Bike Tours lets you see the best Sydney sights without having to worry about heavy traffic. The half-day Classic Sydney Tour cruises past the Opera House, winds around the harbor, and cycles through the Royal Botanic Gardens. A bike and helmet are included on all tours. ✉ *30 Harrington St., The Rocks* ☎ *02/9247–8800* 🌐 *www.bonzabiketours.com* 🎫 *From A$129.*

★ BridgeClimb
This unique tour affords the ultimate view of the harbor and city center from Sydney Harbour Bridge. The hugely popular tours take 3½ hours and start at A$168, with sunrise, day, sunset, and nighttime tours available. They are all worth doing, but for sheer romance, the night tour is hard to beat. An option for those on a budget or with a fear of heights is the 90-minute BridgeClimb Sampler, which takes climbers within the bridge's inner arch to a point around halfway to the top. Prices are higher during the peak season December 25–January 14 inclusive. ✉ *5 Cumberland St., The Rocks* ☎ *1300/908–057* 🌐 *www.bridgeclimb.com* 🎫 *From A$168.*

★ Dave's Sydney Pub Tours
This tour lets visitors drink in Sydney's history at five historic—and unique—pubs in The Rocks, and dine on some unusual pizzas during a 3½-hour jaunt. Operated by locals with a passion for handcrafted beers, the walking tour sets off from Harts Pub at 11:30 am, 2:30 pm, and 6:30 pm. It is designed for those who want to learn more about The Rocks' fascinating history (rather than party types). The tour guide regales folks with tales of 19th-century rum smuggling and the quirky characteristics of each watering hole. There's a visit to one of the cellars, which is normally off-limits to the public. Adventurous diners might like to order the kangaroo or even crocodile pizza at the Australian Heritage Hotel. Non–beer drinkers are offered wine or a soft drink at each pub. ✉ *Harts Pub, Essex St. and Gloucester St., The Rocks* ☎ *04/9293–8244* 🌐 *www.daves.com.au* 🎫 *A$99.*

Sydney Seaplanes
A flight on Sydney Seaplanes is a wonderful way to see Sydney's sights and soar over beaches. Short flights take in the harbor, Bondi Beach, and all the way up to the Northern Beaches, including the picture-perfect Palm Beach. The on-site restaurant serves breakfast and lunch with views of the seaplanes taking off from Rose Bay. It's also a fully licensed premises offering cocktails and champagne. ✉ *1 Vickery Ave., Rose Bay* ☎ *1300/732–752* 🌐 *www.seaplanes.com.au* 🎫 *From A$290.*

SYDNEY BY BOAT

Aboriginal Culture Cruise
Former Sydney tugboat the *Mari Nawi* is owned by the Tribal Warrior Association, an organization committed to empowering disadvantaged Aboriginal people. They operate cultural cruises year-round, showing passengers the sights and telling stories associated with tribes including the Eora, Cadigal, and Wangal, who inhabited areas around Sydney Harbour. After departing from Circular Quay, the cruises head to Clark Island for a traditional welcoming ceremony and dance performance. Back on board, passengers are shown cultural landmarks, fishing spots, and ancient rock carvings. The two-hour cruises cost A$66 per person and depart Saturday April–September at 1 pm and October–March at 3 pm. The cruise departs from Eastern Pontoon, Circular Quay. ✉ *Eastern Pontoon, Circular Quay, Sydney Harbour* ☎ *02/9699–3491* 🌐 *www.tribalwarrior.org* 🎫 *From $A66.*

★ Captain Cook Cruises

The best introduction to Sydney Harbour is Captain Cook's two-hour Harbour Story Cruise (A$45), which follows the southern shore to Watsons Bay, crosses to the north shore to explore Middle Harbour, and returns to Circular Quay. Other options include breakfast, lunch, and dinner cruises; and the popular 24-hour Hop-on-Hop-Off ferry service (A$49) to nine stops around the harbor. ✉ *Circular Quay* ☎ *02/9206–1111* 🌐 *www.captaincook.com.au* 🎫 *From A$49.*

Fantasea Yellow Water Taxis

A fun and fast way to get around is by water taxi. Circular Quay to Manly, for example, costs A$80 and A$10 for each extra person. Minitours of the harbor in these little yellow taxi boats begin at A$60 per person for 45 minutes. ✉ *Cockle Bay Wharf, Darling Harbour, Sydney* ☎ *1300/326–822* 🌐 *yellowwatertaxis.com.au* 🎫 *From $60.*

★ Manly Ferry

There is no finer introduction to the city than a trip aboard one of the commuter ferries that ply Sydney Harbour. The hub of the ferry system is Circular Quay, and ferries dock at the almost 30 wharves around the harbor between about 6 am and 11:30 pm. One of the most popular sightseeing trips is the Manly Ferry, a 30-minute journey from Circular Quay that provides glimpses of harborside mansions and the sandstone cliffs and bushland along the north shore. The one-way Manly Ferry fare is A$7.60, and the Manly Fast Ferry, operated by a private company, costs A$9.90 one-way. ✉ *Wharf 2, Circular Quay* ☎ *131–500* 🌐 *www.transportnsw.info* 🎫 *From A$8.*

WALKING TOURS

Ghost Tours

The Rocks' dark alleyways can be scary, and The Rocks Ghost Tours make sure people are suitably spooked, as the guides, dressed in long black cloaks and carrying lanterns, regale them with stories of the murders and other nasty goings-on in the early days of the colony. Tours depart nightly at 6:45 (April–September) and 7:45 (October–March) from Cadmans Cottage. ✉ *Cadmans Cottage, George St. at Argyle St., Circular Quay* ☎ *02/9241–1283* 🌐 *www.ghosttours.com.au* 🎫 *A$45.*

Rocks Walking Tours

Discover Sydney's first European settlement, with an emphasis on the buildings and personalities of the convict period on tours with this operator. The 1½-hour tours leave daily at 10:30 and 1:30. ✉ *Clocktower Sq., Argyle St. at Harrington St., Shop 4a, The Rocks* ☎ *02/9247–6678* 🌐 *www.rockswalkingtours.com.au* 🎫 *$A32.*

Visitor Information

There are information kiosks at locations throughout the city, including Circular Quay (Alfred and Pitt Streets), Martin Place (at Elizabeth Street), and Town Hall (at George and Bathurst Streets).

The Sydney Visitor Centre is the major source of information for Sydney and New South Wales. There are two locations: The Rocks and Darling Harbour.

CONTACTS Sydney Visitor Centre. ✉ *Level 2, The Rocks Centre, Argyle St. at Playfair St., The Rocks* ☎ *02/9251–0643* 🌐 *www.therocks.com.*

Sydney Harbour

On a bright, sunny day there's no more magical sight than glistening Sydney Harbour. The white sails of the Opera House are matched by the dozens of sailing boats skimming across the blue expanse. It's both a hive of activity and blissfully peaceful: it's easy to get away from the bustle in one of this area's many remote little corners. Explore by taking a ferry, walking across the bridge, or hiking around its native bushland edges. But whatever you do, get up close and enjoy the view.

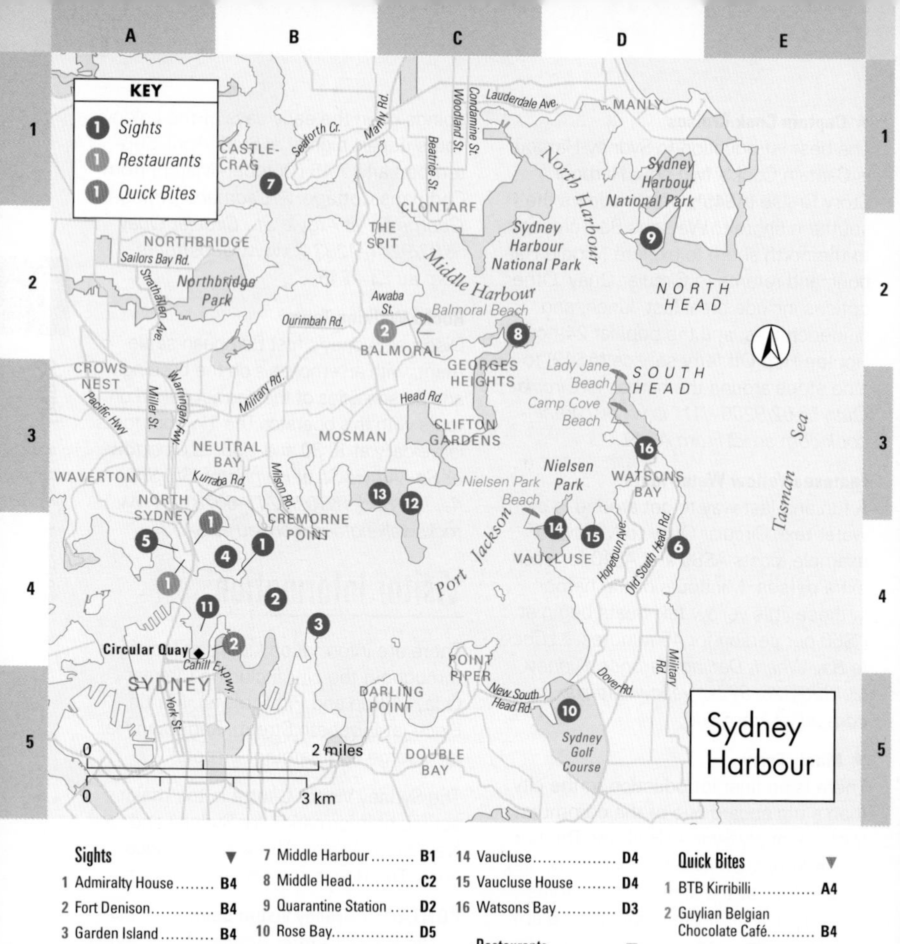

Sights

1 Admiralty House........ **B4**
2 Fort Denison............ **B4**
3 Garden Island........... **B4**
4 Kirribilli................... **B4**
5 Luna Park................ **A4**
6 Macquarie Lighthouse............... **D4**
7 Middle Harbour......... **B1**
8 Middle Head............. **C2**
9 Quarantine Station..... **D2**
10 Rose Bay................. **D5**
11 Sydney Cove............ **A4**
12 Sydney Harbour National Park............. **C3**
13 Taronga Zoo............. **C3**
14 Vaucluse................. **D4**
15 Vaucluse House........ **D4**
16 Watsons Bay............ **D3**

Restaurants

1 Aqua Dining............. **A4**
2 Bathers' Pavilion......... **C2**

Quick Bites

1 BTB Kirribilli............. **A4**
2 Guylian Belgian Chocolate Café.......... **B4**

GETTING HERE AND AROUND

Sydney is well served by public transport. Buses travel from a base in Circular Quay through the city center to the inner suburbs of Kings Cross, Darlinghurst, and Surry Hills, and to the Eastern Suburb beaches. Trains travel from Central Station through the city on a circle line (calling at Circular Quay and Town Hall), out to Bondi Junction, over the bridge to the north shore, and out to the west. Ferries leave Circular Quay for Manly, Balmain, Darling Harbour, and other suburbs, while the free 555 shuttle bus does a circuit through the city, calling at the main sights.

Sights

Admiralty House

HISTORIC HOME | The Sydney residence of the governor-general, the Queen's representative in Australia, this impressive residence is occasionally open for inspection and can be viewed (from the water) during harbor cruises. ✉ *109 Kirribilli Ave., Kirribilli.*

Fort Denison

ISLAND | For a brief time in the early days of the colony, convicts who committed petty offenses were kept on this harbor island, where they existed on such a meager diet that the island was named Pinchgut. Fortification of the island was completed in 1857, when fears of Russian expansion in the Pacific spurred the government on. Today the firing of the fort's cannon doesn't signal imminent invasion, but merely the hour—one o'clock. New South Wales National Parks and Wildlife Service runs half-hour tours at Fort Denison. Purchase tickets (from $A28) from either the NSW National Parks office (1300/072–757) or at Captain Cook Cruises' booth at Jetty 6, Circular Quay; the ferries depart for the island from 10:30 am to 4 pm daily from Jetty 6. ✉ *Circular Quay, Alfred St., Jetty 6, Sydney Harbour* ☎ *1300/072–757* 🌐 *www.nationalparks.nsw.gov.au, www.fortdenison.com.au* 🎟 *Tours from A$28.*

Garden Island

ISLAND | Although it's still known as an "island," this promontory was connected with the mainland in 1942. During the 1941–45 War of the Pacific (WWII and a number of preceding conflicts), Australia's largest naval base and dockyard was a frontline port for Allied ships. Part of the naval base is now open to the public. Access, seven days a week, to the site is via ferry from Circular Quay (take the Watsons Bay ferry). Visitors can view the museum and picnic on the hill. The Naval Historical Society runs tours to the "secure" section of Garden Island but these must be booked well in advance. The 90-minute tours (A$25) run every Thursday. ✉ *Garden Island* ✣ *Take ferry from Circular Quay to Watsons Bay and ask to be let off at Garden Island. No buses go directly to Garden Island.* ☎ *02/9359–2243* 🌐 *www.navyhistory.org.au.*

Kirribilli

NEIGHBORHOOD | Residences in this attractive suburb opposite the city and Opera House have million-dollar views—and prices to match. Two of Sydney's most important mansions stand here. The more modest of the two is **Kirribilli House,** the official Sydney home of the prime minister, which, along with Admiralty House, is open to the public once a year, usually around May. ✉ *Kirribilli.*

Luna Park

AMUSEMENT PARK/CARNIVAL | **FAMILY** | Opened in 1935, this classic amusement park, with its supersize clown-face entrance, can be seen from any angle of Sydney Harbour. It's a fun afternoon no matter your age, with traditional fair rides, like the ghost train and dodgems. The tourist attraction reopened in 2021 after a A$30 million face-lift, with brand-new rides and stylish places to eat. It's located just at Milsons Point Wharf, with regular ferries departing from Circular

Quay. ✉ *1 Olympic Dr., Sydney Harbour* ☎ *02/9922–6644* 🌐 *www.lunaparksydney.com* 🎫 *A$34.*

Macquarie Lighthouse

VIEWPOINT | When the sun shines, the 15-minute cliff-top stroll along South Head Walkway between The Gap and the Macquarie Lighthouse affords some of Sydney's most inspiring views. Convict-architect Francis Greenway (jailed for forgery) designed the original lighthouse here, Australia's first, in 1818. Visitors climb the 100 stairs to the top of the lighthouse on guided tours (20 minutes duration; A$6) that are run every two months by the Sydney Harbour Federation Trust. Call or check the website for dates and bookings. ✉ *Old South Head Rd., Vaucluse* ✣ *To reach Watsons Bay either take ferry from Circular Quay or Bus 324 or 325 from Circular Quay. Bus 324 goes past lighthouse* 🌐 *www.harbourtrust.gov.au.*

Middle Harbour

BRIDGE | Except for the yachts moored in the sandy coves, the upper reaches of Middle Harbour are almost exactly as they were when the first Europeans set eyes on Port Jackson more than 200 years ago. Tucked away in idyllic bushland are tranquil suburbs just a short drive from the city. ✉ *Middle Harbour* ✣ *The focal point of Middle Harbour is Spit Bridge. To get there, take train from either Central or Town Hall station to Milsons Point then take Bus 229 to Spit Bridge. From Spit Bridge walk to Manly and view most of beautiful Middle Harbour.*

Middle Head

CITY PARK | Despite its benign appearance today, Sydney Harbour once bristled with armaments. In the mid-19th century, faced with expansionist European powers hungry for new colonies, the authorities erected artillery positions on the headlands to guard harbor approaches. One of Sydney's newest open spaces, Headland Park, has opened on a former military base. A walking track winds past fortifications, tunnels, and heritage buildings, several of which are now used as cafés, including the Tea Room Gunners' Barracks. ✉ *1200 Middle Head Rd., Mosman* ✣ *Several buses travel from central Sydney to Mosman, Balmoral, and Chowder Bay, which are all suburbs within Middle Head area and close to Headland Park. They include Buses 245, 246, and 247* ☎ *02/8969–2100 Harbour Trust* 🌐 *www.harbourtrust.gov.au* 🎫 *Free.*

Quarantine Station

HOSPITAL | From the 1830s onward, ship passengers who arrived with contagious diseases were isolated on this outpost in the shadow of North Head until pronounced free of illness. You can access the station as part of a guided tour, and now stay overnight in the four-star hotel and cottage accommodation known as Q Station; there are also two waterfront restaurants. There are day tours and five different evening ghost tours (the station reputedly has its fair share of specters) that depart from the visitor center at the Quarantine Station, and a "ghostly sleep-over" for those who want to spend the night in reputedly haunted rooms. Reservations are essential. **TIP→ Visitors can also visit the site without taking a tour; however, if you want to dine, you must make prior restaurant reservations.** ✉ *North Head, North Head Scenic Dr., Manly* ✣ *Take ferry to Manly from Circular Quay, then Bus 135 to site. Or catch Q Station's complimentary bus shuttle opposite Manly Wharf* ☎ *02/9466–1500, 02/9466–1551 tour bookings* 🌐 *www.qstation.com.au* 🎫 *Tours from A$20.*

Rose Bay

BEACH | This large bay, the biggest of Sydney Harbour's 66 bays, was once a base for the Qantas flying boats that provided the only passenger air service between Australia and America and Europe. The last flying boat departed from Rose Bay in the 1960s, but the "airstrip" is still used by floatplanes on scenic flights

Giraffes at Sydney's world-class Taronga Zoo

connecting Sydney with the Hawkesbury River and the central coast. It's a popular place for joggers, who pound the pavement of New South Head Road, which runs along the bay. ✉ *New South Head Rd., Rose Bay* ✣ *Take Bus 325 from Circular Quay, or take ferry to Watsons Bay (it stops at Rose Bay).*

★ Sydney Cove

BODY OF WATER | Sydney Harbour is spotted with many coves, but perhaps the most famous is Sydney Cove, an inlet better known as Circular Quay. With the Sydney Opera House and Bennelong Point, offering stunning restaurants and incredible views to the east, The Rocks to the west, and Harbour Bridge looming over it all, this spot really captures the essence of the city of Sydney. A walkway loops around the cove and is busy no matter what time of day. ✉ *Sydney Cove, Sydney Cove* ✣ *Take train from Central or Town Hall to Circular Quay railway station; or take any number of buses to Circular Quay from all over Sydney. Ferries travel to Circular Quay from many different parts of Sydney, including north side of harbor, Rose Bay, Balmain, and Parramatta. Circular Quay is right in middle of Sydney Cove.*

★ Sydney Harbour National Park

GARDEN | This massive park is made up of 958 acres of separate foreshores and islands, most of them on the north side of the harbor. To see the best areas, put on your walking shoes and head out on the many well-marked trails. The Hermitage Foreshore Walk skirts through bushland around Vaucluse's Nielsen Park. On the north side of the harbor, Bradleys Head and Chowder Head Walk is a 5-km (3-mile) stroll that starts from Taronga Zoo Wharf. The most inspiring trail is the 9½-km (6-mile) Manly Scenic Walkway, which joins the Spit Bridge with Manly by meandering along sandstone headlands, small beaches, and pockets of rain forest, and past Aboriginal sites and the historic Grotto Point Lighthouse. You can take day tours of two harbor islands, Fort Denison and Goat Island, which have interesting colonial history and buildings.

The boardwalk around Sydney Cove on a typical sunny day

Call The New South Wales National Parks and Wildlife Service for tickets. You can also visit Shark Island (off Rose Bay) on a cruise with Captain Cook Cruises (A$20) departing daily from Jetty 6 at Circular Quay. ✉ *Jetty 6, Alfred St., The Rocks* ☎ *1300/072–757* 🌐 *www.nationalparks.nsw.gov.au.*

Taronga Zoo

ZOO | FAMILY | Sydney's zoo, in a natural bush area on the harbor's north shore, houses an extensive collection of Australian fauna, including everybody's favorite marsupial, the koala. The zoo has taken great care to create spacious enclosures that simulate natural habitats. The hillside setting is steep in parts, and a complete tour can be tiring, but you can use the map distributed free at the entrance gate to plan a leisurely route. The views of the harbor are stunning. Use of children's strollers (the basic model) is free. The best way to get here from the city is by ferry from Circular Quay or Darling Harbour. From Taronga Wharf a bus or the cable car will take you up the hill to the main entrance. The ZooPass, a combined ferry–zoo ticket (A$65) is available at Circular Quay. You can also stay overnight at the zoo in what's billed as the "wildest slumber party in town." The "Roar and Snore" program includes a night tour, two behind-the-scenes tours, drinks, dinner, breakfast, and luxury tent accommodation at A$288 per adult on weeknights and A$320 per adult on Friday/Saturday. Other special programs include being a "Keeper for a Day." ✉ *Bradleys Head Rd., Mosman* ☎ *02/9969–2777* 🌐 *www.taronga.org.au* 🎫 *A$44.*

Vaucluse

TOWN | The palatial homes in this glamorous harbor suburb provide a glimpse of Sydney's high society. The small beaches at Nielsen Park and Parsley Bay are safe for swimming and provide wonderful views. Both beaches are packed with families in summer. ✉ *Vaucluse.*

Vaucluse House

HISTORIC HOME | The suburb takes its name from the 1803 Vaucluse House, one of Sydney's most illustrious remaining historic mansions. The 15-room Gothic Revival house and its lush gardens, managed by Sydney Living Museums (previously called Historic Houses Trust), are open to the public. The tearooms, built in the style of an Edwardian conservatory, are popular spots for lunch and afternoon tea on weekends. ✉ *Wentworth Rd., Vaucluse* ✥ *Take Bus 325 from Circular Quay bus stand* ☎ *02/9388–7922* 🌐 *www.vauclusehouse-tearooms.com.au* *A$12.*

★ Watsons Bay

BEACH | Established as a military base and fishing settlement in the colony's early years, Watsons Bay is a charming suburb, with a popular waterfront pub, that has held on to its village ambience despite the exorbitant prices paid for tiny cottages here. Unlike Watsons Bay's tranquil harbor side, the side that faces the ocean is dramatic and tortured, with the raging sea dashing against the sheer, 200-foot sandstone cliffs of The Gap. ✉ *Military Rd., Watsons Bay.*

Beaches

Balmoral Beach

BEACH | This 800-yard-long beach—among the best of the inner-harbor beaches—is in one of Sydney's most exclusive northern suburbs. There's no surf, but it's a great place to learn to windsurf (sailboard rentals are available). The Esplanade, which runs along the beachfront, has a handful of upscale restaurants, as well as several snack bars and cafés that serve award-winning fish-and-chips. In summer you can catch performances of Bard on the Beach. You could easily combine a trip to Balmoral with a visit to Taronga Zoo. To reach Balmoral, take the ferry from Circular Quay to Taronga Zoo and then board Bus 238. Or take Bus 247 from the city (near Wynyard Station) to Mosman and then walk down Raglan Street hill to the Esplanade, the main street running along Balmoral Beach. **Amenities:** food and drink; showers; toilets. **Best for:** swimming; walking; windsurfing. ✉ *Raglan St., Balmoral.*

Camp Cove

BEACH | Just inside South Head, this crescent beach is where Sydney's fashionable people come to watch and be seen. The gentle slope and calm water make it a safe playground for children. A shop at the northern end of the beach sells salad rolls and fresh fruit juices. The grassy hill at the southern end of the beach has a plaque to commemorate the spot where Captain Arthur Phillip, the commander of the First Fleet, first set foot inside Port Jackson. Parking is limited, and keep in mind it's a long walk to the beach. Dive company Abyss (☎ *02/9588–9662*) operates an easy dive off the beach here. Take Bus 324 or 325 from Circular Quay to Watsons Bay and walk along Cliff Street. **Amenities:** food and drink; toilets. **Best for:** solitude; sunset; swimming. ✉ *Cliff St., Watsons Bay.*

Lady Jane

BEACH | Officially called Lady Bay, Lady Jane is the most accessible of the nude beaches around Sydney. It's also a popular part of Sydney's gay scene. Only a couple of hundred yards long and backed by a stone wall, the beach has safe swimming with no surf. From Camp Cove, follow the path north and then descend the short, steep ladder leading down the cliff face to the beach. Take Bus 234 or 325 from Circular Quay to Watsons Bay. From there walk along Cliff Street toward Camp Cove. **Amenities:** toilets. **Best for:** nudists; solitude; swimming. ✉ *Cliff St., Watsons Bay.*

Nielsen Park

BEACH | By Sydney standards, this beach at the end of the Vaucluse Peninsula is small, but behind the sand is a large, shady park that's ideal for picnics. The headlands at either end of the beach are especially popular for their magnificent views across the harbor. The beach is protected by a semicircular net, so don't be deterred by the beach's correct name, Shark Beach. The casual café is open daily and sells drinks, snacks, and meals; there is also a more upscale restaurant open for lunch daily. Parking is often difficult on weekends. Historic Greycliffe House—built in 1840 and now used as National Park offices—is in the park, while the more elaborate and stately Vaucluse House is a 10-minute walk away. Take Bus 325 from Circular Quay. **Amenities:** food and drink; showers; toilets. **Best for:** swimming; walking. ✉ *Greycliffe Ave., off Vaucluse Rd., Vaucluse.*

Restaurants

Aqua Dining

$$$$ | AUSTRALIAN | Tucked beneath the Sydney Harbour Bridge with views of the harbor and Sydney Olympic Pool, this is a popular restaurant for both lunch and dinner. And it is open seven days a week for both. **Known for:** smooth service; incredible views; outstanding seafood. *Average main: A$89* ✉ *Northcliff St. and Paul St., Sydney Harbour* ☎ *02/9964–9998* 🌐 *www.aquadining.com.au.*

★ **Bathers' Pavilion**

$$$ | AUSTRALIAN | Balmoral Beach is blessed. Not only does it have an inviting sandy beach and great water views, but it also has one of the best eating strips north of the Harbour Bridge. **Known for:** superior seafood; casual dining at the café; great views. *Average main: A$50* ✉ *4 The Esplanade, Balmoral* ☎ *02/9969–5050* 🌐 *www.batherspavilion.com.au.*

Coffee and Quick Bites

BTB Kirribilli

$ | AUSTRIAN | Fresh is the name of the game with this café. Zesty avocado on toast, slow-cooked pulled-pork rolls, fresh juices, and rich coffee. **Known for:** friendly staff; fresh eats; great coffee. *Average main: A$20* ✉ *2 Ennis Rd., Sydney Harbour* 🌐 *www.btbkirribilli.sydney.*

Guylian Belgian Chocolate Café

$ | BELGIAN | FAMILY | This Belgian chocolate shop has an on-site café offering ice-cold chocolate milk shakes, frothy hot chocolates, and plenty of sweet treats. Circular Quay is packed with restaurants, but this is only one of a few cafés in the area and with views of the harbor if you get a window seat. **Known for:** water views; artisanal chocolate; sweet treats. *Average main: A$15* ✉ *Opera Quays, Shop 10/3 Macquarie St., Sydney Harbour* ☎ *02/8274–7900* 🌐 *guyliancafe.com.au.*

Nightlife

BARS AND DANCE CLUBS

The Oaks

BARS | For a northern Sydney landmark, The Oaks encapsulates the very best of the modern pub. The immensely popular watering hole, named after the huge oak tree in the center of the large beer garden, is big and boisterous. The pub has a restaurant and several bars with varying levels of sophistication. It's packed on Friday and Saturday night. ✉ *118 Military Rd., Neutral Bay* ☎ *02/9953–5515* 🌐 *www.oakshotel.com.au.*

Performing Arts

BALLET, OPERA, AND CLASSICAL MUSIC

★ **Sydney Opera House**

CONCERTS | This venue showcases all the performing arts in its five theaters, one of which is devoted to opera. The Australian Ballet, the Sydney Dance Company, and the Australian Opera Company also call the Opera House home. The complex includes two stages for theater and the 2,700-seat Concert Hall, where the Sydney Symphony Orchestra and the Australian Chamber Orchestra perform. The box office is open Monday to Saturday 9–8:30 and until 5 on Sunday. ✉ *Bennelong Point, Sydney Harbour* ☎ *02/9250–7111* 🌐 *www.sydneyoperahouse.com.*

DANCE

★ Bangarra Dance Theatre

THEATER | An acclaimed Aboriginal modern dance company, Bangarra Dance Theatre celebrated its 30th anniversary in 2020. The company stages dramatic productions based on contemporary Aboriginal social themes. The performances are described as a fusion of contemporary dance and storytelling; some will have you transfixed by the sheer energy, lighting, and special effects. ✉ *Pier 4, 15 Hickson Rd., Walsh Bay* ☎ *02/9251–5333* 🌐 *www.bangarra.com.au.*

Sydney Dance Company

BALLET | Sydney Dance Company is an innovative contemporary dance troupe with an international reputation. Spanish choreographer Rafael Bonachela is the artistic director. The company performs in Sydney at the Wharf Theatre, the Sydney Opera House, and the new Sydney Theatre, and also runs casual drop-in dance classes for A$22: see the website for class schedules. ✉ *The Wharf, Pier 4, Hickson Rd., Walsh Bay* ☎ *02/9221–4811* 🌐 *www.sydneydancecompany.com.*

THEATER

★ Wharf Theatre

THEATER | Wharf Theatre, on a redeveloped wharf in the shadow of Harbour Bridge, is the headquarters of the Sydney Theatre Company (STC), one of Australia's most original and highly regarded performance groups. Contemporary British and American plays and the latest shows from leading Australian playwrights such as David Williamson and Nick Enright are the main attractions. The company also performs at the Sydney Opera House and at the new Sydney Theatre just a few doors away, located opposite Pier 6/7 at No. 22 Hickson Road. ✉ *Pier 4, Hickson Rd., Walsh Bay* ☎ *02/9250–1777* 🌐 *sydneytheatre.com.au.*

The Rocks

The Rocks is the birthplace not just of Sydney, but of modern Australia. Here the 11 ships of the First Fleet, the first of England's 800-plus ships carrying convicts to the penal colony, dropped anchor in 1788. This stubby peninsula enclosing the western side of Sydney Cove became known simply as The Rocks.

Most of the architecture here dates from the Victorian era, by which time Sydney had become a thriving port. Warehouses lining the waterfront were backed by a row of tradesmen's shops, banks, and taverns, and above them, ascending Observatory Hill, rose a tangled mass of alleyways lined with the cottages of seamen and wharf laborers.

Today The Rocks is a hot spot of cafés, restaurants, and quaint boutiques, and it's one of the city's most popular destinations. And because it's Sydney's most historic area, the old architecture has been beautifully maintained.

GETTING HERE AND AROUND

You can take the train or any number of buses to Circular Quay and then walk to The Rocks. From Bondi and Paddington, take the 380, 382, or 333 bus to Circular Quay via Elizabeth Street. From Clovelly, take the 339 bus all the way to The Rocks, via Central Station. Once there, the best way to get around is on foot—there are quite a few sandstone steps and narrow alleyways to navigate, and your feet are your best friends.

Sights

Argyle Cut

HISTORIC SIGHT | Argyle Street, which links Argyle Place and George Street, is dominated by the Argyle Cut and its massive walls. In the days before the Cut (tunnel) was made, the sandstone ridge here was a major barrier to traffic crossing between Circular Quay and Millers Point.

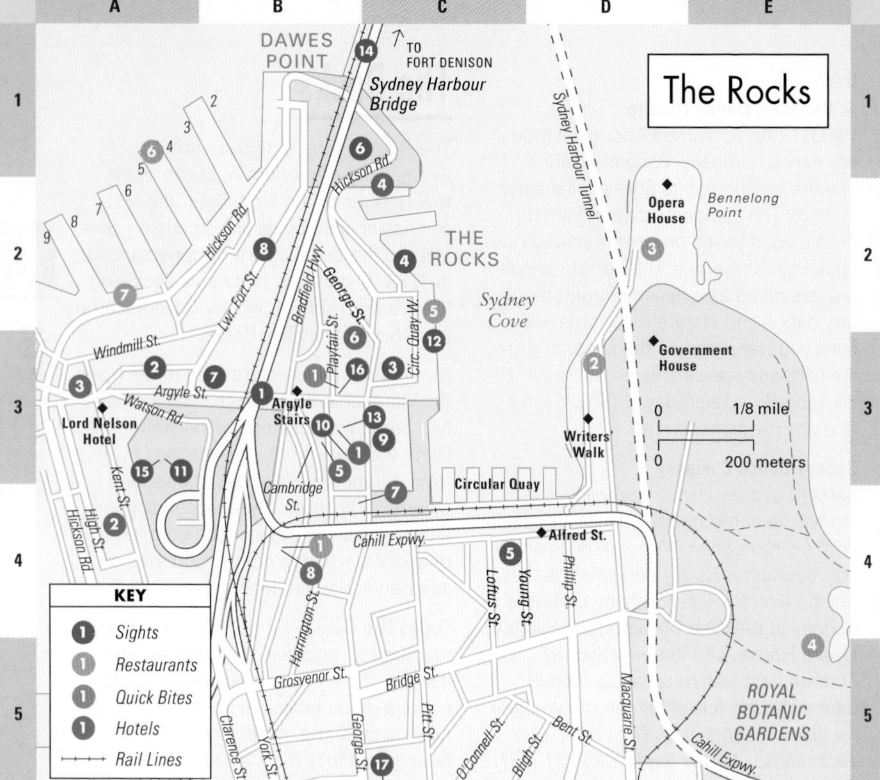

Sights

1. Argyle Cut B3
2. Argyle Place A3
3. Cadman's Cottage C3
4. Campbell's Cove C2
5. Customs House C4
6. Dawes Point Park C1
7. Holy Trinity Garrison Church B3
8. Lower Fort Street B2
9. Museum of Contemporary Art C3
10. Nurses Walk B3
11. Observatory Hill A3
12. Overseas Passenger Terminal C3
13. Suez Canal B3
14. Sydney Harbour Bridge C1
15. Sydney Observatory A3
16. Sydney Visitor Centre at the Rocks B3
17. Upper George Street C5

Restaurants

1. Altitude B4
2. Aria D3
3. Bennelong D2
4. Botanic House E5
5. Quay C2
6. Theatre Bar at the End of the Wharf A1
7. Walsh Bay Kitchen A2

Quick Bites

1. Pancakes On The Rocks B3

Hotels

1. Harbour Rocks Hotel B3
2. The Langham Sydney A4
3. Lord Nelson Brewery Hotel A3
4. Park Hyatt Sydney C2
5. Rendezvous Hotel Sydney The Rocks B3
6. Rydges Sydney Harbour B3
7. The Russell B4
8. Shangri-La Sydney B4

Exploring The Rocks on Foot

Begin at Circular Quay, the lively waterfront ferry terminal, and walk west toward Harbour Bridge, passing the Museum of Contemporary Art, and climb the few stairs into George Street. Pass the historic Fortune of War pub, then as you round the corner head down the sandstone stairs on the right to **Campbell's Cove** and its warehouses. The waterfront restaurants and cafés are pleasant spots for a drink or meal. Continue along Hickson Road toward the Sydney Harbour Bridge until you are directly beneath the bridge's massive girders. Walk under the bridge to **Dawes Point Park** for excellent views of the harbor, including the Opera House and the small island of Fort Denison.

Now turn your back on the bridge and walk south and west, via Lower Fort Street. Explore Argyle Place and continue walking south, past the **Sydney Observatory.** While you're in the neighborhood, be sure to pick up brochures and city information at the **Sydney Visitor Centre at The Rocks,** on the corner of Argyle and Playfair Streets. Turn right at **Nurses Walk,** another of the area's historic and atmospheric backstreets, then left into Surgeons Court, and left again onto George Street. On the left is the handsome sandstone facade of the former Rocks Police Station, now a crafts gallery. From this point, Circular Quay is only a short walk away.

In 1843 convict work gangs hacked at the sandstone with hand tools for 2½ years before the project was abandoned due to lack of progress. Work restarted in 1857, when drills, explosives, and paid labor completed the job. On the lower side of the Cut an archway leads to the **Argyle Stairs,** which begin the climb from Argyle Street up to the Sydney Harbour Bridge walkway. There's a spectacular view from the South East Pylon. ✉ *Argyle Pl., Millers Point.*

Argyle Place

HISTORIC HOME | With all the traditional requirements of an English green—a pub at one end, a church at the other, and grass in between—this charming enclave in the suburb of Millers Point is unusual for Sydney. Argyle Place is lined with 19th-century houses and cottages on its northern side and overlooked by Observatory Hill to the south. ✉ *Argyle Pl., Millers Point.*

Cadman's Cottage

HISTORIC HOME | Sydney's oldest building, completed in 1816, has a history that outweighs its modest dimensions. John Cadman was a convict who was sentenced for life to New South Wales for stealing a horse. He later became superintendent of government boats, a position that entitled him to live in the upper story of this house. The water once practically lapped at Cadman's doorstep, and the original seawall still stands at the front of the house. The small extension on the side of the cottage was built to lock up the oars of Cadman's boats, since oars would have been a necessity for any convict attempting to escape by sea. The cottage can only be viewed from the outside. ✉ *110 George St., The Rocks* ☎ *02/9337–5511* 🌐 *www.nationalparks.nsw.gov.au.*

Campbell's Cove

LIGHTHOUSE | Robert Campbell was a Scottish merchant who is sometimes referred to as the "father of Australian commerce." Campbell broke the stranglehold that the British East India Company exercised over seal and whale products, which were New South Wales's only exports in those early days. The cove's atmospheric sandstone **Campbell's Storehouse,** built from 1838 onward, now houses waterside restaurants. The pulleys that were used to hoist cargoes still hang on the upper level of the warehouses. The cove is also the mooring for Sydney's fully operational tall ships, which conduct theme cruises around the harbor. ✉ *Campbell's Storehouse, 7–27 Circular Quay West, The Rocks* ☎ *No phone.*

Customs House

GOVERNMENT BUILDING | The last surviving example of the elegant sandstone buildings that once ringed Circular Quay, this former customs house now features an amazing model of Sydney under a glass floor. You can walk over the city's skyscrapers, all of which are illuminated by fiber-optic lights. The Customs House has an excellent two-level library, art galleries, and ground-floor bar. The rooftop Café Sydney, the standout in the clutch of restaurants and cafés in this late-19th-century structure, overlooks Sydney Cove. The building stands close to the site where the British flag was first raised on the shores of Sydney Cove in 1788. ✉ *Customs House Sq., 31 Alfred St., Circular Quay* ☎ *02/9242–8551* 🌐 *www.sydneycustomshouse.com.au.*

Dawes Point Park

VIEWPOINT | The wonderful views of the harbor (and since the 1930s, the Harbour Bridge) have made this park and its location noteworthy for centuries. Named for William Dawes, a First Fleet marine officer and astronomer who established the colony's first basic observatory nearby in 1788, this park was also once the site of a fortification known as Dawes Battery. The cannons on the hillside pointing toward the Opera House came from the ships of the First Fleet. ✉ *Hickson Rd., The Rocks.*

Holy Trinity Garrison Church

CHURCH | FAMILY | Every morning, redcoats would march to this 1840 Argyle Place church from Dawes Point Battery (now Dawes Point Park), and it became commonly known as the Garrison Church, although now officially called the Church Hill Anglican. As the regimental plaques and colors around the walls testify, the church still retains a close military association. Sunday services are held at 9:30 am and 4 pm. ✉ *Argyle Pl., Argyle St. at Lower Fort St., The Rocks* ☎ *02/9247–1071.*

Lower Fort Street

NEIGHBORHOOD | At one time the handsome Georgian houses along this street, originally a rough track leading from the Dawes Point Battery to Observatory Hill, were among the best addresses in Sydney. Elaborate wrought-iron lacework still graces many of the facades. ✉ *Lower Fort St., The Rocks.*

Museum of Contemporary Art

ART GALLERY | This ponderous art deco building houses one of Australia's most important collections of modern art, as well as two significant collections of Aboriginal art, a sculpture garden, and continually changing temporary exhibits. Free tours, talks, and hands-on art workshops are conducted regularly. ✉ *140 George St., The Rocks* ☎ *02/9245–2400* 🌐 *www.mca.com.au* 🎫 *Free.*

Nurses Walk

HISTORIC SIGHT | Cutting across the site of the colony's first hospital, Nurses Walk acquired its name at a time when "Sydney" and "sickness" were synonymous. Many of the 736 convicts who survived the voyage from Portsmouth, England, aboard the First Fleet's 11 ships arrived suffering from dysentery, smallpox, scurvy, and typhoid. A few days after he landed at Sydney Cove, Governor Phillip established a tent hospital to care for the worst cases. ✉ *Between Harrington and George Sts., The Rocks* 🌐 *www.therocks.com.*

Observatory Hill

CITY PARK | The city's highest point, at 145 feet, was known originally as Windmill Hill, since the colony's first windmill occupied this breezy spot. Its purpose was to grind grain for flour, but soon after it was built the canvas sails were stolen, the machinery was damaged in a storm, and the foundations cracked. The signal station at the top of the hill was built in 1848. This later became an astronomical observatory. This is a great place for a picnic with a view. ✉ *Upper Fort St., The Rocks.*

Overseas Passenger Terminal

BUSINESS DISTRICT | Busy Circular Quay West is dominated by this multilevel steel-and-glass port terminal, which is often used by visiting cruise ships. There are several excellent waterfront restaurants in the terminal, all with magnificent harbor views. Even if you're not dining in the terminal, it's worth taking the escalator to the upper deck for a good view of the harbor and Opera House. ✉ *Circular Quay West, The Rocks* 🌐 *www.cityofsydney.nsw.gov.au.*

Suez Canal

NEIGHBORHOOD | So narrow that two people can't walk abreast, this alley acquired its name before drains were installed, when rainwater would pour down its funnel-like passageway and gush across George Street. Lanes such as this were once the haunt of the notorious late-19th-century Rocks gangs, when robbery was rife in the area. ✉ *Harrington St. at George St., The Rocks* 🌐 *www.therocks.com.*

★ **Sydney Harbour Bridge**

VIEWPOINT | Despite its nickname "the coat hanger," the bridge has a fond place in all Sydneysiders' hearts. Its opening on March 19, 1932 (during the height of the Great Depression), lifted the spirits of citizens and provided some very unexpected theater. As NSW Premier Jack Lang waited to cut the ribbon, Captain Francis de Groot, a member of the paramilitary New Guard, galloped up on his horse, drew his sword, and slashed the ribbon first.

There are several ways to experience the bridge and its spectacular views. One way is through the South East Pylon. To reach this city-side pylon of the Sydney Harbour Bridge, walk along the bridge's pedestrian pathway. Access is from stairs on Cumberland Street, The Rocks (near BridgeClimb). This structure houses a display on the bridge's construction, and you can climb the 200 steps to the lookout and its unbeatable harbor panorama.

A second (more expensive) way is through the BridgeClimb tour. Not for those afraid of heights, the BridgeClimb tour takes you on a guided walking tour to the very top of Harbour Bridge, 439 feet above sea level. The cost is A$374 per person for a night climb midweek and A$349 for a day climb, with slightly higher prices on weekends.

The third option is to walk to the midpoint of the bridge to take in the views free of charge, but be sure to take the eastern footpath, which overlooks the Sydney Opera House. Access is via the stairs on Cumberland Street (near the BridgeClimb meeting point) and close to the Shangri-La Hotel. ✉ *Cumberland St., The Rocks.*

Sydney Observatory

OBSERVATORY | **FAMILY** | Originally a signaling station for communicating with ships anchored in the harbor, this handsome building on top of Observatory Hill is now an astronomy museum. During evening observatory shows you can tour the building, watch videos, and get a close-up view of the universe through a 16-inch mirror telescope. The digital Sydney Planetarium showcases the virtual night sky to just 20 visitors at a time in a small theater. Reservations are required for the evening shows only. ✉ *Watson Rd., Millers Point* ☎ *02/9217–0222* 🌐 *www.maas.museum/sydney-observatory* 🎫 *Museum free, shows from A$10; Sydney Planetarium A$10.*

Did You Know?

Listed in the *Guinness World Records* book as the widest long span bridge in the world, the Sydney Harbour Bridge was the tallest structure in the city until 1967. It's the sixth-longest single-span steel arch bridge in the world. The top three are all in China: the longest is the Chaotianmen Bridge in Chongquing.

Sydney Visitor Centre at the Rocks

VISITOR CENTER | Known as The Rocks Centre, this ultramodern space is packed with free maps and brochures, and the friendly staff dispenses valuable information and will book tours, hotel rooms, and bus travel. It's near the popular Löwenbräu Keller, where many tourists gather for a beer. ✉ *The Rocks Centre, Argyle St. at Playfair St., The Rocks* ☎ *02/9251–0643* 🌐 *www.visitorcentre.com.au.*

Upper George Street

MARKET | The restored warehouses and Victorian terrace houses that line this part of George Street make this a charming section of The Rocks. The covered Rocks Market takes place here on weekends and it's a great spot to find Aboriginal art, trinkets, and antiques. ✉ *George St., The Rocks.*

Restaurants

Altitude

$$$$ | **MODERN AUSTRALIAN** | The lure of this decadent restaurant high above Sydney Harbour on the 36th floor of the luxurious Shangri-La Hotel, is the view through the floor-to-ceiling windows, but the Mod Oz dishes presented with a strong European influence are equally impressive. The produce hails from local farmers. **Known for:** high-end prices; stylish dining; locally sourced produce. Ⓢ *Average main: A$73* ✉ *Shangri-La Hotel, 176 Cumberland St., Level 36, The Rocks* ☎ *02/9250–6123* 🌐 *www.shangri-la.com* ⏲ *Closed Sun.*

★ **Aria**

$$$$ | **AUSTRALIAN** | With windows overlooking the Opera House and Harbour Bridge, Aria could easily rest on the laurels of its location. Instead, celebrity chef Matthew Moran creates a menu of extraordinary dishes that may be your best meal Down Under. **Known for:** incredible views of the harbor; foodie favorite; seafood like Skull Island prawns and surf clams and eel. Ⓢ *Average main: A$145* ✉ *1 Macquarie St., Circular Quay* ☎ *02/9240–2255* 🌐 *www.ariarestaurant.com* ⏲ *No lunch weekends* 👔 *Jacket required.*

Art and Angst

If you like a bit of controversy with your culture, head to the Art Gallery of New South Wales to view the finalists in the annual **Archibald Prize**. Each year since 1921, the competition has attracted plenty of drama as everyone debates the merits of the winners. Prizes are announced in early March, and the exhibition hangs until mid-May.

★ **Bennelong**

$$$$ | **AUSTRALIAN** | One of Australia's most renowned chefs, Peter Gilmore, oversees the kitchen at possibly the most superbly situated dining room in town. Tucked into the side of the Opera House, the restaurant affords views of Sydney Harbour Bridge and the city lights. **Known for:** Opera House–shape pavlova; incredible views; high-end dining experience. Ⓢ *Average main: A$135* ✉ *Bennelong Point, Sydney Opera House, Circular Quay* ☎ *02/9240–8000* 🌐 *www.bennelong.com.au* ⏲ *No lunch weekdays* 👔 *Jacket required.*

Botanic House

$$$$ | **ASIAN** | With wide verandas providing tranquil views over the gardens, the sound of birdsong filling the air, and a menu created by celebrated chef Luke Nguyen, Botanic House is a top choice for a long lunch or a sunset dinner. The menu is modern Asian, leaning more toward Vietnamese, with dumplings, *bao*, and grilled meats usually on the menu. **TIP→ The restaurant is within the Royal Botanic Gardens; it can be accessed from either the Palace Gate on Macquarie Street or from Lion Gate on Mrs. Macquarie's Road.** **Known for:** great service; pretty

Botanic Gardens setting; fresh Vietnamese meals. $ *Average main: A$70* ✉ *Macquarie St., Royal Botanic Gardens* ☎ *1300/558–980* 🌐 *www.botanichouse.com.au* 🕑 *No dinner Mon.-Thurs.*

★ Quay

$$$$ | MODERN AUSTRALIAN | Quay has been Sydney's top restaurant for 30 years and it's still going strong with chef Peter Gilmore's experimental Mod Oz cuisine created with seasonal, local produce. The menu has carefully created seafood dishes, like greenlip abalone. **Known for:** harbor views; experimental cuisine; White Coral dessert. $ *Average main: A$210* ✉ *West Circular Quay, Overseas Passenger Terminal, upper level, The Rocks* ☎ *02/9251–5600* 🌐 *www.quay.com.au* 🕑 *No lunch weekdays.*

Theatre Bar at the End of the Wharf

$ | MODERN AUSTRALIAN | Most people come to this buzzy bar at the end of Pier 4 for a quick bite before a show at the adjacent Sydney Theatre Company, but the views of the Harbour Bridge are so spectacular that it's worth coming here any time. It gets busy before a show starts, but then the crowd vanishes, leaving it a pleasant place to linger over a quiet glass of wine or cocktail and soak in the amazing view. **Known for:** lively atmosphere; incredible views; huge variety of meals. $ *Average main: A$25* ✉ *Hickson Rd., end of Pier 4, Walsh Bay* ☎ *02/9250–1761* 🌐 *www.sydneytheatre.com.au* 🕑 *Closed Sun.*

Walsh Bay Kitchen

$$$ | ASIAN FUSION | Found inside the Roslyn Packer Theatre, the Walsh Bay Kitchen offers light Asian fusion fare, with flavors of miso and wasabi-crumbed fish often found on the menu. It gets busy here before a show, due in part to the fact that the food here is so much cheaper than at neighboring restaurants, usually costing around A$50 for two courses and a glass of wine. **Known for:** affordable for the area; pretheater dinner; buzzy atmosphere. $ *Average main: A$50* ✉ *Roslyn Packer Theatre Walsh Bay, 22 Hickson Rd., Walsh Bay* ☎ *1300/360–801* 🌐 *www.walshbaykitchen.com.au* 🕑 *Closed Sun.*

Coffee and Quick Bites

Pancakes on The Rocks

$ | AMERICAN | Founded by two Australians who had been on a road trip to the United States, the pair returned and launched Pancakes on The Rocks in the 1950s. Seven decades later and it's still an iconic eatery in Sydney. **Known for:** friendly staff; lively atmosphere; open 24 hours a day. $ *Average main: A$15* ✉ *22 Playfair St., The Rocks* ☎ *02/9247–6371* 🌐 *pancakesontherocks.com.au.*

Hotels

★ Harbour Rocks Hotel

$$ | HOTEL | Formerly a wool-storage facility, this four-story hotel is an Accor MGallery property, which is a select portfolio of distinctive and individual hotels in Australia. **Pros:** great location near harbor; unique courtyard in the city; ultrastylish. **Cons:** no pool; Wi-Fi is an additional charge; heritage rooms could be larger. $ *Rooms from: A$270* ✉ *34 Harrington St., The Rocks* ☎ *02/8220–9999* 🌐 *www.harbourrocks.com.au* 🍴 *Free Breakfast* 🛏 *59 rooms.*

★ The Langham Sydney

$$$ | HOTEL | More English country manor than inner-city hotel, this gorgeous property feels like a decadent, luxurious sanctuary. **Pros:** afternoon tea; sumptuous Venetian- and Asian-inspired decor; excellent in-house restaurant. **Cons:** a bit isolated; lack of views; expensive. $ *Rooms from: A$450* ✉ *89–113 Kent St., The Rocks* ☎ *02/9256–2222* 🌐 *www.sydney.langhamhotels.com.au* 🛏 *100 rooms* 🍴 *Free Breakfast.*

Building Sydney

Descended from Scottish clan chieftains, Governor Lachlan Macquarie was an accomplished soldier and a man of vision. Macquarie, who was in office from 1810 to 1821, was the first governor to foresee a role for New South Wales as a free society rather than an open prison. He laid the foundations for that society by establishing a plan for the city, constructing significant public buildings, and advocating that reformed convicts be readmitted to society.

Macquarie's policies of equality may seem perfectly reasonable today, but in the early 19th century they marked him as a radical. When his vision of a free society threatened to blur distinctions between soldiers, settlers, and convicts, Macquarie was forced to resign. He was later buried on his Scottish estate, his gravestone inscribed with the words "the Father of Australia."

Macquarie's grand plans for the construction of Sydney might have come to nothing had it not been for Francis Greenway. Trained as an architect in England, where he was convicted of forgery and sentenced to 14 years in New South Wales, Greenway received a ticket of prison leave from Macquarie in 1814 and set to work transforming Sydney. Over the next few years he designed lighthouses, hospitals, convict barracks, and many other government buildings, several of which remain to bear witness to his simple but elegant eye. Greenway was eventually even depicted on one side of the old A$10 notes, which went out of circulation early in the 1990s. Only in Australia, perhaps, would a convicted forger occupy pride of place on the currency.

Lord Nelson Brewery Hotel
$$ | **B&B/INN** | If your idea of heaven is sleeping above a pub that brews its own boutique beers (or ales, as they're rightly called), this is the place. **Pros:** cheap rates; great location near harbor; free Wi-Fi; fun pub. **Cons:** limited breakfast options; may be noisy on weekend nights; some rooms are small. *Rooms from: A$210 19 Kent St., The Rocks 02/9251–4044 www.lordnelsonbrewery.com 9 rooms Free Breakfast.*

★ **Park Hyatt Sydney**
$$$$ | **HOTEL** | A multimillion-dollar total rebuild, which included the addition of an entire top floor, has seen the iconic Park Hyatt Sydney reemerge as Sydney's best address. **Pros:** superior dining options; fantastic location; gorgeous views. **Cons:** expensive; a distance from the CBD; very quiet. *Rooms from: A$880 7 Hickson Rd., The Rocks 02/9241–1234 www.hyatt.com No Meals 155 rooms.*

Rendezvous Hotel Sydney The Rocks
$ | **HOTEL** | Situated in the heart of the historic Rocks precinct, the lodging has a boutique-hotel style. **Pros:** spacious rooms; great location; good value. **Cons:** no restaurant or bar; simply appointed rooms; discreet street entrance can be difficult to find. *Rooms from: A$170 75 Harrington St., The Rocks 02/9251–6711 www.rendezvoushotels.com No Meals 68 rooms.*

Rydges Sydney Harbour
$$ | **HOTEL** | Even though it's been around for a few decades, this hotel with its low-key facade is still a bit of a secret. **Pros:** top-story pool; fantastic location near harbor; good value. **Cons:** street-facing rooms very noisy; not family-friendly; basic rooms.

Rooms from: A$220 ✉ 55 George St., The Rocks ☎ 02/9255–1800 🌐 www.rydges.com 🍽 No Meals 🛏 174 rooms.

The Russell

$$ | HOTEL | For charm, character, and central location, it's hard to beat this ornate Victorian hotel. **Pros:** warm ambience; location; includes breakfast; personal service. **Cons:** bit dated; not all rooms have en suite bathrooms; near a pub and busy area, so can be noisy. *Rooms from: A$250 ✉ 143A George St., The Rocks ☎ 02/9241–3543 🌐 www.therussell.com.au 🍽 Free Breakfast 🛏 50 rooms No credit cards.*

★ Shangri-La Hotel Sydney

$$$ | HOTEL | Towering above Walsh Bay from its prime position alongside the Sydney Harbour Bridge, this sleek hotel is *the* place for a room with a bird's-eye view. **Pros:** great in-house restaurant; breathtaking views; soothing ambience. **Cons:** expensive; impersonal and busy feel at times; low-level rooms have limited views. *Rooms from: A$350 ✉ 176 Cumberland St., The Rocks ☎ 02/9250–6000 🌐 www.shangri-la.com 🍽 No Meals 🛏 565 rooms.*

Nightlife

BARS AND DANCE CLUBS

Blu Bar on 36

WINE BARS | Blu Bar on 36 has a stellar view! Situated on the 36th floor of the Shangri-La Hotel, this is a sophisticated place to relax after work or enjoy a late-night drink while taking in the sweeping views of Sydney Harbour and the Opera House. Get here early (just after 5 pm) for a ringside seat. *✉ Shangri-La Hotel, 176 Cumberland St., The Rocks ☎ 02/9250–6000 🌐 www.shangri-la.com.*

Hacienda

COCKTAIL LOUNGES | Set above Circular Quay in the Quay Grand Sydney Harbour, this cocktail bar offers incredible views with outstanding tipples. Rum cocktails are the specialty drink of choice. On the weekends, this place comes alive in the afternoon for sundowners. During the week, it's a bit more of a relaxed crowd, enjoying a predinner drink in a more chill atmosphere than the nearby Opera Bar, which is always packed, day and night. Arrive early and also enjoy some Latin American small bites, including the buttermilk-fried-chicken tortilla. *✉ 61 Macquarie St., Circular Quay ☎ 2/9256–4000 🌐 haciendasydney.com.au.*

★ Opera Bar

PUBS | Perched beneath the concourse of the Opera House and at eye level with Sydney Harbour, Opera Bar has the best location in all of Sydney. Cozy up for a drink in the enclosed bar area or grab a waterside umbrella table and take in the glimmering skyline. Live music plays under the stars nightly from either 5:30 or 8 pm on weeknights, and from 2 pm on weekends. The bar has a full menu, though the attraction here is the scenery, not the cuisine. *✉ Sydney Opera House, Circular Quay ☎ 02/9247–1666 🌐 operabar.com.au.*

JAZZ CLUBS

The Push

PIANO BARS | Every Friday and Saturday evening, this lively piano bar comes alive with a friendly crowd that loves to shout requests to whomever is playing that night. There are classic cocktails, Australian wines, and cheese platters and tapas. Stay late enough and it's likely you'll end up dancing with the local patrons. *✉ 143 George St., The Rocks ☎ 02/9241–2999 🌐 www.pushbar.com.au.*

PUBS WITH MUSIC

Mercantile Hotel

LIVE MUSIC | In the shadow of Harbour Bridge, Mercantile Hotel is Irish and very proud of it. Fiddles, drums, and pipes rise above the clamor in the bar, and lilting accents rejoice in song every night of the week except Monday, from 8:30 pm until late, and on weekends from 3 pm. *✉ 25 George St., The Rocks ☎ 02/9247–3570 🌐 www.themercantilehotel.com.au.*

Shopping

ART GALLERY

The Ken Done Gallery

ART GALLERIES | This is a great place to find the striking artworks of prominent artist Ken Done, who catches the sunny side of Sydney with vivid colors and bold brushstrokes. His gallery also carries a line of bed linens, sunglasses, beach towels, beach and resort wear, and T-shirts. ✉ *1 Hickson Rd., The Rocks* ☎ *02/8274–4599* 🌐 *www.kendone.com.au.*

CLOTHING

Aribella

WOMEN'S CLOTHING | Here you'll find a unique mix of high-grade silk caftans and resort wear. Each is handcrafted, with-high-quality crystals and beads threaded onto each piece. No two garments are the same. ✉ *79 George St., The Rocks* 🌐 *aribella.com.au.*

JEWELRY AND ACCESSORIES

Hathi Jewellery

JEWELRY & WATCHES | Here you'll find a beautiful collection of handmade jewelry including earrings, necklaces, and bracelets. Most pieces are one of a kind. ✉ *19 Playfair St., The Rocks* ☎ *02/9252–4328* 🌐 *www.hathijewellery.com.au.*

MARKETS

★ The Rocks Market

MARKET | This sprawling covered bazaar transforms the upper end of George Street into a multicultural collage of music, food, arts, crafts, and entertainment. It's open weekends 10–5. Be sure to check out the new Rocks Foodies Market with delicious fare, on Friday 9–3. ✉ *Upper George St., near Argyle St., The Rocks* 🌐 *www.therocks.com.*

Domain and Macquarie Street

Some of Sydney's most notable Victorian-era public buildings, as well as one of its finest parks, can be found in this area. In contrast to the simple, utilitarian stone convict cottages of The Rocks, these buildings were constructed at a time when Sydney was experiencing a long period of prosperity thanks to the gold rushes of the mid-19th century and an agricultural boom. The sandstone just below the surface of many coastal areas proved an ideal building material—easily honed into the ornamentation so fashionable during the Victorian era. Macquarie Street is Sydney's most elegant boulevard. It was shaped by Governor Macquarie, who planned the transformation of the cart track leading to Sydney Cove into a stylish street of dwellings and government buildings. An occasional modern high-rise breaks up the streetscape, but many of the 19th-century architectural delights here escaped demolition.

GETTING HERE AND AROUND

The area is served by two train stations—Martin Place and St. James—but they are not on the same line. You can catch trains to both stations from Central and Town Hall. St. James is right next to Hyde Park, and Martin Place has an exit on Macquarie Street. From Macquarie Street it's a short walk to the Domain via the passageway that cuts through Sydney Hospital. A number of buses (including the 380/382 and 333 from Bondi Beach and 555 free shuttle) travel along Elizabeth Street.

Sights

★ Art Gallery of New South Wales

MUSEUM VILLAGE | Apart from Canberra's National Gallery, this is the best place to explore the evolution of European-influenced Australian art, as well as the

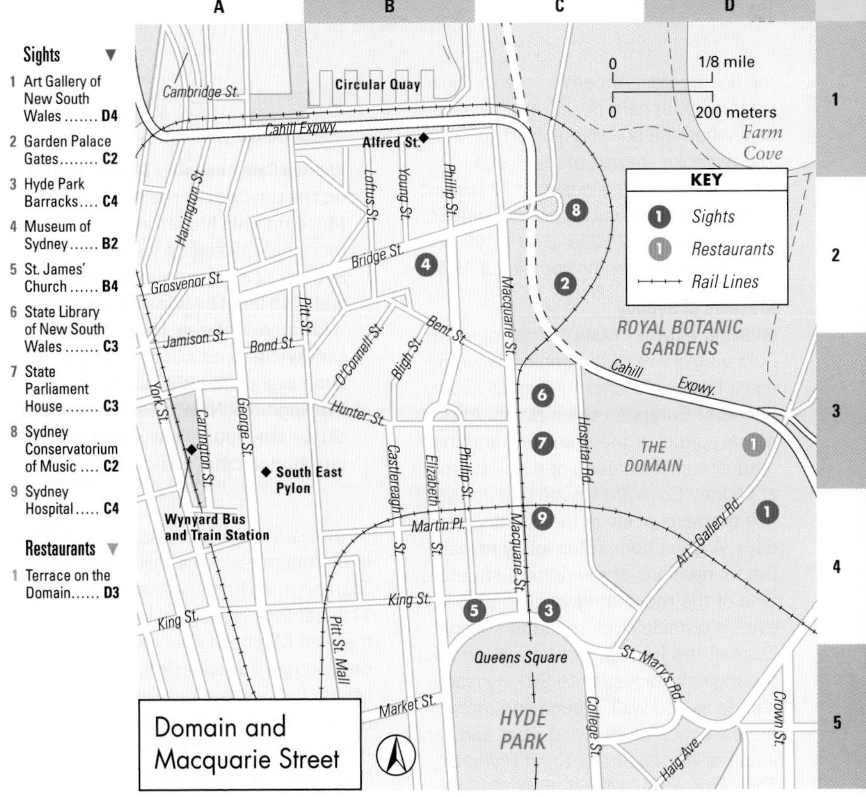

distinctly different concepts that underlie Aboriginal art. All the major Australian artists of the last two centuries are represented in this impressive collection. The entrance level, where large windows frame spectacular views of the harbor, exhibits 20th-century art. Below, in the gallery's major extensions, the Yiribana Gallery displays one of the nation's most comprehensive collections of Aboriginal and Torres Strait Islander art. There are monthly free audio tours and free talks. ✉ *Art Gallery Rd., The Domain* ☎ *02/9225–1700, 1800/679–278* 🌐 *www.artgallery.nsw.gov.au* 🎫 *Free; fee for special exhibits.*

Garden Palace Gates

HISTORIC SIGHT | These gates are all that remain of the Garden Palace, a massive glass pavilion that was erected for the Sydney International Exhibition of 1879 and destroyed by fire three years later. On the arch above the gates is a depiction of the Garden Palace's dome. Stone pillars on either side of the gates are engraved with Australian wildflowers. ✉ *Macquarie St., between Bridge and Bent Sts., The Domain.*

Hyde Park Barracks

JAIL/PRISON | Before Governor Macquarie arrived, convicts were left to roam freely at night. Macquarie was determined to establish law and order, and in 1819 he commissioned convict-architect Francis Greenway to design this restrained, classically Georgian-style building. Today the Barracks houses compelling exhibits that explore behind the scenes of the prison. For example, a surprising number of relics from this period were preserved by rats, which carried away scraps of clothing and other artifacts for their nests beneath the floorboards. A room on the top floor is strung with hammocks, exactly as it was when the building housed convicts. The barracks are part of the Sydney Living Museums collection of 12 historic buildings. ✉ *Queens Sq., Macquarie St., The Domain* ☎ *02/8239–2311* 🌐 *www.sydneylivingmuseums.com.au* 🎟 *A$24.*

Museum of Sydney

MUSEUM VILLAGE | **FAMILY** | This museum built on the site of the original Government House documents Sydney's early period of European colonization. Aboriginal culture, convict society, and the gradual transformation of the settlement at Sydney Cove are woven into an evocative portrayal of life in the country's early days. A glass floor in the lobby reveals the foundations of the original structure. One of the most intriguing exhibits, however, is outside (and free): the striking Edge of the Trees sculpture, where Koori (Aboriginal) voices recite Sydney placenames as you walk around and through the collection of 29 wood, iron, and sandstone pillars. ✉ *Bridge St. at Phillip St., The Domain* ☎ *02/9251–5988* 🌐 *www.sydneylivingmuseums.com.au* 🎟 *A$15.*

St. James' Church

CHURCH | Begun in 1819, the colonial Georgian–style St. James' is the oldest surviving church in the city of Sydney, and another fine Francis Greenway design. Now lost among the skyscrapers, the church's tall spire once served as a landmark for ships entering the harbor. Plaques commemorating Australian explorers and administrators cover the interior walls. Half-hour lunchtime concerts are presented every Wednesday from late February to late December at 1:15. ✉ *Queens Sq., 173 King St., Hyde Park* ☎ *02/8227–1300* 🌐 *www.sjks.org.au.*

State Library of New South Wales

LIBRARY | This large complex is based around the Mitchell and Dixson libraries, which make up the world's largest collection of Australiana. Enter the foyer through the classical portico to see one of the earliest maps of Australia, a copy in marble mosaic of a map made by Abel Tasman, the Dutch navigator, in the mid-17th century. Through the glass doors lies the vast Mitchell Library reading room, but you need a reader's ticket (establishing that you are pursuing legitimate research) to enter. You can, however, take a free escorted history and heritage tour weekdays at 10:30 am. The library continuously runs free exhibitions, and the opulent Shakespeare Room is open to the public Tuesday 10–4. ✉ *Macquarie St., between Royal Botanic Gardens and Parliament House, The Domain* ☎ *02/9273–1414* 🌐 *www.sl.nsw.gov.au.*

Need A Break? 

Rooftop Cafe Australian Museu. Found on the top floor of the Australian Museum, this hidden gem offers incredible sweeping views of Sydney's cityscape and harbor, as well as a lengthy wine list and a wide menu ranging from simple sandwiches and salads to a hearty lamb ragout. ✉ *1 William St., Darlinghurst NSW 2010, The Domain* ☎ *02/9320–6000* 🌐 *www.australianmuseum.net.au/food-and-dining.*

State Parliament House

GOVERNMENT BUILDING | The simple facade and shady verandas of this Greenway-designed 1816 building, formerly the Rum Hospital, typify Australian colonial architecture. From 1829, two rooms of the old hospital were used for meetings of the executive and legislative councils, which had been set up to advise the governor. These advisory bodies grew in power until New South Wales became self-governing in the 1840s, at which time Parliament occupied the entire building.

State Parliament generally sits between mid-February and late May, and again between mid-September and late

Sydney has enough museums and art galleries to appeal to just about every taste.

November. You can visit the public gallery and watch democracy in action. When parliament is not sitting, you can take a free escorted tour (they are conducted on the first Thursday of the month at 1 pm) or walk around at your leisure. You must reserve ahead for tours and to sit in the public gallery. ✉ *6 Macquarie St., The Domain* ☎ *02/9230–2111* 🌐 *www.parliament.nsw.gov.au.*

Sydney Conservatorium of Music

COLLEGE | Providing artistic development for talented young musicians, this institution hosts lunchtime concerts (entry by small donation) and free student performances throughout the year and other musical events. Guided tours take place every Wednesday at 11 am and 2 pm and Saturday at 10 am and 1 pm, with tickets to be purchased online or by phone in advance (A$25). The conservatory's turreted building was originally the stables for nearby Government House. The construction cost caused a storm among Governor Macquarie's superiors in London, and eventually helped bring about the downfall of both Macquarie and the building's architect, Francis Greenway. ✉ *Bridge St. at Macquarie St., The Domain* ☎ *02/9351–2222* 🌐 *music.sydney.edu.au* 🎫 *A$25.*

Sydney Hospital

HOSPITAL | Completed in 1894 to replace the main Rum Hospital building, which had stood on the site since 1811, this institution provided an infinitely better medical option. By all accounts, admission to the Rum Hospital was only slightly preferable to death itself. Convict nurses stole patients' food, and abler patients stole from the weaker. The kitchen sometimes doubled as a mortuary, and the table was occasionally used for operations.

In front of the hospital is a bronze figure of a boar. This is *Il Porcellino,* a copy of a statue that stands in Florence, Italy. According to the inscription, if you make a donation in the coin box and rub the boar's nose, "you will be endowed with good luck." Sydney citizens seem to be a superstitious bunch, because the boar's nose is very shiny indeed. ✉ *8 Macquarie St., The Domain* ☎ *02/9382–7111.*

Restaurants

Terrance on the Domain

$ | ITALIAN | Found within the Royal Botanic Garden Sydney, this is a popular choice from breakfast all the way up to a late dinner. There are three menus in total, with brunch, main meals, and cocktails with light bites. **Known for:** open every day until late; surrounded by stunning gardens; fun atmosphere. *Average main: A$25* ✉ *1 Art Gallery Rd., The Domain* ☎ *1300/300–278* *www.terraceonthedomain.com.au.*

The Opera House and the Royal Botanic Gardens

Bordering Sydney Cove, Farm Cove, and Woolloomooloo Bay, this section of Sydney includes the iconic Sydney Opera House, as well as extensive and delightful harborside gardens and parks.

The colony's first farm was established here in 1788, and the botanical gardens were laid out in 1816. The most dramatic change to the area occurred in 1959, however, when ground was broken on the site for the Sydney Opera House at Bennelong Point. This promontory was originally a small island, then the site of 1819 Fort Macquarie, later a tram depot, and finally the Opera House, one of the world's most striking modern buildings. The area's evolution is an eloquent metaphor for Sydney's own transformation.

GETTING HERE AND AROUND

The best way to get to the Opera House is to take one of the many ferries, buses, or trains that go to Circular Quay and then walk the pedestrian concourse. Some buses travel down Macquarie Street to the Opera House, which involves a slightly shorter walk. To get to the Royal Botanic Gardens, take the CityRail suburban train from the Town Hall, Central, or Bondi Junction station to Martin Place station, exit on the Macquarie Street side, and walk a few hundred yards.

Sights

Andrew (Boy) Charlton Pool

SPORTS VENUE | FAMILY | This heated saltwater eight-lane swimming pool overlooking the navy ships tied up at Garden Island has become a local favorite. There's also a covered splash pool for younger children. Complementing its stunning location is a radical design in glass and steel. The pools also have a chic terrace café above Woolloomooloo Bay, serving breakfast and lunch. There's a kiosk for smoothies and fresh coconuts. It's open from September 1 until April 30. ✉ *1c Mrs. Macquaries Rd., The Domain* ☎ *1300/198–412* *www.abcpool.org* *A$7.*

Farm Cove

VIEWPOINT | The shallow bay east of the Opera House is called Farm Cove. The original convict-settlers established their first gardens on this bay's shores. The enterprise was not a success: the soil was too sandy for agriculture, and most of the crops fell victim to pests, marauding animals, and hungry convicts. The long seawall was constructed from the 1840s onward to enclose the previously swampy foreshore. The area is now home to the Royal Botanic Gardens, a wonderful place to escape the city bustle. ✉ *Sydney* ✣ *Enter Botanic Gardens through gates near Opera House and in Macquarie St. From Opera House, turn right and walk along harbor foreshore (seawall is on your left, Botanic Gardens on your right). To enter Macquarie St. gates, take train to Martin Pl. railway station, exit station, turn left, and walk few hundred yards down Macquarie St.*

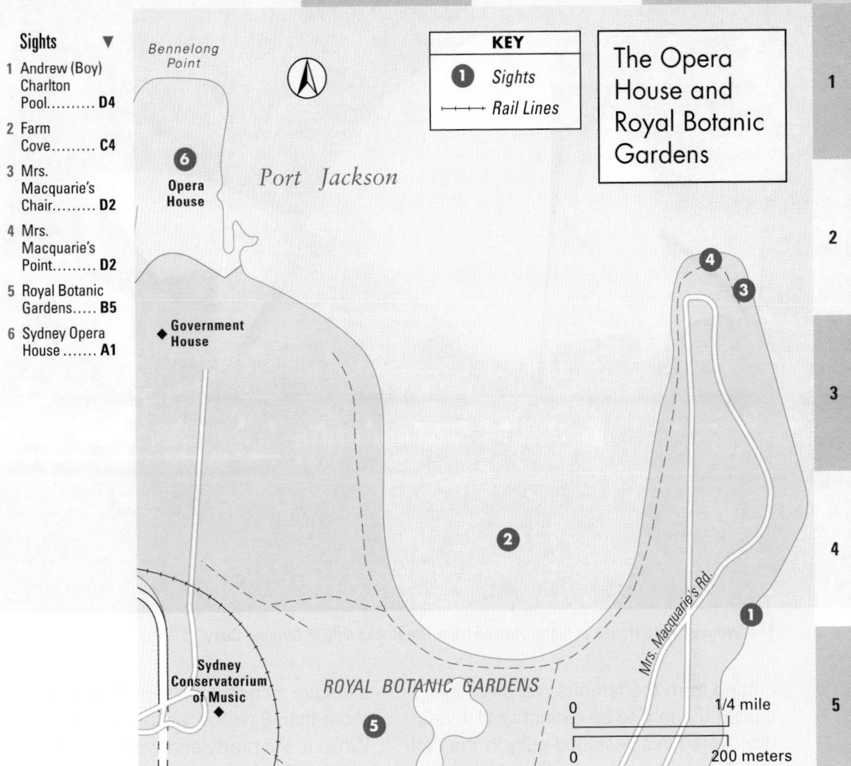

Mrs. Macquarie's Chair

HISTORIC SIGHT | During the early 1800s, Elizabeth Macquarie often sat on the point in the Domain at the east side of Farm Cove, at the rock where a seat has been hewn in her name. The views across the harbor are sensational. ✉ *Mrs. Macquaries Rd., Royal Botanic Gardens.*

Mrs. Macquarie's Point

VIEWPOINT | The inspiring views from this point, to the east of Bennelong Point (site of the Opera House), combine with the shady lawns to make this a popular place for picnics. The views are best at dusk, when the setting sun silhouettes the Opera House and the Harbour Bridge. ✉ *Mrs. Macquaries Rd., Royal Botanic Gardens.*

★ Royal Botanic Gardens

GARDEN | More than 80 acres of sweeping green lawns, groves of indigenous and exotic trees, duck ponds, greenhouses, and some 45,124 types of plants—many of them in bloom—grace these gardens. The elegant property, which attracts strollers and botany enthusiasts from all over the country, is a far cry today from what it once was: a failed attempt by convicts of the First Fleet to establish a farm. Though their early attempts at agriculture were disastrous, the efforts of these first settlers are acknowledged in the Pioneer Garden, a sunken garden built in their memory. Among the many other feature gardens on the property are the Palm Grove—home to some of the oldest trees in Sydney—the Begonia Garden, and the Rare and Threatened Plants Garden. Not to be missed is a

The Sydney Opera House at night, viewed from The Rocks side of Circular Quay

cutting from the famous Wollemi Pine, a plant thought to be extinct until it was discovered in a secluded gully in the Wollemi National Park in the Blue Mountains in 1994. Plants throughout the gardens have various blooming cycles, so no matter what time of year you visit, there are sure to be plenty of flowers. The gardens include striking sculptures and hundreds of species of birds. There are spectacular views over the harbor and the Opera House from the garden's sea wall and two lovely restaurants are open for lunch and snacks. ■ TIP→ **For those who don't want to walk, the ChooChoo Express toylike train offers a 25-minute ride through the gardens, making four stops (A$10).** ✉ *Mrs. Macquaries Rd., The Domain* ☎ *02/9231–8111* 🌐 *www.rbgsyd.nsw.gov.au or www.choochoo.com.au* 🎫 *Free.*

★ Sydney Opera House

NOTABLE BUILDING | One of the most iconic and recognizable buildings in the world, and listed as a World Heritage site in 2007, the Sydney Opera House is a multivenue performing arts center and a unique architectural sight that wows more than 8 million visitors annually. While it sits pretty and worry-free today, this famous landmark had a long and troubled backstory. What should have taken Danish architect Joern Utzon four years and A$7 million to complete when commissioned in 1959, in fact took 15 years, A$102 million, and an additional team of Australian architects. Although you can access the building throughout the day and early evening, all you really get to see is the main foyer area, which is less than inspiring. To see the best of "the house" join one of the guided tours, which include the one-hour Sydney Opera House Tour, departing daily from the lower forecourt level between 9 and 5; and the two-hour backstage tour, departing daily at 7 am. Or book in to see many of the shows running in its five theaters. ✉ *2 Macquarie St., Circular Quay* ☎ *02/9250–7111, 02/9250–7250 tour bookings* 🌐 *www.sydneyopera-house.com* 🎫 *Tours from A$40.*

Darling Harbour and Barangaroo

Until the mid-1980s this horseshoe-shape bay on the city center's western edge was a wasteland of disused docks and railway yards. Then, in an explosive burst of activity the whole area was redeveloped and opened in time for Australia's bicentenary in 1988. Now there's plenty to take in at the Darling Harbour complex: the National Maritime Museum, SEA LIFE Sydney Aquarium, WILD LIFE Sydney Zoo, and the gleaming Exhibition Centre, whose masts and spars recall the square-riggers that once berthed here. At the harbor's center is a large park shaded by palm trees. To the right is Barangaroo Reserve, Sydney's latest harbor playground, with world-class eateries and stunning walks. Waterways and fountains lace the complex together.

GETTING HERE AND AROUND

Take the train to either Town Hall or Central Station. From Town Hall it's a short walk down Druitt Street; from Central you walk through Haymarket and Chinatown. The Light Rail tram (A$2.20 one-way) connects Central Station with Darling Harbour and The Star casino a little farther to the west.

Sights

Australian National Maritime Museum

MUSEUM VILLAGE | FAMILY | The six galleries of this soaring, futuristic building tell the story of Australia and the sea. In addition to figureheads, model ships, and brassy nautical hardware, there are antique racing yachts and the jet-powered *Spirit of Australia,* current holder of the world water speed record, set in 1978. The USA Gallery displays objects from such major U.S. collections as the Smithsonian Institution, and was dedicated by President George Bush Sr. on New Year's Day 1992. An outdoor section showcases numerous vessels moored at the museum's wharves, including the HMAS *Vampire,* a retired Royal Australian Navy destroyer, and the historic tall ship the *James Craig.* You can also climb to the top of the 1874 Bowling Green lighthouse. ✉ *Maritime Heritage Centre, 2 Murray St., Wharf 7, Darling Harbour* ☎ *02/9298–3777* 🌐 *www.sea.museum* 🎫 *Free.*

★ **Barangaroo Reserve**

OTHER ATTRACTION | Barangaroo is Sydney's newest shopping and eating precinct, an ongoing redevelopment of the an old wharf area once known as "The Hungry Mile," between Walsh Bay and The Rocks and a fast favorite with locals because of its central location, easy access, and multiofferings. The harbor front is punctuated with all levels of dining, from high-end to trendy burger bars, and in the newly cobbled streets that run behind them, toward the CBD, there's a maze of fashion boutiques. There's also a boardwalk that currently links Barangaroo to its neighbors, with Darling Harbour to its south and Walsh Bay and the Harbour Bridge to its north. The park's name, Barangaroo Precinct, honors the powerful companion of Benelong, the Indigenous man known to the first European settlers, whose name was given to the point on the other side of the city where the Opera House stands. Barangaroo was an outspoken woman who advocated against the colonization of Sydney. Learn more about the origins of the Barangaroo Precinct and the 15-acre headland that surrounds it on a daily Aboriginal culture tour ($36.30), leaving at 10:30 am. ✉ *Millers Point* 🌐 *www.barangaroo.com.*

Chinatown

NEIGHBORHOOD | Bounded by George Street, Goulburn Street, and Paddy's Market, Chinatown takes your senses on a galloping tour of the Orient. Within this compact grid are aromatic restaurants, traditional apothecaries, Chinese grocers, clothing boutiques, and shops selling Asian-made electronics. The best way to

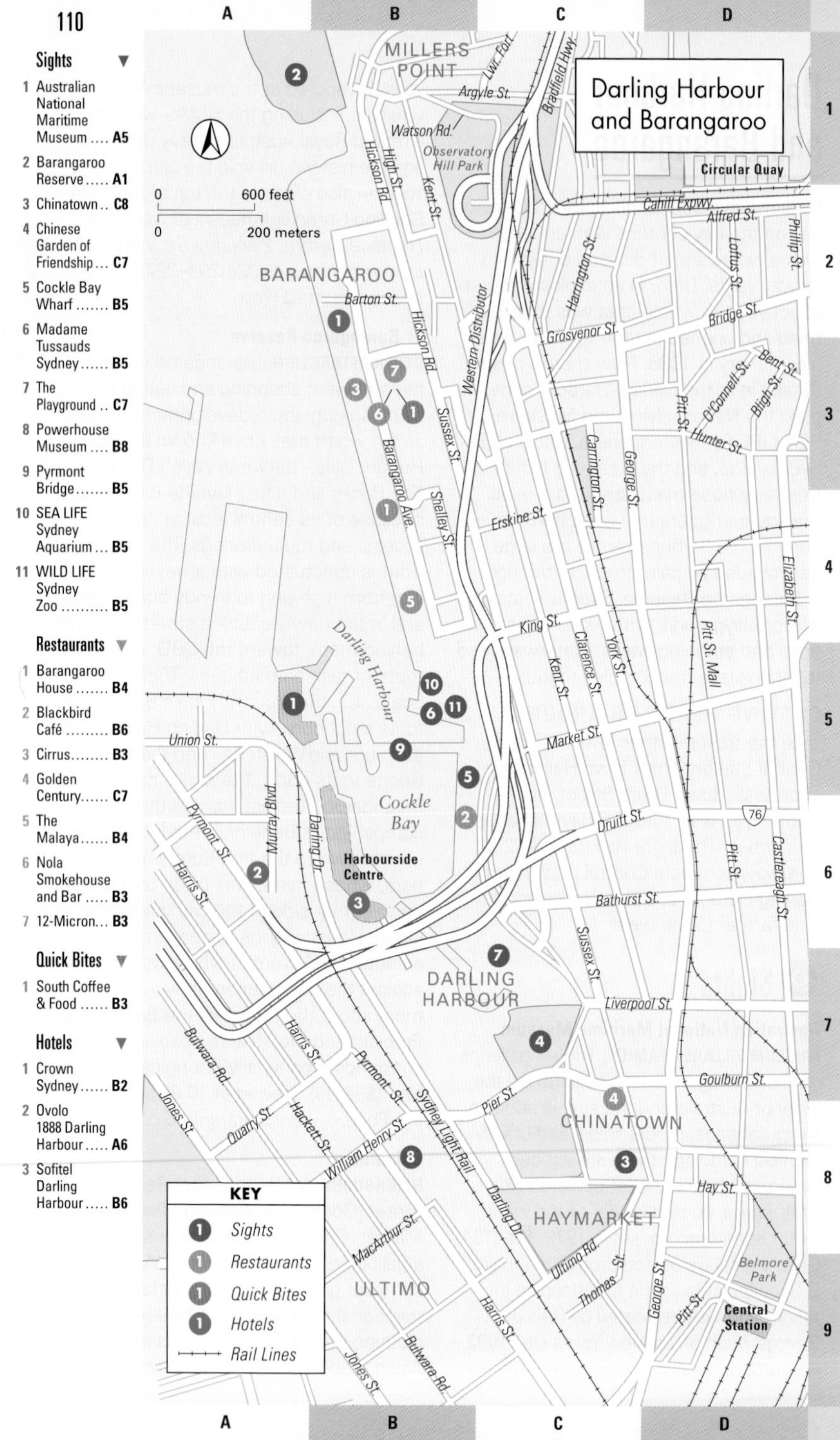
Sights
1 Australian National Maritime Museum A5
2 Barangaroo Reserve A1
3 Chinatown .. C8
4 Chinese Garden of Friendship ... C7
5 Cockle Bay Wharf B5
6 Madame Tussauds Sydney B5
7 The Playground .. C7
8 Powerhouse Museum B8
9 Pyrmont Bridge B5
10 SEA LIFE Sydney Aquarium ... B5
11 WILD LIFE Sydney Zoo B5
Restaurants
1 Barangaroo House B4
2 Blackbird Café B6
3 Cirrus........ B3
4 Golden Century...... C7
5 The Malaya...... B4
6 Nola Smokehouse and Bar B3
7 12-Micron... B3
Quick Bites
1 South Coffee & Food B3
Hotels
1 Crown Sydney...... B2
2 Ovolo 1888 Darling Harbour..... A6
3 Sofitel Darling Harbour..... B6
Darling Harbour and Barangaroo
A
B
C
D
1
2
3
4
5
6
7
8
9
0
600 feet
0
200 meters
MILLERS POINT
Argyle St.
Lwr. Fort
Bradfield Hwy.
Watson Rd.
Observatory Hill Park
Circular Quay
Cahill Expwy.
Alfred St.
Phillip St.
Loftus St.
High St.
Hickson Rd.
Kent St.
BARANGAROO
Barton St.
Harrington St.
Bridge St.
Western Distributor
Grosvenor St.
Bent St.
O'Connell St.
Bligh St.
Pitt St.
Hunter St.
Sussex St.
Barangaroo Ave.
Carrington St.
George St.
Shelley St.
Erskine St.
Elizabeth St.
King St.
Clarence St.
York St.
Kent St.
Pitt St. Mall
Darling Harbour
Union St.
Market St.
Cockle Bay
Murray Blvd.
Darling Dr.
Pyrmont St.
Harris St.
Harbourside Centre
Druitt St.
76
Pitt St.
Castlereagh St.
Bathurst St.
Sussex St.
DARLING HARBOUR
Liverpool St.
Bulwara Rd.
Harris St.
Pyrmont St.
Goulburn St.
Jones St.
Quarry St.
Hackett St.
Sydney Light Rail
Pier St.
CHINATOWN
William Henry St.
Hay St.
Darling Dr.
HAYMARKET
MacArthur St.
Ultimo Rd.
Thomas St.
George St.
Belmore Park
ULTIMO
Pitt St.
Central Station
Harris St.
Jones St.
Bulwara Rd.
KEY
Sights
Restaurants
Quick Bites
Hotels
Rail Lines

get a sense of the area is to take a stroll along Dixon Street, now a pedestrian mall with a Chinese Lion Gate at either end. Sydney's Chinese community was first established here in the 1800s, in the aftermath of the gold rush that originally drew many Chinese immigrants to Australia. For the last few years, the area has enjoyed getting a bit of a face-lift including new lighting, artwork, and more pedestrian walkways. Most Sydneysiders come here regularly to dine, especially on weekends for dim sum (called *yum cha*). ✉ *Dixon St., Haymarket.*

Chinese Garden of Friendship

GARDEN | Chinese prospectors came to the Australian goldfields as far back as the 1850s, and the nation's long and enduring links with China are symbolized by the Chinese Garden of Friendship, the largest garden of its kind outside China. Designed by Chinese landscape architects, the garden includes bridges, lakes, waterfalls, sculptures, and Cantonese-style pavilions—the perfect place for a refreshing cup of tea from the café. Free 35-minute guided tours run daily. ✉ *38 Harbour St., Darling Harbour* ☏ *02/9240–8888* 🌐 *www.darlingharbour.com* 🎫 *A$6* ☞ *Tours run daily 10:30 and 2:30 Oct.–Apr., noon May–Sept.*

Cockle Bay Wharf

MARINA/PIER | Fueling Sydney's addiction to fine food, most of this sprawling waterfront complex, on the city side of Darling Harbour, is dedicated to gastronomy, as well as a few bars and nightclubs. If you have a boat you can dock at the marina—and avoid the hassle of parking a car in one of the city's most congested centers. ✉ *201 Sussex St., Darling Harbour* ☏ *02/9269–9800* 🌐 *www.cocklebaywharf.com.au.*

Madame Tussauds Sydney

MUSEUM VILLAGE | **FAMILY** | Hugh Jackman as Wolverine, songstress Kylie Minogue, and Olympic champion Cathy Freeman are among the contingent of Australian wax figures at the Madame Tussauds Sydney, the only version of the well-known museum in Australia. Located between SEA LIFE Sydney Aquarium and WILD LIFE Sydney Zoo at Darling Harbour, the museum has nine interactive themed areas where patrons can, for example, jump on a surfboard with world champion female surfer Layne Beachley or sing in the band with legendary Aussie rocker Jimmy Barnes. The 70 figures are grouped in themes such as world leaders, cultural icons, and music and film stars. ✉ *Aquarium Wharf, near Wheat St., Darling Harbour* ☏ *02/8251–7800* 🌐 *www.madametussauds.com.au/sydney/en* 🎫 *A$37.*

The Playground

CITY PARK | **FAMILY** | Found just a short walk from Darling Harbour is Darling Quarter, a bustling cultural precinct set around a large open space, punctuated by manicured gardens and surrounded by restaurants that specialize in alfresco dining. At the heart of this area is The Playground, an ever-popular spot for families and those needing a five-minute break from touring on foot. The park offers an intricate water play area for children, with jets of water illuminated by colorful rays of light. This spot really comes to life on a sunny Sydney day, when you will find live music and cultural events on the green, including yoga for all ages every Friday. ✉ *1–25 Harbour St., Darling Harbour* 🌐 *darlingquarter.com.*

Powerhouse Museum

MUSEUM VILLAGE | **FAMILY** | Learning the principles of science is a painless process with this museum's stimulating, interactive displays ideal for all ages. Exhibits in the former 1890s electricity station that once powered Sydney's trams include a whole floor of working steam engines, space modules, airplanes suspended from the ceiling, state-of-the-art computer gadgetry, and a 1930s art deco–style movie-theater auditorium. The museum also stages many excellent exhibitions that are not science-based

Off The Beaten Path

Sydney Fish Market. Second in size only to Tokyo's giant Tsukiji fish market, Sydney's is a showcase for the riches of Australia's seas. An easy 10-minute walk from Darling Harbour (and with its own stop on the Metro Light Rail network), the market is a great place to sample sushi, oysters, octopus, spicy Thai and Chinese fish dishes, and fish-and-chips at the waterfront cafés overlooking the fishing fleet. Behind the scenes guided tours, including the auction, begin at 6:40 am and run until 8:30 am on Monday, Wednesday, Thursday, and Friday ($A50). They also offer cooking classes. Call ahead for advance reservations or book on the website. ✉ *Pyrmont Bridge Rd., at Bank St., Pyrmont West* ☎ *02/9004–1100* 🌐 *www.sydneyfishmarket.com.au.*

on everything from fashion and crochet and jewelry to computer games. ✉ *500 Harris St., Ultimo, Darling Harbour* ☎ *02/9217–0111* 🌐 *www.maas.museum/powerhouse-museum* 🎫 *A$15.*

Pyrmont Bridge

BRIDGE | Dating from 1902, this is the world's oldest electrically operated swing-span bridge. The structure once carried motor traffic, but it's now a walkway that links Darling Harbour's western side with Cockle Bay on the east. The center span still swings open to allow tall-masted ships into Cockle Bay, which sits at the bottom of the horse-shoe-shape shore. ✉ *Darling Harbour.*

SEA LIFE Sydney Aquarium

AQUARIUM | **FAMILY** | Bay of Rays and Shark Valley are among 14 themed areas at SEA LIFE Sydney Aquarium at Darling Harbour. Home to some 13,000 creatures, the huge aquarium also has two of only five dugongs (large, rare marine mammal [similar to a manatee] mainly found off the coast of northern Australia) that are on display anywhere in the world. The Sydney Harbour exhibit shows you what's underneath Sydney's huge expanse of water, while the new open coral tank is dazzlingly colorful. Fish and mammal feedings take place throughout the day, along with talks on some of these amazing creatures. A behind-the-scenes tour is a good value at A$18 over the online admission price. The aquarium is part of the Merlin Entertainments group and good combination ticket deals are available for the company's other attractions that include WILD LIFE Sydney Zoo, the new Madame Tussauds (both located next door to the Aquarium), and the Sydney Tower Eye (A$63). ✉ *Aquarium Pier, 1–5 Wheat Rd., Darling Harbour* ☎ *1800/199657* 🌐 *www.sydneyaquarium.com.au* 🎫 *A$40.*

WILD LIFE Sydney Zoo

ZOO | **FAMILY** | This Sydney attraction brings thousands of Australian animals right to the heart of Sydney. Kangaroos, koalas, and dozens of other species come together under the one huge roof—in nine separate habitats—next door to the SEA LIFE Sydney Aquarium and the new Madame Tussauds. All three attractions are run by the same operator, Merlin Entertainments, and all are able to be visited on one combination ticket. In Devil's Den you'll see the famed Tasmanian devils; in Wallaby Cliffs there are yellow-footed wallabies and hairy-nosed wombats, while you can walk among the eastern grey kangaroos and agile wallabies with their joeys and the spiky echidnas in Kangaroo Walkabout. Watch out for Rex, the 16-foot saltwater crocodile in the Kakadu Gorge habitat. A popular spot is Gum Tree Alley where you'll meet koalas, while the endangered (and very cute) greater bilby is in the Nightfall nocturnal zone. **TIP→ The best deals for stand-alone tickets or combination tickets with other Merlin Entertainments attractions are online. There are savings of around A$12 for a single ticket, while the current combo ticket is A$69.** ✉ *Aquarium Pier, Wheat Rd., Darling Harbour* ☎ *1800/206–158* 🌐 *www.wildlifesydney.com.au* 🎟 *A$37.*

Restaurants

★ Barangaroo House

$$ | AUSTRALIAN | Sitting at the edge of newly completed Barangaroo like an elegant stack of wide, plant-filled bowls clad in charred timber, this three-level spaceship has a seating capacity of 900 people and a variety of spaces for casual and fine dining. The House Bar at the pedestrian promenade level offers craft beers and share plates, like barramundi bites; In the middle is Bea, a sprawling fine-dining restaurant with elevated Australian fare and both indoor and outdoor dining; the buzzy rooftop bar, Smoke, has good views across the harbor. **Known for:** lively rooftop bar; excellent design; Bea's whole roast duck from the Southern Highlands. $ *Average main: A$45* ✉ *35 Barangaroo Ave., Barangaroo, Sydney* ☎ *02/8587–5400* 🌐 *www.barangaroohouse.com.au.*

Blackbird Café

$ | AUSTRALIAN | FAMILY | Blackbird Café is great place to take a break while exploring Darling Harbour. The weekday lunch specials are all under A$20 and a good value. **Known for:** balcony with views; family-friendly; great value. $ *Average main: A$20* ✉ *Cockle Bay Wharf, 201 Sussex St., balcony level, Darling Harbour* ☎ *02/9283–7385* 🌐 *www.blackbirdcafe.com.au.*

★ Cirrus

$$ | AUSTRALIAN | It's named after a cloud, but with its floor-to-ceiling-windows looking out on Cockle Bay, timber fencing (both on the floor and strung in different lengths from the ceiling) akin to what you might see in sand dunes, a suspended/flying vintage speedboat named Alvin, and perhaps the best and freshest seafood offerings in Sydney, Cirrus may as well be named for the sea it floats above. The five-course, degustation-style menu is very popular but the seafood platter of oysters, fat Skull Island prawns, strawberry clams, ocean bugs, and *pipis* (triangular clams) with seaweed mayo ponzu and red-wine vinaigrette is a must. **Known for:** views of the harbor; five-course menu; seafood platter. $ *Average main: A$44* ✉ *23 Barangaroo Ave., Barangaroo, Sydney* ☎ *02/9220–0111* 🌐 *www.cirrusdining.com.au.*

Golden Century

$ | CHINESE | For two hours—or as long as it takes for you to consume delicately steamed prawns, luscious mud crab with ginger and shallots, and *pipis* with black-bean sauce—you might as well be in Hong Kong. This place is heaven for seafood lovers, with wall-to-wall fish tanks filled with crab, lobster, abalone, and schools of barramundi, parrotfish, and coral trout. **Known for:** large range of seafood; lengthy queue; late-night dining. $ *Average main: A$30* ✉ *393–399 Sussex St., Haymarket* ☎ *02/9212–3901.*

The Malaya

$ | MALAYSIAN | The cocktails are legendary, the view is captivating, and the food, a traditional Chinese/Malay fusion, is extraordinary. After 50 years in the business (first opened in 1963), in different venues around Sydney, this modern Asian restaurant still does a roaring trade. **Known for:** Szechuan eggplant; great views; beef Rendang. $ *Average main: A$30* ✉ *King Street Wharf, 39 Lime St., Darling Harbour* ☎ *02/9279–1170* 🌐 *www.themalaya.com.au* ▭ *No credit cards* ⏲ *Closed Mon.*

Nola Smokehouse and Bar

$$$ | AMERICAN | A bit of a hidden gem, to enter this New Orleans–inspired smokehouse you have to come through a door in an alleyway just off Barangaroo waterfront. Take the elevator up two floors and when the doors open you'll be hit by that incredible American barbecue smell. **Known for:** incredible views; extensive whiskey range; authentic smoked meats. *Average main: A$ 65* *100 Barangaroo Ave., Darling Harbour* *02/9188–3039* *www.nolasydney.com.*

12-Micron

$$$ | AUSTRALIAN | Head chef Justin Wise's focus here is celebrating the elements of air, land, and sea in a menu that celebrates local farmers and fine Australian wines. Menu highlights include the pork jowl with black pudding and riberries and lamb neck with potato and broad beans. **Known for:** tasting menu; dessert bar; superior wine pairing. *Average main: A$55* *Tower 1, 100 Barangaroo Ave., Level 2, Sydney* *02/8322–2075* *12micron.com.au* *No lunch Mon.*

Coffee and Quick Bites

South Coffee & Food

$ | AUSTRALIAN | Darling Harbour and Barangaroo are undoubtedly two of the busiest areas of Sydney so for a quiet reprieve step into this tucked-away café. With an impressive wooden art installation snaking around the ceiling, outstanding coffee and freshly baked croissants and muffins, this is the perfect place to recharge before more adventuring. **Known for:** quiet; incredible coffee; arty interiors. *Average main: A$15* *Tower 1/100 Barangaroo Ave., Darling Harbour* *02/9290–3904* *www.southcoffeefood.com.au* *Closed weekends.*

Hotels

★ Crown Sydney

$$$$ | HOTEL | Opened in 2020, the Crown Sydney is perhaps the city's most ambitious development costing a whopping A$2.2 million. **Pros:** convenient location; luxury; incredible views. **Cons:** service hit-and-miss; expensive; some rooms have no views. *Rooms from: A$ 700* *1 Barangaroo Ave., Darling Harbour* *02/8871–7171* *www.crownsydney.com.au* *No Meals* *350 rooms.*

Ovolo 1888 Darling Harbour

$$ | HOTEL | This former wool warehouse has been turned into one of Sydney's most cutting-edge designer hotels. **Pros:** contemporary and cool design; close to Darling Harbour and the city center; free Wi-Fi and free phone calls (in Australia). **Cons:** small rooms; vegan-only menu might not suit all; some rooms next to busy road. *Rooms from: A$250* *139 Murray St., Darling Harbour* *02/8586–1888* *www.ovolohotels.com.au/ovolo1888darlingharbour* *90 rooms* *Free Breakfast.*

Sofitel Darling Harbour

$$$ | HOTEL | FAMILY | When it comes to views, it doesn't get much better than the Sofitel Darling Harbour, especially from the top floor, where the floor-to-ceiling windows offer sweeping vistas of the beaches in the Eastern Suburbs. **Pros:** quality finishes; incredible views in all rooms; central location. **Cons:** no train nearby; Wi-Fi isn't free; busy lobby. *Rooms from: A$330* *12 Darling Dr., Darling Harbour* *02/8388–8888* *www.accorhotels.com* *Free Breakfast* *590 rooms.*

Nightlife

BARS AND DANCE CLUBS

Bungalow 8

DANCE CLUBS | With its primo waterside location at the northern end of King Street Wharf, and famous mussels from its open kitchen, Bungalow 8 invites a night of posing and partying. This is the place to be seen bobbing your head to the spinning of several ultracool resident DJs. *King St. Wharf, 3 Lime St., Darling Harbour* *02/8322–2006* *bungalow8sydney.com.au.*

Marquee - The Star Sydney

DANCE CLUBS | Nightclubbers are heading to Marquee—on the top level of the relaunched casino and entertainment complex, The Star Sydney—to dance the night away. The huge nightclub heaves with 1,500 twentysomethings who take to the dance floors in the Main Room and the smaller Boom Box, or chill out in the opulent Library bar. R&B artists and local and international DJs perform on weekends, with tickets from $A10 if you get in before 11 pm. When it's time to cool down, there are great outdoor balconies overlooking the city and Darling Harbour. ✉ *80 Pyrmont St., Darling Harbour* ☎ *02/9657–7737* 🌐 *www.marqueesydney.com.*

Performing Arts

Sydney Lyric

MUSIC | At The Star casino and entertainment complex, Sydney Lyric is one of the city's most spectacular performing-arts venues. Despite its size, there's no better place to watch big-budget musicals. Every seat in the lavishly spacious, 2,000-seat theater is a good one. ✉ *20–80 Pyrmont St., Pyrmont, Darling Harbour* ☎ *02/9505–3600 tickets* 🌐 *sydneylyric.com.au.*

Shopping

MARKETS

Paddy's Market

MARKET | **FAMILY** | Paddy's Market is a huge fresh produce and flea market held under the Market City complex near the Sydney Entertainment Centre in the Chinatown precinct. There has been a market on this site since 1834, and much of the historic exterior remains. The Metro Light Rail stops at the door. ✉ *9–13 Hay St., Haymarket* 🌐 *www.paddysmarkets.com.au.*

Sydney City Center

Shopping is the main reason to visit Sydney's city center, but there are several buildings and other places of interest among the office blocks, department stores, and shopping centers.

GETTING HERE AND AROUND

Buses from the Eastern Suburbs run along Elizabeth Street on the western side of Hyde Park; buses from the inner Western Suburbs such as Balmain travel to and from the Queen Victoria Building. The main train stations are Town Hall and Martin Place, while Hyde Park is served by both St. James and Museum Station on the City Circle rail line. There are the Light Rail trams that are easy to hop on and off, running the length of George Street. The free shuttle bus (No. 555) completes a circuit around the city center, stopping at the main attractions.

Sights

Anzac Memorial

HISTORIC SIGHT | In the southern section of Hyde Park (near Liverpool Street) stands the 1934 art deco Anzac Memorial, a tribute to the Australians who died in military service during World War I, when the acronym ANZAC (Australian and New Zealand Army Corps) was coined. The 120,000 gold stars inside the dome represent each man and woman of New South Wales who served. The lower level exhibits war-related photographs, and a beautiful, poignant sculpture of an ANZAC soldier and shield. ✉ *Hyde Park* ☎ *02/8262–2900.*

Australian Museum

MUSEUM VILLAGE | **FAMILY** | The strength of this natural history museum, a well-respected academic institution, is its collection of plants, animals, geological specimens, and cultural artifacts from the Asia-Pacific region. Particularly notable are the collections of artifacts from Papua New Guinea and from Australia's

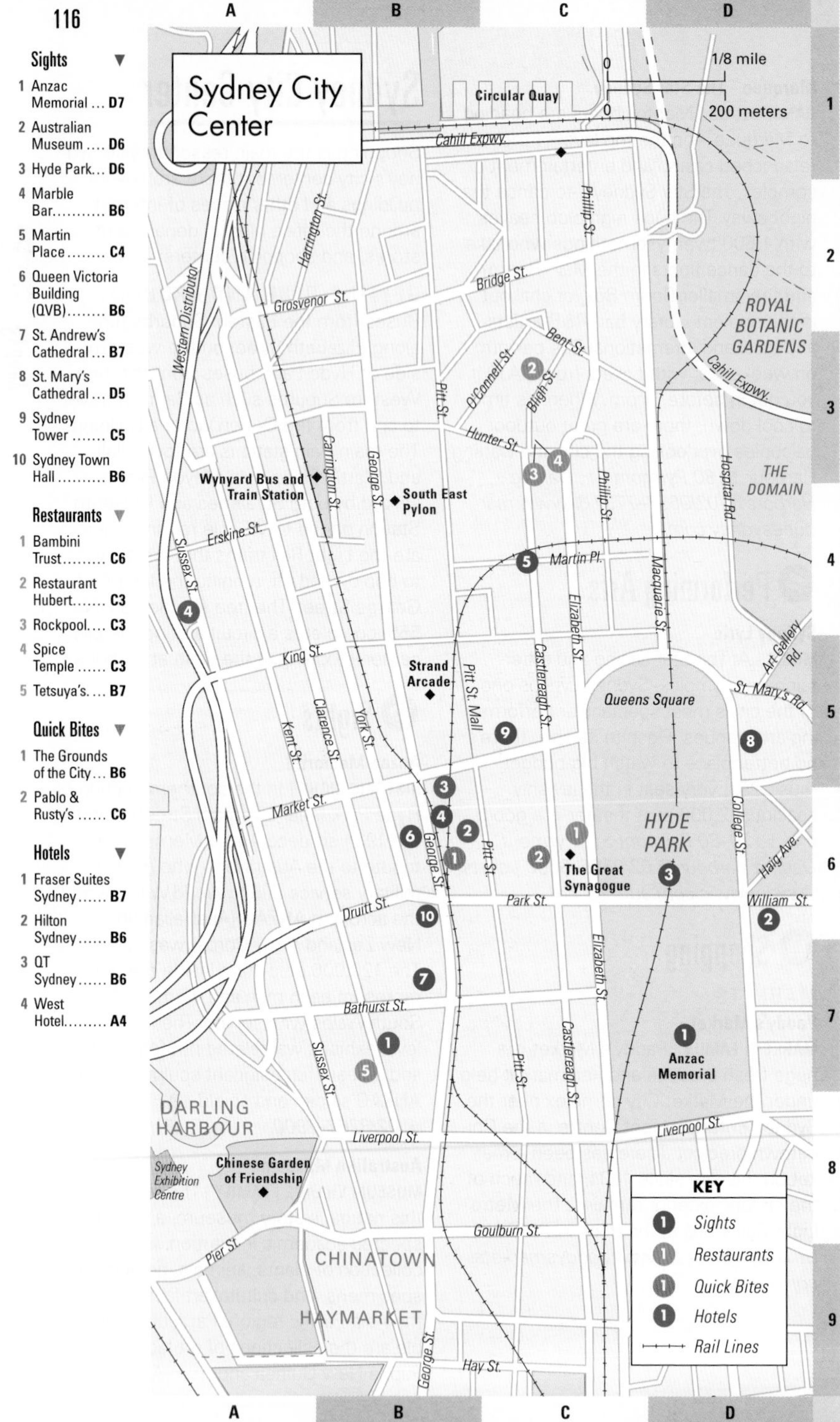

Sights
1 Anzac Memorial ... D7
2 Australian Museum D6
3 Hyde Park... D6
4 Marble Bar........... B6
5 Martin Place........ C4
6 Queen Victoria Building (QVB)........ B6
7 St. Andrew's Cathedral ... B7
8 St. Mary's Cathedral ... D5
9 Sydney Tower C5
10 Sydney Town Hall B6
Restaurants
1 Bambini Trust......... C6
2 Restaurant Hubert....... C3
3 Rockpool.... C3
4 Spice Temple C3
5 Tetsuya's.... B7
Quick Bites
1 The Grounds of the City... B6
2 Pablo & Rusty's C6
Hotels
1 Fraser Suites Sydney...... B7
2 Hilton Sydney...... B6
3 QT Sydney...... B6
4 West Hotel......... A4
Sydney City Center
A
B
C
D
1
2
3
4
5
6
7
8
9
0
1/8 mile
0
200 meters
Circular Quay
Cahill Expwy.
Harrington St.
Phillip St.
Western Distributor
Grosvenor St.
Bridge St.
ROYAL BOTANIC GARDENS
Bent St.
O'Connell St.
Bligh St.
Cahill Expwy.
Pitt St.
Hunter St.
Carrington St.
George St.
Wynyard Bus and Train Station
South East Pylon
Phillip St.
Hospital Rd.
THE DOMAIN
Erskine St.
Sussex St.
Martin Pl.
Macquarie St.
Elizabeth St.
Castlereagh St.
Art Gallery Rd.
King St.
Strand Arcade
Pitt St. Mall
Queens Square
St. Mary's Rd.
Clarence St.
York St.
Kent St.
Market St.
HYDE PARK
College St.
George St.
Pitt St.
The Great Synagogue
Haig Ave.
Druitt St.
Park St.
William St.
Elizabeth St.
Bathurst St.
Sussex St.
Pitt St.
Castlereagh St.
Anzac Memorial
DARLING HARBOUR
Liverpool St.
Liverpool St.
Sydney Exhibition Centre
Chinese Garden of Friendship
Pier St.
Goulburn St.
CHINATOWN
HAYMARKET
George St.
Hay St.
KEY
Sights
Restaurants
Quick Bites
Hotels
Rail Lines

Aboriginal peoples. One of the most popular exhibits is "Dinosaurs" on Level 2, containing 10 complete skeletons, eight life-size models, and interactive displays, while "Surviving Australia" (about Australian animals) and "Indigenous Australia" are the most popular with overseas visitors. There are behind-the-scenes tours (A$98), an excellent shop, and a lively café. ✉ *6 College St., near William St., Hyde Park* ☎ *02/9320–6000* 🌐 *www.australianmuseum.net.au* 🎫 *Free* ☞ *Free guided tours daily, usually at 11 and 2 although subject to change.*

Hyde Park

NATIONAL PARK | Declared public land by Governor Phillip in 1792 and used for the colony's earliest cricket matches and horse races, this area was turned into a park in 1810. The gardens are formal, with fountains, statuary, and tree-lined walks, and its tranquil lawns are popular with office workers at lunchtime. The park has two sections, with Park Street (a traffic street) dividing the two halves. Several events, such as the Night Noodle Markets (open-air Asian food markets) in October, are held in the park. ✉ *Elizabeth, College, and Park Sts., Hyde Park* 🌐 *www.cityofsydney.nsw.gov.au.*

Marble Bar

HOTEL | Stop in at the Marble Bar to experience a masterpiece of Victorian extravagance. The 1890 bar was formerly in another building that was constructed on the profits of the horse-racing track, thus establishing the link between gambling and majestic public architecture that has its modern-day parallel in the Sydney Opera House. Threatened with demolition in the 1970s, the whole bar was moved—marble arches, color-glass ceiling, elaborately carved woodwork, paintings of voluptuous nudes, and all—to its present site in the basement of the Hilton Sydney Hotel. There is live music most weekends. ✉ *Hilton Sydney, 488 George St., City Center* ☎ *02/9266–2000* 🌐 *www.marblebarsydney.com.au* 🕒 *Closed Sun., Mon., and Tues.*

Martin Place

BUSINESS DISTRICT | Sydney's largest pedestrian precinct, flanked by banks, offices, and shopping centers, is the hub of the central business district. There are some grand buildings here—including the beautifully refurbished Commonwealth Bank and the 1870s Venetian Renaissance–style General Post Office building with its 230-foot clock tower (now a Westin hotel). Toward the George Street end of the plaza the simple 1929 cenotaph war memorial commemorates Australians who died in World War I. ✉ *Between Macquarie and George Sts., City Center* 🌐 *www.cityofsydney.nsw.gov.au.*

Queen Victoria Building (QVB)

STORE/MALL | Originally the city's produce market, this huge 1898 sandstone structure was handsomely restored with sweeping staircases, enormous stained-glass windows, and the 1-ton Royal Clock, which hangs from the glass roof. The clock chimes the hour from 9 am to 9 pm with four tableaux: the second shows Queen Elizabeth I knighting Sir Frances Drake; the last ends with an executioner chopping off King Charles I's head. The complex includes more than 200 boutiques and restaurants including the lovely Tea Room on Level 3. Boutiques on the upper floors are generally more upscale. Guided tours cost A$25 and depart Thursday and Saturday at noon; bookings are essential. ✉ *455 George St., City Center* ☎ *02/9265–6800* 🌐 *www.qvb.com.au.*

St. Andrew's Cathedral

CHURCH | The foundation stone for Sydney's Gothic Revival Anglican cathedral—the country's oldest—was laid in 1819, although the original architect, Francis Greenway, fell from grace soon after work began. Edmund Blacket, Sydney's most illustrious church architect, was responsible for its final design and completion—a whopping 50 years later in 1868. Notable features of the sandstone construction include ornamental windows depicting Jesus's life and a great east window with images relating to St. Andrew. ✉ *George St. at Bathurst St., next to Town Hall, City Center* ☎ *02/9265–1661* 🌐 *www.sydneycathedral.com.*

St. Mary's Cathedral

CHURCH | The first St. Mary's was built here in 1821, but fire destroyed the chapel. Work on the present cathedral began in 1868. The spires weren't added until 2000, however. St. Mary's has some particularly fine stained-glass windows and a terrazzo floor in the crypt, where exhibitions are often held. The cathedral's large rose window was imported from England. Separate tours take in the cathedral, the crypt, and the bell tower. Free guided tours depart after Sunday mass. ✉ *College St. at Cathedral St., Hyde Park* ☎ *02/9220–0400* 🌐 *www.stmaryscathedral.org.au* 🎫 *Tours free.*

★ **Sydney Tower**

VIEWPOINT | Short of taking a scenic flight, a visit to the top of this 1,000 foot, golden-turret-topped spike is the best way to see Sydney's spectacular layout. This is the city's tallest building, and the views from its indoor observation deck encompass the entire Sydney metropolitan area. You can often see as far as the Blue Mountains, more than 80 km (50 miles) away. You can view it all from the Sydney Tower Eye Observation Deck 820 feet above the city streets. The building houses two restaurants in the turret. ✉ *100 Market St., between Pitt and Castlereagh Sts., City Center* ☎ *02/9333–9222* 🌐 *www.sydneytowereye.com.au* 🎫 *Observation deck A$32, cheaper tickets available online.*

Sydney Town Hall

GOVERNMENT BUILDING | Sydney's Town Hall—an elaborate sandstone structure—is one of the city's most ornate Victorian buildings. A centerpiece of the building is the massive 8,000-pipe Grand Organ, one of the world's most powerful, which is used for lunchtime concerts. Tours, conducted by the "Friends of Town Hall" for A$5, can be booked through the website. Mingle with locals on the marble steps of the front entrance. ✉ *483 George St., City Center* ☎ *02/9265–9333 general inquiries* 🌐 *www.sydneytownhall.com.au* 🎫 *Free.*

Restaurants

Bambini Trust

$$ | ITALIAN | It's hidden behind huge black doors in one of the city's historic sandstone buildings, but once you're inside you'd swear you were in Paris. Darkwood paneling, black-and-white photographs, and mirrors bearing the day's specials in flowing script lend a bistro feel. **Known for:** open late; great location; outdoor dining options. 💲 *Average main: A$38* ✉ *185 Elizabeth St., City Center* ☎ *02/9283–7098* 🌐 *www.bambinitrust.com.au* ⏲ *Closed Sun. No breakfast or lunch Sat.*

Restaurant Hubert

$$$ | FRENCH | This French restaurant oozes old-school glamour, with live jazz playing each night as diners tuck into traditional French fare, like soufflé and beef tartare. There are five rooms that make up this classy eatery, which include two bars serving classic cocktails, two dining rooms, and an old-school theater where classes and workshops are held. **Known for:** live jazz music; low-lighting ambience; fine dining. 💲 *Average main: A$60* ✉ *The Basement of 15 Blight St., City Center* ☎ *02/9232–0881* 🌐 *www.restauranthubert.com* ⏲ *Closed Sun. No dinner Thurs. and Fri.*

★ **Rockpool**

$$$$ | MODERN AUSTRALIAN | A meal at Rockpool is a crash course in what Mod Oz cooking is all about, conducted in a glamorous, long dining room with a catwalk-like ramp. Chefs Neil Perry and Corey Costelloe weave Thai, Chinese,

The fountain in Hyde Park with the Australian Museum in the background

Mediterranean, and Middle Eastern influences into their repertoire with effortless flair and originality. **Known for:** dramatic interiors; date tart; wide caviar selection. *Average main: A$185 11 Bridge St., City Center 02/8099–7077 www.rockpool.com Closed Sun., Mon., and Tues. No lunch Sat. Jacket required.*

Spice Temple

$$ | CHINESE | The culinary focus of this chic basement eatery—another of the restaurants owned by Neil Perry of Rockpool fame—is regional China. There are dishes from far-flung Yunnan, Hunan, and Sichuan provinces, and as the names suggests, they all have a kick. **Known for:** extensive cocktail list; trendy; great atmosphere. *Average main: A$40 10 Bligh St., City Center 02/8099–7088 www.spicetemple.com.au Closed Sun., Mon., and Tues. No lunch Sat.*

★ Tetsuya's

$$$$ | MODERN AUSTRALIAN | It's worth getting on the waiting list—there's *always* a waiting list—to sample the unique blend of Western and Japanese-French flavors crafted by Sydney's most applauded chef, Tetsuya Wakuda. The serene, expansive dining room's unobtrusive Japanese aesthetic leaves the food as the true highlight. **Known for:** quiet atmosphere; incredible Japanese fare; degustation meals. *Average main: A$220 529 Kent St., City Center 02/9267–2900 www.tetsuyas.com Closed Mon.–Wed. No lunch Tues.–Fri.*

Coffee and Quick Bites

The Grounds of the City

$ | FRENCH | This hidden gem is the city offering of the popular Grounds of Alexandria, a dog- and kid-friendly eatery with a on-site urban farm that's found just outside of the city. This French-style café is less country rustic and more city slick. **Known for:** hidden gem; vintage glamour interiors; outstanding service. *Average main: A$35 Shop RG 12, 500 George St., City Center 02/9699–2225 thegrounds.com.au.*

Pablo & Rusty's

$ | AUSTRALIAN | Started as a specialty coffee creator, Pablo & Rusty opened a sit-down café back in 2010 and it has been a popular spot for coffee meetups ever since. The interiors are stylish and hip, there are single-origin espressos and sophisticated breakfasts and lunches. **Known for:** outdoor seating; exceptional coffee; trendy interiors. *Average main: A$20* *161 Castlereagh St., City Center* *02/9807–6293* *pabloandrustys.com.au* *Closed weekends.*

Hotels

Fraser Suites Sydney

$$ | HOTEL | This serviced-apartment hotel is one of Sydney's swankiest places to stay. **Pros:** free Wi-Fi throughout; cutting-edge design; well priced for longer stays. **Cons:** no balconies; minimalist design may not be to everyone's taste; impersonal due to size. *Rooms from: A$250* *488 Kent St., City Center* *02/8823–8888* *sydney.frasershospitality.com* *No Meals* *201 rooms.*

Hilton Sydney

$$ | HOTEL | At this landmark hotel in downtown Sydney you enter a spacious, light-filled lobby displaying a stunning four-story sculpture. **Pros:** excellent service; hip bar; lavishly appointed rooms. **Cons:** located on busy street; no views; impersonal and busy. *Rooms from: A$270* *488 George St., City Center* *02/9266–2000* *www.hiltonsydney.com* *577 rooms* *No Meals.*

QT Sydney

$$$ | HOTEL | This hotel is the answer for those seeking color and quirkiness, teamed with style and super-efficient service. **Pros:** historic restored building; great location; catchy design. **Cons:** super-soft beds; funkiness may not be to all tastes; no pool or balconies. *Rooms from: A$330* *49 Market St., at George St., City Center* *02/8262–0000* *www.qthotels.com.au* *No Meals* *200 rooms.*

West Hotel

$$ | HOTEL | Situated in a perfect little pocket of Sydney between Darling Harbour, Barangaroo Reserve, and the city center, in a jewel-like building of glass panels that capture and reflect light, West Hotel offers modern, elegant rooms with luxurious finishes in marble, brass, velvets, and gem tones, and a central atrium filled with greenery. **Pros:** exceptional bar and dining options; excellent location for exploring; elegant, comfortable base. **Cons:** inconsistent service; Wi-Fi fee; no swimming pool. *Rooms from: A$270* *65 Sussex St., City Center* *02/8297–6500* *www.westhotel.com.au* *Free Breakfast* *182 rooms.*

Nightlife

BARS AND DANCE CLUBS

★ The Arthouse Hotel

DANCE CLUBS | A former School of the Arts building, The Arthouse Hotel has been renovated into a modern, belle epoque–style hot spot, with four bars and a restaurant spread over three cavernous floors. Art is the focus here, whether it's visual—life-drawing classes are given on Monday, a burlesque drawing class biweekly on Tuesday—aural, or edible, and there is a full-time curator dedicated to programming music, events, and exhibitions. *275 Pitt St., City Center* *02/9284–1200* *www.arthotel.com.au.*

★ Bambini Wine Room

WINE BARS | Bambini Wine Room is a sparkling little jewel box encased in marble-clad walls and topped with lovely chandeliers. You can sip cocktails, whiskeys and any number of fine wines late into the night and feast on affordable bar snacks. *185 Elizabeth St., City Center* *02/9283–7098.*

Hemmesphere

GATHERING PLACES | One of a string of swanky venues in the area, Hemmesphere is still drawing a hip crowd more than a decade after it first opened. Named for Justin Hemmes, son of iconic 1970s fashion designers Jon and Merivale Hemmes, this is where Sydney's hippest pay homage to cocktail culture from low, leather divans. The mood is elegant and sleek, and so are the well-dressed guests, who often include whichever glitterati happen to be in town. It's on the fourth level of the Establishment Hotel complex and draws those seeking an escape from the rowdy action downstairs. ✉ *252 George St., Level 4, City Center* ☎ *02/9714–7313* 🌐 *merivale.com.au/hemmesphere.*

Ivy

DANCE CLUBS | This multilevel complex of bars, pubs, and eateries is in an ultrahip George Street complex. Cocktails are great but expensive, and the crowd varies depending on the night. If you don't fancy this bar, then there's the decadent Pool Club bar on the top floor, where if you get there early you can recline in your own cabana overlooking the swimming pool. Also on-site are the Den (a lavish bar with chaise longue furniture, chandeliers, and cigar menu), the casual Royal George pub, and the Ash Street Cellar bistro. ✉ *330 George St., City Center* ☎ *02/9240–3000* 🌐 *merivale.com.au/ivy.*

Lobo Plantation

BARS | This Cuban-theme bar is a hit in Sydney. Patrons love the palm trees, the cane furniture, and the wall lined with Cuban banknotes. Cocktails are all rum based, with funky names like Ol Grogram with Lobo's own spiced rum, fresh lemon, sugar, and stout vermouth. The affordable bar menu is limited, with empanadas or tacos on offer, but it helps soak up the alcohol. ✉ *209 Clarence St., basement, City Center* ☎ *02/9240–3000* 🌐 *www.thelobo.com.au.*

★ O Bar and Dining

PIANO BARS | This is the place to come at sunset for the view, tapas, and cocktails—and the '70s kitsch of a revolving restaurant. Located on Level 47 of the Australia Square building, O Bar has floor-to-ceiling windows, so no matter which seat you have, the view is great, and constantly changing. It's perfect for a predinner drink, or dinner, too. It's open daily from 5 pm and Friday lunch. ✉ *Australia Sq., 264 George St., Level 47, City Center* ☎ *02/9247–0777* 🌐 *obardining.com.au.*

Performing Arts

THEATER

Belvoir Street Theatre

THEATER | Belvoir Street Theatre has two stages that host innovative and challenging political and social drama. The smaller downstairs space showcases a lineup of brave new Australian drama. The theater is a 10-minute walk from Central Station. ✉ *25 Belvoir St., Surry Hills* ☎ *02/9699–3444* 🌐 *www.belvoir.com.au.*

Capitol Theatre

CONCERTS | This century-old city landmark was refurbished with such modern refinements as fiber-optic ceiling lights that twinkle in time to the music. The 2,000-seat theater specializes in Broadway blockbusters, such as *The Lion King* and *Mary Poppins*, and also hosts pop and rock concerts. Guided behind-the-scenes tours are available (A$38.50); bookings are essential. ✉ *13 Campbell St., Haymarket* ☎ *02/9320–5000* 🌐 *www.capitoltheatre.com.au.*

SBW Stables Theatre

THEATER | This small 120-seat venue is home of the Griffin Theatre Company, which specializes in new Australian writing. ✉ *10 Nimrod St., Kings Cross* ☎ *02/9361–3817* 🌐 *www.griffintheatre.com.au.*

★ State Theatre

CONCERTS | State Theatre is the grande dame of Sydney theaters. It operates as a cinema in June each year, when it hosts the two-week-long Sydney Film Festival; at other times this beautiful space hosts local and international performers. Built in 1929 and restored to its full-blown opulence, the theater has a vaulted ceiling, mosaic floors, marble columns and statues, and brass and bronze doors. A highlight of the magnificent theater is the 20,000-piece chandelier that is supposedly the world's second largest, which Robin Williams once likened to "one of Imelda Marcos's earrings." Even if you don't see a show here, it's worth popping into the lobby for a look around, or join a guided tour to get a good look at the theater's many treasures (A$25). ✉ *49 Market St., City Center* ☎ *02/9373–6655* 🌐 *www.statetheatre.com.au* ☞ *Guided tours Mon.–Wed. 10 am and 1 pm.*

Theatre Royal

THEATER | After being closed for over two decades, the Theatre Royal reopened in late 2021 after a multimillion-dollar facelift. First opened in 1976, it's now the home to some of the biggest Broadway shows to come out of the United States, including the award-winning*by Alanis Morissette.* ✉ *108 King St., City Center* ☎ *1300/163–808* 🌐 *www.theatreroyalsydney.com.*

Shopping

BOOKS

Ariel Booksellers

BOOKS | This is a large, bright, browser's delight, and the place to go for literature, pop culture, avant-garde, and art books. They also hold book readings and other literary events. ✉ *98 Oxford St., City Center* ☎ *02/9332–4581* 🌐 *www.arielbooks.com.au.*

Dymocks

BOOKS | This big, bustling bookstore is packed to its gallery-level coffee shop and is the place to go for all literary needs. ✉ *424 George St., City Center* ☎ *02/9235–0155* 🌐 *www.dymocks.com.au.*

CLOTHING

Country Road

WOMEN'S CLOTHING | The fashion here stands somewhere between Ralph Lauren and Timberland, with an all-Australian assembly of classic, countrified his 'n' hers, plus an ever-expanding variety of soft furnishings in cotton and linen for the rustic retreat. You'll find Country Road clothes in most department stores, but the biggest range is here in this flagship store. ✉ *142–144 Pitt St., City Center* ☎ *02/9394–1818* 🌐 *www.countryroad.com.au.*

★ **Paddy Pallin**

OTHER SPECIALTY STORE | This should be the first stop for serious bush adventurers heading for wild Australia and beyond. Maps, books, and mounds of gear are tailored especially for the Australian outdoors. ✉ *507 Kent St., City Center* ☎ *02/8029–0125* 🌐 *www.paddypallin.com.au.*

★ **R. M. Williams**

OTHER SPECIALTY STORE | The place to go for riding boots, Akubra hats, Drizabone raincoats, and moleskin trousers—the type of clothes worn by Hugh Jackman and Nicole Kidman in the movie *Australia.* ✉ *389 George St., City Center* ☎ *02/9262–2228* 🌐 *www.rmwilliams.com.au.*

DEPARTMENT STORES AND SHOPPING CENTERS

★ **David Jones**

DEPARTMENT STORE | The city's largest department store maintains a reputation for excellent service and high-quality goods. Clothing by many of Australia's finest designers is on display here, and the store also sells its own fashion label at reasonable prices. ✉ *Elizabeth St. at Market St., City Center* ☎ *02/9266–5544* 🌐 *www.davidjones.com.au.*

Myer

DEPARTMENT STORE | Buy clothing and accessories by Australian and international designers at this department store opposite the Queen Victoria Building. ✉ *436 George St., City Center* ☎ *02/8015–6580* 🌐 *www.myer.com.au.*

Pitt Street Mall

MALL | The heart of Sydney's shopping area includes the Mid-City Centre, the huge Westfield Sydney Shopping Centre, Skygarden, Myer, and the charming and historic Strand Arcade—five multilevel shopping plazas crammed with more than 500 shops, from mainstream clothing stores to designer boutiques. **TIP→ Just a short walk away is the iconic David Jones store on Elizabeth Street.** ✉ *182 Pitt St., City Center* ✥ *Between King and Market Sts.* ☎ *02/8236–9200.*

★ Queen Victoria Building

MALL | This is a splendid Victorian-era building with more than 200 boutiques, cafés, and antiques shops. The building is open 24 hours, so you can window-shop even after the stores have closed. Guided history tours, which run 45 minutes, cost A$15 and depart 11:30 am Tuesday, Thursday, and Saturday. Book at the concierge on the ground floor. ✉ *George, York, Market, and Druitt Sts., City Center* ☎ *02/9265–6800* ⊕ *www.qvb.com.au.*

★ Strand Arcade

MALL | This ornate three-story shopping arcade built in 1891 runs between George Street and Pitt Street Mall and is one of Sydney's most elegant shopping strips. Beautiful Victorian-era floor tiles, magnificent cedar staircases, and charmingly old-fashioned shopfronts help make the shopping here refreshingly chain-store free. The upstairs galleries are home to high-end Australian fashion designers and jewelers, while the ground floor has a charming mix of cozy specialty tea and cake shops, beauty and gift stores, and fashion boutiques. Strand Hatters is the best men's hat store in the city and the place to buy an Akubra or fedora. The arcade is bookended by two of the country's iconic chocolate stores—Haigh's Chocolates at George Street and Koko Black on Pitt Street—and both are virtually irresistible. ✉ *412–414 George St., Sydney* ☎ *02/9265–6800* ⊕ *www.strandarcade.com.au.*

JEWELRY AND ACCESSORIES

Dinosaur Designs

OTHER SPECIALTY STORE | This fun store sells luminous bowls, plates, and vases, as well as fanciful jewelry crafted from resin and Perspex in eye-popping colors. There's another location at 339 Oxford Street in Paddington. ✉ *Strand Arcade, George St., City Center* ☎ *02/9361–3776* ⊕ *www.dinosaurdesigns.com.au.*

The National Opal Collection

JEWELRY & WATCHES | This is the only Sydney opal retailer with total ownership of its entire production process—mines, workshops, and showroom—making prices very competitive. In the Pitt Street showroom, you can prearrange to see artisans at work cutting and polishing the stones or visit the on-site museum and learn about the process of opal development and opalized fossils. ✉ *60 Pitt St., City Center* ☎ *02/9247–6344* ⊕ *www.nationalopal.com.*

Paspaley Pearls

JEWELRY & WATCHES | The jewelers here order their exquisite material from pearl farms near the remote Western Australia town of Broome. Prices start high and head for the stratosphere, but if you're serious about a high-quality pearl, this gallery requires a visit. ✉ *Paspaley Bldg., 2 Martin Pl., City Center* ☎ *02/9232–7633* ⊕ *www.paspaley.com.*

Percy Marks Fine Gems

JEWELRY & WATCHES | Here you'll find an outstanding collection of high-quality Australian gemstones, including dazzling black opals, pink diamonds, and pearls from Broome. ✉ *70 Casterleigh St., City Center* ☎ *02/9233–1355* ⊕ *www.percy-marks.com.au.*

Rox Gems and Jewellery

JEWELRY & WATCHES | Come here for serious one-off designs at the cutting edge of lapidary chic. ✉ *Shop 31, Strand Arcade, George St., City Center* ☎ *02/9232–7828* ⊕ *www.rox.com.au.*

MUSIC

Birdland Records

OTHER SPECIALTY STORE | This institution for music lovers has an especially strong selection of jazz, blues, African, and Latin American music in multiple formats, including vinyl and super audio CDs, as well as an authoritative staff ready to lend some assistance. ✉ *Dymocks Bldg., Level 4, 428 George St., City Center* ☎ *02/9231–1188* 🌐 *www.birdland.com.au.*

Inner City and the Eastern Suburbs

Sydney's inner city and Eastern Suburbs are truly the people's domain. They are the hip zones of Sydney featuring the foodie precincts as well as some of the most expensive real estate, great shopping, and the most accessible beaches. Architecture ranges from the mansions of the colonial aristocracy and the humble laborers' cottages of the same period to the modernized terrace houses of Paddington, one of Sydney's most charming and most desirable suburbs. A good way to explore the area is to take the Bondi & Bays Explorer bus that stops at 10 sites including Bondi Beach, Double Bay, Paddington, and Rose Bay.

GETTING HERE AND AROUND

The inner city and Eastern Suburbs are well served by buses, although the journey out to the Eastern Suburbs beaches can be quite long at rush hour. Most depart from Circular Quay (Alfred Street). Travel to Paddington and Bondi is on Nos. 380, 333, and 382; and to Watsons Bay and Vaucluse (via Double Bay and Rose Bay) on Nos. 323, 324, and 325. Buses 380, 382, and 333 travel along Oxford Street, the main artery of the alternative (and gay) neighborhood of Darlinghurst. It is quicker to take the train to Edgecliff or Bondi Junction stations to connect with buses traveling to many of the Eastern Suburbs, including Coogee and Clovelly. A ferry operates between Circular Quay and Watsons Bay, calling at Garden Island, Darling Point, Double Bay, and Rose Bay. It is an easy walk to Darlinghurst and Surry Hills from the city center, while Kings Cross has its own train station, just one stop from the city center. And there's also CBD and South East Light Rail that connects Georgie Street in the CBD to Randwick, which is close to Coogee.

Sights

Centennial Park

CITY PARK | More than 500 acres of palm-lined avenues, groves of Moreton Bay figs, paperbark tree–fringed lakes, and cycling and horse-riding tracks make this a popular park and Sydney's favorite workout circuit. In the early 1800s the marshy land at the lower end provided Sydney with its fresh water. The park was proclaimed in 1888, the centenary of Australia's founding as a colony. The Centennial Park Café is often crowded on weekends, but a mobile canteen between the lakes in the middle of the park serves snacks and espresso. Bikes and blades can be rented from the nearby Clovelly Road outlets, on the eastern side of the park. The Moonlight Cinema screens movies during the summer months. ✉ *Oxford St., at Centennial Ave., Centennial Park* ☎ *02/9339–6699* 🌐 *www.centennialparklands.com.au.*

Elizabeth Bay

NEIGHBORHOOD | Much of this densely populated but still-charming harbor-side suburb was originally part of the extensive Elizabeth Bay House grounds. Wrought-iron balconies and French doors on some of the older apartment blocks give the area a Mediterranean flavor. During the 1920s and 1930s this was a fashionably bohemian quarter, and it remains a favorite among artists and writers. ✉ *Elizabeth Bay Rd., Elizabeth Bay.*

Elizabeth Bay House

HISTORIC HOME | This 1835–39 mansion was regarded in its heyday as the "finest house in the colony." It retains little of its original furniture, although the rooms have been restored in Georgian style. The most striking feature is an oval-shape salon with a winding staircase, naturally lighted by glass panels in the domed roof. The view from the front-facing windows across Elizabeth Bay is stunning. A variety of soirees and talks are held in the house throughout the year. ✉ *7 Onslow Ave., Elizabeth Bay* ☎ *02/9356–3022* 🌐 *sydneylivingmuseums.com.au/elizabeth-bay-house* 🎫 *A$15.*

Harry's Café de Wheels

RESTAURANT | The attraction of this all-day dockyard food stall is not so much the delectable meat pies and coffee served as the clientele. Famous opera singers, actors, and international rock stars have been spotted here rubbing shoulders with shift workers and taxi drivers. This "pie cart" has been a Sydney institution since 1945, when the late Harry "Tiger" Edwards set up his van to serve sailors from the nearby Garden Island base. Drop in any time from 8:30 am (9 am on weekends) until the wee hours for a Tiger Pie, made with mushy peas, mashed potatoes, and gravy. Harry's now has nine other locations in Sydney. ✉ *1 Cowper Wharf Rd., Woolloomooloo* ☎ *02/8346–4100* 🌐 *www.harryscafedewheels.com.au.*

Paddington

NEIGHBORHOOD | Most of this suburb's elegant two-story terrace houses were built during the 1880s, when the colony experienced a long period of economic growth following the gold rushes that began in the 1860s. The balconies are trimmed with decorative wrought iron, sometimes known as Paddington lace, which initially came from England and later from Australian foundries. Rebuilt and repainted, the now-stylish Paddington terrace houses give the area its characteristic villagelike charm. The Oxford Street shopping strip is full of upscale and funky boutiques, cafés, and several good pubs. ✉ *Oxford St., between Boundary and Queen Sts., Paddington.*

Sydney Jewish Museum

MUSEUM VILLAGE | Artifacts, interactive displays, and audiovisual displays chronicle the history of Australian Jews and commemorate the 6 million killed in the Holocaust. Exhibits are brilliantly arranged on eight levels, which lead upward in chronological order, from the handful of Jews who arrived with the First Fleet in 1788 to the 30,000 concentration-camp survivors who came after World War II—one of the largest populations of Holocaust survivors to be found anywhere. A free 40-minute guided tour starts at noon on Monday, Wednesday, Friday, and Sunday. ✉ *148 Darlinghurst Rd., Darlinghurst* ☎ *02/9360–7999* 🌐 *www.sydneyjewishmuseum.com.au* 🎫 *A$15.*

Victoria Barracks

MILITARY SIGHT | If you're curious about the Australian military, you'll enjoy the free tours of this Regency-style barracks (built from 1841), which take place every Thursday at 10 am sharp. The tour includes entry to the Army Museum of New South Wales, which has exhibits covering Australia's military history from the days of the Rum Corps to the Malayan conflict of the 1950s. ✉ *Oxford St., at Oatley Rd., Paddington* ☎ *02/8335–5330* 🌐 *www.armymuseumnsw.com.au* 🎫 *Tours free, museum A$5.*

Beaches

★ Bondi Beach

BEACH | Wide, wonderful Bondi (pronounced *bon*-dye) is the most famous and most crowded of all Sydney beaches. It has something for just about everyone, and the droves that flock here on a sunny day give it a bustling, carnival atmosphere unmatched by any other Sydney beach. Facilities include toilets, open-air showers for rinsing sandy feet and salty bodies, and a kiosk on the beach that rents out sun loungers, beach umbrellas, and even swimsuits. Cafés, ice-cream outlets, restaurants, and boutiques line Campbell Parade, which runs behind the

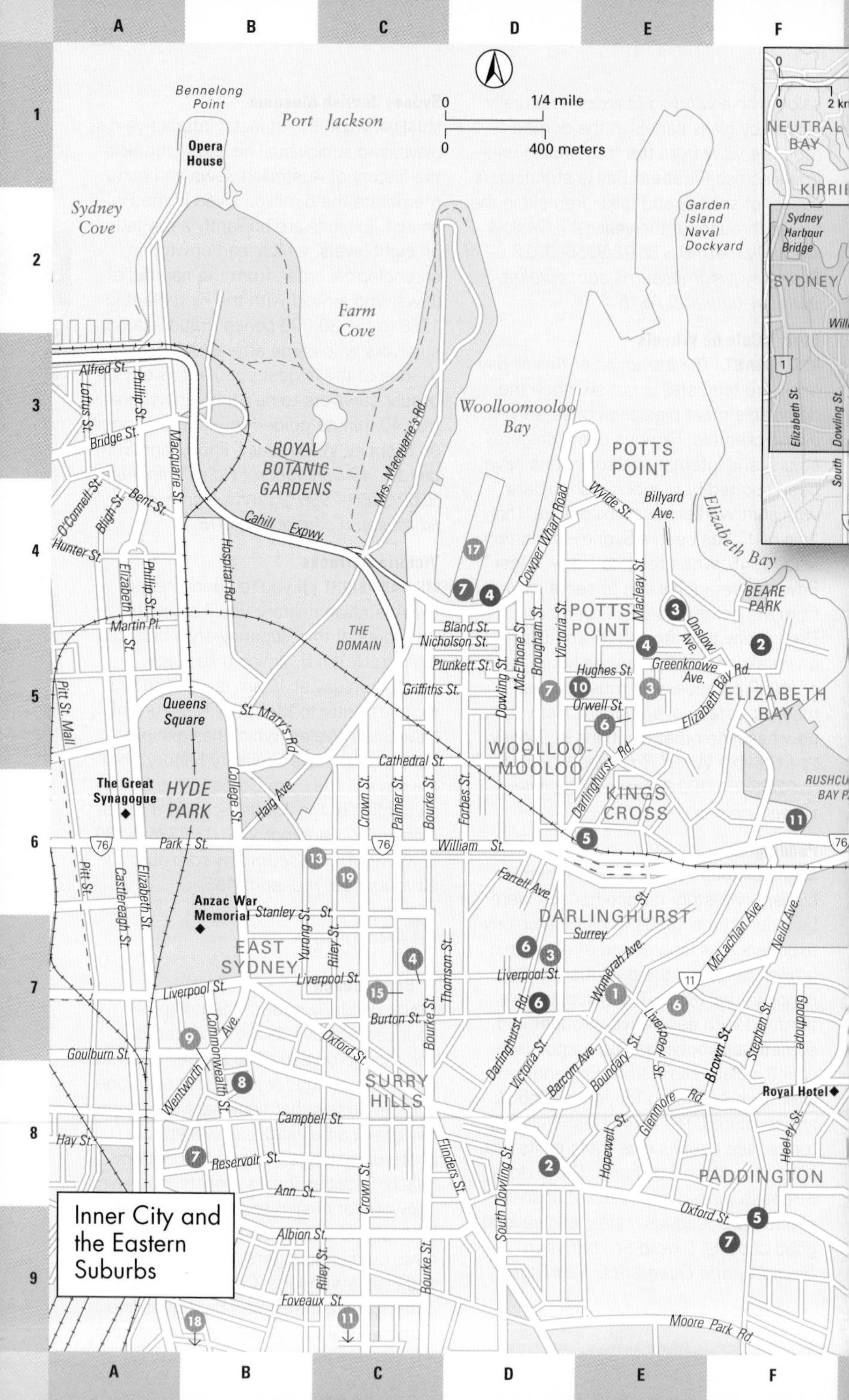

A
B
C
D
E
F
1
2
3
4
5
6
7
8
9
0
1/4 mile
0
400 meters
Bennelong Point
Port Jackson
Opera House
Sydney Cove
Farm Cove
Garden Island Naval Dockyard
NEUTRAL BAY
KIRRIB
Sydney Harbour Bridge
SYDNEY
0
2 km
Elizabeth St.
Dowling St.
South
Alfred St.
Loftus St.
Phillip St.
Bridge St.
Macquarie St.
ROYAL BOTANIC GARDENS
Mrs. Macquarie's Rd.
Woolloomooloo Bay
POTTS POINT
O'Connell St.
Bligh St.
Bent St.
Hunter St.
Cahill Expwy.
Hospital Rd.
Cowper Wharf Road
Wylde St.
Billyard Ave.
Elizabeth Bay
Elizabeth St.
Phillip St.
Martin Pl.
THE DOMAIN
Bland St.
Nicholson St.
Plunkett St.
Griffiths St.
Macleay St.
Victoria St.
Brougham St.
McElhone St.
Dowling St.
POTTS POINT
BEARE PARK
Onslow Ave.
Greenknowe Ave.
Hughes St.
Elizabeth Bay Rd.
Orwell St.
ELIZABETH BAY
Pitt St. Mall
Queens Square
St. Mary's Rd.
Cathedral St.
WOOLLOO-MOOLOO
Darlinghurst Rd.
KINGS CROSS
RUSHCU BAY P
The Great Synagogue
HYDE PARK
College St.
Haig Ave.
Crown St.
Palmer St.
Bourke St.
Forbes St.
Park St.
William St.
Pitt St.
Castlereagh St.
Elizabeth St.
Anzac War Memorial
Stanley St.
Yurong St.
Riley St.
Farrell Ave.
DARLINGHURST
Surrey St.
EAST SYDNEY
Liverpool St.
Thomson St.
Liverpool St.
Womerah Ave.
McLachlan Ave.
Neild Ave.
Liverpool St.
Commonwealth St.
Burton St.
Goulburn St.
Wentworth Ave.
Oxford St.
Bourke St.
Darlinghurst Rd.
Victoria St.
Barcom Ave.
Boundary St.
Liverpool St.
Brown St.
Stephen St.
Goodhope
SURRY HILLS
Glenmore Rd.
Royal Hotel
Campbell St.
Hopewell St.
Heeley St.
Hay St.
Reservoir St.
Crown St.
Flinders St.
South Dowling St.
PADDINGTON
Ann St.
Oxford St.
Albion St.
Riley St.
Bourke St.
Foveaux St.
Moore Park Rd.
Inner City and the Eastern Suburbs

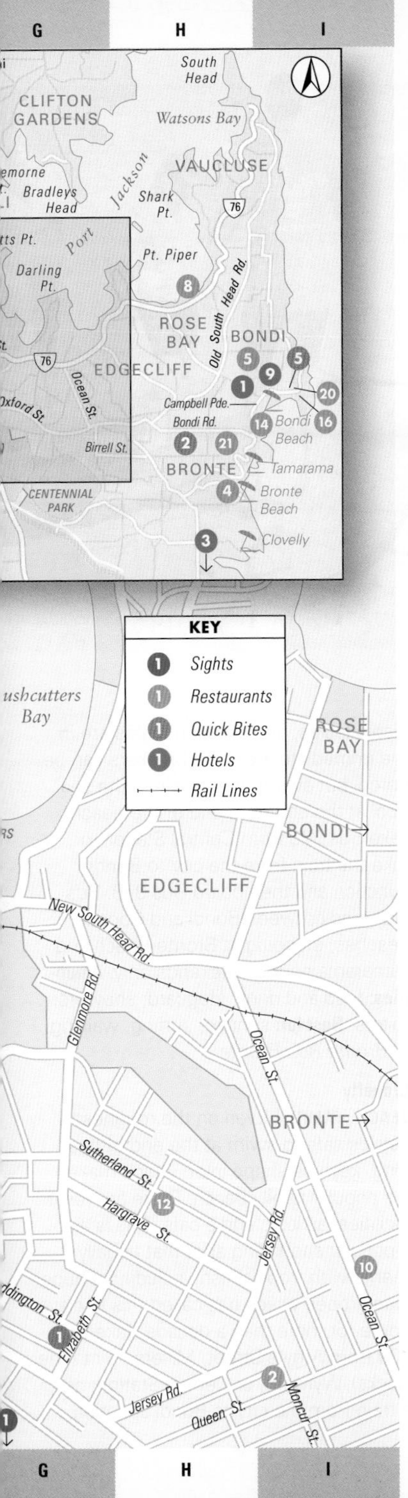

Sights

1 Centennial Park........ G9
2 Elizabeth Bay........... F5
3 Elizabeth Bay House E5
4 Harry's Café de Wheels.............. D4
5 Paddington F9
6 Sydney Jewish Museum D7
7 Victoria Barracks........ F9

Restaurants

1 bills E7
2 Bistro Moncur............I9
3 Bistro Rex................ E5
4 Bronte Belo............. H3
5 Brown Sugar........... H2
6 Buon Ricordo............ E7
7 The Butler D5
8 Catalina Restaurant H2
9 Chin Chin Sydney....... B8
10 Chiswick..................I8
11 Four Ate Five C9
12 Four in Hand............ H8
13 Hyde Park House B6
14 Icebergs Dining Room and Bar I3
15 Joe's Table...............C7
16 North Bondi Fish..........I3
17 Otto Ristorante.......... D4
18 Porteno B9
19 Red Lantern on Riley C6
20 Sean's Panaroma.........I3
21 Totti's H3

Quick Bites

1 Barbetta G9
2 Bennett St Dairy H3
3 Gelato Messina......... D7
4 The Mayflower...........C7
5 Porch and Parlour........I3
6 Room Ten E5
7 Single O.................. B8

Hotels

1 Adina Apartment Hotel Bondi Beach H3
2 Arts Hotel Sydney D8
3 Crowne Plaza Coogee Beach H4
4 DeVere Hotel............ E5
5 Larmont Sydney by Lancemore........... E6
6 Medusa D7
7 Ovolo Woolloomooloo D4
8 Paramount House Hotel..................... B8
9 QT Bondi...................I3
10 Spicers Potts Point...... E5
11 Vibe Hotel Rushcutters F6

Surf school at Bondi Beach

beach. But despite its popularity, it's also a dangerous beach, with an estimated 30 swimmers saved by the seven lifeguards who man this spot every day, even in winter. Families tend to prefer the calmer waters of the northern end of the beach. Surfing is popular at the south end, where a path winds along the sea-sculpted cliffs to Tamarama and Bronte beaches. Take Bus 380, 382, or 333 all the way from Circular Quay, or take the train from the city to Bondi Junction and then board Bus 380, 381, 382, or 333. **Amenities:** food and drink; lifeguards; parking (fee); showers; toilets; water sports. **Best for:** partiers; sunrise; surfing; swimming; walking. ✉ *Campbell Parade, Bondi Beach.*

★ Bronte Beach

BEACH | **FAMILY** | If you want an ocean beach that's close to the city and has a terrific setting, with both sand and grassy areas, this one is hard to beat. A wooded park of palm trees and Norfolk Island pines surrounds Bronte. The park includes a playground and sheltered picnic tables, and excellent cafés are in the immediate area. The breakers can be fierce, but swimming is safe in the sea pool at the southern end of the beach. Take Bus 378 from Central Station, or take the train from the city to Bondi Junction and then board Bus 378. Bus 362 runs between Bondi and Coogee beaches, stopping at Bronte Beach and Tamarama on the weekends only. **Amenities:** food and drink; lifeguard; showers; toilets. **Best for:** sunrise; surfing; walking. ✉ *Bronte Rd., Bronte.*

Clovelly

BEACH | **FAMILY** | Even on the roughest day it's safe to swim at the end of this long, keyhole-shape inlet, which makes it a popular family beach. There are toilet facilities, a kiosk, and a café. This is also a popular snorkeling spot that usually teems with tropical fish, including a huge blue groper, which has called this enclave home for more than a decade. Take Bus 339 from Argyle Street, Millers Point (The Rocks), Wynyard, or Central Station; or a train from the city to Bondi Junction, then board Bus 360. **Amenities:** food and drink; lifeguards; parking (fee); showers; toilets. **Best for:** snorkeling; sunrise; swimming. ✉ *Clovelly Rd., Clovelly.*

Coogee

BEACH | FAMILY | A reef protects this lively beach (pronounced *kuh*-jee), creating slightly calmer swimming conditions than those found at its neighbors. For smaller children, the southern end offers a small enclosed pool, or keep following the coastal path, and there's a small women's-only natural pool that costs just 20 cents entry. The grassy headland overlooking the beach has an excellent children's playground. Cafés in the shopping precinct at the back of the beach sell ice cream, pizza, and the ingredients for picnics. Take Bus 373 or 374 from Circular Quay or Bus 372 from Central Station. Or, take theCBD and South East Light Rail to Randwick and walk down to Coogee Beach, taking 25 minutes. **Amenities:** food and drink; lifeguards; parking (fee); showers; toilets. **Best for:** sunrise; swimming; walking. ✉ *Coogee Bay Rd. at Arden St., Coogee.*

Tamarama

BEACH | This small, fashionable beach—aka "Glam-a-rama"—is one of Sydney's prettiest, but the rocky headlands that squeeze close to the sand on either side make it less than ideal for swimming. The sea is often hazardous here, and surfing is prohibited. A café in the small park behind the beach sells sandwiches, fresh juices, and fruit whips. Take the train from the city to Bondi Junction and then board Bus 360 or 361, or walk for 10 minutes along the cliff path from the south end of Bondi Beach. **Amenities:** food and drink; lifeguard; showers; toilets. **Best for:** sunrise; surfing. ✉ *Tamarama Marine Dr., Tamarama.*

Restaurants

DARLINGHURST

★ bills

$ | CAFÉ | Named after celebrity chef and cookbook author Bill Granger, this sunny corner café is so addictive it should come with a health warning. It's a favorite hangout of everyone from local nurses to semi-disguised rock stars, and you never know who you might be sitting next to at the newspaper-strewn communal table. **Known for:** great service; ricotta hotcakes; hip atmosphere. $ *Average main: A$25* ✉ *433 Liverpool St., Darlinghurst* ☎ *02/9360–9631* 🌐 *www.bills.com.au* ⏲ *No dinner.*

Hyde Park House

$$$ | JAPANESE | Once a bit of a run-down pub known as Hotel William, in 2018 it reopened with a new name after a A$5 million refurbishment, and it's since became one of the classiest restaurants in Sydney. There are four levels in total: the ground offers traditional Australian pub fare, the second is a private dining area that can seat up to 250 people, and then there's a swanky cocktail bar but the real jewel here is the rooftop bar and restaurant offering trendy cocktails and a modern Japanese menu of sushi, sashimi, and sizzling plates. **Known for:** fun cocktails; rooftop restaurant; fresh sashimi. $ *Average main: 50* ✉ *47 William St., City Center* ☎ *02/8377–3650* 🌐 *www.hydeparkhouse.com.*

Joe's Table

$ | VIETNAMESE | A lot of care goes into the creations in this popular Southeast Asian spot: the pork hock is braised for four hours each night before being pressed and then tossed with homemade chili jam, while coconut milk is smoked overnight and then churned into ice cream in the morning. As delicious and affordable as the sandwiches and dumplings are, be sure to save space for this true star of the show, which is served enveloped in smoke under a glass dome and topped with tender young coconut shavings and a simple pinch of salt. **Known for:** delicious Southeast Asian fare; smoking coconut ice cream; jumbo lunch sandwiches. 💲 *Average main: A$20* ✉ *1/28 Kings La., Darlinghurst, Darlinghurst* ☎ *02/8385–7110* 🌐 *www.facebook.com/joestablesydney.*

KINGS CROSS AND POTTS POINT

Bistro Rex

$$ | **FRENCH** | Incredibly chic, this is where the hippest of the city come for early dinner during the week or a late-night nibble with cocktails on the weekend. The feel is Parisian bistro, with a lively atmosphere and traditional French cuisine like steak frites. **Known for:** lively atmosphere; chic interiors; delicious eats. 💲 *Average main: A$ 45* ✉ *50 Macleay St., Potts Point* ☎ *02/9332–2100* 🌐 *bistrorex.com.au* ⏲ *No lunch. Closed Sun. and Mon.*

The Butler

$ | **LATIN AMERICAN** | Tucked away on a pretty backstreet in Potts Point, this restaurant is packed with the beautiful people on the weekend soaking in its buzzy atmosphere, sweeping vistas of Sydney's cityscape, extensive cocktail list, and excellent menu. Prebook a table on the balcony as they go quickly, and then pick a few sharing plates. **Known for:** great views; buzzy atmosphere; great small plates. 💲 *Average main: A$35* ✉ *123 Victoria St., Potts Point* ☎ *02/8354–0742* 🌐 *butlersydney.com.au.*

Red Lantern on Riley

$$ | **VIETNAMESE** | Owned by Vietnamese TV chef Luke Nguyen, this restaurant is popular with his legions of TV fans. Diners should always start with the country's great export, rice paper rolls. **Known for:** great cocktail list; relaxed atmosphere; full tasting menu. 💲 *Average main: A$45* ✉ *60 Riley St., Darlinghurst* ☎ *02/9698–4355* 🌐 *www.redlantern.com.au* ⏲ *No lunch.*

WOOLLOOMOOLOO

Otto Ristorante

$$ | **ITALIAN** | Few restaurants have the magnetic pull of Otto, a place where radio shock jocks sit side by side with fashion-magazine editors and confirmed foodies. Yes, it's a scene, but fortunately one with good Italian food prepared by chef Richard Ptacnik. **Known for:** incredible pasta; great waterfront location; buzzy weekend atmosphere. 💲 *Average main: A$44* ✉ *Wharf at Woolloomooloo, Area 8, 6 Cowper Wharf Rd., Eastern Suburbs* ☎ *02/9368–7488* 🌐 *www.ottoristorante.com.au.*

PADDINGTON

Buon Ricordo

$$$ | **ITALIAN** | Walking into this happy, bubbly place is like turning up at a private party in the backstreets of Naples. Host, chef, and surrogate uncle Armando Percuoco invests classic Neapolitan and Tuscan techniques with inventive personal touches to produce such dishes as the thinly sliced kingfish with gin and orange and truffled egg pasta. **Known for:** standout menu; friendly staff; great service. 💲 *Average main: A$48* ✉ *108 Boundary St., Paddington* ☎ *02/9360–6729* 🌐 *www.buonricordo.com.au* ⏲ *Closed Sun. and Mon. No lunch Tues.–Thurs.*

Four in Hand

$$ | **AUSTRALIAN** | At this cute, popular little pub in Paddington, chef Colin Fassnidge (an Irishman who emerged as the most controversial guest judge on Australian TV cooking show *My Kitchen Rules*) has been wowing patrons for years with his shared dish for two of slow-braised lamb shoulder with kipfler potatoes, baby carrots, and salsa verde. His whole suckling pig is also a popular Sunday long-lunch treat. **Known for:** boozy Sundays; relaxed dining; pub-style atmosphere. 💲 *Average main: A$39* ✉ *105 Sutherland St., Paddington* ☎ *02/9326–2254* 🌐 *www.fourinhand.com.au* ⏲ *Closed Mon.*

WOOLLAHRA

Bistro Moncur

$$ | **FRENCH** | This bistro in the Woollahra Hotel spills over with happy-go-lucky patrons—mostly locals from around the leafy suburb of Woollahra—who have been coming back for more than 20 years now. The best dishes are inspired takes on Parisian fare, like the grilled Sirloin Café de Paris, French onion soufflé gratin, and port sausages with potato puree and Lyonnaise onions, although the signature dish you must try is the much-loved, twice-cooked soufflé. **Known for:** caters to a long lunch; great atmosphere; friendly staff. *Average main: A$42 Woollahra Hotel, 116 Queen St., Woollahra 02/9327–9713 woollahrahotel.com.au.*

Chiswick

$ | **MODERN AUSTRALIAN** | Few central Sydney restaurants have access to their own homegrown produce, but here in trendy and leafy Woollahra—just a few kilometers east of the city—is an all-white and refreshingly bright restaurant surrounded by formal gardens and a large kitchen garden. Chiswick is all about stylish casual dining using the freshest of produce and a wonderful place to linger over a long lunch on a sunny day. **Known for:** great wine list; hearty meals; lively atmosphere. *Average main: A$34 65 Ocean St., Woollahra 02/8388–8688 www.chiswickrestaurant.com.au.*

SURRY HILLS

Chin Chin Sydney

$$$ | **ASIAN** | For a long time, those wanting to experience Chin Chin had to head to Melbourne. But in 2016, a sister restaurant finally opened its doors in Surry Hills, and it has since elbowed its way to epicurean cult status among foodies. **Known for:** cult following so packed on weekends; superior Southeast Asian food; buzzy atmosphere. *Average main: A$50 69 Commonwealth St., Surry Hills 02/9281–3322 www.chinchinrestaurant.com.au/sydney.*

Four Ate Five

$ | **CAFÉ** | This buzzy little café serves some of the best breakfasts in Surry Hills, which is really saying something as there is plenty of stiff competition in this part of town. Come here for the house-made muesli and organic yogurt or fuel up with the 485—egg, hummus, feta, pilpelchuma chili paste, Israeli pickles, and red cabbage salad on a bagel or pretzel—and wash it down with some ginger turmeric kombucha. **Known for:** relaxed atmosphere; espresso coffee; desserts. *Average main: A$16 485 Crown St., Surry Hills 02/9698–6485 fourate-five.com No dinner.*

Porteno

$$$ | **SOUTH AMERICAN** | This South American–inspired restaurant offers a wide range of flame-grilled and charcoal-roasted meats that come with a variety of fresh sides, like chargrilled vegetables or light salads. But it's the wine list that is the star of the show here, with over 300 wines from South America, Italy, and Australia to choose from. **Known for:** incredible wine list; chargrilled meats; lively atmosphere. *Average main: A$ 50 50 Holt St., Surry Hills 02/8399–1440 porteno.com.au No lunch. Closed Sun. and Mon.*

BONDI BEACH

Bronte Belo

$ | **BRAZILIAN** | One of eight or nine eateries in the buzzy café strip opposite Bronte Beach, this is a great place to refuel after the Bondi-to-Bronte cliff-top walk. All share the same postcard-perfect view, but Belo is worth seeking out for its consistently good coffee and spicy sticky chai. **Known for:** brilliant breakfast spot; gets busy; relaxed dining experience. *Average main: A$25 469 Bronte Rd., Bronte 02/9369–5673 brontebelo.com.*

Continued on page 140

Australia's
Modern
Cuisine

It may be referred to as the land down under, but the culinary movement that's sweeping Australia means this country has come out on top. Modern Australian cuisine has transformed the land of Vegemite sandwiches and shrimp-on-the-barbie into a culinary Promised Land with local flavors, organic produce, and bountiful seafood, fashioned by chefs who remain unburdened by restrictive traditions.

Australia is fast proving to be one of the most exciting destinations in the world for food lovers. With its stunning natural bounty, multicultural inspirations, and young culinary innovators, it ticks off all the requisite foodie boxes.

In Sydney, chefs are dishing up new twists on various traditions, creating a Modern Australian (Mod Oz) cuisine with its own compelling style. Traditional bush tucker, for example, has been transformed from a means of survival into a gourmet experience. Spicy Asian flavors have been borrowed from the country's neighbors to the north, and homage has been paid to the precision and customs brought by Australia's early European settlers.

The diversity of the modern Australian culinary movement also means that it is more than just flavors: it's an experience. And one that can be obtained from the award-winning luxury restaurant down to the small Thai-style canteens, pubs, and outdoor cafés.

While purists might argue that Mod Oz cuisine is little more than a plagiarism of flavors and cultures, others will acknowledge it as unadulterated fare with a fascinating history of its very own. Either way, it still offers a dining experience that's unique from anywhere else in the world.

MENU DECODER

Barbie: barbeque | Snags: sausages | Chook: chicken | Vegemite: salty yeast spread | Lamington: small chocolate sponge cake with coconut | Pavlova: meringue dessert topped with cream and fruit | Floater: meat pie with mushy peas and gravy | Damper: simple bread cooked on a campfire | Sanga: sandwich | Cuppa: cup of tea | Tucker: food | Chips: French fries | Tomato sauce: ketchup | Muddy: mud crab | Prawn: shrimp

Seared tuna with avocado, cilantro, and black sesame seeds, topped with caviar

BUSH TUCKER

Bush Tucker food; Tropical rainforest fruits on paper bark

BACK THEN

Native Australian plants and animals have played a vital role in the diets of the Aboriginal people for more than 50,000 years. Generally referred to as bush tucker, these native fruits, nuts, seeds, vegetables, meats, and fish are harvested around the country—from arid deserts to coastal areas and tropical rainforests.

Once little more than a means of survival, today they're touted as gourmet ingredients. And you certainly don't need to go "walkabout" to find them.

RIGHT NOW

Bush tucker has undergone much transformation over the decades, experiencing a renaissance in recent years. Heavily influenced by multicultural cooking techniques, game meats such as emu and wallaby have been elevated from bush-stew ingredients to perfectly seared cuts of meat garnished with seasonal herbs and vegetables. Kangaroo is making its way into stir-fries and curries, while crocodile—once cooked over coals on the campfire—is now served as carpaccio, tempura, or curry, among the many preparations. Seafood, like rock lobster and barramundi, can be found in humble fish-and-chip shops and top-notch eateries.

Of course, bush tucker isn't just about the protein. Native spices, wild fruits, and indigenous nuts have found favor in countless culinary applications. Lemon myrtle leaves lend a lemony flavor to baked goods and savory dishes. Alpine pepper, a crushed herb, gives foods a fiery zing. Quandong is a wild plum-like fruit with subtle apricot flavor. It once was dried as a portable energy source but now is made into jams and pie fillings. Kakadu plums are made into "super" juices with enormous vitamin C content. Bush tomatoes also have become popular in jams and sauces, and are available in

Witchetty grub

Tandoori kangaroo

supermarkets. Native nuts include the bunya nut, which is chestnut-like with pine notes, the shells of which are used for smoking meat. Macadamia nuts, meanwhile, are among the country's biggest exports.

WHERE TO FIND IT

Despite the presence of numerous bush ingredients in Sydney restaurants, the modern bush tucker dining experience is more prominent in the northern parts of the country. You are most likely to find dishes such as kangaroo, and occasionally crocodile, on the menu of restaurants in the city's main tourist precincts of The Rocks and Circular Quay.

In Queensland and the Northern Territory, you'll find full degustation menus combining local meats and seafood with native herbs, spices, and berries. Some even offer tasting tours of their kitchen gardens where you can sample popular flavors like lemon myrtle, tarragon, and hibiscus flower straight from the bush.

INDIGENOUS MEATS

CAMEL: With some one million camels in Australia, camel is fast being served up on many menus, though most are in the Northern Territory. The meat is often compared to mutton and has a similar taste and texture to beef.

CROCODILE: This meat may be fish-like in texture and appearance, but it tastes similar to chicken. The most popular cut is the tail, however legs and meat from the body are also consumed. Crocodile is growing in popularity because of its delicate flavor and versatility. It is often fried and grilled, but may be served raw in carpaccio or sushi rolls.

EMU: Although it's fowl, emu meat is similar in texture and flavor to beef with a light flavor and slight gamey tones on the palate. The meat is high in iron and very low in fat and cholesterol. Typical cuts include rump, strip loin, and oyster filet. It may be served pan-seared or lightly grilled.

KANGAROO: A dark red meat, it is extremely lean with only about 2% fat. The filet or rump is best eaten rare to medium rare, and is typically seared, barbecued, or stir-fried. Young kangaroo meat tastes like beef, while aged cuts take on a gamier flavor.

WALLABY: A cousin to the kangaroo, this meat has a somewhat milder flavor. It is a rich burgundy color and is best prepared with simple, delicate cooking styles, such as barbecuing or pan frying.

WITCHETTY GRUB: The larvae of ghost moths, these grubs are eaten raw or barbecued. People describe the taste as similar to egg, with the texture of a prawn.

A meal of crocodile fillet with vegetables

UPDATED EUROPEAN FARE

Seafood Salad

BACK THEN

Although the foundation of Mod Oz cuisine stems from the arrival of early British settlers, the food scene has certainly steamed ahead since the days of boiled beef and damper.

The real progression of modern Australian food came after World War II, when European immigrants brought a new wave of cooking to the country. It was the French and Italians who really opened the eyes of Australians with their distinguished flavors, commitment to freshness, and masterful culinary techniques. They also laid the foundations for some of the finest vineyards and cheese makers in the country.

RIGHT NOW

Though small, there are still degrees of British influence in modern Australian cooking, albeit slightly updated. The quintessential English meat pie is now filled with ingredients such as Murray cod, lamb, bush tomato, and kangaroo. Traditional Sunday roasts and fish-and-chips spring up in pubs and cafes, but often with a twist. And tea is still a staple on the breakfast table with a true Aussie favorite, Vegemite on toast.

Poaching, roasting, and braising are now popular methods to cook everything from reef fish and yabbies to lamb, suckling pig, and rabbit. Omelettes, cassoulets, and soufflés as well as pasta, risotto, and gnocchi are very well suited to the country's prize-winning meats, vegetables, and seafood. And the rigorous use of garlic, saffron, basil, and tarragon is common in many kitchens.

Greeks, Germans, and Spaniards have also greatly influenced dining, with tapas bars, tavernas, and schnitzel houses well represented throughout the country. Middle Eastern and North African flavors are also beginning to leave their marks.

Even casual pubs are updating dishes to reflect ethnic influences

Aussie meat pie

and local products. It's not unusual to see items like spicy chorizo pizza and Peking Duck pizza on their menus.

Another hallmark of Mod Oz cuisine—and one that parallels America's current culinary trends—is its fascination with seasonal vegetables and organic meats. Specialist farms raising free-range poultry and livestock have become extremely popular with many restaurants throughout the country. Menus often cite an ingredient's producer, i.e. "Blackmore's wagyu bresaola," and also note whether ingredients are "pasture-raised" or "locally grown."

The "paddock to plate" philosophy is getting more attention from top restaurateurs. This means a restaurant aims to source its produce from farmers and producers within their community, ensuring transport miles stay low while food is fresh and region-specific. Some establishments go a step further by growing and harvesting produce on-site in their own kitchen gardens.

AUSTRALIA'S NATURAL BOUNTY

CHEESE FRUIT: Grown in tropical areas, this fruit high in vitamin C has long been used for medicinal purposes. It's eaten while still green since it has a distinct rotting cheese smell when ripe. Leaves can also be eaten raw or cooked.

ILLAWARRA PLUMS: Usually used in jams and chutneys or as a rich sauce to accompany kangaroo, venison, or emu. High in antioxidants, they have a subtle plum flavor with a hint of pine.

LEMON MYRTLE: A native tree with a citrus fragrance and flavor. Leaves can be used fresh or dried and ground in sweet and savory styles of cooking.

MACADAMIA NUTS: Known as Kindal Kindal by native Australians, the macadamia is a round white nut with a hard brown shell and creamy flavor.

MUNTRIES: Small berry-like fruit that have a distinct apple flavor. Also known as emu apples, they can be eaten fresh in salads or added to desserts.

PAPER BARK: Papery leaves from the Melaluca tree, used to cook meat and seafood.

QUANDONG: A bright red fruit similar to a native peach. It's commonly used to make jams and sauces.

WARRIGAL GREENS: A herb-like vegetable with a flavor similar to spinach. They must be well cooked to eliminate their toxic oxalate content.

WATTLESEED: Also known as acacia seeds. They have a nutty to coffee-like flavor and are very high in protein. Often ground down and used in baking.

Macadamia nuts

ASIAN FUSION

Chicken laksa

BACK THEN

Much has changed in the way of Asian food in Australia. Sixty years ago sushi didn't exist in the vocabulary, now there are Japanese restaurants on almost every street.

The Gold Rush of the mid-19th century brought an influx of Chinese immigrants to Australia, prompting Asian cuisine's humble beginnings here. Thai, Vietnamese, Indian, Malaysian, and Japanese migrants followed in various waves in the 20th century. Before long, a cuisine that had started out in family-run restaurants in the outer suburbs of Sydney had become a burgeoning new trend. And by the late 1990s the children of the first wave of immigrants had formed the new guard.

RIGHT NOW

Traditional Chinese, Thai, and Japanese restaurants are very popular in Australia. But Asian fusion restaurants are leading the charge in creating Australia-specific taste innovations. Asian fusion cuisine combines the traditional flavors of Thai, Chinese, Japanese, and Vietnamese cooking, using local Australian ingredients and Western culinary techniques. Chic contemporary interiors, often with long communal tables and shared dishes, are the latest trend. Robust herbs such as mint and coriander, fiery chili, zesty black vinegar, ginger, and pickled vegetables are core ingredients, often wok-fried with fresh Australian ingredients such as Barossa Valley chicken, Thirlmere duck, or Bangalow pork.

Leading the charge is world-renowned, Sydney-based chef Tetsuya Wakuda. His signature dish, a confit of Petuna Tasmanian Ocean Trout with konbu, apple, daikon, and wasabi is a prime example of Asian fusion, uniquely blending French techniques with his Japanese heritage and excellent Australian products.

Yet, smaller modern canteen-style eateries are also serving up

Red chile peppers

Rock lobsters

contemporary Asian fare that provides excellent quality at a fraction of the price. It's in these bustling restaurants that flavors and dishes such as shucked oyster with chili and galangal vinaigrette, roasted duck in coconut curry, wagyu-beef hotpot, soft-shell crab with chili jam, and green curry of barramundi bounce off their plates.

While the majority of Asian fusion food in Australia relies heavily on light cooking styles and fresh ingredients, clay pot cooking as well as heavier-style Malaysian and Indian curries, such as rendang and vindaloo made with local lamb and beef, are also becoming popular.

Asian influences have also made their mark on traditional seafood restaurants, where ginger, lime, coriander, and chili add extra zing to alfresco menus. Exquisite dishes include Japanese-inspired butter-grilled scallops, steamed mussels in Thai-style coconut broth, or ocean trout grilled with garlic, soy, and chili.

LOCAL FISH AND SEAFOOD

ABALONE: A large sea snail with an edible muscular foot. It has a firm, rubbery texture with a very delicate flavor and can retail for about $100 per kilogram. Abalone are often seared or fried.

BALMAIN OR MORETON BAY BUGS: A smaller relative of the rock lobster with a short tail, flat head, and bug-like eyes. They have a sweet taste and a medium texture. A favorite served cold in salads and seafood platters, or split down the middle and grilled.

BARRAMUNDI: A member of the perch family, it's a highly versatile fish with a medium to firm flesh and white to light pink tones. Native to Australia, it lives in both fresh and salt waters and is farmed as well as caught in the wild.

ROCK LOBSTERS: A spiny lobster with long antennae and no claws. The four main types—eastern, southern, western, and tropical—each offer slightly different flavours and textures. The tropical are excellent as sashimi, while the eastern, southern and western lend themselves to baking and barbecue.

SYDNEY ROCK OYSTERS: Despite their name, these bivalves are commonly found throughout the east coast. They're prized for their distinct rich and creamy flavor, and are smaller in size than Pacific oysters. Try eating them raw with a squirt of lemon.

YABBIES: A fresh-water crayfish with firm white flesh and a sweeter taste than rock lobster. Small in size, they can be tricky to eat but are worth the effort. They're often cooked simply in a pot of salted, boiling water.

Salad of yabby tails

Brown Sugar

$ | **MODERN AUSTRALIAN** | You have to seek out this Bondi Beach restaurant, as it's situated several hundred feet back from the beach. You'll quickly find out, however, why locals love this place: organic, seasonal, handcrafted food. **Known for:** great location near beach; focus on health; wholesome food. *Average main: A$35 ✉ 106 Curlewis St., Bondi Beach ☎ 02/9130–1566 🌐 www.brownsugarbondi.com.au ⏲ Closed Mon. No breakfast or lunch Tues.–Thurs.*

Catalina Restaurant

$$$ | **SEAFOOD** | This harbor-front restaurant occupies the site of the old "airport" (back in the days when the fastest way to get to England was by flying boat), and has ringside views of the harbor and Shark Island. Patrons can watch modern seaplanes take off and land just meters away while dining on fine seafood. **Known for:** incredible views; special occasions; formal dining. *Average main: A$48 ✉ Lyne Park, New South Head Rd., Rose Bay ☎ 02/9371–0555 🌐 www.catalinarosebay.com.au ⏲ No dinner Sun.*

★ **Icebergs Dining Room and Bar**

$$$ | **ITALIAN** | The fashionable and famous (including celebrities like Mick Jagger and Paris Hilton) just adore perching like seagulls over the swimming pool at the south end of Australia's most famous beach. It is one of the must-visit restaurants in Sydney, for both the sensational view and the exquisite food. **Known for:** superior food and drinks; Bondi institution; amazing views of Bondi and the beach. *Average main: A$48 ✉ 1 Notts Ave., Bondi Beach ☎ 02/9365–9000 🌐 idrb.com ⏲ Closed Mon.*

North Bondi Fish

$ | **AUSTRALIAN** | Celeb-chef Matt Moran's much-celebrated beachfront fish-and-chips offering is so much more than just standard fish-and-chips. The ocean views enhance a small and select seafood menu that includes fresh Sydney rock oysters, charcoal-grilled snapper, prawns, salmon, and whole fish of the day. **Known for:** fun atmosphere; oceanfront location; busy and popular spot. *Average main: A$35 ✉ 120 Ramsgate Ave., North Bondi ☎ 02/9130–2155 🌐 www.northbondifish.com.au.*

Sean's Panaroma

$$ | **AUSTRALIAN** | North Bondi Beach wouldn't be the same without Sean's Panaroma ("Sean's" to locals), perched on a slight rise a stone's throw from the famous beach. It's been there since the mid-1990s and owner Sean Moran loads his menu with fresh produce grown on his farm in the Blue Mountains, aptly named "Farm Panaroma." Dishes change regularly and are only featured on a blackboard: they may include baked blue-eye fish with roasted cauliflower, or a ravioli of zucchini, mozzarella, and lemons. **Known for:** nice atmosphere; great seafood dishes; average service. *Average main: A$45 ✉ 270 Campbell Parade, Bondi Beach ☎ 02/9365–4924 🌐 www.seansbondi.com ⏲ No lunch Mon.–Thurs.*

Totti's

$$ | **ITALIAN** | Found a little farther up Bondi Road, away from the beach, this restaurant has been a bit of an unexpected hit since opening in 2018. Unexpected because it's housed above a run-down pub called The Royal. **Known for:** incredible casual eats; trendy crowd; classy interiors. *Average main: A$45 ✉ 283 Bondi Rd., Bondi Beach ☎ 02/9114–7371 🌐 merivale.com/venues/tottis.*

Coffee and Quick Bites

Barbetta

$ | **ITALIAN** | The creation of three Italian brothers, this trendy Paddington eatery is a winner at both breakfast or at lunch. The menu has truly unique creations, like the breakfast burger with poached eggs, truffled mushrooms, and crushed peas. **Known for:** warm and welcoming atmosphere; substantial mains; unique meals.

$ Average main: A$25 ✉ 2 Elizabeth St., Paddington ☎ 02/9331–0088 🌐 barbetta.com.au.

Bennett St Dairy

$ | **AUSTRALIAN** | Bondi is known for being the health epicenter of Sydney and, unsurprisingly, the cafés are all about packing as much healthy food into a dish as possible. Breakfast bowls packed with eggs, vegetables, toasted seeds, and gluten-free toast is a popular option here. **Known for:** fresh juice; healthy eats; convenient location. *$ Average main: A$20 ✉ 73 Bondi Rd., Bondi Beach ☎ 02/8592–4415 🌐 www.bennettstdairy.com.*

★ Gelato Messina

$ | **ICE CREAM** | There's a reason why there's always a queue snaking down the street. This is undoubtedly the best gelato in Sydney, with unique flavors that change all the time. **Known for:** friendly staff; unique flavors; authentic gelato. *$ Average main: A$10 ✉ 241 Victoria St., Darlinghurst ☎ 02/9331–1588 🌐 gelatomessina.com.*

The Mayflower

$ | **AUSTRALIAN** | Fast but fancy fare, that's what this Darlinghurst café has become known for since opening in 2020. The cheese toastie comes topped with black truffle, there are poached lobster rolls and caviar sandwiches. **Known for:** trendy café; something special; outstanding service. *$ Average main: A$35 ✉ 303A Liverpool St., Darlinghurst ☎ 04/9730–5475 🌐 the-mayflower.com.au.*

Porch and Parlour

$ | **CAFÉ** | You'll probably have to wait to get one of the tiny tables in this rustic hole-in-the-wall café and wine bar on the northern end of Bondi Beach, but it's worth waiting for as it's one of the best (and healthiest) breakfasts in Bondi. Once you've got a seat and a cup of the fabulous coffee, the service is fast and efficient. **Known for:** all-day dining; fast service; healthy eats. *$ Average main: A$22 ✉ 110 Ramsgate Ave., Bondi Beach ☎ 02/9300–0111 🌐 www.porchandparlour.com.au.*

Room Ten

$ | **AUSTRALIAN** | It might look like nothing more than a hole-in-the-wall but this modest café has been hailed by locals as serving the best coffee in the Potts Point and Kings Cross area. And the seating outside is always packed every morning of the week. **Known for:** fast but delicious eats; specialized coffee; trendy. *$ Average main: A$15 ✉ 10 Llankelly Pl., Potts Point ☎ 04/3244–5342 🌐 www.facebook.com/room10espresso.*

Single O

$ | **AUSTRALIAN** | In 2019, this café opened Sydney's first self-serve batch-brew bar, with craft beer–style taps where you can drink as much single-origin coffee as your heart desires or can handle. But this is more than just an übertrendy spot for coffee: the menu is filled with quirky dishes, with many vegan offerings. **Known for:** huge variety of coffee; vegan and gluten-free options; plenty of seating. *$ Average main: A$20 ✉ 60–64 Reservoir St., Surry Hills ☎ 02/9211–0665 🌐 singleoriginroasters.com.au.*

Hotels

PADDINGTON

Arts Hotel Sydney

$ | **HOTEL** | On a quiet stretch in the trendy shopping precinct of Paddington, this small, friendly, family-run hotel has simple accommodations at an outstanding price. **Pros:** warm feel; great value; personal service. **Cons:** dated interiors throughout; simply appointed rooms; limited breakfast options. *$ Rooms from: A$150 ✉ 21 Oxford St., Paddington ☎ 02/9361–0211 🌐 www.artshotel.com.au ⇆ 64 rooms 🍽 No Meals.*

DARLINGHURST

Medusa

$ | HOTEL | If you're tired of the standard travelers' rooms, this renovated Victorian terrace house may be just the tonic. **Pros:**; flashy design; good location; warm service. **Cons:** urban location may get noisy; funky interiors might not be to everyone's taste; not much privacy due to small size. $ *Rooms from: A$160* ✉ *267 Darlinghurst Rd., Darlinghurst* ☎ *02/9331–1000* 🌐 *www.medusa.com.au* 🍽 *No Meals* 🛏 *18 rooms.*

KINGS CROSS

Larmont Sydney by Lancemore

$ | HOTEL | Found at the top of a hill that leads up from the CBD past Hyde Park and into Kings Cross, Larmont's location offers incredible views of the cityscape. **Pros:** great value for money; large spacious rooms; convenient location. **Cons:** hard to find staff; foyer is impersonal; desk is sometimes unmanned. $ *Rooms from: A$180* ✉ *2–14 Kings Cross Rd., Kings Cross* ☎ *02/9295–8888* 🌐 *www.lancemore.com.au/larmont* 🍽 *No Meals* 🛏 *103 rooms.*

SURRY HILLS

★ Paramount House Hotel

$$$ | HOTEL | Set in Sydney's trendy dining and drinking hot spot of Surry Hills and sharing the former headquarters of Paramount Pictures with the Golden Age Cinema and Bar, Paramount Coffee Project, a rooftop recreation center, and a coworking office space, Paramount House Hotel's loftlike rooms with plant-filled balconies is the coolest place to stay and play in Sydney. **Pros:** close to dining and nightlife; stylish design throughout; superior cocktails, coffee, and cinema on-site. **Cons:** no on-site restaurant for dinner; reception is through busy café; no nearby rail. $ *Rooms from: A$350* ✉ *80 Commonwealth St., Surry Hills* ☎ *02/9211–1222* 🌐 *paramounthousehotel.com* 🍽 *No Meals* 🛏 *29 rooms.*

POTTS POINT

DeVere Hotel

$ | HOTEL | "Simply comfortable and affordable" is the slogan at this 1920s-style hotel at the leafy end of Potts Point, and it's hard to disagree on either count. **Pros:** friendly staff; good value; spacious rooms. **Cons:** basic facilities; breakfast, although available on-site, is no longer included in rate; noisy on weekends. $ *Rooms from: A$127* ✉ *44–46 Macleay St., Potts Point* ☎ *02/9358–1211* 🌐 *www.devere.com.au* 🍽 *No Meals* 🛏 *118 rooms.*

★ Spicers Potts Point

$$$ | B&B/INN | Set over three adjoining Victorian terraces on a tree-lined street close to Kings Cross and Potts Points, Spicers Potts Point combines heritage charm with modern elegance for a cool and calming retreat right in the middle of things. **Pros:** convenient to the harbor and CBD; modern, elegant design; inner-city sanctuary. **Cons:** not family-friendly; street parking; no gym or restaurant on-site. $ *Rooms from: A$400* ✉ *122 Victoria St., Potts Point* ☎ *1300/525–442* 🌐 *www.spicerspottspoint.com* 🍽 *No Meals* 🛏 *20 rooms.*

RUSHCUTTERS BAY

Vibe Hotel Rushcutters

$ | HOTEL | This good-value hotel fronting a lovely harborside park is a more peaceful alternative to staying in Kings Cross, but still within walking distance of the restaurants and bars of the buzzy nightlife strip. **Pros:** quieter alternative to Kings Cross; bay-side location; good value. **Cons:** 50-minute walk into the city; small rooms; no overflow car park and no street parking. $ *Rooms from: A$187* ✉ *100 Bayswater Rd., Rushcutters Bay* ☎ *02/8353–8988* 🌐 *www.tfehotels.com* 🍽 *No Meals* 🛏 *245 rooms.*

WOOLLOOMOOLOO

Ovolo Woolloomooloo

$$$ | **HOTEL** | This ultrahip hotel occupies a former wool shipping shed that includes authentic structures of the former wharf (pulleys, giant trusses, and brontosaurus-like machinery), a great location (a stone's throw from the Opera House), and the chance to be on the harbor but in a quieter location. **Pros:** great location, close to Botanic Gardens; large bathrooms, high-end tech; trendy bar, trendier location. **Cons:** foyer is freezing in the winter; a bit of walk into the city; breakfast is an expensive add-on. *Rooms from: A$365 Wharf at Woolloomooloo, 6 Cowper Wharf Rd., Woolloomooloo 02/9331–9000 www.ovolohotels.com.au/ovolowoolloomooloo No Meals 136 rooms.*

BONDI BEACH

Adina Apartment Hotel Bondi Beach

$$$ | **HOTEL** | This hotel apartment complex, several hundred feet from Bondi Beach, includes more than a dozen restaurants, bars, and stores. **Pros:** part of a trendy complex; spacious apartments; great location. **Cons:** noisy in high season; no views from some rooms; fee for parking. *Rooms from: A$349 69–73 Hall St., Bondi Beach 02/9300–4800 www.adinahotels.com.au No Meals 111 rooms.*

QT Bondi

$$$ | **HOTEL** | Boutique hotel meets cool apartment: QT Bondi is for the modern traveler who cares less about spas, gyms, and room service, and more about a great location, creative design, and considered home-away-from-home amenities (which at QT Bondi means everything from kitchenettes with dishwashers and washing machines to shoehorns and beach bags). **Pros:** quirky, cool design; close to beach and great cafés and restaurants; kitchenettes. **Cons:** no swimming pool; can be noisy; no restaurant on-site. *Rooms from: A$410 6 Beach Rd., Bondi Beach 2/8362–3900 www.qthotels.com No Meals 69 rooms.*

COOGEE

Crowne Plaza Coogee Beach

$$ | **HOTEL** | Live like a local at Coogee Beach, which is just as gorgeous as nearby Bondi, but without the crowds. **Pros:** good value for beachfront accommodations; great location; some rooms have balconies with ocean views. **Cons:** fee for parking; rooms a little dated; incredibly busy foyer. *Rooms from: A$280 242 Arden St., Coogee 02/9315–7600 www.ihg.com No Meals 209 rooms.*

Nightlife

BARS AND DANCE CLUBS

Beach Road Hotel

PUBS | This Bondi institution is famous for its Sunday Sessions, when locals come to enjoy a barbecue, drink, and dance in the outdoor courtyard. There's music every night in summer (except Monday), good affordable food, and a A$20 roast with all the trimmings on Sunday night. *71 Beach Rd., Bondi Beach 02/9130–7247 www.beachroadbondi.com.au.*

Shady Pines Saloon

PUBS | This underground bar offers an authentic saloon experience, with Johnny Cash songs playing, whiskey flowing, and peanut shells found all over the ground. The vibe is friendly, with cocktail hour between 4 pm and 6 pm being a massive hit thanks to A$10 cocktails. Always a fun place to let your hair down, with live music playing on weekends. Open every night of the week. *Shop 4 256 Crown St., Darlinghurst 04/0562–4944 shadypinessaloon.com.*

COMEDY CLUBS

The Comedy Store

COMEDY CLUBS | The city's oldest comedy club is in a plush 300-seat theater in the Entertainment Quarter, which most people still refer to as Fox Studios (its former name). The difficult-to-find theater is at the rear of the complex, close to the parking lot. Shows are Thursday–Saturday at 8:30 pm, and admission is usually around A$30. ✉ *Entertainment Quarter, 122 Lang Rd., Bldg. 207, Centennial Park* ☎ *02/9550–3666* 🌐 *www.comedystore.com.au.*

LBGTQ

Most of the city's gay and lesbian venues are along Oxford Street, in Darlinghurst. The free *Sydney Star Observer,* available along Oxford Street, has a roundup of Sydney's gay and lesbian goings-on, or check the magazine's website (*www.starobserver.com.au*). A monthly free magazine, *Lesbians on the Loose* (*www.lotl.com*), lists events for women.

ARQ

DANCE CLUBS | Sydney's biggest, best-looking, and funkiest gay nightclub, ARQ attracts a clean-cut crowd who like to whip off their shirts as soon as they hear the beat. (Some women head here, too.) There are multiple dance floors, a bar, and plenty of chrome and sparkly lighting. It's open from 9 pm until whenever Thursday through Sunday; a Thursday night drag contest is free and so is entry on a Friday night, while shows have a cover charge ranging from A$15 to A$25 (and sometimes a little more). ✉ *16 Flinders St., Darlinghurst* ☎ *02/9380–8700.*

Stonewall Hotel

LIVE MUSIC | Set over three floors, with drag acts, DJs, and incredible dancers putting on shows throughout the evening until the early hours of the morning, the Stonewall is *the* place to get your dance on. While the drinks are cheap, the service is slow, so pack your patience. Admission varies depending on the time of arrival. Get in before midnight and it's free, unless there's an extra-special show on that night. ✉ *175 Oxford St., Darlinghurst* ☎ *02/9360–1963* 🌐 *stonewallhotel.com.*

Pride Parade

If you're in Sydney in late February and early March, check out the Sydney Gay and Lesbian Mardi Gras parade. This festival, which began as a gay rights protest march in 1978, is one of Australia's major events. Dozens of floats covered with buff dancers make their way from College Street, near St. Mary's Cathedral, up Oxford Street to Taylor's Square. Thousands of spectators watch this amazing party parade.

JAZZ CLUBS

Low 302

LIVE MUSIC | This jazz bar is one of the few late-night bars available in the city, opening until 2 am every night but Monday and Tuesday. There's jazz played but also live instrumental. The vibe is relaxed and the crowd friendly. The menu and drinks are simple with pizza, pasta, and cocktails available and all at a reasonable price. There is a large variety of whiskies available. ✉ *302 Crown St., Surry Hills* ☎ *02/9368–1548* 🌐 *low302.com.au.*

PUBS WITH MUSIC

Kings Cross Hotel

LIVE MUSIC | Spread out over four levels, this towering venue hosts live bands almost every night of the week. There's even a weekly open-mic night on the rooftop bar, where some of the city's best jump on stage and sing covers or originals. There's also a pub menu available, with plenty of seating if you're not one for dancing. ✉ *244–248 William St., Kings Cross* ☎ *02/9331–9900* 🌐 *www.kingscrosshotel.com.au.*

Aboriginal artwork is a visual representation of ancestral stories from "The Dreaming."

Shopping

ART AND CRAFT GALLERIES

Cooee Aboriginal Art

ART GALLERIES | This gallery, open Tuesday–Saturday 10–5, exhibits and sells high-end Aboriginal paintings, sculptures, and limited-edition prints. It's a five-minute walk from Bondi Beach. ✉ *31 Lamrock Ave., Bondi Beach* ☎ *02/9300–9233* 🌐 *www.cooeeart.com.au.*

BOOKS

Gertrude & Alice Café Bookshop

BOOKS | Need something to read on Bondi Beach? Take a stroll to Gertrude & Alice Café Bookshop, named in honor of lovers Gertrude Stein and Alice B. Toklas. Always buzzing with people, it's a great place to sip coffee or chai lattes, or have lunch while perusing the mostly second-hand books. ✉ *46 Hall St., Bondi Beach* ☎ *02/9130–5155* 🌐 *www.gertrudeandalice.com.au.*

CLOTHING

Belinda

WOMEN'S CLOTHING | This is where Sydney's female fashionistas go when there's a dress-up occasion looming. From her namesake store that scores high marks for innovation and imagination, former model Belinda Seper sells nothing but the very latest designs off the catwalks. ✉ *8 Transvaal Ave., Double Bay* ☎ *02/9327–2873* 🌐 *www.belinda.com.au.*

Scanlan & Theodore

WOMEN'S CLOTHING | This is the Sydney outlet for one of Melbourne's most distinguished fashion houses. Designs take their cues from Europe, with superbly tailored women's knitwear, suits, and stylishly glamorous evening wear. ✉ *Bay St., Double Bay, Paddington* ☎ *02/9328–4886* 🌐 *www.scanlantheodore.com.*

DEPARTMENT STORES AND SHOPPING CENTERS

Oxford Street

NEIGHBORHOODS | Nicknamed the "Style Mile," Paddington's main artery, from South Dowling Street east to Queen Street, Woollahra, is dressed to thrill. Lined with boutiques, home-furnishings stores, and cafés, it's a perfect venue for watching the never-ending fashion parade. Take Bus No. 380, 382, or 333 from Circular Quay. ✉ *Oxford St., Paddington.*

MARKETS

★ Bondi Markets

MARKET | This relaxed and friendly beachside market at Bondi is the place to go for clothes—vintage and by up-and-coming designers—plus handmade jewelry, organic cosmetics, art, retro furniture, and secondhand goods. Look closely at the faces in the crowd—you'll often find visiting celebrities lurking behind messy bed hair and dark glasses. The markets are on every Sunday 10–4. ✉ *Bondi Beach Public School, Campbell Parade, Bondi Beach* ☎ *02/9315–7011* 🌐 *www.bondimarkets.com.au.*

★ Paddington Markets

MARKET | About 200 stalls crammed with clothing, plants, crafts, jewelry, and souvenirs fill this busy churchyard market (sometimes called Paddington Bazaar). Distinctly New Age and highly fashion-conscious, the market is an outlet for a handful of avant-garde clothing designers. Go early as it can get very crowded. ✉ *Paddington Uniting Church, 395 Oxford St., Paddington* ☎ *02/9331–2923* 🌐 *www.paddingtonmarkets.com.au.*

Activities

AUSTRALIAN RULES FOOTBALL

Sydney Cricket Ground

FOOTBALL | A fast, demanding game in which the ball can be kicked or punched between teams of 22 players, Australian Rules Football has won a major audience in Sydney, even though the city has only one professional team—the Sydney Swans—compared to the dozen that play in Melbourne, the home of the sport. Sydney Cricket Ground (SCG) hosts games April to September. ✉ *Centennial Park, Moore Park Rd., Paddington* ☎ *02/9360–6601* 🌐 *www.scgt.nsw.gov.au.*

BICYCLING

Sydney's favorite cycling track is Centennial Park's Grand Parade, a 3¾-km (2¼-mile) cycle circuit around the perimeter of this grand, gracious Eastern Suburbs park.

Centennial Park Cycles

BIKING | Rent bicycles here for around A$25 per hour, A$75 per day. There is an additional location inside Centennial Park on Grand Drive. ✉ *50 Clovelly Rd., Randwick* ☎ *02/9398–5027* 🌐 *www.cyclehire.com.au.*

Sydney Bike Sharing

BIKING | **FAMILY** | There are 2,500 dockless bikes around the city, which can be located and activated via a smartphone app (🌐 *www.reddygo.com.au*). ✉ *Elizabeth St., City Center* ☎ *02/9265–9333* 🌐 *www.cityofsydney.nsw.gov.au/explore/getting-around/cycling/dockless-bike-sharing.*

BOATING AND SAILING

EastSail

BOATING | Rent bareboat sailing and motored yachts from this operator for A$850 per half day (four hours); a manned yacht costs around A$1,865 for four hours and includes the skipper. It also conducts sailing schools. ✉ *D'Albora Marina, New Beach Rd., Rushcutters Bay, Eastern Suburbs* ☎ *02/9327–1166* 🌐 *www.eastsail.com.au.*

★ Sydney Harbour Kayaks

BOATING | Sydney Harbour Kayaks rents one- and two-person kayaks. The location beside Spit Bridge has calm water for novices, as well as several beaches and idyllic coves. Prices per hour start from

A$25 for a one-person kayak and A$40 for a double. Guided four-hour tours depart every Saturday and Sunday at 8:30 am (A$155 per person). Novices can take part in three-hour free lessons (A$50 for kayak hire). ✉ *81 Parriwi Rd., Mosman* ☎ *02/9969–4590* 🌐 *www.sydneyharbour-kayaks.com.au.*

CRICKET

Cricket is Sydney's summer sport, and it's often played in parks throughout the nation. For Australians the pinnacle of excitement is the Ashes, when the national cricket team takes the field against England. It happens every other summer, and the two nations take turns hosting the event. Cricket season runs from October through March.

Sydney Cricket Ground

CRICKET | International and interstate games are played at the Sydney Cricket Ground (commonly called the SCG). ✉ *Centennial Park, Moore Park Rd., Paddington* ☎ *02/9360–6601* 🌐 *www.scgt.nsw.gov.au.*

RUGBY LEAGUE

Sydney Football Stadium

RUGBY | Known locally as football (or footy), rugby league is Sydney's winter addiction. This is a fast, gutsy, physical game that bears some similarities to North American football, although the action is more constant and the ball cannot be passed forward. The season falls between March and September. Sydney Football Stadium (now known by its corporate sponsorship name of Allianz Stadium) is the home ground of the Sydney Roosters. Other games are played at ANZ Stadium (Sydney Olympic Park) and stadiums throughout the suburbs. ✉ *Centennial Park, Moore Park Rd., Paddington* ☎ *02/9360–6601* 🌐 *www.scgt.nsw.gov.au.*

SCUBA DIVING

Pro Dive

SCUBA DIVING | Pro Dive is a PADI operator conducting courses and shore- or boat-diving excursions around the harbor and city beaches. Some of the best dive spots—with coral, rock walls, and lots of colorful fish—are close to the Eastern Suburb beaches of Clovelly and Coogee. The company also has a center in Manly. A four-hour boat dive with a guide costs around A$120, including rental equipment; a learn-to-dive course is A$199. Check the website for specials. ✉ *27 Alfreda St., Coogee* ☎ *02/9665–6333* 🌐 *www.prodive.com.au.*

SURFING

Lets Go Surfing

SURFING | This is a complete surfing resource for anyone who wants to hang five with confidence. Lessons are available for all ages and you can rent or buy boards and wet suits. The two-hour beginner surfer lesson, in a small group, is A$140. ✉ *128 Ramsgate Ave., North Bondi* ☎ *02/9365–1800* 🌐 *www.letsgo-surfing.com.au.*

Rip Curl

SURFING | This store has a huge variety of boards and surfing supplies, including cool clothes. It's right at Bondi Beach. ✉ *82 Campbell Parade, Bondi Beach* ☎ *02/9130–2660* 🌐 *www.ripcurl.com.au.*

Greater Sydney

The Greater Sydney area has numerous attractions that can be easily reached by public transport. These include historic townships, the Sydney 2000 Olympics site, national parks where you can explore and enjoy the Australian bush, and wildlife and theme parks that appeal to children.

Other points of interest are the north-side beaches, particularly Manly, and the historic city of Parramatta, founded

A bird's-eye view of the boats in Parramatta River

in 1788 and 26 km (16 miles) to the west; and the magnificent Hawkesbury River, which winds its way around the city's western and northern borders. The waterside suburb of Balmain has pubs and restaurants, an atmospheric Saturday flea market, and backstreets full of character.

GETTING HERE AND AROUND

Trains travel from Central Station to Parramatta daily, and directly to Sydney Olympic Park on weekdays. To reach Olympic Park on weekends, take the train to Lidcombe and then change trains for the short ride to Olympic Park station. The RiverCat ferry travels from Circular Quay to Parramatta, calling at Sydney Olympic Park on the way. Trains depart from Central Station for the Hawkesbury River (alight at Hawkesbury River station in the town of Brooklyn). They also travel to the Royal National Park (alight at Engadine or Heathcote stations, or Loftus, where a tram travels from the station to the park on Sunday only).

TIMING

Each of the sights here could easily fill the better part of a day. If you're short on time, try a tour company that combines visits within a particular area—for example, a day trip west to the Olympic Games site, Featherdale Wildlife Park, and the Blue Mountains.

Sights

Elizabeth Farm

HISTORIC HOME | The oldest European building in Australia, Elizabeth Farm was built by John and Elizabeth Macarthur in 1793. With its simple but elegant lines and long, shady verandas, the house became a template for Australian farmhouses that survives to the present day. It was here, too, that the merino sheep industry began, since the Macarthurs were the first to introduce the tough Spanish breed to Australia. Although John Macarthur has traditionally been credited as the father of Australia's wool industry, it was Elizabeth who largely ran the farm while her husband pursued his official and more-lucrative unofficial duties as an officer in the colony's Rum Corps. Inside are personal objects of the Macarthur family, as well as a re-creation of their furnishings. Free tours are at 11, noon, 1, and 2 each day. ✉ *70 Alice St., Rosehill* ☎ *02/9635–9488* 🌐 *sydneylivingmuseums.com.au/elizabeth-farm* 🎟 *A$15.*

Experiment Farm Cottage

MUSEUM VILLAGE | The site of the first private land grant in Australia, Experiment Farm was settled in 1789 by James Ruse, a former convict who was given 1½ acres by Governor Phillip on condition that he become self-sufficient—a vital experiment if the colony was to survive. Luckily for Phillip, his gamble paid off. The bungalow, with its wide verandas, was built by colonial surgeon John Harris in the 1830s; it contains a fine collection of Australian colonial furniture, and the cellar now houses an exhibition on the life and work of James Ruse. The surrounding ornamental garden is most beautiful in early summer, when the floral perfumes are strongest. ✉ *9 Ruse St., Harris Park* ☎ *02/9635–5655* 🌐 *www.nationaltrust.org.au* 🎟 *From A$10.*

Featherdale Sydney Wildlife Park

ZOO | **FAMILY** | This is the place to see kangaroos, dingoes, wallabies, and echidnas (and even feed some of them) in native bush settings 40 km (25 miles) west of Sydney. The daily crocodile feeding sessions are very popular. Take the train to Blacktown Station and then board the 725 bus for the park. **TIP→ The park is on the way to the Blue Mountains.** ✉ *217 Kildare Rd., Doonside* ☎ *02/9622–1644* 🌐 *www.featherdale.com.au* 🎟 *A$35.*

Koala Park Sanctuary

ZOO | **FAMILY** | At this private park in Sydney's northern outskirts you can feed a kangaroo or get close to a koala. (Koala presentations are daily at 10:20, 11:45, 2, and 3.) The sanctuary also has dingoes, wombats, emus, penguins, and wallaroos. There are sheep-shearing and boomerang-throwing demonstrations. ✉ *84 Castle Hill Rd., West Pennant Hills* ☎ *02/9484–3141* 🌐 *koalapark-sanctuary.com.au* 🎟 *A$30.*

Ku-ring-gai Chase National Park

NATIONAL PARK | Nature hikes here lead past rock engravings and paintings by the Guringai Aboriginal tribe, the area's original inhabitants for whom the park is named. Created in the 1890s, the park mixes large stands of eucalyptus trees with moist, rain-forest-filled gullies where swamp wallabies, possums, goannas, and other creatures roam. The delightful trails are mostly easy or moderate, including the compelling 3-km (2-mile) Garigal Aboriginal Heritage Walk at West Head, which takes in ancient rock-art sites. From Mt. Ku-ring-gai train station you can walk the 3-km (2-mile) Ku-ring-gai Track to Appletree Bay, while the 30-minute, wheelchair-accessible Discovery Trail is an excellent introduction to the region's flora and fauna. Leaflets on all of the walks are available at the park's entry stations and from the Wildlife Shop at Bobbin Head. ✉ *Ku-ring-gai Chase National Park, Bobbin Head Rd., Mount Colah* ☎ *1300/072–757* 🌐 *www.nationalparks.nsw.gov.au* 🎟 *A$12 per vehicle, per day.*

Old Government House

GOVERNMENT BUILDING | On the bank of the Parramatta River, Old Government House (which was the country residence of Sydney's 10 early governors) is Australia's oldest surviving public building, and the World Heritage–listed building is a notable work from the Georgian period. Built by governors John Hunter and Lachlan Macquarie, the building has been faithfully restored in keeping with its origins, and contains the nation's most significant collection of early Australian furniture. In the 260-acre parkland surrounding the house are Governor Brisbane's bathhouse and observatory and the Government House Dairy. The house is often home to special exhibitions.

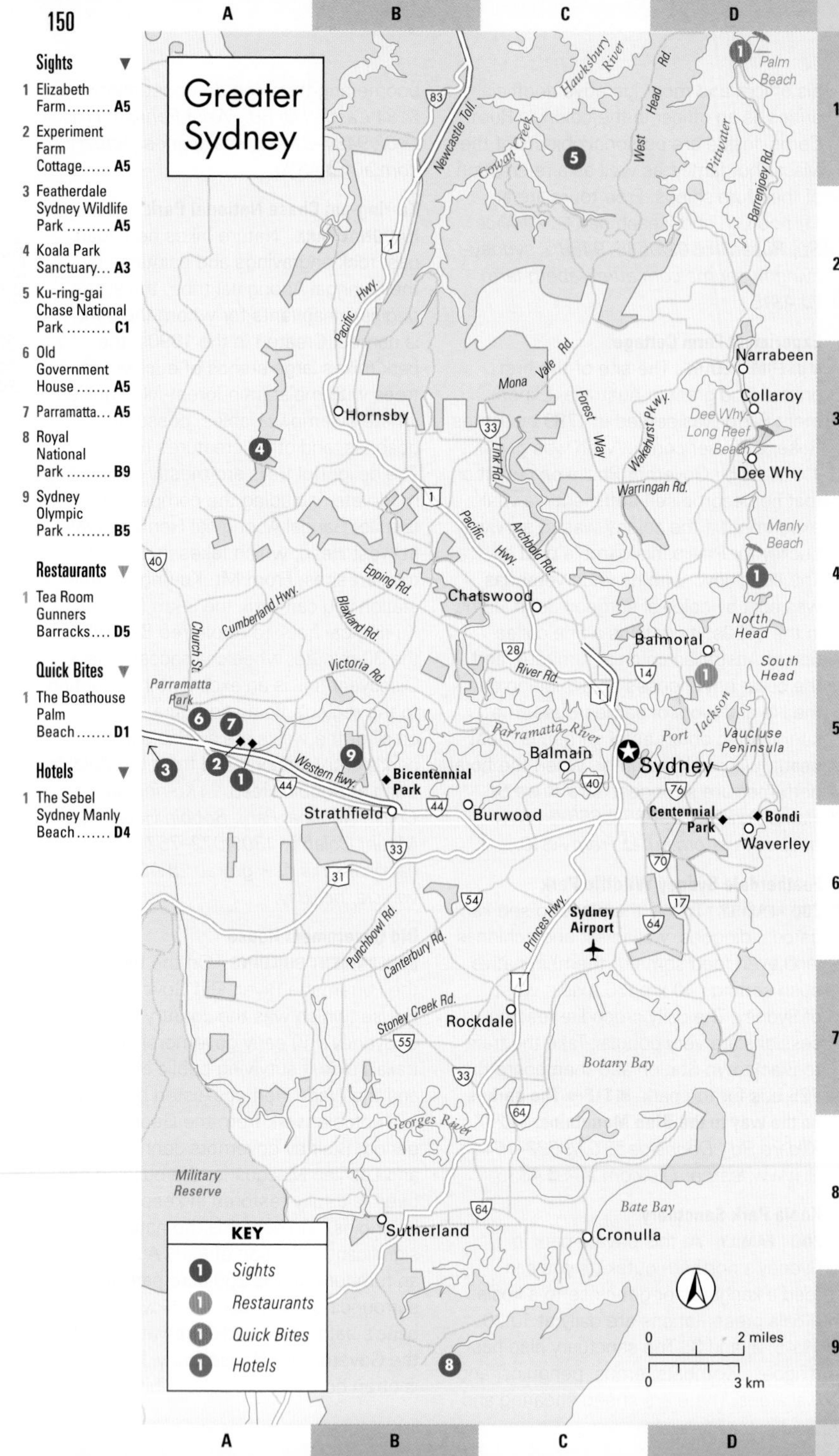
Sights
1 Elizabeth Farm......... A5
2 Experiment Farm Cottage...... A5
3 Featherdale Sydney Wildlife Park A5
4 Koala Park Sanctuary... A3
5 Ku-ring-gai Chase National Park C1
6 Old Government House A5
7 Parramatta... A5
8 Royal National Park B9
9 Sydney Olympic Park B5
Restaurants
1 Tea Room Gunners Barracks.... D5
Quick Bites
1 The Boathouse Palm Beach....... D1
Hotels
1 The Sebel Sydney Manly Beach....... D4
Greater Sydney
A
B
C
D
1
2
3
4
5
6
7
8
9
Palm Beach
Hawksbury River
West Head Rd.
Pittwater
Barrenjoey Rd.
Newcastle Toll.
Cowan Creek
Pacific Hwy.
Narrabeen
Collaroy
Dee Why
Long Reef Beach
Dee Why
Mona Vale Rd.
Forest Way
Wakehurst Pkwy.
Hornsby
Link Rd.
Warringah Rd.
Manly Beach
Archbold Rd.
Epping Rd.
Chatswood
Cumberland Hwy.
Blaxland Rd.
Church St.
North Head
Balmoral
South Head
Victoria Rd.
River Rd.
Parramatta Park
Port Jackson
Vaucluse Peninsula
Parramatta River
Balmain
Sydney
Western Fwy.
Bicentennial Park
Strathfield
Burwood
Centennial Park
Bondi
Waverley
Punchbowl Rd.
Canterbury Rd.
Princes Hwy.
Sydney Airport
Stoney Creek Rd.
Rockdale
Botany Bay
Georges River
Military Reserve
Bate Bay
Sutherland
Cronulla
KEY
Sights
Restaurants
Quick Bites
Hotels
0
2 miles
0
3 km

✉ *Inside Parramatta Park, Parramatta* ✣ *Pitt St. entrance* ☎ *02/9635–8149* 🌐 *www.nationaltrust.org.au* 🎫 *A$15.*

Parramatta

TOWN | This bustling satellite city 26 km (16 miles) west of Sydney is one of Australia's most historic precincts. Its origins as a European settlement are purely agrarian. The sandy, rocky soil around Sydney Cove was too poor to feed the fledgling colony, so Governor Phillip looked to the banks of the Parramatta River for the rich alluvial soil they needed. In 1789, just a year after the first convicts-cum-settlers arrived, Phillip established Rosehill, an area set aside for agriculture. The community developed as its agricultural successes grew, and several important buildings survive as outstanding examples of the period. The two-hour self-guided Harris Park Heritage Walk, which departs from the RiverCat Ferry Terminal, connects the key historic sites and buildings. The ferry departs at frequent intervals from Sydney's Circular Quay, and is a relaxing, scenic alternative to the drive or train ride from the city. A free shuttle bus travels in a loop around Parramatta. ✉ *Parramatta* 🌐 *www.discoverparramatta.com.*

Royal National Park

NATIONAL PARK | Established in 1879 on the coast south of Sydney, the Royal has the distinction of being the first national park in Australia and the second in the world, after Yellowstone National Park in the United States. Several walking tracks traverse the grounds, most of them requiring little or no hiking experience. The Lady Carrington Walk, a 10-km (6-mile) trek, is a self-guided tour that crosses 15 creeks and passes several historic sites. Other tracks take you along the coast past beautiful wildflower displays and through patches of rain forest. You can canoe the Port Hacking River upstream from the Audley Causeway; rentals are available at the Audley boat shed on the river. The Illawarra train line, from Central Station, stops at Loftus, Engadine, Heathcote, Waterfall, and Otford stations, where most of the park's walking tracks begin. There are three campsites in the park. ✉ *Royal National Park, Sydney* ✣ *Royal National Park Visitor Centre, 35 km (22 miles) south of Sydney via Princes Hwy. to Farnell Ave., south of Loftus, or McKell Ave. at Waterfall* ☎ *1300/072–757* 🌐 *www.nationalparks.nsw.gov.au* 🎫 *A$12 per vehicle per day, overnight camping from A$10; booking required.*

Run for Your Life 

Pack your jogging shoes for the biggest footrace in the country. **City to Surf** attracts more than 50,000 people each August—some taking it very seriously, others donning a gorilla suit or fairy outfit. The race starts at Hyde Park and winds through the Eastern Suburbs 14 km (9 miles) to Bondi Beach, via the notorious "Heartbreak Hill" at Rose Bay. For some reason, it never seems to rain on the second Sunday in August.

Sydney Olympic Park

SPORTS VENUE | **FAMILY** | The center of the 2000 Olympic and Paralympic Games lies 14 km (8½ miles) west of the city center. Sprawling across 1,900 acres on the shores of Homebush Bay, the site is a series of majestic stadiums, arenas, and accommodation complexes. Among the park's sports facilities are an aquatic center, archery range, tennis center, and the centerpiece: the 85,000-seat ANZ Olympic Stadium. Since the conclusion of the 2000 Games it has been used for major sporting events like the 2003 Rugby World Cup and concerts for international acts including the Rolling Stones. Don't miss the adjacent Bicentennial Park, made up of 247 acres of swamps, lakes, and parks dotted with

Sydneysiders have more than 30 beaches to choose from.

picnic grounds and bike trails. The most scenic and relaxing way to get to Sydney Olympic Park is to take the RiverCat from Circular Quay to Homebush Bay. You can also take a train from Central Station, Sydney, to Olympic Park. ✉ *1 Herb Elliot Ave., Homebush Bay* ☎ *02/9714–7888* 🌐 *www.sydneyolympicpark.com.au, www.anzstadium.com.au.*

Beaches

Dee Why–Long Reef

BEACH | Separated from Dee Why by a narrow channel, Long Reef Beach is remoter and much quieter than its southern neighbor. However, Dee Why has better surfing conditions, a big sea pool, and several good restaurants. To get here, take Bus 136 from Manly. **Amenities:** food and drink; lifeguard; parking (fee); showers; toilets. **Best for:** swimming; walking. ✉ *The Strand, Dee Why.*

★ Manly Beach

BEACH | The Bondi Beach of the north shore, Manly caters to everyone except those who want to get away from it all. On sunny days Sydneysiders, school groups, and travelers from around the world crowd the 2-km-long (1-mile-long) sweep of white sand and take to the waves to swim and ride boards. The beach is well equipped with changing and toilet facilities and lockers. The promenade that runs between the Norfolk Island pines is great for people-watching and rollerblading. Cafés, souvenir shops, and ice-cream parlors line the nearby shopping area, the Corso. Manly also has several nonbeach attractions, including Oceanworld, an aquarium about 200 yards from the ferry wharf. The ferry ride from the city makes a day at Manly feel more like a holiday than just an excursion to the beach. Take a ferry or the Manly Fast Ferry from Circular Quay. From the dock at Manly the beach is a 10-minute walk. The visitor center is located on the Forecourt of Manly Wharf. The Novotel Sydney Pacific Hotel and the Sebel Manly Beach Hotel are two upscale properties located on the beachfront. **Amenities:** food and drink; lifeguards; parking (fee);

showers; toilets. **Best for:** sunrise; surfing; swimming; walking. ✉ *Steyne St., Manly* 🌐 *www.hellomanly.com.au.*

★ Palm Beach

BEACH | The golden sands of Palm Beach glitter as much as the bejeweled residents of the stylish nearby village. The beach is on one side of the peninsula separating the large inlet of Pittwater from the Pacific Ocean. Bathers can easily cross from the ocean side to Pittwater's calm waters. You can take a circular ferry trip around this waterway from the wharf on the Pittwater side. The view from the lighthouse at the northern end of the beach is well worth the walk. Shops and cafés sell light snacks and meals. North Palm Beach is only patrolled by lifeguards in summer (December to February). Take Bus 190 from Wynyard bus station. **Amenities:** food and drink; lifeguards; showers; toilets. **Best for:** surfing; swimming. ✉ *Ocean Rd., Palm Beach.*

Restaurants

Tea Room Gunners Barracks

$$$ | AUSTRALIAN | Housed in a beautiful sandstone building that served a number of military purposes for more than 130 years, the Tea Room Gunners Barracks has breathtaking views of the harbor and the surrounding gardens and bushland. Their traditional afternoon tea (A$50) is a great way to relax after exploring the armaments of Middle Head. **Known for:** stunning grounds; idylic views; beautiful desserts. 💲 *Average main: A$50* ✉ *202 Suakin Dr., Mosman* ☎ *02/8962–5900* 🌐 *www.gunnersbarracks.com.au.*

Coffee and Quick Bites

The Boathouse Palm Beach

$ | AUSTRALIAN | Located on a jetty that juts out into the ocean, this café is a favorite with Sydneysiders who travel up on weekends and tuck into hearty breakfasts, like poached eggs on sourdough with avocado and pesto, and its trademark coffee that comes with a cocoa anchor on top. It's licensed with many enjoying a long champagne lunch with fresh seafood. **Known for:** trendy crowd; delicious fresh breakfast; water views. 💲 *Average main: A$35* ✉ *Governor Phillip Park, Greater Sydney* ☎ *02/9974–5440* 🌐 *www.theboathousepb.com.au.*

Hotels

The Sebel Sydney Manly Beach

$$ | HOTEL | Right on the beachfront of beautiful Manly, this boutique hotel is a mixture of studios and one- and two-bedroom suites, all with private balconies; the more-spacious accommodations have hot tubs, kitchenettes, and high-tech goodies. **Pros:** friendly staff; beachside locale; well-appointed rooms. **Cons:** expect crowds in summer; busy place; no Wi-Fi in rooms. 💲 *Rooms from: A$280* ✉ *8–13 S. Steyne, Manly* ☎ *02/9977–8866* 🌐 *www.thesebelmanlybeach.com.au* 🍽 *No Meals* 🛏 *83 rooms.*

Shopping

ART AND CRAFT GALLERIES

Kate Owen Gallery + Studio

ART GALLERIES | This gallery showcases quality Indigenous art over three levels in Rozelle, a suburb about 15 minutes west of the city center. Take the M50 or M52 bus from the bus station behind the Queen Victoria Building; alight at the corner of Victoria Road and Darling Street. ✉ *680 Darling St., at Victoria Rd., Rozelle* ☎ *02/9555–5283* 🌐 *www.kateowengallery.com.*

DEPARTMENT STORES AND SHOPPING CENTERS

Birkenhead Point

MALL | A factory outlet with more than 100 clothing, shoe, and housewares stores on the western shores of Iron Cove, about 7 km (4 miles) west of Sydney, Birkenhead Point is a great place to shop for discounted labels including Alannah Hill, Witchery, Bendon (Elle Macpherson's lingerie range), Rip Curl, and David Jones warehouse. Take Bus 504, 506, 518, or the M52 from Druitt Street near Town Hall station and also Circular Quay. Water taxis depart from the site for Circular Quay and Darling Harbour. ✉ *Roseby St., near Iron Cove Bridge, Drummoyne* ☎ *02/9182–8800* 🌐 *www.birkenheadpoint.com.au.*

MARKETS

Balmain Market

MARKET | In a leafy churchyard less than 5 km (3 miles) from the city, Balmain Market has a rustic quality that makes it a refreshing change from city-center shopping. Crafts, handmade furniture, plants, bread, toys, tarot readings, and massages are among the offerings at the 140-odd stalls. Inside the church hall you can buy international snacks. Take Bus No. 442 from the Queen Victoria Building in York Street. ✉ *St. Andrew's Church, Darling St., Balmain* ☎ *04/1104–7655.*

Glebe Markets

MARKET | Handmade and secondhand are the order of the day at this colorful market at the top end of Glebe Point Road. One of the best markets for lovers of all things vintage, Glebe also hosts live music on the lawn and good food stalls as well. The markets are open every Saturday 10–4. ✉ *Glebe Public School, Derby Pl. at Glebe Point Rd., Glebe* 🌐 *www.glebemarkets.com.au.*

Activities

SCUBA DIVING

Dive Centre Manly

SCUBA DIVING | Located at the popular northern Sydney beach, Dive Centre Manly runs all-inclusive shore dives each day, which let you see weedy sea dragons and other sea creatures. PADI certification courses are also available. The cost for a shore dive is A$295. ✉ *10 Belgrave St., Manly* ☎ *02/9977–4355* 🌐 *www.divesydney.com.au.*

SURFING

Manly Surf School

SURFING | This company conducts courses for adults and children, and provides all equipment, including wet suits. Adults can join a two-hour group lesson (four per day) for A$75. Private instruction costs A$115 per hour. Stand-up paddling (on a board) lessons are also available, and are held on the calm waters of Balmoral and Narrabeen lakes. ✉ *North Steyne Surf Club, North Steyne, Manly Beach, Manly* ☎ *02/9932–7000* 🌐 *www.manlysurfschool.com.*

WINDSURFING

Balmoral Water Sports Center

WINDSURFING | Balmoral Water Sports Center runs classes from its base at this north-side harbor beach. Private windsurfing lessons are A$189 per hour. Stand-up paddleboards and kayaks can be rented out for A$35 and A$28 per hour respectively. ✉ *The Esplanade, Balmoral* ☎ *02/9960–5344* 🌐 *www.balmoralwatersportscenter.com.au.*

Rose Bay Aquatic Hire

WINDSURFING | Rose Bay Aquatic Hire offers kayaks and paddleboards at A$25 an hour. Whatever mode of transport chosen, an hour or two on Sydney's beautiful harbor is time well spent. ✉ *1 Vickery Ave., Rose Bay* ☎ *04/1623–9543* 🌐 *www.rosebayaquatichire.com.*

Chapter 4

NEW SOUTH WALES

4

Updated by
Amy Nelmes Bissett

Sights ★★★★★ | Restaurants ★★★★☆ | Hotels ★★★★☆ | Shopping ★★★☆☆ | Nightlife ★★★☆☆

WELCOME TO NEW SOUTH WALES

TOP REASONS TO GO

★ **Getting in Touch with Nature:** Exotic birds are prolific in the Blue Mountains and North Coast and South Coast regions.

★ **The Great Australian Bite:** There are lots of fine restaurants in the Hunter Valley and in the North Coast towns of Coffs Harbour and Byron Bay. Seafood and world-famous oysters in the South Coast are a must.

★ **Outdoor Adventure:** The region's mountains and national parks offer opportunities for walks and hikes, horseback riding, rappelling, canyoning, and rock climbing.

★ **World-Class Wineries:** The Hunter Valley has an international reputation for producing excellent Chardonnay, Shiraz, and a dry Sémillon.

★ **Deserted Beaches:** The coastline has some of the most beautiful white-sand beaches in the country. Most of them are wonderfully undeveloped and crowd-free, with hardly a skyscraper in sight.

Despite being Australia's most populous state, the rich variety of landscapes is the biggest selling point. The Blue Mountains, a World Heritage site, lie approximately 100 km (60 miles) to the west of Sydney; the Hunter Valley is about 160 km (100 miles) or two hours north of Sydney. The North Coast and South Coast are exactly where their names suggest, while Lord Howe Island is offshore, 700 km (435 miles) northeast of Sydney.

1 **Wentworth Falls.** A charming village with some of the finest scenery and bushwalks in the Blue Mountains.

2 **Leura.** One of the prettiest town centers in the Blue Mountains.

3 **Katoomba.** Amazing viewpoints and a scenic railway, walkway, and skyway.

4 **Blackheath.** Great hiking trails and trendy dining.

5 **Mount Victoria.** A popular base for activities

6 **Pokolbin and Nearby.** Home to some of Australia's best-known wine labels.

7 **Newcastle.** Beautiful beaches and ocean baths.

8 **Port Macquarie.** Pristine rivers, lakes, and beaches.

9 **Bellingen.** A relaxing getaway and great base for exploring.

10 **Coffs Harbour.** A popular vacation spot with great beaches.

11 **Byron Bay.** Gorgeous beaches, breathtaking bushwalks, and lively town.

12 **Lord Howe Island.** Island paradise with vivid coral reefs, sheltered beaches, great trails, and famous twin peaks.

13 **Berry.** Popular weekend escape from Sydney with good dining and relaxing vibe.

14 **Jervis Bay.** Some of the most pristine white-sand beaches in all of Australia, if not the world.

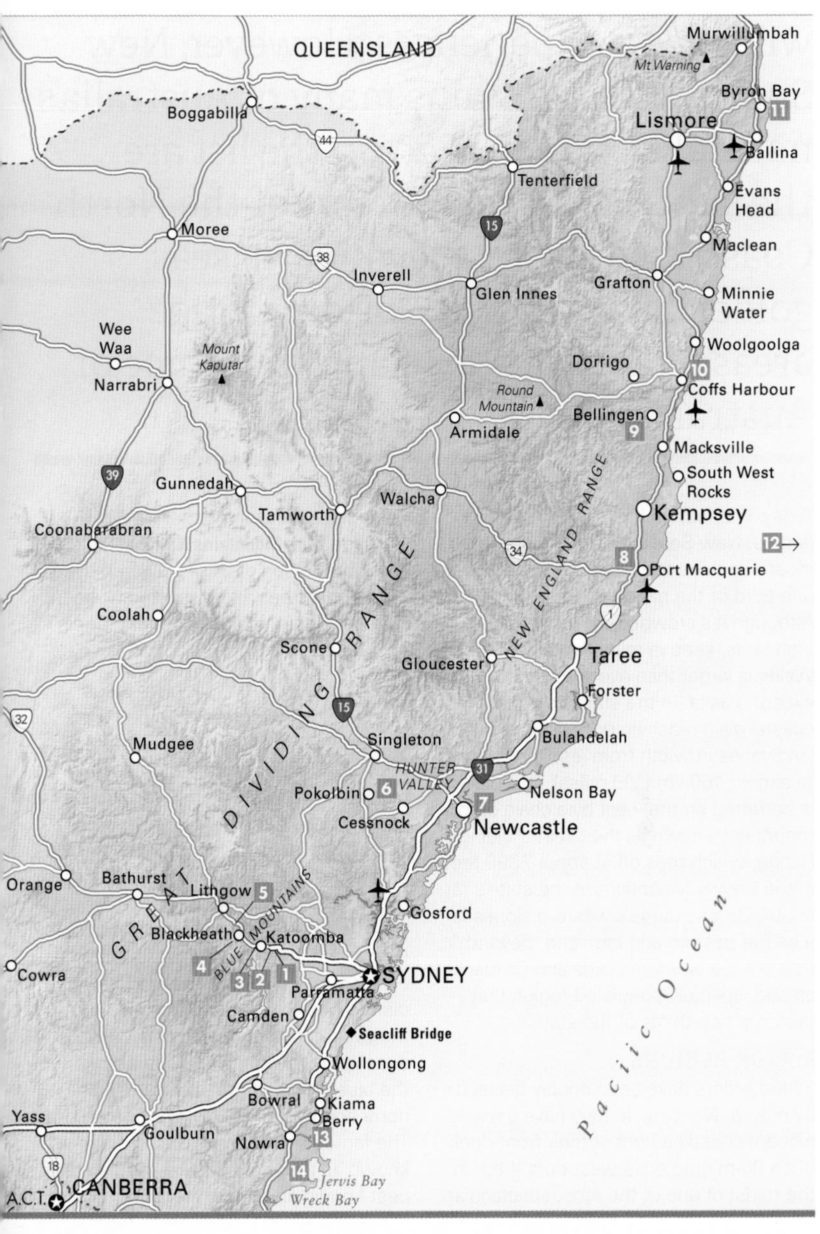
QUEENSLAND
Murwillumbah
Mt Warning
Byron Bay
11
Lismore
Ballina
Boggabilla
44
Tenterfield
Evans Head
15
Moree
Maclean
38
Inverell
Glen Innes
Grafton
Minnie Water
Wee Waa
Mount Kaputar
Woolgoolga
Dorrigo
10
Narrabri
Coffs Harbour
Round Mountain
Bellingen
Armidale
9
Macksville
39
Gunnedah
Walcha
South West Rocks
Tamworth
NEW ENGLAND RANGE
Kempsey
Coonabarabran
12
34
8
Port Macquarie
Coolah
1
Taree
Scone
GREAT DIVIDING RANGE
Gloucester
Forster
32
15
Bulahdelah
Mudgee
Singleton
HUNTER VALLEY
31
Pokolbin
6
Nelson Bay
7
Cessnock
Newcastle
Orange
Bathurst
Lithgow
5
BLUE MOUNTAINS
Gosford
Blackheath
Katoomba
4
3
2
1
Cowra
SYDNEY
Parramatta
Camden
Seacliff Bridge
Pacific Ocean
Wollongong
Bowral
Kiama
Yass
Berry
Goulburn
Nowra
13
18
14
Jervis Bay
A.C.T.
CANBERRA
Wreck Bay

For many travelers Sydney is New South Wales, and they look to the other, less-populous states for Australia's famous wilderness experiences. However, New South Wales contains many of Australia's natural wonders. High on the list are the subtropical rain forests of the North Coast, lush river valleys, warm seas, golden beaches, the World Heritage areas of Lord Howe Island, and some of Australia's finest vineyards.

Today, with approximately 8.16 million people, New South Wales is Australia's most populous state—it's home to about one-third of the nation's population. Although it's crowded by Australian standards, keep in mind that New South Wales is larger than every U.S. state except Alaska. In the state's east, a coastal plain reaching north to Queensland varies in width from less than a mile to almost 160 km (100 miles). This plain is bordered on the west by a chain of low mountains known as the Great Dividing Range, which tops off at about 7,300 feet in the Snowy Mountains in the state's far south. On this range's western slopes is a belt of pasture and farmland. Beyond that are the western plains and Outback, an arid, sparsely populated region that takes up two-thirds of the state.

MAJOR REGIONS

Sydneysiders have been doubly blessed by nature. Not only do they have a magnificent coastline right at their front door, but a 90-minute drive west puts them in the midst of one of the most spectacular wilderness areas in Australia—World Heritage **Blue Mountains National Park.** This rippling sea of hills is covered by tall eucalyptus trees and dissected by deep river valleys—the area is perfect terrain for hiking and adventure activities.

Standing 3,500-plus feet high, these "mountains" were once the bed of an ancient sea. Gradually the sedimentary rock was uplifted until it formed a high plateau, which was etched by eons of wind and water into the wonderland of cliffs, caves, and canyons that exist today. Now the richly forested hills, crisp mountain air, cool-climate gardens, vast sandstone chasms, and little towns of timber and stone are supreme examples of Australia's diversity. The mountains' distinctive blue coloring is caused by the evaporation of oil from the dense eucalyptus forests. This disperses light in the blue colors of the spectrum, a phenomenon known as Rayleigh Scattering. The famous sandstone rock formations known as the Three Sisters are the area's best-known attraction. Wentworth Falls is home to the most stunning natural falls in the mountains. The prettiest of mountain towns, Leura, offers a dazzling 19-km (12-mile) journey along Cliff Drive that skirts the rim of the valley—often only yards from the cliff edge—providing truly spectacular Blue Mountains views.

To almost everyone in Sydney, **the Hunter Valley** conjures up visions of one thing: wine. The Hunter is the largest grape-growing area in the state, with more than 150 wineries producing excellent varieties. The Hunter is divided into seven subregions, each with its own unique character. The hub is the Pokolbin/ Rothbury region, where many of the large operations are found, along with several boutique wineries.

The Hunter Valley covers an area of almost 25,103 square km (9,692 square miles), stretching from the town of Gosford north of Sydney to 177 km (110 miles) farther north along the coast, and almost 300 km (186 miles) inland. The meandering waterway that gives this valley its name is also one of the most extensive river systems in the state.

The North Coast is one of the most glorious and seductive stretches of terrain in Australia, stretching almost 680 km (422 miles) from Newcastle up to the Queensland border. An almost continuous line of beaches defines the coast, with the Great Dividing Range rising to the west the farther you travel north. These natural borders frame a succession of rolling green pasturelands, mossy rain forests, towns dotted by red-roof houses, and waterfalls that tumble in glistening arcs from the escarpment. A journey along the coast leads through several rich agricultural districts, beginning with grazing country in the south and moving into plantations of bananas, sugarcane, mangoes, avocados, and macadamia nuts. Dorrigo National Park, outside Bellingen, and Muttonbird Island, in Coffs Harbour, are two parks good for getting your feet on some native soil and for seeing unusual birdlife.

The tie that binds the North Coast is the Pacific Highway, but despite its name, this highway rarely affords glimpses of the Pacific Ocean. You can drive the entire length of the North Coast in a single day, but allow at least three—or, better still, a week—to properly sample some of its attractions.

Visitors have always had a magical pull to NSW's North Coast but for Sydneysiders, it has always been about the region's **South Coast.** There's an understated beauty here, with mile upon mile of rolling green hills alongside the country's most idyllic beaches. From Sydney to the Victoria border, it's a seven-hour drive over 546 km (339 miles) but most just dip their toes into the vast riches southern NSW has to offer by heading to Berry, a rural country town just three hours south of the city, before continuing to Jervis Bay, a truly majestic beach town that boasts to having the world's whitest sand.

Planning

When to Go

For visitors from the northern hemisphere the Australian summer (approximately December–February) has great pull. The best times to visit the Hunter Valley are during the February–March grape harvest season and the June Hunter Food and Wine Festival. The spring flower celebration, Floriade, lasts from mid-September to mid-October. The North Coast and South Coast resort regions are often booked solid between Christmas and the first half of January, but autumn and spring are good times to visit.

Planning Your Time

It's wise to decide in advance whether you'd like to cover a lot of ground quickly or choose one or two places to linger a while. If you have less than four days, stick close to Sydney. In a busy four- to seven-day period you could visit the Blue Mountains and the Hunter Valley as well.

Start with a visit to the **Blue Mountains.** You could arrange a round-trip itinerary from Sydney in a fairly hectic day or, preferably, spend a night in **Katoomba, Blackheath,** or **Leura** and make it a two-day excursion. Return to Sydney, and then head north to the **Hunter Valley.** A two-day/one-night driving visit here allows you enough time to see the main sights and spend time touring the wineries before traveling back to Sydney on the second day.

If you have more time in the region, continue to the North Coast. In three days of driving you won't likely get much farther than **Coffs Harbour** (with overnights there and in **Port Macquarie**), and this requires rushing it, but it's possible to fly back to Sydney from Coffs. Alternatively, travel south with a pit stop at the historical village of Berry before traveling to Jervis Bay, which is a four-hour drive from Sydney and offers 20 km (12½ miles) of some of the country's most pristine beaches.

Getting Here and Around

AIR

New South Wales is peppered with airports, so flying is the easiest way to get around if you're traveling long distances. You can score the best fares during the quieter seasons. From Sydney, REX (Regional Express) Airlines services Ballina and Lismore (both about 30 minutes from Byron Bay). Qantas flies into Port Macquarie, Coffs Harbour, and Lord Howe Island; its low-cost subsidiary Jetstar flies into Ballina, while Virgin Australia goes to Newcastle, Canberra, Port Macquarie, Ballina, and Coffs Harbour.

AIRLINE CONTACTS Jetstar. ☎ *131–538* 🌐 *www.jetstar.com.* **Qantas Airways.** ☎ *131–313* 🌐 *www.qantas.com.au.* **REX Airlines.** ☎ *131–713* 🌐 *www.rex.com.au.* **Virgin Australia.** ☎ *136–789* 🌐 *www.virginaustralia.com.*

CAR RENTAL

Hiring your own car is the most convenient way of getting around the region, especially the South Coast. The scenic Blue Mountains and Hunter Valley routes and attractions are outside the towns, so having your own set of wheels is helpful. When visiting the wine country, be aware that Australia has very strict rules against drunk driving and there are many tours available that show the best the region has to offer, with a few even departing from Sydney. Most towns have major car-rental companies. You can pick up a car at one point and drop off at another for an extra fee.

TRAIN

As in the States, most people drive here, so train services aren't great and can often cost more than other options. It is possible to travel by train to the Blue Mountains with the Sydney Trains (aka CityRail) commuter network. NSW TrainLink (aka CountryLink) connects Sydney to towns in the Hunter Valley and along the North Coast. The South Coast's Jervis Bay cannot be reached by train; it's quicker and more convenient to drive.

TRAIN INFORMATION Sydney Trains. ☎ *131–500* 🌐 *www.sydneytrains.info.*

Restaurants

Dining varies dramatically throughout New South Wales, from superb city-standard restaurants to average country-town fare. As popular weekend retreats for Sydneysiders, the Blue Mountains have a number of fine restaurants and cozy tearooms that are perfect for light meals. In the Hunter Valley several excellent restaurants show off the region's fine wines. Unsurprisingly, seafood dominates on the North Coast and the South Coast, and again, thanks to holidaying Sydneysiders with high standards, you should be able to tuck into some memorable meals.

Hotels

Accommodations include everything from run-of-the-mill motels and remote wilderness lodges to historic, cliff-perched properties and expansive seaside resorts. Rates are often much lower on weekdays, particularly in the Blue Mountains and the Hunter Valley, as traffic from Sydney is heavier on weekends. The North Coast and the South Coast are popular during summer and Easter school holidays, so book as far ahead as possible.

Restaurant and hotel reviews have been shortened. For full information, visit Fodors.com.

What It Costs In Australian dollars

	$	$$	$$$	$$$$
RESTAURANTS				
	under A$21	A$21–A$35	A$36–A$50	over A$50
HOTELS				
	under A$151	A$151–A$200	A$201–A$300	over A$300

Wentworth Falls

95 km (59 miles) west of Sydney.

This attractive township is home to the Blue Mountains' most stunning natural waterfalls and bushwalking trails. The Falls themselves straddle the highway, but most points of interest and views of the Jamison Valley and Blue Mountains National Park are a short way south.

GETTING HERE AND AROUND

From Sydney, head west onto Parramatta Road, then take the M4, following signs to the Blue Mountains. You'll pay a toll at the end of the motorway. It's also easy to catch a train to Wentworth Falls; the journey from Sydney Central Station takes 1¾ hours, with trains leaving roughly every hour. The Blue Mountains Bus Company (☎ *02/4751–1077* 🌐 *www.bmbc.com.au*) connects towns within the region with Routes 685 and 695, connecting Wentworth Falls to Leura and Katoomba.

Sights

Norman Lindsay Gallery and Museum

HISTORIC HOME | If driving from Sydney, be sure to stop at the National Trust–listed Norman Lindsay Gallery and Museum, dedicated to the Australian artist and writer. Considered one of the cultural highlights of the Blue Mountains, Lindsay lived in this house during the latter part of his life until he died in 1969. Lindsay is best known for his paintings, etchings, and drawings (many of voluptuous nudes), but he also built model boats, sculpted, and wrote poetry and children's books, among which *The Magic Pudding* has become an Australian classic. The delightful landscaped gardens contain several of Lindsay's sculptures, and you can also take a short but scenic bushwalk beyond the garden or take refreshments in the café. Daily tours of Lindsay's studios run from 10 am to 4 pm and are included in the price, while dedicated art fans can stay in the cottage on the grounds for A$175 a night midweek or A$220 a night Friday and weekends. ✉ *14 Norman Lindsay Crescent, Faulconbridge* ☎ *02/4751–1067* 🌐 *www.normanlindsay.com.au* 🎫 *A$17.*

Restaurants

Cafe 92 at The Conservation Hut

$ | **AUSTRALIAN** | From its prime spot in Blue Mountains National Park, on a cliff overlooking the Jamison Valley, this spacious, mud-brick bistro serves simple, savory fare. Lovely brunch dishes include herbed mushrooms with a poached egg and roasted tomatoes on sourdough toast. **Known for:** great brunch spot; views; hearty meals. *Average main: A$18 88 Fletcher St., Wentworth Falls 02/4757–3827 No dinner.*

2773 Cafe

$$ | **MODERN AUSTRALIAN** | **FAMILY** | In Glenbrook, one of the first Blue Mountains towns you'll reach coming from Sydney, this is a great place for breakfast or a relaxing lunch before continuing to Wentworth Falls, about a 30-minute drive west. Dinner is served Thursday through Saturday, with the menu firmly focusing on local produce, especially organic meat from Lithgow Valley (on the other side of the mountains). **Known for:** relaxing atmosphere; organic farm-to-table menu; fair-trade coffee. *Average main: A$28 19 Ross St., Glenbrook 02/4739–5908 www.2773glenbrook.com.au No dinner Mon.–Wed.*

Coffee and Quick Bites

Mountain High Pies

$ | **AUSTRALIAN** | **FAMILY** | Considered the best pie shop in the Blue Mountains National Park, just over 500 pies are served here every day. There's 35 different pies to choose from. **Known for:** easy eats; takeaway; friendly service. *Average main: A$7 293 Great Western Hwy., Wentworth Falls 02/4757–3737 www.mountainhighpies.com.au.*

Activities

HIKING

Falls Reserve

HIKING & WALKING | From a lookout in Falls Reserve, south of the town of Wentworth Falls, you can take in magnificent views both out across the Jamison Valley to the Kings Tableland and of the 935-foot-high **Wentworth Falls** themselves. To find the best view of the falls, follow the trail that crosses the stream and zigzags down the sheer cliff face, signposted "national pass." If you continue, the trail cuts back across the base of the falls and along a narrow ledge to the delightful Valley of the Waters, where it ascends to the top of the cliffs, emerging at the Conservation Hut. The complete circuit takes at least three hours and is a moderately difficult walk. *End of Falls Rd., Wentworth Falls.*

Leura

5 km (3 miles) west of Wentworth Falls.

Leura, the prettiest and chicest of the mountain towns, is bordered by bush and lined with excellent cafés, restaurants, and gift shops. From the south end of the main street (the Mall), the road continues past superb local gardens as it winds down to the massive cliffs overlooking the Jamison Valley. The dazzling 19-km (12-mile) journey along Cliff Drive skirts the rim of the valley—often only yards from the cliff edge—providing truly spectacular Blue Mountains views.

GETTING HERE AND AROUND

The train station at Leura is one stop beyond Wentworth Falls, and the station is walking distance from all the town's shops and galleries. By car, Leura is a few miles west of Wentworth Falls on the Great Western Highway. Alternatively, catch a Blue Mountains Bus Company bus—Routes 685 and 695 connect the town with Wentworth Falls and Katoomba.

Sights

Everglades Historic House and Gardens

GARDEN | Everglades Gardens, a National Trust–listed, cool-climate arboretum and nature reserve established in the 1930s, is one of the best public gardens in the Blue Mountains region. This former home of a Belgian industrialist is surrounded by 13 acres of native bushland and exotic flora, a rhododendron garden, an alpine plant area, and formal European-style terraces. The views of the Jamison Valley are magnificent. ✉ *37 Everglades Ave., Leura* ☎ *02/4784–1938* 🌐 *www.nationaltrust.org.au/places/everglades-house-gardens* 🎟 *A$15.*

Leuralla

HISTORIC HOME | **FAMILY** | This imposing 1911 mansion still belongs to the family of Dr. H. V. ("Doc") Evatt (1894–1965), the first president of the General Assembly of the United Nations and later the leader of the Australian Labor Party. A 19th-century Australian art collection and a small museum dedicated to Dr. Evatt are inside the home. Baby boomers and their children (and grandchildren) will love the collection in the New South Wales Toy and Railway Museum, which is both inside the house and in the gardens. The museum comprises an extensive collection of railway memorabilia, antique curios from yesteryear (including lots of dolls depicting *Alice in Wonderland* scenes), and exhibitions on iconic dolls like Barbie. Directly across the street from the mansion are the Leuralla Public Gardens (entry A$2), with spectacular views of the Jamison Valley. ✉ *36 Olympian Parade, Leura* ☎ *02/4784–1169* 🌐 *www.toyandrailwaymuseum.com.au* 🎟 *A$15; gardens only A$10.*

Sublime Point Lookout

VIEWPOINT | This viewpoint just outside Leura lives up to its name with a great view of the Jamison Valley and the generally spectacular Blue Mountains scenery. It's a quiet vantage point that provides a different perspective from that of the famous **Three Sisters** lookout at nearby Katoomba. ✉ *Sublime Point Rd., Leura.*

Restaurants

★ Leura Garage

$$ | **EUROPEAN** | This buzzy and award-winning eatery housed in an old garage opposite the railway station in Leura serves top-notch food in a delightfully informal setting. Dishes are designed to share and although they might sound simple in name, they are simply astounding. **Known for:** buzzy atmosphere; fresh menu that regularly changes; trendy eatery. 💲 *Average main: A$25* ✉ *84 Railway Parade, Leura* ☎ *02/4784–3391* 🌐 *leuragarage.com.au.*

★ Silk's Brasserie

$$$$ | **AUSTRALIAN** | Thanks to its Sydney-standard food, wine, and service, Silk's still rates as one of the finest Blue Mountains restaurants after more than 20 years. The restaurant is housed in a Federation-era building, and in colder months a log fire warms the century-old simple but elegant interior, where yellow ocher walls reach from black-and-white checkerboard floor to sky-high ceiling. **Known for:** sophisticated experience; fine dining; epicurean institution. 💲 *Average main: A$75* ✉ *1 Lake St., Leura* ☎ *02/4784–2534* 🌐 *www.silksdining.com.au.*

Coffee and Quick Bites

Sparrows Leura

$ | **AUSTRALIAN** | Prides itself on serving specialty coffee, with beans from trendy Melbourne and Sydney roasters. There are pastries available that are baked on-site each day and an extensive breakfast menu. **Known for:** trendy interiors; specialty coffee; fresh eats. 💲 *Average main: A$10* ✉ *82 Railway Parade, Leura* ☎ *0412/881–995* 🌐 *www.facebook.com/sparrowsleura.*

Hotels

Bygone Beautys Cottages

$$$ | **B&B/INN** | These two country cottages, at Wentworth Falls and in the nearby village of Bullaburra, provide self-contained accommodations for couples, families, or small groups. **Pros:** wood-burning fireplaces; antiques collectors love the connected tearoom; romantic setting. **Cons:** bathrooms can be chilly in winter; old-world design isn't for everyone; distance from the Blue Mountains. *Rooms from: A$295 ✉ Grose St. at Megalong St., Leura ☎ 02/4784–3117 🌐 www.bygonebeautys.com.au Free Breakfast 2 cottages.*

Fairmont Resort Blue Mountains MGallery by Sofitel

$$$ | **HOTEL** | Perched on a cliff, the Fairmont offers a sweeping vista of the valley below, and you'll want to wake up early to see the Blue Mountains creak to life with birds breaking into their morning chorus. **Pros:** incredible views; cascading swimming pools; luxury spa. **Cons:** property a little tired in places; not rustic nor luxurious; can be overrun with families. *Rooms from: A$225 ✉ 1 Sublime Point Rd., Leura ☎ 02/4785–0000 🌐 www.fairmontresort.com.au/accommodation No Meals 222 rooms.*

Shopping

Josophan's

FOOD | This gorgeous chocolate boutique in Leura's main shopping street has fast become *the* place to stop for luscious handmade chocolates and drinking chocolate. You can also take part in classes (how does making chocolate truffles sound?) and take away lovely gift boxes of sweets. For a light snack and yummy chocolate desserts, walk across the road to Cafe Madeline (*187a The Mall*), which is also owned by Josophan's proprietor and chocolatier Jodie Van der Velden. *✉ 132 The Mall, Leura ☎ 02/4784–2031 🌐 www.josophans.com.au.*

Katoomba

2 km (1 mile) west of Leura.

The largest and busiest town in the Blue Mountains, Katoomba developed in the early 1840s as a coal-mining settlement, turning its attention to tourism later in the 19th century. The town center on Katoomba Street has shops, restaurants, and cafés, but the marvels at the lower end of town are an even greater draw.

GETTING HERE AND AROUND

Katoomba is just a few minutes' drive from Leura on the Great Western Highway. A train station connects the town with the rest of the region, as does the Blue Mountains Bus Company. A$50 buys a day's access to the red double-decker Explorer buses that travel around Katoomba and Leura stopping at 29 places.

TOURS

Blue Mountains Adventure Company

The well-established Blue Mountains Adventure Company runs abseiling (rappelling), rock-climbing, canyoning, bushwalking, and mountain-biking trips. Lunch, snacks, and all the equipment are generally included. Introductory and intermediate canyoning tours go to such places as Empress Falls or Serendipity Canyon. *✉ 84A Bathurst Rd., Katoomba ☎ 02/4782–1271 🌐 www.bmac.com.au From A$220.*

High n Wild

This outfitter conducts rappelling, canyoning, rock-climbing, and mountain-biking tours throughout the year. Half-day rappelling trips cost A$150; one-day trips are A$250; combination rappelling and canyoning tours cost A$225. The company's office is based at the YHA youth hostel, a short walk from the station. *✉ 207 Katoomba St., Katoomba ☎ 02/4782–6224 🌐 www.high-n-wild.com.au From A$135.*

VISITOR INFORMATION

CONTACTS Blue Mountains Visitor Information Centre. ✉ *Echo Point Rd., Katoomba* ☎ *1300/653–408* 🌐 *www.bluemountainscitytourism.com.au.*

Blue Mountains Chocolate Company

STORE/MALL | If you have a sweet tooth, try this artisanal-chocolate shop. Here you can watch chocolate being made and taste it for free. There are 60 different varieties of handmade chocolates, as well as hot chocolate (perfect for chilly mountain days) and homemade ice cream (chocolate, of course) for those sultry summer days. ✉ *176 Lurline St., Katoomba* ☎ *02/4782–7071* 🌐 *www.bluemountainschocolate.com.au.*

★ Echo Point

VIEWPOINT | Overlooking the densely forested Jamison Valley and three soaring sandstone pillars, this lofty promontory has the best views around Katoomba. The formations—called the Three Sisters—take their name from an Aboriginal legend that relates how a trio of siblings was turned to stone by their witch-doctor father to save them from the clutches of a mythical monster. The area was once a seabed that rose over a long period and subsequently eroded, leaving behind tall formations of sedimentary rock. From Echo Point—where the visitor center is located—you can clearly see the horizontal sandstone bedding in the landscape. There is a wide viewing area as well as the start of walks that take you closer to the Sisters. At night the Sisters are illuminated by floodlights. There are cafés and a visitor information center near the site. ✉ *Echo Point Rd., off Katoomba St., Katoomba.*

★ Scenic World

TRAIL | FAMILY | Thrill-seekers can choose their own adventure on the Scenic Railway, whose trains descend 1,000 feet down the mountainside—the seats allow passengers to adjust the incline angle from 52 to a hair-raising 64 degrees. The railway is one of three attractions at Scenic World, which has carried more than 25 million passengers to the valley floor since it opened in 1945. Once at the base, visitors can hike on easy trails through the rain forest or make the 20-minute hike to Cableway, a huge cable car that whisks passengers back up the mountain. You can also hike back up, but it's a steep, strenuous climb. The third attraction is Scenic Skyway, a glass-enclosed and-floored cabin that travels from one cliff to another, some 920 feet above the ravines below. The A$49.50 day pass provides unlimited rides on all three attractions. ✉ *Cliff Dr., at Violet St., Katoomba* ☎ *02/4780–0200* 🌐 *www.scenicworld.com.au* 🎫 *From A$50.*

Darley's Restaurant

$$$$ | AUSTRALIAN | Found in Lilianfels Blue Mountains Resort & Spa, Darley's focuses on fine dining in a sophisticated setting that exudes old-school charm, with the walls covered in framed photos showing how the Blue Mountains have transformed over the years. The menu always features seafood, a meaty main, and caters to plant-based diets, with the likes of beetroot pastrami to start. **Known for:** weekend tables booked far in advance; high-end dining; seafood dishes. $ *Average main: A$135* ✉ *Lilianfels Ave., Katoomba, Katoomba* ☎ *02/4780–1200* 🌐 *www.darleysrestaurant.com.au.*

Jamison Views Restaurant

$$$$ | AUSTRALIAN | Housed inside the Hotel Mountain Heritage, the restaurant's large bay windows and balcony allows for the best views of the Blue Mountains mountain range and Jamison Valley. The menu is compact, with just three starters and three mains that change seasonally. **Known for:** romantic; live entertainment; outstanding views. $ *Average main: A$59* ✉ *Corner of Apex and Lovel Sts., Katoomba* 🌐 *www.*

Great Hikes in Katoomba

Echo Point to Scenic Railway

In the 1930s, the **Giant Staircase** was hewn out of the cliff by teams of park rangers. The top of the steps are the **Three Sisters Lookout** and the walk down is very steep and narrow in places. It's difficult going but the views make it all worthwhile. Look out for the encouraging halfway sign. At the bottom, keep your eyes peeled for echidnas, brush-tailed and ring-tail possums, bandicoots, quolls, and grey-headed flying foxes. If you're keen for more exertion once you've reached the Railway, take the **Furber Steps.** It's a challenging but rewarding track that has great views of **Katoomba Falls** and **Mt. Solitary** across the valley.

Prince Henry Cliff Walk

If you prefer to hike in the mountains rather than along the forest floor, you'll enjoy this section of the Cliff Walk with superb vistas across the valley. From the Leura Cascades picnic area on Cliff Drive, the trail descends beside Leura Falls creek toward **Bridal Veil Falls.** Be sure to slow down and take in the great views over the **Leura Forest.** Continue on Prince Henry Drive; at **Tarpeian Rock** you can see Mt. Solitary. Keep going uphill toward Olympian Rock and Elysian Rock. From here, follow the cliff line to **Millamurra** and **Tallawarra Lookouts.** The last part of the climb to the **Three Sisters** is perhaps the most challenging but also the most rewarding. Take a few minutes and savor the sweeping views of the valley.

mountainheritage.com.au/restaurant ⏲ *No dinner Sun.–Thurs.*

Pins on Lurline

$$$$ | **AUSTRALIAN** | Head chef Adam Shaw creates a brand-new menu every day, focusing on what produce is available from nearby farms. There's a set 6- or 10-course degustation menu, featuring meaty dishes like pork belly or slow-cooked lamb. **Known for:** pretty surrounding gardens; fine dining; romantic atmosphere. [$] *Average main: A$100* ✉ *132 Lurline St., Katoomba* 🌐 *www.pinsonlurline.com.au* ⏲ *No dinner Mon.-Wed. No lunch Mon.-Fri.*

Coffee and Quick Bites

Katoomba Street Cafe

$ | **CAFÉ** | **FAMILY** | Located in the center of Katoomba township, this café offers casual breakfast eats, freshly baked bakery items, and roasts its own coffee blend on-site. The menu is a mix of big, hearty eats or smaller, simpler items, like raisin toast and Bircher muesli. **Known for:** excellent coffee; casual eats; quick bite. [$] *Average main: 20* ✉ *175 Katoomba St., Katoomba.*

The Yellow Deli

$ | **AUSTRALIAN** | Found on the ground floor of a three-story Federation era building, this café has a bit of a '70s hippy vibe. Inside is filled with mix-matched upcycled furniture. **Known for:** nice views; great atmosphere; healthy eats. [$] *Average main: 10* ✉ *214 Katoomba St, Katoomba* ☎ *02/4782–9744* 🌐 *www.yellowdeli.com.*

Hotels

The Carrington

$$$ | **HOTEL** | Established in 1880, this is one of the grande dames of the Blue Mountains, a Victorian-era relic that, in

its heyday, was considered one of the four great hotels of the British Empire. **Pros:** free Wi-Fi in rooms; drinks on their veranda are a pleasant way to end the day; breakfast included. **Cons:** some rooms have shared bathrooms; the newer rooms lack character; very quiet outside of the weekend. *Rooms from: A$215 15–47 Katoomba St., Katoomba 02/4782–1111 www.thecarrington.com.au Free Breakfast 115 rooms.*

Echoes Boutique Hotel & Restaurant
$$$$ | **HOTEL** | Perched on the edge of the Jamison Valley, this stylish boutique hotel has one of the best views in the Blue Mountains. **Pros:** brilliant restaurant; spectacular views from the terrace; slick, contemporary design. **Cons:** isolated location; little pricey; small. *Rooms from: A$335 3 Lilianfels Ave., Katoomba 02/4782–1966 www.echoeshotel.com.au Free Breakfast 14 rooms.*

★ **Hydro Majestic Blue Mountains**
$$$ | **HOTEL** | This iconic and much-loved cliff-top hotel in Medlow Bath recaptured its former art deco splendor when it reopened a few years ago and is once again a destination hotel. **Pros:** delightful high tea; heritage glamour and living history; most rooms have amazing views. **Cons:** expensive; rooms are small; packed on weekends. *Rooms from: A$295 Great Western Hwy., Medlow Bath 02/4782–6885 www.hydromajestic.com.au 57 rooms No Meals.*

★ **Lilianfels Blue Mountains Resort & Spa**
$$$$ | **HOTEL** | Teetering close to the brink of Echo Point, this glamorous boutique hotel adds a keen sense of manor-house style to the standard Blue Mountains guesthouse experience. **Pros:** lovely drawing room with views; luxurious and restful bathrooms; friendly five-star service. **Cons:** restaurant is very expensive; 19th-century style is not for everyone; can feel impersonal. *Rooms from: A$499 5–19 Lilianfels Ave., at Panorama Dr., Katoomba 02/4780–1200 www.lilianfels.com.au Free Breakfast 85 rooms.*

★ **Lurline House**
$ | **B&B/INN** | This historic little B&B is arguably the town's best. **Pros:** warm and welcoming; rooms have four-poster beds; manicured gardens. **Cons:** not for those who like private hotel stays; younger trendsetters might find the place not to their taste; not all rooms have private courtyard. *Rooms from: A$75 122 Lurline St., Katoomba 02/4782–4609 Free Breakfast 8 rooms.*

Mountain Heritage Hotel & Spa
$$$$ | **HOTEL** | This hotel overlooking the Jamison Valley is steeped in history: it served as a "coffee palace" during the temperance movement, a rest-and-relaxation establishment for the British navy during World War II, and a religious retreat in the 1970s. **Pros:** public areas are charming with great valley views; friendly service; manicured gardens. **Cons:** some rooms are small; furniture is a little dated; not in walking distance to anything. *Rooms from: A$330 Apex St. at Lovel St., Katoomba 02/4782–2155 www.mountainheritage.com.au 37 rooms, 4 suites Free Breakfast.*

Activities

A good hiking brochure can be picked up at Blue Mountains Visitor Centre at Echo Point, which lists walks varying in length from a half hour to three days.

ECO-TOURS

Tread Lightly Eco Tours
HIKING & WALKING | This eco-minded company operates small-group tours of Blue Mountains National Park and guided day and night walks, as well as four-wheel-drive tours and breakfast trips to view wildlife. Half- and full-day walking tours take in such areas as Fern Bower, Blue Gum Forest, and the Ruined Castle. *100 Great Western Hwy., Medlow Bath 04/1497–6752 www.treadlightly.com.au From A$145.*

HIKING

★ **Blue Mountains Adventure Company**
GUIDED TOURS | Established in 1984, the hiking tours offered are well established. There's an introductory Blue Mountains hike, taking two hours and costing A$150. Or there are 10 different full-day walks throughout the mountain range to choose from. There are also self-guided tours, where the team helps create a hiking route for you to navigate by yourself. And for those who are well-seasoned hikers, there are multiday hikes. There's really something for every level of fitness here. ✉ *84a Bathurst Rd., Katoomba* ☎ *02/4782-1271* 🌐 *www.bmac.com.au.*

Blue Mountains Walkabout
HIKING & WALKING | Experience the Blue Mountains from an Aboriginal perspective on this outfitter's challenging one-day walks, which follow a traditional walkabout song line. Indigenous guides take you on a 7-km (4½-mile) off-track walk through rain forests, while giving some background on Aboriginal culture. You'll also taste bush tucker (food). The walk involves some scrambling, so you need to be fit. The tours depart from Faulconbridge Railway Station (near Springwood, in the lower Blue Mountains), about a 30-minute drive east of Katoomba. ✉ *Springwood* ☎ *0408/433–822* 🌐 *www.bluemountainswalkabout.com* 🎫 *A$95.*

Blackheath

12 km (7½ miles) north of Katoomba.

Magnificent easterly views over the Grose Valley—which has outstanding hiking trails—delightful gardens, good restaurants, and antiques shops head the list of reasons to visit the village of Blackheath, at the 3,495-foot summit of the Blue Mountains.

GETTING HERE AND AROUND

Blackheath is an easy drive north from Katoomba, traveling on the Great Western Highway, passing Medlow Bath on the way. There's also a train station on the Blue Mountains line, and the town is also serviced by Blue Mountains Bus Company on Route 698 between Katoomba and Mount Victoria.

VISITOR INFORMATION

CONTACTS Blue Mountains Heritage Centre. ✉ *Govetts Leap Rd. at Mel Ave., Blackheath* ☎ *02/4787–8877* 🌐 *www.nationalparks.nsw.gov.au.*

Sights

Govetts Leap Lookout
VIEWPOINT | Blackheath's most famous view is from the Govetts Leap Lookout, with its striking panorama of the Grose Valley and Bridal Veil Falls. Govett was a surveyor who mapped this region extensively in the 1830s. This lookout is the start or finish of several excellent bushwalks. Brochures are available at the Blue Mountains Heritage Centre. ✉ *End of Govett's Leap Rd., Blackheath* 🌐 *www.nationalparks.nsw.gov.au.*

Trains, Planes and Automobiles
STORE/MALL | **FAMILY** | Children and adults will enjoy a browse around this store that bills itself as the best antique toy shop in the world. ✉ *1 Goldsmith Pl., Blackheath* ☎ *02/4787–7974* 🌐 *www.antiquetoys.com.au.*

Restaurants

★ **Cinnabar Kitchen**
$$ | **WINE BAR** | This lively wine bar–style eatery has attracted quite a bit of hype, and the attention of Sydney-based foodies who have been arriving each weekend in droves, since its opening in early 2018. It's so popular, in fact, the restaurant is now demanding a $48 minimum spend from each diner on the weekend. **Known for:** Jamaican spiced prawns; trendy spot; $48 minimum spend from each diner on the weekend. 💲 *Average main: A$28* ✉ *246 Great Western Hwy.,*

Great Hikes in Blackheath

Grand Canyon Walk

From the parking lot at Evans Lookout, 4.5 km (2.8 miles) from Blackheath, follow the Grand Canyon signs as the path zigzags down the hillside, and the vegetation becomes more like a rain forest. The trail takes you down into the canyon and over a creek. It winds past a few overhanging rocks, then starts a steep decline toward a sandy overhang called the **Rotunda.** After a break here, follow the signs to **Evans Lookout,** which leads you through a tunnel and past two waterfalls. You eventually reach the 33-foot **Beauchamp Falls** in the center of the creek. From here head up through a gap in the cliffs, weaving through boulders, again following signs to Evans Lookout. From Evans Lookout, you can follow a 6.5-km (4-mile) cliff-side walk to **Pulpit Rock** along the Cliff Top Track. The entire loop is 6 km (3.75 miles) and takes around 3½ hours.

Perrys Lookdown to Blue Gum Forest

This is a hard, but rewarding, four-hour walk. From the Perry Lookdown parking lot (turn east into Hat Hill Road from the Great Western Highway at Blackheath), follow the signs pointing out the trail down the hill to **Perrys Lookdown.** You'll have fine views over the **Grose Valley** with its sheer sandstone cliffs with the **Blue Gum Forest** below. Next, head down the hill and do a quick detour to **Docker's Lookout** with its view of Mt. Banks to the north. Head back following the Perrys Lookdown-Blue Gum Forest walk signs. The descent to Blue Gum Forest will take about 90 minutes. Once you've explored the forest floor and its dense canopy, head back up the steep track to Perrys Lookdown.

Blackheath ☎ *02/4787–7269* 🌐 *www.cinnabar.kitchen* ⏲ *Closed Sun.–Tues.*

Hotels

The George Boutique Hotel

$$$ | **HOTEL** | Designed for those wanting a quiet retreat, this small hotel is surrounded by native bushland. **Pros:** surrounded by nature; quiet; incredible native birds. **Cons:** rooms can be on small side; some might find it dated; no wardrobes in some rooms. $ *Rooms from: A$210* ✉ *194 Great Western Hwy., Blackheath* 🌐 *www.thegeorgebluemountains.com.au* 🍽 *No Meals* 🛏 *9 rooms.*

Parklands Country Garden & Lodges

$$$$ | **HOTEL** | Parklands is a four-star sophisticated stay surrounded by manicured gardens. **Pros:** stunning grounds; convenient location; luxury interiors. **Cons:** can feel quiet; no restaurant; expensive breakfast. $ *Rooms from: A$450* ✉ *132 Govetts Leap Rd., Blackheath* 🌐 *www.parklands.com.au* 🍽 *No Meals* 🛏 *28 rooms.*

Activities

HIKING

Auswalk

HIKING & WALKING | This environmentally conscious company, which also leads walks in other parts of Australia, has three-day guided hiking tours through the region, staying at historic inns along the way, with all meals and admission to some local attractions included. The seven-day walk is A$1,845 per person (double occupancy). The owners advise that you be in reasonable shape before starting.

⊠ *Blackheath* ☎ *03/9597–9767* 🌐 *www.auswalk.com.au* 🎫 *From A$1845.*

HORSEBACK RIDING

Megalong Australian Heritage Centre

HORSEBACK RIDING | This rural farm in a deep mountain valley off the Great Western Highway is the place to saddle up and explore the many mountain and valley trails. Both adults and children can go horseback riding around the farm's 2,000 acres, with prices starting at A$75 for an hour's wilderness ride to A$95. The most popular is the picnic horse-riding experience where you ride for 90 minutes before enjoying a cheese and wine platter for A$100. ⊠ *993 Megalong Rd., Megalong* ✥ *15 km (9 miles) south of Blackheath* ☎ *02/4787–8188* 🌐 *www.megalongcc.com.au* 🎫 *From A$75.*

Mount Victoria

7 km (4½ miles) northwest of Blackheath.

The settlement of Mount Victoria is the highest point in the Blue Mountains, and there's a Rip van Winkle air about it—drowsy and only just awake in an unfamiliar world. A walk around the village reveals many atmospheric houses, stores, a charming old post office, and a stately old hotel with the patina of time spelled out in the fading paint of these buildings. Mount Victoria is at the far side of the mountains at the western limit of this region, and the village serves as a good jumping-off point for a couple of out-of-the-way attractions.

GETTING HERE AND AROUND

Mount Victoria is an easy drive north of Blackheath on the Great Western Highway, and it's also on the main Blue Mountains railway line linking Sydney with Lithgow. The 698V bus route connects the village with Katoomba, but only on weekdays.

Sights

★ **Jenolan Caves**

CAVE | FAMILY | Stalactites, stalagmites, columns, and lacelike rock on multiple levels fill the fascinating Jenolan Caves, a labyrinth of vast limestone caverns sculpted by underground rivers. There are as many as 320 caves in the Jenolan area. Two caves (Nettles Cave and Devil's Coachhouse) near the surface can be explored on your own, but a guide is required to reach the most intriguing formations. Standard tours lead through the most popular caves—many say that Orient Cave is the most spectacular—while the more rigorous adventure tours last up to seven hours. The one- to two-hour walks depart every 15 to 30 minutes, on weekends less frequently. Prices start at A$55 for a standard tour. Concerts and murder mystery nights are also held in this spooky environment. Cave House, on the same site, is a nostalgic retreat and has been providing lodging since 1887. To get here, follow the Great Western Highway north out of Mount Victoria, then after Hartley, turn southwest toward Hampton. ⊠ *4655 Jenolan Caves Rd., Jenolan Caves* ✥ *59 km (37 miles) southwest of Mount Victoria* ☎ *1300/763–311* 🌐 *www.jenolancaves.org.au* 🎫 *From A$55.*

Pokolbin and Nearby

163 km (100 miles) north of Sydney.

The Lower Hunter wine-growing region is centered on the village of Pokolbin, where there are antiques shops, good cafés, and dozens of wineries. In peak season, wineries are very busy with tour groups, so if you can visit midweek or off-season, all the better.

GETTING HERE AND AROUND

A car is the best way to visit the wineries and off-the-beaten-path attractions unless you are on a guided tour. Leave

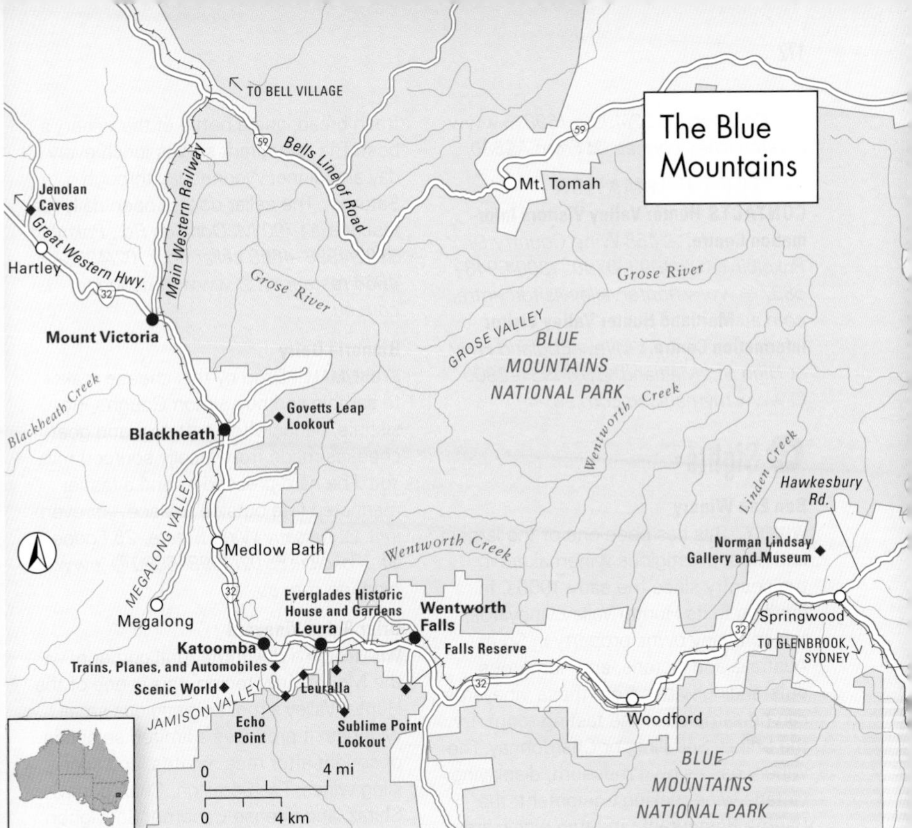

Sydney via the Harbour Bridge or Harbour Tunnel and get onto the Pacific Highway (keep following the signs for Newcastle). Just before Hornsby the road joins the Sydney–Newcastle Freeway, known as the M1. Take the exit from the freeway signposted "Hunter Valley vineyards via Cessnock." From Cessnock, the route to the vineyards is clearly marked. Allow 2½ hours for the journey.

TOURS

Any tour of the area's vineyards should begin at Pokolbin's **Hunter Valley Wine Country Visitors Information Centre,** which has free maps of the vineyards, brochures, and a handy visitor's guide.

AAT Kings

From Sydney, AAT Kings operates a daylong wine-tasting bus tour of the Hunter Valley and another to Hunter Valley Gardens. Buses collect passengers from city hotels from 7 am. ☎ *1300/228–546* 🌐 *www.aatkings.com.au* 🎫 *From A$199.*

Heidi's Hunter Valley

Local operator Heidi's Hunter Valley operates personalized day tours to the wineries and restaurants in a sleek four-wheel-drive vehicle. Heidi Duckworth, who worked for the Hunter Valley Wine Tourism organization for 12 years, knows all the best places in the valley. ☎ *0408/623–136* 🌐 *www.heidishuntervalley.com.au* 🎫 *From A$275 for up to 4 guests.*

Rover Coaches

To avoid driving after sampling too many wines, hop aboard one of the Wine Rover buses, which will pick you up from most accommodations in Pokolbin or Cessnock to visit several wineries. Rover also runs an Ale Trail tour, visiting several Hunter Valley breweries. ✉ *231–233 Vincent*

St., Cessnock ☎ 02/4990–1699 🌐 www.rovercoaches.com.au 💲 From A$580.

VISITOR INFORMATION

CONTACTS Hunter Valley Visitors Information Centre. ✉ *455 Wine Country Dr., Pokolbin* ☎ *02/4993–6700, 1300/6948–6837* 🌐 *www.huntervalleyvisitorcentre.com.au.* **Maitland Hunter Valley Visitor Information Centre.** ✉ *New England Hwy. at High St., Maitland* ☎ *02/4931–2800* 🌐 *www.mymaitland.com.au.*

Sights

Ben Ean Winery

WINERY | This has been one of the largest and most prestigious winemakers in the country since the early 1900s. In addition to its Hunter Valley vineyards, the company owns property in South Australia and Victoria, and numerous outstanding wines from these vineyards can be sampled in the tasting room. Try the Shiraz, Sémillon, or Chardonnay. The winery has its own museum, displaying vintage wine-making equipment; the Baume Restaurant; and two picnic areas, one near the parking lot and the other next to the willow trees around the dam. ✉ *McDonalds Rd., just south of DeBeyers Rd., Pokolbin* ☎ *02/4993–3700* 🌐 *www.benean.com.au.*

Bimbadgen Winery

WINERY | This winery is particularly well-known for its very popular Day on the Green concerts, which are held several times between October and March. Artists have included Tom Jones and Leonard Cohen. Beyond the shows, the winery also produces some very good wines—try the signature Chardonnay or Sémillon. It is also home to one of the Hunter's best restaurants, Esca, which has fantastic views across the vineyards towards the Brokenback Mountains. To take full advantage of the views, you could also prebook a picnic (A$100), which comes with deli meats, cheeses, fresh bread, and a bottle of the winery's best. The restaurant serves lunch every day and dinner Wednesday through Saturday. The cellar door is open daily for tastings. ✉ *790 McDonalds Rd., Pokolbin* ☎ *02/4998–4650 cellar door, 02/4998–4666 restaurant* 🌐 *www.bimbadgen.com.au.*

Binnorie Dairy

STORE/MALL | Drop by this cheese maker to sample and buy Simon Gough's irresistible, handcrafted soft cow and goat cheeses made from locally sourced milk. You'd be hard-pressed to find a tastier marinated feta outside Greece—or even in it. ✉ *Tuscany Wine Estate, 25 Lodge St., Pokolbin* ☎ *02/4998–6660* 🌐 *www.binnorie.com.au.*

Briar Ridge Vineyard

WINERY | In a delightful rural corner of the Mount View region, this is one of the Hunter Valley's most prestigious small wineries. It produces a limited selection of sought-after reds, whites, and sparkling wines. The Sémillon, Chardonnay, Shiraz, and intense Cabernet Sauvignon are highly recommended. The vineyard is on the southern periphery of the Lower Hunter vineyards, about a five-minute drive from Pokolbin. ✉ *593 Mt. View Rd., Mount View* ☎ *02/4990–3670* 🌐 *www.briarridge.com.au.*

★ Hunter Valley Gardens

GARDEN | FAMILY | Garden lovers and those who admire beauty in general should flock to the Hunter Valley Gardens, in the heart of the Pokolbin wine-growing district. The 12 separate gardens occupy 50 acres and include European formal gardens, a Chinese Moongate garden, and a delightful children's storybook garden featuring characters such as the Mad Hatter and Jack and Jill. The gardens have a dazzling Christmas lights display each year; the park is open at night during the holiday season (mid-November–late January) from 6 to 10. The adjacent complex houses restaurants, a popular

Continued on page 181

HIKING THE BLUE MOUNTAINS

Kanangra Falls

Head west of Sydney along the M4, or simply hop a bus or train, and within an hour you'll be on a gradual climb along a traditional Aboriginal pathway into the heart of the Blue Mountains—a sandstone plateau formed 150 million years ago that tops out at 3,600 feet. Dramatic valleys, canyons, and cliff faces to the north and south of the main road have been carved by wind and water over millennia. And the blue? That's light refracting off the fine oil mist from the world's most ecologically diverse tract of eucalypt forest.

(top) Looking out over the Jamison Valley.

A WORLD HERITAGE WONDERLAND

Part of the Greater Blue Mountains World Heritage Area, Blue Mountains National Park encompasses 2,678 sq km (1,034 sq ft) of prime hiking country. Most tracks skirt the cliff edges or run along the bottom of the canyons; paths that connect the two levels are often at points along the cliff that offer breathtaking panoramas of the Jamison, Megalong, or Grose Valleys.

While the geological landscape is worth the trip alone, the flora and fauna are some of the country's most unique. Within just a few square miles, the world's widest variety of eucalypts in one contiguous forest have evolved to thrive in everything from open scrub plains to dense valley rainforests. The Wollami pine, a tree that grew alongside dinosaurs, can only be found in a few small areas here. Then there are the rare or threatened creatures like the Blue Mountains water skink, the yellow-bellied glider, and the long-nosed potoroo. It seems only fitting that both Charles Darwin and John Muir visited here. In 1932 it became one of the first formally protected tracts of land in Australia.

Towns dot the main highway through the Blue Mountains, but Katoomba is the unofficial capital, fully outfitted with resources for visitors and the starting point for some of the most iconic walks. Less-bustling Blackheath, minutes up the road from Katoomba, has our favorite eco-lodges and is closest to the best walks of the Grose Valley. You can get a feel for the region on a day trip from Sydney, but if your schedule permits, stay a night (or three) to fit in a few different hikes.

HIKING LITE: THREE WAYS TO SEE THE JAMISON VALLEY WITHOUT BREAKING A SWEAT

Scenic Skyway

SCENIC CABLEWAY

Less crowded than the Scenic Railway, the world's steepest cable car feels gentle in comparison. The enclosed gondola glides between the valley floor and the cliff rim with views of the Three Sisters.

SCENIC SKYWAY

This Swiss-style, glass-bottom cable car takes you on a 720 m (1/2 mi) long journey 270 m (886 ft) above the gorge for great 360 degree views across the Jamison Valley, the Katoomba Falls, and the famous Three Sisters.

KATOOMBA SCENIC RAILWAY

An incline of 52 degrees makes this former coal-haul railway the world's steepest. Grab a seat in the front. Be prepared for lines at peak visiting times. The railway runs every 10 minutes until 4:50 pm.

Claustral Canyon

Lookout at Echo Point

BLUE MOUNTAIN TRAIL OVERVIEW

KATOOMBA-ECHO POINT	TRAIL TIPS	HIGHLIGHTS
ECHO POINT TO SCENIC RAILWAY: This may not be a long walk, but thanks to the 900 steps of the Giant Staircase, don't underestimate it.	This route is very popular, especially on weekends, so set off early. Be aware that the last railway and cable car up leave at 4:50 pm. If you miss them, you'll have to walk.	• Expansive views across the Jamison Valley and beautiful forest vistas. • Brings you right up against the Three Sisters. • Scenic Railway boarding area is at the end of the trail, so you don't have to walk back up.
PRINCE HENRY CLIFF WALK: Start at the Leura Cascades picnic area and head up the mountain to Echo Point. This is a tough hike and not for the faint of heart.	Olympian Rock and Elysian Rock are perfect spots to picnic.	• Thanks to the level of difficulty, you'll be able to escape the crowds at Katoomba. • Spot lyre birds, kookaburras, and glossy black cockatoos.
BLACKHEATH	**TRAIL TIPS**	**HIGHLIGHTS**
GRAND CANYON WALK: Possible for anyone who's reasonably fit (though there are some steps) and well worth the effort.	A great choice for hot days: the canyon's cool temperatures will come as welcome relief.	• A winding path through lush vegetation and around plummeting waterfalls. • Spectacular views of gorges, forest, and cliff lines at Evans lookout.
PERRY'S LOOKDOWN TO BLUE GUM FOREST: This track starts at Perry's Lookdown parking lot, 9 km (5.5 mi) northeast of Blackheath, and takes you down a steep track into the lovely Blue Gum Forest.	Stop by the Heritage Centre in nearby Blackheath for excellent information on historic sites and hiking trips.	• Experience for yourself why the ecologically unique Blue Gum Forest attracted conservationists' attention in Australia. • You might spot possums, gliders, bandicoots, brown antechinuses, and swamp wallabies.
GLENBROOK	**TRAIL TIPS**	**HIGHLIGHTS**
RED HANDS CAVE TRACK: This moderately difficult circuit walk goes up the Red Hands Creek Valley along a creek and through the rainforest.	It's best to park at the Visitors Centre on Bruce Road and then walk for 10 minutes following the signs to the Glenbrook causeway, as there is no easy parking at the causeway itself.	• Bring your binoculars, because there are many birdwatching opportunities. • See the Blue Mountains' most sacred Aboriginal site, Red Hands Cave. The cave is named after the displays of Aboriginal hand stencils on its walls.

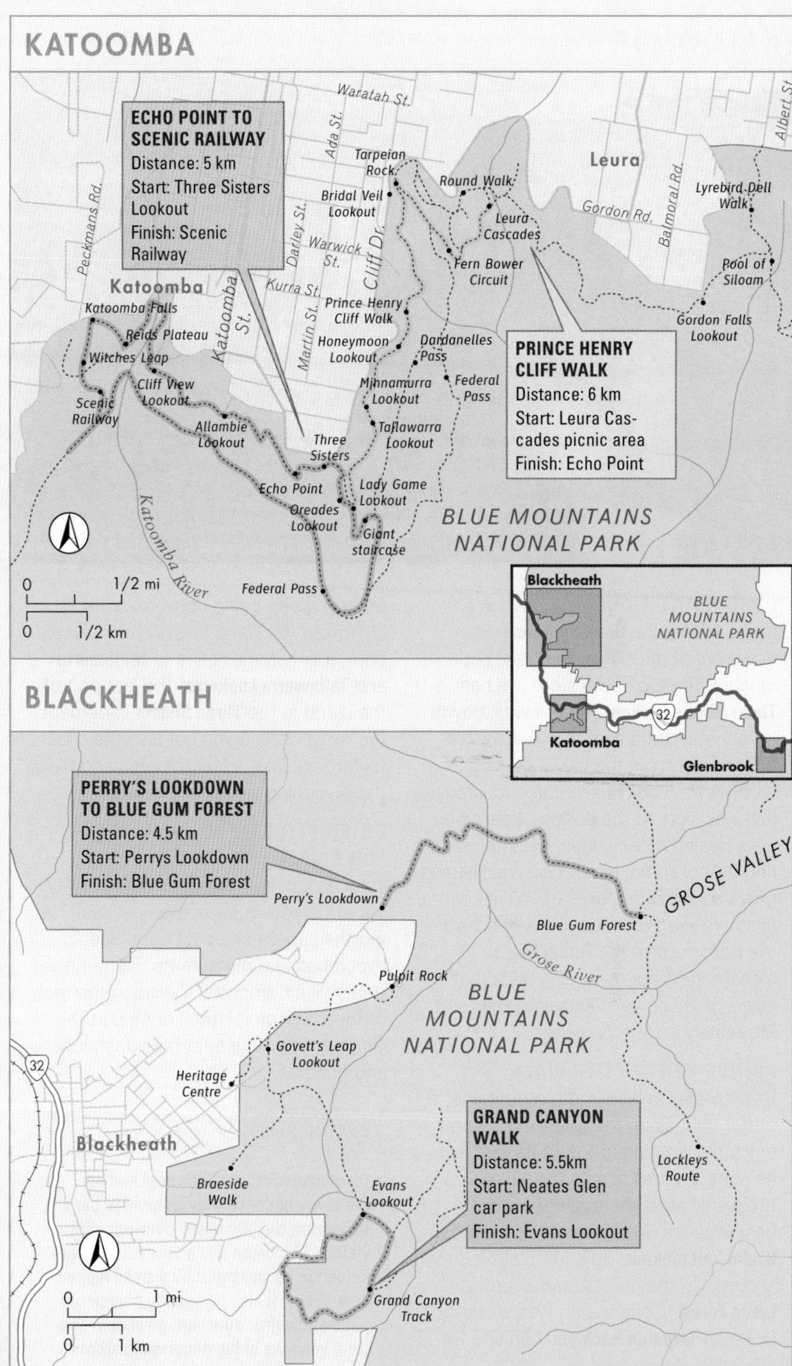
KATOOMBA
ECHO POINT TO SCENIC RAILWAY
Distance: 5 km
Start: Three Sisters Lookout
Finish: Scenic Railway
Waratah St.
Ada St.
Tarpeian Rock
Bridal Veil Lookout
Round Walk
Leura
Gordon Rd.
Balmoral Rd.
Albert St.
Lyrebird Dell Walk
Leura Cascades
Peckmans Rd.
Darley St.
Warwick St.
Cliff Dr.
Fern Bower Circuit
Pool of Siloam
Katoomba
Kurra St.
Katoomba St.
Martin St.
Prince Henry Cliff Walk
Gordon Falls Lookout
Katoomba Falls
Reids Plateau
Witches Leap
Honeymoon Lookout
Dardanelles Pass
Federal Pass
Cliff View Lookout
Scenic Railway
Allambie Lookout
Minnamurra Lookout
Tallawarra Lookout
Three Sisters
PRINCE HENRY CLIFF WALK
Distance: 6 km
Start: Leura Cascades picnic area
Finish: Echo Point
Echo Point
Lady Game Lookout
Oreades Lookout
Giant staircase
BLUE MOUNTAINS NATIONAL PARK
Katoomba River
Federal Pass
0 1/2 mi
0 1/2 km
Blackheath
BLUE MOUNTAINS NATIONAL PARK
32
Katoomba
Glenbrook
BLACKHEATH
PERRY'S LOOKDOWN TO BLUE GUM FOREST
Distance: 4.5 km
Start: Perrys Lookdown
Finish: Blue Gum Forest
Perry's Lookdown
GROSE VALLEY
Blue Gum Forest
Grose River
Pulpit Rock
BLUE MOUNTAINS NATIONAL PARK
Govett's Leap Lookout
32
Heritage Centre
Blackheath
GRAND CANYON WALK
Distance: 5.5km
Start: Neates Glen car park
Finish: Evans Lookout
Lockleys Route
Braeside Walk
Evans Lookout
Grand Canyon Track
0 1 mi
0 1 km

KATOOMBA

View of Three Sisters from Echo Point lookout

ECHO POINT TO SCENIC RAILWAY

In the 1930s, the **Giant Staircase** was hewn out of the cliff by teams of park rangers. The top of the steps are near **Three Sisters Lookout** and the walk down is very steep and narrow in places. It's difficult going but the views make it all worthwhile. Look out for the encouraging half way sign. At the bottom, keep your eyes peeled for echidnas, brushtailed and ring-tail possums, bandicoots, quolls, and grey-headed flying foxes. If you're keen for more exertion once you've reached the Railway, take the **Furber Steps**. It's a challenging but rewarding track that offers great views of **Katoomba Falls** and **Mt. Solitary** across the valley.

PRINCE HENRY CLIFF WALK

If you prefer to hike in the mountains rather than along the forest floor, you'll enjoy this section of the Cliff Walk with its superb vistas across the valley. From the picnic area, the trail descends beside Leura Cascades creek towards **Bridal Veil lookout**. Be sure to slow down and take in the great views over the **Leura Forest**. Continue on Prince Henry Drive; at **Tarpeian Rock** you can see Mt. Solitary. Keep going uphill towards Olympian Rock and Elysian Rock. From here, follow the cliff line to **Millamurra** and **Tallawarra Lookouts**. The last part of the climb to the **Three Sisters** is perhaps the most challenging but also the most rewarding. Take a few minutes and savor the sweeping views of the valley.

QUICK BITES/SUPERMARKETS FOR PICNIC GOODIES

You can stock up at either Coles or ALDI supermarkets in Katoomba or Woolworths supermarket in Leura. Scenic World has two restaurants. For gourmet treats visit Carrington Cellars at the rear of the Carrington Hotel, or stop at The Gingerbread House for breakfast, lunch, and goodies.

STAY HERE IF:

On weekends tour buses descend on the town, but once they've headed back to Sydney, the place isn't over-run with vistors. Katoomba has a very relaxed feel helped in no small part by a small hippy community. It also has plenty of nice old pubs and cafés, cute vintage shops, and rural versions of big department stores.

BLACKHEATH

Mount Hay, Grose Valley

GRAND CANYON WALK

From the parking lot, 4.5 km (2.8 mi) from Blackheath, follow the Grand Canyon track signs as the path zig-zags down the hillside and the vegetation becomes more like a rainforest. The trail takes you down into the canyon and over a creek. It winds past a few overhanging rocks, then starts a steep decline towards a sandy overhang called the **Rotunda**. After a break here, follow the signs to **Evans Lookout**, which will lead you through a tunnel and past two waterfalls. You eventually reach the 10-meter-tall (33 ft) **Beauchamp Falls** in the center of the creek. From here head up through a gap in the cliffs, weaving through boulders, again following signs to Evans Lookout. From Evans Lookout, you can do a 6.5 km (4 mi) Cliffside walk to **Pulpit Rock** along the Cliff Top Track.

PERRYS LOOKDOWN TO BLUE GUM FOREST

From the parking lot, follow the signs pointing out the trail down the hill to **Perrys Lookdown**. You'll have fine views over the **Grose Valley** with its sheer sandstone cliffs with the Blue Gum Forest below. Next, head down the hill and do a quick detour to **Docker's Lookout** with its view of Mt. Banks to the north. Head back following the Perrys Lookdown–Blue Gum Forest walk signs. The descent to **Blue Gum Forest** will take about 90 minutes. Once you've explored the forest floor and its dense canopy, head back up the steep track to Perrys Lookdown.

QUICK BITES/SUPERMARKETS FOR PICNIC GOODIES

Blackheath has something of a gourmet reputation. This Little Piggy Deli has plenty of cured meats, artisan cheeses, and fresh breads.

STAY HERE IF:

Blackheath is smaller and less-visited than Katoomba, but the old weatherboard houses give it a similar feel. There's also enough quirky shops and quaint cafes and restaurants to keep it entertaining. Several Sydney restaurateurs relocated here, so there's a breadth of excellent dining venues.

GLENBROOK

Glenbrook

An echidna

Kookaburras

RED HANDS CAVE TRACK

Red Hands Cave has some well preserved Aboriginal hand stencillings. The stencils are behind Plexiglas (called Perspex here) to protect them from graffiti. There are a few good placards explaining the history and describing the artifacts found in the area. The walk starts on the southern side of the causeway, and after about 2 km (1.2 mi) of gentle steps down the gully, the well-defined track forks: take the right-hand path just after a large rocky outcrop near the edge of a gully. ■ **TIP→ Take care near the edge, there's a significant dropoff.** Up the hill near **Camp Fire Creek**, keep an eye out for axe grinding grooves (oval-shaped indentations in sandstone outcrops that Aboriginal peoples used to shape and sharpen stone axes). The trail passes through several types of forest, including dry eucalypt forest, so there's a good variety of birds in the area. Watch for echidnas in the open forest and chestnut-rumped heathwrens and rock warblers in the sandstone area near the Red Hands Cave.

RED HANDS CAVE TRACK
Length: 6 km
Start: Glenbrook Visitor Centre
Finish: Red Hands Cave

BITES/SUPERMARKETS FOR PICNIC GOODIES

Glenbrook doesn't have the same variety of food and lodging options as Katoomba and Blackheath, but there's a small supermarket on Park Street. Ross Street has a few nice cafes; check out **Kickaboom's** delicious breakfasts.

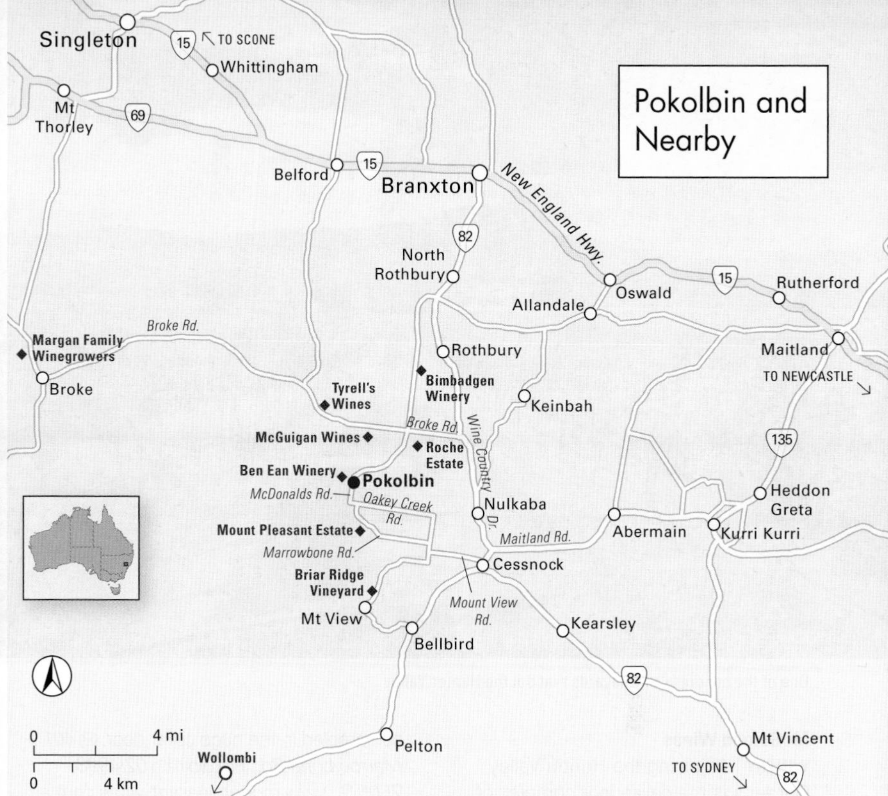

pub, a hotel, a cute wedding chapel, the underground **Hunter Cellars,** and a selection of boutiques selling gifts as well as wonderful chocolates and fudge. ✉ *2090 Broke Rd., Pokolbin* ☎ *02/4998–4000* 🌐 *www.huntervalleygardens.com.au* 🎫 *A$32.*

Margan Family Winegrowers

WINERY | A leading light in the new wave of Hunter winemakers, Margan Family Winegrowers produces some of the valley's best small-volume wines. Try their full-bodied Verdelho, rosé-style Saignée Shiraz, and Certain Views Cabernet Sauvignon. A riper-than-most Sémillon is the flagship. Many items on the fine-dining lunch menu in the restaurant are sourced from the chef's vegetable and herb garden on-site, along with fresh eggs. ✉ *1238 Milbrodale Rd., Broke* ☎ *02/6579–1372 cellar door* 🌐 *www.margan.com.au.*

Matilda Bay Brewhouse Hunter Valley

BREWERY | This brewhouse is part of a large complex that includes a resort, wine school, cooking school, candy making classes, day spa, horseback riding, and Segway tours. There are 12 craft beers produced in this boutique brewery, including the brewer's acclaimed "three-hop" beers: premium lager, premium light lager, and pilsner, along with its alcoholic ginger beer. You can order a chef's beer tasting "paddle" with small glasses of each, complete with tasting notes. Soak up the alcohol with fish-and-chips, meatballs, pizzas, and other light fare, and there's live music most days. ✉ *Hermitage Rd. at Mistletoe La., Pokolbin* ☎ *02/4998–7777* 🌐 *www.hunterresort.com.au.*

One of the hundreds of vineyards that dot the Hunter Valley

McGuigan Wines

WINERY | Adjoining the Hunter Valley Gardens is the cellar-door complex of McGuigan Wines, one of the most well-known wine labels in the Hunter Valley. Here you can taste and buy wines, such as Vineyard Select and Personal Reserve labels, that are not available in suburban wine shops. Winery tours depart at noon every day. While you're there try some of the superb cheeses at the adjacent Hunter Valley Cheese Company—look out for the washed-rind Hunter Valley Gold and the deliciously marinated soft cows'-milk cheese. You can also see the cheeses being made by hand. ✉ *Broke Rd. at McDonalds Rd., Pokolbin* ☎ *02/4998–4111* 🌐 *www.mcguiganwines.com.au.*

Mount Pleasant Estate

WINERY | At this estate chief winemaker Jim Chatto (only the fourth since the winery was founded in 1921) continues the tradition of producing classic Hunter wines. The flagship Maurice O'Shea Shiraz and Chardonnay, and the celebrated Elizabeth Sémillon, are among the wines that can be sampled in the huge cellar door. ✉ *401 Marrowbone Rd., Pokolbin* ☎ *02/4998–7505* 🌐 *www.mountpleasantwines.com.au* 🎟 *A$20 for tasting and tour.*

★ **Roche Estate**

WINERY | You can't miss this ultramodern facility in the heart of Pokolbin. This futuristic winery is a joint venture between two leading Hunter Valley families: the Roches (owners of Hunter Valley Gardens) and the McGuigans, who have made wine for four generations. The winery is best known for its Pinot Gris; however, you can sample a wide variety, including Sémillon, Sauvignon Blanc, Chardonnay, and Shiraz in the stylish tasting room. There's also a Goldfish Wine Bar and Oishii, an on-site fine-dining Japanese-Thai restaurant. If you can, stop in at the winery's branch of the Hunter Valley Smelly Cheese Shop. In the summer the winery hosts major concerts in its 10,000-seat amphitheater—past performers have included Elton John, Rod Stewart, and the Beach Boys. ✉ *Broke Rd. at McDonalds Rd., Pokolbin*

☎ *02/4998–4098 cellar door* 🌐 *www.rocheestate.com.au.*

Tyrrell's Wines

WINERY | Founded in 1858, Tyrrell's Wines is one of the Hunter Valley's oldest family-owned vineyards. This venerable establishment crafts a wide selection of wines, and was the first to produce Chardonnay commercially in Australia. Its famous Vat 47 Chardonnay is still a winner. Enjoy the experience of sampling fine wines in the rustic tasting room, or take a picnic lunch to a site overlooking the valley. Guided tours (A$10) are given daily at 10:30. ✉ *1838 Broke Rd., Pokolbin* ☎ *02/4993–7028* 🌐 *www.tyrrells.com.au.*

Restaurants

★ **Bistro Molines**

$$$ | **FRENCH** | Local French-born celebrity chef Robert Molines, who used to run Roberts Restaurant, has a restaurant on the grounds of the lovely Tallavera vineyard, which has one of the best views in the valley. Make sure you nab a table on or near the veranda. **Known for:** must-visit cellar door; incredible views; overnight accommodation if needed. $ *Average main: A$42* ✉ *Tallavera Grove, 749 Mount View Rd., Mount View* ☎ *02/4990–9553* 🌐 *www.bistromolines.com.au* ⏲ *Closed Tues. and Wed. No dinner Mon. and Thurs.*

Cafe Enzo

$$ | **CAFÉ** | This breakfast and lunch café is at Peppers Creek Village, a charming little shopping and dining enclave in Pokolbin with a village green atmosphere. Housed in a sandstone building, with a lovely attached sun-drenched courtyard overlooking a fountain, this is a great spot for a hearty lunch after a visit to neighboring David Hooks winery and the clothing and antiques shops. **Known for:** very busy; rustic fare; seafood specials. $ *Average main: A$30* ✉ *Peppers Creek Village, Broke Rd. at Ekerts Rd., Pokolbin* ☎ *02/4998–7233* 🌐 *www.enzohuntervalley.com.au* ⏲ *No dinner.*

Circa 1876

$$$$ | **MODERN AUSTRALIAN** | This restaurant in grapevine-covered, 1876-built Pepper Tree Cottage wins the ambience award hands down. The seasonal Mod Oz menu draws inspiration from regional recipes of France and Italy and applies it to local game, seafood, beef, and lamb. **Known for:** stunning interiors; European vineyard feel; special occasion. $ *Average main: A$110* ✉ *64 Halls Rd., Pokolbin* ☎ *02/4998–4999* 🌐 *convent.com.au.*

Il Cacciatore

$$ | **ITALIAN** | Serving up a vast selection of northern Italian specialties, the outdoor terrace at Il Cacciatore is the perfect place for a leisurely weekend lunch. The exterior is classic Australian, with a veranda overlooking the vineyards. **Known for:** boutique hotel on-site; vineyard setting; northern Italian menu. $ *Average main: A$35* ✉ *609 McDonalds Rd., at Gillard Rd., Pokolbin* ☎ *02/4998–7639* 🌐 *www.hermitagelodge.com.au* ⏲ *No lunch weekdays.*

Muse Kitchen

$$$$ | **EUROPEAN** | Located at the entrance to Pokolbin, this award-winning European-style restaurant is found in the picturesque Keith Tulloch Wines courtyard. The menu is focused on Hunter Valley's finest local produce. **Known for:** farm-to-table dining; fine-dining menu; expansive views. $ *Average main: A$85* ✉ *Keith Tulloch Winery, 989 Hermitage Rd., Pokolbin* ☎ *02/4998–7899* 🌐 *www.muse-kitchen.com.au/hunter-valley* ⏲ *Closed Mon. and Tues. No lunch Sat.*

Coffee and Quick Bites

Sabor Dessert Bar

$ | **CAFÉ** | **FAMILY** | During peak season in the Hunter Valley, the queue here snakes around the building. That's all down to the extensive array of desserts available. **Known for:** takeaway options; great service; delicious desserts. $ *Average main: A$5* ✉ *2342 Broke Rd., Pokolbin* ☎ *1300/958–939* 🌐 *www.sabordessert-bar.com.au.*

Hotels

Carriages Boutique Hotel

$$$ | B&B/INN | On 36 acres at the end of a quiet country lane, this rustic-looking but winsome guesthouse, set on a small vineyard, is all about privacy. **Pros:** private; romantic in winter with roaring fireplaces in some rooms; lovely verandas overlooking the grounds. **Cons:** wedding groups sometimes book out most of the place; no children allowed; isolated. $ *Rooms from: A$275* ✉ *112 Halls Rd., Pokolbin* ☎ *02/4998–7591* 🌐 *www.thecarriages.com.au* *10 rooms* *Free Breakfast.*

Cedars Mount View

$$$$ | B&B/INN | This property nestled in the hills above the valley might tempt you to forget about wine tasting for a few days. **Pros:** private and luxurious; luxury toiletries; bathrooms have decadent sunken whirlpool baths. **Cons:** no pool; no room service; location a bit too remote for some. $ *Rooms from: A$485* ✉ *60 Mitchells Rd., Mount View* ☎ *02/4990–9009* 🌐 *www.cedars.com.au* *4 villas, 1 cottage* *Free Breakfast.*

The Convent

$$$ | B&B/INN | This former convent, built in 1909 and transported 605 km (375 miles) from its original home in western New South Wales, is ideal for those who love traditional guesthouses. **Pros:** balconies are a superb place to watch the sunset; romantic and secluded; short walk to Circa 1876 restaurant. **Cons:** a bit noisy; standard rooms are on the small side; busy on weekends. $ *Rooms from: A$275* ✉ *88 Halls Rd., Pokolbin* ☎ *02/4998–4999* 🌐 *www.convent.com.au* *No Meals* *17 rooms.*

The Cooperage Bed and Breakfast

$$ | B&B/INN | This lovely B&B is in the heart of Kelman Vineyards Estate, a working vineyard with a cellar door just a stone's throw from the rooms. **Pros:** free Wi-Fi; big comfy beds; guesthouse rooms have private decks. **Cons:** can be booked out months ahead; not suitable for children under 10; decor not to everyone's taste. $ *Rooms from: A$199* ✉ *41 Kelman Vineyards, off Oakey Creek Rd., Pokolbin* ☎ *02/4990–1232* 🌐 *www.cooperage.com* *Free Breakfast* *5 rooms.*

Mercure Resort Hunter Valley Gardens

$$$ | HOTEL | This good-value hotel is hard to beat when it comes to location: it's next door to the Hunter Valley Gardens and boutiques and within walking distance to half a dozen wineries, including Roche and Hope estates, which both host big-name musicians such as Elton John and Fleetwood Mac at regular concert events. **Pros:** rooms have balconies or terraces; great location; walking distance to major wineries. **Cons:** more business hotel than resort in style; can get busy with conference groups; not really country rustic inside. $ *Rooms from: A$250* ✉ *2090 Broke Rd., Pokolbin* ☎ *02/4998–2000* 🌐 *www.mercurehuntervalley.com.au* *72 rooms* *No Meals.*

Activities

BICYCLING

Hunter Valley Cycling

BIKING | Your bike, helmet, and a map of the area will be delivered to your hotel door by owner Mark or one of his friendly staff. Half-day rentals are A$27, and a full day costs A$35. ✉ *266 De Beyers Rd., Pokolbin* ☎ *0418/281–480* 🌐 *www.huntervalleycycling.com.au.*

HELICOPTER TOURS

Aero Logistics Helicopters

LOCAL SPORTS | Soaring over a patchwork of wineries and the dramatic Brokenback Range is a thrilling experience—and can be a relatively inexpensive one (as helicopter rides go) with flights starting at A$99 per person for eight minutes, although you can splurge A$399 for a one-hour flight to the beaches of Newcastle and the Central Coast. All flights require a minimum of two people. ✉ *230 Old Maitland Rd., Hexham* ☎ *0408/649–696* 🌐 *www.slatteryhelicopters.com.au* 🎫 *From A$135.*

HORSEBACK RIDING

Hunter Valley Horse Riding and Adventures

HORSEBACK RIDING | These friendly folks welcome equestrians of all levels and ages and have a nice selection of guided rides around the valley, from a one-hour ride to the popular sunset ride (A$80), when you're most likely to see wildlife. ✉ *288 Talga Rd., Rothbury* ☎ *02/4930–7111* 🌐 *www.huntervalleyhorses.com.au* 🎫 *From $A60.*

HOT-AIR BALLOONING

★ Balloon Aloft Hunter Valley

BALLOONING | It's an early start to the day, but drifting above the vineyards at sunrise in a hot-air balloon is an absolutely magical way to see the Hunter Valley. Balloon Aloft has been operating since the late '70s and runs hour-long sunrise flights, which culminate with a celebratory champagne breakfast at Petersons Winery. ✉ *Wine Country Dr., Pokolbin* ✣ *Meet at Petersons Champagne House* ☎ *02/4990–9242* 🌐 *www.balloonaloft.com* 🎫 *From A$269.*

Newcastle

160 km (100 miles) north of Sydney.

Once known as the Steel City, today Newcastle is one of Australia's hippest cities. It's flanked by the Pacific Ocean and six beaches on its eastern side and a harbor on its west side. Gentrification began when the steel mills closed in 1999. Nowadays the old wharves and warehouses form part of the lively riverside Honeysuckle precinct, which buzzes with hotels, cafés, and restaurants.

GETTING HERE AND AROUND

This city of about 550,000 is easy to navigate, as the harbor area and city center are just 3 km (2 miles) from the beaches, and buses run between them. Hunter Street—the main artery—runs parallel to the harbor, and it's only a five-minute walk from harbor to downtown. Trains from Sydney stop at Hamilton and Broadmeadow, and shuttle buses take you into the city center. Buses also travel from Hunter Street to Darby Street, the main shopping and dining area.

 Sights

Fort Scratchley

NOTABLE BUILDING | This was one of several forts built on headlands along Australia's shore in the mid- to late-19th century to defend the colony against a possible Russian attack. Built in 1882, its guns had never been fired in anger until June 8, 1942, when the fort returned fire from Japanese submarines in a little-known World War II confrontation called "the shelling of Newcastle"—the city sustained 34 shells but neither damage nor loss of life. The fort, situated on Flagstaff Hill in Newcastle's east end (not far from the railway station), was occupied by the Australian Army until 1972, after which it became a historic site. Although admission is free, a tour of the fort's tunnels is A$13, and a tunnel and fort tour is A$16. Tours run from 10:30, with the last one at 2:30. ✉ *Nobby's Rd., Newcastle* 🌐 *www.fortscratchley.org.au* 🎫 *A$13.*

★ Merewether Baths

POOL | The largest ocean baths (swimming pools) in the southern hemisphere, Mereweather Baths are a Newcastle icon perfect for swimming and splashing all year round. Opened in 1935 at one of the city's six fabulous beaches, they comprise two pools, with one suitable for children. Complete with barbecues and picnic tables, the baths are the ideal place for a family outing. **■TIP→ The baths are patrolled by lifeguards during the**

The North Coast
BRISBANE
QUEENSLAND
Southport
Gold Coast
Coolangatta
Point Danger
Kingscliff
Murwillumbah
Uki
Warwick
Woodenbong
Stanthorpe
The Channon
Mullumbimby
Kyogle
Cape Byron Lighthouse
Cape Byron
Byron Bay Hinterland
Byron Bay
Lismore
Bangalow
Texas
Tabulam
Lennox Head
Casino
Ballina
Bonshaw
Tenterfield
Baryulgil
Evans Head
Deepwater
Cangai
Angourie Point
Maclean
Dundee
Jackadgery
Brooms Head
Grafton
Inverell
Glen Innes
Minnie Water
NORTH SOLITARY ISLAND
Woolgoolga
The Big Banana
SOLITARY ISLANDS
Guyra
Muttonbird Island
Dorrigo
Coffs Harbour
Ebor
Round Mountain
Armidale
Dorrigo National Park/ Rainforest Centre
Bellingen
NEW ENGLAND RANGE
Nambucca Heads
Macksville
Scotts Head
Bellbrook
South West Rocks
Walcha
Willawarrin
Hat Head
Tamworth
Crescent Head
Point Plomer
Port Macquarie Historical Museum
Port Macquarie
Sea Acres Rainforest Centre
Koala Hospital
Nowendoc
Laurieton
Wingham
Crowdy Head
Lord Howe Island
Taree
South Pacific Ocean
Scone
Gloucester
Aberdeen
Krambach
Nabiac
Muswellbrook
TO SYDNEY
Cape Hawke
Forster
Dungog
Stroud
Bulahdelah
Seal Rocks
Singleton
Raymond Terrace
BROUGHTON ISLANDS
Branxton
Tea Gardens
Newcastle
Maitland
Nelson Bay
0
40 mi
0
40 km

summer months only, from around late September to late April. ✉ *Henderson Parade, Newcastle* 🎫 *Free.*

Newcastle Museum

HISTORY MUSEUM | FAMILY | In the former headquarters of the Great Northern Railway, right on Newcastle Harbour, this museum tells the story of the city's coal mining and steel production. Visitors can don a hard hat to witness the Fire and Earth exhibition, which re-creates life in a steel mill complete with furnaces, theatrical drama, and interactive displays that shed light on the workers' challenging lives. Newcastle's other faces are captured with exhibits on Aboriginal history, the gorgeous beaches, and the earthquake that struck the city in 1989. A popular draw for kids, the Supernova Hands-on Science Centre explains how a heavy car is lifted, a tornado occurs, and magnetic fields work. ✉ *Workshop Way, Newcastle* ☎ *02/4974–1400* 🌐 *www.newcastlemuseum.com.au* 🎫 *Free.*

Nobby's Lighthouse

LIGHTHOUSE | A Newcastle landmark, Nobby's Lighthouse (on Nobby's Headland) was the third to be built in New South Wales when it opened in 1854. It's at the end of a long narrow spit (a longshore drift) and is accessed by a nearly 1-km (½-mile) path. Before it was converted to electricity in 1935, the original 20,000-candle light was tended by three keepers. The grounds of the lighthouse, and one of the lightkeeper's cottages, are open Sunday 10–4. It's a terrific vantage point for avid photographers. ✉ *Nobby's Headland, Newcastle* 🌐 *www.newcastle.nsw.gov.au* 🎫 *Free.*

Restaurants

The Landing Bar & Kitchen

$$ | MODERN AUSTRALIAN | Enjoy the passing parade of tugboats and tankers coming and going in Newcastle Harbour from this buzzy bar and restaurant on the Honeysuckle strip. Locals come here for casual catch-ups over cocktails, pizzas, and shared plates on the deck, but the serious foodies head inside for the larger Mod Oz plates, mostly designed to share. **Known for:** cheap eats; relaxed atmosphere; sundowners. 💲 *Average main: A$28* ✉ *1 Honeysuckle Dr., Newcastle* ☎ *02/4927–1722* 🌐 *thelanding.com.au* ⏲ *Closed Mon. and Tues.*

Merewether Surfhouse

$$ | MODERN AUSTRALIAN | Opened on the site of the Merewether Beach's original surfhouse (a lifeguard station), this stunning three-story venue has fantastic ocean views from all three of its eateries. The ground floor café, pizza, and gelato bar are steps from the beach, while the top-level restaurant has expansive panoramas and is open for lunch and dinner. **Known for:** good coffee; always fun environment; different types of cuisine. 💲 *Average main: A$30* ✉ *Henderson Parade, Newcastle* ☎ *02/4918–0000* 🌐 *www.surfhouse.com.au.*

★ Nagisa

$$ | JAPANESE | Overlooking the harbor's edge, here you'll find fresh produce and traditional Japanese fare. Serving up sashimi, sushi, and noodles, Nagisa is a popular weekend restaurant with a buzzy atmosphere. **Known for:** traditional Japanese menu; cocktail bar; fun weekend atmosphere. 💲 *Average main: A$28* ✉ *N2/1 Honeysuckle Dr., Newcastle* ☎ *02/4929–4122* 🌐 *www.nagisa.com.au.*

Rustica

$$$ | MEDITERRANEAN | Meaning "rural" in Italian, this lushly decorated restaurant with stunning views over Newcastle Beach is one of the shining stars in the city's expanding dining scene. The restaurant serves cuisine inspired by the Mediterranean, from the shores of northern Africa to the foothills of Tuscany. **Known for:** popular local spot; Moroccan vegetable and chickpea tagine; stunning views. 💲 *Average main: A$36* ✉ *2/1 King St., Newcastle* ☎ *02/4929–3333* 🌐 *www.rustica.com.au* ⏲ *No lunch Mon.–Wed. No dinner Sun.*

Scratchleys on the Wharf

$$ | **MODERN AUSTRALIAN** | This swank establishment is as close as Newcastle comes to having an iconic restaurant. Enclosed on three sides by glass and perched over the harbor on the busy esplanade, Scratchley's opened not long after the Honeysuckle precinct transformed Newcastle into a hip and happening place more than a decade ago. **Known for:** romantic; incredible seafood; great views. *Average main: A$32* *200 Wharf Rd., Newcastle* *02/4929–1111* *www.scratchleys.com.au.*

★ **Subo Newcastle**

$$$$ | **MODERN AUSTRALIAN** | A bright, intimate star in Newcastle's dining scene, Subo is one of the hottest spots in town and is often booked out weeks ahead. A stylish bistro in the central business district, Subo serves a A$100 five-course tasting plate that changes every six weeks and might include prawn carpaccio and foie gras, confit of chicken wings with blackened corn, Wagyu beef with smoked leeks, and chocolate-orange mousse with rum-and–orange syrup cake. **Known for:** must-have desserts; stylish and trendy; extensive cocktail list. *Average main: A$100* *551d Hunter St., Newcastle* *02/4023–4048* *Closed Sun., Mon., and Tues.*

Coffee and Quick Bites

Estabar Newcastle Beach

$ | **CAFÉ** | Perched right on Newcastle Beach, Estabar is known for its great coffee, organic foods, superb Spanish hot chocolate drinks, and wonderful gelato. Open all day from breakfast until sundown, it's a small space with little tables and a short menu, but it draws a big local following. **Known for:** local hot spot; great coffee; views over Newcastle Beach. *Average main: A$17* *61 Shortland Esplanade, at Ocean St., Newcastle* *04/4730–0896* *www.estabar.com* *No dinner.*

Three Monkeys

$ | **AUSTRALIAN** | Named by locals as the best brunch in Newcastle, this iconic café has been in action for over 20 years and is still as popular today. The menu is extensive, with everything from loaded cookies to savory beef mince on toast with poached eggs. **Known for:** iconic café; lively atmosphere; unique menu. *Average main: A$20* *131 Darby St., Newcastle* *02/4926–3779* *www.threemonkeyscafe.com.au.*

Hotels

Brezza Bell B&B

$$ | **B&B/INN** | This lovely timber cottage with a white-picket fence is the ideal place for a quiet, romantic escape near the beach, a girls' weekend away, or a safe and friendly overnight when traveling solo. **Pros:** posh amenities; home cooking at its best; romantic. **Cons:** no secure parking available; limited facilities; just two rooms. *Rooms from: A$200* *1 Rown Crescent, Newcastle* *02/4963–3812* *www.brezzabella.com.au* *Free Breakfast* *2 rooms.*

Ibis Newcastle

$ | **HOTEL** | Set about a kilometer from Newcastle's downtown, the Ibis is a value-priced chain hotel with parking and a restaurant. **Pros:** good price; good location. **Cons:** expensive in-room Wi-Fi; not on beach or waterfront; small rooms with very small bathrooms. *Rooms from: A$135* *700 Hunter St., Newcastle* *02/4925–2266* *www.ibis.com* *No Meals* *97 rooms.*

Novotel Newcastle Beach

$$$ | **HOTEL** | **FAMILY** | Just a few minutes' walk from the east end of the beach, Novotel has sweeping views of the ocean and of the city. **Pros:** free parking; spacious rooms; great location. **Cons:** no balconies; Wi-Fi isn't free; breakfast is additional. *Rooms from: A$276* *5 King St., Newcastle* *02/4032–3700*

www.novotelnewcastlebeach.com.au No Meals 88 rooms.

Rydges Newcastle

$$$ | **HOTEL** | Newcastle's most upscale hotel, the Rydges Newcastle, formerly known as the Crowne Plaza, is in the trendy Honeysuckle Precinct and has the best location of any hotel in town. **Pros:** great location; ocean views; free Wi-Fi. **Cons:** parking is expensive; not family friendly; basic rooms. *Rooms from: A$245 Merewether St. at Wharf St., Newcastle 02/4907–5000 www.rydges.com 175 rooms No Meals.*

Activities

BICYCLING

Metro Cycles

BICYCLE TOURS | **FAMILY** | Hiring a bike for the day is a great way to get around Newcastle. You can rent a bike from a day to a week. There's everything from tandem bikes to kids bikes available. And bikes with child seats. Cost starts at A$30 a day. Hotel drop-off is available. *2 Bellevue St., Newcastle www.metrocycles.com.au.*

KAYAKING

Newcastle Kayak Tours

KAYAKING | As the world's largest export coal port, Newcastle has a genuine working harbor. It's fascinating to watch the huge freighters as they line up beyond the harbor in the open sea, come through the heads, fill up with coal, and depart. Since the steelworks closed down in 1999, the harbor has opened up to visitors and is lined with smart apartments, hotels, and restaurants. For a close-up look at the giant ships and smaller boats, hop into a kayak for a guided excursion with Newcastle Kayak Tours. The two-hour (A$90) blue tour is the easiest and most popular—it begins at Dog Beach (so named because dogs are allowed), skirts past Queen's Wharf, and then meanders up Throsby Creek and past Newcastle Marina. Limited to 12 paddlers, the tour takes in all the highlights, and you may even be fortunate enough to spot dolphins. Longer and more challenging tours are also available. *Tully St., Newcastle 0432/913–318 www.newcastlekayaktours.com.au From A$90 Tours run in summer only.*

Port Macquarie

390 km (243 miles) northeast of Sydney.

Port Macquarie was founded as a convict settlement in 1821 and is the third-oldest settlement in Australia. Set at the mouth of the Hastings River, the town was chosen for its isolation to serve as an open jail for prisoners convicted of second offenses in New South Wales. By the 1830s the pace of settlement was so brisk that the town was no longer isolated, and its usefulness as a jail had ended.

Today's Port Macquarie has few reminders of its convict past and is flourishing as a vacation area. With its pristine rivers and lakes and 13 regional beaches, including beautiful Town Beach and Shelley Beach, which both have sheltered swimming, it's a great place to get into water sports, catch a fish for dinner, and watch migrating humpback whales in season, usually May to August and September to November.

GETTING HERE AND AROUND

It's a five-hour drive from Sydney heading north on the Pacific Highway. Greyhound and Premier Motor Service run coaches from Sydney Central Station. NSW TrainLink trains operate three services daily between Sydney and the North Coast, though there is no direct train to Port Macquarie. Passengers depart at Wauchope station and then take a bus to Port Macquarie (a 20-minute journey). Timetables are available at the Greater Port Macquarie Visitor Centre or online. Qantas and Virgin Australia have flights from Sydney; Virgin Australia also flies to and from Brisbane.

VISITOR INFORMATION

CONTACTS Visitor Information Centre. ✉ *The Glasshouse, Clarence St. at Hay St., Port Macquarie* ☎ *02/6581–8000, 1300/303–155* 🌐 *www.portmacquarieinfo.com.au.*

Sights

★ Koala Hospital

OTHER ATTRACTION | FAMILY | Operated by the Koala Preservation Society of New South Wales, the town's Koala Hospital is both a worthy cause and a popular attraction. The Port Macquarie region is home to many of these extremely appealing marsupials, and the hospital cares for 250 to 300 sick and injured koalas each year. The staff is passionate about their furry patients and happy to tell you about the care the animals receive. You can walk around the grounds to view the recuperating animals; you can even adopt one (but you can't take it home). Try to visit during feeding times at 8 in the morning or 3 in the afternoon. There are guided tours daily at 3. ✉ *Macquarie Nature Reserve, Lord St., Port Macquarie* ☎ *02/6584–1522* 🌐 *www.koalahospital.org.au* 🎟 *Donation requested.*

Port Macquarie Historical Museum

HISTORY MUSEUM | FAMILY | Housed in a two-story convict-built house dating from 1836, this eclectic museum displays period costumes, memorabilia from World Wars I and II, farm implements, antique clocks and watches, and relics from the town's convict days. ✉ *22 Clarence St., Port Macquarie* ☎ *02/6583–1108* 🌐 *www.portmuseum.org.au* 🎟 *A$7.*

★ Sea Acres Rainforest Centre

NATURE SIGHT | This interpretive center comprises 178 pristine acres of coastal rain forest on the southern side of Port Macquarie. There are more than 170 plant species here, including 300-year-old cabbage-tree palms, as well as native mammals, reptiles, and prolific birdlife. An elevated boardwalk allows you to stroll through the lush environment without disturbing the vegetation. The center has informative guided tours, as well as a gift shop and a pleasant rain-forest café, a lovely place for a bite to eat while listening to the birdsong. ✉ *Pacific Dr., near Shelley Beach Rd., Port Macquarie* ☎ *02/6582–3355* 🌐 *www.nationalparks.nsw.gov.au* 🎟 *Free.*

St. Thomas Church

CHURCH | This 1828 church, the country's fifth-oldest house of worship, was built by convicts using local cedar and stone blocks cemented together with powdered seashells. ✉ *Hay St. at William St.,* ☎ *02/6584–1033.*

Restaurants

The Boathouse Bar & Restaurant

$$ | AUSTRALIAN | FAMILY | With views of moored yachts and tropical gardens, there's a real vacation vibe to this eatery. There are espresso coffees available at breakfast and espresso martinis at night, with live bands playing on the weekend as rowdy tables pop champagne bottles. **Known for:** fun Sunday afternoons; buzzy atmosphere; sundowner cocktails. 💲 *Average main: A$32* ✉ *20 Park St., Port Macquarie* ☎ *02/6589–5100* 🌐 *www.facebook.com/boathousebarrestaurant.*

Thar she blows!

Whales travel up and down the New South Wales coast by the hundreds, so book a whale-watching cruise to catch all the action at close range. Southern right whales and humpbacks travel up from Antarctica from May to August and down again from September to November. Dolphins can be seen almost any time of the year—you never know when an agile pair will shoot through a wave or bob up near your boat.

Orange fungi growing on the Rainforest Tree at Dorrigo National Park

The Corner

$$ | **AUSTRALIAN** | This stylish, contemporary café packs in the crowds, thanks to its fabulously tasty meals, though you may need to exercise a little patience, as service can be a bit slow at times. Try the Corner Breakfast (A$24), which has everything from eggs the way you like them to ham hock–braised beans. **Known for:** slow service; great brunch; buzzy atmosphere. *Average main: A$33* ✉ *Clarence St. at Munster St., Port Macquarie* ☎ *02/6583–3300* 🌐 *www.thecornerrestaurant.com.au* *No dinner Sun.*

★ **The Stunned Mullet**

$$$ | **MODERN AUSTRALIAN** | Opposite Town Beach, Port Macquarie's best restaurant also has the best views, but don't let that distract you from the food. With so much sea in front of you it's only natural that the menu also features lots of seafood—all of it sustainably line caught or farmed. **Known for:** extensive dessert menu with wine pairing; superior seafood; incredible views. *Average main: A$39* ✉ *24 William St., Port Macquarie* ☎ *02/6584–7757* 🌐 *thestunnedmullet.com.au.*

Hotels

Beachcomber Resort

$$$ | **RESORT** | This self-catering resort opposite Town Beach is a great option if you are staying for a few days or traveling with a family. **Pros:** swimming pool with kids' wading pool; well-maintained barbecue area; great location opposite the beach. **Cons:** design a bit dated and tired; no elevators; can be noisy during peak time. *Rooms from: A$205* ✉ *54 William St., Port Macquarie* ☎ *02/6584–1881, 800/001–320* 🌐 *www.beachcomberresort.com.au* *No Meals* *39 rooms.*

Ibis STYLE Port Macquarie

$$ | **HOTEL** | Although the building dates from the late 1960s—when its sawtooth shape was considered very stylish—it's filled with up-to-the-minute amenities: designer furnishings, luxurious linens, marble bathrooms, and private balconies

with ocean and river views. **Pros:** beautiful breakfast room on the top floor with ocean views; a good continental breakfast is brought to your room; toasters in rooms; free Wi-Fi. **Cons:** a few rooms overlook car park; some street noise. *Rooms from: A$159* ✉ *1 Stewart St., Port Macquarie* ☎ *02/6583–1200* 🌐 *www.accorhotels.com* *No Meals* *45 rooms.*

★ **Mantra The Observatory**

$$$ | HOTEL | The most stylish digs in Port Macquarie are just a short walk across leafy parkland to the city's main beach. **Pros:** pool; close to beach; great restaurants. **Cons:** can be impersonal due to size; packed with families in summer; communal areas a little dated. *Rooms from: A$220* ✉ *40 William St., Port Macquarie* ☎ *02/6586–8000* 🌐 *www.mantra.com.au* *No Meals* *81 rooms, 2 penthouses.*

Activities

Unsurprisingly, most of the outdoor activities in this area revolve around the town's crystal clear waters.

FISHING

Ocean Star

FISHING | Deep-sea anglers will enjoy the daylong trips on this 40-foot custom Randel charter boat. Typical catches include snapper, pearl perch, dolphinfish, and grouper. If you have cooking facilities, the crew is happy to clean, ice, and pack your catch. ✉ *Town Wharf, 74 Clarence St., Port Macquarie* ☎ *0416/240–877* 🌐 *www.portmacquariefishingcharters.com.au.*

HORSEBACK RIDING

Port Macquarie Horse Riding Centre

HORSEBACK RIDING | FAMILY | Found just outside of Port Macquarie, this riding school welcomes experts and beginners with short trail rides and overnight treks. The most popular is the express trial ride, taking you through the beautiful vineyards on the grounds. It takes 20 minutes in total and costs A$55. The grounds also have their own on-site restaurant and cellar door with wine tastings every day. ✉ *Enter via Cassegrain Wine, 10 Winery Dr., Port Macquarie* ☎ *04/8700–4483* 🌐 *www.portmacquariehorseriding.com.au.*

SURFING

Port Macquarie Surf School

SURFING | Head back to school and learn to ride the waves from some very competent coaches, all of whom are fully accredited, licensed, and insured with Surfing Australia. There are daily group lessons (A$50 for two hours), or you can opt for one-on-one tutoring (A$85 per hour). Surfboards, wet suits, rash vests, and sunscreen are provided. ✉ *46 Pacific Dr., Port Macquarie* ☎ *02/6584–7733* 🌐 *www.portmacquariesurfschool.com.au* *From A$50.*

WHALE-WATCHING

Port Cruise Adventures

RAFTING | Majestic humpback whales migrate past Port Macquarie nonstop from May to the end of November, and Port Cruise Adventures gets you up close with great-value cruises (A$75) for up to two hours, depending on how far offshore the whales are. The company also has both long and short cruises to see local bottlenose dolphins, which can be spotted year-round. ✉ *Short St. Wharf, Port Macquarie* ☎ *02/6583–8811* 🌐 *portjet.com.au* *From A$75.*

Bellingen

210 km (130 miles) north of Port Macquarie, 520 km (323 miles) from Sydney.

In a river valley a few miles off the Pacific Highway, artsy Bellingen is one of the prettiest towns along the coast. Many of Bellingen's buildings have been classified by the National Trust, and the museum, cafés, galleries, and crafts outlets are favorite hangouts for artists, craft workers, and writers. You'll find food, entertainment, and 250 stalls at the community markets that take place on the third Sunday of every month.

GETTING HERE AND AROUND

It's a seven-hour drive from Sydney along the Pacific Highway, but the town is just 30 minutes from Coffs Harbour and its airport. NSW TrainLink trains run from Sydney to Brisbane twice daily, stopping at Urunga, 10 km (6 miles) away. Both Greyhound and Premier Motor Service also run buses between Sydney and Urunga. From Urunga, either catch a taxi or a local Busways bus to Bellingen—though the bus is quite infrequent. There is also a Busways bus service from Coffs Harbour to Bellingen.

VISITOR INFORMATION

CONTACTS Waterfall Way Visitor Centre. ✉ *29–31 Hyde St., Bellingen* ☎ *02/6655–1522, 1800/705–735.*

★ Dorrigo National Park

VIEWPOINT | From Bellingen a meandering and spectacular road leads inland to Dorrigo and then travels back east eventually reaching the Pacific Highway, close to Coffs Harbour. This circular scenic route, beginning along the Bellinger River, climbs more than 1,000 feet up the heavily wooded escarpment to the Dorrigo Plateau. At the top of the plateau is Dorrigo National Park, a small but outstanding subtropical rain forest that is included on the World Heritage list. Signposts along the main road indicate walking trails. The Satinbird Stroll is a short rain forest walk, and the 6-km (4-mile) Cedar Falls Walk leads to the most spectacular of the park's many waterfalls, but the most dramatic of all is the free Skywalk lookout, a 230-foot boardwalk above the canopy that has panoramic views out to the coast. The national park is approximately 31 km (19 miles) from Bellingen. ✉ *Dorrigo Rainforest Centre, Dome Rd., Dorrigo* ☎ *02/6657–2309* 🌐 *www.nationalparks.nsw.gov.au.*

Dorrigo Rainforest Centre

FOREST | The excellent Dorrigo Rainforest Centre, open daily 9–4:30, has a good display on the natural heritage of the park and a small café that serves good coffee. From here you can walk out high over the forest canopy along the **Skywalk** boardwalk. ✉ *142 Dome Rd., Dorrigo Mountain* ☎ *02/6657–2309* 🌐 *www.nationalparks.nsw.gov.au.*

Koompartoo Retreat

$$$ | **B&B/INN** | These self-contained hardwood cottages on a hillside overlooking Bellingen are superb examples of local craftsmanship, particularly in their use of timbers from surrounding forests. **Pros:** each cottage has a small library; from the chalet verandas you can see kookaburras; peaceful surroundings. **Cons:** dated decor; heating is noisy; no wheelchair access. *$ Rooms from: A$249* ✉ *Rawson St. at Dudley St., Bellingen* ☎ *0473/631–754* 🌐 *www.koompartoo.com.au* *No Meals* *4 cottages.*

HIKING

Bellingen Nature Tours

GUIDED TOURS | Local ecologist Mark Graham leads this deeply immersive tour through conservation areas, subtropical rain forests within the Bellinger Valley to the highest peaks atop the Great Escarpment at the edge of the Dorrigo Plateau. He not only teaches about the unique ecology of the area but delves into the life of the traditional custodians of the land, looking at the traditions of the local Gumbaynggirr people. Price varies as Mark tailors the tour to fit groups of four and above. ✉ *Bellingen* 🌐 *www.bellingennaturetours.com.au* *Price on contact.*

HORSEBACK RIDING

Valery Trails

HORSEBACK RIDING | FAMILY | This large equestrian center is 10 km (6 miles) from Bellingen on the edge of Bongil Bongil National Park. They have 45 horses, and a variety of treks through the local rain forests. Choose from the popular two-hour rides (A$95), breakfast and afternoon barbecue rides, and a two-day ride to Bellingen to stay in the Federal Hotel for (A$450). ✉ *758 Valery Rd., Valery* ☎ *02/6653–4301* 🌐 *www.valerytrails.com.au* 🎫 *From A$85.*

Coffs Harbour

35 km (22 miles) northeast of Bellingen via the Pacific Hwy., 103 km (64 miles) from Bellingen via the inland scenic route along the Dorrigo Plateau, 534 km (320 miles) from Sydney.

The area surrounding Coffs Harbour is the state's "banana belt," where long, neat rows of banana palms cover the hillsides. Set at the foot of steep green hills, the town has great beaches and a mild climate. This idyllic combination has made it one of the most popular vacation spots along the coast. Coffs is also a convenient halfway point on the 1,000-km (620-mile) journey between Sydney and Brisbane.

GETTING HERE AND AROUND

Coffs Harbour is a comfortable 7½-hour drive from Sydney and a six-hour drive from Brisbane. Regular Greyhound and Premier Buses connect the town to Sydney. There is a train station with daily NSW TrainLink services to and from Sydney and Brisbane. And the local airport, 6 km (4 miles) from the central Ocean Parade, is served by Qantas, Virgin Australia, and Tigerair. For more information, contact the visitor center, which is open 9–5 daily.

AIRPORT INFORMATION Coffs Harbour Airport. ✉ *Hogbin Dr., Coffs Harbour* ☎ *02/6648–4767* 🌐 *www.coffsharbourairport.com.*

VISITOR INFORMATION

CONTACTS Coffs Coast Visitors Information Centre. ✉ *253 Pacific Hwy., Coffs Harbour* ☎ *02/6652–4366* 🌐 *www.coffscoast.com.au.*

Sights

★ The Big Banana

NOTABLE BUILDING | FAMILY | Just north of the city, impossible to miss, is the Big Banana—the symbol of Coffs Harbour. This monumental piece of kitsch has stood at the site since 1964. It welcomes visitors to the Big Banana complex, which takes a fascinating look at the past, present, and future of horticulture. There's a multimedia display called "World of Bananas" and a walkway that meanders through the banana plantations and banana packing shed. The park is fantastic for kids and has varied rides all with different prices, including toboggan rides (A$7), a waterslide (A$19.50 for 90 minutes), an ice-skating rink (A$16.50), and laser tag (A$9.90). There's a café on the premises, as well as the Banana Barn, which sells the park's own jams, pickles, fresh tropical fruit, and frozen chocolate-covered bananas on a stick. ✉ *351 Pacific Hwy., Coffs Harbour* ☎ *02/6652–4355* 🌐 *www.bigbanana.com* 🎫 *Entry to Big Banana free; rides and tours extra.*

Dolphin Marine Conservation

OTHER ATTRACTION | FAMILY | Near the port in Coffs Harbour, the Dolphin Marine Conservation aquarium includes colorful reef fish, turtles, seals, penguins, baby crocodiles, and dolphins. Shows take place daily at 10 and 1, and visitors are advised to arrive 30 minutes earlier to get a good seat and receive free "dolphin kisses" from the cute critters before each show. Children may help feed and "shake hands" with dolphins, as well as interact with the seals. You can swim, pat, and play ball with the dolphins and seals in special group encounters if you book in advance. These sessions vary in price depending on time of year—during peak holiday season, dolphin encounters run around A$399 per four-person group. The company's official name is Dolphin Marine Conservation, but many of the locals still call it by its old name, the Pet Porpoise Pool. ✉ *65 Orlando St., beside Coffs Creek, Coffs Harbour* ☎ *02/6659–1900* 🌐 *www.dolphinmarinemagic.com.au* 🎟 *A$38.*

Muttonbird Island

ISLAND | The town has a lively and attractive harbor in the shelter of Muttonbird Island, and a stroll out to this nature reserve is delightful in the evening. To get here, follow the signs to the Coffs Harbour Jetty, then park near the marina. A wide path leads out along the breakwater and up the slope of the island. The trail is steep, but the views from the top are worth the effort. The island is named after the muttonbirds (also known as shearwaters) that nest here between September and April. Between June and September Muttonbird Island is also a good spot for viewing migrating humpback whales. ✉ *Coffs Harbour* 🌐 *www.nationalparks.nsw.gov.au.*

Restaurants

Shearwater Restaurant

$$ | ECLECTIC | This waterfront restaurant with views of Coffs Creek (which is spotlighted at night—look for stingrays swimming by) is open for breakfast, lunch, and dinner, and leaves no culinary stone unturned in its search for novel flavors. The menu in the open-air dining room includes lunch dishes like prawn and scallop red curry. **Known for:** busy on weekends; great service; extensive menu. $ *Average main: A$32* ✉ *The Promenade, 321 Harbour Dr., Coffs Harbour* ☎ *02/6651–6053* 🌐 *www.shearwaterrestaurant.com.au* ⏲ *No dinner Sun.–Tues.*

Coffee and Quick Bites

★ **Fishermen's Co-op**

$ | SEAFOOD | Fish-and-chips don't come any fresher than those served at the fishermen's co-op near the breakwall on the northern side of the harbor in Coffs—everything on the menu is straight off the trawler. Although most of the retail space is given to sales of fresh seafood, you can buy freshly cooked (grilled, battered, or crumbed) fish-and-chips here, as well as calamari, fish cocktails, and salads. **Known for:** relaxed dining; cheap eats; great at lunchtime. $ *Average main: A$15* ✉ *69 Marina Dr., Coffs Harbour* ☎ *02/6652–2811* 🌐 *coffsfishcoop.com.au.*

Hotels

BreakFree Aanuka Beach Resort

$$ | RESORT | FAMILY | Teak furniture and antiques collected from Indonesia and the South Pacific fill the accommodations at this resort, which sits amid palms, frangipani, and hibiscus. **Pros:** home away from home; brilliant setting in a private beachfront cove; great value for families. **Cons:** kid-phobes might not appreciate all the families; some rooms need updating; a little isolated. $ *Rooms from: A$186* ✉ *11 Firman Dr., Coffs Harbour* ☎ *02/6652–7555* 🌐 *www.aanukabeachresort.com.au* 🛏 *27 studios, 39 suites, 12 villas* 🍴 *Free Breakfast.*

Smugglers on the Beach

$$ | RESORT | Five minutes' drive north of Coffs Harbour's busy city center is this small resort with just 16 self-contained one- to three-bedroom apartments, some with hot tubs, spread out among tropical gardens. **Pros:** beautiful beachside location; some rooms have hot tubs; good deals if staying for more than five nights. **Cons:** isolated; two-night minimum, checkout is at 9:30 am; busy with young kids in summer. $ *Rooms from: A$190* ✉ *36 Sandy Beach Rd., Coffs Harbour* ☎ *02/6653–6166* 🌐 *www.smugglers.com.au* 🍴 *No Meals* 🛏 *16 apartments.*

Activities

SCUBA DIVING

The warm seas around Coffs Harbour make this particular part of the coast, with its moray eels, manta rays, turtles, and gray nurse sharks, a scuba diver's favorite. Best are the Solitary Islands, 7 km–21 km (4½ miles–13 miles) offshore.

Jetty Dive Centre
SCUBA DIVING | This outfitter rents gear, schedules scuba and snorkeling trips, and hosts certification classes. A one-day learn-to-dive course is A$345. There are also whale- and dolphin-watching cruises from June to October from A$59. ✉ *398 Harbour Dr., Coffs Harbour* ☎ *02/6651–1611* 🌐 *www.jettydive.com.au.*

Byron Bay

247 km (154 miles) north of Coffs Harbour, 772 km (480 miles) north of Sydney.

Byron Bay is the easternmost point on the Australian mainland, and perhaps earns Australia its nickname the "Lucky Country." Fabulous beaches, storms that spin rainbows across the mountains behind the town, and a sunny, relaxed and somewhat hippie style cast a spell over practically everyone who visits. For many years Byron Bay lured surfers with abundant sunshine, perfect waves on Watego's Beach, and tolerant locals who allowed them to sleep on the sand. These days a more upscale crowd frequents Byron Bay.

Byron Bay is also one of the must-sees on the backpacker circuit, and the town has a youthful energy that fuels late-night partying. There are many art galleries and crafts shops, a great food scene, and numerous adventure tours. The town is at its liveliest on the first Sunday of each month, when Butler Street becomes a bustling market.

GETTING HERE AND AROUND

Byron is the North Coast's most popular destination, and is well served by buses and trains from Sydney and Coffs Harbour. If driving, the journey takes 11 hours from Sydney and 3½ hours from Coffs Harbour. The closest airports are at Ballina and Lismore, both a 30-minute drive away. Virgin Australia, Jetstar, and REX fly to Ballina; REX also flies from Sydney to Lismore. All the usual car companies are there, or you can get a taxi into Byron or take a Ballina-Byron shuttle bus (operated by Byron Easy Bus) for A$20 one-way.

AIRPORT SHUTTLE Byron Easy Bus. ✉ *Byron Bay* ☎ *02/6685–7447* 🌐 *www.byronbayshuttle.com.au.*

VISITOR INFORMATION

CONTACTS Byron Visitor Centre. ✉ *Old Station Master's Cottage, 80 Jonson St., Byron Bay* ☎ *02/6680–8558* 🌐 *www.visitbyronbay.com.*

Sights

★ **Byron Bay Hinterland**
SCENIC DRIVE | Undulating green hills that once boasted a thriving dairy industry are dotted with charming villages and small organic farms growing avocados, coffee, fruits, and macadamia nuts. The best way to discover this gorgeous part of the world—nicknamed the Rainbow Region—is to grab a map and just drive. From Byron, take the road toward the regional town of Lismore for about 15 km (9 miles) to the pretty village of **Bangalow.** Walk along the lovely main street lined with 19th-century storefronts. Carefully follow your map and wind your way northwest for about 20 km (13 miles) to **Federal.** Meander, via the cute towns of **Rosebank** and **Dunoon,** to **The Channon,** where on the second Sunday of every month you'll find a wonderful market with dozens of stalls and entertainment. ✉ *Byron Bay* 🌐 *www.tropicalnsw.com.au.*

The waters surrounding Byron Bay offer top conditions for water sports.

Cape Byron Lighthouse

LIGHTHOUSE | The most powerful beacon on the Australian coastline, Cape Byron Lighthouse dominates the southern end of the beach at Byron Bay and attracts huge numbers of visitors, who want to tick standing at Australia's most easterly point off their bucket list. You can tour the lighthouse (no children under five) daily from 10 am, with the last tour departing at 3 pm. The tours are led by volunteers, and there's $8 entry fee. Whale-watching is popular between June and September, when migrating humpback whales come close to shore. Dolphins swim in these waters year-round, and you can often see pods of them from the cape. You can stay in either of the two six-person assistant lightkeeper's cottages for A$360 a night in low season; prices rise from mid-December to late January and a two-week period over Easter (book well in advance during this period). There's a three-night minimum stay. ✉ *Lighthouse Rd., Byron Bay* ☎ *02/6620–9300* 🌐 *www.nationalparks.nsw.gov.au* 🎫 *A$8.*

Cape Byron Walking Track

TRAIL | This popular trail circumnavigates a 150-acre reserve, passes through grasslands and rain forest, and has sensational seas views as you circle the peninsula and the lighthouse. From several vantage points along the track you may spot dolphins in the waters below. The track begins east of the town on Lighthouse Road. ✉ *Off Lighthouse Rd., Byron Bay* 🌐 *www.nationalparks.nsw.gov.au.*

Beaches

Several superb beaches lie in the vicinity of Byron Bay. In front of the town, Main Beach provides safe swimming, and Clarkes Beach, closer to the cape, has better surf. The most famous surfing beach, however, is Wategos, the only entirely north-facing beach in the state. To the south of the lighthouse Tallow Beach extends for 6 km (4 miles) to a rocky stretch of coastline around Broken Head, which has a number of small sandy coves. Beyond Broken Head is lonely Seven Mile Beach.

Topless sunbathing is popular on many Byron Bay beaches.

Main Beach

BEACH | As the name suggests Main Beach is right in the heart of Byron Bay, across the road from the much-loved Beach Hotel (a popular pub that has good restaurants and accommodation). It stretches southward for some 3 km (2 miles) where its name changes to Clarkes Beach and then The Pass, the latter a legendary surfing spot. Always busy in the summer months, the beach is most easily reached on foot from the town center. There's a sea wall and swimming pool at the northern end, and about 300 feet offshore lies the wreck of the *Tassie II*, a small ammunition supply boat that sunk around the end of Word War II. Swimmers should always swim beside the flags as rips and currents can make this beach hazardous at times—an average of about nine swimmers annually require rescue. There are barbecues and picnic tables in the leafy park flanking the beach. **Amenities:** food and drink; lifeguards (summer only); showers; toilets. **Best for:** snorkeling; swimming; walking. ✉ *Jonson St. at Bay St., Byron Bay.*

Wategos Beach

BEACH | Named for a farming family who grew bananas and vegetables in the hinterland (now a residential area) just behind the beach, Wategos is a lovely 2,000-foot strip of golden sand backed by pandanus palms. It's sheltered from the winds and popular with all comers. If you fancy a walk, you can reach the beach from the city center via the 4-km (2½-mile) Cape Byron Track. Otherwise, drive here and look for parking in the lot or on the street (it can be challenging during busy times). Coin-operated barbecues and picnic tables make this a perfect spot for do-it-yourself lunching, all in the shadow of the majestic Cape Byron Lighthouse, which looms over the beach. The upscale boutique hotel, Raes on Wategos, is nearby. **Amenities:** lifeguards (summer only); parking (fee); toilets. **Best for:** swimming; sunrise. ✉ *Marine Parade, off Palm Valley Dr., Byron Bay.*

 Restaurants

Barrio

$$ | **AUSTRALIAN** | The menu works around the restaurant's wood-fire oven and open-flame grill, with everything from hearty meats from local farms to seafood and smoked vegetables. The wine list is extensive, focusing on Australian wines from all corners of the country. **Known for:** trendy interiors; fresh local produce; extensive wine list. *Average main: A$35* ✉ *Industrial Estate, 1 Porter St., Byron Bay* *www.barriobyronbay.com.au* *No dinner Sat.–Wed.*

Beach Byron Bay

$$ | **CAFÉ** | A Byron Bay legend, this open-air café is a perfect place to sit in the morning sun and watch the waves. Breakfast runs the gamut from wholesome (award-winning locally produced Brookfarm Macadamia muesli with yogurt and banana) to hearty (corned-beef hash, sautéed spinach, fried egg with béarnaise sauce). **Known for:** fresh fare; perfect for day and night; great coffee. *Average main: A$32* ✉ *Clarkes Beach, near parking lot at end of Lawson St., Byron Bay* ☎ *1300/583–766* *www.beachbyronbay.com.au.*

★ Fig Tree Restaurant & Rooms

$$$$ | **AUSTRALIAN** | In this century-old farmhouse with distant views of Byron Bay the draw is upmarket Mod Oz cuisine blending Asian and Mediterranean flavors. Produce fresh from the owners' farm is featured on the lunch platter menu. **Known for:** local produce; big with weddings so check on weekends; incredible grounds with native plants. *Average main: A$90* ✉ *4 Sunrise La., Ewingsdale* ☎ *02/6684–7273* *www.figtreerestaurant.com.au* ☞ *Only lunch available if prebooked.*

Three Blue Ducks

$$$ | **AUSTRALIAN** | **FAMILY** | Found at The Farm, a working property near the main entry point into Byron Bay, Three Blue Ducks is the sister restaurant to the hugely successful Sydney eatery of the same name. This is the perfect spot for breakfast or lunch, with the coffee counter always heaving. **Known for:** farm-to-table fare; rustic restaurant; sustainable menu. *Average main: A$39* ✉ *11 Ewingsdale, Byron Bay* ☎ *02/6684–7795* 🌐 *www.threeblueducks.com/byron.*

 Coffee and Quick Bites

The Byron Bay General Store

$ | **AUSTRALIAN** | Serving tourists and locals since the 1940s, this is an iconic store-turned-café. You'll find beachy interiors, a vegan-friendly menu, and fresh juices. **Known for:** superior coffee; fresh healthy eats; trendy interiors. *Average main: A$15* ✉ *The General Store, 26 Bangalow Rd., Byron Bay* ☎ *02/6680–9236* 🌐 *www.byrongeneralstore.com.*

Folk Byron Bay

$ | **AUSTRALIAN** | This friendly vibrant café is found just outside of Byron and is a firm favorite with locals. It's surrounded by a beautiful garden and native trees with plenty of birds. **Known for:** countryside feel; outstanding coffee; local favorite. *Average main: A$10* ✉ *399 Ewingsdale Rd., Byron Bay* 🌐 *www.folkbyronbay.com.*

 Hotels

Bower at Byron

$$$ | **HOTEL** | With a heated mineral pool, poolside bar, luxury rooms and airport transfer, Bower at Byron is one of the most sophisticated hotels in the Byron Bay region. **Pros:** mineral pool; luxurious; outstanding service. **Cons:** books up quickly; no on-site restaurant; some rooms are next to busy footpath. *Rooms from: A$300* ✉ *28 Bangalow Rd., Byron Bay* ☎ *02/6680–9577* 🌐 *www.thebowerbyronbay.com.au* *No Meals* *29 rooms.*

★ **Elements of Byron**

$$$$ | **RESORT** | **FAMILY** | Since opening in 2016, the A$190 million Elements of Byron has been an instant success in Bryon Bay thanks to high-end technology and finishes and an open and free-flowing design that pulls the surrounding rain forest in. **Pros:** rain forest–facing terraces with fireplaces and lounges; beach and rain-forest location; huge adults-only pool. **Cons:** a little distance from Byron; breakfast is extra; solar train to Byron Bay is not free. *Rooms from: A$520* ✉ *144 Bayshore Dr., Byron Bay* ☎ *02/6639–1500* 🌐 *elementsofbyron.com.au* *No Meals* *68 villas.*

Julian's Apartments

$$$ | **B&B/INN** | These studio apartments just opposite Clarkes Beach are neat, spacious, and well equipped. **Pros:** close to beach; perfect for families (cots and baby supplies can be rented); this is the quiet end of Byron Bay town. **Cons:** popular, so book early; taxi, or hike into town, required; has seen better days. *Rooms from: A$240* ✉ *124 Lighthouse Rd., Byron Bay* ☎ *02/6680–9697* 🌐 *www.juliansbyronbay.com* *11 apartments* *No Meals.*

Raes on Wategos

$$$$ | **B&B/INN** | A high-design boutique hotel, Raes' luxurious Mediterranean-style villa surrounded by a tropical garden offers individually decorated rooms with an eclectic mix of antiques, Indonesian art, Moroccan tables, and fine furnishings. **Pros:** rooms have fireplaces and private terraces; perfect for a romantic break; superb food and spa. **Cons:** breakfast is pricey; have to take a taxi to town; minimum two-night stay on weekends. *Rooms from: A$550* ✉ *Wategos Beach, 8 Marine Parade, Byron Bay* ☎ *02/6685–5366* 🌐 *www.raes.com.au* *No Meals* *7 suites.*

Nightlife

Beach Hotel

LIVE MUSIC | This lounge in the iconic Beach Hotel often hosts live bands. ✉ *Bay St. at Jonson St., Byron Bay* ☎ *02/6685–6402* 🌐 *www.beachhotel.com.au.*

The Northern

LIVE MUSIC | Bands perform most evenings at this old-school pub. ✉ *Jonson St. at Byron St., Byron Bay* ☎ *02/6685–6454* 🌐 *www.thenorthern.com.au.*

Railway Friendly Bar

LIVE MUSIC | Live music rocks this pub, known locally as The Rails, every night; it's built on the old railway station site. ✉ *Jonson St. Railway Station, Byron Bay* ☎ *02/6685–7662* 🌐 *www.therailsbyronbay.com.*

Shopping

Byron Bay Hat Co.

HATS & GLOVES | This local shopping institution carries great hats and bags perfect for the beach. ✉ *4 Jonson St., Byron Bay* ☎ *02/6685–8357.*

Activities

KAYAKING

Go Sea Kayak

KAYAKING | Owned and operated by local surf lifesavers (volunteer lifeguards), this new company runs three-hour kayak tours in two-person kayaks that venture out into the open ocean in search of viewing bottlenose dolphins, sea turtles, and even whales in the season. Guides weave in local Aboriginal history and point out the sights. ✉ *Apex Park, opposite 56 Lawson St., Byron Bay* ☎ *0416/222–344* 🌐 *www.goseakayakbyronbay.com.au* 🎫 *From A$75.*

SCUBA DIVING

The best local diving is at Julian Rocks Marine Reserve, some 3 km (2 miles) offshore, where the confluence of warm and cold currents supports a profusion of marine life and is one of the few sites south of the Great Barrier Reef where you can snorkel with both tropical fish and deep-water animals from the Southern Ocean.

Byron Bay Dive Centre

SCUBA DIVING | This dive center runs snorkeling and scuba-diving trips for all levels of experience, plus gear rental and instruction. The five-hour introductory diving course costs A$215; a single dive with all equipment and guide and some 50 minutes of diving near Julian Rocks costs A$105. A 60-minute snorkel trip, complete with wet suit, is A$99. ✉ *9 Marvel St., Byron Bay* ☎ *02/6685–8333* 🌐 *www.byronbaydivecentre.com.au* 🎫 *From A$99.*

Sundive

SCUBA DIVING | This PADI dive center has courses for all level of divers, as well as boat dives and snorkel trips. The first dive, with all equipment, is A$110; snorkeling trips are available, too. ✉ *9–11 Middleton St., Byron Bay* ☎ *02/6685–7755* 🌐 *www.sundive.com.au* 🎫 *From A$70.*

Lord Howe Island

Fringed by the world's southernmost coral reef as well as gorgeous, sheltered beaches, dominated by two dramatic peaks, and inhabited by just around 400 permanent residents—Lord Howe Island is a secluded slice of paradise that lies about 600 km (370 miles) east of mainland Australia. As a UNESCO World Heritage island, it welcomes just 400 visitors at any time, so it never feels overcrowded. It's a great place for a digital detox—there is no mobile phone coverage anywhere on the island and Internet access is patchy at best. Most visitors rent bicycles and spend their time snorkeling in the lagoon, hand-feeding fish, hiking, and bird-watching, while hardy types climb the summit of 2,870-foot Mt. Gower for sensational views.

En Route

Fifty-three km (33 miles) northwest of Byron Bay is the towering, conical **Mt. Warning**, a 3,800-foot extinct volcano that dominates the pleasant town of Murwillumbah. Its radical shape can be seen from miles away, including the beaches at Byron.

A well-marked **walking track** winds up Mt. Warning, which is a World Heritage national park, from the Breakfast Creek parking area at its base. The 4½-km (2½-mile) track climbs steadily through fern forest and buttressed trees where you can often see native brush turkeys and pademelons (small wallaby-like marsupials). The last 650 feet of the ascent is a strenuous scramble up a steep rock face using chain-link handrails. The local Aboriginal name for the mountain is Wollumbin, which means "cloud catcher," and the metal walkways on the summit are sometimes shrouded in clouds. On a clear day, however, there are fabulous 360-degree views of the massive caldera, one of the largest in the world: national parks crown the southern, western, and northern rims, and the Tweed River flows seaward through the eroded eastern wall. Many people undertake the Mt. Warning ascent before dawn, so they can catch the first rays of light falling on mainland Australia.

GETTING HERE AND AROUND

Qantas subsidiary Qantas Link flies to Lord Howe Island from Sydney, Brisbane, and Port Macquarie. The flight from Sydney is 1 hour and 50 minutes. Flights from the other destinations are 10 minutes or so shorter. As Qantas is the only carrier, and only 400 tourists can visit the island, fares can be quite high—typically more than A$600 one-way. The most economical way to travel to Lord Howe is with an air-and-hotel package deal.

Just 10 km (6 miles) long and with a width varying from 1,000 feet to 2 km (1 mile), crescent-shape Lord Howe Island is compact and easy to navigate. The lagoon hugs the western shore of the island. The town, known as Old Settlement, is midway along the lagoon, and most accommodations are within an easy cycle ride or walk from there. The airport is slightly south of the town, and the two volcanic peaks—Mt. Lidgbird and Mt. Gower—dominate the island's southeast extremity.

Beaches

★ Ned's Beach

BEACH | FAMILY | This beautiful beach on the northeast side of the island is a mecca for fish because fishing bans protect them here. Brightly colored tropical creatures, such as parrotfish and their less-spectacular mullet mates (which are occasionally chased by a harmless reef shark), swim up to shore and greet visitors at the daily 4 pm fish feed. However, visitors can also feed them at other times—you can buy fish food to toss to them from a beach kiosk. This feeding frenzy is fun to watch. Bring snorkel gear to explore the coral a little farther out, or bring a picnic and relax on this beach that's one of the cleanest in Australia. The beach is an easy drive, cycle, or walk from town and the northern hotels. **Amenities:** none. **Best for:** snorkeling; sunrise; swimming; walking. ✉ *Ned's Beach Rd., Ned's Beach, Lord Howe Island* 🌐 *www.lordhoweisland.info.*

Restaurants

★ Arajilla

$$$$ | MODERN AUSTRALIAN | Dining at Arajilla Retreat at least once during a stay on Lord Howe Island is a must. The cuisine, which changes daily, uses fish straight from the ocean and lovely homegrown vegetables. **■ TIP→ In-house guests take precedence over those not staying at the resort, so bookings are essential. Known for:** sophisticated dining; fresh and quality produce; healthy. *Average main: A$95 Lagoon Rd., Old Settlement Beach, Lord Howe Island 0265/632–002 www.arajilla.com.au Only dinner open to nonguests.*

★ Lord Howe Golf Club

$$ | AUSTRALIAN | This is a fine place to socialize with the locals and tourists and enjoy some honest, unpretentious food. The on-site Sunset Bar & Grill is open for dinner on Thursday, Friday, and Sunday, and the menu includes a variety of roasts (such as roast chicken or lamb), steak with garlic butter, schnitzel, fish, and salads, plus pizza on Sunday nights. **Known for:** friendly staff; the place to go on a Friday and Saturday; relaxed dining. *Average main: A$25 Sturt Rd., Lord Howe Island 02/6563–2179 www.lhi.golf Closed Mon.–Thurs.*

Pinetrees Lodge

$$$$ | ECLECTIC | For four generations Pinetrees has been opening its doors to visitors, and staff have certainly honed the art of hospitality. Pop into the lagoon-front lodge for a buffet lunch of assorted salads with the dish of the day, or drop in for dinner; the local kingfish is always a highlight. **Known for:** local institution; signature fish fry buffet; afternoon tea. *Average main: A$65 Pinetrees Lodge, Lagoon Rd., Lord Howe Island 02/262–6585 www.pinetrees.com.au.*

Coffee and Quick Bites

Coral Cafe

$ | AUSTRALIAN | Located at the Lord Howe Island Museum and Visitor's Centre, this is a popular café with those exploring Lord Howe's history. There's traditional bacon and eggs for breakfast and light salads for lunch. **Known for:** convenient location; cheap eats; friendly staff. *Average main: A$10 Lord Howe Island Museum and Visitor's Centre, Lagoon Rd. and Middle Beach Rd., Lord Howe Island 02/6563–2488.*

Hotels

★ Arajilla Lord Howe Island

$$$$ | RESORT | One of the most luxurious accommodations on Lord Howe, Arajilla Retreat contains 10 spacious suites and two two-bedroom suites. **Pros:** rates include all meals, minibar, and predinner drinks; exclusive and secluded; free bike use. **Cons:** interiors might not be to everyone's taste; expensive. *Rooms from: A$700 Old Settlement Beach, Lagoon Rd., Lord Howe Island 02/6563–2002 www.arajilla.com.au 12 suites All-Inclusive.*

Capella Lodge

$$$$ | B&B/INN | In the shadow of Mt. Gower, Capella Lodge is Lord Howe Island's most posh lodging. **Pros:** pure luxury; great location; rates include breakfast, dinner, and drinks; fantastic views. **Cons:** some rooms small; steep rates; isolated. *Rooms from: A$750 Lagoon Rd., Lord Howe Island 02/9918–4355 www.capellalodge.com.au 9 suites Free Breakfast.*

Ocean View Apartments

$$ | HOTEL | If you want to get the low-down on Lord Howe Island history, take a room at this apartment complex owned and operated by fifth- and sixth-generation descendants of the island's original settlers, T. B. and Mary Wilson. **Pros:** great location with easy walk into town;

Did You Know?

Masked boobies, brown noddies, providence petrels, red-tailed topic birds, and sooty terns will be more than just the cute names of feathered friends after a few days on LHI (as the locals call Lord Howe Island). The skies are full of birds gliding and swooping on the warm currents, while at ground level Lord Howe wood hens will be picking at your feet. It's a bird-lover's paradise.

kitchenettes; saltwater swimming pool. **Cons:** dated furnishings; basic facilities; noisy rooms. *Rooms from: A$180* ✉ *Ocean View Dr., Old Settlement Beach, Lord Howe Island* ☎ *02/6563–2041* 🌐 *oceanviewlordhoweisland.com.au* *16 apartments* *No Meals.*

Pinetrees Lodge

$$$$ | **HOTEL** | Right on Lagoon Beach and a short walk from the popular bowling club, the Pinetrees Lodge has a terrific location and is the largest accommodation on Lord Howe Island—with motel rooms, suites, and garden cottages. **Pros:** great amenities; excellent location; good five-night packages available online. **Cons:** can be noisy with families in peak times; no key to rooms; can feel a bit like living in other guests' pockets. *Rooms from: A$790* ✉ *Lagoon Rd., Lord Howe Island* ☎ *02/9262–6585* 🌐 *www.pinetrees.com.au* *34 rooms, 4 suites* *All-Inclusive.*

BIRD-WATCHING

Lord Howe Island Birdwatching

BIRD WATCHING | Lord Howe Island is home to 14 species of seabirds, which breed there in the hundreds and swoop and dive over the two bulbous peaks, Mt. Gower and Mt. Lidgbird. A good viewing spot that's also easier to climb are the Malabar cliffs, on the northeast corner of the island. Here from September to May, you'll see red-tailed tropic birds performing their courting rituals. This is also the time that shearwaters (also known as mutton birds) return to the island daily at dusk, making for an extraordinary avian spectacle. One of the rarest birds, the providence petrel, returns to the island to nest in winter (June to August), while sooty terns are also a regular sight at Ned's Beach and the Northern Hills between September and January. The island also hosts more than 130 species of permanent and migratory birds, such as the flightless Lord Howe Island wood hen. Author and naturalist **Ian Hutton** (*lordhoweisland.info/experiences/bird-watching*) conducts nature tours and seabird cruises. ✉ *Lord Howe Island*

DIVING AND SNORKELING

Lord Howe Island Marine Park

DIVING & SNORKELING | UNESCO World Heritage lists Lord Howe Island's beautiful lagoon, which is sheltered by the world's southernmost coral reef, stretching for some 6 km (4 miles) along the western coast. Contained within Lord Howe Island Marine Park, the lagoon harbors some 500 species of fish and 90 species of coral. There are several ways to explore the lagoon and the coral-filled beaches of the eastern coast, which are only about 3 km (2 miles)—by glass-bottom boat, snorkeling, or scuba diving. Ned's Beach, the site of the island's fish-frenzy, is perfect for snorkelers. Another great spot is the wreck of the ship *The Favourite*, at North Bay, the lagoon's northernmost point. Divers have more than 50 sites to choose from, ranging from shallow resort dives near the beach, to spectacular trenches, caves, and volcanic drop-offs. Experienced divers love the waters around Ball's Pyramid, which abound with kingfish and Galapagos sharks up to 14 feet long. **TIP→ If you don't bring your own snorkeling gear, you can rent it from local resorts.** ✉ *Lord Howe Island Visitor Center, Middle Rd. at Lagoon Rd., Lord Howe Island* ☎ *02/6563–2114* 🌐 *www.lordhoweisland.info.*

FISHING

Fishing at Ball's Pyramid

FISHING | Towering some 1,800 feet above the ocean, Ball's Pyramid is a unique rock stack and one of the world's tallest monoliths in water. Located 23 km (14 miles) south of Lord Howe Island, it's part of the pristine Lord Howe Island Marine Park, in which commercial fishing is banned and huge species of fish abound, making it a top destination for sportfishing. The boat trip to Ball's Pyramid takes 75 minutes and is a perfect way to soak up stunning views back toward the island before you start reeling in the catch. Several dedicated fishing charter operators, including Blue Billie (a fifth-generation family of fishermen), run tours to the pyramid, offering half- and full-day expeditions with rates starting from around A$200 per person. ✉ *Lord Howe Island Marine Park, Lord Howe Island* 🌐 *www.lordhoweisland.info.*

HIKING

★ Mt. Gower

HIKING & WALKING | The larger of the two volcanic peaks located at the southern end of Lord Howe Island, Mt. Gower rises 2,870 feet above sea level. The hike to the summit is arduous and can only be undertaken with a guide. Covering a distance of about 14 km (9 miles) round-trip and taking about 8½ hours to complete, it's a wonderful experience and affords sensational views across the island, the reef, and out to Ball's Pyramid, 23 km (14 miles) away. Along the way, guides point out rare plants and birdlife. Fifth-generation islander Jack Shick, of Lord Howe Island Tours, is a highly experienced guide and takes tours twice a week (Monday and Thursday); the cost is about A$110 per person. ✉ *Lord Howe Island* ☎ *02/6563–2260 Jack Shick* 🌐 *www.lordhoweislandtours.net* 🎫 *A$110.*

Berry

142 km (88 miles) south from Sydney.

For the past decade, Sydneysiders have decamped to Berry for a weekend away from the city. There's something incredibly relaxing about this small country village, surrounded by countryside and a short distance from the ocean. And while it might be small in size, with only 2,600 locals calling this spot home, it sure packs a punch, with award-winning restaurants, boutique shops, and stunning walking tracks. There's also an abundance of antiques shops that line the main high street. It's the perfect one-night pit stop before winding further down the South Coast.

GETTING HERE AND AROUND

To get to Berry, the only viable way is to drive. There's no train service and the bus from Sydney has many changes and is an arduous task that's not really time- or cost-effective. Once there, the village itself is easy to navigate on foot, running just a short 1 km (½ mile) in length.

Sights

Berry Museum

NOTABLE BUILDING | FAMILY | This cute little museum features an extensive collection of artifacts, memorabilia, photographs, and records donated by the local community to provide a great introduction to Berry's local history and its agricultural roots. Kids love the "Please Do Touch" room. ✉ *135 Queen St., Berry* ☎ *02/4464–3097* 🌐 *www.berryhistory.org.au.*

Boat Harbour Rock Pool

HOT SPRING | FAMILY | In the hotter months, locals all head out to this lesser-known swimming spot in Gerringong, found on the coast, to cool down. It's about 1 km (½ mile) from the main high street that runs through Berry. Just follow the directions to Gerringong and you'll soon find the boat ramp that runs close to the pool. It's a small pool that once lived its life as a local swim spot for women only. But today, anyone is welcome and it's an especially great spot for young children. There's no charge but also no facilities. Best time to go is at high tide as it can get a little shallow during low tide. ✉ *Gerringong, Berry.*

Restaurants

Silos Estate

$$ | AUSTRALIAN | This swank estate ticks all the boxes. The restaurant offers farm-style fare in a rustic environment, with share plates, like the overflowing charcuterie. **Known for:** must-visit cellar door; casual dining and share plates; hit with arty types. *Average main: A$35* *B640 Princes Hwy., Berry* *02/4448–6082* *www.silosestate.com* *No dinner.*

SOUTH on albany

$$ | **AUSTRALIAN** | This casual but elegant restaurant is always busy and that's truly down to the menu being packed with seasonal and local fare. Each dish is a taste sensation but arrives looking so pretty that you'll want to stare in awe for a while. **Known for:** incredible desserts; trendy; busy, so prebook. *Average main: A$30* *3/65 Queen St.* *02/4464–2005* *southonalbany.com.au* *No dinner Sun.-Tues. No lunch (except two Sundays per month).*

Coffee and Quick Bites

★ The Famous Berry Donut Van

$ | **AUSTRALIAN** | For almost 60 years, The Famous Berry Donut Van has been just that, a famous must-visit spot for those visiting Berry. The quality of their cinnamon doughnuts is unrivaled. **Known for:** local institution; cinnamon doughnuts; made-to-order doughnuts. *Average main: A$5* *73 Queen St.* *02/4464–1968* *Berry.*

Hotels

Raintree B&B

$$$$ | **B&B/INN** | Nestled in the rain forest just south of Berry, the outstanding Raintree is a secluded retreat that fully immerses guests in nature. **Pros:** spacious guest rooms; luxurious retreat; peaceful nature setting. **Cons:** out of town; incredibly quiet; hot breakfast is extra. *Rooms from: A$620* *160 Red Cedar La.* *04/3824–1150* *www.raintreebnb.com.au* *No Meals* *8 rooms.*

Jervis Bay

197 km (122 miles) from Sydney.

Jervis Bay is the name of both the oceanic bay and the village that surrounds it, and it is the unrivaled white-sand oasis of the South Coast, found in the Shaolhaven region about four hours south of Sydney and an hour south of Berry. The bay is nine times bigger than Sydney Harbour and is, in fact, the deepest bay in Australia. Here you'll find 22 km (14 miles) of the most pristine white-sand beaches the country has to offer.

GETTING HERE AND AROUND

Jervis Bay is a comfortable four-hour drive from Sydney, winding through the many small country towns along the way. The views over Kiama, about halfway down the coast, is a true breathtaking moment. The easiest way to adventure through the South Coast is by car. There's no train service and there's no direct bus service.

VISITOR INFORMATION

CONTACTS Visitor Information. *Dent St. at Woollamia Rd.* *02/4441–5999.*

Sights

★ Booderee National Park

NATIONAL PARK | Booderee is the Aboriginal word meaning "bay of plenty" and there really is plenty to see and do at this incredibly beautiful national park, located at the southernmost part of Jervis Bay. Camping sites are available throughout the park. Cave Beach has on-site showers and a small walk down to a vast beach that's a safe spot for swimming. Green Patch Beach is a good location for snorkelers with its bounty of interesting fish on its tranquil shores. The historic Cape St George Lighthouse is the perfect location for whale- and bird-watching. *Jervis Bay Rd.* *02/4443–0977* *parksaustralia.gov.au/booderee.*

Point Perpendicular Lighthouse

VIEWPOINT | FAMILY | This modest white lighthouse may be decommissioned but its scenic approach, winding through natural scrub and a spattering of colorful wildflowers, and unrivalled views and whale-watching on Jervis Bay make it a must visit if you are nearby. Built in 1898 with a concrete-block construction that was a first at the time, Point Perpendicular Lighthouse was a working lighthouse until 1993. The best time to visit is at sunrise when the skies swirl with purples and pinks. You'll often see dolphins playing in the waters below the dramatic cliff's edge. ✉ *Lighthouse Rd., Beecroft Peninsula, Lot 51.*

Beaches

Chinamans Beach

BEACH | Just north of Hyams Beach, this smaller beach has the same enviable white sands and incredible clear waters minus the crowds. During high season, it's worth heading to this quieter spot to enjoy all that Jervis Bay has to offer. The water is safe for swimming and the coastal path that runs along it takes you to Greenfield Beach. **Amenities:** toilets. **Best for:** swimming; water sports. ✉ *Aster St.*

Greenfield Beach

BEACH | Set in Jervis Bay National Park, Greenfield Beach offers powdery white sands, access to walking trails, and an abundance of wildlife including kangaroos and wallabies, and it's a safe swimming spot, even for those with little experience in the sea. **Amenities:** showers; toilets. **Best for:** swimming. ✉ *Cyrus St.*

★ Hyams Beach

BEACH | FAMILY | Of the 22 km (14 miles) of beautiful beaches that Jervis Bay has to offer, Hyams Beach is the most famous. The white sands are apparently the whitest in the world (per Guinness World Records), and while such hype can often lead to disappointment, this beach lives up to expectations. The sands are magnificently white, the waters are crystal clear turquoise, and the combination is paradise found. In the summer months, it can get a little busy here but nothing like the Sydney beaches. In the spring and autumn months, there's a little more room to breathe. **Amenities:** showers; toilets; food and drink. **Best for:** swimming; water sports. ✉ *Cyrus St.*

Restaurants

★ Gunyah

$$$$ | AUSTRIAN | Set in the remarkable Paperbark Camp glamping spot filled with high-end tree houses that are available for two-night minimum stays on the weekend, this restaurant is a romantic and warmly lit tree house for grown-ups. The menu is a set, three-course affair (A$80) featuring meats in the autumn months and light zesty fish and seafood in the summer. **Known for:** very romantic; great for a special occasion; advance reservations. $ *Average main: A$70* ✉ *Paperbark Camp, 571 Woollamia Rd.* ☎ *02/4441–7299* 🌐 *www.paperbarkcamp.com.au.*

Hyams Beach Store and Cafe

$ | AUSTRALIAN | Manned by a dog named Albert, and frequented by locals who declare it serves the best burger in town, this beach-vibe café has exactly what's needed after a full day of activities in Jervis Bay. This is a casual eats spot, for a great breakfast or lunch. **Known for:** delightful desserts; hearty, unfussy meals; meat-heavy menu. $ *Average main: A$20* ✉ *Hyams Beach, 76 Cyrus St.* ☎ *02/4443–3874* 🌐 *www.hyamsbeachcafe.com.au.*

Wildginger

$$$ | THAI | The chef here cut his teeth at one of Sydney's top Thai restaurants so it's no surprise that this Thai-inspired, Asian-fusion restaurant is one of the most popular spots in the area. The banquet option is very popular, allowing you to try a mix of the many dishes available here. **Known for:** three-hour braised beef cheeks in southern-style green curry; seafood specialties; banquet tasting menu. $ *Average main: A$40* ✉ *42 Owen St.* ☎ *02/4441–5577* 🌐 *www.wild-ginger.com.au.*

Hotels

★ Hyams Beach Seaside Cottages
$$$ | **B&B/INN** | Built in the 1920s by a group of fisherman who wanted to be close to the water, these pint-size, one-bedroom cottages painted in baby blue, pink, and yellow will appeal to tiny-home fans. **Pros:** unique experience; beachfront location; amazing views. **Cons:** no breakfast; book out fast; can feel a little small. $ *Rooms from: A$295* ✉ *55/53 Cyrus St.* ☎ *02/4411–7000* 🌐 *www.hyamsbeachseasidecottages.com.au* 🍽 *No Meals* *7 cottages.*

Jervis Bay Holiday Park
$$ | **RESORT** | The name might suggest a caravan park, but don't be fooled: Jervis Bay has fantastically finished villas along the waterfront, with a balcony and patio with either pool views or river views. **Pros:** waterfront views; lots of amenities; great for families. **Cons:** not on the beach; can be noisy; a short drive into Jervis. $ *Rooms from: A$180* ✉ *785 Woollamia Rd.* ☎ *02/4441–5046* 🌐 *jervisbayholidaypark.com.au* *12 rooms* 🍽 *No Meals.*

Activities

Jervis Bay Stand Up Paddle
CANOEING & ROWING | Jervis Bay is the perfect place to go paddleboarding, and for beginners, there's a daily stand-up class with tour (reservations are essential). ✉ *1/2 Erina Rd.* ☎ *0403/354–716* 🌐 *www.jervisbaystanduppaddle.com.au.*

Sea Kayak Jervis Bay
CANOEING & ROWING | Guide Tracy Gibson has plenty of funny tales to tell about the area in between helpful guidance to get more power from your paddle. ✉ *2/3 Snapper Rd.* ☎ *0418/649–082* 🌐 *www.seakayakjervisbay.com.*

Chapter 5

MELBOURNE

Updated by
Belinda Jackson

Sights ★★★★★ | Restaurants ★★★★★ | Hotels ★★★★☆ | Shopping ★★★★☆ | Nightlife ★★★★★

WELCOME TO MELBOURNE

TOP REASONS TO GO

★ **Fabulous Markets:** Melbourne has nearly a dozen major markets including the huge Queen Victoria Market, with more than 600 stalls.

★ **International Cuisine:** The country's most cosmopolitan city boasts a feted smorgasbord of cuisines, its own, freewheeling contemporary Australian cuisine, and a rising awareness of native Australian ingredients.

★ **Sizzling Nightlife:** Discover the city center's late-night cocktail bars and dining scene. Melbourne's famous live music scene is found in the historic pubs and buzzing clubs of Fitzroy, Collingwood, St. Kilda, and Brunswick.

★ **Sports Galore:** The Melbourne Cup horse race in November brings the entire city to a standstill. The same is true of Australian Rules football.

★ **Arts and Culture:** Renowned for its rich, lively arts scene, performances range from small, experimental theater productions to international comedy, fashion, literary, and theater festivals.

The Yarra River cuts through the city center; the main business district is on the northern side, and the southern side has arts, entertainment, and restaurant precincts. Several exclusive suburbs hug the southeastern shore of the bay. The Yarra Valley wineries and the Dandenong Ranges are an hour's drive to the east. The beaches and vineyards of the Mornington Peninsula are a 90-minute drive south.

1 **City Center.** The place to be for arts, funky back alleys, shopping, street art, and Australia's best food. Explore the laneways for top restaurants and tiny bars, the arts precinct around the National Gallery of Victoria, and the King's Domain gardens.

2 **Richmond.** Heaven for foodies. Come here for a Vietnamese soup kitchen, a Korean barbecue, a Laotian banquet, or a Thai hole-in-the-wall.

3 **East Melbourne.** The harmonious streetscapes in this historic enclave of Victorian houses, which date from the boom following the gold rushes of the 1850s, are a great excuse for a stroll.

4 **South Melbourne.** This leafy, charming suburb is home to South Melbourne Market and a thriving café scene.

5 **St. Kilda.** Dozens of alfresco restaurants overflow into the streets, and the cafés and bars are buzzing with young fashionistas.

6 **Fitzroy.** Come here if you're looking for an Afghan camel bag, a secondhand paperback, or live music and a craft beer in a backstreet beer garden.

7 **Brunswick.** Melbourne's eclectic and multicultural heart with Mediterranean and Middle Eastern markets, craft coffee shops, and a lively nightlife scene.

8 **Carlton.** Known for its beautiful old town houses, authentic Italian food, and proximity to the city center, this lively suburb is also home to Carlton Garden, which houses the modern Melbourne Museum.

9 **South Yarra and Prahran.** Two neighboring suburbs, both are crammed with upmarket bars, cafés, and great shopping.

10 **Brighton.** Colorful bathing boxes and a pretty beach and town are the draw here.

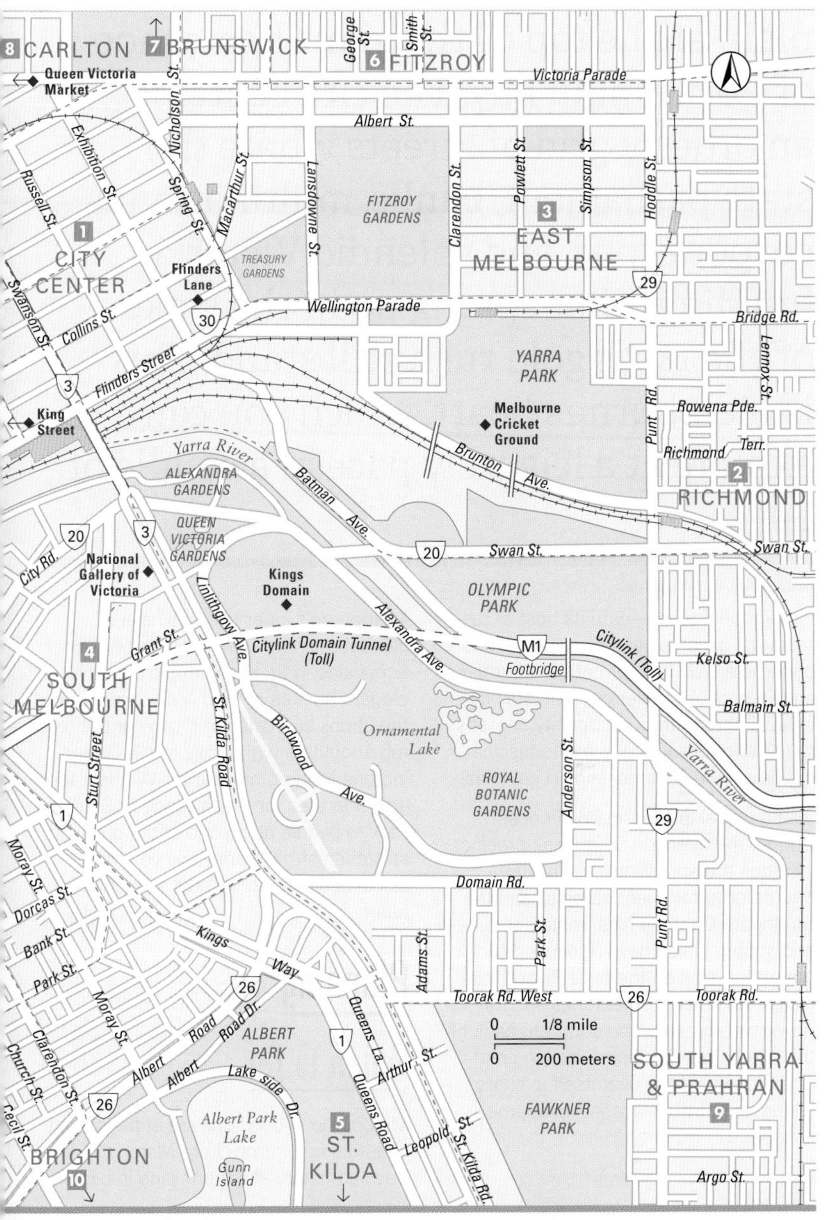
8 CARLTON
7 BRUNSWICK
6 FITZROY
Queen Victoria Market
George St.
Smith St.
Victoria Parade
Albert St.
Exhibition St.
Nicholson St.
Russell St.
Spring St.
Macarthur St.
Lansdowne St.
FITZROY GARDENS
Clarendon St.
Powlett St.
Simpson St.
Hoddle St.
1 CITY CENTER
3 EAST MELBOURNE
TREASURY GARDENS
Flinders Lane
Swanson St.
Collins St.
30
29
Wellington Parade
Bridge Rd.
Lennox St.
YARRA PARK
Flinders Street
3
King Street
Melbourne Cricket Ground
Punt Rd.
Rowena Pde.
Richmond Terr.
Brunton Ave.
Yarra River
Batman Ave.
ALEXANDRA GARDENS
2 RICHMOND
QUEEN VICTORIA GARDENS
20
City Rd.
National Gallery of Victoria
Kings Domain
Swan St.
OLYMPIC PARK
Linlithgow Ave.
Alexandra Ave.
4 SOUTH MELBOURNE
Grant St.
Citylink Domain Tunnel (Toll)
M1
Footbridge
Citylink (Toll)
Kelso St.
Balmain St.
St. Kilda Road
Birdwood Ave.
Ornamental Lake
ROYAL BOTANIC GARDENS
Anderson St.
Sturt Street
1
Moray St.
Dorcas St.
Bank St.
Park St.
Domain Rd.
Kings Way
Adams St.
Park St.
Punt Rd.
26
Toorak Rd. West
Toorak Rd.
0 1/8 mile
0 200 meters
Clarendon St.
Church St.
Cecil St.
Albert Road
Albert Road Dr.
ALBERT PARK
Queens La.
Arthur St.
Lake side Dr.
Queens Road
SOUTH YARRA & PRAHRAN
FAWKNER PARK
9
Albert Park Lake
Gunn Island
5 ST. KILDA
Leopold St.
St. Kilda Rd.
Argo St.
BRIGHTON
10

Consistently rated among the "world's most liveable cities" in quality-of-life surveys, Melbourne is built on a coastal plain at the top of the giant horseshoe of Port Phillip Bay. The city center is an orderly grid of streets where the state parliament, banks, multinational corporations, and splendid Victorian buildings that sprang up in the wake of the 1850s gold rush still stand. This is Melbourne's heart, which you can explore at a leisurely pace in a couple of days.

Federation Square—with its host of restaurants, galleries, and museums—has become a civic hub for both Melburnians and visitors. A subtler city icon, its "laneways" thread through the city center's major streets and are home to fascinating bars, cafés, shops, and art galleries.

Just a hop-skip over nearby Princes Bridge, the riverside Southbank precinct includes the sprawling Crown Melbourne entertainment complex and the Southgate Centre's bars, restaurants, and shops, which have refocused Melbourne's vision on the Yarra River. Once a blighted stretch of factories and rundown warehouses, the southern bank of the river is now a vibrant, exciting part of the city, and the river itself is finally taking its rightful place in Melbourne's psyche.

Melbourne's inner suburbs have a character all their own. Stroll along the Esplanade in St. Kilda, amble past the elegant houses of East Melbourne, enjoy the shops and cafés of Fitzroy or Carlton, rub shoulders with locals at the Queen Victoria Market, nip into the Windsor for afternoon tea, or rent a canoe at Studley Park to paddle along one of the prettiest stretches of the Yarra—and you may discover Melbourne's soul as well as its heart.

Planning

When to Go

Melbourne and Victoria are at their most beautiful in autumn, from March to May. Days are crisp, and the foliage in parks and gardens is glorious. Melbourne winters can be gloomy, although the wild seas and leaden skies from June to August provide a suitable backdrop for the dramatic coastal scenery of the Great Ocean Road. By September the weather begins to clear, and the football finals are on. Book early to visit Melbourne during the Spring Racing Carnival and the Melbourne International Arts Festival (late October/early November) and during mid-January when the Australian Open tennis tournament is staged.

Planning Your Time

The free, maroon City Circle Tram (No. 35) is an easy hop-on/hop-off way to see many of the city's sights in a short time without exhausting yourself. The Parliament House tram stop goes to the Princess Theatre, the grand Windsor Hotel, Parliament House, the "Paris End" of Collins Street, and St. Patrick's Cathedral. Get off at Flinders Street to take a peek at the infamous *Chloe* painting in Young and Jackson's pub, and then continue over the Yarra via the Princes Bridge to the Royal Botanic Gardens to the Shrine of Remembrance. There, you can stroll the banks of the Yarra, looking back at Federation Square, before checking out the riverside restaurants, shops, and the casino in the Southbank precinct. A trip to the Eureka Skydeck, the southern hemisphere's highest viewing platform, puts the city into perspective.

On your second day, see why Melbourne's street art has so many fans, with a stroll through the laneways that splinter off Flinders Lane—Hosier Lane is the most famous. Recharge on Melbourne's famed coffee in one of hundreds of hole-in-the-wall cafés, before choosing dinner in this lane full of renowned choices. Afterward, take a tram along St. Kilda Road to the hip Acland Street area, in the seaside suburb of St. Kilda, for dinner.

On Day 3, put the walking shoes on—or hop on and off the No. 78 tram—for a long wander down Chapel Street for its markets, restaurants, cafés, and bars. On the way back to the city, you might squeeze in a bit more exploring at the Treasury Gardens and Captain Cook's Cottage in the adjoining Fitzroy Gardens, or meet the sharks at the Melbourne Aquarium, opposite Southbank, or head northeast to Fitzroy for an amble along groovy Brunswick Street, or north to Carlton to immerse yourself in Little Italy.

If you have additional time, head east to the Yarra Valley for an organized winery tour or ride on the Puffing Billy steam train, which leaves from Belgrave and travels through the fern gullies and forests of the Dandenong Ranges. On the way back, stop at a teahouse in Belgrave or Olinda and browse the curio stores. If possible, take an evening excursion to Phillip Island for the endearing Penguin Parade at sunset. Just 90 minutes from the city center, a trip to Melbourne's playground—the beaches and wineries of the Mornington Peninsula—is another great day out.

Getting Here and Around

Melbourne is most easily reached by plane, as it's hours by car from the nearest big city. International airlines flying into Melbourne include Air New Zealand, United, Singapore Airlines, Emirates, Etihad, Thai Airways, Malaysia Airlines, Virgin Australia, and Qantas.

TIP→ Make sure to check which airport your flight arrives into, as Avalon is a 40-minute drive southwest of the city but Tullamarine is much closer.

BUS AND TRAM

To use public transportation in Melbourne, you need a ticket called a Myki (a stored-value smart card). It can be purchased (A$6 for the card itself) at 7-Eleven stores, train stations, vending machines at major tram stops, and the Melbourne Visitors Hub at Town Hall. Each time you enter a train station, or hop on a tram or bus, you must touch the Myki card to a validator. The standard two-hour fare of A$4.50 is activated the first time you touch on, and you can change between any bus, tram, or train during this period. Daily travel is capped at two, two-hour fares (A$9), at which point you can travel as much as you like without extra charge. Trams run until midnight (1 am on Friday and Saturday) and can be hailed wherever you see a green-and-white tram-stop sign.

TIP→ All tram journeys are free in the Free Tram Zone, from Queen Victoria Market to Docklands, Spring Street, Flinders Street Station, and Federation Square, in the city center.

CAR

Melbourne's regimented layout makes it easy to negotiate by car, but two unusual rules apply because of the tram traffic. At intersections in the city center, trams should be passed by swinging to the far left before turning right (known as the "hook turn"); and when a tram stops to allow passengers to disembark across a roadway to the curb, the cars behind it also must stop. Motorists using various tollways have 72 hours to pay the toll after using the highway. To pay by credit card, call *133–331*. Alternatively, you can buy passes online. A weekend pass is around A$19.70. *www.linkt.com.au.*

CRUISE

Cruise ships stopping in Melbourne dock in Port Melbourne at Station Pier. Tour buses, taxis, and a shuttle bus can collect visitors, and the stop for the city-bound Tram 109 is just beyond the start of the pier. The area around Station Pier has numerous restaurants and attractive water views. The lively entertainment and dining hub of St. Kilda is a pleasant 5-km (3-mile) walk southeast from here, alongside attractive bay beaches.

TRAIN

The main entrance to Southern Cross Railway Station is at Spencer and Little Collins Streets. From here the statewide V/Line rail company sells tickets for 11-hour rail trips to Sydney, as well as services to many regional centers in Victoria. V/Line buses connect with the trains to provide transport to coastal towns; take the train to Geelong to connect with a bus to Lorne, Apollo Bay, and Port Campbell, or travel by train to Warrnambool and take a bus to Port Fairy.

Restaurants

Melbourne teems with top-quality restaurants, particularly in the city center, St. Kilda, South Yarra, Fitzroy, and Southbank. Lygon Street is a favorite with those who love great coffee, pasta, and Italian bakeries, Chinatown serves up top-quality dumplings and noodles and the city center also has many back alleys (known as "laneways") containing popular cafés that serve meals as well as good coffee (a Melbourne trademark)—Flinders Lane is a dining hot spot. Reservations are generally advised (though not possible for some places). Although most places are licensed to sell alcohol, the few that aren't usually allow you to bring your own. Many places serve food throughout the day, but lunch menus usually operate noon–2:30 pm, and dinner is usually served 7–10:30 pm. Tipping is not customary in Australia, but if you receive good service a 10% tip is welcome. Note there may be a corkage fee in restaurants, which allows you to bring in your own alcoholic drinks.

Hotels

Staying in the heart of Melbourne, on Collins or Flinders Streets and their nearby laneways, or at Southbank, is ideal for those who like dining and shopping. Another fashionable area close to the city center is South Yarra, which has excellent shopping. Wherever you stay, make sure you're near a tram or train line.

Restaurant and hotel reviews have been shortened. For full information, visit Fodors.com.

What It Costs in Australian Dollars

$	$$	$$$	$$$$
RESTAURANTS			
under A$21	A$21–A$35	A$36–A$50	over A$50
HOTELS			
under A$151	A$151–A$200	A$201–A$300	over A$300

Tours

The free City Circle tram operates every 12 minutes from 10 to 9 Thursday–Saturday and 10–6 Sunday–Wednesday around the edge of the Central Business District and Docklands, with stops on Flinders, La Trobe, Victoria, and Spring Streets, and Harbour Esplanade. Look for the burgundy-and-cream trams. Metropolitan buses operate daily until around 9 pm to all suburbs, while the NightRider bus service runs between 2 am and 5 am on Saturday and 2 am and 6 am on Sunday.

AAT Kings
This tour agency runs a half-day Magnificent Melbourne tour (from A$71) that explores such sights as historical locations, city gardens, and the iconic Melbourne Cricket Ground. The company also organizes longer tours outside Melbourne. ✉ *Federation Sq., Flinders St. at Russell St., City Center* ☎ *1300/228–546* 🌐 *www.aatkings.com* 🎟 *From A$71.*

Chocoholic Tours
Chocoholic Tours runs city tours for chocolate lovers every day of the week. Take the two-hour tour or go deeper on its Melbourne Lanes and Arcades Chocolate Walking Tour, which offers 10 tastings throughout the city's famous laneways. The Yarra Valley Chocolate and Winery Tour is another popular option, taking tourists on a unique journey through Victoria's produce. Private tours are also available. Bookings are essential. ✉ *Block Arcade, 282 Collins St., City Center* ☎ *13/0091–5566* 🌐 *www.chocoholic-tours.com.au* 🎟 *From A$49.*

★ **Golden Mile Heritage Walk**
Hidden Secrets Tours runs guided walks of Melbourne's Golden Mile Heritage Trail, visiting the city's architectural and historic sites. The 2½-hour tours depart daily at 10 am from the steps of St Paul's Cathedral (opposite Flinders Street Station), following the trail of glitter and grunge that the 1850s gold rush brought to the city. Other tours explore Melbourne's café culture, its lanes and arcades, and even a Progressive Degustation Walking tour, an ever-changing tasting tour into some of the city's best restaurants. ✉ *Flinders St. and Swanston St., Melbourne* ☎ *03/9663–3358* 🌐 *www.hiddensecretstours.com* 🎟 *From A$59.*

Gray Line
Explore Melbourne and its environs on Gray Line's guided bus and boat tours. The Melbourne Morning City Tour visits the city center's main attractions including Chinatown and the ornate Victorian architecture, and also its parks and the Queen Victoria Markets. The four-hour tour departs daily from locations around the city. ✉ *City Center* ☎ *1300/858–687* 🌐 *www.grayline.com.au* 🎟 *From A$71.*

Localing Tours
Spend a day getting under Melbourne's skin with a private tour of the city, led by a Melburnian. Street art, coffee, football, fashion, architecture, and food are all on the list of topics covered, but are customized to the guests' interest. A day tour includes coffee, tastings, transport. ✉ *City Center* ☎ *03/9088–8001* 🌐 *www.localingtours.com* 🎟 *A$1020 for 2 guests.*

Melbourne River Cruises
One of the best ways to see Melbourne is from the deck of a boat on the Yarra River. Melbourne River Cruises' fleet of modern, glass-enclosed boats operate one- and two-hour Yarra River cruises daily (A$27 and A$45, respectively), traversing either west through the commercial heart of the city or east through the parks and gardens, or a combination of the two. Cruises run roughly every hour from 11 to 3, depending on weather and tide conditions. Tours depart from Southbank Promenade Berth 2. ✉ *Berth 2, Southbank Promenade, City Center* ☎ *03/8610–2600* 🌐 *www.melbcruises.com.au* 🎫 *From A$27.*

Visitor Information

The Melbourne Visitor Hub at Town Hall is set in the city's center, and offers local knowledge about Melbourne and regional Victoria. It can offer customized itineraries, free walking maps, guides, and brochures.

The Melbourne Visitor Booth in the Bourke Street Mall provides free information on where to shop, eat, and experience in Melbourne. It can supply free walking and public transport maps. Large-screen videos and touch screens add to the experience. The booth is open daily from 10 am–4 pm.

City Ambassadors can be identified by their bright red uniforms, and can provide directions, information to events and answer public transport inquiries. They are found across the city center and in Federation Square.

If you can't make it into a visitor center, you can book a free 20 minute consultation by phone, or online platforms, weekdays from 10:30 am to 3:30 pm. *(03) 9658–9658.*

CONTACTS

City of Melbourne Ambassadors Program
City Ambassadors—usually mature men and women easily spotted by their red uniforms—are volunteers for the City of Melbourne and rove the central retail area providing directions and information for people needing their assistance (Monday–Saturday 10–4, Sunday 11:30–3). ✉ *90–130 Swanston St. at Little Collins St., City Center* ☎ *03/9658–9658.*

Melbourne Visitor Hub
Find information and booking services at the information center, open daily 9–6. ✉ *Town Hall, Little Collins St. at Swanston St., City Center* ☎ *03/9658–9658* 🌐 *www.visitmelbourne.com.*

City Center

The City Center (CBD) is designed in a grid formation, with myriad alleyways twisting between them, often containing restaurants, galleries, and bars. The CBD is bounded by Spring Street in the east, Victoria Street to the north, Flinders Street to the south, and Spencer Street to the west. Federation Square, opposite the Flinders Street Station, is considered the CBD's heart and is an ideal starting point. The most popular shopping areas are the elegant eastern end of Collins Street and the busy pedestrian mall of Bourke Street. Spring Street holds many of the city's historic buildings from the mid-1800s.

GETTING HERE AND AROUND

Melbourne and its suburbs are well served by trams, trains, and buses. All trams in the CBD are free, and the City Circle tram, with its commentary, is perfect for sightseeing. Trams run east–west and north–south across the city, and travel to the popular St. Kilda and Docklands. The Metro train network operates a City Loop service with stops at Flinders Street, Parliament, Flagstaff, Melbourne Central, and Southern Cross stations, where you'll find connections with a network of trains to outer areas, including the Dandenong Ranges.

★ Arts Centre Melbourne

ARTS CENTER | Melbourne's most important cultural landmark is the venue for performances by the Australian Ballet, Opera Australia, Melbourne Theatre Company, and Melbourne Symphony Orchestra. It encompasses Hamer Hall, the Arts Centre complex, the original National Gallery of Victoria, and the outdoor Sidney Myer Music Bowl. Take a 60-minute tour of the five floors of the complex, plus the current gallery exhibition and refreshment at the café, or its longer Sunday backstage tour. Neither tour is suitable for children under 12 and both must be booked in advance. At night, look for the center's spire, which creates a magical spectacle with brilliant fiber-optic cables. ✉ *100 St. Kilda Rd., City Center* ☎ *03/9281–8000, 1300/182–183 bookings* 🌐 *www.artscentremelbourne.com.au.*

★ Block Arcade

STORE/MALL | Melbourne's most elegant 19th-century shopping arcade dates from the 1880s, when "Marvelous Melbourne" was flush with the prosperity of the gold rushes. A century later, renovations scraped back the grime to reveal a magnificent mosaic floor. Take a guided walking tour back to the Block's origins, back in 1892; reservations are essential. ✉ *282 Collins St., City Center* ☎ *03/9654–5244* 🌐 *www.theblock.com.au* 🎫 *Free.*

Cooks' Cottage

Once the on-leave residence of the Pacific navigator Captain James Cook, this modest two-story home, built in 1755 by Cook senior, was transported stone by stone from Great Ayton in Yorkshire, England, and rebuilt in the lush Fitzroy Gardens in 1934. It's believed that Cook lived in the cottage between his many voyages. The interior is simple, a suitable domestic realm for a man who spent much of his life in cramped quarters aboard sailing ships. ✉ *Fitzroy Gardens, Lansdowne St. at Wellington Parade, City Center* ☎ *03/9658–7203* 🎫 *A$8* ⏲ *Closed Tues. and Wed.*

Eureka Skydeck

VIEWPOINT | Named after the goldfields uprising of 1854, the Eureka Tower (which houses the 88th-level Eureka Skydeck) is the highest public vantage point in the southern hemisphere. The funky-shape blue-glass building with an impressive gold cap is the place to get a bird's-eye view of Melbourne and overcome your fear of heights, especially on the Skydeck. An enclosed all-glass cube, known as the Edge (A$12 additional charge), projects about 10 feet out from the viewing platform—here you can stand, seemingly suspended, over the city on a clear glass floor. ✉ *7 Riverside Quay, City Center* ☎ *03/9693–8888* 🌐 *www.eurekaskydeck.com.au* 🎫 *A$25.*

Federation Square

PLAZA/SQUARE | Encompassing a whole city block, the bold, abstract-style landmark was designed to be Melbourne's official meeting place, with a variety of attractions and restaurants within it. The square incorporates the second branch of the National Gallery of Victoria (Ian Potter Centre), which exhibits Aboriginal and modern Australian art, as well as the Australian Centre for the Moving Image; the Edge amphitheater, a contemporary music and theater performance venue; and the Koorie Heritage Trust, which runs exhibitions and programs relating to Aboriginal Melbourne, and sells Victorian Aboriginal products and designs. Regular events are held in the square and along the path beside the Yarra River. Crowds often gather to watch live performances and events televised on the giant "Fed TV" in the center of the square. ✉ *Flinders St., between Swanston and Russell Sts., City Center* ☎ *03/9655–1900* 🌐 *www.fedsquare.com* 🎫 *Free.*

The picturesque Yarra River is lined with picnic spots, fishing jetties, and bike paths.

Fitzroy Gardens

CITY PARK | FAMILY | This 64-acre expanse of European trees, manicured lawns, garden beds, statuary, and sweeping walks is Melbourne's most popular central park. Among its highlights is its 90-year-old Conservatory and the Avenue of Elms, a majestic stand of 130-year-old trees, one of the few in the world that has not been devastated by Dutch elm disease. ✉ *Lansdowne St. at Wellington Parade, City Center* 🌐 *www.fitzroygardens.com* 🎫 *Free.*

Flinders Street Station

TRAIN/TRAIN STATION | Much more than just a train station, Flinders Street Station is a Melbourne icon and a popular meeting place. The term "meet me under the clocks" is widely used, indicating the timepieces on the front of this grand Edwardian hub of Melbourne's suburban rail network. When it was proposed to replace them with television screens, an uproar ensued. Today there are both clocks and screens. ✉ *Flinders St. and St. Kilda Rd., City Center.*

★ Hosier Lane Street Art

STREET | Melbourne's best-known laneway for its vibrant street art scene, Hosier Lane is easily accessible off Flinders Lane, and may whet your appetite for further exploration. The ever-changing nature of the art means you can wander at will, or join a walking tour. With tours run by street artists, Blender Studios also conducts walks past the large-scale murals of Fitzroy, and even runs street art workshops for adults and kids. ✉ *Hosier La., City Center* 🌐 *melbournestreettours.rezdy.com* 🎫 *From A$69, 3-hr tour.*

★ Ian Potter Centre: NGV Australia

ART GALLERY | The Aboriginal and modern Australian art collection of the National Gallery of Victoria hangs on the walls of this gallery in Fed Square. Key pieces include pioneering Indigenous artist Emily Kam Kngwarray's vast work, Anwerlarr Anganenty (Big Yam Dreaming) 1995, as well as paintings from the famous Heidelberg school, such as Frederick McCubbin's *Lost* and Tom Roberts's *Shearing the Rams*. Other displays include textiles, sculpture, and photography. A gallery highlight is the Indigenous collection, which changes every six months and includes both traditional and contemporary art. ✉ *The Atrium, Federation Sq., Flinders St. at Russell St., City Center* ☎ *03/8620–2222* 🌐 *www.ngv.vic.gov.au* 🎫 *Free; special exhibitions have varying ticket prices.*

National Gallery of Victoria

ART MUSEUM | This massive, moat-encircled, bluestone-and-concrete edifice houses works from renowned international painters including Picasso, Renoir, and Van Gogh. Its Winter Masterpieces series of international blockbuster exhibitions require tickets. In the Great Hall, it's considered perfectly reasonable to stretch out on the floor in order to properly appreciate the world's largest stained-glass ceiling, by Leonard French. A second campus of the NGV, in nearby Federation Square, exhibits Australian art only. ✉ *180 St. Kilda Rd., City Center* ☎ *03/8620–0222* 🌐 *www.ngv.vic.gov.au* 🎫 *Free; special exhibitions have varying ticket prices.*

Old Melbourne Gaol

JAIL/PRISON | This bluestone building, the city's first jail, is now a museum that has three tiers of cells with catwalks around the upper levels and is rumored to be haunted. Its most famous inmate was the notorious bushranger Ned Kelly, who was hanged here in 1880. The Hangman's night tours (reservations essential) are a popular, if macabre, facet of Melbourne nightlife. ✉ *Russell St., between LaTrobe and Victoria Sts., City Center* ☎ *03/9656–9889* 🌐 *www.oldmelbournegaol.com.au* 🎫 *From A$30* 🕓 *Closed Mon. and Tues.*

Royal Arcade

PUBLIC ART | Opened in 1870, this is the country's oldest shopping arcade, and despite alterations it retains an airy, graceful elegance that often transfixes passersby. Browse beautiful curios, diamonds, or magic spells in its ornate shops. At the heart of the arcade, the statues of mythical monsters Gog and Magog toll the hour on either side of Gaunt's Clock. ✉ *335 Bourke St., City Center* ☎ *04/3889–1212* 🌐 *www.royalarcade.com.au.*

SEA LIFE Melbourne Aquarium

AQUARIUM | **FAMILY** | Become part of the action as you stroll through a transparent tunnel surrounded by water and the denizens of the deep on the prowl. Or press your nose to the glass in the Antarctica exhibition and watch king and gentoo penguins waddling around on ice and darting through water. You can also don snow gear and sit among the penguins. If you're feeling brave, do a shark dive—they're held twice daily, include scuba equipment, and are led by an instructor. No diving experience is required. The aquamarine building illuminates a previously dismal section of Yarra River bank, opposite Crown Casino. ✉ *Flinders St. at King St., City Center* 🌐 *www.visitsealife.com* 🎫 *Entry A$37; shark dives A$319; Penguin Passport A$159.*

Southgate

PROMENADE | On the river's edge next to the Arts Centre, Southgate is a prime spot for lingering—designer shops, celebrity chefs' restaurants, bars, and casual eating places help locals and visitors while away the hours. The promenade links with the forecourt of Crown Casino and its hotels. ✉ *Southbank Blvd., City Center* ☎ *03/9960–8100* 🌐 *www.southgatemelbourne.com.au.*

St. Patrick's Cathedral

PUBLIC ART | Construction of the Gothic Revival building began in 1858 and took 82 years to finish. A statue of the Irish patriot Daniel O'Connell stands in the courtyard, testament to the fact that Ireland supplied Australia with many of its early immigrants, especially during the Irish potato famine in the mid-19th century. ✉ *Cathedral Pl., City Center* ☎ *03/9662–2233* 🌐 *www.cam.org.au/cathedral.*

St. Paul's Cathedral

CHURCH | This 1892 headquarters of Melbourne's Anglican faith is one of the most important works of William Butterfield, a leader of the Gothic Revival style in England. Located opposite Flinders Street Station, the cathedral underwent a massive restoration in 2006. Outside is a statue of Matthew Flinders, the first seaman to circumnavigate Australia, between 1801 and 1803. ✉ *Flinders St. and Swanston St., City Center* ☎ *03/9653–4220* 🌐 *www.cathedral.org.au.*

State Library of Victoria

LIBRARY | On a rise behind lawns and heroic statuary, this handsome 1853 building was constructed during the gold-rush boom and houses more than 1½ million volumes as well as bushranger Ned Kelly's famous armor. Large reading areas—including the splendid domed reading room up the grand staircase—make this a comfortable place for browsing, and three galleries display works from the library's Pictures Collection. ✉ *328 Swanston St., at La Trobe St., City Center* ☎ *03/8664–7000* 🌐 *www.slv.vic.gov.au* 🎫 *Free.*

Young and Jackson Hotel

HOTEL | Pubs are not generally known for their artwork, but climb the steps to the first-floor bar of the 160-year-old hotel to see *Chloe*, a painting that has scandalized and titillated Melburnians for many decades. The larger-than-life nude, painted by Jules Joseph Lefebvre in Paris in 1875, has adorned the walls of Young and Jackson's Hotel (which now specializes in Australian craft beers) since 1909. ✉ *1 Swanston St., opposite Flinders St. Station, City Center* ☎ *03/9650–3884* 🌐 *www.youngandjacksons.com.au.*

King's Domain Gardens

This expansive stretch of parkland includes Queen Victoria Gardens, Alexandra Gardens, the Shrine of Remembrance, the Pioneer Women's Garden, the Sidney Myer Music Bowl, and the Royal Botanic Gardens. The temple-style **Shrine of Remembrance** is designed so that a beam of sunlight passes over the Stone of Remembrance in the Inner Shrine at 11 am on Remembrance Day—the 11th day of the 11th month, when in 1918 the armistice marking the end of World War I was declared.

Restaurants

Becco

$$$ | **ITALIAN** | Every city center needs a place like this, with a drop-in bar and lively dining room. At lunchtime no-time-to-dawdle business types tuck into Italian classics, while those with a sweet tooth will go weak at the knees over a decadent tiramisu. **Known for:** macchiato cocktail; great service; gnocchi osso buco. 💲 *Average main: A$39* ✉ *11–25 Crossley St., City Center* ☎ *03/9663–3000* 🌐 *www.becco.com.au* 🕒 *Closed Sun. and Mon. No lunch Sat.*

Chin Chin

$$ | **ASIAN** | Shared plates of Southeast Asian dishes form the basis of Chin Chin's popular menu. Modeled on hawker-style dining, come for early or late for lunch or dinner to avoid the rush. **Known for:** sophisticated curries; kingfish sashimi; Feed Me menu. 💲 *Average main: A$28* ✉ *125 Flinders La., City Center* ☎ *03/8663–2000* 🌐 *www.chinchin.melbourne.*

★ Farmer's Daughters

$$$$ | **AUSTRALIAN** | You'll find your place in one of the three levels at Farmer's Daughters, in the fine-dining restaurant, in the deli, or up on the rooftop—its focus is the produce drawn from the rich farmlands of Gippsland, a region the size of Switzerland, to Melbourne's east.

Share small plates in the deli or opt for the chef's selection (A$70), choose the Gippsland Getaway set menu in the restaurant (A$110), or take a cocktail made with locally sourced spirits up on the roof, for a true farm-to-plate experience. **Known for:** locally grown ingredients; excellent cocktails; offers fine dining and a more casual deli. *Average main: A$70 ✉ 95 Exhibition St., City Center ☎ 03/9116–8682 🌐 www.farmersdaughters.com.au ⏲ Closed Sun.*

★ Florentino

$$$$ | ITALIAN | Since 1928, dining at Florentino has meant experiencing the pinnacle of Melbourne hospitality. After taking a seat in the famous mural room, with its huge chandeliers, wooden panels, and Florentine murals, you can sample dishes like suckling pig, and spanner crab risotto. **Known for:** Tuscan dishes; food and wine pairings; romantic atmosphere. *Average main: A$65 ✉ 80 Bourke St., City Center ☎ 03/9662–1811 🌐 www.florentino.com.au ⏲ No lunch Sat. Closed Sun.*

★ Flower Drum

$$$ | CANTONESE | Superb Cantonese cuisine is the hallmark of one of Australia's truly great Chinese restaurants, which is still receiving awards after opening in 1975. The restrained elegance of the design, deftness of the service, and intelligence of the wine list puts most other restaurants to shame. **Known for:** sautéed pearl meat; Peking duck; retro decor. *Average main: A$40 ✉ 17 Market La., City Center ☎ 03/9662–3655 🌐 flowerdrum.melbourne ⏲ No lunch Sun.*

★ Higher Ground

$ | AUSTRALIAN | Serving restaurant meals at breakfast and brunch, Higher Ground leads the pack for early morning dining. Grab a well-crafted pour-over and pastries, or linger over eggs paired with cauliflower, market fish, or the best ricotta hotcakes in town. **Known for:** soaring interiors; excellent coffee; innovative food pairings. *Average main: 18 ✉ 650 Little Bourke St., City Center ☎ 03/8899–6219 🌐 darlinggroup.com.au ⏲ No dinner Sun.–Wed.*

★ HuTong Dumpling Bar

$$ | CHINESE | The name means "alleyway" and in a sea of dumpling houses in Melbourne, down this little alleyway, you'll find the best of them all. The boiled pork dumplings are popular (A$14.20 for 12), though the panfried variations of pork, chicken, prawn, and chives hold up well, too. **Known for:** extensive menu; wantons with hot chili sauce; bustling atmosphere. *Average main: A$26 ✉ 14–16 Market La., City Center ☎ 03/9650–8128 🌐 www.hutong.com.au.*

Krimper

$ | AUSTRALIAN | Designed to showcase the building's warehouse origins, Krimper's design is rough-hewn but warm. Hidden away among former motorcycle repair shops and a burgeoning dining laneway, Krimper serves innovative food, excellent coffee, and hot chocolate from local company, Mork. **Known for:** classic breakfast with a twist; great coffee; hip vibe. *Average main: A$20 ✉ 20 Guildford La., City Center ☎ 03/9043–8844 🌐 www.krimper.com.au.*

MoVida Next Door

$ | SPANISH | As the name suggests, this popular Spanish tapas restaurant is next door to something—in this case the grown-up parent restaurant called MoVida. This is the casual little sister for those wanting a quick refuelling of sherry and seafood. **Known for:** great for pre- and posttheater; large specials menu; lively scene. *Average main: A$19 ✉ 164 Flinders St., City Center ✣ At Hosier La. ☎ 03/9663–3038 🌐 www.movida.com.au ⏲ Closed Mon. and Tues. No lunch Wed. and Thurs.*

★ Rockpool Bar & Grill

$$$$ | STEAKHOUSE | Taking his inspiration from the steak houses of North America, Rockpool is prolific Australian chef Neil Perry's flagship brand. Start with the

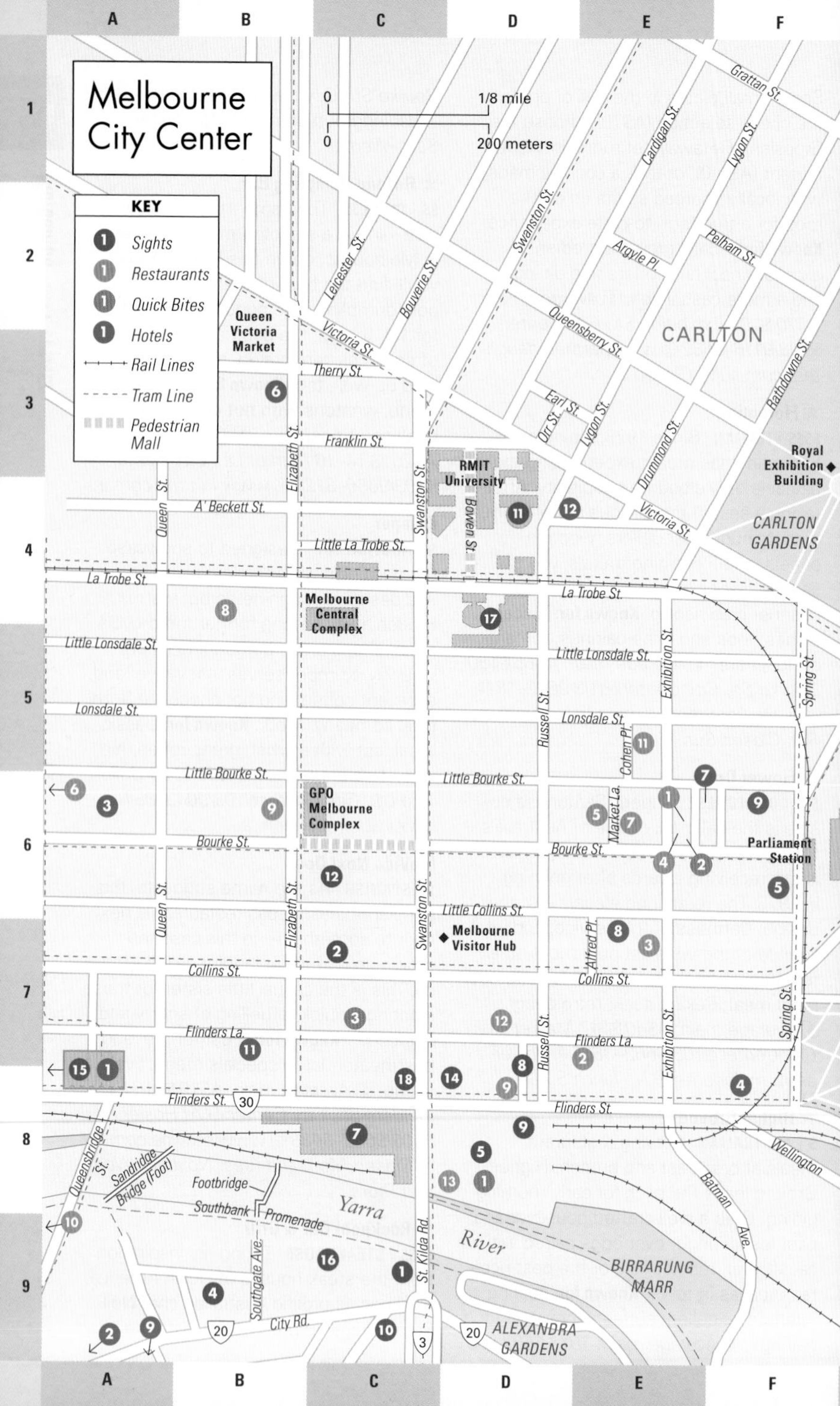

Melbourne City Center
KEY
Sights
Restaurants
Quick Bites
Hotels
Rail Lines
Tram Line
Pedestrian Mall
0
1/8 mile
0
200 meters
A
B
C
D
E
F
1
2
3
4
5
6
7
8
9
Grattan St.
Cardigan St.
Lygon St.
Swanston St.
Argyle Pl.
Pelham St.
Leicester St.
Bouverie St.
Queen Victoria Market
Victoria St.
Queensberry St.
CARLTON
Rathdowne St.
Therry St.
Earl St.
Orr St.
Lygon St.
Drummond St.
Franklin St.
Elizabeth St.
RMIT University
Royal Exhibition Building
Queen St.
A' Beckett St.
Bowen St.
Victoria St.
CARLTON GARDENS
Little La Trobe St.
La Trobe St.
La Trobe St.
Melbourne Central Complex
Little Lonsdale St.
Little Lonsdale St.
Exhibition St.
Spring St.
Lonsdale St.
Russell St.
Lonsdale St.
Cohen Pl.
Little Bourke St.
Little Bourke St.
GPO Melbourne Complex
Market La.
Bourke St.
Bourke St.
Parliament Station
Little Collins St.
Melbourne Visitor Hub
Alfred Pl.
Collins St.
Collins St.
Flinders La.
Flinders La.
Flinders St.
Flinders St.
30
Queensbridge St.
Sandridge Bridge (Foot)
Footbridge
Southbank
Promenade
Yarra
River
St. Kilda Rd.
Wellington
Batman Ave.
BIRRARUNG MARR
Southgate Ave.
City Rd.
20
20
3
ALEXANDRA GARDENS

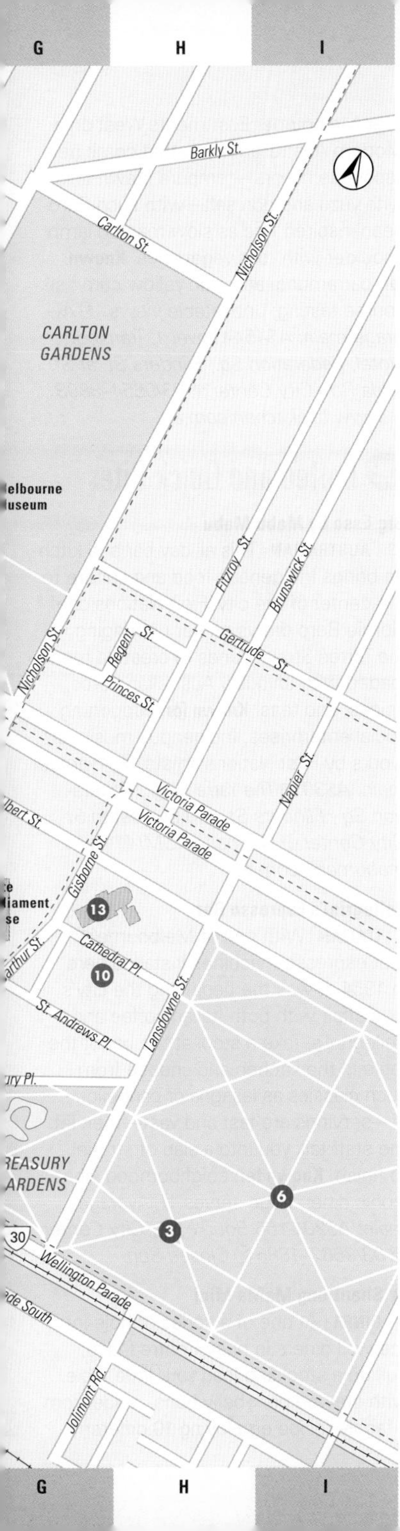

G H I

Carlton St.
Nicholson St.
Barkly St.
CARLTON GARDENS
Melbourne Museum
Fitzroy St.
Brunswick St.
Gertrude St.
Regent St.
Princes St.
Nicholson St.
Victoria Parade
Victoria Parade
Napier St.
Gisborne St.
Cathedral Pl.
St. Andrews Pl.
Lansdowne St.
TREASURY GARDENS
Wellington Parade
Jolimont Rd.

Sights

1 Arts Centre Melbourne ... C9
2 Block Arcade ... C7
3 Cooks' Cottage ... H8
4 Eureka Skydeck ... B9
5 Federation Square ... D8
6 Fitzroy Gardens ... I8
7 Flinders Street Station ... C8
8 Hosier Lane Street Art ... D7
9 Ian Potter Centre: NGV Australia ... D8
10 National Gallery of Victoria ... C9
11 Old Melbourne Gaol ... D4
12 Royal Arcade ... C6
13 St Patrick's Cathedral ... G6
14 St Paul's Cathedral ... D8
15 SEA LIFE Melbourne Aquarium ... A8
16 Southgate ... C9
17 State Library of Victoria ... D4
18 Young and Jackson Hotel ... C8

Restaurants

1 Becco ... E6
2 Chin Chin ... E7
3 Farmer's Daughters ... E7
4 Florentino ... E6
5 Flower Drum ... E6
6 Higher Ground ... A6
7 HuTong Dumpling Bar ... E6
8 Krimper ... B4
9 MoVida Next Door ... D8
10 Rockpool Bar & Grill ... A9
11 Seamstress Restaurant & Bar ... E5
12 Supernormal ... D7
13 Taxi Kitchen ... D8

Quick Bites

1 Big Esso by Mabu Mabu ... D8
2 Pellegrini's Espresso Bar ... E6
3 ShanDong MaMa Mini ... C7

Hotels

1 Best Western Melbourne City ... A8
2 Crown Metropol ... A9
3 Hilton Melbourne Little Queen Street ... A6
4 Hotel Lindrum ... F8
5 The Hotel Windsor ... F6
6 Jasper Hotel ... B3
7 Lancemore Crossley St ... E6
8 Next Hotel Melbourne ... E6
9 Ovolo Laneways ... F6
10 Park Hyatt Melbourne ... G6
11 The Sebel Melbourne Flinders Lane ... B7
12 Space Hotel ... D4

G H I

whole grilled king prawns and move onto a range of beef cuts—which have been aged and butchered in-house—from the wood-fire grill. **Known for:** wines by the glass; expert service; premium dry-aged beef. 💲 *Average main: A$72* ✉ *Crown Complex, 8 Whiteman St., City Center* ☎ *03/9081–0532* 🌐 *www.rockpoolbarand-grill.com.au.*

Seamstress Restaurant & Bar
$$ | **ASIAN** | This bar-restaurant occupies a heritage-listed four-story building that has housed an undergarment manufacturer, a 1900s sweatshop, a brothel, and even a Buddhist temple (but not at the same time). Tasty Asian dishes, in small, medium, and large portions, are designed to be shared. **Known for:** braised beef short rib, plum-hoisin sauce; generous banquets; A$45 three-course set lunch. 💲 *Average main: A$34* ✉ *113 Lonsdale St., City Center* ☎ *03/9663–6363* 🌐 *www.seamstress.com.au* 🕑 *Closed Sun. No lunch Sat.*

Supernormal
$$$ | **ASIAN** | Chef Andrew McConnell's dominance of the Melbourne food scene cannot be ignored: besides this playful Pan-Asian restaurant, his stable includes glossy late-night European restaurant Gimlet on nearby Russell Street, the formal Cutler & Co in Fitzroy, and Cumulus Inc., beloved by the breakfast crowd. Fight off the competition for a seat at Supernormal's bar and eat your way through Tokyo, Shanghai, Seoul, and Hong Kong: share plates of *bao,* dumplings, and the raw kingfish; McConnell's New England lobster rolls have a cult following. **Known for:** adventurous wine and cocktails list; lobster rolls; Wagyu strip loin. 💲 *Average main: A$39* ✉ *180 Flinders La., Melbourne* ☎ *03/9650–8688* 🌐 *supernormal.net.au.*

Taxi Kitchen
$$$ | **MODERN AUSTRALIAN** | Occupying an innovative steel-and-glass space above Federation Square, Taxi boasts both extraordinary food and spectacular views over Melbourne. East meets West on a Modern Australian menu that combines Japanese flavors—tempura prawn tails with yuzu and nori salt—with such European-inspired fare as slow-roasted lamb shoulder with root vegetables. **Known for:** barramundi and crab yellow curry; six-course tasting; unbeatable views. 💲 *Average main: A$45* ✉ *Level 1, Transport Hotel, Federation Sq., Flinders St. at St. Kilda Rd., City Center* ☎ *03/9654–8808* 🌐 *www.taxikitchen.com.au.*

Coffee and Quick Bites

Big Esso by Mabu Mabu
$$ | **AUSTRALIAN** | This all-day bar and kitchen brings Indigenous food and culture to the center of the city. First Nations chef Nornie Bero draws on her upbringing in the Torres Strait Islands to create a menu loaded with uniquely Australian herbs, spices, and teas. **Known for:** supporting social enterprises; Indigenous music; artworks by First Nations artists. 💲 *Average main: A$30* ✉ *The Yarra Bldg., Federation Sq., Flinders St. and Swanston St., City Center* ✣ *Opposite ACMI* 🌐 *www.mabumabu.com.au.*

Pellegrini's Espresso Bar
$ | **ITALIAN** | With one of Melbourne's first espresso machines installed here in 1954, it was the beginning the city's love affair with both Italian coffee and Pellegrini's. Take a stool at the bar or the table in the kitchen and choose from such classics as lasagna or cannelloni—servings are fast and vast—then let the staff talk you into a slab of strudel to finish. **Known for:** neighborhood vibe; iconic diner; huge serves. 💲 *Average main: A$20* ✉ *66 Bourke St., City Center* ☎ *03/9662–1885* 🕑 *Closed Sun.*

★ **ShanDong MaMa Mini**
$ | **DINER** | At one of a series of hole-in-the-wall diners in busy Centre Place, pull up a stool and load your little table with stewed pork-belly buns, made from a family recipe employing 10 different

Melbourne's restaurant scene is a global potpourri of ethnic influences.

spices. The little diner and its mother restaurant, in the Midcity Centre arcade, are also justly famed for their dumplings filled with a fine mackerel-and-coriander mousse. **Known for:** pork-belly buns; craft beer; quick service. *$ Average main: A$14 ✉ 5 Centre Pl., City Center ☎ 041/1666–2992 🌐 www.shandong-mamamini.com.au.*

Hotels

Best Western Melbourne City

$ | **HOTEL** | This 114-room hotel with a dash of industrial chic (exposed brick walls and black, brown, and red minimalist decor) is just the sort of lodging you'd expect in hip central Melbourne. **Pros:** hip, but homey; good value; near Southern Cross Station for intercity arrivals. **Cons:** industrial design may not be to everyone's liking; a little removed from restaurants in the city center; some rooms lack views. *$ Rooms from: A$120 ✉ 16 Spencer St., City Center ☎ 03/9621–3333 🌐 www.bestwesternmelbourne.com.au 114 rooms No Meals.*

Crown Metropol

$$$ | **HOTEL** | There are three five-star hotels in the riverside Crown Casino complex in Southbank, and while the Metropol may be the largest (it has 658 rooms, making it one of the country's biggest), it still retains an elegant boutique-type feel. **Pros:** extensive dining options; luxury spa; fabulous pool. **Cons:** vertiginous views; impersonal feel; casino area might not appeal to all. *$ Rooms from: A$268 ✉ 8 Whiteman St., City Center ☎ 03/9292–6211 🌐 www.crownmetropolmelbourne.com.au 625 rooms, 33 lofts, 1 apartment Free Breakfast.*

Hilton Melbourne Little Queen Street

$$$$ | **HOTEL** | Located in the grand 1930s Equity Chambers building and a modern tower behind it, the new Hilton draws upon that golden era of travel for a touch of glamour. **Pros:** fine-dining in-house restaurant; large-scale mural by local artist collective; 1930s style throughout. **Cons:** some rooms without views; no pool; secretive entrance. *$ Rooms from:*

A$325 ✉ 18 Little Queen St., City Center ☎ 03/9116–8888 🌐 www.hilton.com 🍴 No Meals 🛏 244 rooms.

Hotel Lindrum

$$$ | **HOTEL** | Housed in the Heritage-listed Lindrum family billiards center, a short walk from Federation Square, this is one of Melbourne's savviest boutique properties. **Pros:** full in-room entertainment systems; warm feel; exceptional service. **Cons:** some may find the traditional decor outdated; small restaurant and bar; on busy thoroughfare. *$ Rooms from: A$265 ✉ 26 Flinders St., City Center ☎ 03/9668–1111 🌐 www.hotellindrum.com.au 🛏 59 rooms 🍴 Free Breakfast.*

The Hotel Windsor

$$$ | **HOTEL** | Built in 1883, this aristocrat of Melbourne hotels combines Victorian-era character with modern comforts, and is a must for history lovers (it also has a terrific can't-miss afternoon tea). **Pros:** high tea; elegant heritage feel; central location. **Cons:** basic breakfast; some rooms lack views; heritage rooms decor may be too "old world" for some. *$ Rooms from: A$219 ✉ 111 Spring St., City Center ☎ 03/9633–6000 🌐 www.thehotelwindsor.com.au 🛏 160 rooms, 20 suites 🍴 Free Breakfast.*

Jasper Hotel

$$ | **HOTEL** | A former YWCA, the Jasper has undergone a radical face-lift, redesigned and polished to a shine. **Pros:** budget rates; close to the Victoria Markets; lovely courtyard. **Cons:** slightly removed from city center; neutral decor; may be noisy in the morning, being near the markets. *$ Rooms from: A$159 ✉ 489 Elizabeth St., City Center ☎ 03/8327–2777, 1800/468–359 🌐 www.jasperhotel.com.au 🛏 80 rooms, 10 suites 🍴 No Meals.*

★ Lancemore Crossley St.

$$$ | **HOTEL** | There's an unexpected sense of space and lots of light in this compact boutique hotel at the top of Melbourne's Chinatown. **Pros:** rooftop terrace; located in the theater district; playful vibe. **Cons:** dark lobby; no pool; unfriendly entertainment system. *$ Rooms from: A$249 ✉ 51 Little Bourke St., City Center ☎ 03/9639–1639 🌐 www.lancemore.com.au/crossley-st 🛏 113 rooms 🍴 No Meals.*

Next Hotel Melbourne

$$$ | **HOTEL** | Woven into Melbourne's new 80 Collins precinct, the entrance to Next is so discreet, it's almost as though you're slipping into your secret Melbourne home—albeit one with a Clef d'Or concierge. Set amongst the skyscrapers of the "Paris End" of Collins Street, its rooms are thoughtfully designed with luxurious beds and Melbourne-made toiletries, and its in-house restaurant, La Madonna, showcases the skills and the origins of its two head chefs, from Hong Kong and Sicily. Test the hotel's own barrel-aged spirits at the cocktail bar, or take your drink into one of the many deep armchairs hidden around the intimate public areas, with its clubby, members-only feel. **Pros:** renowned restaurant; innovative cocktails; excellent location. **Cons:** no pool; mostly city views; not family-friendly. *$ Rooms from: A$280 ✉ 103 Little Collins St., City Center ☎ 03/9118–3333 🌐 www.nexthotelmelbourne.com 🍴 No Meals 🛏 255 rooms.*

Ovolo Laneways

$$$ | **HOTEL** | Much effort has gone into making this 43-room boutique hotel uniquely stylish and comfortable, including its laneway location, which is ideal for those who want to be in the heart of the action. **Pros:** free Wi-Fi; latest entertainment technology in the rooms; central location. **Cons:** no restaurant; small lobby; area can be noisy late at night. *$ Rooms from: A$206 ✉ 19 Little Bourke St., City Center ☎ 03/8692–0777 🌐 www.ovolohotels.com 🛏 43 rooms 🍴 Free Breakfast.*

Park Hyatt Melbourne

$$$$ | **HOTEL** | Set right next to Fitzroy Gardens and opposite St. Patrick's Cathedral, this is one of Melbourne's most elegant

hotels. **Pros:** surrounded by gardens; lavish appointments; world-class service. **Cons:** breakfast buffet is underwhelming; slightly corporate atmosphere; a little removed from the city center. *Rooms from: A$315 1 Parliament Sq., City Center 03/9224–1234 www.hyatt.com/en-US/hotel/australia/park-hyatt-melbourne/melph 216 rooms, 24 suites Free Breakfast.*

The Sebel Melbourne Flinders Lane

$$$ | HOTEL | FAMILY | The smallest of the city's upscale hotels, the Sebel has a central location and a mix of lovely one- and two-bedroom suites, which sleep four to eight people. **Pros:** ideal location; elegant design; swanky feel. **Cons:** rooms book out quickly; no restaurant; not for the budget-conscious. *Rooms from: A$293 321 Flinders La., City Center 03/9629–4088 www.accorhotels.com 58 suites No Meals.*

Space Hotel

$ | HOTEL | FAMILY | Located just minutes from bustling Lygon Street, Carlton Gardens, and Queen Victoria Market, this family-run venue targets budget travelers who like a bit more comfort. **Pros:** easy to meet other travelers; central location; great value. **Cons:** slightly outdated rooms; shared facilities; can get noisy with lively patrons. *Rooms from: A$89 380 Russell St., City Center 0303/9662–3888 spacehotel.com.au 128 rooms No Meals.*

Nightlife

BARS

The Atrium Bar on 35

COCKTAIL LOUNGES | This cocktail bar on the 35th floor of the Sofitel Melbourne on Collins has spectacular views; a great way to end a night at one of the nearby theaters. *25 Collins St., City Center 03/9653–0000 www.sofitel-melbourne.com.*

Cookie

BARS | Located in a lofty warehouse-style space with exposed ceiling pipes and a balcony, Cookie focuses on domestic and international craft beer and great Thai food. *Curtin House, 252 Swanston St., 1st fl., City Center 03/9663–7660 cookie.net.au.*

Embla

WINE BARS | Welcoming but still sophisticated, Embla is a throwback to and an improvement on Melbourne's original small bar scene. An accessible but often obscure wine list is accompanied by wholesome gourmet snacks from the wood-fired oven that are cooked to perfection. *122 Russell St., City Center 0455/122-121 www.embla.com.au.*

★ **Gin Palace**

WINE BARS | Reminiscent of Hollywood's golden era, Gin Palace is a must-visit for gin lovers, with knowledgeable staff and more than enough types of martinis to satisfy any taste, and a brace of gin and tonics featuring Australian and international craft gins and exotic tonics. *10 Russell Pl., off Bourke St., City Center 03/9654–0533 www.ginpalace.com.au.*

Melbourne Supper Club

WINE BARS | Age-buffed leather sofas, cigars, and an exhaustive wine list characterize this classy club. For views and cocktails, continue upstairs to the rooftop terrace bar Siglo, which overlooks the neoclassic architecture of Victoria's state parliament building. *161 Spring St., 1st fl., City Center 03/9654–6300.*

Mitre Tavern

PUBS | One of the oldest pubs in town, pulling pints since 1868, locals love the unpretentious vibe of this British-style establishment in the city's financial district. It's especially popular with nine-to-fivers who like an after-work drink in the beer garden. *5 Bank Pl., City Center 03/9670–5644 www.mitretavern.com.au.*

Section 8

BARS | A shipping container located in an old parking lot in Chinatown, set in an alleyway filled with street art, Section 8 is all things Melbourne. The reliably trendy bar is popular with the artsy student crowd enjoying a drink (and maybe a dance) in this mostly outdoor bar. ✉ *27–29 Tattersalls La., City Center* ☎ *0430/291–588* 🌐 *www.section8.com.au.*

COMEDY CLUBS

Comic's Lounge

COMEDY CLUBS | This comedy club is a good place for a laugh. ✉ *26 Errol St., North Melbourne* ☎ *03/9348–9488* 🌐 *the-comicslounge.com.au.*

MUSIC CLUBS

Cherry Bar

LIVE MUSIC | This iconic and intimate, this rowdy rock 'n' roll bar is located on AC/DC Lane. The address alone says it all. ✉ *AC/DC La., City Center* ☎ *03/9639–8122* 🌐 *www.cherrybar.com.au.*

Max Watt's House of Music

LIVE MUSIC | This popular venue is known for live local and lesser-known international rock bands, and as a stand-up venue during the International Comedy Festival. ✉ *125 Swanston St., City Center* ☎ *1300/843–443 tickets* 🌐 *maxwatts.com.au.*

Performing Arts

MUSIC AND DANCE

Australian Ballet

In the 2,000-seat State Theatre at the Arts Centre, the Australian Ballet stages six programs annually, and presents visiting celebrity dancers from around the world. ✉ *The Arts Centre, 100 St. Kilda Rd., Southbank* ☎ *1300/182–183* 🌐 *www.australianballet.com.au.*

Melbourne Symphony Orchestra

MUSIC | The Melbourne Symphony Orchestra performs year-round in the 2,500-seat Hamer Hall. ✉ *The Arts Centre, 100 St. Kilda Rd., Southbank* ☎ *03/9929–9600* 🌐 *www.mso.com.au.*

Sidney Myer Music Bowl

MUSIC | Open-air concerts take place December through March at the Sidney Myer Music Bowl. ✉ *King's Domain, near Swan St. Bridge, City Center* ☎ *1300/130–300 Ticketmaster.com.au.*

THEATER

Comedy Theatre

THEATER | Revues and plays are staged at the Comedy Theatre, which along with the Princess, Regent, and Forum theaters is owned by the Marriner Group and uses the same telephone numbers. ✉ *240 Exhibition St., City Center* ☎ *03/9299–9800, 1300/111–011 tickets* 🌐 *www.marrinergroup.com.au.*

fortyfivedownstairs

THEATER | A cutting-edge, not-for-profit theater, visit for independent theater, cabaret, and exhibitions. ✉ *45 Flinders La., City Center* ☎ *03/9662–9966* 🌐 *www.fortyfivedownstairs.com.*

Halftix

THEATER | This ticket booth sells tickets to theater attractions at half price on performance days. It's open Tuesday–Friday, 11

A Funny Night Out

Melburnians love a laugh, and the annual Melbourne International Comedy Festival is a great opportunity to enjoy top Australian and international comedians. The monthlong event takes place in the Melbourne Town Hall and venues across town, with free events in open spaces. In addition to hosting comedy stars, the festival seeks out new talent and culminates with the Raw Comedy award for the best new Australian stand-up performer. If you're in town in April, you won't be laughing if you miss it.

Melbourne is known for its robust theater scene.

am–4 pm. Phone for information about shows on sale (recorded message), or see listings on the website. ✉ *Melbourne Town Hall, 208 Little Collins St., City Center* ☎ *03/9650–9420* 🌐 *www.halftix-melbourne.com.*

Regent Theatre

THEATER | An ornate 1920s building, the Regent originally opened to screen movies but nowadays presents mainstream theater productions, including *The Lion King* and *Moulin Rouge! The Musical.* ✉ *191 Collins St., City Center* ☎ *1300/111–011 www.ticketmaster.com.au* 🌐 *www.marrinergroup.com.au.*

Shopping

BOOKS

Books for Cooks

BOOKS | A fantastic array of cookbooks stock the shelves of Books for Cooks, including many from local chefs. Located at the Queen Victoria Market, the shop's only steps from plenty of fresh produce, meat, and fish to support any sudden inspirations. ✉ *Queen Victoria Market, 115 Victoria St., City Center* ☎ *03/8415–1415* 🌐 *www.booksforcooks.com.au.*

JEWELRY

Craft Victoria

CRAFTS | Craft Victoria fosters creativity with seminars and exhibits, and has a top-notch selection of Australian pottery, textile works, and jewelry for sale. The not-for-profit design group also runs free exhibitions and interviews with makers of contemporary, sustainable craft and design. ✉ *Watson Pl., off Flinders La., City Center* ☎ *03/9650–7775* 🌐 *www.craft.org.au.*

MARKETS

★ **Queen Victoria Market**

MARKET | **FAMILY** | This market has buzzed with food and bargain shoppers since 1878. With more than 600 mostly open-air stalls, this sprawling, spirited bazaar is the city's prime produce outlet—many Melburnians come here to buy strawberries, honey, fresh flowers, imported cheeses, meat, and eye-bright fresh fish. There is a section for certified organic produce, and the beautiful Dairy Produce Hall is a plethora of cheeses, fresh pasta and breads, coffee, and deli delights. On Sunday there is less food and more great deals on jeans, T-shirts, and souvenirs. Food trucks and live music on weekends lend the market a festive air. ✉ *Elizabeth St. at Victoria St., City Center* ☎ *03/9320–5822* 🌐 *www.qvm.com.au.*

SHOES AND LEATHER GOODS

Hassett

LEATHER GOODS | Bespoke shoemaker Hassett sells handmade leather belts, satchels, and wallets, many made from kangaroo leather. Much of Theo Hassett's leather is sourced from Greenhalgh Tannery in Ballarat, which specializes in tanning with wattle tree bark. On the premises you'll also find a café and a barbershop. ✉ *Captains of Industry, 2 Somerset Pl., Levels 1/2, City Center* ✣ *Off Little Bourke St.* ☎ *0424/030–464* 🌐 *www.hassettgoods.com.*

SHOPPING CENTERS

Block Arcade

MALL | An elegant 19th-century shopping plaza with mosaic-tile floors, Block Arcade contains the venerable Hopetoun Tea Rooms— serving high tea since 1892—jewelers including French Jewelbox, specialty Australian chocolatier Haigh's, the underground, long-standing record shop Basement Discs, Australian plant essences company Essensorie, Gewurzhaus spice merchant, and Australian By Design, hidden away on the third level (take the lift opposite the Hopetoun Tea Rooms). ✉ *282 Collins St., City Center* ☎ *03/9654–5244* 🌐 *theblock.com.au.*

Bourke Street Mall

MALL | Once the busiest east–west thoroughfare in the city, Bourke Street Mall is a pedestrian-only zone—but watch out for those trams! Two of the city's biggest department stores are here; an essential part of growing up in Melbourne is being taken to Myer at Christmas to see the window displays. ✉ *Bourke St., City Center.*

Collins and Little Collins Streets

ANTIQUES & COLLECTIBLES | A precinct of stores frequented by shoppers lured by labels, Little Collins Street is still worth a visit. In between frock shops you'll find musty stores selling classic film posters, antique and estate jewelry, and Australian opals. The glittering St. Collins Lane draws less mainstream, higher-end designers, while the eastern end of Collins Street, beyond the cream-and-red Romanesque facade of St. Michael's Uniting Church, is the Paris End, a name coined by Melburnians to identify the elegance of its fashionable shops as well as its general hauteur. Here you find big-name international designer clothing, bags, and jewelry. Its newest precinct, the 80 Collins Street, hosts such curios as sustainable cobblers and luxury eyewear designers between cafés, new hotels, and swanky restaurants. ✉ *Little Collins St., City Center.*

David Jones

DEPARTMENT STORE | This big, upmarket department store has a large array of luxury brands for both men and women. ✉ *310 Bourke St., between Elizabeth and Swanston Sts., City Center* ☎ *03/9643–2222* 🌐 *www.davidjones.com.au.*

Emporium Melbourne

MALL | Many international brands established their first Australian outlets at this major shopping mall in the city center. The mall is filled with fashion, technology, food, and art outlets, and joined via aboveground glass walkways to the Myer and David Jones department stores and the Bourke Street mall to the south, and Melbourne Central shopping center heading north. International stores include Michael Kors and Victoria's Secret, and Australian designers are well represented, including RM Williams, Scanlan Theodore, sass & bide, and Camilla. Coffee is always close to hand and there are several upmarket food courts—on the fourth floor, Tetsujin's sushi train has great city views. ✉ *Lonsdale St., City*

Center ☎ *03/8609–8221* 🌐 *emporium-melbourne.com.au.*

Flinders Lane

NEIGHBORHOODS | Dotted with chic boutiques fighting for space amongst top-end cafés, bars, and restaurants, many of them selling merchandise by up-and-coming Australian designers, Flinders Lane will keep fashionistas happy. Between Swanston and Elizabeth Streets, look for Cathedral Arcade, home to vintage and designer stores, in the bottom of the Nicholas Building. The lift leads to an eclectic collection of tiny shops full of unique fashion and accessories. Flinders Lane will try to divert you with walls of colorful street art. ✉ *Flinders La., City Center.*

Melbourne Central

MALL | Here you'll find a dizzying complex of predominantly high-street brands that's huge enough to enclose an 1880s redbrick shot tower (once used to make bullets) in its atrium. The Ella (Elizabeth and La Trobe Streets) corner is a tangle of hole-in-the-wall eats, coffee roasters, the excellent Blackhearts & Sparrows bottle shop, and acclaimed cocktail bar BYRDIE (try the wattleseed Negroni). ✉ *300 Lonsdale St., City Center* ☎ *03/9922–1122* 🌐 *www.melbournecentral.com.au.*

Myer

DEPARTMENT STORE | Myer is one of the country's largest department stores, carrying myriad casual and luxury brands for men and women. ✉ *314–336 Bourke St., between Elizabeth and Swanston Sts., City Center* ☎ *136–937* 🌐 *www.myer.com.au.*

Royal Arcade

MALL | Opened in 1870, this is Melbourne's oldest shopping plaza. It remains a lovely place to browse and is home to the splendid Gaunt's Clock, which tolls away the hours. ✉ *355 Bourke St., City Center* 🌐 *www.royalarcade.com.au.*

Southgate

MALL | The shops and eateries at this spectacular riverside location are a short walk from both the city center, across the Ponyfish Island pedestrian bridge (slip down the stairs halfway across the bridge to find one of the city's best-placed bars, Ponyfish), and the Arts Center. There's outdoor seating next to the Southbank promenade. ✉ *4 Southbank Promenade, City Center* ☎ *03/9686–1000* 🌐 *www.southgatemelbourne.com.au.*

Activities

BICYCLING

Bicycle Network

BIKING | This bike-advocacy group can provide advice on cycling in Melbourne and Victoria, including information about the road rules in relation to cyclists. The office sells some maps and books for cycling tours. Its website has trail maps. ✉ *4/246 Bourke St., City Center* ☎ *03/8376–8888* 🌐 *www.bicyclenetwork.com.au.*

Real Melbourne Bike Tours

BIKING | **FAMILY** | The bike tours offered by this company promise to show the best of Melbourne. The four-hour rides depart at 10 am from Federation Square and include coffee and cakes in Little Italy and lunch. The company also rents bicycles for A$25 for two hours (A$50 per day) and electric bikes from A$40 for one hour (A$100 per day), including helmets, locks, kids' seats, and a map of five top rides, with suggestions of where to eat and drink. Founded in 1976, it's on the edge of the Yarra River just near Princes Bridge and Federation Square. ✉ *Vault 14, Federation Sq., City Center* ✣ *On riverbank level, near Riverland Bar under Princes Bridge* ☎ *0417/339–203* 🌐 *www.rentabike.net.au* 🎟 *From A$120.*

TENNIS

Melbourne Park Tennis Centre

TENNIS | FAMILY | This center has 24 outdoor and eight hard indoor Plexicushion courts, plus eight clay courts. Play is canceled during the Australian Open in January. ✉ *National Tennis Centre (Level 2), Entrance D, Olympic Blvd., City Center* ☎ *1300/836–647* 🌐 *www.tennisworld.net.au* 🎫 *Court hire from A$31/hr.*

Richmond

Home of Victoria Street—Melbourne's "little Vietnam"—and the hipster café and bar stretch of Swan Road, Richmond is 2 km (1 mile) east of the city center (take Tram 70 from Flinders Street for Swan Street or Tram 109 from Collins Street for Victoria Street). If you're looking for a new wardrobe, a Vietnamese soup kitchen, a Korean barbecue, a Laotian banquet, or a Thai hole-in-the-wall, this is the place to come.

GETTING HERE AND AROUND

Several tram lines connect central Melbourne with Richmond. Take Tram 70 from Flinders Street Station to Swan Street, Richmond, or take Tram 109 from Collins Street to Victoria Street. Trams 48 and 75 take you from Flinders Street to Bridge Road, while Tram 78 travels along Chapel Street (in South Yarra) north along Church Street, through the heart of Richmond. Trains connect Flinders Street Station with several useful local stations: Richmond, East Richmond and Burnley (for Swan Street), West Richmond (for Bridge Road), and North Richmond (for Victoria Street). If driving, or even walking, proceed east along Flinders Street, which becomes Wellington Parade, past the prominent Melbourne Cricket Ground, then cross Hoddle Street.

Sights

Bridge Road

NEIGHBORHOOD | Once a run-down area of Richmond, this street is now a bargain shopper's paradise. Track down factory outlets selling fashion and leather goods, refuel at independent brewery Burnley Brewing or Oster Italian osteria. Take Tram 48 or 75 from the city. ✉ *Bridge Rd., Richmond* 🌐 *www.bridgerd.com.au.*

Victoria Street

STREET | One of Melbourne's most popular "eat streets," this 2-km (1-mile) stretch has restaurants ranging from simple canteens to tablecloth-and-candlelight dining spots. The street is packed with Vietnamese grocers, kitchenware stores, several art galleries, and a handful of chichi drinking spots and historic neighborhood hotels. Once a year at Tet, Vietnamese New Year (in January and February but the exact date varies from year to year), the street comes to life with a daylong Lunar Festival, with dragon dances, music, and more food! ✉ *Victoria St., Richmond.*

Restaurants

★ **I Love Pho**

$ | VIETNAMESE | Tucking into a steaming bowl of pho (traditional noodle soup) at this Victoria Street restaurant is like channeling the backstreets of Hanoi and Saigon. Each order comes with a piled plate of Vietnamese mint, bean shoots, and lemon wedges, and there are bottles of chili paste and fish sauce on every mock-marble plastic table. **Known for:** friendly service; best pho in town; rice-paper rolls. [$] *Average main: A$10* ✉ *264 Victoria St., Richmond* ☎ *03/9427–7749* 🌐 *pholove.com.au.*

Nightlife

MUSIC CLUBS

Corner Hotel

LIVE MUSIC | The Corner Hotel has alternative, reggae, rock, blues, and jazz gigs with an emphasis on homegrown bands. Tasty pub meals can be had on the rooftop for a pre-gig dinner or in the beer garden, 'Round the Corner. ✉ *57 Swan St., Richmond* ☎ *03/9427–7300 bar, 1300/724–867 tickets* 🌐 *www.cornerhotel.com.*

East Melbourne

The harmonious streetscapes in this historic enclave of Victorian-era houses, which date from the boom following the gold rushes of the 1850s, make East Melbourne a great neighborhood for a stroll.

GETTING HERE AND AROUND

East Melbourne's attractions are an easy walk from the city center. The Free City Circle tram travels along Spring Street, stopping at Parliament House and the Old Treasury building. Trams 48 and 75 travel along Flinders Street and Wellington Parade to East Melbourne sights: Fitzroy Gardens is on the north side of Wellington Parade, and the MCG is on the south side.

Sights

★ **Melbourne Cricket Ground (MCG)**

SPORTS VENUE | A tour of this complex is essential for an understanding of Melbourne's sporting obsession. You can get the stories behind it all at the National Sports Museum. The site is a pleasant 10-minute walk from the city center or a tram ride (Nos. 48 and 75) to Jolimont Station. ✉ *Jolimont Terr., East Melbourne* ☎ *03/9657–8888* 🌐 *www.mcg.org.au* 🎫 *A$30.*

Activities

CRICKET

Melbourne Cricket Ground

CRICKET | All big international and interstate cricket matches in Victoria are played at the Melbourne Cricket Ground from October to March, and the biggest international bands also play here to maximum audiences. The stadium has lights for night games and can accommodate 100,000 people—the MCG app helps you find your own seat, public transport options, and where you left the car. Tickets are available at the gate or through Ticketek. ✉ *Yarra Park, Brunton Ave., Richmond* ☎ *03/9657–8867 stadium, 132–849 Ticketek* 🌐 *www.mcg.org.au.*

GOLF

Yarra Bend Golf Course

GOLF | **FAMILY** | Despite being just 4 km (2½ miles) northeast from the city, this challenging course seems a world away, due to its length and surrounding parkland. Ten thousand bats have also made their home on the back 9. A golf range is ideal to practice your game before the round. The course even has a 36-hole adventure minigolf course (A$25), suitable for children and adults, and offers budget midweek and twilight rates. ✉ *Yarra Bend Rd., Fairfield* ☎ *03/9481–3729* 🌐 *www.yarrabendgolf.com* 🎫 *Weekdays: 18 holes A$41, 9 holes A$30; weekends: 18 and 9 holes, up to A$48* ⛳ *18 holes, 5915 yards, par 70.*

TENNIS

★ **Australian Open**

TENNIS | The Australian Open, held in January, is one of the world's four Grand Slam tournaments, and the excitement is felt throughout the city. You can buy tickets at the event or from Ticketek. Major games are broadcast on the big screens at Federation Square, free. ✉ *Batman Ave., Melbourne* ☎ *03/9039–9407 tickets* 🌐 *www.ausopen.com.*

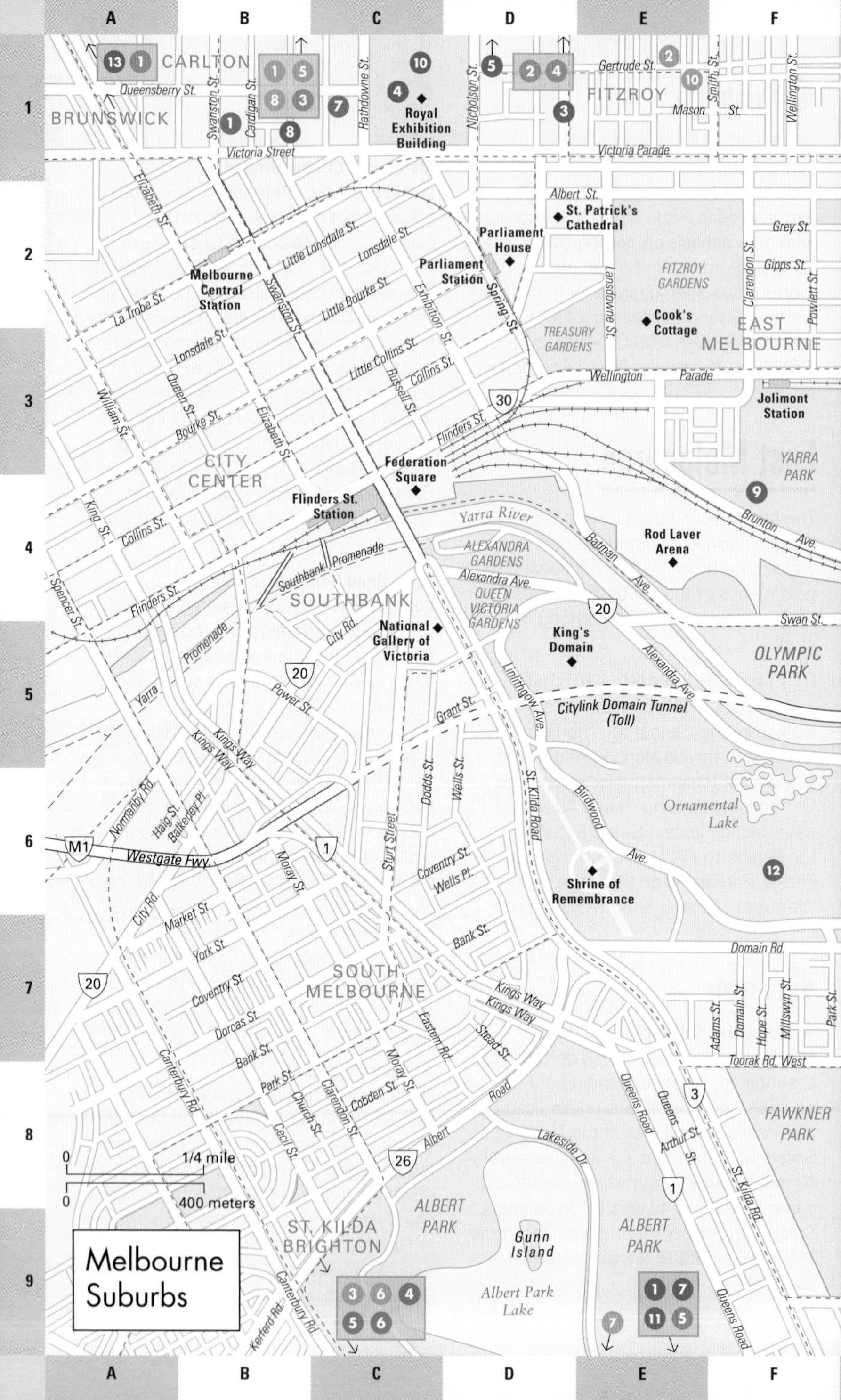
Melbourne Suburbs
CARLTON
BRUNSWICK
FITZROY
Royal Exhibition Building
St. Patrick's Cathedral
Parliament House
Parliament Station
Melbourne Central Station
FITZROY GARDENS
TREASURY GARDENS
Cook's Cottage
EAST MELBOURNE
Jolimont Station
YARRA PARK
CITY CENTER
Federation Square
Flinders St. Station
Yarra River
ALEXANDRA GARDENS
QUEEN VICTORIA GARDENS
Rod Laver Arena
SOUTHBANK
National Gallery of Victoria
King's Domain
OLYMPIC PARK
Citylink Domain Tunnel (Toll)
Ornamental Lake
Shrine of Remembrance
SOUTH MELBOURNE
FAWKNER PARK
ALBERT PARK
Gunn Island
Albert Park Lake
ST. KILDA BRIGHTON
Westgate Fwy.
Queensberry St.
Victoria Street
Victoria Parade
Gertrude St.
Mason St.
Swanston St.
Cardigan St.
Rathdowne St.
Nicholson St.
Smith St.
Wellington St.
Albert St.
Grey St.
Gipps St.
Clarendon St.
Powlett St.
Lansdowne St.
Wellington Parade
Elizabeth St.
Little Lonsdale St.
Lonsdale St.
Little Bourke St.
Exhibition St.
Spring St.
La Trobe St.
Little Collins St.
Collins St.
Russell St.
Queen St.
William St.
Bourke St.
Flinders St.
King St.
Spencer St.
Southbank Promenade
Promenade
Batman Ave.
Brunton Ave.
Alexandra Ave.
Swan St.
City Rd.
Power St.
Yarra
Linlithgow Ave.
Grant St.
Kings Way
Normanby Rd.
Haig St.
Balkerley Pl.
Dodds St.
Wells St.
St. Kilda Road
Birdwood Ave.
Sturt Street
Moray St.
Coventry St.
Wells Pl.
Bank St.
Market St.
York St.
Dorcas St.
Domain Rd.
Adams St.
Domain St.
Hope St.
Millswyn St.
Park St.
Toorak Rd. West
Eastern Rd.
Stead St.
Canterbury Rd.
Church St.
Clarendon St.
Cobden St.
Cecil St.
Albert Road
Lakeside Dr.
Queens Road
Arthur St.
St. Kilda Rd.
Kerferd Rd.
0 1/4 mile
0 400 meters
A B C D E F
1 2 3 4 5 6 7 8 9

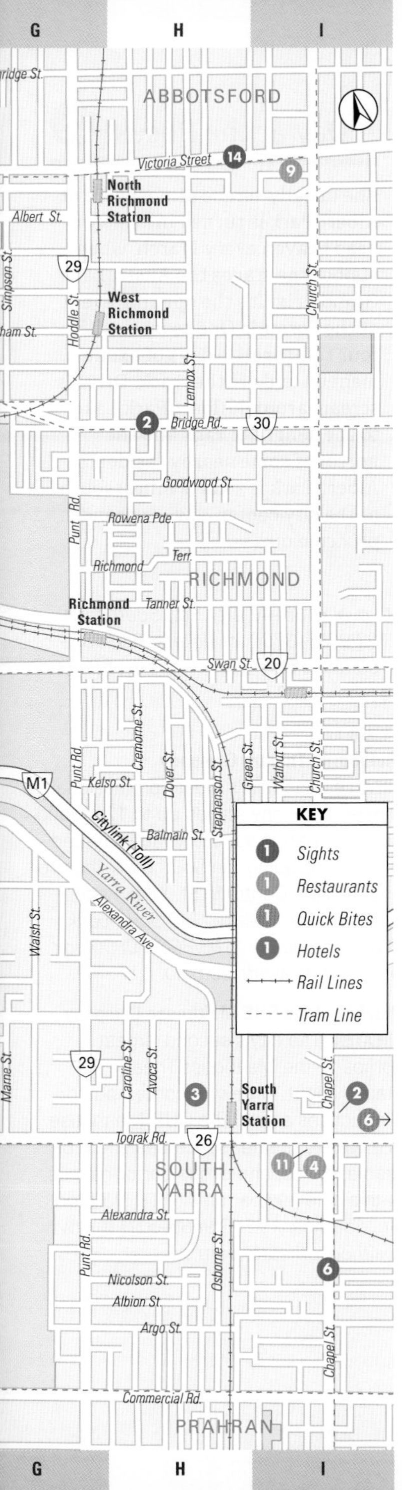

Sights

1 Acland Street E9
2 Bridge Road H3
3 Brunswick Street....... D1
4 Carlton Gardens C1
5 CERES Community Environment Park....... D1
6 Chapel Street............. I8
7 Luna Park................ E9
8 Lygon Street............ B1
9 Melbourne Cricket Ground (MCG)........... F4
10 Melbourne Museum C1
11 Rippon Lea Estate E9
12 Royal Botanic Gardens.................. F6
13 Sydney Road A1
14 Victoria Street.......... H1

Restaurants

1 Abla's..................... C1
2 Añada E1
3 Café di Stasio C9
4 Caffe e Cucina I8
5 D.O.C. Pizza & Mozzarella Bar C1
6 Donovan's C9
7 Fitzrovia E9
8 400 Gradi.................. C1
9 I Love Pho I1
10 Ladro E1
11 Lona Misa I8

Quick Bites

1 A1 Bakery................ A1
2 Babka D1
3 Brunetti C1
4 Lune Croissanterie D1
5 Monarch Cakes.......... E9
6 The Stables of Como I7

Hotels

1 Arrow on Swanston.... B1
2 The Como Melbourne.... I7
3 The Lyall Hotel and Spa H7
4 Middle Park Hotel C9
5 The Prince................ C9
6 Tolarno Hotel............ C9
7 Zagame's House C1

Powlett Reserve Tennis Centre

TENNIS | This center has five synthetic-grass outdoor courts. ✉ *Powlett Reserve, Albert St. and Simpson St., East Melbourne* ☎ *03/9417–3682* 🌐 *www.victennisacademy.com.au* 🎫 *Court hire from A$25/hr.*

South Melbourne

With leafy streets and heritage buildings restored to house chic boutiques, cafés, and restaurants, South Melbourne is one of Melbourne's oldest, and most charming, suburbs. The highlight here is the bustling South Melbourne Market but in the warmer months, the area's shops, bars, cafés, and restaurants spill out onto the streets between Southbank and the grassy expanses of Albert Park.

Hotels

Middle Park Hotel

$$ | **HOTEL** | In the picturesque suburb of Middle Park, toward the lively St. Kilda area, this 25-room hotel has been stylishly designed by renowned local architects Six Degrees, giving the 125-year-old building new life. **Pros:** sophisticated decor; historic surroundings; close to the Grand Prix track. **Cons:** no elevator; small rooms in a historic building; might be too far from city for some. 💲 *Rooms from: A$155* ✉ *102 Canterbury Rd., City Center* ☎ *03/9810–0079* 🌐 *middleparkhotel.com.au* 🛏 *23 rooms, 1 suite, 1 apartment* 🍽 *Free Breakfast.*

Performing Arts

MUSIC AND DANCE

Opera Australia

OPERA | Opera Australia has regular seasons, often with performances by world-renowned stars. The length and time of seasons vary, but all performances take place within the Arts Centre. ✉ *Level 4, 35–47 City Rd., Southbank* ☎ *03/9685–3700 for tickets, 03/9685–3700 box office* 🌐 *www.opera.org.au* 🎫 *From A$79.*

A Day at the Races

The usually serene atmosphere of Albert Park is turned into motorhead heaven every March, when Melbourne stages the Australian Grand Prix. It's the opening event of the Formula One season, with four full-throttle days of excitement on and off the track. Drivers scream around Albert Park Lake to the delight of fans and the horror of some nearby residents. Albert Park is 3 km (2 miles) south of the city center. 🌐 *www.grandprix.com.au.*

THEATER

Melbourne Theatre Company

THEATER | Australia's oldest professional theater company stages up to 12 productions per year in various venues around the city, including the Southbank Theatre and the Arts Centre in St. Kilda Road. ✉ *Southbank Theatre, 140 Southbank Blvd., Southbank* ☎ *03/8688–0800 box office* 🌐 *www.mtc.com.au.*

Playbox at the CUB Malthouse Company

THEATER | The city's second-largest company, the Malthouse Theatre, stages about 10 new or contemporary productions a year. The CUB Malthouse is a flexible theater space designed for drama, dance, and circus performances, with a café and bar on-site. ✉ *113 Sturt St., Southbank* ☎ *03/9685–5111* 🌐 *www.malthousetheatre.com.au.*

Shopping

MARKETS

★ South Melbourne Market

MARKET | Established in 1867, South Melbourne Market is Melbourne's second-oldest market, beloved by grandmothers and the suburb's hipster set. You'll find a huge selection of fresh produce and foodstuffs (the Dim Sims are famous), an incubator section for upcoming local housewares and accessories designers, and a food hall. ✉ *Cecil St. at Coventry St., South Melbourne* ☎ *03/9209–6295* 🌐 *www.southmelbournemarket.com.au.*

SHOPPING CENTERS

South Wharf

OUTLET | This shopping precinct near the Exhibition Centre and the *Polly Woodside* historic ship hosts riverside restaurants and cafés in heritage sheds, and discount outlet shopping of international and local fashion, outdoor, and footwear brands, including Billabong, Kathmandu, sass & bide, and Tigerlilly Swimwear. ✉ *South Wharf Promenade, Southbank* 🌐 *southwharf.com.au.*

St. Kilda

Most nights of the week, the streets of this Victorian seaside suburb come alive with visitors, and its many restaurants, cafés, and bars buzz with energy. The holiday atmosphere continues on Sunday at open-air markets on the beach, while the tree-lined promenade and pier extending into Port Phillip Bay are perfect for strolling and people-watching. The quaintly named St. Kilda Sea Baths (now a modern swimming pool–spa complex) are housed in a turn-of-the-20th-century building. Although no one wanted to live there in the 1970s and '80s, St. Kilda is now a very smart address. Many visitors choose to stay here and hop on a tram to the city center.

GETTING HERE AND AROUND

Several trams travel to St. Kilda from central Melbourne. Trams 96 (from Bourke Street) and 12 (from Collins Street) head east–west through the city center, then go all the way south to St. Kilda. Tram 16 runs to St. Kilda from Melbourne University along Swanston Street, as does Tram 3A at weekends. A good place to board these latter two trams is the stop between Flinders Street Station and Federation Square. It's a pleasant ride down St. Kilda Road into Fitzroy Street and past the bay.

Sights

Acland Street

STREET | An alphabet soup of Chinese, French, Italian, and Lebanese eateries—along with a fantastic array of cake shops dating from the 1930s—lines the sidewalk of St. Kilda's ultrahip restaurant row. The street faces Luna Park. ✉ *Acland St., between Barkly St. and Shakespeare Grove, St. Kilda.*

★ Luna Park

AMUSEMENT PARK/CARNIVAL | **FAMILY** | A much-photographed Melbourne landmark, the park's entrance is a huge, gaping mouth, swallowing visitors whole and delivering them into a world of ghost trains, pirate ships, and carousels. Built in 1912, the **Scenic Railway** is the park's most popular ride. It's said to be the oldest continually operating roller coaster in the world. The railway is less roller coaster and more a relaxed loop-the-loop, with stunning views of Port Phillip Bay between each dip and turn. Luna Park is a five-minute stroll southeast of St. Kilda. ✉ *Lower Esplanade, St. Kilda* ☎ *03/9525–5033, 1300/888–272* 🌐 *www.lunapark.com.au* 🎟 *A$15 entry and first ride, subsequent rides from A$12.*

The groovy cafés of St. Kilda

Beaches

St. Kilda Beach

BEACH | While there is no surf to speak of, this half-mile stretch of sand still remains one of the country's liveliest beaches as it's close to bars, restaurants, and hotels. While most people like to hang out on the sand, windsurfing, sailing, roller-blading, and beach volleyball are other popular activities. Two iconic landmarks—St. Kilda Baths and St. Kilda Pier—are close by and give visitors something to do on those blistering hot summer afternoons. The Sunday foreshore market is just minutes away as well. **Amenities:** food and drink; parking (fee); toilets. **Best for:** partiers; swimming; windsurfing. ✉ *Marine Parade, St. Kilda.*

Restaurants

★ Café di Stasio

$$$$ | **ITALIAN** | This upscale bistro treads a very fine line between mannered elegance and decadence. A sleek marble bar and modishly ravaged walls contribute to the sense that you've stepped into a scene from *La Dolce Vita.* Happily, the restaurant is as serious about its food as its sense of style. **Known for:** crayfish omelet; expert staff; long lunches. $ *Average main: A$95* ✉ *31 Fitzroy St., St. Kilda* ☎ *03/9525–3999* 🌐 *www.distasio.com.au.*

★ Donovan's

$$$ | **AUSTRALIAN** | Grab a window table at this very popular bay-side restaurant (housed in the former 1920s bathing pavilion), and enjoy wide-open views of St. Kilda beach and its passing parade of in-line skaters, skateboarders, dog walkers, and ice-cream lickers. Start with the day's oysters, move to the fish and meats cooked superbly over char-coal, and slow it down over wine and cheese at this long-standing St. Kilda icon. **Known for:** extensive wine list; top-notch seafood; ocean views. $ *Average main: A$48* ✉ *40 Jacka Blvd., St. Kilda* ☎ *03/9534–8221* 🌐 *www.donovans.com.au.*

Fitzrovia

$$ | MODERN AUSTRALIAN | With a philosophy of celebrating local produce, Fitzrovia is known for fresh flavors with a European twist. The building, one of Melbourne's historical mansions overlooking Albert Park, is suitably grand while the food is hearty and sophisticated. **Known for:** laid-back lunches; vegetarian-friendly dishes; door-stop sandwich (bacon, mozzarella, and pear relish). *$ Average main: A$30 ✉ 2/155 Fitzroy St., St. Kilda ☎ 03/9537–0001 ⊕ www.fitzrovia.com.au ⏲ No dinner.*

Coffee and Quick Bites

Monarch Cakes

$ | CAFÉ | Past the yoga rooms and juice bars, Acland Street's timeless drawcard is its old-school cake shops, and Monarch has been doling out its creamy glories since 1934. Fresh cakes and slices are displayed behind glass windows that lure the crowds, before being packed carefully in boxes to go, for an instant picnic treat. **Known for:** glorious window displays; Monarch's famous plum cake; cupcakes of all hues. *$ Average main: A$10 ✉ 103 Acland St., St. Kilda ☎ 03/9534–2972 ⊕ www.monarchcakes.com.au.*

Hotels

The Prince

$$ | HOTEL | Cutting-edge design, contemporary artworks and sculptural furniture, and spare yet inviting luxury make this boutique hotel perfect for aficionados of unfussy elegance. **Pros:** great location; super comfortable rooms; gallery feel. **Cons:** hotel can be noisy due to functions; the area can get unsavory at night; the modern shapes and neutral hues might not appeal to some. *$ Rooms from: A$189 ✉ 2 Acland St., St. Kilda ☎ 03/9536–1111 ⊕ www.theprince.com.au ➪ 39 rooms 🍽 No Meals.*

Tolarno Hotel

$ | HOTEL | Set in the heart of St. Kilda's café, bar, and club precinct, Tolarno Hotel was once a restaurant and gallery owned by beloved Melbourne artist Mirka Mora and her husband Georges, and it still has an idiosyncratic artistic bent. **Pros:** heart-of-breezy–St. Kilda location; great restaurant; cool vibe. **Cons:** no elevator; can be noisy late at night; area can have a dubious crowd. *$ Rooms from: A$99 ✉ 42 Fitzroy St., St. Kilda ☎ 03/9537–0200 ⊕ www.tolarnostkilda.com.au ➪ 32 rooms, 5 suites 🍽 No Meals.*

Nightlife

BARS

★ Esplanade Hotel

LIVE MUSIC | Not only is this hallowed live music venue a great place to see local bands, but the Esplanade, or "Espy," is a historic pub—built in 1878—listed with the National Trust. Following a three-year renovation, she has retained her iconic band room, and added a swag of new bar spaces and three restaurants including My Tiger for Cantonese cuisine, in vibrant, beautiful settings: grab a table on the terrace to be seen. *✉ 11 The Esplanade, St. Kilda ☎ 03/9639–4000 ⊕ www.hotelesplanade.com.au.*

CONCERT VENUE

Palais Theatre

LIVE MUSIC | This theater, which first opened in 1927, features film, music festival openings, and concerts by Australian and international acts such as the Soweto Gospel Choir and Joe Bonamassa. *✉ Lower Esplanade, St. Kilda ☎ 03/8537–7677, 136–100 Ticketmaster ⊕ www.palaistheatre.com.au.*

MUSIC CLUBS

Prince of Wales

LIVE MUSIC | For rock and roll, punk, and grunge, head to the Prince Bandroom at the Prince of Wales, which attracts a straight and gay crowd. Ticket prices vary widely, depending on the gig. *✉ 29*

Fitzroy St., St. Kilda ☎ *03/9636–1111* 🌐 *princebandroom.com.au.*

Shopping

MARKETS

The Esplanade Market St. Kilda

MARKET | Open since 1970, this market started as an outlet for local artists. Today, it has up to 200 stalls selling contemporary paintings, crafts, pottery, jewelry, and homemade gifts. It's open every Sunday from 10 am to 4 pm. ✉ *Upper Esplanade, St. Kilda* ☎ *03/9209–6634* 🌐 *www.stkildaesplanademarket.com.au.*

Activities

AUSTRALIAN RULES FOOTBALL

★ **Melbourne Cricket Ground**

FOOTBALL | The Melbourne Cricket Ground is the prime venue for AFL games and is also home to the National Sports Museum. ✉ *Brunton Ave., Yarra Park* ☎ *03/9657–8867* 🌐 *www.mcg.org.au.*

HORSE RACING

Champions: Thoroughbred Racing Gallery

HORSE RACING | **FAMILY** | Horse-racing information, displays, and a minishrine to Australia's most famous race house, Phar Lap, take center stage at this gallery in the National Sports Museum. ✉ *Melbourne Cricket Ground, Brunton Ave., Gate 3, Yarra Park* ☎ *03/9657–8879* 🌐 *www.australiansportsmuseum.org.au* 🎫 *A$30.*

KITEBOARDING

The Zu Boardsports

WATER SPORTS | The Zu Boardsports runs kiteboarding lessons at St. Kilda. Private lessons are A$209 for two hours. ✉ *330 Beaconsfield Parade, at Pier Rd., St. Kilda* ☎ *03/9525–5655* 🌐 *www.thezu.com.au* 🎫 *A$209 per 2-hr lesson.*

Australian Rules Football

This fast, vigorous game, played between teams of 18, is one of four kinds of football Down Under. Aussies also play Rugby League, Rugby Union, and soccer, but Australian Rules, widely known as "footy," is the one to which Victoria, South Australia, the Northern Territory, and Western Australia subscribe. The ball can be kicked or punched in any direction, but never thrown. Players make spectacular leaps vying to catch ("mark") a kicked ball before it touches the ground, for which they earn a free kick. *www.afl.com.au*

Fitzroy

Melbourne's bohemian quarter is 2 km (1 mile) northeast of the city center. If you're looking for an Afghan camel bag or a secondhand paperback, or perhaps to hear some tunes while sipping a pint in a backstreet beer garden, Fitzroy is the place. Take Tram 11 or 86 from the city.

GETTING HERE AND AROUND

Fitzroy is an easy place to access, both from the city and nearby suburbs. From the city, take the No. 11 from Collins Street. It will take you all the way up Brunswick Street. From Bourke Street, hop on the No. 86 tram for a ride to Gertrude Street.

Sights

Brunswick Street

STREET | Along with Lygon Street in nearby Carlton, Brunswick Street is one of Melbourne's favorite places to dine. You might want to step into a simple kebab shop serving tender meats for less than A$12, or opt for dinner at one of the stylish, highly regarded bar-restaurants. The street also has many galleries, bookstores, bars, arts-and-crafts shops, and clothes shops (vintage fashion is a feature). ✉ *Brunswick St., between Alexandra and Victoria Parades, Fitzroy.*

Restaurants

★ Añada

$$ | SPANISH | A chalkboard on the exposed brick wall lists eight dry and six sweet sherries to start (or finish), and there are Spanish and Portuguese wines to accompany your selection of tapas and *raciones* (larger shared plates). Seated at a table or on a stool at the bar, begin with anchovy tapa, and go on to the authentic paella. Just leave room for dessert; the churros and chocolate are sinful. **Known for:** Andalucian fare; obscure meats; aged jamon. *$ Average main: A$25* ✉ *197 Gertrude St., Fitzroy* ☎ *03/9415–6101* 🌐 *anada.com.au* ⏲ *No lunch weekdays.*

Ladro

$$ | ITALIAN | A local favorite, this stellar Italian bistro emphasizes flavor over starchy linen and stuffy attitude. Delicious wood-fired pizzas, that some insist are the best in the city, put this suburban gem on the map (thankfully, it's only a short walk from the city). **Known for:** cannoli specials; sustainability initiatives; puttanesca pizza. *$ Average main: A$26* ✉ *224 Gertrude St., Fitzroy* ☎ *03/9415–7575* 🌐 *ladro.com.au* ⏲ *No lunch.*

Coffee and Quick Bites

Babka

$ | CAFÉ | Food lovers in the know are often found loitering at this tiny, bustling café. Try the excellent pastries, fresh-baked breads, or more substantial offerings like the Russian borscht (beetroot and cabbage soup) or *menemen*—scrambled eggs with chili, mint, tomato, and a sprinkling of feta cheese. **Known for:** bustling atmosphere; incredible sandwiches; freshly baked bread. *$ Average main: A$13* ✉ *358 Brunswick St., Fitzroy* ☎ *03/9416–0091* ⏲ *Closed Mon. No dinner.*

★ Lune Croissanterie

$ | BAKERY | Locals and tourists alike can be found queueing outside Lune each morning for the city's most beloved pastries including what some say are the world's best croissants, which take three days to create. Not afraid to experiment, seasonal flavors may include pumpkin pie or Persian love cake. **Known for:** legendary kouign amann; world-famous croissant flavors; great coffee. *$ Average main: A$7* ✉ *119 Rose St., Fitzroy* ☎ *03/9419–2320* 🌐 *www.lunecroissanterie.com.*

Nightlife

BARS

★ The Everleigh

COCKTAIL LOUNGES | One of the city's best cocktail bars, the Everleigh also makes a perfect spot for couples, with dark lighting, soft tunes, and glamorous, 1920s decor. Expect hand-cut ice, fine spirits, and genuinely expert bartenders. ✉ *150–156 Gertrude St., upstairs, Fitzroy* ☎ *03/9416–2229* 🌐 *www.theeverleigh.com.*

MUSIC CLUBS

The Night Cat

LIVE MUSIC | Bands and DJs play Afro-Cuban and disco dance music here Thursday to Saturday evening, and the Latin big band on Sunday night is legendary. ✉ *141 Johnston St., Fitzroy* ☎ *03/9417–0090* 🌐 *www.thenightcat.com.au.*

The Rainbow

PUBS | Most nights of the week, for the past few decades, this great pub, located down a backstreet, has been showcasing local acts. There's also a great range of craft beers available, which you can enjoy in the beer garden during the warmer months. Established in 1869, this neighborhood pub has budget steak nights on top of its regular menu, and over 100 beers for you to work your way through. ✉ *27 St. David St., Fitzroy* ☎ *03/9419–4193* 🌐 *therainbow.com.au.*

Shopping

ART AND CRAFT GALLERIES

The Rose St. Artists' Market

CRAFTS | Works from Melbourne's best artists and designers are on display at this popular artists' market, from oil paintings to sustainable bags, housewares to clothing and jewelry; ideal for unique, eclectic gifts and mementos.The organizers also arrange other makers' markets in various sites across the city. For more art, wander the nearby streets to see some of the city's best large-scale murals. ✉ *60 Rose St., Fitzroy* ☎ *03/9419–5529* 🌐 *www.rosestmarket.com.au.*

BOOKS

Brunswick Street Bookstore

BOOKS | Brunswick Street Bookstore specializes in art, design, and architecture publications, and also stocks modern Australian literature. ✉ *305 Brunswick St., Fitzroy* ☎ *03/9416–1030* 🌐 *www.mylocalbookshop.com.au.*

CLOTHING

The Social Studio

WOMEN'S CLOTHING | This not-for-profit store provides work experience, employment, and passageways for refugee youth. There are limited-edition women's fashion designs made using only reclaimed materials sourced from the local fashion industry, and products by Indigenous designers. It's located in Collingwood Yards, a social enterprise incubator for emerging artists. ✉ *Collingwood Yards, Unit 101, 30 Perry St., Collingwood* ☎ *03/9417–2143* 🌐 *www.thesocialstudio.org.*

SHOPPING CENTERS

Brunswick Street

NEIGHBORHOODS | Northeast of the city in Fitzroy, Brunswick Street has hip and grungy restaurants, coffee shops, gift stores, and clothing outlets selling the latest look, as well as retro and vintage finds, from fashion to housewares, signs to delightful bric-a-brac. ✉ *Brunswick St., Fitzroy.*

Smith Street

NEIGHBORHOODS | Perhaps Melbourne's hippest street, this colorful strip is dotted with bars, restaurants, and many vintage-style clothing shops. Toward the northern end are clothing factory outlets. ✉ *Smith St., Fitzroy.*

Brunswick

Just 4 km (2 miles) north of the city center, Brunswick is Melbourne's multicultural heart. Here Middle Eastern spice shops sit next to avant-garde galleries, Egyptian supermarkets, Turkish tile shops, Japanese yakitori eateries, Lebanese bakeries, Indian haberdasheries, and secondhand bookstores. Take Tram 19 from the city.

GETTING HERE AND AROUND

Tram 19 travels from Flinders Street Station in the city along Elizabeth Street and Brunswick's main thoroughfare, Sydney Road. You can also catch a train to Brunswick; take the Upfield Railway Line from Flinders Street Station and alight at either Jewell, Brunswick, or Anstey stations—they're all in Brunswick.

Sights

CERES Community Environment Park

OTHER ATTRACTION | **FAMILY** | On the banks of the Merri Creek in East Brunswick, this award-winning sustainability center is home to a permaculture and bush-food nursery. Buy local produce and crafts here, eat at the Merri Table Cafe, and explore the green technology displays. The Merri Creek bike path passes CERES. ✉ *45 Roberts St., at Stewart St., Brunswick East* ☎ *03/9389–0100* 🌐 *ceres.org.au* *Free.*

Sydney Road

STREET | Cultures collide on Sydney Road as Arabic mingles with French, Hindi does battle with Bengali, and the muezzin's call to prayer argues with Lebanese pop music. Scents intoxicate and colors beguile. Cafés serving everything from pastries to tagines (Moroccan stews) to Turkish delight sit shoulder to shoulder along the roadside with quirky record shops, antiques auction houses, and Bollywood video stores. ✉ *Sydney Rd., between Brunswick Rd. and Bell St., Brunswick.*

Restaurants

400 Gradi

$ | **ITALIAN** | This is the place for authentic Italian pizza: chef Johnny Di Francesco trained in Naples to make pizza to the Associazione Verace Pizza Napoletana rules, and has consistently won titles of world's best margherita, and also best pizzeria in Oceania. Besides pizza, the restaurant serves excellent pasta and other Italian dishes in a buzzing section of Lygon Street. **Known for:** slick decor; world's best margherita pizza; house-made gelato. [$] *Average main: A$20* ✉ *99 Lygon St., Brunswick East* ☎ *03/9380–2320* 🌐 *www.400gradi.com.au.*

Coffee and Quick Bites

★ **A1 Bakery**

$ | **LEBANESE** | For the freshest rounds of Lebanese bread, go to the source of the best *khobz* (bread) in the city: A1 Bakery has been running the ovens here since 1992. Sit in for Lebanese pizzas and kibbe (deep-fried lamb mince in cracked wheat) or order a platter of dips and *kofta* and a falafel wrap to go. **Known for:** delicious bread; baklava; inexpensive. [$] *Average main: A$10* ✉ *643–645 Sydney Rd., Brunswick* ☎ *03/9386–0440* 🌐 *www.a1bakery.com.au.*

Nightlife

BARS

Alehouse Project

BREWPUBS | Regarded as having one of the best craft beer lists in the city, with a strong emphasis on Australian brews, this local favorite also has an excellent menu, matched especially to the beers on offer. Head to the beer garden out back in the warmer months. ✉ *98 Lygon St., Brunswick East* ☎ *03/9387–1218* 🌐 *www.facebook.com/thealehouseproject.*

Retreat Hotel

BEER GARDENS | This expansive pub has local bands performing most nights of the week. It also has one of the city's best beer gardens. ✉ *280 Sydney Rd., Brunswick* ☎ *03/9380–4090* 🌐 *retreathotelbrunswick.com.au.*

Union Hotel

BREWPUBS | This family-friendly pub showcases local music on weekends. The atmosphere is always friendly and welcoming. ✉ *109 Union St., Brunswick West* ☎ *03/9388–2235* 🌐 *unionhotelbrunswick.com.au.*

Carlton

To see the best of Carlton's Victorian-era architecture, walk along Drummond Street, with its rows of gracious terrace houses (notably Rosaville at No. 46, Medley Hall at No. 48, and Lothian Terrace at No. 175), and Canning Street, which has a mix of workers' cottages and grander properties.

BOUNDARIES

Carlton is just 2 km (1 mile) north of the city. It is bounded by Elizabeth Street (which becomes Royal Parade) to the west, Princes Street to the north, Victoria Street (which becomes Victoria Parade) to the south, and Nicholson Street to the east. Carlton is directly west of Fitzroy.

GETTING HERE AND AROUND

Carlton is served by the many Swanston Street tram routes that terminate at Melbourne University (located in Parkville, just west of Carlton). Tram 1 extends north beyond the university, turning into the top end of Lygon Street. Alternatively, catch a bus (No. 200 or 207) from Lonsdale Street to Carlton.

Sights

Carlton Gardens

GARDEN | FAMILY | Sixty-four acres of tree-lined paths, artificial lakes, and flower beds in this English-style 19th-century park are the backdrop for the outstanding Melbourne Museum, and the World Heritage–listed Royal Exhibition Building, erected in 1880. ✉ *Victoria Parade, at Nicholson, Carlton, and Rathdowne Sts., Carlton* ☎ .

Lygon Street

STREET | Known as Melbourne's Little Italy, Lygon Street is a perfect example of the city's multiculturalism: where once you'd have seen only Italian restaurants, there are now Thai, Egyptian, Caribbean, and Greek eateries. The city's famous café culture was also born here, with the arrival of one of Melbourne's first espresso machines at one of the street's Italian-owned cafés in the 1950s. ✉ *Lygon St., between Victoria and Alexandra Parades, Carlton.*

Melbourne Museum

HISTORY MUSEUM | FAMILY | A spectacular, postmodern building (in Carlton Gardens) offers visitors insights into Victoria's histories, cultures and natural environments. Visit such globally recognized exhibitions such as *Te Vainui O Pasifika, Bugs Alive!, 600 Million Years, The Mind,* and *Dinosaur Walk,* along with brilliant temporary and touring exhibitions from near and far. In the Bunjilaka Aboriginal Cultural Center, *First Peoples* presents the Koorie experience and hosts three exhibitions a year of works by Koorie artists, while the Melbourne Story tells the history of this city. ✉ *Carlton Gardens, 11 Nicholson St., Carlton* ☎ *131–102 local, 03/8341–7777 international* 🌐 *museumsvictoria.com.au/melbournemuseum* 🎫 *A$15.*

Restaurants

Abla's

$$ | LEBANESE | Matriarch Abla Amad has been re-creating the much-loved family recipes from her homeland of Lebanon since 1979. This intimate restaurant resembles a lounge room of a family house, which with Abla walking around talking to diners, adds to the feeling of being looked after. **Known for:** homemade baklava; chicken and rice; family owned. [$] *Average main: A$30* ✉ *109 Elgin St., Carlton* ☎ *03/9347–0006* 🌐 *www.ablas.com.au* ⏲ *Closed Sun. No lunch.*

D.O.C. Pizza & Mozzarella Bar

$$ | ITALIAN | A major player in Melbourne's pizza wars, D.O.C. has perfected the art of using fresh, simple ingredients to create something special. The real treat lies in the pizza of the day. **Known for:** passionate service; pizza specials; mozzarella degustation. [$] *Average main: A$25* ✉ *295 Drummond St., Carlton* ☎ *03/9347–2998* 🌐 *www.docgroup.net.*

Coffee and Quick Bites

★ Brunetti

$$ | CAFÉ | First opened in 1974, this iconic Romanesque bakery has moved around Carlton on several occasions, and the masses have followed. Its biggest undertaking is in the heart of Lygon Street and still filled with perfect biscotti, mouthwatering cakes, and great service. **Known for:** Italian-style espresso; chocolate eclairs; decadent cake display. [$] *Average main: A$23* ✉ *380 Lygon St., Carlton* ☎ *03/9347–2801* 🌐 *www.brunetti.com.au.*

Hotels

Arrow on Swanston

$ | **HOTEL** | Location and great value make up for the limited space in this CBD-edge hotel. **Pros:** amenities suitable for longer stays; easy walk to eateries and CBD attractions; budget-friendly. **Cons:** only basic housekeeping; plain decor; limited space. *Rooms from: A$110 ✉ 488 Swanston St., Carlton ☎ 03/9225–9000 🌐 www.arrowonswanston.com.au 47 rooms, 38 apartments No Meals.*

Zagame's House

$$$ | **HOTEL** | There's a story of Melbourne in every room of this boutique hotel on Lygon Street, with its food, wines, oversized art, and even bottled cocktails all sourced locally. **Pros:** urbane design; close to Little Italy; pet-friendly. **Cons:** no views; the area gets noisy at night; no lifts. *Rooms from: A$229 ✉ 66 Lygon St., Carlton ☎ 03/9084–7777 🌐 www.zagameshouse.com.au No Meals 97 rooms.*

Shopping

BOOKS

Readings

BOOKS | An independent retailer with an exceptional range of books, magazines, and film and music CDs, Readings is a Melbourne institution. The Carlton store has operated since 1969, and there are now six suburban branches and another shop in the State Library in the city center. *✉ 309 Lygon St., Carlton ☎ 03/9347–6633 🌐 www.readings.com.au.*

South Yarra and Prahran

One of the most chic and fashion-conscious areas to be on any given day (or night) is in the strip of inner-city suburbs of South Yarra, Prahran, and Windsor. The area is chock-full of bars, eateries, and upscale boutiques.

GETTING HERE AND AROUND

Several trams, including Nos. 6, 72, 78, 5, and 64 travel to either South Yarra, Prahran, or Windsor. Running east–west, No. 58 traverses Toorak Road, South Yarra; No. 72 runs along Commercial Road, Prahran, No. 6 travels down High Street, Prahran and Nos. 5 and 64 run through Windsor along Dandenong Road. Tram 78 runs north–south along Chapel Street from Richmond, cutting through all three suburbs. You can also catch a train to South Yarra, Prahran, and Windsor stations; take the Sandringham line from Flinders Street Station.

Sights

★ Chapel Street

NEIGHBORHOOD | The heart of the trendy South Yarra–Prahran–Windsor area, this long road is packed with pubs, bars, notable restaurants, and upscale boutiques—more than 1,000 shops can be found within the precinct. Australian icons like Dinosaur Designs and Scanlan Theodore showcase their original work at the fashion-conscious, upscale Toorak Road end of the street (nearest to the city). Catch the 78 tram or walk south along Chapel Street to Greville Street and visit a small lane of hip bars, clothing boutiques, and record stores. Past Greville Street, moving into Windsor at the south end of Chapel Street, things get hipper, with cafés and vintage shops; this part of Chapel Street has three great markets selling everything from fresh produce to vintage records. *✉ Chapel St., between Toorak and Dandenong Rds., Prahran ☎ 03/9529–6331 🌐 www.chapelstreet.com.au.*

Rippon Lea Estate

HISTORIC HOME | Construction of Rippon Lea, a sprawling polychrome brick mansion built in the Romanesque style, began in the late 1860s. By the time it was completed in 1903, the original 15-room house had expanded into a 33-room mansion. Notable architectural features include a grotto, a tower that overlooks a lake, and humpback bridges. There is also a fernery and an orchard with more than 100 varieties of heritage apples and pears. Access to the house is for exhibitions or, between exhibitions, by guided tour only, but a self-guided tour of the grounds only is available. To get here, take a Sandringham line train from Flinders Street Station to Rippon-lea Station; it's a 15-minute ride south of the city center. ⊠ *192 Hotham St., Elsternwick* ☎ *03/9523–6095* ⊕ *www.ripponleaestate.com.au* 🎫 *House and garden: A$15.*

Royal Botanic Gardens

GARDEN | FAMILY | Within its 93 acres are 8,000 species of native and imported plants and trees, sweeping lawns, and ornamental lakes populated with ducks and swans that love to be fed. The Children's Garden is a fun and interactive place for kids to explore. Summer brings alfresco performances of classic plays, usually Shakespeare, and children's classics like *Wind in the Willows,* as well as the popular Moonlight Cinema series. There is also a garden shop and several cafés including The Terrace, which serves high tea. The present design and layout were the brainchild of W.R. Guilfoyle, curator, botanist, and director of the gardens from 1873 to 1910. Take an Aboriginal Heritage walk through the gardens, a significant site for the local Kulin Nation. Your Aboriginal guide will identify native plants and describe their use and the connection to Country (A$35). ⊠ *Birdwood Ave., South Yarra* ☎ *03/9252–2300* ⊕ *www.rbg.vic.gov.au* 🎫 *Free.*

Restaurants

Caffe e Cucina

$$ | ITALIAN | FAMILY | If you're looking for a quintessential Italian dining experience in a place where it's easy to imagine yourself back in the old country, this is it. Fashionable, look-at-me types flock here for coffee and pastries downstairs, or more-leisurely meals upstairs in the warm, woody dining room. **Known for:** traditional menu; decadent tiramisu; knowledgeable staff. $ *Average main: A$35* ⊠ *581 Chapel St., South Yarra* ☎ *03/9827–4139* ⊕ *caffeecucina.com.au.*

Lona Misa

$$ | LATIN AMERICAN | Vegan and vegetarian fare is the focus of this restaurant, set in the new Ovolo South Yarra hotel. With a strong Latin American vibe, choose the vegan versions of chicken tamales, the Brazilian seafood stew *moqueca* or the queso con chorizo, and vegetable dishes from its charcoal oven. **Known for:** some alcohol-free options; vegan dining; some vegetarian options. $ *Average main: A$26* ⊠ *234 Toorak Rd., South Yarra* ☎ *03/9116–2000* ⊕ *www.ovolohotels.com.*

Coffee and Quick Bites

The Stables of Como

$ | CAFÉ | There's a Gallic devil-may-care attitude to brunch in these former stables, with Bloody Marys and Mumm champagne listed beside the granola and eggs on sourdough. Or you could try matching its cocktails—espresso martinis or a Pimms with the French toast and *croque fromage.* **Known for:** cocktails; lemonade scones; lunches to go for picnics. $ *Average main: A$19* ⊠ *Williams Rd. at Lechlade Ave., South Yarra* ☎ *03/9827–6886* ⊕ *www.thestablesofcomo.com.au.*

Hotels

The Como Melbourne

$$$ | HOTEL | With its opulent and funky modern furnishings, this luxury hotel is as popular with business travelers as it is with visiting artists and musicians. **Pros:** great service; lavishly appointed rooms; great shopping and restaurants nearby. **Cons:** parking not included; breakfast not included; outside the city center. $ *Rooms from: A$250* ⊠ *630 Chapel St., South Yarra* ☎ *03/9825–2222* ⊕ *www.*

comomelbourne.com.au 111 rooms No Meals.

★ The Lyall Hotel and Spa

$$$$ | **HOTEL** | "Understated elegance" is the catchphrase of The Lyall, located in a quiet, leafy street in one of the city's most prestigious neighborhoods. **Pros:** leafy outlook; an extravagant spa; huge rooms. **Cons:** location may be too quiet for some; some rooms lack views; outside city center. *Rooms from: A$380* *14 Murphy St., South Yarra* *03/9868–8222* *www.thelyall.com* *40 rooms* *No Meals.*

Nightlife

BARS

Revolver Upstairs

DANCE CLUBS | This bar caters predominantly to young partygoers, with early-morning recovery sessions—a time for revelers around town to keep on partying—that are especially popular. *229 Chapel St., Prahran* *revolverupstairs.com.au.*

Shopping

CLOTHING

Eco D

WOMEN'S CLOTHING | International and Australian designers mix and mingle here, so you can find local fashion icons like Scotch & Soda, Silk Laundry, and American Vintage here. There are eight boutiques, including its Prahran, South Yarra, Brighton, and Hawthorn stores. *123 Toorak Rd., South Yarra* *03/9819–5416* *www.ecod.com.au.*

JEWELRY

★ Dinosaur Designs

CRAFTS | Celebrated Australian design duo Louise Olsen and Stephen Ormandy create luminous bowls and vases, and bold resin, gold, and silver jewelry. Each piece is distinctive and unique. *562 Chapel St., South Yarra* *03/9827–2600* *www.dinosaurdesigns.com.au.*

MARKETS

Camberwell Sunday Market

MARKET | A popular haunt for seekers of the old and odd, this market, about 6 km (4 miles) northeast of Chapel Street, South Yarra, has more than 300 stalls selling antiques, preloved clothing, books, and knickknacks. Food vans provide sustenance. *Station St., Camberwell* *www.camberwellsundaymarket.org.*

Chapel Street Bazaar

MARKET | Everything from estate jewelry and stylish secondhand clothes to porcelain and curios is on sale at these wooden cubicles and glass-fronted counters. *217–223 Chapel St., Prahran* *03/9529–1727* *www.chapelstreet.com.au.*

Prahran Market

MARKET | A fantastic, mouthwatering array of high-quality foods imported from all over the world is available at this popular market, including organic produce and sustainable seafood. The guided Market Discovery Trail runs the third Saturday of each month, including tastings and coffee (A$25). *163 Commercial Rd., South Yarra* *03/8290–8220* *www.prahranmarket.com.au.*

MUSIC

★ Greville Records

MUSIC | A Melbourne music institution, Greville Records carries rare releases in rock, alternative, and vinyl. *152 Greville St., Prahran* *03/9510–3012* *www.grevillerecords.com.au.*

SHOPPING CENTERS

Chapel Street

NEIGHBORHOODS | This street is where you can find some of the ritziest boutiques in Melbourne, as well as cafés, art galleries, bars, and restaurants. *Chapel St., between Toorak and Dandenong Rds., Prahran.*

High Street

ANTIQUES & COLLECTIBLES | Located between the suburbs of Prahran and Armadale, to the east of Chapel Street, High Street has the best collection of antiques shops in Australia. ✉ *High St., between Chapel St. and Orrong Rd., Prahran.*

The Jam Factory

MALL | This historic redbrick brewery-turned-factory complex houses cinemas, fashion, food, and gift shops. ✉ *500 Chapel St., South Yarra* ☎ *03/8578–6504* 🌐 *www.thejamfactory.com.au.*

Activities

GOLF

Albert Park Golf Course

GOLF | Two kilometers (1½ miles) south of the city, Albert Park Golf Course is an 18-hole, par-72 course beside Albert Park Lake, where the Formula 1 Grand Prix is held in March. Clubs, buggies, and carts can be hired at the course. Golf lessons for everyone from beginners to advanced players, starting at A$70 for a half-hour lesson for a single player. ✉ *Queens Rd., Albert Park* ☎ *03/9510–5588* 🌐 *www.albertparkgolf.com.au* *18 holes A$42, 9 holes A$30* *18 holes, 6280 yards, par 72.*

TENNIS

Fawkner Park Tennis Centre

TENNIS | Play tennis here on six synthetic-grass outdoor courts. ✉ *Fawkner Park, Toorak Rd. W, South Yarra* ☎ *03/9820–0100* 🌐 *www.victennisacademy.com.au* *Court hire from A$25/hr.*

Brighton

One of Melbourne's most iconic tourist destinations, Brighton boasts a beautiful and scenic beach with a line of 82 colorful bathing boxes, which date back to about the 1900s.

Beaches

★ **Middle Brighton Beach**

BEACH | Most commonly known for its colorful and culturally significant bathing boxes, which were built more than a century ago in response to Victorian ideas of morality and seaside bathing, Brighton Beach is also ideal for families since its location in a cove means that it's protected from the wind. Perfect for those looking for a quieter spot to bathe than St. Kilda Beach, the Middle Brighton Baths (*www.middlebrightonbaths.com.au*) is a nice place to view the boats and have a bite to eat. Good views of the bathing boxes and Melbourne's skyline can be enjoyed from the gardens at Green Point. **Amenities:** parking (fee); toilets. **Best for:** solitude; swimming. ✉ *Esplanade, Brighton.*

Chapter 6

SIDE TRIPS FROM MELBOURNE AND GREATER VICTORIA

Updated by
Belinda Jackson

Sights	Restaurants	Hotels	Shopping	Nightlife
★★★★★	★★★★★	★★★★☆	★☆☆☆☆	★☆☆☆☆

WELCOME TO SIDE TRIPS FROM MELBOURNE AND GREATER VICTORIA

TOP REASONS TO GO

★ **The Amazing Outdoors:** Victoria has outstanding national parks. Bushwalking, canoeing, fishing, rafting, and horse riding are all on the menu.

★ **Golden Country:** You can still pan for gold—and find it—in rivers northwest of Melbourne. But the gold-rush era's most attractive remnants are beautiful 19th-century towns constructed from its riches.

★ **Wonderful Wineries:** You'll find hundreds of wineries across the state, particularly in the Yarra Valley, Rutherglen, and on the Mornington Peninsula.

★ **Unique Wildlife:** With parrots in Sherbrooke, Phillip Island's Penguin Parade, and platypuses and dingoes at the Healesville Sanctuary, Victoria teems with native fauna.

★ **Foodie Heaven:** Victoria has a reputation for excellent local produce and wine. Even in rural towns, cafés and restaurants focus on fresh seasonal items.

The Yarra Valley wineries and the Dandenong Ranges are an hour's drive east of Melbourne. The Great Ocean Road begins at Torquay, southwest of Melbourne, and continues along the Southern Ocean coast to Portland. The Goldfields are between one- and two hours northwest of Melbourne. The Grampians and the Murray River region and its wineries are about a three-hour drive north to northeast of the city.

1 Yarra Valley and Healesville. Small towns with good cafés and shops, and a good base for travel to Yarra Valley wineries and the Dandenongs Region.

2 The Dandenong Ranges. Winding roads connect national parks, formal gardens, and walking trails.

3 Mornington Peninsula. Seaside villages, pretty beaches, art galleries, and wall-to-wall wineries.

4 Phillip Island. Breathtaking natural beauty and the famous Penguin Parade.

5 Queenscliff. Seaside town and popular detour on the drive to the start of the Great Ocean Road.

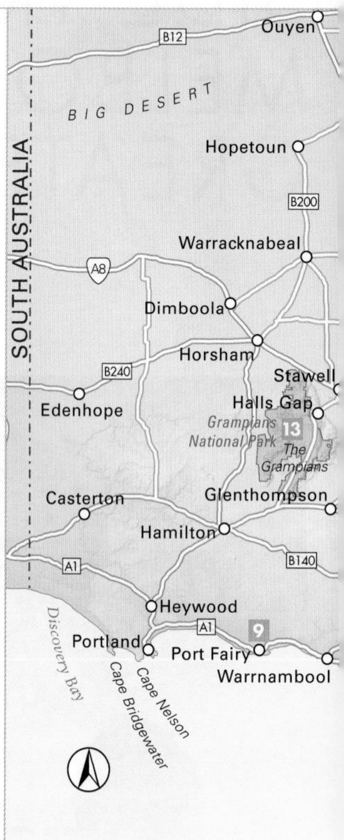

6 Lorne. Lively holiday town on the Great Ocean Road.

7 Apollo Bay. A quieter town on Great Ocean Road and base for nearby national parks.

8 Port Campbell National Park. Home to some of Australia's most famous geological formations.

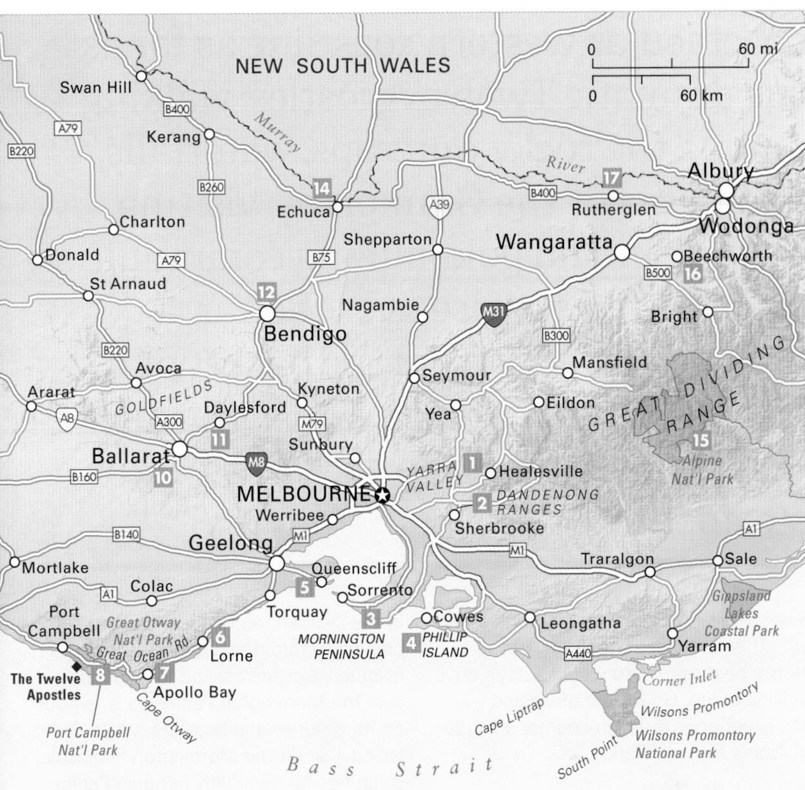

9 Port Fairy. The state's prettiest village.

10 Ballarat. Former gold-rush town with impressive museums and Victorian architecture.

11 Daylesford and Hepburn Springs. Known for its natural springs and spas, and contemporary art scene.

12 Bendigo. Bustling small city with historic mines and great galleries and wineries.

13 Grampians National Park. Stunning mountain scenery, great bushwalks, and Aboriginal rock art sites.

14 Echuca. Historic Murray River town with the world's largest fleet of active paddle steamers.

15 Alpine National Park. Gorgeous alpine scenery, grassy plains, and lots of outdoor activities.

16 Beechworth. A town with Ned Kelly associations and within easy reach of national parks.

17 Rutherglen. The source of Australia's finest fortified wines.

Without venturing too far from the Melbourne city limits, you can indulge in all sorts of pastimes—exploring the spectacular western coastline as far as the dramatic Twelve Apostles; walking among the rocky outcrops, waterfalls, and fauna of the Grampians; visiting historic inland gold-mining communities; toasting the sunrise over the Yarra Valley vineyards from the basket of a hot-air balloon; or taking in a Murray River sunset from the deck of a paddle steamer.

Sweeping landscapes are quilted together in this compact state. Many of the state's best sights are within a day's drive of Melbourne. Go further afield and you can experience the high-country solitude of Alpine National Park.

MAJOR REGIONS

Victoria's relatively compact size makes the state's principal attractions appealingly easy to reach, and the state's excellent road system makes driving the best option. There are a handful of enticing destinations within a 60- to 90-minute drive of the city. Victoria is blessed with 22 distinct wine regions (and around 600 cellar doors, where you can try and buy the product). The Yarra Valley, 65 km (40 miles) east of Melbourne, is Victoria's oldest wine region and a pleasant place to spend a day on an organized tour. About 35 km (22 miles) south of the Yarra Valley is Olinda, a cute village at the heart of the Dandenong Ranges. This area of beautifully forested hills and valleys is a favorite weekend escape for Melburnians. The Mornington Peninsula is famous for its wineries and beaches, while Phillip Island, just off the Mornington Peninsula, is famous for its nightly Penguin Parade. On the western shore of Port Phillip Bay, the Bellarine Peninsula also has a burgeoning winery industry, but it's the grand 19th-century hotels of Queenscliff that most attract day-trippers.

The **Great Ocean Road,** which snakes along Victoria's rugged and windswept southwestern coast, is arguably Australia's most spectacular coastal drive. The road, built by returned soldiers after World War I along majestic cliffs, occasionally dips down to sea level. Here, in championship surfing country, some of the world's finest waves pound mile after mile of uninhabited, golden, sandy beaches and rocky headlands. Although the route is officially deemed to be 243 km (152 miles), and runs between the towns of Torquay in the east and Allansford (near Warrnambool) in the west, most people think of it as the much longer route that continues farther west to Port Fairy, Portland and to the South Australian border, and inland to small towns such as Colac. Its many twists and turns and wonderful sights along the way take many hours to explore. Allow time to stop in the attractive towns of Lorne and Apollo Bay, and to explore Port Campbell National Park and Port Fairy.

Driving is the most convenient way to see the region, and the only way to really enjoy the many sights along Great Ocean Road. However, the winding road is notorious for its motor accidents (you'll notice roadside signs along the route reminding visitors that Australia drives on the left), so take care on the bends and slow down. The speed limit is 80 kmph (50 mph), but the going may be slow on the most scenic routes, especially during the summer holiday period. Allow plenty of time to pull over to take photographs and at least two to three days to see all the attractions along the Great Ocean Road and its hinterland.

Victoria was changed forever in the early 1850s by the discovery of gold in the center of the state. News of fantastic gold deposits caused immigrants from every corner of the world to pour into Victoria's **Gold Country** to seek their fortunes as "diggers"—a name that has become synonymous with Australians ever since. Few miners became wealthy from their searches, however. The real money was made by those supplying goods and services to the thousands who had succumbed to gold fever. Gold towns like Ballarat and Bendigo sprang up like mushrooms to accommodate these fortune seekers, and prospered until the gold rush receded. Afterward, they became ghost towns or turned to agriculture to survive. However, many beautiful buildings were constructed from the spoils of gold, and these gracious old public buildings and grand hotels survive today and make a visit to Bendigo and Ballarat a pleasure for those who love classic architecture. Between Ballarat and other historic gold towns to the north are the twin hot spots of Daylesford and Hepburn Springs—which together constitute the spa capital of Australia.

Although Victoria was not the first Australian state to experience a gold rush, when gold was discovered here in 1851 it became a veritable El Dorado. During the boom years of the 19th century, 90% of the gold mined in Australia came from the then British colony. The biggest finds were at Bendigo and Ballarat, whose diggings proved to be among the richest alluvial goldfields in the world.

For leisurely exploration of the Gold Country, a car is essential. Public transportation adequately serves the main centers, but access to smaller towns is less assured and even in the bigger towns attractions are spread out.

The Grampians. Encompassing a series of rugged sandstone ranges covered with native bushland, Grampians National Park is a wilderness area three hours from the heart of Melbourne. Spectacular rock formations including the Balconies, the Pinnacle, and the Fortress can be visited via walking trails. The Wonderland Range forms a wall behind the township of Halls Gap, which is a popular hangout for kangaroos.

Murray River Region. The mighty Murray River forms the border between Victoria and New South Wales, and is an aquatic playground. Houseboats, speedboats, and old paddle wheelers share the river, and golf courses, farms, historic towns like Echuca, and stands of majestic eucalyptus trees hug its banks. Wineries produce internationally acclaimed fortified wines and full-bodied reds.

Victoria's dramatic **High Country** is just under the NSW-Victorian border, and includes the state's main ski resorts and Alpine National Park. In spring and fall, some of the prettiest drives are along its mountain roads, including the C522, dubbed the Snow Road for its winter parade of skiers and snowboarders heading up to the ski resorts around Mt. Hotham and Falls Creek. Slow down to enjoy the drive between gorgeously picturesque villages such as Chiltern and Beechworth, photograph rustic tobacco kilns set against snowy peaks, and keep an eye out for roadside shops and cafés selling delicious local produce, as the High Country enjoys a revival thanks to food, wine, and adventure-loving travelers. Steeped in history and natural beauty, the High Country region is a gourmet foodies' heaven known for its fruit, olives, honey, and cheeses, and is also a renowned wine region. Victoria exports more than A$200 million worth of wine annually, and this region's muscats and ports are legendary. The Rutherglen area, in particular, produces the country's finest fortified wines (dessert wines or "stickies").

Planning

When to Go

Victoria is at its most beautiful in fall, March through May, when days are crisp, sunny, and clear and the foliage in parks and gardens is glorious. Winter, with its wild seas and leaden skies, stretches June through August in this region, providing a suitable backdrop for the dramatic coastal scenery. It's dry and sunny in the northeast, however, thanks to the cloud-blocking bulk of the Great Dividing Range. Northeast summers, December through February, are extremely hot, so it's best to travel here and through the Goldfields regions in spring (September through November) and fall.

Planning Your Time

From Melbourne, head for the town of Belgrave. Here you can ride the Puffing Billy steam train through the fern gullies and forests of the Dandenongs. In the afternoon, travel to Phillip Island for the endearing sunset Penguin Parade. Stay the night, and on the third morning meander along the coastal roads of the Mornington Peninsula through such stately towns as Sorrento and Portsea. Stop at a beach, or lunch at a winery before returning to Melbourne that afternoon.

If you have more time to spend in the area, make your way west from Melbourne to Queenscliff on the Bellarine Peninsula, before setting off down the Great Ocean Road. (If you are starting from the Mornington Peninsula, you take the Sorrento-Queenscliff car and passenger ferry, which crosses Port Phillip Bay in 45 minutes.) The Great Ocean Road is one of the world's finest scenic drives, with stops at some irresistible beaches. Overnight in Lorne, beneath the Otway Ranges, then drive west to Port Campbell Marine National Park. Here you can view the Twelve Apostles rock formations and stroll along the beach. Continue to Port Fairy for the night, making sure that you check out the wonderful Bay of Islands and Bay of Martyrs rock stacks (in the sea) along the way. On Day 4 wander along the banks of Port Fairy's Moyne River and amble around Griffiths Island. You can then drive northeast to the Goldfields center of Ballarat. That evening, explore the town's 19th-century streetscapes, then catch the sound-and-light show at Sovereign Hill. Spend the night here, and in the morning head to the wineries and spas around Daylesford and Hepburn Springs before returning to Melbourne.

Getting Here and Around

The best way to explore Victoria is by car. The state's road system is excellent, with clearly marked highways linking the Great Ocean Road to the Mornington Peninsula and Wilson's Promontory, the Yarra Valley, and the Murray River region. Distances are not as extreme as in other states. Many scenic places (Bendigo, Ballarat, Beechworth, and Echuca, for instance) are less than three hours from Melbourne; the vineyards of the Yarra Valley and the Mornington Peninsula are an easy 90-minute drive. Buses and trains, which cost less but take more time, also run between most regional centers.

Restaurants

Chefs in Victoria take pride in their trendsetting preparations of fresh local produce. International flavors are found in both casual and upscale spots: some of the best bargains can be found in local cafés, and several of the state's top restaurants are located in small country towns. On Sunday, be sure to join in the Victorian tradition of an all-day "brekky."

Hotels

Lodgings in Victoria include grand country hotels, simple roadside motels, secluded bushland or seaside cabins, friendly bed-and-breakfasts, backpacker hostels, and "glamping" (glamorous camping). Although you don't find many sprawling resorts in this state, most of the grand old mansions and country homes have air-conditioning, home-cooked meals, and free parking. Rates are usually reduced after school and national holidays. The state government's tourism board (*www.visitvictoria.com*) has a list of Victoria's accommodations to help you plan.

Restaurant and hotel reviews have been shortened. For full information, visit Fodors.com.

What It Costs in Australian Dollars

	$	$$	$$$	$$$$
RESTAURANTS	under A$21	A$21–A$35	A$36–A$50	over A$50
HOTELS	under A$151	A$151–A$200	A$201–A$300	over A$300

Yarra Valley and Healesville

65 km (40 miles) northeast of Melbourne.

The Yarra Valley spreads eastward from Melbourne's suburban fringe, and is a popular area with both locals and international visitors. Because Melburnians often use the valley for weekend breaks, the best time to visit is on working weekdays when the crowds are thinner. The small, attractive towns are dotted with good cafés, restaurants, and shops; in the rolling countryside between them you'll find numerous fine wineries that have excellent restaurants with impressive food and views.

Healesville is a good base for travel to Yarra Valley wineries and the Dandenongs Region, as it's an easy drive from both. This pleasant town with a tree-lined main street is also home to the Healesville Sanctuary, an open-plan zoo that showcases all manner of Australian native wildlife. Two popular areas within Yarra Ranges National Park—Badger Weir Walk and Maroondah Reservoir—are ideal for bushwalking and picnics.

GETTING HERE AND AROUND

Healesville, on the eastern side of the Yarra Valley, is 65 km (40 miles) from Melbourne. Take the Eastern Freeway (M3)

from Melbourne to its junction with the Maroondah Highway (B360) and follow the signs to Lilydale and on to Healesville. Trains, operated by Metro, travel from central Melbourne to Lilydale, and McKenzie's buses connect Lilydale with Yarra Glen and Healesville via Route 685. It's advisable to have a car to explore the wineries, or take a half- or full-day tour. Most tours will pick you up at your hotel.

CONTACTS McKenzie's Tourist Services. ☎ *03/5962–5088* 🌐 *www.mckenzies.com.au.* **Metro.** ☎ *1800/800–007* 🌐 *www.ptv.vic.gov.au.*

TOURS

Several companies operate winery tours from Melbourne or the Yarra Valley itself. Tours generally include visits to four to five wineries and lunch.

Swans on Doongalla Horse Drawn Carriages
Daily from 11 to 4, visit four wineries in horse-drawn carriages along St. Huberts Road for a minimum of four people. Includes a wine tasting and a light lunch served at Yering Farm winery. The meeting place is St. Huberts Winery. ☎ *03/9762–1910, 0419/877–093* 🌐 *www.swansondoongalla.com.au* 🎫 *From A$200.*

Wine Tours Victoria
These full-day tours depart from Melbourne to visit four to five wineries in either the Yarra Valley, Mornington Peninsula, Mt. Macedon, or Bellaraine Peninsula wine regions. Includes a two-course lunch with wine at one of the cellar doors. ☎ *03/5428–8500, 1800/946–386 toll-free in Australia* 🌐 *www.winetours.com.au* 🎫 *From A$180.*

Yarra Valley Railway
Rail enthusiasts can still enjoy the tracks even though regular passenger train services to Healesville ceased in 1980. You can travel along part of the track in railmotors (all-in-one motor and carriage) operated by the Yarra Valley Railway. The railmotors travel from Healesville through picturesque country, over Watts River, under bridges, and through the historic Tarrawarra brick tunnel and back again—a round-trip of about 8 km (5 miles) that takes about 45 minutes. Trains depart every hour, on the hour, 10–4 Sunday and public holidays, with extra services on school holidays. ✉ *Healesville-Kinglake Rd., Healesville* ☎ *03/5962–2490 reservations* 🌐 *www.yvr.com.au* 🎫 *From A$18.*

Yarra Valley Transfers
Design your own bespoke cellar door tour with this company, which also offers airport transfers and tours to other Victorian wine regions. ☎ *1800/146–706* 🌐 *www.yarravalleytransfers.com.au* 🎫 *Day tours from A$250 per person.*

Zoobus
The Zoobus runs a daily return bus service from Federation Square in Melbourne's city center to Healesville Sanctuary. ☎ *0455/054–545* 🌐 *www.zoobus.com.au* 🎫 *Return fares from A$70.*

VISITOR INFORMATION

CONTACTS Yarra Valley Visitor Information. ✉ *Healesville* ☎ *03/8739–8000* 🌐 *www.visityarravalley.com.au.*

Sights

The Yarra Valley is known for its wonderful produce—fruit, vegetables, herbs, bread, and cheeses—on sale at the monthly regional farmers' markets, including one at Yering Station.

De Bortoli
WINERY | A family-owned winery for four generations, De Bortoli was established (in New South Wales) in 1928, four years after the founder, Vittorio De Bortoli, and his wife, Giuseppina, migrated to Australia from northern Italy. Today, this Yarra Valley winery specializes in Chardonnay, Pinot Noir, Cabernet Sauvignon, and Shiraz, along with a changing array of less famous wines including Gamay, Pinot Blanc, and Nebbiolo. Wine tastings start from A$10 and can include the famous Noble One Botrytis Semillon, De Bortoli's most awarded wine since its release in 1982. Choose from Trophy Room premium wine tastings or cheese and wine tastings (for a minimum of two people) with prices on application. The restaurant, which has stunning views of the surrounding vines, landscaped gardens, and mountains, serves Italian dishes using Yarra Valley produce; the fixed-price two-course lunch is A$70 a head and the three-course option is A$85. ✉ *58 Pinnacle La., Dixon's Creek* ☎ *03/5965–2271* 🌐 *www.debortoliyarra.com.au.*

Wine and Song

Catch a little jazz at lunch or spend the whole day watching great performances by local and international headline acts. From opera to rock, Victoria's wineries provide an array of entertainment for music connoisseurs in summer, so check out the events with local tourist offices. Make sure you book early for the popular Day on the Green concert series held at Rochford Wines in the Yarra Valley, Mt. Duneed Estate near Geelong, All Saints Winery in Rutherglen, and Mitchelton Wines in Nagambie. *www.adayonthegreen.com.au*

★ **Domaine Chandon**
WINERY | Established by French champagne house Moët & Chandon, this vineyard has one of the most spectacular settings in the Yarra Valley; its Chandon tasting bar has enormous floor-to-ceiling windows providing fantastic views over

the vineyards and the Yarra Ranges. Apart from sparkling wines, the winery produces Shiraz, Pinot Noir, Meunier, and Chardonnay. Take a free self-guided tour of the winery's history and production methods from 10:30 to 4:30 daily, or sign up for a wine discovery class on Sunday with a maximum of 12 people (bookings essential) to get a closer look at wine appreciation. The restaurant's three-course gathering-style menu is designed to share, and changes seasonally (A$85 per person). The French-inspired menu starts with charcuterie and dips, then onto small bites followed by heartier mains including market fish and a lamb rump. A vegetarian option is available. Otherwise, the lounge menu has build-your-own platters of pâtés, olives, dips, and cured fish and meats, A$8 per item. ✉ *727 Maroondah Hwy., Coldstream* ☎ *03/9738–9200* 🌐 *www.chandon.com.au.*

Healesville Sanctuary

WILDLIFE REFUGE | FAMILY | Come face-to-face with wedge-tailed eagles, grumpy wombats, nimble sugar gliders, and shy platypuses at Healesville Sanctuary, a lovely, leafy, native wildlife sanctuary. Don't miss the twice-daily Spirits of the Sky show, during which raptors and parrots fly close overhead. You can get up close and personal with a koala, kangaroo, or echidna on a Close-Up Encounter (from A$31 extra), or for A$102, take a two-hour VIP tour with a ranger. Another highlight is the Land of Parrots aviary, where you can feed and interact with colorful birds. You can also view the animal hospital to see wildlife recovering from injury or illness. The Future Vets play space lets kids—and their parents—dress up as vets and role-play caring for animals, and kids can also join the Sanctuary Food Tour to see what it takes to feed over 1,400 animals. Take a break and refuel at the zoo's three cafés, including the largest, Sanctuary Harvest café, which serves full meals made with Yarra Valley's seasonal produce. ✉ *Badger Creek Rd., Healesville* ☎ *03/5957–2800, 1300/966–784* 🌐 *www.zoo.org.au* 🎫 *A$40.*

Rochford Wines

WINERY | This winery occupies a striking-looking property; its cellar door building crafted almost entirely of glass overlooks the vineyards and rolling green paddocks. The family-owned winery produces renowned Pinot Noir and Chardonnay, and its huge amphitheater plays host to international and local performers during the annual A Day on the Green concert series (acts have included Alicia Keys and Elton John). Isabella's fine-dining restaurant serves French Mediterranean meals and light platters 11:30–4, seven days a week, and pizzeria Il Vigneto is open for lunch and dinner on weekends and lunch only on Monday. Rochford has also teamed up with a group of distillers to create a range of gins, which you can weave into cocktails at its on-site gin bar, and its cellar door is open seven days. ✉ *878 Maroondah Hwy., Coldstream* ☎ *03/5957–3333* 🌐 *www.rochfordwines.com.au.*

Yering Station

WINERY | Victoria's first vineyard still has plenty of rustic charm, and it's a delightful place to eat, drink, and stay. An 1859 redbrick building is home to the busy cellar door, where you can taste its renowned Pinot Noirs and Shiraz Vioginers, or take a guided tasting, from A$10. The property's architectural and gastronomical pièce de résistance is the winery building, which houses the Wine Bar Restaurant. It's a sweeping, hand-hewn stone building with floor-to-ceiling windows overlooking spectacular valley scenery. Yering hosts an annual sculpture exhibition from October to December, and a farmers' market takes place on the third Sunday of the month. ✉ *38 Melba Hwy., Yarra Glen* ☎ *03/9730–0100* 🌐 *www.yering.com.*

"Just a short drive from Melbourne is the captivating beauty of the Yarra Valley." —photo by lisargold, Fodors.com member

Restaurants

Innocent Bystander

$$ | **PIZZA** | Despite the lofty, modern, steel-and-glass interior, this spacious contemporary restaurant in the town of Healesville has a warm, welcoming feel, and serves excellent food. It also hosts a winery's cellar door, along with a gourmet food shop and bakery. **Known for:** reservations required for indoor dining; variety of pizzas; local wine and beer. *Average main: A$24* ✉ *316 Maroondah Hwy., Healesville* ☎ *03/5999–9222* 🌐 *www.innocentbystander.com.au.*

Stones of the Yarra Valley

$$$$ | **MODERN AUSTRALIAN** | Housed in an old weather-beaten barn that has been beautifully restored, Stones of the Yarra Valley is set amid vines and apple orchards and surrounded by century-old oak trees with views of the Yarra Ranges. The Barn is a great place for weekend lunches (Saturday serves two courses for A$60 or three for A$75, Sunday's La Famiglia share table costs $85), and the historic Stables restaurant also serves weekend lunch and chef's shared plates tasting dinner on Friday and Saturday (lunch A$70, dinner A$100). **Known for:** boutique guesthouse next door; beautiful setting; weekend lunch. *Average main: A$70* ✉ *14 St. Huberts Rd., Coldstream* ☎ *03/8727–3000* 🌐 *stonesoftheyarravalley.com.*

★ **TarraWarra Estate**

$$$ | **AUSTRALIAN** | Turning off a country lane, TarraWarra Estate is a series of bold architectural statements: step through a hobbitlike door set into the green hills of its subterranean cellar door to taste the flagship chardonnays and Pinot Noir (open 11–5). Then wander between towering sculptures to the sunny restaurant for innovative Australian cuisine inspired by the bountiful kitchen gardens, set on the estate of nearly a thousand rolling acres of vines (serving noon–3, three courses A$85, four courses A$95, includes a plant-based menu). **Known for:** contemporary architecture; plant-based cuisines with a strong vegan focus; renowned art and sculpture

gallery. $ *Average main: A$38* ✉ *311 Healesville-Yarra Glen Rd., Healesville* ☎ *03/5962–3311* 🌐 *www.tarrawarra.com.au, www.twma.com.au* ⏲ *Closed Mon.*

Coffee and Quick Bites

Matilda Bay Brewery

$ | **PIZZA** | **FAMILY** | For a pick-me-up, head into this breezy brewpub, a staple on the Yarra Valley scene. It serves tasty dishes using local and organic produce to accompany its renowned range of craft beers, including crisped Italian pizzas, vegan burgers, and its signature Matilda Bay Burger. **Known for:** easy pizzas; renowned craft beers; signature burger. $ *Average main: A$15* ✉ *336 Maroondah Hwy., Healesville* ☎ *03/5957–3200* 🌐 *matildabay.com.*

My Little Kitchen

$ | **CAFÉ** | **FAMILY** | A real local's café, you'll find families and their pets mingling, with good coffee, an array of tasty brunch dishes including zucchini fritters with grilled haloumi, brekkie rolls (bacon and eggs), tacos, and steak sandwiches. **Known for:** quality coffee; Yarra Valley produce; kid-friendly. $ *Average main: A$19* ✉ *274 Maroondah Hwy., Healesville* ☎ *03/5611–3686* 🌐 *www.mylittlekitchen.com.au.*

Hotels

Balgownie Estate Vineyard Resort and Spa

$$$ | **HOTEL** | This resort has it all—stylish suites and apartment-style accommodations overlooking the Yarra Valley and Dandenong Ranges, plus a ton of other amenities. **Pros:** great day spa; excellent facilities; on-site cellar door. **Cons:**; service inconsistent; holds conferences, so may get busy at times. $ *Rooms from: A$250* ✉ *1309 Melba Hwy., at Gulf Rd., Yarra Glen* ☎ *03/9730–0700* 🌐 *www.balgownie.com.au* *15 rooms, 55 spa suites* *Free Breakfast.*

Chateau Yering

$$$$ | **HOTEL** | Once an 1850s homestead, whose grounds later became the Yarra Valley's first vineyard, this luxury hotel features opulent suites that have antique furniture and deep claw-foot or spa bathtubs. **Pros:** beautiful setting and valley views; grand living; excellent dining options. **Cons:** service inconsistent; needs some updates; high tea is a little disappointing. $ *Rooms from: A$395* ✉ *42 Melba Hwy., Yarra Glen* ☎ *03/9237–3333, 1800/237–333* 🌐 *www.chateauyering.com.au* *32 rooms* *Free Breakfast.*

Healesville Hotel

$ | **HOTEL** | This famous local lodge in a restored 1910 pub has a renowned dining room and seven colorful, modern rooms upstairs, with high ceilings, tall windows, and genteel touches such as handmade soaps. **Pros:** historic hotel; range of accommodation styles; great food. **Cons:** shared bathrooms within the main building; limited facilities. $ *Rooms from: A$130* ✉ *256 Maroondah Hwy., Healesville* ☎ *03/5962–4002* 🌐 *www.healesvillehotel.com.au* *7 rooms, 1 house, 2 apartments* *No Meals.*

Shopping

Four Pillars

WINE/SPIRITS | The bellwether of Australia's craft gin movement, Four Pillars' industrial-style distillery bustles with admirers: its Navy Strength Gin is a six-time winner of best its class at the world Gin Masters. Pop in for a tasting paddle of gins and a light snack and watch the distillers at work behind a glass window, or go deeper with a tour of the distillery. Like what you taste? All its standard gins and limited-edition gins (such as the Christmas gin, available from November), as well as its preferred tonic waters, are available for purchase, along with stylish cookbooks and chic drinking paraphernalia. ✉ *2a Lilydale Rd., Healesville* ☎ *800/374–446* 🌐 *www.fourpillarsgin.com.au.*

Yarra Valley Chocolaterie

CHOCOLATE | FAMILY | Resident European chocolatiers create a vast array of high-quality treats in all shapes and styles—more than 300 of them, in fact—at this artisan chocolate and ice-cream maker. Many items include locally grown ingredients such as rosemary and lavender, and there's a bush tucker range of chocolates incorporating native plant products such as lemon myrtle, jindilli nut, and wattleseed. They even have a range of beauty products, if the adults want an excuse to smear chocolate-inspired goodness all over their faces. The Chocolaterie has year-round events including kids' chocolate-making classes. It also has outposts on the Mornington Peninsula and Great Ocean Road. **TIP→ The on-site café has a beautiful view over hilly green farmland and is a great place to eat chocolate and made-on-the-premises ice cream, and also serves light meals; we also suggest you buy a selection of chocolates to enjoy later.** ✉ *35 Old Healesville Rd., Yarra Glen* ☎ *03/9730–2777* 🌐 *www.yvci.com.au.*

Activities

There are plenty of opportunities to get out in the fresh air in the Yarra Valley. Those with cash to spare can go ballooning; others may just like to walk or ride a bike along the trails or play a round of golf. Wine tasting is a given.

BALLOONING

★ Global Ballooning

BALLOONING | This hot-air-balloon operation runs flights over the Yarra Valley. Take off at dawn and drift peacefully over the vineyards for an hour. For A$30 extra, enjoy a breakfast with sparkling wine after the flight at Balgownie Estate. Check the website for accommodation packages. ✉ *Balgownie Estate, 1309 Melba Hwy., Yarra Glen* ☎ *1800/627–661* 🌐 *www.globalballooning.com.au* 🎫 *From A$405.*

BIKING

Ride Time Yarra Valley

BIKING | FAMILY | With bases in both Lilydale and Warburton, you can rent all types of bikes—including mountain, electric, kids, and road bikes—and compulsory helmet from A$60 a day (adult bikes). Ride Time will steer you to the best cycling routes in the valley. It also offers one-way pickup and delivery services for an additional fee on the popular, (mostly) flat 38-km (24-mile) Warburton Rail Trail, which traverses from Lilydale to Warburton via vivid green gullies, national park, forests, and vineyards. Keep an eye out for kangaroos on the way. ✉ *108 Main St., Lilydale* ✣ *Across road from Lilydale Railway Station* ☎ *03/5966–9649* 🌐 *yarravalleycycles.com.*

BUSHWALKING

Yarra Ranges National Park

HIKING & WALKING | About 80 km (50 miles) east of Melbourne, this nearly 200,000-acre national park extending north of the Yarra River has plenty to keep your legs busy. Cross a 1,148-foot-long elevated walkway (known as the Rainforest Gallery) to see 400-year-old Mountain Ash and Myrtle Beech trees, trek all or a section of the 29-km (18-mile) O'Shannassy Aqueduct Trail, or climb the lookout tower at the peak of Mt. Donna Buang. Afterward, unpack lunch at one of several picnic areas, which can be reached by car. ✉ *Yarra Ranges National Park* ☎ *131–963* 🌐 *www.parks.vic.gov.au.*

GOLF

Warburton Golf Club

GOLF | This gem of a course is hidden among the Yarra Ranges. For A$35 for 18 holes on weekends (A$30 on weekdays), you can golf over meandering streams and bushland blooming with wildflowers. Although it's a semiprivate club, visitors are very welcome to come and play 9 or 18 holes if they call and book in advance. Rental clubs are available (A$10) if you didn't pack your own. The course is hilly and golf carts can be hired for A$40.

Warburton is 30 km (19 miles) southeast of Healesville. ✉ *17 Dammans Rd., Warburton* ☎ *03/5966–2306* 🌐 *www.warburtongolf.com.au* 💳 *18 holes: weekdays A$30, weekends A$35; 9 holes: A$23/ A$28* ⛳ *18 holes, 5925 yards, par 69.*

The Dandenong Ranges

Melburnians come to the beautiful Dandenong Ranges, also known simply as the Dandenongs, for a breath of fresh air, especially in fall when the deciduous trees turn golden and in spring when the public gardens explode into color with tulip, daffodil, azalea, and rhododendron blooms. At Mt. Dandenong, the highest point (2,077 feet), a scenic lookout known as SkyHigh Mt. Dandenong affords spectacular views over Melbourne and the bay beyond. Dandenong Ranges National Park, which encompasses five smaller parks, including Sherbrooke Forest and Ferntree Gully, has dozens of walking trails.

The many villages (which include Olinda, Sassafras, Kalorama, Sherbrooke, and Kallista) have curio shops, art galleries, food emporiums, cafés, and restaurants, and are dotted with lovely B&Bs. Visitors should be aware that the Dandenong Ranges and the high point of Mt. Dandenong are completely different from Dandenong, an outer suburb of Melbourne (30 km [19 miles] southeast of downtown and on the Pakenham railway line).

GETTING HERE AND AROUND

Motorists can either take the Yarra Valley route (*see above*), turn off at Lilydale, and head south to Montrose and on to Olinda, or take the Eastern Freeway or M3 (a toll applies) and exit at the Ringwood Bypass (State Route 26), which becomes the Mt. Dandenong Road (C415) and on to Olinda. Trains travel from Flinders Street Station to Belgrave on the Belgrave line. This town is on the southern edge of the Dandenongs and is the home of the steam train called Puffing Billy.

Other towns on the same railway line are Ferntree Gully and Upper Ferntree Gully.

Bus 688 runs from Upper Ferntree Gully Station through the trees to Sassafras and Olinda, then passes William Ricketts Sanctuary; while Bus 694 links Belgrave Station to the Mt. Dandenong Lookout, via the villages of Sherbrooke, Sassafras, and Olinda. Alternatively, take the train from Flinders Street Station to Croydon (on the Lilydale line), then take the 688 bus south to William Ricketts Sanctuary and Olinda.

TOURS

Melbourne's Best Day Tours
This tour company takes visitors to major sights in the region, including its Puffing Billy and Wineries tour. ✉ *Federation Sq., Flinders St. at Russell St., City Center* 🌐 *www.melbournetours.com.au* 💳 *From A$175.*

VISITOR INFORMATION

CONTACTS Dandenong Ranges Information. ✉ *Upper Ferntree Gully* ☎ *03/8739–8000* 🌐 *www.visitdandenongranges.com.au.*

Sights

★ **Cloudehill Gardens & Nursery**
GARDEN | These glorious gardens are divided into 25 "garden rooms" that include the Maple Court, the Azalea Steps, and 100-year-old European beech trees. They were first established in the late 1890s as commercial and cut-flower gardens by the Woolrich family. The internationally famous gardens are dotted with artworks by local artists and the Diggers Garden Shop hosts workshops and sells seeds, plants, and books. A central terraced area, with manicured hedges and a sculpture of a huge vase, is stunning, as is the view across the mountain ranges from the garden café. The Seasons café serves breakfast, lunch, and afternoon tea daily, with some

ingredients coming from its own kitchen garden. A popular dish is the "Chatter Platter," a selection of cheeses, terrine, dips, garlic prawns, and salad (A$30 per person). ✉ *89 Olinda-Monbulk Rd., Olinda* ☎ *03/9751–1009* 🌐 *www.cloudehill.com.au* 🎫 *A$10.*

★ Dandenong Ranges Botanic Garden

GARDEN | The expansive gardens contain the largest collection of rhododendrons in the southern hemisphere, with around 15,000 rhododendrons, and thousands more azaleas and camellias; the garden's premier season is spring, when they put on a show of spectacular white, mauve, yellow, and pink blooms. Several miles of walking trails lead to vistas over the Yarra Valley, and the gardens are a short stroll from Olinda village. Otherwise, jump on board the Garden Explorer minibus for a short, guided tour. For a perfect afternoon, combine your visit with tea and scones in the park's garden's café or back down in the village. ✉ *The Georgian Rd., Olinda* ☎ *131–963* 🌐 *parks.vic.gov.au* 🎫 *Free.*

George Tindale Memorial Garden

GARDEN | Azaleas, camellias, and hydrangeas spill down the hillsides in this 6-acre, English-style garden. While at its most colorful in spring, when the flowers are in bloom, and in autumn, when the trees turn gold and yellow, it is also beautiful in winter with a touch of snow. It's located just 8 km (5 miles) north of Belgrave in the little forest settlement of Sherbrooke, where whipbird calls echo through the trees. ✉ *33 Sherbrooke Rd., Sherbrook* ☎ *131–963* 🌐 *parks.vic.gov.au* 🎫 *Free.*

Puffing Billy

TRAIN/TRAIN STATION | **FAMILY** | This gleaming narrow-gauge steam train, based 46 km (28 miles) from Healesville in the town of Belgrave, runs on a line originally built in the early 1900s to open up the Dandenong Ranges to 20th-century pioneers. It's a great way to see the foothill landscapes. Daily trips between Belgrave and Emerald Lake pass through picturesque forests and over spectacular wooden trestle bridges. The 13-km (8-mile) trip takes an hour; it's another hour if you continue to the historic town of Gembrook. There are also on-board lunch and train-and-picnic packs, plus special music and children's events, and the new, architecturally impressive visitor center includes a café and interactive activities sharing the little train's long history. ✉ *1 Old Monbulk Rd., Belgrave* ☎ *03/9757–0700* 🌐 *www.puffingbilly.com.au* 🎫 *From A$36.*

SkyHigh Mount Dandenong

VIEWPOINT | **FAMILY** | This lookout at the top of Mt. Dandenong has breathtaking views over Melbourne to the Mornington Peninsula and Port Phillip Bay. You can picnic or barbecue on the grounds, eat at the bistro (breakfast, lunch, and dinner), or stroll along the pleasant English Garden Walk while the kids get lost in the hedge maze (additional entry fee). Other fun attractions include a Wishing Tree and the Giant's Chair. Bistro open for breakfast, lunch, and dinner daily. On Sunday, book ahead for its popular roast lunch and afternoon teas: the lookout charges a gate fee upon entrance. ✉ *26 Observatory Rd., Mt. Dandenong* ☎ *03/9751–0443* 🌐 *www.skyhighmtdandenong.com.au* 🎫 *A$7 per car; maze A$6.*

★ William Ricketts Sanctuary

GARDEN | Fern gardens, moss-covered rocks, waterfalls, towering mountain ash, and 92 kiln-fired sculptures of Indigenous Australians and Australian native animals fill this 4-acre property on Mt. Dandenong. William Ricketts, who established the sanctuary in the 1930s, meant it to stand as an embodiment of his philosophy: that people must act as custodians of the natural environment as Australia's Indigenous people have for many millennia. Take an audio tour around the gardens (A$5) or download the podcast (free). ✉ *1402 Mt. Dandenong Tourist Rd., Mt. Dandenong* ☎ *131–963 Parks Victoria* 🌐 *parks.vic.gov.au* 🎫 *Free.*

All aboard the steam train

Restaurants

Olinda, Sassafras, and Sherbrooke each have a handful of good restaurants and cafés, and many specialty boutique stores selling curios and gifts. It's a short drive to the Dandenong Ranges Botanical Garden, Olinda Falls picnic grounds, Cloudehill Gardens, and various hiking trails to walk it all off.

Miss Marple's Tea Room

$ | **CAFÉ** | This determinedly old-fashioned and charming establishment is modeled after an English tearoom and is renowned for its afternoon teas. Named after the famous Agatha Christie detective, this place is a holdout from the era when the Dandenong Ranges were visited by genteel folk looking for polite conversation over a civilized cup of tea. **Known for:** scones with jam and cream; afternoon tea; long lines on weekends. *Average main: A$17 ✉ 382 Mt. Dandenong Tourist Rd., Sassafras ☎ 03/9755–1610 🌐 www.missmarplestearoom.com.*

Ranges

$$ | **EUROPEAN** | This popular café-restaurant, right in the heart of Olinda, buzzes all day and is the perfect place for a snack or meal after browsing the adjacent curio shops or gardens. It's open daily for breakfast, lunch, and morning and afternoon tea. **Known for:** afternoon tea; lively spot; daily savory pies. *Average main: A$25 ✉ 5 Olinda-Monbulk Rd., Olinda ☎ 03/9751–2133 🌐 www.ranges.com.au ⏲ No dinner Sun. and Mon.*

★ **Ripe Cafe**

$$ | **AUSTRALIAN** | With crackling open fires in winter and a covered deck for summer grazing, this buzzy cottage café-cum-providore is the perfect place for a heartwarming casual lunch or afternoon tea. The menu changes daily, but may include baguettes, fish, or pasta, with a focus on vegan, vegetarian, and gluten-free choices. **Known for:** open fire in winter; home-baked cakes; locally made relishes and condiments for sale. *Average main: A$22 ✉ 376 Mt. Dandenong Tourist*

Rd., Sassafras ☎ 03/9755–2100 🌐 ripecafesassafras.com ⊗ No dinner.

 Coffee and Quick Bites

Proserpina Bakehouse

$ | BAKERY | FAMILY | All the baked goods in this popular café began from Victorian biodynamic wheat flour that's milled here in the bakery. Proserpina bakes its breads daily, including the popular *pane di'casa* wheat bread and the sprouted grain spelt and rye. **Known for:** tarts and pastries made on the premises; organic breads; reasonable prices. *$ Average main: A$12 ✉ 361 Mt. Dandenong Tourist Rd., Sassafras ☎ 03/9755–3332 ⊗ Closed Tues.*

Olinda is the main village in the Dandenong Ranges region and a good base for exploring the area. It's actually two villages (Lower and Upper Olinda, though Lower Olinda is better known by the name of the peak it sits beneath, Mt. Dandenong). The two are connected by Monash Avenue, along which you'll find a lot of the town's B&Bs and self-catering cottages.

Yarra Ranges Getaways

$$$ | HOUSE | FAMILY | Curl up with a book in front of the open fire in a charming 1880s cottage, or take over a sprawling house on 10 acres of landscaped gardens—there are 21 properties in this group, ranging from one-bedroom cottages to a four-bedroom house. **Pros:** live like a local; historic properties; a wide range of properties to suit. **Cons:** no breakfast in some properties; busy on weekends; two-night minimum stay. *$ Rooms from: A$215 ✉ 361 Mt. Dandenong Tourist Rd., Sassafras ☎ 1300/488–448 🌐 www.valleyrangesgetaways.com.au 21 cottages and houses No Meals.*

Perfect Picnics 

The Dandenongs are heaven for fresh-air freaks, flower fanatics, and foodies. Pick up some goodies at one of the region's Saturday morning produce markets and work up an appetite taking the 2 km (1½-mile) loop walk to Sherbrooke Falls from O'Donohue Picnic Ground. Ask the tourist office about other great walks and picnic spots.

 Activities

HIKING

Dandenong Ranges National Park

HIKING & WALKING | Several reserves, including the Sherbrooke Forest—home to Sherbrooke Falls—make up this beautiful leafy and hilly national park. Trails include the Olinda Forest Trail (from Mt. Dandenong to Kallista), the Western Trail from the top of Mt. Dandenong to Ferntree Gully, the Sherbrooke Falls Loop, and the Tourist Track from Sassafras to Emerald. Brochures and a trail map are available on the park's website. *✉ Dandenong Ranges, Olinda ☎ 131–963 🌐 www.parks.vic.gov.au.*

Mornington Peninsula

The Mornington Peninsula circles the southeastern half of Port Phillip Bay. A much larger piece of land than it first appears, the peninsula is lapped by water on three sides, with 192 km (121 miles) of coastline, and measures about 65 km (40 miles) by 35 km (22 miles). Along the bay's coast is a string of seaside villages stretching from the larger towns of Frankston and Mornington to the summer holiday towns of Mount Martha, Rosebud, and Rye, with upmarket Sorrento and Portsea at its tip. On the Western Port Bay side, the smaller settlements of Flinders, Somers, and Hastings have quieter beaches without the crowds.

Together with Main Ridge and Merricks, Red Hill is one of the state's premium producers of cool-climate wines, particularly Pinot Noir and Chardonnay. The majority of the peninsula's 60 wineries are clustered around Red Hill and Red Hill South; however, there are another dozen or more dotted around areas farther north, including Moorooduc, Dromana, and Merricks. For an afternoon of fine wine, excellent seafood, and spectacular coastal views, plan a route that winds between vineyards. Red Hill has a busy produce-and-crafts market, which has been operating for decades and shows no signs of abating. It's held on the first Saturday morning of each month from September to May. A good website for getting all the lowdown on peninsula wineries is *www.morningtonpeninsulawineries.com.au*.

Sorrento is one of the region's prettiest beach towns and one of the most popular day-tripper spots on the peninsula. It's also the peninsula's oldest settlement, and thus is dotted with numerous historic buildings and National Trust sites (among them the Collins Settlement Historical Site, which marks the first settlement site at Sullivan Bay; and the Nepean Historical Society Museum, with its displays of Aboriginal artifacts and settlers' tools). In summer the town transforms from a sleepy seaside village into a hectic holiday hot spot. Sorrento Back Beach, with its rock pools and cliff-side trails, is one of the most popular hangouts.

GETTING HERE AND AROUND

Renting a car in Melbourne is the most practical way of seeing the Mornington Peninsula. The simplest way is via the tolled M1 and M3 freeways, so you won't pass a single traffic light or roundabout. They connect to the Mornington Peninsula Freeway (M11), which continues south to the various bay-side towns. Otherwise, drive south along the Nepean Highway and at Frankston take the Frankston-Moorooduc Highway or stay on the Nepean Highway—eventually they both merge into the M11. A train runs from Flinders Street Station to Frankston. At Frankston, connect with a diesel-train service to towns on the east of the peninsula including Hastings, Bittern, Point Crib, and Stony Point. Buses also run from Frankston to the bay-side towns; the No. 781 bus goes to Mornington and Mount Martha and the Nos. 782 and 783 buses travel to Hastings and Flinders on the Western Port side.

Ferries run passenger services to Phillip Island and French Island from Stony Point (on the eastern side of the Mornington Peninsula) and back again on this foot ferry (bicycles permitted A$4 extra, one-way). Parking is available, and trains run to the Stony Point terminus. An adult one-way ferry fare is A$13.50.

A car and passenger ferry crosses Port Phillip Bay, sailing between Sorrento (Mornington Peninsula) and Queenscliff (Bellarine Peninsula), departing every hour on the hour 7 am–6 pm, later in peak holiday season. One-way fares are A$13 (foot passenger), and a car costs from A$72, plus fares for any passengers.

The SkyBus shuttle bus runs from Melbourne Airport's Terminal 4 (T4) to Rosebud on the Mornington Peninsula with stops along the bay. One-way fares range from A$22 to A$55. The buses have free Wi-Fi, no prebooking required.

TRANSPORTATION

SkyBus - Peninsula Express
Ride from Melbourne Airport's Terminal 4 (T4) to Rosebud on the Mornington Peninsula with 16 stops along the bay including Frankston and Mordialloc train station. One-way fares range from A$22 to A$55. The buses have free Wi-Fi, no

prebooking required. ☎ *1300/759–287* 🌐 *www.skybus.com.au.*

Sorrento-Queenscliff Ferry
This car and passenger ferry crosses Port Phillip Bay, sailing between Sorrento (Mornington Peninsula) and Queenscliff (Bellarine Peninsula), departing every hour on the hour 7 am–6 pm, later in peak holiday season. One-way fares are A$13 (foot passenger), and a car costs from A$72, plus fares for any passengers. ✉ *Sorrento* ☎ *03/5257–4500* 🌐 *www.searoad.com.au.*

Western Port Ferries
Cross from Stony Point (on the eastern side of the Mornington Peninsula) to Phillip Island and French Island and back again on this foot ferry (bicycles permitted A$4 extra, one-way). Parking is available, and trains run to the Stony Point terminus. An adult one-way ferry fare is A$13.50 ☎ *03/5257–4565* 🌐 *www.westernportferries.com.au.*

WINERY TOURS

Amour of the Grape
Choose a personal tour to create your own itinerary or a set winery tour for groups of two to seven passengers. A day's outing includes tastings at four or five preselected cellar doors, and a gourmet lunch and a glass of wine at a boutique winery café. Beer and cider tours, scenic, and spa packages to the Peninsula Hot Springs are also available, and bigger groups can be accommodated on request. ☎ *0414/704–801* 🌐 *www.amourofthegrape.com.au* 🎫 *From A$150 per person Mornington Peninsula pickup; central Melbourne pickup from A$275 per person (for 2 people).*

Localing Tours
Go beyond the bus tour and meet the winemakers of the Mornington Peninsula, or walk a coastal track to work up an appetite for lunch at one of Victoria's great regional restaurants. With their private tours, Localing Tours helps visitors find that gallery hidden down a country lane, the café everyone's talking about, the deserted beach. Multiday and self-drive tours also available. ✉ *City Center* ☎ *03/9088–8001* 🌐 *www.localingtours.com* 🎫 *A$1320 for up to 2 guests (excludes lunch).*

Wine Tours Victoria
This operator runs tours of four to five wineries using minivans for up to 10 people, with a winery lunch, and coffee also on the menu. It services all four regions that surround the Port Phillip Bay: Mornington Peninsula, Yarra Valley, Macedon Ranges, and the up-and-coming Bellarine Peninsula, with its coastal views, and is available for private charter to any other Victorian wine region. ✉ *9 The Willows, Gisborne, Melbourne* ☎ *03/5428–8500, 1800/946–386* 🌐 *www.winetours.com.au* 🎫 *From A$180 per person, minimum 2 people.*

VISITOR INFORMATION

CONTACTS Mornington Peninsula Visitor Information Centre. ✉ *359B Point Nepean Rd., Dromana* ☎ *03/5950–1579, 1800/804–009 toll-free* 🌐 *www.visitmorningtonpeninsula.org.*

Sights

★ **Arthurs Seat Eagle**
AMUSEMENT RIDE | FAMILY | There's been a chairlift climbing up to Arthurs Seat since 1960. Now, the new Eagle's gondolas take 14 minutes to drift slowly above the eucalyptus forests up to Arthurs Seat, at 1,030 feet above sea level. The gondolas are surprisingly quiet, so you'll hear the birdcall among the trees: keep an eye out for the wedge-tailed eagle, after which the Eagle chairlift is named. You can travel one way or return, starting from either the base station, or down from the summit station at Arthur's Seat. It's not a mountain, but the peak affords magnificent views back to Melbourne and across Port Phillip Bay. Take coffee or

Continued on page 276

In recent decades, Australia has emerged as an international wine powerhouse. The country's varied climate has proven favorable for growing high-quality grapes, and winemakers now produce some of the world's best Shiraz (Syrah) wines, as well as acclaimed Pinot Noirs and Rieslings. Wine sales currently contribute about **$6.5** billion to the country's economy, and Australia is the third largest supplier to the United States behind France and Italy.

Touring wineries here is easy, as most properties have tasting rooms with regular hours. Whether you're sipping in situ at a winery or tasting wines at a shop in Sydney, here's how to get the most from your wine experience.

(top) Pinot noir grapes (right) Vineyard in One Tree Hill, South Australia.

Wines of Australia

WINE TRENDS: THEN AND NOW

(top left) Wine bottles await labels, (bottom left) Hunter Valley vista, (right) tasting in Barossa Valley

Although the first grapes in Australia arrived with British settlers in 1787, it really wasn't until the mid 1960s that a more refined tradition of wine making began to take hold. Prior to 1960, Australia's wine repertoire extended little beyond sherry and port, but after WWII, an influx of European immigrants, notably from Germany and Italy, opened the country's eyes to new tastes and production methods.

Australia now produces many classic varietals at prices from **A$10** to **A$80,000** (for a 1951 Penfolds Grange Hermitage, made by Australian pioneer **winemake**r Max Schubert). There are more than 60 wine regions dotted across the country and many of the smaller producers in lesser-known areas are beginning to flourish.

Although the industry has experienced rapid growth, it hasn't been without its problems. The health of the global economy, international competition, global warming, disease, drought, and bushfire have each presented challenges along the way.

These days, Australian vintners are known for combining old traditions with new ideas and technical innovations. While oak barrels are still widely used, stainless steel and plastic tanks are now recognized as suitable fermentation and storage methods. Screw caps, introduced more than **two decades** ago, are becoming more popular with winemakers and consumers.

The industry's latest trends also include a growing interest in environmental sustainability, with organic and biodynamic wines appearing from numerous producers. The internet has revolutionized business, giving even the smallest vintners access to an international stage.

Like well-cellared wine, the palate of modern Australia is continually maturing. Whether your taste is for robust reds from Coonawarra and Barossa or the delicate and versatile whites of the Hunter Valley and Margaret River, Australia's winemakers are producing beautiful wines perfect to enjoy now or later.

AUSTRALIA'S DOMINANT VARIETALS

REDS

SHIRAZ

Australia's classic varietal. A full-bodied wine that, in hot areas, makes an earthy expression with softer acidity. Cooler regions produce a leaner, peppery style.

CABERNET SAUVIGNON

Dark red with blackcurrant and black cherry flavors, often with firm tannins and more acidity than Shiraz.

MERLOT

Intensely purple colored, full-bodied wine characterized by moderate tannins, aromas of plum, and a velvety mouth-feel.

PINOT NOIR

Lighter-bodied with gentle tannins and fruity aromas of red berries.

WHITES

CHARDONNAY

Full-bodied wine that is often high in alcohol and low in acidity. Most Australian versions are oaked.

RIESLING

Lighter-bodied wines with citrus and honey notes. Most are unoaked and dry or slightly off-dry.

SAUVIGNON BLANC

Makes crisp, dry wines with high acid and aromas of peach and lime.

SEMILLON

Light-bodied wines that have crisp acidity and complex flavors, including herbs, nuts, and honey.

WHITE BLENDS

Chardonnay-Semillon and Sauvignon Blanc-Semillon blends are popular. Semillon adds bright notes.

WINE TOURING TIPS

Large vintners like Rosemount, McGuigan Wines, Jacobs Creek, Yalumba, and Wolf Blass are well equipped for visitors and many offer vineyard tours, as well as restaurants or cafes. Some require appointments.

Many boutique producers also have "cellar doors," a.k.a. tasting rooms, open seven days a week, but it is advisable to check their websites for details. The average tastings cost around A$10 to A$15 for a flight of up to five different styles. Some include cheese, cracker, and fruit plates.

Wine barrels

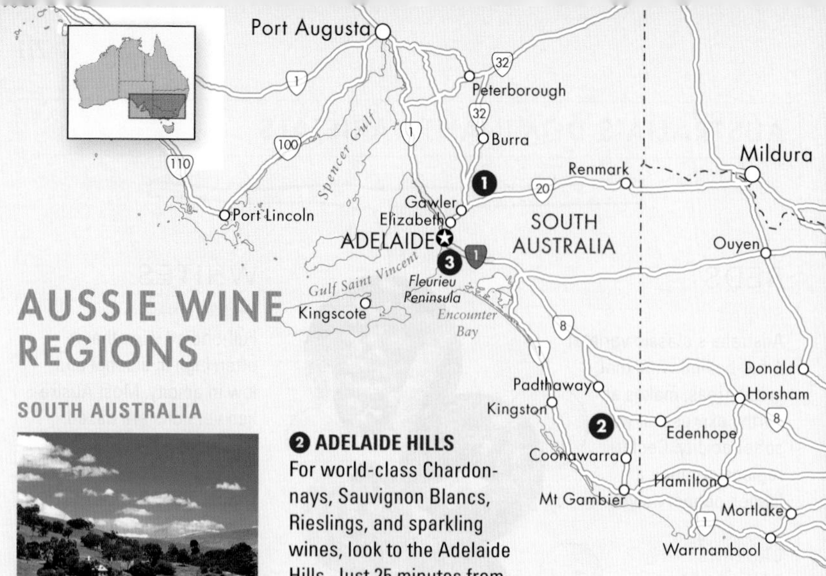

AUSSIE WINE REGIONS

SOUTH AUSTRALIA

Barossa Valley

❶ BAROSSA VALLEY

The country's best-known wine region, Barossa Valley has more than 550 grape growers, including some fifth- and sixth-generation families. Shiraz is highly celebrated, particularly the lauded Penfolds Grange. Cabernet Sauvignon, Grenache, Merlot, Riesling, Semillon, and Chardonnay are all well suited to Barossa's temperate climate, which is slightly cooler on its peaks and in neighboring Eden Valley. Big producers Jacobs Creek and Wolf Blass both have visitors centers with modern tasting rooms and restaurants. For a history lesson, take a tour at Langmeil Winery. An impressive property is Yalumba, with a stone winery and clock tower. So, too, is the well-established Peter Lehmann Estate on the banks of the North Para River.

❷ ADELAIDE HILLS

For world-class Chardonnays, Sauvignon Blancs, Rieslings, and sparkling wines, look to the Adelaide Hills. Just 25 minutes from the center of Adelaide, this high-altitude region, amid Mount Lofty and down through the Piccadilly Valley, has nurtured elegantly refined white wines. The cooler climate also means that it's one of South Australia's leading producers of the temperamental Pinot Noir. There are about 25 cellars that offer tastings, including Petaluma Cellar, well known for its sparkling wines, Rieslings, and Chardonnays as well as its modern Bridgewater Mill restaurant. To try Italian varietals, head to Chain of Ponds. For excellent Sauvignon Blanc, stop into Shaw and Smith's 46-hectare estate.

Adelaide Hills

❸ MCLAREN VALE

Situated in the Fleurieu Peninsula region, McLaren Vale is an easy 40-minute trip south of Adelaide. Uniquely located by the coast, it's regarded as one of the more unpretentious regions thanks to laid-back beach lifestyle, passionate vintners, and family-owned wineries. This fusion of ideals, together with its warm climate, has most likely sparked its interest in experimenting with more exotic varieties such as Tempranillo, Zinfandel, and Mourvedre, as well as Viognier and Sangiovese. There are more than 60 cellar tasting rooms, ranging from the large producers such as Rosemount Estate and Tintara Winery to boutique producers such as Wirra Wirra, D'Arenberg, and Gemtree, each offering sales and wine flights that include the chance to sample local foods.

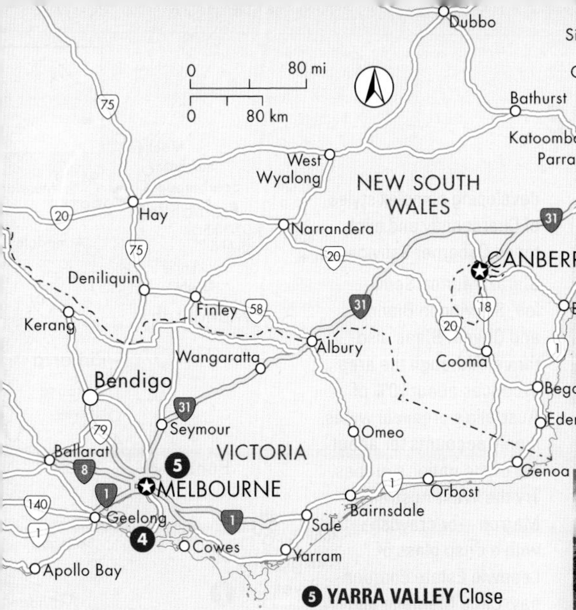

VICTORIA

❹ MORNINGTON PENINSULA

An hour south of Melbourne, the peninsula is a magnet for lovers of Pinot Noir and cool-climate Chardonnay. This is not the place for big brands, but little laneways leading to tiny vineyards – in fact, there are more than 50 cellar doors on this slip of a peninsula, many boasting exceptional restaurants for perfect food and wine matching, followed by a swim at a sandy beach and a night sleeping amidst the vines. Try T'Gallant for its approachable pizza and pinot grigio or belweather Crittenden Estate for adventures with Italian varietals. Make time to wander the lauded sculpture gardens of Montalto and Pt Leo Estate.

❺ YARRA VALLEY Close proximity to Melbourne makes the Yarra an easy choice if your touring time is limited. A cool climate and diverse mix of volcanic and clay soils have allowed Chardonnay and Pinot Noir to flourish. Other notable varieties here include Viognier, Gewürztraminer, Pinot Gris, and Sauvignon Blanc, as well as Malbec, Sangiovese, and Nebbiolo. Sparkling wine is also a winner and Domaine Chandon is a magnificent spot to enjoy some perfect bubbly. For a laidback experience, Lilydale is also a good choice. But upping the style stakes is the magnificent Yering Station with its modern Australian restaurant and gallery space. Elsewhere, De Bortoli sells delicious top-end wines.

Yarra Valley

Hunter Valley

NEW SOUTH WALES

❻ HUNTER VALLEY

Despite being a producer of award-winning Chardonnay, Verdelho, and Shiraz, it's the honeyed Semillon, which can mature for up to two decades, that Hunter Valley does best. Split into upper and lower regions, it has more that 150 years of winemaking up its sleeve and 120 cellar doors. It's safe to say the Hunter knows how to entertain. From large-scale music concerts at Bimbadgen Estate and Tempus Two to the annual Jazz in the Vines event and other small food and wine festivals year-round, the region is constantly buzzing. Pokolbin, Broke, Wollombi, Lovedale, Rothbury and Mt View are the main areas to sample the regions best offerings. Autumn is an excellent time to visit.

AUSSIE WINE REGIONS

WESTERN AUSTRALIA

❼ MARGARET RIVER REGION With the first vines planted in 1967, Margaret River might be one of the country's younger wine areas but that hasn't stopped it from producing exceptionally high quality vintages.

Cool breezes from the Indian Ocean and a steady, Mediterranean-style climate offer perfect conditions for developing complex styles of Chardonnay and minty-toned Cabernet Sauvignons. Shiraz, Merlot, Semillon, Sauvignon Blanc, and Chenin Blanc also thrive. Although the area produces about 20% of Australia's premium wines, it only accounts for about **2%** of the nation's grapes. Try the West Australian Marron—or crayfish—with a crisp glass of Leeuwin Estate chardonnay. Cape Mentelle and **Cullen** are also among the region's highlights, with many of their special releases sold only through their cellar doors.

READING THE LABEL

According to Australia's Label Integrity Program, when a wine label states region, grape variety, or vintage, then 85% of the wine contained in the bottle must come from that region, variety, or vintage.

❶ The producer of the wine.

❷ The vintage year, meaning the year the grapes were picked, crushed, and bottled.

❸ Australian GIs, or Geographic Indications, identify the region where the wine grapes were grown.

❹ The varietal, or type of grapes used to make the wine.

❺ The wine in this bottle contains 12% alcohol content by volume.

❻ The wine's country of origin.

❼ The volume of wine in the bottle.

MORE TASTING OPPORTUNITIES

Wine tasting at Mitchell Winery, Clare Valley

SIPPING IN SHOPS AND BARS

Even when you're not ensconced in the country's lush vineyards, high-quality wine isn't far away. The capital cities serve as a gateway for many of the wine country's top tastes.

In Sydney, try city center wine bars like **Ash Street Cellar** or **Glass Brasserie wine bar** at the Hilton Hotel, or visit **10 William St** in Paddington and the beautiful little **Love Tilly Devine** in Darlinghurst. The **Australian Wine Centre** wine merchants in Circular Quay offer private tastings (with prior notice).

Heading south, visit Melbourne's **Prince Wine Store** at one of its three locations, or soak up the atmosphere at **The Melbourne Supper Club** and the **Carlton Wine Room**. **Juliet wine bar** puts female winemakers in the spotlight, while the vast wine list in **Marion** will find a fit for all budgets, with an exciting array available by the glass in this neighborhood wine bar on **Gertrude St**, Fitzroy.

The upscale **Leigh Street Wine Room** in Adelaide's centre has a huge range of natural wines, and smaller vineyards are well represented at the city's stalwart **East End Cellars. Petition**, in Perth's State Buildings, is a good bet with its shelves of wines, stacked up the ceiling.

WINE FESTIVALS

Festivals offer chance to interact with the winemakers as well as sample local produce, especially cheese, fruit, and seafood. **The Barossa Vintage Festival** is one of the largest and longest running wine events in South Australia. Held in April each year it has everything from rare wine auctions to family friendly events. Other notables are **Adelaide's Tasting Australia** (April), **Coonawarra After Dark Weekend** (April), and **McLaren Vale Sea** and **Vines Festival** (June). In Western Australia, the **Western Australia Gourmet Escape** (November) celebrates culinary and winemaking talents while the month-long **Melbourne Food & Wine Festival** extends right across the state (March).

RESEARCH & PLANNING

A little planning will allow you to make the perfect choices when it comes to deciding which regions to visit and where to taste. The websites of Australia's tourism commissions are filled with helpful planning informations. Not only do they offer winery information but also options for tours, accommodation and other sights to see while in the area. These include 🌐 *www.visitvictoria.com*, 🌐 *www.southaustralia.com*, 🌐 *www.visitnsw.com.au*, 🌐 *www.westernaustralia.com*

Once on the ground, visitors centers such as the **Margaret River Wine Centre, Adelaide's National Wine Centre of Australia, and Hunter Valley Wine Country Tourism** can offer sound advice, especially on the best varietals and history of the regions.

Barossa Vintage Festival

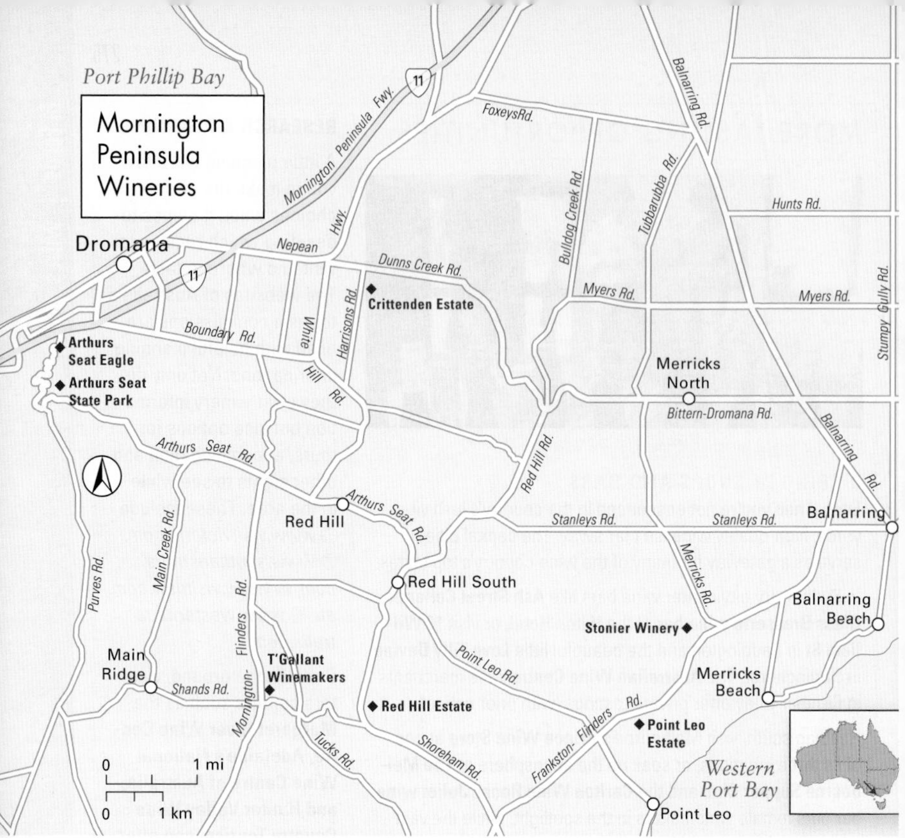

lunch at the café at the top before your return journey. There is plenty of parking at the base, as well as a small café, but limited parking at the peak, and the entire facility is wheelchair-friendly. From the summit, take the 1.8-km (1.1-mile) circuit walk, which passes several scenic viewing points. ✉ *Base station, 1085 Arthurs Seat Rd., Dromana* ☎ *03/5987–0600* 🌐 *www.aseagle.com.au* 🎫 *From $18.*

Arthurs Seat State Park

VIEWPOINT | **FAMILY** | Sweeping views of the surrounding countryside can be seen from this park, taking in Port Phillip Bay, Port Phillip Heads, and—on a clear day—the city skyline, the You Yangs, and Mt. Macedon. The mountain, which gives Arthurs Seat State Park its name, is the highest point on the Mornington Peninsula and named after Arthurs Seat in Edinburgh. A marked scenic drive snakes its way up to the summit, and walking tracks meander through the park's stands of eucalyptus. Seawinds, a public garden established by a local gardener in the 1940s, also forms part of the park and is a 10-minute walk or about 500 yards away. The road from Mornington is open at all times, so you can enjoy the spectacular mountaintop view by day or at night to see the lights. ✉ *Arthurs Seat Rd., Arthur's Seat* ☎ *131–963* 🌐 *www.parks.vic.gov.au* 🎫 *Free.*

Crittenden Estate

WINERY | One of the region's most picturesque wineries with a lovely lakeside setting, Crittenden Estate produces Chardonnay, Pinot Noir, Pinot Grigio, and some Spanish and Italian styles. The flagship Crittenden Estate Pinot Noir and Chardonnay are made from vines that are among the oldest on the peninsula.

The cellar door is open for tastings daily, and winery tours can be arranged by appointment. The restaurant, Stillwater at Crittenden ($$$), is lovely year-round, and when the weather is fine, diners sit out on a terrace under shady umbrellas while enjoying views over the lake. It is open weekends for dinner and daily for lunch, except in winter when it closes Monday and Tuesday. Want to linger awhile? The estate has three stylish overwater bungalows, a minute's amble along the lake's edge from the cellar door and restaurant. ✉ *25 Harrisons Rd., Dromana* ☎ *03/5981–9555 restaurant, 03/5987–3800 cellar door, 0400/339–995 accommodations* 🌐 *www.crittendenwines.com.au, www.lakesidevillas.com.au.*

★ Point Leo Estate

WINERY | The once private estate of one of the wealthiest men in Australia, Point Leo Estate opened to the public in late 2017 with a fine dining restaurant and winery experience set against dramatic coastal views and enhanced by an ambitious collection of more than 50 large-scale contemporary international and local works dotted along winding paths. Download the audio walk app from Point Leo's website before you visit and plan to spend an entire afternoon exploring. If all that sculpture gets you thirsty, take a break for a wine tasting at the cellar door (or take a glass on your walk). If you can plan ahead, make a reservation at Laura, considered one of Victoria's top restaurants, at the bistro next door, Pt. Leo Restaurant, or outside on the Wine Terrace, which often has live music and always has glorious views of the vineyard, sculptures, and the bay. ✉ *3649 Frankston-Flinders Rd., Merricks* ☎ *03/5989–9011* 🌐 *www.ptleoestate.com.au* 🎟 *A$16 for wine tasting and sculpture park entry.*

Red Hill Estate

WINERY | This winery, which has won numerous medals for its Chardonnay, Pinot Noir, and Shiraz, has an equally impressive view. Not only are there sweeping vistas over the 23-acre vineyard, but the magnificent waters of Western Port are spread out in the distance. On clear days you can see as far as Phillip Island as you wander around the gardens. The award-winning cuisine and fabulous floor-to-ceiling windows make Max's Restaurant the perfect place to while away at least half the day. Order from the à la carte menu (two-course à la carte lunch A$70, three-course à la carte lunch A$85), available Wednesday–Saturday. The fixed three-course Sunday roast lunch costs A$85. Dinner is served on Saturday night, including the five-course degustation menu, A$110 or A$155 with matching wines. Otherwise, go casual on the lawn with cheese plates, charcuterie boards, and small plates including Coffin Bay oysters and Yarra Valley caviar (A$4 each). Although it may be a little chilly, winter is a good time to visit, as several events are staged, including art shows and the region's Winter Wine Weekend in June. ✉ *53 Shoreham Rd., Red Hill South* ☎ *03/5989–2838 cellar door, 03/5931–0177 restaurant* 🌐 *www.redhillestate.com.au, www.maxsrestaurant.com.au.*

Stonier Winery

WINERY | This preeminent Mornington Peninsula producer of wines uses grapes from the region's oldest vines. The establishment specializes in Chardonnay and Pinot Noir (from vines first planted in 1978 and 1982, respectively) and also makes a sparkling Chardonnay and Pinot Noir. Although there's no restaurant, you can order a platter featuring local Red Hill cheeses to enjoy on the lawns. Visitors may be invited on an informal tour of the fermentation and barrel rooms. Several events take place during the year, such as the dedicated Sparkling Day in December. ✉ *2 Thompsons La., Merricks* ☎ *03/5989–8300* 🌐 *www.stonier.com.au.*

★ T'Gallant Winemakers
WINERY | **FAMILY** | Home to the peninsula's first Pinot Grigio vines, this popular Italian-theme winery also contains a restaurant. T'Gallant produces excellent Pinot Noir, Prosecco, and Pinot Gris. If you're an art lover as well as a wine fan, you'll also admire the beautiful artwork on its bottle labels. The on-site pizza bar is always buzzing and the food is exceptional, with dishes made from local ingredients, including items from the house herb garden. Tuck into a signature Italian wood-fired pizza or a chocolate ganache brownie paired with its pink Moscato. Open seven days a week, there's live music every weekend at lunchtime. Their annual winter Mushrooms in May festival is very popular and bookings are essential. ✉ *1385 Mornington–Flinders Rd., Main Ridge* ☎ *03/5931–1300* 🌐 *www.tgallant.com.au.*

Beaches

Rosebud Beach
BEACH | **FAMILY** | Backing onto the suburb of Rosebud, this popular beach has been rated one of the safest in Victoria. The white-sand flats extend a long way offshore and sand bars keep the area protected for swimming, while trees provide natural shade. The beach reserve includes a jetty (from which many locals fish), boat ramp, and camping ground. A picnic and barbecue area and adventure playground make the beach a hit with families, and the nearby Bay Trail walking and cycling track is popular. Accommodation around here tends to be motels and cottages for rent. **Amenities:** food and drink; lifeguards; parking (free); restrooms; showers. **Best for:** swimming; walking. ✉ *Point Nepean Rd., end of Jetty Rd., Rosebud.*

Restaurants

★ Laura
$$$$ | **AUSTRALIAN** | Named for the Jaume Plensa sculpture of a girl's head, which is in full view of the best tables, this award-winning restaurant sits at the heart of a A$60-million-plus sculpture park, and its set menus celebrate the peninsula's bounty and its connections with local farmers. The decor is calm and elegant, with white-linen tablecloths and neutral, soothing tones that do not distract from the stunning setting framed by its walls of windows. **TIP→ If you can't get a reservation at this 45-seat hot ticket, the vibrant Pt. Leo Dining Room (separated only by glass from Laura) is larger and more casual, but also excellent.** **Known for:** elegant setting and views; modern fine dining; Relais & Châteaux appointment. 💲 *Average main: A$150* ✉ *3649 Frankston-Flinders Rd., Merricks* ☎ *03/5989–9011* 🌐 *www.ptleoestate.com.au.*

★ Montalto Vineyard & Olive Grove
$$$$ | **AUSTRALIAN** | Overlooking a vineyard of rolling green hills, this restaurant has an à la carte menu, which changes regularly based on available local produce. The wine list borrows from the best of the estate's vintages, as well as classic wines from other regions. **Known for:** sculpture gardens and bird-watching; beautiful setting; picnic hampers in summer. 💲 *Average main: A$105* ✉ *33 Shoreham Rd., Red Hill South* ☎ *03/5989–8412* 🌐 *www.montalto.com.au.*

Coffee and Quick Bites

Cellar & Pantry
$ | **SANDWICHES** | Busy produce store-cum-deli, this is the perfect place to pick up the makings of a picnic lunch or a dinner in self-contained accommodation. It is packed full of crusty loaves, cured and fresh meats, fruits and vegetables, aromatic cheeses, olives, relishes and chutneys, and countless other goodies. **Known for:** veranda seating; picnic

supplies; local wines and coffee. *Average main: A$11 ✉ 141 Shoreham Rd., Red Hill South ☎ 03/5989–2411 🌐 www.cellarandpantry.com.au.*

★ Merricks General Store

$$ | AUSTRALIAN | FAMILY | Good food, local wines and notable art mix at this beautiful community hub, which has been a general store for a century. Pull up a chair at a farmhouse table and order the buttermilk hotcakes for brunch, or settle in for a long lunch—start with the salumi and move on to elegant mains—beneath the vines on the terrace. **Known for:** kid-friendly dining options; well-curated wine store; fresh pastries and sandwiches for picnics. *Average main: A$25 ✉ 3460 Frankston-Flinders Rd., Merricks ☎ 03/5989–8088 🌐 mgwinestore.com.au.*

Hotels

Hotel Sorrento

$$ | HOTEL | Built in 1872, this historic hotel has attractive rooms with exposed limestone walls, stylish interiors, and water views. **Pros:** beside the Queenscliff ferry terminal; great location; impressive views from some rooms. **Cons:** jam-packed on weekends. *Rooms from: A$180 ✉ 5–15 Hotham Rd., Sorrento ☎ 03/5984–8000 🌐 www.hotelsorrento.com.au ⇨ 37 rooms, 13 suites ¶◎¶ No Meals.*

★ Lakeside Villas at Crittenden Estate

$$$$ | B&B/INN | FAMILY | Wine and dine to your heart's content, then amble home to a stylish overwater bungalow on a tranquil lake. **Pros:** breakfast hamper with eggs, bacon, and local muesli; beautiful setting; free wine tastings. **Cons:** limited availability; nearby Stillwater Restaurant is open for dinner only on Friday and Saturday. *Rooms from: A$400 ✉ 25 Harrisons Rd., Dromana ☎ 0400/339–995 🌐 www.lakesidevillas.com.au ⇨ 3 villas ¶◎¶ Free Breakfast.*

Precious Resource

Victoria has weathered major droughts, and Australians are very conscious about the probability of another dry stretch. As a result, signs are displayed in many places, including hotels, suggesting water-saving measures. Do as the locals do and use water carefully wherever you can.

★ Lindenderry at Red Hill

$$$$ | HOTEL | A stalwart of 30 years on the peninsula, Lindenderry's multimillion-dollar makeover sees the boutique hotel channel a stylish country house, with generously sized rooms, each with doors leading out to Mediterranean-style terraces or gardens overlooking a landscape of Australian bushland and manicured vines. **Pros:** short walk to Red Hill markets and other wineries; beautiful setting on 30-acre estate; spacious rooms with a chic, muted palette. **Cons:** no natural light in the bathrooms. *Rooms from: A$390 ✉ 142 Arthurs Seat Rd., Red Hill South ☎ 03/5989–2933 🌐 www.lancemore.com.au/lindenderry ⇨ 40 rooms ¶◎¶ Free Breakfast.*

Activities

DIVING AND SNORKELING

Bayplay Adventure Tours

DIVING & SNORKELING | This adventure tour company runs a variety of activities, including diving, snorkeling, bike riding, and sea kayaking. You can explore colonies of weedy seadragons, dive through an octopus's garden, or feel the wash when dolphins leap over your kayak. Dives start from A$130, while a three-hour sea kayaking tour to a dolphin sanctuary costs A$110 per person. *✉ 3755 Port Nepean Rd., Portsea ☎ 03/5984–0888 🌐 www.bayplay.com.au.*

HIKING

The Mornington Peninsula is a memorable walking destination. There are walks for all levels of fitness and interest, from cliff-top strolls to the ultimate 26-km (16-mile) Two Bays Walking Track. Stop in at the visitor information center at Dromana or Sorrento to see what walking maps they have on hand, or contact Parks Victoria, the government body that manages the state's national parks.

Arthurs Seat State Park: There is a one-hour circuit walk to Kings Falls; otherwise, the relaxing Seawinds Gardens walk is less than a mile in length and takes only about half an hour.

Bushrangers Bay Walk: An exhilarating 6-km (4-mile) return walk along Western Port begins at Cape Schanck Lighthouse and winds past basalt cliffs and Bushranger Bay, to finish at Main Creek.

Coppin's Track: A pleasant 3-km (2-mile) round-trip walk that stretches from Sorrento ocean beach (or Back Beach as it's known) to Jubilee Point along the Bass Strait coastline.

Two Bays Walking Track: A hard-core 26-km (16-mile) walking track that links Dromana, on Port Phillip Bay, with Cape Schanck on Western Port Bay.

Parks Victoria

HIKING & WALKING | This government agency manages all of Victoria's national parks. Its informative website includes park descriptions and trail maps that can be downloaded, as well as information on safety considerations, special events, and park attractions. ✉ *Melbourne* ☎ *131–963* 🌐 *www.parks.vic.gov.au.*

HORSEBACK RIDING

The Ranch

HORSEBACK RIDING | **FAMILY** | Ride along the edge of St. Andrews Beach on a group horse ride with The Ranch. Catering to both beginners and experienced riders, The Ranch runs horse and pony rides on weekends and during school holidays (which includes the December to January summer vacation). Scenic rides traverse the 200-acre property, while the Forest and Bush'n'Beach rides go further afield. There are scenic trail and forest rides for intermediate and experienced riders, while short and simple pony rides give the under-sixes some fun as well. ✉ *810 Boneo Rd., Cape Schanck* ☎ *03/5988–6262* 🌐 *www.ace-hi.com.au* 🎟 *From A$97, 45-minute scenic ride.*

SPAS

★ Peninsula Hot Springs

SPAS | Set among tranquil bushland, this fabulous bathing experience sees more than 20 natural thermal mineral water pools ranging from deliciously steamy to truly chilling plunge pools. Inspired by bathing traditions and rituals from around the world, you'll find Japanese bathing experiences, a Moroccan hammam, body clay painting, treatments using Indigenous ingredients, and the Fire & Ice experience, which includes an ice cave and Deep Freeze going as low as –25°C, before getting toasty in the 50°C wet and dry saunas. Some sections are family-friendly, while the Spa Dreaming center and private bathing areas are for bathers over 16 years. Budget for a half day of dipping, perhaps enjoy a massage or facial in the private spa sanctuary, and lunch in the on-site café. Wildly popular on summer weekends, the best time to visit is midweek mornings. Winter bathing is a special experience, when mist and steam intermingle, and moonlit bathing is available between 11 pm and 5 am (A$65). Basic bathing packages start from A$30, and A$110 for private bathing experiences. ✉ *Springs La., Fingal, Mornington* ☎ *03/5950–8777* 🌐 *www.peninsulahotsprings.com.*

Phillip Island

124 km (77 miles) southeast of Melbourne.

South of Melbourne and just off the Mornington Peninsula, Phillip Island has long been a playground for Victorians. Amid the striking coastal landscapes and bushland interior live more than 200 bird species, wallabies, and native flora. The perennial highlight, however, is the famous Penguin Parade, in which the little birds march ashore each evening to the delight of onlookers.

Take a walk along the extensive boardwalks that cover the coastal cliffs, visit the blowhole, and view the silver gull rookery. Short-tailed shearwaters (also known as mutton birds) arrive on Phillip Island around the last week of September after a 12,000-km (7,450-mile) migration from the Aleutian Islands, near Alaska, where they'll return in April. Further out, Seal Rocks host Australia's largest colony of fur seals; up to 20,000 creatures bask on the rocky platforms and cavort in the water here year-round. Boat tours cruise past these playful creatures.

GETTING HERE AND AROUND

To reach the island from Melbourne, take the Princes Freeway (M1) southeast to the South Gippsland Highway (M420), and follow this to the Bass Highway (B420). The bridge at San Remo crosses over to Phillip Island. V/Line runs combined train and bus service directly to Cowes, or a train to Stony Point on the Mornington Peninsula, where a daily passenger ferry runs to Phillip Island and French Island.

TRANSPORTATION

V/Line

This combination train and bus service goes from Southern Cross Station to Cowes (with change at Dandenong or Koo Wee Rup railway stations), a journey of 2½ to 3½ hours. You can also get the V/Line train from suburban Frankston to Stony Point, and take the ferry to Cowes. ☎ *1800/800–007* 🌐 *www.vline.com.au.*

Western Port Ferries

Cross from Stony Point (on the eastern side of the Mornington Peninsula) to Phillip Island and French Island and back again on this foot ferry (bicycles permitted A$4 extra, one-way). Park for A$2 or get to the terminus via train. Parking is available, and trains from Melbourne run to the Stony Point terminus. An adult one-way ferry fare is A$13. ☎ *03/5257–4565* 🌐 *www.westernportferries.com.au.*

TOURS

Gray Line

This operator runs various day tours of the Penguin Parade, often combined with such experiences as Seal Rocks or the Koala Conservation Reserve, to see more extraordinary wildlife. ☎ *1300/858–687* 🌐 *www.grayline.com.au.*

Wildlife Coast Cruises

This operator runs two-hour cruises from Cowes Jetty to the Nobbies and Seal Rocks, spending 30–40 minutes viewing the seal colony. Full-day and half-day cruises run daily all year round, including a twilight bay cruise. Its whale-watching cruises run from June to November, and it also operates one-hour trips to Cape Woolamai. The company also runs wildlife cruises to view the rich marine life off Wilson's Promontory. ✉ *13 The Esplanade, Cowes* ☎ *1300/763–739* 🌐 *www.wildlifecoastcruises.com.au* 🎫 *From A$33.*

VISITOR INFORMATION

CONTACTS Phillip Island Visitor Information Centre. ✉ *895 Phillip Island Rd., Newhaven* ☎ *1300/366–422* 🌐 *www.visitphillipisland.com.*

Sights

Antarctic Journey and The Nobbies

WILDLIFE REFUGE | FAMILY | Phillip Island's marine wildlife attraction is just 3 km (2 miles) from the Penguin Parade, perched on the very edge of Point Grant on the island's far west end. It's an ultramodern interpretative center, with an interactive, multimedia Antarctic Journey, which includes a freezing "chill zone." Outside, a series of wooden boardwalks wind around the rocky headland to the nearby blowhole, with fantastic views of Nobbies headland and Seal Rocks beyond it. ✉ *1320 Ventnor Rd., Phillip Island* ☎ *03/5951–2800* 🌐 *www.penguins.org.au/attractions/antarctic-journey* 🎫 *A$14.*

Cowes

TOWN | The seaside town of Cowes is the hub of Phillip Island; the pier is where you can board sightseeing cruises and the passenger ferry that travels across Western Port to French Island and Stony Point on the Mornington Peninsula. It has a lively café scene and several quality gift shops interspersed with the traditionally cheaper tourist fare. Restaurant and hotel bookings are essential in the busy summer months. ✉ *Cowes.*

Koala Conservation Reserve

WILDLIFE REFUGE | **FAMILY** | At this excellent wildlife center you can stroll along treetop-high boardwalks and view koalas in their natural habitat. At the visitor center, learn some fascinating things about the cute furry creatures—such as how they sleep 21 hours a day. It is located just a short drive from the tourist information center at Newhaven; follow the signs along Phillip Island Tourist Road. ✉ *1810 Phillip Island Rd., Cowes* ☎ *03/5951–2800* 🌐 *www.penguins.org.au/attractions/koala-reserve/* 🎫 *A$14.*

★ Penguin Parade

WILDLIFE REFUGE | **FAMILY** | Phillip Island's main draw is the nightly parade of little penguins, also called fairy penguins, waddling from the sea to their burrows in nearby dunes. The parade of miniature penguins attracts onlookers year-round and crowds on summer weekends and holidays. There are several ways to view the Penguin Parade: general admission, with viewing from concrete bleachers; the Penguin Plus experience, which puts you on a smaller viewing platform that is closer to the action. There's even a small underground section to watch the penguins as they go to their nests. The Guided Ranger tour puts you on an intimate beachfront viewing stand with a ranger, while the VIP Tour gets you into a private, elevated "Skybox" overlooking the beach. The Ultimate Adventure Tour, for private groups, includes headphones and night-vision equipment and a secluded spot on a separate beach. The spectacle begins at around sunset each night; booking ahead is essential in summer and during public holidays. Wear closed shoes and warm clothing—even in summer—and rain protection gear. Make sure to arrive an hour before the tour begins. ✉ *1019 Ventnor Rd., Phillip Island* ☎ *03/5951–2800* 🌐 *www.penguins.org.au* 🎫 *From A$28.*

Rhyll

TOWN | Quieter than Cowes, Rhyll is a charming fishing village on the eastern side of Phillip Island. You can rent a boat from the dock or take a sightseeing cruise from the pier. The local wetlands are internationally significant for their resident and migratory birdlife, and a short mangrove boardwalk leads to Conservation Hill and the Koala Conservation Reserve. ✉ *Rhyll.*

Beaches

Cape Woolamai Surf Beach

BEACH | Phillip Island's only surf lifesaving club is based on this long, exposed stretch of prime surfing beach, recognised as a National Surfing Reserve. The hazardous 4.2-km (2.6-mile) beach has strong undertows, so it's for experienced surfers and swimmers only, and only between the safety flags when lifeguards are on patrol, from December to mid-April: check the surf lifesaving club's website for patrol times. Walkers can take in the views here on a ramble to The Pinnacles.

The Woolamai Beach Road runs off Phillip Island Road and is 14 km (9 miles) from Cowes. The nearest accommodation is generally cottage-style; Black Dolphin has a luxury penthouse and a cottage on the Cape, on Corona Road. **Amenities**: food and drink; lifeguards; parking (free); restrooms; showers. **Best for:** surfing; swimming; walking. ✉ *Woolamai Beach Rd., Cape Woolamai* 🌐 *www.woolamai-beach.org.au.*

Kitty Miller Bay

BEACH | Regarded as one of Victoria's best little beaches, this south-facing beach provides excellent swimming and snorkeling, and a walking trail to view the remains of the wreck of the SS *Speke* at low tide. Sheltered by Watts Point and Kennon Head, the curved beach has low waves, with undertows only appearing when the waves whip up at high tide, which is the best time for surfing. There's not much shade and no kiosk, so bring water, food, and sunscreen with you. The beach is at the intersection with Watts Road. From Cowes, go either via Ventnor Road to Back Beach Road, or via Phillip Island Road and Back Beach Road, turning onto Kitty Miller Road. The beach is around 10 km (6 miles) from Cowes. The low-key nature of Phillip Island and the remote nature of the beach means that accommodation is usually B&B-style. Try the Kitty Miller Bay B&B on Watts Road (kittymillerbaybedandbreakfast.com.au). **Amenities :** parking (free). **Best for:** snorkeling; surfing; swimming; walking. ✉ *Kitty Miller Rd., Phillip Island.*

Restaurants

Cape Kitchen

$$ | AUSTRALIAN | Serving regional and Victorian produce from breakfast to late lunch, Cape Kitchen is a wildly popular brunch spot. The exciting breakfast menu, served until 11:30 am, includes house-cured ocean trout, corn cakes with chili jam and eggs, and locally smoked salmon. **Known for:** great coffee; regional produce; surf beach views. [$] *Average main: A$30* ✉ *1215 Phillip Island Rd., Newhaven* ☎ *03/5956–7200* 🌐 *www.thecapekitchen.com.au.*

★ **Isola Di Capri**

$$ | ITALIAN | FAMILY | Isola Di Capri has been serving up generous plates of seafood since 1972. Start with a shared antipasto platter or lobster toast before moving on to the fish of the day or locally sourced rib-eye steak. **Known for:** sea and pier views; delicious house-made gelato; antipasto platters. [$] *Average main: A$35* ✉ *2 Thompson Ave., Cowes, Phillip Island* ☎ *03/5952–2435* 🌐 *www.isoladicapri.com.au.*

Coffee and Quick Bites

★ **Wild Food Farm Cafe**

$ | AUSTRALIAN | Taste Australia's unique ingredients at this exciting café—try wattleseed scones, a zingy finger lime aioli on the side of a lemon-myrtle tempura barramundi fish fillet, a sweet crumble with quandong and macadamia nuts. Classic breakfast and lunch dishes such as smashed avocado on toast or bacon and eggs are lifted with the addition of wild lime olive oil or mushrooms with native thyme. **Known for:** Australian native ingredients; bush barbecues; smashed avo. [$] *Average main: A$20* ✉ *30 Rhyll-Newhaven Rd., Phillip Island* ☎ *0406/153-143* 🌐 *www.wildfoodfarm.com.au.*

Hotels

Five Acres

$$$$ | RESORT | Three design-led cabins sit on this 5-acre block of land in Ventnor, 10 minutes from Cowes on the northeastern edge of Phillip Island. **Pros:** farmland setting; sustainably built; close to beaches. **Cons:** car required; pricey; no children. [$] *Rooms from: A$540* ✉ *46 Mchaffies La., Phillip Island* ☎ *0433/093–902* 🌐 *www.fiveacres.com.au* 🍴 *Free Breakfast* 🛏 *3 cabins.*

Glen Isla House

$$$ | **B&B/INN** | A beautiful, safe swimming beach is right at the doorstep of this luxurious B&B, which contains six individually themed rooms. **Pros:** short drive to penguins; gorgeous furnishings; on a pristine beach. **Cons:** not suitable for young children; breakfast is extra; the heritage style may be too traditional for some. *Rooms from: A$255* *230 Church St., Cowes* *03/5952–1882* *www.glenisla.com* *6 rooms, 1 cottage* *No Meals.*

Activities

AUTO-RACING

Phillip Island Grand Prix Circuit

AUTO RACING | **FAMILY** | The island has had a long involvement with motor sports: the first Australian Grand Prix was run on its local, unpaved roads back in 1928, before a circuit was built in the 1950s. The track was completely redeveloped in the 1980s, and in 1989 hosted the first Australian Motorcycle Grand Prix. The circuit holds regular races as well as big-ticket events, such as the Australian Motorcycle Grand Prix and Superbike World Championship.

Speed freaks can buckle up for hot laps in a racing car driven by a professional driver year-round (from A$360 for three laps, see website for dates and times) or drive a go-kart around a 750-meter replica of the actual track. There are 60-minute guided walking tours of the track daily that also go behind the scenes up in the control tower (subject to availability); Australia's largest slot car Grand Prix Circuit replica racing track; and a museum showcasing the island's motor racing history. *Back Beach Rd., Phillip Island* *03/5952–9400* *www.phillipislandcircuit.com.au* *Tours A$28; museum A$18; slot cars A$8.*

En Route

From Queenscliff, follow Great Ocean Road signs for 45 km (28 miles) to **Torquay,** Australia's premier surfing and windsurfing resort, and Bell's Beach, famous for its Easter surfing contests and its October international windsurfing competitions. The Great Ocean Road, a positively magnificent coastal drive, officially begins at Torquay. The seaside towns of Anglesea, Aireys Inlet, and Fairhaven are other good warm-weather swimming spots.

HIKING

Walking Tracks on Phillip Island

HIKING & WALKING | Walking tracks and viewing platforms around Phillip Island have splendid views, with routes to suit all fitness levels. The Cape Woolamai trail at the island's eastern tip is a reminder of the island's volcanic past, and the Bush to Bay Trail can be broken down into sections. Churchill Island has several good walking tracks, and there are great views from the boardwalks around the Nobbies. For information on all the good walking trails, visit the Phillip Island Visitor Information Centre at Newhaven, the small town you encounter as you come across the bridge from the mainland. *Phillip Island Visitor Information Centre, 895 Phillip Island Rd., Newhaven* *www.visitphillipisland.com.au.*

Queenscliff

103 km (64 miles) southwest of Melbourne.

In the late 19th century, Queenscliff, on the Bellarine Peninsula, was a favorite weekend destination for well-to-do Melburnians who traveled by paddle steamer or train to stay at the area's grand hotels, some of which are still in business today. Be sure to check out Fort Queenscliff, another landmark from bygone days. Good restaurants and quiet charm are also traits of Queenscliff. The playground of families during the day and dog walkers come dusk, Queenscliff is a restful alternative to the resort towns of Sorrento and Portsea on the other side of the bay. At the end of November, the annual Queenscliff Music Festival (*www.qmf.net.au*) draws thousands of visitors to town.

GETTING HERE AND AROUND

The lovely coastal village of Queenscliff and nearby smaller sibling Point Lonsdale make for a worthy—and well-signposted—detour on the drive from Melbourne to the start of the Great Ocean Road.

It's about a 60- to 90-minute drive from Melbourne to Geelong via the Princes Freeway (M1), then to Queenscliff via the Bellarine Highway (B110). Trains run from Melbourne's Southern Cross Station to Geelong, where buses (Nos. 75 and 76) continue on to Queenscliff.

It's easy to walk around Queenscliff's main attractions; ask at the visitor center in Hesse Street for maps.

The narrow-gauge Bellarine Railway tourist train runs the 16 km (10 miles) between the towns of Queenscliff and Drysdale several times a week. The volunteer-run steam train also offers heritage train rides and train driver experiences. Most Saturdays, and occasional Friday nights between October and May, the popular Blues Train (*www.thebluestrain.com.au*) mixes dinner with live blues entertainment. For gourmands, the route becomes a moveable feast, with the restaurant train offering fine dining journeys with a six-course degustation on the Q Train (*www.theqtrain.com.au*).

The Port Phillip Ferries passenger-only ferry service sails two return services daily between Docklands, in the heart of Melbourne city, to the town of Portarlington, on the northern side of the Bellarine Peninsula, 30 km (18 miles) from Geelong. (A$16.50 one-way.)

The Queenscliff-Sorrento car and passenger ferry travels between these two towns on opposite sides of the Port Phillip Bay, sailing between Sorrento (Mornington Peninsula) and Queenscliff (Bellarine Peninsula), departing every hour, on the hour from 7 to 6, later in peak holiday season. One-way adult fares are A$13 (foot passenger), and a car costs A$72 one-way, plus fares for any passengers.

TRANSPORTATION

Bellarine Railway

This narrow-gauge tourist train runs the 16 km (10 miles) between the towns of Queenscliff and Drysdale several times a week. On Saturday, and occasional Friday nights, between August and May, the popular Blues Train (*www.thebluestrain.com.au*) mixes dinner with live blues entertainment; tickets cost A$118 per person. For gourmands, the route becomes a moveable feast, with the restaurant train offering a four-hour fine dining journey with a six-course degustation during the first week of the month, as well as every second Thursday, on the Q Train (*www.theqtrain.com.au*). Tickets from $119 per person. ✉ *Queenscliff Railway Station, 20 Symonds St., Queenscliff* ☎ *03/5258–2069* 🌐 *bellarinerailway.com.au.*

Port Phillip Ferries

This passenger-only ferry service sails two return services daily between Docklands, in the heart of Melbourne city, to the town of Portarlington, on the northern side of the Bellarine Peninsula, 28 km (17 miles) from Geelong. (A$14.50 one-way.) ☎ *03/9514–8959* 🌐 *www.portphillipferries.com.au.*

Queenscliff–Sorrento Ferry

This car and passenger ferry travels between these two towns on opposite sides of the Port Phillip Bay, sailing between Sorrento (Mornington Peninsula) and Queenscliff (Bellarine Peninsula), departing every hour, on the hour from 7 to 6, later in peak holiday season. One-way adult fares are A$12 (foot passenger), and a car costs A$65 one-way, plus fares for any passengers. ✉ *Queenscliff* ☎ *03/5258–3244* 🌐 *www.searoad.com.au.*

V/Line
Catch a V/Line train to Geelong, and connect to a local bus to Queenscliff. ☎ *1800/800–007* 🌐 *www.vline.com.au.*

VISITOR INFORMATION

CONTACTS Queenscliffe Visitor Information Centre. ✉ *18 Hesse St., Queenscliff* ☎ *03/5258–4843, 884–843* 🌐 *www.queenscliff.com.au.*

Coffee and Quick Bites

★ The Rolling Pin
$ | **AUSTRALIAN** | **FAMILY** | Consistently covered in glory at the annual (and hotly contested) Australia's Best Pie awards, the pie to order here is the Surf 'n Turf. The national title–winning pie is made from chunky beef from cattle raised in Tasmania's pristine air, and topped with prawns and a creamy garlic sauce. **Known for:** wholemeal vegetarian pasty; Surf 'n Turf pie; breakfast (bacon, egg, sausage, tomato) pie. 💲 *Average main: A$7* ✉ *40 Hesse St., Queenscliff* ☎ *03/5258–1533* 🌐 *www.rollingpin.com.au.*

Hotels

Vue Grand Hotel
$$$ | **HOTEL** | Built in 1881, this stylish hotel blends old-world elegance with modern touches in its recently restored grand premises. **Pros:** balconies overlook main street; grand experience; wonderful dining room. **Cons:** on-street parking only; no lifts; not on the seaside. 💲 *Rooms from: A$225* ✉ *46–48 Hesse St., Queenscliff* ☎ *03/5258–1544* 🌐 *www.vuegrand.com.au* *29 rooms, 3 suites* 🍴 *No Meals.*

Light Up Your Trip

There are seven historic lighthouses of varying shapes and sizes on the coast—from Point Lonsdale in the east to Portland in the west. Don't miss the tall red-capped white **Split Point Lighthouse** at Aireys Inlet, while **Cape Otway Lighthouse,** the oldest surviving lighthouse on mainland Australia, marks the point where the Southern Ocean and Bass Strait collide. Farther west at Portland is majestic **Cape Nelson Lighthouse.** Guided tours are available, and you can also arrange to sleep in a lighthouse.

Lorne

148 km (92 miles) southwest of Melbourne, 95 km (59 miles) southwest of Queenscliff, 50 km (31 miles) southwest of Torquay.

Located between sweeping Loutit Bay and the Great Otway National Park, pretty Lorne is one of the most popular towns on the Great Ocean Road, with a definite surf-and-holiday feel. It's the site of both a wild celebration every New Year's Eve and the popular Pier-to-Pub Swim held on the first weekend in January. Some people make their reservations a year or more in advance. It's also the starting point for the Great Ocean Road Running Festival held each May (the footrace ends in Apollo Bay). The town has a lively café and pub scene, as well as several upscale restaurants, trendy boutiques, and a day spa.

GETTING HERE AND AROUND

You really need a car to get to Lorne and other Great Ocean Road towns; the next best option is to take an organized tour. Public transport is available, but it's a long process: take the V/Line train to

Geelong, then transfer to a bus to Apollo Bay, which stops at Lorne (about five hours). If driving, take the Princes Highway (M1) west from Melbourne across the Westgate Bridge to Geelong. From there, follow signs along the Surf Coast Highway to Torquay, where you'll connect with the Great Ocean Road.

VISITOR INFORMATION

CONTACTS Lorne Visitor Information Centre. ✉ *15 Mountjoy Parade, Lorne* ☎ *03/5289–1152, 1300/891–152* 🌐 *www.lovelorne.com.au.*

Beaches

Lorne Beach

BEACH | This stretch of the Victorian coast is sometimes called The Shipwreck Coast, with reputedly up to 700 ships at rest offshore. Lorne itself has a shipwreck plaque walk along the foreshore, giving the history of local disasters and near-misses dating from 1854. The Lorne Surf Life Saving Club patrols the southern end of popular Lorne Beach, which runs south from the Erskine River for 1.2 km (¾ mile). Care must be taken when the waves are high as the undertow and rips can be dangerous: swim in the patrolled areas between the flags. The beach has parking for 250 cars, a lookout, shade trees and shelters, barbecue and play areas, and a cycle track. The Lorne Beach Pavilion has a swimming pool, large playground, outdoor trampoline, and skate park as well. A camping ground and caravan park are also near the beach. Parking is available at the junction of Bay Street, Mountjoy Parade, and the Great Ocean Road, or along the Great Ocean Road itself. Other entrances to the beach are via **Grove Street** or **William Street**. The Mantra Lorne resort, with 12 acres of gardens and a range of rooms and apartments, is directly on the beach. **Amenities:** food and drink; lifeguards; parking (free); restrooms; showers. **Best for:** surfing; swimming; walking. ✉ *Great Ocean Rd., at Bay St., Lorne.*

Restaurants

★ **Brae**

$$$ | **AUSTRALIAN** | Up in the hinterland above the Great Ocean Road, in a village at a crossroads, sits one of Australia's most celebrated restaurants. Chef Dan Hunter's Brae serves a daily set menu renowned for its fine organic fare, much drawn from its own farm, which surrounds the dining room, the rest from ethical, sustainable suppliers of the highest quality. **Known for:** six guest rooms on-site in high demand; destination dining; organic fare from its own farm. [$] *Average main: A$275* ✉ *4285 Cape Otway Rd., Birregurra, Lorne* ☎ *03/5236–2226* 🌐 *www.braerestaurant.com* ⏲ *Closed Tues. and Wed.*

Marks

$$$ | **SEAFOOD** | Fresh seafood—from fried calamari to roasted flathead—is the draw at this Lorne institution, which has been going strong since 1989. The design is "funky seaside," with bright walls, blue chairs, and a smattering of local art and sculpture for sale. **Known for:** chocolate mousse; catch of the day; oysters. [$] *Average main: A$36* ✉ *122 Mountjoy Parade, Lorne* ☎ *03/5289–2787* 🌐 *www.marksrestaurant.com.au* ⏲ *Closed Sun.-Mon. Closed July and Aug.*

Coffee and Quick Bites

Salonika

$ | **BAKERY** | This café's Portuguese tarts, which are made in-house, have a dedicated following amongst Lorne's café society. If you miss out, console yourself with a bag of *loukoumades* (Greek doughnuts), while those with a savory tooth will appreciate the fresh sourdough loaves by renowned Irrewarra bakery, and this modern Greek café's classic spanakopita. **Known for:** Greek doughnuts; Portuguese tarts; beach views. [$] *Average main: A$5* ✉ *122 Mountjoy Parade, Lorne* 🌐 *www.salonika.com.au* ⏲ *Closed Tues. and Wed.*

Hotels

★ **La Perouse Lorne**

$$$$ | B&B/INN | Small and perfectly formed, this four-room hotel on the Great Ocean Road has its heart in France. **Pros:** intimate; Australian artwork; fireplaces and verandas. **Cons:** books up quickly; pricey; no sea views. *Rooms from: A$450 ✉ 26 William St., Lorne ☎ 0418/534–422 🌐 www.laperouselorne.com Free Breakfast 4 rooms.*

Mantra Lorne

$$ | RESORT | FAMILY | You can fall asleep listening to waves rolling ashore at this huge complex on 12 acres near the water's edge in Lorne. **Pros:** 18-hole putting green; beachfront location; lots of facilities. **Cons:** no privacy in ground-floor apartments; 10 am checkout; superbusy in summer holidays. *Rooms from: A$190 ✉ Mountjoy Parade, Lorne ☎ 03/5228–9777 🌐 www.mantralorne.com.au 142 rooms, 135 apartments No Meals.*

Activities

HIKING

The Great Ocean Road and the "Surf Coast" section of it around Torquay, Lorne, and Aireys Inlet have fantastic walks providing great cliff-top views, while inland a little way there are waterfalls and picnic grounds to explore.

The 44-km (27-mile) Surf Coast Walk, which begins near Jan Juc car park (1 mile west of Torquay) and ends around Moggs Creek Picnic Area at Aireys, can be done in short segments.

Inland is the vast Great Otway National Park, which has many picturesque walks, including the 12-km (7½-mile) Currawong Falls Track walk from Distillery Creek Picnic Area, which can be quite strenuous. There are 10 waterfalls within 10 km (6 miles) from Lorne, including short, easier walks to Erskine Falls and Sheoak Falls (*www.lovelorne.com.au*). The Torquay and Lorne visitor centers have trail maps.

Apollo Bay

45 km (28 miles) west of Lorne.

A small attractive town on a wide curving bay, Apollo Bay is midway on the Great Ocean Road. There are many places to eat and plenty of opportunities for aquatic activities. It's most popular as a base to explore the famous rock formations of the Twelve Apostles Marine National Park, and the greenery of Great Otway National Park.

GETTING HERE AND AROUND

Driving is the most convenient way to get here. Otherwise take the combined V/Line train-bus option, which involves riding a train from Melbourne's Southern Cross Station to Geelong and then a bus along the Great Ocean Road to Apollo Bay, via Lorne and other Surf Coast towns.

Sights

★ **Kennett River Koala Walk**

NATURE PRESERVE | This little hamlet on the Great Ocean Road is home to a colony of wild koalas who hang, like ripe fruit, from the trees just off the highway. Located halfway between Lorne and Apollo Bay, pull in where you see Kennett River's Koala Cafe, and get the camera out. This location is also well-known for flocks of colorful king parrots, kookaburras, and wallabies. Don't try to touch or feed any of the wildlife and keep dogs in the car: koalas are more active (and therefore easier to spot) in the early morning and late afternoon. *✉ Kennett River, Kennett River Free.*

Sea kayaking in Apollo Bay

Beaches

Apollo Bay Beach

BEACH | FAMILY | At 195 km (121 miles) from Melbourne, you'll find one of Victoria's most popular holiday beaches. Protected by a working fishing harbor and Point Bunbury, the waves are gentler toward the southern end of the bay: care must be taken with an undertow that gets stronger as you go north. The local surf lifesaving club patrols between flags at the southern end. The 3-km (almost 2-mile) beach runs parallel to the Great Ocean Road (also called Collingwood Street within the town), and there's a reserve with shady trees, a barbecue, playground, and a picnic area near the main shopping area. Behind the street is a row of shops and cafés, and on most Saturdays, the Apollo Bay market sees stall holders lining the foreshore path to sell local produce and crafts. Behind the town, the green hills of the Otways provide a change of scenery. Walk up the pathway to Marriners Lookout for idyllic views, though a sunken steamship lurks beneath the waters. If you want to get closer to the sea, Apollo Bay Surf and Kayak runs kayaking tours to see the local seal colony, as well as providing surfing and paddle-boarding lessons. The Seaview Motel and Apartments are near the beach, and some rooms have balconies looking over the view. **Amenities:** food and drink; lifeguards (in summer); parking (free); toilets; showers. **Best for:** surfing; swimming; walking. ⊠ *Great Ocean Rd., Apollo Bay.*

Coffee and Quick Bites

Apollo Bay Fisherman's Co-op

$ | SEAFOOD | FAMILY | Seafood fresh from the fishing trawlers is the reason to visit this long-standing fisherman's co-op, located in Apollo Bay's working harbor. Rock lobster, shark, and barracouta are regulars on the menu, and scallop, octopus, giant crab, squid, and even abalone make an appearance. **Known for:** fish straight from the fishing boats; rock lobster; seafood platter. $ *Average main: A$7* ⊠ *2 Breakwater Rd., Apollo Bay* ☎ *03/5237–1067* 🌐 *www.apollobayfish-coop.com.au* Ⓜ *3233.*

Hotels

★ Chris's Beacon Point Restaurant and Villas
$$$ | HOTEL | FAMILY | Set high in the Otway Ranges overlooking the Great Ocean Road and the sea, this is a wonderful place to dine or bed down for the night. **Pros:** spacious studios; sensational views; spot koalas from the property's windows. **Cons:** book ahead or miss out; pricey restaurant; steep walk to some rooms. *Rooms from: A$250* ✉ *280 Skenes Creek Rd., Apollo Bay* *Take Skenes Creek Rd. turnoff about 3 km (2 miles) from Apollo Bay and wind up hill to Beacon Point* ☎ *03/5237–6411* *www.chriss.com.au* *4 villas, 5 studios* *No Meals.*

Activities

Wildlife Wonders
HIKING & WALKING | Take a walk on the wild side through the Otways bushland, just outside Apollo Bay, with a guide who will show you the wildlife and landscapes of the Great Ocean Road. Suitable for prams and wheelchairs, the 75-minute walk is just 1.4 km (0.85 miles) long, and passes through land fenced off from feral predators, making it a haven for native animals. You'll also visit Wildlife Wonders' research station, which tracks animals and habitats on its grounds, including quolls, pademelons, bettongs, and cockatoos. Between May and July, you may even see passing southern right and humpback whales. Finish up with coffee at Wildlife Wonders' cafe. All profits go toward conservation of the Otways' environment. ✉ *475 Great Ocean Rd., Apollo Bay* ☎ *1300/099–467* *www.wildlifewonders.org.au* *A$59.*

Port Campbell National Park

271km (168 miles) southwest of Melbourne via the Great Ocean Rd., 90 km (56 miles) west of Apollo Bay, 135 km (83 miles) west of Lorne.

It is possible to visit Port Campbell National Park on an organized day trip from Melbourne, but better to stay overnight at one of the nearby towns and explore the region at your leisure. Port Campbell township is a logical place to base yourself, with a range of accommodation and dining options. The 30-km (19-mile) coastal drive is crammed with amazing sea sculptures, and you'll be stopping in the car parks along the way to get out and walk along the boardwalks to viewing platforms and steps that lead down to the coast.

GETTING HERE AND AROUND

The scenic route to Port Campbell National Park (which is actually a few miles east of the town of Port Campbell) is via the Great Ocean Road from Torquay, via Lorne and Apollo Bay. A car is the best way to go. A shorter drive is via the Princes Highway (M1) from Melbourne to Warrnambool, then the Great Ocean Road east to Port Campbell. A V/Line train operates to Warrnambool, and then a bus can be taken to Port Campbell. The journey takes about five hours.

TRANSPORTATION V/Line. ☎ *1800/800–007* *www.vline.com.au.*

VISITOR INFORMATION

CONTACTS Port Campbell Visitor Information Centre. ✉ *26 Morris St., Port Campbell* ☎ *1300/137–255* *www.visit12apostles.com.au.*

Sights

★ Port Campbell National Park

Stretching some 30 km (19 miles) along Victoria's southeastern coastline, Port Campbell National Park is the site of some of the most famous and most beautiful geological formations in Australia. The ferocious Southern Ocean has gnawed at the limestone cliffs along this coast for eons, creating a sort of badlands-by-the-sea, where strangely shaped formations stand offshore amid the surf. The most famous of these formations is the Twelve Apostles, as much a symbol for Victoria as the Sydney Opera House is for New South Wales (the name has always been a misnomer, as there were originally only nine of these stone columns—or sea stacks as they are correctly termed. Collapses in 2005 and 2009 mean that eight remain). If you happen to be visiting the Twelve Apostles just after sunset, you're likely to see bands of little penguins returning to their burrows on the beach. There's a population of around 3,000 of these cute creatures in the area.

Loch Ard Gorge, named after the iron-hulled clipper that wrecked on the shores of nearby Muttonbird Island in 1878, is another spectacular place to walk. Four of the *Loch Ard*'s victims are buried in a nearby cemetery, while a sign by the gorge tells the story of the ship and its crew. This stretch of coast is often called the Shipwreck Coast for the hundreds of vessels that have met untimely ends in the treacherous waters. The Historic Shipwreck Trail, with landmarks describing 25 of the disasters, stretches from Moonlight Head to Port Fairy.

Spectacular all year round, it is busiest in the warmer months, November to April, so expect to share key sights with many other visitors. This is also the best time to witness the boisterous birdlife on nearby Muttonbird Island. Toward nightfall, hundreds of hawks and kites circle the island in search of baby mutton birds emerging from their protective burrows. The birds of prey beat a hasty retreat at the sight of thousands of adult shearwaters approaching with food for their chicks as the last light fades from the sky. Other amazing sea stacks and stone formations farther west along the Great Ocean Road are also not to be missed. These include the Grotto, London Bridge (now an arch after an earlier collapse), and the spectacular Bay of Islands and Bay of Martyrs.

A self-guided, 1½-hour Discovery Walk begins near Port Campbell Beach, where it's safe to swim between the surf patrol flags. The pounding surf and undertow are treacherous at other nearby beaches. ✉ *Port Campbell National Park, Port Campbell.*

Restaurants

Waves

$$ | **AUSTRALIAN** | A relaxed main street eatery with a spacious sundeck and friendly staff, open for breakfast from 6 am, there are daily fish and soup specials, and Devonshire teas with fresh scones. Waves also has self-contained rooms including some with spa baths. **Known for:** tea and scones; casual dining; simple, hearty meals. *Average main: A$30* ✉ *29 Lord St., Port Campbell* ☎ *03/5598–6111* 🌐 *www.wavesportcampbell.com.au.*

Coffee and Quick Bites

★ Timboon Fine Ice Cream

$ | **ICE CREAM** | **FAMILY** | Possibly Victoria's best ice cream is made in the vivid green hills behind Port Campbell. You won't regret the 15-minute drive to the village of Timboon to taste its all-natural ice creams and sorbets, made with milk from local dairies. **Known for:** orange and cardamom ice cream; exceptional ice cream; vegan and gluten-free options. *Average main: A$10* ✉ *1A Barrett*

Loch Ard Gorge in Port Campbell National Park, Great Ocean Road

St., Timboon ☎ 03/5501–9736 🌐 www.timboonfineicecream.com.au.

Hotels

Daysy Hill Country Cottages

$ | **HOUSE** | **FAMILY** | Set in manicured gardens with lavender-lined walkways, these five attractive sandstone-and-cedar cottages look over the Newfield Valley. **Pros:** family-friendly; good price; great location. **Cons:** car required; self-catering only; limited facilities. *$ Rooms from: A$150 ✉ 2585 Cobden-Port Campbell Rd., Port Campbell ☎ 03/5598–6226 🌐 www.daysyhillcottages.com.au 5 cottages, 3 cabins No Meals.*

Southern Ocean Villas

$$$ | **HOUSE** | Ideally situated on the edge of Port Campbell National Park, within short walking distance of the town center and beach, these villas are stylishly furnished and fitted with polished wood floors, picture windows, and high ceilings. **Pros:** set in secluded gardens; near Twelve Apostles; good for longer stays. **Cons:** no views; difficult to find; located in sleepy town. *$ Rooms from: A$280 ✉ 2 McCue St., Port Campbell ☎ 03/5598–4200 🌐 www.southernocean-villas.com 20 villas No Meals.*

Activities

DIVING

The Twelve Apostles Marine National Park and the nearby Arches Marine Sanctuary both provide fantastic diving opportunities. Local wrecks that can be explored with experienced guides include the *Napier* at Port Campbell, the famous *Loch Ard* (off Muttonbird Island), the *Schomberg* at Peterborough, and the *Fiji* near Moonlight Head. All wrecks are protected by federal law, and are not to be disturbed in any way. *See Port Campbell boat charters in Tours.*

HIKING

The Port Campbell National Park area, which is home to the Twelve Apostles, Loch Ard George, and other amazing landforms, has many good short walks.

Most are along wooden boardwalks; some also include steep stairs down to the beach. Most are sections of the much larger Great Ocean Walk, a one-way, long-distance 110-km (68-mile) walk from Apollo Bay to the Twelve Apostles.

Inland from Port Campbell is the Camperdown-Timboon Rail Trail (also known as the Crater to Coast Rail Trail). It passes by lakes and streams and open volcanic plains. It is suitable for walkers and mountain bikers. The 36-km (22-mile) trail has good signage. The visitor center at Port Campbell and other visitor information centers have all the details.

Port Fairy

377 km (215 miles) southwest of Melbourne via the Great Ocean Rd.; it is considerably shorter if you take the inland route along the Princes Fwy (M1).

Port Fairy is widely considered to be the state's prettiest village. The second-oldest town in Victoria, it was originally known as Belfast, and there are indeed echoes of Ireland in the landscape and architecture. More than 50 of the cottages and sturdy bluestone buildings that line the banks of the River Moyne have been classified as landmarks by the National Trust, and few towns repay a leisurely stroll so richly. Huge Norfolk Island pines line many of the streets, particularly Gipps Street, and the town is dotted with good cafés, pubs, and art galleries.

The town still thrives as the base for a fishing fleet, and as host to the Port Fairy Folk Festival, one of Australia's most famous musical events, held every March. The town has a large colony of short-tailed shearwaters that nest on Griffiths Island. Amazingly, these birds travel here from the Aleutian Islands near Alaska, always arriving within three days of September 22. You can take a 45-minute walk around the island on marked trails to the historic lighthouse.

GETTING HERE AND AROUND

The most convenient form of transport is by car; the 377-km (234-mile) trip along the Great Ocean Road from Melbourne takes about 6½ hours, and it's advisable to break up the journey, as there's so much to see along the way. It's a shorter trip if you take the Princes Highway (M1).

TRANSPORTATION
V/Line
Travel from Melbourne's Southern Cross Station to Warrnambool (3½ hours) on V/Line trains, and then make the short distance (29 km [18 miles]) on V/Line buses to Port Fairy. ☎ *1800/800–007* 🌐 *www.vline.com.au.*

VISITOR INFORMATION

CONTACTS Port Fairy Visitor Information Centre. ✉ *Railway Pl., 4 Bank St., Port Fairy* ☎ *1300/656–564* 🌐 *www.portfairy-australia.com.au.*

Sights

Port Fairy Historical Society
HISTORY MUSEUM | The historical society's museum contains relics from the 19th-century whaling days, when Port Fairy was a whaling station with one of the largest ports in Victoria. It also highlights the stories of the many ships that have come to grief along this dangerous coast. ✉ *Old Courthouse, 30 Gipps St., Port Fairy* ☎ *03/5568–2263* 🌐 *www.historicalsociety.port-fairy.com* 🎫 *A$5* 🕙 *Closed Sun.–Tues., Thurs., and Fri.*

Tower Hill State Game Reserve
WILDLIFE REFUGE | This reserve—Victoria's largest dormant volcano—is packed with native Australian animals in their natural state. The Worn Gundidj Visitor Centre in the reserve conducts cultural interpretative walks. Take its 90-minute personalized bush and nature walk to learn about Indigenous lifestyles, bush food, and medicine, and hear about the local

inhabitants, which include emus, sugar gliders, koalas, kangaroos, birds, and reptiles. The standard tour is A$35; also ask about the availability of other occasional specialist tours, including twilight visits, to experience Aboriginal culture firsthand. Parks Victoria's website also has a map of the reserve and self-guided walking trails. ✉ *Tower Hill State Game Reserve, Princes Hwy., between Port Fairy and Warrnambool, Tower Hill* ☎ *131–963 Parks Victoria, 03/5565–9202, 03/5561–5315 Tower Hill Tours* 🌐 *parks.vic.gov.au* ☞ *See www.towerhill.org.au for tour information.*

Restaurants

★ Coffin Sally's

$ | PIZZA | FAMILY | Down a bluestone alleyway, Coffin Sally is the good-time girl of Port Fairy, a fun, grown-up pizza bar doling up quality beers, wines, and cocktails alongside piping hot pizzas. The signature pizza, Buffalo Sally, features local Shaw River buffalo mozzarella, cherry tomatoes, and fresh basil. **Known for:** historic, bluestone walls; great quality pizzas; good service. *$ Average main: A$20* ✉ *33 Sackville St., Port Fairy* ☎ *03/5568–2618* 🌐 *www.coffinsally.com.au* ⏲ *Closed Tues. and Wed.*

Time & Tide

$$$$ | CAFÉ | "High Tea by the High Sea" is the reason to visit this luscious café, as well as its appetite-stimulating Southern Ocean view. Take a seat on a high-backed chair and indulge in three tiers of savory tarts, finger sandwiches, brownies, filled meringues, and more, including tea or coffee. **Known for:** grand high tea; books up fast; ocean views. *$ Average main: A$79* ✉ *21 Thistle Pl., Port Fairy* ☎ *03/5568–2134* 🌐 *www.timeandtidehightea.com* ⏲ *Closed weekdays.*

Coffee and Quick Bites

Oak & Anchor

$ | CAFÉ | Enter this whitewashed stone hotel to find its café serving breakfast from 7 am, as well as lunch and dinner. The Oak & Anchor might have been around since 1857, but the food is fresh and light—try the quinoa porridge for breakfast or the Australian king prawns with sourdough for lunch. **Known for:** historic building; share platters for dinner; local cheeses. *$ Average main: A$16* ✉ *9 Bank St., Port Fairy* ☎ *03/4508–4206* 🌐 *oakandanchorhotel.com.*

Hotels

★ Drift House

$$$$ | HOTEL | Drift House doesn't need to boast; behind the unassuming facade are six beautifully designed suites that make you wish you could move in forever. **Pros:** fabulous breakfast; walking distance to restaurants; impeccable design. **Cons:** small pool; pricey; two-night minimum applies. *$ Rooms from: A$475* ✉ *98 Gipps St., Port Fairy* ☎ *03/5568–3309* 🌐 *www.drifthouse.com.au* *Free Breakfast* *6 suites.*

Merrijig Inn

$$ | B&B/INN | One of Victoria's oldest inns, this beautifully restored 1841 Georgian-style building overlooks Port Fairy's working wharf from King George Square. **Pros:** roaring fire in winter; cute and cozy; great food. **Cons:** books out fast; restaurant is closed midweek; upstairs rooms have character, but they're small. *$ Rooms from: A$160* ✉ *1 Campbell St., Port Fairy* ☎ *03/5568–2324* 🌐 *www.merrijiginn.com* *8 rooms* *Free Breakfast.*

★ Oscars Waterfront Boutique Hotel

$$$$ | B&B/INN | With an absolute waterfront location, overlooking a marina of yachts, this hotel gives French provincial style an Australian edge. **Pros:** great breakfasts; fantastic location; elegant decor. **Cons:** no on-site restaurant; no elevator; town is dead in the off-season. $ *Rooms from: A$325* ✉ *41B Gipps St., Port Fairy* ☎ *03/5568–3022* 🌐 *www.oscarsportfairy.com* 🛏 *7 suites* 🍽 *Free Breakfast.*

Activities

HIKING

There are several walks around Port Fairy that highlight the town's historical aspects and the area's great beauty. Pick up a Historic Walks map from the visitor center and follow a trail past some 30 beautiful buildings; it takes about an hour. The Port Fairy Maritime & Shipwreck Heritage Walk is a 2-km (1-mile) trail that passes the sites of several shipwrecks: the barque *Socrates,* which was battered by huge seas in 1843; the barque *Lydia,* which was wrecked off the coast in 1847; the schooner *Thistle,* which went down in 1837; and the brigantine *Essington,* which sank while moored at Port Fairy in 1852. Other historic attractions en route include the town port, the lifeboat station, riverside warehouses, cannons and gun emplacements at Battery Hill, and Griffiths Island Lighthouse. The walk is well marked.

Griffiths Island is another good place to walk. You can stroll around the entire island in about an hour, visiting the lighthouse and perhaps spotting a black wallaby along the way.

Ten minutes or 14 km (9 miles) east of Port Fairy is Tower Hill State Game Reserve, nested in an extinct volcano. There are several walking trails and plenty of chances to see emus and kangaroos. About 40 minutes northeast is Budj Bim National Park which is comanaged by the Gunditjmara Traditional Owners and Parks Victoria. Another extinct volcano, the landscape is UNESCO World Heritage listed for its significant Aboriginal cultural values. There are four walks, including one to the crater rim and lava caves.

Ballarat

116 km (73 miles) northwest of Melbourne.

In the local Aboriginal language, the name Ballarat means "resting place." In pre-gold-rush days, nearby Lake Wendouree provided the area with a plentiful supply of food. Once the gold boom hit, however, the town became much less restful; in 1854 Ballarat was the scene of the Battle of the Eureka Stockade, a skirmish that took place between miners and authorities over gold license fees that miners were forced to pay, though they had no vote. More than 30 men died in the battle. Today their flag—the Southern Cross—is a symbol of Australia's egalitarian spirit and can be viewed in the Eureka Centre.

Despite the harsh times, fortunes made from the mines (and from the miners) resulted in the grand Victorian architecture on Sturt and Lydiard Streets—note the post office, the town hall, Craig's Royal Hotel, and Her Majesty's Theatre. The Old Colonists' Hall and the Mining Exchange (at 16 and 8 Lydiard Street, respectively) now house shops and cafés. The visitor center has a self-guided heritage walk.

GETTING HERE AND AROUND

It's an easy 90-minute drive to Ballarat along the Western Highway (M8) from Melbourne. The road, however, is the main artery between Melbourne and Adelaide, and many huge trucks also use the road. Take care and drive within the speed limit. From Ballarat you can easily drive north to the spa-country towns of Daylesford–Hepburn Springs and Bendigo on the Midland Highway. The city itself is well signposted. The city center is built around a well-planned grid and has ample parking. Local bus services run from Sturt Street, the main thoroughfare, to most of Ballarat's attractions.

Great Ocean Road Tours

AAT Kings. This operator has a seven-day tour from Melbourne to Adelaide that travels the length of the Great Ocean Road and also includes visits to Mt. Gambier and Kangaroo Island. ✉ *Federation Sq., at Flinders and Russell Sts., City Center* ☎ *1300/228–546* 🌐 *www.aatkings.com.au* 🎫 *From A$3508.*

Mulloka Cruises. Explore Port Fairy Bay on a half-hour boat cruise—a quick way to get your sea legs and see Port Fairy from a different angle and learn more about it from the boat's friendly owners. The Mulloka takes a maximum of 12 guests, and there are no set times, so call ahead to book. ✉ *Martins Point, end of wharf, Port Fairy* ☎ *0408/514–382* 🌐 *www.facebook.com/mullokacruises/* 🎫 *From A$15.*

Split Point Lighthouse tours. Explore the majestic, and still operational, Split Point Lighthouse at Aireys Inlet, also known as the White Queen. You can see her for miles as you approach this section of the Great Ocean Road west of Anglesea—just look for the huge white tower with the red cap—and the views from the top are amazing. Take a self-guided tour via the information panels; there are also guides on hand to talk you through the lighthouse's history. Allow 30 minutes, plus extra time to see if you can spy a pod of dolphins, or even whales during their migratory season from April to October. Book entry online or pay at the door. ✉ *Split Point Lighthouse, Federal St., Aireys Inlet* 🌐 *www.splitpointlighthouse.com.au* 🎫 *From A$10.*

Spring Creek Horse Rides. Ride through beautiful Otway National Park on horseback for a leisurely hour or two; its all-day ride includes riding to and from the local pub for lunch via the Anglesea River. ✉ *245 Portreath Rd., Bellbrae* ☎ *0423/456–922 mobile* 🌐 *www.springcreekhorserides.com.au* 🎫 *From A$71.*

12 Apostles Helicopters. One exciting way to appreciate the awesome force of the Southern Ocean and this amazing natural sculpture park is by helicopter. Fifteen-minute flights take in the Twelve Apostles and Loch Ard Gorge; longer flights travel farther up the coast to the west and inland. ✉ *12 Apostles Information Centre, Great Ocean Rd., at Booringa Rd., Port Campbell* ☎ *03/5598–8283* 🌐 *www.12apostleshelicopters.com.au* 🎫 *From A$145.*

Autopia Tours. Take a day trip from Melbourne down the Great Ocean Road with this small-group, eco-conscious tour operator, mixing wildlife experiences, adventure, and delicious local food. If a day is not enough, Autopia also offers multiday trips along the coast, visiting the Twelve Apostles and the Grampians; and its three-day journeys continue all the way to Adelaide. Accommodation is either shared dorms or private en suite rooms. ✉ *Port Fairy* ☎ *03/9393–1333* 🌐 *www.autopiatours.com.au* 🎫 *From A$150, 1-day eco-tour.*

Trains run between Ballarat and Melbourne, and buses operate from Ballarat throughout the Goldfields region including Daylesford and Bendigo.

TRANSPORTATION

V/Line

Take trains between Ballarat and Melbourne, and buses from Ballarat to other Gold Country destinations such as Daylesford and Bendigo. ☎ *1800/800–007* 🌐 *www.vline.com.au.*

VISITOR INFORMATION

CONTACTS Ballarat Visitor Information Centre. ✉ *225 Sturt St., Ballarat* ☎ *1800/446–633* 🌐 *www.visitballarat.com.au.*

Sights

Art Gallery of Ballarat

ART GALLERY | This impressive art museum has a large collection of Australian art, from 19th-century works to contemporary pieces. Keep an eye out for its paintings by landscape artist Eugene von Guerard, who captured Ballarat as it appeared in the raucous early gold rush days. ✉ *40 Lydiard St., Ballarat* ☎ *03/5320–5858* 🌐 *www.artgalleryofballarat.com.au* 🎫 *Free.*

Ballarat Botanical Gardens

GARDEN | On the shores of Lake Wendouree, the Ballarat Botanical Gardens are identifiable by the brilliant blooms and classical statuary. At the rear of the gardens, the Conservatory hosts events during the town's Begonia Festival held each March, with other events taking place near the lake. ✉ *Gillies St. N at Lake Gardens Ave., Ballarat* ☎ *03/5320–5135* 🌐 *www.ballaratbotanicalgardens.com.au.*

Ballarat Wildlife Park

ZOO | FAMILY | All sorts of native animals, including kangaroos and emus (which roam free), saltwater crocodiles, snakes, Tasmanian devils, wombats, tree kangaroos, and echidnas can be found at this wildlife sanctuary. Daily tours of the park are led at 11, with a koala show at 2 and a wombat show at 2:30. Sunday at 3 is "crunch time," when Crunch the crocodile gets a feed. If you're also hungry, the park has a café and picnic areas. ✉ *250 Fussell St. at York St., Ballarat East* ☎ *03/5333–5933* 🌐 *www.wildlifepark.com.au* 🎫 *A$35.*

★ **Eureka Centre**

HISTORY MUSEUM | FAMILY | The Eureka Centre stands on the site of the 1854 Eureka Stockade revolt, in which gold miners staged an armed rebellion against police corruption and for the establishment of democracy in Victoria. The museum brings history to life via impressive interactive technology. Visitors learn about democracy around the world and can admire the tattered but beautiful remains of the original Eureka Flag, which flew above the site of the battle. A simple on-site café serves coffee and cake. ✉ *102 Stawell St. S, Ballarat* ☎ *03/5333–0333* 🌐 *www.eurekacentreballarat.com.au* 🎫 *A$6.*

★ **Sovereign Hill**

HISTORIC DISTRICT | FAMILY | Built on the site of the former mines of the gold rush era, this living museum town provides an authentic look at life, work, and play during Ballarat's gold rush era. Highlights of the main street include an operational hotel, blacksmith's shop, bakery, stores, and even a post office—all perfectly preserved relics of their time. You can have your photo taken in period costumes, take a mine shaft tour, pan for real gold (and find some), ride in a stagecoach, or head to the lolly shop to taste old-fashioned candy. Return at night for "Aura," a 90-minute sound-and-light spectacular that tells the story of the Eureka uprising. Your entry ticket gives you entrance to all Sovereign Hill's included activities, and you can add on such experiences as themed dining and accommodation, for full immersion in the period. ✉ *Bradshaw St., Ballarat* ☎ *03/5337–1199* 🌐 *www.sovereignhill.com.au* 🎫 *From A$39* ⊙ *Closed Mon.*

Restaurants

The Forge

$$ | PIZZA | FAMILY | This former industrial building now houses a pizzeria that serves top-notch wood-fired pizzas in a big dining room with long timber tables, wooden beams, and exposed brick walls. The pizzas are excellent, with light crusts and tasty toppings; try the Volcano (hot salami, chili pepper, Gorgonzola, feta, olives, and anchovies) for an entrée with a zing. **Known for:** pizza strips with dip appetizer; industrial-cool decor and setting; Volcano pizza. 💲 *Average main: A$24* ✉ *14 Armstrong St. N, Ballarat* ☎ *03/5337–6635* 🌐 *www.theforgepizzeria.com.au.*

Coffee and Quick Bites

★ **FIKA**

$ | CAFÉ | Taking its name from the Swedish word for coffee break, this sleek contemporary café decked out with blond wood and industrial light fittings serves excellent coffee. There's also a light meal menu with a healthy twist, including macadamia chia pudding for breakfast and a caprese salad for lunch—counterbalanced with BLAT sandwiches (bacon, lettuce, avocado, and tomato) and single-origin coffee. **Known for:** Scandinavian design; single-origin coffee; healthy options. 💲 *Average main: A$12* ✉ *36a Doveton St., Ballarat* ☎ *0427/527–447* 🌐 *www.fikacoffeebrewers.com.au.*

Hotels

The Ansonia

$ | **HOTEL** | Built in the 1870s as professional offices, this building now houses a boutique hotel. **Pros:** free parking; cozy; arty. **Cons:** small rooms; noise from rooms above; rooms opening onto the atrium lack privacy. *Rooms from: A$150* *32 Lydiard St., Ballarat* *03/5332–4678* *www.theansonianlydiard.com.au* *16 rooms, 3 apartments* *Free Breakfast.*

Mercure Ballarat Hotel

$$ | **HOTEL** | **FAMILY** | This single-story accommodation is spread out over a large property dotted with gum trees next to Sovereign Hill; rooms are furnished in classic style, with dark green and timber notes, or contemporary white. **Pros:** walking distance to Sovereign Hill open-air museum; spacious; atmospheric. **Cons:** windows don't open; lodge rooms are dated; about 2½ km (1½ miles) from the city center. *Rooms from: A$155* *613 Main Rd., Ballarat* *03/5327–1200* *www.mercureballarat.com.au* *88 rooms, 9 apartments* *No Meals.*

Daylesford and Hepburn Springs

109 km (68 miles) northwest of Melbourne, 45 km (28 miles) northeast of Ballarat.

Nestled in the slopes of the Great Dividing Range, Daylesford and its nearby twin, Hepburn Springs, are a spa-lover's paradise. The water table here is naturally aerated with carbon dioxide and rich in soluble mineral salts, making it ideal for indulging in mineral baths and other rejuvenating treatments. The natural springs were first noted during the gold rush, and Swiss-Italian immigrants established a spa at Hepburn Springs in 1875. There are now about 70 natural springs in the area. The best time to visit the area is autumn, when the deciduous trees turn bronze and you can finish up a relaxing day next to an open fire with a glass of local red.

Liquid Gold

The promise of gold "in them thar hills" drew mobs of prospectors in the 1850s, but today's visitors aren't looking to quench their thirst for riches. Ballarat's climate produces great Pinot Noir and Chardonnay, while the Grampians is the birthplace of Great Western, Australia's first and best-known sparkling wine. The Pyrenees region is known for its classic Shiraz.

GETTING HERE AND AROUND

The twin towns of Daylesford and Hepburn Springs are easily reached by car from Melbourne. Take the Western Highway (M8) to Ballarat, then take the Midland Highway for another 40 km (25 miles) to Daylesford (via Creswick). Hepburn Springs is a mile or two from Daylesford. V/Line operates trains from Southern Cross Station, Melbourne, to Ballarat or Woodend (near Mount Macedon), and V/Line buses connect with the trains to take passengers to Daylesford.

TRANSPORTATION

V/Line

Trains operate from Southern Cross Station in Melbourne to Ballarat or Woodend (near Mount Macedon), where buses connect to Daylesford. *1800/800–007* *www.vline.com.au.*

VISITOR INFORMATION

CONTACTS Daylesford Regional Visitor Information Centre. *98 Vincent St., Daylesford* *1800/454–891* *www.visithepburnshire.com.au.*

Sights

★ Bromley & Co

ARTS CENTER | This impressive art gallery displays the stylish, contemporary work of David Bromley—one of Australia's top contemporary artists—along with other artists. The narrow shopfront belies a fascinating interior, with art pieces scattered down the long, narrow interior, to spaces upstairs, and out to a garden. ✉ *45a Vincent St., Daylesford* ☎ *03/5348–3979* 🌐 *www.bromleyandco.com* 🕑 *Closed Mon.–Thurs.*

Convent Gallery

ART GALLERY | Perched on a hillside overlooking Daylesford, this gallery occupies a former 19th-century nunnery that has been restored to its lovely Victorian-era state. It houses three levels of fine art and a nun-related museum, and occasionally stages live arts performances. At the front of the gallery is Bad Habits, a sunny café that serves light lunches and snacks, while Altar Bar is a hip place for a drink. The second-story penthouse suite is the ultimate in decadence, with its own hydrotherapy bath and a boudoir-style bedroom. For groups, the 1920s Monastiraki guesthouse lets you sleep among yet more art from the Convent's owner, Tina Banitska, which displays a wicked sense of humor, or the two-bedroom art house, "Love and Madness," opposite the Convent Gallery. ✉ *Hill St. at Daly St., Daylesford* ☎ *03/5348–3211* 🌐 *www.theconvent.com.au* 🎫 *A$5 entrance to the art gallery and museum.*

Mineral Springs Reserve

HOT SPRING | Above the Hepburn Bathhouse and Spa, a path winds past a series of mineral springs in this 74-acre reserve, created in 1865. Each spring has a slightly different chemical composition—and a significantly different taste. You can bring empty bottles and fill them for free with the mineral water of your choice. The reserve includes walking trails, playgrounds, and a café. ✉ *Mineral Springs Reserve, Hepburn Springs* 🎫 *Free.*

Hotels

★ The Dudley Boutique Hotel

$$$$ | **B&B/INN** | Restrained and elegant, The Dudley provides a country house for explorations in this spa town. **Pros:** short walk to Hepburn Bathhouse; tranquil garden setting; great heritage character. **Cons:** no on-site restaurant; adults only; limited number of rooms may limit available booking dates. $ *Rooms from: A$329* ✉ *10 Forest Ave., Hepburn Springs* ☎ *03/5348–3033* 🌐 *www.thedudley.com.au* *6 rooms* 🍽 *Free Breakfast.*

★ Lake House

$$$$ | **HOTEL** | Featuring one of Australia's best restaurants, this rambling lakeside hotel adds a distinct glamour to spa country. **Pros:** tree house hot tubs with lake views; renowned food; tranquil garden setting. **Cons:** service can be inconsistent; some suites don't have views; two-night minimum stay on weekends. $ *Rooms from: A$875* ✉ *King St., Daylesford* ☎ *03/5348–3329* 🌐 *www.lakehouse.com.au* *33 rooms* 🍽 *All-Inclusive.*

Activities

SPAS

★ Hepburn Bathhouse & Spa

SPAS | A destination for relaxation and wellness since the 19th century, this facility is the centerpiece of Australia's premier spa destination, and one of the largest and most spectacular spas in the country. The complex encompasses the original Edwardian Bathhouse (circa 1895), which houses private mineral baths and more than 20 wet-and-dry treatment rooms, and a stunning, contemporary building, where you find the public bathhouse and the private sanctuary area. Patrons can buy two-hour passes for the bathhouse or the sanctuary. The bathhouse includes a relaxation mineral pool and a spa pool (A$55), while the sanctuary has underwater spa couches (for the ultimate in hydrotherapy), an aroma steam room, and a salt therapy pool. There is also the day spa area, where you can choose from a long list of therapies, including body wraps and polishes, facials, and other treatments using the mineral waters. Products used in the spa include a Hepburn Collection range specifically designed for Hepburn Bathhouse & Spa. ✉ *1 Mineral Springs Crescent, Hepburn Springs* ☎ *03/5321–6000* 🌐 *www.hepburnbathhouse.com.*

Bendigo

150 km (93 miles) northwest of Melbourne, 92 km (57 miles) south of Echuca.

Gold was discovered in the Bendigo district in 1851, and it skyrocketed as the richest city in the world until 1900. The city's magnificent public buildings bear witness to the richness of its mines. Today Bendigo has reinvented itself as a cultural destination, with distinguished buildings lining both sides of Pall Mall in the city center. These include the Shamrock Hotel, the Old Post Office, and the Bendigo Town Hall, all majestic examples of late-Victorian architecture. Although these glorious relics of a golden age dominate the landscape, the city is far from old-fashioned. You'll also find a lively café and restaurant scene, 30 boutique wineries, some of which can be visited on organized winery tours, and a strong arts scene led by one of the best regional art galleries in Australia.

GETTING HERE AND AROUND

To reach Bendigo, take the Calder Highway northwest from Melbourne; the trip takes about 1 hour and 40 minutes. V/Line operates trains to Bendigo from Melbourne's Southern Cross Station, a journey of about two hours. It also operates buses between Bendigo and Daylesford, and on to Ballarat. Bendigo Airport Service also runs an airport shuttle bus between Melbourne Airport to Bendigo.

TRANSPORTATION

Bendigo Airport Service
This coach service runs daily between Melbourne Tullamarine Airport and Bendigo, with stops along the way. Bookings are essential, and online bookings can be made up to three hours before departure. A one-way ticket costs A$49. ✉ *Platform 2, Bendigo Railway Station, Bendigo* ☎ *03/5444–3939* 🌐 *www.bendigoairportservice.com.au.*

V/Line
There are up to 20 train services a day from Melbourne's Southern Cross Station to Bendigo, a journey of about two hours. V/Line buses also travel between Bendigo and Daylesford, and on to Ballarat. ☎ *1800/800–007* 🌐 *www.vline.com.au.*

TOURS

Vintage Talking Tram
A good introduction to Bendigo is a tour aboard this hop-on, hop-off streetcar, which includes a taped commentary on the town's history. The half-hourly tram runs on an 8-km (5-mile) circuit between the Central Deborah Gold Mine and the Joss House temple, making six stops at historic sites. For a different perspective, the Dja Dja Warrung Tram journeys 40,000 years back into the traditions of the local Dja Dja Warrung people and their stories of creation and histories. One ticket covers both tram journeys. ✉ *Bendigo* ☎ *03/5442–2821* 🌐 *www.bendigotramways.com* 🎫 *From A$10.*

VISITOR INFORMATION

CONTACTS Bendigo Visitor Centre. ✉ *51 Pall Mall, Bendigo* ☎ *03/5434–6060, 1800/813–153* 🌐 *www.bendigotourism.com.au.*

Sights

★ Bendigo Art Gallery
ART GALLERY | A notable collection of contemporary Australian painting can be found in this beautiful gallery, including the work of Rupert Bunny, Emily Kame Kngwarreye, and Arthur Boyd. The gallery

also has some significant 19th-century French realist and impressionist works, bequeathed by a local surgeon. International exhibitions are regularly hosted. There are free guided tours every day at 11 am and 2 pm. ✉ *42 View St., Bendigo* ☎ *03/5434–6088* 🌐 *www.bendigoartgallery.com.au* 🎫 *Entry to permanent exhibition free; touring exhibitions cost from A$10.*

Bendigo Joss House Temple

TEMPLE | An active place of worship on the outskirts of the city, this small temple was built by Chinese miners in 1871, during the gold rush days. At the height of the boom in the 1850s and 1860s, about a quarter of Bendigo's miners were Chinese. These men were usually dispatched from villages on the Chinese mainland, and they were expected to work hard and return as quickly as possible with their fortunes. Sadly, tensions with white miners were a feature of that era, along with anti-Chinese riots. Luckily this attractive element of their presence has endured from those turbulent times. ✉ *3 Finn St., Bendigo* ☎ *03/5442–1685* 🌐 *www.bendigojosshouse.com* 🎫 *Entry by donation* ⏲ *Closed weekdays.*

Bendigo Pottery

ARTS CENTER | Australia's oldest working pottery workshop turns out distinctive brown-and-cream pieces that many Australians have in their kitchens. Founded in 1858, the historic workshop hosts demonstrations. You can even get your hands dirty creating your own clay piece during an affordable wheel-throwing lesson (bookings essential during school holidays); there's also a clay play area for small children. Impressive beehive brick kilns, which you can step inside, are star exhibits in the museum. It's 6½ km (4 miles) northeast of Bendigo on the way to Echuca, and there is a small café also on the premises. ✉ *146 Midland Hwy., Epsom* ☎ *03/5448–4404* 🌐 *www.bendigopottery.com.au* 🎫 *Free, museum A$8, wheel-throwing lessons from A$30.*

★ **Central Deborah Gold Mine**

FACTORY | **FAMILY** | This historic mine, with a 1,665-foot shaft, yielded almost a ton of gold before it closed in 1954. Aboveground you can pan for gold, see the old stamper battery, and climb up the poppet head, but the thrill of mining is felt belowground. The one-hour underground tour takes you 200 feet below the surface in an industrial lift to widened tunnels, letting you experience the conditions miners worked in during the gold rush era. Hear the roar of the traditional mining equipment and see gold in its natural state. The tour is wheelchair accessible. ✉ *76 Violet St., Bendigo* ☎ *03/5443–8255* 🌐 *www.central-deborah.com* 🎫 *A$7 (aboveground only); self-guided tours (including entry) from A$32.*

Golden Dragon Museum

OTHER MUSEUM | The Chinese community's important role in Bendigo life, past and present, is explored within this museum. Its centerpieces are the century-old Loong imperial ceremonial dragon and the Sun Loong imperial dragon, which, at more than 106 yards in length, is said to be the world's longest. When carried in procession, the body alone requires 52 carriers and 52 relievers, and more to carry the head, neck, and tail; the head alone weighs 64 pounds. Also on display are other ceremonial objects, costumes, and historic artifacts. The lovely Yi Yuan Gardens, opposite, with ponds and bridges, are part of the museum. ✉ *1–11 Bridge St., Bendigo* ☎ *03/5441–5044* 🌐 *www.goldendragonmuseum.org* 🎫 *A$12* ⏲ *Closed Mon.*

Restaurants

★ **The Woodhouse**

$$ | **STEAKHOUSE** | This excellent restaurant in a former blacksmith's workshop serves quality, locally sourced food in a casual dining environment. The atmospheric interior has exposed brick walls and timber beams, with a wood-fired pizza oven visible at one end of the bar. **Known for:** craft beers; high-quality steaks;

woodfired pizzas. $ *Average main: A$33* ✉ *101 Williamson St., Bendigo* ☎ *03/5443–8671* 🌐 *www.thewoodhouse.com.au* ⏲ *Closed Mon. and Tues. No lunch Wed.–Fri.*

Coffee and Quick Bites

Bridgewater Bakehouse

$ | **BAKERY** | **FAMILY** | It's worth the country drive from Bendigo to this bakery to taste an Australian obsession—the vanilla slice—and Bridgewater Bakehouse is twice-winner of the annual, fiercely contested, national competition. The perfect slice is a thick slab of firm custard, wedged between two slivers of flaky pastry and iced with a glossy fondant. **Known for:** roast lamb and gravy pie; vanilla slice; multiple outposts. $ *Average main: A$10* ✉ *Shop 9, 20 Bath La., Bendigo* ☎ *03/5443–0737* 🌐 *www.bridgewaterbakehouse.com.au.*

Hotels

★ Balgownie Estate Bendigo

$ | **RESORT** | Spend the night beneath canvas in a luxuriously appointed bell tent, set on 81 acres in the region's oldest winery. **Pros:** taste local wine; romantic bushland setting; outdoor bath. **Cons:** shared bathrooms for standard tents; walk to bathroom; booked out on weekends. $ *Rooms from: A$137* ✉ *46 Hermitage Rd., Maiden Gully, Bendigo* ☎ *03/5449–6222* 🌐 *www.balgownieestatebendigo.com* 🍴 *Free Breakfast* 🛏 *15 rooms.*

Hotel Shamrock

$$ | **HOTEL** | **FAMILY** | The lodgings at this landmark Victorian hotel in the city center range from traditional guest rooms to spacious suites. **Pros:** family rooms; historic gold era building; central location. **Cons:** some rooms have no views; restaurant service is hit-and-miss; limited facilities. $ *Rooms from: A$160* ✉ *Pall Mall, at Williamson St., Bendigo* ☎ *03/5443–0333* 🌐 *www.hotelshamrock.com.au* 🛏 *36 rooms and suites* 🍴 *Free Breakfast.*

★ Mercure Schaller Bendigo

$ | **HOTEL** | Named after Australian artist Mark Schaller, this art hotel is a cutting-edge addition to the Bendigo accommodation scene. **Pros:** walking distance to the city center; art-led design; lively lobby. **Cons:** tiny balconies; queen beds are the largest size available; small rooms. $ *Rooms from: A$149* ✉ *Lucan St., at Bayne St., Bendigo* ☎ *03/4433–6100* 🌐 *www.accor.com* 🛏 *120 rooms* 🍴 *No Meals.*

Activities

BIKING

There are some great bike trails and four self-guided winery cycle tours ranging in length from 21 km to 50 km (13 miles to 31 miles). The Mandurang Valley Wine Trail is the shortest and leads to the Chateau Dore Winery and Lynnevale Estate. You can also cycle along the O'Keefe Rail Trail and the Bendigo Bushland Trail; maps and brochures are available at the visitor center.

Moroni's Bikes

BIKING | This long-established company rents out mountain bikes and can advise on popular rides including the rail trails that stretch as far as the wine region of Heathcote and on the Goldfields Trail to Castlemaine. Ask the owners—keen mountain bikers themselves—directions to such popular mountain biking areas as Spring Gully and Harcourt. ✉ *104 Mitchell St., Bendigo* ☎ *03/5443–9644* 🌐 *www.moronisbikes.com.au* 🎫 *Bike rental from A$45 per day.*

HIKING AND WALKING

There are many excellent self-guided walks around Bendigo, and trails interconnect with the popular biking trails. You can do your own theme walk following in the gold-rush trail or admiring the city's grand old buildings. Popular bushland walks include One Tree Hill, Wildflower

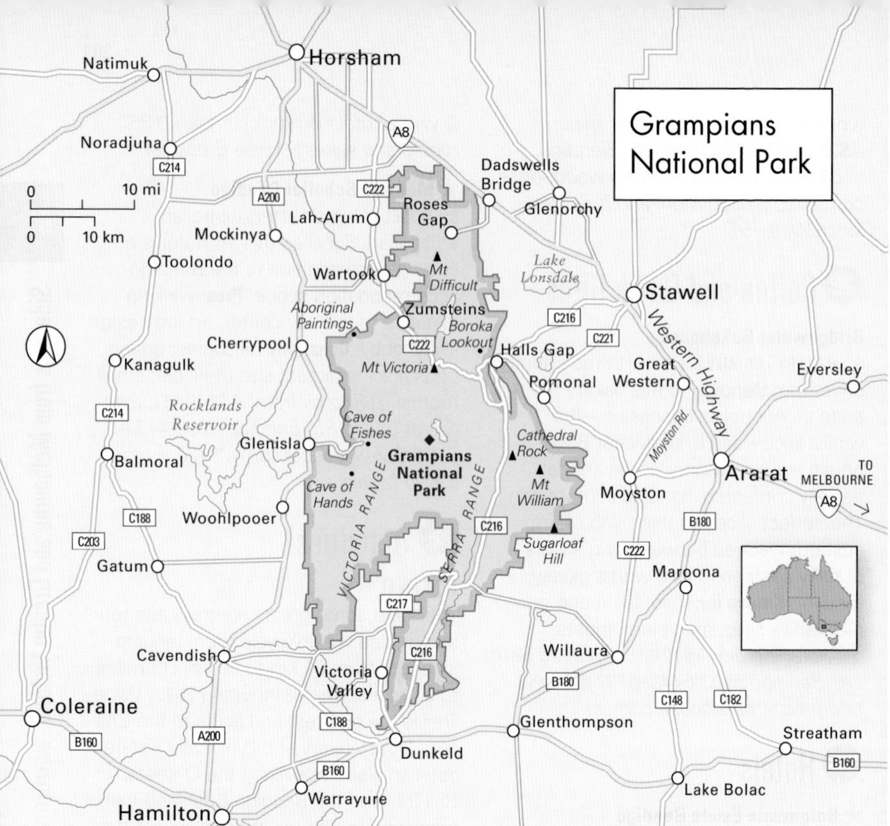

Drive, and the Old Tom Mine Walk in the Greater Bendigo National Park. The visitor center on Pall Mall has maps and brochures, as does its website.

Grampians National Park

260 km (162 miles) west of Melbourne, 100 km (62 miles) north of Hamilton.

Bushwalking is by far the most popular activity in Gariwerd, the Aboriginal name for the Grampians. Some of the best walks include Mackenzie Falls, the walk to Mt. Murdadjoog/Mt. Abrupt, the Mount Wudjub-Guyun/Hollow Mountain walk, and another to Silverband Falls. Even if you're not a big walker you can still see many of the best-known rock formations. Elephant Hide, the Balconies, the Pinnacle, and the Fortress are only a short walk from a car park. Canoeing is another great way to get away from the crowds and experience the lakes and rivers of the Grampians.

The most popular attractions of the central Grampians region can be visited in one day. However, if you want to visit few wineries and really take in the scenery, allow yourself another day or two. From the town of Halls Gap it's a 15-km (9-mile) drive (plus a 100-yard walk from the car park) to the spectacular Boroka Lookout.

GETTING HERE AND AROUND

Halls Gap (the base town for the Grampians National Park) is reached via Ballarat and Ararat on the Western Highway (M8). The town is 260 km (162 miles) northwest of Melbourne, 97 km (60 miles) northeast of Hamilton, and 140 km (87 miles) west of Ballarat. V/Line operates trains to Ballarat from Melbourne. V/Line buses connect with the trains to take passengers to Halls Gap. For timetables and fares, contact V/Line.

TOURS

Hangin' Out

For those who love experiencing the great outdoors from different angles, Hangin' Out runs rock climbing and abseiling tours to suit beginners and more experienced climbers for some of the best climbing in the world. They also conduct an informative, all-day guided adventure walk from Gunigalg/Mt. Stapylton to Wudjub-Guyun/Hollow Mountain in the north of Gariwerd/the Grampians, a unique walk that aims to connect people with the country. All tours aim to help people respect the rich cultural heritage and unique ecology of the Gariwerd region. ☎ *0407/684–831* 🌐 *www.hanginout.com.au* *From A$85.*

VISITOR INFORMATION

CONTACTS Halls Gap Visitor Information Centre. ✉ *117 Grampians Rd., Halls Gap* ☎ *1800/065–599* 🌐 *www.visitgrampians.com.au.* **Stawell and Grampians Visitor Information Centre.** ✉ *8 Main St., Stawell* ☎ *1800/330–080* 🌐 *www.visitgrampians.com.au.*

Sights

★ Grampians National Park

NATIONAL PARK | Comprising four mountain ranges—Mt. Difficult, Mt. William, Serra, and Victoria—the impressive Grampians National Park spills over 413,000 acres. Its rugged peaks, towering trees, waterfalls, creeks, and plethora of wildlife attract bushwalkers, rock climbers, and nature lovers. Spectacular wildflowers carpet the region in spring, while a number of significant Aboriginal rock art sites make it an ideal place to learn about Victoria's Indigenous history. The township of Halls Creek (population 600) sits within the national park, and with its 10,000 tourist beds it becomes quite a busy place in summer and at Easter. If you're staying in a self-catering accommodation, it's wise to stock up on groceries and wine in the big towns of Ballarat, Ararat, Hamilton, or Horsham, since prices at the Halls Gap general store are inflated. One of the most picturesque drives in the park is the 60-km-stretch (37-mile-stretch) from Halls Gap to Dunkeld. Some areas in the park can be affected by fire and flood from year to year, so check with Parks Victoria for current road and camping conditions. ✉ *Grampians National Park, Halls Gap* ☎ *131–963* 🌐 *parks.vic.gov.au.*

Restaurants

Kookaburra Hotel

$$$ | **AUSTRALIAN** | In the heart of Halls Gap, this is one of the town's best dining options and serves an imaginative range of dishes. The restaurant and bar provides a casual, gastropub experience, with signature dishes like the spinach crepe, baked duckling, blackened barramundi, and the kangaroo fillet. **Known for:** gets busy, so book ahead; kangaroo fillet; regional wines. $ *Average main: A$36* ✉ *125 Grampian Rd., Halls Gap* ☎ *03/5356–4222* 🌐 *www.kookaburrahotel.com.au* *Closed Mon. No lunch Tues.–Fri.*

★ Royal Mail Hotel

$$$ | **MODERN AUSTRALIAN** | Expansive views of the southern Grampians peaks compete with the extraordinary food plated up at the hotel in the tiny town of Dunkeld, 64 km (40 miles) south of Halls Gap. One of Victoria's signature dining experiences, the menu changes daily depending on the harvest from one of the country's largest working restaurant kitchen gardens, specializing in organic and heirloom vegetables. **Known for:** stylish accommodations on-site; exceptional dining; produce sourced from on-site gardens and farm. $ *Average main: A$46* ✉ *98 Parker St., Dunkeld*

Sitting on edge of Boroka Lookout in the Grampians National Park

☎ *03/5577–2241* 🌐 *www.royalmail.com.au* ☞ *Sat. dinner degustation only.*

Coffee and Quick Bites

Dunkeld Old Bakery
$ | **BAKERY** | Flipping dough into the same oven since 1887, this Grampians bakery earns its name. Stock up on croissants, baguettes and a gourmet pie (A$7)—such as beef and ale or the crowd-pleasing lamb ragu—to eat on the road, or grab a little table in the sun at the front of the bakery. **Known for:** vegetarian, vegan, and gluten-free options; eggs Benedict; fresh croissants. $ *Average main: A$7* ✉ *97 Martin St., Dunkeld* ☎ *03/5556–3606* 🌐 *www.dunkeldoldbakery.com.au.*

Hotels

★ **Boroka Downs**
$$$$ | **HOTEL** | On 100 acres of bush, scrub, and grassland, bordering the Grampians National Park, Boroka's five villas are nothing short of spectacular. **Pros:** eco-friendly and luxurious; floor-to-ceiling windows frame mountain views; kangaroos at the windows. **Cons:** own car required; two-night minimum stay; pricey. $ *Rooms from: A$450* ✉ *51 Birdswing Rd., Pomonal, Halls Gap* ☎ *0458/064–231* 🌐 *www.borokadowns.com.au* *5 villas* *Free Breakfast.*

Activities

CANOEING

Absolute Outdoors
CANOEING & ROWING | **FAMILY** | If you want to experience the Grampians wilderness via its serene lakes, a half-day guided canoeing trip may be the answer. The company, which operates from a shop that sells outdoor equipment in Halls Gap, hosts outings on Lake Bellfield, a little to the southeast of the township. It also runs rock climbing, abseiling, and mountain bike adventures within the park—its Rock Adventure combines family-friendly climbing and abseiling. ✉ *105 Main Rd. (aka Grampians Rd.), Halls Gap* ☎ *1300/526–258* 🌐 *www.*

absoluteoutdoors.com.au From A$80 for a half-day canoeing tour.*

HIKING

★ Park Trek Walking Holidays

HIKING & WALKING | This four-day walk traverses the little-explored northern region of the Grampians, along the newly opened section of the long-distance Grampians Peak Trail. Open only to licensed tour operators, you'll be away from the hubbub of the southern region of this beautiful national park, staying in new, purpose-built huts. A good level of fitness is required for this walk, with its exhilarating, 360-degree views over the ancient country. Groups are a maximum of 10 or 12, with two guides who serve up meals, snacks, and regional knowledge. ✉ *117–119 Grampians Rd., Halls Gap* ☎ *03/5639–2615* 🌐 *www.parktrek.com.au* *4-day walk from A$2150 a person.*

Echuca

206 km (128 miles) north of Melbourne, 194 km (120 miles) west of Rutherglen, 92 km (57 miles) north of Bendigo.

The name Echuca comes from a word in the Indigenous Yorta Yorta language meaning "meeting of the waters," a reference to the town's location at the confluence of the Murray, Campaspe, and Goulburn rivers. In the second half of the 19th century, Echuca was Australia's largest inland port. Many reminders of Echuca's colorful heyday remain in the restored paddle steamers, barges, and historic hotels, and in the Red Gum Works, the town's sawmill, now a working museum.

GETTING HERE AND AROUND

Echuca is a three-hour drive from Melbourne, reached most directly by the Calder Freeway (M79) or the Northern Highway (B75). V/Line trains take 3½ hours to reach Echuca from Melbourne's Southern Cross Station once or twice a day.

VISITOR INFORMATION

CONTACTS Echuca Visitor Information Centre. ✉ *Old Pump Station, 2 Heygarth St., Echuca* ☎ *1800/039–043* 🌐 *www.echucamoama.com.*

Sights

★ Historic River Precinct

NAUTICAL SIGHT | The inland river port of Echuca is a heritage town, home to a large paddle steamer fleet and its historic wharf. Among the vessels docked at the wharf is the PS *Adelaide* (built in 1866), the world's oldest operating wooden-hulled paddle steamer. Other historic buildings include the Bridge Hotel, built by ex-convict Henry Hopwood and the "father of Echuca," who had the foresight to establish a punt, and then to build a bridge at this commercially strategic point on the river. The Star Hotel, built in the 1860s, has an underground bar and escape tunnel, which was used by after-hours drinkers in the 19th century to evade the police. The Port of Echuca Discovery Centre is now open and full of historical displays. It's also a booking office, where you can get tickets to paddle steamer cruises and other historic sights, plus a spooky Port After Dark tour (A$15). The center itself runs daily tours (A$12.50) covering its displays and the recently revitalized wharf areas (warehouses, old railroad tracks, and riverboats included), and the Star Hotel.

One-hour river excursions are a refreshing treat at the end of a hot summer's day. Step aboard the *Adelaide*, the historic *Pevensey*, or the *Alexander Arbuthnot* for a one-hour cruise. Book tickets at the Port of Echuca Discovery Centre. Otherwise, Murray River Paddle Steamers runs hour-long excursions on the PS *Canberra*, and the *Emmylou*, a 19th-century-style boat built in 1980–82 for a historic television series, does overnight and multiday cruises from two to six night. A one-hour cruise on the PS *Canberra* costs A$30. ✉ *74 Murray Esplanade, Echuca*

☎ *03/5481–0500, 1300/942–737* 🌐 *www.portofechuca.org.au.*

Coffee and Quick Bites

The Sweet Meadow

$ | **CAFÉ** | Load the brunch table with French toast, waffles, breakfast wraps, and a big fry at this too-cute weatherboard café on Echuca's main street. The café serves all plant-based foods, from its milky coffees to its sweet smoothie bowls and refined sugar-free slices. **Known for:** sustainably sourced produce; all-vegan menu; handmade ceramics and artworks for sale. $ *Average main: A$19* ✉ *640 High St., Echuca* ☎ *03/5482–4099* 🌐 *www.thesweetmeadow.com.*

Hotels

★ **PS Emmylou**

$$$$ | **B&B/INN** | Departing from Echuca around sunset, this handsome steamer chugs down the Murray River on cruises ranging from two to six nights, sailing through ancient wetlands, stopping to visit wineries, sites of Aboriginal cultural significance, and the 1860s Perricoota Station homestead. **Pros:** lovely river scenery; fabulous sense of history; lots of birdlife. **Cons:** 60% single supplement; often sold out; some rooms better than others. $ *Rooms from: A$1040* ✉ *57 Murray Esplanade, Echuca* ☎ *03/5482–5244* 🌐 *www.murrayrivercruises.com.au* *8 cabins.*

Activities

BOATING

Murray River Houseboats

BOATING | **FAMILY** | A popular pursuit on the Murray is to rent a houseboat and drift slowly down the river, and this operator's top-tier vessels are five-star floating experiences; at the top of the range, expect all en suite cabins, Jacuzzis, state-of-the-art kitchens, and the latest appliances. They can sleep from 2 to 12 people and be rented from three days to a week and longer. There are six boats for rent. Prices start from A$1,380 for three nights on weekends or four nights midweek, for two to seven people. ✉ *Riverboat Dock, Echuca* ☎ *03/5480–2343* 🌐 *www.murrayriverhouseboats.com.au.*

CANOEING

River Country Adventours

BOATING | If you want to canoe up a lazy river—the Goulburn, which is a tributary of the Murray—you can arrange for a half- or full-day guided safari with this tour company. They also travel further afield, with their two-day, outback flight tours to the beautiful inland Lake Eyre, with meals and accommodation at outback pubs including the remote William Creek Pub (from A$2,795 per person). ✉ *13 Mackie St., Kyabram* ☎ *03/5852–2736, 0428/585–227 mobile* 🌐 *www.adventours.com.au* *From A$75 per person.*

HIKING AND BIKING

There are many popular hiking and bicycling trails in the area, including the 6-km (3.7-mile) Banyule State Forest trail, which starts at the Echuca Visitor Center; the 5-km (3-mile) Campaspe River walk; and a series of short loop walks from 30 minutes to two hours in the Barmah National Park, which pass through the world's largest river red gum forest. This region is significant to Yorta Yorta and other Aboriginal groups, who lived here for over 40,000 years. The visitor center has all the details and maps.

Alpine National Park

323 km (200 miles) northeast of Melbourne, 40–50 km (25–31 miles) south to southeast of Mt. Buffalo.

The Alpine National Park stretches from central Gippsland in Victoria, all the way to the New South Wales border where it adjoins Kosciuszko National Park. Within the park are some of Australia's most

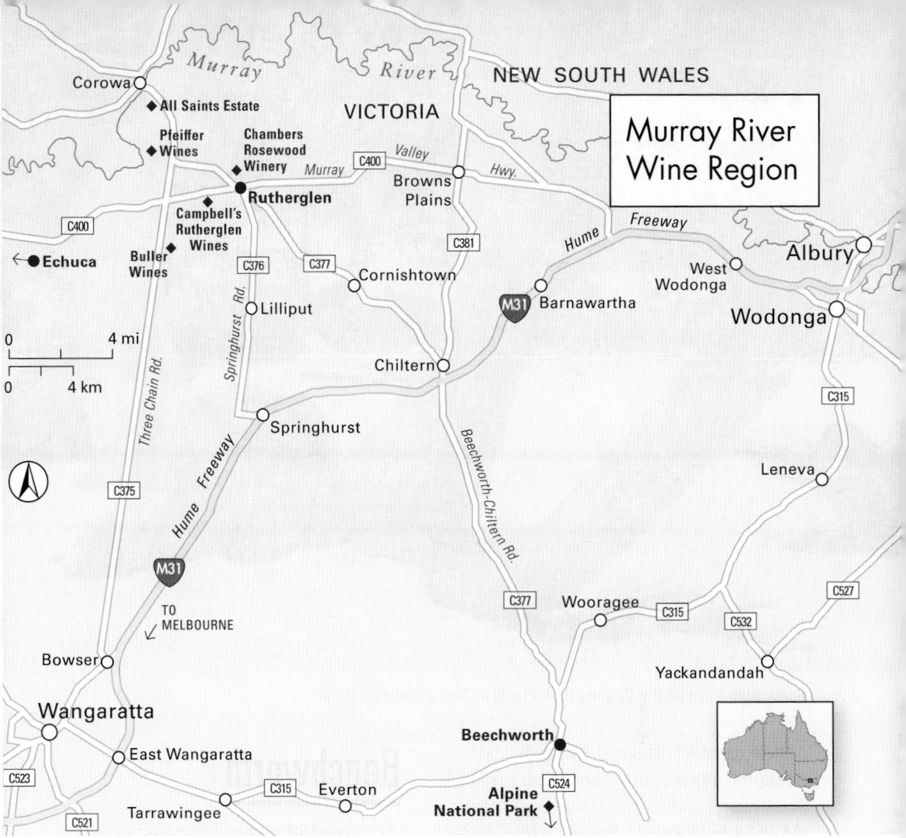

Murray River Wine Region

stunning alpine landscapes, including mountain peaks, escarpments, and grassy high plains.

Sights

Alpine National Park

NATIONAL PARK | This national park covers three loosely connected areas in eastern Victoria, which follow the peaks of the Great Dividing Range. One of these areas, formerly Bogong National Park, contains some of the highest mountains on the continent. As such, it is a wintertime destination for skiers who flock to the resorts at Falls Creek, Mt. Hotham, and Dinner Plain. The land around here is rich in history. "*Bogong*" is a word in the local Dhudhuroa language for "big moth," and it was to Mt. Bogong that local Indigenous tribes came each year after the winter thaw in search of bogong moths, considered a delicacy. They were eventually displaced by cattle ranchers who brought their cattle here to graze. The main townships in the area are Bright and Mount Beauty, both of which have visitor information centers. ✉ *Alpine National Park* ☎ *131–963* 🌐 *parks.vic.gov.au.*

Restaurants

Reed & Co Distillery

$$ | **AUSTRALIAN** | A bright restaurant and café, the real reason to pop in is Reed & Co's artisanal gin, The Remedy—employing such Australian botanicals as eucalyptus and pine—for a quality afternoon G&T or gin cocktail at its bar. The craft gin, created by two former chefs, is complemented by Koji Bird, barbecue chicken served with kimchi, pickles, and smoked mayo. **Known for:** on-site

Snow Gum trees on the Bogong High Plains in Alpine National Park

coffee roaster; artisanal Remedy Gin; seasonal ingredients from other small Australian producers. $ *Average main: A$25* ✉ *15 Wills St., Bright* ☎ *03/5750–1304* 🌐 *www.reedandcodistillery.com* ⏲ *Closed Tues.–Thurs.*

Coffee and Quick Bites

Sixpence Coffee
$ | **CAFÉ** | Coffee aficionados make a beeline for here for house-roasted coffee and sensational pastries: the café caters to early birds, opening at 7 am. **Known for:** beans to go; small-batch coffee roastery; delicious pastries. $ *Average main: A$5* ✉ *15 Wills St., Bright* ☎ *0423/262–386* 🌐 *www.sixpencecoffee.com.au* ⏲ *Closed weekends.*

Beechworth

271 km (168 miles) northeast of Melbourne, 96 km (60 miles) northwest of Alpine National Park, 44 km (26 miles) south of Rutherglen.

One of the prettiest towns in Victoria, Beechworth flourished during the gold rush. When gold ran out, the town of 30,000 was left with all the trappings of prosperity—fine banks, imposing public buildings, breweries, parks, and hotels wrapped in wrought iron—but with scarcely two nuggets to rub together. However, poverty protected the town from such modern improvements as aluminum window frames, and many historic treasures that might have been destroyed in the name of progress have been retained.

Ned Kelly

The English have Robin Hood, the Americans Jesse James. Australians have Ned Kelly, an Irish-descended working-class youth whose struggles against police injustice and governmental indifference made him a legend (though whether he was a hero or villain can still be a hot topic of conversation). The best way to learn about this local legend is to visit the town of Beechworth, where a Ned Kelly Guided Walking Tour, run by two local historians, departs from the old clock tower in the main street (A$20, *www.facebook.com/beechworthtours*). You'll see the courthouse where he was tried and the jail where he was imprisoned during his many scrapes with the law. The Burke Museum displays one of his death masks, made shortly after he was hanged at Old Melbourne Gaol. If you long to hear more, visit Glenrowan (40 km [25 miles] southwest of Beechworth), the scene of his famous "last stand" in 1880. It was here that Kelly, clad in his legendary iron armor, walked alone down the main street, fending off police bullets. He was finally shot in the leg, arrested, and hanged in Old Melbourne Gaol. A huge statue, and a sound-and-light show that has received rather mixed reviews, commemorate Australia's most infamous outlaw.

GETTING HERE AND AROUND

Beechworth and Rutherglen are on opposite sides of the Hume Freeway, the main Sydney–Melbourne artery. The 44-km (26-mile) Rutherglen-Beechworth Road (C377) connects both towns. Beechworth is about a three-hour drive from Melbourne, four hours from Canberra, and six hours from Sydney. Beechworth can also be reached by taking a train from Melbourne's Southern Cross Station to Wangaratta, then changing to a bus service to the town; it's about a 3½-hour journey.

The visitor information center can book accommodation and tours, and provide information on local attractions including the Burke Museum, the Historic Courthouse, and the Telegraph Station, and lets you join the Echoes of History and the Ned Kelly walking tours.

VISITOR INFORMATION

CONTACTS Beechworth Tourist Information Centre. ✉ *Old Town Hall, 103 Ford St., Beechworth* ☎ *03/5728–8065, 1300/366–321* 🌐 *www.explorebeechworth.com.au.*

Sights

★ Beechworth Honey

STORE/MALL | FAMILY | So much more than just a honey shop, Beechworth Honey is a leading producer of pure honey, including single varietal honeys, a working beehive, and a little educational tour great for kids. Shop its raw and pure honey varieties, made from 100% natural, locally produced honey. Peruse the great-smelling honey- and beeswax-based skin care and the high-quality, locally made handcrafts, which make great gifts. The group's Bee Cause project contributes 1% of all global sales revenue toward supporting bees and their environment. ✉ *31 Ford St., Beechworth* ☎ *02/6033–2322* 🌐 *www.beechworthhoney.com.au* Ⓜ *3747.*

Billson's Breweries

BREWERY | The 1920s temperance movement helped to turn this brewery's focus to the brewing of nonalcoholic cordials. The cordials are produced using old-time recipes and seasonal flavors, such as Sicilian blood orange, using the area's

The mighty Murray River is the lifeblood of the region.

natural spring water. Temperance is no longer an issue, and Billson's also creates a range of craft beers, whiskey, its own gin, and even a coffee liqueur. Their range of premixed drinks still uses the original cordials: try the full range, including the popular vodka with portello (grape and berry cola flavor). The brewery has several venues and serves a simple menu of pub grub, including burgers and steak sandwiches. Choose from the Tasting Room, the dog-friendly beer garden, and the more upmarket Speakeasy, where you can sip a cocktail and order a grazing board of local olives, meats, and cheeses. On the same site is the Beechworth Carriage Museum, a collection of 20 horse-drawn vehicles and Australian Light Horse Infantry memorabilia from World War I. Open daily 10–5, A$1. Tastings are free. ✉ *29 Last St., Beechworth* ☎ *03/5728–1304, 1800/990–098* 🌐 *www.billsons.com.au* 🎫 *Free.*

Burke Museum

HISTORY MUSEUM | FAMILY | This 160-year-old museum takes its name from Robert O'Hara Burke who, with William Wills, became one of the first European explorers to cross Australia from south to north in 1861. Burke served as superintendent of police in Beechworth from 1856 to 1859. The museum also displays a reconstructed streetscape of Beechworth in the 1880s, a section dedicated to the Chinese population during the gold rush years, and a natural history collection of taxidermy animals, including a rare thylacine, or Tasmanian tiger, extinct since 1936. ✉ *Loch St., Beechworth* ☎ *03/5728–8067* 🌐 *www.burkemuseum.com.au* 🎫 *A$5.*

Ford Street

STREET | A stroll along Ford Street is the best way to absorb the historic character and charm of Beechworth. Between fabulous cafés, housewares shops, and the town's signature Beechworth Honey business (stop in for free tastings and to sample the honey-based hand creams), the distinguished buildings are Tanswell's Commercial Hotel, the Town Hall, and the Courthouse. It was in the latter that the committal hearing for the famous bushranger Ned Kelly took place in August 1880. His feisty mother, Ellen Kelly, was also sentenced to three years in jail at this court. The town bustles on Saturday mornings, especially when the excellent farmers' market is held on the grounds of the Christ Church Anglican Church, on the first Saturday of the month. ✉ *Ford St., Beechworth* 🌐 *www.explorebeechworth.com.au.*

Restaurants

★ Bridge Road Brewers

$$ | **PIZZA** | **FAMILY** | Taste great craft beer and eat amazing pizza at this busy brewer, one of eight craft breweries of the High Country Brewery Trail. Tucked away down a little lane off the main street, the brewery is housed in an 1850s coach house built during the gold rush era. **Known for:** family-friendly; convenient to rail trail; award-winning brews. [$] *Average main: A$22* ✉ *Old Coach House Brewers La., 50 Ford St., Beechworth* ☎ *03/5728–2703* 🌐 *www.bridgeroadbrewers.com.au.*

★ Provenance

$$$$ | **JAPANESE FUSION** | Set in an ornate old bank which dates to 1856, this feted restaurant sees classic Australian ingredients such as kangaroo or local goat presented with Japanese preparation and accoutrements. There is a strong showing of sake on the drinks menu, which has a good selection of wines from the Beechworth region. **Known for:** stylish accommodation on-site; native Australian ingredients with a Japanese twist; wide range of sake. [$] *Average main: A$150* ✉ *86 Ford St., Beechworth* ☎ *03/5728–1786* 🌐 *www.theprovenance.com.au* ⏲ *Closed Tues.–Thurs.*

Coffee and Quick Bites

Beechworth Bakery

$ | **BAKERY** | **FAMILY** | For a delicious breakfast on the go, this widely admired bakery's eggs Benedict wrap is a great start. For the rest of the day, hit the deli sandwich bar, order a Beechworth steak pie or the robust Ned Kelly pie, a meat pie topped with bacon, egg, and cheese. **Known for:** sit inside or takeaway; Ned Kelly pie; vegan options. [$] *Average main: A$7* ✉ *27 Camp St., Beechworth* ☎ *1300/233–784* 🌐 *www.beechworthbakery.com.au.*

Beechworth Ice Creamery

$ | **CAFÉ** | **FAMILY** | On a hot summer's day, after a bike ride on the rail trail, pull up for a handmade sorbet from this family business, which has been making its sorbets in the back kitchen for 20 years. There is a standard list of 22 flavors, but the real winners are those blended with seasonal, locally grown fruits: the raspberry sorbet is a firm favorite. **Known for:** gluten-, egg-, and dairy-free sorbets; local institution; seasonal sorbets. [$] *Average main: A$6* ✉ *3 Camp St., Beechworth* ☎ *03/5728–1330* 🌐 *www.facebook.com/beechworthicecreamery.*

Activities

BICYCLING

The area from the Murray River to the mountains of northeast Victoria is ideal for cyclists of all persuasions, including casual pedalers and mountain bike enthusiasts.

Murray to Mountains Rail Trail

BIKING | **FAMILY** | A 98-km (61-mile) paved trail stretches from Wangaratta to Bright, with a spur to Milawa and a branch line to Beechworth and Yackandandah. Bicycle rentals are available at Wangaratta, Beechworth, Bright, and Myrtleford. A trail map is available from the visitor centers at each of these towns, and can also be downloaded from the trail website. ✉ *100 Murphy St., Beechworth* ☎ *1800/801–065 Wangaratta Visitor Information Centre* 🌐 *www.murraytomountains.com.au.*

HIKING

There are several national parks within easy reach of Beechworth: Chiltern–Mt. Pilot National Park, Beechworth Historic Park, Mount Buffalo National Park, Mount Granya State Park, and Warby-Ovens National Park. The Beechworth visitor center and Parks Victoria have information on bushwalks. The town of Beechworth is the perfect place to get out and about and stretch your legs while admiring late-19th-century architecture. You can pick up a copy of "Echoes of History," a self-guided walking tour of the town from the visitor information center.

Parks Victoria
HIKING & WALKING | This government organization has information on Victoria's national parks and walking trails. ☎ *131–963* 🌐 *www.parks.vic.gov.au.*

Rutherglen

294 km (182 miles) northeast of Melbourne, 40 km (25 miles) northwest of Beechworth.

The surrounding red-loam soil signifies the beginning of the Rutherglen wine district, the source of Australia's finest fortified wines. If the term conjures up visions of cloying ports, you're in for a surprise. In his authoritative *Australian Wine Compendium,* James Halliday says, "Like Narcissus drowning in his own reflection, one can lose oneself in the aroma of a great old muscat."

The main event in the region is Tastes of Rutherglen, held over two consecutive weekends in March (*www.tastesofrutherglen.com.au*). The festival is a celebration of food, wine, and music—in particular jazz, folk, and country. Events are held in town and at all surrounding wineries. Another popular day in the vineyards is the Rutherglen Winery Walkabout held in June, when wine, food, and music are again on the menu (*www.winerywalkabout.com.au*).

The friendly tourism office stocks local produce including olives and oils and has a good selection of Rutherglen wines for sale, along with the usual services. Book accommodations through them, buy tickets to events, or rent bicycles from A$25 for a half day to cycle the flat rail trail amid the vineyards.

GETTING HERE AND AROUND

See Beechworth.

Rutherglen is 294 km (182 miles) north of Melbourne, about a 3½- to 4-hour drive along the Hume Freeway. V/Line train and bus services also come to Rutherglen.

TRANSPORTATION

V/Line
This train and bus service operates daily on V/Line from Melbourne's Southern Cross Station via Seymour and Wangaratta, a journey of about 3 hours and 25 minutes. ☎ *1800/800–007* 🌐 *www.ptv.vic.gov.au.*

TOURS

Rutherglen Bus and Tour
Rutherglen Bus and Tour has winery tours for a minimum of six people, with visits to five to six wineries on half-day tours and eight to nine estates on day tours. Half-day tours cost A$40 per person, and day tours cost from A$55 per person (with pickup from Rutherglen accommodations only, though pickups from other towns can be arranged for A$15 per person). ✉ *42 Ready St., Rutherglen* ☎ *0417/328–774* 🌐 *www.rutherglenbusandtour.com* 🎫 *From A$40.*

VISITOR INFORMATION

CONTACTS Rutherglen Wine Experience and Visitor Information Centre. ✉ *57 Main St., Rutherglen* ☎ *1800/622–871* 🌐 *www.explorerutherglen.com.au.*

Sights

All Saints Estate

WINERY | In business since 1864, this winery has a splendid, turreted castle that was built in the 1880s with capacious storage areas for its product. The old bottling hall and cellar have been revamped as a cheese tasting room, and a corrugated iron former Chinese dormitory is the property's third heritage-listed building, which you can visit to see in its original state—bunks and all—on guided tours of the winery. Tours are conducted at 11 am on weekends; book in advance (A$50, includes wine and cheese tasting). The winery produces Muscat and Muscadelle from 60-year-old vines, and a range of crisp whites and full-bodied reds. The on-site Indigo Food Company providore sells regional cheeses and condiments ideal for a lavish picnic hamper. The menu at the Terrace restaurant—considered the best in the region—changes seasonally; desserts are excellent, especially when combined with a formidable northeast fortified wine. The cellar door and cheese room are open daily; the restaurant is open for lunch from Wednesday to Sunday. The winery hosts a huge A Day on the Green music festival each February (*www.adayonthegreen.com.au*). ✉ *All Saints Rd., Wahgunyah* ✣ *9 km (5½ miles) northeast of Rutherglen* ☎ *1800/021–621* 🌐 *www.allsaintswine.com.au* 🎫 *Free.*

★ Buller Wines

WINERY | Established by Reginald Langdon Buller in 1921, this Rutherglen winery produces delicious fortified wines and gutsy, full-bodied reds, the flagship being its Shiraz. As the old Shiraz vines are not irrigated, the annual yields are low, but the fruit produced has intense flavor, which winemaker Dave Whyte crafts into wines of great depth and elegance. Tastings and sales are at the cellar door, free, or pay A$15 for tastings of four of its Muscat or Topaque, from 4, 10, 25, and 50 years old! Treat yourself to a grazing platter and Rare Muscat straight from the barrel (A$35) or the Three Chain Road gins, distilled here (A$25). The winery is also home to its on-site restaurant, Pavilion, overlooking the vineyards. ✉ *2804 Federation Way, Rutherglen* ☎ *02/6032–9660* 🌐 *www.bullerwines.com.au* 🎫 *Free.*

Campbell's Rutherglen Wines

WINERY | Wines have been made here by five generations of the Campbell family, dating back to 1870. Brothers Colin and Malcolm Campbell, the winemaker and viticulturist respectively, have been at the helm for the past 40 years, and Colin's daughter Julie joins him as winemaker. Famed for its award-winning Bobbie Burns Shiraz and Merchant Prince Rare Rutherglen Muscat, the property covers a picturesque 160 acres. You can wander freely through the winery on a self-guided tour and taste wines at the cellar door, including rare and aged vintages. Vintage Reserve wines are available only at the cellar door. Private tastings and guided tours can be booked. The winery does not have a restaurant but sells baskets of local gourmet goodies. The winery also takes part in the annual Tastes of Rutherglen wine festival, when food and music are on the agenda. ✉ *4603 Murray Valley Hwy., Rutherglen* ✣ *3 km (2 miles) west of Rutherglen* ☎ *02/6033–6000, 1800/359–458* 🌐 *www.campbellswines.com.au* 🎫 *Free.*

Chambers Rosewood Winery

WINERY | Established in the 1850s, this is one of Australia's heavyweight producers of fortified wines. Stephen Chambers's Muscats are legendary, with blending stocks that go back more than a century. Stephen, a sixth-generation winemaker, runs a very relaxed winery, which is genuinely rustic, being just a few corrugated iron sheds in an off-the-beaten-track road. The cellar door is renowned for great value and plenty of tastings; you can take home reasonably priced red and white wine and a full range of fortified wines—from the clean-skin variety (no-label stock) to big two-liter flagons. There's no restaurant, just a cellar door, which also sells homemade jams and condiments. ✉ *Barkley St., off Corowa Rd., Rutherglen* ☎ *02/6032–8641* 🌐 *www.chambersrosewood.com.au* 🎫 *Free.*

Pfeiffer Wines

WINERY | Since its first vines were planted in 1895, this winery has made exceptional fortified wines such as Topaque and Muscat, and varietal wines, including Shiraz and Durif. It also has one of the few Australian plantings of Gamay, the classic French grape used to make Beaujolais, and produces a large range of vegan wines. Cheese platters (A$30) are available anytime. Winemaker Jen Pfeiffer also makes a cheeky wine cocktail called Pfeiffer Seriously Pink, which makes a great aperitif. ✉ *167 Distillery Rd., Wahgunyah* ⊕ *9 km (5½ miles) northwest of Rutherglen* ☎ *02/6033–2805* 🌐 *www.pfeifferwinesrutherglen.com.au* 🎫 *Free.*

Coffee and Quick Bites

Parker Pies

$ | **BAKERY** | **FAMILY** | Self-billed as Australia's Greatest Pie Shop, Parkers really are that good. Not just your average pie, here's your chance to try a kangaroo pie—with mushrooms and caramelized onion—or perhaps an emu or buffalo pie, when in stock. **Known for:** fast service; award-winning beef pies; good takeaway coffee. $ *Average main: A$8* ✉ *88 Main St., Rutherglen* 🌐 *www.parkerpies.com.au.*

Pickled Sisters Cafe

$$ | **CAFÉ** | **FAMILY** | A Rutherglen favorite for over 20 years, expect robust, flavorsome Aus-European dishes that include pâtes, terrines, confit duck, and hearty vegetarian tagines. Each menu item is matched with a local wine—a handy way to taste your way around the region, without having to drive. **Known for:** prosecco on the brunch menu; lavish vineyard platter; exploratory wines by the glass. $ *Average main: A$25* ✉ *121b Main St., Rutherglen* ☎ *02/6033–2377* 🌐 *www.pickledsisters.com.au* ⏲ *Closed Tues.–Thurs.*

Hotels

★ **Mount Ophir Estate**

$$$$ | **APARTMENT** | **FAMILY** | Impossibly romantic, the Tower at Mount Ophir Estate was built in 1903, part of a French provincial–style winery in an unmistakably Australian landscape. **Pros:** unique accommodations; impeccable design and styling; magnificent historical buildings. **Cons:** two-night minimum in the Tower; steep staircases in the Tower suit agile adults only; requires a car. $ *Rooms from: A$550* ✉ *168 Stillards La., Rutherglen* ☎ *02/6035–2222* 🌐 *www.mountophirestate.com.au* 🛏 *5 cottages, 1 tower* 🍽 *No Meals.*

Tuileries

$$$ | **HOTEL** | Incorporating a vineyard, olive groves, and a renowned restaurant, this accommodation, now owned by De Bortoli Wines, feels like a private enclave. **Pros:** set beside Rutherglen Estates' exciting Indigenous art gallery; beautifully appointed suites; tranquil vineyard and garden setting. **Cons:** self-drive essential; books out during the major wine festivals; next to no nightlife in Rutherglen. $ *Rooms from: A$225* ✉ *13–35 Drummond St., Rutherglen* ☎ *02/6033–6100* 🌐 *www.tuileriesrutherglen.com.au* 🛏 *16 rooms* 🍽 *Free Breakfast.*

Chapter 7

TASMANIA

Updated by
Dan Broun

Sights ★★★★★ | Restaurants ★★★★☆ | Hotels ★★★★☆ | Shopping ★★☆☆☆ | Nightlife ★★☆☆☆

WELCOME TO TASMANIA

TOP REASONS TO GO

★ **Beautiful Walks:** Tasmania has some of Australia's best walking terrain. Stunning walks of varying lengths can be experienced all over the state.

★ **Colonial Homes and Cottages:** Many of the Georgian mansions and cottages from Tasmania's colonial period are now lovely accommodation and entertainment venues.

★ **Tassie Tastes:** Hungry Tasmanians and tourists alike are well served, thanks to the state's world-famous produce, whisky, and wine.

★ **Stunning Capital:** Nipaluna/Hobart, nestled beneath kunanyi/Mt. Wellington and hugging the Derwent Estuary, has long attracted lovers of nature and the arts.

★ **Pure Wilderness:** The Tasmanian Wilderness World Heritage Area is a vast and varied world-famous attraction.

1 **Hobart.** A historic walkable little city with cool cafés, bars, and MONA.

2 **The Huon Valley.** Known for emerald green valleys and forest walks and coastal villages.

3 **Richmond.** Popular colonial village with antiques stores, cafés, and excellent vineyards.

4 **Port Arthur and the Tasman Peninsula.** Convict history and stunning coastline.

5 **East-Coast Resorts.** Coastal scenery, beaches, and fishing towns.

6 **Freycinet National Park.** Renowned among adventure seekers and those who appreciate stunning scenery.

7 **Launceston.** Pleasant parks, groovy cafés, historic mansions, and the Tamar Valley Wine Route.

8 **Devonport and Nearby.** A base for exploring the beautiful and varied northwest region.

9 **Stanley.** Tasmania's version of Uluru and the gateway to The Tarkine.

10 **Cradle Mountain-Lake St. Clair National Park.** Spectacular alpine scenery and popular hiking trails.

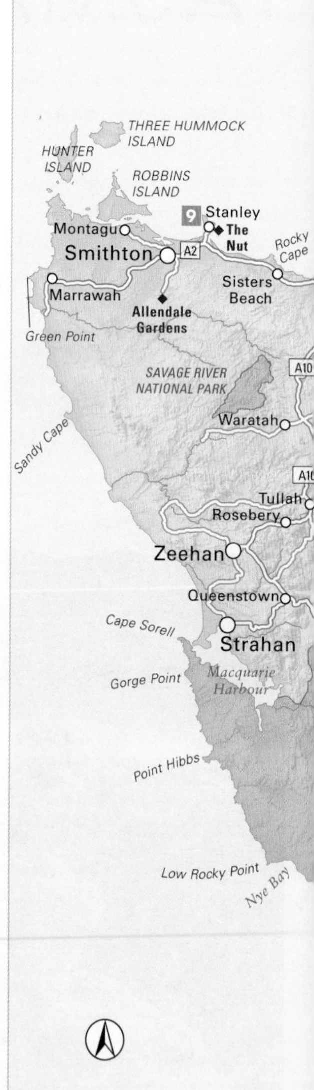

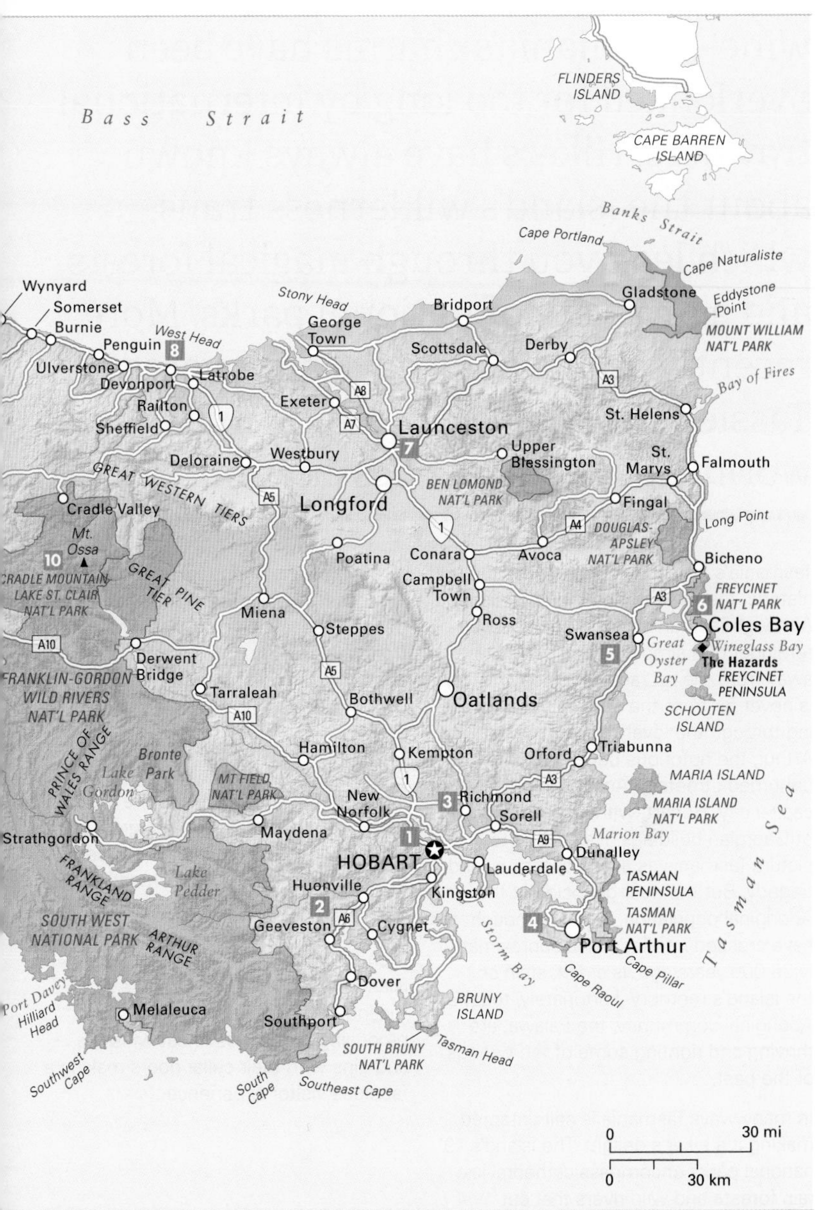
Bass Strait
FLINDERS ISLAND
CAPE BARREN ISLAND
Banks Strait
Cape Portland
Cape Naturaliste
Eddystone Point
MOUNT WILLIAM NAT'L PARK
Bay of Fires
Gladstone
Bridport
Stony Head
Wynyard
Somerset
Burnie
Penguin
8
West Head
George Town
Scottsdale
Derby
Ulverstone
Devonport
Latrobe
A8
A3
Exeter
Railton
Sheffield
1
A7
Launceston
7
St. Helens
Upper Blessington
St. Marys
Falmouth
Deloraine
Westbury
GREAT WESTERN TIERS
BEN LOMOND NAT'L PARK
Longford
A5
Fingal
Cradle Valley
Mt. Ossa
10
CRADLE MOUNTAIN-LAKE ST. CLAIR NAT'L PARK
GREAT PINE TIER
Long Point
A4
DOUGLAS-APSLEY NAT'L PARK
Poatina
Conara
Avoca
Bicheno
Campbell Town
FREYCINET NAT'L PARK
6
Miena
Ross
Coles Bay
Steppes
Swansea
Great Oyster Bay
Wineglass Bay
The Hazards
A10
Derwent Bridge
5
FREYCINET PENINSULA
FRANKLIN-GORDON WILD RIVERS NAT'L PARK
Tarraleah
Bothwell
Oatlands
SCHOUTEN ISLAND
A10
PRINCE OF WALES RANGE
Bronte Park
Lake Gordon
Hamilton
Kempton
Orford
Triabunna
MARIA ISLAND
MT FIELD NAT'L PARK
New Norfolk
3
Richmond
MARIA ISLAND NAT'L PARK
Tasman Sea
Strathgordon
Maydena
Sorell
1
A9
Marion Bay
HOBART
Dunalley
Lauderdale
FRANKLAND RANGE
Lake Pedder
Huonville
Kingston
TASMAN PENINSULA
2
SOUTH WEST NATIONAL PARK
ARTHUR RANGE
A6
Geeveston
Cygnet
TASMAN NAT'L PARK
4
Port Arthur
Storm Bay
Cape Pillar
Cape Raoul
Dover
Port Davey
Hilliard Head
Melaleuca
BRUNY ISLAND
Southport
Tasman Head
SOUTH BRUNY NAT'L PARK
Southwest Cape
South Cape
Southeast Cape
0
30 mi
0
30 km

Wild and dramatic landscapes, empty white beaches, unique art and music festivals, and heavenly food, spirits, and wine—Tasmania's charms have been overlooked for too long by international travelers. Hikers have always known about the island's wilderness trails, which lead you through magical forests and a diversity of national parks. More recently gourmands have discovered Tassie's superb local produce, making it a world-class gourmet destination, too.

Tasmania's attractions encompass the historic, the healthy, and the hedonistic. Although Tasmania now is an unspoiled reminder of a simpler, slower lifestyle away from the rat race, its bloody history is never far from the surface. Today, walking through the lovely grounds in Port Arthur, the notorious penal colony, or the unhurried streets of Australia's smallest capital city, Hobart, with its profusion of Georgian buildings, it's difficult to picture Tasmania as a land of turmoil and tragedy. But the near genocide of the Aboriginal population, who are thought to have crossed into Tasmania approximately 36,000 years ago, is a dark stain on the island's memory. Fortunately, today's Aboriginal community, the Palawa, are thriving and righting some of the wrongs of the past.

In many ways Tasmania is still untamed, making it a hiker's delight. The island's 19 national parks encompass cathedral-like rain forests and wild rivers that cut through chains of untracked mountains. The coastlines are scalloped with endless desolate beaches—some pristine white, fronting serene turquoise bays, and some rugged and rocky, facing churning, choppy seas.

These beautiful surroundings form part of Tasmania's newest claim to fame as a gourmet haven. Thanks to the island's many microclimates, you can grow or harvest virtually anything from superb dairy produce to wonderful meat, and its clear seas abound in wonderful seafood. Oenophiles have also discovered the island's cool-climate wines, and the island's wine routes are worth a slow meander. The island's distilleries are producing the worlds finest whiskies and gins with their cellar doors making a fabulous visitor experience.

MAJOR REGIONS

Perhaps Australia's most beautiful state capital, the compact city of **Hobart** has a vibrant culture with beautifully preserved colonial-era architecture in genteel surroundings. **Side trips from Hobart** include short drives to some of Tasmania's most scenic and historic places, including the Huon Valley with its orchards, walking trails, and quaint towns, the charming colonial village of Richmond, and Port Arthur and the Tasman Peninsula with its world-renowned, historic penal colony and spectacular landscape. You can take these side trips in a day, but if you can, stay a night or two to experience their delights at a leisurely pace.

The east coast enjoys Tasmania's mildest climate, pristine beaches, and excellent fishing spots. The stretches of white sand along **Freycinet National Park and east coast resorts** are often so deserted that you can pretend you're Robinson Crusoe. The east coast resorts and towns in this region are quiet but historically interesting; in Triabunna, for example, you can catch a ferry to the Maria Island National Park, once a whaling station, farms, and a penal settlement in the mid-19th century. Farther north, the town of Swansea has numerous stone colonial buildings that have been restored as hotels and restaurants, as well as the unusual Spiky Bridge (so named because of its vertically placed stone "spikes") and the convict-built Three Arch Bridge, both of which date from 1845. The jewel of the eastern coast is Freycinet National Park, renowned among adventure seekers and those who appreciate stunning scenery. The spectacular granite peaks of the Hazards and the idyllic protected beach at Wineglass Bay have been dazzling visitors to this peninsula since it became a park in 1916. Tasmania's second-biggest city, Launceton, is a pleasant place to while away time, thanks to its attractive parks, historic colonial mansions, and farmers' market.

Tasmania's **Northwest** region is one of the most beautiful and least explored areas of the state. For its sheer range of landscapes, from jagged mountain contours to ancient rain forests and alpine heathlands in the Cradle Mountain area alone, the northwest can't be matched. The region's beauty saw it designated the Tasmanian Wilderness World Heritage Area, protecting one of the last true wilderness regions on Earth. These regions are a major draw for hikers and sightseers. The port town of Devonport is worth a visit as is the town of Stanley, one of the prettiest towns in Tasmania. The western side of the northwest tip of Tasmania, a region known as The Tarkine, or takayna in the language of the First Nations people of the region, bears the full force of the roaring forties winds coming across the Indian Ocean, and this part of Tasmania contains some of the island's most dramatic scenery and most fascinating Aboriginal cultural heritage. Mining was a major industry a century ago, and although some mines still operate, the townships have a rather forlorn look these days, but the natural landscapes more than compensate the curious traveler.

Planning

When to Go

Cold weather–phobes beware: Tasmanian winters can draw freezing blasts from the Antarctic, so this is not the season to explore the highlands or wilderness areas, unless, of course, you like a little snow play. It's wiser in the colder months to investigate the many art galleries or enjoy the cozy interiors of colonial cottages and the open fireplaces of welcoming pubs.

Summer can be hot—bushfires do occasionally occur—but temperatures tend to be lower than on the Australian mainland.

The best seasons to visit are autumn, summer, and spring; early autumn is beautiful, with deciduous trees in full color and still conditions. Spring, with its splashes of pastel wildflowers and mild weather, is equally lovely. Tassie really comes alive in summer, when it's warm enough to swim at the many gorgeous beaches, the fresh summer produce is bountiful, and the lavender farms are in bloom. Winter, however, is home to pagan-inspired festivals such as Dark MOFO and the Festival of Voices—warm yourself around the fires with mulled cider and song.

Tasmania is a relaxing island with few crowds, except during the mid-December to mid-February school holiday period and at the end of the annual Sydney-to-Hobart yacht race just after Christmas, but you can always find a secluded beach or nature walk even at peak tourist season. Most attractions and sights are open year-round.

Planning Your Time

If you have limited time in Tasmania, spend your first morning in Hobart, where you can stroll around the docks, Salamanca Place, and Battery Point, and have some fish-and-chips from the harbor's floating chippies. After lunch, drive to Richmond and explore its 19th-century streetscape, then stay in a local bed-and-breakfast. On the second day head for Port Arthur, and spend the morning exploring the fascinating former penal colony. Spend the afternoon taking in the dramatic scenery of the Tasman Peninsula, noting the bizarre Tessellated Pavement, Devils Kitchen, and Tasman Arch blowhole near Eaglehawk Neck, or take one of the four-hour return walks to spectacular Cape Huay or Cape Raoul. Return to Hobart for the night, then on the third morning take a leisurely drive around the scenic Huon Valley—the towns of Franklin or Cygnet are particularly delightful. On return to Hobart, finish your tour with a trip to the summit of kunanyi/Mt. Wellington or a wander around the amazing Museum of Old and New Art (MONA).

If you have more time, continue on to Freycinet National Park. Climb the steep path to the outlook over Wineglass Bay, then descend to the sands for a picnic and swim. Stay two nights in the park, visit Friendly Beaches, and then meander back through the east coast wine regions. Return to the capital, topping off the day with city views from kunanyi/Mt. Wellington.

Getting Here and Around

Tasmania is compact—the drive from Hobart in the south to the northern city of Launceston takes little more than two hours. The easiest way to see the state is by car, as you can plan a somewhat circular route around the island. Begin in Hobart or Launceston, where car rentals are available from the airport and city agencies, or in Devonport if you arrive on the ferry from Melbourne. Allow plenty of time for stops along the way, as there are some fabulous sights to be seen. Bring a sturdy pair of shoes and warm clothing for impromptu mountain and seaside walks; you'll most often have huge patches of forest and long expanses of white beaches all to yourself.

In some cases the street addresses for attractions may not include building numbers (in other words, only the name of the street will be given). Don't worry—this just means either that the street is short and the attractions are clearly visible or that signposts will clearly lead you there.

If you are exploring several national parks in the space of a few weeks or months it is recommended to buy a Holiday Vehicle Pass that is valid for two months for

A$80 per vehicle and allows access to all the national parks of Tasmania.

AIR

Hobart International Airport is 22 km (14 miles) east of Hobart, one hour by air from Melbourne or two hours from Sydney. Although most interstate flights connect through Melbourne, Qantas, Jetstar, and Virgin Australia also run direct flights to some other mainland cities. Launceston airport is at Western Junction, 16 km (10 miles) south of central Launceston. It's served by Jetstar, Qantas, and Virgin Australia.

On the island, King Island Airlines, Regional Express Airlines (REX), or Sharp Airlines can get you to the northwest and King or Flinders Islands. Par Avion flies from Cambridge, south of Hobart to popular tourist locations, such as Melaleuca, Strahan, Maria Island, Bruny Island, and Flinders Island. Tickets can be booked through the airlines or through the Tasmanian Travel and Information Centre. Skybus has an airport shuttle service for A$19.50 per person between the airport and city hotels. Metered taxis and Ubers are available at the stand in front of the terminal. The fare to downtown Hobart is approximately A$45.

CAR

Port Arthur is an easy 90-minute drive from Hobart via the Arthur Highway. A private vehicle is essential if you want to explore parts of the Tasman Peninsula beyond the historic settlement. A vehicle is absolutely essential on the west coast. The road from Hobart travels through the Derwent Valley and past lovely historic towns before rising to the plateau of central Tasmania. Many of the roads in western Tasmania are twisty and even unpaved in the more remote areas, but two-wheel drive is sufficient for most touring. Be prepared for sudden weather changes: snow in the summertime is not uncommon in the highest areas. Lake St. Clair is 173 km (107 miles) northwest of Hobart, and can be reached via the Lyell Highway, or from Launceston via Deloraine or Poatina. Cradle Mountain is 85 km (53 miles) south of Devonport, and can be reached by car via Claude Road from Sheffield or via Wilmot. Both lead 30 km (19 miles) along Route C132 to Cradle Valley.

Restaurants

Although there are elegant dining options in the larger towns—especially Hobart—most eateries serve meals in a casual setting. Fiercely proud of their local produce, Tasmanian restaurateurs have packed their menus with home-grown seafood, beef, lamb, and cheeses, washed down with their famous cold-climate wines or craft beers. Tasmanian wine is nearly unknown in the rest of the world—however, the secret is out, with Tasmanian Pinots and sparkling wine wowing wine judges around the world. The Tasmanian whisky and gin scene is also thriving with boutique distilleries emerging all the time.

Hotels

The hospitality industry is thriving in Tasmania, so in popular areas you'll find a wide range of accommodation options, from inexpensive motels and cabins to genteel B&Bs, rustic lodges to luxury hotels. Most hotels will have air-conditioning, but bed-and-breakfast lodgings often do not. Apart from a few hotels right in the main city center, most Hobart accommodations have free parking. No smoking is allowed inside any Tasmanian public building.

Restaurant and hotel reviews have been shortened. For full information, visit Fodors.com.

What It Costs in Australian Dollars

$	$$	$$$	$$$$
RESTAURANTS			
under A$25	A$25–A$44	A$45–A$70	over A$70
HOTELS			
under A$151	A$151–A$200	A$201–A$300	over A$300

Hobart

Straddling the Derwent River at the foot of kunanyi/Mt. Wellington's forested slopes, nipaluna/Hobart was founded as a penal settlement in 1803. It's the second-oldest city in Australia after Sydney, and it certainly rivals its mainland counterpart as Australia's most beautiful state capital. Close-set colonial brick-and-sandstone shops and homes line the narrow, quiet streets, creating a genteel setting for this historic city of 240,000. Life revolves around the River Derwent and its port, one of the deepest harbors in the world. Here warehouses that once stored Hobart's major exports of fruit, wool, apples, and products from the city's former whaling fleet still stand alongside the wharf today, only today they house cafés, boutiques, and art galleries.

Hobart sparkles between Christmas and New Year—summer Down Under—during the annual Sydney-to-Hobart yacht race. The event dominates conversations among Hobart's citizens, who descend on Constitution Dock to welcome the yachts and join in the boisterous festivities of the crews. The New Year also coincides with a major food and wine festival, when the dockside area comes alive with the best Tasmanian produce. In recent years, the eclectic Museum of Old and New Art (MONA) has invigorated Hobart's cultural life. The "MONA effect" has triggered a mini-explosion of cool, new places to eat, drink, and play. The pagan-inspired Dark Mofo festival in the dead of winter now attracts tens of thousands each year to a hedonistic celebration of all things dark and mysterious. Otherwise, Hobart is a placid city whose nightlife is largely confined to excellent restaurants, jazz clubs, and whisky bars.

The Hobart Tasmanian Travel and Information Centre hours are daily 9–5.

GETTING HERE AND AROUND

Hobart, being teeny-tiny, is eminently walkable; once you're in the city center, no attraction is more than 15 minutes' walk away, apart from the Cascade Brewery and the Museum of Old and New Art (MONA). Because of the many one-way streets, it's best to park a car and leave it for the day as you explore. If you prefer two wheels to two legs, you can hire trendy electric bicycles from Hobart Bike Hire on Brooke Street for A$50 for the day, A$35/day in winter. There are also open-topped double-decker buses with a hop-on, hop-off ticket, valid for 24 hours, available from A$35. There are also ferry options if you'd like to go to MONA or to the village of Bellerive on the Eastern Shore by water. Both leave from Brooke Street Pier.

VISITOR INFORMATION

CONTACTS Tasmanian Travel and Information Centre. ✉ *20 Davey St., at Elizabeth St., Hobart Waterfront* ☎ *03/6238–4222* 🌐 *www.hobarttravelcentre.com.au.*

Sights

★ **Brooke Street Pier**

MARINA/PIER | The busy waterfront at Brooke Street Pier is the city's key departure point for harbor and MONA cruises. The translucent building has an excellent cocktail bar and restaurant as well as plenty of tourist information and a trading space for Tasmanian artisans. ✉ *Brooke Street Pier, 12 Franklin Wharf, Hobart* ✥ *On waterfront at end of Brooke St.* 🌐 *www.brookestreetpier.com* 🎟 *Free.*

Cascade Brewery

BREWERY | This is Australia's oldest and most picturesque brewery, producing fine Tasmanian beers since 1824. You can see its inner workings on the 90-minute tours, which require lots of walking and climbing, but you're rewarded with three free drinks at the end. Note that appropriate attire (long pants and closed-toe shoes only) is required, and tour reservations are essential. It's a 30-minute walk from the city center, or buses leave from Franklin Square every 35 minutes from 9:15 am. The Cascade Hotel often has live music and is a great place to sample the wares after the tour. ✉ *140 Cascade Rd., South Hobart* ☎ *03/6224–1117* 🌐 *www.cascadebreweryco.com.au* 🎫 *A$30.*

★ **Constitution Dock**

MARINA/PIER | **FAMILY** | Yachts competing in the annual Sydney-to-Hobart race moor at this colorful marina dock from the end of December through the first week of January. Buildings fronting the dock are century-old reminders of Hobart's trading history. Nearby Hunter Street is the original spot where British ships anchored at the time of colonization. There's a multitude of eateries, from fish punts to five star. ✉ *Argyle St. at Davey St., Hobart Waterfront* ☎ *No phone* 🎫 *Free.*

Maritime Museum of Tasmania

NAUTICAL SIGHT | **FAMILY** | The old state library building houses one of the best maritime collections in Australia, including figureheads, whaling implements, models, and photographs dating from as far back as 1804. It's a small museum though, so don't plan on spending more than an hour. Upstairs the Carnegie Gallery has rotating exhibitions in a magnificent space. ✉ *Carnegie Bldg., Argyle St. at Davey St., Hobart Waterfront* ☎ *03/6234–1427* 🌐 *www.maritimetas.org* 🎫 *A$10.*

★ **Museum of Old and New Art** *((MONA))*

OTHER MUSEUM | **FAMILY** | Australia's largest privately funded museum is home to a diverse array of exhibits from Tasmanian millionaire David Walsh's private collection. The unusual collection contains more than 400 often provocative pieces, including Sidney Nolan's *Snake*—an impressive mural made of more than 1,500 individual paintings—and Wim Delvoye's *Cloaca Professional*, an interesting contraption that transforms food into excrement. Each year, the museum also hosts the Mona Foma Festival, Tasmania's largest contemporary music festival. MONA's two-week winter festival, Dark Mofo, celebrates the dark through large-scale public art, food, music, and light. Sometimes compared with Bilbao's Guggenheim Museum, MONA has an eclectic mix of antiquities and contemporary art. The unusual building itself is set into cliffs on the Berriedale peninsula, and visitors to the museum use touch-screen devices to learn about the exhibits as they wander around. There is often music on the lawns with large-scale public art throughout the site. To reach MONA, it's a 15-minute drive, or you can take the MONA-ROMA minibus from the Hobart waterfront or airport. There is also the MONA fast catamaran from the Hobart waterfront. ✉ *651–655 Main Rd., Berriedale* ☎ *03/6277–9900* 🌐 *www.mona.net.au* 🎫 *A$30 (grounds are free)* ⏲ *Closed Tues.–Thurs.*

Penitentiary Chapel Historic Site

NOTABLE BUILDING | "The Tench," as it was known by its inhabitants, was the prisoners' barracks for Hobart Town. The buildings, only a short walk from Hobart's CBD, vividly portray Tasmania's penal, judicial, and religious heritage in their courtrooms, old cells, and underground tunnels. If you want to get spooked, come for the nighttime ghost tour (reservations necessary). ✉ *Brisbane St. at Campbell St., City Center* ☎ *03/6231–0911* 🌐 *nationaltrusttas.rezdy.com* 🎫 *From A$25.*

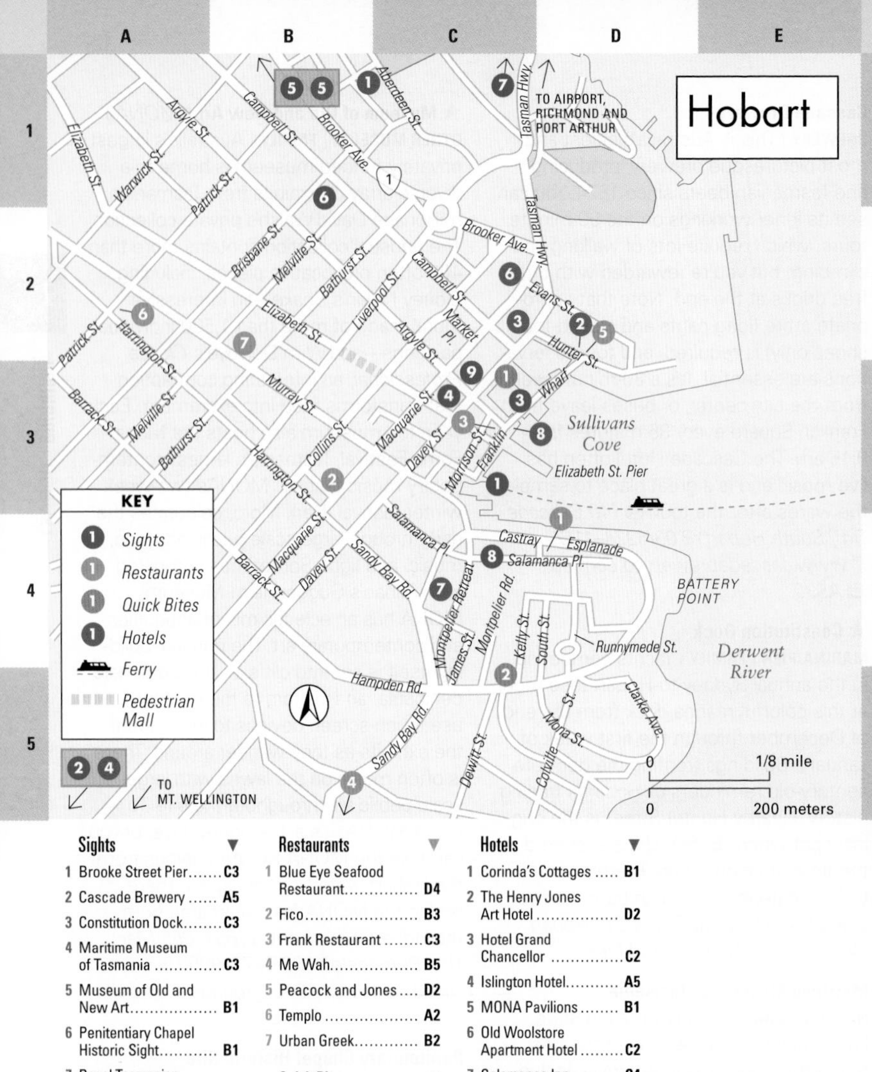

Sights

1 Brooke Street Pier C3
2 Cascade Brewery A5
3 Constitution Dock C3
4 Maritime Museum of Tasmania C3
5 Museum of Old and New Art.................. B1
6 Penitentiary Chapel Historic Sight............ B1
7 Royal Tasmanian Botanical Gardens....... C1
8 Salamanca Place........ C4
9 Tasmanian Museum and Art Gallery........... C3

Restaurants

1 Blue Eye Seafood Restaurant............... D4
2 Fico....................... B3
3 Frank Restaurant C3
4 Me Wah................. B5
5 Peacock and Jones D2
6 Templo A2
7 Urban Greek............ B2

Quick Bites

1 Flippers Cooked Seafood................... C3
2 Jackman & McRoss..... C5

Hotels

1 Corinda's Cottages B1
2 The Henry Jones Art Hotel D2
3 Hotel Grand Chancellor C2
4 Islington Hotel........... A5
5 MONA Pavilions B1
6 Old Woolstore Apartment Hotel C2
7 Salamanca Inn........... C4
8 Sullivans Cove Apartments............... C3

Royal Tasmanian Botanical Gardens
GARDEN | FAMILY | The largest area of open land in Hobart, these well-tended gardens are rarely crowded and provide a welcome relief from the city. Plants from all over the world are here—more than 6,000 exotic and native species in all. The collection of Tasmania's unique native flora is especially impressive. The café serves wholesome meals with some produce grown on-site. The gardens also host regular concerts and events throughout the summer. A sub-Antarctic chamber contains specimens from islands far to the south of Tasmania. ✉ *Lower Domain Rd., Queen's Domain* ☎ *03/6236–3075* 🌐 *www.rtbg.tas.gov.au* 🎫 *Free.*

★ **Salamanca Place**
PEDESTRIAN MALL | FAMILY | Many of the sandstone warehouses once used by whalers and traders from ships docking at Salamanca Place have been converted into delightful craft shops, art galleries, and restaurants. At the boisterous Saturday market, which attracts all elements of Tasmanian society, from hippies to the well-heeled, dealers in Tasmanian arts and crafts, fresh produce, clothing, rare books, and much more display their wares between 8:30 and 3. Keep an eye open for items made from beautiful Tasmanian timber, particularly Huon pine. ✉ *Salamanca Pl., Hobart Waterfront* 🌐 *www.salamanca.com.au* 🎫 *Free.*

★ **Tasmanian Museum and Art Gallery**
ART MUSEUM | Housed in a series of colonial-era buildings overlooking Constitution Dock, this art and artifact gallery is a good starting point for uncovering Tasmania's rich history. With one of Australia's largest and most diverse collections it's a great place in Hobart to learn about the island's Aboriginal culture, European history, and unique wildlife. There are free guided tours Wednesday to Sunday at 11 am, 1 pm, and 2 pm and a great café and gift shop. ✉ *Dunn Pl., Hobart Waterfront* ☎ *03/6165–7000* 🌐 *www.tmag.tas.gov.au* 🎫 *Free.*

kunanyi / Mt. Wellington

kunanyi is the Tasmanian Aboriginal (Palawa) name for Mt. Wellington, the ever-present behemoth that hovers over Hobart. The Mountain, as most locals refer to it, is a place for recreation and wonder for Hobartians. There are a multitude of walking tracks from the city to the summit. Other tracks are designed specifically for mountain biking. kunanyi/Mt. Wellington is also a drawcard for rock climbers and is clad in mixed forest types, dozens of creeks and waterfalls, giant boulder fields, and an alpine moorland.

Beaches

Hobart, which is surrounded by water, has a number of spectacular sandy beaches, most of them close to the city center or on the Derwent estuary.

Cornelian Bay Beach
BEACH | FAMILY | Just five minutes' drive from Hobart's city center, this safe and quiet beach lies immediately north of the Queen's Domain urban parkland. Assorted sailing boats sit offshore in Cornelian Bay, while a popular trail, the Queen's Walk, runs directly behind the beach. The Cornelian Bay trail is popular among the locals. Charming Heritage-listed boathouses, picnic sites, a children's playground, and barbecues line the shore. The waterfront-facing Cornelian Bay Boathouse Restaurant is known for creative locally caught seafood and fresh Tasmanian produce. **Amenities:** food and drink; parking (free). **Best for:** solitude; walking. ✉ *Cornelian Bay, Queen's Domain.*

Seven Mile Beach

BEACH | FAMILY | One of Hobart's favorite beaches, this long, sandy stretch of sand is less than a 20-minute drive outside of Hobart, close to the airport. It is both isolated and stunning to look at, although it can be noisy with planes taking off and landing nearby. Considered a great family beach, it's rarely crowded and ideal for long walks along sand that's peppered with many unusual shells. The small surrounding community includes playgrounds, golf courses, and a café. Seven Mile Beach Cabin and Caravan Park is set within a beautiful park alongside the beach. There are numerous day-use areas—No. 1 has unsheltered tables and a lawn area suitable for picnicking. **Amenities:** food and drink; parking (free); showers; toilets. **Best for:** solitude; swimming; walking. ✉ *Seven Mile Beach.*

Restaurants

Constitution Dock is the perfect place for watching the yachts and locals drift by, as well as savoring fresh fish-and-chips from one of the punts (floating fish-and-chips shops) moored on the water. Ask for the fish of the day or try some freshly shucked oysters. The city's main restaurant areas include the docks, the streets around Salamanca Place through midtown to North Hobart.

★ Blue Eye Seafood Restaurant

$$ | SEAFOOD | FAMILY | Located on Castray Esplanade opposite Princes Wharf, Blue Eye offers up a wide variety of fresh Tasmanian seafood, cooked to perfection. The barbecue Pirates Bay octopus is a highlight, as is the mixed grill, washed down with a cool Tasmanian craft beer or crisp Pinot. **Known for:** local craft beers; barbecue Pirates Bay octopus; Bruny Island oysters. $ *Average main: A$38* ✉ *1 Castray Esplanade, Battery Point* ☎ *03/6223–5297* 🌐 *www.blueeye.net.au* 🕓 *Closed Sun.*

★ Fico

$$$ | ITALIAN | Fico is influenced by the tables of Europe where food and conviviality go hand in hand. They proudly source our produce from local farmers, growers, fishers, and butchers. While the menu is ever-changing it is consistently creative and interesting. **Known for:** expertly roasted pigeon; modern Italian; tasting menu. $ *Average main: A$45* ✉ *151 Macquarie St., City Center* ☎ *03/6245–3391* 🌐 *www.ficofico.net* 🕓 *Closed Mon.–Thurs.* ✍ *Reservations Essential.*

★ Frank Restaurant

$$ | ARGENTINE | South American food culture has inspired the menu of this eclectic but sophisticated eatery on Hobart's waterfront. Blending fresh Tasmanian produce with centuries of South American flavor refinement, Frank is a lively spot for a reason. **Known for:** eclectic decor; South American–influenced menu; waterfront location. $ *Average main: A$38* ✉ *1 Franklin Wharf, Hobart Waterfront* ☎ *03/6231–5005* 🌐 *www.frankrestaurant.com.au.*

Me Wah

$$$ | CHINESE | FAMILY | Featuring a superb range of wines from around the world, this sumptuously decorated Sandy Bay eatery rivals many of the better Chinese restaurants in Sydney and Melbourne. There is a broad menu, ranging from the pricey "candy heart" dried abalone to traditional favorites, such as Me Wah's delicious steamed dumplings; there's also a banquet option. **Known for:** traditional Cantonese tea service; steamed dumplings; broad menu. $ *Average main: A$45* ✉ *16 Magnet Ct., Sandy Bay* ☎ *03/6223–3688* 🌐 *www.mewah.com.au* 🕓 *Closed Mon.*

Peacock and Jones

$$$ | AUSTRALIAN | Tucked away in the sandstone buildings of Hunter Street, Peacock and Jones offers intimate fine

Continued on page 334

FOLLOWING THE CONVICT TRAIL

For many, Tasmania conjures up grim images of chain-ganged prisoners: British convicts banished from the motherland to languish on a distant island in a faraway colony.

Its humble (and brutal) beginning as a penal colony is a point of pride for many Australians. It's no small feat that a colony comprised of, among others, poor Irish, Scottish, and Welsh convicts—many imprisoned for crimes as petty as stealing a loaf of bread—were able to build what is now Australia. It epitomizes a toughness of character that Australians prize. Many here can accurately trace their lineage back to the incarcerated. Kevin Rudd, the country's former Prime Minister, is himself descended from six convicts, including Mary Wade, the youngest female prisoner transported to Australia at the age of 11.

Tasmania has a number of remarkably well-preserved convict sites, most of which are set on the isolated Tasman Peninsula, some 75 km (47 mi) southeast of Hobart. Here, the region's beautifully rugged landscape belies the horrors of the past. Exploring Tasmania's convict heritage and the dramatic beauty of the island are two sides of the same coin. The region's isolation, impenetrable rain forests, and sheer cliffs falling into the sea made it a perfect island prison. By following signs on what's called the Convict Trail, you'll go home with provocative insight into what life was like for the almost 75,000 souls sent to Tasmania between 1803 and 1853.

The rugged and beautiful Tasmanian Coast.

TASMANIA'S CONVICT PAST

Port Arthur Historic Site

"It is impossible to convey, in words, any idea of the hideous phantasmagoria of shifting limbs and faces which moved through the evil-smelling twilight of this terrible prison-house. Callot might have drawn it, Dante might have suggested it, but a minute attempt to describe its horrors would but disgust. There are depths in humanity which one cannot explore, as there are mephitic caverns into which one dare not penetrate."

—Marcus Clarke's description of Port Arthur's Separate Prison in his famous novel *For the Term of his Natural Life.*

They came in chains to this hostile island, where the seasons were all the wrong way around and the sights and smells were unfamiliar. In the 50 years following the establishment of the first settlement in Tasmania (Van Diemen's Land) in 1803, 57,909 male and 13,392 female prisoners were sent to the island. From 1830 on, many ended up at the newly built penal settlement at Port Arthur, where the slightest infraction would be punished by 100 lashes or weeks of solitary confinement on a diet of bread and water. Life was spent in chains, breaking up rocks or doing other menial tasks—all meant to keep criminal tendencies at bay.

The location of the settlement on the Tasman Peninsula was ideal for a prison. Joined to the rest of the island by a narrow neck of land with steep cliffs pounded by surging surf, it was easy to isolate and guard with half-starved dogs on the infamous dogline. Even though convicts were sentenced for a specific number of years, conditions were so brutal that even a few years could become a life sentence. With no chance of escape, some prisoners saw suicide as the only way out.

As the number of prisoners increased, more buildings went up. In time, the penal colony became a self-sufficient industrial center where prisoners sawed timber, built ships, laid bricks, cut stone, and made tiles, shoes, iron castings, and clothing.

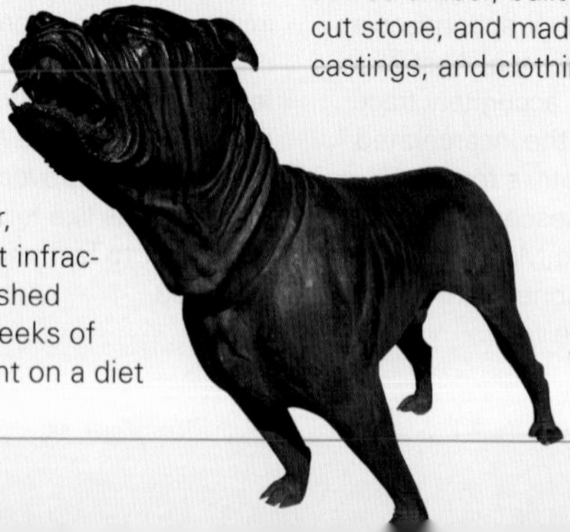

A sculpture representing the infamous dogline at Eaglehawk Neck, Tasman Peninsula.

HOW TO EXPLORE

GETTING HERE

To fully experience the trail, you'll need a car. It's possible to get to Port Arthur via operators such as Tassielink, but you can't access the whole trail by public transportion.

From Hobart head north to the well-preserved village of Richmond before continuing southeast on the Arthur Highway (A9) to the small town of Sorrell. Not far from here is the infamous Eaglehawk neck, marking the start of the Tasman Peninsula. The Convict Trail runs in a circle around the peninsula, with signs clearly marking the many sites along the way.

TIMING

Port Arthur is 120 km (75 mi) or an hour and a half away from Hobart, but will take longer if you intend on making stops at Richmond and Sorell (which you should).

This trip can be done in one long day, but if you want to thoroughly explore the Tasman Peninsula, allow for two or three days. The Convict Trail booklet is available from visitor information centers across Tasmania and details the key sites and attractions along the route.

Isle of the Dead

Richmond Bridge and Church

EXPLORING

It's easy to forget that Port Arthur wasn't an isolated settlement. The whole of the Tasman Peninsula was part of a larger penal colony, so, for the full experience, don't overlook the smaller sights. There are plenty of cafés and accommodations along the way, so take your time.

STUNNING VIEWS

Don't miss the vistas at the Tasman National Park Lookout. The walk along dramatic sea cliffs, which are among the highest and most spectacular in Australia, is easy and rewarding. The views of Pirates Bay, Cape Hauy, and the two islands just off the coast called The Lanterns are spectacular.

EN ROUTE

Take a break at the famous Sorell Fruit Farm where from November to May it's pick-you-own-berry season (✉ *174 Pawleena Road, Sorell* ☎ *03/6265–2744* 🌐 *www.sorellfruitfarm.com* ⏲ *Oct., Mar., Apr., and May 10–4; Nov., Dec., Jan., and Feb. 8:30–5*).

TOURING THE CONVICT TRAIL

It's hard to absorb this disturbing story of human suffering. Around 73,000 convicts were transported here, and about 1 in 5 served time in Port Arthur, on Tasmania's southernmost tip.

Stone bridge at Richmond

❶ RICHMOND BRIDGE. Australia's oldest bridge was built by convict labor in 1825 and is a lasting symbol of the island's convict heritage. Don't miss the village's gaol, which predates Port Arthur by five years.

❷ SORELL. This early settlement is where bloody bushranger battles were fought in the colony's formative years. Bushrangers were actually outlaws who lived in the bush. A walk around the town reveals some interesting heritage buildings; there are also plenty of antiques shops and cafes to keep you occupied.

Sorell Berry Farm

❸ THE DOGLINE. Statues of snarling hounds represent the dogs that prevented the convicts from escaping and mark the infamous dogline along the narrow strip of land linking the Tasman Peninsula with the rest of Tasmania.

Norfolk Bay

❹ NORFOLK BAY. This is the site of a human-powered tramway. Goods were unloaded from ships at the Convict Station and then transported to Port Arthur by a tram dragged by convicts across the peninsula. This saved the ship a dangerous journey across the peninsula's stormy bays.

❺ PORT ARTHUR. Walking among the peaceful ruins and quiet gardens, it's difficult to imagine that this place was hell-on-earth for the convicts. When the settlement closed in 1877, the area was renamed Carnarvon in an attempt to disconnect the land from the horrors associated with its former name. However, in 1927 it was reinstated as Port Arthur and opened to a public keen to embrace this aspect of the Australian story.

TRAIL MARKERS

The Convict Trail is marked with a broad arrow symbol that was stamped on convict-made goods. It's framed in yellow to reference the color of convict clothing.

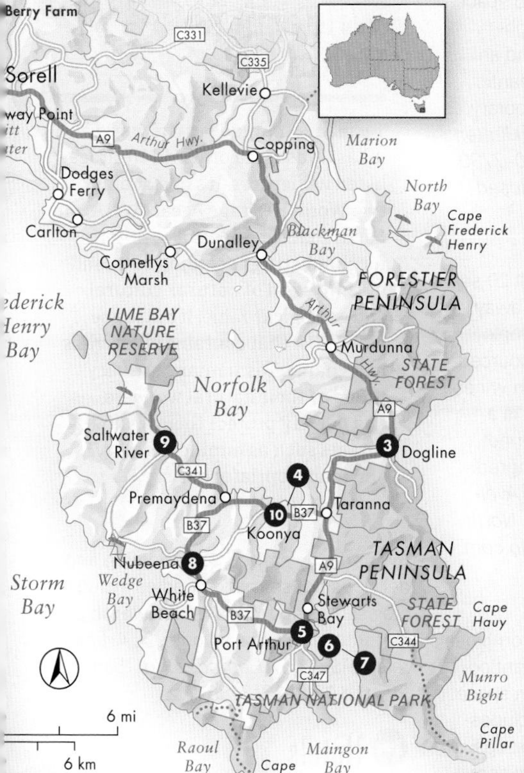

6 POINT PUER BOYS PRISON. More than 3,000 boys, some as young as age nine, passed through here from 1834 to 1849. Located just across the harbor from the main Port Arthur settlement, this was the first jail in the British Empire built exclusively for juvenile male convicts. But just because they were young doesn't mean they were spared from hard labor like stone-cutting and construction. The prison was also infamous for its stern discipline—solitary confinement, days at a time on a tread wheel, and whipping were standard punishments for even a trivial breach of the rules.

The Penitentiary Block

Sandstone church at Port Arthur

7 ISLE OF THE DEAD CONVICT CEMETERY. A small island in the harbor near Port Arthur is the final resting place for about a thousand people, most of them convicts and ex-convict paupers who were buried mostly in unmarked graves.

8 NUBEENA was established as an outstation of Port Arthur and for many years was an important convict farming community. It was also the sight of a semaphore station, used to raise the alarm if a convict made a bid for freedom.

9 SALTWATER RIVER. Exploring the abandoned mines reveals the terrible conditions in which the convicts suffered: restored tiny underground cells, totally without light and filled with fetid air give horrifying insight.

10 KOONYA. The probation station here was once an important convict outpost known as the Cascades. It operated between 1843 and 1846 and you'll find a few isolated houses and a well-restored penitentiary that once held 400 men, at least a quarter of them in chains.

dining in a contemporary-art-filled space. The stars of the show are the highest-quality Tasmanian produce and an enticing wine list. **Known for:** romantic vibe; seasonal produce; contemporary art. *$ Average main: A$45 ✉ 33 Hunter St., Hobart Waterfront ☎ 03/6210–7730 ⊕ peacockandjones.com.au ⏲ Closed Sun.–Tues.*

★ Templo

$$$ | MODERN AUSTRALIAN | A small 20-seat neighborhood restaurant tucked away in the back streets of Hobart, Templo celebrates seasonal and locally sourced produce and minimal-intervention wines from small producers. This place is a gem you'll need to book weeks if not months ahead. **Known for:** local ingredients; intimate; excellent food. *$ Average main: A$50 ✉ 96 Patrick St., North Hobart ☎ 03/6234–7659 ⊕ templo.com.au ⏲ Closed Tues. and Wed.*

Urban Greek

$$ | GREEK FUSION | Urban Greek combines the flavors of the old world with antipodean audacity, all set in a modern space. The variety of seating options includes communal benches, tables for groups, or kitchen-bar placement. **Known for:** communal seating; traditional Greek cuisine with modern Australian twist; affordable eats. *$ Average main: A$30 ✉ 103 Murray St., North Hobart ☎ 03/6109–4712 ⊕ www.urbangreekhobart.com.*

Coffee and Quick Bites

Flippers Cooked Seafood

$ | SEAFOOD | This fish-shape floating chip shop on Constitution Dock is one of the top places in town for an alfresco waterfront fish-and-chips meal. **Known for:** fish-and-chips; waterfront location; popular. *$ Average main: A$15 ✉ 1 Constitution Wharf, Hobart ☎ 03/6234–3101 ⊕ www.flippersfishandchips.com.au.*

★ Jackman & McRoss

$ | BAKERY | This Hobart institution in Battery Point is still a can't-miss spot for the perfectly crafted cup of coffee and delicious house-made goodies including croissants and fruit tarts. **Known for:** coffee; fruit tarts; local favorite. *$ Average main: A$7 ✉ 57 Hampden Rd., Battery Point ☎ 03/6223–3186.*

Wilderness Value

Tasmania is unique in the world as it has a vast area of World Heritage–listed wilderness. It's one of only two World Heritage Areas (WHA) on Earth that satisfies 7 of 10 criteria for that listing, including outstanding universal of natural, cultural, and geological value. It's also the only WHA that contains wilderness in its name. Tasmanians are very proud of their natural wonders and fiercely protect them against threats such as mining, forestry, and inappropriate tourism.

Hotels

Hobart has some lovely lodgings in old, historic houses and cottages, most of which have been beautifully restored. If you're seeking more modern conveniences, there are plenty of newer hotels. Airbnb also has a large presence in Hobart and inner city suburbs.

Corinda's Cottages

$$$$ | B&B/INN | This complex comprises a charming residence built in the 1880s for Alfred Crisp, a wealthy timber merchant who later became Lord Mayor of Hobart, as well as two pavilions and three lovingly restored outbuildings in which each of the accommodations are located—these include a gardener's residence, servants' quarters, and coach house. **Pros:** walking distance to CBD and waterfront; wonderfully restored historic accommodation; generous buffet breakfast. **Cons:**

steep steps in the Gardener's Cottage; low accessibility; no leisure facilities. *Rooms from: A$445 17 Glebe St., Glebe 03/6234–1590 www.corinda.com.au 7 rooms, 3 cottages, 2 pavilions Free Breakfast.*

★ The Henry Jones Art Hotel

$$$ | HOTEL | Arguably one of Australia's best hotels, right on the Hobart waterfront, this row of historic warehouses and a former jam factory have been transformed into a sensational, art-theme hotel, where the work of Tasmania's finest contemporary artists is displayed. **Pros:** excellent location; incredible art collection; stunning rooms worth lingering in. **Cons:** some rooms look into atrium so no natural light; tours, restaurants, cocktail bar are all pricey; breakfast is A$35. *Rooms from: A$280 25 Hunter St., City Center 03/6210–7700 www.thehenryjones.com 56 rooms No Meals.*

Hotel Grand Chancellor

$$$ | HOTEL | Across the street from the old wharves and steps from some of the most exciting restaurants in Hobart, this imposing glass-and-stone building offers sumptuous accommodation in one of the city's best locations. **Pros:** offers familiar chain comforts; steps away from the city's museums; adjacent to concert hall. **Cons:** fee for parking; stark lobby; some traffic noise. *Rooms from: A$225 1 Davey St., Hobart Waterfront 03/6235–4535, 1800/753–379 www.ghihotels.com 244 rooms No Meals.*

★ Islington Hotel

$$$$ | HOTEL | Built in 1847, this elegant Regency mansion was converted to a five-star luxury boutique hotel and is now one of the finest urban lodgings in Australia. **Pros:** fully tailored hospitality experience; sophisticated service from staff; free parking. **Cons:** 20-minute walk to city center; no leisure facilities; only accommodates children 15 years and over. *Rooms from: A$415 321 Davey St., South Hobart 03/6220–2123 www.islingtonhotel.com 11 rooms Free Breakfast.*

★ MONA Pavilions

$$$$ | HOTEL | These eight high-style pavilions are easily Tasmania's most cutting-edge accommodations—the pavilions are on the grounds of Tasmania's world-class experimental art museum, the Museum of Old and New Art (MONA). **Pros:** private museum tours; stunning setting and views; individually themed rooms with featured art. **Cons:** restaurant closed Tuesday; limited availability; high-tech features can be confusing. *Rooms from: A$950 655 Main Rd., Berriedale 03/6277–9900 mona.net.au/stay/mona-pavilions 8 chalets Free Breakfast.*

Old Woolstore Apartment Hotel

$$ | HOTEL | FAMILY | With a mix of standard rooms as well studios and one- and two-bedroom apartments, this property just a block from Hobart's iconic waterfront occupies one of the city's oldest and most historic buildings, the Roberts Limited Woolstore. **Pros:** central location; large rooms; historic ambience. **Cons:** busy neighborhood; confusing drive-in entrance; small balconies. *Rooms from: A$190 1 Macquarie St., City Center 1800/814–676, 03/6235–5355 www.oldwoolstore.com.au 59 rooms, 177 apartments, 6 suites No Meals.*

Salamanca Inn

$$ | B&B/INN | FAMILY | These elegant, self-contained apartments blend in well with the surrounding historic district and are perfect for families, as they have queen-size beds, modern kitchens, and free laundry facilities. **Pros:** spotlessly clean; in the heart of the restaurant and shopping district; excellent reception staff. **Cons:** Wi-Fi in the rooms can be slow; no views; some roads are blocked off during the Saturday markets. *Rooms from: A$200 10 Gladstone St., Battery Point 03/6223–3300,*

1800/030–944 🌐 *www.salamancainn.com.au* *60 suites* *No Meals.*

Sullivans Cove Apartments

$$$$ | APARTMENT | FAMILY | This is an impressive collection of 47 handsome, self-catered apartments and penthouses spread across five waterfront precincts in Hobart. **Pros:** wide selection of apartment styles; close to Salamanca Place shops and waterfront; stunning interiors. **Cons:** some noise from adjoining businesses; no leisure facilities; need to book early to reserve. $ *Rooms from: A$410* ✉ *Sullivans Cove Apartments and Check-in, 5/19a Hunter St., Hobart Waterfront* ☎ *03/6234–5063* 🌐 *www.sullivanscoveapartments.com.au* *47 apartments* *No Meals.*

Nightlife

Hobart's nightlife isn't exactly what you'll find in the bigger cities of the world, but some excellent bars and live music venues have emerged over recent years. Venues are small but very cool, with excellent food, wine, craft beers, and local spirits on offer.

BARS AND DANCE CLUBS

★ **The Glass House**

COCKTAIL LOUNGES | One of Hobart's best-placed venues, The Glass House brings a collection of the most enticing cocktails and delicious food together in a unique translucent floating facility with impressive views of the Derwent. This venue is also the home pier for the ferry service to and from MONA. ✉ *Brooke St. Pier, Hobart Waterfront* ☎ *03/6223–1032* 🌐 *www.theglass.house.*

★ **In The Hanging Garden**

BEER GARDENS | Break bread, drink, and gather in the garden, hidden in plain sight. Enjoy delicious food from their local kitchen collaborators, and drinks from all over Tasmania and the mainland, too. The menu and produce change with the seasons. Venture down from the garden and into the Cathedral, an unholy beer garden and live music venue. The 59-foot-tall structure is a sheltered meeting ground for garden gatherings. ✉ *112 Murray St., Battery Point* 🌐 *www.inthehanginggarden.com.au.*

★ **Preachers**

BEER GARDENS | This cute and cozy Heritage-listed cottage hides Hobart's best beer garden in its backyard, home to a full-size bus. Warm in winter, bright and breezy in summer, with good food, a great relaxed vibe, and a selection of local craft beers and ciders—Preachers ticks all the boxes, especially on a sunny day. ✉ *5 Knopwood St., Battery Point* ☎ *03/6223–3621.*

Republic Bar and Cafe

BARS | The cool kids head to this raucous, art deco pub warmed by roaring log fires to watch nightly live music, including plenty of top Tasmanian and touring bands. The food on offer is excellent and good value. ✉ *299 Elizabeth St., North Hobart* ☎ *03/6234–6954* 🌐 *pubbanc.com.au.*

★ **Room For A Pony**

CAFÉS | FAMILY | By day it's an alfresco restaurant offering café fare, and by night a bar and beer garden with shareable snacks and live music. This cool, converted gas station is a flexible and light-filled hot spot with bespoke wood furniture and room for several ponies. The name is a tongue-in-cheek reference to a British '90s sitcom, *Keeping Up Appearances,* and the space is appropriately friendly with touches of quirk and humor. ✉ *338 Elizabeth St., North Hobart* ☎ *03/6231–0508* 🌐 *www.roomforapony.com.au.*

★ **Shambles Brewery**

BREWPUBS | Nestled between Hobart's CBD and the café strip of North Hobart, Shambles occupies a fond place in Hobartians' hearts for its excellent beer (brewed on-site), its relaxed, urbane atmosphere, and long benches for large groups or smaller nooks for a more intimate experience. Give their Dirty Copper amber ale a try. ✉ *222 Elizabeth St., North Hobart* ☎ *03/6289–5639* 🌐 *www.shamblesbrewery.com.au.*

T42

CAFÉS | FAMILY | Officially called Tavern 42 Degrees South, this lively waterfront spot is popular for both dining and drinking—it's something of a Hobart institution. Patrons have the choice of sitting inside or out, noshing on tapas, sipping wine, and looking out over the harbor. The T42 house breakfast is a great kick-start to a day of exploring Hobart. ✉ *Elizabeth St. Pier, Hobart Waterfront* ☎ *03/6224–7742* 🌐 *www.tav42.com.au.*

LIVE MUSIC

Altar

LIVE MUSIC | A temple of live music, in the heart of Hobart. Plus, electronic DJs and nocturnal artists take over High Altar for a late-night dance party every Friday and Saturday. ✉ *112 Murray St., Hobart* 🌐 *www.altarhobart.com.au.*

Performing Arts

★ Federation Concert Hall

MUSIC | The permanent home of the acclaimed Tasmanian Symphony Orchestra, this 1,100-seat tiered auditorium welcomes touring musicians and speakers and is adjacent to the Hotel Grand Chancellor. The acoustics here are excellent. ✉ *1 Davey St., Hobart Waterfront* ☎ *03/6235–4535* 🌐 *www.tso.com.au.*

Theatre Royal

THEATER | This 1834 architectural gem with portraits of composers painted on its magnificent dome stages classic and contemporary plays by Australian and international playwrights. The renovation and development of the site has seen extra theaters added to the precinct. It's fabulous. ✉ *29 Campbell St., Hobart Waterfront* ☎ *03/6233–2299* 🌐 *www.theatreroyal.com.au.*

Shopping

Tasmanian artisans and craftspeople work with diverse materials to fashion unusual pottery, metalwork, and wool garments. Items made from regional timber, including myrtle, sassafras, and Huon pine, are popular. The wonderful scenery around the island is an inspiration for numerous artists.

Along the Hobart waterfront at Salamanca Place are a large number of shops that sell arts and crafts. On Saturday (between 8 and 3) the area turns into a giant market, where still more local artists join produce growers, bric-a-brac sellers, and itinerant musicians to sell their local wares.

Art Mob

ART GALLERIES | Set close to the waterfront by the Henry Jones Art Hotel, Art Mob exhibits and sells a wide range of local Tasmanian Aboriginal art and crafts, including jewelry, from many communities and artists. The collection includes rare necklaces and exquisite baskets as well as fine prints and paintings by noted Aboriginal artists. ✉ *29 Hunter St., City Center* ☎ *03/6236–9200* 🌐 *www.artmob.com.au.*

Gallery Salamanca

CRAFTS | This retail shop and gallery specializes in high-quality products made in Tasmania, including ceramics, glass, jewelery, sculpture, and textiles. The mission here is showcase the talents of Tasmania's emerging and established artists. Located within the Salamanca Arts Centre just off Salamanca Place, the gallery represents more than 90 artisans. ✉ *65 Salamanca Pl., Battery Point* ☎ *03/6223–5022* 🌐 *www.gallerysalamanca.com.au.*

Handmark Gallery

ART GALLERIES | Featuring the work of some of Tasmania's finest artists, this gallery is one of the gems of Salamanca Place. Inside you'll find Hobart's best wooden jewelry boxes as well as art deco jewelry and pottery, paintings, works on paper, and sculpture. The gallery also runs a number of exhibitions each year in conjunction with its sister gallery in Evandale, Northern Tasmania. Some of the exhibiting artists here have gone on to show at national and international galleries. The works of Tasmanian Aboriginal elder Lola Greeno are a very special feature. ✉ *77 Salamanca Pl., Battery Point* ☎ *03/6223–7895* 🌐 *www.handmark.com.au.*

Red Parka

OTHER SPECIALTY STORE | A funky shopfront for local artists working across varied disciplines, you will find ceramics, textiles, books, and many other treasures. Often with a local twist, featuring native flora and fauna or made from local materials, this is a must for the souvenir hunter that values original and clever design. ✉ *22 Criterion St., City Center* 🌐 *redparka.com.au.*

★ Wild Island Shop

ART GALLERIES | This gallery and shop sells environmental art, cards, calendars, diaries, jewelry, clothing, and ceramics, all inspired by Tasmania, the "'Wild Island." All wares are made in Australia and all support the Australian environment. Regular exhibitions feature local artists who use the Tasmanian wilderness as their muse, a must-visit for original souvenirs. ✉ *The Galleria, 8/33 Salamanca Pl., Battery Point* ☎ *03/6224–0220* 🌐 *www.wildislandtas.com.au.*

Activities

Hobartians are an outdoorsy lot who make the most of the city's waterfront location by fishing, cruising, and sailing or heading inland to kunanyi/Mt. Wellington to explore the many trails that start there.

BICYCLING

Hobart Bike Hire

BIKING | FAMILY | This conveniently located outfitter for renting bikes makes for a fun way to get around the city, particularly via the old railway lines along the western bank of the Derwent River. In addition to pedal bikes for adults and kids, tandem bikes and automatic electric bikes are available. ✉ *1a Brooke St., Hobart Waterfront* ☎ *0447/556–189* 🌐 *www.hobartbikehire.com.au* 🎫 *From A$25 daily.*

BOAT TOURS

★ Pennicott Wilderness Journeys

BOAT TOURS | FAMILY | From Hobart, this operator runs a range of cruises, including a 2½-hour trip that explores Hobart's waterways, a full-day seafood-focused tour on which you cruise down to Bruny Island, taste oysters shucked straight from the water, and watch your guide dive for abalone and sea urchin. You can also choose to drive yourself to Adventure Bay on Bruny Island (the Bruny Island Ferry can take any size vehicle) and join a three-hour wilderness cruise, where you can spot seals and, if you're lucky, dolphins and whales. Another stunning adventure tour on the Tasman Peninsular is so spectacular it must be experienced to be believed. ✉ *Constitution Dock Bridge, Franklin Wharf, Hobart Waterfront* ☎ *03/6234–4270* 🌐 *www.pennicottjourneys.com.au* 🎫 *From A$125.*

Peppermint Bay Cruises

BOATING | FAMILY | This catamaran races through the majestic waterways of the Derwent River and the D'Entrecasteaux Channel to Peppermint Bay at Woodbridge for lunch and provides a fantastic way to spy some of Tasmania's epic wildlife. And it is abundant, from sea eagles and falcons soaring above the weathered cliffs to pods of dolphins swimming alongside the boat. ✉ *Brooke St. Pier, Sulivans Cove, Hobart Waterfront* ☎ *1300/137–919* 🌐 *www.peppermintbay.com.au* 🎫 *A$130.*

FISHING

Tasmania's well-stocked lakes and streams are among the world's best for trout fishing. The season runs from August through May, and licensed trips can be arranged through the Tasmanian Travel and Information Centre.

Several professional fishing guides are based on the island. For information on these guides, as well as related tours, accommodations, and sea charters, check out *www.troutguidestasmania.com.au* or inquire at the Tasmanian Travel and Information Centre for a professional guide in the area you are visiting.

Mr Flathead

FISHING | If you fancy taking to the ocean to explore local fishing hot spots, check with this company that runs half- and full-day family-friendly tours on which you'll find scores of flathead, whiting, and salmon. All rods, reels, and equipment are supplied and the head guide, Mark, aka Mr Flathead, is as entertaining as the fishing! *Dodges Ferry boat ramp, Tiger Head Rd., Dodges Ferry 0439/617–200 www.mrflathead.com.au $A150 half day.*

Rod & Fly Tasmania

FISHING | Tasmania is home to some world-class fishing, and if you'd like to catch some local trout in the region's wonderfully clear rivers and highland lakes, this friendly operator is a good choice for setting up an outing, with more than 30 years of experience. *35 Misty Hill Rd., Mountain River 03/6266–4480, 0408/469–771 www.rodandfly.com.au.*

GOLF

Tasmania is fast becoming *the* place to play golf in Australia and there are about 85 golf courses around Tasmania, and visitors are welcome to play on many of them. Greens fees range from A$10 for 9 holes at the smaller country courses all the way up to A$90 for 18 holes at the more exclusive, larger clubs. Accessibility may vary (for example, some courses may require that you be introduced by a member), so it's always best to check first by phoning ahead.

There are several excellent golf courses within the Hobart area with new ones appearing all the time.

Claremont Golf Club

GOLF | Situated on a stunning peninsula jutting into the River Derwent and within close proximity of Hobart and its surroundings, this is the only public 18-hole golf club situated in the northern suburbs of the city. *1 Bournville Crescent, Hobart 03/6249–1000 www.claremontgolf.com.au A$50 18 holes, 5747 yards, par 69.*

★ **Ratho Farm Golf Links**

GOLF | This quirky 9-hole layout, about 75 km (47 miles) north of Hobart in the village of Bothwell, was established in 1822, making it the oldest golf course outside Scotland, where the sport originated—it's part of a working farm. Ratho also has a welcoming, warm homestead with dining, bar facilities, and 16 attractive en suite rooms in lovingly restored old farm buildings. *2122 Highland Lakes Rd., Bothwell 03/6259–5628 www.rathofarm.com A$15 for 9 holes, A$40 for 18 holes 18 holes, 5660 yards, par 70.*

HIKING

Pick up a kunanyi/Mt. Wellington Walk Map from the tourist office on Elizabeth Street in Hobart to make the most of the mountain park that towers over Hobart. Although shops around town stock and hire outdoor equipment, you should bring your own gear if you're planning any serious bushwalking. There are hundreds of walking tracks in Wellington Park and thousand of miles across Tasmania. Sneakers are adequate for most trails and along beaches, however some of the walks cross exposed alpine environments where the weather can change from bad to worse very quickly; prepare

The extremely popular Saturday Salamanca Market

accordingly. A car is necessary to access several of the trails around the Wellington Range although there is a bus from the city to the summit.

★ Trek Tasmania

HIKING & WALKING | Trek Tasmania is a boutique tour company focused on taking small groups into the wilds of Tasmania, onto the paths less traveled and into the heart of the Tasmanian wilderness. Their specialty is offering quality, deep immersion wilderness experiences with a commitment to sustainable eco-tourism principles. ☎ *0400/882–742* 🌐 *www.trektasmania.com.au.*

WALKING TOURS

Hobart Historic Tours

HIKING & WALKING | This tour company leads history walks through old Hobart, around the waterfront and maritime precinct, and to historic pubs. ✉ *Hobart Travel Centre, Davey St. at Elizabeth St., Hobart Waterfront* ☎ *03/6234–5550* 🌐 *www.hobarthistorictours.com.au* 🎫 *From A$33.*

YACHTING

If the annual Sydney-to-Hobart race has inspired you to find your sea legs, you're in the right place. Hobart is a city for sailors.

★ Hobart Yachts

BOATING | Hobart Yachts runs a range of cruises, from three-hour twilight sailings on the River Derwent to weeklong charters up the east coast or to Port Davey. ✉ *Hobart Waterfront* ☎ *0438/399–477* 🌐 *www.hobartyachts.com.au.*

The Huon Valley

40 km (25 miles) south of Hobart.

En route to the vast wilderness of South West National Park is the tranquil Huon Valley. Sheltered coasts and sandy beaches are pocketed with thick forests and small farms. William Bligh planted the first apple tree here, founding one of the region's major industries. Other fruit, nut, and berry farms dot the valley with some of the tastiest cherries in the world plentiful. Trout caught fresh from churning tannin-rich rivers are also a regional delicacy.

The valley is also famous for its boatbuilding industry, using local timbers, and as an emerging wine region the Huon holds attractions aplenty.

Sights

Tahune AirWalk Tasmania

FOREST | FAMILY | Beyond Geeveston, the cantilevered, 1,880-foot-long Tahune AirWalk rises to 150 feet above the forest floor, providing a stunning panorama of the Huon and Picton rivers and the Hartz Mountains. The best views are from the platform at the end of the walkway, and if you have time, follow one of the trails that leads from the center through the surrounding forests. If one day isn't enough you can stay the night on-site in the reasonably priced Tahune Lodge or in a self-contained cabin. There's also a shop and a café with free Wi-Fi. ✉ *Arve Rd., Geeveston* ☎ *03/6251–3903* 🌐 *tahuneairwalk.com.au* 🎫 *A$30.*

★ Willie Smith's Apple Shed

FARM/RANCH | En route to Huonville, this museum, cider house, and café showcases the best of the local product. It's housed in a former apple-packing shed and is a remarkable time capsule, depicting the lives of the early Huon Valley settlers. Over the years this venue has evolved to offer regular events, great food, and even better cider. The Sunday Session is a great way to end a weekend in the valley. ✉ *2064 Huon Hwy., Grove* ☎ *03/6266–4345* 🌐 *www.williesmiths.com.au* 🎫 *Free.*

Beaches

Cockle Creek

BEACH | Cockle Creek is the southernmost "town" in Australia. It consists of a a ranger station and a campground, but also a series of stunning beaches. The neighboring hamlet of Catamaran is similarly dotted with picturesque bays and beaches, surrounded by forests and mountains. French explorers landed here before English settlement and aspects of that history can be explored also. There are walking tracks including the awe-inspiring Lion Rock at South Cape Bay. **Amenities:** toilets. **Best for:** walking; swimming. ✉ *Cockle Creek Rd., Hastings* 🌐 *parks.tas.gov.au/explore-our-parks/southwest-national-park/cockle-creek.*

Kingston Beach

BEACH | FAMILY | This is the first main swimming beach southwest of Hobart—it's less than 30 minutes' drive from the Huon Valley. The beach sits in front of the fairly developed town of Kingston, on the Derwent River at the mouth of Browns Rivulet. Shopping and housing sit behind and to the south of the beach, and a narrow reserve, picnic area, and playground back the sand. Kingston Beach is patrolled by the local Surf Life Saving Club; however, you should still keep clear of any boating activity in the south corner—the waters are quite deep directly off the beach. **Amenities:** food and drink; lifeguards; parking (free); showers; toilets. **Best for:** surfing; swimming; walking. ✉ *Beach Rd. at Osbourne Esplanade, Kingston Beach.*

Restaurants

Home Hill Winery Restaurant

$$$ | AUSTRALIAN | Large plate-glass windows open to the Home Hill winery's endless hillside vineyards at this boutique vineyard, cellar door, and restaurant—a true Tasmanian country retreat. The seasonal menu features many local producers. **Known for:** morning and afternoon tea; pretty setting; slow-cooked lamb shoulder. 💲 *Average main: A$45* ✉ *38 Nairn St., Ranelagh* ☎ *03/6258–1120* 🌐 *homehillwines.com.au.*

★ Port Cygnet Cannery

$$ | **AUSTRALIAN** | Port Cygnet Cannery is situated 50 minutes' drive south of Hobart in the historic port town of Cygnet, Tasmania. The building was formerly an apple canning factory and is now evolving into a hub of food, beverage, and agricultural businesses. **Known for:** located in a historic port town; wood-fired pizza; in-house wine. *Average main: A$38* *60 Lymington Rd., Port Cygnet* *03/6211–8332* *www.portcygnetcannery.com.*

Hotels

★ Herons Rise Vineyard

$$ | **B&B/INN** | Mornings in any of the vineyard's three self-contained cottages are bucolic and gorgeous; you'll wake to glorious water views out over the flower gardens, where you might see rabbits nibbling while you soak up the tranquility of this peaceful environment. **Pros:** convenient to Bruny Island; peaceful surroundings; beautiful views of the Tasman Sea and rural landscape. **Cons:** breakfast not included (but bountiful provisions available); smoke from fireplaces might be a problem for some; no leisure facilities. *Rooms from: A$170* *Saddle Rd., Kettering* *0412/152–164* *www.heronsrise.com.au* *2 cottages* *No Meals.*

Richmond

24 km (15 miles) northeast of Hobart.

Twenty minutes' drive from Hobart and a century behind the big city, this colonial village in the Coal River valley is a major tourist magnet. Visitors stroll and browse through the craft shops, antiques stores, and cafés along the main street. Richmond is also home to a number of vineyards, all of which produce excellent cool-climate wines.

Restaurants

★ Frogmore Creek

$$$ | **AUSTRALIAN** | Wine tasting and an art gallery complement this unpretentious but upscale restaurant with floor-to-ceiling windows looking out to views over the vineyards of Frogmore Creek and Barilla Bay. In the restaurant creative yet simple dishes make choosing a meal difficult. **Known for:** fresh oysters; vineyard views; tapas-style menu. *Average main: A$45* *699 Richmond Rd., Cambridge* *03/6274–5844* *www.frogmorecreek.com.au* *No dinner.*

Pooley's Vineyard

$$ | **AUSTRALIAN** | An idyllic set of sandstone buildings dating back to the 1830s, built in the Georgian style, nestled among rolling hills of grapevines, pasture, and pine trees, this property is truly stunning. A wide variety of excellent wines coupled with gourmet wood-fired pizzas on a warm spring day is the perfect way to while away an afternoon after browsing the high street of Richmond. **Known for:** wood-fired pizza; beautiful location; nice variety of wine. *Average main: A$28* *1431 Richmond Rd., Richmond* *www.pooleywines.com.au.*

Hotels

Riversdale Estate

$$ | **B&B/INN** | This working estate produces sumptuous wines from its 98 acres of vines, but also has cropping and livestock activities which add an authentic farm-stay feel. **Pros:** family-friendly; peaceful setting; French provincial decor. **Cons:** service can be inconsistent; restaurant is disappointing; working vineyard, so there can be equipment noise. *Rooms from: A$180* *222 Denholms Rd., Cambridge* *03/6248–5555* *riversdaleestate.com.au* *Minimum two-night stay* *7 cottages* *No Meals.*

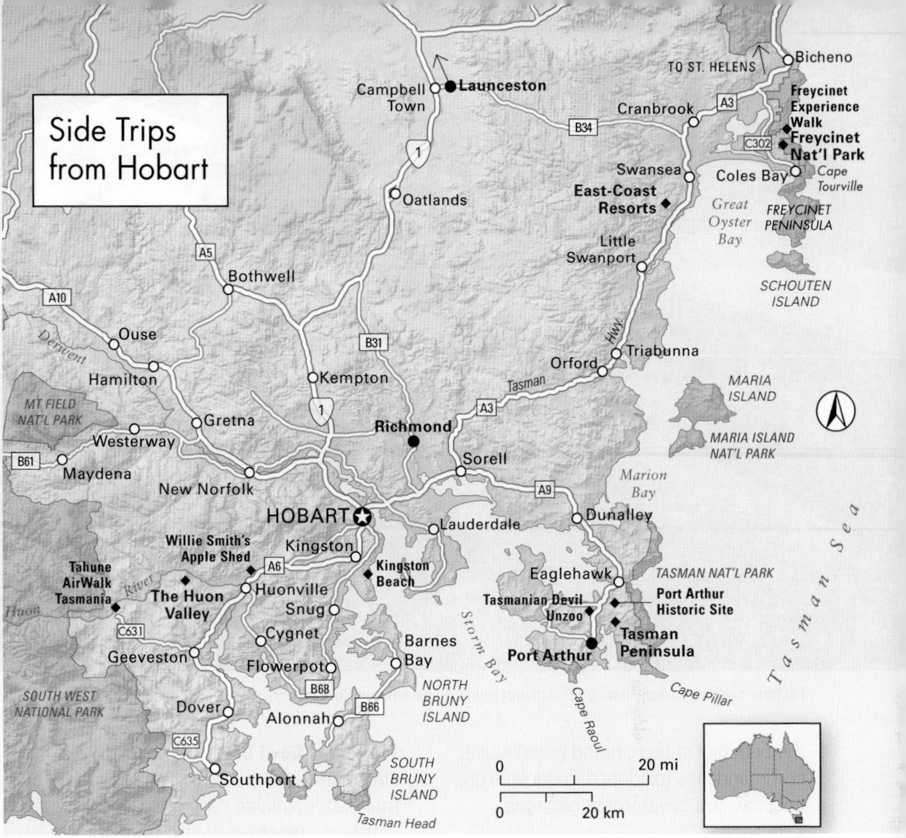

Side Trips from Hobart

Port Arthur and the Tasman Peninsula

102 km (63 miles) southeast of Hobart.

When Governor George Arthur, lieutenant-governor of Van Diemen's Land (now Tasmania), was looking for a site to dump his worst convict offenders in 1830, the Tasman Peninsula was a natural choice. Joined to the rest of Tasmania only by the narrow Eaglehawk Neck, the spit was easy to isolate and guard. Between 1830 and 1877, more than 12,000 convicts served sentences at Port Arthur in Britain's equivalent of Devil's Island. Dogs patrolled the narrow causeway, and guards spread rumors that sharks infested the waters. Reminders of those dark days remain in some of the area names—Dauntless Point, Stinking Point, Isle of the Dead.

Today, as many people visit the peninsula for the spectacular coastal scenery and to hike the Three Capes Track as visit the Port Arthur Historic Site.

Sights

★ Port Arthur Historic Site

MUSEUM VILLAGE | FAMILY | This property, formerly the grounds of the Port Arthur Penal Settlement, is now a lovely—and quite large—historical park with a fascinating convict past central to Tasmania's history. Be prepared to do some walking between widely scattered sites. Begin at the excellent visitor center, which introduces you to the experience by "sentencing, transporting, and assigning" you before you set foot in the colony. Most of the original buildings were damaged by bushfires in 1895 and 1897, shortly after the settlement was abandoned, but you can still see

Historic buildings from Tasmania's convict past can be seen in Port Arthur.

the beautiful church, round guardhouse, commandant's residence, model prison, hospital, and government cottages.

The old **lunatic asylum** is now an excellent museum, with a scale model of the Port Arthur settlement, a video history, and a collection of tools, leg irons, and chains. Along with a walking tour of the grounds and entrance to the museum, admission includes a harbor cruise, of which there are eight scheduled daily in summer. There's a separate twice-daily cruise to and tour of the **Isle of the Dead,** which sits in the middle of the bay. It's estimated that 1,769 convicts and 180 others are buried here, mostly in communal pits. Ghost tours (reservations are essential) leave the visitor center at dusk and last about 90 minutes. Buy your tickets at the site, or at the Brooke Street Pier, at Franklin Wharf in Hobart. ✉ *Arthur Hwy., Port Arthur* ☎ *1800/659–101* 🌐 *www.portarthur.org.au* 🎫 *From A$39.*

Tasmanian Devil Unzoo

PUBLIC ART | FAMILY | This "unzoo" offers a four-in-one wildlife nature experience that combines up-close animal encounters, wildlife adventures, a Tasmanian native garden, and original art. It is also the best place to come face-to-face with real live Tasmanian devils. Spot these burrowing carnivorous marsupials (about the size of a small dog), as well as quolls, boobooks (small, spotted brown owls), masked owls, eagles, and other native fauna. The philosophy of the "unzoo" is to challenge the way native animals are presented to the public. ✉ *5990 Port Arthur Hwy., Taranna* ⊕ *11 km (7 miles) north of Port Arthur* ☎ *1800/641–641* 🌐 *tasmaniandevilunzoo.com.au* 🎫 *A$39.*

Beaches

White Beach

BEACH | FAMILY | It's less than a 10-minute drive from the historic former penal colony of Port Arthur to the pristine white sands of beautiful White Beach, a wild, unspoiled, crescent-shape beach often named one of the most beautiful beaches in Australia. The breathtaking views from the beach are among the most beautiful in all of Tasmania, stretching as far as the eye can see across Wedge Bay to Storm Bay and then beyond to the Hartz Mountains. The local trails are worth exploring, not far from the usually deserted 3-km (2-mile) beach, although world-class diving is also available at Eaglehawk Neck and decent surfing at Roaring Beach. White Beach Tourist Park fronts directly onto the beach, and the general area has a number of cafés and restaurants offering excellent local Tasmanian cuisine. **Amenities:** food and drink; parking (free); toilets. **Best for:** snorkeling; solitude; sunrise; sunset; surfing; swimming; walking. ✉ *White Beach Rd., Port Arthur.*

Restaurants

1830
$$ | AUSTRALIAN | FAMILY | Feast on wonderfully fresh Tasmanian seafood and game in the heart of the Port Arthur Historic Site at this small but lovely restaurant. Standout appetizers include the area's local oysters. **Known for:** a tad overpriced; pretour dinner; fresh oysters. *$ Average main: A$38* ✉ *Port Arthur Historic Site, Port Arthur* ☎ *03/6251–2310, 1800/659–101* 🌐 *www.portarthur.org.au.*

Hotels

Stewarts Bay Lodge
$$ | B&B/INN | FAMILY | Less than five minutes' drive from the Port Arthur Historic Site, this cabin park is located on the edge of a gorgeous bay with white sandy beach ringed by tall eucalypt forest. **Pros:** good on-site restaurant; natural setting; private beach is stunning. **Cons:** on-site restaurant is only dining option; booked up far in advance in peak season; marked difference between cabin styles. *$ Rooms from: A$200* ✉ *6955 Arthur Hwy., Port Arthur* ☎ *03/6250–2888* 🌐 *stewartsbaylodge.com.au* *19 cabins, 21 chalets* *No Meals.*

East-Coast Resorts

From Hobart, the east-coast Tasman Highway travels cross-country to Orford, then passes through beautiful coastal scenery with spectacular white-sand beaches, usually completely deserted, before reaching Swansea. Bicheno, just north of Freycinet National Park, and the Bay of Fires, which is farther north, are both fishing and holiday towns with quiet, sheltered harbors. The area has arguably the best beaches in the world.

Sights

★ **Freycinet Experience Walk**
WALKING TOURS | Freycinet Experience Walk is an eco-certified, fully inclusive walking tour in Tasmania. Over four days, you will cover the entire length of the Freycinet Peninsula, including the iconic Wineglass Bay. Spend your days taking in stunning coastal vistas and the beauty of Tasmania's flora and fauna. By night, dine on freshly prepared Tasmanian produce before resting your head at the sustainably built Friendly Beaches Lodge in the heart of Freycinet National Park. ✉ *Coles Bay* ☎ *1800/506–003* 🌐 *www.freycinet.com.au* *A$2750.*

Beaches

Bicheno Beach
BEACH | FAMILY | Extending 650 feet along the southern shore of Waubs Bay, this gentle beach is in the heart of pretty Bicheno. A secondary north-facing beach sits on the western side of the bay. Rounded granite rocks border and separate the two beaches. There is a car park and toilet facilities at the middle of the beach where Beach Street meets

the sand, while the town itself sits on the slopes at the south end. A popular shoreline walking track follows the rocky coast around the headland. If the swell is up, be sure to look for the blowhole. **Amenities:** food and drink; parking (free); toilets. **Best for:** surfing; swimming; walking. ✉ *Bicheno.*

Friendly Beaches

BEACH | **FAMILY** | Contained within the boundaries of the Freycinet National Park, this long, sweeping, beautiful beach is accessed from Coles Bay Road, 9 km (6 miles) south of the turnoff on the Tasman Highway. Enjoy going barefoot as the sand is extremely soft, fine, and bright as a result of its high silicon content. The signature orange-lichen-encrusted granite boulders contrast beautifully against the white sand and turquoise water. The waves are excellent for surfers, but there are strong rip and tidal currents, so exercise care. Start at the small parking area, take the short stroll to the beach, and bring water and sunscreen, as there are no nearby facilities. **Amenities:** parking (free); toilets. **Best for:** solitude; surfing; swimming; walking. ✉ *Coles Bay Rd., Coles Bay.*

Hotels

★ **Avalon Coastal Retreat**

$$$$ | **HOUSE** | This gorgeous three-bedroom house is the ultimate in exclusivity: it sits entirely alone on Tasmania's east coast, with just the occasional passing white-bellied sea eagle for company. **Pros:** fully stocked; unadulterated privacy; gorgeous views. **Cons:** limited availability; three-night minimum stay; expensive. $ *Rooms from: A$900* ✉ *11922 Tasman Hwy., Swansea* ☎ *1300/361–136 Australia, 428/250–399 international* 🌐 *avalonretreats.com.au* *1 3-bedroom house* 🍴 *Free Breakfast.*

Diamond Island Resort

$$ | **RESORT** | Direct access to a deserted beach, island walks, and penguin-viewing platforms are among the draws of this peaceful hideaway 1½ km (1 mile) north of Bicheno and overlooking the Tasman Sea. Twelve two-bedroom duplexes are nestled within 7 acres of landscaped gardens; there are also 14 smaller one-bedroom units. **Pros:** kitchenettes in all units; minutes from a superb beach; access to wildlife. **Cons:** feels a little dated; no leisure facilities; not great value for what you get. $ *Rooms from: A$180* ✉ *69 Tasman Hwy., Bicheno* ☎ *03/6375–0100, 800/030–299* 🌐 *diamondisland.com.au* *26 rooms* 🍴 *Free Breakfast.*

Eastcoaster

$$ | **RESORT** | **FAMILY** | This seaside complex in the town of Louisville is a great jumping-off point for exploring Maria Island National Park; the resort's catamaran, the *Eastcoaster Express,* makes three or four trips a day to the island. **Pros:** family-friendly resort; inexpensive and unpretentious; leisure facilities. **Cons:** somewhat dated design; some distance from other attractions; not the best beach in the area. $ *Rooms from: A$170* ✉ *1 Louisville Rd., Orford* ☎ *03/6257–1172* 🌐 *eastcoaster-resort.com.au* *48 rooms, 8 cabins, 30 caravan sites* 🍴 *No Meals.*

Hamptons on the Bay

$$$ | **HOTEL** | **FAMILY** | These water-facing cabins have dramatic views over Great Oyster Bay and the Freycinet Peninsula through full-length windows in living and bedroom areas. **Pros:** 10-minute drive to Swansea's restaurants; friendly property manager; incredible views over the ocean. **Cons:** no on-site dining; no Wi-Fi in rooms; barbecue area is between Cabins 5 and 6, which could impact privacy. $ *Rooms from: A$260* ✉ *12164 Tasman Hwy., Swansea* ☎ *0417/481–777* 🌐 *www.hamptonsonthebay.com.au* *6 1-bedroom cabins, 1 2-bedroom cabin, 1 3-bedroom house* 🍴 *No Meals.*

Meredith House and Mews

$$ | **B&B/INN** | Exquisite red-cedar furnishings and antiques decorate this grand 1853 refurbished residence in the center of Swansea. **Pros:** excellent service from affable hosts; superb freshly cooked

"We had driven from Friendly Beach further into the Park when we came across this beautiful area." —
photo by Gary Ott, Fodors.com member

breakfasts; authentic colonial-era building. **Cons:** books up well in advance; not appropriate for young families; no leisure facilities. $ *Rooms from: A$190* ✉ *15 Noyes St., Swansea* ☎ *03/6257–8119* 🌐 *www.meredith-house.com.au* *11 rooms* *Free Breakfast.*

Activities

AIR TOURS

Freycinet Air

LOCAL SPORTS | This company flies from the Friendly Beaches Airfield, located 18 km (11 miles) north of Coles Bay, and has scenic flights with unparalleled views of Wineglass Bay, the Hazards, and the Peninsula. Freycinet Air offer a range of flights in fixed-wing planes and helicopters. ✉ *Friendly Beaches Airfield, Rosny Park* ☎ *03/6375–1694* 🌐 *www.freycinetair.com.au* *From A$155.*

CRUISES

★ **Wineglass Bay Cruises**

BOATING | **FAMILY** | Another way to experience the wonders of the Freycinet Peninsula is on a scenic cruise with Wineglass Bay Cruises. Guides endeavor to show you whales, dolphins, seals, white-bellied sea eagles, and albatrosses on the four-hour tour—you'll also experience stunning scenery and a rare, intimate perspective on an extraordinary Tasmanian location. Tour prices include lunch, and drinks can be purchased from the fully licensed bar, with an indulgent upper deck option in the Sky Lounge providing all drinks and freshly shucked oysters in the fare. ✉ *Jetty, Jetty Rd., Coles Bay* ☎ *03/6257–0355* 🌐 *www.wineglassbaycruises.com* *From A$145.*

KAYAKING

Frecyinet is Tasmania's premier sea-kayaking destination, and it's possible to do guided tours or hire your own kayak and cruise around at your own pace.

★ **Freycinet Adventures**

KAYAKING | **FAMILY** | Providing a memorable way to explore the spectacular coastline at a leisurely pace, this family-run company runs half-day kayaking tours around the peninsula, as well as two day trips. Along the way guides point out local marine life, such as sea eagles and dolphins. Tour packages cater to all skill levels. ✉ *2 Freycinet Dr., Coles Bay* ☎ *03/6257–0500* 🌐 *www.freycinetadventures.com.au* 🎫 *From A$120.*

WILDLIFE WATCHING

Bicheno Penguin Tours

WILDLIFE-WATCHING | FAMILY | At Bicheno, a very popular tour is the nightly hour-long vigil to see the penguins emerge from the water and clamber up to their nesting area. The daily tours begin at dusk, and penguin numbers often exceed 50. It's a magical opportunity to view these creatures up close. ✉ *70 Burgess St., Bicheno* ☎ *03/6375–1333* 🌐 *www.bichenopenguintours.com.au* 🎫 *A$40.*

Hiking Freycinet

The Freycinet Peninsular offers dozens of hiking options, from gentle strolls along stunning beaches to adventure scrambles over rugged peaks. Some standouts are the walk to Wineglass Bay, the climb up Mt. Amos, or the 30-km circuit around the peninsula. For easier options try Honeymoon Bay, Cape Tourville, or Sleepy Bay.

Freycinet National Park

238 km (149 miles) north of Port Arthur, 214 km (133 miles) southwest of Launceston, 206 km (128 miles) northeast of Hobart.

The road onto the Freycinet Peninsula ends just past the township of Coles Bay; from that point the stunning Freycinet National Park begins and covers 24,700 acres.

ESSENTIALS

Freycinet National Park Offices

Parks passes are required for entering all Tasmanian national parks; they can be purchased here or at Service Tasmania offices. ✉ *Coles Bay Rd., Coles Bay* ☎ *03/6256–7000* 🌐 *www.parks.tas.gov.au.*

Sights

★ **Freycinet National Park**

NATIONAL PARK | FAMILY | Highlights of the dramatic scenery here include the mountain-size granite formations known as the Hazards. On the ocean side of the peninsula there are also sheer cliffs that drop into the deep-blue ocean; views from the lighthouse at Cape Tourville are unforgettable. A series of tiny coves, one called Honeymoon Bay, provide a quieter perspective on the Great Oyster Bay side. Wineglass Bay, a perfect crescent of dazzling white sand, is best viewed from the lookout platform, about a 30-minute walk up a gentle hill from the parking lot; if you're feeling energetic, though, the view from the top of Mt. Amos, one of the Hazards, is worth the effort. A round-trip walk from the parking lot to Wineglass Bay takes about 2½ hours, and there are longer hiking options in the park. The park's many trails are well signposted. Daily entry to the park costs A$20 per person and A$40 per vehicle. ✉ *Coles Bay Rd., Coles Bay* ☎ *03/6256–7000* 🌐 *www.parks.tas.gov.au.*

Beaches

Nine Mile Beach

BEACH | FAMILY | A stone's throw from the historic town of Swansea, this long, sweeping beach is a favorite for swimming, fishing, and simply soaking up the views and peaceful surroundings—visitors enjoy uninterrupted views across Great Oyster Bay to Schouten Island, The Hazards, and the Freycinet Peninsula. Dangerous rips can be a concern here—take care, especially near the sand bar. The western end of the beach has a variety of lodgings and holiday rentals. Great Swanport lagoon and wetlands form the back side of the beach. There's parking for about 100 cars in the lot. **Amenities:** parking (free). **Best for:** solitude; surfing; swimming; walking. ✉ *Dolphin Sands Rd., Swansea.*

Edge of the Bay

$$$ | **HOUSE** | The outstanding views from these modern, minimalist-style water-view suites and cottages set along 27 acres of untouched wilderness stretch for miles across Great Oyster Bay to the Hazards. **Pros:** animals wander freely around the resort; excellent on-site restaurant; idyllic setting. **Cons:** two-night minimum; books up well in advance; no breakfast is served but breakfast baskets can be ordered. *Rooms from: A$270* ✉ *2308 Main Rd., Coles Bay* ☎ *03/6257–0102* 🌐 *www.edgeofthebay.com.au* *14 suites, 7 cottages* *No Meals.*

★ Freycinet Lodge

$$$ | **HOUSE** | With cabin-style accommodations scattered through the densely wooded forest overlooking Great Oyster Bay, this cushy eco-lodge has a remote setting that allows for an intimate connection with the surrounding scenic environment. **Pros:** proximity to the national park; superb food in fine-dining restaurant; perfect for getting away from it all. **Cons:** rooms can be on the cold side; only the premier spa cabin has a TV; utilitarian furniture for the price. *Rooms from: A$299* ✉ *Freycinet National Park, Coles Bay Rd., Coles Bay* ☎ *03/6256–7222* 🌐 *www.freycinetlodge.com.au* *60 cabins* *Free Breakfast.*

Saffire Freycinet

$$$$ | **RESORT** | Blame it on jaw-dropping views of Great Oyster Bay and the Hazards Mountains that frame the resort, or the modernist architecture, this far-flung luxe getaway screams style. **Pros:**; views from every inch of the property; comfy, modern suites; great excursions. **Cons:** very pricey; one restaurant; extremely remote (transfers are not included). *Rooms from: A$2400* ✉ *Coles Bay Rd., Freycinet Peninsula, Coles Bay* ☎ *03/6256–7888* 🌐 *www.saffire-freycinet.com.au* *20 suites* *All-Inclusive.*

Launceston

200 km (124 miles) north of Hobart.

Nestled in a fertile agricultural basin where the South Esk and North Esk rivers join to form the Tamar, the city of Launceston (pronounced *Lon*-sess-tun), or Lonnie to locals, is the commercial center of Tasmania's northern region. Many unusual markets and shops are concentrated downtown (unlike Hobart, which has most of its stores in the historic center, set apart from the commercial district).

Launceston is far from bustling, and has a notable number of pleasant parks, late-19th-century homes, historic mansions, and private gardens. The sumptuous countryside that surrounds the city—rolling farmland and the rich loam of English-looking landscapes—set off by the South Esk River meandering through towering gorges, is also appealing.

Cataract Gorge

CANYON | **FAMILY** | Almost in the heart of the city, the South Esk River flows through the stunningly beautiful Cataract Gorge on its way toward the Tamar River. A 1-km (½-mile) path leads along the face of the precipices to the Cliff Gardens Reserve, where there are picnic tables, a swimming pool, and a restaurant. Take the chairlift in the first basin for a thrilling aerial view of the gorge—at just over 900 feet, it's the longest single span in the world. Self-guided nature trails wind through the park, and it's a great place for a picnic or to catch some live music. ✉ *Basin Rd., Launceston* ☎ *03/6331–5915*

The Midlands

You can speed between Hobart and Launceston on the 200-km (124-mile) Highway 1 (Midlands Highway, also known as the Heritage Highway) in less than 2½ hours. Doing so, however, means bypassing one of Tasmania's most charmingly lovely pastoral regions and rural villages.

Heading north from Hobart, the first community you'll encounter (it's about 85 km [53 miles] outside the city) is the Georgian town of **Oatlands,** set on the shore of Lake Dulverton. Built in the 1820s as a garrison for the local farming community, the town still retains many original buildings that were built from the glorious golden sandstone of the region. There are also some fine old churches and a wind-powered mill that produces the finest stone-ground flour, which you can sample in its best form at the local bakery.

The quaint village of **Ross,** about 55 km (34 miles) northeast of Oatlands, also has some wonderful historic buildings dating from the mid-19th century. The town's most iconic landmark, though, is the 1836 Ross Bridge, whose graceful sandstone arches are adorned with decorative carving.

A short detour from the Midlands Highway will bring you to **Longford** (it's 72 km [45 miles] northwest of Ross). Settled in 1813, Longford was one of northern Tasmania's first towns, and is now a National Trust historic site. Of particular early historic interest here is Christ Church, built in 1839. Although it's only open on Sunday, the church has a beautiful west window that is regarded as one of the country's finest. Nearby Woolmers Estate is a fascinating property to explore and book a stay at.

There are a number of other **historic villages** in the vicinity of Longford that are worth a visit. Hadspen, Carrick, Hagley, Perth, and Evandale are all within a short 25-km (16-mile) radius of the town, and all have their own special charms. Near Evandale on the road toward Nile, Clarendon House is one of the great Georgian houses of Australia, restored by the National Trust.

Spending the night in one of the towns along the Midlands Highway will let you more fully indulge in the historic-charm experience; many of the lodgings in the region occupy beautiful old buildings. Perhaps most impressive of all is **Brickendon** (*03/6391–1383; 03/6391–1251*) in Longford, whose restored cottages have antique tubs, fireplaces, and private gardens. The compound is a true colonial village, with a chapel, a trout lake, and more than 20 National Trust–classified buildings.

🌐 *www.launcestoncataractgorge.com.au* 🎫 *Gorge free, chairlift from A$15.*

James Boag Brewery Experience

BREWERY | Since 1881, this operation has been brewing some of Australia's finest beer in an imposing brick building, in which weekday brewery tours are run. Visitors learn the entire process, from brewhouse to packaging, and end with beer tastings (plus a cheese platter if you book the more expensive option). Bookings are essential. ✉ *39 William St., Launceston* ☎ *03/6332–6300* 🌐 *www.jamesboag.com.au/agegate* 🎫 *Tour A$35* 🕒 *Closed Mon.–Wed.*

Queen Victoria Museum and Art Gallery
ART MUSEUM | FAMILY | Opened in 1891, the gallery presents fascinating insights into the city's history, including the rich Aboriginal and colonial past. There's also a large natural-history collection of stuffed birds and animals (including the now-extinct thylacine, or Tasmanian tiger). Regular tours and history talks are a great way to dig a little deeper into the museum's collection. ✉ *2 Invermay Rd., Launceston* ☎ *03/6323–3777* 🌐 *www.qvmag.tas.gov.au* *Free.*

★ **Tamar Valley Wine Route**
SCENIC DRIVE | Along both sides of the Tamar River north of Launceston, the soil and cool weather are perfect for grape growing. Here in the Tamar Valley wine region, some of the outstanding varieties grown include Pinot Noir, Riesling, and Pinot Grigio; the sparkling wines produced here are world-leading. A map of the route, available for download at their website, will help you to plan your visit. Noteworthy stops along the route are Pipers Brook Vineyard, Joseph Cromy, Holm Oak, Holyman wines at Stoney Rise, Clover Hill, and The Jansz Wine Room. ✉ *Launceston* 🌐 *www.tamarvalleywineroute.com.au.*

Restaurants

Hallam's Waterfront
$$$ | SEAFOOD | The menu at this iconic restaurant with its fabulous location by the Tamar River highlights fresh local seafood, mainly from the east coast. Try such dishes as Cape Grim porterhouse steak with crispy sweet potato and pepper jus, or seafood (it might be prawns, scallops, mussels, clams, or fish). **Known for:** great location; local seafood; fun crowd. $ *Average main: A$45* ✉ *13 Park St., Launceston* ☎ *03/6334–0554* 🌐 *www.hallamswaterfront.com.au* *Closed Sun.*

★ **Stillwater**
$$$ | AUSTRALIAN | Part of Ritchie's Mill—a beautifully restored 1830s flour mill beside the Tamar River—this much-lauded restaurant and Launceston institution, serves wonderfully creative seafood dishes, usually with an Asian twist, such as the confit of Macquarie Harbour ocean trout with wasabi mash, trout crackle, and citrus and flying fish roe emulsion, or try the scallop sashimi. The five-course tasting menu includes wine pairings from the great selection of Tasmanian wines. **Known for:** wine bar and gallery on premises, too; fish of the day; five-course tasting menu. $ *Average main: A$45* ✉ *Ritchie's Mill, 2 Bridge Rd., Launceston* ☎ *03/6331–4153* 🌐 *www.stillwater.com.au* *No dinner Sun. and Mon.*

Hotels

Hotel Grand Chancellor
$$ | HOTEL | This modern six-story building in the city center has large rooms that blend classic if slightly bland furnishings with modern conveniences. **Pros:** check-in is a breeze; central location; perfect as a business stay. **Cons:** no leisure facilities; accessibility problems with some rooms; rooms look faded compared to the lobby. $ *Rooms from: A$165* ✉ *29 Cameron St., Launceston* ☎ *03/6334–3434, 800/753–379* 🌐 *www.grandchancellorhotels.com* *165 rooms, 7 suites* *No Meals.*

Peppers Seaport Hotel
$$$ | HOTEL | Superbly situated on the Tamar riverfront, this popular urban-chic hotel is part of the Seaport Dock area and is shaped like a ship. **Pros:** lovely waterfront views from some rooms; immaculate lobby and service; free Wi-Fi. **Cons:** parking costs extra; a long walk to other attractions; the waterfront scene isn't very lively. $ *Rooms from: A$230* ✉ *28 Seaport Blvd., Launceston* ☎ *03/6345–3333* 🌐 *www.peppers.com.au* *60 rooms* *No Meals.*

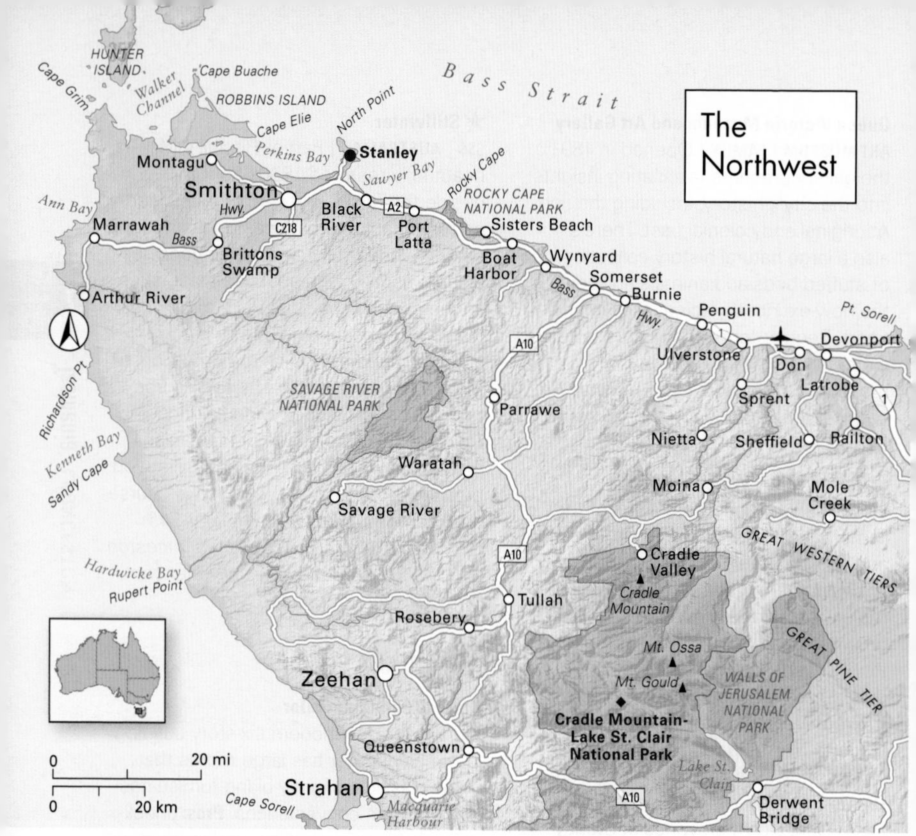

The Northwest

★ **TwoFourTwo**
$$$ | APARTMENT | Three contemporary apartments and a town house built within a historic Launceston property have all modern conveniences, including espresso machines and iPod docks, plus the wonderful timber design work of Alan Livermore, one of the owners. **Pros:** rooms are stylish and well laid out; great hosts; personal touches like fresh flowers. **Cons:** no leisure facilities; no on-site parking; average views. *Rooms from: A$220* *242 Charles St., Launceston* *03/6331–9242* *www.twofourtwo.com.au* *4 apartments* *No Meals.*

Nightlife

The local *Examiner* newspaper is the best source of information on local nightlife and entertainment, but be warned: no one goes to Launceston to party.

★ **Saint John**
BREWPUBS | The Saint John craft brewery and bar joins a proliferation of trendy tearooms, cafés, and bars to solidify Launceston's evolution to hipster status. Try the beers on tap and bar snacks. *133 Saint John St., Launceston* *03/6333–0340* *saintjohncraftbeer.com.au.*

Shopping

Launceston is a convenient place for a little shopping, with most stores central on George Street and in nearby Yorktown Mall. The market each Sunday is a pleasant place for a morning souvenir hunt.

★ **Aspire Adventure Equipment**
SPORTING GOODS | This outdoor adventure store is the perfect place to stock up on all the things you will need for a camping

trip around Tasmania or if you just need an emergency "Tassie tuxedo" to survive the winter. The staff are extremely knowledgeable, and this store stocks a wide variety of quality equipment. ✉ *136 York St., Launceston* ☎ *03/6331–8708* 🌐 *www.aspireadventureequipment.com.au.*

★ **Design Tasmania**

ART GALLERIES | Carrying beautiful items made from Tasmanian wood, this studio carries custom-designed furniture and locally crafted pottery, glass, and clothing. It's also known for its inspiring contemporary art exhibitions and design collections. The center often has an artist in residence and is just a short walk from the city center. ✉ *Brisbane St., Launceston* ☎ *03/6331–5506* 🌐 *www.designtasmania.com.au.*

Activities

There are plenty of opportunities to spot wildlife, fish, or birds in the lovely countryside surrounding Launceston and the Tamar Valley. The Tamar Wetlands is close to Launceston with bird hides and a boardwalk.

BIRD-WATCHING

Tamar Island Wetlands

BIRD WATCHING | **FAMILY** | This bird sanctuary on the banks of the Tamar River just outside Launceston is the ideal place to see purple swamp hens and black swans from boardwalks over the wetlands while scanning the sky for white-breasted sea eagles or forest ravens. Cape Barren Geese have been known to visit on occasion. ✉ *West Tamar Hwy., Riverside* ☎ *03/6327–3964* 🌐 *www.parks.tas.gov.au* 🎫 *Free.*

WALKING

Launceston Historic Walks

HIKING & WALKING | **FAMILY** | This professional outfit conducts a leisurely one-hour sightseeing stroll through the historic heart of the city. The guided walks leave from the 1842 Gallery and present an engaging look at Launceston's charming architecture and the city's colorful past. ✉ *Cimitiere St., Launceston* ☎ *03/6331–2213* 🎫 *A$18.*

ZIP LINING

★ **Hollybank Treetops Adventure**

ZIP LINING | **FAMILY** | Just 15 minutes' drive northeast of Launceston, this popular attraction that's especially appealing to kids, or kids at heart, offers three-hour zip-lining tours through a verdant forest canopy high above the Pipers River. Other on-site activities include Segway and mountain bike tours. ✉ *66 Hollybank Rd., Underwood* ☎ *03/6395–1390* 🌐 *www.treetopsadventure.com.au* 🎫 *From A$125.*

Stanley

140 km (87 miles) northwest of Devonport, 400 km (248 miles) northwest of Hobart.

Stanley is one of the prettiest villages in Tasmania, and a must for anyone traveling in the northwest. A gathering of historic cottages at the foot of the Nut, Tasmania's version of Uluru (Ayers Rock), it's filled with friendly tearooms, interesting shops, and old country inns. Stanley is the gateway to the wild and mysterious Tarkine rain forest.

Sights

Highfield Historic Site

HISTORIC HOME | **FAMILY** | At this atmospheric site you can explore the town's history at the fully restored Regency house and grounds where Van Diemen's Land Company, who settled the estate in 1824, once stood. Day tours are self-guided, but guides in period costumes are on hand to answer any questions. Views over the town and surrounding areas make the trip to Highfield worthwhile. ✉ *Green Hills Rd., Stanley* ☎ *03/6458–1100* 🎫 *A$12.*

The Nut

NATURE SIGHT | **FAMILY** | This sheer volcanic plug that's some 12½ million years old rears up right behind the village—it's almost totally surrounded by the sea. You can ride a chairlift to the top of the 500-foot-high headland, where the views are breathtaking; or, you can make the 20-minute trek on a footpath leading to the summit, where walking trails lead in all directions. It's a stunning place to view birdlife and the whole northwest coastline. ✉ *Browns Rd., Stanley* ☎ *03/6458–1286* 🎫 *Chairlift A$12.*

Beaches

Godfreys Beach

BEACH | FAMILY | Just north of the Nut is Stanley's curving Godfreys Beach, at which you can detect how elements of the region have formed by volcanic activity—note the basalt rock formations. The 1-km (½-mile) beach is largely protected from the region's strong westerly winds, which can lead to waves of 3 feet or higher. A favorite location for serious photographers, this is also a lovely stretch of sand for strolling, but it's a bit chilly for swimming. You can park at the lot near town, at the south end of the sand, where you'll also find a playground. **Amenities:** parking (free); showers; toilets. **Best for:** solitude; walking. ✉ *Green Hill Rd., Stanley.*

Restaurants

Stanley's on the Bay

$$ | AUSTRALIAN | Set on the waterfront in the fully restored old Bond Store, this unpretentious restaurant specializes in succulent steaks and freshly cooked seafood. Try the eye fillet of beef—Australian terminology for the top-quality beef cut—topped with prawns, scallops, and locally caught fish fillets, served in a creamy white-wine sauce. **Known for:** juicy steaks; fresh seafood; nice waterfront location. $ *Average main: A$35* ✉ *15 Wharf Rd., Stanley* ☎ *03/6458–1404* 🌐 *www.stanleyvillage.com.au* ⏲ *Closed Sun. and July and Aug. No lunch.*

Hotels

Beachside Retreat West Inlet

$$ | B&B/INN | FAMILY | These unique, environmentally friendly cabins are located directly on waterfront sand dunes overlooking the sea with kilometers of absolutely private beach frontage. **Pros:** breathtaking views from cabins; guests with special needs are well catered to; wildlife at your door. **Cons:** limited food availability on-site; accessibility issues around getting on the beach; two-night minimum. $ *Rooms from: A$180* ✉ *253 Stanley Hwy., Stanley* ☎ *03/6458–1350* 🌐 *www.beachsideretreat.com* 🛏 *4 cabins* 🍽 *No Meals.*

★ Tarkine Wilderness Lodge

$$$$ | B&B/INN | This superb country lodge sits atop a grassy rise amid ancient rain forest. **Pros:** friendly hosts; ancient rain forest on the property; wildlife experiences. **Cons:** no Wi-Fi; two-night minimum; some distance to any services. $ *Rooms from: A$600* ✉ *Newhaven Track, Meunna, Stanley* ☎ *03/6445–9184* 🌐 *tarkinelodge.com.au* 🛏 *3 rooms* 🍽 *Free Breakfast.*

Activities

★ Tarkine Drive

FOUR-WHEELING | The best way to explore the richness of the Tarkine is by taking a journey of discovery on the northwest section of the Tarkine Drive and South Arthur Drive. There's no better way to enjoy the sights: pretty coastal hamlets, rich agricultural land, cool temperate rain forest, and wild places. Your journey can be as relaxed or as energetic as you like. ✉ *Arthur River* 🌐 *discoverthetarkine.com.au/tarkine-drive* 🎫 *Free.*

★ Tarkine Trails

HIKING & WALKING | Tarkine Trails offers small-group walking experiences into the wilds of the takayna/Tarkine wilderness of Tasmania. Experience ancient rain forest and wild coastlines imbued with the spirit of the oldest living culture on Earth. Their specialty is fostering a quality,

Looking out across Cradle Mountain–Lake St. Clair National Park

deep-immersion wilderness experience in this special place. ⊠ *Stanley* ⊕ *www.tarkinetrails.com.au* 🎫 *$A1995.*

Cradle Mountain–Lake St. Clair National Park

173 km (107 miles) northwest of Hobart to Lake St. Clair at the southern end of the park, 85 km (53 miles) southwest of Devonport, 181 km (113 miles) from Launceston, 155 km (97 miles) northeast from Strahan to Cradle Mountain at the northern end of the park.

This expansive, remote park contains some of the most spectacular alpine scenery and mountain trails in Australia. Popular with hikers of all abilities, the park has several high peaks, including Mt. Ossa, the highest in Tasmania (more than 5,300 feet).

ESSENTIALS

VISITOR CENTERS Cradle Mountain Visitor Centre. ⊠ *4057 Cradle Mountain Rd., Cradle Mountain* ☎ *03/6492–1110* ⊕ *www.parks.tas.gov.au.* **Lake St. Clair Visitor Centre.** ⊠ *Lake St. Clair National Park, Derwent Bridge* ☎ *03/6289–1172* ⊕ *www.parks.tas.gov.au.*

Sights

★ Cradle Mountain–Lake St. Clair National Park

MOUNTAIN | FAMILY | The Cradle Mountain section of the park lies in the north. The southern section of the park, centered on Lake St. Clair, is popular for boating and hiking. Many walking trails lead from the settlement at the southern end of the lake, which is surrounded by mountain peaks and dense forest. Visitors are advised to park their cars in the free lot and then make use of the shuttle bus that runs from the Cradle Mountain Visitor Centre and makes stops at all the trails.

One of the most famous trails in Australia, the Overland Track traverses 65 km (40 miles) between the park's northern and southern boundaries. The walk usually takes six days, depending on the weather, and on clear days the mountain scenery seems to stretch forever. Hikers are charged A$200 to do the Overland during peak walking season (October to May). ✉ *Cradle Mountain–Lake St. Clair National Park, Cradle Mountain* ☎ *03/6492–1110* 🌐 *parks.tas.gov.au/explore-our-parks/cradle-mountain* 🎫 *A$20 per person.*

Hotels

Cradle Mountain Hotel

$$ | RESORT | Five minutes' drive from the entrance to the national park is this upmarket lodge, complete with rooms that face the woods and have perching posts for local birds. **Pros:** tours from the door; delicious meals in fine-dining restaurant; on-site art gallery. **Cons:** no mobile reception on-site; only average views; can be packed with corporate events. $ *Rooms from: A$200* ✉ *3718 Cradle Mountain Rd., Cradle Mountain* ☎ *03/6492–1404* 🌐 *www.cradlemountainhotel.com.au* *60 rooms* *No Meals.*

Discovery Holiday Parks, Cradle Mountain

$ | HOUSE | FAMILY | Near the forest at the northern edge of the park, Discovery Holiday Parks is the best budget accommodation in the area, with campgrounds, RV sites, four-bed bunkhouses with cooking facilities, and self-contained cabins with kitchens. **Pros:** free Internet; family-friendly and good-value accommodation; wildlife abounds on-site. **Cons:** Wi-Fi doesn't reach most cabins; most expensive spa cabins are pricey; reception closes early. $ *Rooms from: A$45* ✉ *3832 Cradle Mountain Rd., Cradle Mountain* ☎ *03/6492–1395* 🌐 *www.discoveryholidayparks.com.au* *38 unpowered sites, 10 powered sites, 75 bunkhouse beds, 36 cabins* *No Meals.*

★ **Peppers Cradle Mountain Lodge**

$$$ | RESORT | FAMILY | This charming lodge with its collection of wood cabins dotted around the wilderness of Cradle Mountain Valley is a firm favorite with park visitors. **Pros:** great spa; good range of food options; fireplaces are a hit in winter. **Cons:** Internet restricted to the lobby; no TVs; no room service. $ *Rooms from: A$240* ✉ *4038 Cradle Mountain Rd., Cradle Mountain* ☎ *1300/806–192* 🌐 *www.cradlemountainlodge.com.au* *58 rooms, 28 suites* *Free Breakfast.*

Chapter 8

SOUTH EAST QUEENSLAND

8

Updated by
Melissa Fagan

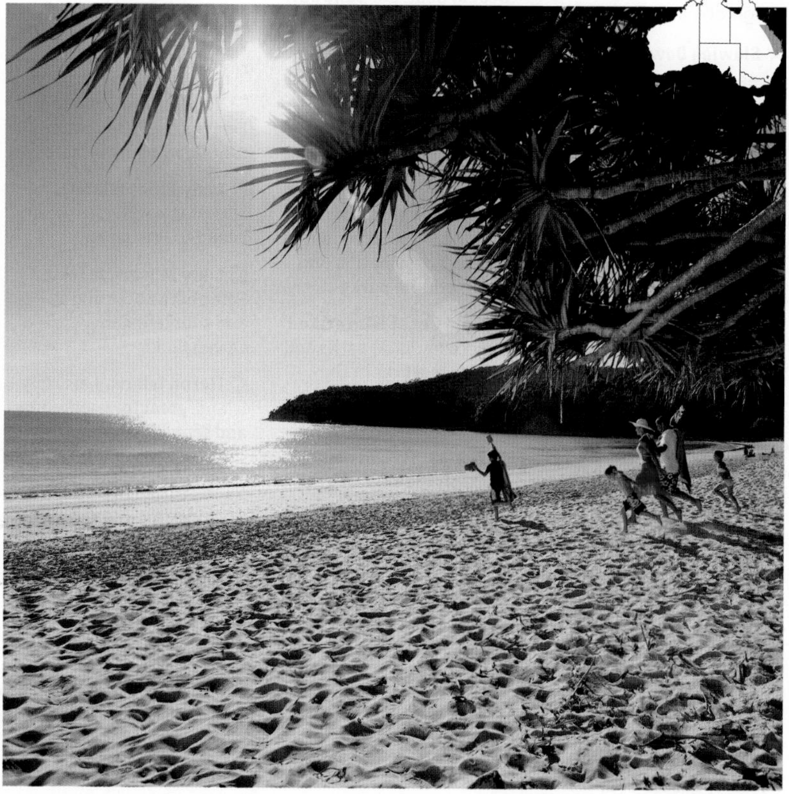

Sights	Restaurants	Hotels	Shopping	Nightlife
★★★★★	★★★★☆	★★★★☆	★★★☆☆	★★★☆☆

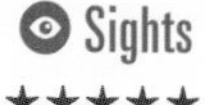

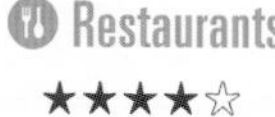

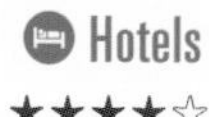

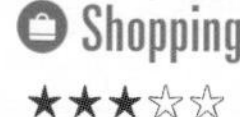

WELCOME TO SOUTH EAST QUEENSLAND

TOP REASONS TO GO

★ **Getting Wild:** Reefs teeming with fish, rays, and turtles; pristine rain forests filled with rare birds and reptiles; unspoiled beaches and islands; meandering rivers and dramatic gorges; and of course, kangaroos and koalas.

★ **Slowing Down:** Queensland has a relaxed and welcoming vibe, even at the upmarket hotels and fine-dining restaurants.

★ **Going Local:** From Indigenous-led tours, to wineries, microbreweries, local produce-driven restaurants, and a thriving local music scene, the region is ripe with homegrown goodness.

★ **Being Forever Young:** The Gold Coast's theme parks provide endless thrills; the region is also an outdoor adventure-lover's playground, with some of the world's best surf breaks, diving, hiking, and more.

★ **Savoring the Arts:** Brisbane's Gallery of Modern Art and the Gold Coast's Home of the Arts, performance centers, galleries, and art spaces are world-class.

1 **Brisbane.** Queensland's lively capital and 2032 Olympic city.

2 **Southern Downs.** Home to Queensland's best viticultural regions.

3 **Coomera and Oxenford.** These northern Gold Coast suburbs are all about theme parks.

4 **Southport and Main Beach.** Boat, bike, and surf along the Gold Coast's northern peninsula.

5 **Surfers Paradise and Broadbeach.** Glittering strip of high-rises towering above white sand beaches.

6 **Burleigh Heads and Beyond.** Popular foodie and surf destination and great wildlife parks.

7 **Gold Coast Hinterland.** Superb national parks and nature reserves in the heart of the Gondwana rain forests.

8 **Noosa.** Stylish resort town on the edge of a national park.

9 **Peregian and Coolum.** A great base for exploring the Sunshine Coast.

10 **Maroochydore.** Popular beach town with great beaches.

11 **Mooloolaba.** Cute town with a lively Esplanade.

12 **Caloundra.** Nine beaches from family-friendly to surfer-friendly, with views over the Glass House Mountains.

13 **Glass House Mountains Area.** Home to famous Australia Zoo and ancient volcanic mountains.

14 **Montville.** Artsy mountain village.

15 **Maleny.** Eclectic rural village with scenic reserve.

16 **Yandina and Eumundi.** Famous markets, restaurants, and a ginger factory.

17 **Lady Elliot Island.** The closest Great Barrier Reef island to Brisbane.

18 **Lady Musgrave Island.** Some of the best diving and snorkeling in Queensland.

19 **Heron Island.** Leisurely island, great for snorkeling and scuba diving.

20 **Great Keppel Island.** Palm-fringed beaches, great hiking, and unspoiled coral.

21 **K'gari (Fraser Island).** Unique island with multicolor sand cliffs, rain forest, whale-watching, and Aboriginal sites.

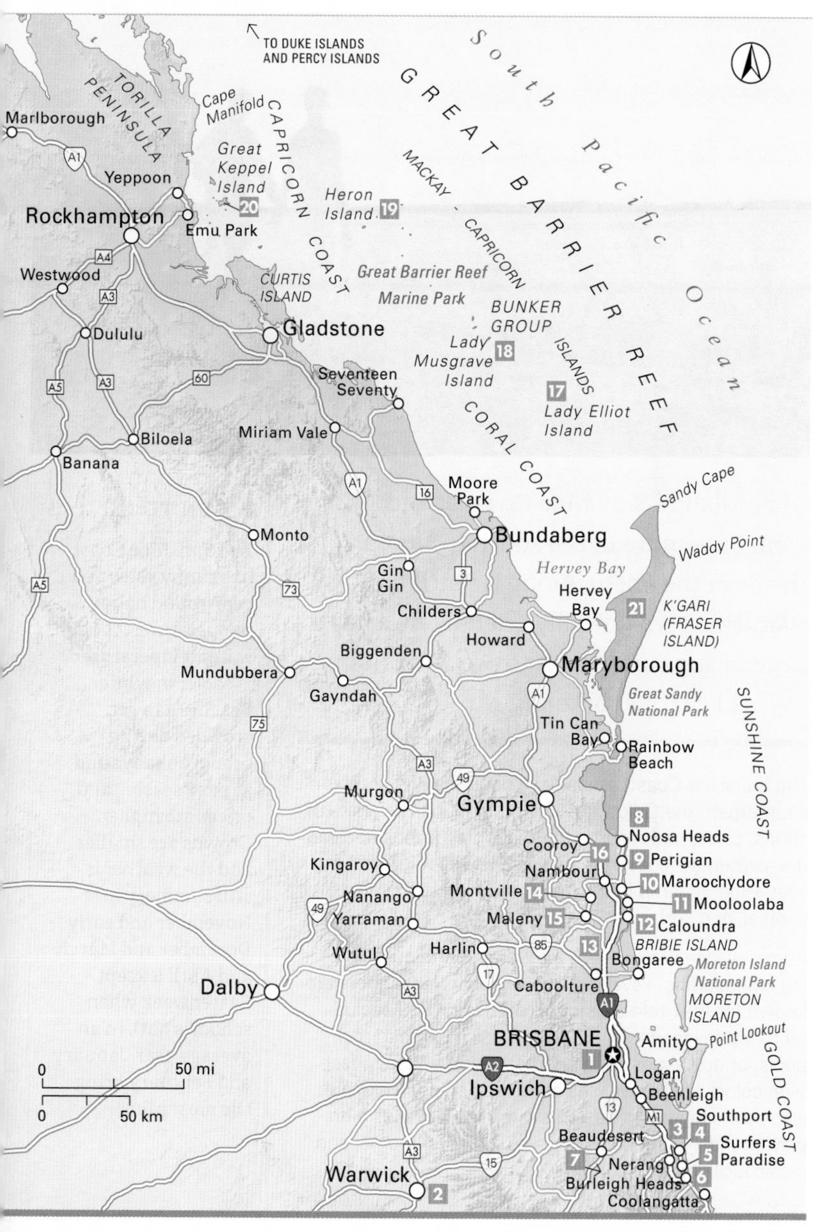

TO DUKE ISLANDS AND PERCY ISLANDS
South Pacific Ocean
GREAT BARRIER REEF
TORILLA PENINSULA
Cape Manifold
CAPRICORN COAST
Marlborough
Great Keppel Island
20
MACKAY CAPRICORN
Heron Island
19
Yeppoon
Rockhampton
Emu Park
Westwood
CURTIS ISLAND
Great Barrier Reef Marine Park
BUNKER GROUP ISLANDS
Dululu
Gladstone
Lady Musgrave Island
18
Seventeen Seventy
17
Lady Elliot Island
CORAL COAST
Miriam Vale
Biloela
Banana
Moore Park
Sandy Cape
Monto
Bundaberg
Waddy Point
Hervey Bay
Gin Gin
Hervey Bay
21
K'GARI (FRASER ISLAND)
Childers
Howard
Biggenden
Maryborough
Mundubbera
Gayndah
Great Sandy National Park
SUNSHINE COAST
Tin Can Bay
Rainbow Beach
Murgon
Gympie
8
Noosa Heads
Cooroy
16
9 Perigian
Kingaroy
Nambour
10 Maroochydore
Montville 14
Nanango
11 Mooloolaba
Maleny 15
Yarraman
12 Caloundra
BRIBIE ISLAND
Harlin
13
Wutul
Bongaree
Moreton Island National Park
Caboolture
MORETON ISLAND
Dalby
BRISBANE
Amity
Point Lookout
1
GOLD COAST
0
50 mi
Logan
Ipswich
Beenleigh
0
50 km
Southport
3 4
Beaudesert
Surfers Paradise
5
7
Nerang
Warwick
Burleigh Heads
6
2
Coolangatta
A1
A4
A3
A5
60
16
73
3
75
49
A2
85
17
13
M1
15

SUNSHINE COAST'S TOP BEACHES

Queensland's Sunshine Coast stretches from Caloundra in the south to Noosa Heads in the north. Along it you'll find everything from family-friendly beaches to thundering surf breaks to pretty sheltered coves ideal for snorkeling.

The Sunshine Coast is less developed than its southern counterpart, the Gold Coast. Although it has its share of shops, cafés, and resorts, there are still dozens of clean, uncrowded beaches where you can sunbathe, stroll, cast a line, or jump in the unspoiled waters to swim, snorkel, and surf.

Some beaches are perfect for water sports such as sailing, windsurfing, kayaking, or wakeboarding. Others are known for their reliable surf breaks. You'll find secluded rocky coves where you can "fossick" among rock pools, or don a mask and snorkel to come face-to-face with colorful fish, rays, sea stars, and squid. There are also safe, lifeguard-patrolled swimming beaches with playgrounds, skate parks, kiosks, changing rooms, and picnic facilities ideal for families.

WHEN TO GO

The Sunshine Coast has sunny skies and year-round balmy temperatures, though water temperature is cooler in winter. Beaches can get crowded during school holidays and at peak season, and prices are higher. Crowds are smaller and the weather is still summery in November and early December and March and April (except Easter week when school is out). In an average year, January and February bring the most rain.

SUNSHINE BEACH

Lovely Sunshine Beach, the last easterly facing beach before Noosa, is patrolled year-round. Beach breaks, reliable swell, a rocky headland sheltering it from winds, and clear, glassy water make Sunshine popular with surfers. When northeasterlies blow, surf the protected northern pocket. Fish off the beach year-round for dart, bream, and flathead, or cast a long line into deep water to hook numerous seasonal species. Use covered picnic areas, barbecues, toilets, and parking.

MOOLOOLABA BEACH

This super-safe, family-friendly swimming beach is patrolled year-round, and has just enough swell to make it fun. There are shady picnic areas with barbecues, playgrounds, showers, toilets, and parking—as well as the local meeting point, the Loo with a View. Stroll south along the coastal path to the river mouth and rock wall (off which you can fish, year-round, for bream); north to Alexandra Headland for views of the bay; or along Mooloolaba Esplanade, lined with casual eateries and boutiques. Surfers might want to check out the point break just over the northern side of Alexandra Headland.

COOLUM BEACH

Coolum Beach is a popular choice for families, boasting a surf club, skate park, playgrounds, changing rooms, toilets, kiosks, shorefront parks, and picnic areas. A long, white-sand beach, Coolum is patrolled year-round, and has a nice beach break and some decent waves off the headland. Fish from the beach in the evening for grouper, tailor, bream, and dart; catch bream around the headland, especially in winter. Walk south along the boardwalk to the headland park for magnificent coastal views, or north to quieter Peregian Beach with its patrolled surf, playground, and adjacent Environmental Park.

SAFETY

Most popular Sunshine Coast beaches are patrolled by lifeguards in school holiday and peak periods and on weekends throughout the warmer months. On some Sunshine Coast beaches, sandbanks, strong currents, and riptides make surf conditions challenging. Even on patrolled beaches, swimming unaccompanied is not recommended.

Swim between the red-and-yellow flags, and follow lifeguards' directives. Locals are often the best sources of advice on where and when to dive in.

Sharks are rarely a problem; however, lifeguards keep watch and issue warnings if they're sighted. A more constant hazard is the harsh Queensland sun: apply SPF50-plus sunscreen at regular intervals. Get information on local beaches at coastalwatch.com, and surf reports on Surf Life Saving Queensland's website, *lifesaving.com.au*. Contact SLSQ Lifesaving at 07/3846–8000.

COASTAL AND WILDERNESS WALKS

South East Queensland lays claim to some of the world's most superb wilderness areas. In the hinterlands of the Gold and Sunshine coasts are national parks, forests, and nature reserves dense with trails and walkways. Several also trace scenic sections of the coastline.

In parts of the Gold Coast, trails wind along the beachfront, trace rain-forest-clad headlands, and meander through waterfront reserves. The Sunshine Coast's Coastal Pathway stretches the entire length of the coast, 73 km (45 miles) in total, giving walkers and cyclists access to beaches, lookouts, and coastal towns, as well as world-class scenery.

There are a string of national parks and wilderness areas across South East Queensland, with trails of varying lengths and degrees of difficulty. Walkers are rewarded with memorable sights: dramatic waterfalls and pristine pools, tracts of ancient rain forest, and glowworm caves; wildflowers, wildlife, and exceptional views, some stretching as far as the coast.

SAFETY

For bushwalking you'll need sturdy shoes with grip, a hat, sunscreen, insect repellent, wet- and cold-weather gear, drinking water, food, camping equipment and permits (if overnighting), and a map and compass. Leech-proof yourself by wearing long socks over your pant legs and carrying a lighter to burn off any hitchhikers. Let others know your planned route and timing, even for day hikes.

QUEENSLAND'S GREAT WALKS

If your schedule allows it, tackle one of Queensland's Great Walks. A A$10-million state government initiative, the Great Walks aim to allow visitors of all ages and of average fitness to explore significant wilderness areas in a safe, eco-sensitive way.

A standout is the 54-km (34-mile) Gold Coast Hinterland Great Walk, linking the species-rich, Gondwana Rainforests of Australia World Heritage Area of Lamington and Springbrook plateaus via the glorious Numinbah Valley. En route, you'll traverse ancient volcanic terrain and pristine rain forest, passing torrential streams and waterfalls and 3,000-year-old hoop pines. Allow three days for the full walk, camping at designated sites en route, or trek just one section.

The Sunshine Coast Hinterland Great Walk, a 58-km (36-mile) hike traversing the Blackall Range northwest of Brisbane, includes sections of Kondalilla and Mapleton Falls national parks, Maleny Forest Reserve, and Delicia Road Conservation Park. The four- to six-day hike takes you past waterfalls and through open eucalypt and lush subtropical rain forest teeming with native birds, reptiles, and frogs.

The Cooloola Great Walk meanders through Great Sandy National Park north of Noosa. A 90-km (55-mile) network of graded walking tracks passes the spectacular multihue sand dunes of Rainbow Beach, and includes walks of varying distances and difficulty across a range of conditions.

K'gari (Fraser Island) Great Walk rewards hikers with exceptional scenery—wide, white-sand beaches, pristine deep-blue lakes, rain-forest tracts, and plenty of birds, reptiles, wallabies, and dingoes.

SHORTER OPTIONS

Coastal Trails. Compact Burleigh Head National Park, midway between Surfer's Paradise and Coolangatta, includes coastal rain forest and heath that's home to wallabies, koalas, lizards, snakes, and brush turkeys. Trek the 2 km (1-mile) Rainforest Circuit for excellent views, or the shadier, shorter, 1 km (.75-mile) Oceanview Walk. Noosa National Park offers a range of options, from the 1 km (.7-mile) return Palm Grove walk to the 10 km return Coastal Walk, which takes you around bush-covered headlands and pristine bays.

Hinterland Trails. Mt. Tamborine, Springwood, Witches Falls-Joalah, and Lamington national parks in the Gold Coast Hinterland are all ideal for exploring on foot. Several wilderness retreats in the region include guided bushwalks as part of the package. West of the Sunshine Coast, short scenic walking trails in Kondallilla National Park take you past waterfalls, boulder-strewn streams, and lush rain forest.

The sunny climes of South East Queensland attracts everyone from families, partygoers, nature-lovers, to escapists. Whether you want to surf or soak in the Pacific Ocean, enjoy fresh cuisine with local flourishes, sip from your favorite cocktail or microbrewed beer, chill out at a health retreat, hike through subtropical rain forests, or join seabirds and turtles on a pristine coral isle—it's all here.

Local license plates deem Queensland "The Sunshine State"—a laid-back stretch of beaches and sun where many Australians head for their vacations. The state has actively promoted tourism, and areas such as the Gold Coast, an hour south of Brisbane, and the Sunshine Coast, a roughly equivalent distance north of the capital, offer high-rise hotels, nightclubs, trendy bars, markets and cafés, shopping precincts, and a variety of water-based activities. These thriving coastal strips are the major attraction of southern Queensland for Australians and foreign tourists alike—along with a scattering of islands, notably Fraser Island, off Hervey Bay, and the Mackay-Capricorn islands lying on the southern end of the Great Barrier Reef.

Queensland is a vibrant and cosmopolitan place to visit, and while elsewhere in Australia, Queenslanders may have a reputation for being parochial and even backward, the state—especially the South East—is home to an increasingly diverse population. Still, as with many regions blessed with abundant sunshine, the lifestyle here is relaxed.

MAJOR REGIONS

Brisbane. Queensland's capital city is a breezily cheerful, increasingly sophisticated city with cultural attractions, great restaurants, nightlife, and galleries all centered on the city's sprawling river. If the Brisbane cityscape gives you a thirst for pastoral rolling hills—and fabulous wine—you're in luck, because some of Queensland's best viticultural regions like **Southern Downs** lie within a two-hour drive of the city

The Gold Coast. An hour's drive south of Brisbane, Queensland's first coastal resort has a bit of everything—from the high-rise glitz of Surfers Paradise to the retro holiday vibes of Burleigh and Palm Beach, action-packed theme parks, upmarket eateries, hidden bars, and hectic clubs. Take a surf lesson on some of world's best-known breaks, walk down to the beach and curl your toes in the sand, or for something different drive west and spend a day (or several) exploring the lush Gold Coast Hinterland.

The Sunshine Coast is a 60-km (37-mile) stretch of white-sand beaches, inlets, lakes, and mountains that begins at the Glass House Mountains, an hour's drive north of Brisbane, and extends to Rainbow Beach in the north. Kenilworth is its inland extreme, 40 km (25 miles) from the ocean. For the most part, the Sunshine Coast is less developed than its southern cousin, the Gold Coast. Although there are plenty of stylish restaurants and luxurious hotels, this coast is best loved for its national parks, secluded coves, and relaxed beachside towns like Noosa, Peregian, Coolum, Maroochydore, Mooloolaba, and Caloundra.

The Sunshine Coast Hinterland, extending from the Glass House Mountains just northwest of Brisbane to Eumundi and Yandina, west of the northern Sunshine Coast town of Noosa, is ideal terrain for day-trippers. Tracts of subtropical rain forest and mountainous areas linked by scenic drives and walking trails are interspersed with charming hillside villages, their main streets lined with cafés, galleries, gift shops, and guesthouses. Here you'll also find thriving markets; renowned restaurants and cooking schools; ginger, nut, and pineapple farms; theme and wildlife parks; and luxury B&Bs. The hinterland's southerly extent is the nine distinctive conical outcrops of the Glass House Mountains—the eroded remnants of ancient volcanoes—rising dramatically from a flattish landscape 45 km (27 miles) northwest of Brisbane. Meander north through the mountains to reach the arty village of Maleny and the quaint, European-style Montville. Continue north to the towns of Yandina and Eumundi, where among other treasures, you'll find much-lauded restaurant Spirit House and the Ginger Factory, and thriving markets.

Despite its name, **the Mackay–Capricorn Islands,** a group of islands lying offshore between Bundaberg and Rockhampton, is closer to the southern half of Queensland than it is to the city of Mackay. They comprise the section of the Great Barrier Reef known as Capricorn Marine Park, which stretches for 140 km (87 miles) and cuts through the Tropic of Capricorn, Heron Island being the closest point. Heron, Wilson, Lady Musgrave, Lady Elliot, and Great Keppel islands are great for wildlife: turtles use several of the islands as breeding grounds; seabirds nest here; and humpback whales pass through on their migration to Antarctica each spring—generally between July and October.

A gigantic sand island off Hervey Bay, **K'gari (F raser Island)** is paradise for the active visitor. What it lacks in luxe amenities it makes up for in scenery: miles of white-sand beaches, deep-blue lakes, and bushland bristling with wildlife—including some of the world's most purebred dingoes.

Planning

When to Go

Temperatures average 15.6°C (60°F) between May and September with chillier nights, and 20°C (68°F) to 29°C (80°F) December to February. From December through March, expect high humidity and periods of heavy rain. Temperatures run slightly cooler inland. Sea- and reef-side Queensland tends to fill up from mid-December through January and can also be heavily booked in July, September, and throughout Easter. There's no daylight saving time in the state.

Planning Your Time

If you're after a quick, Miami Beach–style holiday, fly into Brisbane and head straight for the glitzy Gold Coast, overnighting in Surfers Paradise. You could end the spree with a final night and morning in nearby Lamington National Park, renowned for its subtropical wilderness and birdlife.

If you have a bit more time, do three days on shore and two days on the reef. Stay a night in Brisbane, then head to the Sunshine Coast for a hike in the Glasshouse Mountains on the way to Noosa Heads. When you've had your fill of beaches and surf, take a leisurely drive through the Sunshine Coast's lovely hinterland villages for quaint shops and cafés and stunning natural scenery. Then make your way north to Bundaberg or Gladstone for a flight to Lady Elliot, Heron, or Wilson islands to wildlife-watch, dive, and snorkel; or a ferry to K'gari (Fraser Island), off Hervey Bay, where you can swim in pristine lakes, 4WD along beaches stretching 80 km (50 miles), and see wild dingoes.

Unless you're keen to see everything, limit yourself to a few areas—**Brisbane,** its surrounding **Sunshine and Gold coasts,** K'gari, or the coral isles of the Mackay-Capricorn group—taking three to four days to explore each. Extended stays also allow for bushwalking expeditions in national parks, trips to resorts on the reef, traipsing around the wineries of Queensland's **Southern Downs,** and enjoying the state's many theme parks.

Getting Here and Around

AIR

Qantas (*www.qantas.com.au*), Virgin Australia (*www.virginaustralia.com*), and a number of other carriers fly direct from U.S. cities to Australian capitals and regional tourist hubs. Qantas, Virgin Australia, and Jetstar (*www.jetstar.com.au*) link several regional centers throughout Queensland. Rex (*www.rex.com.au*), has an extensive network across regional Queensland.

BOAT

Ferries and charter boats ply the waters between the South East Queensland mainland and its various islands and offshore resorts. Most make daily or more frequent return trips; some carry vehicles as well as passengers.

BUS

Buses service most major towns and tourist areas around South East Queensland, and are reliable and affordable—though on many routes it's as cheap, and faster, to fly. During holiday periods on popular routes buses are often heavily booked; buy tickets in advance, and don't expect to stretch out, even on overnight services. Tourist offices can advise which companies go where.

CAR

Traveling outside of cities is often simplest and most comfortable by car. Roads are generally good, but signage varies in clarity; study maps and work out highway exits in advance (although most hire cars will have GPS installed). Be prepared for heavy traffic between Brisbane and the Gold and Sunshine coasts in peak periods. Expect temporary road closures and detours after heavy rains. Roads are narrow and winding in some parts of the hinterlands. You'll need a 4X4 to get around Fraser Island, the sand islands of Moreton Bay, and some national park roads and Outback tracks. You can rent a small runabout from about A$25 per day, a decent touring car from about A$30 a day, an SUV or four-wheel drive from A$35 a day, and a passenger van from about A$80 per day (based on a weekly rental period). Gas costs vary, and tend to be pricier away from major towns and highways.

TRAIN

Frequent trains service routes between the capital and the Gold and Sunshine coasts, connecting with G:Link light-rail for access to beach resorts on the Gold Coast. In the Sunshine Coast, transfers are required to major beach resorts. The Queensland Rail network links regional towns and tourist centers, and is a scenic way to travel (though on longer routes it's often cheaper to fly). The *Spirit of Queensland* and high-speed *Tilt Train* ply the coast between Brisbane and Cairns, servicing towns that act as launching pads for island resorts.

Restaurants

South East Queensland has come into its own as a foodie hub. Cosmopolitan Brisbane boasts its share of Modern Australian, Mediterranean, and Asian-influenced menus capitalizing on fresh regional produce, as well as local wines and local microbrew beers. The cuisine at many of Queensland's high-end resorts now rivals the standards of big-city fine dining. Open-air market-style dining is available year-round in Brisbane, and increasingly, on the coasts—featuring food trucks, live music, and a convivial atmosphere. Coastal tourist towns are full of casual open-air restaurants that take advantage of the tropical climate—an increasing number of them helmed by city-class chefs. If you're on the road, an old-fashioned pub meal is more than satisfying and a great way to get to know the locals.

Hotels

Accommodations in this region run the gamut from rain-forest lodges, boutique hotels, Outback pubs, backpacker hostels, and colonial "Queenslander" bed-and-breakfasts—beautiful timber houses built high on stilts, with wraparound verandas and character windows—to deluxe beachside resorts and big-city hotels. The luxury resorts are clustered around the major tourist areas of the Gold and Sunshine coasts and nearby islands such as Heron and Wilson. In smaller coastal towns, accommodation is mostly in motels, apartments, and B&Bs. There is a range of eco-friendly accommodation options, which utilize green technologies such as renewable energy and water conservation systems to minimize their impact on the environs. Many of Queensland's island resorts fall into this category.

Restaurant and hotel reviews have been shortened. For full information, visit Fodors.com.

What It Costs in Australian Dollars

$	$$	$$$	$$$$
RESTAURANTS			
under A$21	A$21–A$35	A$36–A$50	over A$50
HOTELS			
under A$151	A$151–A$200	A$201–A$300	over A$300

Tours

Guided day tours are a simple way to see Brisbane if your schedule is tight. View the city's many attractions from the comfort of a chauffeured coach, with a driver giving insider information. Buses are also great for covering the relatively short distances between Brisbane and nearly all of the mainland attractions. Within an hour or two you can be taste-testing your way through the Tambourine or Scenic Rim wineries, or making friends with local wildlife—feeding dolphins, whale-watching, or having your photo taken with a koala!

Most day tours include admission to sights, refreshments, and on full-day tours, lunch, as well as commentary en route and time to explore.

JPT Tour Group
Also known as Australian Day Tours, this company conducts transfers, half-, full-, and multiday tours across popular sites in Brisbane, Moreton Island, the Gold and Sunshine coasts, K'gari (Fraser Island), and more. ✉ *Shop 6, 9 Trickett St., Surfers Paradise* ☎ *07/5630–1602 outside Australia, 1300/781–362* 🌐 *www.daytours.com.au* 🎫 *From A$60.*

Queensland Day Tours
This group runs day tours to some of South East Queensland's most popular beach and hinterland destinations, including the Gold Coast, Springbrook and Mt. Tamborine, as well as Minjerribah (North Stradbroke Island), and Moreton Island. Tour options include wildlife encounters, whale- and dolphin-watching, brewery tours, and more. ☎ *0488/332–257* 🌐 *www.qdtours.com.au* 🎫 *From A$169.*

Brisbane

Called Meanjin by the local Jagera and Turrbal people, the city of Brisbane was first occupied by white settlers in 1824 as a penal colony. Today the city sprawls out along the wide, meandering Brisbane River (Maiwar). Many beautiful timber Queenslander homes, built in the 1800s, still dot the riverbanks and inner suburbs, and in spring the city's numerous parks erupt in a riot of colorful jacaranda, poinciana, and bougainvillea blossoms. Today the Queensland capital is one of Australia's most up-and-coming cities: glittering high-rises mark its polished business center, slick fashion boutiques, restaurants, and start-up businesses abound, and numerous outdoor attractions beckon. In summer, the city swelters with high daytime temperatures and stifling humidity—which may explain the ongoing popularity of air-conditioned cinemas. Wear SPF 50-plus sunscreen and a broad-brimmed hat outdoors, even on overcast days.

Brisbane's inner suburbs, a 5- to 10-minute drive or 15- to 20-minute walk from the city center, have a mix of intriguing eateries, funky watering holes, and quiet accommodations. Fortitude Valley combines Chinatown with a cosmopolitan mix of clubs, cafés, and boutiques. Spring Hill has several high-quality hotels, and Paddington, New Farm, Petrie Terrace, West End, and Woolloongabba feature an eclectic mix of restaurants, bars, and markets. Brisbane is also a convenient base for trips to the Sunshine and Gold coasts, the mountainous hinterlands, and the Moreton Bay islands.

GETTING HERE AND AROUND

AIR

Brisbane is Queensland's major transit hub. Qantas, Virgin Australia, Jetstar, and Rex fly to all Australian capital cities and many regional hubs around Queensland, including the Gold, Sunshine, and Whitsunday coasts.

Brisbane International Airport is 9 km (5½ miles) from the city center. Con-x-ion operates a bus service to meet all flights and drops passengers door to door at major hotels throughout Brisbane, the Gold Coast, Noosa and Hervey Bay. The one-way fare is A$15 to Brisbane, A$35 to Surfers Paradise hotels, and A$51 to Noosa, with cheaper deals available for families.

Airtrain has rail services to stations throughout Brisbane and the Gold Coast. The one-way fare is A$19.50 per person, or A$37 for a round-trip from the airport to the city (discounts apply for groups and tickets purchased online). Trains depart up to four times an hour, taking 20 minutes to reach the city center. Kids (5–14 years) travel free. Taxis to downtown Brisbane cost A$45 to A$55, depending on time of day.

CONTACTS Brisbane Airtrain. ☎ *07/3216–3308, 1800/119–091* 🌐 *www.airtrain.com.au.* **Brisbane International Airport.** ✉ *Airport*

Dr., Brisbane Airport ☎ *07/3406–3000* 🌐 *www.bne.com.au.*

BOAT AND FERRY

CityCat boats and City Ferries dock at 25 points along the Brisbane River from Hamilton to St. Lucia, running every 15 minutes or more for most of the day (the last service is at 11:45 pm). There is also a peak-hour SpeedyCat express service with limited stops. The ferries are terrific for a quick survey of the Brisbane waterfront, from the city skyline to luxury homes and beautiful parkland. If you're staying within the CBD and South Bank, try the free CityHopper ferry, which runs every 30 minutes between 6 am and midnight every day.

CONTACTS CityCat ferries. ☎ *131–230* 🌐 *www.translink.com.au.*

BUS

Greyhound Australia, the country's only nationwide bus line, travels to around 1,100 destinations. Bus stops are well signposted, and vehicles usually run on schedule. It's 1,716 km (1,064 miles), a 30-hour journey, between Brisbane and Cairns. Book in person at Greyhound's Roma Street office, by phone, or online. Purchase point-to-point tickets or flexible passes that allow multiple stops. Most buses are also equipped with USB ports and Wi-Fi.

Crisps Coaches operates a morning and afternoon service from Brisbane to the Southern Downs and towns to the city's south and west. TransLink's help line and website can help you find bus lines that run to your destination.

BUS CONTACTS Con-x-ion. ☎ *1300/266–946* 🌐 *www.con-x-ion.com.* **Crisps Coaches.** ✉ *78 Grafton St., Warwick* ☎ *07/4661–8333* 🌐 *www.crisps.com.au.* **Greyhound Australia—Brisbane Travel Center.** ✉ *Brisbane Transit Centre, Level 3, 151–171 Roma St., City Center* ☎ *07/3736–2601, 1300/473–946* 🌐 *www.greyhound.com.au.* **TransLink.** ☎ *131–230* 🌐 *www.translink.com.au.*

RENTAL CAR

Most major car rental companies have offices in Brisbane, including Avis, Thrifty, Budget, and Hertz. Four-wheel-drive vehicles, motor homes, and camper vans (sleeping two to six people) are available from Britz, and Maui Rentals. If you're heading north along the coast or northwest into the bush, you can rent in Brisbane and drop off in Cairns or other towns. One-way rental fees usually apply.

Brisbane is 1,002 km (621 miles) from Sydney, a 12-hour drive along the Pacific Highway (Highway 1). Another route follows Highway 1 to Newcastle, then heads inland on the New England Highway (Highway 15). Either drive can be made in a long day, although two days or more are recommended for ample time to rest and sightsee.

RENTAL CONTACTS Britz Australia Campervan Hire and Car Rentals. ✉ *21 Industry Ct., Eagle Farm* ☎ *07/3868–1248, 1300/738–087* 🌐 *www.britz.com.au.* **Maui Australia Motorhome Rentals and Car Hire.** ✉ *21 Industry Ct., Eagle Farm* ☎ *07/3868–1248, 1800/827–821* 🌐 *www.maui-rentals.com/au.*

TAXI

Taxis are metered and relatively inexpensive. They are usually available at designated taxi stands outside hotels, downtown, and at Brisbane Transit and Roma Street stations, although it is often best to phone for one. Ride-sharing service Uber is also available to anyone with the smartphone app. Fares are often cheaper than traditional taxis.

TAXI CONTACTS Black and White Cabs. ☎ *133–222* 🌐 *www.blackandwhitecabs.com.au.* **13 Cabs.** ✉ *Brisbane* ☎ *132–227* 🌐 *book.13cabs.com.au.* **Uber.** ✉ *Brisbane* 🌐 *www.uber.com/cities/brisbane.*

TRAIN

CountryLink trains make the 14-hour journey between Sydney and Brisbane. Rail services from Brisbane city and airport to the Gold Coast run regularly

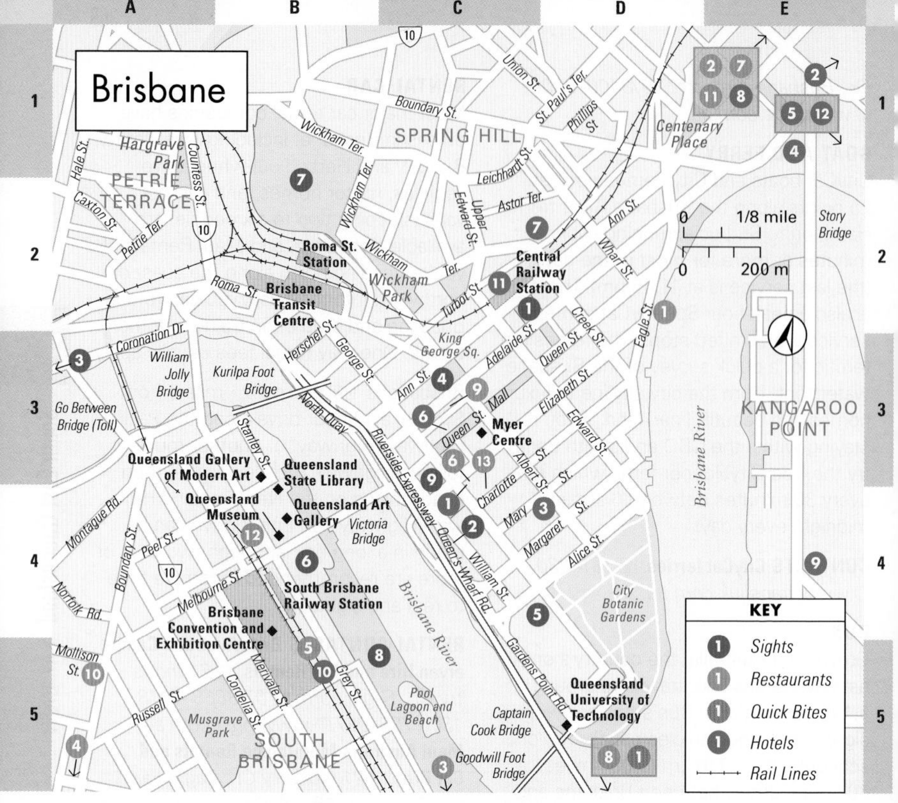

Sights

1 Anzac Square and the Shrine of Remembrance **C2**
2 The Commissariat Store Museum **C4**
3 Lone Pine Koala Sanctuary................ **A3**
4 Museum of Brisbane.... **C3**
5 Parliament House........ **C4**
6 Queensland Cultural Centre.................... **B4**
7 Roma Street Parkland **B2**
8 South Bank Parklands................. **C5**
9 Treasury Casino & Hotel.................... **C3**

Restaurants

1 Blackbird Bar & Grill........................ **D2**
2 Breakfast Creek Hotel... **E1**
3 Cafe O-Mai **C5**
4 Caravanserai........... **A5**
5 The Charming Squire... **B5**
6 Donna Chang............ **C3**
7 e'cco **E1**
8 Enoteca 1889........... **D5**
9 Felix for Goodness....... **C3**
10 The Gunshop Cafe...... **A5**
11 Happy Boy................ **E1**
12 Julius Pizzeria........... **B4**
13 The Pancake Manor **C3**

Quick Bites

1 Banneton Bakery and Cafe **D5**

Hotels

1 Adina Apartment Hotel Brisbane **C3**
2 The Calile **E1**
3 Capri by Fraser.......... **D4**
4 Crystalbrook Vincent.... **E1**
5 Edward Lodge............ **E1**
6 Hyatt Regency Brisbane.................. **C3**
7 Ovolo Incholm............ **C2**
8 Ovolo The Valley **E1**
9 The Point Brisbane **E4**
10 Rydges South Bank..... **B5**
11 Sofitel Brisbane Central **C2**
12 Spicers Balfour **E1**

from 5:30 am until midnight. The *Spirit of Queensland* makes the 24-hour trip along the state's coast from Brisbane to Cairns five times a week, with stops at Mackay, Townsville, the Whitsunday coast, and more. All trains include the option of luxurious RailBed carriages with convertible lie-down bed seats, personal entertainment systems, and meals. The speedy, state-of-the-art *Tilt Train* runs from Brisbane to Bundaberg and Brisbane to Rockhampton six days a week, passing through various regional centers along the way.

Other long-distance passenger trains from Brisbane include the *Westlander*, to and from Charleville (twice weekly); and the *Spirit of the Outback*, to and from Longreach, via Rockhampton (twice weekly). Trains depart from Roma Street Station.

TRAIN CONTACTS Queensland Rail Travel. ✉ *Brisbane Central Travel Center, 305 Edward St., Brisbane* ☎ *07/3072–2222* 🌐 *www.queenslandrail.com.au.*

TOURS

At the Brisbane Visitor Information and Booking Center, pick up a self-guided Brisbane CityWalk map (also available from tourist information offices and online), as well as brochures and maps detailing other designated Brisbane walking trails.

Blackcard Cultural Tours
Explore Meanjin (Brisbane) with knowledgeable Aboriginal tour guides. Discover Aboriginal history, art, and bush tucker on a 90-minute walking tour. ✉ *Southbank* ☎ *04/3706–6028* 🌐 *www.theblackcard.com.au* 🎫 *From A$99.*

★ Brisbane Greeters
Discover Brisbane through the eyes of the friendly Brisbane Greeters, a complimentary walking tour service staffed by passionate volunteer tour guides. "Greeters Choice" tours depart daily at 10 am from Brisbane City Hall, and can be booked up to three hours in advance. Or with seven days' notice, you can design your own "Your Choice" tour. Available in more than 20 different languages. ✉ *Brisbane City Hall, King George Sq. entrance, City Center* ☎ *07/3006–6290* 🌐 *www.brisbane.qld.gov.au/whats-on-in-brisbane/brisbane-greeter-tours.*

JPT Tours
JPT Tours (also known as Australian Day Tours) conducts half- and full-day tours of Brisbane, Moreton Island, K'gari (Fraser Island), Springbrook National Park, Mt. Tamborine, Byron Bay, and northward to Australia Zoo in Beerwah, with options to include meals and attractions. Check online to view current rates, last-minute specials, and promotions. ✉ *9 Trickett St., Shop 6, Surfers Paradise* ☎ *07/5630–1602, 1300/781–362* 🌐 *www.jpttours.com* 🎫 *From A$83.*

Kookaburra Showboat Cruises
Enjoy a full day of sightseeing, lunch, dinner, or high tea on a paddle wheeler cruise along the Brisbane River. Lunch cruises include scenic and historic commentary; live entertainment and dancing are highlights of dinner cruises. ✉ *Eagle St. Pier, 45 Eagle St., City Center* ☎ *07/3221–1300* 🌐 *www.kookaburrariverqueens.com* 🎫 *From A$75.*

River City Cruises
Daily sightseeing tours through and around South Bank, the City Center, and Kangaroo Point cliffs, including morning and afternoon tea options. Tours depart from Jetty A at South Bank Parklands, in front of the Wheel of Brisbane. ✉ *Jetty A, South Bank Parklands, Brisbane* ☎ *0428/278–473* 🌐 *www.rivercitycruises.com.au* 🎫 *From A$33.*

Story Bridge Adventure Climb
Energetic visitors might want to scale Brisbane's Story Bridge for a 360-degree view of the city and beyond. Regular departures during the day, at dawn, twilight, and at night. Express Climb and Climb & Abseil options also available. ✉ *170 Main St., Kangaroo Point*

Lone Pine Koala Sanctuary, Brisbane

07/3188–9070 www.storybridgeadventureclimb.com.au From A$129.

VISITOR INFORMATION

CONTACTS Brisbane Visitor Information and Booking Center. *The Regent, 167 Queen St. Mall, Queen St., City Center 07/3006–6290 www.visitbrisbane.com.au/the-city/visitor-information/brisbane-visitor-information-centre.*

Sights

Brisbane's city-center landmarks—a mix of Victorian, Edwardian, and slick contemporary architecture—are best explored on foot. Most lie within the triangle formed by Ann Street and the bends of the Brisbane River.

TIP→ **Streets running toward the river are named after female British royalty; those parallel to the river after male royalty.**

The well-tended South Bank precinct has riverfront parklands and cultural centers, alfresco cafés, a man-made beach, and weekend markets. Upriver, the quiet, leafy suburb of Fig Tree Pocket is home to Australia's best-known koala sanctuary.

Anzac Square and the Shrine of Remembrance

MILITARY SIGHT | Paths stretch across manicured lawns toward the Doric Greek Revival shrine made of Queensland sandstone. An eternal flame burns here for Australian soldiers who died in World War I. In the Shrine of Remembrance, a subsurface crypt stores soil samples from key battlefields. On April 25, Anzac Day, a moving dawn service is held here in remembrance of Australia's fallen soldiers. *Adelaide St., between Edward and Creek Sts., City Center Free.*

The Commissariat Store Museum

NOTABLE BUILDING | Convict-built in 1829 on the site of the city's original timber wharf, this was Brisbane's first stone building. It has served as a customs house, storehouse, and immigrants' shelter, and is currently the headquarters of The Royal Historical Society of Queensland. The RHSQ library and Commissariat Store museum is open to visitors

Tuesday to Friday, and holds exhibitions, historical documents, manuscripts, and artifacts dating back to Brisbane's early colonial days. Group tours of the museum are welcome. ✉ *115 William St., City Center* ☎ *07/3221–4198* 🌐 *www.commissariatstore.org.au* 🎫 *A$10.*

★ Lone Pine Koala Sanctuary

WILDLIFE REFUGE | FAMILY | Founded in 1927, Queensland's most famous fauna park is recognized by the *Guinness Book of World Records* as the world's first and largest koala sanctuary. As well as more than 130 koalas, you'll find emus, wombats, crocodiles, bats, platypuses, and lorikeets. You can hand-feed baby kangaroos, have a snake wrapped around you, or have your photo taken next to a koala. There are sheepdog shows, regular bird feedings, and animal presentations. Intimate encounters and behind-the-scenes tours can also be arranged for small groups. For an extra-special visit, book a combo ticket (from A$85) via Mirimar Cruises (*www.mirimarcruises.com.au*) and travel to Lone Pine along the Brisbane River. ✉ *708 Jesmond Rd., Fig Tree Pocket* ☎ *07/3378–1366 Lone Pine Sanctuary, 0412/749–426 Mirimar Cruises* 🌐 *www.koala.net* 🎫 *A$49.*

★ Museum of Brisbane

OTHER MUSEUM | FAMILY | Housed in City Hall in the center of Brisbane City, the museum offers a rotating schedule of innovative and interactive exhibitions throughout the year that celebrate the city, its people, culture, and history. There are also a range of free tours including a daily Museum highlights tour at noon, and self-guided Museum Tours and Clock Tower Tours every 15 minutes 10:15 am–4:45 pm. Free except for special exhibitions or programs. ✉ *City Hall, Level 3, 64 Adelaide St., City Center* ☎ *07/3339–0800* 🌐 *www.museumofbrisbane.com.au.*

Parliament House

GARDEN | Opened in 1868, this splendid, stone-clad, French Renaissance building with a Mount Isa copper roof earned its colonial designer a meager 200-guinea (A$440) fee. The interior is fitted with polished timber, brass, and frosted and engraved glass. Free half-hour tours run on weekday afternoons, depending on demand. The adjacent, kid-friendly City Botanic Gardens have native and exotic plants and theme areas, including the Bamboo Grove and Weeping Fig Avenue, along with sculptures, ponds, and an on-site café. ✉ *George St. at Alice St., City Center* ☎ *07/3553–6000* 🌐 *www.parliament.qld.gov.au* 🎫 *Free.*

★ Queensland Cultural Centre

PUBLIC ART | On the southern bank of the Brisbane River, you'll find a variety of world-class facilities nestled together among landscaped lawns and cafés. The world-famous Gallery of Modern Art (GoMA) with its ever-changing exhibitions and events is a must-visit, as is the equally impressive Queensland Art Gallery, Queensland Museum, and Sciencentre. The State Library of Queensland has a host of free, interactive children's activities and the Queensland Performing Arts Centre (QPAC) bustles with concerts and stage shows. There's also a host of restaurants, cafés, gift and book shops, a ticketing agent (in QPAC), public-access computer terminals, and various public spaces. Regular special events and festivals are also held in front of the Cultural Centre, particularly on weekends. Green Cabs (modern rickshaws) are a fun and unique way to get around and sightsee in this area. Starting at the Wheel of Brisbane adjacent QPAC, they'll ferry passengers anywhere between West End and Fortitude Valley. ✉ *Melbourne St. at Grey St., South Bank, South Brisbane* ☎ *07/3840–7303 galleries, 07/3840–7555 Museum and Sciencentre, 07/3840–7666 State Library, 07/3840–7444 QPAC* 🌐 *www.qagoma.qld.gov.au* 🎫 *Free (excluding Sciencentre and certain GoMA exhibitions).*

Roma Street Parkland

GARDEN | FAMILY | The world's largest subtropical garden within a city is a gentle mix of forest paths, floral displays, and structured plantings surrounding a fish-stocked lake. Highlights include the Lilly Pilly Garden, with native evergreen rain-forest plants, interesting children's play areas, and the friendly resident birds and lizards. Free hour-long guided garden tours focus on various themes, including bush tucker. Self-guided tour maps are available at the Roma Street Parkland Information Hub; The Sound Society is a monthly live music event, from 11:30 on Sunday. ✉ *1 Parkland Blvd., City Center* ☎ *1300/137–468* 🌐 *www.visitbrisbane.com.au/roma-street-parkland-and-spring-hill* 🎫 *Free.*

★ **South Bank Parklands**

CITY PARK | FAMILY | This vibrant community space on the banks of the Brisbane River includes parklands, shops, hotels, a maritime museum, walking and cycling paths, a sprawling man-made beach, a stunning Nepalese pagoda, and excellent city views. The weekend Collective Markets is the place to discover handmade goods, live entertainers, buskers, artists, and emerging designers. Almost every week you'll find a new festival or event lighting up the Cultural Forecourt. Nearby Grey Street is lined with trendy shops and cafés, as well as contemporary international restaurants, bars, and a cinema. The Wheel of Brisbane (A$19), a giant Ferris wheel at the northern entrance of South Bank, has some of the most spectacular views of the city. South Bank Parklands stretches along the riverbank south of the Queensland Cultural Centre. ✉ *Grey St., south of Melbourne St., Brisbane* ☎ *07/3156–6366 Parklands, 07/3844–3464 Wheel of Brisbane, 07/3844–5361 Maritime Museum* 🌐 *www.visitbrisbane.com.au/south-bank* 🎫 *Parklands free, museum A$18.*

Treasury Casino & Hotel

CASINO | With a "neat and tidy" dress code geared to securing an upscale clientele, The Treasury is a European-style casino with three levels of gaming beneath a stunning four-story atrium. Beneath a seduction of light and color, the facility comes alive at night with more than 80 gaming tables and more than 1,300 machines, as well as six restaurants and six bars. Open 24 hours. ✉ *130 William St., City Center* ☎ *07/3306–8888* 🌐 *www.treasurybrisbane.com.au.*

Restaurants

Brisbane offers a wide range of dining options, from casual eateries to cutting-edge fine dining. Top chefs have decamped to Brisbane's best eateries and are busy putting put a fresh subtropical spin on Modern Australian, Pan-Asian, and Mediterranean cuisine.

Imaginative dishes capitalize on abundant regional produce: fine fresh seafood—notably the local delicacy, the Moreton Bay bug (a sweet-fleshed crustacean)—premium steak, Darling Downs lamb, cheeses, macadamia nuts, avocados, olives, and fruit, matched with fine regional wines.

Most of the city's hip cafés, bars, and smart fine-dining establishments are clustered in the CBD, South Bank, West End, Fortitude Valley, New Farm, Teneriffe, and Petrie Terrace; you'll also find some excellent eateries around the suburbs, particularly Rosalie, Paddington, Milton, Ascot and Woolloongabba. For terrific fresh seafood, head for Brisbane's bay-side suburbs, such as Manly, Redcliffe, and Sandgate.

Typically, dining ambience is relaxed, seating is alfresco, and well-mannered children are welcomed. Given its year-round temperate climate, open-air night market dining is increasingly popular.

Modern sculpture at the Queensland Cultural Centre, South Bank, Brisbane

Blackbird Bar & Grill

$$$ | **AUSTRALIAN** | With its prime riverfront location at Eagle Street Pier, overlooking the Story Bridge, floor-to-ceiling windows, and designer interiors inspired by *The Great Gatsby,* Blackbird is a great place for a special night out. With a focus on sustainable local produce, menu highlights include sumptuous shellfish platters, as well as a choice of seven varieties of steak, suckling pig, and local fish cooked to perfection on an open wood-fired grill. **Known for:** riverside location with views; steaks cooked on a wood-fired grill; sustainably sourced seafood. *Average main: A$50* ✉ *Riverside Center, 123 Eagle St., City Center* ☎ *07/3229–1200* 🌐 *www.blackbirdbrisbane.com.au.*

Breakfast Creek Hotel

$$$ | **AUSTRALIAN** | Perched on the wharf at Breakfast Creek, this iconic, Heritage-listed hotel is renowned for its breezy tropical beer garden and superb trademark steaks. Non-steak eaters also have plenty of options, including vegetarian dishes, salads, and fresh seafood. **Known for:** iconic location; classic pub food; historic architecture. *Average main: A$38* ✉ *2 Kingsford Smith Dr., Albion* ☎ *07/3262–5988* 🌐 *www.breakfastcreekhotel.com.*

★ **Cafe O-Mai**

$ | **VIETNAMESE** | This family-run café on Brisbane's south side is always busy, serving dishes that combine traditional Vietnamese flavors and techniques with local ingredients, great coffee, desserts, and fresh juices. Baguettes are baked in-house daily, and specialties like pork sausages and spring rolls are handmade in-store. **Known for:** authentic pho; handmade pork sausages; freshly squeezed juices. *Average main: A$16* ✉ *15 Cracknell Rd., South Brisbane* ☎ *07/3255–9778* 🌐 *www.cafeomai.com.au.*

Caravanserai

$$ | **TURKISH** | Decked out in traditional woven kilims and Mediterranean lanterns, this Turkish restaurant is a treat for the senses, with its rich, generously portioned servings of contemporary Middle

Eastern fare served among cozy nooks of candlelit tables and breezy views over West End. **Known for:** river views from back veranda; authentic Turkish atmosphere; sultan's banquet. *Average main: A$30* *1–3 Dornoch Terr., West End* *04/1324–8259* *www.caravanserai.restaurant* *Closed Mon.*

The Charming Squire

$$ | MODERN AUSTRALIAN | Named after legendary convict brewmaster James Squire, this stylish new brewery and restaurant in South Bank's cultural precinct boasts a large, open-plan bar area—featuring sweeping ceilings, polished concrete flooring, repurposed timber, and trendy copper accents. Enjoy local beef, lamb, and pork slow-cooked on the Iron Bark coal pit, alongside traditional pub favorites like fish-and-chips, burgers, pizza, salads, and antipasto-style share plates. **Known for:** slow cooking on the Iron Bark coal pit; Australian pub cuisine; wide selection of craft beers and ciders. *Average main: A$35* *133 Grey St., Southbank* *07/3077–7254* *www.jamessquire.com.au/brewhouses/the-charming-squire.*

★ **Donna Chang**

$$$ | CHINESE | An exciting addition to Brisbane's dining scene, this modern Chinese restaurant offers delicious, fresh food and a wonderful wine list amid the grandeur of a renovated 1920s bank. Beneath soaring ceilings and chandeliers, choose from a menu that includes traditional favorites (with a focus on spice) and more adventurous combinations like Moreton Bay bugs with salted duck egg and fermented chili. **Known for:** fine dining without the fuss; modern Chinese menu; stunning heritage setting. *Average main: A$38* *171 George St., Shop 3, City Center* *07/3243–4888* *www.donnachang.com.au.*

★ **e'cco**

$$$ | MEDITERRANEAN | Beloved Brisbane institution e'cco serves innovative fare to a loyal following in a relaxed setting. The menu consists of seasonally changing Mediterranean- and Asian-inspired Mod Oz dishes, with a focus on fresh, local ingredients. **Known for:** tasting menu with wine pairings; celebrated chef; visually appealing food with bold flavors. *Average main: A$45* *63 Skyring Terr., New Farm* *07/3831–8344* *www.eccobistro.com* *Closed Sun. and Mon.*

★ **Enoteca 1889**

$$$ | ITALIAN | Specializing in "vera cucina Romana" (real Roman food), this award-winning Italian restaurant in Woollangabba's antique quarter is well worth crossing the Brisbane River for. The menu favors simplicity over complexity: elegant starters like lightly fried zucchini flowers stuffed with cheese and anchovies, freshly made pasta or fish of the day for main, tiramisu or panna cotta for dessert. **Known for:** historic 1889 Moreton Rubber building; traditional Roman fare; seasonal four-course set menu. *Average main: A$40* *10–12 Logan Rd., Woolloongabba* *07/3392–4315* *www.1889enoteca.com.au* *No lunch Tues.–Thurs. Closed Mon.*

★ **Felix for Goodness**

$$ | AUSTRALIAN | Hidden away in Burnett Lane just off Queen Street, Felix for Goodness has dished up delectable made-from-scratch breakfasts, lunches, snacks, and cakes (with an emphasis on organic) since 2014. In terms of decor, think exposed brick and concrete, natural light, and clean lines. **Known for:** extensive range of gluten-free and vegetarian options; rustic, homemade goodness; all-day brunch. *Average main: A$22* *50 Burnett La., City Center* *Restaurant is at mezzanine level, through a narrow doorway and up a set of stairs* *07/3161–7966* *felixforgoodness.com* *No dinner.*

The Gunshop Cafe

$ | CAFÉ | Named after its previous life as an actual gun shop, this trendy West End café is the place to go for breakfast and brunch on weekends. Unfinished brick walls where guns once hung set the stage for an eclectic menu, coffee, and spicy chai tea with honey from the café's own rooftop bees. **Known for:** breakfast until 3 pm; potato-feta hash cakes; flourless chocolate fudge cake. *Average main: A$20 53 Mollison St., West End 07/3844–2241 www.thegunshopcafe.net No dinner.*

Happy Boy
$$ | CHINESE | With its minimal decor and open-air fairy-lit deck, this bustling little wine bar and eatery in Fortitude Valley is not your average Chinese restaurant. Locals and foodies alike flock to experience its delicious, regional Chinese fare. **Known for:** extensive, sommelier-selected wine list; innovative Chinese food; chef's banquet for $A45 per person. *Average main: A$22 East St., between Ann and Wickham Sts., Fortitude Valley 0413/246–890 www.happyboy.com.au Closed Mon.*

★ **Julius Pizzeria**
$$ | PIZZA | FAMILY | Ideally positioned for a quick pre- or posttheater dinner, this always-busy pizzeria combines breezy yet attentive service with low-fuss dining—and delicious Italian food. Pizzas feature crisp wood-fired bases, with a variety of Rosse (tomato sauce–based) and Bianche (without sauce) toppings that follow the less-is-more approach. **Known for:** Bambini menu for children; open kitchen featuring a wood-fired oven; friendly but efficient service. *Average main: A$25 77 Grey St., South Brisbane 07/3844–2655 juliuspizzeria.com.au Closed Mon. No lunch Tues. and Wed.*

The Pancake Manor
$ | CAFÉ | FAMILY | Housed inside the historic, Heritage-listed St. Luke's Cathedral, this elegant 24-hour pancake parlor is a Brisbane institution. Guests can take a seat in one of the Manor's converted church pew booths and chow down on a tempting menu of snacks, breakfasts, salads, steaks, and sweets beneath the building's grand redbrick arches. **Known for:** kid-friendly dining 24/7; housed in a Heritage-listed cathedral; grilled bananas in creamy butterscotch sauce. *Average main: A$16 18 Charlotte St., City Center 07/3221–6433 www.pancakemanor.com.au.*

Coffee and Quick Bites

Banneton Bakery and Cafe
$ | BAKERY | Tucked away in a semi-industrial area in inner-city Woolloongabba, Banneton is home to some of Brisbane's tastiest bread and pastries. For those with savory taste buds, there are pies and quiches, as well as a range of filled baguettes and croissants, all made in-house. **Known for:** tarte au citron, tangy but silky smooth; hearty pies including the ever-popular steak and Guinness; sourdough, rye, baguettes, and ciabatta bread. *Average main: A$8 25 Balaclava St., Brisbane 07/3393–2111 banneton.com.au.*

Hotels

Inner-city Brisbane is home to an ever-growing array of luxury and designer hotels, boutique accommodations, and smartly serviced apartments. Many have good-value packages and seasonal and last-minute specials. Jump online for the best deals.

Adina Apartment Hotel Brisbane
$$ | HOTEL | With its central, riverside location opposite Queen Street's Myer Building, this apartment hotel in a renovated 1920s bank building offers a range of well-equipped rooms from studios with kitchenette to three-bedroom apartments with sweeping river or city views. **Pros:** external rooms feature balcony; excellent location; combines heritage charm with modern amenities. **Cons:** interior design is stylish and functional but lacks flair; free Wi-Fi only 1 MBS (extra for high-speed); internal rooms can be dark. *Rooms from: A$186 171 George St.,*

City Center ☎ *07/3155–1000* 🌐 *www.adinahotels.com/en/apartments/brisbane* 🛏 *220 rooms* 🍽 *No Meals.*

★ **The Calile**

$$$$ | **HOTEL** | More Byron than Brisbane, the Calile offers a luxury resort-like experience in the heart of inner-city Brisbane, with James Street's designer boutiques and restaurants at your doorstep. **Pros:** understated sophistication; vacation vibes in an urban setting; large outdoor pool. **Cons:** breakfast extra; parking $A25 extra; a little out of the city center. 💲 *Rooms from: A$329* ✉ *48 James St., Fortitude Valley* ☎ *07/3607–5888* 🌐 *www.thecalilehotel.com* 🛏 *175 rooms* 🍽 *No Meals.*

Capri by Fraser

$$ | **HOTEL** | Contemporary design meets superior comfort at this newly completed, health-focused hotel, perfectly positioned between the Queen Street Mall and the Botanic Gardens in CBD. **Pros:** quality, healthy buffet breakfast; great service and location; free, fast Wi-Fi. **Cons:** rooms on the small side; clean and comfortable but minimal atmosphere; pricey parking. 💲 *Rooms from: A$189* ✉ *80 Albert St., City Center* ☎ *07/3013–0088* 🌐 *brisbane.capribyfraser.com* 🛏 *239 rooms* 🍽 *Free Breakfast.*

Crystalbrook Vincent

$$$ | **HOTEL** | Tucked under the Story Bridge amid the rejuvenated entertainment precinct at the Howard Smith Wharves, the five-star Crystalbrook Vincent (formerly the Fantauzzo) is both sophisticated and sustainable. **Pros:** artwork by Vincent Fantauzzo; riverside location in the heart of the Howard Smith Wharves precinct; sustainable focus. **Cons:** breakfast not included; rooftop bar area can get crowded on weekends; lower floor rooms can be noisy at night. 💲 *Rooms from: A$275* ✉ *5 Boundary St., Brisbane* ☎ *07/3515–0700* 🌐 *www.crystalbrookcollection.com/vincent* 🍽 *No Meals.*

Edward Lodge

$ | **B&B/INN** | This charming, inner-suburban, art deco B&B is set among Asian-style tropical gardens and close to cafés and restaurants, New Farm Park, Brisbane Powerhouse, and the CityCat ferry. **Pros:** guest kitchen and laundry; vibrant area; free continental breakfast. **Cons:** 15-minute walk from the city; no room service; no pool. 💲 *Rooms from: A$142* ✉ *75 Sydney St., New Farm* ☎ *07/3358–2680* 🌐 *www.edwardlodge.com.au* 🛏 *9 rooms, 1 apartment* 🍽 *Free Breakfast.*

★ **Hyatt Regency Brisbane**

$$$ | **HOTEL** | Formerly Next Hotel Brisbane, Hyatt Regency Brisbane combines innovative, plush design and an unbeatable location on the Queen Street Mall. **Pros:** free unlimited Wi-Fi; clean, comfortable, and quiet; central location. **Cons:** on-site dining is expensive—better options nearby; queen rooms on the small side; limited parking. 💲 *Rooms from: A$229* ✉ *72 Queen St., City Center* ☎ *07/5647–1234* 🌐 *www.hyatt.com* 🛏 *292 rooms* 🍽 *No Meals.*

Ovolo Incholm

$$$ | **HOTEL** | This delightful art deco hotel in inner-city Spring Hill has received an Ovolo face-lift—all the old-world glamour remains, including the original elevator, but public spaces have been tastefully and artistically remodeled, and rooms upgraded. **Pros:** pet-friendly; old-world charm meets modern comfort; personalized service and lots of freebies. **Cons:** breakfast is an additional charge; '80s music in public areas can get a bit much; no pool. 💲 *Rooms from: A$218* ✉ *73 Wickham Terr., Brisbane* ☎ *07/3226–8888* 🌐 *www.ovolohotels.com.au/ovoloinchcolm* 🛏 *50 rooms* 🍽 *No Meals.*

Ovolo The Valley

$$$ | **HOTEL** | Ovolo The Valley embraces the Valley's quirky history while adding a funky sophistication and all the latest tech touches. **Pros:** rooftop pool with views; superb design and facilities; close to nightlife. **Cons:** can be noisy—ask for a room away from street; expensive parking; outside the city center. *Rooms from: A$228 1000 Ann St., Fortitude Valley 07/3253–6999 thevalley-brisbane.com.au 103 rooms Free Breakfast.*

The Point Brisbane

$$ | **HOTEL** | Across the river from central Brisbane, this modern hotel on picturesque Kangaroo Point has great city skyline and river views from each balcony. **Pros:** terrific on-site facilities including 24-hour room service; free parking; wheelchair-accessible rooms. **Cons:** free Wi-Fi but can be slow; rooms on freeway side of hotel may be noisy; a 20-minute walk to the city. *Rooms from: A$175 21 Lambert St., Kangaroo Point 07/3240–0888, 1800/088–388 www.gettothepoint.com.au 201 rooms Free Breakfast.*

Rydges South Bank

$$$ | **HOTEL** | **FAMILY** | Surrounded by Brisbane's famous South Bank Parklands and Cultural Precinct, within walking distance of numerous attractions, this tasteful, well-maintained hotel is an excellent choice if location's your focus. **Pros:** riverside rooms feature great city views; lively location; excellent restaurant and facilities. **Cons:** pool is on the small side; not all rooms have balconies so be sure to request one; steep fees for parking. *Rooms from: A$239 9 Glenelg St., at Grey St., South Brisbane 07/3364–0800 www.rydges.com/southbank 304 rooms No Meals.*

Sofitel Brisbane Central

$$$ | **HOTEL** | This decadent, French-flavored hotel is a quiet and classy choice in a central location. **Pros:** superb buffet breakfast; prompt, pleasant service; luxurious rooms and facilities incuding an award-winning spa. **Cons:** compact bathrooms; expensive Wi-Fi and parking; pricey meals and minibar. *Rooms from: A$249 249 Turbot St., City Center 07/3835–4444 www.sofitelbrisbane.com.au 416 rooms Free Breakfast.*

★ Spicers Balfour

$$$ | **HOTEL** | A distinctly local experience perfect for weary travelers looking for a home away from home, this elegant boutique hotel has nine suites housed inside a traditional Queenslander mansion, complete with flowing verandas, tropical gardens, and breezy river views. **Pros:** free Wi-Fi, parking, and à la carte breakfast included in rate; attentive and personalized service; close to public transport and ferry. **Cons:** some rooms on the small side; off-street parking is limited; outside the city center. *Rooms from: A$239 37 Balfour St., New Farm 07/3358–8888 spicersretreats.com 17 rooms Free Breakfast.*

Nightlife

You'll find a range of nightlife options throughout Brisbane, from sophisticated riverfront cocktail bars, to hidden laneway bars, suburban microbreweries, live music venues, and traditional pubs. Many bars in the city center close at midnight; after that all the action is on Caxton Street and Fortitude Valley, which can get raucous in the wee hours. Some late night venues require patrons to present photo identification for entry after 10 pm, so if you're looking for a late night drink be sure to carry your passport. For up-to-date information visit *www.visitbrisbane.com.au/things-to-do/nightlife.*

BARS

Cloudland

WINE BARS | An "urban oasis" with fanciful design, a retractable glass roof, and street-front waterfall flowing over its contemporary architectural facade, Cloudland restaurant and nightclub woos well-heeled locals and tourists alike with an extensive drinks menu, cut-above food, and an exciting, expensive ambience. *641 Ann St., Fortitude Valley 07/3872–6600 www.cloudland.tv.*

Cru Bar + Cellar

WINE BARS | Sleek and sophisticated, Cru Bar + Cellar has leather ottomans, a long onyx bar, circa-1800 French chandeliers, and a fine-wine-loving clientele. Cru's huge cellar houses hundreds of top Australian vintages, to drink on-site or later; the cocktail menu is also extensive and impressive. Cheese tasting plates are available all day. The dinner menu, designed by an award-winning chef, has a focus on Australian ingredients. ✉ *James St. Market, 22 James St., Fortitude Valley* ☎ *07/3252–2400* 🌐 *www.crubar.com.*

★ **Lefty's Old Time Music Hall**

BARS | This award-winning saloon-style bar on bustling Caxton Street mixes old-school American charm with modern craft brews and a hefty range of spirits (including more than 100 rye whiskies). Decked out in vintage taxidermy and moody chandeliers, the retro Americana vibe continues with the Southern-theme bar food, including po'boys, corn dogs, and popcorn shrimp and the latest addition, Ben's burgers. A rollicking mix of country and rockabilly tunes burst from the stage and speakers. ✉ *15 Caxton St., Petrie Terrace* 🌐 *www.leftysmusichall.com.au.*

Performing Arts

The Saturday edition of the *Courier–Mail* newspaper (*www.couriermail.com.au*) lists live gigs and concerts, ballet, opera, theater, jazz, and other events in its Life section, while Friday's *CM2* insert has a comprehensive entertainment guide for the weekend ahead. *Must Do Brisbane* (*www.mustdobrisbane.com.au*) has suburb-by-suburb listings of Brisbane's best cafés, restaurants, shopping, and nightlife spots, as well as weekly updates on new events and establishments in the city and surrounding areas. Alternately, visit *Brisbane Art* (*www.bneart.com*) for up-to-date listings of arts events and galleries around the city.

ARTS CENTERS

Brisbane Powerhouse

ARTS CENTERS | Housed in a grand, former coal power station, the Heritage-listed Brisbane Powerhouse hosts frequent, often-free, art exhibitions, live performances, and children's events in its flexible 200- and 400-seat theaters. Cafés, restaurants, bikeways, boardwalks, and picnic areas complement the spacious, contemporary riverside hub, which also adjoins beautiful New Farm Park. A recent renovation added a new café-bar, a roof terrace, and enlarged theater spaces. ✉ *119 Lamington St., New Farm* ☎ *07/3358–8600 box office, 07/3358–8622 reception* 🌐 *www.brisbanepowerhouse.org.*

Shopping

For more information on shopping in Brisbane, visit 🌐 *www.visitbrisbane.com.au/things-to-do/shopping.*

ANTIQUES

Camp Hill Antique Center and Tart Cafe

ANTIQUES & COLLECTIBLES | Located in a refurbished 1950s cinema, Brisbane's largest antiques center houses 70-plus stalls, an on-site tart café, and everything from fine china, collectibles, and the kitschiest of curiosities, to clothing, records, prints, paintings, home wares, games, and a vast collection of Australiana. Open weekdays 9–5 and weekends 8–5. ✉ *545 Old Cleveland Rd., Camp Hill, Brisbane* ☎ *07/3392–1114* 🌐 *www.camphillantiquecentre.com.*

Empire Revival

ANTIQUES & COLLECTIBLES | Located in a converted theater, Empire Revival (formerly Paddington Antique Centre) is brimming with antiques, furniture, collectibles, various bric-a-brac as well as colorful vintage clothing. Around 50 dealers operate within the center, alongside an on-site café. It's open daily 9–5, closing an hour earlier on Sunday. ✉ *167 Latrobe Terr., Paddington*

State library, Queensland Cultural Centre

☎ *07/3369–8088* 🌐 *www.empirerevival.com.au.*

ART GALLERIES

Woolloongabba Art Gallery

ART GALLERIES | The gallery represents and exhibits contemporary artists, including Aboriginal and Torres Strait Islanders. Works cost between A$50 and A$10,000, and come with certificates of authenticity. It's open Tuesday through Friday 9–6 and Saturday 9–3, with regular exhibitions. ✉ *613 Stanley St., Woolloongabba* ☎ *07/3891–5551* 🌐 *www.wag.com.au* ☞ *Open Tues.–Sat.; Sun. and Mon. by appointment.*

MALLS AND ARCADES

Brisbane Arcade

ANTIQUES & COLLECTIBLES | Heritage-listed Brisbane Arcade, circa 1923, joins Queen Street Mall and Adelaide Street and houses designer boutiques, jewelry shops, and upscale gift, art, and antiques stores. ✉ *160 Queen St. Mall, City Center* 🌐 *www.brisbanearcade.com.au.*

James Street

NEIGHBORHOODS | This new upmarket lifestyle precinct in Fortitude Valley has an ever-growing array of local fashion, housewares, jewelry, and design stores, alongside trendy cafés and bars. ✉ *James St., Fortitude Valley* ☎ *07/3850–0111* 🌐 *www.jamesst.com.au.*

MacArthur Central

MALL | Historic MacArthur Central, the WWII headquarters of U.S. General Douglas MacArthur, houses boutiques and specialty shops, a food court, and a museum. Located at the bottom of the Queen Street Mall, the streets surrounding the center also feature a range of high-end fashion boutiques including Louis Vuitton, Hermès, and Tiffany & Co. The MacArthur Museum is open to the public Tuesday, Thursday, and Sunday 10–2:30. ✉ *201 Edward St., City Center* ☎ *07/3211–7052 museum* 🌐 *www.mmb.org.au.*

Queen Street Mall

MALL | FAMILY | Fun and lively Queen Street Mall is nearly a third of a mile long, and incorporates 700 retailers and five major shopping centers, including the Myer Centre, Wintergarden, and Queens Plaza, as well as two large department stores, Myer and David Jones. There are also four arcades: historic Tattersall's Arcade and MacArthur Central, Heritage-listed Brisbane Arcade, and Broadway on the Mall, all housing designer boutiques and a range of specialty stores. On weekends, free entertainment and performances can often be found on the mall's two open stages. ✉ *Queen St., City Center* ☎ *07/3006–6200* 🌐 *www.visitbrisbane.com.au/the-city/things-to-do/shopping/queen-street-mall.*

MARKETS

Brisbane Powerhouse Farmers Market

MARKET | The Brisbane Powerhouse hosts a local produce farmers' market from 6 am to noon every Saturday. Enjoy a fresh, leisurely breakfast on the lawn by the river, and afterward, stroll through nearby New Farm Park. ✉ *119 Lamington St., New Farm* ☎ *07/3358–8600* 🌐 *www.janpowersfarmersmarkets.com.au/powerhouse-farmers-markets.*

Collective Markets South Bank

MARKET | South Bank Parklands hosts a weekend Collective Markets, showcasing high-quality and emerging designer clothing, accessories, artwork, craft, food, and music. It runs Friday 5–9, Saturday 10–9, and Sunday 9–4 in Stanley Street Plaza. ✉ *Grey St., At Stanley St. Plaza, City Center* ☎ *07/3844–2440* 🌐 *www.collectivemarkets.com.au.*

Eat Street Markets

MARKET | FAMILY | Located on a revamped shipping wharf at riverside Hamilton, this bustling interactive market gives visitors a taste of Brisbane's best street food from more than 70 funky shipping container "restaurants." Open Friday and Saturday evening 4 pm–10 pm and Sunday 4 pm–9 pm, there's also a regular lineup of live music and entertainment, and hip wares from local artists and makers. Entry costs A$5. ✉ *221D Macarthur Ave., Hamilton, Brisbane* ☎ *07/3358–2500* 🌐 *www.eatstreetmarkets.com.*

Riverside Markets

MARKET | FAMILY | This eclectic arts-and-crafts bazaar in Brisbane's Botanic Gardens sells everything from pressed flowers to hand-painted didgeridoos and homemade treats and clothing. It's open Sunday 8–3. ✉ *City Botanic Gardens, Alice St. at Albert St., City Center* ☎ *07/3870–2807* 🌐 *www.queenslandmarkets.com.au/riverside-markets/.*

OUTDOOR GEAR OUTFITTERS

Paddy Pallin

SPORTING GOODS | With stores throughout Australia, Paddy Pallin sells quality outdoor and travel gear, including hats, footwear, clothing, backpacks, and equipment. On staff are dedicated bushwalkers, rock climbers, and travelers. ✉ *120 Wickham St., Fortitude Valley* ☎ *07/3839–3811* 🌐 *www.paddypallin.com.au.*

Activities

Brisbane offers a host of outdoor activities. You can kayak or paddleboard on the Brisbane River, and numerous scenic bushwalking, climbing, and rappelling sites lie less than 90 minutes by car from Brisbane. Government-run Outdoors Queensland (QORF) (*www.qorf.org.au*) gives regional information and lists businesses offering adventure activities from hiking to horse riding.

BICYCLING

An extensive network of bicycle paths crisscrosses Brisbane. One of the best paths follows the level and impeccably maintained Bicentennial Bikeway southeast along the Brisbane River, across the Goodwill Bridge, then along to South Bank Parklands or Kangaroo Point cliffs. The Kurilpa Bridge and Go Between Bridge are also both cyclist-friendly ways to cross the river between the city and

South Brisbane. The city's famous Riverwalk gives cyclists and pedestrians a scenic route from New Farm to the CBD.

Cycling Brisbane

BIKING | This Brisbane City Council website provides safety tips and information on cycling as an online interactive map and downloadable maps of the city's bikeway network. You'll also find information on the CityCycle network, which has bikes available from 150 designated points around the inner city. ✉ *Brisbane* 🌐 *www.cyclingbrisbane.com.au.*

GOLF

St. Lucia Golf Links and Golf World

GOLF | One of Brisbane's oldest golf courses, St. Lucia Golf Links and Golf World is an 18-hole, par-70, pay-and-play course open to visitors. Work up an appetite on the fairways, then dine on-site at the Hillstone clubhouse's Hundred Acre Bar, overlooking the 18th green. ✉ *Indooroopilly Rd., at Carawa St., St. Lucia* ☎ *07/3403–2556 golf course, 07/3870–3433 Hillstone Clubhouse* 🌐 *www.hillstonestlucia.com.au* 🎫 *From $A20 (9/18 holes no cart), $A39/45 (9/18 holes with cart)* 🏌 *18 holes, 5917 yards, par 69.*

MULTISPORT OUTFITTERS

Riverlife Adventure Centre

KAYAKING | **FAMILY** | A one-stop-shop for adventure in the inner city, Riverlife runs guided rock-climbing and abseiling sessions off Kangaroo Point cliffs, cycling and Segway tours around Brisbane attractions, day and night kayaking and stand-up paddleboarding trips on the Brisbane River (followed by barbecue dinner and seafood options). The Mirrabooka Aboriginal Cultural Experience includes a traditional performance by the Yuggera Aboriginal Dancers and hands-on instruction in fire-starting, instrument playing, boomerang throwing, and painting. The center also rents bicycles, rollerblades, kick bikes, and scooters. ✉ *Naval Stores, Lower River Terr., Kangaroo Point* ☎ *07/3891–5766* 🌐 *www.riverlife.com.au* 🎫 *From A$25.*

WATER SPORTS

Moreton Bay

WATER SPORTS | A half-hour's drive east of Brisbane city brings you to Moreton Bay, stretching 125 km (78 miles) from the Gold Coast to the Sunshine Coast. A number of operators based in Brisbane's bay-side suburbs—Manly, Redcliffe, Sandgate—run sailing, diving, sightseeing, and whale- and dolphin-watching trips around the Bay, and trips to its various islands. Some cruises include tours of St. Helena Island's historic prison ruins; others visit Moreton Island, where you can toboggan down massive white sand dunes. ✉ *Moreton Island National Park* 🌐 *www.moretonbay.qld.gov.au.*

Moreton Bay Escapes

WATER SPORTS | **FAMILY** | This operator runs tours and charters around Moreton Island National Park that includes 4WD driving, snorkeling, kayaking, bodyboarding, hiking, and sand boarding. Tailored excursions incorporate bird-watching, fishing, swimming with dolphins, and more. Admission includes ferry trip, park entry fees, and meals. ✉ *Brisbane* ☎ *1300/559–355* 🌐 *www.moretonbayescapes.com.au* 🎫 *From A$129.*

Southern Downs

From Brisbane, the Granite Belt is 225 km (140 miles) west, Mt. Tamborine is 62 km (39 miles) southwest, and Scenic Rim wineries are around 135 km (85 miles) southwest.

Drive two hours west on the Cunningham Highway and you'll reach the Southern Downs, where spring brings the scent of peach and apple blossoms and fall finds the region's 50-plus vineyards, concentrated around Stanthorpe, ripe for harvest. Winter is ideal for wine-country excursions, with clear days and tastings by fireplace by night. This area, extending from Cunninghams Gap in the east to Goondiwindi in the west, Allora in the north to Wallangarra in the south, is known as the Granite Belt.

The local Italian community pioneered viticulture here, planting the first Shiraz grapes in 1965. Today the Granite Belt is the state's largest wine region, with nearly 2,000 acres under vines and more than 50 cellar doors (wine-tasting rooms), most attached to family-run and boutique wineries. Thanks to its altitude (2,500–4,000 feet above sea level) and decomposed-granite soils, the region enjoys unique growing and ripening conditions, enabling the production of outstanding, full-bodied reds and extra-crisp whites.

Just over an hour's drive southwest of Brisbane, inland from the Gold Coast, you'll find the world's largest caldera and one of the state's most exciting emerging wine regions: the Scenic Rim. The region's rich volcanic soils, first planted with vines in the late 19th century, now produce fine red and white varieties. On the region's easterly edge, you'll find a dozen wineries and a distillery within a compact area around Mt. Tamborine.

GETTING HERE AND AROUND

Driving yourself is an option but may not be the best idea if you are wine tasting. However, for the self-guiders out there, the Granite Belt and Scenic Rim tourism boards provide downloadable maps. Find Granite Belt winery and walking trails at *www.granitebeltwinecountry.com.au*, and Scenic Rim winery and trail maps at *www.visitscenicrim.com.au*.

Arguably, the safest way to sample the offerings of the region's wineries is via guided tour. More than half a dozen companies run tours of wineries in the Scenic Rim and Mt. Tamborine areas, but some require groups of at least six people.

TOURS

Cork 'n Fork Winery Tours

Family-run Cork 'n Fork Winery Tours runs daily and overnight viticultural tours for couples and small groups to Mt. Tamborine and the Scenic Rim. Their popular full-day tour includes hotel pickups from the Gold Coast or Tamborine Mountain, two-course lunch, and four winery visits with guided tastings. ✉ *Mt. Tamborine* ☎ *0415/454–313* 🌐 *corknforktours.com* 🎫 *From A$149.*

Filippo's Tours

This popular operator runs an assortment of specialist food, wine, and brewery tours across the Granite Belt, with departures from both Stanthorpe and Brisbane. Small, customized, group tours are also available. ☎ *1800/020–383* 🌐 *www.filippostours.com.au* 🎫 *From A$110.*

Granite Highlands Maxi Tours

This local operator runs half-day, full-day, and weekend tours of Granite Belt wineries, specializing in the verdant vineyards of Stanthorpe. Departing Brisbane and various regional centers, most tours also include meals, sightseeing, and local attractions. ☎ *07/4681–3969, 1800/852–969* 🌐 *www.maxitours.com.au* 🎫 *From A$95.*

Sights

Ballandean Estate Wines

WINERY | Just south of Glen Aplin is the town of Ballandean, home to award-winning Ballandean Estate Wines, the oldest family-owned and-operated vineyard and winery in Queensland. The first grapes were grown on the Granite Belt site in 1931, and the tasting room is the original brick shed built in 1950. The Barrel Room Cafe behind it—with massive, 125-year-old wooden barrels lining one wall—serves modern Italian cuisine, showcasing local produce and quality coffee (lunch Thursday–Monday, dinner Friday and Saturday). There are 45-minute tours of the facility daily at 11 am for A$5 per person. ✉ *354 Sundown Rd., Ballandean* ☎ *07/4684–1226* 🌐 *www.ballandean-estate.com* 🎫 *A$5 cellar door.*

Girraween National Park

FOREST | FAMILY | One of the most popular parks in southeast Queensland—meaning "place of flowers"—sits at the end of the New England Tableland, a stepped plateau area with elevations ranging from 1,968 to 4,921 feet. The 17 km (11 miles) of walking tracks, most starting near the information center and picnic area, wind past granite outcrops, giant boulders, eucalyptus forests, and spectacular wildflowers in spring. Along the way you might encounter kangaroos, echidnas, brush-tailed possums, and turquoise parrots. To camp, you'll need a permit (*www.parks.des.qld.gov.au*). ✉ *Ballandean* ✣ *11 km (7 miles) north of Wallangarra or 26 km (16 miles) south of Stanthorpe, off New England Hwy.* ☎ *137–468* 🌐 *www.parks.des.qld.gov.au/parks/girraween/.*

Sirromet Wines at Mount Cotton

WINERY | Queensland's largest winery sits midway between Brisbane and the Gold Coast. Sirromet's much-lauded wines—distinctive reds, crisp whites, and some terrific blended varieties—can be sampled at their impressive cellar door, alongside coffee and cake, Devonshire tea, and lunchtime platters (bookings required). Additional dining options are Restaurant Lurleen's and The Tuscan Terrace. ✉ *850–938 Mount Cotton Rd., Mount Cotton* ☎ *07/3206–2999* 🌐 *www.sirromet.com* 🎫 *Tastings from A$5; guided tours from A$20.*

Spicers Peak Lodge

$$$$ | RESORT | This luxurious, all-inclusive mountain retreat offers a range of lavishly appointed suites, most with stone fireplaces, and all with views and complimentary minibars. **Pros:** stunning, serene location; world-class restaurant with terrific wine list; thoughtful, impeccable service. **Cons:** two-night minimum stay on weekends; remote location not suited to day trips; all-inclusive package pricey. [$] *Rooms from: A$1399* ✉ *Wilkinsons Rd., Maryvale* ☎ *1300/198–386* 🌐 *www.spicersretreats.com/spicers-peak-lodge* *12 suites and private lodges* 🍴 *All-Inclusive.*

★ **Vineyard Cottages and Café**

$$$ | B&B/INN | Built around a turn-of-the-20th-century church that's now the Vineyard Café and restaurant, this popular property boasts seven period-style cottages set amid 2 acres of manicured gardens, only two blocks from Ballandean village. **Pros:** accessible; warm ambience with excellent food and wine; close to top wineries. **Cons:** free Wi-Fi in public areas only; some road noise—request a cottage in back to avoid; 20 minutes to Stanthorpe. [$] *Rooms from: A$245* ✉ *New England Hwy., near Bents Rd., Ballandean* ☎ *07/4684–1270* 🌐 *www.vineyardcottages.com.au* *4 cottages, 3 suites* 🍴 *Free Breakfast.*

Coomera and Oxenford

48–51 km (30–32 miles) south of Brisbane.

The biggest draws of these two northern Gold Coast suburbs are their family-oriented theme parks—Dreamworld, Warner Bros. Movie World, Wet 'n' Wild Water World, Paradise Country, the Australian Outback Spectacular, and WhiteWater World. The sprawling complexes have many attractions: each takes about a day for a leisurely visit. An array of ticketing options are available, including multiday and multipark passes. For more information visit *themeparks.com.au*or *www.dreamworld.com.au.*

Australian Outback Spectacular

PERFORMANCE VENUE | FAMILY | The Australian Outback Spectacular lets visitors experience "the heart and soul of the Australian Outback." The evening show features state-of-the-art visual effects and performances from top local stunt riders, interactive team racing, and live country and orchestral music. Guests get a hearty, three-course dinner and complimentary drinks during the 90-minute, A$23-million production, plus a souvenir stockman's hat. There is also a monthly matinee performance on Sunday. ✉ *Pacific Motorway, Oxenford* ☎ *133–386 bookings and information* 🌐 *outbackspectacular.com.au* 🎫 *From A$100.*

Dreamworld

FAIRGROUND | FAMILY | At Coomera's Dreamworld, the main draw is the high-tech thrill rides including the aptly named Giant Drop, a nearly 400-foot vertical plummet akin to skydiving; the nine-story, 360-degree pendulum swing of Claw; and Tail Spin, a soaring mini airplane adventure. Animal lovers will enjoy Tiger Island where Bengal tigers and their gorgeous cubs swim and play, Koala Country, and the conservation-focused on-site Wildlife Sanctuary (including crocs). There are also Family Rides, a range of rides for young children, pools and waterslides of Whitewater World, and Corroboree, an interactive celebration of Aboriginal and Torres Strait Island heritage and culture. Purchase tickets online for discounts and specials. ✉ *1 Dreamworld Pkwy., Coomera* ☎ *07/5588–1111, 1800/073–300* 🌐 *www.dreamworld.com.au* 🎫 *Entry from A$69.*

Paradise Country

FARM/RANCH | FAMILY | Billed as "an authentic Australian farm experience," the park appeals to families with wildlife tours, animal feedings, koala cuddling, sheep shearing, boomerang throwing, and displays of horsemanship. Meanwhile, adults can book a private wine tasting session. You can also stay overnight in an on-site tent, including eco tents, or your own motor home. The park is directly behind the Australian Outback Spectacular. Car parking spaces are limited. ✉ *Pacific Motorway, Oxenford* ☎ *07/5519–6200* 🌐 *paradisecountry.com.au* 🎫 *From A$39.*

Warner Bros. Movie World

FILM/TV STUDIO | FAMILY | Mixing old Hollywood ambience with live character shows, interactive adventures, and thrill rides for young and old, Warner Bros. offers something for everyone. Rides include the Batman-themed DC Rivals HyperCoaster—the southern hemisphere's longest, fastest and highest. With a large portion of its area now covered by a 43,055-square-foot roof, this park is a smart choice in bad weather. It's adjacent to Australian Outback Spectacular. ✉ *Pacific Motorway, Oxenford* ☎ *133–386* 🌐 *www.movieworld.com.au* 🎫 *From A$89* ⏱ *Closed Anzac Day (Apr. 25) and Christmas Day.*

Wet 'n' Wild Water World

WATER PARK | FAMILY | Oxenford's Wet 'n' Wild Water World boasts magnificent, adrenaline-pumping waterslides including the tallest water-park tower in Australia, the Double Barrel two-person body slide, and the Surfrider that simulates the sensation of surfing the world's biggest waves. Kids love Buccaneer Bay, a pirate-themed aquatic playground with multiple levels, and the new Wet 'n' Wild Junior area, featuring another eight kid-friendly slides, including mini versions of the park's most popular thrill rides. Select pools and slides are heated May through September, when days are often still sunny and warm. The park is ½ km (¼ mile) down the Pacific Highway from Warner Bros. Movie World. ✉ *Pacific Hwy., Oxenford* ☎ *133–386* 🌐 *www.wetnwild.com.au* 🎫 *From A$79.*

Southport and Main Beach

16 km (10 miles) southeast of Oxenford.

South of Oxenford, look for the turnoff to the Spit, a natural peninsula that stretches 4 km (2½ miles) north, almost to the tip of South Stradbroke Island. Seaworld Drive runs the full length of the Spit, from Mariner's Cove (a popular covered area with affordable restaurants and fast-food outlets) to a nature reserve. This narrow peninsula is bordered by the Pacific Ocean to the east and the calm waters of the Broadwater (a long lagoon) to the west. Two of the Gold Coast's most opulent hotels face each other across Seaworld Drive and are connected to Marina Mirage, arguably the most elegant shopping precinct on the Gold Coast. An assortment of adventure sports operators can also be found in this area, including jet boating and skiing, helicopter flights, fishing charters, electric bike rentals, surf schools, and sailing lessons.

Restaurants

Misono Japanese Steakhouse

$$$$ | JAPANESE | FAMILY | Run by charismatic chefs, who clearly love to please a crowd, this popular teppanyaki restaurant at the JW Marriott Gold Coast Resort & Spa is as much about the spectacle of the meal as the quality ingredients and perfectly executed flavors. Try the succulent fillet steak with teriyaki chicken, traditional tofu and hibachi vegetables, or salmon and lobster tail. **Known for:** signature cocktails; theatrical experience with charistmatic chefs; deluxe seafood and Wagyu banquets. *Average main: A$65 JW Marriott Hotel, Level 3, 158 Ferny Ave., Surfers Paradise 07/5592–9800 www.misonorestaurant.com Closed Mon. and Tues. No lunch.*

Omeros Bros Seafood Restaurant

$$$ | SEAFOOD | This iconic seafood restaurant perched on the waterfront at the lovely Marina Mirage center has dishes spanning the seafood spectrum—from bouillabaisse and classic surf and turf to local barramundi, lobster, oysters, mud crab, and Moreton Bay bugs. This is also a tempting selection of meat, vegetarian, and pasta dishes, and an extensive dessert menu and wine list. **Known for:** fresh local seafood; spectacular waterfront views and sunsets; excellent service. *Average main: A$40 Marina Mirage, Seaworld Dr., Shop 55/74, Southport 07/5591–7222 www.omerosbros.com.*

Hotels

Palazzo Versace

$$$$ | HOTEL | The famous Italian fashion house lent its flair to this expansive, opulent waterfront hotel—the first of its kind in the world. **Pros:** all rooms include a spa bath; five-star service and dining; palm-fringed 206-foot-long lagoon pool. **Cons:** still an icon, but may have seen better days; opulent style may not be to all tastes; pricey. *Rooms from: A$499 94 Seaworld Dr., adjoining Marina Mirage, Southport 07/5509–8000 www.palazzoversace.com 200 rooms Free Breakfast.*

Shopping

Marina Mirage Gold Coast

MALL | The sleek Marina Mirage Gold Coast features 80-plus stores, including high-end gift and housewares, jewelry, and designer fashion boutiques like Christensen Copenhagen and Calvin Klein, along with famous Australian brands, fine waterfront restaurants, beauty salons and day spas, and marina facilities. On Saturday morning (6:30 am–noon), buy fresh gourmet produce at the Marina Mirage Gourmet Farmers' Markets. *74 Seaworld Dr., Main Beach, Southport www.marinamirage.com.au.*

Activities

BOAT TOURS

★ Paradise Jet Boating

ADVENTURE TOURS | FAMILY | The thrill-seekers' way to sightsee, these high-speed jet boats rocket through the Gold Coast's scenic beaches and waterways, treating passengers to 360-degree spins, high-speed drifting, and other exciting maneuvers along the way. ✉ *Mariners Cove Marina, 60 Seaworld Dr., Shop 7B, Southport* ☎ *07/5526–3089, 1300/538–262* 🌐 *www.paradisejetboating.com.au* 🎫 *From A$42.*

CYCLING

Beach Bikes Gold Coast

BIKING | This family-run business is the longest running bike hire operation on the Gold Coast. Hire includes delivery to anywhere on the Gold Coast, pickup, helmet, and lock. E-bikes are also available. ✉ *28 Cronin Ave.* ☎ *0413/119–909* 🌐 *www.bikehiregoldcoast.com.au* 🎫 *Bike rental from A$30 for ½-day hire.*

SURFING

Get Wet Surf School

SURFING | Get Wet Surf School holds group lessons (up to six students per coach) at a sheltered, crowd-free beach off the Spit, just north of Surfers Paradise. They also host private lessons and multiday surf tours. ✉ *Seaworld Dr., Main Beach, Southport* ☎ *1800/438–938* 🌐 *www.getwetsurf.com* 🎫 *From A$65.*

Surfers Paradise and Broadbeach

5 km (3 miles) south of Southport.

Before the Gold Coast, now Australia's sixth-largest city, there was Surfers Paradise: a stunning 3-km (2-mile) stretch of beach, 5 km (3 miles) south of Southport. Now a strip of high-rises, it's still a vibrant beachside town, with plentiful shopping options and an emergent arts and fine-dining culture (check out the 4217 for some of the region's up-and-coming artisans and providores (*www.the4217.com*). For stunning 360-degree views of the entire coast and hinterland, venture up to the SkyPoint observation deck and Seventy7 Café + Bar located on the 77th floor of Surfers' famous Q1 Tower, the tallest building in the southern hemisphere. For the latest on events, nightlife, new eateries, and more visit *www.surfersparadise.com.*

Two miles farther south, Broadbeach is one of the most popular areas on the Gold Coast. It's also home to some great cafés, trendy nightspots, and the mega-shopping mall Pacific Fair. For up-to-date information visit *broadbeachgc.com.*

Hotels

★ Peppers Soul

$$$$ | HOTEL | FAMILY | With its central location right on Cavill Avenue and across the road from a patrolled beach, the 77-story Peppers Soul offers some of the most stunning views on the Gold Coast. **Pros:** central Surfers Paradise location; all rooms have ocean views; breakfast is a cut above. **Cons:** not a good choice for those with vertigo; can get hectic during school holidays; due to number of floors, elevator can be slow from higher floors. $ *Rooms from: A$419* ✉ *8 The Esplanade, Surfers Paradise* ☎ *07/5635–5700* 🌐 *www.peppers.com.au/soul-surfers-paradise* 🛏 *287 rooms* 🍽 *No Meals.*

QT Gold Coast

$$$ | HOTEL | One of Queensland's most popular destination hotels, this vibrant retro-meets-modern resort boasts 360-degree views of the beach and hinterland, on-site restaurants and bars, and enough quirk and energy to make it stand brightly apart. **Pros:** incredible views; lively atmosphere and design; excellent on-site dining and bar options. **Cons:** area can be noisy at night (ask for a room on a higher level); self-parking costs A$20 per night; breakfast extra and expensive. *Rooms from: A$252* *7 Staghorn Ave., Surfers Paradise* *07/5584–1200* *www.qtgoldcoast.com.au* *297 rooms* *No Meals.*

The Star Gold Coast

$$$ | RESORT | This massive, glitzy resort in Broadbeach houses The Star Grand and The Darling hotels: the former offering tasteful rooms with a calming palette and the latter, spacious suites and penthouses designed with decadence in mind. **Pros:** free parking for guests; modern, luxury furnishings and facilities; close to shopping centers. **Cons:** pool at The Star Grand is on the small side; no complimentary water in rooms; 15-minute walk to the beach. *Rooms from: A$248* *Broadbeach Island, Casino Dr., off Gold Coast Hwy., Broadbeach* *07/5592–8100* *www.star.com.au/goldcoast* *The Star Grand: 596 rooms; The Darling: 56 suites* *Free Breakfast.*

The Wave Resort

$$$ | RESORT | This ultramodern high-rise apartment resort is one of Broadbeach's most luxurious. **Pros:** well-maintained and soundproofed rooms; free parking and unlimited Wi-Fi; helpful staff. **Cons:** checkout is 10 am; in-room provisions not replenished; no one-night stays in peak periods. *Rooms from: A$252* *89–91 Surf Parade, Broadbeach* *07/5555–9200* *www.thewaveresort.com.au* *118 apartments* *No Meals.*

Shopping

★ Pacific Fair

MALL | A sprawling indoor/outdoor shopping hub, Pacific Fair is Queensland's largest mall, featuring Myer and David Jones department stores, major retailers, and more than 400 specialty stores and services (including travel agencies, fashion outlets, and sports and outdoor gear). For a breather, head to the landscaped grounds with restaurants and cafés dotted around sparkling pools and water features, a children's park, and village green, or take in a movie at the 12-screen cinema complex. *Hooker Blvd., at Gold Coast Hwy., opposite The Star Casino and Hotel, Broadbeach* *www.pacificfair.com.au.*

Surfers Paradise Beachfront Markets

MARKET | Every Friday and Saturday night crowds flock to haggle for handmade crafts and gifts at the busy Surfers Paradise Beachfront Markets. More than 100 market stalls line the beachfront from 4 pm. *The Esplanade, between Hanlan St. and Elkhorn Ave., Surfers Paradise* *www.surfersparadisemarkets.com.au.*

Burleigh Heads and Beyond

At the southern end of the Gold Coast, between Broadbeach and the New South Wales border, you'll find a burgeoning strip of funky restaurants, bars, and cafés, high-rise apartment blocks sitting cheek by jowl alongside old-school seaside shacks and motels, and some of the world's most renowned surf breaks. Foodies will feel well at home; many of the Gold Coast's best restaurants are to be found here. Families will love Currumbin Wildlife Sanctuary, and the calm waters of Tallebudgera Beach. Hotel accommodation is limited—you're more likely to find holiday apartment rentals. For all the latest information about Burleigh Heads visit *www.queensland.com.*

Sights

★ Currumbin Wildlife Sanctuary

WILDLIFE REFUGE | FAMILY | A Gold Coast institution and perhaps the most ecologically minded wildlife facility in the region, Currumbin Wildlife Sanctuary is a 70-acre, not-for-profit National Trust Reserve featuring more than 60 koalas and an on-site wildlife hospital. Established in 1947 as a lorikeet sanctuary, it now shelters a wide variety of Australian species, including kangaroos, crocodiles, wombats, dingoes, Tasmanian devils, echidnas, emus, and rare birds. There are more than 10 daily animal feedings, shows, and performances, friendly 'roos (often with joeys in their pouches!) love to be petted and hand-fed, and the fleet of young koalas make for perfect cuddle and photo opportunities. All revenue goes toward Currumbin's work protecting, treating, and rehabilitating local wildlife. **TIP→ Tickets are much cheaper if bought online in advance, especially in low season.** ✉ *28 Tomewin St., off Gold Coast Hwy., Currumbin ✣ 14 km (8½ miles) south of Broadbeach ☎ 07/5534–1266, 1300/886–511 🌐 currumbinsanctuary.com.au 🎫 From A$50.*

David Fleay Wildlife Park

OTHER ATTRACTION | FAMILY | Located in the town of Burleigh Heads—7 km (4½ miles) south of Broadbeach—and named for an Australian wildlife naturalist, the park features a daily program of ranger-led walks and presentations, a boardwalk trail, and picnic facilities. See koalas, kangaroos, dingoes, platypuses, and crocodiles, grouped together in separate zones according to their natural habitat, or discover threatened species and the elusive platypus in the state-of-the-art nocturnal house. There's also a café and a gift shop. **TIP→ Daily presentations are included in the ticket price; the platypus feeding at 10:30 am is a must-see.** ✉ *Tallebudgera Creek Rd., near W. Burleigh Rd., Burleigh Heads ☎ 07/5579–2051 🌐 www.npsr.qld.gov.au/parks/david-fleay 🎫 From A$26.*

Restaurants

The Collective

$ | CONTEMPORARY | FAMILY | This market-style collaboration has been at the forefront of a new wave of dining establishments hitting the Gold Coast since 2016. With five kitchens operating under the one roof, patrons can choose from contemporary Australian, Mexican, Italian, Asian, or American-inspired cuisines, in this airy, light-filled space. **Known for:** fun, noisy vibe; huge variety of dishes including gluten-free and vegetarian options; rooftop bar perfect for sunset drinks. *$ Average main: A$20 ✉ 1128 Gold Coast Hwy., Palm Beach ☎ 07/5618–8229 🌐 www.thecollective-palmbeach.com.au.*

Francies Pizzeria

$$ | PIZZA | At the far southern end of the Gold Coast, this bustling hole-in-the-wall punches well above its weight, serving Neapolitan-style pizzas from 5 pm every night to a friendly crowd of in-the-know locals and visitors. With quirky pop- and rock-inspired names like The Fennel Countdown, Sage Against the Machine, and the Dollop Parton, the menu includes a full range of vegan pizzas, with plenty of gluten-free options. **Known for:** thin-crust pizzas, oven-baked focaccia, and share plates; friendly, no-fuss service and great vibes; full range of vegan pizza options. *$ Average main: A$22 ✉ Shop 2, 102 Griffith St., Coolangatta ☎ 0411/415–554 🌐 www.francies.com.au ⏲ No lunch.*

Coffee and Quick Bites

Zephyr Coffee

$ | AUSTRALIAN | Tucked away down a side street, across the road from beautiful Kirra beach, Zephyr Coffee is the kind of unpretentious local café you wish was in your neighborhood. With house-roasted beans, coffee is the major drawcard, but the food is also delicious, with tasty options including acai bowls, homemade banana bread, and jaffle toasted sandwiches, all perfect for a beachside snack. **Known for:** healthy breakfast bowls, including dairy-free and vegan options; air-roasted coffee beans in a range of house blends; range of sweet and savory jaffles. *$ Average main: A$10 ✉ 1 Churchill St., Coolangatta ☎ 07/5659–2745 🌐 www.zephyrcoffeeco.com.au ⏲ No dinner.*

Hotels

★ Bon Sol

$$$$ | **APARTMENT** | Featuring interior styling by Anna Spiro, responsible for the makeover of Cabarita's Halcyon House, these unassuming 1960s two-bedroom apartments—currently two in total—offer a completely different Gold Coast experience. **Pros:** luxe fittings, designer interiors, and personalized service; unlike anywhere else on the Gold Coast; in the heart of groovy Burleigh Heads. **Cons:** not suitable for children under 13; minimum three-night stay; expensive. *Rooms from: A$770 ✉ 44 The Esplanade, Burleigh Heads ☎ 0419/465–563 🌐 bonsol.com.au 2 apartments No Meals.*

The Mysa Motel

$$$ | **MOTEL** | The Mysa Motel captures the essence of old-school quirk, a stroll away from white sand beaches in Palm Beach on the southern Gold Coast. **Pros:** touches like self check-in and complimentary welcome pack; luxurious and cozy, with distinct retro Gold Coast vibes; close to Palm Beach cafés, restaurants, and bars. **Cons:** no on-site manager; beach is close, but you have to cross a main road to get there; may be some traffic noise in some rooms. *Rooms from: A$220 ✉ 1100 Gold Coast Hwy., Palm Beach ☎ 07/467–976 🌐 themysamotel.com No Meals 7 rooms.*

Activities

SURFING

★ Walkin' on Water

SURFING | **FAMILY** | Learn to surf amid the pristine beach and point breaks of Greenmount and Coolangatta. Walkin' on Water offers group beginner lessons and private lessons daily, as well as a SurfGroms program especially for kids. Board and rash vest are included in the price, as is a wet suit if you need one. Two-hour group lessons from A$55 per person. *✉ Marine Parade, in carpark opposite Greenmount Surf Club, Coolangatta ☎ 0418/780–311 🌐 www.walkinonwater.com From A$55.*

Gold Coast Hinterland

No visit to the Gold Coast would be complete without an excursion to the region's verdant hinterland. The natural grandeur of the area lies in dramatic contrast to the human-made excesses of the coastal strip. The Gold Coast Hinterland's superb national parks and nature reserves protect magnificent waterfalls, natural rock pools, mountain lookouts with expansive views of the surrounding terrain and coast, and an array of wildlife. Walking trails traverse rain forest dense with ancient trees. Among the parks lie boutique wineries and quaint villages where a high-rise is anything over one story. The parks form part of a unique, ancient geological region known as the Scenic Rim: a chain of mountains running parallel to the coast through southeast Queensland and northern New South Wales. Because it rises to 3,000 feet above sea level, some parts of the hinterland are 4°C–6°C (7°F–11°F) cooler than the coast.

GETTING HERE AND AROUND

The hinterland's main areas—Tamborine Mountain, Lamington National Park, and Springbrook—can be reached from the Pacific Highway or via Beaudesert from Brisbane, and are a 30- to 40-minute drive inland from the Gold Coast. To reach Tamborine, around 80 km (50 miles) south of Brisbane and 36 km (24 miles) from Southport, take Exit 57 off the Pacific Motorway to the Oxenford–Tamborine Road; or take Exit 71 off the Pacific Motorway, the Nerang–Beaudesert Road, to Canungra. From Canungra, follow the signs to Tamborine, 4 km (2½ miles) along Tamborine Mountain Road. The Gold Coast Hinterland is ideal for touring by car: rent a vehicle, arm yourself with local maps, fill the tank, and take to the hills.

TOURS

Araucaria Ecotours

This eco-certified company runs single and multiday guided tours of Mt. Tamborine and the Scenic Rim, taking in its rich diversity of wildlife and habitat. Travel options include camping, bird-watching, glowworm cave tours, wine tasting, and more. ✉ *1770 Running Creek Rd.* ☎ *07/5544–1283* 🌐 *www.learnaboutwildlife.com* 🎫 *From A$165.*

JPT Tour Group

This tour company (also known as Australian Day Tours) picks up passengers from Gold Coast hotels and the Brisbane Transit Centre daily at 8:15 am and travels via Tamborine Mountain to the Hinterland and O'Reilly's Rainforest Retreat, before returning to the Gold Coast at 5:15 pm (Brisbane at 6:15 pm). Tour highlights include the Mt. Tamborine Gallery Walk, and lunch with optional bird feeding at O'Reilly's. The company also runs nightly tours and guided walks through local hinterland caves, which, when the sun is down, light up spectacularly with populations of glowworms. ✉ *9 Trickett St., Shop 6, Surfers Paradise* ☎ *1300/781–362, 07/5630–1602* 🌐 *www.jpttours.com* 🎫 *From A$110.*

Southern Cross Day Tours

This father-and-son team leads expeditions to the natural wonders of the area, keeping away from the crowds. Tours include several national parks, plus wildlife spotting and cultural activities along the way. ✉ *Circle on Cavill, Cavill Ave., Shop T34, Surfers Paradise* ☎ *1300/762–665 in Australia, 07/5655–0716 international* 🌐 *southerncrossdaytours.com.au* 🎫 *From A$99.*

Sights

★ Lamington National Park

FOREST | Part of the Gondwana Rainforests of Australia World Heritage Area, beautiful Lamington National Park is a lush, subtropical-temperate zone that shelters abundant and highly diverse plant and animal life. Forming part of the largest subtropical rain forest in the world, find Antarctic beech trees dating back more than 3,000 years, as well as waterfalls, mountain pools, breathtaking views, bright wildflowers, and more than 160 native bird species. The Park is laced with 160 km (100 miles) of bushwalking tracks, ranging from 1.2 km (¾ mile) to 54 km (34 miles), with campsites along the way. All park camping areas require nightly permits, obtained in advance. ✉ *Binna Burra* ☎ *137–468* 🌐 *parks.des.qld.gov.au* 🎫 *Free day entry, paid permit required for overnight stays.*

Springbrook National Park

FOREST | The peaks of Springbrook National Park rise to around 3,000 feet, dominating the skyline west of the Gold Coast. The World Heritage–listed park has four regions: scenic Springbrook plateau, Mt. Cougal, Natural Bridge, and Numinbah. Highlights include waterfalls and cascades, Jurassic age hoop pines, ancient rain forest, and abundant native birds and wildlife. Thanks to steep, winding roads and longish distances between sections, it takes at least a full day to explore this large park. It's about 30 km (19 miles) from the tiny hamlet of Springbrook to Natural Bridge—a waterfall that cascades through a cavern roof into an icy pool, which is home to Australia's largest glowworm colony. Several waterfalls, including the area's largest, Purling Brook Falls, can be reached via a steepish 4-km (2½-mile) path (allow 15 minutes for each half mile). The 54-km Gold Coast Hinterland Great Walk extends from the Settlement campground to Green Mountains campsite in Tamborine National Park. For those short on time or energy, the lookout near the parking lot has beautiful waterfall views. Camping is permitted only in designated private campgrounds. Book online in advance (*qpws.usedirect.com*). ✉ *Springbrook* ☎ *137–468* 🌐 *parks.des.qld.gov.au/parks/springbrook* 🎫 *Free, paid permit required for overnight stays.*

Tamborine National Park

FOREST | More than 20 million years ago, volcanic eruptions created rugged landscapes, while fertile volcanic soils produced the luxuriant tracts of rain forest that make up the enchanting Tamborine National Park. It's worth spending at least a day or two here. Apart from the natural environment, there are wineries, lodges, restaurants, and the famed Gallery Walk, a 1-km-long (½-mile-long) street lined with art galleries. Some of the simplest (under two hours) and best trails here are the Cedar Creek Falls Track with waterfall views, Palm Grove Rainforest Circuit, and Macdonald Rainforest Circuit, a quieter walk popular with bird-watchers. Start your visit with a stop at Tamborine Mountain Visitor Information Centre (open 10 am to 3 pm weekdays and until 4 pm weekends), and don't forget to stop by the local Botanic Gardens for a rest and a picnic. ✉ *Main Western Rd., Mt. Tamborine* ☎ *07/5545–3200 information center* 🌐 *visittamborinemountain.com.au* 🎫 *Free.*

Hotels

Binna Burra Mountain Lodge & Campsite

$ | **B&B/INN** | **FAMILY** | At the doorstep of Lamington National Park, this historic, eco-certified property has reemerged from the ravages of the 2019 wildfires, and remains a bird-watcher's paradise, with sweeping views across Heritage-listed rain forest and more than 160 km (99 miles) of walking trails. **Pros:** great choice for families; beautiful setting, views, and wildlife; old-fashioned, communal atmosphere. **Cons:** while rooms are heated, the area can be cold and damp in winter; Sky Lodge in need of refurbishment; remote location means food options limited to on-site dining. $ *Rooms from: A$75* ✉ *Binna Burra Rd., via Beechmont, Lamington National Park* ☎ *07/5533–3622, 1300/246–622* 🌐 *www.binnaburralodge.com.au* *18 sky lodges, 18 safari tents, 18 campsites* 🍽 *No Meals.*

★ Gwinganna Lifestyle Retreat

$$$$ | ALL-INCLUSIVE | Gwinganna means lookout in the local Yugambeh language, and true to its name, this 500-acre property sits high on a plateau in the Tallebudgera Valley, with views out to the ocean—just 60 minutes from Brisbane Airport. **Pros:** simple, yet delicious cuisine with a focus on organic ingredients; tranquil location with spectacular views; award-winning spa and experiences like equine therapy. **Cons:** no alcohol or caffeine, except for some weekend programs; communal vibe and meals may be off-putting for some; set arrival dates apply. $ *Rooms from: A$1210* ✉ *192 Syndicate Rd., Tallebudgera Valley* ☎ *1800/219–272, 07/5589–5000* 🌐 *www.gwinganna.com* *60 rooms* 🍽 *All-Inclusive.*

O'Reilly's Rainforest Retreat, Villas & Lost World Spa

$$ | RESORT | FAMILY | One thousand meters (3,280 feet) above sea level and immersed in the subtropical rain forests of World Heritage–listed Lamington National Park, the eco-certified O'Reilly's Rainforest Retreat boasts a range of accommodation options, from simple garden- and mountain-view rooms, to one- and two-bedroom canopy suites, and luxury, multiroom mountain villas (complete with balcony Jacuzzis). **Pros:** proximity to wildlife including kangaroos; breathtaking location; infinity pool features stunning mountain views. **Cons:** restaurant meals are expensive; Wi-Fi available in public areas but can be slow; long drive up mountain—use a coach or transfer service if you're not confident on Australian roads. $ *Rooms from: A$180* ✉ *Lamington National Park Rd., Canungra* ☎ *07/5544–0644, 1800/688–722* 🌐 *www.oreillys.com.au* *120 rooms* 🍽 *Free Breakfast.*

Pethers Rainforest Retreat

$$$$ | RESORT | Set on 12 acres of privately owned rain forest, this secluded, couples-only resort comprises 10 spacious tree houses with timber floors, French doors opening onto verandas, fireplaces, hot tubs, and open-plan interiors furnished with Asian antiques. **Pros:** luxurious appointments; glorious environs; complimentary Wi-Fi, parking, and breakfast. **Cons:** limited mobile phone coverage; degustion dinner menu may not appeal to everyone; no on-site dinner Sunday. $ *Rooms from: A$325* ✉ *28B Geissmann St., North Tamborine* ☎ *07/5545–4577* 🌐 *www.pethers.com.au* *10 tree houses* 🍽 *Free Breakfast.*

Activities

HIKING

Bushwalking is a popular pastime in the national parks and nature reserves of the Gold Coast Hinterland, where an extensive network of well-maintained scenic trails caters to recreational walkers, serious hikers, campers, and wildlife lovers. The region's many protected wilderness tracts, including World Heritage–listed Gondwana Rainforests of Australia (within Springbook National Park), contain hundreds of well-marked trails that vary from easy half-hour strolls to steep half-day hikes and multiday treks. Most Hinterland walks offer spectacular views and sights.

However, conditions can be challenging and changeable, so before setting out on longer hikes, get suitably equipped. Download local trail maps and detailed park info from the Queensland Parks and Forests website or regional visitor information offices, and follow the guidelines.

Luke's Bluff Lookout on O'Reilly's Plateau, Lamington National Park

When walking, wear sturdy shoes, sunscreen, and protective gear; carry maps and a compass; and pack drinking water, emergency food supplies, and a well-charged mobile phone. If possible, walk in a group, especially on long hikes. Check local weather conditions with the Bureau of Meteorology and trail conditions on the Parks and Forests website before you go.

If exploring the national parks by car, check road conditions with the RACQ's website and be sure you have local maps, good tires, sound brakes, water, and a full tank of gas before setting out.

Department of Environment and Science, Parks and Forests Portfolio
CAMPGROUND | ☎ *137–468 camping permits and information* 🌐 *parks.des.qld.gov.au.*

Royal Automobile Club of Queensland (RACQ)
CAMPGROUND | ☎ *131–905* 🌐 *www.racq.com.au.*

Noosa

39 km (24 miles) northeast of Nambour, 17 km (11 miles) north of Coolum, 140 km (87 miles) north of Brisbane.

Set along the calm waters of Laguna Bay at the northern tip of the Sunshine Coast, Noosa is one of Australia's most stylish resort areas. Until the mid-1980s the town consisted of little more than a few shacks—then surfers discovered the spectacular waves that curl around the headland of Noosa National Park. In 2020, Noosa officially became the tenth World Surfing Reserve. Today Noosa is an enticing mix of surf, sand, natural beauty and sophistication, with a serious reputation for distinctive, always-evolving cuisine. Views along the trail from Laguna Lookout to the top of the headland take in miles of magnificent beaches, ocean, and dense vegetation.

Sights

Teewah Coloured Sands

NATURE SIGHT | About 3 km (2 miles) northeast of Noosa Heads you'll find the Teewah Coloured Sands, an area of multicolor dunes created in the Ice Age by natural chemicals in the soil. Teewah's sands stretch inland from the beach to a distance of about 17 km (11 miles); some of the 72 distinctly hued sands even form cliffs rising to 600 feet. A four-wheel-drive vehicle and permit are essential for exploring this area and sites to the north, such as Cooloola National Park—home to 1,300-plus species of plants, 700 native animals, and 44% of Australia's bird species—and Great Sandy National Park. Access is by ferry across the Noosa River at Tewantin. Tour operators run day trips that take in these sights; some include visits to K'gari (Fraser Island), north of Rainbow Beach. You can also explore the area on foot. One of Queensland's Great Walks winds through Cooloola National Park. ✉ *Noosa Heads.*

Beaches

Noosa Main Beach

BEACH | FAMILY | With gentle waves and year-round lifeguard patrol, Noosa's Main Beach is a perfect swimming spot, ideal for families or those who aren't confident in the bigger swells. The beach backs onto leafy Hastings Street with its bustle of upmarket cafés, bars, restaurants, and shopping spots. For a quieter scene, head to Noosa Spit, a popular picnic spot and off-leash dog beach. Or for wild beauty and great surf, Tea Tree Bay in the national park is a 20-minute walk away. **Amenities:** food and drink; lifeguards; parking; showers; toilets. **Best for:** sunrise; sunset; swimming; surfing; walking. ✉ *Hastings St., Noosa Heads* 🌐 *www.visitnoosa.com.au.*

★ Sunshine Beach

BEACH | Incorporating 16 km (10 miles) of beachfront that stretches north to Noosa national park, lovely Sunshine Beach is patrolled year-round. Beach breaks, reliable swell, a rocky headland sheltering it from winds, and clear, glassy water make Sunshine popular with surfers. End a long day of swimming with a beer or a meal at The Sunshine Beach Surf Club. **Amenities:** food and drink; lifeguards; parking; showers; toilets. **Best for:** sunrise; sunset; surfing; swimming; walking. ✉ *Belmore Terr., Sunshine Beach.*

Restaurants

Bistro C

$$$ | MODERN AUSTRALIAN | Spectacular views of the bay from the open dining area make a stunning backdrop for this fashionable restaurant's Mod Oz cuisine. The fresh, tropical menu highlights local seafood, though landlubbers can partake of several meat and vegetarian dishes (think lamb rump, caramelized pork belly, duck confit, or risotto verde). **Known for:** special tapas and drinks menu 3 pm to 5 pm daily; beachfront location; award-winning cuisine. $ *Average main: A$37* ✉ *49 Hastings St., on Beach Complex, Noosa Heads* ☎ *07/5447–2855* 🌐 *www.bistroc.com.au.*

Ricky's River Bar + Restaurant

$$$ | MODERN AUSTRALIAN | A dining room overlooking the Noosa River makes this picturesque restaurant the perfect spot for a relaxed lunch or a romantic dinner. The menu features "modern Noosa cuisine," which mingles Mediterranean flavors beautifully with Australian ingredients. **Known for:** delicious dessert cocktails; stunning Noosa riverfront location; tasting menu with matching wines. $ *Average main: A$45* ✉ *Noosa Wharf, Quamby Pl., Noosa Heads* ☎ *07/5447–2455* 🌐 *www.rickys.com.au.*

Sunshine Beach Surf Club

$$ | AUSTRALIAN | With its prime oceanfront position, and a large all-weather open deck overlooking the beach, the Sunshine Beach Surf Club is the kind of place you could sit for hours just soaking up the view. Fortunately, the food is also excellent, with highlights including salt-and-pepper squid, fish tacos, and their signature *nasi goreng* (Indonesian fried rice), as well as a range of classic pub fare like burgers, steak, chicken parmy, nachos, and pizza. **Known for:** nasi goreng with pork belly, shrimp, coriander salad, and fried egg; one of the best oceanfront locations on the Sunshine Coast; fresh seafood, including the ever-popular salt-and-pepper squid. *Average main: 24* ✉ *Corner of Duke St. and Belmore Terr., Sunshine Beach* ☎ *07/5447–5491* 🌐 *surf-club.sunshinebeachslsc.com.au.*

Coffee and Quick Bites

★ Moonstruck Coffee & Gin
$ | **CAFÉ** | By day, grab an outdoor table and watch the world drift by with a perfectly balanced flat white, as Moonstruck, a Hastings Street hole-in-the-wall, has excellent coffee. At night, soak up the art deco decor and mood lighting with a dirty martini (or two)—it has a 50-plus list of Australian boutique gins and great cocktails. **Known for:** array of all-local boutique gins make it a fun nighttime spot; house-roasted coffee; outdoor table. *Average main: A$15* ✉ *5 Hastings St., Noosa Heads* 🌐 *www.moonstrucknoosa.com.*

Hotels

Sofitel Noosa Pacific Resort
$$$$ | **RESORT** | Facing fashionable Hastings Street on one side, the river on the other, the Sofitel is the place to stay in Noosa. **Pros:** spacious, well-kept rooms; close to beach and shops; beautiful pool area. **Cons:** pool can get busy during school holidays; pricey; parking available but not included. *Rooms from: A$400* ✉ *14–16 Hastings St., Noosa Heads* ☎ *07/5449–4888* 🌐 *www.sofitelnoosa-pacificresort.com.au* *176 rooms* *No Meals.*

Hope Island

This isn't your average island. Like several Gold Coast islands, it is actually a mile or two inland and circled by the Coomera River and a series of canals. The resort has a marina full of luxury launches and yachts, two golf courses, a swanky hotel, beautiful condos, and upscale restaurants, nightclubs, and shops. Stop by if you're passing through for a glimpse into jet-set culture, Queensland style.

Hope Island is accessed via bridges from the west or east. Route 4, also known as the Oxenford–Southport Road, passes straight through.

Activities

RIVER CRUISING

Everglades Ecosafaris
BOATING | Everglades Ecosafaris runs half- and full-day river cruises and guided canoe trips through the serene wilderness of the Noosa Everglades. For the full experience, spend the night "glamping" at the Habitat Ecocamp. ✉ *Everglades Ecosafaris, 204 Lake Flat Rd., Noosaville* ☎ *07/5485–3165* 🌐 *www.evergladesecosafaris.com.au* *From A$79.*

SURFING

Go Ride a Wave
SURFING | This operator rents equipment and runs surfing lessons for beginners at Noosa Heads Main Beach. Book in advance to secure two-hour beginner, group, or private lessons, with surfboard, wet suit, and all other equipment included in the fee (A$75/$65). Discounts apply for multiple lessons. ✉ *On beach, Hastings St., near Haul St., Noosa Heads* ☎ *1300/132–441* 🌐 *www.gorideawave.com.au.*

Peregian and Coolum

11 km (7 miles) south of Noosa, with Coolum 17 km (11 miles) south of Noosa and 25 km (16 miles) northeast of Nambour.

At the center of the Sunshine Coast, Coolum makes an ideal base for exploring the countryside. It has one of the finest beaches in the region, a growing reputation for good food and quality accommodations, and all the services you might need: banks with ATMs, medical centers, gas stations, pharmacies, supermarkets, gyms, beauty salons, and day spas—even a beachfront playground, kiosk, and skate park. Ten minutes north of Coolum is Peregian, a quaint little seaside town with numerous fashionable shops, eateries, and facilities, a string of stunning beaches, and a local produce and crafts market on the first and third Sunday of the month.

Beaches

★ Coolum Beach

BEACH | FAMILY | A popular choice for families, beautiful **Coolum Beach** boasts a surf club, skate park, playgrounds, change rooms, toilets, kiosk, shorefront parks, and well-maintained picnic areas. A long, white-sand beach, Coolum is patrolled year-round and has a nice beach break and some decent, uncrowded waves off the headland. Walk south along the boardwalk to the headland park for magnificent coastal views, or north to quieter **Peregian Beach** with its patrolled surf, playground, and adjacent Environmental Park. **Amenities:** food and drink; lifeguards; parking; showers; toilets. **Best for:** sunset; surfing; swimming; walking. ✉ *David Low Way, Coolum* 🌐 *www.visitsunshinecoast.com.*

Restaurants

Coolum Beach Surf Club

$$ | AUSTRALIAN | FAMILY | This lively oceanfront restaurant serves fresh seafood and simple, pub-style fare in its large dining room overlooking Coolum Beach. Reasonable prices, rotating meal specials, live entertainment, and a friendly, casual atmosphere ensure it is always well attended by locals and visitors alike. **Known for:** casual dining with a spectacular oceanfront setting; wood-fired chargrill steaks, locally sourced; ultimate brekky tower—big breakfast for 3–4 people. 💲 *Average main: A$24* ✉ *1775–1779 David Low Way, Coolum* ☎ *07/5446–1148* 🌐 *www.coolumsurfclub.com.*

★ Pitchfork

$$ | MODERN AUSTRALIAN | Positioned within the café and shopping strip along Peregian Beach, this contemporary seaside bistro entices crowds with its imaginative, subtropical Mod Oz cuisine and modern, rustic styling. Booking in advance is highly recommended. **Known for:** entire menu available for takeout; rotating seasonal menu; kid-friendly menu. 💲 *Average main: A$35* ✉ *5/4 Kingfisher Dr., Peregian Beach* ☎ *07/5471–3697* 🌐 *pitchforkrestaurant.com.au* ⏲ *Closed Mon.*

Hotels

Coolum Seaside Resort

$$ | APARTMENT | FAMILY | These sleek and spacious self-contained studios and one- to four-bedroom apartments are just around the corner from Coolum's restaurants, shops, and beach. **Pros:** central to beach and restaurants; good on-site facilities; complimentary Wi-Fi, cable TV, and parking. **Cons:** about a 10-minute walk to the beach; minimum two-night stay; dated design in some units. 💲 *Rooms from: A$190* ✉ *6–8 Perry St., Coolum* ☎ *07/5455–7200, 1800/809–062* 🌐 *www.coolumseaside.com* 🛏 *44 apartments* 🍽 *No Meals.*

Activities

SURFING

Coolum Surf School

SURFING | Run by an expert surfer and local lifeguard, Coolum Surf School runs two-hour group and 90-minute private lessons, as well as board and gear hire. You'll find it north of Coolum Surf Lifesaving Club, next to the skate park. ✉ *Coolum Boardriders Clubhouse, Tickle Park, David Low Way, Coolum* ☎ *0438/731–503* 🌐 *www.coolumsurfschool.com.au* 🎫 *Classes from $60 (prices include gear).*

Maroochydore

18 km (11 miles) south of Coolum, 18 km (11 miles) east of Nambour.

Maroochydore, at the mouth of the Maroochy River, has been a popular beach resort town for years, and has its fair share of high-rise towers. Its draw is excellent surfing and swimming beaches.

Beaches

Alexandra Headland

BEACH | FAMILY | South of Maroochydore's main beach and just north of Mooloolaba, Alexandra Headland offers a reliable surf break in moderate to high swell. The beach is patrolled year-round, but swimmers need to take care to avoid the headland rocks at the southern end of the beach where there is often a strong rip. A shady park, barbecue and picnic area, kiosk, playground, skate park, and walking and cycling tracks color the foreshore, with many alfresco cafés and restaurants also nearby. **Amenities:** food and drink; lifeguards; parking; showers; toilets. **Best for:** sunset; surfing; swimming; walking. ✉ *Alexandra Parade, Alexandra Headland* 🌐 *www.visitsunshinecoast.com.*

Maroochydore Beach

BEACH | FAMILY | Patrolled year-round by one of Queensland's oldest surf lifesaving clubs, rips are common along this strip, so stay in the central area between the red-and-yellow flags. A busy walking and cycling track runs adjacent to the beachfront, connecting visitors to both Cotton Tree and Alexandra Headland. A few minutes north is Maroochy River, a popular fishing spot and water sports activities hub. As with almost all Sunshine Coast beaches, an array of shops, cafés, and eateries line the esplanade. **Amenities:** food and drink; lifeguards; parking; showers; toilets; water sports. **Best for:** sunset; surfing; swimming; walking. ✉ *Alexandra Parade, Maroochydore* 🌐 *www.visitsunshinecoast.com.*

Coffee and Quick Bites

Raw Energy

$ | CAFÉ | Keep your fuel up for long days of swimming and surfing with a stop at Raw Energy, where freshly made smoothies and juices, hearty burgers and wraps, and fair-trade coffee will give you just the boost you need. So successful that it sparked a chain, here you'll find light and healthy fare including protein- and superfood-packed smoothies; seasonal, locally flavored fruit, veggie, and green juices; and an array of burgers stacked sky-high with fresh ingredients. **Known for:** free-range and locally grown produce; healthy energy bowls and smoothies; all-day breakfast. $ *Average main: A$16* ✉ *20 Memorial Ave., Maroochydore* ☎ *07/5443–7322* 🌐 *www.rawenergy.com.au/cotton-tree.*

Hotels

The Sebel Maroochydore

$$$ | APARTMENT | FAMILY | Each spacious one- or two-bedroom apartment in this stylish, view-rich, 15-level hotel has a curved feature wall and full gourmet kitchen bristling with modern European appliances, and most have separate media rooms. **Pros:** free parking; 25-meter (82-foot) pool and separate kids pool; hot tub in every room. **Cons:** decor a little outdated; beach is across a four-lane road; noise from pool area and traffic at night. *Rooms from: A$275* *20 Aerodrome Rd., Maroochydore* *07/5479–8000* *www.thesebel.com/queensland/the-sebel-maroochydore* *28 apartments* *No Meals.*

Mooloolaba

5 km (3 miles) south of Maroochydore.

Mooloolaba stretches along a lovely beach and riverbank, both an easy walk from town. The Esplanade has many casual cafés, upscale restaurants, and fashionable shops. Head to the town outskirts for picnic spots and prime coastal views.

Sights

SEA LIFE Sunshine Coast

NAUTICAL SIGHT | FAMILY | This all-weather sea life sanctuary has back-to-back marine presentations, including stingray feedings, guided shark tours, and seal and otter shows, all accompanied by informative talks. Eleven theme zones spread over three levels, including Australia's largest and most interactive jellyfish display, a seahorse sanctuary, and a famous underwater tunnel that gets you face-to-face with the majestic creatures of the deep. A souvenir shop and a café are also on-site, as well as a three-level indoor playground for kids. The aquarium is part of Mooloolaba's Wharf Complex, which features a marina, restaurants, and a tavern. **TIP→ Save up by booking a fully flexible ticket valid for up to 12 months online in advance.** *10 Parkyn Parade, The Wharf, Mooloolaba* *07/5458–6280* *www.visitsealife.com/sunshine-coast* *A$44.*

Beaches

★ Mooloolaba Beach

BEACH | FAMILY | A super-safe, family-friendly swimming beach, Mooloolaba Beach is patrolled year-round and has just enough swell to make it fun. Surfers might want to check out the left-hand break that sometimes forms off the rocks at the northern end. There are shady picnic areas with barbecues, playgrounds, and exercise areas—as well as the local meeting point, the Loo with a View. Stroll south along the coastal path to the river mouth and rock wall (off which you can fish, year-round, for bream); north to Alexandra Headland for views of the bay; or along Mooloolaba Esplanade, lined with casual eateries and boutiques. **Amenities:** food and drink; lifeguards; parking; showers; toilets. **Best for:** sunrise; sunset; swimming; walking. *Beach Terr., Mooloolaba* *www.visitsunshinecoast.com.*

Restaurants

Bella Venezia Italian Restaurant & Bar

$$$ | ITALIAN | A large mural of Venice, simple wooden tables, and terra-cotta floor tiles decorate this popular restaurant in an arcade off the Esplanade. You can eat in or take out traditional and modern Italian cuisine with an extensive selection of pizza, pasta, and risotto, including vegan options, matched with an award-winning wine list. **Known for:** modern spin on Italian classics; Sunshine Coast's longest-established restaurant; pasta made from scratch in-house. *Average main: A$38* *95 The Esplanade, Mooloolaba* *07/5444–5844* *www.bellavenezia.com.au.*

Hotels

Mantra Sirocco

$$$$ | APARTMENT | Located across the road from the beach and surrounded by trendy restaurants and cafés, this popular, upscale apartment complex on

Mooloolaba's main drag has spacious, self-contained two- and three-bedroom apartments, an impressive pool and Jacuzzi area, and a large fitness center. **Pros:** free parking; fantastic views from big balconies; in-room Jacuzzis. **Cons:** interiors in need of updating; Wi-Fi costs extra; minimum two-night stay on weekends. *$ Rooms from: A$499 ✉ 59–75 The Esplanade, Mooloolaba ☎ 07/5444–1400, 1800/811–454 reservations 🌐 www.mantrasirocco.com.au 43 apartments No Meals.*

Caloundra

29 km (18 miles) south of Maroochydore, 63 km (39 miles) south of Noosa, 91 km (56 miles) north of Brisbane.

This unassuming southern seaside town is a bit of a hidden gem. Popular with families, Caloundra has nine beaches of its own, which include everything from placid wading beaches (King's Beach and Bulcock Beach are best for families) to bays with thundering surf, such as Dicky, Buddina, and Wurtulla beaches.

Beaches

Bulcock Beach

BEACH | Flanked by a timber boardwalk with stunning views across the coastline, Bulcock Beach is one of Caloundra's most popular swimming spots. Surf the break at nearby Happy Valley, or enjoy boogie boarding or bodysurfing. Rips can form through the channel, so stay between the flags and only swim when the beach is patrolled (September–May). Head across the road for cafés, restaurants, shops, and a place to cool off. **Amenities:** lifeguards; parking; toilets. **Best for:** sunrise; sunset; surfing; walking. *✉ The Esplanade, Caloundra.*

★ King's Beach

BEACH | **FAMILY** | With rock pools, water fountains, an oceanfront saltwater swimming pool, and gentle, patrolled swimming areas, it's no surprise that festive King's Beach is one of the Sunshine Coast's most popular choices for families. **Amenities:** food and drink; lifeguards; parking; showers; toilets. **Best for:** sunset; surfing; swimming; walking. *✉ Ormond Terr., Caloundra.*

Restaurants

★ Sandbar Cafe

$$ | **AUSTRALIAN** | Offering delicious breakfasts, tasty lunches, and some of the best fish-and-chips on the Sunshine Coast, Sandbar Cafe has something for everyone. Its breezy location, right on Bulcock Beach, makes it a great place to escape the heat while treating yourself to some smashed avo on toast, a breakfast burger, or the signature Chef's Brekky, with roasted pork belly, chili beans, goat cheese, and toasted sourdough. **Known for:** sea views over Bulcock Beach toward Bribie Island; award-winning fish-and-chips; Chef's Brekky, and full breakfast menu till 2 pm. *$ Average main: A$22 ✉ 26 The Esplanade, Caloundra ☎ 07/5491–0800 🌐 sandbarcaloundra.com.au.*

Hotels

Rolling Surf Resort

$$$ | **RESORT** | **FAMILY** | The stunning white sands of Kings Beach front this modern, airy resort comprised of well-equipped one- to three-bedroom oceanfront and poolside apartments enveloped in tropical gardens. **Pros:** free parking; huge pool; right on the beach. **Cons:** limited complimentary Wi-Fi; can be noisy; two-night minimum stay in high season. *$ Rooms from: A$240 ✉ 10 Levuka Ave., Kings Beach, Caloundra ☎ 07/5491–9777, 1800/775–559 🌐 www.rollingsurfresort.com.au 66 apartments No Meals.*

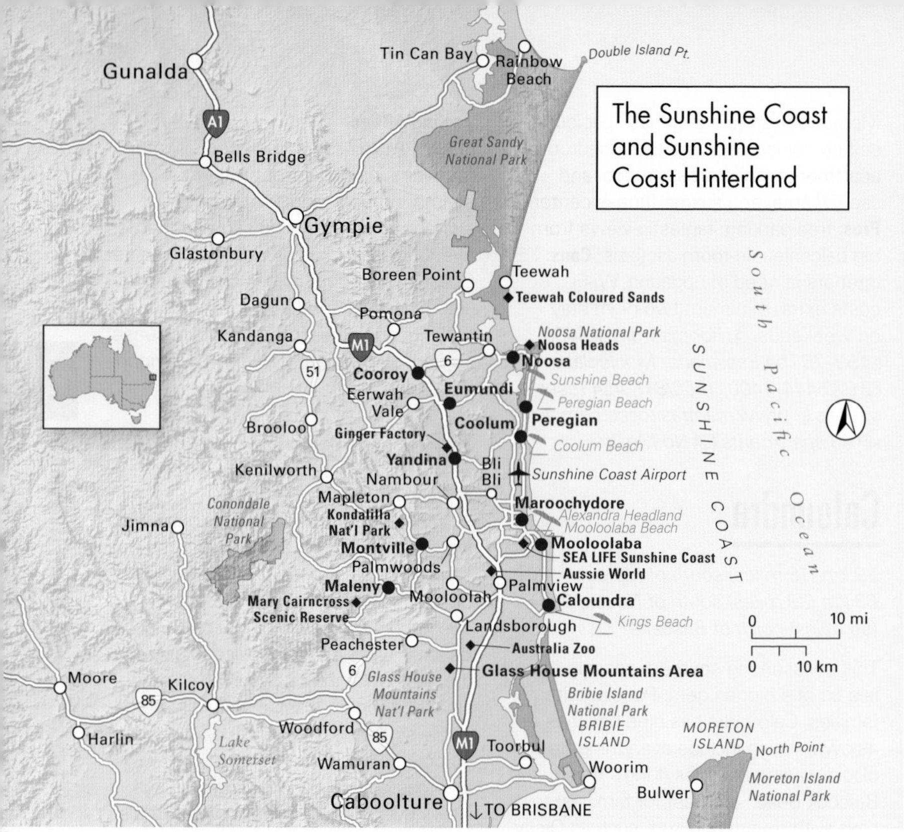

The Sunshine Coast and Sunshine Coast Hinterland

★ Rumba Beach Resort

$$$ | **RESORT** | **FAMILY** | This family-friendly resort in the heart of Caloundra's Bulcock Beach, offers one- to three-bedroom apartments, many with stunning views over Pumicestone Passage toward Bribie Island, and inland to the Glass House Mountains. **Pros:** central location, close to restaurants and cafés; large unheated lagoon pool and heated lap pool; beachside location offering views across to Bribie Island. **Cons:** no breakfast; room orientation is long and narrow, so back bedrooms can be dark; popular with families, so pools can get crowded in holidays. *Rooms from: A$265* *10 Leeding Terr., Caloundra* *07/5492–0555* *www.rumbaresort.com.au* *No Meals* *65 apartments.*

Activities

SURFING

★ Caloundra Surf School

SURFING | **FAMILY** | The only operator with exclusive permits to operate in three of Caloundra's beaches, Caloundra Surf School specializes in private and group sessions. Owner-operator John takes a no-nonsense, safety-first approach to introduce you to the thrill of surfing in Caloundra's gentle surf. Surfboard and bodyboard hire also available. *Caloundra* *0413/381–010* *A$50 group lesson.*

Glass House Mountains Area

35 km (22 miles) north of Brisbane on Bruce Hwy. to the Glass House Mountains Rd. exit; 4 km (2½ miles) south of Beerwah.

More than 20 million years old, the Glass House Mountains consist of nine conical outcrops—the eroded remnants of volcanoes—that rise dramatically from a flattish landscape northwest of Brisbane. Get a great view of the mountains from Glass House Mountains Lookout. Access is 10 km (6 miles) from the village via Glass House Mountains Tourist Route. The lookout is also the starting point for a scenic 25-minute walk. Several longer walks begin from nearby vantage points, such as Mt. Beerburrum and Wild Horse Mountain Lookout.

Sights

Aussie World

AMUSEMENT PARK/CARNIVAL | FAMILY | The Sunshine Coast's colorful Aussie World amusement park features several games rooms, a hall for "Funnybone Flicks," and a bustling fairground with 30-plus rides, including bumper cars, a retro merry-go-round, Ferris wheel, roller coaster, log ride, minigolf—even a sideshow alley. Admission is cheap, the "old school" carnival vibe is fun and friendly, and the park is far less crowded than its Gold Coast equivalents. An eclectic range of specialty stores are also housed within the complex, as well as the iconic Banana Bender Pub: a quirky, much-photographed watering hole full of kitsch Australiana and classic Aussie pub meals. ✉ *73 Frizzo Rd., Palmview* ☎ *07/5494–5444* 🌐 *www.aussieworld.com.au* 🎫 *From A$44.*

★ Australia Zoo

ZOO | FAMILY | Made famous by the late Steve Irwin, this popular, 110-acre park is home to all manner of Australian animals: koalas, kangaroos, wallabies, dingoes, Tasmanian devils, snakes, wombats, lizards—and, naturally, crocodiles. There are also otters, lemurs, tigers, red pandas, and a giant rain forest aviary. Daily shows feature crocs, birds of prey, koalas, and more. There are also plenty of extras that let you get up close and personal with the residents, including petting and hand-feeding red pandas (A$99), getting cozy with cheetahs (A$69) and rhinos (A$99), or cuddling a koala (A$49). Get around the park on foot or try the free hop-on, hop-off mini-trains. Private guided tours and Segway adventures (A$60) are also available. ✉ *1638 Steve Irwin Way, Beerwah* ✣ *5 km (3 miles) north of Glass House Mountains* ☎ *07/5436–2000* 🌐 *www.australiazoo.com.au* 🎫 *From A$59.*

Montville

16 km (10 miles) northwest of Forest Glen.

This charming mountain village, settled in 1887, is known as the creative heart of the Sunshine Coast, as many artists live here. There are panoramic views of the coast from the main street, a charming mix of Tudor, Irish, and English cottages constructed of log or stone; Bavarian and Swiss houses; quaint B&Bs; and old Queenslander homes. Shops are a browser's delight, full of curiosities and locally made crafts, while galleries showcase more serious pieces by local artists.

Sights

Kondalilla National Park

VIEWPOINT | FAMILY | With its swimming hole, 295-foot waterfall, picnic grounds, and walking trails, Kondalilla National Park is a popular local attraction. Three bushwalks begin near the grassy picnic area: Picnic Creek Circuit, Rock Pools Walk, and the Kondalilla Falls Circuit. They're all rated easy to moderate and range from

Fishing at Bulcock Beach, Caloundra, Sunshine Coast

2 km (1 mile) to 5 km (3 miles) in length. The **Sunshine Coast Hinterland Great Walk** (58 km [34 miles]) is accessible from the Falls Loop track, and links with parks farther north. Download maps from the Queensland Government Parks and Forests website. Camping is not permitted within the park. ✉ *Kondalilla Falls Rd., off Montville–Mapleton Rd., near Flaxton, Montville* ☎ *137-468* 🌐 *parks.des.qld.gov.au/parks/kondalilla* 🎫 *Free.*

Restaurants

★ Altitude

$$$ | AUSTRALIAN | With stunning 180-degree views from across the range to the coast, Altitude combines low-key fine dining with straight-up delicious food—and wines to match. The interior is modern, with a bush-inspired palette. **Known for:** menu combines local produce with pan-cultural flavors; three-course menu (A$65) is excellent value; casual fine dining with stunning views. $ *Average main: 37* ✉ *94–96 Main St., Montville* ☎ *07/5478–5889* 🌐 *altitudeonmontville.com.au* ☞ *Courtesy bus to local accommodations available 5:30 pm–9:30 pm.*

Montville Café Bar Grill

$$ | AUSTRALIAN | Twinkling with fairy lights by night and window-box blooms by day, this friendly, "ye olde English"–style family pub on Montville's main street provides a free courtesy bus to and from local accommodations every evening. Start with the salt-and-pepper calamari, and work your way up to a generous Darling Downs eye fillet, with a quality range of Australian wines to accompany. **Known for:** local institution; live entertainment on weekends; convivial pub atmosphere. $ *Average main: A$32* ✉ *Main St., Montville* ☎ *07/5278–5535* 🌐 *www.montvillepub.com.au* ☞ *Courtesy bus to local accommodation 5:30–10 pm nightly.*

Hotels

Misty View Cottages

$$$$ | B&B/INN | For a romantic escape, this exclusive retreat set high on a ridge just outside Montville offers luxury and seclusion in a stunning natural setting. **Pros:** large spa bath overlooking the valley is the ultimate indulgence; each cottage is private, with stunning views over the valley; romantic getaway. **Cons:** no Wi-Fi or Bluetooth set up; 10 am checkout; expensive. *Rooms from: A$500 284 Western Ave., Montville 07/5442–9522 mistyview.com.au Free Breakfast 4 cottages.*

★ Narrows Escape Rainforest Retreat

$$$$ | B&B/INN | In a fecund valley on the Montville outskirts, this tranquil, couples-only retreat features six self-contained, generously appointed cottages nestled deep in the hinterland rain forest. **Pros:** no children or large groups; beautiful, peaceful setting; excellent service. **Cons:** most pavilions have queen-size beds; secluded bushland setting—no views; a little way out of town. *Rooms from: A$475 78 Narrows Rd., Montville 07/5478–5000 www.narrowsescape.com.au 6 cottages Free Breakfast.*

The Spotted Chook & Amelie's Petite Maison

$$$$ | B&B/INN | FAMILY | Just over a mile from Montville, this whimsical, French-provincial-style B&B feels a world away with its picturesque country gardens and sweeping views over Obi Obi Gorge. **Pros:** wheelchair-friendly cottage, ramps, and walkways; warm and welcoming ambience; delicious French-style country breakfasts included in rate. **Cons:** books up quickly in wedding season; furnishings a little tired in some rooms; two-night minimum stay. *Rooms from: A$330 176 Western Ave., Montville 07/5442–9242 www.spottedchook.com.au 4 suites, 1 cottage Free Breakfast.*

Treetops Montville

$$$ | B&B/INN | Convenient to beautiful Kondalilla Falls, these cutting-edge-design tree houses perched on an escarpment are the ideal location for a romantic escape. **Pros:** close to town and walking tracks; stunning views; peaceful setting. **Cons:** limited phone reception; no Wi-Fi in rooms; minimum two-night stay on weekends. *Rooms from: A$260 4 Cynthia Hunt Dr., off Kondalilla Falls Rd., Flaxton 07/5478–6618, 1800/087–330 www.treetopsmontville.com.au 4 tree houses, 4 cabins Free Breakfast.*

Maleny

14 km (8½ miles) west of Montville.

The hinterland village of Maleny is a lively mix of rural life, the arts, wineries, cafés, and cooperative ventures. First settled around 1880, eclectic Maleny is now a popular tourist center with a strong community spirit, as well as a working dairy town.

Sights

Mary Cairncross Scenic Reserve

TRAIL | One of the area's most popular picnic spots, Mary Cairncross Scenic Reserve is 5 km (3 miles) southeast of Maleny at the intersection of the Landsborough–Maleny Road and Mountain View Road. The 130 acres of subtropical rain forest shelter an array of wildlife that includes bandicoots, goannas, echidnas, wallabies—and even pythons. There are two easy walks and a A$4.7-million Rainforest Discovery Center offers interactive displays, as well as sensory experiences and exhibits. Eat in the café (serving fair-trade coffee and homemade cakes) or at picnic tables for magnificent views of the Glass House Mountains. *148 Mountain View Rd., Maleny 07/5494–2826 mary-cairncross.sunshinecoast.qld.gov.au.*

Restaurants

Maple 3 Café

$ | **CAFÉ** | This local favorite changes its menu daily, but there are always fresh salads, focaccias, pastas, and plenty of dessert options. Come in for breakfast or brunch, grab a sandwich and a huge slice of homemade cake, and head down to Lake Baroon for a picnic. **Known for:** three resident water dragons (lizards) that sit by the tables; local institution with great coffee and hearty breakfasts; dessert selection, including cheesecake and chocolate brownies. *Average main: A$19 ✉ 3 Maple St., Maleny ☎ 07/5499–9177 🌐 www.facebook.com/maple3cafe.*

Coffee and Quick Bites

Maleny Food Co.

$ | **DESSERTS** | Maleny Food Co. started life as a café and fromagerie, making artisanal gelato and sorbet on the side. While the cheese and café offerings are worth sampling, it's the gelato that most people come for. **Known for:** award-winning gelato in over a hundred flavors; take-away cheese boxes and grazing boards; showcasing food from local farmers and producers. *Average main: A$10 ✉ 29 Maple St., Maleny ☎ 07/5494–2860 🌐 www.malenyfoodco.com ⏲ Closed Mon. No dinner.*

Hotels

Blue Summit Cottages

$$$ | **B&B/INN** | With four luxurious cottages and a grand house that sleeps up to 14, all on a view-rich mountaintop property set among 10 acres of immaculate gardens and rolling hills, this is the perfect place to get away from it all. **Pros:** free Wi-Fi and cable TV; breathtaking location; complete privacy and serenity. **Cons:** weekends can be expensive—book midweek for better deals; books out quickly in high season; a 10-minute drive to town. *Rooms from: A$300 ✉ 547 Maleny-Kenilworth Rd., Maleny ☎ 07/5435–8410 🌐 www.bluesummitcottages.com.au 4 cottages, 1 house Free Breakfast.*

Maleny Tropical Retreat

$$ | **B&B/INN** | At the end of a steep driveway, ensconced in a misty rain-forest valley, lies this romantic B&B retreat. **Pros:** large DVD and games library; top location and service; quality cooked breakfast. **Cons:** interiors in some rooms could do with a refresh; patchy phone reception and Wi-Fi in some villas and cottages; higher rates and two-night minimum stay on weekends. *Rooms from: A$179 ✉ 540 Maleny–Montville Rd., Maleny ☎ 07/5435–2113 🌐 www.malenytropicalretreat.com 9 rooms and cabins Free Breakfast.*

Yandina, Eumundi, and Cooroy

Yandina is 110 km (68 miles) north of Brisbane on the Bruce Hwy., Eumundi is 12 km (7½ miles) north of Yandina.

Yandina and Eumundi, just 12 km (7½ miles) apart, are home to some of the most iconic attractions in the area. Don't miss the Ginger Factory in Yandina, where you can learn—and eat—lots while enjoying the mini-amusement-park-like attractions; or stop in at the tranquil Spirit House for a meal, cooking class, or cocktail at the Hong Sa Bar. The Eumundi Market (on Wednesday and Saturday) is also a must.

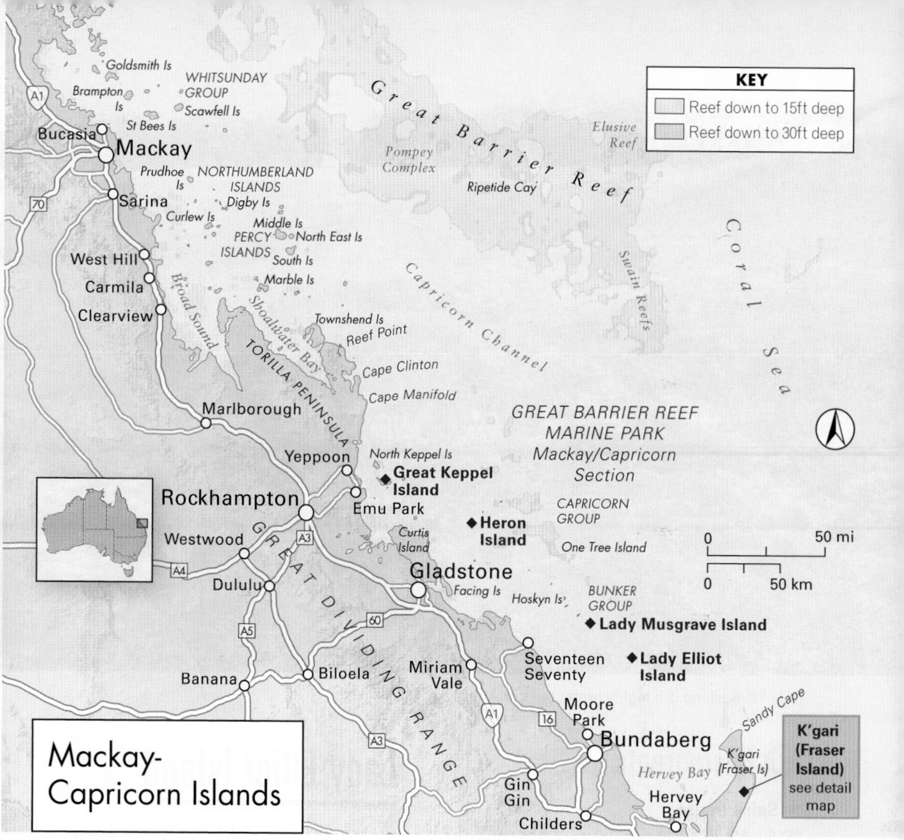

Mackay-Capricorn Islands

KEY
Reef down to 15ft deep
Reef down to 30ft deep

GREAT BARRIER REEF MARINE PARK
Mackay/Capricorn Section

Sights

★ Eumundi Markets

MARKET | FAMILY | The big attraction of this area is the twice-weekly Eumundi Markets—the best and largest street market on the Sunshine Coast, and one of the largest in Australia. More than 600 stall holders gather along Memorial Drive in the picturesque town of Eumundi to sell arts, crafts, clothing, accessories, and fresh and gourmet produce. Buses run to Eumundi from Noosa and other Sunshine Coast towns on market days, when the town swells to near-cosmopolitan proportions. Live musicians, poets, and masseurs keep the crowd relaxed. ✉ *80 Memorial Dr., Eumundi* ☎ *07/5442–7106* 🌐 *www.eumundimarkets.com.au.*

The Ginger Factory

OTHER ATTRACTION | FAMILY | This legendary Queensland establishment goes far beyond its original factory-door sale of ginger. You can still take a 40-minute guided tour of the world's only publicly accessible ginger processing plant. A café and shop sell ginger in all forms—incorporated into jams, cookies, chocolates, ice cream, wine, and herbal products. There's also a train trip and a boat ride, a miniature rain forest for kids, a live beehive tour that includes a honey tasting, and plenty of shops to browse. Just up the road, you'll find the beautiful Yandina Historic House. ✉ *50 Pioneer Rd., Yandina* ☎ *07/5447–8431, 1800/067–686* 🌐 *www.gingerfactory.com.au* 🎫 *Free entry; tours, demos, and rides from A$8.*

Lady Elliot Island is a highly protected coral cay.

Restaurants

★ Spirit House

$$$$ | ASIAN | This iconic Yandina restaurant does a remarkable job re-creating contemporary Thai cuisine on Queensland soil. The menu, which includes three four-course and degustation options, changes seasonally, with most ingredients sourced locally. **Known for:** all staff spend time in Thailand as part of their training; signature whole crispy fish with tamarind-chili sauce; contemporary Thai food in a serene garden setting. *[$] Average main: A$95 ✉ 20 Ninderry Rd., Yandina ☎ 07/5446–8977 🌐 www.spirithouse.com.au ⏲ Closed Mon. and Tues. ☞ Three-course minimum.*

Lady Elliot Island

80 km (50 miles) off the Queensland coast.

The closest Great Barrier Reef island to Brisbane, Lady Elliot Island is a highly protected coral cay approximately 85 km (53 miles) northeast of Bundaberg. The 111-acre island is a sanctuary for more than 1,200 species of marine life, which—along with its crystal clear waters and healthy coral—make it one of the top snorkeling and diving destinations on the reef.

GETTING HERE AND AROUND

Lady Elliot is the only Barrier Reef coral cay with its own airstrip. There is no boat access, but small chartered aircraft transfers are available from Bundaberg (30 minutes), Hervey Bay (40 minutes), Brisbane

(80 minutes), and the Gold Coast (120 minutes). Plane size varies from 9-seater Britten Norman Islander to 19-seater Twin Otter. Strict luggage limits for both hand and checked baggage allow 15 kilograms (33 pounds) per person for overnight guests. Excess luggage charges apply.

You can day-trip to Lady Elliot, too. The cost includes scenic flight, buffet lunch, reef walking, glass-bottom boat ride, snorkeling, and island tour. Tours require a minimum of two passengers.

AIRLINES Seair Pacific. ☎ *07/5599–4509, 1300/473–247* 🌐 *www.seairpacific.com.au.*

Sights

★ Lady Elliot Island

ISLAND | One of just six island resorts actually on the reef, Lady Elliot Island is a high-level Marine National Park Zone. Wildlife here easily outnumbers the guests (a maximum of 150 overnight guests and 100 day visitors are permitted at any one time)—and that reality is underscored by the ammoniacal odor of hundreds of nesting seabirds and, in season, the sounds and sights of them courting, mating, and nesting.

Divers enjoy the easy access to the reef and the variety of diving sites around Lady Elliot. Fringed on all sides by coral reefs and blessed with a stunning white-sand, coral-strewn shore and bright azure waters, this oval isle seems to have been made for diving. There's a busy dive shop and a reef education center with marine-theme exhibits (plus an educational video library—great for rainy days). Inclement weather and choppy waves can lead to canceled dives and washed-out underwater visibility. When the waters are calm, you'll see turtles, morays, sharks, rays, and millions of tropical fish. Many divers visit Lady Elliot specifically to encounter the resident population of manta rays that feed off the coral.

From October to April, Lady Elliot becomes a busy breeding ground for crested and bridled terns, silver gulls, lesser frigate birds, and the rare red-tailed tropic bird. Between November and March, green and loggerhead turtles emerge from the water to lay their eggs; hatching takes place after January. During the hatching season, staff biologists host guided turtle-watching night hikes. From about July through October, pods of humpback whales are visible from the beachfront restaurant.

Lady Elliot is one of the few islands in the area where camping—albeit modified—is part of the resort, and a back-to-basics, eco-friendly philosophy dominates the accommodations. ✉ *Lady Elliot Island* 🌐 *www.ladyelliot.com.au.*

Hotels

Lady Elliot Island Eco Resort

$$$ | **RESORT** | **FAMILY** | All accommodation on the island is provided by Lady Elliot Island Eco Resort, where you'll feel more like a marine biologist at an island field camp than a tourist enjoying a luxury resort. **Pros:** hearty meals; eco-friendly and unbeatable proximity to nature; plenty of activities. **Cons:** minimum three-night stay over holidays; limited leisure options for rainy, nondiving days; no Wi-Fi, TV, or phone reception in rooms. *$ Rooms from: A$219* ✉ *Lady Elliot Island* ☎ *07/5536–3644 head office, 07/4156–4444 resort* 🌐 *www.ladyelliot.com.au* *44 rooms* *Free Breakfast.*

Lady Musgrave Island

40 km (25 nautical miles) north of Lady Elliot Island, 96 km (53 nautical miles) northeast of Bundaberg.

This island sits at the southern end of the Great Barrier Reef Marine Park, about 40 km (25 miles) north of Lady Elliot Island and 96 km (60 miles) northeast of Bundaberg. The cay, part of Capricornia Cays National Park, has a 2,945-acre surrounding reef, about one-third of which is a massive yet calm lagoon, a true coral cay of 39.5 acres. Like nearby Lady Elliot Island, it has some of the best diving and snorkeling in Queensland.

From October through April the island is a bird and turtle rookery, with black noddies, wedge-tailed shearwaters, bridled terns, more timid black-naped and roseate terns, and green and loggerhead turtles. There's also an abundance of flora, including casuarina and pisonia trees.

There is no permanent accommodation on the island; however, it is possible to camp at certain times of the year. Permits are required and there is a limit of 40 campers at any time. While there are a range of options for day trips to the island, campers are able to fully immerse themselves in the experience of living simply on a coral cay, amid the myriad sea life.

GETTING HERE AND AROUND

Lady Musgrave Experience

The Lady Musgrave Experience operates transfers and day tours from Bundaberg, a four-hour drive from Brisbane, aboard a three-level, high-speed luxury catamaran. It takes approximately 2½ hours to reach Lady Musgrave Island, and the full day tour includes morning tea and lunch, and activities include snorkeling, glass-bottom boat tours, and guided island walks. With a resident marine biologist on hand to answer all your questions about the Great Barrier Reef and its marine life, tours are educational and eco-conscious, as well as being a great day out. Tour price is A$228 (adults) and A$158 (children). Scuba diving is from A$110 per dive. Return transfers for campers also available: A$440. ✉ *15–17 Marina Dr., Shop 5, Burnett Heads* ☎ *07/4151–5225* 🌐 *ladymusgraveexperience.com.au.*

VISITOR INFORMATION

CONTACT Capricornia Cays National Park. 🌐 *parks.des.qld.gov.au/parks/capricornia-cays.*

Activities

At the resort dive shop you can rent equipment and arrange dive courses to more than a dozen excellent sites, including Lighthouse Bommie, home to a 40-strong manta ray colony, and the Blow Hole and Hiro's Cave. Refresher pool dives, a shore snorkeling trip, and guided reef, nature, and historical walks are free for resort guests. Off-boat snorkeling and glass-bottom boat rides are A$36 for adults or A$22 for children. Boat dives and night dives range A$80–A$105. Open-water certification courses cost A$745; "Discover Scuba Diving" short courses are A$200; and referral courses, available to those who've completed the classroom and pool portions of a certification course prior to arrival, are also available.

Diving here is weather-dependent, so plan accordingly if you intend to do a dive course over multiple days. Special five-night packages, including buffet breakfast and dinner, a glass-bottom boat tour, snorkeling tours, and reef tax, start at A$1,171 per person including flights. Several other special deals and packages are available.

Scuba diving off Heron Island

Heron Island

72 km (45 miles) northeast of the mainland port of Gladstone.

Most resort islands lie well inside the shelter of the distant reef, but Heron Island, some 72 km (45 miles) northeast of the mainland port of Gladstone, is actually part of the reef. The waters off this 40-acre island are spectacular, teeming with fish and coral, and ideal for snorkeling and scuba diving. The water is generally clearest in June and July and cloudiest during the rainy season, January and February. Heron Island operates on "island time"—an hour ahead of Australian Eastern Standard Time—and at its own leisurely pace. You won't find much in the way of nightlife, as the island's single resort accepts a cozy maximum of 250 people—and there are no day-trippers. But these might be reasons why you decide to come here.

GETTING HERE AND AROUND

Once in Gladstone, passengers can board the high-speed, 112-foot Heron Islander from the city's marina. The launch makes the two-hour run to Heron Island from Gladstone, on the Queensland coast, for A$64 one-way, departing at 2 pm daily and arriving at 4:30 pm. The return boat departs from Heron Island for the mainland at 10 am EST (9 am island time) and arrives at 12:30 pm. This can be a rough journey: take ginger or antinausea medicine a half hour before departure. A courtesy shuttle bus transfers guests from Gladstone Airport, leaving at 12:40 pm daily, and meets all afternoon boats. (Fly to Gladstone from Brisbane, Mackay, Rockhampton, Townsville, and Cairns with Qantas or Virgin Australia.) You can also arrange transfers to and from Gladstone Station; get here on Queensland Rail's fast *Tilt Train* or *Spirit of Queensland* from the north or south (🌐 *www.queenslandrail.com.au*).

Australia by Seaplane
If you're short on time, Australia by Sea plane makes scenic, 25-minute flights to Heron Island from Gladstone from A$349 one-way, operating daily (except Christmas Day, Boxing Day, and New Year's Day). The baggage restriction is 33 pounds per person, with soft suitcases preferred. Lockup facilities for excess baggage are provided free. ✉ *Heron Island* ☎ *0412/623–554, 0419/669–575* 🌐 *www.australiabyseaplane.com.au.*

Marine Helicopter Charter
Daily transfers to Heron Island with Marine Helicopter Charter take 30 minutes each way and include expert commentary from your pilot. Baggage allowance is 33 pounds per person with soft luggage preferred. Adult tickets are A$449 each way if you book a return ticket. Single one-way tickets are A$530. ✉ *Heron Island* ☎ *07/4978–0129* 🌐 *www.heronislandhelicopters.com.*

Heron Island Resort
$$$$ | RESORT | Set among palm trees and connected by sand paths, this secluded, eco-certified resort has a range of accommodation types, from the deluxe Beach House with private outdoor shower and beach boardwalk to the comparatively compact, garden-level Turtle Rooms. **Pros:** complete island getaway and immersion in natural environment; lots of free activities; eco-friendly. **Cons:** no TVs in rooms; Wi-Fi is limited and costs extra; no mobile phone coverage. $ *Rooms from: A$358* ✉ *Heron Island* ☎ *1300/731–551* 🌐 *www.heronisland.com* *109 rooms* *Free Breakfast.*

You can book snorkeling, scuba diving, and fishing excursions as well as turtle-watching tours and sunset cruises through Heron Island Marine Centre & Dive Shop. Snorkeling lessons are free, refresher dive courses from A$10. Snorkeling trips are A$50.

DIVING

Various diving options include a resort diving course for beginners, including training and one guided dive, for A$200 (subsequent dives, A$155). For certified divers it's A$75 per dive, and just A$55 per dive upward of five dives. Night dives, including light stick and flashlight, are A$100. Three-, five-, and seven-night dive packages include multiple dives throughout Heron and Wistari reefs, as well as accommodation, breakfast, buffet lunch, dinner, and all tanks and weights. Price is upon application. Half- and full-day dive boat charters are also available.

For all dives, prebooking is essential, and gear costs you extra. Children under 8 aren't permitted on snorkeling trips, under-12s can dive but only with a private guide, and under-14s must be accompanied by an adult (and if diving, must be certified).

FISHING

Heron Island Marine Centre & Dive Shop
DIVING & SNORKELING | In addition to diving, snorkeling, and semisubmersible trips (A$60), Heron Island Marine Centre & Dive Shop runs kayaking and paddleboarding tours, and research station tours. Toast the sunset on an hour-long wine-and-cheese cruise (A$50). ✉ *Heron Island* ☎ *1800/875–343* 🌐 *www.heronisland.com.*

SNORKELING AND SEMISUBMERSIBLE
Nondivers wanting to explore their underwater environs can take a half-day snorkeling tour of Heron and Wistari reefs, or an hour-long, naturalist-guided semisubmersible tour. Guided reef and birdlife walks and movies under the stars are free. Visits to the island's Marine Research Station are A$10 per adult.

Great Keppel Island

40 km (25 miles) from the Great Barrier Reef.

Positioned at the southern end of the Great Barrier Reef near the Tropic of Capricorn, idyllic Great Keppel Island boasts crystal clear waters, palm-fringed white sand beaches, scenic hiking trails, and some of the most diverse and unspoiled coral on the reef. The 593-acre island is also home to a rich diversity of flora and fauna, including more than 90 species of birds.

GETTING HERE AND AROUND
AIR

Virgin Australia flies to Rockhampton from Brisbane, with connections to all major Australian cities. Qantas has direct flights to Rockhampton from Brisbane, Townsville, and Mackay, connecting to other capitals.

AIRLINES Peace Aviation. ☎ *07/4927–4355, 0429/616–758* 🌐 *www.peaceaviation.com.* **Qantas.** ☎ *131–313* 🌐 *www.qantas.com.* **Virgin Australia.** ☎ *136–789* 🌐 *www.virginaustralia.com.*

BOAT AND FERRY

Freedom Fast Cats

These ferries transfer guests to the island from Pier 1 at Rosslyn Bay Harbour, near Yeppoon (across the bay from the marina). Departures are early to mid-morning (check schedules) daily, and return trips back to the mainland are early to mid-afternoon. The cost is A$45 per adult, round-trip (A$30 for early crossing). Glass-bottom boat tours (A$78 per adult) and various cruise packages are also available. Depending on the time of your flight arrival, you may need to stay overnight in Rockhampton or Yeppoon before and after your island stay. ✉ *Great Keppel Island* ☎ *07/4933–6888* 🌐 *www.freedomfastcats.com.*

Keppel Bay Marina

Keppel Bay Marina runs day cruises to secluded coves and beaches: choose a romantic sunset cruise (A$50) or a full-day cruise including snorkeling, fishing, beachcombing, and a full buffet lunch on board (A$115). Three-day adventure cruises (including accommodation), as well as private charters, are also available by request. ✉ *Great Keppel Island* ☎ *07/4933–6244* 🌐 *www.keppelbaymarina.com.au.*

Sights

Great Keppel Island

ISLAND | Although Great Keppel is large, at 8 km (5 miles) by 11 km (7 miles), it lies 40 km (25 miles) from the Great Barrier Reef, which makes for a long trip from the mainland. There's lots to do, with walking trails, 17 stunning safe swimming beaches, excellent coral gardens in many sheltered coves, plenty of friendly local wildlife, and dozens of beach and water-sports activities available. An abundance of bushwalking tracks allows visitors to explore the island's interior and access secluded beaches. The island has a marina and an airstrip, and a number of places to stay, including Great Keppel Island Holiday Village. ✉ *Great Keppel Island.*

Hotels

Great Keppel Island Holiday Village

$ | **HOUSE** | **FAMILY** | Surrounded by stunning beaches and untouched bush, this is a modest, quiet alternative for travelers looking to get back to basics and enjoy the environs the "old-fashioned" way.

Pros: great value; beautiful and peaceful location; relaxed and friendly atmosphere. **Cons:** minimum three-night stay; no Wi-Fi or TV (except in Keppel House); patchy mobile phone coverage. *Rooms from: A$100* *Great Keppel Island* *07/4939–8655, 1800/537–735* *www.gkiholidayvillage.com.au* *16 rooms* *No Meals.*

WATER SPORTS

Keppel Water Sports

WATER SPORTS | Based at the water-sports hut on Fisherman's Beach, this operator runs guided kayak and motorized canoe trips, and water taxi drop-offs to and pickups from surrounding beaches and islands. They also rent out water-sports equipment, including kayaks and paddleboards, and have banana and tube rides. *Fisherman's Beach, Great Keppel Island* *0407/116–973* *keppelwatersports.com.au.*

K'gari (Fraser Island)

200 km (125 miles) north of Brisbane.

K'gari (Fraser Island), at 1,014 square km (391 square miles), is the largest of Queensland's islands and the most unusual. K'gari is the world's largest sand island—instead of coral reefs and coconut palms, it has wildflower-dotted meadows; 100-plus freshwater lakes; dense, tall stands of rain forest; towering dunes; sculpted, multicolor sand cliffs; up to 40,000 migratory shorebirds; and rare and endangered species including dugongs, turtles, Illidge's ant-blue butterfly, and eastern curlews—a lineup that won the island a place on UNESCO's World Heritage list.

The island's Butchulla people have occupied the island for at least 5,000 years, and their sacred sites are dotted around the island. The surf fishing is legendary, and humpback whales and their calves winter in Hervey Bay between May and September.

Hervey Bay is the name given to the expanse of water between K'gari and the Queensland coast, and to four nearby coastal towns—Urangan, Pialba, Scarness, and Torquay—that have merged into a single settlement. Hervey Bay and Rainbow Beach are the main jumping-off points for offshore excursions. (Maps and road signs usually refer to individual town names.)

GETTING HERE AND AROUND

AIR

Several direct air services on Jetstar, Qantas, and Virgin Australia connect Sydney and Fraser Coast (Hervey Bay) Airport. Bay 2 Dore shuttle buses link the airport to Urangan, meeting flights upon request.

AIRPORT CONTACT Fraser Coast (Hervey Bay) Airport. *Don Adams Dr., Hervey Bay* *07/4194–8100* *www.frasercoastairport.com.au.*

BOAT AND FERRY

Numerous vehicular ferries service Fraser Island from Rainbow Beach and Hervey Bay. Manta Ray Fraser Island Barges runs a regular service from 6 am to 5:30 pm between Inskip Point, near Rainbow Beach, and Hook Point at the island's southern end. The company's two to three barges make up to 40 round-trips daily, so if you miss one barge, the next will be along soon. Buy tickets online (recommended) or as you board.

Fraser Island Barges' *Fraser Venture* makes the half-hour trip between River Heads, 20 minutes' drive south of Hervey Bay, and Wanggoolba Creek, opposite Eurong Bay Resort on the island's west coast, three times a day. The Kingfisher Bay Passenger and Vehicle Ferry also connects River Heads with Kingfisher Bay Resort in 50 minutes up to six times a day.

BOAT AND FERRY CONTACTS Fraser Island Barges. ✉ *54 Ariadne St.* ☎ *07/4194–9300, 1800/249–122* 🌐 *www.fraserislandferry.com.au.* **Kingfisher Bay Ferry.** ✉ *Urangan* ☎ *07/4194–9300, 1800/227–437* 🌐 *www.fraserislandferry.com.au/barges/kingfisher-bay-ferry.* **Manta Ray Fraser Island Barges.** ✉ *66 Rainbow Beach Rd.* ☎ *07/5486–3935, 0418/872–599* 🌐 *www.mantarayfraserislandbarge.com.au.*

CAR AND BUGGY

K'gari's east coast favors two Australian passions: beaches and vehicles. Unrestricted access has made this coast a giant sandbox for four-wheel-drive vehicles, busiest in school-holiday periods.

The southernmost tip of K'gari is just more than 200 km (125 miles) north of Brisbane. The simplest access is via barge from Rainbow Beach or Hervey Bay, 90 km (56 miles) farther north. For Rainbow Beach, take the Bruce Highway toward Gympie, then follow signs to Rainbow Beach. For Hervey Bay, head to Maryborough, then follow the signs to River Heads.

Every vehicle entering the island by barge from the mainland must have a one-month Vehicle Access Permit (A$51.60). To obtain these and island camping permits (A$6.55 per person, per night), contact QPWS 🌐 *www.nprsr.qld.gov.au.*

You can rent four-wheel-drive vehicles from Aussie Trax 4WD Hire at Kingfisher Bay Resort and Village for upward of A$91 per person per day, or from various rental companies at Urangan and Hervey Bay Airport for considerably less.

Four-wheel-drive rentals may be cheaper on the mainland, but factoring in the ferry ticket makes rental on-island a viable option. Most commodities, including gas, are pricier on-island.

Wet weather and sandy surfaces can make island driving challenging and hazardous. Consult QPWS's website for detailed information on safe driving and local hazards. Basic mechanical assistance and tow-truck services are available from Eurong. Orchid Beach has emergency towing only. If you can't get the mechanical assistance you need, phone Eurong Police.

Getting Help

While there is a permanent paramedic on the island, K'gari does not have a resident doctor. Emergency medical assistance can be obtained at the ranger stations in Eurong, Waddy Point, and Dundubara, but these have variable hours—if no answer, phone the base station at Nambour on the mainland. Kingfisher Bay Resort has first-aid facilities and resident nursing staff.

CAR RENTAL Budget Car Rental. ✉ *Hervey Bay Airport, Airport Terminal, Hervey Bay* ☎ *07/4125–6906* 🌐 *www.budget.com.au.*

ESSENTIALS

VEHICLE PERMITS Queensland Parks and Forests. ☎ *137–468 info and permits* 🌐 *parks.des.qld.gov.au.*

VISITOR INFORMATION Hervey Bay Visitor Information Centre. ✉ *227 Maryborough-Hervey Bay Rd., Hervey Bay* ☎ *1800/811–728* 🌐 *www.visitfrasercoast.com.*

TOURS

Air Fraser Island

Air Fraser Island runs day trips, transfers, and scenic and whale-watching flights (in season) from Hervey Bay, using the pristine beaches of Fraser Island as its landing strip. Overnight packages, including 4WD rentals, are also available. ✉ *Fraser Island* ☎ *1300/172–706* 🌐 *www.airfraserisland.com.au* 🎟 *From A$80.*

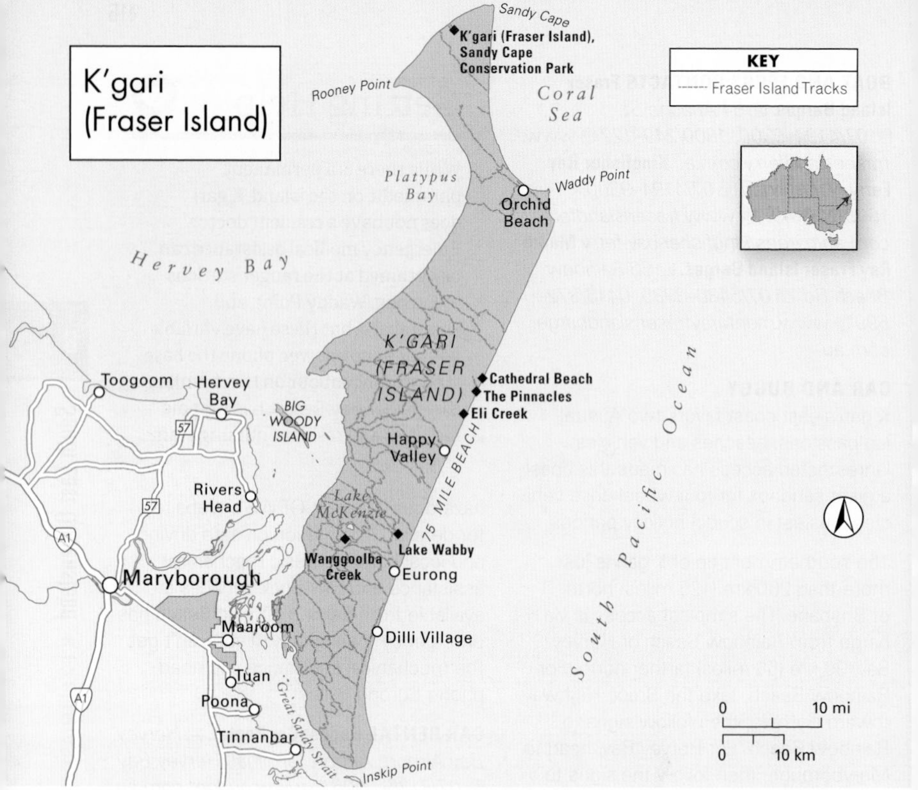

K'gari (Fraser Island)

KEY
------ Fraser Island Tracks

Sandy Cape
K'gari (Fraser Island), Sandy Cape Conservation Park
Rooney Point
Coral Sea
Platypus Bay
Waddy Point
Orchid Beach
Hervey Bay
K'GARI (FRASER ISLAND)
Cathedral Beach
The Pinnacles
Eli Creek
Toogoom
Hervey Bay
BIG WOODY ISLAND
Happy Valley
75 MILE BEACH
South Pacific Ocean
Rivers Head
Lake McKenzie
Lake Wabby
Wanggoolba Creek
Eurong
Maryborough
Maaroom
Dilli Village
Tuan
Poona
Tinnanbar
Great Sandy Strait
Inskip Point
0 10 mi
0 10 km

Fraser Explorer Tours
This group operates one- to five-day 4WD tours across World Heritage–listed Fraser Island, taking in its pristine beaches and colored sands, freshwater lakes, verdant forests, and abundant marine life. Departing both Hervey Bay and Rainbow Beach, tours include barge transfers, meals, national park fees, and audio guides in various languages. *1 Eastern St., Fraser Island* *07/4194–9222, 1800/678–431* *www.fraserexplorertours.com.au* *From A$198.*

★ **Nomads Fraser Island**
Take a two- or three-day 4WD tour of the island led by experienced, local guides. Eco-certified Nomads Fraser Island Tours share the incredible natural attractions of the island while also providing a background on the legends, stories, and beliefs of the Butchulla people. Enjoy bushwalks, swims, and food and lodging while also learning which sites on the island were used for Butchulla ceremonies, rituals, gatherings, childbirth, fishing, and disputes. *Fraser Island* *07/3041–3256* *nomadsfraserisland.com.*

Sights

Highlights of a drive along the east coast, which is known as Seventy-Five Mile Beach for its sheer distance, include **Eli Creek,** a great freshwater swimming hole. North of this popular spot lies the rusting hulk of the *Maheno,* half buried in the sand, a roost for seagulls and a prime hunting ground for anglers when the tailor are running. Once a luxury passenger steamship that operated between Australia and New Zealand (and served as a hospital ship during World War I), it was wrecked during a cyclone in 1935 as it was being towed to Japan to be sold for scrap metal. North of the wreck are the **Pinnacles**—dramatic, deep-red cliff formations. About 20 km (12 miles) south of Eli Creek, and surrounded by massive sand-blow (or dune), is **Lake Wabby,** the deepest of the island's lakes.

Note that swimming in the ocean off the island is not recommended because of the rough conditions and sharks that hunt close to shore. Stick to the inland lakes.

K'gari (Fraser Island), Sandy Cape Conservation Park

NATURE SIGHT | This park covers the top third of K'gari. Beaches around Indian Head are known for their shell middens—shell heaps that were left behind after Buchamba feasting. The head's name is another kind of relic: Captain James Cook saw some Buchamba people standing on the headland as he sailed past, and he therefore named the area after inhabitants he believed to be "Indians." Farther north, past Waddy Point, is one of K'gari's most magnificent variations on sand: wind and time have created enormous dunes. Nearby at Orchid Beach are a series of bubbling craters known as the Champagne Pools. ✉ *Fraser Island* ☎ *137–468* 🌐 *parks.des.qld.gov.au/parks/kgari-fraser.*

Wanggoolba Creek

FOREST | A boardwalk heads south from Central Station to Wanggoolba Creek, a favorite spot for photographers. The little stream snakes through a green palm forest, trickling over a bed of white sand between clumps of rare angiopteris fern. The 1 km (½-mile) circuit takes 30 minutes to an hour. ✉ *Fraser Island.*

Hotels

★ Kingfisher Bay Resort

$$ | **RESORT** | **FAMILY** | This stylish, high-tech marriage of glass, stainless steel, dark timber, and corrugated iron nestles in tree-covered dunes on the island's west coast. **Pros:** excellent location; terrific facilities, tours, and activities; eco-friendly. **Cons:** charge for Wi-Fi; west-coast beaches unsuitable for 4WD vehicles; many rooms in need of updating. *$ Rooms from: A$199* ✉ *North White Cliffs, 75 Mile Beach, Fraser Island* ☎ *07/4120–3333, 1800/072–555* 🌐 *www.kingfisherbay.com* *152 rooms* *No Meals.*

Activities

FISHING

Hervey Bay Fly and Sportfishing

FISHING | This family-run business caters to all levels of experience with its half- and full-day fishing trips through the waters off K'gari (Fraser Island). Morning tea, lunch, refreshments, bait, tackle, and fish cleaning are all included. Private and overnight charters are also available upon request. ✉ *51 Tristania Crescent, Urangan* ☎ *0407/627–852* 🌐 *herveybaysportfishing.com.au* *From A$167.*

Offshore fishing, K'gari (Fraser Island)

FISHING | All freshwater fish are protected on K'gari, so you can't fish in lakes or streams, but just offshore is one of Australia's richest, most diverse fishing areas, with whiting, flathead, trevally, red emperor, snapper, sea perch, coronation trout, cod, and, in summer, mackerel, cobia, amberjack, and more. This is partly due to the diversity of habitat; choose between estuary, surf beach, reef, sport, and game fishing. On reef-fishing trips dolphins are commonly sighted, as are whales in season. When angling off K'gari beaches and jetties, follow Parks and Forests' guidelines. To discourage dingoes and other undesirable visitors, clean fish away from campsites and dispose of scraps carefully (bury fish scraps at least a foot below the tide line). Some beaches are closed to fishing during August and September, and bag and size limits apply to some species; for details, go to www.parks.des.qld.gov.au/parks/kgari-fraser ✉ *Fraser Island* 🌐 *parks.des.qld.gov.au/parks/kgari-fraser.*

HIKING

Central Station

HIKING & WALKING | The island's excellent network of walking trails converges at Central Station, a former logging camp at the center of the island. Services here are limited to a map board, parking lot, and campground. It's a promising place for spotting dingoes. Comparative isolation has meant that K'gari's dingoes are the most purebred in Australia. They're also wild animals, so remember: don't feed them, watch from a distance, don't walk alone after dark, store food and dispose of rubbish carefully, and keep a close eye on children, especially between late afternoon and early morning. Most of the island's well-marked trails are sandy tracks. Guides advise wearing sturdy shoes, wearing sunscreen, and carrying first-aid supplies and drinking water on all walks. ✉ *Central Station, Fraser Island.*

Pile Valley

HIKING & WALKING | One trail from Central Station leads through rain forest—growing, incredibly enough, straight out of the sand—to Pile Valley, which has a stand of giant satinay trees. Allow two hours to walk the full 4½-km (2¼-mile) circuit. ✉ *Fraser Island.*

SWIMMING

Lake McKenzie

SWIMMING | The center of K'gari is a quiet, natural garden of paperbark swamps, giant satinay and brush box forests, wildflower heaths, and 40 freshwater lakes. The spectacularly clear Lake McKenzie, ringed by a beach of incandescent white sand, is arguably the most stunning of the lakes and is the perfect place for a refreshing swim, day or night. ✉ *Lake McKenzie, Fraser Island.*

Chapter 9

THE GREAT BARRIER REEF

Updated by
Ben Groundwater

Sights ★★★★★ | Restaurants ★★★★★ | Hotels ★★★★★ | Shopping ★★★☆☆ | Nightlife ★★★★☆

WELCOME TO THE GREAT BARRIER REEF

TOP REASONS TO GO

★ **Reef Explorations:** There are thousands of spectacular dive sites scattered along the coral spine of the Great Barrier Reef.

★ **Wildlife Watching:** Flora and fauna on the islands themselves can be fascinating: rain forests, hills and rocky areas, and postcard-perfect beaches provide diverse habitat.

★ **Cultural Immersion:** The Kuku Yalanji people have lived in the area between Port Douglas and Cookdown for millennia. A highlight of visiting the region is experiencing this unique landscape from the perspective of its traditional owners.

★ **Ancient Rain Forest:** The UNESCO World Heritage–listed Daintree rain forest is a rich and ancient ecosystem in which you'll find sustainable resorts, jungle zip lines, and deserted beaches.

★ **Outback Adventures:** West of Port Douglas lie vast tracts of savannah dotted with termite mounds and teeming with kangaroos, wallabies, reptiles, and birds.

If you're visiting the reef only briefly, it's simplest to day-trip from the mainland. Some reef-island resorts are accessible by boat; others can be reached only by plane, and both airfare and rates can be expensive. Day trips depart from major coastal cities including Cairns and Port Douglas.

1 **Cairns.** A "tourist town" and perfect base for exploring the Great Barrier Reef.

2 **Palm Cove.** A beachside suburb of Cairns and idyllic base for exploring northern Queensland.

3 **Port Douglas.** It's all about rain forest and reef here as well as Four Mile Beach and a lively yet laid-back little town.

4 **Mossman.** A sugarcane town at the foot of the mountains and stop-off on the way to Mossman Gorge and Daintree.

5 **Cape Tribulation.** The activities and lodging base for the spectacular Daintree National Park.

6 **Cooktown.** At the edge of wilderness, with pristine beaches, magical views, and nearby Indigenous rock art sites.

7 **Airlie Beach.** A lively town and the gateway to the Whitsunday Islands and the Great Barrier Reef.

8 **Long Island.** Mostly national parkland with great trails, excellent snorkeling, and some peaceful retreats.

9 **Hamilton Island.** Buzzing with activity but also offering beautiful beaches and views.

10 **Orpheus Island.** A national park and a true Great Barrier Reef island with unspoiled beaches.

11 **Bedarra Island.** A tiny and quiet island with dense rain forest and luxe hotel resort.

12 **Fitzroy Island.** A popular day trip from Cairns with extensive fringing coral reef and access to water activities.

13 **Lizard Island.** Excellent walking trails, spectacular views, and luxe beachfront accommodations.

14 **Townsville.** A lively coastal city with turn-of-the-20th-century colonial structures.

15 **Magnetic Island.** Twenty-three island beaches, nine offshore shipwrecks, and a haven for wildlife.

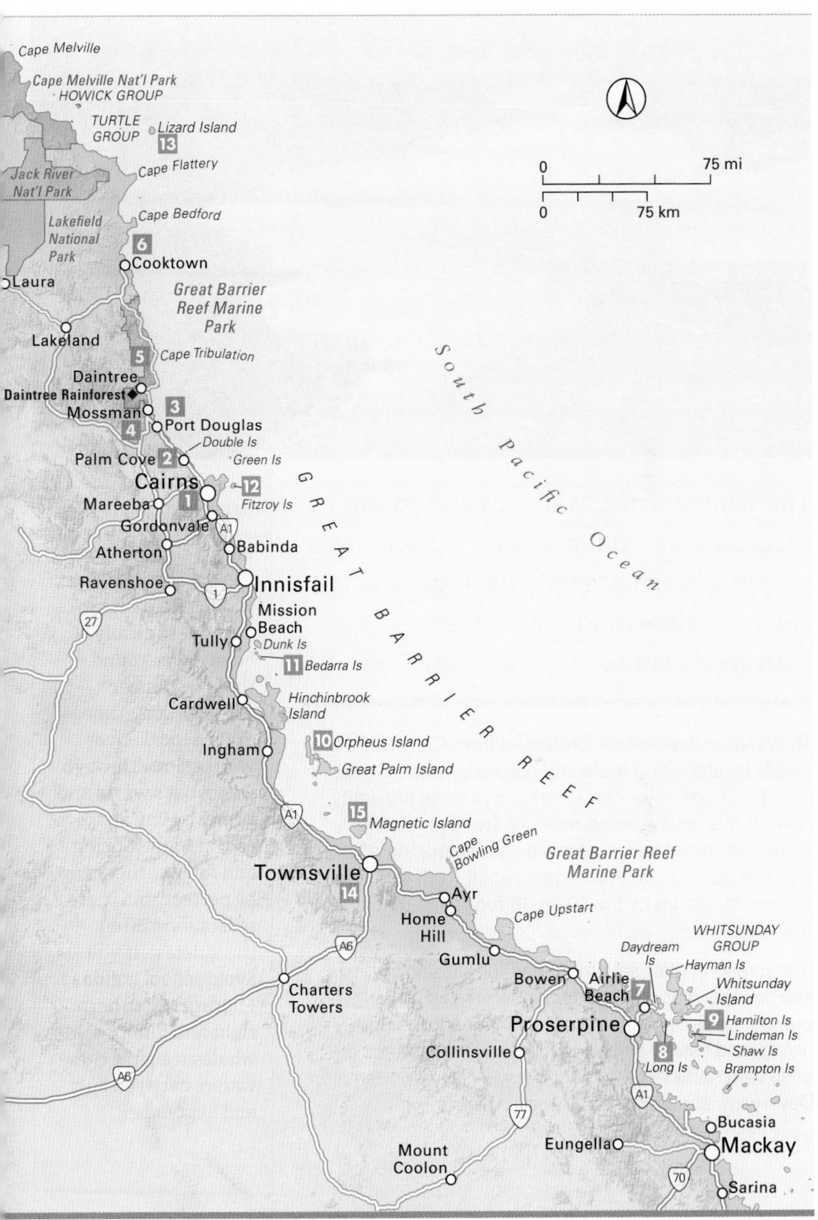
Cape Melville
Cape Melville Nat'l Park
HOWICK GROUP
TURTLE GROUP
Lizard Island
13
Cape Flattery
Jack River Nat'l Park
Lakefield National Park
Cape Bedford
6
Cooktown
Laura
Great Barrier Reef Marine Park
Lakeland
5
Cape Tribulation
Daintree
Daintree Rainforest
Mossman
3
Port Douglas
4
Double Is
Palm Cove
2
Green Is
Cairns
12
Fitzroy Is
1
Mareeba
Gordonvale
A1
Atherton
Babinda
Ravenshoe
1
Innisfail
27
Mission Beach
Tully
Dunk Is
11
Bedarra Is
Cardwell
Hinchinbrook Island
10
Orpheus Island
Ingham
Great Palm Island
A1
15
Magnetic Island
Cape Bowling Green
Townsville
14
Great Barrier Reef Marine Park
Ayr
Home Hill
Cape Upstart
Gumlu
A6
Charters Towers
Bowen
Airlie Beach
7
Proserpine
Collinsville
WHITSUNDAY GROUP
Daydream Is
Hayman Is
Whitsunday Island
9
Hamilton Is
Lindeman Is
Shaw Is
8
Long Is
Brampton Is
A6
A1
77
Bucasia
Eungella
Mackay
Mount Coolon
70
Sarina
South Pacific Ocean
GREAT BARRIER REEF
0
75 mi
0
75 km

SAILING THE WHITSUNDAY ISLANDS

The Whitsundays, 74 islands and dozens of islets scattered along the Queensland coast off Airlie Beach, are favorite destinations among yachties and beach lovers—and with good reason.

The Whitsunday Islands, protected from Coral Sea swells by sheltering reefs and cooled by trade winds, offer hundreds of yacht anchorages in close proximity, making this ideal cruising territory. The aquamarine waters shimmer and sparkle—a light-scattering effect that results when fine sediment runoff from river systems is stirred up by the 10- to 16-foot tides that sweep the coast.

Island resorts offer safe moorings for passing yachts, and an array of water sports and facilities. Farther out, on the Barrier Reef, you'll find fine snorkeling, diving, and fishing sites. Most Whitsunday Islands are unspoiled national parks; just a few—Hayman, Hamilton, Daydream, and South Long—have resorts.

WHEN TO GO

With a climate moderated by cooling trade winds, the Whitsundays are typically balmy year-round, though summer days can sometimes exceed 100°F. Over winter (June through August) it's warm and sunny by day and cool at night. Spring and fall weather can be perfect, and these seasons are often the quietest, if you avoid school holidays. Migrating southern right and humpback whales traverse these waters between July and September.

WHERE CAN I FIND ...

Underwater adventure? Most Whitsunday resorts have dedicated dive shops offering scuba and snorkeling lessons and rental gear; all either run or can organize day trips to dive and snorkeling spots nearby. Highlights include Hardy Reef and the iconic Heart Reef, where a purpose-built pontoon floats in sheltered waters teeming with tropical fish, turtles, and rays. Not keen to get wet? Take a semisubmersible coral-viewing tour, guided reef walk, or scenic heli-flight. Sheltered coves and coral-fringed beaches around many Whitsunday islands also offer good snorkeling.

Luxury? At Qualia, Hamilton Island's most lavish accommodation, sleek suites have infinity pools and alfresco areas, artfully lighted after dark, and fine food and wine brought in from Hamilton's best restaurants. Bedarra, Orpheus, Hayman, Palm Bay and Lizard Island resorts serve up gourmet meals and exclusive accommodations.

Family-friendliness? Daydream and Hamilton islands have dedicated kids' clubs, playgrounds, and myriad kid-at-heart features and activities. At Fitzroy Island Resort, children's activity programs mean parents can relax or join in the fun, while nature-based activities on Lizard Island are great for older kids.

White beaches? Whitehaven Beach on Whitsunday Island, the largest of the island group, offers those quintessential bleach-white, pure silica sands contrasting against aquamarine waters that vacation dreams are made of. Get here by seaplane or boat from Airlie Beach or charter your own yacht and drop anchor here for a few days.

TOP REASONS TO GO

Aquatic Playground

This is a snorkelers' and divers' paradise and one of the world's top sailing and cruising areas. It's also great for kayaking, windsurfing, and paragliding—and most resorts include the use of nonmotorized water sports equipment in their rates.

Tropical Paradise

Enjoy a mild climate and warm, clear waters whatever the season, plus beautiful fine white-sand beaches.

Gourmet Destination

Several Whitsunday and Barrier Reef island resorts offer cuisine to rival that of high-end city establishments. Island-resort food runs the gamut from four-star gourmet fare to regional cuisine presented with site-specific twists.

Resort Variety

You can divide your time easily between luxurious, leisurely resorts (such as Elysian Retreat on South Long Island) and an activity-oriented isle (such as Hamilton).

OUTDOOR ADVENTURES IN DAINTREE

Daintree National Park—which includes Cape Tribulation—is an ecological wonderland. Here you can see several of the world's most ancient plants and some of Australia's rarest creatures, protected by the Daintree's traditional owners, the Eastern Kuku Yalanji, for millennia.

A two-hour drive north of Cairns, the Daintree is the oldest tropical rain forest in the world. The park extends over approximately 30,000 acres, and the entire Wet Tropics region—which stretches from Townsville to Cooktown—was declared a UNESCO World Heritage site in 1988. Within it, experts have identified several species of angiosperms, the most primitive flowering plants in existence, many of which are found nowhere else on the planet. Stand in awe under the branches of the zamia fern, which has an underground trunk system evolved in defense against dinosaurs.

WHEN TO GO

Sunny days, comfortably cool nights, no stingers in the ocean, and mud-free rain forest: "the Dry" season (May to October) is the most pleasant time to visit.

"The Wet"—roughly November through April—can be wonderful, too: foliage is lush and buds turn to hothouse blooms. Drawbacks include occasional flash flooding and high humidity.

Spring and late fall can be a good compromise: the weather—and the water—are typically warm and clear.

A SACRED SITE

The traditional custodians of the Daintree are the Eastern Kuku Yalanji, who have been coexisting with and subsisting on the forest's abundant flora and fauna for tens of thousands of years. Designating five rather than four seasons in a year, the Eastern Kuku Yalanji used changes in weather and growth cycles to guide hunting and foraging expeditions into the rain forest: when the *jun jun* (blue ginger) came into fruit, they'd catch *diwan* (Australian brush turkey); when *jilngan* (mat grass) flowered, they'd collect *jarruka* (orange-footed scrubfowl) eggs; and year-round, they'd track tree-dwelling animals—*yawa* (possum), *kambi* (flying fox), and *murral* (tree kangaroo). Even today, members of the Kuku Yalanji can tell you which local plants can be eaten, used as medicines, and made into utensils, weapons, and shelter.

The Daintree's Indigenous inhabitants believe many of the area's natural sites have spiritual significance, attributing particular power to Wundu (Thornton Peak), Manjal Dimbi (Mt. Demi), Wurrmbu (The Bluff), and Kulki (Cape Tribulation). Dozens of spots in the rain forest—waterfalls, crags, peaks, and creeks—are deemed by the Kuku Yalanji to have spiritual, healing, or regenerative powers. Take a walk with one of the area's traditional custodians to get an intimate, intriguing perspective on this extraordinary terrain.

Various Indigenous-guided tours and experiences in the Daintree area focus on bush tucker and medicines, wildlife and hunting techniques, culture, history, and ritual. A waterhole just behind Daintree Eco Lodge & Spa is deemed a site of special significance for women: a dip in its healing waters is a female-only ritual.

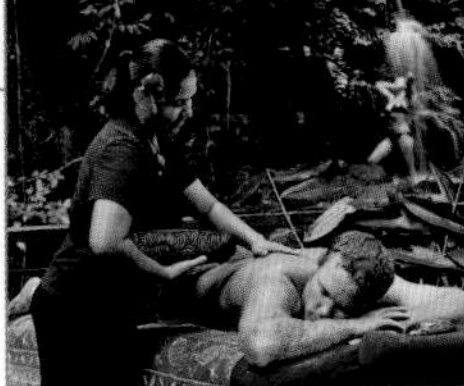

TOP REASONS TO GO

Animals. Watch for the rare Bennett's tree kangaroo, believed to have evolved from possums; the endangered, spotted-tailed quoll, a marsupial carnivore; a giant white-tailed rat (prone to raiding campsites); and the Daintree River ringtail possum, found only around Thornton Peak and the upper reaches of the Daintree and Mossman rivers.

Birds. Daintree National Park shelters hundreds of bird species: azure kingfishers swoop on crabs in the creeks, white-rumped swiftlets dart above the canopy. The pied imperial pigeon flies south from Papua New Guinea to breed here—as does the glorious buff-breasted paradise kingfisher, distinguished by its orange underbelly, blue wings, and long white tail. Year-round, you'll see orange-footed scrubfowl foraging or building gigantic leaf-litter nest-mounds. If you're very lucky, you might even spot the 6-foot-tall, flightless southern cassowary.

A maze of 3,000 individual reefs and 900 islands stretching for 2,300 km (1,429 miles), the Great Barrier Reef is among the world's most spectacular natural attractions. This underwater wonderland is a haven for thousands of species of marine creatures, as well as turtles and birds.

Most visitors explore this section of Australia from one of the dozen-plus resorts strung along the coasts of islands in the southern half of the marine park, many of which can be found in the Whitsunday Islands group. Although most Barrier Reef islands are closer to the mainland than they are to the spectacular outer reef, all island resorts offer (or can organize) boat excursions to various outer-reef sites.

The Great Barrier Reef system began to form approximately 6,000–8,000 years ago, say marine scientists. It's composed of individual reefs and islands, which lie to the west of the Coral Sea and extend south into the Pacific Ocean. Most of the reef is about 65 km (40 miles) off the Queensland coast, although some parts extend as far as 300 km (186 miles) offshore. Altogether, it covers an area bigger than Great Britain, forming the largest living feature on Earth and the only one visible from space. The reef was established as a marine park in 1975, and the United Nations designated the Great Barrier Reef a World Heritage site in 1981. Strict legislation was enacted in 2004, prohibiting fishing along most of the reef—a further attempt to protect the underwater treasures of this vast, delicate ecosystem.

MAJOR REGIONS

A laid-back tropical tourist hub built around a busy marina and swimming lagoon, **Cairns** bristles with hotels, tour agencies, dive-cruise boats, and travelers en route to the rain forest and reef. It has some fine retail stores and markets, plus an extensive waterfront park and entertainment precinct.

Along the pristine coastline **north of Cairns** the Captain Cook Highway runs from Cairns to Mossman, a gorgeous stretch punctuated by charming villages and tourist towns, including Palm Cove, with its European Riviera ambience, and bustling Port Douglas, with its sparkling marina, sprawling resorts, and hip café scene. North of the Daintree River, wildlife parks and sunny coastal villages fade into sensationally wild terrain. UNESCO World Heritage–listed wilderness extends to Cape Tribulation and beyond. If you came to Australia seeking high-octane sun, pristine coral cays, steamy jungles filled with exotic birdcalls and riotous vegetation, and a languid beachcomber lifestyle, head for the coast between Daintree and Cooktown, a frontier destination that tacks two days onto your itinerary. Here you'll find few services but some terrific, eco-friendly rain forest retreats.

Discovered in 1770 by Captain James Cook of the HMS *Endeavour,* the glorious **Whitsunday Islands**—a group of 74 islands situated within 161 km (100 miles) of each other and around 50 km (31 miles) from Shute Harbour, just off the mid-north-Queensland coast—today lure holidaymakers with world-class water sports, sheltered yacht anchorages, and resorts catering to every taste. The Whitsundays are a favorite sailing destination and an easy-access base from which to explore the midsection of the Great Barrier Reef. Only a few of the islands have resorts; others serve as destinations for day trips, beach time, and bushwalks, or simply as backdrop at scenic moorings. Shute Harbour is the principal mainland departure point, but Airlie Beach, the closest mainland town, buzzes with backpackers, who flock to its man-made lagoon, markets, bars, and budget digs. Well-heeled travelers might prefer the boutique retreats and resorts that hug the hillsides above the main drag. Islands include Hamilton, Hayman, Daydream, and Long Island.

North Coast Islands. The upscale, eco-conscious boutique resorts on Orpheus Island and Bedarra Island, off Ingham and Mission Beach respectively, are tailored to foodies and honeymooners, reclusive VIPs, and nature-loving travelers. Fitzroy Island and Lizard Island, off Cairns, offer ready access to world-class dive and game-fishing sites.

Townsville and Magnetic Island. Regional city Townsville has gracious heritage buildings, excellent museums and marine centers, and a well-maintained waterfront with a man-made swimming lagoon. Townsville, along with adjacent twin Thuringowa, make up Australia's largest tropical city, with a combined population of just under 180,000. It's the commercial capital of the north, and a major center for education, scientific research, and defense. Spread along the banks of Ross Creek and around the pink granite outcrop of Castle Hill, Townsville is a pleasant city of palm-fringed malls, historic colonial buildings, extensive parkland, and gardens. It's also the stepping-off point for offshore Magnetic Island, a popular holiday spot, with high-end and budget accommodations and an array of aquatic activities, including sea kayaking and scuba diving.

Planning

When to Go

The bulk of the Great Barrier Reef islands lie north of the Tropic of Capricorn in a monsoonal climate zone. In the hot, wet season (roughly December through April), expect tropical downpours that can limit outdoor activities and mar underwater visibility.

The warm days, clear skies, and pleasantly cool nights of the dry season, especially June through August, are ideal for traveling around and above Cairns. In the Whitsundays, some winter days may be too cool for swimming and nights can be chilly (pack a sweater and long pants).

The islands are warm, even in winter; during the summer months, temperatures regularly top 30°C (85°F), and the farther north you go, the hotter it gets. The water temperature is mild to warm year-round; however, in jellyfish season (typically, November through May), you'll need to wear a full-body stinger suit to swim anywhere but within patrolled, netted areas.

Planning Your Time

Most visitors to the Great Barrier Reef combine stays on one or more islands with time in Queensland's coastal towns and national parks. With a week or more, you could stay at two very different Barrier Reef island resorts: perhaps at an activities-packed Whitsundays resort and one of the more remote northerly islands, allowing a day or two to travel between them. If you want to resort-hop, opt for the Whitsundays, where island resorts lie in relatively close proximity and are well serviced by water and air transport.

If you have limited time, take a boat from Cairns or Port Douglas to a pontoon on the outer reef for a day on the water. A helicopter flight back to the mainland will give you an exhilarating aerial view of the reef and its islands. Alternatively, catch an early boat from Cairns to Fitzroy Island or from Shute Harbour to Daydream Island. Spend a couple of hours snorkeling, take a walk around, then relax on a quiet beach or in the resort bar.

Getting Here and Around

AIR

Jetstar, Virgin Australia, and Qantas have daily direct flights linking capital cities around Australia to Cairns Airport (which also handles international flights). These airlines also have flights to Townsville, Whitsunday Airport (Proserpine), Hamilton Island, and Mackay, linking with east-coast capitals and major regional cities throughout Queensland. From these hubs, regular boat and charter air services are available to most of the Great Barrier Reef resorts. Generally, island charter flights are timed to connect with domestic flights, but double-check.

For information about reaching the islands, see Getting Here and Around under each island's heading.

CONTACTS Airport Connections. ✉ *14 Comport St., Cairns* ☎ *07/4049–2244* 🌐 *www.tnqshuttle.com.* **Cairns Airport.** ✉ *Airport Ave., Cairns Airport, Cairns QLD 4870, Aeroglen* ☎ *0707/4080–6703* 🌐 *www.cairnsairport.com.au.*

BOAT

Usually, island launches are timed to connect with charter flights from island or mainland airports, but do ask. Crossings can be choppy; take ginger tablets for motion sickness ahead of time. If you're based on the mainland or in a hurry, many operators run day trips out to the reef and resort islands.

Several operators provide skipper-yourself (bareboat) and crewed charters to explore the Whitsundays. Almost all have five-day minimum charter periods; most offer discounts for multiday hires and optional extras such as catering. Packages start from around A$1,200 per person, per night, but can be several times that on crewed or luxury vessels.

BUS

Long-distance buses are an economical but often cramped way to travel along the North Queensland coast; don't expect to get much sleep on board. Shuttle buses transfer visitors from regional airports, Cairns, and beaches and towns to as far north as Cape Tribulation. They link airports, railway stations, and local towns to island ferry services departing from Mission Beach, Airlie Beach, and Shute Harbour. Hotel pickups are usually available; call ahead to confirm.

CAR

If you're visiting several North Queensland destinations, it may be simplest to drive. Most popular North Queensland routes are paved, though remote roads may be flooded in the wet season. A 4WD vehicle is advised if you're tackling the Daintree or going further north than Cooktown. Leave extra time if you're crossing the Daintree River or driving between Port Douglas and Cairns—peak-season traffic and roadwork may create congestion. If you're heading farther north along the coast, fill up with gas at or before Wonga Beach, and carry water, tools, and supplies. Past this point, services are infrequent, and gas and goods can be pricey.

Restaurants

Typically, restaurants on Barrier Reef islands are part of each island's main resort, so many resorts' rates include some or all meals. Some larger resorts have a range of restaurants, with formal dining rooms, outdoor barbecues, and seafood buffets; some have premium dining options for which you pay extra. On the mainland you'll find plenty of casual, open-air restaurants, serving mainly Modern Australian–style meals that showcase seafood and regional produce. With a few notable exceptions, Cairns, Palm Cove, and Port Douglas are your best bets for upscale dining.

Hotels

Most inhabited islands have just one main resort, typically offering a range of lodging types and prices. Choose island destinations based on your budget and the kind of vacation you want—active or relaxed, sociable or quiet, or a mix. Offerings range from luxurious enclaves with upscale facilities (Lizard, Orpheus, Bedarra, Hayman islands) to small, eco-focused retreats (Long Island) to activity-packed, family-friendly resorts (Long, Daydream islands and Fitzroy islands). The more rustic, remote resorts may lack modern conveniences such as telephones, televisions, and Internet access. Even on some Barrier Reef resorts close to the mainland, Internet connections can be slow and mobile phone coverage limited, and critters may infiltrate your room.

Restaurant and hotel reviews have been shortened. For full information, visit Fodors.com.

What It Costs in Australian Dollars

	$	$$	$$$	$$$$
RESTAURANTS	under A$36	A$36–A$45	A$46–A$65	over A$65
HOTELS	under A$201	A$201–A$300	A$301–A$450	over A$450

Health and Safety

You'll find large, well-equipped hospitals in Cairns, Townsville, and Mackay; doctors and medical centers in Port Douglas and Airlie Beach, and nearby towns. Emergency services are scarce between the Daintree River and Cooktown. Island resort front-desk staff typically handle emergencies and can summon doctors and aerial ambulance services. Remote islands have "flying doctor" kits and Hamilton Island has its own doctors.

Avoid midday rays, even in winter, and wear a hat and SPF 50-plus sunscreen to prevent sunburn. Rehydrate often and take it easy in the heat.

Avoid touching coral: it is easily damaged, and can cut and sting. Clean cuts thoroughly, scrubbing with a brush and flushing the affected area with saline solution. Toxic and stinging jellyfish frequent waters off the mainland and some Barrier Reef islands over the warmer months. Avoid the ocean at these times, unless you're wearing a stinger suit. If in doubt, ask a local.

Mosquitoes, midges, and leeches can be a problem in wet summer months. Wear insect repellent to avoid being bitten; check extremities, especially between your toes, after walking in damp, forested areas, and remove leeches by applying a flame or salt.

Estuarine crocodiles live in rivers and coastal waters along the North Queensland coast and on some Barrier Reef islands. Don't swim where crocs live (ask a local), especially in breeding season, September to April—and never dangle your limbs over the sides of boats.

Cairns

Tourism is the lifeblood of Cairns (pronounced *Care-ns*). The city makes a good base for exploring the wild top half of Queensland, and international travelers use it as a jumping-off point for activities such as scuba diving and snorkeling trips to the Barrier Reef, as well as boating, fishing, parasailing, scenic flights, and rain-forest treks.

Though the surrounding environment is a tough one, with intense heat in summer—not to mention stealthy saltwater crocodiles, venomous snakes, and jellyfish so deadly they put the region's stunning beaches off-limits to swimmers for nearly half the year—Cairns and tropical North Queensland are far from intimidating places. The people are warm and friendly, the sights spectacular, and the beachside lounging is world-class.

GETTING HERE AND AROUND

AIR

Cairns Airport is a major international gateway, and a connection point for flights to other parts of Queensland, including Townsville, Mackay, Rockhampton, Hamilton Island, and the Northern Territory, as well as all Australia's capital cities.

Airport Connections runs coaches between Cairns International Airport and town—an 8-km (5-mile) trip that takes about 10 minutes and costs A$18. All seats must be prebooked. The company also services Cairns's northern beaches, Palm Cove, Port Douglas, Silky Oaks Lodge (near Mossman), and Daintree Village (A$25 to A$70). Excellence Coaches also offers private transfers from the airport to the city for A$65 for up to five passengers. Port Douglas–based Exemplar Coaches and Limousines provides services direct from the airport to Cairns CBD (A$17), Palm Cove (A$25), and Port Douglas (A$46), just over an hour's drive north of Cairns, by coach or limousine. Private taxis and Uber also operate from Cairns airport.

CAR

Between Brisbane and Cairns, the Bruce Highway rarely touches the coast. Unless you're planning to stop off en route or explore the Great Green Way, fly or take the *Spirit of Queensland* (*www.queenslandrailtravel.com.au*) train to Cairns, renting a vehicle on arrival. Avis, Budget, Hertz, Enterprise, Thrifty, and Europcar all have rental cars and four-wheel-drive vehicles available.

TRAIN

Trains arrive at Cairns Railway Station in the city center. The *Spirit of Queensland* takes 24 hours to make the 1,681-km (1,045-mile) journey between Brisbane and Cairns but is a comfortable ride, whether you're in a reclining Premium Economy seat or on one of the state-of-the-art RailBed seats, which convert to podlike beds (premium economy A$221; RailBed A$390, includes three meals). The *Savannahlander* links Cairns and Forsayth, taking up to four days (with overnight stops en route) to traverse the 425 km (264 miles) of varying terrain including rain forest, savanna land, and arid Outback (A$1,020–A$1,530, accommodation and tours included). You can also take shorter segments of all these journeys.

TRAIN INFORMATION Cairns Railway Station. ✉ *Bunda St., between Spence and Scott Sts., CBD* ☎ *07/4036–9250* 🌐 *www.queenslandrailtravel.com.au.*

TOURS

★ Adventure North Australia: Cape Tribulation Tour

On Adventure North's private Cape Tribulation Tour, you can cruise the Daintree River, enjoy a barbecue lunch, and then explore Cape Tribulation and Mossman Gorge with an experienced driver-guide. ✉ *26 Redden St., Cairns* ☎ *07/4047–9075* 🌐 *www.adventurenorthaustralia.com* 🎫 *From A$1727.*

BTS Tours

BTS Tours runs various trips out of Cairns and Port Douglas, including a popular full-day Daintree tour and half-day Mossman Gorge trip. The Daintree itinerary includes a croc-spotting river cruise, canoeing, swimming in rain-forest pools, guided walks, and a barbecue lunch (A$165–A$175). Or take the Kuku Yalanji–guided tour of the Mossman Gorge, including rain-forest walk, bush tea, and free time to swim and sightsee (an additional A$104). ✉ *53–61 Macrossan St., Shop 8, Port Douglas* ☎ *07/4099–5665* 🌐 *www.btstours.com.au* 🎫 *From A$29.*

Coral Expeditions

This established operator's comfortable expedition-style ships take passengers on 7-, 10-, and 18-night live-aboard trips, departing Cairns. Exclusive outer Barrier Reef moorings mean you see more of the marine life. Itineraries explore either the Barrier Reef exclusively, or head up to Torres Strait and even around to Darwin. Friendly crew, dive guides, and an onboard marine biologist ensure scuba novices are up to speed and snorkelers are catered to. The per-person fare includes complimentary scuba skills sessions, snorkeling gear, twin-berth accommodation, all meals, and most activities. ✉ *Coral Expeditions head office, 246 Hartley St, Portsmith* ☎ *07/4040–9999, 1800/079–545 toll-free in Australia* 🌐 *www.coralexpeditions.com* 🎫 *From A$4750.*

Down Under Tours

Eco-certified Down Under Tours makes half- and full-day trips and four-wheel-drive excursions, as well as reef trips, river cruises, white-water rafting, bungee jumping, and hot-air-ballooning adventures, most departing from Cairns. Popular guided half- and full-day excursions take in the attractions of Kuranda, Hartley's Crocodile Adventures, and Mossman Gorge, the Daintree, and Cape Tribulation. ✉ *26 Redden St., CBD* ☎ *07/4047–9097* 🌐 *www.downundertours.com* 🎫 *From A$99.*

Heritage 4WD Safari Tours

Advanced eco–certified Heritage Tours runs nine-day Gulf Savannah tours departing Cairns (A$4,199 per person, twin-share, or A$5,098 sole use), and 7-day fly/drive to 12-day overland trips to Cape York Peninsula during the dry season, May through early October. Two popular seven-day, fly/drive tours between Cairns and Cape York start at A$4,199 twin-share, or A$5,098 sole use. All tours include transfers, meals and accommodation, have a maximum of 25 guests and are accompanied by a senior guide. ✉ *21 Salter Close, Cairns* ☎ *07/4054–7750, 1800/775–533* 🌐 *www.heritagetours.com.au* 🎫 *From A$3895.*

Kuku Yalanji Cultural Habitat Tours

The Eastern Kuku Yalanji have called the Daintree area home for tens of thousands of years, and have an intimate understanding of the terrain. Today, the Walker brothers—part of the Kubirri Warra clan—pass on a little of that ancestral wisdom on two-hour beach, mudflat, and mangrove walks (daily, 9:30 am and 1:30 pm, A$90). Learn techniques for throwing spears, tracking coastal food sources, and much more from knowledgeable, skillful guides. A medium level of fitness is required. Transfers between the Port Douglas area and Cooya Beach, a 25-minute drive north, are A$30. ✉ *Port Douglas* ☎ *07/4098–3437* 🌐 *www.kycht.com.au* 🎫 *A$90.*

★ Ocean Spirit Cruises
Long-established Ocean Spirit Cruises runs full-day tours to glorious Michaelmas Cay, a remote Great Barrier Reef sand isle encircled by fish-and turtle-filled coral gardens. It's also a protected sanctuary for migratory seabirds. Cruise out to the cay on *Ocean Spirit*, a 105-foot luxury sailing catamaran, for four hours of snorkeling, semisubmersible coral-viewing tours, and marine biologist presentations, with a full buffet lunch, morning and afternoon tea and snorkeling gear included in the A$219 per person cost. *Ocean Spirit* departs daily from Cairns Reef Fleet Terminal. Transfers from Cairns and the northern beaches are available from $A30. ✉ *Reef Fleet Terminal, 1 Spence St., Office 3, Level 1, CBD* ☎ *07/4044–9944* 🌐 *www.oceanspirit.com.au* 🎫 *From A$219.*

Sights

Cosmopolitan Cairns, the unofficial capital of Far North Queensland, is Australia's 15th-largest city, with a burgeoning population pushing 150,000—double that when you include the thriving hinterland. Once a sleepy tropical town sprawled around Trinity Bay and Inlet, the city has expanded hugely in recent decades, and now extends north to Ellis Beach, west to the Atherton Tablelands, and south along the Great Green Way as far as Edmonton.

Australian Butterfly Sanctuary
WILDLIFE REFUGE | More than 1,500 tropical butterflies—including dozens of the electric-blue Ulysses species and Australia's largest butterfly, the green-and-gold Cairns birdwing—flutter within a compact rain-forest aviary, alighting on foliage, interpretative signage, and feeding stations. About 60 butterflies are released into the aviary each day, ensuring the colorful spectacle continues. Free half-hour guided tours of the aviary and caterpillar breeding area are full of fascinating tidbits. ✉ *8 Rob Veivers Dr., Kuranda* ☎ *07/4093–7575* 🌐 *www.australianbutterflies.com* 🎫 *From A$20 entry and guided tour.*

Kuranda Experience

Tropical Kuranda offers several nature-oriented attractions, including the Australian Butterfly Sanctuary, Birdworld Kuranda, and Kuranda Koala Gardens. See these sites individually, or visit on a Kuranda 3 Park Pass (A$51), which gives entry to all three and can be purchased with a return Skyrail Pass (from A$85).

★ Birdworld Kuranda
NATURE PRESERVE | One of your best chances to see the endangered southern cassowary, a prehistoric emu-like bird, is at Birdworld Kuranda. It's home to hundreds of colorful birds from nearly 60 species, more than 20 of them native to vanishing rain-forest areas—walking and flying freely in a gigantic aviary. Many of them are tame enough to perch on your shoulders. Wear a hat and sleeved shirt: birds' claws are scratchy. ✉ *Kuranda Heritage Village, Rob Vievers Dr., Kuranda* ☎ *07/4093–9188* 🌐 *www.birdworldkuranda.com* 🎫 *From A$20.*

Cairns Art Gallery
ART GALLERY | **FAMILY** | Occupying the impressive former Public Office Building constructed in the 1930s, Cairns Art Gallery houses a hodgepodge of local, national, international, and Indigenous artworks, including a fine collection of Australian photography, in its wood-paneled rooms. The shop stocks high-quality Australian giftware, toys, jewelry, prints, books, and cards. There are also kids' programs, classes, talks, and workshops. ✉ *City Place, Shields St. at Abbott St., CBD* ☎ *07/4046–4800* 🌐 *www.cairnsart-gallery.com.au* 🎫 *Free.*

★ The Esplanade

PROMENADE | Fronting Cairns Harbour, this busy boardwalk and recreational zone is the focal point of life in Cairns. Along the walk you'll encounter shady trees and public art, picnic and barbecue facilities, a large saltwater swimming lagoon, volleyball courts, an imaginative kids' playground, a state-of-the-art skate plaza, and areas for fitness, markets, and live entertainment. A shallow, 4,800-square-meter (51,667-square-foot) filtered saltwater lagoon swimming pool with a sandy shore, decking, and shelters, patrolled by lifeguards year-round, provides free, convenient relief from the often sticky air. Along the street opposite and along the marina at the boardwalk's southern end, you'll find hotels, shops, galleries, bars, and eateries. ✉ *Between Spence and Upward Sts., CBD* ☎ *1300/692–247 Cairns City Council* 🌐 *www.cairnsesplanade.com* 🎫 *Free.*

Kuranda Scenic Railway

SCENIC DRIVE | The historic Kuranda Scenic Railway makes a two-hour ascent through rain forest and 15 hand-hewn tunnels to pretty Kuranda village, gateway to the Atherton Tableland. Book a simple Heritage Class seat; get a cool towel and souvenir pack; or splurge on a Gold Class ticket with fine local food and wine, table service, swanky decor, and a souvenir guide. Several tour packages are available, from full-day rain-forest safaris, and visits to local Aboriginal centers and wildlife parks to simple round-trips combining rail and cable-car journeys. ✉ *Cairns Railway Station, Bunda St., CBD* ☎ *07/4231–9045, 1800/577–245* 🌐 *www.ksr.com.au* 🎫 *From A$50.*

★ Skyrail Rainforest Cableway

OTHER ATTRACTION | **FAMILY** | From the Skyrail terminal just north of Cairns, take a six-person cable car on a breathtaking 7½-km (5-mile) journey across pristine, World Heritage–listed rain-forest canopy to the highland village of Kuranda, where you can visit wildlife parks and shop for local crafts and Aboriginal art. At two stations along the way, you can hop off and explore (the Skyrail ticket price includes a short ranger-guided rain-forest tour at Red Peak, and there's an info center and lookout at Barron Falls). Upgrade your ticket to the glass floor Diamond View Gondola for an even better view. The cableway base station is 15 km (9 miles) north of Cairns. Many visitors take the Scenic Railway to Kuranda, the cableway on the return trip. ✉ *6 Skyrail Dr., Smithfield* ☎ *07/4038–5555* 🌐 *www.skyrail.com.au* 🎫 *From A$57.*

Restaurants

★ Bayleaf Balinese Restaurant

$ | **INDONESIAN** | Dining in this spacious, central restaurant, you can enjoy some of the most delicious, innovative cuisine in North Queensland. Choose from an expansive menu that combines traditional Balinese spices and recipes with native Australian ingredients, such as the crocodile satay and mouthwatering *be celeng base manis* (pork in sweet soy sauce). **■ TIP→ Don't eat lunch if you're planning to order the rijstaffel at dinner—it's huge.** **Known for:** local favorite; traditional rijsttafel feast for two; award-winning wine list and long, tropically themed cocktail menu. $ *Average main: A$30* ✉ *Bay Village Tropical Retreat, 227 Lake St., at Gatton St., CBD* ☎ *07/4047–7955* 🌐 *www.bayleafrestaurant.com.au* ⏲ *No lunch Sat.–Mon.*

★ CC's Bar & Grill

$$$ | **STEAKHOUSE** | In a city that loves a steak, this is probably the best of them. CC's Bar & Grill sources most of its beef from farms owned by its parent company, Crystalbrook, whose cattle station is about three hours from Cairns. **Known for:** excellent steaks; great wine list; fine-dining atmosphere. $ *Average main: A$49* ✉ *163 Abbot St., CBD* ☎ *07/4253–4010* 🌐 *www.crystalbrookcollection.com/bailey/ccs-bar-and-grill* ⏲ *Closed Sun.–Wed.*

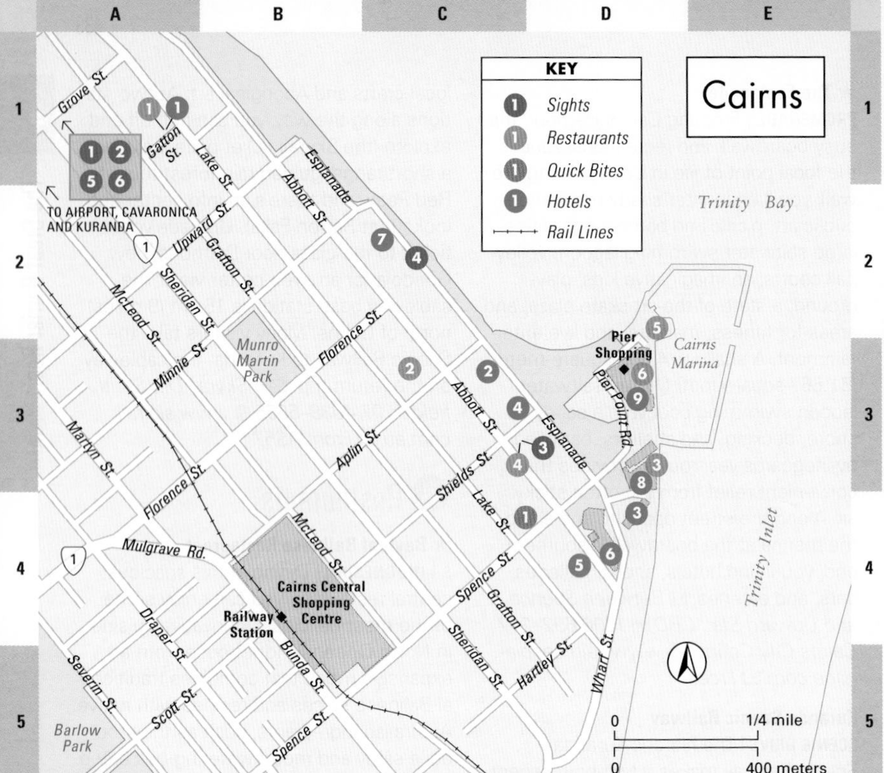

Sights

1 Australian Butterfly Sanctuary **A1**
2 Birdworld Kuranda **A1**
3 Cairns Art Gallery **C3**
4 The Esplanade **C2**
5 Kuranda Scenic Railway **A1**
6 Skyrail Rainforest Cableway **A1**

Restaurants

1 Bayleaf Balinese Restaurant **A1**
2 CC's Bar & Grill **C3**
3 Ochre Restaurant **D3**
4 Perrotta's at the Gallery **C3**
5 Salt House **D2**
6 Waterbar & Grill Steakhouse **D3**

Quick Bites

1 Bang and Grind **C4**

Hotels

1 Bay Village Tropical Retreat & Apartments **A1**
2 Crystalbrook Flynn **C3**
3 Hilton Cairns **D4**
4 Oaks Cairns Hotel **C3**
5 Pullman Cairns International **D4**
6 The Reef Hotel Casino **D4**
7 Riley, a Crystalbrook Collection Resort **C2**
8 The Sebel Cairns Harbour Lights Hotel ... **D3**
9 Shangri-La Hotel, The Marina **D3**

Scenic Drive: The Great Green Way

Babinda Boulders. About an hour's drive from Cairns, Babinda Boulders is a popular swimming hole, and a sacred Aboriginal site. It's 7 km (5 miles) inland on The Boulders Road from the town of Babinda, accessible via the Bruce Highway about 60 km (37 miles) south of Cairns. You can also hike to the boulders, taking the 19-km (12-mile) Goldfield Track (Wooroonooran National Park) that starts in Goldsborough Valley, southwest of Cairns, and ends in Babinda Boulders car park. ✉ *Babinda Information Centre, 1 Munro St., at Bruce Hwy., Babinda* ☎ *07/4067–1008 info center* 🌐 *www.babindainfocentre.com.au.*

Great Green Way. A scenic section of the Bruce Highway locals call the Great Green Way links Cairns with Townsville, taking you through sugarcane, papaya, and banana plantations, past white-sand beaches and an island-dotted ocean. The 348-km (216-mile) drive takes about 4½ hours. Allow time to explore towns, parks, and rainforest tracts along the way. ✉ *Bruce Hwy., between Cairns and Townsville.*

Paronella Park. A sprawling Spanish-style castle and gardens grace this offbeat National Trust site in the Mena Creek Falls rain forest. Explore the park on a self-guided botanical walk or 30-minute guided tour, enjoy Devonshire tea on the café's deck, buy local crafts, and cool off under a 40-foot waterfall. On hour-long flashlight-lit evening tours starting nightly at 6:15, you might spot eels, water dragons, fireflies, and glowworms. Allow at least three hours to explore. ✉ *1671 Japoonvale Rd. (Old Bruce Hwy.), Mena Creek* ☎ *07/4065–0000* 🌐 *www.paronellapark.com.au* 🎫 *A$50.*

Tully Gorge National Park. In the wettest zone of the Wet Tropics World Heritage area, the mighty Tully River is a magnet for white-water rafters, while the gorge's scenic, often mist-shrouded trails suit walkers of all levels. Access Tully Gorge National Park via the town of Tully, 141 km (88 miles) or about two hours' drive south of Cairns, then continue for 54 km (34 miles)—approximately 40 minutes—along Jarra Creek and Cardstone roads to Kareeya Hydroelectric Station parking lot and viewing platform. Other excellent vantage points are the Tully Falls lookout, 24 km (15 miles) south of Ravenshoe, and the Flip Wilson and Frank Roberts lookouts. ✉ *Tully Falls Rd., Koombooloomba* ☎ *07/4068–2288 Tully visitor information, 137–468 parks camping permits and general inquiries* 🌐 *www.nprsr.qld.gov.au/parks/tully-gorge.*

Wooroonooran National Park. Extending south of Gordonvale to the Palmerston Highway near Innisfail, this is one of the most densely vegetated areas in Australia. Rain forest rules, from the lowland tropical variety to the stunted growth on Mt. Bartle Frere (at 5,287 feet, the highest point in Queensland). Walking tracks range from the stroll-in-the-park Tchupala Falls and Josephine Falls circuits (30 minutes each) to the challenging Walshs Pyramid track, just south of Cairns, and the grueling two-day Bartle Frere trail. You may camp throughout the park with permits. ✉ *Josephine Falls Rd., Cairns* ☎ *07/4067–1008 Babinda Information Centre* 🌐 *www.nprsr.qld.gov.au/parks/wooroonooran.*

★ **Ochre Restaurant**

$$ | AUSTRALIAN | FAMILY | Local seafood and native and seasonal ingredients take top billing at this upscale yet relaxed Cairns institution that specializes in bush dining. Expect to find the likes of kangaroo, crocodile, and even green ants, with fine antipodean wines to match. **Known for:** signature dessert—wattle-seed pavlova with Davidson plum sorbet and macadamia biscotti; Australian game; gluten-free and vegetarian options. *$ Average main: A$42 ✉ 6/1 Marlin Parade, CBD ☎ 07/4051–0100 ⊕ ochrerestaurant.com.au ⏲ Closed Sun.*

Perrotta's at the Gallery

$ | MODERN AUSTRALIAN | FAMILY | This outdoor café and wine bar at Cairns Art Gallery serves sumptuous breakfasts as well as lunch and dinner. Lunch fare features a signature duck salad, gourmet sandwiches, and heartier meals, while dinner options include Italian and Modern Australian dishes: antipasto, pasta, and pizza. **Known for:** smoothies; central location; road menu. *$ Average main: A$25 ✉ Gallery Deck, Cairns Art Gallery, 38 Abbott St., at Shield St., CBD ☎ 07/4031–5899 ⊕ www.perrottasatg.com.*

Salt House

$$ | MODERN AUSTRALIAN | Blessed with mountain and ocean views and located in prime position at the Cairns Marina, Salt House serves Modern Australian fare in casual chic environs. A carefully considered menu includes plenty of local seafood, as well as a mouthwatering selection of local cuts of meat cooked on the custom Argentinian grill. **Known for:** stunning waterside location; excellent wine list; local seafood. *$ Average main: A$39 ✉ Marina Point, 6/2 Pierpoint Rd., CBD ☎ 07/4041–7733 ⊕ salthouse.com.au.*

Waterbar & Grill Steakhouse

$$ | STEAKHOUSE | At this busy waterfront eatery, you can gaze at Cairns's bustling marina while chowing down on a locally sourced, chargrilled steak, which come in all cuts and sizes, with thick fries on the side. There's also a nice selection of barbecued lamb ribs, burgers, seafood, and lighter lunch fare, such as pita wraps and salads. **Known for:** prime waterfront location; pork ribs; good cocktail menu. *$ Average main: A$42 ✉ Pier Shopping Centre, Pier Point Rd., Shop G1A, CBD ☎ 07/4031–1199 ⊕ www.waterbarandgrill.com.au ⏲ No lunch Mon.–Thurs.*

Beaches

Because Cairns lacks city beaches, most people head out to the reef to swim and snorkel. North of the airport, neighboring areas including **Machans Beach, Holloways Beach, Yorkey's Knob, Trinity Beach,** and **Clifton Beach** are perfect for swimming from June through September and sometimes even October; check local weather reports. Avoid the ocean at other times, however, when deadly box jellyfish (marine stingers) and invisible-to-the-eye Irukandji jellyfish float in the waters along the coast.

Coffee and Quick Bites

Bang and Grind

$ | AUSTRALIAN | Get immersed in north Queensland coffee culture at Bang and Grind, a lively café in the CBD. The venue is known for its house-blended coffee, which goes perfectly with classic Australian breakfast fare such as avocado toast, eggs Benedict, and pancakes. **Known for:** excellent coffee; good brunches; lively atmosphere. *$ Average main: A$14 ✉ 8/14 Spence St., CBD ☎ 07/4051–7770 ⊕ www.facebook.com/BangandGrind ⏲ Closed Sun.*

The Skyrail Rainforest Cableway outside Cairns

Hotels

Bay Village Tropical Retreat & Apartments
$ | **RESORT** | **FAMILY** | The sociable public areas at this family-friendly complex include a lovely lagoon pool, a guest laundry, and the terrific Bayleaf Balinese Restaurant & Bar. The main complex offers simple but spacious double, family, and studio rooms, some with balconies. **Pros:** a lovely central courtyard with pool, surrounded by tropical gardens; clean, generously sized rooms; excellent restaurant on-site. **Cons:** standard rooms lack ambient lighting and all but simple amenities; pool area and ground-floor rooms can be noisy; no elevator access to second floor. *Rooms from: A$130* *227 Lake St., at Gatton St., CBD* *07/4051–4622* *www.bayvillage.com.au* *81 rooms* *No Meals.*

Crystalbrook Flynn
$$ | **HOTEL** | The Flynn is the third in a series of five-star Cairns properties owned by the Crystalbrook group (which also farms beef), and it's the "fun and energetic" brand. **Pros:** light-filled rooms; sparkling new; high-quality on-site drinking and dining. **Cons:** can be busy; crowd trends younger; Flynn's Italian closed most nights. *Rooms from: A$295* *85 Esplanade, CBD* *07/4253–5000* *www.crystalbrookcollection.com/flynn* *No Meals* *311 rooms.*

★ **Hilton Cairns**
$$ | **HOTEL** | This attractive hotel has an enviable location near the waterfront, a flotilla of services, and classy on-site drinking and dining options. **Pros:** friendly, helpful service; good dining and drinking options; modern rooms with comfortable beds. **Cons:** steep fees for parking; business hotel can feel a little corporate; tour groups can create crowds in public areas. *Rooms from: A$260* *34 Esplanade, CBD* *07/4050–2000* *www.hilton.com* *No Meals* *262 rooms.*

Oaks Cairns Hotel
$ | **HOTEL** | The Oaks is a brand-new hotel and it shows, with smart and very spacious rooms, and one of Cairns' few rooftop bars and restaurants in Oak and

Vine. **Pros:** friendly service; great location; beautiful views from rooftop restaurant. **Cons:** restaurant fills quickly on weekends; not as luxurious as some competitors; no parking on-site. $ *Rooms from: A$199* ✉ *59–63 Esplanade, CBD* ☎ *07/3188–6052, 1300/064–982 reservations* 🌐 *www.oakshotels.com/en/oaks-cairns-hotel* 🍽 *No Meals* *76 rooms.*

Pullman Cairns International
$$ | **HOTEL** | This practicality-meets-luxury hotel near Cairns's waterfront has an impressive three-story lobby, an elegant day spa, and rooms and suites with furnished balconies. **Pros:** recently refurbished rooms; central location; good on-site services and facilities. **Cons:** fees for parking; not all rooms have harbor views; service can be sluggish. $ *Rooms from: A$251* ✉ *17 Abbot St., at Spence St., CBD* ☎ *07/4031–1300* 🌐 *www.pullmancairnsinternational.com.au* 🍽 *No Meals* *321 rooms.*

★ **The Reef Hotel Casino**
$$ | **HOTEL** | Part of a lively entertainment complex in the heart of Cairns, this high-end hotel has spacious rooms and suites, as well as several restaurants and bars, a theater, a casino, an outdoor swimming pool, and a small wildlife sanctuary and ropes course in its rooftop dome. **Pros:** generously sized rooms; several on-site entertainment and dining options; helpful, high-end service. **Cons:** casino on-site; chilly pool; large, busy complex, lacks intimate feel. $ *Rooms from: A$293* ✉ *35–41 Wharf St., CBD* ☎ *07/4030–8888* 🌐 *www.reefcasino.com.au* 🍽 *No Meals* *128 rooms.*

Riley, a Crystalbrook Collection Resort
$$$ | **HOTEL** | This modern, contemporary property on the Cairns Esplanade is in the heart of the city, and rooms come with a view of Cairns, the resort, or the sea. **Pros:** great, central location; Cairns's highest rooftop bar; complimentary parking. **Cons:** public access to bars, pool, and restaurant; some oddly shaped rooms in the tower; suited for younger market. $ *Rooms from: A$344* ✉ *131–141 Esplanade, Cairns* ☎ *07/4252–7777* 🌐 *www.crystalbrookcollection.com/riley* 🍽 *No Meals* *311 rooms.*

The Sebel Cairns Harbour Lights Hotel
$$ | **HOTEL** | The hotel rooms and one- and two-bedroom apartments at this hotel on Cairns's waterfront are a two-minute stroll to Reef Fleet Terminal, making them ideal for early-morning reef trips. **Pros:** great inlet views; terrific central location; good on-site dining options. **Cons:** pool small, and can be chilly in cooler months; fees for parking; lacks personality and feels a little corporate. $ *Rooms from: A$299* ✉ *1 Marlin Parade, CBD* ☎ *07/4057–0800* 🌐 *thesebelcairnsharbourlightshotel.com* 🍽 *No Meals* ☞ *Takeout available from Dundee's on ground floor* *84 rooms.*

Shangri-La Hotel, The Marina
$$ | **HOTEL** | With chic modern decor in blues and blue-grays reflecting the waterfront location and buzzing on-site bars and eateries, this marina-side resort is among Cairns's hippest. **Pros:** proximity to the marina; great views; free Wi-Fi. **Cons:** Horizon Club breakfast can be underwhelming; lower-floor pier-side rooms above the bar can be noisy; guests have to pay for parking. $ *Rooms from: A$264* ✉ *Pierpoint Rd., CBD* ☎ *07/4031–1411, 1800/222–448* 🌐 *www.shangri-la.com/cairns/shangrila* 🍽 *No Meals* *184 rooms.*

Nightlife

Cairns's Esplanade and the CBD streets leading off it come alive at night, with most restaurants serving until late, and wine or a cold beer is a staple with evening meals. Several rowdy pubs catering to backpackers and younger travelers line the central section of City Place; a few bars and hotel venues manage to be upscale while remaining true to the city's easygoing spirit. Unless noted, bars are open nightly and there's no cover charge.

Off The Beaten Path

Undara Experience. This extraordinary complex on the edge of Undara Volcanic National Park, 275 km (171 miles) or a four-hour scenic drive or rail trip from Cairns, supplies the complete Outback experience: bush breakfasts, campfire activities, lava-tube tours, and guided evening wildlife walks, plus a range of distinctive accommodation. Vintage railway cars have been converted into comfortable (if compact), fan-cooled motel rooms with their own en suites. You can also stay in a modern, air-conditioned "Pioneer Hut" with private veranda, fridge, and bathroom (A$195 per night in high season), in a safari tent; or at a powered or unpowered site with shared amenities. One-night "budget" self-drive packages that incorporate tours, campfire activities, and swag-tent accommodation cost A$217 per person in high season, with meals; or from A$321 per person with swankier accommodation. Two-night packages including meals, rail-carriage or Pioneer Hut accommodation, and tours range cost A$497 per person in high season. Other packages include transfers to and from Cairns via coach or on heritage train *The Savannahlander*. Drink and dine on-site at Fettler's Iron Pot Bistro; breakfast at the Ringers' Camp. ✉ *Undara Volcanic Park, Savannah Way, Mt. Surprise* ☎ *07/4097–1900, 1800/990–992* 🌐 *www.undara.com.au.*

Bar36

LIVE MUSIC | Popular with visitors and locals alike, this sleek bar-lounge off the main foyer of The Reef Hotel Casino has live bands (including big-name acts) and great atmosphere. Get a table early and enjoy a quiet drink and some tapas before the crowds pile in. ✉ *The Reef Hotel Casino, 35–41 Wharf St., ground-fl. foyer, CBD* ☎ *07/4030–8888* 🌐 *www.reefcasino.com.au/venue/bar36.*

Hemingway's Brewery

BREWPUBS | Located on the water in the Cruise Liner Terminal, Hemingway's Brewery is in a historic building, has a relaxed vibe, and there's plenty of room for families or groups to spread out. Enjoy Trinity Inlet views over one of the eight in-house beers on tap. There is also a classic food menu featuring local produce served in burgers and salads, or on pizzas, for those who want something to pair with their pale ale. It's a fun venue with lovely views and good beers. ✉ *Cairns Wharf, 4 Wharf St., CBD* ☎ *07/4099–6663* 🌐 *www.hemingwaysbrewery.com/cairns-wharf.*

The Pier Bar

BARS | A prime waterside location and a big, breezy deck draw an upbeat, mixed crowd to The Pier Bar. They flock here for wood-fired pizzas, well-priced drinks, and laid-back Sunday sessions with live music and DJs. The bar gets noisier, younger, and more crowded as the night wears on, but service is friendly and food is palatable, even when the bar's jam-packed. ✉ *The Pier Shopping Centre, 1 Pierpoint Rd., Cairns* ☎ *07/4031–4677* 🌐 *www.thepierbar.com.au.*

Performing Arts

Cairns Performing Arts Centre

ARTS CENTERS | **FAMILY** | This precinct combines two performing arts spaces: the Cairns Performing Arts Centre and the Munro Martin Parklands. Munro Martin Parklands hosts audiences in its open-air amphitheater surrounded by lush tropical gardens, while the CPAC features two indoor theaters. Each showcases local and international talent performing across many genres from dance to theater, ballet, music, and comedy. ✉ *9–11 Florence St., Cairns* ☎ *1300/855–835* 🌐 *www.cairnsperformingartscentre.com.au.*

★ Tanks Arts Centre

ARTS CENTERS | FAMILY | This vibrant arts center is housed in a trio of repurposed World War II–era oil storage tanks in Cairns's lush Flecker Botanic Gardens, 4 km (2 miles) north of the Cairns city center. It has become a vital creative hub for the region, showcasing everything from dance and theater troupes to local folk, blues, jazz, and Indigenous artists. The Centre hosts a colorful arts and food market, with live music and free kids' activities, on the last Sunday of the month from April to November. ✉ *46 Collins Ave., Edge Hill* ☎ *07/4032–6600* 🌐 *www.tanksartscentre.com* 🎟 *Galleries free, venue ticket prices vary.*

Shopping

Cairns Central

MALL | Adjacent to Cairns Railway Station, Cairns Central houses 180-plus specialty stores, a supermarket, department stores, a food court, several coffee shops, and a cinema complex. Strollers are available to rent. It also has the only free parking in Cairns CBD: three hours free. ✉ *McLeod St. at Spence St., CBD* ☎ *07/4041–4111* 🌐 *www.cairnscentral.com.au.*

Cairns Night Markets

MARKET | FAMILY | If you're looking for bargain beachwear, local jewelry, art and crafts, a massage, a meal, a coffee, or souvenirs, the Cairns Night Markets, open daily 4:30 to 10:30 pm, are the place to go. Bring cash—several of the 70-plus merchants charge additional fees for credit cards. ✉ *71–75 The Esplanade, at Aplin St., CBD* ☎ *01/4051–7666* 🌐 *www.nightmarkets.com.au.*

Cairns Night Markets

The food court in the lively, inexpensive Cairns Night Markets between Shield and Spence Streets (*71–75 The Esplanade, www.nightmarkets.com.au*) offers something for every palate, from Korean barbecue to sweet-and-sour chicken, sushi, Thai, and Italian. You can also max out on desserts, with outlets offering crepes, waffles, churros, gelato, ice cream, and Italian-style coffee. The food court's open daily from 10 am to 11 pm; the night markets, 4:30 to 10:30 pm. Most stalls accept credit cards, but bring cash just in case.

Rusty's Markets

MARKET | FAMILY | Cairns's iconic weekend "street" market, Rusty's attracts 180-plus stallholders, who peddle everything from fresh tropical produce to art and crafts, jewelry, clothing, natural health and skin-care products, and food. The market is covered, offering a pleasant respite from the sun. Take advantage of two hours' free parking in Gilligan's/Rusty's carpark, above Rusty's on Sheridan Street. ✉ *57–89 Grafton St., CBD* ☎ *07/4040–2705* 🌐 *www.rustysmarkets.com.au.*

Activities

It's no surprise that lots of tours out of Cairns focus on the Great Barrier Reef. Half-day snorkeling, diving, and fishing trips out of Cairns, most departing from the Reef Fleet Terminal, start from around A$100; full-day trips start from about A$250. Scuba dives and gear generally cost extra. Note that you may also be hit with a Port Authority charge of around A$8.50 per person, per day.

Ask a few pertinent questions before booking diving tours: dive trips vary in size, and some cater specifically to, say, sightseers; others to experienced divers. If you're a beginner or Open Water diver, ensure that you book excursions that visit suitable dive sites, with certified staff on hand to assist you.

Cairns is also a great base for adventure activities and horse riding on the Atherton Tableland, ballooning over the Mareeba Valley, and day tours to the UNESCO World Heritage–listed Daintree rain forest. The offices of adventure-tour companies, tourist offices, and booking agents are concentrated around the Esplanade.

Cairns Canyoning

ADVENTURE TOURS | Get ready for a day of wild and wet adventure with Cairns Canyoning, which runs adventure tours into the various rivers and gorges that surround the city. These are classic canyoning trips, featuring abseiling, sliding, swimming, and leaps of faith off reasonably high cliffs. Different locations provide different levels of difficulty and risk: this is a case of choose your own adventure. ✉ *58 Grafton St., CBD* ☎ *07/4243–3242* 🌐 *www.cairnscanyoning.com* 🎫 *From A$174.*

Cairns Marlin Marina

MARINA/PIER | This floating marina's 261 berths bristle with charter fishing, diving, and private vessels, including superyachts up to 197 feet long. At the Reef Fleet Terminal off Marlin Wharf, you'll find tour offices, shops, cafés, and Wi-Fi connectivity. Big-game fishing is a big business here; fish weighing more than 1,000 pounds have been caught in the waters off the reef. Most of the dive boats and catamarans that ply the Great Barrier Reef dock here or at nearby Trinity Wharf. ✉ *1 Spence St., CBD* ☎ *07/4052–3866* 🌐 *www.portsnorth.com.au/marina.*

Divers Den

DIVING & SNORKELING | Long-established, PADI five-star-rated Divers Den has a roaming permit that allows its guides to visit any part of the Great Barrier Reef, including 17 exclusive moorings on the reef's outer edge frequented by turtles, rays, and colorful reef fish. Open Water and advanced PADI dive courses include live-aboard trips. Daily transfers take divers out to luxury live-aboard vessel, OceanQuest, which operates around the Norman, Saxon, and Hastings reefs. Guests can book in to stay on OceanQuest for as many nights as they like. Day trips include up to three dives or snorkeling opportunities; gear and lunch are included in the price, but photos cost extra. ✉ *319 Draper St., CBD* ☎ *07/4046–7333* 🌐 *www.diversden.com.au* 🎫 *From A$180.*

Dreamtime Dive and Snorkel

CULTURAL TOURS | Here's a reef experience with a refreshing difference. Dreamtime Dive and Snorkel is a local company that adds an Indigenous perspective to a dive or snorkel trip, with traditional owners of the Cairns sea country on board to guide visitors through their Great Barrier Reef experience. Daylong trips stop at two outer reef locations for snorkeling and scuba diving, with guided snorkeling tours, lunch, and the chance to learn from the on-board team all included. ✉ *1 Spence St., CBD* ☎ *07/4030–7920* 🌐 *dreamtimedive.com* 🎫 *From A$249.*

★ **Mike Ball Dive Expeditions**

DIVING & SNORKELING | Mike Ball, an enthusiastic American who's been diving the Great Barrier Reef since 1969, runs multiday, multidive trips along the Queensland coastline on which novice divers are given expert guidance and experienced divers get to set their own bottom times and dive their own plans. Custom-built, twin-hulled live-aboard boats loaded with top-end gear, serious divers, and qualified chefs depart twice weekly to visit renowned dive sites and spot minke whales and sharks. Dive courses cost extra, but there are several available, and the quality of instruction is high. ✉ *3 Abbott St., CBD* ☎ *07/4053–0500, 0407/146–834* 🌐 *www.mikeball.com* 🎟 *From A$2047, with standard gear rental fees from A$44 per day; personal guides from A$50 per dive.*

★ Ocean Spirit Cruises
DIVING & SNORKELING | **FAMILY** | This operator offers daily trips on its sleek sailing catamaran that include four hours at Michaelmas Cay on the Great Barrier Reef, a marine biologist presentation, snorkeling gear, guided snorkeling, a fish-feeding demonstration, a semisubmersible tour, morning and afternoon tea, a buffet lunch, and a glass of wine on the return journey. If you're a beginner, have mobility issues, or aren't a strong swimmer, this might be the best operator for you. ✉ *Reef Fleet Terminal, 1 Spence St., CBD* ☎ *07/4044–9944* 🌐 *www.oceanspirit.com.au* 🎟 *From A$213.*

Pro Dive Cairns
DIVING & SNORKELING | This Advanced Ecotourism–certified operator runs multiday, live-aboard trips on its custom-built dive boat, and offers PADI-five-star-accredited courses at its state-of-the-art training facility in Cairns. Three-day, two-night live-aboard trips take a maximum of 32 divers and snorkelers to Outer Barrier Reef, where they can dive ecologically diverse sites with optimal visibility. Trips include accommodation in serviced twin or double cabins, equipment, transfers, and an initial guided orientation on the first dive. ✉ *Pro Dive Cairns Training Centre, 116 Spence St., CBD* ☎ *07/4031–5255* 🌐 *prodivecairns.com* 🎟 *A$915 for 3-day/2-night live-aboard trip.*

★ Raging Thunder Adventures
RAFTING | **FAMILY** | This operator specializes in white-water rafting trips to two of the area's best rivers: the Tully and the Barron. Half-day trips are available for the Barron, while the Tully requires a full-day commitment. Both have excellent rapids in the wet season. ✉ *19–21 Barry St., CBD* ☎ *07/4030–7990* 🌐 *www.ragingthunder.com.au* 🎟 *From A$153.*

Palm Cove

23 km (14 miles) north of Cairns.

A 35-minute drive north of Cairns, Palm Cove is one of Queensland's jewels: an idyllic, albeit pricey, base from which to explore the far north. It's a quiet place, sought out by those in the know for its magnificent trees, calm waters, exceptionally clean beach, and excellent restaurants.

Prime time for visiting the far north is May through September, when daily maximum temperatures average around 27°C (80°F) and the water is comfortably warm. During the wet season, November through April, expect rain, humidity, and lots of bugs. Highly poisonous box and Irukandji jellyfish make the coastline unsafe for swimming from October through May, but "jellies" hardly ever drift out as far as the reefs, so you're safe to get wet there.

GETTING HERE AND AROUND

Getting here from Cairns is a cinch: by car, follow the signs from the city center to Captain Cook Highway, then head north, taking the Palm Cove turnoff after about 25 km (16 miles). Regular shuttle buses service Palm Cove from the airport, Cairns, and Port Douglas, farther north. Around this compact beach area, though, most people walk or cycle.

Sights

A charming beachside village that sprawls back toward the highway, Palm Cove is navigated easily on foot. Many of the best accommodations, bars, and eateries are strung along the oceanfront strip of Williams Esplanade, fronting what has been dubbed Australia's cleanest beach. At its far north end, a five-minute

Palm Cove is one of many pristine beaches along the tropical Queensland coast.

stroll from the village, there's a jetty and a small marina.

Hartley's Crocodile Adventures

WILDLIFE REFUGE | FAMILY | Hartley's houses thousands of crocodiles as well as koalas, wallabies, quolls, snakes, lizards, southern cassowaries, and tropical birds in natural environs, accessible via boardwalks and boat tours. A lagoon cruise, on which keepers feed big crocs at close range, is included in your entry price. There are daily cassowary, wallaby, quoll, and koala feedings, croc and snake shows, and croc farm tours. Most thrilling is the "Big Croc Feed," a private tour for up to four people. It's your chance to handle squirming baby crocs and pole-feed gigantic ones, and includes a guided tour and commemorative photo. Lily's Bistro showcases local delicacies, including crocodile, of course. If you don't feel like driving, several Cairns-based tour operators include Hartley's on their day-tour itineraries. ✉ *Captain Cook Hwy., Wangetti* ☎ *07/4055–3576* 🌐 *www.crocodileadventures.com* 🎫 *Entry from A$43.*

Restaurants

Beach Almond

$$ | SEAFOOD | This low-key eatery's simple beach-shack setting on Palm Cove's seafront underplays the freshness and flavor of its modern Asian food. The small but satisfying menu is full of fresh spins on favorite dishes from around Southeast Asia, and seafood is the specialty here. **Known for:** Asian-fusion menu; two-person seafood platter; butter prawns. 💲 *Average main: A$39* ✉ *145 Williams Esplanade, Palm Cove* ☎ *07/4059–1908* 🌐 *www.beachalmond.com.*

★ NuNu Restaurant

$$$ | MODERN AUSTRALIAN | Sexy suede lounges, intimate banquettes, and unbroken views of the Coral Sea make lingering easy at this Palm Cove eatery with the region's best and freshest produce. Select from small plates or larger share portions, which include

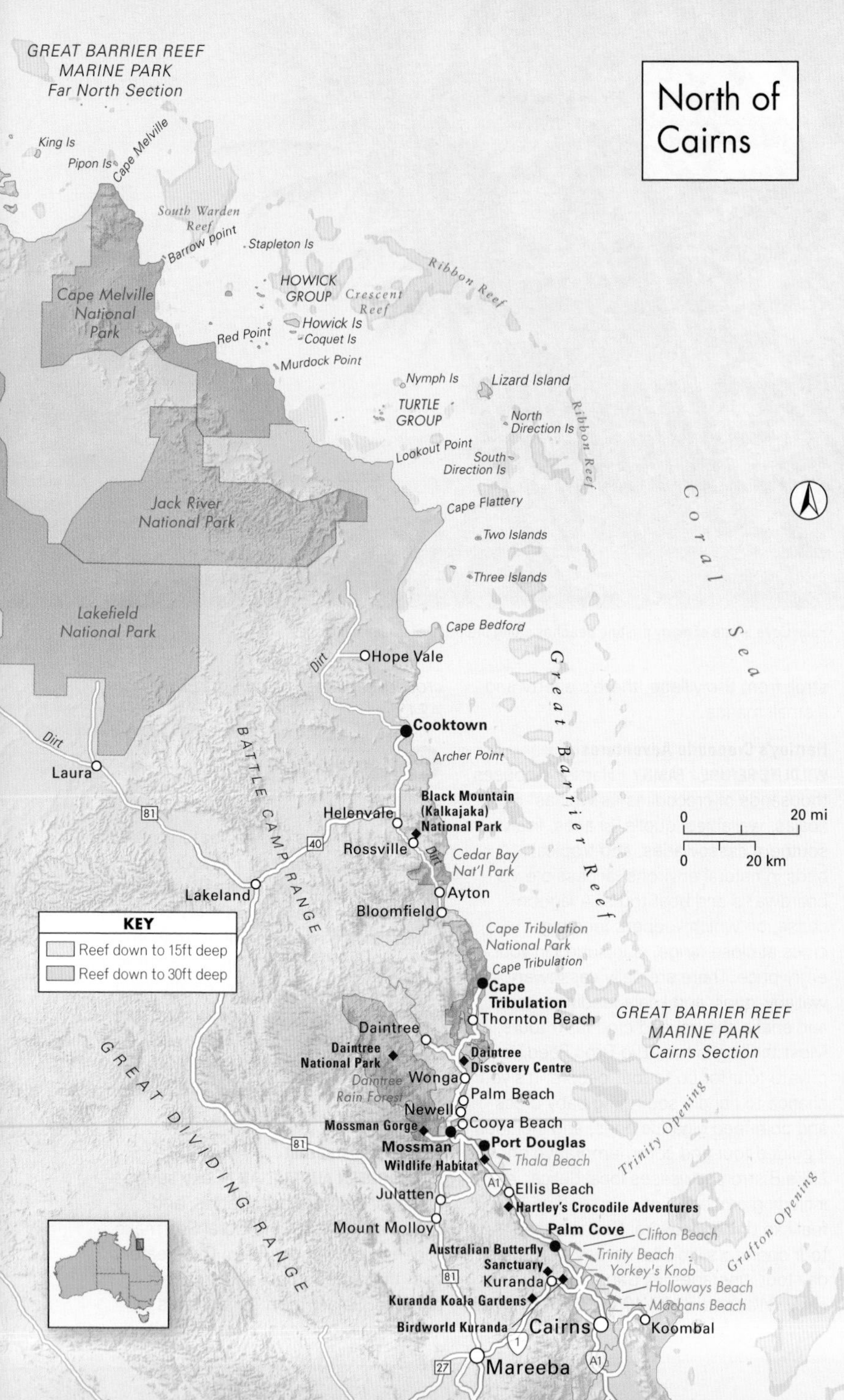

North of Cairns
GREAT BARRIER REEF MARINE PARK Far North Section
King Is
Pipon Is
Cape Melville
South Warden Reef
Barrow point
Stapleton Is
HOWICK GROUP
Crescent Reef
Ribbon Reef
Cape Melville National Park
Howick Is
Coquet Is
Red Point
Murdock Point
Nymph Is
Lizard Island
TURTLE GROUP
North Direction Is
Ribbon Reef
Lookout Point
South Direction Is
Cape Flattery
Jack River National Park
Two Islands
Three Islands
Coral Sea
Lakefield National Park
Cape Bedford
Hope Vale
Dirt
Great Barrier Reef
Cooktown
Dirt
Laura
Archer Point
BATTLE CAMP RANGE
Black Mountain (Kalkajaka) National Park
Helenvale
81
40
Rossville
Dirt
Cedar Bay Nat'l Park
0
20 mi
0
20 km
Lakeland
Ayton
Bloomfield
KEY
Reef down to 15ft deep
Reef down to 30ft deep
Cape Tribulation National Park
Cape Tribulation
Cape Tribulation
Thornton Beach
GREAT BARRIER REEF MARINE PARK Cairns Section
Daintree
Daintree National Park
Daintree Discovery Centre
GREAT DIVIDING RANGE
Wonga
Daintree Rain Forest
Palm Beach
Newell
Cooya Beach
Mossman Gorge
Port Douglas
81
Mossman
Thala Beach
Trinity Opening
Wildlife Habitat
A1
Ellis Beach
Julatten
Hartley's Crocodile Adventures
Mount Molloy
Palm Cove
Clifton Beach
Australian Butterfly Sanctuary
Trinity Beach
Grafton Opening
Yorkey's Knob
81
Kuranda
Holloways Beach
Kuranda Koala Gardens
Machans Beach
Birdworld Kuranda
Cairns
Koombal
1
27
Mareeba
A1

the likes of kimchi butter-poached reef fish, sugarcane-smoked duck, and Sichuan eggplant. **Known for:** duck rice; butter-poached reef fish; Asian fusion cuisine. *Average main: A$46 ✉ Alamanda Palm Cove by Lancemore, 1 Veivers Rd., Palm Cove ☎ 07/4059–1880 🌐 www.nunu.com.au.*

Temple of Tastes

$$ | ASIAN | Knowledgeable staff, an impressive wine and cocktail list, and a torchlit waterfront terrace are among the many reasons to dine at this excellent resort restaurant that is paddock-to-plate dining. You can expect generous servings of fresh Modern Australian food infused with Asian and South Pacific flavors. **Known for:** gluten-free and vegetarian options; Thai red duck curry; cheese platters. *Average main: A$40 ✉ Hotel Pullmann Palm Cove Sea Temple Resort and Spa, 5 Triton St., Palm Cove ☎ 07/4059–9628 🌐 www.pullmanpalmcove.com.au.*

Vivo

$ | MODERN AUSTRALIAN | FAMILY | Enjoy Coral Sea views framed by palms and melaleucas along with Mod Oz dishes at this classy beachside eatery. Diners come for the mix of Southeast Asian and Australian breakfast favorites; the duck salad and battered coral trout at lunch; and seafood with seasonal produce at dinner. **Known for:** relaxed beachside destination; open kitchen; a popular spot for city-strong coffee, and cocktails. *Average main: A$34 ✉ 49 Williams Esplanade, Palm Cove ☎ 07/4059–0944 🌐 www.vivo.com.au.*

Coffee and Quick Bites

27 Degrees

$ | CAFÉ | Ah, 27 degrees. It's pretty much the perfect temperature, isn't it? (When we're talking Celsius.) And it's also pretty much the perfect café when you're in Palm Cove and need a coffee and a decent breakfast. 27 Degrees is a classic, with friendly service, city-quality coffee, and a menu of health-conscious Aussie brunch favorites such as acai bowls, granola, smoothies, and more. **Known for:** brunch favorites; high-quality coffee; health-conscious snacks. *Average main: A$16 ✉ 1 French St., Palm Cove ☎ 0401/391–698 🌐 facebook.com/27degreesqld ⊙ Closed Mon. and Tues.*

Hotels

★ Alamanda Palm Cove by Lancemore

$$$$ | RESORT | Fine landscaping, pools, barbecues, and sunny areas for relaxation enhance this classy colonial-style vacation complex fronting a palm-shaded white-sand beach. **Pros:** free Wi-Fi; terrific location; upscale restaurant. **Cons:** pools on the chilly side; no elevators; Wi-Fi weak in some rooms. *Rooms from: A$899 ✉ 1 Veivers Rd., Palm Cove ☎ 07/4055–3000 🌐 www.lancemore.com.au/alamanda ⇨ 67 suites 🍽 No Meals.*

Hotel Pullman Palm Cove Sea Temple Resort and Spa

$$$ | RESORT | The well-appointed studio rooms and apartments at Pullman's gorgeous Palm Cove property have private balcony or terrace areas, high-definition flat-screen TVs, and comfortable beds with memory-foam pillows. **Pros:** five-star service; gorgeous grounds and pools; excellent on-site restaurant. **Cons:** five-minute walk from Palm Cove's main strip and beach; occasional noise from wedding parties; busy pool area when lots of children staying. *Rooms from: A$305 ✉ 5 Triton St., Palm Cove ☎ 07/4059–9600 🌐 www.pullmanpalmcove.com.au 🍽 No Meals ⇨ 126 rooms.*

Peppers Beach Club & Spa

$$$ | RESORT | FAMILY | Its beachfront location, excellent on-site dining, and tropical suites make this laid-back resort popular with city dwellers seeking upscale relaxation. **Pros:** well-equipped, air-conditioned gym; terrific on-site dining; multiple pools including a quiet pool zone and Serenity wing. **Cons:** main pool area can be busy; patchy Wi-Fi in places; may be too loud for couples looking to relax. *Rooms from: A$316 ✉ 123 Williams Esplanade, Palm Cove ☎ 07/4059–9200 direct line, 1300/737–444 toll-free in Australia, 07/5665–4426 Australia-wide reservations ⊕ www.peppers.com.au/beach-club-spa Free Breakfast 150 rooms.*

The Reef House

$$$$ | **RESORT** | This centrally located small resort, once a private residence, feels positively quaint, and that's a good thing when you're looking for a low-key escape in this resort area. **Pros:** free Wi-Fi and movies; large, well-appointed rooms; complimentary sunset punch and canapés. **Cons:** Wi-Fi and phone reception patchy; not ideal for families; grounds relatively small. *Rooms from: A$549 ✉ 99 Williams Esplanade, Palm Cove ☎ 07/4080–2600 ⊕ www.reefhouse.com.au Free Breakfast 67 rooms.*

Activities

Palm Cove makes a great base for rain-forest and reef activities—hiking, biking, horseback riding, rafting, ballooning, and ATV adventures on the Atherton Tableland; snorkeling, diving, and sailing around the Low Isles and Barrier Reef; sea kayaking just offshore; and scenic flights over just about anywhere a small plane can get on a tank of gas. Though few cruise or tour companies are based in this beachside enclave, many Cairns and Port Douglas–based operators offer Palm Cove transfers.

KAYAKING

★ **Palm Cove Watersports**

KAYAKING | **FAMILY** | Paddling around history-rich Double Island, off Palm Cove Jetty, in a kayak or on a paddleboard is a tranquil, eco-friendly way to get close to the local marine life: you'll often spot dolphins, stingrays, turtles, and colorful fish on this local operator's terrific sunrise tours and half-day snorkeling excursions. Helpful guides impart safety briefings and labor-saving tips on technique before you set out, and there are frequent stops for refreshments, snorkeling (May through November), and wildlife-watching en route. Even if you've never paddled a kayak before you're unlikely to capsize; the single and double kayaks are super-stable. Half-day trips circumnavigate Double Island, stopping off on the fringing reef about 600 meters (½ mile) from shore and on a secluded beach. Transfers from Cairns (A$25 per person) and Port Douglas (A$40 per person) are available; bookings are essential. **TIP→ Safety and snorkeling gear is provided, but bring sunglasses, a hat, and sunscreen.** *✉ 149–153 Williams Esplanade, Palm Cove ☎ 0402/861–011 ⊕ www.palmcovewatersports.com From A$60.*

Port Douglas

67½ km (42 miles) northwest of Cairns.

Known simply as "Port" to locals, Port Douglas offers almost as broad a range of outdoor adventures as Cairns, but in a more compact, laid-back setting. In this burgeoning tourist town there's a palpable buzz, despite tropical haze and humidity. Travelers from all over the world base themselves here, making excursions to the north's wild rain forests and the Great Barrier Reef. Varied lodgings, restaurants, and bars center on and around Port's main strip, Macrossan Street.

Like much of North Queensland, Port Douglas was settled by Europeans after gold was discovered nearby. When local ore deposits dwindled in the 1880s, it became a port for sugar milled in nearby Mossman until the 1950s. The town's many old "Queenslander" buildings give it the feel of a simple seaside settlement, despite its modern resorts and overbuilt landscape. The rain forests and beaches that envelop the town are, for the most part, World Heritage sites—so while Port continues to grow in popularity, the extraordinary environs that draw people here are protected from development.

GETTING HERE AND AROUND

By car, it's a scenic, 75-minute drive north to Port Douglas from Cairns: take Sheridan Street to the Captain Cook Highway, following it for around 60 km (35 miles) to the Port Douglas turnoff. North of Palm Cove, along the 30-km (19-mile) Marlin Coast, the road plays hide-and-seek with an idyllic stretch of shoreline, ducking inland through tunnels of tropical coastal forest and curving back to the surf to reach Port Douglas.

Around town, most people drive, walk, or cycle. It's about 5½ km (3½ miles), or an hour's level walk from the highway to the main street. Regular shuttle buses call in at major hotels and resorts day and night, ferrying travelers to and from Cairns, the airport, and nearby towns and attractions.

Sights

Port Douglas is actually an isthmus, bounded by Four Mile Beach on one side, Dickson Inlet on the other, with the town's main retail, café, and restaurant strip, Macrossan Street, running up the center. The town sprawls as far as the highway, 5½ km (3½ miles) to the west, along Port Douglas Road, which is lined with upmarket resorts and holiday apartment complexes. At the far end of Macrossan Street, on Wharf Street, there's a busy marina.

★ Wildlife Habitat

NATURE PRESERVE | FAMILY | This world-class wildlife sanctuary just off the Captain Cook Highway is divided into "immersion" wetland, rain forest, grassland, and savanna habitats, enabling close creature encounters with everything from koalas to cassowaries and crocs. The park shelters more than 180 species of native wildlife in its 8-acre expanse, including technicolor parrots, emus, kangaroos, echidnas, and reptiles. The breakfast with the birds, served daily 9–10:30 am, is accompanied by avian residents so tame they'll perch on your shoulders—and may steal your food if you're distracted. You can also lunch with the lorikeets from 12:30 daily, then join one of the sanctuary's free expert-guided tours, held several times daily. For something even more special book the nocturnal tour (A$43) or a two-hour animal and dining package (A$170). ✉ *Port Douglas Rd., at Agincourt St., Port Douglas* ☎ *07/4099–3235* 🌐 *www.wildlifehabitat.com.au* 🎫 *From A$38.*

Restaurants

★ Harrisons

$$ | BRITISH | A classic "Queenslander" with a lovely outdoor cocktails area shaded by century-old mango trees and fine dining inside, Harrisons impresses with deftly executed dishes that showcase fresh seafood and small-batch ingredients, sourced locally. There's a six-course tasting menu at A$95 per person, A$145 with matched wines, and on the wine list, you'll find plenty of good mid-priced antipodean drops and a smattering of French ones. **Known for:** Modern Australian menu with a British twist; has won multiple awards for its dining experience; North Queensland crayfish with truffled hollandaise. $ *Average main: A$42* ✉ *22 Wharf St., Port Douglas* ☎ *07/4099–0802* 🌐 *www.harrisonsrestaurant.com.au.*

★ Salsa Bar & Grill

$$ | MODERN AUSTRALIAN | FAMILY | Rub shoulders with local foodies and enjoy intimate dining after sunset on the large wooden deck of this lively waterside institution that serves tropical Modern Australian fare. The dinner menu offers something for everyone, from kingfish ceviche to herb-crusted wild barramundi, to a seafood laksa that utilizes plenty of the local produce. **Known for:** linguine pepperincino with local red claw crayfish; great waterfront location; creative cocktail menu. *Average main: A$39* *26 Wharf St., Port Douglas* *07/4099–4922* *www.salsaportdouglas.com.au* *Closed Tues. and Wed.*

Sassi La Cucina + Bar

$$ | **ITALIAN** | Those craving traditional Italian cuisine utilizing fresh North Queensland ingredients should make themselves a booking at Sassi, a lively, friendly eatery with plenty of outdoor dining space on the main drag. The menu here has all of the hits—spaghetti *con le vongole,* seafood linguine, and the like—along with a solid wine list featuring plenty of Italian varietals. **Known for:** excellent wine list; Italian favorites done well; spaghetti with clams. *Average main: A$44* *4 Macrossan St., Port Douglas* *07/4099–6744* *www.sassi.com.au* *Closed Mon. and Tues.*

Watergate Restaurant & Lounge Bar

$$ | **MODERN AUSTRALIAN** | Atmospheric indoor-outdoor dining, attentive service, and a well-stocked bar are nice, but the primary draw at this relaxed restaurant is the food, which highlights the freshest local ingredients. Enjoy reef fish and prawns straight off Port Douglas's fishing boats, and seasonal fruit, vegetables, and herbs from the Atherton Tableland. **Known for:** to-die-for dessert menu; friendly, warm service; kangaroo loin. *Average main: A$38* *5/31 Macrossan St., Port Douglas* *07/4099–5544* *www.watergateportdouglas.com.au.*

Coffee and Quick Bites

Sparrow Coffee

$ | **AUSTRALIAN** | Sparrow is all about good coffee. There's very little else on sale here except Port Douglas's best flat white or espresso, with an excellent range of alternative milks for those who can't do dairy. **Known for:** excellent coffee; speedy service; laid-back charm. *Average main: A$5* *39 Macrossan St., Port Douglas* *07/4099–5388* *www.facebook.com/sparrowcoffeeco.*

Hotels

Coconut Grove Port Douglas

$$$$ | **APARTMENT** | These well-appointed luxe apartments and penthouses perched above Port Douglas's main strip have state-of-the-art furnishings and appliances, freestanding spa baths, and large entertaining spaces including big, furnished balconies or decks, some with outdoor barbecues and plunge pools. **Pros:** free undercover parking; immaculate living areas; central location. **Cons:** reception closes after business hours; fees for daily housekeeping; 10 am checkout. *Rooms from: A$670* *56 Macrossan St., Port Douglas* *07/4099–0600* *www.coconutgroveportdouglas.com.au* *Reception closes daily 5 pm–8 am* *No Meals* *33 suites.*

★ **Lazy Lizard Inn**

$ | **HOTEL** | **FAMILY** | The clean, spacious, self-contained studios at this friendly low-rise motel just outside of town make it a practical base for those who don't mind a short walk or cycle to Port Douglas's center. **Pros:** easy parking outside your door; friendly hosts; free cable TV and Wi-Fi. **Cons:** no on-site bar or restaurant; reception closes at 6 pm; slightly out of town. *Rooms from: A$129* *121 Davidson St., Port Douglas* *07/4099–5900, 1800/995–950 toll-free in Australia* *www.lazylizardinn.com.au* *No Meals* *22 studios.*

★ **Mandalay Luxury Beachfront Apartments**

$$$ | **APARTMENT** | **FAMILY** | With beautiful Four-Mile Beach just outside and shops and eateries a brisk walk away, these comfortable, expansive, fully equipped apartments are in an excellent location. **Pros:** close to the beach; reasonable rates; plenty of space. **Cons:** street outside is poorly lit at night; no restaurant on site; no reception in off-peak hours. *Rooms from: A$330* *Garrick St. at Beryl St., Port*

Douglas ☎ *07/4099–0100* 🌐 *www.mandalay.com.au* 🍽 *No Meals* 🛏 *41 apartments.*

Sheraton Grand Mirage Resort

$$$ | **RESORT** | **FAMILY** | Centered on a complex of interconnecting saltwater lagoon pools, the Sheraton Grand Mirage is a good choice for families. **Pros:** plenty of on-site facilities; magnificent saltwater lagoon pools and steps from the beachfront; modernized rooms and suites. **Cons:** cost of on-site food and other extras can add up; it's a fair distance from Port Douglas's restaurants and shopping; it can feel overwhelmingly large. [$] *Rooms from: A$364* ✉ *Ave. of Palms, Port Douglas* ☎ *07/4099–5888* 🌐 *www.marriott.com* 🍽 *No Meals* 🛏 *394 rooms.*

★ **Thala Beach Nature Reserve**

$$$ | **RESORT** | Set on 145 acres of private beach, coconut groves, and forest, this eco-certified nature lodge is about low-key luxury. **Pros:** 2 km (1.25 miles) of private access beaches; free Wi-Fi in the restaurant and lobby; free activities include guided walks and bird-watching. **Cons:** 15-minute drive to Port Douglas; hilly property is unsuitable for limited mobility guests; no in-room Internet access. [$] *Rooms from: A$427* ✉ *5078 Captain Cook Hwy., Port Douglas* ✥ *Oak Beach, 38½ km (24 miles) north of Cairns, just south of Port Douglas* ☎ *07/4098–5700, 866/998–4252 toll-free from U.S.* 🌐 *www.thalabeach.com.au* 🍽 *No Meals* 🛏 *83 suites.*

Shopping

★ **Port Douglas markets**

MARKET | **FAMILY** | Local growers and artisans gather on Sunday mornings in Port Douglas's waterfront park to sell fresh tropical produce and gourmet goodies, arts and crafts, handmade garments, precious-stone jewelry, books, and souvenirs. The atmosphere is relaxed, the crowd is colorful, and there's plenty of variety. ✉ *Anzac Park, Wharf St., end of Macrossan St., Port Douglas* 🌐 *douglas.qld.gov.au.*

Activities

Port Douglas is a great base for activities on the mainland and reef. Several tour companies conduct day trips into the rain forest and beyond in four-wheel-drive buses and vans; most include river cruises for crocodile-spotting and stops at local attractions. Various reef operators either base vessels at or pick up from Port Douglas Marina. You can also horseback ride, bungee jump, raft, go off-roading, hike, mountain bike, and balloon on and around the Atherton Tablelands.

FISHING

MV *Norseman*

FISHING | **FAMILY** | Long-established MV *Norseman* is one of the best game-fishing boats on the Great Barrier Reef for novice and experienced anglers alike. Head out to the best spots on the reef's edge on a 60-foot, purpose-designed, high-tech vessel to fish for large pelagic species including Spanish mackerel, tuna, wahoo, and the elusive giant trevally. Closer in, find sea perch, mangrove jack, red and spangeled emperor, and coral trout. It's A$285 per adult for a full day on the water (bait, equipment, instruction, lunch, and refreshments, fuel levy, rod, and reel; reef taxes included). Port Douglas accommodation transfers are free. ✉ *Crystalbrook Superyacht Marina, 44 Wharf St., Berth E11, at Inlet Road, Port Douglas* ☎ *0419/015–262* 🌐 *www.mvnorseman.com.au* 🎟 *From A$285 per person.*

RAIN FOREST AND REEF TOURS

★ **Back Country Bliss Adventures**

LOCAL SPORTS | **FAMILY** | Amazing wilderness locations, high-quality equipment, excellent staff, and Wet Tropic World Heritage Tour Operator accreditation give the Bliss team the edge. Based in Port Douglas but ranging much farther afield, the company runs customized, culturally and eco-sensitive small-group trips that take you to nature and adventure hot spots in the Port Douglas area. They'll take you hiking, drift-snorkeling in rain-forest streams, and "jungle surfing" in the rain-forest canopy. ✉ *6460 Captain Cook Hwy.* ☎ *07/4099–3677* 🌐 *www.backcountrybliss.com.au* 🎫 *From A$120* ☞ *Tour prices include pickups from and drop-offs to local accommodations and resorts.*

Daintree Tours

FOUR-WHEELING | FAMILY | This operator conducts daylong, well-guided trips in top-of-the-line 4WD vehicles and custom-built trucks to the Daintree rain forest and beyond, with plenty of stop-offs en route to eat, drink, swim, and explore. Visit the Mossman Gorge, the Daintree rain forest, and Cape Tribulation. You can also arrange a daylong private charter to Kuranda, the Atherton Tablelands, and the rugged track to Bloomfield Falls. Ample lunch and refreshments, included in all excursions, ensure you keep your strength up. Port Douglas pickups and drop-offs make the early-morning starts simple. ✉ *Tropical Journeys, 11–17 Macrossan St., Port Douglas* ☎ *07/4231–8012* 🌐 *www.daintreetours.com* 🎫 *From A$209.*

Reef and Rainforest Connections

SNORKELING | FAMILY | This long-established, eco-friendly operator offers day trips exploring Kuranda's attractions and local wildlife parks; excursions to Cape Tribulation, the Daintree rain forest, and Mossman Gorge; and Great Barrier Reef cruises with Quicksilver Connections. The popular Kuranda day tour includes trips on the historic Scenic Railway and Skyrail Rainforest Cableway, and a stroll around charming Kuranda Village, with its markets, curio stores, and wildlife attractions. ✉ *40 Macrossan St., Port Douglas* ☎ *07/4047–9085* 🌐 *www.reefandrainforest.com.au* 🎫 *From A$155.*

★ **Tony's Tropical Tours**

HIKING & WALKING | FAMILY | This company gives entertaining small-group day tours in luxe Land Cruisers that take in rain forest sights and attractions as far as Cape Tribulation or, if you're prepared to get up earlier, the renowned and ruggedly beautiful Bloomfield Track. Well-informed, witty commentary from local experts, and non-rushed, well-chosen stops and activities—from interpretative rain-forest walks and Daintree River wildlife (croc) cruises, to handmade ice-cream and tropical-fruit tasting—make these trips crowd-pleasers. Refreshments, included in the cost, are a cut above the norm. Tony's also runs off-road tours through the Daintree as far as the Bloomfield Falls and terrific charter tours to the crater lakes and the Atherton Tablelands on which you might see kangaroos, birdlife, and the famed Curtain Fig tree. ✉ *Port Douglas* ☎ *07/4099–3230* 🌐 *www.tropicaltours.com.au* 🎫 *From A$205.*

RIVER CRUISES

Crocodile Express

BOATING | FAMILY | Bird-watchers and photographers flock to Crocodile Express's flat-bottom boats to cruise the Daintree River on crocodile-spotting excursions; you may also see rare birds and outsize butterflies, flying foxes, snakes, and lizards en route. Sixty-minute cruises leave the Daintree Gateway, 500 meters (1,640 feet) before the ferry crossing, at regular intervals from 8:30 am to 3:30 pm; or you can board at Daintree Village Jetty and cruise the Upper Daintree regularly between 10 and 3:30. Extra cruises from both access points are scheduled in peak periods. ✉ *5 Stewart St., end of Mossman–Daintree Rd., Daintree* ☎ *07/4098–6120* 🌐 *www.crocodileexpress.com* 🎫 *From A$27.*

SNORKELING AND DIVING

Eye to Eye Marine Encounters

DIVING & SNORKELING | John Rumney, who pioneered swim-with-whales in Queensland, brings 30-plus years of experience on the Reef and extensive ecological knowledge and nautical expertise to his revered minke whale expeditions, working with highly skilled divers, scientists, and skippers to ensure each trip is as exciting as it is eco-friendly.

Marine Encounters also specializes in private, curated diving trips in the region. ✉ *10 Captain Cook Hwy., Port Douglas* ☎ *07/4098–5417, 0417/726–622* 🌐 *www.marineencounters.com.au.*

Quicksilver Cruises

DIVING & SNORKELING | **FAMILY** | Quicksilver's fast, modern catamarans speed you from Port Douglas's marina to a large commercial activity platform on the outer Barrier Reef. There, you can dive and snorkel with the reef residents, and make leisurely sail-and-snorkel trips to Low Isle coral cays. Options at Agincourt Reef include marine-biologist-guided snorkeling tours (A$68–A$87), introductory or certified scuba dives (extra A$132–A$183), 10-minute scenic heli-tours (A$199), and "Ocean Walker" sea-bed explorations (A$183). There's also a semisubmersible underwater observatory, included in the A$266 rate. Day trips include a varied lunch buffet, morning and afternoon tea, snorkeling gear, and stinger suits. Transfers are available from Port Douglas accommodations and farther afield (A$18–A$34). ✉ *The Reef Marina, 44 Wharf St., off Inlet Dr., Port Douglas* ☎ *07/4087–2100* 🌐 *www.quicksilver-cruises.com* 💵 *From A$266.*

The Silver Series: *Silversonic*

DIVING & SNORKELING | **FAMILY** | High-end, high-speed catamaran *Silversonic* whisks visitors to three pristine dive-snorkel sites on Agincourt Reef, known for its high-visibility waters. There, you can spend five hours amid spectacular corals on the edge of the Coral Sea trench, with turtles, rays, tropical fish, large pelagic species, and, in season, the odd minke whale. Full-day outer reef cruises run daily, weather permitting; the A$255 tariff includes a tropical buffet lunch, morning and afternoon tea, snorkeling, and gear; all scuba dives are guided at no extra cost. Coach transfers from local accommodations are included in the cruise fare; transfers to and from Palm Cove, the northern beaches, and Cairns are available for a surcharge. ✉ *The Reef Marina, 1 Wharf St., off Inlet Dr., Port Douglas* ☎ *07/4087–2100* 🌐 *www.silverseries.com.au* 💵 *From A$255.*

Mossman

20 km (12 miles) northwest of Port Douglas, 75 km (47 miles) north of Cairns via the Captain Cook Hwy.

This sleepy sugarcane town of just a couple of thousand residents has shops, a medical center, and gas stations, but most visitors merely pass through en route to Mossman Gorge, the Daintree, and rain-forest accommodations. There's little here to explore, but it's a good place to stop for supplies and has a few good eateries.

The spectacular wilderness around Mossman is ideal terrain for adventure sports and outdoor activities. If you have a day—or even a few hours—to spare, you can explore beaches, rain forest, and bushland trails on horseback, mountain bike, or ATV; take a scenic trek through Mossman Gorge; or drift-snorkel in the Upper Mossman River. The region's Indigenous guardians, the Kuku Yalanji, run guided tours of Mossman Gorge and their coastal hunting grounds near Wonga Beach, in the World Heritage–listed Daintree rain forest.

TOURS

ABORIGINAL TOURS

★ Kuku Yalanji Cultural Habitat Tours

(*Daintree Dreaming tour*)

On these relaxed, two-hour coastal walks, Kubirri Warra brothers Linc and Brandon Walker, members of the Kuku Yalanji *bama* (people), take turns guiding groups through three diverse ecosystems along Cooya Beach, demonstrating traditional plant use, pointing out bush tucker ingredients, recounting Dreamtime legends, and sharing their prodigious cultural and local knowledge, with plenty of jokes thrown in. Wear wading shoes, light clothing, a hat, insect repellent, and sunscreen. ✉ *Cooya Beach Rd., Mossman* ☎ *07/4098–3437* 🌐 *www.kycht.com.au* 🎫 *From A$90.*

★ **Walkabout Adventures**

Personable Indigenous guide Juan Walker and his team take small groups on fascinating half- and full-day rain-forest safari and coastal hunting trips, and personalized tours on request. These excursions can include a visit to the world's oldest rain forest, Mossman Gorge, and coastal mudflats, mangroves, and beaches, with swims in rain-forest streams, foraging mangrove walks, plus mud crab feasts cooked up on the beach. ✉ *Cooya Beach Rd., Daintree* ☎ *0429/478–206 Juan Walker* 🌐 *www.walkaboutadventures.com.au* 🎫 *From A$180, including transfers from Port Douglas, Mossman, and Daintree Village.*

ESSENTIALS

VISITOR INFORMATION Destination Daintree. ✉ *Daintree* 🌐 *www.destination-daintree.com.*

Sights

Daintree Village, a half-hour drive north along the Mossman-Daintree Road, has restaurants, cafés, galleries, and access to croc river cruises. Drive 20 minutes northeast of Mossman to reach Wonga Beach, where you can stroll along the sand or go walkabout with Indigenous guides.

★ **Mossman Gorge**

CANYON | **FAMILY** | Just 5 km (3 miles) outside Mossman are the spectacular waterfalls and swimming-hole-studded river that tumble through sheer-walled Mossman Gorge. The Kuku Yalanji–run Mossman Gorge Centre is the starting point for various walks, tours, and activities. There are several boulder-studded, croc-free swimming holes within the gorge, and a 2½-km (1½-mile) rain-forest walking track and suspension bridge. (Swimming in the river itself is hazardous, crocs or not, due to swift currents, slippery rocks, and flash flooding.) Keep your eyes peeled for tree and musky rat-kangaroos, Boyd's water dragons, scrub fowl, turtles, and big, bright butterflies—and try to avoid stinging vines (plants with serrated-edge, heart-shaped leaves, found at rain-forest edges). If you intend to hike beyond the river and rain-forest circuits, inform the information desk staff at the Mossman Gorge Centre, which also has café/restaurant, gift shop, Indigenous art gallery, restrooms, showers, and visitor parking. ✉ *Mossman Gorge Centre, 212r Mossman Gorge Rd., Mossman* ☎ *07/4099–7000* 🌐 *www.mossmangorge.com.au* 🎫 *Free entry to Mossman Gorge Centre; A$12 return bus trip out to gorge; tour prices vary.*

Hotels

Daintree EcoLodge & Spa

$$$ | **RESORT** | At this 30-acre boutique eco-resort in the ancient Daintree rain forest, elevated boardwalks protect the fragile environs and link the day spa, heated pool, restaurant/bar, and 15 free-standing tree houses or "bayans." All are air-conditioned and equipped with ceiling fans, satellite TVs, and king-size canopy beds. **Pros:** lower rates with longer stays or early bookings; alfresco spa treatments; eco-friendly. **Cons:** noise from public areas carries to proximate rooms and spa; no in-room Internet access; no one at reception desk from 8 pm to 8 am. 💲 *Rooms from: A$380* ✉ *3189 Mossman-Daintree Rd., Mossman* ✣ *3 km (2 miles) past Daintree village, 110 km (68 miles) north of Cairns* ☎ *07/4777–7377* 🌐 *www.daintree-ecolodge.com.au* 🍽 *Free Breakfast* 🛏 *15 suites.*

★ **Silky Oaks Lodge**

$$$$ | **RESORT** | This beautiful, retreat-like resort and Advanced Ecotourism–certified hotel in the heart of the rain forest has luxe tree houses and suites clustered around an expansive open-sided lodge,

Silky Oaks Lodge, near Daintree National Park

day spa, and lagoon pool. **Pros:** well-marked walking trails around the resort; really special and unique property; helpful tour desk and lots of included activities. **Cons:** steep paths to some rooms (though you can call for a buggy pickup); no in-room Internet; access road can flood after heavy rain, January through March. *Rooms from: A$690* *Finlayvale Rd., Mossman* *07/4098–1666* *www.silkyoakslodge.com.au* *All-Inclusive* *43 suites.*

Cape Tribulation

35 km (22 miles) north of the Daintree River crossing, 140 km (87 miles) north of Cairns.

Set dramatically at the base of Mt. Sorrow, Cape Tribulation was named by Captain James Cook after a nearby reef snagged the HMS *Endeavour,* forcing him to seek refuge at the site of present-day Cooktown. Today, the tiny settlement, little more than a general store and a few lodges, is the activities and accommodations base for the surrounding national park.

GETTING HERE AND AROUND

The 140-km (86-mile) drive from Cairns to Cape Tribulation takes just under three hours. If you're renting a car, it's simplest to do so in Cairns or Port Douglas. This can be tough driving territory. The "highway" is narrow with just two lanes; many minor roads are rough and unpaved; and even major thruways in this area may be closed in the wet season due to flooding.

Mason's Cape Tribulation Tourist Information Centre, grocery store, bottle shop, and PK's Jungle Village, a little farther north on the opposite side of Cape Tribulation Road, are the last stops for food, supplies, and fuel as you head north. At PK's there's a supermarket, a bar serving meals and drinks, and an ATM.

ATMs are scarce beyond Mossman. Get cash and gas at the service station and convenience store on the Mossman-Daintree Road at Wonga Beach, or at PK's. North of the Daintree River, mobile phone coverage is limited (except in and around Mossman and Daintree Village and around Thornton Beach Kiosk), and you'll be lucky to get any signal once you get as far as Cape Tribulation.

Sun Palm Transport's daily services link Cairns airport with Cairns, Palm Cove, and Port Douglas. Charter services to Mossman, Daintree, Cow Bay, and Cape Trib can also be arranged. The journey from Cairns to Port Douglas takes around two hours, with stops at most resorts on request.

FERRY TRAVEL

Daintree Ferry

The Daintree–Mossman Road winds through sugarcane plantations and towering green hills to the Daintree River, a short waterway fed by monsoonal rains that makes it a favorite inland haunt for saltwater crocodiles. On the river's northerly side, a sign announces Cape Tribulation National Park. There's just one cable ferry, carrying a maximum 27 vehicles, so although the crossing takes five minutes, the wait can be 15 minutes or more, especially between 11 am and 1 pm, and all afternoon during holidays. There's no need to prebook your passage, but bring cash if you'll be crossing after dark. Return fare for a car is A$28 (one-way A$16); for a motorbike, it's A$11/A$6; a multiday car pass (five trips) is A$56; and walk-on passengers pay just A$2. ✉ *Daintree River ferry crossing, Daintree-Mossman Rd., Daintree* ✣ *Ferry turnoff is just under 30 kms (18 miles) north of Mossman on Daintree-Mossman Rd.* ☎ *07/4099–9444 Douglas Shire Council offices* 🌐 *www.douglas.qld.gov.au/community/daintree-ferry.*

ESSENTIALS

VISITOR INFORMATION Mason's Cape Tribulation Tourist Information Centre, Shop, & Mason's Tours. ✉ *3781 Cape Tribulation Rd., Cape Tribulation* ☎ *07/4098–0070* 🌐 *www.masonstours.com.au.*

Cape Tribulation Road winds through rain forest north of Cow Bay, veering east to join the coast at Thornton Beach, then skirting a string of near-deserted beaches en route to Cape Trib. Accommodations, attractions, and access points for beaches, croc cruise boats, and mangrove and rain-forest boardwalks are well signposted from the main road.

These rugged-looking yet fragile environs, Kuku Yalanji tribal lands, are best explored with experienced, culturally sensitive, and eco-conscious guides. Excursions by 4WD and on horseback, bicycle, boat, and foot are offered by a few dozen local operators and resorts.

If exploring off-road on your own, arm yourself with detailed local maps, supplies, and up-to-date information. Let a reliable person know your intended route and return time, and don't underestimate the wildness of this terrain.

Daintree Discovery Centre

VISITOR CENTER | FAMILY | This World Heritage–accredited Wet Tropics Visitor Centre's elevated boardwalks and a high viewing tower enable you to overlook an astoundingly diverse tract of ancient rain forest. You can acquire information en route from handheld audio guides, expert talks, and the on-site interpretative center. Four audio-guided trails include a Bush Tucker Trail and a Cassowary Circuit, on which you might spot one of these large but well-camouflaged birds. Take the Aerial Walkway across part of the bush, then the stairs to the top of the 76-foot-high Canopy Tower. Keen students of botany and ecology might want to prebook a guided group tour. The shop sells books, cards, souvenirs, and clothing. There's also an on-site café. ✉ *Tulip Oak Rd., off Cape Tribulation Rd., Cow Bay* ☎ *07/4098–9171* 🌐 *www.daintree-rec.com.au* 🎫 *A$37 (includes 68-page guidebook/return entry for 7 days).*

★ **Daintree National Park**

NATIONAL PARK | The world's oldest tropical rain forest is an ecological wonderland: 85 of the 120 rarest species on Earth are found here, and new ones are still being discovered. The 22,000-acre park, part of the UNESCO World Heritage–listed Wet Tropics region, stretches along the coast and west into the jungle from Cow Bay, 40 km (25 miles) or around an hour's drive northwest of Mossman. The traditional owners, the Eastern Kuku Yalanji, who live in well-honed harmony with their rain-forest environs, attribute powerful properties to many local sites—so tread sensitively. Prime hiking season here is May through September, and many local operators offer guided Daintree rain-forest walks, longer hikes, and nighttime wildlife-spotting excursions. Gather information and maps from local rangers or the Queensland Parks and Wildlife Service's ParksQ website before hiking unguided, and stay on marked trails and boardwalks to avoid damaging your fragile surroundings. Whatever season you go, bring insect repellent. ✉ *Daintree* ☎ *137–468* 🌐 *www.nprsr.qld.gov.au/parks/daintree.*

Restaurants

On The Turps Bar & Restaurant

$ | MODERN AUSTRALIAN | At this open-air restaurant in the Daintree rain forest, wallabies, bandicoots, and musky rat kangaroos might join you at the table as you tuck into a Mod Oz meal that highlights local, seasonal ingredients including fresh seafood, and wines from the well-stocked bar. On The Turps also does "tropical continental" breakfasts and varied, good-value lunches, as well as leisurely morning and afternoon Devonshire teas. **TIP→ Arrive early for a dip in the creek, a rain forest stroll, or a spa treatment. Known for:** good range of vegetarian and vegan meals; delicious local barramundi; home-style cooking. $ *Average main: A$34* ✉ *Turpentine Rd., Lot 236, R36, Cape Tribulation* ↔ *18 km (about 11 miles) north of Daintree River crossing, turn left at Turpentine Rd.* ☎ *07/4098–9321* 🌐 *www.heritagelodge.net.au/restaurant.*

★ **Whet Cafe, Bar and Restaurant**

$ | MODERN AUSTRALIAN | FAMILY | Stylish and hip yet comfortable, Whet Cafe, Bar and Restaurant draws visitors and locals with its outdoor deck, perfect for long lunches, sunset cocktails, and romantic dinners. It has Modern Australian food using regional and seasonal ingredients and friendly service, and is a fully self-sustained, off-grid operation. **Known for:** melt-in-your-mouth steaks and local-caught barramundi; jungle dining; local seafood with Mediterranean influences. $ *Average main: A$28* ✉ *Cape Tribulation Rd., Lot 1, Cape Tribulation* ☎ *07/4098–0007* 🌐 *www.whet.net.au.*

Hotels

Privately run campgrounds and small resorts can be found along Daintree Road at Myall Creek and Cape Tribulation.

Cape Tribulation Farmstay B&B

$ | B&B/INN | FAMILY | A handful of simple but comfortable, solar-powered cabins sit among rambutan, mangosteen, and breadfruit trees on this 40-hectare exotic fruit farm. **Pros:** free Internet (but only in the central farmhouse); beach and rain-forest trails adjoin the property; breakfast basket of fresh tropical fruit. **Cons:** modest accommodations; no swimming pool; few in-room modern conveniences. $ *Rooms from: A$170* ✉ *3939 Cape Tribulation Rd., Cape Tribulation* ☎ *07/4098–0042* 🌐 *www.capetribfarm.com.au* *5 rooms* *Free Breakfast.*

Cockatoo Hill Retreat

$$$ | B&B/INN | The elegant solar-powered tree houses at this impeccably run boutique retreat invite relaxation and romance. **Pros:** magnificent views; helpful, thoughtful host; eco-friendly. **Cons:**

no on-site food apart from breakfast; 4WD required after heavy rain for the steep driveway; phone/Internet access only if you have Telstra service. $ *Rooms from: A$395* ✉ *2060 Cape Tribulation Rd., Diwan* ✣ *Midway between Daintree and Cape Tribulation* ☎ *07/4098–9277* 🌐 *www.cockatoohillretreat.com.au* *4 rooms* *Free Breakfast.*

Activities

CANOPY TOURS

Jungle Surfing Canopy Tours

ZIP LINING | FAMILY | It's an exhilarating perspective on the rain forest and reef: suspended above the canopy on flying-fox zip lines, your speed controlled by guides as you whiz along over lush rain forest and Mason's Creek, stopping at tree platforms for killer bird's-eye views. Sessions last two hours and depart up to 12 times a day starting at 7:50 am. Nightly guided Jungle Adventures Nightwalks explore the critter-filled 45-acre grounds, departing PK's Jungle Village reception at 7:30 pm. You can also buy tickets covering zip-lining and the night tour. Transfers from most local accommodations are free, or self-drive to the central departure point. Day-tour packages from Port Douglas include lunch. Note that Jungle Surfing is unsuitable for anyone weighing more than 120 kilograms (260 pounds), and that anyone under 18 needs to sign a medical declaration and waiver before they'll be allowed to zip-line. ✉ *Jungle Adventure Centre, Cape Tribulation Rd., Lot 2, Cape Tribulation* ✣ *Free parking at pickup point. Arrive 10 mins prior to designated departure time to complete paperwork* ☎ *07/4098–0043* 🌐 *www.junglesurfing.com.au* *From A$49.*

GREAT BARRIER REEF TOURS

★ **Ocean Safari**

SNORKELING | FAMILY | Eco-certified Ocean Safari runs half-day small-group tours that include snorkeling two pristine sites on the Great Barrier Reef, just half an hour's thrilling motorboat ride off Cape Trib Beach. Well-chosen sites on magnificent Mackay and Undine reefs teem with "Nemos" (clown fish), turtles, rays, barracuda, potato cod, giant clams, nudibranchs, and an astounding array of corals. A maximum of 25 passengers and a rigid inflatable boat (with covered seating area and bathroom facilities). Snorkeling equipment, expert guidance, and reef tax are included in the price; you can rent wet suits/sunsuits (A$8) and prescription masks (A$15), and buy soft drinks, chocolate, and underwater cameras on board. Meet at Ocean Safari's office, on-site at the Turtle Rock Cafe opposite PK's; pickups from Cape Trib accommodations are free. Package deals that include safari-hut accommodation at Jungle Lodge and an Ocean Safari excursion are available. ✉ *Ocean Safari office (at Turtle Rock Cafe), Cape Tribulation Rd., Lot 4, Cape Tribulation* ✣ *Opposite PK's Jungle Village* ☎ *07/4098–0006* 🌐 *www.oceansafari.com.au* *From A$163.*

Cooktown

103 km (64 miles), around 2 hours' drive, north of Cape Tribulation; 324 km (203 miles) or 4 hours' drive north of Cairns.

Traveling north, Cooktown is the last major settlement on the east coast of the continent, sitting at the edge of a difficult wilderness. Its wide main street consists mainly of two-story pubs with four-wheel-drive vehicles parked out front. Despite the frontier air, Cooktown has an impressive history. It was here in 1770 that Captain James Cook beached HMS *Endeavour* to repair her hull. Any tour of Cooktown should begin at the waterfront, where a statue of Cook gazes out to sea, overlooking the spot where he landed.

GETTING HERE AND AROUND

By car from Cairns, take the inland highway, Peninsula Developmental Road, a 200-odd-mile stretch of fully paved road that barrels you through Australia's Outback—watch for errant cattle and 'roos on the drive. From Cape Tribulation, head up the Cooktown Developmental Road, or take the 4WD-only Bloomfield Track, just 97 km (60 miles), but challenging and sometimes flooded in the Wet. The Bloomfield Track journey, which roughly traces a series of Indigenous story-line trails known as the Bama (People's) Way, takes around three hours, longer in wet weather; the Developmental Road is smoother but less scenic. Getting around Cooktown, a compact town, is a comparative cinch: drive, walk, or cycle.

TOURS

CULTURAL TOURS

★ Adventure North Australia

This company's one- to three-day excursions during the dry season (May through November) offer a mix World Heritage–listed attractions, Indigenous cultural highlights, and Aussie-style adventure. Adventure North also runs short fly/drive tours, and a three-day rain-forest and Outback 4WD tour that takes the rugged coast road from Cairns to Cooktown through the Daintree, returning through Far North Queensland's Outback on the Mulligan Highway. On every tour, experienced, affable driver-guides offer a wealth of local tidbits. Rates include tours, entry fees, some meals, flights and, on multiday trips, budget or premium accommodation. ✉ *26 Redden St., Cairns* ☎ *07/4047–9075* 🌐 *www.adventurenorthaustralia.com* 🎫 *From A$560* 🕒 *Closed in wet season (Dec.–Apr.).*

Sights

Cooktown has some lovely old buildings and a cemetery dating from the 1870s gold rush. Stroll along botanic garden trails and uncrowded beaches, check out the environment interpretative center and visitor-info hub Nature's PowerHouse, cool off in the public swimming pool, and scale Grassy Hill around sunset for stupendous views.

Black Mountain (Kalkajaka) National Park

NATIONAL PARK | Just south of Cooktown within the Wet Tropics World Heritage Area, Black Mountain (Kalkajaka) National Park protects a unique mix of gigantic granite boulders, wet-tropics species, and savanna woodland vegetation harboring abundant wildlife, including threatened species. Lucky visitors might spot the scanty frog, rainbow skink, Black Mountain gecko, Godman's rock-wallaby, or a rare ghost bat. Kalkajaka means "place of the spear"; Black Mountain was a significant meeting place for the Eastern Kuku Yalanji. The boulders are treacherous, so climbing and hiking is not allowed, but the lookout point provides a fairly close-up view. ✉ *Mulligan Hwy., Rossville* ☎ *137–468* 🌐 *www.nprsr.qld.gov.au/parks/black-mountain.*

Cooktown History Centre

MUSEUM VILLAGE | Cooktown's historical museum, aptly housed in a former postal and telegraph office built in 1875, is staffed by affable volunteers and houses an extensive collection of photographs dating from 1873. The building also holds Cooktown's archives and is a research center for local history. It also houses semipermanent displays. ✉ *121 Charlotte St., Cooktown* ☎ *07/4069–6640* 🌐 *www.cooktownandcapeyork.com* 🎫 *A$5* 🕒 *Closed Sun.*

Grassy Hill Lighthouse

HISTORIC SIGHT | A strenuous, not especially scenic walk or short drive from Cooktown lie Grassy Hill and the lighthouse, spectacular lookouts affording panoramic views of Cooktown, the Endeavour River, and the Coral Sea. Follow in the footsteps of Captain James Cook, who scaled the slope to view the reef and navigate his boat's safe passage out. The lighthouse, shipped from England in 1885, helped boats avoid the reef for a century before being rendered obsolete; it was then restored as a historical relic. ✉ *Grassy Hill, at eastern end of Hope St., Cooktown.*

James Cook Museum

HISTORY MUSEUM | Cooktown, in its heyday, was a gold-mining port, with 64 pubs lining the 3-km-long (2-mile-long) main street; a significant slice of this colorful history, including mementos of Cook's voyage and Indigenous artifacts, is preserved at this National Trust–run museum. The former convent houses relics of the Palmer gold-mining and pastoral eras, including a Chinese joss house; canoes; and the anchor and one of six cannons jettisoned when the HMS *Endeavour* ran aground. The surprisingly good on-site shop sells books and souvenirs. It's recommended that you allow at least an hour to pore over the exhibits. ✉ *Helen St. at Furneaux St., Cooktown* ☎ *07/4069–5386* 🌐 *www.nationaltrust.org.au/qld/JamesCookMuseum* 🎫 *A$18.*

Nature's Powerhouse & Cooktown Botanic Gardens

GARDEN | This interpretive center and museum at the entrance to Cooktown's Heritage-listed Botanic Gardens is home to a valuable collection of local botanical illustrations by internationally recognized artist Vera Scarth-Johnson, and impressive displays of Cape York Peninsula wildlife, bequeathed by local fauna expert Charlie Tanner. Take extra time to wander through the gardens, which, with its stone-pitched waterways and shady paths, include 154 acres of colorful native and exotic plants. A popular attraction in the gardens is a 7-meter python carved locally from ironwood. You can enjoy afternoon tea or a light lunch at the Vera Café; browse the shop of botanically themed gifts and souvenirs, including beautiful scarves, prints and postcards, wooden bowls, and authentic Indigenous art; and get regional travel tips from the on-site Cooktown and Cape York Peninsula Visitor Information Centre. ✉ *Walker St., Cooktown* ✣ *Follow road to end of Walker St.* ☎ *07/4069–5763* 🌐 *www.facebook.com/naturespowerhouse* 🎫 *Botanic Gardens free, Nature's Powerhouse free.*

Hotels

★ The Sovereign Resort Hotel

$$ | **HOTEL** | **FAMILY** | This attractive, two-story colonial-style hotel in the heart of town is the best bet in Cooktown. **Pros:** terrific gardens, barbecue area, and pool; furnished balconies overlooking tropical gardens; airport/wharf transfers. **Cons:** front desk closes early; furniture needs updating; restaurant closed in wet season (November–March). 💲 *Rooms from: A$240* ✉ *128 Charlotte St., at Green St., Cooktown* ☎ *07/4043–0500* 🌐 *www.sovereignresort.com.au* 🛏 *38 rooms* 🍽 *No Meals.*

Activities

FISHING

The closest town on the Queensland coast to the Great Barrier Reef, Cooktown offers fast, easy access to some of the reef's best fishing (and dive) sites. Boats bristling with game-fishing gear depart from the marina daily, bound for famed fishing grounds on the outer reef, and at Egret and Boulder, 10 miles offshore. The likely catch: Spanish mackerel, sailfish, coral trout, red and spangled emperor, and black marlin.

★ Gone Fishing

FISHING | **FAMILY** | Specializing in three-quarter- and full-day fishing charters on the Endeavour River and the estuaries and islands offshore, Gone Fishing also offers small-group, two-hour river tours and crocodile-spotting expeditions. ✉ *Wilkinson St., Lot 3, Cooktown* ☎ *07/4069–5396, 0427/695–980* 🌐 *www.fishingcooktown.com* 🎫 *From A$275 per person.*

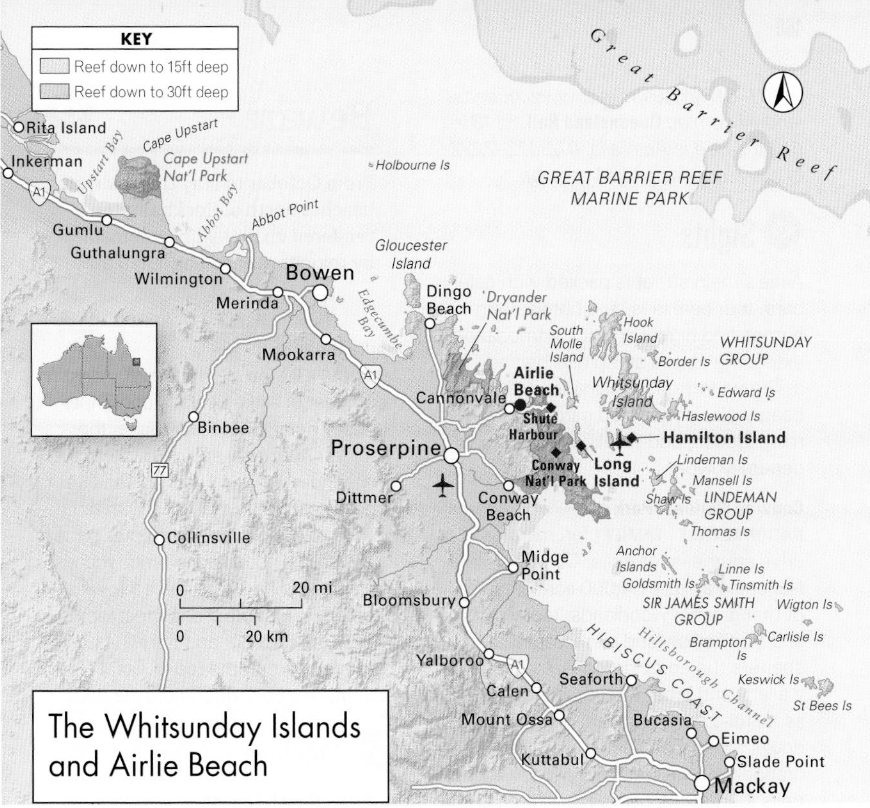

Airlie Beach

1,119 km (695 miles) or 13½ hours' drive north of Brisbane, 623 km (387 miles) south of Cairns via the Bruce Hwy.

Airlie Beach's balmy climate and its proximity to the Whitsunday Islands, a resort and water-sports playground, make it hugely popular with partying backpackers and holidaymakers en route to the islands and reef.

GETTING HERE AND AROUND

Whitsunday Coast Airport, near Proserpine, 36 km (23 miles) southeast of Airlie Beach, has direct flights to and from Brisbane and Sydney. Whitsunday Transit buses connect the airport and Proserpine Railway Station to Airlie Beach, Cannonvale, and Shute Harbour (about A$22 one-way), with services timed to meet all flights and passenger trains (drive time 30–40 minutes). It's A$14, one-way, to or from Proserpine railway station. Greyhound Australia offers services into Airlie Beach from Sydney, Brisbane, and towns between, and from Cairns. Queensland Rail operates several long-distance trains weekly, northbound and southbound, that stop at Proserpine Railway Station, about 25 km (15 miles) from Airlie Beach.

AIRPORT Whitsunday Coast Airport. ✉ *Sir Reginald Ansett Dr., Proserpine* ☎ *07/4945–0200 airport.*

BUS CONTACTS Greyhound Australia. ☎ *1300/473–946 toll-free in Australia, 07/4690–9850* 🌐 *www.greyhound.com.au.* **Whitsunday Transit.** ☎ *07/4946–1800* 🌐 *www.whitsundaytransit.com.au.*

TRAIN CONTACTS Proserpine Railway Station. ✉ *6 Hinschen St., Proserpine*

☎ *131–617 in Australia* 🌐 *www.queenslandrail.com.au.* **Queensland Rail.** ☎ *131–617 toll-free in Australia, 07/3072–2222* 🌐 *www.queenslandrail.com.au.*

Sights

Airlie's main street is packed with cafés, bars, tour agencies, and hotels, with homes and higher-end accommodations extending up the steep hills behind it. The waterfront Esplanade, with its boardwalk, landscaped gardens, swimming lagoon, and weekend markets, is generally lively.

Conway National Park

NATIONAL PARK | FAMILY | Ten minutes' drive southeast of Airlie, Conway National Park is a 54,000-acre expanse of mangroves, woodlands, rocky cliffs, and tropical lowland rain forest that shelters the endangered Proserpine rock wallaby and other rare species, as well as sulfur-crested cockatoos, emerald doves, Australian bush-turkeys, and orange-footed scrubfowl. Most walking trails start at the park's picnic area at the end of Forestry Road, about 10 km (6 miles) from Airlie. Mount Rooper Walking Track, a 5.4-km (3-mile) circuit, meanders uphill through bushland to a lookout with breathtaking Whitsundays views. If time permits, and you're sufficiently fit, you can cycle, run, or walk the 27-km (17-mile) Conway circuit, starting at Forestry Road carpark and ending in Airlie Beach. Swamp Bay track follows the creek to a coral-strewn beach with a bush camping area. ✉ *Shute Harbour Rd., at Mandalay Rd., Airlie Beach* ✣ *Travel 10 km (6 miles) west along Shute Harbour Rd., then turn left onto Brandy Creek Rd. Follow it to Forestry Rd. and carpark (start of the Conway circuit)* ☎ *137–468* 🌐 *www.nprsr.qld.gov.au/parks/conway* 🎫 *Camping permits, A$7 per person, per night* ☞ *Camping permits must be prebooked.*

Beware

From October to May the ocean off beaches north of Rockhampton is rendered virtually unswimmable by toxic-tentacled box jellyfish.

Shute Harbour

MARINA/PIER | Ten kilometers (6 miles) southeast of Airlie Beach along Shute Harbour Road, Shute Harbour is the main ferry terminal and gateway to the Whitsunday Islands and the reef. The large, sheltered inlet teems with boats—it's one of the busiest commuter ports in Australia. Though accommodation is available, the harbor is geared toward transferring visitors. For a great view over Shute Harbour and the Whitsunday Passage, drive to the top of Coral Point. ✉ *Shute Harbour Rd., Shute Harbour.*

Beaches

★ Airlie Beach Lagoon

BEACH | FAMILY | Hugely popular with locals and visitors, especially in stinger season, this stinger-free swimming enclosure on Airlie's shorefront has dedicated lap-swimming lanes, real-sand "beaches," adjoining children's pools, and sensor-activated lighting after dark. There are toilets, showers, and change rooms nearby, and all pools are patrolled by trained lifeguards year-round. Surrounding the lagoon are a children's playground and a tropical garden, crisscrossed with walkways and dotted with public art, picnic tables, and free electric barbecues. **Amenities:** food and drink; lifeguards; showers; toilets. **Best for:** swimming. ✉ *The Esplanade, at Broadwater Ave., parallel to Shute Harbour Rd., Airlie Beach* ☎ *07/4945–0200 Whitsunday Council, 1300/972–753* 🌐 *www.tourismwhitsundays.com.au.*

Restaurants

Fish D'Vine and Rum Bar

$$ | **SEAFOOD** | The menu here showcases seafood in all its forms—from beer-battered fish-and-chips to seafood chowder and wild-caught barramundi (the chef will even cook your catch). The bar is stocked with 500-plus rums and has a mean cocktail list. **Known for:** mojitos; beachy flavor; signature seafood indulgence, loaded with mud crab, and reef fish. *Average main: A$40 12 Airlie Esplanade, Airlie Beach 07/4948–0088 fishdvine.com.au.*

Northerlies Bar and Grill

$ | **MODERN AUSTRALIAN** | **FAMILY** | Overlooking a tranquil bay just outside of Airlie Beach, Northerlies has become a local favorite. A farm-to-table ethos shapes the menu, so expect fresh-from-the-boat seafood, single-farm origin steaks, and house-smoked meats paired with local produce. **Known for:** shuttle service to and from Airlie Beach; aged bone-in rib eye; quiet, waterfront location with alfresco dining. *Average main: A$34 Pringle Rd., Lot 116 1800/682–277 www.northerlies.com.au.*

Coffee and Quick Bites

★ Cafe One 3

$ | **AUSTRALIAN** | **FAMILY** | This cozy, friendly café makes a point of supporting local farmers, with a locavore breakfast menu featuring the best of Whitsunday produce. There are plenty of vegan, vegetarian, and gluten-free options, plus high-quality coffee. **Known for:** use of local produce; vegan options; friendly service. *Average main: A$12 13 Waterson Way, Airlie Beach 0419/783–313 Closed weekends.*

Hotels

Airlie Beach Hotel

$ | **HOTEL** | **FAMILY** | With the town's small beach at its doorstep, three eateries and bars downstairs, and the main street directly behind it, this hotel makes a comfy and convenient base. **Pros:** close to main strip, Airlie Lagoon, and waterfront; interiors rebuilt in 2018; lots of on-site food and drink options. **Cons:** basic hotel with basic facilities; rooms can be noisy; no room service. *Rooms from: A$199 16 The Esplanade, at Coconut Grove, Airlie Beach 07/4964–1999, 1800/466–233 toll-free in Australia www.airliebeachhotel.com.au 80 rooms No Meals.*

Mantra Boathouse Apartments

$$$ | **RESORT** | **FAMILY** | Perched on the Port of Airlie Marina with enviable views of the boats swaying in the bay, the Mantra Boathouse Apartments are generously sized two- and three-bedroom apartments, ideal for those looking for self-contained accommodations. **Pros:** full-size fully stocked kitchens; large balconies; complimentary parking. **Cons:** no room service; housekeeping only comes weekly; short walk to restaurants. *Rooms from: A$405 33 Port Dr., Airlie Beach 07/5665–4450 www.mantra.com.au 44 apartments No Meals.*

Pinnacles Resort

$$$ | **APARTMENT** | **FAMILY** | Occupying prime position at the top of a hill overlooking the bay and the Whitsunday Islands, Pinnacles is a stylish retreat with plenty to offer those looking for self-contained accommodation. **Pros:** beautiful pool; stunning ocean views; spacious apartments with excellent kitchens. **Cons:** lacks the feel of a hotel; no restaurants on-site; can be a hike to upper part of the resort. *Rooms from: A$351 16 Golden Orchid Dr., Airlie Beach 07/4948–4800 www.pinnaclesresort.com.au No Meals 29 apartments.*

★ **Whitsunday Moorings B&B**
$ | **B&B/INN** | Overlooking Abel Point Marina, this meticulously run B&B has everything you need: stupendous marina views, charming hosts, and terrific gourmet breakfasts, often accompanied by colorful chirping parrots. **Pros:** free Wi-Fi; charming, knowledgeable host; fabulous breakfasts on harbor-facing terrace. **Cons:** reception closed between 7 pm and 6 am; required two-night stay for East or West rooms; uphill walk from main street. *Rooms from: A$180 ✉ 37 Airlie Crescent, Airlie Beach ☎ 07/4946–4692 🌐 www.whitsundaymooringsbb.com.au 3 rooms 🍽 Free Breakfast.*

Shute Harbour Road, the main strip, is where it all happens in Airlie Beach. Most main-street establishments cater to the backpacker crowd, with boisterous, college-style entertainment, live music, and a late-opening dance club. Older and more sophisticated visitors gravitate to quieter establishments with pleasant outdoor areas, such as the bars and restaurants attached to some of the hillside resorts.

BOAT TOURS

Cumberland Charter Yachts
BOAT TOURS | This company's fleet includes sailing yachts and catamarans and can accommodate groups. *✉ Abel Point Marina, Shingley Dr., Shop 18, Airlie Beach ☎ 07/4946–7500, 1800/075–101 🌐 www.ccy.com.au.*

Queensland Yacht Charters (*Whitsunday Yacht Charters*)
BOAT TOURS | Queensland Yacht Charters, established in 1980, offers sailing charters starting at five nights on a fleet of boat that include catamarans, monohulls, and powerboats. *✉ Abel Point Marina, Shingley Dr., Unit 9, Airlie Beach ☎ 07/4946–7400, 1800/075–013 toll-free in Australia 🌐 www.yachtcharters.com.au.*

Whitsunday Rent A Yacht
BOAT TOURS | This company specializes in skipper yourself (also known as bareboat) yacht charters in the Whitsundays. *✉ Shute Harbour, 6 Bay Terr., Airlie Beach ☎ 07/4946–9232, 1800/075–000 toll-free in Australia 🌐 www.rentayacht.com.au.*

Whitsunday Sailing Adventures
BOAT TOURS | Whitsunday Sailing Adventures runs several sailing, scuba, and snorkeling trips around the islands and Great Barrier Reef on a dozen-plus owner-operated vessels, including modern sailing cats and tall ships. Choose from sailing, diving, kayaking, and snorkeling excursions. A two-night, three-day liveaboard outer reef trip starts at A$749 per person in a private double room, with one scuba dive and all gear and meals included. One- and two-night performance sailing adventures start at A$450. If time is limited, there's an eco-friendly sail-and-snorkel day trip (A$179). Book well ahead for holiday periods. *✉ 344 Shute Harbour Rd., Airlie Beach ☎ 07/4940–2000, 1300/653–100 toll-free in Australia 🌐 www.whitsundaysailingadventures.com.au From A$179.*

Long Island

12 km (7 miles) west of Hamilton Island, 13 km (7½ miles) east of the mainland.

Although it's 9 km (5½ miles) long and no more than 2 km (1 mile) wide—around 3,000 acres total—this aptly named island has several walking trails through tracts of dense rain forest. Most of the island is national parkland, sheltering birds, butterflies, goannas, and wallabies. Some of its beaches are picturesque; others rocky and windblown. Though its waters are less clear than those off the outer reef islands, there are some excellent snorkeling spots on the island's fringing reef, where you'll share the balmy water with soft and hard corals, tropical fish, and turtles. You may also see dolphins and migrating humpback whales July through September.

GETTING HERE AND AROUND

You can reach Long Island via water taxi from Shute Harbour or private watercraft. The trip takes around 20 minutes by water taxi, and is cheaper if you have more passengers (maximum of nine people per boat). It makes several scheduled trips a day, departing the harbor at 8:30 am, 10:30 pm, 2 pm, and 5 pm and travels directly to Palm Bay Resort on Long Island. It returns from Palm Bay at 8:30 am, 11 am, 2:30 pm, and 5:30 pm. Prebooking is essential.

Various regional operators, including Air Whitsunday and Hamilton Island Air, offer seaplane or helicopter transfers to Long Island resorts from regional airports including Great Barrier Reef (Hamilton Island), Whitsundays Airport near Airlie Beach, and Whitsunday Coast (Proserpine) Airport. Transfers are scheduled to coincide with incoming and outgoing flights. If your vacation time is limited, this is the fastest way to get here—but per-person costs can be steep. Trips require minimum passenger numbers, strict baggage limits apply, and prebooking is essential.

Air Whitsunday flies from Shute Harbour Airport to Palm Bay Resort on demand in a six-seater aircraft, carrying two or four passengers plus luggage (A$290). Flights can be booked via Air Whitsunday or Palm Bay Resort.

If you're keen to visit other resort isles from Hamilton Island, the on-island helicopter service, Hamilton Island Air, can transport you there for A$660. Helicopters take off on demand from Great Barrier Reef (Hamilton Island) Airport, flying to Long Island and to Airlie Beach on the mainland. Prebookings are essential for all charter flights; baggage is limited to 15 kg (33 pounds) per passenger, in soft-sided bags, and anyone weighing more than 110 kg (250 pounds) pays a seat surcharge.

Virgin Australia and Jetstar have direct flights between Hamilton Island and Melbourne, Sydney, and Brisbane.

AIR TRAVEL

Air Whitsunday

This local seaplane operator flies from Shute Harbour Airport to Palm Bay Resort on demand in a six-seater aircraft, carrying two or four passengers plus luggage (A$290). Flights can be booked via Air Whitsunday or Palm Bay Resort. ✉ *Air Whitsunday Airport, 12 Whitsunday Rd., Terminal 1, Flametree* ☎ *07/4946–9111 Air Whitsunday, 0477/770–133 Palm Bay Resort* 🌐 *www.airwhitsunday.com.au.*

Hamilton Island Air

From Hamilton Island airport, you can take a scenic helicopter flight to Palm Bay Resort for $660 (one or two passengers, plus limited baggage). ✉ *Great Barrier Reef (Hamilton Island) Airport, Palm Valley Way, Hamilton Island* ☎ *07/4969–9599* 🌐 *www.hamiltonislandair.com.*

BOAT TRAVEL

Whitsunday Water Taxi

(*Shute Harbour Water Taxi*) The local water-taxi operator at Shute Harbour makes three scheduled trips a day, departing the harbor at 8:30 am, 10:30 pm, 2 pm, and 5 pm and traveling directly to Palm Bay Resort on Long Island. It returns from Palm Bay at 8:30 am, 11 am, 2:30 pm, and 5:30 pm. Prebooking is essential, especially in peak periods. There is a maximum of nine people per boat. ✉ *Shute Harbour Jetty, Shute Harbour* ☎ *1800/202–909* 🌐 *www.whitsundayislandtaxi.com.au.*

Hotels

★ Elysian Retreat

$$$$ | **ALL-INCLUSIVE** | Opened in early 2019, this luxurious, eco-friendly Paradise Bay retreat on the southern point of Long Island is nestled in a private cove between ocean and rain forest, and its large windows and private balconies with uninterrupted water views maximize

on the setting. **Pros:** magnesium pool; stunning setting with oceanfront villas; dedicated boat takes guests to Whitehaven Beach. **Cons:** Telstra mobile reception only; 20 guests max so limited availability; adults only. 💲 *Rooms from: A$1270* ✉ *Long Island* ☎ *1800/765–687* 🌐 *www.elysianretreat.com.au* 🛏 *10 villas* 🍽 *All-Inclusive.*

Palm Bay Resort

$$$ | RESORT | This beachfront property houses self-catering travelers at alluringly reasonable rates. **Pros:** lovely accommodations in glorious tranquil environs; friendly, helpful staff; island grocery/food store and bottle shop. **Cons:** restaurant closed some days; self-catering, though staff clean your dishes; can be noisy at night. 💲 *Rooms from: A$345* ✉ *Long Island* ✣ *Get to and from Palm Bay Resort (one-way rates): from A$55* ☎ *1300/655–126 toll-free in Australia* 🌐 *www.palmbayresort.com.au* 🛏 *25 suites* 🍽 *No Meals.*

Hamilton Island

16 km (10 miles) southeast of Shute Harbour.

Though it's the most heavily populated and developed island in the Whitsunday group, more than 70% of Hamilton Island has been preserved in its natural state. The 1,482-acre island abounds in beautiful beaches (such as long, curving, palm-dotted Catseye Beach), bush trails, and spectacular lookouts. Yet for all its natural beauty, Hamilton is more an action-packed, sociable holiday isle than it is a place to get away from it all.

Around 35 minutes by ferry from Shute Harbour, Hamilton buzzes with activity. Guests of the resort, and its various types of accommodation, including hotel-style and self-catering establishments, make up most of the itinerant population, but there are private residences here—as well as throngs of day-trippers from the mainland, other islands, and cruising yachts, who wander the island's bustling marina and village each day.

For a family-friendly, one-stop Whitsundays experience, Hamilton Island is a smart choice. Many of the resort accommodations allow kids under age 12 to stay free, provided they stay with parents and use existing beds (no roll-aways or cribs). Under-12s can even eat free at some island restaurants when staying at resort hotels, choosing from kids' menus.

The resort's set up like a small city, with its own school, post office, banking outlets, medical center, pharmacy, supermarket, hair and beauty salon, and DVD-rental store, plus two day spas, shops, restaurants, bars, and a nightclub. But little on Hamilton is free; prices—for food, activities, Internet use, even grocery items—can be steep. The ubiquitous golf carts that visitors rent to zip around the island are A$49 an hour, A$65 for three hours, and A$87 for 24 hours from Hamilton Island Buggy Rentals. Save a few bucks by using the free Island Shuttle service that runs around the island on two set routes at regular (15- to 40-minute) intervals between 6:50 am and 11 pm.

GETTING HERE AND AROUND

Virgin Australia and Jetstar fly directly to Hamilton Island from Sydney, Melbourne, and Brisbane. You can take a Cruise Whitsundays ferry to the island from Abel Point Marina, Airlie Beach, or nearby Shute Harbour (A$60), or arrange a seaplane transfer from regional mainland airports at Proserpine or Mackay, or from Airlie Beach's Whitsunday Airport with Hamilton Island Air. From Hamilton Island, the "hub" of the Whitsundays, you can catch a ferry to neighboring resort isles Daydream and Hayman via fast ferry with Cruise Whitsundays Resort Connections, timed to coincide with incoming and outgoing flights from Hamilton's airport. You can get there

Wind- and motor-powered water sports are popular on many Whitsunday Islands.

faster by seaplane with Air Whitsunday or helicopter with Hamilton Island Air.

Sunsail Australia
This operator has various yachts available for bareboat charter at Hamilton Island's marina. You can book a five-day-minimum charter yacht and sail around the Whitsundays' sheltered waters. Optional extras include professional skipper and cook, kayaks, and dinghy. Rates vary according to the number of days, number of passengers, vessel, and season. Sunsail Whitsundays also offers certified sailing courses. ✉ *Front St., Hamilton Island* ☎ *07/4948–8250, 1800/803–988 toll-free in Australia* 🌐 *www.sunsail.com.au.*

BUGGY RENTAL Hamilton Island Buggy Rental. ✉ *Front St., Hamilton Island* ☎ *07/9433–9444, 137–333 toll-free in Australia, 866/209–0891 in U.S., 424/206–5274 toll-free in U.S., 07/4946–8263 buggy hire* 🌐 *www.hamiltonisland.com.au/getting-around-island/buggy-hire.*

FERRY Cruise Whitsundays. ✉ *4 The Cove Rd., Airlie Beach* ☎ *07/4846–7000* 🌐 *www.cruisewhitsundays.com.*

HELICOPTER Hamilton Island Air. ✉ *Great Barrier Reef (Hamilton Island) Airport, Palm Valley Way, Hamilton Island* ☎ *07/4969–9599* 🌐 *www.hamiltonislandair.com.*

SEAPLANE Air Whitsunday. ✉ *Whitsunday Airport, 12 Air Whitsunday Ave., Terminal 1, Flametree* ☎ *07/4946–9111* 🌐 *www.airwhitsunday.com.au.*

Sights

Hamilton Island Wildlife
WILDLIFE REFUGE | FAMILY | This charming wildlife sanctuary houses kangaroos, wallabies, wombats, dingoes, birds, and reptiles, including a resident croc. Guided tours run daily, at 10 am and 3 pm, and there are daily breakfasts with the koalas. ✉ *1 Resort Dr., Hamilton Island* ☎ *07/4946–9078 sanctuary, 07/4946–8305 HI tour desk* 🌐 *www.hamiltonisland.com.au* 🎟 *From A$30.*

Castaway Cuisine

On Hamilton, the Whitsundays' largest inhabited island, guests can eat and drink at a variety of restaurants and bars. Virtually all of them are managed by the Hamilton Island consortium, whose owners, the Oatley family, made their millions out of wine. The Oatleys are keen to further the island's reputation for quality wining and dining—recruiting big-city chefs, improving supply lines, scheduling epicurean events, and adding to the island's vast central cellar and produce store. Opportunities for young guns to work their way up through Hamilton's hierarchy, training under culinary heavyweights, bring a continuing stream of fresh talent to the island. The bad news? Staff don't always stay and as a result, food and service standards can be inconsistent—and as there's a virtual monopoly on dining options, prices tend to be steep.

Restaurants

Hamilton Island Resort has lots of dining options, including casual cafés and takeaway outlets, a pub serving counter meals, a dinner-cruise boat, and several restaurants.

coca chu

$$ | **ASIAN FUSION** | **FAMILY** | Offering hawker-style street food dining, coca chu appeals to all with its relaxed vibe, Catseye Beach views, and a varied dinner menu that showcases regional produce and Southeast Asian flavors. The twice-cooked Sichuan duck with chili, coriander, ginger, and soy black vinegar sauce is a worthy signature dish. **Known for:** Sichuan duck with aromatics; casual Asian family-style dining perfect for groups; part of the Kids Stay & Eat Free offering on the island. *Average main: A$38* *Main resort complex, Catseye Beach, Hamilton Island* *07/4946–9999* *www.hamiltonisland.com.au/restaurants/coca-chu* *No lunch.*

Manta Ray

$ | **ECLECTIC** | **FAMILY** | This could be the island's best all-round dining establishment. It's great for breezy alfresco lunches, sunset drinks on the deck, and relaxed dinners. **Known for:** well-priced menu to suit the whole family; children (up to 12) with adults can eat free; great burgers. *Average main: A$26* *Front St., Hamilton Island* *07/4946–9999 resort restaurant reservations* *www.hamiltonisland.com.au/restaurants/manta-ray.*

Romano's

$$ | **ITALIAN** | The full-frontal marina views from the broad balconies of this two-level waterfront eatery make it a favorite for family celebrations and romantic dining. The menu is loaded with traditional Italian fare like saltimbocca as well as more inventive dishes, such as tagliatelle with Queensland prawns and spanner crab. **Known for:** lighter alfresco dining menu available beginning at 3 pm; sophisticated waterfront dining; Italian-style comfort fare. *Average main: A$40* *Marina Village, Front St., Hamilton Island* *07/4946–9999 resort restaurant reservations* *www.hamiltonisland.com.au/restaurants/romanos* *No lunch. Closed Sun., Mon., and Tues.*

TAKO

$ | **MODERN MEXICAN** | **FAMILY** | Hamilton Island's latest concept restaurant, TAKO, takes its influence from a range of Mexican regions to create tasty but approachable dishes. The exciting menu features lots of shareable dishes: the likes of tostadas, tacos, and quesadillas inspired by the various regions of Mexico. **Known for:** unlike anything else on Hamilton Island; approachable cuisine; lively environment. *Average main: A$26 Front St., Hamilton Island 07/4946–8032 www.hamiltonisland.com.au/restaurants/tako No credit cards Closed Mon., Tues., and Wed. No lunch.*

Coffee and Quick Bites

Popeye's Takeaway

$ | **SEAFOOD** | There's nothing fancy about Popeye's—but then, that's the point. This fish-and-chips joint is set up as a casual, reasonably priced alternative to some of the more upmarket dining options on Hamilton Island, with all of the favorites: battered or grilled fish, family-friendly "fisherman's baskets," potato scallops and more. **Known for:** fresh seafood; reasonable prices; marina outlook. *Average main: A$15 Front St., Hamilton Island 07/4948–9422 www.hamiltonisland.com.au No dinner.*

Hotels

There are a variety of places to stay in Hamilton Island whether you're traveling with the family or looking for your private getaway. You also can find an apartment-style retreat. Among the accommodation options on the island are the more than 100 self-catering properties managed by Hamilton Island Holiday Homes (*137–333; www.hamiltonislandholidayhomes.com.au*). They include one- to five-bedroom vacation properties in prime locations around the island, including studio, split-level, and two-story designs. All have air-conditioning, TVs, balconies, and access to the resort's communal swimming pools and fitness center. Homes sleep between 1 and 12 people. Each rental comes with island airport transfers and the use of a four-seater golf buggy, nonmotorized watercraft at Catseye Beach, and the Hamilton Island sports complex facilities. There is a minimum stay of four or more nights in holiday periods and a two- or three-night minimum at other times, depending on the property. Some accommodations are a bit dated and there is no housekeeping. The upsides are the privacy, the full kitchen and laundry facilities, and the complimentary use of many resort facilities.

Hamilton Island Beach Club

$$$$ | **RESORT** | The upscale amenities and no-kids policy mean this hotel swarms with couples, who can cool off in the infinity-edge pool, enjoy meals poolside, or admire the Catseye Beach and Coral Sea views from their private balconies or courtyards. **Pros:** adults only; beachfront location; free Wi-Fi. **Cons:** rates are quite high; checkout time is 10 am; service standards vary. *Rooms from: A$741 9 Resort Dr., Hamilton Island 02/9007–0009 HI accommodation, 137–333 toll-free in Australia www.hamiltonisland.com.au 57 rooms Free Breakfast.*

Hamilton Island Palm Bungalows

$$$ | **RESORT** | **FAMILY** | Spacious, self-contained, and with a relaxed island vibe, these steep-roofed, freestanding bungalows are great for families and self-sufficient travelers. **Pros:** close to main pool, beach, and wildlife park; free use nonmotorized watercraft; complimentary airport transfers. **Cons:** no Wi-Fi in rooms; up a steepish hill; no ocean views. *Rooms from: A$396 3 Resort Dr., Hamilton Island 02/9007–0009 HI accommodation, 137–333 toll-free in Australia www.hamiltonisland.com.au 49 rooms No Meals.*

Hamilton Island Reef View Hotel

$$$ | **HOTEL** | **FAMILY** | All hotel rooms here are comfortable, with private balconies, but only hotel rooms on the fifth floor and above live up to the name, with their unbroken Coral Sea vistas. **Pros:** better-than-usual service; good buffet breakfast; some suites have private patios with plunge pools. **Cons:** rooms a little dated; cockatoos fly in open windows;

lower-level rooms can be noisy. $ *Rooms from: A$351 ✉ 12 Resort Dr., Hamilton Island ☎ 02/9007–0009, 137–333 toll-free in Australia ⊕ www.hamiltonisland.com.au ⇨ 363 rooms 🍽 Free Breakfast.*

★ Qualia

$$$$ | RESORT | Catering to a privileged few, Hamilton Island's most exclusive resort has a tranquil and decadent ambience, private beach, infinity-edge pools, and a complex of luxe, well-appointed freestanding pavilions. **Pros:** high-end everything; Windward Pavilions have their own plunge pools; fine food and wine. **Cons:** service not as polished as some may expect; located well away from the main resort complex and marina; two-night minimum stay in peak periods. $ *Rooms from: A$1350 ✉ 20 Whitsunday Blvd., Lot 10, Hamilton Island ☎ 02/9007–0009, 137–777 toll-free in Australia ⊕ www.qualia.com.au ⇨ 60 suites 🍽 Free Breakfast.*

Nightlife

Hamilton Island has several resort bars as well as a handful of independent ones: all except Qualia's are open to visitors. Find live music at the Reef Lounge, harborside tables at the Marina Tavern and Mariners, sundowner cocktails on the Bommie Deck at Hamilton Island Yacht Club or with panoramic island views at One Tree Hill, and post-sunset drinks at The Garden Bar.

Shopping

Hamilton Island's Marina Village, along Front Street, houses shops selling resort and surf wear, children's clothes, souvenirs, and gifts. You'll also find an art gallery, design store, jeweler, florist, small supermarket, general store, pharmacy, newsstand, post office, golf pro shop, real-estate agent, bakery, bottle shop, and a hair salon on the island. In general, you'll pay more for goods and services here than for their equivalents on the mainland.

FISHING

Topnotch Game Fishing

FISHING | The outer Great Barrier Reef offers world-class fishing for species like black marlin, wahoo, Spanish mackerel, and tuna—and you have a better-than-average chance of landing one off the deck of purpose-built flybridge game boat. Take a small-group sportfishing trip with Topnotch Game Fishing, with all equipment included. A half-day shared charter is A$200; full-day private charters, maximum of 10 people, start from A$3,200. Full-day tours include all catering, and on any tour the crew will clean and prepare your fish for you, or organize for it to be cooked at a local restaurant. If time or your budget is tight, you can hire a dinghy for puttering about closer to shore. Organize it directly or book through Hamilton Island's Tour Desk. ✉ *Front St, Hamilton Island ☎ 07/4946–8305 ⊕ www.hamiltonisland.com.au 🎫 From A$200.*

GOLF

★ Hamilton Island Golf Club

GOLF | This Peter Thomson–designed championship course has sweeping Whitsundays views from all 18 holes. You can rent clubs, take lessons, and practice your swing on the driving range at the Hamilton Island–run complex, which incorporates a swanky clubhouse, pro shop, restaurant, and bar. Clubs, shoes, and lessons are also available. Ferries to Dent Island depart all day from 7 am from Hamilton Island Marina; allow five hours to play 18 holes and half that to play nine. Prices include GPS-fitted golf carts and ferry transfers. ✉ *Main St., Dent Island ☎ 07/4948–9760 ⊕ www.hamiltonislandgolfclub.com.au 🎫 A$165; A$50 club rental; A$15 shoe rental ⛳ 18 holes, 6692 yards, par 71.*

GREAT BARRIER REEF TOURS

★ Heart Island

DIVING & SNORKELING | FAMILY | It has to be one of the most photographed landmarks on the Great Barrier Reef: Heart Reef, the perfectly shaped outcrop near Hardy Reef Lagoon. And there's now a new way to experience it, with *Heart Island,* an exclusive, floating pontoon with all of the luxury fittings, accessible via helicopter ride from Hamilton Island. A maximum six guests at a time here are given 90 minutes to enjoy the pontoon and explore the lagoon—either snorkeling or in a glass-bottom boat—and then take a boat ride around Heart Reef, before being whisked back to Hamilton. ✉ *Depart Hamilton Island Airport and Airport Jetty, Palm Valley Way, Hamilton Island* ☎ *07/4946–8305 tour desk* 🌐 *www.hamiltonisland.com.au* 🎫 *From A$1100.*

★ Reefsleep

DIVING & SNORKELING | FAMILY | Stay overnight on *Hardy Reef* pontoon on Cruise Whitsundays' terrific two-day Reefsleep package: it includes all meals, use of the pontoon's extensive facilities, and the chance to enjoy turtles, reef sharks, and colorful tropical fish without the day-tripping crowd. The cost includes fast transport to and from the pontoon, two full days on the reef, and one night sleeping in a swag under the stars. Breakfast, morning and afternoon teas, buffet lunches both days, and a barbecue are all included. Use of snorkeling gear, wet suits, bath towels, and Reefworld's many facilities, including reef presentations and semisubmersible tours, is free. Optional extras include guided "Snorkel Safari" tours (A$59); guided scuba dives for beginners (A$139), with second dives an additional A$59; night dives; and scenic heli-flights over the reef. The cost of the Reefsleep Swags Under the Stars is A$795 for a single swag or A$595 per person in a double swag (a low tent with viewing panel, mattress, and bedding), with reef tax included. ✉ *24 The Cove Rd., Airlie Beach* ☎ *07/4846–7000* 🌐 *www.cruisewhitsundays.com* 🎫 *From A$595.*

MULTISPORT OPERATORS

Hamilton Island Activities

WATER SPORTS | FAMILY | Hamilton Island Resort has the widest selection of activities in the Whitsundays—game fishing, snorkeling, scuba diving, waterskiing, jet skiing, wakeboarding, sea kayaking, and speedboat adventure rides are all on the agenda. Everything can be booked through the island's central tour desk. The use of nonmotorized watercraft is free to resort guests through the Beach Sports Hut on Catseye Beach, with staff ready to give assistance, tips, and—for a fee—lessons. If the Coral Sea doesn't tempt you, there are well-marked walking trails, quad-bike and ATV tours, go-karts, a nine-pin bowling center, an aquatic driving range, public-access swimming pools, and an 18-hole golf course on nearby Dent Island. The island's sports and fitness complex incorporates a state-of-the-art gym, a whirlpool spa and sauna, squash and floodlit tennis courts, and a minigolf course. You can also sign up for various tours, cruises, and special events. ✉ *Main resort complex, off Resort Dr., Hamilton Island* ☎ *07/4946–8305 HI tour desk, 137–333 toll-free in Australia* 🌐 *www.hamiltonisland.com.au.*

Orpheus Island

24 km (15 miles) offshore of Ingham, 80 km (50 miles) northeast of Townsville, 190 km (118 miles) south of Cairns.

Volcanic in origin, this narrow island—11 km (7 miles) long and 1 km (½ mile) wide, 3,500 acres total—uncoils like a snake in the waters between Halifax Bay and the Barrier Reef. It's part of the Palm Island Group, which consists of 10 islands, eight of which are home to local Indigenous communities. Orpheus is a national park, occupied only by a marine

Continued on page 480

WHAT LIVES ON THE REEF?

Equivalent to the Amazon Rainforest in its biodiversity, the Reef hosts the earth's most abundant collection of sea life. Resident species include (but aren't limited to):

- More than 1,500 species of fish
- 5,000 species of mollusk
- 400 species of hard and soft coral
- 30 whale and dolphin species
- More than 500 species of sea plants and grasses
- 14 sea-snake species
- Six sea-turtle species
- 200 sea-bird species
- More than 150 species of shark

DIVING THE REEF

To astronauts who've seen it from space, the Great Barrier Reef resembles a vast, snaking wall—like a moat running parallel to Australia's entire northeastern coast. Almost unimaginably long at 1,430-odd miles, it's one of the few organic structures that can be seen from above the earth's atmosphere without a telescope.

(above) pink coral;
(left) glass fish

Up close, though, what looks (and from its name, sounds) like a barrier is in fact a labyrinthine complex with millions of points of entry. Mind-boggling in size and scope, encompassing more than 4,000 separate reefs, cays, and islands, the Reef could rightly be called its own subaqueous country.

An undersea enthusiast could spend a lifetime exploring this terrain—which ranges from dizzying chasms to sepulchral coral caves, and from lush underwater "gardens" to sandy sun-dappled shallows—without ever mapping all its resident wonders. Not only is the Reef system home to thousands upon thousands of sea-life species, the populations are changing all the time.

So how is a visitor—especially one with only a week to spend—supposed to plan a trip to this underwater Eden? How to choose among the seemingly endless spots for dropping anchor, donning fins and tanks, and plunging in?

With this many options, figuring out what you want to experience on the Reef is essential. If you've dreamed of floating among sea turtles, you'll likely need to head to a different location than if you want to swim with sharks; if you're an experienced deep-water diver with a taste for shipwrecks, you'll probably need to make separate arrangements from your friends who prefer to hover near the surface. There really is a spot for every kind of diver on the Reef; the trick is knowing where they are.

Luckily, many veteran divers agree about some of the Reef's most reliably excellent sites (and the best ways to access them). The selection compiled here should help you to—ahem—get your feet wet.

BEST DIVING EXPERIENCES

Potato cod and diver

BEST WRECK DIVE

The coral formations of the Reef, while dazzling for divers, have proven treacherous to ship captains for centuries. More than 1,500 shipwrecks have been found on the Reef thus far—and there are almost certainly more waiting to be discovered.

S.S. *YONGALA*

The hulk of this 360-foot steamship, which sank during a cyclone in 1911, is easily the most popular wreck dive on the Reef. Part of the appeal is its easy accessibility; the Yongala lies just a half-hour's boat ride off the coast of Townsville, and though some sections are fairly deep (around 90 feet), others are just 45 feet below the surface.The entire wreck is now encrusted with coral, and swarms with a profusion of species including giant grouper, sea snakes, green sea turtles, and spotted eagle rays.

Difficulty level: Intermediate. Divers should have some previous deep-water experience before visiting this site.

How to get there: Yongala Dive (www.yongaladive.com.au), based in Alva Beach (south of Townsville), runs trips to the wreck several times per week.

BEST SITE TO GET YOUR HEART RATE UP

For some thrill-seeking divers, the wonders of the Great Barrier Reef are even better when accompanied by an extra shot of adrenaline—and a few dozen sharks.

OSPREY REEF

More than 200 miles north of Cairns (and only accessible via a live-aboard dive trip), Osprey is peerless for divers hell-bent on a rendezvous with the ocean's most famous predators. The northernmost section of the reef, where two ocean currents converge (it's known as the North Horn), is an especially thronged feeding ground for white-tipped reef, gray reef, hammerhead, and tiger sharks.

Difficulty level: Intermediate. Though the North Horn's best shark-viewing areas are only at about 60 feet, even seasoned divers may feel understandably anxious.

How to get there: Mike Ball Dive Expeditions (www.mikeball.com) offers multi-day packages to Osprey Reef from Cairns and Port Douglas.

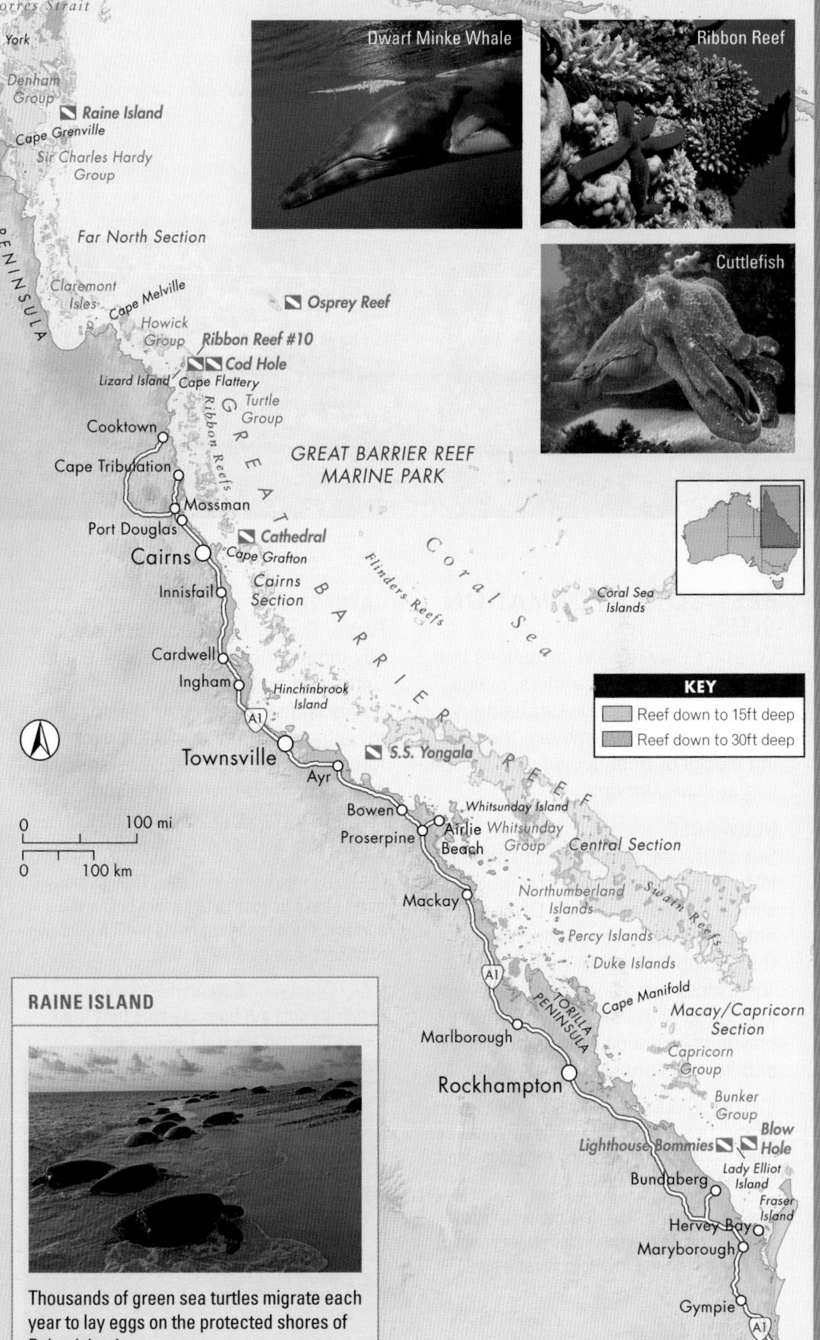

Thousands of green sea turtles migrate each year to lay eggs on the protected shores of Raine Island.

Scuba isn't the only option; snorkelers have plenty of opportunities to get up close to coral, too.

BEST CORAL-FORMATION SITES

Whether they're hard formations that mimic the shapes of antlers, brains, and stacked plates, or soft feathery Gorgonians and anemones, the building blocks of Reef ecology are compelling in their own right.

BLOWHOLE

Set off the eastern coast of Lady Elliot Island, this cavern-like coral tube is almost 60 feet in length. Divers can enter from either end, and swim through an interior festooned with Technicolor hard and soft corals—and swarming with banded coral shrimp, crayon-bright nudibranchs (sea slugs), and fluttery lionfish.

Difficulty level: Easy. Unless you're claustrophobic. Divers need only be Open-Water certified to visit this site, which ranges in depth from about 40 to 65 feet.

How to get there: The dive center at Lady Elliot Island Resort (www.ladyelliot.com.au) runs dives to the BlowHole several times daily.

CATHEDRAL

Part of Thetford Reef, which lies within day-tripping distance of coastal Cairns, Cathedral is a wonderland of coral spires and swim-through chasms. The towering coral heads include thick forests of blue staghorn, sea fans, and sea whips; in between are sandy-bottomed canyons where shafts of sunlight play over giant clam beds.

Difficulty level: Intermediate. Though many coral peaks lie just 15 to 20 feet below the surface, the deeper channels (which go down to 85 feet) can be disorienting.

How to get there: Silverseries (www.silverseries.com.au) runs day-long trips from Cairns that visit several Thetford sites.

Divers explore a swim-through coral formation.

BEST GUARANTEED CLOSE-ENCOUNTER SITES

While just about any dive site on the Reef will bring you face-to-face with fantastic marine creatures, a few particular spots maximize your chances.

RIBBON REEF NUMBER 10

The northernmost of the Ribbon Reefs (a group that extends off the Cairns coast all the way to the Torres Strait) is home to some famously curious sea creatures. At Cod Hole, divers have been hand-feeding the enormous, 70-pound resident potato cod for decades. Ribbon Reef Number 10 is also one of the only places on earth where visitors can have breathtakingly close contact with wild dwarf minke whales. These small, playful baleen whales stop here every June and July—and they often approach within a few feet of respectful divers.

Difficulty level: Easy. Divers need only be Open-Water certified to dive at the 50-foot Cod Hole; dwarf minke encounters are open to snorkelers.

How to get there: Several dive operators run live-aboard trips to the Ribbon Reefs, including Mike Ball Expeditions (www.mikeball.com), Pro Dive Cairns (www.prodivecairns.com), and Eye to Eye Marine Encounters (www.marineencounters.com.au).

LIGHTHOUSE BOMMIES

Part of the southerly Whitsunday group, Lady Elliot Island is surrounded by shallow, pristine waters that teem with life. In particular, the Lighthouse Bommies—freestanding coral formations set off the island's northwest coast—host a large population of manta rays, some of which have a wingspan twelve feet across.

Difficulty level: Easy. Divers need only be Open-Water certified to visit this site; the depth averages about 50 feet.

How to get there: The dive center at Lady Elliot Island Resort (www.ladyelliot.com.au) runs dives to the Bommies daily.

Sea turtle and diver

RAINE ISLAND

In the far north reaches of the Coral Sea off Cape York, this coral cay is one of the Reef's greatest—and most inaccessible—treasures. Its beaches comprise the world's largest nesting ground for endangered green sea turtles; during November and December more than 20,000 turtles per week mob the shores to lay their eggs. Because Raine is a strictly protected preserve, seeing this annual phenomenon is an exceedingly rare privilege. In fact, only one dive operator, Eye to Eye Marine Encounters, is sanctioned by the Marine Park Authority to visit the site—and only twice a year.

Difficulty level: Intermediate to Expert. The dive trips involve a heavy research component; participants not only dive among the turtles, but also collect data on them and fit them with satellite tags (some also tag tiger sharks, another rare endemic species).

How to get there: The 18 spots on these ten-day trips are in high demand; learn more at www.marineencounters.com.au.

SCUBA DIVING 101

(left) ProDive is one of several great dive companies on the Reef; (right) snorkelers receive instruction.

Visiting the Reef can be a snap even if you've never dived before; most local dive operators offer Open Water (entry-level) certification courses that can be completed in just three to five days. The course involves both classroom and pool training, followed by a written test and one or more open-water dives on the Reef. Once you're certified, you'll be able to dive to depths of up to 60 feet; you'll also be eligible to rent equipment and book dive trips all over the world.

TIGHT SCHEDULE?

If time is of the essence, ask about doing your Open Water class and in-pool training near home; some Reef operators may allow you to complete your certification (and get right to the good part—the actual ocean dives) once you arrive in Australia.

Though most serious divers insist that certification is necessary for scuba safety, if you're short on time you may find yourself tempted to take advantage of what are generally called "resort courses"—single-day instruction programs that allow you to dive at limited depths under strict supervision. As long as you choose a reputable operator (like Mike Ball Dive Expeditions, www.mikeball.com) and do exactly as your dive guides say, you'll likely be fine.

FLYING

No matter how you get yourself under-water, you'll need to make sure you don't schedule a flight and a dive in the same day. Flying too soon after diving can lead to "the bends"—an excruciating buildup of nitrogen bubbles in the bloodstream that requires a decompression chamber to alleviate. Since that's not anything you'd want to develop at the beginning of a transatlantic flight, be sure to wait 12 hours before flying after a single dive, 18 hours after multiple dives, and 24 hours if your dive(s) required decompression stops.

Regulators up! Reef visitors learn scuba basics.

LOGISTICS

CERTIFYING ORGANIZATIONS

You'll find that all reliable dive operators—on the Reef and elsewhere—are affiliated with one of the three major international dive-training organizations: PADI (www.padi.com), NAUI (www.naui.org), or SSI (www.divessi.com). The certification requirements for all three are similar, and most dive shops and outfitters consider them interchangeable (i.e., they'll honor a certification from any of the three).

COSTS

The price for taking a full Open Water certification course (usually over four or five days of training) averages around A$600—but in many cases, rental equipment, wetsuits, and instruction manuals cost extra. Some dive shops have relationships with hotels, and offer dive/stay packages. One-day scuba resort courses usually cost around $250-$350, with all gear included.

EMERGENCIES

Before diving on the Reef, it's a good idea to purchase divers' insurance through the Divers Alert Network (DAN), an international organization that provides emergency medical assistance to divers. (Learn more about the different plans at www.diversalertnetwork.org). DAN also has a 24-hour emergency hotline staffed by doctors, emergency medical technicians, and nurses; for help with diving injuries or immediate medical advice, call (001) 919-684-4326 from Australia.

SNORKELING TIPS

Snorkelers explore Fitzroy Reef Lagoon.

- If you're a beginner, avoid snorkeling in areas where there's chop or strong currents.
- Every few minutes, look up and check what's floating ahead of you—you'll want to avoid boats, jellyfish, and other surface-swimmers.
- Give corals, plants, and sea creatures a wide berth—for their protection and yours.
- Wear a "rashie"—a light, UV-blocking top—or plenty of high-SPF, waterproof sunscreen; the water's reflection greatly intensifies the sun's rays.

DIVING TIPS

- Before heading off on a dive trip, have your doctor rule out any possible health complications.
- Be sure your dive operator is affiliated with an internationally known training organization, such as PADI or NAUI.
- Stick to dive trips and sites that are within your expertise level—the Reef is not the place to push safety limits.
- Remember that in Australia, depths and weights use the metric system—so bring a conversion table if you need to.
- Always dive with a partner, and always keep your partner in sight.
- Never dive when you're feeling ill—especially if you're experiencing sinus congestion.
- Never dive after consuming alcohol.
- If you feel unwell or disoriented while diving, signal to your partner that you need to surface so she or he can accompany you.

DANGERS OF THE REEF

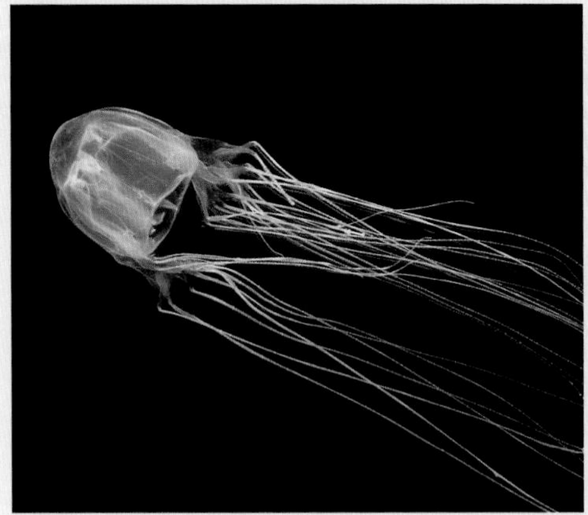

(left) The Irukandji box jellyfish sting causes severe pain; (right) small sharks inhabit areas of the Reef.

Like any other wild natural habitat, the Reef is home to creatures that are capable of causing you harm—and possibly even killing you. But surprisingly, the most lethal Reef inhabitants aren't of the Shark Week variety. In fact, they're just about invisible.

THE DEADLIEST REEF DWELLER

Chironex fleckeri—better known as box jellyfish—are native to the same waters as the Reef. They also just happen to be the most poisonous sea creatures on the planet. Cube-shaped and transparent (which makes them difficult to see in the water), these jellies have tentacles whose stinging cells release an enormously potent venom on contact. A box-jelly sting causes excruciating pain, often followed very quickly (within three or four minutes) by death.

The good news about box jellies is that they're only rarely encountered on the outer Reef and islands (they're much more prevalent close to the mainland shore, especially in summer—which is why you may see beautiful North Queensland beaches completely empty on a hot December day). While the only sure way to prevent a box jellyfish sting is to stay out of the sea altogether, there are measures you can take to lessen the already minimal risks. First, consider wearing a full-length Lycra "stinger suit" when you dive. Second, make sure your dive operator carries a supply of Chironex antivenom onboard your dive boat, just in case.

OTHER (LESS DEADLY) DANGERS

Although box jellyfish are by far the most dangerous creatures on the Reef, there are other "biteys" and "nasties" to be aware of. In particular, you should be aware of a tiny box-jelly variety called Irukandji (whose sting causes delayed but often intense pain); cone snails, which, though not aggressive, contain the most potent neurotoxin known to man; Millepora, or stinging coral (which causes irritation and welts when it touches bare skin); sea snakes (who seldom bite humans, but whose poison can cause paralysis); and, yes, sharks (although you'll likely only see small ones on the Reef—the much more hyped hammerheads, tiger sharks, and great whites prefer deeper and colder waters).

PROTECTING THE REEF

(left) Even the tiniest coral can serve as protective habitat; (right) A diver explores a large coral formation.

Enormous though it may be, the Great Barrier Reef's ecosystem is one that requires a delicate balance. The interdependence of species here means that harming even a single food source—like a particular type of plankton—can have wide-ranging and even devastating effects.

The majority of the Reef is an official marine preserve that's managed and protected by the Great Barrier Reef Marine Park Authority. This government agency has developed a series of long-range programs to help protect the Reef—including population-monitoring of sealife species, water-temperature and salinity studies, and screening of all commercial fishing and tourism/recreational operations.

Since almost 2 million tourists visit the Reef each year, even day-trippers should be mindful of their impact on this fragile environment. Specifically, if you're planning to dive and snorkel here, you should:

- Make sure your dive gear is secure, with no loose straps or dangling hoses that might snag on corals.
- Swim slowly to avoid brushing against corals (and be especially mindful when wearing swim fins).
- Avoid picking up or touching any corals, plants, or creatures (for your protection and theirs). No souvenirs, even empty shells or dead-looking coral.
- Keep clear of all free-swimming sea creatures like sea turtles, dolphins, dugongs, or whales.

VOLUNTEERING ON THE REEF

If you'd like to do more to protect the Reef, the following organizations offer volunteer programs that allow you to help collect study data and monitor the health of reef species:

- The Australian Marine Conservation Society: www.amcs.org.au
- Reef Check Australia: www.reefcheckaustralia.org
- UNESCO (United Nations Educational, Scientific, and Cultural Organization): whc.unesco.org

research station and the island's resort, which has a large vegetable garden, a solar hot-water system, and a 21,134-gallon water tank, as well as an infinity-edge pool and several beachfront villas linked by a rear boardwalk.

Although there are patches of rain forest in the island's deeper gullies and around its sheltered bays, Orpheus is a true Barrier Reef island, ringed by seven unspoiled sandy beaches and superb coral reefs. Amazingly, 340 of the known 359 species of coral inhabit these waters, as do more than 1,100 types of tropical fish and the biggest giant clams in the southern hemisphere. The local marine life is easily accessed and extraordinary.

GETTING HERE AND AROUND

Nautilus Aviation helicopters depart daily at 2 pm from Townsville Airport's Domestic Gate Lounge 10, returning Orpheus guests to the mainland from 2:30 (A$400 per person, one-way). You can also charter flights from other mainland ports and islands. Baggage should be soft-sided and is strictly limited to a maximum of 15 kilograms (33 pounds) per person. Excess baggage can be stored at Townsville Airport for free, and the resort offers complimentary laundry (excluding dry cleaning). Book flights with Orpheus Island Resort.

SEAPLANE Nautilus Aviation. ✉ *Townsville Airport, Gypsy Moth Court, Hangar 15, Townsville* ☏ *07/4034–9000 Nautilus Aviation, 07/4725–6056 Nautilus Aviation Townsville Airport Base* 🌐 *www.nautilusaviation.com.au.*

★ **Orpheus Island Lodge**

$$$$ | **RESORT** | This unpretentious, eco-friendly resort epitomizes laid-back luxury, with sleekly appointed beachfront rooms, suites, and villas; romantic alfresco dining; boutique wines; and numerous outdoor activities included in the rate. **Pros:** excellent underwater sites nearby; the signature alfresco "Dining with the Tides" experience; free Wi-Fi in public areas. **Cons:** no fitness center; occasional geckos and insects indoors; no in-room Internet. $ *Rooms from: A$1600* ✉ *Orpheus Island Resort, Orpheus Island* ✈ *Accessible via air from Townsville or Cairns* ☏ *07/4777–7377* 🌐 *www.orpheus.com.au* *14 rooms* *All-Inclusive.*

Orpheus Island Resort is surrounded by walking trails, and there are spectacular snorkeling and diving sites right off the beaches, with manta rays (July to early November), humpback whale migration (June to September), and the annual coral spawning (mid- to late October to late November) among the underwater highlights. Resort guests get complimentary use of snorkeling and light fishing gear, as well as kayaks, stand-up paddleboards, catamarans, and motorized dinghies in which to buzz from cove to cove. The coral around Orpheus is some of the best in the area, and cruises to the outer reef can be arranged through the resort for an additional fee. Whereas most Great Barrier Reef resort islands are more than 50 km (31 miles) from the reef, Orpheus is just 15 km (9 miles) away. Dive operators on the island provide scuba courses and various boat-diving options.

BOAT CRUISES

Hinchinbrook and Palm Islands Tours

BOATING | Orpheus Island resort guests can take helicopter flights over Hinchinbrook Island National Park, Australia's largest protected island wilderness; or cruise the Hinchinbrook-Cardwell channel, and nearby Palm Islands, with stops for wildlife-spotting, snorkeling, and bushwalks. On a daylong Hinchinbrook-Cardwell channel cruise, you'll seek out saltwater crocs in island estuaries and anchor in secluded coves for guided rain-forest treks to Zoe and Mulligan waterfalls. Or take a leisurely cruise around the Palm Islands on the resort's own vessel, the *Maree Ann*, with stops to snorkel, explore significant sites, and take guided nature walks. Sunset cruises on the *Maree Ann* include drinks and canapés on deck. ✉ *Orpheus Island* ☎ *07/4777–7377* 🌐 *www.orpheus.com.au* 🎫 *From about A$300 per person depending on charter, vessel, and number of guests.*

FISHING

Orpheus Island Fishing

FISHING | The tropical waters off Orpheus Island offer prized game and reef fish species. On group trips or solo dinghy excursions via motorized dinghy (free for guests' use, as is light tackle), tasty reef fish (red emperor and coral trout, sweetlip, and giant trevally) can be caught right off the island. On excursions to the outer reef, you'll get the chance to land large pelagics including wahoo, Spanish mackerel, and dog-tooth tuna. Prebooking fishing charters is essential and all expeditions are subject to weather and tidal conditions. ✉ *Orpheus Island Jetty, Orpheus Island* ☎ *07/4777–7377* 🌐 *www.orpheus.com.au* 🎫 *From A$1200 for outer reef private charter; from A$100/hr for local island private boat charter.*

GREAT BARRIER REEF EXCURSIONS

Orpheus Island Diving & Snorkeling

SCUBA DIVING | **FAMILY** | Orpheus Island is encircled by fringing reef, with world-class dive and snorkeling sites an easy boat or dinghy ride away; free pool scuba refresher courses and various off-island boat-diving options are available for beginner and PADI-certified divers. The resort can arrange half-day dive and snorkeling trips around the neighboring Palm Islands, and full-day charter dive and snorkeling excursions to sites on the Outer Barrier Reef teeming with turtles, colorful fish, and coral species—and, in season, massive manta rays and masses of coral spawning. Costs depend on passenger numbers and inclusions; booking ahead is essential. Resort guests can also preorder gourmet picnic hampers and use the resort's motorized dinghies to visit secluded, boulder-strewn coves and snorkeling spots on the island's fringing reef. Often, you can snorkel directly off the beach into fish-filled coral gardens. ✉ *Orpheus Island Resort Jetty, Orpheus Island* ☎ *07/4777–7377* 🌐 *www.orpheus.com.au* 🎫 *From A$300.*

Bedarra Island

5 km (3 miles) off the coast of Mission Beach.

This tiny, 247-acre island has natural springs, dense rain-forest tracts, and eight unspoiled beaches. Bedarra Island Resort has upscale facilities, services, and dining options. It is geared for relaxation, but there's still plenty for active guests to do. You can play tennis, work out at the resort gym, sail catamarans around the coves, fish from motorized dinghies, or paddleboard with turtles off the island's main beach. You can sunbathe and picnic on rain-forest fringed beaches (gourmet hamper provided), and go bird-watching and wildlife-spotting along the island's walking trails. Deep-sea game fishing, sailing, and diving excursions on the outer Great Barrier Reef can be arranged through the resort and customized to suit. It's possible to snorkel around the island, but it's not on the reef, and the water can be cloudy during rain.

GETTING HERE AND AROUND

Bedarra Island lies about 77.3 km (48 miles) from Orpheus Island. Fast launch transfers from Mission Beach on the mainland (two hours' drive south of Cairns and about three hours north of Townsville) depart daily on demand at 12:30 pm (A$198 per couple, one-way). Departing guests can take the daily Bedarra–Mission Beach launch at 10:30 am; launch

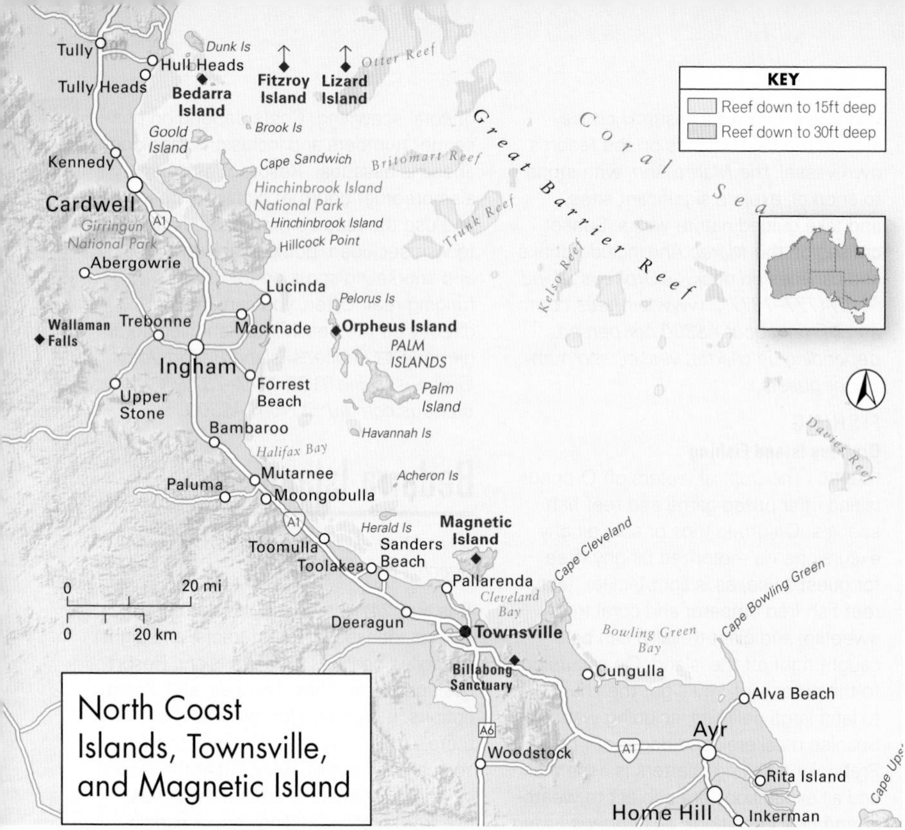

North Coast Islands, Townsville, and Magnetic Island

transfers can be arranged at other times at an additional rate. If your time is more limited than your credit card, it's a 45-minute helicopter transfer from Cairns to Bedarra's beachside helipad. Prebook all transfers through the resort.

Hotels

★ **Bedarra**

$$$$ | **RESORT** | Billing itself as "the ultimate in barefoot luxury," the laid-back, exclusive, child-free Bedarra Island Resort hosts no more than 20 guests in modern, eco-friendly accommodations, spoiling them with fine food and service, and upscale amenities. **Pros:** secluded, spectacular environs; relaxed but attentive service; sailing trips can be arranged. **Cons:** no room service; reception only open 7 am to 7 pm; Wi-Fi can be slow and cell phone signals intermittent. *Rooms from: A$1490* *Bedarra Island* *07/4068–8233* *www.bedarra.com.au* *Closed late Jan.–early Mar.* *10 rooms* *All-Inclusive.*

Fitzroy Island

6 km (4 miles) from Cairns.

This ruggedly picturesque, heavily forested island is 94% national park, with vegetation ranging from rain forest to heath, and an extensive fringing coral reef. Only 6 km (4 miles)—less than an hour's cruise—from Cairns, the 988-acre island, once connected to the mainland, was a hunting, gathering, and ceremonial ground for the Gungandji people, who called it Kobaburra before Cook renamed it in 1770. Today Fitzroy Island houses a modern resort and budget cabins, as well as facilities for the day-trippers who flock here year-round to snorkel, dive, and kayak with turtles and tropical fish. From June to September, migrating manta rays and humpback whales pass right by the island. We recommend it as a day trip.

GETTING HERE AND AROUND

Various ferries service Fitzroy Island daily: *Fitzroy Flyer* and *Sunlover* cruise out of Cairns's Reef Fleet Terminal daily at 8 and 9:30 am, respectively, departing the island for the return trip at 5 and 4:20 pm. Sunlover Reef Cruises offers Fitzroy Island transfers as part of snorkeling day-trip packages.

FERRY CONTACTS Fitzroy Flyer. ✉ *Departs from Cairns Reef Fleet Terminal, 1 Spence St., Cairns* ☎ *07/4044–6700* 🌐 *www.fitzroyisland.com.* **Sunlover Reef Cruises.** ✉ *Departs from Reef Fleet Terminal, 1 Spence St., Cairns* ☎ *07/4050–1333* 🌐 *www.sunlover.com.au.*

Activities

Half a dozen marked walking trails traverse Fitzroy Island National Park; they range from half-hour rain-forest strolls to steep, challenging three-hour hikes. Take drinking water; wear sturdy closed shoes, insect repellent, sunscreen, and a hat; and watch for snakes (and in estuaries and mangroves, crocs). For maps and detailed information, visit the **Queensland Government Department of Environment and Sciences)** website (*www.environment.des.qld.gov.au*).

But most visitors to the island are keen to get on or under the water, and there are plenty of options for doing that. Day-trippers and resort guests can book guided dives and tuition, rent scuba gear at Fitzroy Island Dive & Adventure Centre, and rent snorkeling and water sports equipment by the jetty on Welcome Beach. The island has some terrific snorkeling spots—some right off the beach, others accessible by sea kayak—and excellent beginner dive sites close to shore. Go sea kayaking, paddleboarding, or glass-bottom boat touring for more chances to spot turtles, rays, reef sharks, and thousands of bright-hued fish.

Fitzroy Island Sports Hub

DIVING & SNORKELING | FAMILY | Day-trippers, resort guests, divers, and campers can rent kayaks, paddle-skis, and stand-up paddleboards here, as well as stinger suits, diving gear and equipment, tanks, and snorkeling gear. You can also book guided dive and snorkeling trips, sea-kayaking explorations, introductory dives, and glass-bottom boat tours. ✉ *Fitzroy Island Resort, next to Fitzroy Island Jetty, near Welcome Bay, Fitzroy Island* ☎ *07/4044–6700* 🌐 *www.fitzroyisland.com* *From A$20.*

Lizard Island

240 km (150 miles) off the North Queensland coast.

The small, upscale resort on secluded Lizard Island is the farthest north of any Barrier Reef hideaway. At 2,500 acres, virtually all of it protected as a national park, the island is larger than and quite different from other islands in the region. Composed mostly of granite, Lizard has a remarkable diversity of vegetation and terrain: grassy hills give way to rocky slabs interspersed with valleys of rain forest.

Ringed by two dozen white-sand beaches, the island has some of the best fringing coral in the region. Excellent walking trails lead to lookouts with spectacular views of the coast. The island's highest point, Cook's Look (1,180 feet), is the historic spot from which, in August 1770, Captain Cook finally spotted a safe passage through the reef that had held his vessel captive for a thousand miles. Large monitor lizards, after which the island is named, often bask in this area.

GETTING HERE AND AROUND

Lizard Island has its own small airstrip. Hour-long flights to the island depart five days a week from Cairns, at 2 pm, with return flights at 11 am; taking an hour and costing A$385 per person each way. Allow 2½ hours transit time for connecting international flights, 90 minutes for domestic flight transits: check-in is 30 minutes prior to flight time at the East Air Terminal. You can also arrange charter flights to the island, with prices varying depending on the size of aircraft available (07/4040–1333).

AIR CONTACTS Hinterland Aviation. ✉ *Tom McDonald Dr., Cairns* ☎ *07/4040–1333 international, 1300/359–428 toll-free in Australia* 🌐 *www.hinterlandaviation.com.au.*

Sights

★ Cod Hole

REEF | For divers and snorkelers, the usually crystal clear waters off Lizard Island are a dream. Cod Hole, 20 km (12 miles) from Lizard Island, ranks among the best dive sites on Earth. Massive potato cod swim up to divers like hungry puppies; it's an awesome experience, considering these fish can weigh 300 pounds and reach around 6 feet in length. The island lures big-game anglers from all over the world from September to December, when black marlin are running. ✉ *Lizard Island, Lizard Island.*

Hotels

★ Lizard Island Resort

$$$$ | **RESORT** | Beloved by honeymooners, divers, and well-heeled travelers, this outer Great Barrier Reef resort ticks all the high-end tropical-island vacation boxes: luxurious beachfront accommodation, fine food and wine, and world-class diving and fishing. **Pros:** use of nonmotorized watercraft and dinghies; superb diving and fishing; quality food and wine (included in the rate). **Cons:** no cell-phone coverage; lighting inadequate for reading; successive cyclones have damaged the island's vegetation. $ *Rooms from: A$2029* ✉ *Lizard Island, Lizard Island* ☎ *1800/837–204 bookings, toll-free in Australia, 07/4043–1999 resort, 844/887–6724 toll-free in U.S.* 🌐 *www.lizardisland.com.au* *40 suites* *All-Inclusive.*

Activities

The lodge has catamarans, outboard dinghies, paddle-skis (including glass-bottom ones), fishing supplies, snorkeling gear, and lessons. There is superb snorkeling around the island's fringing coral, or you can cruise over it on a glass-bottom sea kayak. Self-guided bushwalking trails and nature slideshows get guests in touch with the local flora and fauna. Arrange a picnic hamper with the kitchen staff and take a dinghy out for an afternoon on your own private beach. All these activities are included in your room rate.

Other activities cost extra: inner and outer reef dive/snorkel trips, night dives, scuba courses, and game- and bottom-fishing excursions (black marlin season runs September through December). For pricing, details, and to prebook activities, contact Lizard Island Activities Desk (*800/837–204; www.lizardisland.com.au*).

FISHING

Lizard Island is one of the big game-fishing centers in Australia, with several world records set here since the mid-1990s. Game fishing is generally best in spring and early summer, and giant black marlin weighing more than 1,000 pounds are no rarity. September through December, the folk from Lizard Island run full-day game-fishing trips to the outer reef; January through August, you can book half-day bottom-fishing excursions.

★ Lizard Island Sportfishing

FISHING | Even though fishing is banned in the waters immediately off Lizard Island, world-renowned fishing grounds lie less than an hour away. From September through December, fishing enthusiasts arrive in droves to land tuna, sailfish, mahimahi, and, if they're lucky, the legendary "Grander" black marlin. From January to August, you might nab trevally, mackerel, or queenfish. Lizard Island Resort arranges small-group, high-adrenaline trips to the outer reef and half- and full-day inner reef excursions on its 51-foot Riviera Platinum Model Flybridge cruiser, *Fascination III*. Outer-reef game-fishing day trips include heavy tackle, lunch, and light refreshments; half-day excursions include bait, light tackle, and refreshments. Prices vary according to season, weather, and availability. Prebooking essential. ✉ *Lizard Island Resort Jetty, Lizard Island* ☎ *1800/837–204 toll-free in Australia, 884/833–7862 in U.S.* 🌐 *www.lizardisland.com.au* 🎫 *From A$2300.*

SCUBA DIVING

The reefs around Lizard Island have some of the best marine life and coral on the planet. The resort runs expertly guided scuba-diving and snorkeling trips on its custom-built dive boat to pristine sites on the Great Barrier Reef, including the Ribbon Reefs and globally renowned Cod Hole, as well as local dives, snorkeling excursions, and scuba courses.

★ Lizard Island Snorkeling & Diving

DIVING & SNORKELING | Lizard Island is a short boat ride from some of the richest, least spoiled sites on the Great Barrier Reef. Within an hour, you can dive the Ribbon reefs or renowned Cod Hole, eyeballing giant potato cod, pelagic fish, turtles, rays, and sharks. You can also take guided dives to explore fish-filled coral gardens just offshore. Lizard Island Resort's 55-foot dive boat MV *Serranidae* makes reef excursions as well as dive-snorkel trips, and privately guided dives to local fringing reefs and the Cobia Hole. Need scuba skills or gear? The resort has PADI Referral courses, and a wide range of modern dive equipment for rent. Use of snorkeling masks, snorkels, and fins is complimentary. ✉ *Lizard Island Resort, Lizard Island* ☎ *1800/837–204 toll-free in Australia, 884/833–7862 in U.S.* 🌐 *www.lizardisland.com.au* 🎫 *From A$95* ☞ *All divers must bring certification card and current dive medical certificate.*

Townsville

1,358 km (844 miles) north of Brisbane, 348 km (216 miles) south of Cairns.

This coastal city has little in the way of sandy beaches or surf, but it does have shady parks, charming old buildings, and a boardwalk-flanked waterfront esplanade with a terrific man-made beach and picnic facilities. The historic town center has thrived in the past decade, with an influx of lively eateries and bars. There is also an excellent museum and a world-class aquarium.

Queensland Parks and Wildlife Service has an office on Magnetic Island, but Tourism Townsville's information kiosk in Flinders Square and the Townsville Bulletin Square Visitor Information Centre near the Museum of Tropical Queensland (MTQ), on the mainland, are the best sources of visitor info about the island.

GETTING HERE AND AROUND

Qantas flies frequently from Townsville Airport to Brisbane, Cairns, Cloncurry, Mount Isa, and Mackay, as well as to capital cities around Australia and overseas destinations. Jetstar has services to Brisbane, Sydney, and Melbourne; Virgin Australia connects Townsville with Brisbane, Sydney, and Melbourne. Townsville Taxis are available at the airport. The average cost of the ride to a city hotel is between A$25 and A$30, more after 7 pm.

There are no air connections to Magnetic Island; you need to take a ferry from Townsville (one-way, it's A$17 for a walk-on passenger; from A$101 each way for a vehicle with up to four passengers).

Townsville is a flat, somewhat dull 1,358-km (844-mile), 16-hour drive from Brisbane. The 348-km (216-mile), 4½-hour journey from here to Cairns, with occasional Hinchinbrook Island views, is more scenic. Greyhound Australia coaches travel regularly to Cairns, Mount Isa, Rockhampton, Brisbane, and other destinations throughout Australia from the SeaLink Terminal on Townsville's Breakwater, also the departure point for Magnetic Island ferries, day cruises, and dive trips. Regular long-distance Queensland Rail services, offering reclining seats or podlike RailBeds, connect Townsville with Brisbane, Cairns, Mount Isa, and dozens of towns en route.

The modern train, *Spirit of Queensland*, plies the coast between Brisbane and Cairns five times weekly in each direction, stopping at Townsville en route. It has reclining premium economy seats, and podlike fold-flat RailBed seats with numerous mod cons: reading lights, entertainment consoles, USB and AC power plugs, bedding, towels, and toiletries. From Brisbane to Townsville, one-way, a RailBed ticket is A$332.

Once in town, you can flag a Townsville Taxis cab on the street, find one at taxi stands, hotels, and the island's ferry terminal, or book one online.

FERRY CONTACTS Magnetic Island Ferries. ✉ *Ross St., South Townsville, South Townsville* ☎ *07/4796–9300* 🌐 *www.fantaseacruisingmagnetic.com.au.* **SeaLink Queensland.** ✉ *Breakwater Terminal, 18 Sir Leslie Thiess Dr., Townsville* ☎ *07/4726–0800* 🌐 *www.sealinkqld.com.au.*

TAXI CONTACTS Townsville Taxis. ✉ *11–15 Yeatman St., Townsville* ☎ *131–008 local bookings, 07/4778–9555 interstate bookings.*

VISITOR INFORMATION

CONTACTS Flinders Square Visitor Information Centre. ✉ *Flinders Sq., 334–336 Flinders St., Townsville* ☎ *07/4721–3660* 🌐 *www.townsvillenorthqueensland.com.au.*

Sights

Billabong Sanctuary

ZOO | FAMILY | This eco-friendly, interactive sanctuary on 22 acres of bushland shelters koalas, wombats, dingoes, wallabies, endangered bilbies, snakes, crocodiles, lizards, and numerous birds, most featuring in daily wildlife shows, presentations, and feedings. The sanctuary has daily free-flight birds of prey shows, crocodile and cassowary feedings, venomous snake presentations, and turtle racing. Visitors can snap a selfie with a koala, or have their photo taken holding a wombat, snake, or baby croc. Thrill-seekers can book a personal croc-feeding experience, with or without souvenir photo. ✉ *Bruce Hwy., Nome* ✦ *17 km (11 miles) south of Townsville* ☎ *07/4778–8344* 🌐 *www.billabongsanctuary.com.au* 🎫 *A$40 entry.*

Castle Hill

VIEWPOINT | The summit of pink-granite monolith Castle Hill, 1 km (½ mile) from the city center, provides great views of the city and Magnetic Island. While you're perched on top, think about the proud local resident who, with the aid of several scout troops, spent years in the 1970s piling rubble onto the peak to try to add the 23 feet that would make Castle Hill a mountain, officially speaking—which means a rise of at least 1,000 feet. These days, most people trek to the top along a steep walking track that doubles as one of Queensland's most scenic jogging routes. ✉ *Castle Hill Lookout, Castle Hill Rd., Townsville* ☎ *07/4721–3660 Townsville visitor information.*

Flinders Street

HISTORIC DISTRICT | A stroll along Flinders Street from the Strand to Stanley Street takes you past some of Townsville's most impressive turn-of-the-20th-century colonial structures. **Magnetic House** and several other historic buildings along the strip have been beautifully restored. The grand old **Queens Hotel** is a fine example of the early Victorian Classical Revival style, as is the **Perc Tucker Regional Gallery,** circa 1885, originally a bank. **Tattersalls Hotel,** circa 1865, is typical of its era, with wide verandas and fancy wrought-iron balustrades; today, it houses the rambunctious **Molly Malones** Irish pub. Once the town's post office, what's now **The Brewery** had an impressive masonry clock tower when it was erected in 1889. The tower was dismantled in 1942 so it wouldn't be a target during World War II air raids, and re-erected in 1964. **The Exchange,** Townsville's oldest pub, was built in 1869, burned down in 1881, and was rebuilt the following year. ✉ *Flinders St., Townsville.*

Museum of Tropical Queensland

MUSEUM VILLAGE | **FAMILY** | Centuries-old relics from the HMS *Pandora* (the ship sent by the British Admiralty to capture the mutinous *Bounty* crew), which sank in 1791 carrying 14 crew members of Captain Bligh's infamous ship, are among the exhibits at this repository of the region's maritime, natural, and Indigenous history. There's a fun introduction to North Queensland's culture and lifestyle, a shipwreck exhibit, and the ecology-focused Enchanted Rainforest. Displays of tropical wildlife, dinosaur fossils, local corals, and deep-sea creatures round out a diverse public collection. ✉ *70–102 Flinders St. E, Townsville* ☎ *07/4726–0600* 🌐 *www.mtq.qm.qld.gov.au* 🎫 *A$15.*

Queens Gardens

GARDEN | **FAMILY** | Offering shade and serenity less than a mile from the CBD, Townsville's colonial-era botanic gardens occupies 10 verdant acres at the base of Castle Hill. Bordered by frangipani (plumeria) and towering Moreton Bay fig trees, whose unique dangling roots veil the entry to the grounds, the gardens are a wonderful place to picnic, stroll, or amuse the kids. There are play areas, a hedge maze, formal rose garden, fountains, and a lovely rain-forest walk. A compact aviary houses bright-plumed peacocks, lorikeets, and sulfur-crested cockatoos. ✉ *Gregory St. at Paxton St., North Ward* ☎ *1300/878–001 toll-free in Australia* 🎫 *Free.*

Townsville Town Common Conservation Park

NATURE PRESERVE | **FAMILY** | Spot wallabies, echidnas, dingoes, goannas, and hundreds of bird species at this terrific wetlands conservation park crisscrossed by walking and biking trails, and dotted with bird blinds and a wildlife-viewing tower. You can take the easy, hour-long Forest Walk to see kingfishers and honey-eaters, the Pallarenda to Tegoora Rock circuit for wetlands overviews, or several other walking and biking trails (with estimated walk times ranging from 30 minutes to five hours). The 5-km (3-mile), two-plus-hour-long trail from Bald Rock to Mount Marlowl is worth the uphill trek for the glorious regional panorama at the summit. Most trails start from Bald Rock parking lot, 7 km (4½ miles) from the park entrance on unpaved roads. ✉ *Freshwater Lagoon Rd., off Cape Pallarenda Rd., near Rowes Bay Golf Club, Pallarenda* ☎ *07/4721–3660 Townsville tourist information* 🌐 *www.nprsr.qld.gov.au/parks/townsville.*

Wallaman Falls

NATIONAL PARK | **FAMILY** | Surrounding the highest sheer-drop waterfall in Australia is glorious Girringun National Park, in which ancient rain forests accessible via scenic walking trails shelter rare plants and animals that include the endangered southern cassowary, platypus, and musky rat-kangaroo. You might also spot eastern water dragons, saw-shelled turtles, and crocodiles here. The park is the start of the Wet Tropics Great Walk, suitable for experienced hikers. For day-trippers, there are two spectacular lookouts and some scenic short walks, such as the 45-minute Banggurru circuit along Stony Creek's bank, or the steeper, two-hour walk to the base of the falls. ✉ *Lava Plains Mount Fox Rd.* ✣ *From Townsville, take Bruce Hwy. (A1) north for just under 100 km (60 miles), then turn left onto Lannercost St. (signposted for Abergowrie/Wallaman Falls), taking Abergowrie-Ingham Rd. to Abergowrie, then Stone Rd. and Mount Fox Rd. to park entrance* ☎ *137–468 ParksQ infoline* 🌐 *www.nprsr.qld.gov.au/parks* 🎟 *Free.*

Townsville is blessed with a golden, 2-km (1-mile) beach that stretches along the city's northern edge. The beach, with its associated pools, water park, and adjacent parklands, is hugely popular with the locals, especially over school holidays and summer.

★ The Strand

BEACH | FAMILY | Dubbed Australia's Cleanest Beach, this palm-flanked stretch of sand—lined with jogging tracks and cycleways, picnic-friendly parklands, and hip beachfront bars—has two swimming enclosures and a long pier perfect for fishing. The beach and its permanent swimming enclosure, Strand Rock Pool, are fitted with temporary nets during box-jellyfish season, November through May. There's also a free, kid-friendly Strand Water Park. All are patrolled by lifeguards daily, with hours varying seasonally. **Amenities:** food and drink; lifeguards; toilets. **Best for:** swimming. ✉ *The Strand, Townsville* ☎ *134–810 Townsville City Council* 🌐 *www.townsville.qld.gov.au.*

JAM Corner

$$ | MODERN AUSTRALIAN | This fine-dining restaurant sources terrific organic and tropical produce for its Modern Australian menus, which change seasonally, but always feature fresh seafood and premium Australian meats in artful, beautifully balanced dishes, with fine antipodean wines to complement them. For special occasions, there's a luxurious, chandelier-lighted private dining room. **■ TIP→ Reservations aren't essential, but it's a smart idea to book ahead. Known for:** great wine list; one of the fancier restaurants in town; affordable, pared-back lunch menu. 💲 *Average main: A$39* ✉ *1 Palmer St., South Townsville* ☎ *07/4721–4900* 🌐 *www.jamcorner.com.au* 🕙 *Closed Sun. and Mon.*

★ A Touch of Salt

$$ | MODERN AUSTRALIAN | This Modern Australian eatery fits the bill: location (riverfront), service (impeccable), ambience (relaxed), food (exciting and flavorful), and wine (top-flight). The menu is a carefully curated collection of local meat, seafood, and vegetable creations, with something to suit every palate, including a comprehensive "plant-based" section to the menu. **Known for:** excellent, largely Australian wine list; perfect pick for date night; expansive waterfront deck. 💲 *Average main: A$38* ✉ *86 Ogden St., Townsville* ☎ *07/4724–4441* 🌐 *www.atouchofsalt.com.au* 🕙 *No lunch Sat.–Thurs.*

Grand Hotel Townsville

$ | HOTEL | With a terrific location in Townsville's liveliest bar-restaurant precinct, this stylish, secure, and spotless hotel-apartment complex has everything you need: chic, well-appointed accommodation; a clean pool and terrific gym; business center; accommodating staff; and charge-back arrangements with local eateries. **Pros:** 24-hour room service;

close to many bars, eateries, and attractions; helpful, friendly staff. **Cons:** free on-site car-parking spots limited; Palmer Street–facing rooms can be noisy, especially on weekends; lower-floor rooms are small and lack views. *$ Rooms from: A$135 ✉ 8–10 Palmer St., Townsville ☎ 07/4753–2800 🌐 www.grandhotel-townsville.com.au 106 rooms No Meals.*

Oaks Metropole Hotel

$ | HOTEL | The smartly configured studios and suites at this hotel are a five-minute walk from Palmer Street's bar and dining precinct, and an easy stroll across the footbridge from Flinders Street and the ferry port. **Pros:** discounts for longer stays; excellent in-room facilities; central location. **Cons:** smokers in outdoor common areas; service standards vary; feels a tad clinical. *$ Rooms from: A$129 ✉ 81 Palmer St., Townsville ☎ 07/4753–2900 reception, 1300/559–129 toll-free in Australia 🌐 www.oakshotels.com 104 rooms No Meals.*

★ The Brewery

BREWPUBS | Townsville's historic post office now houses this sociable gastropub, which serves upmarket, bistro-style meals and boutique beers brewed on-site. The owners have combined modern finishes with the building's original design, incorporating old post-office fittings, such as the main bar, once the stamp counter, to create a venue with character and polish. *✉ 252 Flinders St., Townsville ☎ 07/4724–2999 🌐 www.townsvillebrewery.com.*

The Ville Resort Casino

BARS | Dominating Townsville's waterfront, this high-rise casino-hotel complex is an entertainment hub, containing a luxury hotel, six on-site restaurants and bars, performance space featuring regular live shows, and more than 370 slot machines and 20-plus gaming tables. If you choose to stay over, the 194-room hotel has well-appointed rooms, suites, and a two-bedroom apartment. *✉ Sir Leslie Thiess Dr., Townsville ☎ 07/4722–2333 🌐 www.the-ville.com.au.*

KAYAKING

Magnetic Island Sea Kayaks

KAYAKING | FAMILY | On these eco-friendly kayaking trips around Magnetic Island's quieter bays, you might spot turtles, dolphins, dugongs, sea eagles, ospreys, and, mid-July through mid-September, migrating whales and their calves. The company runs two different excursions: a leisurely 4½-hour morning tour of beaches, coves, and bays (A$95) and a twilight paddle around Horseshoe Bay with a stop for drinks (A$65). Rates include the use of single or double kayaks and safety gear, expert instruction and guidance, commentary on the island's ecology, breakfast or sunset drinks, reef tax, and national park entry fees. *✉ Horseshoe Bay boat ramp, end of Pacific Dr., off Horseshoe Bay Rd., Magnetic Island ☎ 07/4778–5424 🌐 www.seakayak.com.au From A$65.*

SCUBA DIVING

Surrounded by tropical islands and warm waters, Townsville is a top-notch diving center. Diving courses, day trips, and multiday excursions tend to be less crowded than those in the hot spots of Cairns or the Whitsunday Islands.

About 16 km (10 miles) offshore, a 60-km (37-mile) boat ride southeast of Townsville, is the wreck of the mighty SS *Yongala,* a steamship that sank in 1911 and now lies 49 to 91 feet beneath the surface. It teems with marine life and is considered one of Australia's best dive sites. It can be explored on one- and two-day trips. All local dive operators conduct excursions to the wreck.

Adrenalin Dive

DIVING & SNORKELING | This local outfit runs day and live-aboard trips to diverse sites on the Great Barrier Reef, including the wreck of the SS *Yongala*. The *Yongala* trip includes weight belt, tanks, two dives, and lunch; it's an extra A$10 for the introductory guided dive that's compulsory for novice divers. Snorkel/dive day trips to sheltered sites on the GBR's Lodestone Reef are A$274 for snorkelers, A$359 for certified divers. On a three-night, live-aboard eco-trip, you can make up to 10 dives, including two night dives and two dives on the *Yongala* (A$920 for a snorkeler, A$1,020 for a diver in a double room, including diving, gear, and meals). Cheaper twin and dorm berths are available. On all dive trips, optional extras include PADI Adventure Dives (A$25 per dive); enriched-air nitrox (A$50 for two tanks, nitrox-certified divers only); and camera rental (A$65). ✉ *66–70 Perkins St. W, Townsville* ☎ *07/4724–0600* 🌐 *www.adrenalindive.com.au* 🎫 *From A$274.*

Magnetic Island

10 km (6 miles) from Townsville.

More than half of Magnetic Island's 52 square km (20 square miles) is national parkland, laced with miles of walking trails and rising to 1,640 feet at the Mt. Cook summit. The terrain is littered with huge granite boulders and softened by tall hoop pines, eucalyptus forest, and rain-forest gullies. A haven for wildlife, the island shelters rock wallabies, echidnas, frogs, possums, fruit bats, nonvenomous green tree snakes, and northern Australia's largest population of wild koalas. Its beaches, mangroves, sea-grass beds, and fringing reefs support turtles nesting, fish hatching, and a significant dugong population. You can take time out on 23 island beaches and dive nine offshore shipwrecks.

More than 2,500 people call "Maggie" home; most live on the island's eastern shore at Picnic Bay, Arcadia, Nelly Bay, and Horseshoe Bay. Many artists and craftspeople reside here, drawn by the serenity and scenic environs; you can see and buy their work at studios and galleries around the island.

GETTING HERE AND AROUND

Magnetic Island Ferries

The 40-minute Magnetic Island Ferry service has several scheduled services daily from the mainland to Maggie's Nelly Bay Ferry Terminal, 10 km (6 miles) offshore. The first ferry leaves Townsville at 5 am weekdays, 7 am on weekends, with the last return service departing the island at 5 pm. One-way fares are from A$108 for a vehicle with up to six people, A$15 for a person with no vehicle (bicycles free). SeaLink Queensland has a daily 25-minute catamaran service linking Townsville and Nelly Bay on Magnetic Island. Bus and island transfers meet the ferry during daylight hours. Up to 17 SeaLink ferries a day cruise out of Townsville between 5:30 am (6:30 Sunday) and 9:20 pm (10:30 pm Wednesday to Saturday), returning between 6 am (7 am Sunday) and 10 pm (11 pm Wednesday to Saturday); a one-way ticket costs A$17.50. ✉ *22 Ross St., Townsville* ☎ *07/4796–9300* 🌐 *www.magneticislandferries.com.au.*

Magnetic Island Sunbus

Get an overview of Magnetic Island riding the cheap, reliable local buses, which ply the coast road between Picnic Point, Nelly Bay, Arcadia, and Horseshoe Bay from dawn till late, and can be hailed from the roadside. Single-fare tickets (A$2.40 to A$3) as well as unlimited-travel day and weekly passes are available from the driver. The bus departs Picnic Bay Jetty at regular intervals throughout the week. ✉ *Nelly Bay, 44 Mandalay Ave., Magnetic Island* ☎ *07/4778–5130* 🌐 *www.sunbus.com.au.*

Did You Know?

Bigeye trevally (Caranx sexfasciatus), a type of jack, can form schools of up to 1,500 fish during the day. At night these schools break up, and individuals or small groups hunt seaborne insects, crustaceans, jelly-fish, and smaller species of fish.

Migaloo the Albino Whale

Migaloo was the world's only documented white humpback whale when he was first spotted in 1991, making his way up the Queensland coastline. A witty Indigenous Elder suggested the name Migaloo, an Aboriginal word for "white fella."

Every year, thousands eagerly watch for a glimpse of Migaloo's distinctive pure-white dorsal fin, as the 46-foot whale makes his annual migration from the Antarctic to tropical waters in June and July. He's been spotted as far up Australia's east coast as Port Douglas, north of Cairns—usually from the decks of dive and cruise boats (which are forbidden by law from going within 1,640 feet of the rare cetacean). Sometimes Migaloo travels solo; on other journeys, he's accompanied by dolphins or fellow humpbacks. With humpback numbers on Australia's east coast increasing by about 10% each year, hopefully you will spot Migaloo with more of his friends during your visit.

Migaloo's not the only albino whale you might spot on your visit to Australia. In 2018, an adorable albino humpback calf was spotted off the NSW coast.

Magnetic Island Taxi Service
This local taxi company services the entire island. Go to its website to prebook cabs and get fare estimates. ✉ *33 Keane St, Magnetic Island* ☎ *13–1008 toll-free in Australia, 07/3363–2317* 🌐 *www.131008.com.*

VISITOR INFORMATION

CONTACTS Queensland Parks and Wildlife Service, Magnetic Island. ✉ *22 Hurst St., Picnic Bay* ☎ *137–468 ParksQ hotline, toll-free in Australia* 🌐 *www.nprsr.qld.gov.au/parks/magnetic-island.*

Hotels

Magnetic Island began "life" as a holiday-home getaway for Townsville residents; only in the past decade has it attracted the kind of large-scale development that has transformed other islands near the Barrier Reef. Accommodations here are a mix of functional 1970s properties; small budget lodges; and newer, upmarket but relatively small apartment complexes and resorts. Luxurious Peppers Blue on Blue Resort is one of a handful of exceptions to the rule.

Peppers Blue On Blue Resort
$ | **RESORT** | **FAMILY** | The hotel and studio rooms, apartments, and penthouse suites at waterfront Blue on Blue are stylishly designed, with high-end entertainment systems, luxe amenities, and balconies overlooking the ferry port, pool, or the island's private marina. **Pros:** convenient launchpad for excursions; fine on-site food and wine; big buffet breakfasts include eggs made to order. **Cons:** not all rooms suitable for self-catering; lower-floor, ferry-side rooms can be noisy; some suites lack full elevator access. [$] *Rooms from: A$195* ✉ *123 Sooning St., adjacent to ferry terminal, Nelly Bay* ☎ *07/4758–2400 reception, 1300/987–600 reservations, toll-free in Australia* 🌐 *www.peppers.com.au/blue-on-blue* 🛏 *60 twin rooms, 127 apartment suites and penthouses* 🍴 *No Meals.*

Activities

The island has 24 km (15 miles) of hiking trails, most of which are relatively easy. The popular Forts Walk leads to World War II gun emplacements overlooking Horseshoe and Florence bays. At a leisurely pace, it takes about 45 minutes each way from the Horseshoe–Radical Bay Road. Look up en route and you may spot a sleepy koala.

Some of the island's best views are on the 5-km (3-mile) Nelly Bay to Arcadia Walk. Look out for shell middens created over thousands of years by the island's Aboriginal owners, the Wulgurukaba, or "Canoe People."

Swimming and snorkeling are other popular activities, but from November to May, box jellyfish ("stingers") are a hazard: swim at Picnic and Horseshoe bays, which have stinger nets, and wear a protective suit. At other times, Alma Bay and Nelly Bay, as well as Picnic, Florence, Radical, Horseshoe, and Balding bays, are all suitable for swimming. Horseshoe has daily lifeguard patrols and a stinger-free swimming enclosure; Alma and Picnic bays are patrolled over weekends and school holiday periods, September to May.

Geoffrey Bay has a well-trafficked unofficial snorkel trail. Other good snorkeling spots include Nelly Bay, Alma Bay (which has its own snorkel trail), and the northern ends of Florence and Arthur bays. Near the northeastern corner of the island, Radical Bay has a small, idyllic beach flanked by tree-covered rock outcrops. Horseshoe Bay, the island's largest beach, is lined with boat-rental outlets and water-sports equipment.

SNORKELING AND SCUBA DIVING

Pleasure Divers

DIVING & SNORKELING | FAMILY | The local guides at Pleasure Divers run good-value dive trips to the SS *Yongala* shipwreck and pristine Lodestone Reef on the outer Barrier Reef as well as snorkeling and diving in the waters off Magnetic Island. Day trips include two dives and buffet lunch. Optional introductory dives, adventure diving, and guided dives (compulsory for those with fewer than 15 logged dives) cost extra. Reef dive and snorkel trips run Tuesday, Thursday, Friday, and Sunday; *Yongala* trips run Wednesday and Saturday, departing Nelly Bay Ferry Terminal and Townsville. Pleasure Divers runs various SSI/PADI-accredited courses from the island, including refresher sessions and three-day, four-dive Open Water courses. ✉ *10 Marine Parade, Arcadia* ☎ *07/4778–5788* 🌐 *www.pleasuredivers.com.au* 🎟 *From A$50.*

TOAD RACES

Arcadia Village Hotel Toad Races

LOCAL SPORTS | FAMILY | A Magnetic Island institution, the Arcadia Village Hotel's weekly cane-toad races offer cut-price, Aussie-style hilarity. After each race, the winners kiss their toads and collect the proceeds, with funds raised going to the Arcadia Surf Life Saving Club. The Arcadia's cane-toad races have been held every Wednesday night from 8 pm for nearly three decades, despite several changes in the hotel's ownership. Even when the toads aren't racing, the hotel is pumping, with three well-patronized bars, regular live bands, pool tables, a big lagoon pool, and bistro meals. ✉ *Arcadia Village Motel, 1 Marine Parade, Arcadia* ☎ *07/4778–5177* 🌐 *www.arcadiavillagehotel.com.*

WATER SPORTS

Horseshoe Bay Watersports

WATER SPORTS | FAMILY | This outfitter can take you tube riding, wakeboarding, waterskiing, and sailing on a Hobie cat in the translucent waters of Horseshoe Bay. All tube rides are for a minimum of two people and start from A$15 per person for an exhilarating 10 minutes; an extra person can ride for free in the ski boat to take pictures. Horseshoe Bay Watersports also rents out an array of water-sports gear and equipment. Find them beside the boat ramp at the center of Horseshoe Bay, weather permitting. ✉ *Boat ramp, Pacific Dr., at Horseshoe Bay Rd., Horseshoe Bay* ☎ *07/4758–1336* 🎫 *From A$15.*

★ Magnetic Jet Ski Tours

WATER SPORTS | FAMILY | This operator offers tours through Magnetic Island's clear waters on SeaDoo four-stroke Jet Skis. Choose between the three-hour island circumnavigation (A$395 per ski) and the two-hour "Top End" tour (A$250 per ski), with up to two people on each ski. All equipment and instruction are included in the rate; no licenses required. ✉ *9 Pacific Dr., Horseshoe Bay* ☎ *07/4778–5533* 🌐 *www.facebook.com/MagneticJet* 🎫 *From A$250.*

Chapter 10

SOUTH AUSTRALIA

Updated by
Alexis Buxton-Collins

Sights ★★★★☆ | Restaurants ★★★★★ | Hotels ★★★★☆ | Shopping ★★★☆☆ | Nightlife ★★★★☆

WELCOME TO SOUTH AUSTRALIA

TOP REASONS TO GO

★ **Arts and Music:** South Australia has fantastic events: the Adelaide Fringe Festival, DreamBIG Children's Festival, and WOMADelaide's four-day celebration of music and dance, to name a few.

★ **Bush Tucker:** The Australian palate has been reeducated in the pleasures of bush tucker: taste kangaroo alongside native botanicals like sweet muntries, tart desert lime, and salty, succulent karkalla.

★ **Historic Homes:** Stay in historic properties in North Adelaide and the Adelaide Hills that offer easy access to the city, rustic villages, and vineyards.

★ **Wonderful Wines:** The top-notch wines of the Barossa Valley, McLaren Vale, Adelaide Hills, and Clare Valley are treasured by connoisseurs.

★ **Wildlife:** Kangaroo Island is Australia's third largest island and home to colonies of fur seals, sea lions, and penguins, along with tens of thousands of koalas, kangaroos, and wallabies.

1 **Adelaide.** South Australia's lively capital.

2 **Mt. Lofty.** Panoramic views of Adelaide.

3 **Bridgewater.** Home to an historic mill.

4 **Lyndoch.** A perfect base for Barossa.

5 **Tanunda.** Distinctly German-feeling town.

6 **Angaston.** Historic and alcoholic attractions.

7 **Nuriootpa.** Commercial center of Valley.

8 **Marananga.** Wineries and restaurants.

9 **Sevenhill.** Explore vineyards and wineries.

10 **Clare.** A bustling town in Clare Valley.

11 **McLaren Vale.** Great wineries and scenery.

12 **Goolwa.** Upmarket vacation destination.

13 **Victor Harbor.** SA's favorite seaside getaway.

14 **Kingscote.** Base for exploring Kangaroo Island (KI).

15 **Penneshaw.** A tiny ferry port on KI.

16 **Seal Bay Conservation Park.**

17 **Flinders Chase National Park.**

18 **Coober Pedy.** An underground town.

19 **Ikara-Flinders Ranges National Park.**

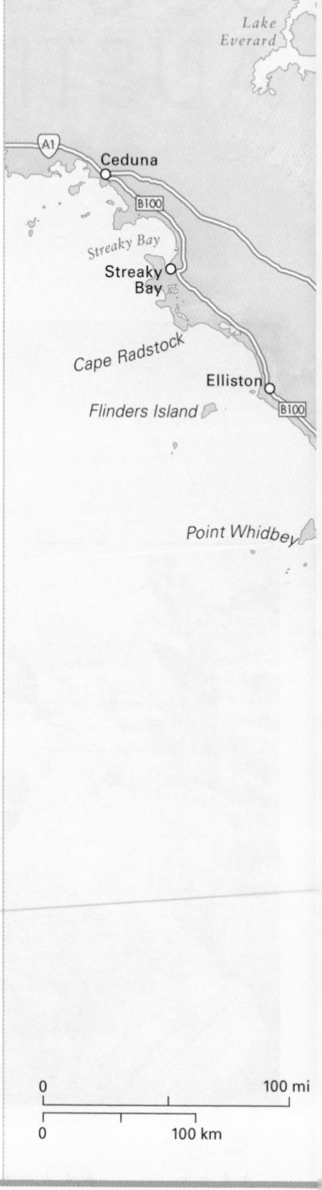

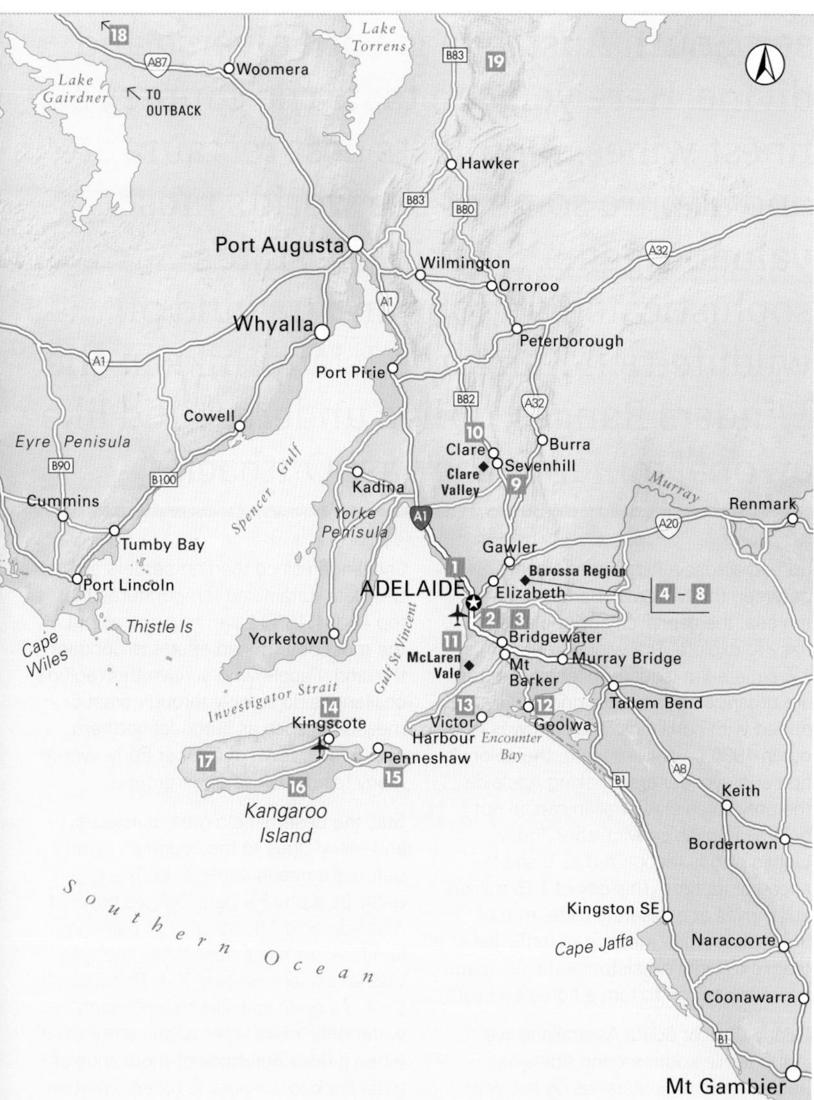
18
Lake Torrens
B83
19
Lake Gairdner
A87
Woomera
TO OUTBACK
Hawker
B83
B80
Port Augusta
A32
Wilmington
Orroroo
A1
Whyalla
Peterborough
A1
Port Pirie
B82
A32
Cowell
10
Burra
Eyre Penisula
Clare
Sevenhill
Clare Valley
9
B90
B100
Spencer Gulf
Kadina
Murray
Cummins
Yorke Penisula
A1
Renmark
A20
Tumby Bay
Gawler
1
Barossa Region
Port Lincoln
ADELAIDE
Elizabeth
4 - 8
2
3
Thistle Is
Cape Wiles
Yorketown
11
Bridgewater
Gulf St Vincent
McLaren Vale
Mt Barker
Murray Bridge
Investigator Strait
14
13
12
Tallem Bend
Kingscote
Victor Harbour
Encounter Bay
Goolwa
17
Penneshaw
15
16
A8
B1
Kangaroo Island
Keith
Bordertown
Southern Ocean
Kingston SE
Cape Jaffa
Naracoorte
Coonawarra
B1
Mt Gambier

Renowned for its celebrations of the arts, its highly developed food culture, and bountiful harvests from vines, land, and sea, South Australia is both diverse and divine. Here you can taste the country's finest wines, sample its best restaurants, and admire some of the world's most valuable gems. Or skip the state's sophisticated options and unwind on wildlife-rich Kangaroo Island, hike in the Flinders Ranges, or live underground like an opal miner in the vast Outback.

Spread across a flat saucer of land between the Mt. Lofty Ranges and the sea, the capital city of Adelaide is easy to explore. The wide streets of its 1½-square-km (square-mile) city center are organized in a simple grid that's ringed with parklands. The plan was laid out in 1836 by William Light, the colony's first surveyor-general, making Adelaide the only colonial Australian capital not built by English convict labor. Today Light's plan is recognized as being far ahead of its time. This city of 1.15 million still moves at a leisurely pace, free of the typical urban menace of traffic jams thanks to Light's insistence that all roads be wide enough to turn a horse and cart.

Nearly 90% of South Australians live in the fertile south around Adelaide, because the region stands on the very doorstep of the harshest, driest land in the most arid of Earth's populated continents. Jagged hills and stony deserts fill the parched interior, which is virtually unchanged since the first settlers arrived. Desolate terrain and temperatures that top 48°C (118°F) have thwarted all but the most determined efforts to conquer the land. People who survive this region's challenges do so only through drastic measures, such as in the far-northern opal-mining town of Coober Pedy, where many residents live underground.

Still, the deserts hold great surprises, and many clues to the country's history before European settlement. The ruggedly beautiful Flinders Ranges north of Adelaide hold Aboriginal cave paintings and fossil remains from when the area was an ancient seabed. Kati-Thanda-Lake Eyre is a great salt lake that fills with water only a few times each century, but when it does hundreds of thousands of birds flock to the area to breed, creating an unforgettable spectacle. The Nullarbor ("treeless") Plain stretches west across state lines in its tirelessly flat, ruthlessly arid march into Western Australia.

Yet South Australia is, perhaps ironically, gifted with the good life. It produces most of the nation's wine, and the sea ensures a plentiful supply of rock lobster and famed King George whiting. Cottages and guesthouses tucked away in the countryside around Adelaide are among the most charming and relaxing in Australia. Farther afield, unique experiences like watching seal pups cuddle with their mothers on Kangaroo Island would warm any heart. South Australia may not be grand in reputation, but its attractions are extraordinary, and after a visit you'll know you've indulged in one of Australia's best-kept secrets.

MAJOR REGIONS

Adelaide retains the atmosphere of a large country town despite being a major urban center and Australia's premier festival city. Sitting on southern Australia's coast, Adelaide has fascinating museums, inventive restaurants, and is the entry point to four major wine regions. It also is a starting point for some tours to Kangaroo Island.

Secluded green slopes and flowery gardens turn the **Adelaide Hills** into a pastoral vision in this desert state. The patchwork quilt of vast orchards, neat vineyards, and avenues of tall conifers resembles the Tuscan countryside, while 19th-century German immigrants also left their mark. In summer the hills are consistently cooler than the city, although the charming towns and wineries are pleasant to visit any time of year. Towns in the Adelaide Hills region include Mt. Lofty and Bridgewater.

The **Barossa wine region,** which is just over an hour's drive northeast of Adelaide, was settled by Silesian immigrants who left the German–Polish border region in the 1840s to escape religious persecution. These farmers brought traditions that you can't miss in the solid bluestone architecture, the tall slender spires of the Lutheran churches, and the *kuchen,* a cake as popular as the Devonshire tea introduced by British settlers. It's also one of the country's best-known wine regions—almost 200 wineries across the region's two wide, shallow valleys produce celebrated wines. Most wineries in the Barossa operate sale rooms (called cellar doors) that can have up to a dozen varieties of wine available for tasting. You are not expected to sample the entire selection; to do so would overpower your taste buds. It's far better to give the tasting-room staff some idea of your personal preferences and let them suggest wine for you to sample. Many also offer premium experiences that must be booked in advance. Towns in the Barossa wine region include Lyndoch, Tanunda, Angaston, Nuriootpa, and Marananga.

Smaller and less well known than the Barossa, the **Clare Valley** nonetheless holds its own among Australia's wine-producing regions. Its robust reds and delicate whites are among the country's finest, and the Clare Valley is generally regarded as the best area in Australia for fragrant, flavorsome Rieslings. On the fringe of the vast inland deserts, the Clare Valley is a narrow sliver of fertile soil about 30 km (19 miles) long and 5 km (3 miles) wide, with a microclimate and varied soil profiles that make it ideal for premium wine making. The first vines were planted here as early as 1842, but it took a century and a half for the Clare Valley to take its deserved place on the national stage. The mix of small family wineries and large-scale producers, 150-year-old settlements and grand country houses, snug valleys and dense native forests, has rare charm. The most iconic way to explore the valley is via the gentle cycling trail that meanders along its length. Clare Valley towns include Sevenhill and Clare.

The **Fleurieu Peninsula** has traditionally been seen as Adelaide's backyard. McLaren Vale wineries attract connoisseurs, and the beaches and bays bring in surfers, swimmers, and sun-seekers. Generations of local families have vacationed in the string of beachside resorts between Victor Harbor and Goolwa, near the mouth of the Murray River. The countryside, with its rolling hills and dramatic cliff scenery, is a joy to drive through. Although the region is within easy reach of Adelaide, you should consider spending the night if you want to enjoy all it has to offer. You can also easily combine a visit here with one or more nights on Kangaroo Island.

Remote, beautiful, and just falling on the right side of isolated, **Kangaroo Island** remains a paradise for animal lovers despite the 2020 bushfires that affected its western half. Australia's third-largest island is barely 16 km (10 miles) from the Australian mainland, yet the island belongs to another age—a folksy, friendly, less sophisticated time when you'd leave your car unlocked and knew everyone by name. The island is most beautiful along the coastline, where the land is sculpted into a series of bays and inlets teeming with bird and marine life. The stark interior has its own charm, however, with pockets of red earth between stretches of bush and farmland. Wildlife is probably the island's greatest attraction; you can stroll along a beach crowded with sea lions and watch kangaroos, koalas, pelicans, and little penguins in their native environments. You could easily spend a week here, but if you only have one day, start with the southern coast, where the standout sights are, and tour the island in a clockwise direction, leaving the north-coast beaches for the afternoon. Before heading out, fill your gas tank and pack a picnic lunch. Shops are few and far between outside the towns, and general stores are the main outlets for food and gas. The island is home to Seal Bay Conservation Park and Flinders Chase National Park as well as towns including Kingscote and Penneshaw.

Heading north of Adelaide, a trip to South Australia's **Outback** gives visitors a glimpse into an arid and dramatic landscape that is unmistakably Australian. An expanse of desert vegetation, this land of scrubby salt bush and hardy eucalyptus trees is brightened after rain by wildflowers—including the state's floral emblem, the blood-red Sturt's desert pea, with its black, olive-like heart. The terrain is marked by geological uplifts, abrupt transitions between plateaus at the edges of ancient, long-inactive fault lines. Few roads track through this desert wilderness—the main highway is the Stuart, which runs all the way to Alice Springs in the Northern Territory. The people of the Outback are as hardy as their surroundings. They are also often eccentric, colorful characters who happily bend your ear over a drink in the local pub. Remote, isolated communities attract loners, adventurers, fortune-seekers, and people simply on the run. In this unyielding country, you must be tough to survive. Ikara-Flinders Ranges National Park is in South Australia's Outback, as is the town of Coober Pedy.

Planning

When to Go

Adelaide has the least rainfall of all Australian capital cities, and the midday summer heat is oppressive. The Outback in particular is too hot for comfortable touring during this time, but Outback winters are pleasantly warm during the day while at night temperatures plummet. South Australia's national parks are open year-round. The best times to visit are in spring and autumn. In summer extreme fire danger may close walking tracks, and in winter heavy rain can make some roads impassable. Boating on the Murray River and Lake Alexandrina is best from October to March, when the long evenings are bathed in soft light, though you can expect crowds during the summer holidays which last from mid-December until the end of March. The ocean is warmest from December to March.

Planning Your Time

Many of the state's attractions are an easy drive from Adelaide. However, for a taste of the real South Australia a trip to a national park or to the Outback is definitely worth the extra travel time. Short flights between destinations make any journey possible within a day or overnight, but the more time you leave yourself to explore the virtues of this underrated state, the better.

If you have limited time, spend your first day in Adelaide enjoying the museums and historic sights as well as the bustling Central Market. Take a sunset stroll along the Torrens, then have dinner and drinks at one of the city's vibrant restaurants or laneway bars before retiring for the night. On Day 2 tour the Adelaide Hills, strolling the streets of 19th-century villages and taking in the panorama from atop Mt. Lofty. Stay the night in a charming B&B in one of the region's small towns, or come back down to North Adelaide and rest among the beautiful sandstone homes. Save Day 3 for wine tasting in the Barossa Valley.

If you have more time, expand your horizons beyond Adelaide and take a tram-car ride to the beach at touristy Glenelg or its neighbors at laid-back Brighton or posher Henley Beach, where you can laze on the white sands and watch the sun set over the ocean. Spend the night here or at a B&B on the Fleurieu Peninsula, then take Day 3 to explore the vineyards of McLaren Vale and catch the ferry to Kangaroo Island. After a night here, use Day 4 to explore and appreciate the island's wildlife and untamed beauty. Return to Adelaide in the afternoon on Day 5 and drive up to the Adelaide Hills for sunset at Mt. Lofty.

Getting Here and Around

AIR

Adelaide Airport, 15 minutes from the city center, is a pleasant place to fly into and the state's main hub. The international and domestic terminals share a modern building complete with cafés, a tourist office, and free Wi-Fi.

International airlines serving Adelaide include Singapore Airlines, Malaysia Airlines, Cathay Pacific, Air New Zealand, Qatar Airways, China Southern Airways, and Emirates. Qantas also connects Adelaide with many international cities (usually via Melbourne or Sydney). Domestic airlines flying into Adelaide include Qantas, Jetstar, Rex Airlines, and Virgin Australia. You can also fly to Coober Pedy, Port Augusta, and Kangaroo Island from here.

BUS

Adelaide's Central Bus Station is the state's main hub for travel across the region as well as interstate services to Melbourne and Sydney. It's difficult and time-consuming to travel by bus to the wine regions, however; we recommend either renting a car or taking a tour.

CAR

The best way to experience this diverse state is by road. In general driving conditions are excellent, although minor roads may be unpaved in regional areas. It's one hour from Adelaide to the wineries of McLaren Vale or the Barossa, while Clare, the southern coast, and most other major sights can be reached in under two hours. The most direct route to the Flinders Ranges is via the Princes Highway and Port Augusta, but a more interesting route takes you through the Clare Valley vineyards.

TRAIN

If you love train travel, you might find yourself stopping in Adelaide, as two classic train journeys also wind through this state: the *Ghan,* which runs north via

Alice Springs to Darwin, and the *Indian Pacific,* which crosses the Nullarbor Plain on its way from Sydney to Perth. More prosaically, you can catch a train to Sydney or Melbourne, though often budget airlines are much cheaper.

Restaurants

Foodies are spoiled for choice in South Australia; the region is famous throughout the country for its excellent produce. Make sure you try some of Adelaide's Mod Oz cuisine, with dishes showcasing oysters, crayfish, and King George whiting prepared with Asian and Mediterranean flavors. Native Australian ingredients are also used in some eateries; look out for kangaroo, lemon myrtle, samphire, and wattleseed.

Many restaurants close for a few days a week, so call ahead to check. Some upscale institutions require booking well in advance, and tables are tight during major city festivals and holidays.

Hotels

As well as all the standard chains, South Australia is packed with delightful lodgings in contemporary studios, converted cottages, and grand mansions. Modern resorts sprawl along the coastal suburbs, the Barossa Valley, and other tourist centers, but intimate properties for 10 or fewer guests can easily be found.

There is plenty of competition in Adelaide, so shop around for great deals. Outside the city, weekday nights are usually less expensive and two-night minimum bookings often apply.

Restaurant and hotel reviews have been shortened. For full information, visit Fodors.com.

What It Costs in Australian Dollars

$	$$	$$$	$$$$
RESTAURANTS			
under A$21	A$21–A$35	A$36–A$50	over A$50
HOTELS			
under A$151	A$151–A$200	A$201–A$300	over A$300

Wineries

Oenophiles rejoice: in South Australia you've arrived in wine heaven. SA is the country's wine powerhouse, producing most of the nation's wine and boasting some of the oldest vineyards in the world. Thanks to its diverse geography and climate, the region produces a huge range of grape varieties—from cool-climate Rieslings in the Clare Valley to the big, full-bodied Shiraz wines of the world-famous Barossa. Less well known, McLaren Vale now punches above its weight with an exceptional variety of grapes, including exquisite Grenache and Mediterranean varietals like Tempranillo, Nero d'avila, and Vermentino, while just a 20-minute drive from Adelaide is Adelaide Hills, where temperatures are lower than the rest of the region, leading to great sparkling wines and Pinot Noir.

Although you can drive yourself to any of these regions, strict drunk-driving laws mean that the unfortunate designated driver will be restricted to a few sips, if that. We highly recommend that you leave the driving to professionals.

D'Arenberg Cube
In South Australia's McLaren Vale wine region, the avant-garde d'Arenberg Cube offers public and private tasting rooms, wine-blending workshops, virtual fermenters, master classes, and an art gallery in a multistory structure resembling a half-solved Rubik's cube. The winery itself, of course, is now its unmissable epicenter. There are multiple daytime dining options

on-site, including Polly's Wine Lounge and d'Arry's Verandah Restaurant, the latter of which is located inside a restored 19th-century house, both open for lunch daily. Entrance to the Cube is A$15 and includes a tasting flight. ✉ *58 Osborn Rd., McLaren Vale* ☎ *8/8329–4888* 🌐 *www.darenberg.com.au.*

A Taste of South Australia
For a luxurious tour option in the region, go with Mary Anne Kennedy, the owner of A Taste of South Australia, who is one of the most knowledgeable regional food and wine guides. Her boutique tours of any region you choose with lunch included are a tasty treat. ☎ *0419/861–588* 🌐 *www.tastesa.com.au* *Tours from A$495.*

Adelaide

Australians think of Adelaide as a city of churches, but Adelaide has outgrown its reputation as a sleepy country town dotted with cathedrals and spires. The Adelaide of this millennium is infinitely more complex, with a large, multiethnic population and thriving urban art and music scenes supported by an activation program that encourages pop-up shops, markets, performances, street food, minifestivals, art exhibitions, and other "off-the-cuff" experiences in the city's underutilized streets and public spaces.

GETTING HERE AND AROUND

Bright and clean, leafy and beautiful Adelaide is a breeze to explore, with a grid pattern of streets encircled by parkland. The heart of the greenbelt is divided by the meandering River Torrens, which turns into a lake beside the the Festival Centre in its prettiest stretch.

A car gives you the freedom to discover the country lanes and villages in the hills region outside the city, and Adelaide also has excellent road connections with other states. But South Australia is a big place, and we recommend flying if you're looking to save time. Adelaide has an excellent bus system, including the no-cost Adelaide Free City Connector buses, which make about 30 downtown stops. Free guides to Adelaide's public bus lines are available from the Adelaide Metro Info Centre. The city's only surviving tram route now runs between the Entertainment Centre in Hindmarsh through the city to the beach at Glenelg. Ticketing is identical to that on city buses; travel between South Terrace and the Entertainment Centre on Port Road is free.

To reach the Adelaide Hills region from Adelaide, head toward the M1 Princes Highway or drive down Pulteney Street and on to Glen Osmond Road, which becomes the M1. From here signs point to Crafers and the freeway.

Ride apps are more common these days—those commonly in use in Adelaide are Ola, Uber, and Didi.

TAXI Suburban Taxis. ☎ *131–008* 🌐 *www.suburbantaxis.com.au.* **Yellow Cabs.** ☎ *132–227* 🌐 *www.yellowadelaide.com.au.*

WHEN TO GO

FESTIVALS

Adelaide Festival of Arts
Australia's oldest arts festival takes place annually for 2½ weeks in February and March. It's a cultural smorgasbord of outdoor opera, classical music, jazz, art exhibitions, film, a writers' festival, and cabaret presented by some of the world's top artists; it's held across the city at a variety of venues. ✉ *City Center* ☎ *08/8216–4444* 🌐 *www.adelaidefestival.com.au.*

Adelaide Fringe Festival
The Fringe Festival, held over four weeks during mid-February and mid-March, is the second largest of its kind in the world. It's an open-access arts festival, featuring cabaret, street performances, comedy, circus, music, visual art, theater, puppetry, dance, and design, all across Adelaide and its surroundings, while regional offshoots take the

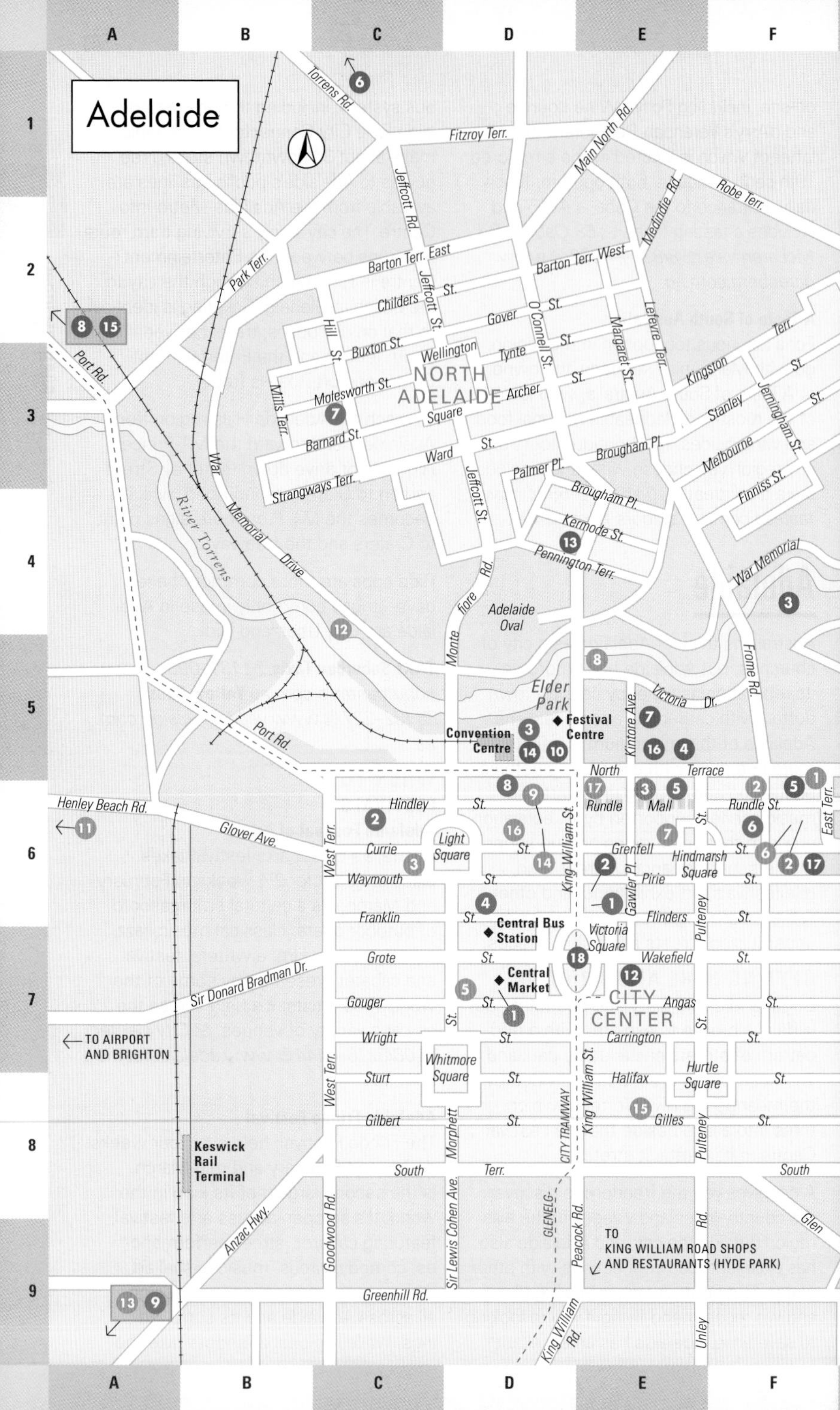

Adelaide
NORTH ADELAIDE
CITY CENTER
Adelaide Oval
Elder Park
Convention Centre
Festival Centre
Central Bus Station
Central Market
Light Square
Victoria Square
Hindmarsh Square
Whitmore Square
Hurtle Square
Keswick Rail Terminal
River Torrens
TO AIRPORT AND BRIGHTON
TO KING WILLIAM ROAD SHOPS AND RESTAURANTS (HYDE PARK)
CITY TRAMWAY
GLENELG
Torrens Rd.
Fitzroy Terr.
Main North Rd.
Robe Terr.
Medindie Rd.
Jeffcott Rd.
Park Terr.
Port Rd.
Barton Terr. East
Barton Terr. West
Childers St.
Gover St.
Buxton St.
Wellington Square
Tynte St.
Molesworth St.
Archer St.
Barnard St.
Ward St.
Strangways Terr.
Mills Terr.
Hill St.
Jeffcott St.
O'Connell St.
Margaret St.
Lefevre Terr.
Kingston Terr.
Stanley St.
Melbourne St.
Jerningham St.
Finniss St.
Brougham Pl.
Palmer Pl.
Kermode St.
Pennington Terr.
War Memorial Drive
Montefiore Rd.
Frome Rd.
Victoria Dr.
Kintore Ave.
North Terrace
Hindley St.
Rundle Mall
Rundle St.
East Terr.
Henley Beach Rd.
Glover Ave.
West Terr.
Currie St.
Grenfell St.
Waymouth St.
Pirie St.
Franklin St.
Flinders St.
Grote St.
Wakefield St.
Gouger St.
Angas St.
Wright St.
Carrington St.
Sturt St.
Halifax St.
Gilbert St.
Gilles St.
South Terr.
Sir Donald Bradman Dr.
King William St.
Gawler Pl.
Pulteney St.
Morphett St.
Anzac Hwy.
Goodwood Rd.
Sir Lewis Cohen Ave.
Peacock Rd.
Greenhill Rd.
King William Rd.
Unley Rd.
Glen
A B C D E F
1 2 3 4 5 6 7 8 9

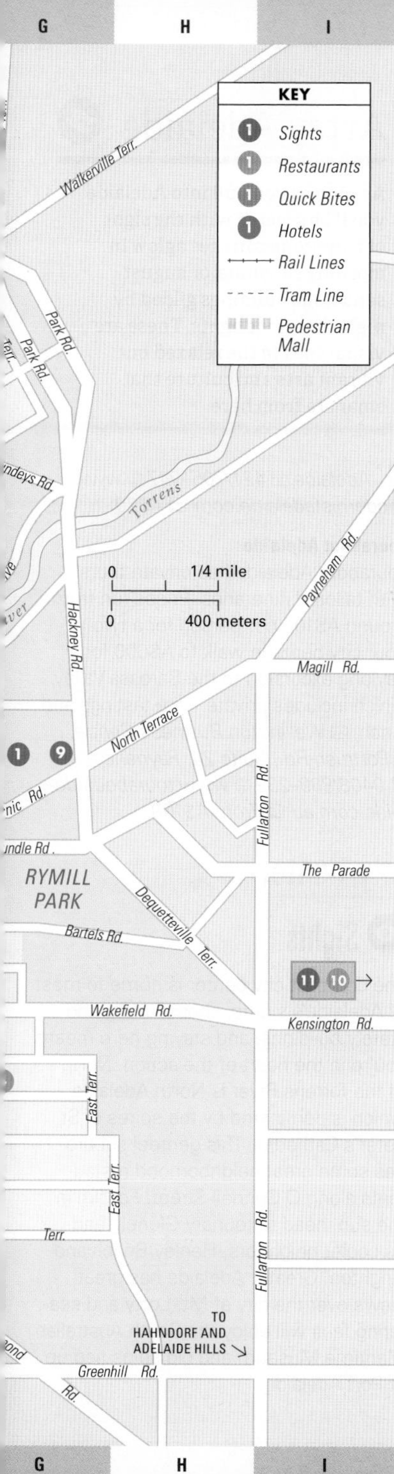

Sights

1 Adelaide Botanic Garden G5
2 Adelaide Town Hall...... E6
3 Adelaide Zoo F4
4 Art Gallery of South Australia E5
5 Ayers House............. F6
6 Coopers Brewery........ C1
7 Migration Museum...... E5
8 National Railway Museum A2
9 National Wine Centre of Australia G5
10 Parliament House....... D5
11 Penfolds Magill Estate ... I7
12 St. Francis Xavier's Cathedral E7
13 St. Peter's Cathedral.... D4
14 SKYCITY Adelaide Casino D5
15 South Australian Maritime Museum...... A2
16 South Australian Museum E5
17 Tandanya National Aboriginal Cultural Institute F6
18 Victoria Square/ Tarntanyangga.......... D7

Restaurants

1 Africola F5
2 Amalfi Pizzeria Ristorante................ F6
3 Aurora.................... C6
4 Chianti.................... G7
5 Concubine D7
6 Hey Jupiter F6
7 Jasmin Indian Restaurant................ E6
8 Jolleys Boathouse....... E5
9 Leigh Street Wine Room.............. D6
10 Magill Estate I7
11 Parwana A6
12 Red Ochre Barrel and Grill........... C4
13 Sammy's on the Marina.............. A9
14 Shobosho................ D6
15 Sibling.................... E8
16 Sunny's Pizza............ D6
17 2KW E6

Quick Bites

1 Big Table.................. D7
2 Exchange Coffee F6
3 Monday's E6

Hotels

1 Adina Apartment Hotel Adelaide Treasury E6
2 BreakFree on Hindley................... C6
3 Eos by SkyCity........... D5
4 The Franklin Boutique Hotel.......... D6
5 Hotel Richmond.......... E6
6 Majestic Roof Garden Hotel............. F6
7 North Adelaide Heritage Group........... C3
8 Oaks Adelaide Embassy Suites......... D6
9 Oaks Glenelg Plaza Pier Suites........ A9

party all around the state. ✉ *City Center* ☎ *08/8100–2000* 🌐 *www.adelaidefringe.com.au.*

WOMADelaide Festival
The annual four-day festival of world music, arts, and dance takes place in early March and attracts top musicians from all over the world to its multiple stages in the picturesque Botanic Park. ✉ *Botanic Park, Hackney Rd., Adelaide* ☎ *1300/496–623* 🌐 *www.womadelaide.com.au.*

TOURS

Adelaide Sightseeing
Adelaide Sightseeing operates pretty much every kind of tour you can think of. A morning city sights tour from the Central Business District (CBD) is joined by an afternoon bus tour of the Adelaide Hills and the German village of Hahndorf, and various other themed tours, including Nature and Wildlife Tours; Food and Wine Tours; River Cruises, and more. Prices are better if you book online. ✉ *85 Franklin St., Adelaide* ☎ *1300/769–762* 🌐 *www.adelaidesightseeing.com.au* 🎫 *From A$70.*

Gray Line Adelaide
Gray Line Adelaide is a long-standing luxury bus tour that provides morning city tours that take in all the highlights, as well as day-long tours of nearby Barossa Valley wineries, the natural wonderland of Kangaroo Island, and other attractions. ✉ *85 Franklin St., Adelaide* ☎ *1300/858–687* 🌐 *www.grayline.com.au* 🎫 *Tours from A$69.*

★ **Modernist Adelaide Walking Tour**
Architecture buffs and urban historians will love experiencing Adelaide through this walking tour, founded by mid-century modern architecture and design enthusiast Stuart Symons to celebrate Adelaide's modernist architecture. Bookings are essential for the 75-minute weekend walks; private group tours may also be arranged by appointment. See website for available dates and times. ✉ *Tours leave from Crack Kitchen, 13 Franklin St., Adelaide* ☎ *421/705–947* 🌐 *www.modernistadelaide.com* 🎫 *A$20.*

Artsy Adelaide

As soon as you pull into Adelaide you'll be greeted with the sight of tiny stone cottages aglow in morning sunshine, or august sandstone buildings gilded by nighttime floodlights. These are visual cues to the relaxed but vibrant arts and culture that emanate from here.

Tourabout Adelaide
Tourabout Adelaide has private tours with tailored itineraries. Prices run from around A$100 per person for a two-hour city heritage walk to A$600 for a daylong excursion to the Barossa Valley, which includes private wine tastings and lunch. ✉ *Wellington Business Centre, 2 Portrush Rd., Suite 24, Payneham* ☎ *0408/809–232* 🌐 *www.touraboutadelaide.com.au* 🎫 *From A$100.*

City Center

The compact city center is home to most of Adelaide's sights, shops, and grand stately buildings, and staying here means you're in the heart of the action. North of the Torrens River is North Adelaide, which is dominated by the spires of St. Peter's Cathedral. This genteel suburb has some great neighborhood restaurants along O'Connell Street. For fun in the sun, head to touristy Glenelg and its cooler neighbors, Henley Beach and Brighton. Greater Adelaide has great views over the city at Mt. Lofty and seafaring fans will enjoy the South Australian Maritime Museum and old ships tied up at Port Adelaide.

Botanic Gardens of Adelaide

★ Adelaide Botanic Garden

GARDEN | FAMILY | These magnificent formal gardens include an international rose garden, giant water lilies, an avenue of Moreton Bay fig trees, acres of green lawns, and duck ponds. The Bicentennial Conservatory—the largest single-span glass house in the southern hemisphere—provides an environment for lowland rain-forest species such as the cassowary palm and torch ginger. The Santos Museum of Economic Botany contains fascinating exhibits on the commercial use of some species, and on-site Restaurant Botanic utilizes many plants grown on-site in exquisite degustations. In summer the Moonlight Cinema series (*www.moonlight.com.au*) screens new, classic, and cult films in Botanic Park, adjacent the garden at sunset; if you forget a picnic blanket you can hire one as well as buy drinks and snacks. Tickets sell fast, so plan ahead. Check the website for workshops, events, and concerts in the park. ✉ *Botanic Rd., North Terr., City Center* ☎ *08/8222–9311* 🌐 *www.botanicgardens.sa.gov.au* 🎫 *Free.*

Adelaide Town Hall

GOVERNMENT BUILDING | An imposing building constructed in 1863 in Renaissance style, the Town Hall was modeled after buildings in Genoa and Florence. Tours visit the Colonel Light Room, where objects used to map and plan Adelaide are exhibited, and there are frequently traveling art exhibitions. The balcony of the Town Hall is famous for the appearance of the Beatles in 1964, which attracted the venue's largest crowd to date: approximately 300,000 screaming fans. ✉ *128 King William St., City Center* ☎ *08/8203–7590* 🌐 *www.adelaidetownhall.com.au.*

Adelaide Zoo

ZOO | FAMILY | Australia's second-oldest zoo still retains much of its original architecture. Enter through the 1883 cast-iron gates to see such animals as the giant pandas, Sumatran tigers, Australian rain-forest birds, and chimpanzees housed in modern, natural settings. The zoo is world renowned for its captive breeding and release programs, and rare species including the red panda and South Australia's own yellow-footed rock wallaby are among its successes. In 2008, the Australian government and Adelaide Zoo signed a cooperative agreement to help secure the long-term survival of the giant panda, and in 2009 Wang Wang and Fu Ni arrived on loan from China to become the only giant pandas in the southern hemisphere, and the first to live permanently in Australia. Special VIP panda tours are also available, as are Keeper For A Day tours that let you go behind the scenes and interact with a range of animals. Ask at the ticket office about feeding times, and consult the website for opening times for specific areas of the zoo. ✉ *Frome Rd., near War Memorial Dr., City Center* ☎ *08/8267–3255* 🌐 *www.adelaidezoo.com.au* 🎫 *A$39.*

Art Gallery of South Australia
ART MUSEUM | FAMILY | Many famous Australian painters, including Charles Conder, Margaret Preston, Clifford Possum Tjapaltjarri, Russell Drysdale, and Sidney Nolan, are represented in here. Extensive Renaissance and British artworks are on display, and the atrium houses Aboriginal pieces. There is usually a visiting exhibition, too. A café and bookshop are also on-site. ✉ *North Terr., near Pulteney St., City Center* ☎ *08/8207–7000* 🌐 *www.agsa.sa.gov.au.*

Ayers House
HISTORIC HOME | FAMILY | Between 1855 and 1897 this sprawling colonial structure was the home of Sir Henry Ayers, South Australia's premier and the man for whom Uluru was originally named Ayers Rock. Most rooms—including the unusual Summer Sitting Room, in the cool of the basement—have been restored with period furnishings and the state's best examples of 19th-century costumes and lifestyle. Entrance is free on weekends and volunteers lead guided tours when they're available. ✉ *288 North Terr., City Center* ☎ *08/8223–1234* 🌐 *www.ayershousemuseum.org.au* 🎫 *Free.*

Migration Museum
OTHER MUSEUM | Chronicled in this converted 19th-century Destitute Asylum, which later in the 19th century served as a school where Aboriginal children were forced to train as servants to the British, are the origins, hopes, and fates of some of the millions of immigrants who settled in Australia during the past two centuries. The museum is starkly realistic, and the bleak welcome that awaited many migrants is graphically illustrated, while temporary exhibitions point to a more hopeful future. ✉ *82 Kintore Ave., City Center* ☎ *08/8207–7580* 🌐 *migration.history.sa.gov.au* 🎫 *Free.*

National Wine Centre of Australia
WINERY | Timber, steel, and glass evoke the ribs of a huge wine barrel, and a soaring, open-plan concourse make this a spectacular showcase for Australian wines set on the edge of the Botanic Gardens. The A$15 Wine Discovery Journey, offered daily at 11 am, takes you from Neolithic pottery jars to a stainless-steel tank; you can even make your own virtual wine on a touch-screen computer. The center's guided tastings start at A$25 per person. In the Wined Bar, 120 wines drawn from all over Australia can be tasted in flights from state-of-the-art enomatic servers with iconic drops including Penfold's Grange and Henschke's Hill of Grace making regular appearances. The Wined Bar has a good all-day menu, including a great selection of local cheeses and smoked meats. ✉ *Hackney Rd. at Botanic Rd., City Center* ☎ *08/8313–3355* 🌐 *nationalwinecentre.com.au* 🎫 *Free.*

Parliament House
NOTABLE BUILDING | Ten Corinthian columns are the most striking features of this classical parliament building. It was completed in two stages 50 years apart: the west wing in 1889 and the east wing in 1939. Alongside is **Old Parliament**

An exhibition at the Pacific Cultures Gallery, Adelaide

House, which dates from 1843. There's a free guided tour of both houses weekdays at 10 and 2 during nonsitting days. The viewing gallery is open to the public when parliament is sitting. ✉ *North Terr. at King William St., City Center* ☎ *08/8237–9467* 🌐 *www.parliament.sa.gov.au.*

SKYCITY Adelaide Casino

CASINO | Housed in one half of Adelaide's grand neoclassical railway station, SkyCity is the place to go for every type of gaming, from chiming poker machines to high-stakes Texas hold 'em. The complex is also home to four bars, including the elegant Chandelier Bar, and seven restaurants, and is one of the few places in Adelaide that keeps pumping until dawn. ✉ *125 North Terr., City Center* ☎ *08/8212–2811* 🌐 *www.skycityadelaide.com.au.*

South Australian Museum

COLLEGE | **FAMILY** | This museum's Aboriginal Cultures Gallery houses the largest collection of Indigenous Australian cultural material in the world. Old black-and-white films show traditional dancing, and touch screens convey desert life. Also in the museum are an exhibit commemorating renowned Antarctic explorer Sir Douglas Mawson, after whom Australia's main Antarctic research station is named; an Opal-Fossils Gallery housing the world's most expensive opals and the fantastic opalized partial skeleton of a 19-foot-long plesiosaur; and a biodiversity gallery. There's also a café overlooking a grassy lawn. If you are traveling during local school holidays, there are fantastic interactive craft and education activities for children for a small fee. ✉ *North Terr., near Gawler Pl., City Center* ☎ *08/8207–7500* 🌐 *www.samuseum.sa.gov.au* 🎫 *Free.*

St. Francis Xavier's Cathedral

CHURCH | This church faced a bitter battle over construction after the 1848 decision to build a Catholic cathedral. It's now a prominent, decorative church with a soaring nave, stone arches through to side aisles with dark-wood ceilings, and beautiful stained-glass windows. For a self-guided tour, a useful free booklet called "19 minute Cathedral Tour" is available by the entrance. ✉ *17 Wakefield St., at Victoria Sq., City Center* ☎ *08/8232–8688* 🌐 *www.adelcathparish.org.*

St. Peter's Cathedral

CHURCH | The spires and towers of this cathedral dramatically contrast with the nearby city skyline. St. Peter's is the epitome of Anglican architecture in Australia, and an important example of grand Gothic Revival. Free 45-minute guided tours are available Wednesday at 11 and Sunday at 12:30. ✉ *27 King William St., North Adelaide* ☎ *08/8267–4551* 🌐 *www.stpeters-cathedral.org.au.*

★ **Tandanya National Aboriginal Cultural Institute**

COLLEGE | A must-see, Tandanya is the first major Aboriginal cultural facility of its kind in Australia. You'll find worthwhile changing exhibitions of works by contemporary, notable Aboriginal artists, and a theater where you can watch cultural performances and shows by visiting artists from around the country and the Pacific Islands. There's a great gift shop, too, where you can buy Aboriginal-designed household goods, apparel, and artwork. ✉ *253 Grenfell St., City Center* ☎ *08/8224–3200* 🌐 *www.tandanya.com.au* 🎟 *Free* 🕒 *Closed Sun.*

Victoria Square/Tarntanyangga

PLAZA/SQUARE | Known as the "place of the red kangaroo dreaming" to Kaurna traditional owners and designated by William Light as the geographical center of Adelaide, this public space is the city's focal point and a popular meeting spot. The fountain in the square, which is floodlighted at night, celebrates the three rivers that supply Adelaide's water: the Torrens, Onkaparinga, and Murray; each is represented by a stylized man or woman paired with an Australian native bird. The park hosts many events and attracts lunching office workers while shoppers and tourists come and go from the Glenelg-City Tram, which stops here on its way through the city. ✉ *King William, Grote, and Wakefield Sts., City Center* 🌐 *www.adelaidecitycouncil.com.*

Restaurants

Gouger, Hutt, O'Connell, and Rundle Streets are the historic eating strips in Adelaide, while an increasing number of restaurants are clustered in the lively pedestrian-only laneways of Leigh and Peel Streets. Outside the city center, The Parade in Norwood, King William Street in Unley, and Jetty Road in Glenelg also have plenty of options and are fun to stroll around until a restaurant or café catches your fancy.

If you feel like an alfresco picnic, pick up some delicious local produce from the Central Market. On Moonta Street, right next to the Central Market, two food courts are bustling Pan-Asian food halls. They feature modern Asian design with beautiful lighting, lovely green foliage, and ornate timber throughout. Chinatown Plaza includes highlights such as dim sum at Yum Cha, fresh Malaysian food at Kampung Boy, and modern Japanese at Izakaya.

Africola

$$$ | **AFRICAN** | This is one of the city's most original places both in terms of interior design (including a vibrant Technicolor bar and dining space) and the Modern Australian menu, featuring South African–inspired and somewhat kitschy dishes with robust flavors such as the spicy, smoked peri peri chicken and crispy chicken skin "tea sandwich." The wine list is brief but well curated and leans toward natural numbers; alternatively you can bring your own for A$20. **Known for:** great cocktails; eclectic and lively decor and atmosphere; cooking that's way outside the box. $ *Average main: A$50* ✉ *4 East Terr., City Center* ☎ *08/8223–3885* 🌐 *www.africola.com.au* 🕒 *Closed Sun. and Mon.*

Amalfi Pizzeria Ristorante

$$ | **ITALIAN** | This local favorite is rustic and noisy, with professionals and university students engaging in enthusiastic conversation. The terrazzo-tile dining room is furnished with bare wooden tables and paper place-mat menus, which list traditional pizza and pasta dishes in two sizes—appetizer and entrée. **Known for:** stays open late; spaghetti marinara; comfort food with generous portions. *Average main: A$28 29 Frome St., City Center 08/8223–1948 Closed Sun. No lunch Sat.*

Aurora

$$$ | **MODERN AUSTRALIAN** | You wouldn't know it from first glance, but this restaurant is part of a multipurpose art space and there's plenty of creativity on the fine dining menu designed by South African chef Brendan Wessels. Expect nods to his homeland like the large braai in the kitchen that adds a touch of smoke to many dishes. **Known for:** trinchado with spiced chicken livers; highly sustainable ethos; perfect for dinner before (or after) a show in the same venue. *Average main: A$42 63 Light Sq., City Center 08/7089–9600 www.auroraadl.com.au No dinner Sun.-Tues. No lunch Sun.-Wed.*

Chianti

$$$ | **ITALIAN** | Family run since 1985, and located in one of Adelaide's iconic Victorian houses converted to commercial space, Chianti is all things to all people. Sit inside or outside and enjoy the award-winning breakfasts or, in the evenings, the traditional northern Italian trattoria cuisine. **Known for:** attentive service; classic brunches; European wines including a reserve list. *Average main: A$38 160 Hutt St., City Center 08/8232–7955 www.chianti.net.au Closed Sun.*

Concubine

$$ | **CHINESE FUSION** | This restaurant, located in Adelaide's premier Asian dining strip, is a step above its neighbors with modern Chinese dishes that utilize traditional spices and fresh local produce, meat, and fish. The service is professional yet warm and friendly, with an ambience that is second to none thanks to the funky decor and trendy vibe. **Known for:** seasonal, fresh ingredients; opulent space lit by colorful lanterns; good wines and cocktails. *Average main: A$30 132 Gouger St., City Center 08/8212–8288 www.concubine.com.au Closed Mon.*

Hey Jupiter

$$ | **FRENCH** | Owned by a French expat and his Australian wife, Hey Jupiter is in all aspects a Parisian brasserie transported to Adelaide—wicker seats, oyster happy hours, and all—but with better service and a wine list that goes far beyond average. Located on a quiet street near plenty of other shops and bars in Adelaide's bustling East End, Hey Jupiter is a great place to stop for weekend breakfast, lunch, or dinner, as well as a nice place to simply grab a drink after a long afternoon of shopping on Rundle Street. **Known for:** classic French food; patio dining; oyster platter. *Average main: A$35 11 Ebenezer Pl., City Center 0416/050–721 heyjupiter.com.au.*

★ **Jasmin Indian Restaurant**

$$ | **INDIAN** | Located in a basement off Hindmarsh Square, this elegant establishment is beautifully decorated with stylish timber furniture and local artwork. The dim lighting and relaxing background music really set the mood for some quality Indian cuisine, which is what you'll get in spades; in fact, you might want to try everything on the menu, and the Feed Me Menu allows for just that. **Known for:** friendly staff offering exceptional service; great local wine; the Punjabi lamb tandoori and prawn sambal—perennial favorites. *Average main: A$28 31 Hindmarsh Sq., City Center 08/8223–7837 www.jasmin.com.au No dinner Sun. and Mon. No lunch Sat.–Wed.*

Jolleys Boathouse
$$$ | **MODERN AUSTRALIAN** | There's a relaxed, nautical air at this mainstay—which perfectly suits the location on the south bank of the River Torrens. Sliding glass doors open onto a full-width front balcony for alfresco dining. **Known for:** generous portions; views over the River Torrens; seasonal menu with fresh choices. *Average main: A$42* *1 Jolleys La., Victoria Dr. at King William Rd., City Center* *08/8223–2891* *www.jolleysboathouse.com* *Closed Mon. and Tues. No lunch Sat. No dinner Sun.*

Leigh Street Wine Room
$$ | **MODERN AUSTRALIAN** | A restaurant masquerading as a natural wine bar, this former dry cleaner takes its design cues from trendy Parisian bistros. Come for predinner drinks—the walls are lined with 500 bottles of mostly natural wine and the knowledgeable staff are happy to point you in the right direction—then stay for the sophisticated share plates. **Known for:** acoustic baffling means noise levels are perfect; a comprehensive wine selection; the skewers of beef tongue are divine. *Average main: A$28* *9 Leigh St., City Center* *0498/765–855* *leighstreetwineroom.com* *Closed Mon. and Tues. No dinner Wed. and Thurs.*

Red Ochre Barrel and Grill
$$$$ | **MODERN AUSTRALIAN** | A sweeping view of Adelaide is the backdrop for contemporary workings of traditional bush meats such as kangaroo, emu, and wild boar, plus herbs, and fruits at this "floating" riverfront restaurant. The downstairs River Torrens Café, the restaurant's sister venue, is more informal, and offers a modern Italian menu for weekday lunches and dinners. **Known for:** steaks; famous take on pavlova, a classic Australian dessert; beautiful setting to dine. *Average main: A$60* *War Memorial Dr., North Adelaide* *08/8211–8555* *www.redochrebarrelandgrill.com.au* *Closed Sun. and Mon. No lunch.*

★ **Shobosho**
$$$ | **ASIAN FUSION** | If you've ever turned your nose up at Asian fusion, you may reconsider when you come to Shobosho, with its use of organic local ingredients and Korean and Japanese influences in the cooking. Everything about the space, from the approach to service to the immensely creative dishes—often cooked over coals—to the plateware and the atmosphere itself, strikes a balance between sophisticated and relaxed that is difficult to find in Adelaide. **Known for:** private downstairs yakitori bar; sake list features artisanal producers by the glass; yakitori (skewers) are delicious and simple. *Average main: A$40* *17 Leigh St., City Center* *08/8366–2224* *www.shobosho.com.au.*

Sibling
$ | **CAFÉ** | In 2018, Caitlin Duff and husband, Nathaniel Morse, opened this daily coffee shop, café, and coworking space next to the retail shop Ensemble, run by Caitlin's sister, Anny. They serve locally roasted coffee, cold-pressed juices, pots of tea, vegan baked goods, and more, including breakfast and lunch in an airy space flooded with natural light and brightened by hanging plants. **Known for:** ideal for vegetarians and vegans; beautiful mood-lifting atmosphere; healthy smoothies. *Average main: A$18* *96 Gilles St., City Center* *www.siblingcafe.com.au.*

Sunny's Pizza
$$ | **PIZZA** | Sourdough pizzas topped with house-made sauces and fresh local ingredients are the first reason that locals can't stop going to Sunny's any night of the week. Then there's the negronis so perfectly executed you'd swear you were in a piazza in Milano—plus the incredibly friendly service, the fun wine list featuring small producers from the Adelaide Hills and around Australia, DJs on weekend nights, and cold craft beers on draft. **Known for:** long waits for seating on busy nights; simple, contemporary

cocktails; fun atmosphere with lively music. [$] *Average main: A$25* ✉ *17 Solomon St., City Center* ☎ *0455/522–356* 🌐 *www.sunnys.pizza.*

2KW

$$ | **MODERN AUSTRALIAN** | It takes two elevators to get to this rooftop venue, but it's worth it for elegant Modern Australian dishes that make the most of highly seasonal produce—many local producers are name-checked on the menu. After dinner, retire to the adjacent bar overlooking the governor-general's house (and most of North Adelaide) for a nightcap. **Known for:** excellent service; fresh local seafood; fantastic drinks selection. [$] *Average main: A$35* ✉ *2 King William St., City Center* ☎ *08/8212–5511* 🌐 *www.2kwbar.com.au.*

Coffee and Quick Bites

★ Big Table

$ | **CAFÉ** | Simply the best breakfast choice in Adelaide, Big Table has been at the Central Market for over 20 years, and regulars know to get there early for a chance at one of the few tables. Sitting at the counter isn't too bad an option either, especially when you have treats like fresh banana bread with rhubarb conserve and ricotta to look forward to. **Known for:** good coffee; local favorite; breakfast bowls with local meats and seasonal items. [$] *Average main: A$16* ✉ *Adelaide Central Market, Southern Roadway, Stall 39/40, City Center* ☎ *08/8212–3899* 💳 *No credit cards* ⏲ *Closed Sun., Mon., and Wed. No dinner.*

★ Exchange Coffee

$ | **CAFÉ** | Conveniently located on a quiet street off Rundle Mall, this cozy and friendly specialty coffee shop has what it takes to pep customers up. Baristas prepare expertly sourced, single-origin coffees from various roasters, with the option to try espresso, Aeropress, or batch brew, and light, healthy, delicious fare for breakfast and lunch. **Known for:** lots of natural light; seriously good coffee; the signature Wallace sandwich, an upgrade on the classic BLT. [$] *Average main: A$18* ✉ *1–3/12–18 Vardon Ave., City Center* ☎ *0415/966–225* 🌐 *exchangecoffee.com.au.*

Monday's

$ | **CAFÉ** | After working in Melbourne with respected roasters Market Lane and Everyday Coffee, Monday's owner Jarrad Sharrock brought his knowledge back to his hometown of Adelaide and opened his own roastery and minimalist design café in 2017, to the delight of locals.This is his second site and in addition to excellent coffee serves a tight menu of bagels and delicious pastries made fresh at a nearby bakery. **Known for:** healthy, plant-based food options; sleek modern space; fantastic coffee including beans for sale to take home. [$] *Average main: A$12* ✉ *95 Grenfell St., City Center* 🌐 *www.mondays.coffee* ⏲ *Closed weekends.*

Hotels

At first glance, large, international, business-style hotels seem to dominate Adelaide—there's a Hilton, an InterContinental, and a Crowne Plaza—but there's actually a wide choice of places to rest your head. Adelaide's accommodations are a mix of traditional midrise hotels, backpacker hostels, an abundance of self-contained apartments, and charming bed-and-breakfasts, many in century-old sandstone buildings. With a car you'll be within easy reach of a Glenelg beach house or an Adelaide Hills B&B.

★ Adina Apartment Hotel Adelaide Treasury

$$$ | **HOTEL** | Contemporary Italian furnishings in white, slate-gray, and ochre are juxtaposed with 19th-century Adelaide architecture in this stylish Victoria Square hotel. **Pros:** short walk to Central Market; beautiful, classic building; one- and two-bedroom apartments have full kitchen facilities. **Cons:** gym and pool are quite small; building layout can be hard to

navigate; no on-site parking but parking station nearby. *Rooms from: A$249* *2 Flinders St., City Center* *08/8112–0000, 02/9356–5062* *www.adinahotels.com/en/apartments/adelaide-treasury* *79 rooms* *No Meals.*

BreakFree on Hindley

$ | **HOTEL** | Step out your door at this three-story redbrick complex in Adelaide's lively West End and you might think you're in the tropics—open-air walkways and palm trees suggest you're close to the beach. **Pros:** complex is on the Adelaide FREE bus route; great value for money; fully equipped kitchens. **Cons:** pricey parking; bathrooms could do with a face-lift; basic furnishings. *Rooms from: A$129* *255 Hindley St., City Center* *08/8217–2500* *www.breakfree.com.au/adelaide* *116 rooms* *No Meals.*

★ **Eos by SkyCity**

$$$$ | **HOTEL** | With bold contemporary architecture and hundreds of original local artworks adorning both rooms and public spaces this sleek hotel could double as a gallery, and the roomy suites are appropriately stylish. **Pros:** concierge services include an on-call trainer; some of Adelaide's largest rooms; views over the River Torrens from the River View Suites. **Cons:** breakfast not included; rooms can be considerably more expensive on weekends; attached to the casino. *Rooms from: A$450* *Festival Dr., City Center* *08/7077–3588* *www.skycityadelaide.com.au/hotel/eos-by-skycity* *No Meals* *120 rooms.*

The Franklin Boutique Hotel

$ | **B&B/INN** | Situated above the Franklin Hotel—a pub known for its relaxed but quirky atmosphere, good food, and micro beers—in the Central Business District, this hotel has seven uniquely and tastefully decorated rooms with all the amenities you'd expect, plus a Nespresso machine and original, unique artwork from local artists in each room. **Pros:** close to Central Market; free in-room snacks and drinks; fun boutique experience. **Cons:** finding free parking can be difficult; potential for noise from the downstairs pub; limited capacity. *Rooms from: A$149* *92 Franklin St., City Center* *08/8410–0036* *www.thefranklinhotel.com.au* *7 rooms* *No Meals.*

Hotel Richmond

$ | **HOTEL** | Situated in the center of Rundle Mall, the city's main shopping strip, the hotel is an original, 1920s art deco building and offers a boutique experience, trendy rooms, and luxurious suites. **Pros:** stylish lounge bar; beautiful, classic building; location is close to many shops and sights. **Cons:** fee for parking; must walk through mall with luggage to reach hotel; foot traffic in Rundle Mall and the lively Lounge Bar can be noisy. *Rooms from: A$150* *128 Rundle Mall, City Center* *08/8215–4444* *www.hotelrichmond.com.au* *30 rooms* *No Meals.*

Majestic Roof Garden Hotel

$$ | **HOTEL** | **FAMILY** | Modern and stylish, each room features modern bathrooms, king-size beds, and free Wi-Fi. **Pros:** spacious bathrooms; near restaurants and bars; rooftop garden. **Cons:** no pool; on-site restaurant a little pricey; west-facing rooms have no view. *Rooms from: A$180* *55 Frome St., City Center* *08/8100–4400* *www.majesticroofgardenhotel.com.au* *119 rooms* *No Meals.*

Oaks Adelaide Embassy Suites

$$$ | **HOTEL** | This hotel is ideally positioned to explore the River Torrens, visit the Adelaide Casino and Adelaide Convention Centre, or take in the many restaurants and nightlife spots along or surrounding Hindley Street. **Pros:** minutes from River Torrens, parklands, and Hindley Street entertainment precinct; good city views; well serviced by public transport. **Cons:** can be noisy; expensive parking; not much atmosphere. *Rooms from: A$214* *96 North Terr., City Center* *08/8124–9900* *www.oakshotels.com* *110 apartments* *No Meals.*

The Art Gallery of South Australia

Nightlife

Adelaide's nightlife is concentrated in the city center and there's something going on every night but weekends are especially busy. Cover charges are rare except for nightclubs, and vary according to the night and time of entry. Near the end end of Hindley Street, Peel and Leigh Streets are lined with small bars of every persuasion that make them the epicenter of Adelaide's laneway culture, while Rundle Street and Vardon Avenue in the East End are especially popular in the warmer months when outdoor seating is at a premium. The restaurants and karaoke bars on Gouger Street are always busy, Waymouth Street is lined with more traditional pubs, and nightclubs are concentrated on Hindley Street, which gets very rowdy late at night. Vibrant suburban precincts with a mix of bars and restaurants can be found on The Parade in Norwood and Jetty Road in Glenelg, which is especially popular on Saturday night and Sunday afternoon.

BARS AND CLUBS

Bar Torino

BARS | The children of the owners of Chianti, a mainstay Italian restaurant in Adelaide, opened up one of the city's coolest places to hang out and enjoy great cocktails, wine, and beer (right next door to their parents' restaurant, where you may want to have dinner after a drink here). Banquettes and exposed brick walls add sophisticated touches to the chic atmosphere. Don't miss the house vermouth, which features in many of the cocktails. There are more than 20 variations on the classic gin and tonic here, as well as some interesting fortified wines. Small bites include burrata and kingfish crudo and there's a strong Italian influence in the heartier mains. ✉ *158 Hutt St., City Center* ☎ *08/8155–6010* 🌐 *www.bartorino.com.au.*

★ **Clever Little Tailor**

BARS | Adelaide has a fascination with small bars and hole-in-the-wall-style venues, and the Clever Little Tailor was one of the city's first. Named after a German fairy tale, the warmth of this place is undeniable. The bar staff is welcoming and helpful and the venue is cozy and charming with its contemporary interior, exposed red bricks, and hanging ferns. The cocktails are delicious, too, and the boutique wine and beer list is impressive. Plus, the music is soft enough to chat to your heart's content. ✉ *19 Peel St., City Center* 🌐 *cleverlittletailor.com.au.*

East End Cellars

WINE BARS | With a selection measuring in the thousands and a climate-controlled "vault" of sought-after unicorn wines, this is one of Adelaide's best wine shops. The staff are highly knowledgeable and for a A$15 fee will open any of the bottles for you to enjoy on-site. On Friday evening, local winemakers stop by to personally pour some of their bottles and share the stories behind them, and during the annual Fringe Festival the entire laneway turns into a giant party. ✉ *25 Vardon Ave., City Center* ☎ *08/8232–5300* 🌐 *www.eastendcellars.com.au.*

★ **Exeter Hotel**

PUBS | For generations the front bar of this classic pub has welcomed everyone from students downing beers to businesspeople taking advantage of the surprisingly good wine list, and when the sun is out it's nigh impossible to get one of the outside tables. Local DJs and bands still regularly play here and if you're passing by at lunchtime, the steak sandwich is one of Adelaide's best value lunches. ✉ *246 Rundle St., City Center* ☎ *08/8223–2623* 🌐 *www.theexeter.com.au.*

Grace Emily Hotel

PUBS | A classic old-school pub, bartenders spout the mantra "no pokies, no TAB, no food"—pokies are the poker machines found in many pubs, and TAB, Australia's version of OTB, lets you place bets on horse races—at this music-lover's watering hole. Entertainment comes in the form of consistently excellent live music including a legendary Monday open mic night that's been running for two decades. The beer garden is one of the city's best, with secluded spots for those wanting a quiet tipple and larger tables for groups to drink en masse and alfresco. In 2017 the pub was inducted into the South Australian Music Hall of Fame, recognizing its unique commitment to live music culture. ✉ *232 Waymouth St., City Center* ☎ *08/8231–5500.*

La Buvette Drinkery

WINE BARS | **FAMILY** | French expats and locals alike gather in this relaxed yet sophisticated Parisian-inspired wine bar on a quiet lane off Hindley Street for snacks and a unique bottle of wine, whether French or South Australian. Owned by a French expat, of course, La Buvette Drinkery is the ideal spot for observing the French ritual of aperitif before dinner: enjoy a local sparkling wine or well-made spritz alongside artisanal terrine to start the evening well. ✉ *27 Gresham St., City Center* ☎ *0426/017–356* 🌐 *www.labuvettedrinkery.com.au.*

Maybe Mae

COCKTAIL LOUNGES | Don't be embarrassed if you hesitate at the skillfully camouflaged doors to this opulent underground speakeasy; most first-time visitors do. Push through them and you'll find a fully table-serviced bar serving innovative cocktails with an emphasis on sustainability. ✉ *15 Peel St., City Center* ☎ *0424/899–946* 🌐 *www.maybemae.com.*

Rhino Room

COMEDY CLUBS | This is the home of Adelaide comedy, with a rotating lineup of open-mic nights and showcases as well as cabaret performances. Some of Australia's best comedians and high-profile overseas acts have graced the tiny stage, but it's also a great place to catch emerging talents. During the annual Fringe Festival every available space is turned into a venue as it becomes a bustling comedic hub. Check the website for upcoming performances. ✉ *1/131 Pirie St., City Center* ☎ *0419/824–912* 🌐 *www.rhinoroom.com.au.*

Udaberri Pintxos Y Vino

BARS | One of the first of Adelaide's growing trend of "small bars," Udaberri is a cozy, intimate setting where some of the city's best wine and beer selection is served alongside delicious Basque-style tapas. The narrow space is reminiscent of a barn, but it's a very chic barn. DJs spin house beats, but the music is never overpowering as interaction and conversation is encouraged. If you're lucky enough to beat the crowds to the loft, you can unwind on the sofas while enjoying the view. In addition to tapas, heartier plates with Mediterranean flair, like straciatella with figs and pistachio, or semi-cured chorizo, are served. ✉ *11–13 Leigh St., City Center* ☎ *08/8410–5733* 🌐 *www.udaberri.com.au.*

Performing Arts

South Australia truly is the festival state and a number of the largest events coincide at the end of summer during "Mad March," making this the best time to visit. The East End of Adelaide comes alive during this time, as Rundle Street is closed to cars on weekend and the nearby parklands are transformed into giant open-air hubs featuring multiple bars and performance venues.

For a listing of performances and exhibitions, look to the entertainment pages of *The Advertiser,* Adelaide's daily newspaper or the online-only *InDaily.* The free, weekly *Fest Magazine* also runs for the duration of the festival offering reviews, interviews, and recommendations.

Adelaide Entertainment Centre

ARTS CENTERS | Opened in 1991, most major concerts are held at this indoor arena, which also features a mix of everything from music, theater, and other performing arts to conventions and sporting events. ✉ *98 Port Rd., Hindmarsh* ☎ *08/8208–2222* 🌐 *www.theaec.net.*

Adelaide Festival Centre

ARTS CENTERS | This is the city's major venue for the performing arts. The Festival Centre programs four major festivals and the State Opera, the State Theatre Company of South Australia, and the Adelaide Symphony Orchestra also perform here regularly. Performances are in the Playhouse, the Festival and Space theaters, the outdoor amphitheater, and Her Majesty's Theatre at 58 Grote Street. The box office is open weekdays 9–6. ✉ *King William St., near North Terr., City Center* ☎ *08/8216–8600* 🌐 *www.adelaidefestivalcentre.com.au.*

Shopping

If you are wondering where everyone in Adelaide is, you'll find them at Rundle Mall, the city's main shopping strip. Shops in the City Center are generally open Monday through Thursday 9–5:30, Friday 9–9, Saturday 9–5, and Sunday 11–5. Suburban shops are often open until 9 pm on Thursday night instead of Friday. As the center of the world's opal industry, Adelaide has many opal shops, which are around King William Street. Other good buys are South Australian regional wines, crafts, and Aboriginal artwork. For local fashion, head to the boutiques on King William Road in Hyde Park, a 40-minute walk south from Victoria Square.

Adelaide Exchange Jewellers

JEWELRY & WATCHES | Located just off Rundle Mall, the exchange sells high-quality new and antique jewelry. They can also be found in Glenelg, Mitcham, and Modbury. ✉ *10 Stephens Pl., City Center* ☎ *08/8212–2496* 🌐 *www.adelaide-exchange.com.au.*

Australian Opal and Diamond Collection

JEWELRY & WATCHES | One of Australia's leading opal merchants, wholesalers, exporters, and manufacturing jewelers,

Australian Opal and Diamond Collection sells superb handcrafted one-of-a-kind opal jewelry. ✉ *14 King William St., City Center* ☎ *08/8211–9995* 🌐 *www.aodc.net.au.*

★ Central Market

MARKET | FAMILY | One of the largest produce markets in the southern hemisphere, and Adelaide's pride and joy, the Central Market is chock-full of stellar local foods, including glistening-fresh fish, meat, crusty Vietnamese and Continental breads, German baked goods, cheeses of every shape and color, and old-fashioned lollies (candy). You can also buy souvenir T-shirts, CDs, books, cut flowers, and a great cup of coffee. ✉ *44–60 Gouger St., City Center* ☎ *08/8203–7494* 🌐 *www.adelaidecentralmarket.com.au.*

★ Haigh's Chocolates

CHOCOLATE | Ask anyone who no longer lives in Adelaide what they miss most about the city and chances are they'll say "Haigh's." Australia's oldest chocolate manufacturer has tempted sweet tooths with corner shop displays since 1915, and although there are now Haigh's stores in several locations across the city and in other capitals, the Beehive Corner store is the original, and a local icon. The family-owned South Australian company produces exquisite truffles, pralines, and creams—as well as the chocolate bilby (an endangered Australian marsupial), Haigh's answer to the Easter bunny. No trip to Adelaide is complete without at least one chocolate indulgence. **TIP→ Free chocolate-making tours at the Haigh's Visitor Center at 154 Greenhill Road in Parkside run Monday through Saturday beginning at 9 am. Bookings are essential.** ✉ *2 Rundle Mall, at King William St., City Center* ☎ *08/8231–2844* 🌐 *www.haighs-chocolates.com.au.*

★ JamFactory

ART GALLERIES | A contemporary craft-and-design center at the Lion Arts Centre, JamFactory exhibits and sells unique Australian glassware, ceramics, wood, and metal work and you can often see the artists at work. Its fantastic gift shop is the place to pick up a unique handmade piece of art or jewelry, including a description from the artist. ✉ *19 Morphett St., City Center* ☎ *08/8231–0005* 🌐 *www.jamfactory.com.au.*

★ Rundle Mall

MALL | Adelaide's main shopping area is Rundle Mall, a pedestrian plaza lined with boutiques, department stores, and arcades, including Australia's two best-known stores, Myer and David Jones, as well as some of the world's big name and luxury brands sprinkled among the local shops. People of all ages hang out on the mall, relaxing on a bench or browsing the shops. Heritage-listed Adelaide Arcade is a Victorian-era jewel, with a decorative tiled floor, skylights, and dozens of shops behind huge timber-framed windows. ✉ *Rundle St., between King William and Pulteney Sts., City Center* ☎ *08/8203–7200* 🌐 *www.rundlemall.com.*

Urban Cow Studio

ART GALLERIES | For quirky locally made jewelry, pottery, glass, and sculptures, visit Urban Cow Studio, which exhibits works by more than 150 South Australian artists and designers. ✉ *10 Vaughan Pl., City Center* ☎ *08/8232–6126* 🌐 *www.urbancow.com.au.*

Activities

BICYCLING

Adelaide's many parks, flat terrain, and uncluttered streets make it a perfect city for two-wheel exploring.

Santos Tour Down Under

BIKING | FAMILY | As the first stop on the world cycling calendar, the Tour Down Under brings in riders from all over the world as part of the UCI Pro Tour each January. Outside of the Tour de France, the event attracts the biggest crowds in the world for eight days, taking in metropolitan and regional South Australia.

Cycling devotees may be interested in the Breakaway Series, which provides the chance to ride some of the stages, or take it easy with the DeTours events that combine race watching with visits to some of South Australia's premium food and wine regions. ✉ *Victoria Sq., Adelaide* ☎ *08/8463–4701* 🌐 *www.tourdownunder.com.au.*

Greater Adelaide

Sights

★ **Coopers Brewery**

BREWERY | Founded by Thomas Cooper in 1862, this is Australia's only large-scale, independent, family-owned brewery. The Coopers beer story began when Thomas tried to create a tonic for his ailing wife, Ann, but instead created his first batch of beer. Customers grew in numbers as Thomas hand-delivered his all-natural ales and stout by horse and cart; the tradition lives on with guest appearances at special events by Clydesdayles drawing the very same cart that Thomas once used. Visitors can take accessible guided tours (A$33) of the brewhouse and enjoy tastings of the award-winning signature Coopers ales, including Coopers Pale Ale, Coopers Sparkling Ale, and Coopers Stout, in the museum post-tour. Proceeds from the brewery tour ticket price go to the Coopers Brewery Foundation, which then distributes funds to various charities. The museum features a display of the historic horse and cart, vintage Coopers delivery truck, and pictorials showcasing the history of the brewery. ✉ *461 South Rd., Regency Park* ☎ *08/8440–1800* 🌐 *www.coopers.com.au* 🎫 *A$33* ☞ *Must be over 18 and wearing closed-toe shoes.*

National Railway Museum

OTHER MUSEUM | **FAMILY** | Steam-train buffs will love this collection of locomotives and rolling stock in the former Port Adelaide railway yard. The largest of its kind in Australia, the collection includes enormous "mountain"-class engines and the "Tea and Sugar" train, once the lifeline for camps scattered across the deserts of South and Western Australia. For an additional cost take a ride on the historic Semaphore to Fort Glanville Tourist Railway; it runs every Sunday and public holiday from October to end of April and more frequently during school holidays. There are covered outdoor eating areas with tables and chairs at the museum, where visitors may bring their own food and drink. ✉ *76 Lipson St., Port Adelaide* ☎ *08/8341–1690* 🌐 *nrm.org.au* 🎫 *A$17.*

★ **Penfolds Magill Estate**

WINERY | Founded in 1844 by immigrant English doctor Christopher Rawson Penfold, this is the birthplace of Australia's most famous wine, Penfolds Grange, and one of Australia's only city wineries. Introduced in 1951, Grange is the flagship of a huge stable of wines priced from everyday to special-occasion (collectors pay tens of thousands of dollars for complete sets of Grange). Book ahead for the Magill Estate Heritage Tour (A$25, 10 am and 1 pm daily) to hear some of the stories behind the site; if you're a serious wine lover take the Ultimate Penfolds Tour (A$150) and visit the original Penfold family cottage then head into the winery to enjoy some premium wine tastings, or go for the Iconic Penfolds Experience (A$295), which includes a three-course lunch and wine pairings in addition to the tour. ✉ *78 Penfold Rd., Magill* ☎ *08/8301–5569* 🌐 *www.penfolds.com* 🎫 *From A$25.*

South Australian Maritime Museum

HISTORY MUSEUM | **FAMILY** | Inside a restored stone warehouse, this museum in Port Adelaide, a 20-minute drive from central Adelaide, brings maritime history vividly to life with ships' figureheads, shipwreck relics, and intricate scale models including a ketch you can walk through. In the basement you can see a bunk bed aboard an 1840s immigrant ship and hear passengers telling of life and death on their journeys to South Australia. In addition to the warehouse displays, the museum includes a lighthouse (worth climbing the 75 steps up to see the view), and tours of the historic quarantine are sometimes available (if that's not too real). The surrounding suburb of Port Adelaide has plenty of antiques shops to visit, and nearby Semaphore has a street lined with cafés leading to a lovely beach. ✉ *126 Lipson St., Port Adelaide* ☎ *08/8207–6255* 🌐 *maritime.history.sa.gov.au* 🎫 *A$15, includes lighthouse entry.*

Beaches

Whether you want to catch a wave, drop a line, or simply watch the sun set over the ocean, Adelaide's beaches offer something for everyone. From North Haven in the north to Sellicks Beach in the south, most beaches are less than 30 minutes from the city center. At the end of Adelaide's only tram line, the busy beach at Glenelg is framed by restaurants, bars, and an amusement park. Farther south the hills of the Fleurieu Peninsula meet the sea and beaches hidden beneath cliff faces provide great swimming, fishing, and surfing spots.

★ Glenelg Beach

BEACH | FAMILY | Located just 11 km (7 miles) from the Adelaide city center, palindromic Glenelg is a busy seaside suburb known for its sandy beach, historic jetty, serene marinas, bustling shops, hotels, restaurants, bars, and The Beachouse entertainment complex. Trams lead the way to the beach, carrying passengers from the city along Jetty Road while pedestrians weave in and out of the various retail outlets that line the strip. A day trip to Glenelg is a must, but the easygoing beach vibe encourages everyone from backpackers to more discerning travelers to make it their Adelaide base. The beach is large and sandy with a very gentle slope, and the waters are calm. Expect to see large crowds on hotter days and, depending on the season, seaweed can be a problem. **Amenities:** food and drink; lifeguards; parking; showers; toilets; water sports. **Best for:** sunrise; sunset; swimming; walking; windsurfing. ✉ *Jetty Rd., Glenelg* ✣ *Trams run approximately every 10 mins from downtown* ☎ *08/8179–9599 Bay Discovery Centre* 🌐 *www.glenelgsa.com.au.*

Henley Beach

BEACH | FAMILY | The beach in this quiet coastal suburb offers white sand, gently lapping waves, summer entertainment, and a square known for popular dining spots. You'll find families spread out along the sand, and there's plenty of space on the wide lawns to enjoy a picnic or fish-and-chips. The jetty is perfect for walking or fishing—drop a line in the water and try your luck. During summer, Henley Beach Square comes alive with live music and festivals while eateries along Henley Beach Road bring the world to your plate—Asian, African, Mediterranean, and Indian mix with local cuisine and incredible gelato. **Amenities:** food and drink; parking; toilets. **Best for:** swimming; sunrise; sunset; walking; windsurfing. ✉ *Esplanade, Henley Beach* ☎ *08/8408–1111 City of Charles Sturt.*

Restaurants

★ Magill Estate

$$$$ | MODERN AUSTRALIAN | Lovers of Australian wine should not miss a meal at this intimate pavilion-style vineyard restaurant set in the country's most famous winery. Though only 15 minutes from the city it's high enough to afford views over the vineyards and the city skyline toward the coast, and the seasonal, Modern Australian cuisine is just as special. **Known for:** incredible wine pairings; romantic setting; indulgent seven-course tasting menu. $ *Average main: A$220* ✉ *78 Penfold Rd., Magill* ☎ *08/8301–5551* 🌐 *www.magillestaterestaurant.com* ⏲ *Closed Mon. and Tues. No lunch Wed.–Fri. No dinner Sun.*

★ **Parwana**

$ | **AFGHAN** | On the short drive from the airport to the city, this colorful and welcoming family-run restaurant serves up traditional Afghan comfort food that has locals booking weeks ahead. Some items are only available on certain days but the rich, oily eggplant *banjaan borani* is always on the menu and a must try. **Known for:** advance bookings are essential; glistening jeweled rice and fragrant, spiced dishes; friendly service. *Average main: A$20 124B Henley Beach Rd., Adelaide 08/8443–9001 www.parwana.com.au Closed Mon.*

Sammy's on the Marina

$$$ | **SEAFOOD** | Adelaide is a prime spot for enjoying Australia's incredible seafood. At Sammy's on the Marina, enormous fishbowl windows frame views of million-dollar yachts at the far end of Glenelg's glitzy Holdfast Marina and are perfect for watching the setting sun, playing dolphins, or a storm rolling across Gulf St. Vincent as you tuck into a dozen freshly shucked oysters or the popular and generous seafood platter. **Known for:** classy atmosphere; fresh, local seafood including rock lobster and oysters; reliable, friendly service. *Average main: A$40 1–12 Holdfast Promenade, Glenelg 08/8376–8211 www.sammys.net.au.*

Hotels

★ **North Adelaide Heritage Group**

$$$ | **B&B/INN** | In the city's leafy, oldest section atop a hill, antiques dealers Rodney and Regina Twiss have converted Heritage-listed mews houses, a meeting chapel, an arts-and-crafts manor house, and a fire station (complete with 1942 fire engine) into apartments and suites, and filled them with Australian antiques and contemporary furnishings. **Pros:** most properties have large gardens full of birdlife; historic properties in Adelaide's most upscale suburb; friendly owners give helpful tips. **Cons:** setting is suburban rather than picturesque countryside; not child-friendly; some properties can be on the dark side. *Rooms from: A$225 82 Hill St., North Adelaide 08/8267–2020 www.adelaideheritage.com 19 rooms Free Breakfast.*

Oaks Glenelg Plaza Pier Suites

$$ | **APARTMENT** | Sea air wafts through open balcony doors in this all-apartment complex on Adelaide's most popular beach. **Pros:** large rooms with views; steps from the beach; helpful reception staff who are full of advice. **Cons:** expensive parking; the bars can get noisy and messy at peak times; corporate feel to the lobby. *Rooms from: A$199 16 Holdfast Promenade, Glenelg 08/8350–6688, 1300/551–111 www.oakshotels.com/en/oaks-plaza-pier 191 rooms No Meals.*

Nightlife

BARS AND CLUBS

Wellington Hotel

PUBS | First licensed in 1851, the Wellington is a hop lover's heaven with 16 taps pouring beer and cider from around Australia and the world. Order a "schooner" (small glass) or "pint" (larger glass) of your favorite and take it outside to the seats overlooking a large square surrounded by heritage homes. There's live acoustic music on Sunday afternoon and hearty pub food every day of the week. It's a good place to stop on the way to (or from) the nearby Adelaide Oval and gets crowded when there's a sporting event. *36 Wellington Sq., North Adelaide 08/8267–1322 www.facebook.com/wellingtonhotelnthadel.*

Shopping

Harbour Town Adelaide

OUTLET | For discount shopping, hop off the plane and head straight to nearby Harbourtown. You'll find Nine West, Hurley, Levi's, Oakley, Cue, RM Williams, Adidas, and Bonds among the

100 outlets. ✉ *727 Tapleys Hill Rd., West Beach* ☎ *08/8355–1144* 🌐 *www.harbourtownadelaide.com.au.*

Westfield Marion Shopping Centre
MALL | Adelaide's largest shopping complex is easily accessible via public transport and contains more than 300 stores, including major department stores and boutiques, bars, restaurants, and the largest cinema complex in the state. Good air-conditioning means it's crowded on hot summer days. ✉ *297 Diagonal Rd., Marion* ☎ *08/8298–1188* 🌐 *www.westfield.com.au/marion.*

Activities

AUSTRALIAN RULES FOOTBALL AND CRICKET

Adelaide Oval
SPECTATOR SPORTS | **FAMILY** | The stadium received a state-of-the-art upgrade in 2013 and is now the dual home for cricket and Australian Rules Football—South Australia's most popular winter sport. The Aussie Rules season runs March through September, while cricket season is October through March. Tours of the historic stadium are led by expert volunteers and operate on nonevent days; choose between a general tour highlighting celebrated moments in the sporting, musical, and civic history of this world-famous sporting arena, and a special guided tour of cricket museums. Or see if from an unforgettable angle on the RoofClimb that traverses the scalloped shells and includes the chance to lean out from 50 meters above the oval. Overlooking the stadium, the elegant Five Regions restaurant offers modern South Australian cuisine and wines, highlighting one of the state's famed wine regions each month. Dinner is offered Tuesday through Saturday. There's also an on-site hotel. ✉ *War Memorial Dr., North Adelaide* ☎ *08/8211–1100* 🌐 *www.adelaideoval.com.au* 🎟 *Tours from A$25.*

BASKETBALL

Titanium Security Arena
BASKETBALL | The home stadium for the Adelaide 36ers of the National Basketball League and the Adelaide Lightning of the Women's National Basketball League. Located in Findon, an inner western suburb of Adelaide, Adelaide Arena is the largest purpose-built basketball arena in Australia. The NBL season runs from October to March. ✉ *44A Crittenden Rd., Findon* ☎ *08/8268–3592* 🌐 *www.titaniumarena.com.au.*

GOLF

North Adelaide Golf Course
GOLF | A 10-minute walk outside of the city, the North Adelaide Golf Course—one of the most picturesque golf settings in the country with game-distracting views of the city—runs one short (par 3) and two full 18-hole courses. You can rent clubs and carts from the pro shop. Playing hours are dawn to dusk daily. ✉ *Strangways Terr., North Adelaide* ☎ *08/8203–7888* 🌐 *northadelaidegolf.com.au* 🎟 *North Course: from A$22 weekdays, A$27 weekends; South Course: A$32 weekdays, A$39 weekends* 🏌 *North Course: 18 holes, 4958 yards, par 68; South Course: 18 holes, 6435 yards, par 71.*

SOCCER

Coopers Stadium
SOCCER | **FAMILY** | Also known as Hindmarsh Stadium, this is a multipurpose venue and the first purpose-built soccer stadium in Australia. It's the home of the Australian A-League soccer team, Adelaide United. The national A-League season runs from October to May and includes a finals series similar to Australian Rules Football. ✉ *Holden St., Hindmarsh* ☎ *08/8241–7122* 🌐 *www.coopersstadium.com.au.*

WATER SPORTS

Temptation Sailing

WATER SPORTS | FAMILY | The Dolphin Boat, also known as *Temptation,* is the first vessel in South Australia to be given a dolphin swim license, which allows you to swim with the cute and friendly animals. The dolphins and tour guides have developed a close relationship over the years, as the company has been operating since 2002, so you're guaranteed to get up close. In fact, if you don't get into the water to swim with the dolphins, they will refund the difference between the watch and the swim. They also offer afternoon tea and twilight cruises. The waters around Adelaide are beautiful, so these opportunities are worth considering. ✉ *10 Holdfast Promenade, Glenelg* ☎ *0412/811–838* 🌐 *www.dolphinboat.com.au* 🎫 *From A$25; dolphin swims from A$120.*

Mt. Lofty

14 km (9 miles) southeast of Adelaide.

There are splendid views over all the entire city from the lookout atop 2,300-foot Mt. Lofty, the coldest location in Adelaide, where snow occasionally falls in winter months. Energetic types can follow some of the many trails that lead from the summit—they are especially popular on weekend mornings—or alternatively, have a cup of coffee in the café and enjoy the view in the warmth.

GETTING HERE AND AROUND

By car from Adelaide, take the Crafers exit off the South Eastern Freeway and follow Summit Road or from the eastern suburbs via Greenhill Road. You can get to the summit as well as the Mt. Lofty Botanic Gardens and Cleland Wildlife Park in about 40 minutes by catching Bus 864F from Currie or Grenfell Street in the city center. Alight at bus stop 24A and connect to Bus 823.

A 4½-km (3-mile) one-way walk from the Waterfall Gully parking lot in Cleland Conservation Park (15-minute drive from Adelaide) takes you along Waterfall Creek before climbing steeply to the white surveying tower on the summit; the parking lot can get full on weekends and the track is closed on Total Fire Ban days.

Sights

★ **Cleland Wildlife Park**

WILDLIFE REFUGE | FAMILY | A short drive from Mt. Lofty Summit brings you to delightful Cleland Wildlife Park, where many animals roam free in three different forest habitats. Self-guided walking trails crisscross the park and its surroundings, and you're guaranteed to see emus and kangaroos in the grasslands and pelicans around the swampy billabongs. There are also enclosures for wombats and other less sociable animals. Koala cuddling is a highlight of koala close-up sessions (A$33, daily 2 pm and 2:30 pm). Breakfast with the Birds offers the chance to feed a variety of species before the park opens to the public, and private two-hour night walks (A$327 for up to four people) let you wander among nocturnal species such as potoroos and brush-tailed bettongs: check the website for the next scheduled walk. Private guided tours can be arranged for A$135 per hour weekdays, A$270 per hour weekends. Reservations are essential. The park is closed when there's a fire ban (usually between December and February). ✉ *365 Mount Lofty Summit Rd., Mount Lofty* ☎ *08/8339–2444* 🌐 *www.clelandwildlifepark.sa.gov.au* 🎫 *A$30.*

CRFT Wines

WINERY | Get to know one of the newer boutique wineries in the Adelaide Hills by visiting the CRFT Wines cellar door. Located on a beautiful country road with one vineyard after another, it's built from a converted shearing shed and horse stable. CRFT offers a range of unique, single vineyard wines, made by a couple of married winemakers, Candice Helbig and Frewin Ries. Their aim in forming CRFT was to champion the incredible diversity of soils and climates in the subregions of the Adelaide Hills. The tasting room is open to the public every weekend for wine flights (starting from A$15 per person), wines by the glass or bottle, and take-home bottle sales. Complimentary olives are served with each wine flight, and there's a cheese plate you can opt for as well. The fireplace roars on chilly days. ✉ *45 Rangeview Dr., Carey Gully* ☎ *042/528–809* 🌐 *www.crftwines.com.au* 🕑 *Closed Mon.–Thurs.*

Mt. Lofty Botanic Gardens

GARDEN | With its rhododendrons, magnolias, ferns, and native and exotic trees, these gardens are glorious in fall and spring; free guided walks leave the lower parking lot on Thursday at 10:30 am year-round except on extreme fire danger days when the forecast is above 35°C (95°F). ✉ *Picadilly entrance, 16 Lampert Rd., Mount Lofty* ☎ *08/8370–8370* 🌐 *www.botanicgardens.sa.gov.au/visit/mount-lofty-botanic-garden.*

★ **Ngeringa Winery**

WINERY | For more than 20 years this winery on the former Jurlique herb farm has practiced biodynamic farming by following lunar cycles, growing vegetables, raising livestock, and abstaining from chemical treatments. The winery cellar door is open by appointment only, and also occasional events including memorable paddock-to-plate dining experiences showcasing Ngeringa wines like the sprightly pet nat alongside incredible produce grown on-site. The farm supplies most of Adelaide's top restaurants and there is also a dedicated chamber music venue on-site. Tastings by appointment, A$20. ✉ *107 Williams Rd.* ☎ *08/8398–2867* 🌐 *www.ngeringa.com.*

Nice Views

There is no better view of Adelaide—day or night—than the city-and-sea sweep from atop 2,300-foot Mt. Lofty. There's an appropriately named glass-front restaurant here called the Summit, though prices are as elevated as the location.

Restaurants

Lost In A Forest

$$ | PIZZA | Named after a song by The Cure, this "wood oven wine lounge" built into a restored old church is a cozy spot to get local wine and the best pizza in the Adelaide Hills, made with local organic ingredients. It's an ideal destination for dinner after a day of wine tasting or lunch before a short hike. **Known for:** cool and casual vibe to match local winemaker; on cold nights, the fire pit out front is lit; eclectic cocktail list. [$] *Average main: A$25* ✉ *1203 Greenhill Rd., Uraidla* ☎ *08/8390–3444* 🌐 *lostinaforest.com.au* 🕑 *Closed Mon.–Wed. No lunch Thurs. and Fri.*

★ **The Summertown Aristologist**

$$ | MODERN AUSTRALIAN | This is contemporary food that takes Modern Australian cooking to new heights. A chalkboard, listing dishes defined only by their ingredients—most of which are locally grown—greets diners who come to this casual, wine-focused, entirely seasonal restaurant, where chefs in the open kitchen work hard to deliver creatively composed share plates served on handmade ceramic dishware. **Known for:** house-made charcuterie and locally made cheeses; eclectic wine list featuring small-batch organic producers; delicious, chewy house-made sourdough bread. [$] *Average main: A$30* ✉ *1097 Greenhill Rd., Summertown* ☎ *0477/410–105* www.thesummertownaristologist.com *Closed Mon.–Thurs.*

The Summit
$$ | **CAFÉ** | If you suffer from vertigo, think twice about dining here; this glass-front building atop Mt. Lofty is all about dining with altitude. Breakfasts range from a simple grilled cheese sandwich to an imposing "brekkie tower" that feeds four and lunch is upscale café fare. **Known for:** delicious breakfasts; local wines; excellent view. *Average main: A$25* *266 Mt. Lofty Summit Rd., Mount Lofty* *08/8339–2600* *www.mount-loftysummit.com.*

Hotels

Mt. Lofty House
$$$$ | **B&B/INN** | From very English garden terraces below the summit of Mt. Lofty, this refined and iconic country house overlooks a patchwork of vineyards, farms, and bushland. **Pros:** incredible interior decoration; peaceful location in stunning surroundings; extensive wine cellar. **Cons:** no casual dining options; pricey; popular with groups, so book ahead at the restaurant. *Rooms from: A$499* *1 Mawson Dr., Crafers* *08/8339–6777* *www.mtloftyhouse.com.au* *30 rooms* *Free Breakfast.*

SEQUOIA Lodge
$$$$ | **RESORT** | This series of fourteen suites perched tantalizingly above a valley carpeted in vineyards and mixed farmlands represents the pinnacle of luxury in the Adelaide Hills. **Pros:** luxurious experience; wide range of included experiences; incredible views. **Cons:** some experiences cost extra; no children under 18 allowed; rates are high, and go up on weekends. *Rooms from: A$1000* *1 Mawson Dr., Mount Lofty* *08/8130-9230* *www.sequoialodge.com.au* *Free Breakfast* *14 suites.*

Bridgewater

10 km (7 miles) from Mt. Lofty, 22 km (14 miles) southeast of Adelaide.

Bridgewater came into existence in 1841 as a refreshment stop for bullock teams fording Cock's Creek. More English than German, with its flowing creek and flower-filled gardens, this leafy, tranquil village was officially planned in 1859 by the builder of the first Bridgewater flour mill.

GETTING HERE AND AROUND

From the city center, drive onto the Mount Barker Expressway until you see the Stirling exit. From there, travel through lush countryside following the signs to Bridgewater. The town itself is small and walkable. By public transport, take Bus 864 or 864F from Currie or Pulteney Streets in the city to stop 46.

Restaurants

Bridgewater Mill Restaurant
$$$ | **AUSTRALIAN** | **FAMILY** | A stylish yet charmingly casual restaurant in a converted 1860s flour mill, this is a great spot to linger over a long lunch of share plates. Using regional produce, head chef Ben Fenwick creates an imaginative contemporary menu that is a mix of French, Japanese, Middle Eastern, and Modern Australian. **Known for:** dining by an open fire in the winter; extensive range of local wines; historic building. *Average main: A$38* *386 Mt. Barker Rd., Bridgewater* *08/8339–9200* *thebridgewatermill.com.au* *Closed Tues. and Wed. No dinner Mon. and Thurs.*

Coffee and Quick Bites

The Organic Market and Café
$ | **CAFÉ** | **FAMILY** | Pram-wheeling parents, hikers resting their walking poles, and friends catching up on gossip keep this red-and-blue café and adjoining organic supermarket buzzing all day. Reasons to linger include tasty focaccias and soups; rich,

The vineyards of the Barossa Valley

indulgent baked goods like home-baked muffins and cakes; and all kinds of purportedly healthy and unquestionably delicious drinks. **Known for:** an attached grocery store with healthy provisions; excellent coffee, chai, and tea; warm, friendly space. *Average main: A$16 5 Druid Ave., Stirling 3 km (2 miles) from Bridgewater 08/8339–4835 café www.organicmarket.com.au No dinner.*

Hotels

Thorngrove Manor Hotel

$$$$ | B&B/INN | With its opulent suites set amid glorious gardens, this romantic Gothic folly of turrets and towers is *Lifestyles of the Rich and Famous* writ large. **Pros:** very attendant service; perfect for the archetypal romantic getaway; complete luxury. **Cons:** no alcohol sold (BYO welcome); very limited room availability; if you have to ask how expensive it is, you can't afford it. *Rooms from: A$1399 2 Glenside La., Crafers 08/8339–6748 www.thorngrove.com.au 6 rooms Free Breakfast.*

Lyndoch

69 km (43 miles) northeast of Adelaide.

This pleasant little town surrounded by vineyards was established in 1837 and is the Barossa's oldest settlement site. Like the region itself, it owes the spelling of its name to a draftsman's error—it was meant to be named after the British soldier Lord Lynedoch.

GETTING HERE AND AROUND

The most direct route from Adelaide to the Barossa wine region is via the town of Gawler. From Adelaide, drive west through the Parklands and turn right onto busy South Road, which turns into the Northern Expressway (M2) and whisks you quickly out of the city. Follow the signs until it joins the A20 near Gawler then leave the highway and take the Willaston Interchange Ramp and follow the signs to Lyndoch. The entire trip should take about an hour. A more attractive, if circuitous, route to Lyndoch takes you through the Adelaide Hills' Chain of Ponds and Williamstown.

Sights

Burge Family Winemakers

WINERY | You can drink in a leafy vineyard view while tasting from the wine barrels (if you get so lucky) at this understated cellar door. Winemaker Derek Fitzgerald's repertoire includes Semillon, GSM, Shiraz, and Rhône blends. ✉ *1312 Barossa Valley Way, near Hermann Thumm Dr., Lyndoch* ☎ *08/8524–4644* 🌐 *www.burgefamily.com.au* 🕑 *Closed Sun., Tues., and Wed.*

Lyndoch Lavender Farm

GARDEN | **FAMILY** | A family-friendly tribute to the purple flower that adorns the hills, Lyndoch Lavender Farm grows more than 80 varieties on 6 lush acres high above Lyndoch. Light café meals are available, and the farm shop sells essential oils, creams, and other products, including wine from the surrounding vineyards. The most spectacular time to visit is during flowering season from August to September. ✉ *Hoffnungsthal Rd. at Tweedies Gully Rd., Lyndoch* ☎ *08/8524–4538* 🌐 *www.lyndochlavenderfarm.com.au* *Free.*

Hotels

Abbotsford Country House

$$$$ | **B&B/INN** | Tranquility reigns at this antiques-filled property on 50 acres of rolling beef farm with Barossa views and an 800-plant rose garden. **Pros:** hearty breakfast; a serene and luxurious place to recover from all the wine tasting; very welcoming hosts. **Cons:** no children under 12; lack of gym facilities; no on-site lunch or dinner. [$] *Rooms from: A$425* ✉ *219 Yaldara Dr., Lyndoch* ☎ *08/8524–4662* 🌐 *www.abbotsfordhouse.com* *8 suites* *Free Breakfast.*

★ **Kingsford The Barossa**

$$$$ | **B&B/INN** | Set in a historic 1856 homestead on a 225-acre estate, Kingsford The Barossa offers one of the Barossa Valley's most exquisite experiences and is the perfect base for exploring the surrounding wine country. **Pros:** secluded feel yet easily accessible; personable hosts make you feel like family; gourmet farm-to-table seasonal menus. **Cons:** The Matilda Suite books out well in advance; only open Friday and Saturday nights (for now); two-night minimum. [$] *Rooms from: A$695* ✉ *68 Kingsford Rd.* ☎ *08/8524–8120* 🌐 *kingsfordbarossa.com.au* *16 rooms* *Free Breakfast.*

Le Mas

$$$$ | **B&B/INN** | Some Barossa wineries make French-style wines; this delightful retreat is in the style of a classic Provençal farmhouse thanks to owners who have filled an 1857 homestead with French silk curtains, armoires, and objets d'art, and added a light-filled conservatory that overlooks sprawling lawns leading down to a gum-lined creek. **Pros:** plenty of spaces to relax; gorgeous furnishings; an atmosphere of luxury. **Cons:** no children under 16; quite expensive; on-site restaurant is open Wednesday to Sunday only. [$] *Rooms from: A$850* ✉ *1929 Barossa Valley Way, 6 km (4 miles) northeast of Lyndoch, Lyndoch* ☎ *08/8524–4488* 🌐 *lemasbarossa.com.au* *Free Breakfast* *4 rooms.*

Tanunda

13 km (8 miles) northeast of Lyndoch, 70 km (43 miles) northeast of Adelaide.

The cultural heart of the Barossa, Tanunda is its most German settlement. The four Lutheran churches in town testify to that heritage, and dozens of shops selling German pastries, breads, and wursts (sausages)—not to mention wine—line the main street. Many of the valley's best wineries are close by.

ESSENTIALS

VISITOR INFORMATION Barossa Visitor Centre. ✉ *66–68 Murray St., Tanunda* ☎ *1300/852–982* 🌐 *www.barossa.com/info/visitor-information-centres.*

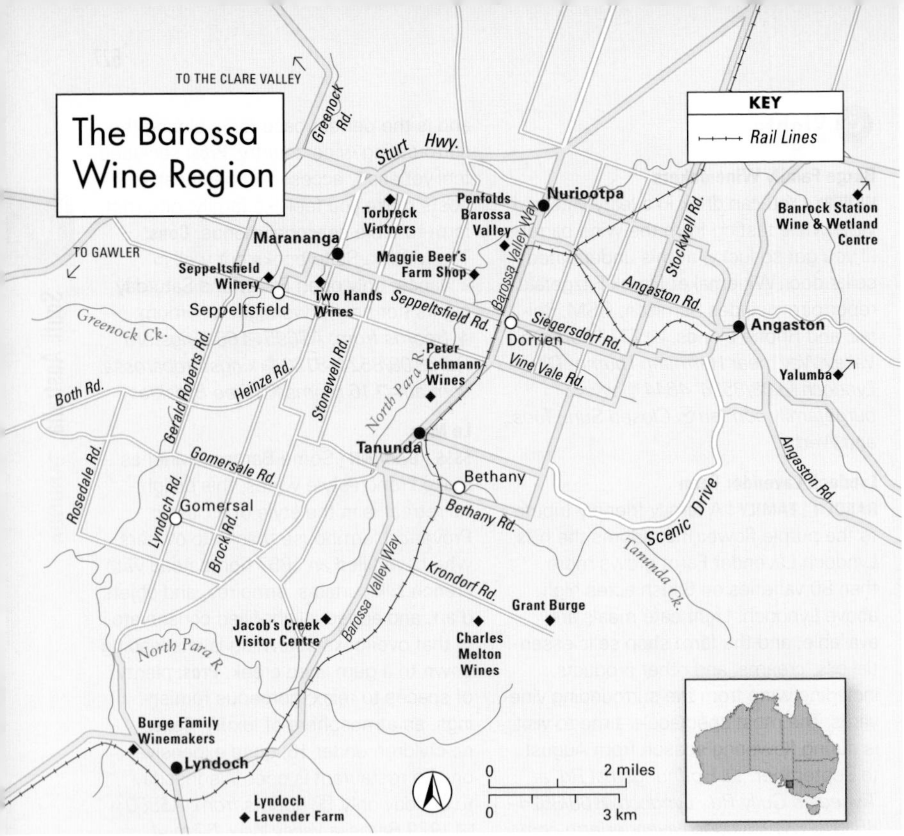

The Barossa Wine Region

Sights

Charles Melton Wines

WINERY | Tasting here is relaxed and casual in a brick-floor, timber-wall cellar door, which is warmed by a log fire in winter. After making sure the resident cats have vacated it first, settle into a director's chair at the long wooden table and let the staff pour. Nine Popes, a huge, decadent red blend, is the flagship wine, and the ruby-red Rose of Virginia is an iconic Australian rosé. You can enjoy a glass of either with a cheese platter on the veranda. Tastings from A$10. ✉ *194 Krondorf Rd., near Nitschke Rd., Tanunda* ☎ *08/8563–3606* 🌐 *www.charlesmelton-wines.com.au.*

Grant Burge

WINERY | This is one of the most successful of the Barossa's younger wine labels. Wines include impressive Chardonnays, crisp Rieslings, and powerful reds such as Meshach Shiraz. Don't miss the Holy Trinity—a highly acclaimed Rhône blend of Grenache, Shiraz, and Mourvedre. The cellar door overlooks the vines at Krondorf, 5 km (3 miles) south of Tanunda and offers regional grazing platters in addition to tastings. Tastings from A$10. ✉ *279 Krondorf Rd., Tanunda* ☎ *08/8563–7675* 🌐 *www.grantburgewines.com.au.*

Jacob's Creek Visitor Centre

WINERY | An impressive block of glass, steel, and recycled timber, Jacob's Creek Visitor Centre overlooks the creek whose name is familiar to wine drinkers around the world. It can sometimes be overrun with large groups, but the informative staff members make it well worth a visit—it's certainly more than your run-of-the-mill visitor center. Inside the building, plasma screens and pictorial displays tell the history of the label. Five tasting flights have themes, including "light & fresh," "low alcohol & organic," and limited release, or staff can tailor a selection of wines for you. The sprawling lawns edged with towering eucalyptus trees are perfect for a picnic, and you can bring your own hamper or purchase one at the cellar door. Tastings from A$5. ✉ *2129 Barossa Valley Way, Tanunda* ✣ *Near Jacob's Creek* ☎ *08/8521–3000* 🌐 *www.jacobscreek.com.*

Peter Lehmann Wines

WINERY | This winery was founded by a larger-than-life Barossa character who had an influence on just about every winemaker in the valley. Art-hung stonework and a wood-burning fireplace make the tasting room one of the most pleasant in the valley and it is the only place to find the Black Queen Sparkling Shiraz. Wooden tables on a shady lawn encourage picnicking on the Weighbridge platter, a selection of local smoked meats, cheeses, and condiments that's big enough for two. Tastings from A$10. ✉ *Para Rd., off Stelzer Rd., Tanunda* ☎ *08/8565–9555* 🌐 *www.peterlehmannwines.com.*

Restaurants

★ FermentAsian

$$ | **ASIAN FUSION** | Whether it's for lunch (more casual) or dinner, the creative modern Southeast Asian cuisine works wonderfully with local and European wines alike, and the selection here is among the best in the region, if not the state. Vietnamese owner chef Tuoi Do incorporates local ingredients into a menu that speaks of her heritage; a tasting menu is available. **Known for:** vegetarian friendly; innovative dishes with beautiful plating; enormous and world-class wine list. $ *Average main: A$35* ✉ *90 Murray St., Tanunda* ☎ *08/8563–0765* 🌐 *fermentasian.com.au* ⏲ *Closed Mon. and Tues. No lunch Wed. No dinner Sun.*

Pace Yourself

Home-smoked meats, organic farmhouse cheeses, and mouth-filling Shiraz—the Barossa is the ultimate picnic basket. Use this fact as an excuse for a long lunch, which will give you time to recover from all that wine tasting. Remember to pace yourself as you taste, and wherever possible, make use of those spittoons you see at each winery. You'll be glad you did.

1918 Bistro & Grill

$$$ | **AUSTRALIAN** | This rustic and whimsical restaurant in a restored villa makes exemplary use of the Barossa's distinctive regional produce in a seasonal Mod Oz menu flavored with tastes from Asia and the Middle East. Local olive oil and seasonal fruits and vegetables influence dishes, and the Barossa-centric wine list includes rare classics and newcomers. **Known for:** garden dining beneath a huge Norfolk pine; satisfying proteins; beautiful heritage decor. $ *Average main: A$38* ✉ *94 Murray St., Tanunda* ☎ *08/8563–0405* 🌐 *www.1918.com.au.*

Coffee and Quick Bites

Apex Bakery

$ | **BAKERY** | **FAMILY** | The wood-fired oven at this popular spot has been running continuously since it was first established in 1924, and the fourth-generation owners still use many of the same recipes with slow-fermenting dough that were in vogue then. Bread and sweet and savory pastries start coming out early each morning, and locals are split as to whether the hearty meat pies or the custard-and-cream-filled *bienenstich* is the better hangover cure. **Known for:** open from 7 most mornings; slow-fermented bread; satisfying meat pies—part of any classic Australian road trip. $ *Average* main: A$6 ✉ 1a Elizabeth St., Tanunda ☎ 08/8563–0000 🌐 www.apexbakery.com.au ⏲ Closed Sun.*

Hotels

Blickinstal Barossa Valley Retreat

$$ | **B&B/INN** | Its name means "view into the valley," which understates the breathtaking panoramas from this lovely B&B. **Pros:** all accommodations have air-conditioning; great-value rooms in convenient location near Tanunda; spa bath and fireplace in the larger rooms. **Cons:** no fine dining on-site; somewhat rustic feeling; don't expect corporate-style facilities or an anonymous stay. *$ Rooms from: A$180 ✉ 261 Rifle Range Rd., Tanunda ☎ 08/8563–2716 🌐 www.blickinstal.com.au 6 rooms Free Breakfast.*

Discovery Park Glamping

$$ | **RESORT** | **FAMILY** | Each of the 12 safari tents at the glamping park within existing Tanunda Valley caravan park features a spacious private deck (some have vineyard views), en suite bathroom, kitchenette, and a large bedroom with split king bed. **Pros:** spacious; beautiful views; heated spa. **Cons:** no restaurant on-site; book in advance; rustic. *$ Rooms from: A$160 ✉ Barossa Valley Way, Tanunda ☎ 08/8218–5505 🌐 www.discoveryholidayparks.com.au/caravan-parks/south-australia/tanunda-barossa-valley 12 rooms No Meals.*

Angaston

10 km (6 miles) northeast of Tanunda, or 14 km (9 miles) via Menglers Hill Road Scenic Drive, 82 km (51 miles) northeast of Adelaide.

Named after George Fife Angas, the Englishman who founded the town and sponsored many of the German and British immigrants who came here, Angaston is full of jacaranda trees, and its quiet main street is lined with stately stone buildings and tiny shops. You can buy a range of delicious regional produce every Saturday morning at the Barossa Farmers Market, behind Vintners Bar & Grill.

Sights

★ Yalumba

WINERY | Australia's oldest family-owned winery, the iconic Yalumba sits within a hugely impressive compound overlooked by an imposing clocktower. It's the only winery in the southern hemisphere with a functioning cooperage on-site, and that can be visited on one of the many tours that start from A$50. A range of tastings are available in the tasting room that is decorated with antique wine-making materials and mementos of the Hill Smith family, whose ancestors first planted vines in the Barossa in 1849. Try the award-winning Viognier and The Signature, a classic Australian "claret" blend of Shiraz and Cabernet. Private tours can be arranged upon request. *✉ 40 Eden Valley Rd., just south of Valley Rd., Angaston ☎ 08/8561–3309 🌐 www.yalumba.com.*

Restaurants

★ Casa Carboni

$$ | **ITALIAN** | Local winemakers and visitors alike love this cozy restaurant and cooking school run by a married couple. Fiona and Matteo Carboni are united by their love for Italy and moved to the Barossa after living in Matteo's native Italy. **Known for:** a lovely gift shop with locally made items; special wine bar on Friday night; local winemakers often dine here. *$ Average main: A$27 ✉ 67 Murray St., Angaston ☎ 0415/157–669 🌐 www.casacarboni.com.au ⏲ Closed Mon.–Wed.*

Vintners Bar & Grill

$$$ | **AUSTRALIAN** | Locals flock to this sophisticated, long-standing favorite, where giant ironwood beams overlook a light-filled dining room and wide windows open out onto rows of vineyards.

An upbeat soundtrack, friendly service, and comfortable charcoal suede chairs make it easy to relax into a leisurely meal, as does the wine list that includes plenty of international options alongside Barossa classics. **Known for:** polished country hospitality; South Australian seafood; a favorite of top winemakers. *[$] Average main: A$38 ✉ 752 Stockwell Rd., Angaston ☎ 08/8564–2488 🌐 www.vintners.com.au ⊙ No dinner Sun.*

Nuriootpa

6 km (4 miles) northwest of Angaston, 74 km (46 miles) northeast of Adelaide.

Long before it was the Barossa's commercial center, Nuriootpa was used as a bartering place by the Kaurna traditional owners, hence its name: Nuriootpa, which may be derived from a word meaning "meeting place." Most locals call it Nurie.

Sights

★ Maggie Beer's Farm Shop

STORE/MALL | Renowned cook and food writer Maggie Beer is an icon of Australian cuisine. Burned-fig jam, ice cream, aged red wine vinegar, verjuice (a golden liquid made from unfermented grape juice and used for flavoring), and her signature Pheasant Farm pâté are some of the delights you can taste and buy at Maggie Beer's Farm Shop. Treat-filled picnic baskets are available all day to take out or dip into on the deck overlooking a tree-fringed pond full of turtles. Book ahead for the paid cooking demonstrations. *✉ 50 Pheasant Farm Rd., Nuriootpa ☎ 08/8562–4477 🌐 www.maggiebeersfarmshop.com.au.*

Penfolds Barossa Valley

WINERY | A very big brother to the 19th-century Magill Estate in Adelaide, this massive wine-making outfit in the center of Nuriootpa lets you taste Shiraz, Cabernet, Merlot, Chardonnay, and Riesling blends—but not the celebrated Grange—at the cellar door. To savor the flagship wine and other premium vintages, book a Taste of Grange Tour (A$150 per person, minimum of two, 24-hour advance notice needed). There are also 90-minute blending workshops for A$85 per person. *✉ 30 Tanunda Rd., Nuriootpa ☎ 08/8568–8408 🌐 www.penfolds.com.*

Marananga

7 km (4 miles) west of Nuriootpa, 71 km (44 miles) northeast of Adelaide.

The tiny hamlet of Marananga inhabits one of the prettiest corners of the Barossa. This area's original name was Gnadenfrei, which means "free by the grace of God"—a reference to the religious persecution the German settlers suffered before they emigrated to Australia. Marananga, the original Kaurna name, was adopted in 1918, when a wave of anti-German sentiment spurred many name changes in the closing days of World War I.

Sights

★ Seppeltsfield Winery

WINERY | Joseph Seppelt was a Silesian farmer who purchased land in the Barossa after arriving in Australia in 1849. Under the control of his son, Benno, the wine-making business flourished, and today Seppeltsfield Winery and its splendid grounds are a tribute to the family's industry and enthusiasm. Fortified wine is a Seppeltsfield specialty; this is the only place in the world where you can find an unbroken lineage stretching back to 1878. Most notable is the exquisite 100-year-old Para Liqueur Tawny. Book ahead for the Centenary Tour that allows you to walk through the cellar and taste it directly from the barrel. The Rosé Grenache and Cabernet are also worth tasting before exploring

Off The Beaten Path

Banrock Station Wine & Wetland Centre. The saltbush and scrub-lined Murray River floodplain 150 km (94 miles) east of Nuriootpa is an unlikely setting for a winery, but it is worth making the journey to this spot at Kingston-on-Murray. Within the eco-friendly rammed-earth building perched above the vineyard and wetlands you can select a wine to accompany an all-day grazing platter or lunch on the outdoor deck—try the baked Murray cod with seasonal quinoa salad. Afterward, you can take one of three self-guided walks (ranging from 2.5 km [1.5 miles] up to 8 km [5 miles]); trail access is by donation) to view the surrounding wetlands (which can be "drylands" during a drought), and learn about the ongoing restoration and conservation work funded by Banrock Station wine sales and walkers' donations. ✉ *Holmes Rd., just off Sturt Hwy., Kingston-on-Murray* ☎ *08/8583–0299* 🌐 *www.banrockstation.com.au.*

the rest of the complex that includes an excellent on-site restaurant, an art gallery and studios that you can visit, a soap factory that runs workshops, and a coffee roaster as well as the Seppelt family mausoleum that overlooks an avenue planted with more than 2,000 palm trees. ✉ *730 Seppeltsfield Rd., 3 km (2 miles) west of Marananga, Seppeltsfield* ☎ *08/8568–6200* 🌐 *www.seppeltsfield.com.au* 🎫 *Tastings from A$10 and tours from A$99.*

★ Torbreck Vintners

WINERY | This is one of Australia's top estate wineries and a good representation of classic, artfully made Barossa wine. The modern and airy tasting room complements its original 1850s settler's cottage cellar door, with subtle color tones and earthy textures. Taste the iconic Shiraz wines on the deck overlooking its renowned Descendant vineyard for A$20, or upgrade to the more premium experience with the renowned RunRig that is blended with Viognier to create a powerful, elegant wine. ✉ *348 Roennfeldt Rd., Marananga* ☎ *08/8568–8123* 🌐 *torbreck.com.*

Two Hands Wines

WINERY | The interior of this 19th-century sandstone cottage is every bit as surprising as the wines produced here. Polished wood and glass surround the contemporary counter where the excellent staff leads you through the tasting of several "out of the box" reds, whites, and blends. The main event is the Garden Series Shiraz sourced from six wine regions;. compare and contrast Shiraz from the Barossa, McLaren Vale, and Adelaide Hills, among others. The Search For The Holy Grail (A$150) takes you into the estate vineyard for a behind-the-scenes look at how the wines are made. ✉ *273 Neldner Rd., Marananga* ☎ *08/8562–4566* 🌐 *www.twohandswines.com* 🎫 *Tastings from A$15.*

Restaurants

★ Hentley Farm

$$$$ | **MODERN AUSTRALIAN** | Lunch at this degustation-only restaurant begins with a walk through the kitchen, and the chefs reappear continually throughout the meal to introduce each new course. It's just one of the personal touches in a memorable meal that relies heavily on locally

Fish Tales

With over 4,000 km (2,485 miles) of coastline and hundreds of miles of rivers, South Australia has almost as many opportunities for fishing as it has varieties of fish. You can join local anglers of all ages dangling hand lines from a jetty, casting into the surf from coastal rocks, hopping aboard charter boats, or spending a day sitting on a riverside log.

The Murray River is the place to head for callop (also called yellow belly or golden perch) and elusive Murray cod—the catch-and-release season lasts from January 1 to July 31. In the river's backwaters you can also net a feed of yabbies, a type of freshwater crayfish, which make a wonderful appetizer before you tuck into the one that didn't get away. In the ocean King George whiting reigns supreme, but there is also excellent eating with mulloway, bream, snapper, snook, salmon, and sweep. The yellowtail kingfish, a great fighter usually found in deep water, can be found in the shallower waters of Coffin Bay on the Eyre Peninsula.

Baird Bay Ocean Eco Experience. Most well-known for their Swim with Sea Lions and Dolphin tours on the Eyre Peninsula—a truly awesome once-in-a-lifetime experience worth every penny of the A$200—this husband-and-wife duo also runs fishing charters on request. Children are welcome. Tours run from September 1 to May 31 when conditions are good. Book ahead to ensure a spot. ✉ *33 Baird Bay Rd., Baird Bay* ☎ *08/8626–5017* 🌐 *www.bairdbay.com* 🎟 *A$200.*

The legendary Kangaroo Island is another top spot for fishing.

Kangaroo Island Fishing Adventures. This tour operator has a fast, clean live-aboard west coaster and specializes in day trips and longer tours along the pristine shores of Kangaroo Island. Anglers can find King George whiting, nannygai, trevally, and tuna in the Investigator Strait, which is rarely fished by private fishing boats, or simply cruise along the island's scenic and secluded north coast. With advance notice he company can also organize accommodation and pick-up when you arrive on the island. ✉ *1170 Western River Rd., Parndana* ☎ *08/8559–3232* 🌐 *www.kangarooislandadventures.com.au.*

grown produce (much of it, including the signature garden leaves that hit the table first, drawn from the on-site gardens). **Known for:** the playful passion-fruit "egg" palate cleanser; extended lunches that showcase the best of this top food and wine region; meaningful interactions with the chefs. $ *Average main: A$210* ✉ *Gerald Roberts Rd. at Jenke Rd., Marananga* ☎ *08/8562–8427* 🌐 *www.hentleyfarm.com.au/dine* ⏲ *Closed Mon.–Wed. No dinner.*

Hotels

The Lodge Country House

$$$$ | **B&B/INN** | Rambling and aristocratic, this bluestone homestead with period-style furniture was built in 1903 for one of the 13 children of Joseph Seppelt, founder of the showpiece winery across the road. **Pros:** views of the vineyards; beautiful gardens; hosts who delight in telling guests about the history of the place. **Cons:** not walkable to town; pricey; no chidren unless booking the entire house. $ *Rooms from: A$380* ✉ *743*

Seppeltsfield Rd., Seppeltsfield ✥ 3 km (2 miles) south of Marananga ☎ 08/8562–8277 🌐 www.thelodgecountryhouse.com.au 🛏 4 rooms 🍽 Free Breakfast.

★ **The Louise**

$$$$ | **RESORT** | Prepare for pampering and privacy at this country estate on a quiet back road with glorious valley views and destination dining at its best. **Pros:** guest comfort is prized here with all sorts of luxury touches; stunning rooms with beautiful private gardens; two on-site dining options. **Cons:** closes every July for renovations; no children under 10; pricey. [$] *Rooms from: A$600 ✉ Seppeltsfield Rd. at Stonewell Rd., Marananga ☎ 08/8562–2722 🌐 www.thelouise.com.au 🛏 15 suites 🍽 Free Breakfast.*

Sevenhill

126 km (78 miles) north of Adelaide.

Sevenhill is the Clare Valley's geographic center, and the location of the region's first winery, established by Jesuit priests in 1851 to produce altar wine. The area had been settled three years earlier by Austrian Jesuits who named their seminary after the seven hills of Rome.

The Riesling Trail, a walking and cycling track that follows an old Clare Valley railway line, runs through Sevenhill. The 35-km (22-mile) trail passes wineries and villages in gently rolling country between Auburn and Clare, and three loop trails take you to vineyards off the main track.

Sights

Kilikanoon Wines

WINERY | Award-winning and internationally known Kilikanoon produces multilayered reds such as the dense, richly colored Oracle Shiraz that has been named best in the world; Prodigal Grenache is another beauty. Tiered tastings allow you to choose 7 or 14 wines highlighting the diversity of soils and microclimates in the Clare Valley, or book ahead for the premium Revelation Experience (A$60) that steps things up a notch with access to Kilikanoon's most exclusive wines including the ultrapremium Revelation Shiraz. *✉ 30 Penna La., 2 km (1 mile) off Main North Rd., Penwortham ☎ 08/8843–4206 🌐 www.kilikanoon.com.au.*

★ **Sevenhill Cellars**

WINERY | **FAMILY** | The area's first winery, Sevenhill Cellars was created by the Jesuits, and they still run the show, with any profits going to education, mission work, and the needy within Australia. In the 1940s the winery branched out from sacramental wine to commercial production, and today make a variety of styles including Riesling (try the St. Francis Xavier label), Verdelho, Grenache, and fortified wines. Enjoy a tasting (A$10, redeemable), then head on a self-guided tour of the grounds that takes in the cellars, the cemetery, and the church crypt where Jesuits have been interred since 1865. *✉ 111C College Rd., just off Main North Rd., Sevenhill ☎ 08/8843–5900 🌐 www.sevenhill.com.au.*

Skillogalee Winery

WINERY | Known for its excellent Riesling, Gewürztraminer, and Shiraz, this boutique winery also has an excellent, if slightly dated, restaurant on-site. Wine tasting takes place in a small room in the 1850s cottage. Don't miss the sparkling Riesling. **TIP→ There's also an on-site, self-contained cottage for rent.** *✉ 45 Trevarrick Rd., Sevenhill ☎ 08/8843–4311 🌐 www.skillogalee.com.au.*

Restaurants

The Rising Sun Hotel

$$ | **MODERN AUSTRALIAN** | People have watched the world go by from the veranda of this landmark hotel in Auburn, 17 km (10 miles) south of Sevenhill, since it was built in 1849. Pull up a chair overlooking the street and partake of the filling comfort food like braised lamb

Off The Beaten Path

Martindale Hall. Just outside the slate-mining hamlet of Mintaro, 10 km (6 miles) southeast of Sevenhill, wealthy bachelor Edmund Bowman built this gracious 32 room manor house in 1879—as legend has it, to lure his fiancée from England to the colonies. He failed, but continued to spend lavishly. In 1891 a near-bankrupt Bowman sold the grand house to the Mortlock family, who in 1965 willed it—and its contents—to the University of Adelaide. Now privately leased, Martindale Hall is a museum of late-19th- and early-20th-century rural life, filled with the Mortlocks' books, beds, furniture, crockery, glassware, and billiard table. The house, which is open for self-guided tours, was featured in director Peter Weir's first film, *Picnic at Hanging Rock.* ✉ *1 Min Man Rd., 3 km (2 miles) south of Mintaro, Mintaro* ☎ *0417/838–897* 🌐 *www.martindalehall-mintaro.com.au* 🎫 *A$15* ⏲ *Closed Tues.*

shanks with wilted greens and creamy mashed potato to go along with an excellent selection of drinks. **Known for:** large list of Clare Valley, Australian, and international beers and ciders; exclusively Clare Valley wines, including old vintages; historical atmosphere. $ *Average main: A$30* ✉ *19 Main North Rd., Auburn* ☎ *08/8849–2015* 🌐 *www.therisingsunhotel.com.au.*

Skillogalee Winery

$$$ | AUSTRALIAN | The dining area at this local favorite spills from a 1850s cottage onto a beautiful veranda overlooking a flower-filled garden and rows of grapevines. The menu changes seasonally, but entrées might include fish tagine with olives, apricots, and Skillogalee figs with saffron and lemon couscous or dukkah-crusted chicken breast. **TIP→ Gourmet picnic baskets can be ordered (24-hours notice required). Known for:** house wines available by the glass; lovely morning and afternoon teas; fireplace in cozy dining room. $ *Average main: A$40* ✉ *Trevarrick Rd., Sevenhill* ☎ *08/8843–4311* 🌐 *www.skillogalee.com.au* ⏲ *No dinner.*

★ Watervale Hotel

$$ | MODERN AUSTRALIAN | It may look like a standard country pub from the outside, but step through the front door and you'll find an entirely different story. Plentiful leather chesterfields, chaise longues, and a shimmering blue-and-gold pressed-tin bar set the scene for the valley's best dining experience. **TIP→ The adjacent six-bedroom house is available for rent and is perfect for larger groups. Known for:** "doggie degustation"—canine-appropriate treats available; hyperseasonal and local produce; an excellent and easy to navigate wine list from Clare and beyond. $ *Average main: A$30* ✉ *37 Main N Rd., 8 km (5 miles) south of Sevenhill, Sevenhill* ☎ *08/8843–0229* 🌐 *watervalehotel.com.au.*

Activities

BICYCLING

Clare Valley Cycle Hire

SCENIC DRIVE | FAMILY | Riding the Riesling Trail from Clare to Auburn is one of the best ways to explore the valley—it takes around 2½ hours to cycle the whole thing (one-way), unless, of course, you get distracted by the wineries along the way. This 35-km-long (22-mile-long) cycling track follows the path of the old rail line that sliced through the hills until it was irreparably damaged by the 1983 Ash Wednesday bushfires. Bikes (including helmets, which are mandatory in Australia) for both adults and kids (and baby seats) can be rented from Clare Valley Cycle Hire. If you want to make life a bit easier, consider an e-bike with a small motor. ✉ *56 Warenda Rd., Clare* ☎ *0475/733–747* 🌐 *www.clarevalleycycle-hire.com.au* 🎫 *From A$25.*

Clare

6 km (4 miles) north of Sevenhill, 136 km (84 miles) north of Adelaide.

The bustling town of Clare is the Clare Valley's commercial center. Unusual for ultra-English South Australia, many of its early settlers were Irish—hence the valley's name, after the Irish county Clare, and place-names such as Armagh and Donnybrook.

GETTING HERE AND AROUND

As with the Barossa wine region, a car is useful for exploring the Clare Valley in any depth as some wineries lay up steep roads on the valley's flanks. Taste wine in moderation if you're driving; as well as keeping yourself and others safe, you'll avoid paying the extremely high penalties for driving while intoxicated.

TOURS

Clare Valley Experiences

Clare Valley Experiences combines wine and beer tasting with food, culture, and cycling on its tour of the region's major wineries and sites (A$295 each for two people, including lunch), departing from Clare. Prices go down with more guests, and there is also a half-day tour available. ✉ *29 Hope St., Clare* ☎ *08/8842–1880* 🌐 *www.clarevalleyexperiences.com* 🎫 *Tours from $140.*

ESSENTIALS

VISITOR INFORMATION Clare Valley Visitor Information Centre. ✉ *8 Spring Gully Rd., 6 km (4 miles) south of Clare, Clare* ☎ *08/8842–2131, 1800/242–131* 🌐 *www.clarevalley.com.au.*

Sights

Knappstein Enterprise Winery & Brewery

WINERY | One of the most recognizable and popular wineries in the Clare Valley, Knappstein is located in the original 19th-century Enterprise Brewery, a Heritage-listed building and a well-known landmark of a township that's oozing with history. The four Rieslings are consistently excellent, and the same could be said for the Cabernet and Shiraz wines lovingly handcrafted here. ✉ *2 Pioneer Ave., Clare* ☎ *08/8841–2100* 🌐 *www.knappstein.com.au.*

Tim Adams Wines

WINERY | The small, no-frills tasting room means there is nothing to distract you from discovering why Tim Adams Wines has a big reputation. The standout in an impressive collection of reds and whites, which includes a celebrated Riesling and delicious Fiano, is the purple-red Aberfeldy Shiraz, made from century-old vines. You can buy wine by the glass or bottle to enjoy with a cheese platter on the large deck. ✉ *156 Warenda Rd. just off Main North Rd., 3 km (2 miles) south of Clare, Clare* ☎ *08/8842–2429* 🌐 *www.timadamswines.com.au.*

Hotels

★ **Bungaree Station**

$$$ | **B&B/INN** | **FAMILY** | Journey back to colonial Australia at this 7,000-acre mixed cropping and sheep farm, where outlying cottages and the Heritage-listed stables beside the stone homestead have been converted into family-friendly, self-contained accommodations, and the reception area and a farm shop selling local wines and produce is located in the original station store. **Pros:** great option for groups, with some cottages sleeping up to 10; fascinating insight into a working homestead; discounts for multiple-night stays. **Cons:** the property lies slightly outside the valley; food options are limited; city types might find it too

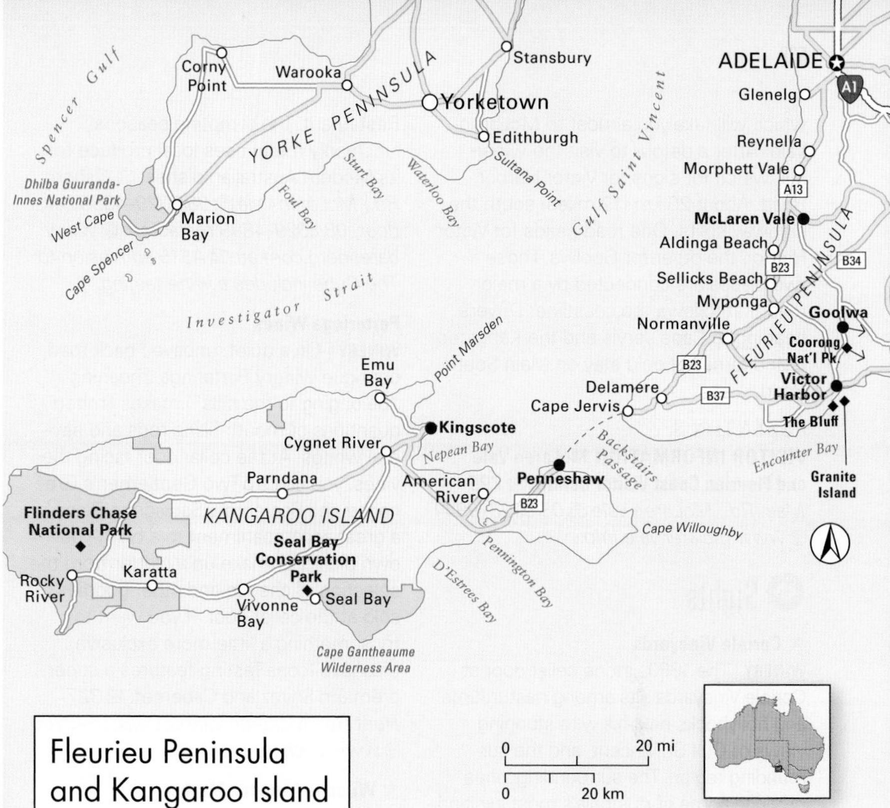

rustic. $ *Rooms from: A$240* ✉ *431 Bungaree Rd., 12 km (7 miles) north of Clare, Clare* ☎ *08/8842–2677* 🌐 *www.bungareestation.com.au* *17 rooms* *Free Breakfast.*

McLaren Vale

39 km (24 miles) south of Adelaide.

Beginning on the outskirts of Adelaide's southern suburbs, the McLaren Vale wine region has a distinctly modern, upscale look, though many of the more than 80 wineries in the area are as old as their Barossa peers. The first vines were planted in 1838 at northern Reynella by Englishman John Reynell, who had collected them en route from the Cape of Good Hope. The McLaren Vale region has always been known for its big—and softer—reds, including Shiraz and Grenache, as well as an increasing number of "alternative" Mediterranean varietals in both red and white. Local microbrewed beer and craft spirits are also becoming popular in the region.

GETTING HERE AND AROUND

The Fleurieu Peninsula is an easy drive south from Adelaide. Renting a car in Adelaide and driving south is the best way to visit the area, especially if you wish to tour the wineries, which aren't served by public transportation. McLaren Vale itself is less than an hour away. Leave central Adelaide along South Terrace or West Terrace, linking with the Anzac Highway, which heads toward Glenelg. At the Gallipoli Underpass intersection with Main South Road, turn left and continue for 6 km (4 miles) before turning onto the Southern Expressway, which will take you almost to McLaren Vale. After a detour to visit the wineries, watch for signs for Victor Harbor Road. About 20 km (12 miles) south the highway splits. One road heads for Victor Harbor, the other for Goolwa. Those two places are connected by a major road that follows the coastline. Drivers heading to Cape Jervis and the Kangaroo Island ferries should stay on Main South Road.

ESSENTIALS

VISITOR INFORMATION McLaren Vale and Fleurieu Coast Visitor Centre. ⌧ *796 Main Rd., McLaren Vale* ☎ *08/8323–9944* 🌐 *www.mclarenvale.info.*

Sights

★ Coriole Vineyards

WINERY | The 1860s stone cellar door at Coriole Vineyards sits among nasturtiums and hollyhocks on a hill with stunning views of Gulf St. Vincent and the surrounding region. The surrounding vines produce some of Australia's most exciting Italian varietal wines, such as Fiano, Sangiovese, and Montepulciano. Coriole also grows olives and makes olive oils, which you can taste along with their wine. Enjoy all three as part of a meal at on-site restaurant Gather, which foregrounds foraged and estate-grown ingredients on a seasonal menu of delicate share plates. The hosted tastings are excellent and should be booked ahead. ⌧ *Chaffeys Rd., near Kays Rd., McLaren Vale* ☎ *08/8323–8305* 🌐 *www.coriole.com.*

d'Arenberg

WINERY | Winemaker Chester Osborn is known for powerful reds and fortified wines as well as quality whites with eye-catching names (the Cenosilicaphobic Cat, anyone?). The winery, family run since 1912, is dominated by the stunning architecture of the d'Arenburg Cube, which is an attraction in itself and overlooks the vineyards, the valley, and the sea, as well as d'Arry's Verandah Restaurant. The tempting seasonal lunch-only menu uses local produce for its Modern Australian dishes. ⌧ *Osborn Rd., McLaren Vale* ☎ *08/8329–4888 cellar door, 08/8329–4848 restaurant* 🌐 *www.darenberg.com.au* 🎫 *A$15 admission to The Cube includes a wine tasting.*

Pertaringa Wines

WINERY | On a quiet, unpaved back road, boutique winery Pertaringa (meaning "belonging to the hills") makes limited quantities of mouth-filling reds and several whites. At the cellar door facing the vines, you can sip Two Gentlemen's Grenache and Scarecrow Sauvignon Blanc, a great accompaniment to a bring-your-own picnic, or make up a platter from the selection of cheese and other goodies sold at the cellar door. If you want to try something a little more exclusive, the A$15 Icons Tasting features a super premium Shiraz and Cabernet. ⌧ *327 Hunt Rd., McLaren Vale* ☎ *08/8383–2700* 🌐 *www.bechardy.com.au.*

★ Wilunga Farmer's Market

MARKET | **FAMILY** | At South Australia's first farmers' market—and arguably its best in terms of the quality of the products and the overall experience—there are more than 60 stalls showcasing local cheese, meat, and produce as well as famous bakeries. There family-friendly, Saturday-morning-only market also has excellent freshly brewed coffee and legendary brisket and pickle sandwiches. Visiting here is a wonderful way to get to know local culture. Occasionally, producers offer workshops on topics such as cheese making. ⌧ *St. Peter's Terr. at High St., Willunga* ☎ *08/8556–4297* 🌐 *www.willungafarmersmarket.com.au.*

Restaurants

Leonards Mill

$$$$ | **MODERN AUSTRALIAN** | In a beautifully restored 160-year-old flour mill, this inviting restaurant on the way to Cape Jervis (and Kangaroo Island) proudly foregrounds local produce. The floor staff know many of the suppliers personally and all ingredients on the prix-fixe menu are sourced within a 50-km (31-mile) radius. **Known for:** evocative heritage setting; a serious commitment to locavore dining; interesting beverage list highlighting lesser-known suppliers. *Average main: A$60 ✉ 7869 Main S Rd., 57 km (35 miles) from McLaren Vale, McLaren Vale ☎ 08/8598–4184 🌐 leonardsmill.com.au ⏲ Closed Mon. and Tues. No lunch Wed., Thurs., and Sun.*

The Little Rickshaw

$$ | **ASIAN** | In the seaside town of Aldinga this cute little spot offers vibrant Southeast Asian cuisine accompanied by an excellent selection of wines, mostly from smaller producers. The restaurant occupies an old blacksmith's shop and adjacent courtyard and is full of charm, while the owners are friendly and accommodating—order the "feed me" option and you won't leave hungry. **Known for:** outdoor courtyard is delightful in the warmer months; friendly, welcoming atmosphere; spices in the dishes complement many lighter local wines. *Average main: A$28 ✉ 24 Old Coach Rd., Aldinga is 10 km (6 miles) southwest of McLaren Vale, McLaren Vale ☎ 0403/784–568 🌐 www.thelittlerickshaw.com.au ⏲ No dinner Sun.–Wed. No lunch Mon.–Sat.*

Maxwell Restaurant

$$$$ | **MODERN AUSTRALIAN** | The multi-course tasting menu at this winery restaurant is the most beautiful food you'll encounter in the Vale. The presentation is often striking and innovative but the dishes themselves are still eminently approachable. **Known for:** mushrooms grown in a limestone cave on-site; memorable, eye-catching dishes; wonderful views. *Average main: A$120 ✉ 19 Olivers Rd., McLaren Vale ☎ 08/8323–8200 🌐 www.maxwellwines.com.au/restaurant ⏲ Closed Mon.–Thurs. No dinner Fri. and Sun.*

★ Salopian Inn

$$ | **MODERN AUSTRALIAN** | Billed as an eclectic regional dining experience, the Salopian Inn sources its food from a home garden (the menu comes with a map of the plot) as well as pasture-fed, locally sourced beef and lamb, free-range poultry and pork, and sustainably caught local seafood. Expect plenty of influences from across Asia in the cooking, which is best sampled on the A$85 tasting menu. **Known for:** delectable pork, ginger, and spring onion dumplings; enjoy a long lunch here any day of the week; focus on sustainability in sourcing ingredients. *Average main: A$30 ✉ Main Rd. at McMurtrie Rd., McLaren Vale ☎ 08/8323–8769 🌐 salopian.com.au ⏲ No dinner Sun.–Wed.*

★ Star of Greece

$$ | **MODERN AUSTRALIAN** | "(Not a Greek restaurant)" warns the menu at this gorgeous restaurant on the cliffs at Port Willunga, 10 km (6 miles) southwest of McLaren Vale. Instead you'll find plenty of seafood drawn from the aqua seas framed by large windows that make this an unforgettable dining experience—the Szechuan pepper squid with seasonal salad is a perennial favorite. **Known for:** popular site for celebrations, with a champagne list to match; stunning beach views; fresh seafood. *Average main: A$35 ✉ 1 Esplanade, Port Willunga ☎ 08/8557–7420 🌐 www.starofgreece.com.au ⏲ Closed Mon. and Tues. No dinner Wed.*

The Victory Hotel

$$ | **MODERN AUSTRALIAN** | **FAMILY** | Local families, winemakers, and travelers all convene here for great seafood and a stellar wine list, all in a relaxed, comfortable setting. There are daily specials not to miss, and the menu ranges from fresh oysters to excellent bar food like classic schnitzel and and salt-and-pepper squid, and also includes more composed Modern Australian dishes with fresh seafood and seasonal vegetables.

■ TIP→ **Proprietor Doug Govan is particularly fond of Burgundy, so you might get to enjoy some very special Pinot Noir if you go down in the cellar to pick out a bottle.** **Known for:** excellent selection of cheeses; incredibly well-stocked wine cellar; patio has views of the gulf. *Average main: A$30 ✉ Old Sellicks Hill Rd., Sellicks Hill ☎ 08/8556–3083 🌐 victoryhotel.com.au.*

Hotels

★ Karawatha Cottages

$$$ | APARTMENT | Since opting for a "treechange" in 2016, hosts Friederike and Georg have embedded themselves in the local community, and guests staying in these cute self-contained cottages can take advantage of the relationships they've built with a range of guest experiences. **Pros:** very peaceful, with wonderful views; multiple wineries within walking distance; friendly owners will help put together an itinerary. **Cons:** at the furthest end of McLaren Vale from the beach; two night minimum; no on-site dining. *Rooms from: A$300 ✉ 285 Blewitt Springs Rd., McLaren Vale ☎ 0434/164–066 🌐 www.karawathacottages.com.au 🍽 Free Breakfast 3 rooms.*

Goolwa

44 km (27 miles) southeast of McLaren Vale, 83 km (51 miles) south of Adelaide.

Beautifully situated near the mouth of the mighty Murray River, which travels some 2,508 km (1,558 miles) from its source in New South Wales, Goolwa grew fat on the 19th-century river paddle-steamer trade. Though it's a lot sleepier these days, its enviable position close to the sea and the combined attractions of Lake Alexandrina and Coorong National Park mean that tourism has replaced river trade as the main source of income.

Sights

Goolwa Wharf

MARINA/PIER | FAMILY | Set sail from here for daily tour cruises upon the *Spirit of the Coorong*, a fully equipped motorboat that offers a 90 minute (A$40) cruise to the Murray Mouth and a 3½-hour (A$95) or 6-hour cruise (A$125) that explore further into Coorong National Park. The 3½-hour tour runs from October to May and both longer cruises include guided walks, lunch, and afternoon tea. Visitors can also enjoy locally brewed craft beer and whiskey at Fleurieu Distillery located in the old railway goods shed on the wharf or go shopping at the Goolwa Wharf Markets on the first and third Sunday of each month. *✉ Goolwa Wharf, Goolwa ☎ 08/8555–2203 🌐 www.coorongcruises.com.au.*

Oscar W

OTHER ATTRACTION | FAMILY | Goolwa is the home port of paddle-steamer *Oscar W*. Built in 1908, it's one of the few remaining wood-fired boiler ships and after plying the river as a trading boat was converted into a tourist attraction in the 1960s. When not participating in commemorative cruises and paddleboat races, the boat is open for inspection and, in warmer weather, one-hour cruises and longer trips that include a lunch stop—check the website for upcoming dates. *✉ Goolwa Wharf, Goolwa ☎ 1300/466–592 🌐 www.oscar-w.info 🎫 Donation requested to inspect boat.*

Victor Harbor

18 km (11 miles) west of Goolwa, 83 km (52 miles) south of Adelaide.

As famous for its natural beauty and wildlife as for its resorts, Victor Harbor is South Australia's favorite seaside getaway. In 1802 English and French explorers Matthew Flinders and Nicolas Baudin met here at Encounter Bay, and by 1830 the harbor was a major whaling center. Pods of southern right whales came here to breed in winter, and they made for a profitable trade through the mid-1800s. By 1878 the whales were hunted nearly to extinction, but the return of these majestic creatures to Victor Harbor in recent decades has established the city as a premier source of information on whales and whaling history.

ESSENTIALS

VISITOR INFORMATION Victor Harbor Visitor Information Centre. ✉ *10 Coral St., Victor Harbor* ☎ *1800/557–094* 🌐 *encountervictorharbor.com.au/visitor-information.*

Sights

The Bluff

VIEWPOINT | FAMILY | Seven kilometers (4½ miles) west of Victor Harbor, the Bluff is where whalers once stood lookout for their prey. Today the granite outcrop, also known as Rosetta Head, serves the same purpose in very different circumstances. It's a steep, 1,400-foot climb to the top via a formed trail to enjoy the bluff views, or you can park near the summit. ✉ *The Bluff, Victor Harbor.*

Cockle Train

TRAIN/TRAIN STATION | FAMILY | Traveling the route of South Australia's first railway line—originally laid between Goolwa and Port Elliot, and extended to Victor Harbor in 1864—the Cockle Train traces the lovely Southern Ocean beaches on its 16-km (10-mile), half-hour journey. The train runs by steam power, subject to availability and weather conditions, daily during summer school holidays (late December to late January), on Easter weekend, and on Wednesday and Sunday in the winter months. A diesel locomotive pulls the heritage passenger cars on days of Total Fire Ban. ✉ *Railway Terr., near Coral St., Victor Harbor* ☎ *08/8263–5621 on days train operates, 1300/466–592* 🌐 *www.steamrangerheritagerailway.org* 🎫 *A$33 round-trip.*

Granite Island

ISLAND | FAMILY | This island is linked to the mainland by a 650-yard causeway, along which Clydesdales pull a double-decker tram. Within Granite Island Nature Park a self-guided walk leads around the island, which is filled with sculptures. **■ TIP→ Look out for seals in the shallows.** ✉ *Granite Island, Victor Harbor* ☎ *1800/557–094* 🌐 *www.parks.sa.gov.au/parks/granite-island-recreation-park* 🎫 *A$20 round-trip tram; A$25 guided nature tours.*

South Australian Whale Centre

VISITOR CENTER | FAMILY | The center tells the often graphic story of the whaling industry along South Australia's coast, particularly in Encounter Bay. Excellent interpretive displays spread over three floors focus on dolphins, seals, penguins, and whales—all of which can be seen in these waters. In whale-watching season the center has a 24-hour information hotline on sightings. ✉ *2 Railway Terr., Victor Harbor* ☎ *08/8551–0750* 🌐 *www.sawhalecentre.com* 🎫 *From A$10.*

Beaches

Boomer Beach

BEACH | The surf here is very big thanks to the exposed reef break. Most waves are dumpers, hence the name Boomer, and can get up to 15 feet high. As a result, this is a beach for surfers and strong swimmers. Waves decrease toward Victor Harbor, providing lower surf and usually calm conditions. In summer the surf tends to be mostly flat, but you need to be vigilant of rocks, rips, and sharks year-round. There is an excellent view down the entire beach from the headland at Port Elliot; from here you can spot the southern right whale, which in winter claims this area as its territory. **Amenities:** lifeguards; parking; toilets. **Best for:** surfing; swimming. ✉ *Port Elliot.*

Horseshoe Bay, Port Elliot

BEACH | **FAMILY** | This wide, sandy beach faces east at the short jetty and swings round to face south against Commodore Point. Because the bay is well protected on either side the waves are relatively low, making this a great swimming destination. However, waves can be heavy during a high swell and surge up the steep beach. The safest swimming is at the western end near the Surf Life Saving Club that also houses a busy restaurant and café. Fishing is popular around the jetty and boundary rocks. **Amenities:** parking; toilets. **Best for:** swimming; walking. ✉ *Basham Parade, Port Elliot.*

Middleton

BEACH | One of South Australia's most popular beaches for beginner and intermediate surfers, Middleton is known for waves that roll in gently rather than breaking violently. As a result it's perfect for those still honing their technique, and several companies offer surf lessons here year-round. The entire beach is composed of fine sand that slopes very gently resulting in predictable, even sets that also suit bodyboarding. Thanks to the very wide surf zone, it is moderately safe to swim in the inner surf zone on the bar, but swimmers are advised not to venture beyond the first line of breakers as strong currents occupy the trough between the sand bars. **Amenities:** parking; toilets. **Best for:** surfing; walking. ✉ *Esplanade, Middleton.*

Activities

BICYCLING

Encounter Bikeway

BIKING | **FAMILY** | Cycling enthusiasts and families alike will love Encounter Bikeway, a paved track that runs 32 km (20 miles) from the Bluff along a scenic coastal route to Laffin Point (east of Goolwa). Almost flat, the bikeway is suitable for riders of most ages and experience levels. **TIP→ When the Cockle Train is operating the Encounter Bikeway users can combine their trip with a journey on the train, traveling one-way on the bike path and returning on the train.** ✉ *Encounter Bikeway, Victor Harbor* 🌐 *encountervictorharbor.com.au/business/encounter-bikeway.*

Off The Beaten Path

Coorong National Park. A sliver of land stretching southeast of the Fleurieu Peninsula, this park hugs the coast for more than 150 km (94 miles). Many Australians became aware of the Coorong's beauty from the 1970s film *Storm Boy*, which told the story of a boy's friendship with a pelican. These curious birds are one reason why the Coorong is a wetland area of world standing. ✉ *Coorong National Park* ✣ *Accessible via Goolwa, Meningie, and Salt Creek off Hwy. 1* ☎ *08/8575–1200* 🌐 *www.parks.sa.gov.au/parks/coorong-national-park.*

Kingscote

119 km (74 miles) southwest of Adelaide.

Kangaroo Island's largest town and main commercial hub, Kingscote is a good base for exploring as there are few food, fuel, or accommodation providers in the island's western half. Reeves Point, just north of the town, is where South Australia's colonial history began. Settlers landed here in 1836 and established the first official town in the new colony. Little remains of the original settlement except Hope Cottage, now a small museum, several graves, and a huge, twisted mulberry tree that grew from a cutting the settlers brought with them. Halfway between Kingscote and the ferry terminal at Penneshaw, American River is named

Remarkable Rocks are one of Kangaroo Island's signature landmarks.

after the American sealers who lived here before colonization and is another accommodation and restaurant hub.

Restaurants

★ Cactus

$ | AUSTRALIAN | This casual diner is a godsend for the island and the fresh, colorful breakfasts and hearty lunches are worth planning a day around. Mexican and Asian influences abound on a menu that's accompanied by local wine, gin, and beer or freshly baked pastries including Portuguese custard tarts that have achieved legendary status. [$] *Average main: A$20* ✉ *54 Dauncey St., Kingscote* ☎ *0473/311–049* ⊕ *facebook.com/cactus.ki.59/.*

Hotels

Aurora Ozone Hotel

$$ | HOTEL | The original Victorian facade on this two-story 1920s hotel is contrasted by modern and spacious rooms that overlook Nepean Bay, and lots of windows, flat-screen TVs, vibrant modern artworks, and some in-room whirlpool tubs make the suites, town houses, and Penthouse Apartments among the island's best. **Pros:** hot and cold buffet breakfast served seven days a week; across the street from the waterfront; friendly staff. **Cons:** gambling on premises might be a no-go for some people; modern design lacks charisma; older rooms are old-fashioned, as is the breakfast. [$] *Rooms from: A$159* ✉ *67 Chapman Terr., Kingscote* ☎ *08/8553–2011, 1800/083–133* ⊕ *www.aurorareSorts.com.au* *78 rooms* *No Meals.*

Kangaroo Island Bayview Villas

$$$ | APARTMENT | FAMILY | Located on a hillside overlooking Nepean Bay and the town of Kingscote, these bayview villas are fully equipped, self-contained accommodations with a private patio and barbecue facilities perfect for the warmer months. **Pros:** good for groups and/or families; panoramic views; modern and spacious. **Cons:** lacks the assistance of a hotel concierge; no on-site dining; stairs may be challenging for those with

Exploring Kangaroo Island

Because Kangaroo Island's main attractions are widely scattered along the breadth of the 145-km-long (90-mile-long) island, the best way to see them is on a guided tour or by car. The main roads form a paved loop, which branches off to such major sites as Seal Bay and Admirals Arch and Remarkable Rocks in Flinders Chase National Park. Stretches of unpaved road lead to lighthouses at Cape Borda and Cape Willoughby, South Australia's oldest. Roads to the island's northern beaches, bays, and camping areas are also unpaved.

Getting to Kangaroo Island

Qantas (*131–313, www.qantas.com.au*) has daily flights between Adelaide and Kingscote, Kangaroo Island's main airport and REX (*131–713, www.rex.com.au*) services the same route twice a week. Flights to the island take about 30 minutes.

SeaLink ferries (*131–301, www.sealink.com.au*) allow visitors to bring cars over to Penneshaw from Cape Jervis, at the tip of the Fleurieu Peninsula, a two-hour drive from Adelaide. There are two daily sailings each way in winter and five in summer, with additional crossings at peak times. SeaLink operates the vehicular passenger ferry *Sea Lion 2000* and *Spirit of Kangaroo Island*, a designated freight boat with passenger facilities. Ferries are the favored means of transportation between the island and the mainland, and reservations are necessary.

Kangaroo Island Tours

Adelaide Sightseeing. Expert local guides will bring you to all the wonderful Kangaroo Island attractions including unique highlights like Remarkable Rocks, Admirals Arch, and Little Sahara. One- and two-day tours with various themes are offered from A$315 and up. ✉ *85 Franklin St., City Center* ☎ *1300/769–762* 🌐 *www.adelaidesightseeing.com.au/kangaroo-island.*

Exceptional Kangaroo Island. Quality four-wheel-drive and bushwalking tours led by a former ranger have a focus on sustainable wildlife encounters in the wild and feature local food served picnic-style. Guides lead guests in conversation on Kangaroo Island's rich history, unique ecology, and contemporary lifestyle. Tailor-made itineraries can also be arranged. ✉ *1139 Playford Hwy., Kingscote* ☎ *08/8553–9119* 🌐 *www.exceptionalkangarooisland.com* 🎫 *From A$496* Ⓜ *Cygnet River.*

Kangaroo Island Odysseys. Luxury four-wheel-drive nature tours range from one to three days: expect lots of wildlife and great food. Tours enter normally restricted areas of the island's national parks for undisturbed nature. ✉ *Addison St., Lot 34, Kingscote* ☎ *08/8553–0386* 🌐 *www.kangarooislandodysseys.com.au* 🎫 *From A$399.*

SeaLink Kangaroo Island. SeaLink Kangaroo Island operates one-day (A$315) bus tours of the island departing from Adelaide, in conjunction with the ferry service from Cape Jervis, leaving at 6:45 am and returning at 10:40 pm. The day tours involve a lot of time on the bus; multiday tours allow more time to enjoy the island, and SeaLink also offers a range ofself-drive packages. ✉ *Level 3, 26 Flinders St., Adelaide* ☎ *131–301* 🌐 *www.sealink.com.au* 🎫 *From A$185.*

mobility issues. $ *Rooms from: A$279* ✉ *2a Reeves St., Kingscote* ☎ *0438/875–812* 🌐 *www.bayview-villas.com.au* *4 apartments* *No Meals.*

Mercure Kangaroo Island Lodge
$ | RESORT | Facing beautiful Eastern Cove at American River, the island's oldest resort, located 39 km (24 miles) southeast of Kingscote, has rooms that overlook open water or the salt-water pool; the most attractive are the "waterview" rooms, which have mud-brick walls, warm terra-cotta tones, and king-size beds. **Pros:** chic bar/lounge area for sipping cocktails and wine; set in beautiful and peaceful surroundings; pool on-site. **Cons:** not many rooms equipped for families; part of a hotel chain, so not as much local charm; dated rooms and basic breakfast. $ *Rooms from: A$139* ✉ *Scenic Dr., American River* ☎ *08/8553–7053, 1800/355–581* 🌐 *www.kilodge.com.au* *38 rooms* *No Meals.*

Wanderers Rest
$$ | B&B/INN | Delightful local artworks dot the walls in this country inn's stylish units, all of which have king-size beds. **Pros:** simple, high-quality accommodations with stunning views; wake up to birdsong; wood fire in the restaurant on cool evenings. **Cons:** rooms aren't particularly unique in design; tours and extras quickly add up; kids under 10 aren't allowed. $ *Rooms from: A$160* ✉ *Bayview Rd., Lot 2, American River* ☎ *08/8553–7140* 🌐 *www.wanderersrest.com.au* *8 suites* *Free Breakfast.*

Penneshaw

59 km (37 miles) east of Kingscote.

This tiny ferry port once had a huge population of penguins—locals would complain about the birds burrowing in their gardens, and you'd often see them around town after dark—but sadly, the colony's numbers have decreased in recent years due to an increased number of seals (and domestic cats and dogs) who prey on the flightless birds. You can still see some on nocturnal tours, but other reasons to visit Penneshaw include a gorgeous shoreline, views of spectacularly blue water, and rolling green hills.

ESSENTIALS

VISITOR INFORMATION Kangaroo Island Visitor Information Centre. ✉ *43 Howard Dr., Penneshaw* ☎ *0417/551–444* 🌐 *www.tourkangarooisland.com.au.*

Sights

Penneshaw Penguin Centre
NATURE PRESERVE | FAMILY | There are now only around 15 pairs of the delightful little (formerly called fairy) penguins in the colony here at Penneshaw. From the indoor interpretive center, where you can read about bird activity—including mating, nesting, and feeding—a boardwalk leads to a viewing platform above rocks and sand riddled with burrows. Because the penguins spend most of the day fishing at sea or inside their burrows, the best viewing is after sunset. The informative guided tours leave from the center after sunset daily except Wednesday and Thursday. You might see penguins waddling ashore, chicks emerging from their burrows to feed, or scruffy adults molting. Although sometimes you may not see any at all. Bookings essential. ✉ *Middle Terr. at Bay Terr., Penneshaw* ☎ *0430/411–487* 🌐 *www.penneshawpenguincentre.com* *Guided tours A$25* ⏲ *Closed Feb. 1–21.*

Beaches

Island Beach
BEACH | Known locally as Millionaires' Row for its fabulous real estate, Island Beach is the quintessential beach holiday location. Framed by dense bushland, the sandy beach is secluded, stretches almost as far as the eye can see, and provides very safe swimming. Walking along the coast toward American River

yields plenty of bird-watching opportunities. **Amenities:** food and drink; parking. **Best for:** solitude; swimming; walking. ✉ *Island Beach* ✢ *Off Island Beach Rd.*

Restaurants

Millie Mae's Pantry

$ | **AUSTRALIAN** | Shaded by a large mulberry tree, this cute café has a short blackboard menu that changes daily to incorporate fresh produce from the colorful on-site garden and beyond. Salvaged materials give the large deck a rustic feel and the eponymous pantry is filled with a huge variety of goods from local producers. *$ Average main: A$15* ✉ *1 Nat Thomas St., Penneshaw* ☎ *0455/680–292* 🌐 *www.milliemaespantry.com.*

Hotels

BIG4 Cape Jervis Accommodation & Caravan Park

$ | **HOTEL** | **FAMILY** | Overlooking the deceptively calm Backstairs Passage and the sea cliffs of Kangaroo Island beyond, this remote spot (it's on the mainland but due to ferry times, it's a popular spot for those heading to the island) feels like it marks the edge of civilization. **Pros:** wonderful views of Kangaroo Island; 24-hour check-in; close to the ferry terminal. **Cons:** no in-house dining and very few nearby options; limited Wi-Fi and cellular service; rooms are a little rustic. *$ Rooms from: A$133* ✉ *9351 Main S Rd., 105 km (65 miles) south of Adelaide, near mainland ferry terminal, Penneshaw* ☎ *08/8598–0288* 🌐 *www.big4.com.au/caravan-parks/sa/fleurieu-peninsula/cape-jervis-accommodation-caravan-park* 🍽 *No Meals* *16 rooms.*

Seafront Kangaroo Island

$$ | **HOTEL** | This hotel has an ideal position near the ferry terminal and overlooking Penneshaw Bay. You can choose an ocean-view room or stay amid tropical gardens in freestanding chalets. **Pros:** nice views; steps away from ferry terminal and penguin viewing; pool. **Cons:** limited disabled access; on-site restaurant lacks atmosphere; quite no-frills in terms of design and decor. *$ Rooms from: A$190* ✉ *49 North Terr., Penneshaw* ☎ *08/8553–1028, 1800/624–624* 🌐 *www.seafront.com.au* *28 rooms.*

Seal Bay Conservation Park

60 km (37 miles) southwest of Kingscote via South Coast Rd.

There are no seals at Seal Bay, but a visit is a highlight of most people's time on Kangaroo Island—it's one of the only places in the world where you can walk along a beach crowded with wild sea lions (in the company of a trained guide). The endangered Australian sea lion is one of the rarest species in the world and Seal Bay is home to around 800—the misleading name is thanks to whalers who couldn't tell the difference between seals and sea lions (the latter have ear flaps and can use their back flippers to "walk" on land, unlike seals). The tours here are some of the best close-up animal encounters of their kind.

Sights

★ **Seal Bay Conservation Park**

WILDLIFE REFUGE | **FAMILY** | This top Kangaroo Island attraction gives you the chance to visit one of the state's largest Australian sea lion colonies. About 300 animals usually lounge on the beach, except on stormy days when they shelter in the dunes. You can visit the beach and get surprisingly close to females, pups, and bulls on a 45-minute tour with an interpretive officer; otherwise, you can follow the self-guided boardwalk to a lookout over the sand. The park visitor center has fun and educational displays, and a touch table covered in sea-lion skins and bones. There is also a souvenir shop. ✉ *Seal Bay*

"Naptime on the beach at Kangaroo Island" —photo by Istarr, Fodors.com member

Conservation Park ✣ End of Seal Bay Rd. ☏ 08/8553–4463 🌐 www.sealbay.sa.gov.au/home 🎫 From A$17.

Beaches

Hanson Bay

BEACH | This beach is off the beaten path. A narrow, winding, unsealed road off South Coast Road, 46 km (29 miles) west of Seal Bay Road, ends at this perfect little sandy cove. Rocky headlands on either side protect the gently sloping beach so swimming is safe. To the east are several secluded beaches; these are more exposed, though, and riptides make swimming dangerous. **Amenities:** parking; toilets. **Best for:** surfing; swimming; walking. ✉ *W. River Rd., off S. Coast Rd., Karatta.*

Flinders Chase National Park

102 km (64 miles) west of Kingscote.

Some of Australia's most beautiful coastal scenery is in Flinders Chase National Park on Kangaroo Island.

Sights

★ **Flinders Chase National Park**

NATIONAL PARK | Much of Kangaroo Island has been given over to farmland but since being declared a national treasure in 1919, a huge area of original vegetation has been protected in Flinders Chase. The catastrophic wildfires that swept through Kangaroo Island in early 2020 burnt 98% of the park but within weeks green shoots had begun to re-emerge and wildlife returned soon afterward. Now the regenerating landscape offers

The effects of the sea are visible in oddly shaped rocks at Flinders Chase National Park.

a unique chance to observe how well adapted Australian flora is to bushfires; many native species need fire to reproduce.

The best way to see the park is on foot and several short walking trails meander through shaded valleys or along spectacular coastal cliffs. But the undoubted highlight is the 61-km (38-mile) Kangaroo Island Wilderness Trail, which adds tannin-stained creeks, mallee scrub, sugar gum forests, and isolated beaches into the mix as well as passing the aforementioned geological marvels. Walkers can hike the full five-day trail or tackle a single section with a range of licensed tour operators. The effects of seas crashing mercilessly onto Australia's southern coast are visible in the oddly shaped rocks on the island's shores. ✉ *S. Coast Rd., Flinders Chase National Park* 🌐 *www.parks.sa.gov.au/parks/flinders-chase-national-park* 🎫 *From A$12.*

 Hotels

★ Ecopia

$$$$ | APARTMENT | Most visitors to Kangaroo Island spot plenty of wildlife, but a stay at these off-grid rammed earth villas near the center of the island makes it a certainty. **Pros:** the remote location means brilliant night skies; lots of wildlife; fully equipped kitchen and outdoor grill. **Cons:** reaching the property involves driving on unsealed roads; it's a long way to the shops for supplies; minimum two-night stay. $ *Rooms from: A$660* ✉ *563B Gregors Rd., 58 km (36 miles) from Flinders Chase, Flinders Chase National Park* ☎ *0414/751–733* 🌐 *www.ecopiaretreat.com.au* 🍽 *No Meals* 🛏 *3 villas.*

 Activities

FISHING

Fishing is excellent on Kangaroo Island's beaches, bays, and rivers. No permit is required for recreational fishing, but minimum lengths and bag limits apply.

You can pick up a fishing guide from the information center in Penneshaw.

Caltex Kingscote
FISHING | This spot sells fishing tackle and bait. ✉ *26 Telegraph Rd., Kingscote* ☎ *08/8553–2725.*

Coober Pedy

850 km (526 miles) northwest of Adelaide.

Known as much for the way some of the 1,700 inhabitants live—underground in dugouts gouged into the hills to escape the relentless heat—as for its opal riches, Coober Pedy is arguably Australia's most singular place. The town is ringed by mullock heaps, pyramids of rock, and sand left over after mine shafts are dug.

Opals are Coober Pedy's reason for existence. Australia has 95% of the world's opal deposits, and Coober Pedy has the bulk of that wealth; this is the world's richest opal field.

GETTING HERE AND AROUND

REX/Regional Express Airlines flies direct to Coober Pedy from Adelaide three times a week. Because it's the only public carrier flying to Coober Pedy, prices are sometimes steep. The airport is open only when a flight is arriving or departing. At other times, contact the Desert Cave Hotel (*see Hotels*).Greyhound Australia buses leave Adelaide's Central Bus Station for Coober Pedy daily. Tickets for the 12-hour overnight ride can cost A$200 each way.The main road to Coober Pedy is the Stuart Highway from Adelaide, 850 km (527 miles) to the south. Alice Springs is 700 km (435 miles) north of Coober Pedy. The drive from Adelaide to Coober Pedy takes about nine hours. From Alice Springs it's about seven hours.A rental car enables you to see what lies beyond Hutchison Street, but you'll need to book well in advance as Budget is the only operator in town and rates are quite high, so an organized tour is a better way to do so. If driving yourself, be aware that although some roads are unpaved—those to the Breakaways and the Dog Fence, for example—surfaces are generally suitable for conventional vehicles. Check on road conditions with the police if there has been substantial rain and avoid driving at dawn and dusk when kangaroos are out in force.The most interesting route to Flinders Ranges National Park from Adelaide takes you north through the Clare Valley vineyards and Burra's copper-mining villages. For a more direct journey to Wilpena Pound, follow the Princes Highway (A1) north to Port Augusta, and then head east toward Quorn and Hawker. A four-wheel-drive vehicle is highly recommended for traveling on the many gravel roads around the national park.

TRANSPORTATION Coober Pedy Airport. ✉ *Airport Rd., off Stuart Hwy., 2 km (1 mile) north of town, Coober Pedy* ☎ *08/8672–5688.***Greyhound Australia.** ✉ *52–56 Hutchinson St., Coober Pedy* ☎ *1300/473–946* 🌐 *www.greyhound.com.au.***Rex Airlines.** ☎ *131–713* 🌐 *www.rex.com.au.*

ESSENTIALS

VISITOR INFORMATION Coober Pedy Visitor Information Centre. ✉ *Coober Pedy District Council Bldg., Hutchison St., Lot 773, Coober Pedy* ☎ *08/8672–4617* 🌐 *www.cooberpedy.com.*

Sights

Fossicking, or searching for opal gemstones—locally called noodling—requires no permit at the Jewellers Shop mining area at the edge of town. Ask at the visitor information center if you need help finding it.

Take care in unmarked areas and always watch your step, as the area is littered with abandoned opal mines that are not marked or fenced off. (Working mines are off-limits to visitors.)

Although most of Coober Pedy's devotions are decidedly material in nature, the town does have its share of spiritual houses of worship. In keeping with the town's layout, they, too, are underground. **St. Peter and St. Paul Catholic Church** is a National Heritage–listed building, and the Anglican **Catacomb Church** is notable for its altar fashioned from a windlass (a winch) and lectern made from a log of mulga wood. The **Serbian Orthodox Church** is striking, with its scalloped ceiling, rock-carved icons, and brilliant stained-glass windows.

Kanku-Breakaways Conservation Park

SCENIC DRIVE | This striking series of buttes and jagged hills centered on the Moon Plain is of great cultural and spiritual significance to the traditional owners but to the untrained eye is reminiscent of most spectacular parts of the American West. There are fossils and patches of petrified forest in this strange landscape, which has appealed to makers of apocalyptic films; *Mad Max 3—Beyond Thunderdome* was filmed here, as was *Ground Zero.* The scenery is especially evocative early in the morning or at sunset when the colors come alive, and can get very windy so be sure to bring appropriate clothing. Kanku-Breakaways Conservation Park is 30 km (19 miles) northeast of Coober Pedy. Permits to explore the area cost A$10 per vehicle and can be purchased at the Coober Pedy Tourist Information Centre in the District Council Office on Hutchinson Street or from Underground Books. ✉ *Coober Pedy* ✣ *Off Stuart Hwy. 33 km (20 miles) north of Coober Pedy* 🌐 *www.parks.sa.gov.au/parks/kanku-breakaways-conservation-park* 🎫 *Permits A$10 per vehicle.*

★ **Mail Run Tour**

INDIGENOUS SIGHT | This 12-hour, 600-km (372-mile) tour through the Outback (A$340) is one of the most unusual experiences anywhere, with stops at outback cattle stations, bush pubs, and the world's longest man-made structure, the Dingo Fence. Tours (maximum of four people per tour; price is per person) depart Monday and Thursday at 8:45 am. ✉ *Post Office Hill Rd., Lot 374, Coober Pedy* ☎ *08/8672–5226* 🌐 *www.mailruntour.com* 🎫 *A$340.*

Old Timers Mine

MINE | **FAMILY** | This is a genuine opal mine turned into a museum. Two fully furnished underground houses give some idea of what an opal miner's life must have been like, while mining memorabilia is exhibited in an extensive network of hand-dug tunnels and shafts. Self-guided tours include the chance to noodle in nearby pits and see a selection of valuable opals under natural and UV light. ✉ *2190 Crowders Gully Rd., Coober Pedy* ☎ *08/8672–5555* 🌐 *oldtimersmine.com.au* 🎫 *A$15.*

★ **Umoona Opal Mine & Museum**

MINE | **FAMILY** | This is an enormous underground complex with an original mine, a noteworthy video on the history of opal mining, exhibits examining the Indigenous and European history of the region, and examples of underground bunk camping and cooking facilities. Learn about the story of opal, different types and qualities of opal, examples of hand-dug and modern dugouts, and the experience of living underground. Guided tours of the mine (A$13) are available at 10, 2, and 4 daily. There is also an opal shop and museum with noteworthy opals and fossils that are free to view. ✉ *14 Hutchison St., Coober Pedy* ☎ *08/8672–5288* 🌐 *www.umoonaopalmine.com.au* 🎫 *A$13.*

Restaurants

Italo-Australian Miners Club

$ | **ITALIAN** | Adorned with photographs from a bygone era, this casual eatery opened in 1964 during the height of opal mining and is a popular spot for viewing the sunset, watching a rugby game on

TV, and unwinding at the end of a day of sightseeing. Comforting dishes like lasagna are served as are beer and Australian wine. **Known for:** generous portions; historical feeling; no-frills and affordable drinking and eating. *Average main: A$20* ✉ *Italian Club Rd., Coober Pedy* ☎ *08/8672–5101* *Closed Sun. and Tues.*

Hotels

★ **Desert Cave Hotel**

$$ | HOTEL | This underground hotel presents a contemporary, blocky face to the desert town. **Pros:** peaceful underground rooms; unique place to stay; pool is welcome relief in the heat. **Cons:** can be pushy with various tour offerings; Umberto's is closed during summer; underground rooms are not for the claustrophobic. *Rooms from: A$170* ✉ *Hutchison St. at Post Office Hill Rd., Lot 1, Coober Pedy* ☎ *08/8672–5688* *www.desertcave.com.au* *50 rooms* *No Meals.*

The Underground Motel

$ | HOTEL | The Breakaways sometimes seem close enough to touch at this hilltop motel, where you can lounge on a veranda watching the sun set on the rock formations 30 km (19 miles) across the desert. **Pros:** small cubby house for children; lovely patio to sit out on and watch the stars; very helpful owners. **Cons:** can be noisy on windy days on account of the air shaft; rooms are a little dated; slightly out of town, which in the heat is a disadvantage. *Rooms from: A$135* ✉ *Catacomb Rd. at Big Johns Rd., Lot 1138, Coober Pedy* ☎ *08/8672–5324* *www.theundergroundmotel.com.au* *9 rooms* *No Meals.*

Ikara-Flinders Ranges National Park

700 km (434 miles) southeast of Coober Pedy, 440 km (273 miles) northeast of Adelaide.

Extending north from Spencer Gulf, the Flinders Ranges mountain chain includes one of Australia's most impressive Outback parks—the 360-square-mile Ikara–Flinders Ranges National Park. Once the bed of an ancient sea, these dry, folded, and cracked mountains and deep valleys today are covered by cypress pine and casuarina, and the creeks are lined with magnificent river red gums. The area is utterly fascinating—for geologists, for bird-watchers, for photographers, and for anyone else who revels in wild, raw scenery and exotic plant and animal life.

ESSENTIALS

VISITOR INFORMATION Wilpena Pound Visitor Centre. ✉ *1 Wilpena Rd., Hawker* ☎ *08/8648–0048* *www.wilpenapound.com.au/do/visitor-Information-centre.*

Sights

★ **Ikara-Flinders Ranges National Park**

NATIONAL PARK | FAMILY | Numerous trails, some of them quite steep, make the Flinders Ranges ideal for bushwalking even though the park has few amenities. Water in this region is scarce, and should be carried at all times. The best time for walking is during the relatively cool months between April and October. This is also the wettest time of year, so you should be prepared for rain. Wildflowers, including the spectacular Stuart's desert pea, can sometimes be found in early spring when male emus look after clutches of cute striped chicks. The park's most spectacular (and strenuous) walking trail leads to the summit of 3,840-foot St. Mary's Peak, the highest point on the Pound's rim and South Australia's second-tallest peak. Visitors are asked not to climb all the way up because of its great spiritual significance to Adnyamathanha traditional owners; fortunately the views from nearby Tanderra Saddle are just as spectacular, stretching far over the surrounding landscape towards vast glittering salt pans in the distance. Give yourself a full day to get up and back. ✉ *Hawker* ✣ *End of Wilpena Rd.* 🌐 *www.parks.sa.gov.au/parks/ikara-flinders-ranges-national-park* 🎫 *A$12 entry fee per vehicle.*

Wilpena Pound

NATURE SIGHT | FAMILY | At the center of the park is Wilpena Pound, a craterlike 80-square-km (31-square-mile) natural bowl ringed by hills that curve gently upward, only to fall away from the rims of sheer cliffs. Geologists will tell you that it is in fact a synclinal basin while for the Adnyamathanha traditional owners it was formed by two giant serpents who went to the sleep. The only entrance to the Pound is a narrow cleft through which Wilpena Creek sometimes runs. The best way to see it is from above—scenic flights are available at Wilpena Pound Resort (from A$186) and are well worth the splurge. ✉ *Wilpena Rd., Hawker* 🌐 *www.parks.sa.gov.au/parks/ikara-flinders-ranges-national-park.*

Hotels

★ **Wilpena Pound Resort**

$$$ | RESORT | You couldn't ask for a more idyllic and civilized nature outpost than this popular resort at the entrance to Wilpena Pound. **Pros:** glamping done right; quiet and peaceful rooms; perfect for animal lovers. **Cons:** necessities are a drive away; permanent tents are overpriced; campsites can be overrun with school groups. $ *Rooms from: A$227* ✉ *1 Wilpena Rd., Hawker* ✣ *156 km (97 miles) off Princes Hwy. via town of Hawker* ☎ *08/8648–0004* 🌐 *www.wilpenapound.com.au* 🛏 *121 rooms* 🍽 *No Meals.*

Chapter 11

THE OUTBACK

Updated by
Amy Nelmes Bissett

Sights	Restaurants	Hotels	Shopping	Nightlife
★★★★★	★★★☆☆	★★★☆☆	★☆☆☆☆	★★☆☆☆

WELCOME TO THE OUTBACK

TOP REASONS TO GO

★ **Red Heart:** Watching the sun rise and set at Uluru is an unforgettable, once-in-a-lifetime experience.

★ **Old Culture:** The Red Centre, Top End, and the Kimberley are the best places to encounter and learn about the oldest continuous culture in the world, that of Australia's Aboriginal people.

★ **National Parks:** With spectacular terrain and one-of-a-kind plant and animal species, the rugged national parks of the Outback tell the story of Australia's age-old landforms, with the Kimberley region an unforgettable highlight.

★ **Wild Rivers:** The waterways and billabongs of the Top End teem with wildlife, including saltwater crocodiles, barramundi, and a multitude of birdlife.

★ **Cable Beach:** Ride a camel into the sunset on one of Australia's most beautiful beaches or sit back and soak it all in.

Big, vast, expansive, huge—whichever way you cut it, Australia's Outback is daunting. This, in many respects, is the "real Australia" as you imagine it—remote, mostly uninhabited, the landscape ground down over millennia.

Getting around by road will absorb weeks, if not years, but fortunately air services can cut the travel times between the gems of this vast area—the Red Centre, the Top End, and the Kimberley—significantly.

1 **Alice Springs.** Often referred to as the headquarters of the Outback, this is the starting point for desert adventures.

2 **East and West MacDonnell Ranges.** The ranges hide some of Australia's most famous landscapes, with incredible geological formations spotted throughout.

3 **Watarrka National Park (Kings Canyon).** Lace up your walking boots and head to the towering red rock cliffs better known as Kings Canyon.

4 **Uluru–Kata Tjuta National Park.** The immense monolith forms part of the traditional belief system to the traditional owners of the land.

5 **Darwin.** Tropical capital city packed with a diverse food scene. The perfect base for Top End adventures.

6 **Kakadu National Park.** The largest national park in Australia offering unspoiled wilderness and ancient Aboriginal art.

7 **Katherine Gorge.** Thirteen impressive gorges stretch for as far as the eye can see. An area best explored by canoe.

8 **Kununurra.** The eastern gateway to East Kimberley, a world where on-land and water adventures await.

9 **Purnululu (Bungle Bungle) National Park.** With unique sandstone formations, this striking geological landmark is best viewed from above.

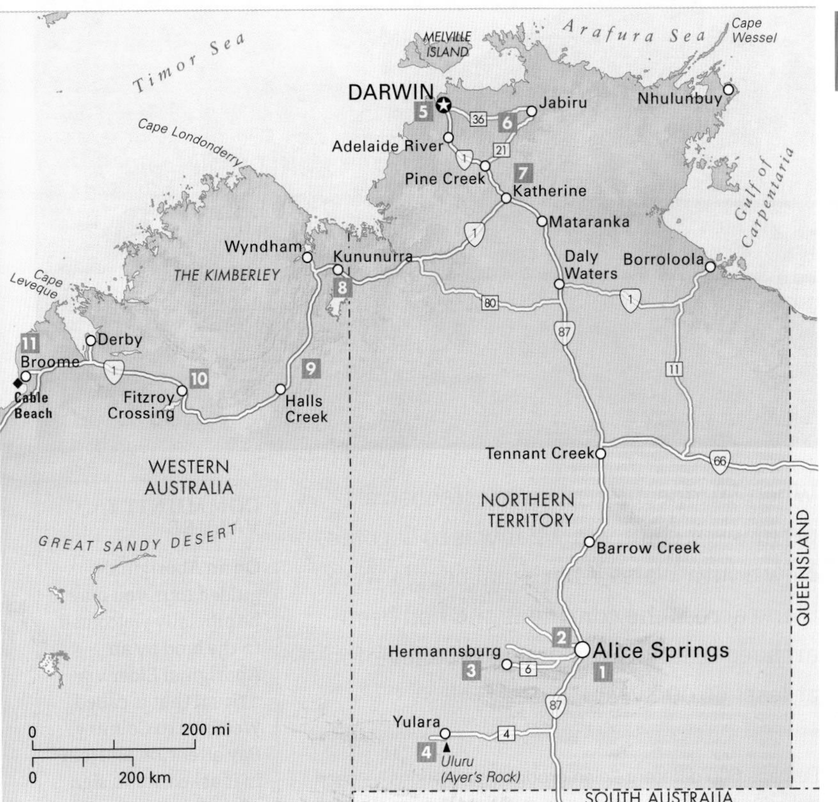

10 Danggu Geikie Gorge National Park. Spectacular multicolor deep cliffs carved by the floodwaters of the Fitzroy River.

11 Broome. Home to the idyllic Cable Beach, sunset camel rides, and pearl farms.

ABORIGINAL CULTURE

When Europeans arrived to establish a permanent colony in what was to become New South Wales, Aboriginal people were living across the continent and had been, archaeologists and geneticists believe, for at least 60,000 years.

Perhaps 600 different "clan groups" or "nations"—each with its own distinctive culture and beliefs—greeted the new settlers in a clash of civilizations that remains largely unresolved today. Despite the efforts of governments of all persuasions and society at large, Aboriginal people by all measures—economic, health, social, education—remain an underprivileged group.

But Aboriginal culture as expressed in oral tradition, art, and lifestyle is of growing interest to travelers. Experiences range from taking organized tours to viewing dance performances, and from shopping for traditional art, to visiting Aboriginal communities. Tourism here represents an important source of income, ensuring that local communities prosper and that their heritage is preserved.

COMMUNITY VALUES

On an Aboriginal-guided tour, you may be officially welcomed to the land by an Aboriginal Elder via a ritual that is called Welcome to Country. Pay attention and join in if asked; it is a sign of good manners and respect to your local hosts.

There were once strict rules about eye contact so you may find that some people won't make eye contact with you. This, or lowering the eyes, are two actions that are a show of respect toward older people.

SACRED SITES

Uluru's (Ayers Rock) traditional owners, the Anangu people, believe they are direct descendants of the beings—which include a python, an emu, a blue-tongue lizard, and a poisonous snake—who formed the land and its physical features during the Tjukurpa (the "Dreamtime," or creation period). Uluru is one of the world's largest monoliths, though such a classification belies the otherworldly, spiritual energy surrounding it.

Kakadu National Park contains some of the best ancient rock art accessible to visitors in Australia. The Anbangbang Gallery features a frieze of Aboriginal rock painting dating back thousands of years, and among the six galleries at Ubirr there is a 49-foot frieze of X-ray paintings depicting animals, birds, and fish. Warradjan Aboriginal Cultural Centre's large display, developed by the local Bininj/Mungguy people, provides detailed information about culture in Kakadu.

Although the Bungle Bungle Range in **Purnululu National Park** was extensively used by Aboriginal people during the wet season, when plant and animal life was abundant, few Europeans knew of its existence until the mid-1980s. The area is rich in Aboriginal rock art, and is home to many burial sites, although these are not typically open to visitors.

Farther west in the **Kimberley Region** the pearling town of **Broome** is the starting point for many adventure tours into the most remote sections of the Outback along the legendary Gibb River Road, as well as for visits to Aboriginal communities like Bardi Creek, Biridu Community, and One Arm Point Community with local Aboriginal guides. Danggu Geikie Gorge, Windjana Gorge, and Tunnel Creek combine wilderness scenery with Indigenous rock art, lifestyles, and stories from the Dreamtime.

TOP SIGHTS

By far the best way to experience Aboriginal culture is on foot with an experienced guide, though at some national parks, interpretive centers, signage, and—occasionally—self-guided audio equipment mean you can visit on your own. Going about it on foot generally requires a level of fitness and surefootedness for trails and pathways; even the best locations are uneven and stony, and can include steep climbs. Boats provide an easier alternative—at Danggu Geikie Gorge and Kakadu guided tours offered along the waterways include information about Aboriginal culture.

From Broome, four-wheel-drive safaris can get you into remote Aboriginal communities where you can meet the locals and listen to tales of the Dreamtime around the campfire.

If mobility is an issue, there are easily accessible interpretive centers at Uluru and Kakadu national parks with extensive displays describing traditional and contemporary Aboriginal life.

Few visitors who explore Australia's remote Red Centre and wild Top End are left unmoved by the stark, expansive beauty of the landscape. The Outback's amazing World Heritage national parks, many on the ancestral homelands of the traditional Indigenous owners, are home to some of Australia's most fascinating and iconic natural attractions.

These include Uluru (Ayers Rock), the magnificent Bungle Bungles, and the vast bird-filled wetlands and raging waterfalls of Kakadu. The Outback contains deeply carved rock canyons, deserts with unending horizons, and prolific wildlife. It is Australia at its wildest, rawest, and most sublime, and it's a landscape that will sear itself onto your memory forever.

The Top End of Australia is a geographic description—but it's also a state of mind. Isolated from the rest of Australia by thousands of miles of desert and lonely scrubland, Top Enders are different and proud of it, making the most of their isolation with a strongly independent and individualistic attitude. The region is a melting pot of cultures and traditions. Darwin and Broome—closer geographically to the cities of Southeast Asia than to any Australian counterparts—host the nation's most racially diverse populations with a multicultural cast of characters sharing a relaxed, tropical lifestyle.

In the west, the Kimberley offers some of the most dramatic landscapes in Australia. A land of rugged ranges and vast cattle stations, this is still the frontier, a place even few Australians get to see.

Like Top Enders, the people of the region see themselves as living in a land apart from the rest of the nation, and it's easy to see why: climate extremes, inaccessibility of the landscape, and great distances combine to make the Kimberley one of the world's few uniquely unpeopled spaces.

For thousands of years, this area of northern and central Australia has been home to Aboriginal communities that have undiminished ties to the land. Stunning examples of ancient rock art remain—on cliffs, in hidden valleys, and in city art galleries and cooperative art centers in remote communities. Aboriginal artwork has now moved into Australia's mainstream art movement, and some expensive canvases by local artists decorate galleries, homes, and corporate boardrooms around the world. But there is more to Aboriginal culture than art, and there is no better place to try and understand it than here, on a guided tour of some of the country's most spiritually significant sites.

MAJOR REGIONS

Red Centre has as its primary areas of interest Alice Springs, which is flanked by the intriguing East and West MacDonnell Ranges, with their cliffs and gorges; Watarrka National Park (Kings Canyon); and Uluru–Kata Tjuta National Park, home to Uluru (pronounced *oo*-loo- *roo* and also called Ayers Rock) and Kata Tjuta (*ka*-ta *tchoo*-ta and also known as The Olgas). Uluru, that magnificent stone monolith rising from the plains, is one of Australia's iconic images and is the main reason people visit the Red Centre. Unless you have more than three days, focus on only one of these Red Centre areas.

The **Top End** of Australia packs in some of the world's great natural environments, and with few people to crowd the views. From Arnhem Land in the east—home to remote Aboriginal people—to the lush tropical city of Darwin, the Top End offers some of the most dramatic landscapes in Australia, along with modern and ancient Aboriginal art and locals with a definite individualistic attitude. It's a land of rugged ranges and tropical wetlands, of vast cattle stations and awe-inspiring national parks, including Kakadu National Park, a wilderness area that is one of Australia's natural jewels and the reason many people come to this part of Australia. Nitmuluk (Katherine Gorge) and Litchfield National Park are also here.

Look no further than the **Kimberley** for a genuine Outback experience. Perched on the northwestern hump of Western Australia only half as far from Indonesia as it is from Sydney, the Kimberley remains a frontier of sorts, remote and with few facilities and people (only 45,000 people living in an area of 423,517 square km [163,521 square miles]). The region contains such spectacular national parks as Kununurra, a good base for exploring Mirima National Park; Purnululu (Bungle Bungle) National Park, a vast area of bizarrely shaped and colored rock formations; and Danggu Geikie Gorge National Park, an ancient flooded reef with red walls from iron oxide—as well as numerous tropical forests, croc-infested rivers, and soaring cliffs, and the town of Broome, rich in pearl history. The region is also dotted with cattle stations. The first European explorers, dubbed by one of their descendants as "kings in grass castles," ventured into the heart of the region in 1879 to establish cattle stations. They subsequently became embroiled in one of the country's longest-lasting conflicts between white settlers and Aboriginals, led by Jandamarra of the Bunuba people.

Planning

When to Go

May to October are the best months to visit the Red Centre and the Top End; nights are crisp and cold, while days are pleasantly warm. Summer temperatures in the Centre—which can rise above 43°C (109°F)—are oppressive, while the wet season (November through April) means Darwin and surroundings are hot, humid, and, well, wet. In the Kimberley, June through August is the preferred season, with usually clear skies and balmy days and nights.

In the Top End, the year is divided into the wet season (the Wet; November through April) and the dry season (the Dry; May through October). The Dry is a period of idyllic weather with warm days and cool nights, while the Wet brings extreme humidity and monsoonal storms that dump an average of 59 inches of rain in a few months, resulting in widespread road closures. You can also catch spectacular electrical storms, particularly over the ocean. The "Build Up," usually sometime between late-September and mid-November, is the Top End's most oppressive weather period in terms of humidity, so be warned.

The Kimberley has a similar wet season; however, the rainfall is less and generally comes in short, heavy storms. Cyclones also occur during this period and can disrupt travel arrangements. Each August in Broome there's a 10-day festival celebrating the town's pearl history.

Planning Your Time

The sheer size of the Outback, which includes the entire Northern Territory and parts of Western Australia, means it is impossible to cover it all on a short visit. You will need to be selective.

If you choose one of Australia's great icons—Uluru, for instance—you could fly directly to Ayers Rock Airport and spend two days there, taking a hike around the rock followed by a look at the Uluru–Kata Tjuta Cultural Centre near its base. The next day, take a sightseeing flight by helicopter or fixed-wing aircraft, then visit Kata Tjuta (the Olgas) to explore its extraordinary domes, and end the day with sunset at the rock. A short flight will get you to Alice Springs, where you can easily take a day trip to either the Eastern or Western MacDonnell Ranges to explore the gorges and take a dip in a waterhole.

If you make Darwin your starting point, head east early on the Arnhem Highway to Fogg Dam to view the birdlife. Continue into Kakadu National Park and picnic at the rock-art site at Ubirr. Take a scenic flight in the afternoon, then a trip to the Bowali Visitors Centre, and overnight in Jabiru. On the second day, head to Nourlangie Rock; then continue to the Yellow Water Billabong cruise at Cooinda and stay there for the night. The next day, drive to Litchfield National Park and take a dip in Florence, Tjaynera (Sandy Creek), or Wangi Falls—be sure to heed the warning signs if crocs have been spotted in the area.

The easiest way to see Purnululu's amazing "beehive" rock formations is from the air. To do this, you'll need to fly to Kununurra from Darwin or Broome, then take a sightseeing flight. If you want to drive from Darwin to Broome, it's 1,162 miles. Ideally, take a week to do the drive, as there is much to see and do along the way.

In the Red Centre region, the primary areas of interest are Alice Springs and the Eastern and Western MacDonnell Ranges, Kings Canyon, and Uluru–Kata Tjuta National Park, with neighboring Ayers Rock Resort. Unless you have more than three days for this region, focus on only one of these areas.

Getting Here and Around

AIR

Darwin is the main international arrival point. Qantas and Virgin Australia are Australia's main domestic airlines, and both operate an extensive network and regular services crisscrossing the country from all the major cities to smaller regional centers like Alice Springs and Broome. Both airlines also have budget subsidiaries—Jetstar (Qantas) and Tigerair (Virgin Australia)—while Air North has an extensive network throughout the Top End and covers some Western Australia legs.

CAR AND BUS

Driving around the Outback is relatively easy, with sealed (paved) two-lane roads and light traffic outside Darwin—several popular unsealed (sand or dirt) roads can certainly make the journey more interesting but are considered unsafe without a proper four-wheel-drive vehicle. Distances can be daunting; for example, Adelaide to Alice Springs via the Stuart Highway is 952 miles, and can take 16 hours. From Darwin to Broome is 1,162 miles, a tiring 21-hour drive (you really want to take a week for it, with many stops along the way). Greyhound

Australia operates an extensive network of long-distance coaches. Although major highways usually remain open, many regional roads are closed during the wet season due to flooding—or occasionally for bush fires if conditions are especially dry and windy.

TRAIN

Great Southern Railways operates *The Ghan* from Adelaide north to Alice Springs, then on to Darwin (and also in the reverse) once or twice a week depending on the time of year.

Restaurants

Restaurants and cafés in the Northern Territory are largely reflective of their location: in the Red Centre, you'll find "bush tucker" menus with crocodile, kangaroo, camel, and native fruits, berries, and plants; in Darwin and Broome, locally caught seafood is prepared with flavor influences from Asia. Many restaurants and cafés offer alfresco dining. And unlike the major cities on the east coast, like Melbourne and Sydney, the vast majority of the eateries in the Outback are more laid-back. Fine-dining options are rare. Tips aren't expected, but an extra 10% for exceptional service is welcome.

Hotels

From five-star to basic, you'll find suitable accommodations throughout the region. The well-known international chains are largely in Darwin, but there are also sublime boutique accommodations set in wilderness or natural settings outside these centers, especially in the Kimberley. You can also experience Outback Australia at homesteads and working cattle stations, while owner-run bed-and-breakfasts provide comfort, charm, and a glimpse of local life. In the cities and the Outback there are plenty of less-than-memorable motels where you can at least get a clean bed for the night. Popular options—especially for families and small groups—are self-contained apartments, villas, and chalets. With two or three bedrooms, living areas, and fully stocked kitchens, they allow you to save on dining costs by cooking your own meals and are best if you're staying more than one night.

Restaurant and hotel reviews have been shortened. For full information, visit Fodors.com.

What It Costs in Australian Dollars

	$	$$	$$$	$$$$
RESTAURANTS				
	under A$21	A$21–A$35	A$36–A$50	over A$50
HOTELS				
	under A$151	A$151–A$200	A$201–A$300	over A$300

Health and Safety

If you are self-driving—especially in remote areas—make sure you have enough fuel, water, and food, and carry a first-aid kit. Let others know where you are going and for how long. If you go off bushwalking or hiking, bring adequate supplies and directions, and let others know your plan.

There are "critters" to avoid—snakes, crocodiles, and box jellyfish, for example. Mosquitoes are prevalent, so cover up and use a good insect repellent; the worst times for mosquitoes are dawn and dusk. And during summer in the Northern Territory, flies are a huge problem with a fly net an essential purchase before visiting.

Respect the Australian sun, especially in summer. Sunburn is a real danger if you don't do what the Australians are urged to do: slip, slap, slop—that is, slip on a hat, slap on sunglasses, and slop on sunscreen. On popular beaches around major cities and towns, lifesavers (lifeguards) are usually on duty and put up flags to swim between, but generally most beaches are unguarded. Take extra care, especially where there are strong currents.

TIP→ Crocodiles are active in many of the Outback's waterways, so obey warning signs and check before swimming.

The emergency contact number for police, fire, and ambulance is 000. From a GSM mobile (cell) phone you can also dial 112, although triple zero will still get through. Telstra is the only service provider that has reliable network coverage outside of major cities; however, be aware that mobile phone coverage outside of town limits is almost nonexistent in the Outback. If traveling in remote areas by car, consider renting a satellite phone, which you can find at many Outback tourist information centers.

Tours

If you want to avoid the hassles of getting yourself around this vast region, a tour group is certainly an option. Hundreds of tours and tour operators cover Western Australia and the Northern Territory, and can introduce you to the many experiences on offer here: four-wheel-drive treks, helicopter flights, bush-tucker-gathering expeditions, Aboriginal-guided walks, fishing safaris, and national park tours to name a few.

You can also take a day tour or shorter overnight tours up to, say, five days, most of which operate from Darwin, Broome, Perth, and Alice Springs.
The benefit is that all your transport, accommodations, meals, and sightseeing arrangements are preset, and you will get to see and do things you may otherwise miss if you try to organize them yourself.

★ Bill Peach Journeys

This agency runs the small airline Aircruising Australia, uses private aircraft to fly you to the iconic attractions of central Australia, and includes overnights in best-available hotels and motels. The 12-day Great Australian Air Tour departs from and returns to Sydney, with stops at Longreach in Queensland; Katherine, Kakadu, and Darwin in the Northern Territory; Kununurra and Broome in Western Australia; and finally Uluru and Alice Springs in the Northern Territory. ✉ *1753 Botany Rd., Suite 4.04* ☎ *1800/252–053 within Australia, 02/8336–2990 international* 🌐 *www.billpeachjourneys.com.au* 🎫 *From A$19,950.*

Kimberley Wild Adventure Tours

This company offers a variety of multiple-day camping safaris, from one and two days up to 22 days, through the Kimberley using four-wheel-drive vehicles. Highlights of the 12-day Wild Kimberly Loop are Western Australia's legendary Gibb River Road, Cable Beach, Broome, Windjana Gorge, Tunnel Creek, Echidna Chasm, Cathedral Gorge, Purnululu National Park (the Bungle Bungles), El Questro Wilderness Park, Kununurra, Lake Argyle, Katherine, and Darwin. There are plenty of chances to see wildlife and Aboriginal rock art along the way. ✉ *9 Bagot St., Broome* ☎ *1300/738–870* 🌐 *kimberleywild.com.au* 🎫 *From A$3695.*

True North

True North operates a small luxury expedition cruise ship which takes just 36 passengers on 7-, 10-, and 13-night sailings between Broome and Wyndham along the otherwise inaccessible Kimberley coastline. Trips are adventure oriented, with daily activities including scenic walks, fishing, diving, snorkeling, and on-shore picnics. The ship also has six expedition craft and its own helicopter for scenic flights. ✉ *The Port of Broome, 401 Port Dr., Broome* ☎ *08/9192–1829* 🌐 *www.truenorth.com.au* 🎫 *From A$20,595.*

Alice Springs

2,028 km (1,260 miles) northwest of Sydney, 1,532-km (952-mile) north of Adelaide, 1,992 km (1,237 miles) northeast of Perth.

Once a ramshackle collection of buildings on dusty streets, Alice Springs—known colloquially as "the Alice" or just "Alice"—is today an incongruously suburban tourist center with a population of more than 29,000 in the middle of the desert, dominated by the MacDonnell Ranges, which change color according to the time of day, from brick red to purple. Alice derives most of its income from tourism, and more than 459,000 people visit annually from within Australia and around the world. Visitors will be struck by the relaxed vibe of the town. Ancient sites, a focus for the Arrernte Aboriginal people's ceremonial activities, lie cheek by jowl with air-conditioned shops and hotels.

GETTING HERE AND AROUND

Alice Springs Airport is 15 km (9 miles) southeast of town. Qantas flies in and out daily with direct flights from Brisbane, Sydney, Melbourne, Adelaide, Perth, Darwin, and Cairns, as well as Ayers Rock Airport. Virgin Australia flies direct from Adelaide and Darwin. It's three hours' flying time from Sydney, Melbourne, and Brisbane; two hours from Adelaide and Darwin; and about 40 minutes from Ayers Rock Airport. Flights run less frequently in the "Wet" summer months.

The Alice Springs Airport Shuttle Bus, operated by Alice Wanderer, meets every flight. The ride to all hotels and residential addresses in town costs A$16.50 each way and can be booked by phone or online through the Alice Wanderer website, *www.alicewanderer.com.au (08/8952–2111).* From the airport, taxi fare to most parts of town is about A$30.

The Stuart Highway, commonly called the Track, is the only road into Alice Springs. The town center lies east of the highway. The 1,532-km (952-mile) drive from Adelaide takes about 16 hours, while the drive from Darwin is about 1,496 km (930 miles), and takes about 16½ hours. Bus tours run between all Red Centre sites, as well as between Alice Springs and Ayers Rock Resort, a journey that can take six hours. Note that Kings Canyon is a further four-hour drive from Ayers Rock Resort—in turn, its own six-hour drive from Alice Springs—so plan accordingly and fly directly into Ayers Rock Airport instead of Alice Springs if you're especially short on time.

Traveling by car will give you the most flexible itinerary—although the trade-off is that you'll travel many long, lonely stretches of one-lane highway through the red-dust desert. Vehicles can be rented at Alice Springs and Ayers Rock Resort. The Central Australian Tourism Industry Association in Alice Springs books tours and rental cars, and provides motoring information.

TAXI

CONTACT Alice Springs Taxis. ✉ *1/13 Whittaker St., Alice Springs* ☎ *08/8952–1877, 131–008 for taxis Australia-wide* 🌐 *www.131008.com.*

TRAIN

The *Ghan*

If you're looking for a unique, relaxing, and memorable way to see the Outback, this is it. The *Ghan* train travels from Adelaide up to Alice Springs and Darwin on a three-day ride through the wilds of Central Australia, giving you a chance to get out and explore Katherine, Alice Springs, and certain South Australia towns along the way. Trains generally run twice a week from Adelaide on Sunday and Wednesday, while there are slight variations in the schedule between June and August, and in November and February. The *Ghan* Expedition series also runs from April to October 2019 and again in March 2020, offering a four-day, three-night journey with full-day excursions of Katherine, Alice Springs, and Coober Pedy as you travel from Darwin to Adelaide. ⊠ *Adelaide Parklands Terminal* ☎ *1800/703–357 within Australia, 08/8213–4401 outside Australia* 🌐 *www.greatsouthernrail.com.au.*

SAFETY AND PRECAUTIONS

Please note that many Aboriginal people living in or around Alice Springs have been asked to leave their native villages by tribal Elders because of their problems with alcohol. As a result, crime and violence stemming from alcohol abuse can make Alice unsafe at night, and it's recommended you travel only by taxi after dark. Sections of the dry Todd riverbed function as makeshift campsites for some folks, so caution is advised when traversing it. Remember to lock up your rental car and hide any interesting looking belongings—like Eskys (coolers)—in the trunk to help discourage theft.

TIMING

The best time to visit is between May and September, when the weather is mild during the day, although often freezing at night; the summer months can be blisteringly hot, and some tourism services are less frequent or stop altogether. Alice Springs is pleasant enough, but note that most of the Red Centre's main attractions are at least a four- to six-hour drive outside the town. If visiting Uluru is the main reason for your visit to the Red Centre, you can skip Alice Springs and fly directly to Ayers Rock Airport to position yourself closer to Uluru–Kata Tjuta National Park and Kings Canyon.

TOURS

AAT Kings

This well-known bus company operates half-day tours that include visits to the Royal Flying Doctor Service headquarters, School of the Air, Alice Springs Reptile Centre, Telegraph Station, and the Anzac Hill scenic lookout. Full-day tours to Palm Valley via four-wheel-drive vehicles and highlights of the West MacDonnell Ranges—including Standley Chasm, Ellery Creek Big Hole, the Ochre Pits, Simpsons Gap, Ormiston Gorge, and lunch at Glen Helen Lodge—are also available. ⊠ *48 Priest St., Alice Springs* ☎ *08/8953–5187, 1300/228–546* 🌐 *www.aatkings.com.au* 🎟 *From A$110.*

ESSENTIALS

VISITOR INFORMATION Alice Springs Visitor Information Centre. ⊠ *Todd Mall at Parsons St., Alice Springs* ☎ *08/8952–5800, 1800/645–199* 🌐 *www.discovercentralaustralia.com.*

Sights

★ Alice Springs Desert Park

NATURE PRESERVE | FAMILY | Focusing on the desert, which makes up 70% of the Australian landmass, this 128-acre site contains 92 types of plants and 37 animal species in several Australian ecosystems—including the largest nocturnal-animal house in the southern hemisphere. An open-air habitat is also open at night, when animals are most active. At daily presentations, Aboriginal guides discuss the different plants and animals that have helped people traditionally survive and thrive in such an arid desert environment. Don't miss the twice-daily birds of prey presentation at 9 am and 3 pm. Allow about four hours to explore the park, which is located about 7 km (4 miles) west of downtown Alice Springs. ⊠ *871 Larapinta Dr., Alice Springs* ☎ *08/8951–8788* 🌐 *www.alicespringsdesertpark.com.au* 🎟 *A$37.*

Alice Springs Reptile Centre

ZOO | FAMILY | Thorny devils, frill-neck lizards, some of the world's deadliest snakes, and "Terry" the saltwater crocodile inhabit this park in the heart of town, opposite the Royal Flying Doctor Service. From May to August, viewing is best from 11 to 3, when reptiles are most active. There's also a gecko cave and free talks conducted daily at 11, 1, and 3:30,

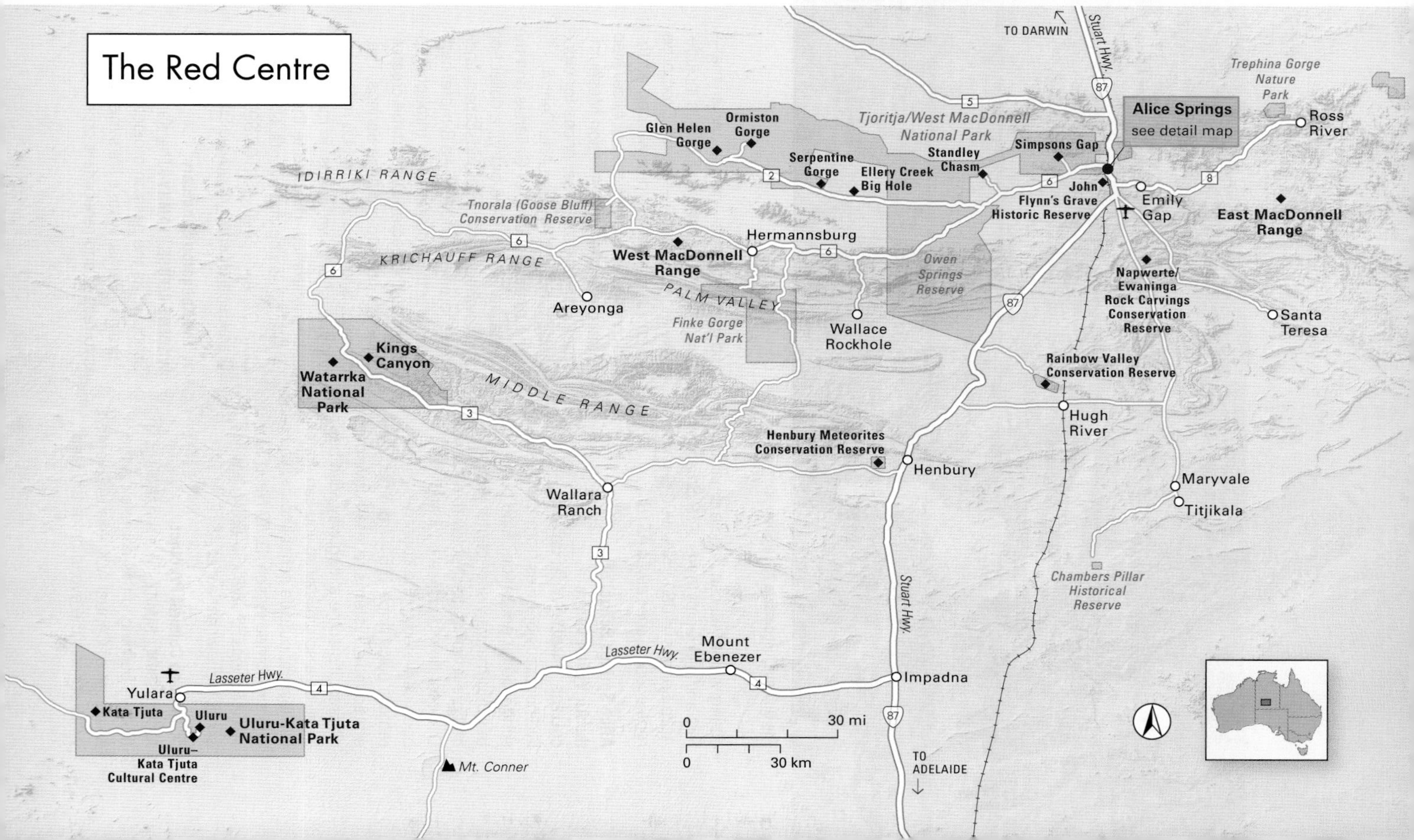

The Red Centre

TO DARWIN
Stuart Hwy.
87
5
Trephina Gorge Nature Park
Alice Springs
see detail map
Ross River
Tjoritja/West MacDonnell National Park
Glen Helen Gorge
Ormiston Gorge
Serpentine Gorge
Ellery Creek Big Hole
Standley Chasm
Simpsons Gap
John Flynn's Grave Historic Reserve
Emily Gap
East MacDonnell Range
8
2
6
IDIRRIKI RANGE
Tnorala (Goose Bluff) Conservation Reserve
Hermannsburg
West MacDonnell Range
KRICHAUFF RANGE
Areyonga
PALM VALLEY
Finke Gorge Nat'l Park
Wallace Rockhole
Owen Springs Reserve
Napwerte/ Ewaninga Rock Carvings Conservation Reserve
Santa Teresa
Kings Canyon
Watarrka National Park
MIDDLE RANGE
Rainbow Valley Conservation Reserve
Hugh River
3
Henbury Meteorites Conservation Reserve
Henbury
Wallara Ranch
Maryvale
Titjikala
Chambers Pillar Historical Reserve
Mount Ebenezer
Lasseter Hwy.
Impadna
4
Yulara
Kata Tjuta
Uluru
Uluru-Kata Tjuta National Park
Uluru–Kata Tjuta Cultural Centre
Mt. Conner
0
30 mi
0
30 km
TO ADELAIDE

The Outback just outside Alice Springs

during which you can handle small critters and pick up pythons. ✉ *9 Stuart Terr., Alice Springs* ☎ *08/8952–8900* 🌐 *www.reptilecentre.com.au* 🎫 *A$18.*

Alice Springs School of the Air Visitor Centre

COLLEGE | FAMILY | What do children who live hundreds of miles from the nearest school do for education? Find out at this informative visitor center, which harbors a working school within its walls. Discover how distance education has been delivered to the country's most remote parts since 1951; from pedal-operated radio systems to interactive online classes, it's come a long way. Visit before 3 pm on a school day so you can watch a live lesson; outside school hours, you can see a recorded lesson. ✉ *80 Head St., Alice Springs* ☎ *08/8951–6834* 🌐 *www.schooloftheair.net.au* 🎫 *A$12.*

★ Araluen Cultural Precinct

ART MUSEUM | FAMILY | The most distinctive building in this complex is the Museum of Central Australia (A$8 entry), which charts the evolution of the land and its inhabitants—human and animal—around central Australia. Exhibits include a skeleton of the 10½-foot-tall *Dromornis stirtoni,* the largest bird to walk on earth, which was found northeast of Alice. Also in the precinct are the Aviation Museum (free), Central Craft (free, prices for workshops vary), and Araluen Arts Centre, home to the Araluen Art Galleries and the Namatjira Gallery (A$8 entry), a collection of renowned Aboriginal landscapes, and the Yeperenye Scuplture—a 3-meter-high caterpillar that you can walk through, representing the sacred Dreamtime creator of the country around Alice Springs. The precinct is located 2.4 km (1½ miles) southwest of town, and is on most tourist bus itineraries. The on-site theater has regular screening and events. ✉ *61 Larapinta Dr., Alice Springs* ☎ *08/8951–1122* 🌐 *araluenartscentre.nt.gov.au* 🎫 *A$8.*

★ The Kangaroo Sanctuary

WILDLIFE REFUGE | FAMILY | The Kangaroo Sanctuary is the passion project of Chris "Brolga" Barns, whose life's mission is to rescue and rehabilitate orphaned kangaroos and educate people about how they can easily do the same—all you need to do is pay attention while you're driving, and if you spot a deceased kangaroo on the side of the road, check to see if there's still a living joey in its pouch, since they'll often survive the impact of a vehicle and can live for up to four more days after it. Your ticket includes door-to-door transfers (no one is allowed to drive straight to the property), a 2½- to 3-hour tour, and gives you a chance to take turns holding baby kangaroos and feed Roger, Brolga's marsupial costar in the popular BBC documentary series *Kangaroo Dundee*, who started it all. ✉ *Alice Springs* ☎ *08/8965–0038* 🌐 *kangaroosanctuary.com* 🎫 *A$85* 🕑 *Closed Sat.–Mon.* ☞ *The tour picks you up and drops you off at your Alice Springs accommodations.*

Lasseters Casino

CASINO | Entry is free at Lasseters Casino, where the action goes late into the night with more than 300 slot machines, plus blackjack, roulette, craps, and baccarat tables. Choose from six restaurants and bars, each with its own style ranging from exotic eats at Tali to tapas at Tempo. The Juicy Rump is known for live music, Stadium 93 for its sports bar atmosphere. The Goat & Bucket is a beer lover's paradise, while Casbah is perfectly positioned should you need a break from betting. ✉ *93 Barrett Dr., Alice Springs* ☎ *08/8950–7777, 1800/808–975* 🌐 *www.lasseters.com.au/casino* 🎫 *Free.*

Royal Flying Doctor Service (RFDS) Alice Springs Tourist Facility

OTHER ATTRACTION | **FAMILY** | This much-visited tourist attraction in Alice Springs has a theater, interactive displays, and a full-scale replica of the fuselage of the service's current Pilatus PC-12 aircraft. The site has long been the radio base for the Royal Flying Doctor Service, which directs doctors (using aircraft) on their house calls to remote settlements and homes hundreds of miles apart, making it a vital part of Outback life. The center features historical displays, a holographic audiovisual show portraying RFDS founder Reverend John Flynn, tours that run every half hour throughout the year, and a lovely café at the back. ✉ *8–10 Stuart Terr., Alice Springs* ☎ *08/8958–8411* 🌐 *www.rfdsalicesprings.com.au* 🎫 *A$19.*

Women's Museum of Australia and Old Gaol Alice Springs

OTHER MUSEUM | **FAMILY** | This fascinating museum—which happens to be housed in the Old Alice Springs Gaol simply because it's a historic building—tells the stories of the brave, strong women of the Red Centre, with exhibits showing the important role women played during WWII, and how women of all races helped shape Australian politics, education, medicine, aviation, sports, and pretty much every aspect of today's society. You'll also be able to tour the old jail, which began as a prison for both sexes but became an all-male prison in the 1980s, and hear the stories of its former inhabitants through an interactive audio display. ✉ *2 Stuart Terr., Alice Springs* ☎ *08/8952–9006* 🌐 *pioneerwomen.com.au* 🎫 *A$15.*

Restaurants

Barra on Todd

$ | **AUSTRALIAN** | **FAMILY** | Barramundi is the name of the game at this venerable and popular restaurant on the banks of the dry Todd River, part of the Mercure Alice Springs Resort. The beer-battered "barra" is a drawcard here, but there's also a wide range of authentic curries to try. **Known for:** waterfront views; Thai-style barramundi spring rolls; curries. 💲 *Average main: A$20* ✉ *34 Stott Terr., Alice Springs* ☎ *08/8951–4545.*

Bean Tree Cafe

$ | **AUSTRALIAN** | This inviting café is set within the grounds of the 16-hectare haven, Olive Pink Botanic Garden. The menu is filled with plenty of vegan options,

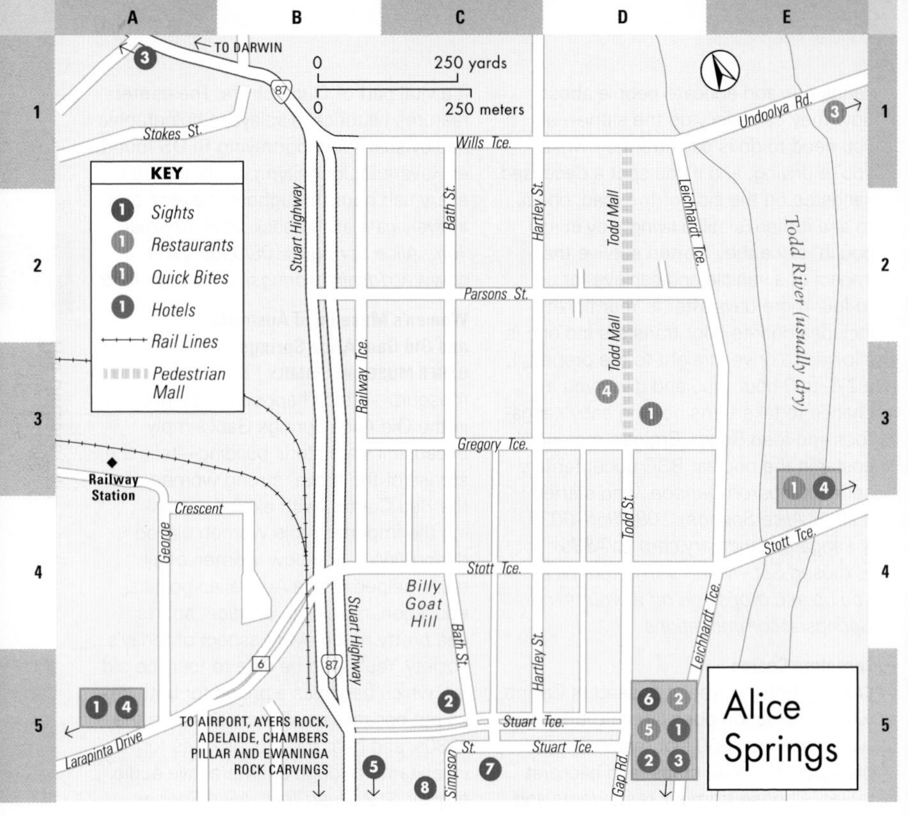

Sights

1 Alice Springs Desert Park.............. A5

2 Alice Springs Reptile Centre............ C5

3 Alice Springs School of the Air Visitor Centre... A1

4 Araluen Cultural Precinct.................. A5

5 The Kangaroo Sanctuary................ B5

6 Lasseters Casino D5

7 Royal Flying Doctor Service (RFDS) Alice Springs Tourist Facility............ C5

8 Women's Museum of Australia and Old Gaol Alice Springs............ C5

Restaurants

1 Barra on Todd........... E3

2 Bean Tree Cafe D5

3 Casa Nostra Pizza and Spaghetti House.... E1

4 Epilogue Lounge........ D3

5 Hanuman D5

Quick Bites

1 Page 27 .... D3

Hotels

1 Crowne Plaza Alice Springs Lasseters D5

2 Desert Palms Alice Springs............ D5

3 DoubleTree by Hilton Hotel Alice Springs..... D5

4 Mercure Alice Springs Resort..................... E3

with vegan breakfast, veggie bowls, and a vegan burger. **Known for:** hidden gem; extensive vegan menu; beautiful views of gardens. $ *Average main: A$20* ✉ *Olive Pink Botanic Garden, 27 Tuncks Rd., Alice Springs* ☎ *04/4727–0949* ⊕ *www.facebook.com/TheBeantreeCafe* ⊙ *Closed Mon.–Wed.*

Casa Nostra Pizza and Spaghetti House

$$ | ITALIAN | FAMILY | Red-and-white checkered tablecloths, Chianti bottles, and plastic grapes festoon this family-run Alice Springs classic spot that continues to draw in locals with traditional Italian meat dishes, pizza, and pasta. Take a tip from the regulars and preorder a serving of vanilla slice for dessert, or you might miss out on this scrumptious cake of layered papery pastry and custard cream. **Known for:** BYO beer and wine; Al's Special; cream-and-black-pepper sauce that the chef took 15 years to perfect. $ *Average main: A$32* ✉ *1 Undoolya Rd., at Sturt Terr., Alice Springs* ☎ *08/8952–6749.*

Epilogue Lounge

$$ | AUSTRALIAN | Transforming from a casual eatery as the sun goes town, this laneway eatery offers tapas-style meals, live music, and a lengthy wine and cocktail list. The ambience is relaxed and welcoming. **Known for:** tasty tapas; buzzy atmosphere; intimate and romantic. $ *Average main: A$25* ✉ *58 Todd St., Alice Springs* ☎ *0429/003–874* ✍ *epiloguelounge@gmail.com* ⊙ *Closed Tues.*

★ Hanuman

$$$ | ASIAN | Beginning his journey in Colombo, Sri Lanka, and becoming one of Australia's most respected experts in Asian flavors, chef Jimmy Shu has assembled teams of traditionally trained chefs who combine their cooking secrets with his contemporary take on Asian cuisine. Hanuman has been a favorite with locals and visitors for three decades. **Known for:** desserts like black-rice brûlée; trumpet mushrooms topped with prawn and pork mince; barramundi poached in coconut sauce. $ *Average main: A$38* ✉ *DoubleTree by Hilton Hotel Alice Springs, 82 Barrett Dr., Alice Springs* ☎ *08/8953–7188* ⊕ *www.hanuman.com.au* ⊙ *No lunch weekends.*

Coffee and Quick Bites

Page 27

$ | AUSTRALIAN | Bursting with charisma, this trendy laneway café has a slight hippie edge. It has all the feels of a Melbourne coffeehouse. **Known for:** quick service; delicious coffee; quirky interiors. $ *Average main: A$20* ✉ *3 Fan Arcade, Alice Springs* ☎ *04/1748–6464* ⊕ *facebook.com/Page27Cafe.*

Hotels

★ Crowne Plaza Alice Springs Lasseters

$$$ | HOTEL | FAMILY | A popular place thanks to great views of the MacDonnell Ranges from guest rooms and the nightlife provided by the casino, the Crowne Plaza is the most luxurious resort in Alice Springs. **Pros:** casino and nightlife on the property; on-site gym facilities; complimentary in-room Wi-Fi. **Cons:** restaurants are on the pricey side; 30-minute walk to town center; adjacent convention center attracts big groups. $ *Rooms from: A$251* ✉ *93 Barrett Dr., Alice Springs* ☎ *08/8950–7777* ⊕ *www.ihg.com* *205 rooms* *No Meals.*

Desert Palms Alice Springs

$ | RESORT | FAMILY | Accommodations at Desert Palms are in self-contained, freestanding A-frame units set up as double, triple, quad, and family villas, each with a private balcony and access to a lovely island pool with a waterfall to help you take your mind off the dry desert heat. **Pros:** free Wi-Fi; private, comfortable villas with fully stocked kitchenettes; golf course adjacent. **Cons:** taxi or car needed to reach town center; villas have thin walls; no-frills bathrooms. $ *Rooms from: A$130* ✉ *74 Barrett Dr., Alice Springs* ☎ *08/8952–5977, 1800/678–037* *reservations ⊕ www.desertpalms.com.au ⇆ 80 apartments ♨ No Meals.*

DoubleTree by Hilton Hotel Alice Springs
$$$ | HOTEL | FAMILY | Landscaped lawns with elegant eucalyptus and palm trees greet you at this upscale international chain about a mile outside town. **Pros:** Wi-Fi is free in the lobby and in rooms if you join Hilton Honors; many rooms have views of the MacDonnell Ranges; excellent on-site restaurants. **Cons:** Wi-Fi is pricey if you're not a Hilton Honors member; no shopping nearby; taxi or car is needed to reach the town center. *[$] Rooms from: A$229 ✉ 82 Barrett Dr., Alice Springs ☎ 08/8950–8000 ⊕ hilton.com ⇆ 236 rooms ♨ No Meals.*

Mercure Alice Springs Resort
$$ | HOTEL | FAMILY | Many of the rooms at this new addition to Accor Hotels' portfolio open directly onto lawns or gardens where dozens of native birds chatter, making you forget you're in the middle of the desert and instead, perhaps inside a tropical garden. **Pros:** free Wi-Fi; 10-minute walk to Todd Mall shops; soft pillows and comfortable beds. **Cons:** small parking lot for hotel and restaurant; no views; convention facilities attract tour groups. *[$] Rooms from: A$165 ✉ 34 Stott Terr., Alice Springs ☎ 08/8951–4545 ⊕ www.accorhotels.com ⇆ 139 rooms ♨ No Meals.*

Nightlife

Maxim's Bar at Todd Tavern
PUBS | Maxim's Bar, located inside Todd Tavern, the only traditional Australian pub in town, has something going on every night. The property also includes a restaurant, bottle shop (liquor store), and gambling facilities. You can bet on horse races across the country with TAB (the Australian equivalent of OTB) or try your luck at keno—but keep some change aside to lose in the slot machines. Shoot some pool, be a pinball wizard, or catch some sports on the TVs. *✉ 1 Todd Mall, Alice Springs ☎ 08/8952–1255 ⊕ www.toddtavern.com.au.*

Art Hunt

The essence of this ancient land is epitomized in the paintings of the renowned Aboriginal landscape artist Albert Namatjira and his followers. Viewed away from the desert, these artists' images of the MacDonnell Ranges may appear at first to be garish and unreal in their depiction of purple-and-red mountain ranges and stark-white ghost gum trees. However, seeing the real thing makes it difficult to imagine executing the paintings in any other way. Galleries abound along Todd Mall; they're filled with bark paintings and didgeridoos.

Shopping

Shopping in Alice Springs is all about Aboriginal artwork. Central Australian Aboriginal paintings are characterized by intricate patterns of dots—and are commonly called sand paintings because they were originally drawn on sand as ceremonial devices.

Mbantua Aboriginal Art Gallery
ART GALLERIES | Supporters of the Aboriginal artists of Central Australia since 1987, the Mbantua Art Gallery's Todd Mall shop houses some of the best samples of Indigenous art in Alice Springs. Learn more about this fascinating culture at the Gallery's Cultural Museum, where you can see boomerangs, spears, and other artifacts and objects collected around the Northern Territory. *✉ 64 Todd St., Alice Springs ☎ 08/8952–5571 ⊕ www.mbantua.com.au.*

Papunya Tula Artists

ART GALLERIES | Encouraged to paint a mural on a blank building wall by a local school teacher in 1971, the Papunya Tula artists were the founders of the modern western and central desert art movement. This gallery showcases the work of some of the area's best. ✉ *63 Todd St., Alice Springs* ☎ *08/8952–4731.*

★ **Red Kangaroo Books**

BOOKS | From bush poetry and traditional bush tucker recipes to anthropological texts on Aboriginal people and their culture, Red Kangaroo Books has an outstanding collection of literature pertaining to all things Australian. ✉ *79 Todd St., Alice Springs* ☎ *08/8953–2137* 🌐 *www.redkangaroobooks.com.*

This Is Aboriginal Art

ART GALLERIES | Stop by the gallery to explore two floors full of artwork by local painters, who typically work from the on-site studio. Finished pieces can also be purchased online through the website. ✉ *87 Todd St., Alice Springs* ☎ *08/8952–1544* 🌐 *www.thisisaboriginal-art.com.au.*

Todd Mall Markets

MARKET | **FAMILY** | Held every other Sunday morning from 9 am until around 1 pm, mid-February to December, the markets feature more than 100 stalls of local arts, crafts, and food, which are displayed while musicians entertain. ✉ *Todd St., Alice Springs* ☎ *04/5855–5506* 🌐 *www.toddmallmarkets.com.au.*

Activities

CAMEL RIDING

Pyndan Camel Tracks

LOCAL SPORTS | Daily one-hour camel rides are offered three times a day at noon, 2:30, and sunset, during which you'll explore a valley of diverse habitat of ironbark and mulga trees, and, of course, take in views of the ancient MacDonnell Ranges. While it's located about 15 km (9 miles) from the town center, the company offers free rides from your Alice Springs accommodation so you can spend some quality time with your new furry friend. ✉ *21259 Jane Rd., Alice Springs* ☎ *04/1617–0164* 🌐 *www.cameltracks.com* 🎫 *From A$39.*

HOT-AIR BALLOONING

★ **Outback Ballooning**

BALLOONING | Floating over the desert spinifex in a hot-air balloon while the sun comes up is a once-in-a-lifetime experience. Outback Ballooning makes hotel pickups about an hour before dawn and returns you between 8 am and 9 am depending on the time of year. The A$305 fee gives you 30 minutes of flying time, mandatory Civil Aviation Safety Authority insurance, and a champagne breakfast; a 60-minute flight will cost you A$395. Those who still want to participate but are sensitive to heights can pay A$50 for what the company calls a Balloon Chase, allowing you to see how the balloons are set up preflight, watch them take off, and follow along with them through the desert alongside crew members before meeting back up with your group for celebratory snacks and bubbles. **TIP→ Take warm clothes to beat the predawn chill.** ✉ *35 Kennett Ct., Alice Springs* ☎ *08/8952–8723* 🌐 *www.outbackballooning.com.au* 🎫 *From A$305.*

East and West MacDonnell Ranges

Alice Springs is flanked by the MacDonnell Ranges. Those to the east of Alice Springs are known as the East MacDonnell Ranges and those to the west are known as the West MacDonnell Ranges.

Eye-catching scenery and Aboriginal rock art in the MacDonnell Ranges east of the Alice are well worth a day or more of exploration. Emily Gap (a sacred Aboriginal site), Jessie Gap, and Corroboree Rock, once a setting for important male-only Aboriginal ceremonies, are within the first 50 km (31 miles) east of Alice Springs. Beyond these are Trephina Gorge, John Hayes Rockhole, and N'Dhala Gorge Nature Park (home to numerous Aboriginal rock carvings).

The West MacDonnell Ranges, which stretch westward from just a few kilometers outside Alice Springs to around 200 km (125 miles) farther away, are a spectacular series of red-rock mountains interspersed by canyons and narrow gorges. Each of the chasms and gorges has its own unique character, and in many, there are waterholes where you can swim. Black-footed rock wallabies are among the wildlife to be spotted. The 223-km (139-mile) Larapinta Trail in the park, the showpiece of central Australian bushwalking, is broken into 12 sections, each a one- to two-day walk.

GETTING HERE AND AROUND

To reach all the major sights of the West MacDonnell Ranges, the Red Centre Way follows Larapinta Drive (the western continuation of Stott Terrace) from Alice Springs and Namatjira Drive westward to Glen Helen, about 130 km (81 miles) from Alice Springs. Roads leading off it access the highlights. To reach key attractions in the East MacDonnell Ranges such as Emily Gap and Jessie Gap, take Ross Highway east from Alice Springs.

SAFETY AND PRECAUTIONS

Take care when bushwalking or hiking, as paths are usually rocky and uneven. Snakes inhabit most areas so it's important to keep on the track and avoid walking through long grass. You should always carry and drink plenty of water; at least one liter of water for every hour of walking in hot weather.

TOURS

Emu Run Experience
One-day tours are offered by air-conditioned bus to all the major West MacDonnell sights, including Simpsons Gap, Standley Chasm, the Ochre Pits, Ormiston Gorge, and Glen Helen, and there's a chance to take a dip in the Ellery Creek Big Hole, a picturesque waterhole popular with the locals. You'll also get morning tea, lunch, afternoon snacks, and door-to-door pickup and drop-off service. ✉ *275 Stuart Hwy., Alice Springs* ☎ *08/8953–7057* 🌐 *www.emurun.com.au* 🎫 *From A$132.*

Trek Larapinta
Whether you're looking for a short three-day excursion into the wilderness (from A$1,695), a six-day trek (from A$3,195), a nine-day journey (from A$3,895), or an epic 16-day adventure covering the entire Larapinta Trail (from A$4,995), this company gives you plenty of options based on how much time you have and how much hiking you really want to do. ✉ *11 Whittaker St., Alice Springs* ☎ *1300/133–278* 🌐 *www.treklarapinta.com.au* 🎫 *From A$1695.*

ESSENTIALS

VISITOR INFORMATION Emily and Jessie Gaps Nature Park Information.
✣ *10 km (6 miles) east of Alice Springs* ☎ *08/8952–1013* 🌐 *nt.gov.au/leisure/parks-reserves/find-a-park-to-visit/yeperenye-emily-jessie-gaps-nature-park.*

Sights

★ Ellery Creek Big Hole
NATURE SIGHT | This is one of the prettiest (and coldest) swimming holes in the Red Centre, so it's quite popular with locals and visitors alike—it's also the deepest and most permanent waterhole in the area, so you may glimpse wild creatures like wallabies or goannas (monitor lizards) quenching their thirst. Take the 3-km (2-mile) Dolomite Walk for a close-up look at this fascinating geological site. ✉ *Namatjira Dr., Alice Springs* ✣ *88 km (55 miles) west of Alice Springs* ☎ *08/8951–8250* 🌐 *northernterritory.com/alice-springs-and-surrounds* 🎫 *Free.*

The Australian Heartland

For most Australians, the Red Centre is the mystical and legendary core of the continent and Uluru is its beautiful focal point. Whether they have been there or not, locals believe its image symbolizes a steady pulse that radiates deep through the red earth, through the heartland, and all the way to the coasts.

Little more than a thumbprint within the vast Australian continent, the Red Centre is harsh and isolated. Its hard, relentless topography (and lack of conveniences) makes this one of the most difficult areas of the country to survive in, much less explore. But the early pioneers—some foolish, some hardy—managed to set up bases that thrived. They created cattle stations, introduced electricity, and implemented telegraph services, enabling them to maintain a lifestyle that, if not luxurious, was at least reasonably comfortable.

The people who now sparsely populate the Red Centre are a breed of their own. Many were born and grew up here, but others were "blow-ins"—immigrants from far-flung countries and folks from other Australian states who fell in love with the area, took up the challenge to make a life in the desert, and stayed on as they succeeded. Either way, the people out here have a few common characteristics. They're laconic and down-to-earth, canny and astute, and likely to try to pull your leg when you least expect it.

No one could survive the isolation without a good sense of humor: Where else in the world would you hold a bottomless-boat race in a dry riverbed? The Henley-on-Todd Regatta, as it is known, is a sight to behold in Alice Springs each August, with dozens of would-be skippers bumbling along within the bottomless-boat frames.

As the small towns grew and businesses quietly prospered in the mid-1800s, a rail link between Alice Springs and Adelaide was planned. However, the undercurrent of challenge and humor that touches all life here ran through this project as well. Construction began in 1877, but things went wrong from the start. No one had seen rain for ages, and no one expected it; hence, the track was laid right across a floodplain. It wasn't long before locals realized their mistake, when intermittent heavy floods regularly washed the tracks away. The railway is still in operation today, and all works well, but its history is one of many local jokes here.

The Red Centre is a special place where you will meet people whose generous and sincere hospitality may move you. The land and all its riches offer some of the most spectacular and unique sights on the planet, along with a sense of timelessness that will slow you down and fill your spirit. Take a moment to shade your eyes from the sun and pick up on the subtleties that nature has carefully protected and camouflaged here, and you will soon discover that the Red Centre is not the dead center.

Glen Helen Gorge

NATURE SIGHT | This gorge, cut by the sporadic Finke River, often described as the oldest river in the world, slices through the MacDonnell Ranges, revealing dramatic rock layering and tilting. Here the river forms a broad, cold, permanent waterhole that's great for a bracing swim. ✉ *Namatjira Dr., Alice Springs ✣ 132 km (82 miles) west of Alice Springs* ☎ *08/8951–8250* 🌐 *northernterritory.com/alice-springs-and-surrounds* 🎫 *Free.*

John Flynn's Grave Historic Reserve

CEMETERY | John Flynn, the Royal Flying Doctor Service founder, is memorialized at this spot along Larapinta Drive just 6½ km (4 miles) west of Alice Springs in view of the majestic West MacDonnell range. ✉ *623 Larapinta Dr., Alice Springs* ☎ *No phone* 🌐 *www.discovercentralaustralia.com* 🎫 *Free.*

★ **Ormiston Gorge**

NATURE SIGHT | This beautiful gorge has something for everyone, whether you're interested in swimming in the waterhole, taking a short hike to Gum Tree Lookout for fantastic views of the 820-foot-high gorge walls rising from the pool below, or experiencing the best of both worlds on the 90-minute, 7 km (4½-mile) Ormiston Pound Walk. ✉ *Namatjira Dr., Alice Springs ✣ 135 km (84 miles) west of Alice Springs* ☎ *08/8956–7799* 🌐 *northernterritory.com/alice-springs-and-surrounds* 🎫 *Free.*

Serpentine Gorge

NATURE SIGHT | Accessible only by four-wheel-drive vehicle, this site is best experienced by taking a refreshing swim through the narrow, winding gorge. According to an Aboriginal myth, a fierce serpent makes its home in the pool, hence the name. ✉ *Namatjira Dr., Alice Springs ✣ 99 km (61 miles) west of Alice Springs* ☎ *08/8951–8250* 🌐 *www.discovercentralaustralia.com/serpentine-gorge* 🎫 *Free.*

Simpsons Gap

NATIONAL PARK | The closest gorge to Alice Springs—there's even a bicycle and walking track from the city center—greets you with views of stark-white ghost gums (Australian evergreen trees), red rocks, and gorgeous, purple-haze mountains that provide a taste of scenery to be seen farther into the ranges. Heed the "No Swimming" signs, as freshwater crocodiles may be present if there's enough water, and come in the morning and late afternoon for a chance to catch a glimpse of rock wallabies. ✉ *Larapinta Dr., Alice Springs ✣ 18 km (11 miles) west of Alice Springs, then 6 km (4 miles) on side road* ☎ *08/8951–8250* 🌐 *nt.gov.au/leisure/parks-reserves* 🎫 *Free.*

Standley Chasm

NATURE SIGHT | At midday, when the sun is directly overhead, the 10-yard-wide canyon glows red from the reflected light, a phenomenon that lasts for just 15 minutes. The walk from the parking lot takes about 20 minutes and is rocky toward the end. For a greater challenge, climb to the top via the steep trail that branches off to the left at the end of the gorge; the views are spectacular. There's also a kiosk selling snacks and drinks at the park entrance. ✉ *Larapinta Dr., Alice Springs ✣ 40 km (25 miles) west of Alice Springs, then 9 km (5½ miles) on Standley Chasm Rd.* ☎ *08/8956–7440* 🌐 *www.standleychasm.com.au* 🎫 *A$12.*

Hotels

Glen Helen Lodge

$$ | **HOTEL** | **FAMILY** | Choose from motel, dorm, or campsite accommodations and enjoy views of Glen Helen Gorge and its wildlife, including many bird species, rock wallabies, dingoes, and lizards. **Pros:** plenty of opportunities to see local fauna; traditional Outback Australia atmosphere; easy access to the Larapinta Walking Trail and Glen Helen Gorge. **Cons:** rooms 10–17 are next to the generator and can be noisy; limited Wi-Fi in the restaurant and at reception; no swimming pool. *Rooms from: A$160* *1 Namatjira Dr., Alice Springs* *135 km (84 miles) west of Alice Springs* *08/8956–7208* *www.discoveryholidayparks.com.au* *25 rooms* *Free Breakfast.*

Activities

HIKING

The **Larapinta Trail,** a 223-km-long (139-mile-long) walking track that runs from Alice Springs into the Western MacDonnell Ranges, is a spectacular, though challenging, track that takes hikers through classically rugged and dry central Australian landscapes. Hikers are encouraged to participate in the voluntary Overnight Walker Registration Scheme, designed to ensure that all trekkers on the trail can be tracked and accounted for in case of an emergency. Contact the **Northern Territory Parks & Wildlife Service** (08/8951–8250) for more information. **Tourism Central Australia** in Alice Springs (08/8952–5800) can also advise you if you're interested in planning bushwalking itineraries. **World Expeditions** runs guided and self-guided, multiday hikes on the best sections of the trail, ranging from 3 to 14 days, with accommodation in permanent campsites and all meals. Prices start at A$920 for a three-day self-guided trek. *www.worldexpeditions.com.*

Watarrka National Park (Kings Canyon)

Several impressive geological sights lie along the route from Alice Springs to Watarrka National Park along the Stuart and Lasseter highways, with the finale being Kings Canyon, the must-see attraction for this area.

GETTING HERE AND AROUND

Watarrka National Park is 450 km (280 miles) southwest of Alice Springs via the Stuart and Lasseter highways and Luritja Road. You also can reach the park from Alice Springs by taking Larapinta Drive through the mountains (the West MacDonnell Ranges); however, if you take this route, you need a four-wheel drive and also a Mereenie Loop Pass, which you can purchase at the Alice Springs Visitor Information Centre (*08/8952–5800*). If you're coming from Uluru or Yulara, take Lasseter Highway and Luritja Road to the park's entrance. Within the park, Luritja Road takes you northwest through the park from Kings Creek Station to Kings Canyon, while Larapinta Drive heads south into the park toward Kings Canyon.

TOURS

Karrke Aboriginal Cultural Experience

Within the Wanmarra Aboriginal community just a few minutes' drive from Kings Creek Station, this one-hour cultural tour gives visitors an up-close look at some of the bush tucker, plants, and other artifacts still important to Indigenous culture today. Let Peter and Christine introduce you to the all-important grinding stone, weapons made from mulga wood, and traditional dot painting techniques—you might even get to sample a witchetty grub, which tastes remarkably like buttered popcorn when cooked on the fire. Tours take place four times a day, Wednesday through Sunday at 9 and 11:30, and operate from mid-January to mid-November. *Wanmara, Petermann NT 0872, Kings Canyon* *3 km (2 miles) northwest of Kings Creek Station. Look for signs and take dirt road just off Luritja Dr.* *08/8956–7620* *www.bourkeaboriginalculturetours.com.au* *A$30, cash only on-site or can be booked with a credit card through Kings Canyon accommodations.*

ESSENTIALS

VISITOR INFORMATION Watarrka National Park (Kings Canyon) Visitor Information. ✉ *Watarrka National Park* ☎ *08/8956–7460 Watarrka Ranger Station* 🌐 *nt.gov.au/leisure/parks-reserves.*

Sights

Henbury Meteorites Conservation Reserve

NATURE SIGHT | The Henbury Meteorites craters, 12 depressions between 6 feet and 600 feet across, are believed to have been formed by a meteorite shower 4,700 years ago—the largest one measures roughly 590 feet wide by 50 feet deep! To get here, you must travel 15 km (9 miles) off the highway on an unpaved road—conventional 2WD sedans will be fine, but be aware that some rental car companies don't cover you if you break down on unsealed roads. ✉ *Ernest Giles Rd.* ✣ *119 km (74 miles) south of Alice Springs and 15 km (9 miles) west of Stuart Hwy.* ☎ *08/8952–1013* 🌐 *nt.gov.au/leisure/parks-reserves* 🎫 *Free.*

★ **Kings Canyon**

CANYON | Inside Watarrka National Park, Kings Canyon is one of the most spectacular sights in central Australia. Sprawling in scope, the canyon's sheer cliff walls shelter a world of ferns and woodlands, permanent springs, and rock pools. The main path is the 6-km (4-mile) Kings Canyon Rim Walk, which starts with a short but steep 15-minute climb straight up from the parking lot to the top of the escarpment; the view 886 feet down to the base of the canyon is amazing. Steep stairs mark your arrival into the scenic Garden of Eden—the only way out along the main trail is via another round of intense stair-climbing back up to the top of the canyon wall, so make sure you're carrying plenty of water for the hike. An easier walk, called the Creek Walk, which starts at the parking lot and winds through the base of the canyon, is just as worthwhile. Alternatively, Kings Canyon Resort offers 8-, 15-, and 30-minute helicopter rides so you can view it all from above (from A$95, A$150, and A$285, respectively). ✉ *Luritja Rd., Alice Springs* ✣ *450 km (280 miles) southwest of Alice Springs (167 km [104 miles] from Lasseter Hwy. turnoff)* ☎ *08/8956–7460* 🌐 *nt.gov.au/leisure/parks-reserves* 🎫 *Free.*

Napwerte / Ewaninga Rock Carvings Conservation Reserve

NATURE SIGHT | More than 3,000 ancient Aboriginal rock engravings (petroglyphs) are etched into sandstone outcrops in Napwerte/Ewaninga Rock Carvings Conservation Reserve, 35 km (22 miles) south of Alice on the road to Chamber's Pillar. Early morning and late-afternoon light are best for photographing the lines, circles, and animal tracks. A 2-km (1-mile) trail leads to several art sites. The reserve is open all day year-round and is accessible by regular (rather than four-wheel-drive) cars; technically, however, the road is unsealed, so check with your rental car company to make sure it's not against their rules to drive on it. ✉ *Old South Rd.* ✣ *35 km (22 miles) south of Alice Springs* ☎ *08/8952–1013* 🌐 *nt.gov.au/leisure/parks-reserves* 🎫 *Free.*

Rainbow Valley Conservation Reserve

NATURE SIGHT | Amazing formations in the sandstone cliffs of the James Range take on rainbow colors in the early-morning and late-afternoon light; the colors are caused by water dissolving the red iron in the sandstone and further erosion that has created dramatic rock faces and squared towers. To reach the reserve, turn left off the Stuart Highway 75 km (46 miles) south of Alice. The next 22 km (13 miles) are on a dirt track, requiring a four-wheel-drive vehicle. ✉ *Stuart Hwy., Alice Springs* ✣ *75 km (46 miles) south of Alice Springs, then 22 km (13 miles) east via an unsealed road* ☎ *08/8952–1013* 🌐 *nt.gov.au/leisure/parks-reserves* 🎫 *Free.*

Hotels

★ Kings Canyon Resort

$$$$ | **RESORT** | **FAMILY** | The best place to stay near Watarrka National Park, this resort is 9 km (6 miles) from Kings Canyon and offers accommodations ranging from budget-friendly rooms with shared bathrooms and campsites to deluxe cabins with luxurious spa tubs overlooking rugged rock formations. **Pros:** game and trivia nights are offered several times a week; dining options for every budget; complimentary activities and tour bookings available at reception. **Cons:** it's about four hours from Uluru and five hours from Alice Springs; Wi-Fi is only available for purchase; own transport needed to get to the canyon (beyond a guided tour). *Rooms from: A$459* *Luritja Rd., Watarrka National Park* *08/7210–9600* *www.kingscanyonresort.com.au* *177 rooms* *No Meals.*

Kings Creek Station

$$$ | **RESORT** | **FAMILY** | This working cattle and camel station just 36 km (22 miles) from Kings Canyon offers affordable, rustic accommodation options ranging from campgrounds and twin-share Safari Cabins to a $1,100-a-night luxury glamping experience. **Pros:** complimentary microwave, fridge, and gas barbecues; cabin rate includes an impressive bushman's-style breakfast; children five and under stay free. **Cons:** accommodations are basic but pricey; it's a 35-minute drive from Kings Canyon; all Safari Cabins have twin beds and shared bathroom facilities. *Rooms from: A$202* *Luritja Rd., Kings Canyon* *Luritja Rd. via Lasseter Hwy. (from Alice Springs or Uluru), 36 km (22 miles) before you reach Kings Canyon* *08/7111–1462* *www.kingscreekstation.com.au* *28 rooms* *Free Breakfast.*

Uluru-Kata Tjuta National Park

It's easy to see why Aboriginal people attach such spiritual significance to Uluru (Ayers Rock). It rises magnificently above the plain and dramatically changes color throughout the day. At 2,831 feet, Uluru is one of the world's largest monoliths, though such a classification belies the otherworldly, spiritual energy surrounding it. The Anangu people are the traditional owners of the land around Uluru and Kata Tjuta. They believe they are direct descendants of the beings—which include a python, an emu, a blue-tongue lizard, and a poisonous snake—who formed the land and its physical features during the Tjukurpa (the "Dreamtime," or creation period).

Kata Tjuta (the Olgas), 58 km (36 miles) west of Uluru, is a series of 36 gigantic rock domes hiding a maze of fascinating gorges and crevasses. The names Ayers Rock and the Olgas are used out of familiarity alone; at the sites themselves, the Aboriginal Uluru and Kata Tjuta are the respective names of preference. The entire area is called Yulara, though the airport is still known as Ayers Rock.

Uluru and Kata Tjuta have very different compositions. Monolithic Uluru is made up of a type of sandstone called arkose, while the rock domes at Kata Tjuta are composed of conglomerate. Both of these intriguing sights lie within Uluru–Kata Tjuta National Park, which is protected as a UNESCO World Heritage site. The whole experience is a bit like seeing the Grand Canyon turned inside out, and a visit here will be remembered for a lifetime.

In terms of where to eat and stay, Ayers Rock Resort, officially known as the township of Yulara, is essentially a complex of lodgings, restaurants, and facilities, and is base camp for exploring Uluru and Kata Tjuta. Note that the accommodations and services here are the only ones in the vicinity of the national park. Uluru is about a 20-minute drive from the resort area (there's a sunset-viewing area on the way); driving to Kata Tjuta will take another 30 minutes. The park entrance fee of A$38 is valid for three days but can be extended to five days free of charge.

The resort "village" includes a bank, newsstand, supermarket, several souvenir shops and restaurants, an Aboriginal art gallery, hair salon, and child-care center.

The accommodations at the resort, which range from luxury hotels to a campground and hostel, are all run by Voyages Indigenous Tourism Australia and share many of the same facilities. Indoor dining is limited to each hotel's restaurants and the less-expensive eateries in the Town Centre, all of which can be charged back to your room. All reservations can be made through Voyages Indigenous Tourism Australia (*www.voyages.com.au*) on-site, or through their central reservations service in Sydney.

GETTING HERE AND AROUND

Qantas's budget subsidiary, Jetstar, operates nonstop flights from Sydney, Brisbane, and Melbourne, while Qantas offers nonstop hops from Cairns and Alice Springs; and Virgin Australia flies nonstop from Sydney. Passengers from other capital cities fly to Alice Springs to connect with flights to Ayers Rock Airport, which is 9 km (6 miles) north of the resort complex.

AAT Kings runs a complimentary shuttle bus between the airport and Yulara, which meets every flight. If you have reservations at the resort, representatives wait outside the baggage-claim area of the airport to whisk you and other guests away on the 10-minute drive.

If you're driving from Alice Springs, it's a five-hour-plus, 440-km (273-mile) trip to Ayers Rock Resort. Like every major Australian highway, the road is paved, but lacks a shoulder and is one lane in each direction for the duration, making it challenging and risky to overtake the four-trailer-long road trains, although the drivers will sometimes flash their blinker, indicating when it's safe for you to pass. The route, long and straight with monotonous desert scenery, often induces fatigue; avoid driving at night, sunrise, and sunset, as wildlife is prolific and you've a good chance of colliding with a kangaroo—they typically sleep all day but wake up just before sunset, thus making nighttime driving a lot more complicated.

From the resort it's 19 km (12 miles) to Uluru or 53 km (33 miles) to Kata Tjuta on winding, sealed roads.

If you prefer to explore Uluru and Kata Tjuta on your own schedule, renting your own car is a good idea; the only other ways to get to the national park are on group bus tours or by chauffeured taxi or coach. Avis, Hertz, and Thrifty all rent cars at Ayers Rock Resort as well as Ayers Rock Airport. Arrange for your rental early, since cars are limited.

TRANSPORTATION CONTACTS

AAT Kings

From complimentary airport transfers to and from Ayers Rock Resort to a multitude of tour packages, AAT Kings is the one tour bus you'll see everywhere in these parts. ✉ *167 Yulara Dr., Yulara* ☎ *08/8956–2171, 1300/228–546* 🌐 *www.aatkings.com.*

Automobile Association of the Northern Territory

Roadside assistance anywhere in the Northern Territory once you sign up for a membership. ✉ *2/14 Knuckey St., Darwin* ☎ *08/8925–5901, 131–111 emergency road assistance* 🌐 *www.aant.com.au.*

NT Road Report

Check conditions before you head out in case of road closures due to flooding or bushfires. ☎ *1800/246–199* 🌐 *roadreport.nt.gov.au.*

Uluru Hop On Hop Off
This nifty hop-on, hop-off shuttle service offers round-trip transfers from Ayers Rock Resort to Uluru (from A$49), Kata Tjuta (from A$95) or one-, two-, and three-day passes to both (from A$120, A$160, and A$210, respectively). ✉ *118 Kali Ct., Yulara* ☎ *08/8956–2019* 🌐 *uluru-hoponhopoff.com.au.*

SAFETY AND PRECAUTIONS
Water is vital in the Red Centre. It is easy to forget, but the dry atmosphere and the temperatures can make you prone to dehydration. If you are walking or climbing, you will need to consume additional water at regular intervals. You should carry at least one liter of water for every hour. Regardless of where you plan to travel, it is essential to carry plenty of water, which means 10 liters minimum if you're driving into the desert.

TIMING
If seeing Uluru is your reason for visiting the Red Centre, there are tours that fly in and out, stopping just long enough to watch the rock at sunset. However, for a more leisurely visit, allow two days so you can also visit Kata Tjuta (The Olgas) nearby.

TOURS
AIR TOURS
Ayers Rock Helicopters
Helicopter flights are A$150 per person for 15 minutes over Uluru, or A$265 for 30 minutes over both Kata Tjuta and Uluru. A slightly longer 36-minute flight for A$375 offers a different angle view of the two sites from the back. ✉ *149 Yulara Dr., Yulara* ☎ *08/8956–2077* 🌐 *www.flyuluru.com.au* 🎫 *From A$150.*

Ayers Rock Scenic Flights
The best views of Uluru and Kata Tjuta are from the air. Light-plane tours, with courtesy door-to-door pickup from Ayers Rock Resort hotels, include 24-minute flights over Uluru (from A$120), 40-minute flights over both sites (from A$240), as well as day tours to Kings Canyon (from A$785) and a huge meteorite crater known as Gosses Bluff (from A$650). For more information and options, visit the tourism information office at Ayers Rock Resort's Town Square. ✉ *149 Yulara Dr., Yulara* ☎ *08/8956–2345* 🌐 *www.flyuluru.com.au* 🎫 *From A$120.*

ABORIGINAL TOURS
Small-group tour company SEIT Outback Australia (*08/8956–3156*) organizes trips through the Uluru and Kata Tjuta region, with two of them led by local Aboriginal guides. These tours, which leave from Ayers Rock Resort and cost A$177 for a full-day experience, include a trip to Cave Hill and into the desert of the Pitjantjatjara Lands of Central Australia, as well as a special trip to traditional homelands to meet the locals and learn firsthand how they fought to establish land rights and make Uluru-Kata Tjuta National Park what it is today. Aboriginal art aficionados can also attend 90-minute dot-painting workshops held twice daily by Maruku Arts and Crafts in Yulara Town Square for a chance to learn about this ancient art form and create your own souvenir (A$69).

CAMEL TOURS
★ **Uluru Camel Tours**
A great way to get out in the open and see the sights is from the back of one of the desert's creatures. Uluru Camel Tours has sunrise and sunset tours that last for 2½ hours and include breakfast or champagne, beer, wine, and snacks depending on which one you do (A$135); 45-minute "express" rides for A$80 and even quicker 10-minute jaunts around the paddock for A$15 offer a brief introduction to this incredible animal. ✉ *10 Kali Circuit, Yulara* ☎ *08/8956–3333* 🌐 *ulurucameltours.com.au* 🎫 *From A$80.*

ESSENTIALS
VISITOR INFORMATION
The Uluru–Kata Tjuta Cultural Centre is on the park road just before you reach the rock. It also contains the park's ranger station. The Cultural Centre is open

daily from 7 am to 6 pm. The Tours and Information Centre at Yulara Town Square is open daily from 8 am to 7 am.

CONTACTS Ayers Rock Resort Central Reservations Service. ✉ *Voyages Indigenous Tourism Australia, 179 Elizabeth St., Sydney* ☎ *1300/134–044* 🌐 *www.ayersrockresort.com.au.* **Uluru–Kata Tjuta Cultural Centre.** ✉ *Uluru Rd., Yulara* ☎ *08/8956–1128* 🌐 *www.parksaustralia.gov.au.* **Yulara Tours and Information Centre.** ✉ *127 Yulara Dr., Yulara* ☎ *08/8957–7324* 🌐 *www.ayersrockresort.com.au.*

Watch the Sky

More stars and other astronomical sights, such as the fascinating Magellanic Clouds, are visible in the southern hemisphere than in the northern, and the desert night sky shows off their glory with diamond-like clarity. Look out for the Southern Cross, the constellation that navigators used for many centuries to find their way—most Australians will proudly point it out for you.

Sights

★ Kata Tjuta

NATURE SIGHT | There are three main walks at Kata Tjuta, the first from the parking lot into Walpa Gorge, a 2.6-km (1.6-mile) hike to the deepest valley between the rocks. The round-trip journey takes about one hour. The gorge is a desert refuge for plants and animals and the rocky track gently rises along a moisture-rich gully, passing inconspicuous rare plants and ending at a grove of flourishing spearwood. More rewarding, but also more difficult, is the Valley of the Winds Walk, which takes you along a stony track to two spectacular lookouts, Karu (2.2 km or 1.3 miles return; allow an hour) and Karingana (5.4 km or 3.3 miles; allow 2½ hours). Experienced walkers can also complete the full 7.4-km (4.6-mile) circuit in about four hours. **TIP→ Note that the Valley of the Winds Walk closes when temperatures rise above 36°C (97°F), which is usually after 11 am in summer.** The Kata Tjuta Viewing Area, 25 km (16 miles) along Kata Tjuta Road is 1,970 feet from the car park, and interpretive panels explain the natural life around you. It's also where tour buses line up for sunrise photos about a half hour before dawn. Be prepared for crowds—and amazing views of Kata Tjuta and Uluru in the distance. ✉ *Lasseter Hwy., Yulara* ⊕ *53 km (33 miles) west of Yulara* 🌐 *www.parksaustralia.gov.au* 🎫 *A$38.*

★ Uluru

NATURE SIGHT | Rising like an enormous red mountain in the middle of an otherwise completely flat desert, Uluru (formerly called Ayers Rock) is a marvel to behold. Two car parks—Mala and Kuniya—provide access for several short walks, or you can choose to do the full 10-km (6-mile) circuit on the Uluru Base Walk, which takes about four hours. Some places are Aboriginal sacred sites and cannot be entered, nor can they be photographed or captured on video—these are clearly signposted—while signs around the base explain the significance of what you're looking at and recount traditional myths and legends. The Mala Walk is 2 km (1 mile) in length and almost all on flat land, taking you to Kanju Gorge from the car park; park rangers provide free tours daily at 8 am from October through April and at 10 am from May through September. The Liru Walk starts at the cultural center and takes you to the base Uluru. Along the way are stands of mulga trees and, after rain, wildflowers. The track is wheelchair accessible and the walk is an easy 1½ hours. On the southern side of Uluru, the Kuniya Walk and Mutitjulu Waterhole trail starts at the Kuniya car park and is an easy 45-minute walk along a wheelchair-accessible trail to the water hole, home of Wanampi, an ancestral snake.

The monumental Uluru as seen from the air

A rock shelter once used by Aboriginal people houses rock art. Another popular way to experience Uluru is to watch the natural light reflect on it from one of the two sunset-viewing areas. As the last rays of daylight strike, the rock positively glows as if lit from within. Just as quickly, the light is extinguished and the color changes to a somber mauve and finally to black. ✉ *Lasseter Hwy., Yulara* 🌐 *www.parksaustralia.gov.au* 🎫 *A$38.*

Uluru–Kata Tjuta Cultural Centre

VISITOR CENTER | The cultural center is the first thing you'll see after entering the park through a tollgate. The two buildings are built in a serpentine style, reflecting the Kuniya and Liru stories about two ancestral snakes who fought a long-ago battle on the southern side of Uluru. Inside, you can learn about Aboriginal history and the return of the park to its traditional owners on October 26, 1985. There's also an excellent park ranger's station where you can get maps and hiking guides, as well as two art shops, Maruku and Walkatjara, where you'll likely see Indigenous artists at work. Pick up a souvenir or grab refreshments at the Ininti Cafe, or rent a bicycle for another fun way to explore this beautiful Outback landscape (from A$50). ✉ *Uluru Rd., Yulara* ☎ *08/8956–1128* 🌐 *www.parksaustralia.gov.au/uluru* 🎫 *Free.*

Restaurants

Gecko's Cafe

$$ | **AUSTRALIAN** | In the center of the Yulara town center, this casual eatery has reasonably priced options, including affordable appetizers, salads, burgers, pastas, pizzas, and sweet treats. Open every day for lunch and dinner, it's one of the most budget-friendly spots in Ayers Rock Resort. **Known for:** kangaroo and Wagyu beef burgers; beer-battered barramundi served with desert lime aioli; crocodile ribs marinated in lemon myrtle. $ *Average main: A$26* ✉ *Yulara Town Sq., 1/127 Yulara Dr., Yulara* ☎ *02/8296–8010* 🌐 *www.ayersrockresort.com.au.*

Ilkari Restaurant

$$$$ | **AUSTRALIAN** | Situated inside the Sails in the Desert hotel, Ilkari Restaurant serves specialties like lamb cutlets and kangaroo skewers at live cooking stations, giving you a sort of dinner-and-a-show experience compared to that of the usual hotel buffet. The buffet items change nightly and the decor reflects local legends with a Kuniya Dreaming mural covering the rear wall. **Known for:** cooked-to-order dishes made with flair; the perennially popular chocolate fountain; South Australian oysters and king prawns. *Average main: A$75 ✉ 1/163 Yulara Dr., Yulara ✥ Located inside Sails in the Desert Hotel ☎ 02/8296–8010 ⊕ www.ayersrockresort.com.au.*

Pioneer BBQ and Bar

$$ | **AUSTRALIAN** | Order steaks, barramundi, emu sausages, crocodile tails, or kangaroo loins from the server, then cook it to your liking Aussie-style on large barbecues. This DIY-dining option and its adjacent bar with live music is one of the most popular in the resort, and with barbecue being practically a national sport here, it's easy to see why. **Known for:** emu sausages; vegetarian options such as tofu and vegetable stir-fry plus salad bar; chicken breast marinated in locally sourced lemon myrtle. *Average main: A$25 ✉ Outback Pioneer Hotel, 2/1 Yulara Dr., Yulara ☎ 08/8957–7605 ⊕ www.ayersrockresort.com.au.*

Pira Pool Bar

$$ | **ECLECTIC** | A lovely spot for a late-afternoon cocktail or mocktail, this casual poolside bar at Sails in the Desert offers an all-day menu of light bites from 11 am to 7 pm. A variety of wines, beers, ciders, soft drinks, coffees, teas, and juices are also available. **Known for:** tandoori chicken sliders; curry of the day; James Squire 150 Lashes beer-battered barramundi. *Average main: A$26 ✉ Sails in the Desert Hotel, 163 Yulara Dr., Yulara ☎ 08/8957–7417 ⊕ www.ayersrockresort.com.au.*

★ Sounds of Silence

$$$ | **AUSTRALIAN** | Australian wines and Northern Territory specialty dishes like bush salads and Australian game are served at a lookout here before you dine on your buffet meal in the middle of the desert and enjoy an astronomer-led stargazing tour of the southern sky. A more intimate and pricier small-group table d'hôte four-course dinner called Tali Wiru is also available for a maximum of 20 diners at a different vantage point. **Known for:** canapés made with locally sourced Indigenous ingredients; complimentary transfers and open bar are included in the price; bush tucker–inspired buffet items. *Average main: A$234 ✉ 171 Yulara Dr., Yulara ☎ 02/8296–8010 ⊕ www.ayersrockresort.com.au/experiences/detail/sounds-of-silence.*

Coffee and Quick Bites

Kulata Academy Cafe

$ | **AUSTRALIAN** | Kulata is a bit more than a grab-and-go café. This is where the trainees of the National Indigenous Training Academy take their first step in their hospitality career. **Known for:** speedy service; fresh sandwiches made daily; friendly staff. *Average main: A$10 ✉ 4/127 Yulara Dr., Yulara ☎ 02/8296–8010 ⊕ www.ayersrockresort.com.au/dining/kulata-academy-cafe.*

Hotels

Desert Gardens Hotel

$$$$ | **HOTEL** | Blond-wood furniture complements desert hues in this hotel's small, neat rooms, which are named after different Australian flora, have a balcony or courtyard, and are surrounded by lovely native gardens. **Pros:** shady gardens among gum trees; views of Uluru; free in-room Wi-Fi. **Cons:** a 10- to 15-minute walk or shuttle ride (free) to Yulara town center; the property looks a little dated; busy resort entrance road passes hotel. *Rooms from: A$400*

An Official End to Climbing Uluru

While the topic of climbing Uluru is a heated subject in Central Australia these days, it was decided in 2017 by the park's management board that the climbing trail will be closed as of October 26, 2019, the 34th anniversary of the handover of the parklands to the Anangu traditional owners. Besides being a strenuous, even dangerous hike—the 1.5-km (1-mile) hike takes about three hours round-trip in extreme heat without a real trail, just a single chain to cling to for folks traveling in both directions—it's considered extremely disrespectful to climb such a sacred Aboriginal site. Several signs posted at the base of the trail remind visitors of the many cultural, environmental, and safety reasons to admire this amazing monolith from the ground level.

With climbing Uluru no longer an option, it's important to remember that there are many other ways to experience it from below—or above. You can rent a bike, ride a Segway, take a motorcycle tour, go on an Aboriginal cultural tour, take a helicopter ride to see it from above, skydive next to it, view it from a blimp, enjoy a fancy dinner under the stars, or view a fabulous art-and-light exhibit (Field of Light, through December) near it, see it at sunrise and sunset from one of the viewing areas, or just take a drive or walk around the base to view it from all possible angles.

✉ *1 Yulara Dr., Yulara* ☎ *02/8296–8010* 🌐 *www.ayersrockresort.com.au/accommodation/desert-gardens-hotel* *218 rooms* *No Meals.*

Emu Walk Apartments
$$$$ | **HOTEL** | **FAMILY** | Perfect for families, large groups, or folks who otherwise just like to cook while they're on the road, Emu Walk Apartments is the only accommodation at Ayers Rock Resort that offers an in-room self-catering option, complete with full kitchens. **Pros:** adjacent to resort dining options; extra beds ideal for families or traveling companions; within walking distance to shops and supermarket. **Cons:** can be noisy with those walking to and from Yulara town center; limited amenities in rooms; room rates are pricey. $ *Rooms from: A$420* ✉ *3 Yulara Dr., Yulara* ☎ *02/8296–8010* 🌐 *www.ayersrockresort.com.au/accommodation/emu-walk-apartments* *60 apartments* *No Meals.*

★ **Longitude 131°**
$$$$ | **RESORT** | With 15 elevated, hard-floored "tents" offering king-size beds and uninterrupted, panoramic views of Uluru thanks to the floor-to-ceiling sliding-glass doors, this desert oasis about 3 km (2 miles) from the Ayers Rock Resort provides the ultimate Outback luxury experience. **Pros:** touring included; luxury tented accommodation, some convertible to twin share; dinner under the stars. **Cons:** minimum two-night stay requirement; no bathtubs; children younger than 13 not allowed. $ *Rooms from: A$1500* ✉ *Yulara Dr., Yulara* ☎ *02/9918–4355* 🌐 *longitude131.com.au* *15 suites* *All-Inclusive.*

The Lost Camel
$$$$ | **HOTEL** | This boutique-hotel-style property is built around a blue-tile, rivet-and-glass-paneled, reverse infinity pool, arguably the fanciest in Ayers Rock Resort. **Pros:** Aboriginal-theme photographs on walls; brightly colored decor; the prettiest, most stylish swimming

pool in the resort. **Cons:** it's next to Yulara town center, so can be busy; rooms can be pricey; unusual bathroom layout. $ *Rooms from: A$330* ✉ *Yulara Dr., Yulara* ☎ *02/8296–8010* 🌐 *www.ayersrockresort.com.au* *99 rooms* *No Meals.*

Outback Pioneer Hotel and Lodge
$$$ | HOTEL | FAMILY | The theme at this affordable and popular hotel is the 1860s Outback, complete with corrugated iron, timber beams, and camel saddles. **Pros:** tennis courts; lodge rooms are cheapest in the resort; free shuttle bus. **Cons:** rooms closer to Pioneer BBQ will hear music until about 11 pm; hotel rooms are basic for the price; some budget-style rooms have communal bathrooms. $ *Rooms from: A$300* ✉ *Yulara Dr., Yulara* ☎ *02/8296–8010* 🌐 *www.ayersrockresort.com.au/accommodation/outback-pioneer-lodge* *167 rooms* *No Meals.*

★ **Sails in the Desert**
$$$$ | RESORT | FAMILY | Architectural shade sails, ghost-gum-fringed lawns, Aboriginal art, and numerous facilities distinguish this upscale hotel with rooms in three-tiered blocks that frame a gorgeous white-tiled pool. **Pros:** complimentary in-room Wi-Fi; Aboriginal artworks featured throughout; kids under 12 stay free. **Cons:** to get to Yulara town center requires a walk or shuttle; this hotel is popular with families and well-to-do tour groups; rooms and dining options are the priciest at Ayers Rock Resort. $ *Rooms from: A$475* ✉ *163 Yulara Dr., Yulara* ☎ *02/8296–8010* 🌐 *www.ayersrockresort.com.au/accommodation/sails-in-the-desert* *228 rooms* *No Meals.*

Shopping

Uluru–Kata Tjuta Cultural Centre
SOUVENIRS | FAMILY | The cultural center not only has information about the Anangu people and their culture, it also houses beautiful art for purchase. The Ininti Cafe carries souvenirs and light food, while Maruku and Walkatjara Art Uluru sell Aboriginal paintings and handicrafts. The Cultural Centre itself is open daily from 10 am to 4 pm (information desk from 10 am to 5 pm); Ininti Cafe is open daily from 10 am to 4 pm; Maruku Arts is open daily 7:30 am to 5:30 pm; Walkatjara Art Uluru is open daily from 8 am to 4 pm. ✉ *Uluru–Kata Tjuta National Park, Uluru Rd., Yulara* ☎ *08/8956–1128* 🌐 *parksaustralia.gov.au/uluru/do/cultural-centre.*

Darwin

3,149 km (1,956 miles) northwest of Sydney, 2,618 km (1,626 miles) north of Adelaide.

Darwin is Australia's most colorful and exotic capital city. Surrounded on three sides by the turquoise waters of the Timor Sea, the streets are lined with tropical frangipani flowers and palm trees. Warm and dry in winter, hot and steamy in summer, it's a relaxed and casual place, as well as a beguiling blend of tropical frontier outpost and Outback hardiness. Thanks to the humidity levels, its close proximity to Southeast Asia, and its multicultural population, it almost seems more like Asia than the rest of Australia.

Darwin is a city that has always had to fight for its survival. Its history of failed attempts date from 1824, when Europeans attempted to establish an enclave in this harsh, unyielding climate. The original 1869 settlement, called Palmerston, was built on a parcel of mangrove wetlands and scrub forest. It was not until 1911, after it had already weathered the disastrous cyclones of 1878, 1881, and 1897, that the town was named after the scientist who had visited Australia's shores aboard the *Beagle* in 1839. During World War II, it was bombed 64 times, as the harbor full of warships was a prime target for the Japanese war planes. Then, on the night of Christmas Eve 1974, the city was almost completely destroyed by Cyclone Tracy, Australia's greatest natural disaster.

It's a tribute to those who stayed and to those who have come to live here after Tracy that the rebuilt city now thrives as an administrative and commercial center for northern Australia. Old Darwin has been replaced by something of an edifice complex—such buildings as Parliament House and the Supreme Court all seem very grand for such a small city, especially one that prides itself on its casual, outdoor-centric lifestyle.

Today, Darwin is the best place from which to explore Australia's Top End.

GETTING HERE AND AROUND

Darwin's International Airport is serviced from overseas by Qantas, Jetstar (and Jetstar Asia), Donghai Airlines, SilkAir, and Air North. Jetstar flies from Darwin to Bali several times a week, while SilkAir and Jetstar Asia connect Darwin with Singapore, and Air North flies to Dili in East Timor.

Qantas, Air North, Virgin Australia, Tigerair, and Jetstar all fly into Darwin regularly from other parts of Australia and operate regional flights within the Top End. Air North flies west to Kununurra and Broome, and east to Gove. The Darwin City Airport Shuttle offers regular service between the airport and the city's hotels for A$18 one-way or A$36 round-trip. The taxi journey downtown costs about A$25–A$30.

The *Ghan* train connects Darwin with Adelaide via Alice Springs on a two-night all-inclusive 2,979-km (1,851-mile) journey a couple of times a week depending on the time of year (*www.greatsouthernrail.com.au*).

The best way to get around Darwin is by car and the Stuart Highway is Darwin's land connection with the rest of Australia. By road, Darwin is 16½ hours from Alice Springs (1,497 km [930 miles]), 21 hours from Broome via the Great Northern Highway (1,871 km [1,162 miles]), 38 hours from Brisbane (3,425 km [2,128 miles]), and 44 hours from Perth (4,041km [2,510 miles]).

For drivers headed outside the Northern Territory, note that one-way drop-off fees for rental vehicles are often twice as much as a weekly rentals. If you don't feel like driving, the bus network in Darwin links the city with its far-flung suburbs, and a choice of minibus operators, including the 24-hour Metro minibuses, run all over town for fixed prices starting at A$4 per person. The main bus terminal (the Darwin Bus Interchange) is on Harry Chan Avenue, near the Bennett Street end of Smith Street Mall; bus fares start at A$3 for a single ride good for up to three hours, and range from A$7 day passes to A$20 weekly and 10-trip tickets. A minibus stand is also located at the front of Darwin's airport terminal. Popular ride-sharing services Uber and Hi Oscar can also be found in Darwin, allowing you to get around town for less.

TAXIS Blue Taxi Company. ✉ *15 Finniss St., Darwin* ☎ *138–294* 🌐 *www.bluetaxi.com.au.* **Darwin Radio Taxis.** ✉ *315 Larkin Ave., Darwin* ☎ *131–008 in local area* 🌐 *www.darwinradiotaxis.com.au.*

SAFETY AND PRECAUTIONS

Swimming in the ocean is not recommended because of the box jellyfish, commonly known as "stingers." Salt and freshwater crocodiles are found in most Top End billabongs and rivers, and are occasionally seen even on Darwin beaches. The accessible rivers and billabongs are generally signposted if saltwater crocodiles are known to inhabit the area, but if you are not sure, don't swim.

Avoid driving outside towns after dark due to the dangers presented by roaming buffalo, cattle, horses, donkeys, and kangaroos. If your vehicle breaks down, stay with it; it is easier to find a missing car than missing people. If you are going for a bushwalk, always tell someone your plan and when you expect to return.

TIMING

Although Darwin has some attractions, many people view the city as the entry point to the Top End's national parks, in particular Kakadu and Litchfield. Two days in the city will be enough to see the main attractions, after which you will want to head to Kakadu.

TOURS

AAT Kings Darwin Day Tours

AAT Kings offers afternoon tours to several popular sights around the city, including the Darwin Aviation Museum, Museum and Art Gallery of the Northern Territory, and George Brown Botanic Gardens, all while guides discuss the culture of the area's Larrakia traditional owners, the city's role in World War II, and how it came to be such a multicultural locale today (A$71). Those in a more adventurous mood should check out the company's Jumping Crocs and Nature Adventure tour, which includes a cruise down the Adelaide River about 90 minutes outside of town that also happens to be home to more than 1,600 crocodiles. You'll also visit the Window on the Wetlands and Fogg Dam Conservation Reserve on this half-day trip (A$115). ✉ *6/52 Mitchell St., City Center* ☎ *1300/228–546* 🌐 *www.aatkings.com/tours* 🎫 *From A$71.*

Darwin City Explorer (Tour Tub)

Known in these parts as the "Tour Tub," the Darwin City Explorer takes you on a half-day guided trip to some of the area's biggest attractions, including the WWII Oil Storage Tunnels, the Defence of Darwin Experience & Darwin Military Museum, the Museum and Art Gallery of the Northern Territory, Fannie Bay Gaol, the Aviation Heritage Centre, and on certain days, the Parap Markets (Saturday) and the Qantas Hangar (weekdays). Your ticket also gives you complimentary transfers from your hotel and covers entrance fees to all listed attractions. ✉ *50 Mitchell St., City Center* ☎ *08/8985–6322* 🌐 *tourtube.com.au* 🎫 *From A$125.*

Spirit of Darwin Sunset Cruises

Embark on a 2½-hour cruise around scenic Darwin Harbour, with a complimentary drink and canapés as you take in views of one of the best sunsets in the Top End. For A$30 more, you can add the dinner option, which includes your choice of main dish, salad, and dessert. ✉ *Dock, 2 Stokes Hill Rd., City Center* ☎ *0417/381–977* 🌐 *spiritofdarwin.com.au* 🎫 *From A$70.*

ESSENTIALS

VISITOR INFORMATION Tourism Top End. ✉ *6 Bennett St., City Center* ☎ *08/8980–6000, 1300/138–886* 🌐 *www.tourism-topend.com.au.*

Sights

Crocodylus Park

ZOO | FAMILY | This research facility has an excellent air-conditioned crocodile museum and education center. There are more than 1,200 crocodiles here, from babies to giants up to 16 feet long. The saurian section of the zoo includes the croc-infested Bellairs Lagoon and pens for breeding and raising. The park also has enclosures with lions, tigers, American alligators, cassowaries, primates, turtles, an emu, and a dingo, among other animals, and holds one of the biggest snakes in Australia: a Burmese python weighing 308 pounds. Tours and feedings are at 10 am, noon, and 2 pm, while a croc boat cruise gets you a little closer to these magnificent creatures twice a day at 11 am and 1 pm. ✉ *815 McMillans Rd., Berrimah* ☎ *08/8922–4500* 🌐 *www.crocodyluspark.com.au* 🎫 *A$40.*

Crocosaurus Cove

ZOO | FAMILY | Right in the heart of Darwin City, this is the place to go swimming with saltwater crocodiles and live to tell the tale. Feeding times for the big crocs (daily at 11:30 am, 2:30 pm, and 4:30 pm) and the Cage of Death, a

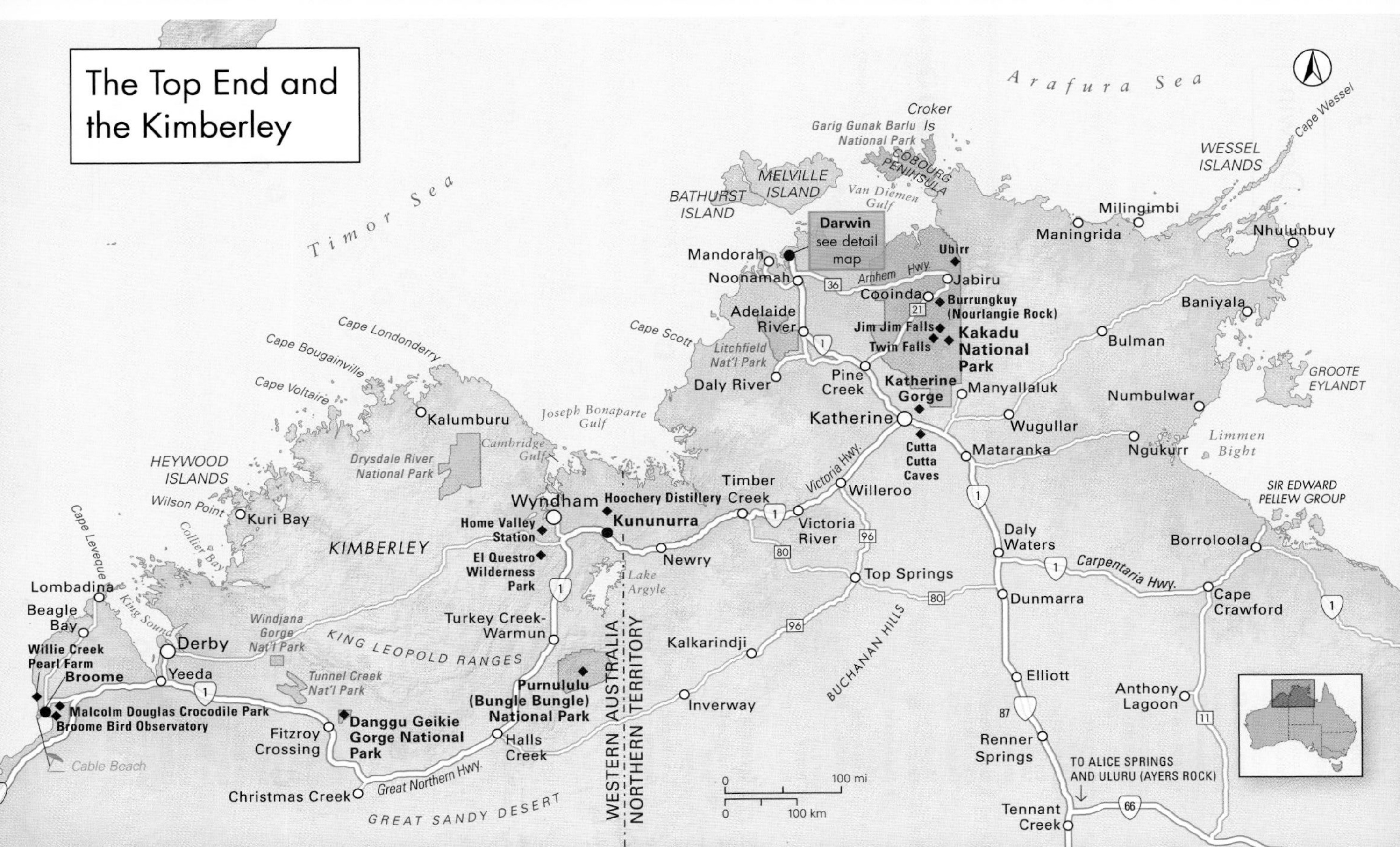
The Top End and the Kimberley
Arafura Sea
Timor Sea
Croker Is
Garig Gunak Barlu National Park
COBOURG PENINSULA
Cape Wessel
WESSEL ISLANDS
MELVILLE ISLAND
BATHURST ISLAND
Van Diemen Gulf
Darwin see detail map
Mandorah
Noonamah
Arnhem Hwy.
Ubirr
Jabiru
Cooinda
Burrungkuy (Nourlangie Rock)
Jim Jim Falls
Twin Falls
Kakadu National Park
Milingimbi
Maningrida
Nhulunbuy
Baniyala
Bulman
GROOTE EYLANDT
Numbulwar
Limmen Bight
Ngukurr
Adelaide River
Cape Scott
Litchfield Nat'l Park
Daly River
Pine Creek
Katherine Gorge
Manyallaluk
Katherine
Wugullar
Mataranka
Cutta Cutta Caves
Cape Londonderry
Cape Bougainville
Cape Voltaire
Kalumburu
Joseph Bonaparte Gulf
Cambridge Gulf
Drysdale River National Park
HEYWOOD ISLANDS
Wilson Point
Kuri Bay
Collier Bay
KIMBERLEY
Wyndham
Hoochery Distillery
Kununurra
Home Valley Station
El Questro Wilderness Park
Timber Creek
Victoria Hwy.
Willeroo
Victoria River
SIR EDWARD PELLEW GROUP
Borroloola
Daly Waters
Newry
Lake Argyle
Top Springs
Carpentaria Hwy.
Cape Crawford
Dunmarra
Cape Leveque
Lombadina
Beagle Bay
King Sound
Derby
Windjana Gorge Nat'l Park
KING LEOPOLD RANGES
Turkey Creek-Warmun
WESTERN AUSTRALIA
NORTHERN TERRITORY
Kalkarindji
BUCHANAN HILLS
Willie Creek Pearl Farm
Broome
Yeeda
Tunnel Creek Nat'l Park
Purnululu (Bungle Bungle) National Park
Elliott
Anthony Lagoon
Malcolm Douglas Crocodile Park
Broome Bird Observatory
Danggu Geikie Gorge National Park
Inverway
Fitzroy Crossing
Halls Creek
Renner Springs
Cable Beach
Great Northern Hwy.
Christmas Creek
GREAT SANDY DESERT
0 100 mi
0 100 km
TO ALICE SPRINGS AND ULURU (AYERS ROCK)
Tennant Creek
1
36
21
80
96
87
11
66

Sights

1 Crocodylus Park **D3**
2 Crocosaurus Cove......... **C7**
3 Darwin Aviation Museum **D3**
4 The Darwin Waterfront Precinct and Stokes Hill Wharf **D8**
5 Defence of Darwin Experience at the Darwin Military Museum **A1**
6 George Brown Darwin Botanic Gardens..... **C5**
7 Mindil Beach Casino....... **B6**
8 Museum and Art Gallery of the Northern Territory..... **B4**
9 Territory Wildlife Park **D3**

Restaurants

1 Crustaceans on the Wharf **D8**
2 Eva's Botanic Gardens Cafe **B5**
3 Hanuman ... **B7**
4 Lola's Pergola...... **A6**
5 MERAKI Greek Taverna **C7**
6 Pee Wee's at the Point **A2**

Quick Bites

1 Kopi Stop ... **B7**
2 Laneway Specialty Coffee....... **C4**

Hotels

1 DoubleTree by Hilton Hotel Esplanade Darwin **B7**
2 Mindil Beach Casino Resort....... **B6**
3 Novotel Darwin CBD Hotel... **B7**
4 Vibe Hotel Darwin Waterfront.. **C8**

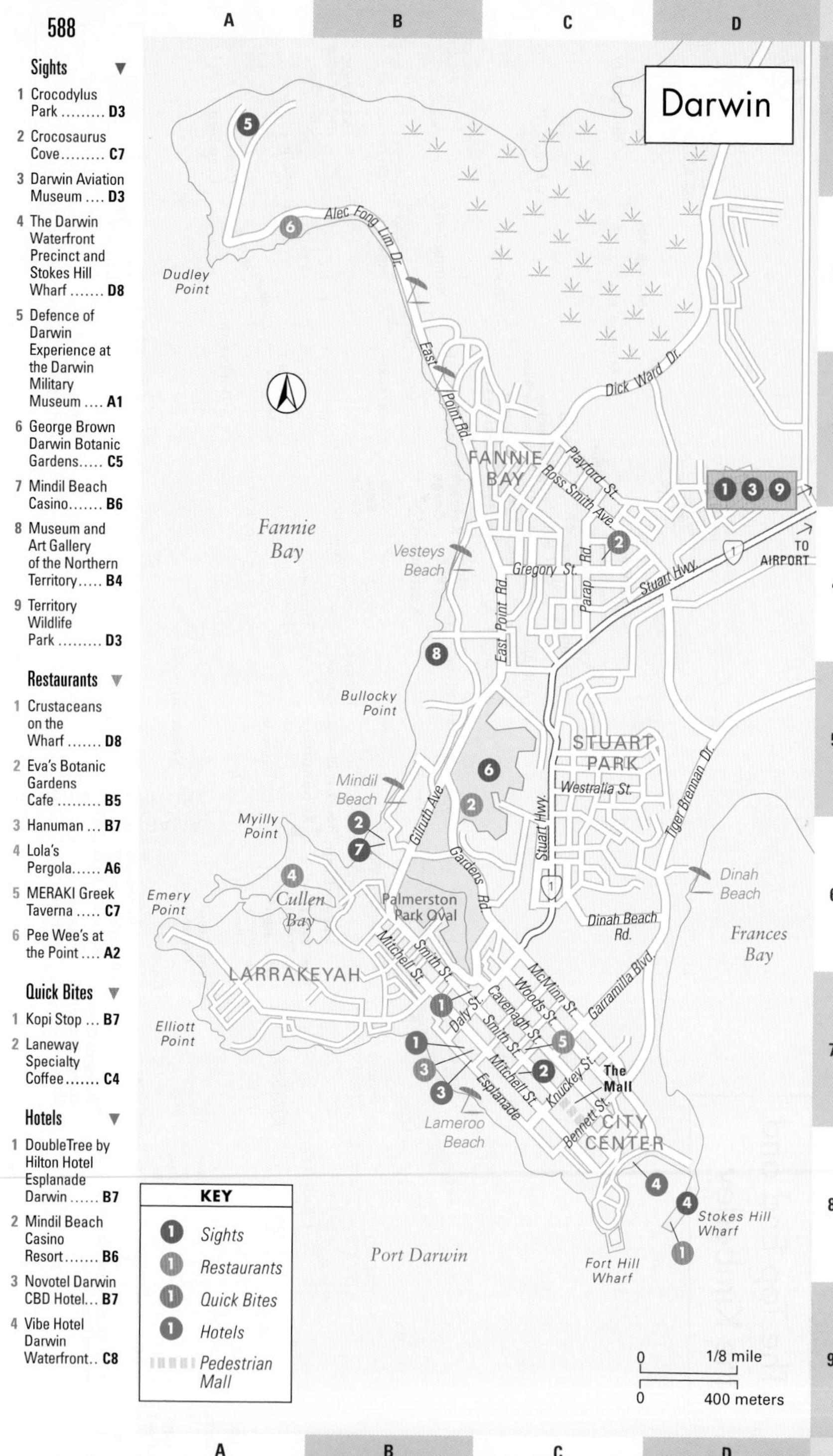

not-for-the-faint-of-heart attraction where visitors are lowered into croc-infested pools in a clear perspex container (A$175), are not to be missed. Bring your swimsuit along and take a photo of you swimming alongside these impressive creatures (again, you're in a completely separate pool). Feedings and presentations happen at different times throughout the day in the four main sections—fish, big crocs, turtles, and nocturnal reptiles—during which you can take your turn feeding young crocs and holding a variety of reptiles. ✉ *58 Mitchell St., Darwin* ☎ *08/8981–7522* 🌐 *www.crocosauruscove.com* 🎫 *A$35.*

Darwin Aviation Museum

MUSEUM VILLAGE | Due to its isolation and sparse population, the Northern Territory played an important role in the expansion of aviation in Australia, and this impressive museum traces the history of flight Down Under. Planes on display include a massive B-52 bomber on permanent loan from the United States and a recently retired RAAF F-111 fighter jet, as well as a Japanese Zero shot down on the first day of bombing raids in 1942. There's also a great exhibition on female aviators, including Amy Johnson, the first to fly solo from the U.K. to Australia in 1930. ✉ *557 Stuart Hwy., Winnellie* ☎ *08/8947–2145* 🌐 *www.darwinaviationmuseum.com.au* 🎫 *A$15.*

The Darwin Waterfront Precinct and Stokes Hill Wharf

MARINA/PIER | **FAMILY** | The best views of Darwin Harbour are from Stokes Hill Wharf, a working pier that receives cargo ships, trawlers, defense vessels, and, occasionally, huge cruise liners. It's also a favorite spot for Darwinites to fish, and when the mackerel are running, you can join scores of locals over a few beers. The cluster of cafés becomes crowded on weekends and when cruise ships arrive. On the city side, in the Waterfront Precinct, is the Wave Lagoon (entry is $7; open daily 10 am to 6 pm) and a free, stinger-free (safe from jellyfish) swimming lagoon. Both are popular on hot days. The Waterfront is also home to some of the city's best restaurants and cafés, and is where free festivals and movie nights are held during the dry season. ✉ *19B Kitchener Dr., Darwin Harbour* ☎ *08/8999–5155* 🌐 *www.waterfront.nt.gov.au.*

Be Croc Smart

The crocodile has long been a dominant predator in the wetland regions of Australia. Powerful and stealthy, the saltwater (estuarine) crocodile has little to fear—and that includes humans. More than 150,000 "salties" and another 100,000 freshwater crocs ("freshies") make their home in the coastal and tidal areas of rivers, as well as floodplains and freshwater reaches of rivers of northern Australia. Attacks on people are rare and deaths few (about one a year), but you should observe all no-swimming and warning signs and treat crocs with respect.

Defence of Darwin Experience at the Darwin Military Museum

MUSEUM VILLAGE | WWII came to Australia when 188 Japanese planes bombed Darwin on February 19, 1942, killing 235 people and injuring an additional 400. This high-tech, newer section of the museum at East Point—opened in 2012 to commemorate the 70th anniversary of the attack—tells the story of the people who were there that day, the events that led up to and followed it, and Darwin's role in the war. The Defence of Darwin Experience is the highlight—when you hear the air raid siren, head to the back of the museum and enter the theater to view an intense, multisensory telling of what happened that day, complete with loud explosive sounds, strobe lights, and flash effects. It's part of the Darwin Military Museum, which has lots of guns and other military equipment on display, as well as some original buildings that were there during World War II. ✉ *5434 Alec Fong Lim Dr., East Point* ☎ *08/8981-9702* 🌐 *www.darwinmilitarymuseum.com.au* 🎫 *A$20.*

George Brown Darwin Botanic Gardens
GARDEN | FAMILY | First planted in 1886 and largely destroyed by Cyclone Tracy, the 103-acre site today displays rain forest, mangroves, and open woodland environments. There are more than 450 species of palms growing in the gardens. A popular walk takes visitors on a self-guided tour of plants that Aboriginal people have used for medicinal purposes for centuries. The Children's Evolutionary Playground traces the changes in plant groups through time, while the plant display house has tropical ferns, orchids, and other exotic plants to check out. Head to Eva's, a lovely café nestled in a Heritage-listed church within the gardens—it's open from 7 am to 3 pm for breakfast and lunch, and offers a variety of tasty baked goods, coffee, and tea in case you need a break. ✉ *Gilruth Ave. at Gardens Rd., Mindil Beach* ☎ *08/8999-4418* 🌐 *www.nt.gov.au* 🎫 *Free.*

Mindil Beach Casino
CASINO | Mindil Beach Casino is one of Darwin's most popular evening spots. More than 700 gaming machines open 24 hours a day, while gaming tables are open from noon until 4 am Thursday and Sunday and until 6 am Friday and Saturday. Fancy a break from the betting? Choose from one of four restaurants—Cove (steak house), Dragon Court (Asian-fusion), il Piatto (Italian), or The Vue (bistro dining). SkyCity's bars—Sandbar, The Sportsbar, Lagoon Bar, and INFINITY, a new beach club–themed bar beside the casino's infinity pool—are just as fabulous. ✉ *Mindil Beach, Gilruth Ave., Mindil Beach* ☎ *08/8943-8888* 🌐 *mindilbeachcasinoresort.com.au.*

A Tropical Summer

Darwin's wet season—when the humidity rises and monsoonal rains dump around 68 inches—runs from November to April. The days offer a predictable mix of sunshine and afternoon showers, along with some spectacular thunder and lightning storms. There are fewer visitors at this time of the year, and Darwin slows to an even more relaxed pace. Across the Top End, waterfalls increase in size, floodplains rejuvenate to a lush green, and flowers bloom.

★ Museum and Art Gallery of the Northern Territory
MUSEUM VILLAGE | Collections at this excellent—and free—museum and art gallery encompass Aboriginal art and culture, maritime archaeology, Northern Territory history, and natural sciences. One gallery is devoted to Cyclone Tracy, where you can listen to a terrifying recording of the howling winds. You can also see "Sweetheart," a 16-foot, 10-inch stuffed saltwater crocodile that was known for attacking fishing boats on the Finniss River in the 1970s. ✉ *19 Conacher St., Fannie Bay* ☎ *08/8999-8264* 🌐 *www.magnt.net.au* 🎫 *Free.*

Territory Wildlife Park
NATURE PRESERVE | FAMILY | With 1,544 acres of natural bushland, this impressive park is dedicated to the Northern Territory's native fauna and flora. In addition to saltwater crocodiles, dingoes, olive pythons, and waterbirds, among other animals, the park also has an underwater viewing area for observing freshwater fish and a nocturnal house kept dark for late-night creatures. The treetop-level walkway through the huge aviary allows you to watch native birds from the

Off The Beaten Path

Litchfield National Park. This beautiful park lies just 120 km (75 miles) southwest of Darwin off the Stuart Highway. Its 1,500 square km (579 square miles) are an untouched wilderness of monsoonal rain forests, rivers, and striking rock formations. The highlights include four separate, spectacular waterfalls—Florence, Tjaynera (Sandy Creek), Wangi, and Tolmer Falls—all of which have secluded plunge pools. *The pools are suitable for swimming but occasionally there are crocs here, so observe any "no swimming" signs.*There is also a dramatic group of large, freestanding sandstone pillars known as the Lost City (accessible only by four-wheel-drive track), and Magnetic Termite Mounds, which have an eerie resemblance to eroded grave markers, which dot the black-soiled plains of the park's northern area. You'll need to camp if you want to stay in the park; campgrounds and RV sites are located near several of the major sights (call the Parks and Wildlife Service of the Northern Territory at *08/8976–0282* for more information on the facilities, as they vary by campsite). There are also a few restaurants and modest hotels in the nearby town of Batchelor, though most folks just visit Litchfield as a day trip from Darwin, about a 90-minute drive away. ✉ *Litchfield Park Rd., Litchfield Park* ✣ *120 km (75 miles) southwest of Darwin* 🌐 *nt.gov.au* 🎫 *Free.*

swamps and forests at close range. Daily events include feedings, guided walks, and a birds of prey display: see the website for daily schedules. There's also a nifty tram to help you get around. ✉ *Cox Peninsula Rd., Berry Springs* ✣ *50 km (31 miles) or about 45 mins south of Darwin* ☎ *08/8988–7200* 🌐 *www.territorywildlifepark.com.au* 🎫 *A$37.*

Restaurants

Crustaceans on the Wharf

$$ | SEAFOOD | FAMILY | Located at the end of Stokes Hill Wharf, and in a great spot to catch the sunset, this casual restaurant specializes in all things seafood, with dishes like local wild-caught barramundi, lobster mornay, and crumbed calamari on the menu. Kids ages 10 and under eat free for every adult main meal purchased. **Known for:** family-friendly; incredible views; superfresh seafood. 💲 *Average main: A$30* ✉ *Stokes Hill Wharf, Darwin Wharf Precinct, Wharf Precinct* ☎ *08/8981–8658* 🌐 *www.crustaceans.net.au.*

Eva's Botanic Gardens Cafe

$ | AUSTRALIAN | Found within Darwin's picturesque Botanic Gardens is Eva's Cafe, inside the Heritage-listed Wesleyan Church. Here you'll find excellent coffee, healthy smoothies, and freshly made juices. **Known for:** incredible surrounds; retro furnishing; menu packed with seasonal dishes. 💲 *Average main: A$15* ✉ *Gardens Rd., City Center* ☎ *04/4747–4776* 🌐 *botanicgardenscafe.com.au* 🕒 *No dinner.*

★ Hanuman

$$ | INDIAN | Hailed as one of the best eateries in Darwin, Hanuman offers an Indian-fusion menu with a firm focus on seafood. Indoor seating is air-conditioned, with low lighting and a sophisticated feel once the sun sets. **Known for:** excellent service; great atmosphere on the weekend; incredible prawns. 💲 *Average main: A$30* ✉ *93 Mitchell St., City Center* ☎ *08/8941–3500* 🌐 *www.hanuman.com.au* 🕒 *No lunch weekends.*

Lola's Pergola

$ | AUSTRALIAN | Named after the owner's daughter, this whimsical waterfront spot along the Cullen Bay Marina serves pub-style favorites like burgers, pizzas, and, of course, chips, in a circus-inspired setting complete with carousel horses (some which can be used) and other retro-style, nostalgia-inducing decor. It's a great place to take the kids and your young-at-heart friends. **Known for:** mango chicken burgers; an excellent craft beer selection; family-friendly atmosphere. *Average main: A$20 48 Marina Blvd., Cullen Bay 08/8941–5711 facebook.com/lolaspergola Closed Mon. and Tues.*

MERAKI Greek Taverna

$$ | GREEK | Darwin's got a vast Greek community and this foodie hot spot is a celebration of Kalymnian cooking traditions handed down from generation to generation. With a simple white and blue decor, the focus here is on the food, and the approach is *mezethes*-style dining, or having plates of food to share with your friends and family. **Known for:** classic Greek sweets like baklava and galatobouriko; live bouzouki music on Friday and Saturday night; tender fried calamari (kalamaraki). *Average main: A$28 4/64 Smith St., Darwin 04/8603–0985 www.merakigreektaverna.com.au Closed Sun. No lunch Sat.*

Pee Wee's at the Point

$$$ | MODERN AUSTRALIAN | Uninterrupted views of Darwin Harbour at East Point Reserve, Modern Australian fare, and a carefully considered wine list make this restaurant a favorite with locals and visitors wanting a special night out. Dine inside with views of the harbor through large glass doors, or sit out on the tiered timber decks beneath the stars. **Known for:** a deliciously decadent dessert called Fifty Shades of Chocolate; oven-baked, wild-caught NT saltwater barramundi; spicy threadfin salmon wings. *Average main: A$45 East Point Reserve, Alec Fong Ling Dr., Fannie Bay 08/8981–6868 www.peewees.com.au Closed Sun. and Mon. Closed during the wet season (late Jan.–mid-Mar.).*

Coffee and Quick Bites

Kopi Stop

$ | AUSTRALIAN | It might not look much from the outside, just a simple hole-in-the-wall. But there's a reason why there's always a queue snaking down the street. **Known for:** quick service; incredible coffee; friendly staff. *Average main: A$15 1/2 Harriet Pl., Darwin 04/6770–8255 www.facebook.com/kopistopdarwin.*

Laneway Speciality Coffee

$ | AUSTRALIAN | The menu might be tight but each dish is packed with the finest and freshest of ingredients. This is one of Darwin's trendiest cafés. **Known for:** freshly made every morning; great coffee; friendly staff. *Average main: A$15 4/1 Vickers St., Parap 08/8941–4511 lanewaycoffee.com.au.*

Hotels

DoubleTree by Hilton Hotel Esplanade Darwin

$$$ | HOTEL | Located at the edge of the CBD next to another completely separate DoubleTree property, this hotel is an easy five-minute walk from all the popular pubs, restaurants, and shopping on Mitchell Street. **Pros:** free parking; great location in the city center; large swimming pool with pool floats and noodles. **Cons:** can't control the room temperature; Wi-Fi not free if you're not a Hilton Honors member; nearby convention center attracts tour groups. *Rooms from: A$245 116 The Esplanade, Darwin 08/8980–0800 doubletree3.hilton.com 197 rooms No Meals.*

★ Mindil Beach Casino Resort

$$$ | RESORT | FAMILY | The most luxurious place to stay in Darwin, the three-story hotel adjacent to the Mindil Beach Casino

Tiwi Islands sculptures at a gallery in Darwin

offers oceanfront accommodations set amid lush lawns and gardens plus 32 resort rooms and suites surrounding a huge lagoon-style swimming pool. **Pros:** next door to Mindil Markets; Darwin's only swim-up bar; award-winning restaurants on-site. **Cons:** parking is not free (A$15 a night); convention center attracts big groups; casino operates 24 hours, so nights can be noisy. *Rooms from: A$299 Gilruth Ave., Mindil Beach 08/8943–8888 mindilbeachcasinoresort.com.au 152 rooms No Meals.*

★ Novotel Darwin CBD Hotel

$$$ | **HOTEL** | Situated along Darwin's magnificent Esplanade, just one block from all the action on Mitchell Street, this hotel offers a green tropical oasis in its lobby, a charming bar and restaurant in the vine-filled atrium, and rooms that overlook the park and the bright blue waters below. **Pros:** close to restaurants, pubs, and shopping; tropical garden in the atrium; some rooms have views overlooking Darwin Harbour. **Cons:** parking is not free; bathrooms are a little on the small side; rooms absorb noise from the central atrium and bar, breakfast area. *Rooms from: A$215 100 The Esplanade, Darwin 08/8963–5000 www.accorhotels.com 141 rooms No Meals.*

Vibe Hotel Darwin Waterfront

$$$ | **HOTEL** | This good-value hotel overlooks the Darwin Wave Pool and Lagoon and puts you right in the heart of the busy Waterfront precinct. **Pros:** surrounded by great pubs and restaurants; great location; nice views of Darwin Waterfront. **Cons:** Wi-Fi is free but slow; parking on-site but not free (A$15 per day); 10-minute walk to city center. *Rooms from: A$252 7 Kitchener Dr., Waterfront 138–423 vibehotels.com/hotel/darwin-waterfront 121 rooms No Meals.*

★ **The Darwin Ski Club**

BARS | This favorite local spot is *the* place to go for a sunset beer in the tropics, and it's right next to the Museum and Art Gallery of the Northern Territory. Its plastic white chairs and tables add to the laid-back, "old Darwin" vibe. There's live music on Friday and Saturday night, too. ✉ *20 Conacher St., Fannie Bay* ☎ *08/8981–6630* 🌐 *www.darwinskiclub.com.au.*

Hotel Darwin

PUBS | Built as an iconic hotel in the 1940s, the original structure survived the bombing of Darwin and Cyclone Tracy only to be torn down in 1999 and rebuilt as the popular bar and restaurant you see today. Stop by for daily lunch specials between 11:30 am and 2:30 pm (or daily dinner specials between 6 pm and 9 pm), catch a game inside the sports bar, try your luck with with the keno and UBET machines, or grab a drink and listen to live music in the spacious outdoor beer garden. ✉ *39 Mitchell St., City Center* ☎ *08/8941–7947* 🌐 *www.thehoteldarwin.com.au.*

★ **Shenannigans**

PUBS | You'll likely hear it before you see it—there's live music nearly every night of the week, and folks are singing or dancing along with it outside on the terrace. This lively and local favorite Irish pub and restaurant offers traditional pub grub as well as a special Sunday roast, with Guinness, Kilkenny, and Harp on tap, among other popular beer selections. Join in on trivia night or karaoke night, held once a week, or dance the night away with everyone else. ✉ *69 Mitchell St., City Center* ☎ *08/8981–2100* 🌐 *www.shenannigans.com.au.*

The Indigenous Arts Scene

Start at the Museum and Art Gallery of the Northern Territory for a comprehensive understanding of Indigenous art and artifacts, then head to one of many arts and crafts outlets in and around Darwin to purchase an authentic and unique piece of art. In many Indigenous communities throughout the tropical Outback—including Maningrida, Oenpelli, the Tiwi Islands, and Yirrikala—you can buy direct from the artist.

Performing Arts

Darwin Entertainment Centre

THEATER | Darwin Entertainment Centre has hosted some of the biggest shows from around the world, including many Broadway-level productions. Tickets generally start around A$35 and go up to A$100 depending on the show. ✉ *93 Mitchell St., City Center* ☎ *08/8980–3333* 🌐 *www.yourcentre.com.au.*

★ **Deckchair Cinema**

FILM | Watching a movie beneath the stars while relaxing on canvas deck chairs with a glass of wine at this outdoor, 400-seat movie theater is one of Darwin's quintessential experiences. Australian, foreign, art house, or classic films are screened every night from April through November. Gates open nightly at 6 pm, and picnic baskets (no BYO alcohol) are permitted, although there is a hot food kiosk and a bar. The first movie usually screens at 7:30 pm, with a second showing at 9 or 9:30 pm on Friday and Saturday nights offered for A$10 instead of the usual A$16. Make sure you hold onto your belongings—especially your food!—while you're watching the movie, as there are possums that roam the grounds and love to rummage through things. ✉ *Jervois Rd., off Kitchener Dr., Wharf Precinct* ☎ *08/8941–4377* 🌐 *www.deckchaircinema.com* 🎟 *A$16.*

Shopping

★ **Mindil Beach Sunset Market**

MARKET | FAMILY | The Mindil Beach Sunset Market is an extravaganza that takes place every Thursday and Sunday from 4 pm to 9 pm from April through October. Come in the late afternoon to snack at one of more than 60 stalls offering food from more than 25 different countries. You can shop at more than 200 local artisans' booths; enjoy performances by singers, dancers, fire artists, and musicians; catch a whip-cracking demonstration, or join the other Darwinites with a bottle of wine to watch the sun plunge into the sea. ✉ *Beach Rd., Mindil Beach* ☎ *08/8981–3454* 🌐 *www.mindil.com.au.*

Nightcliff Market

MARKET | One of the few markets here open year-round, Nightcliff Market takes place on Sunday morning and lasts until around 2 pm in Nightcliff Village, with craft and food stalls and performances by musicians, dancers, and other entertainers; it's a great spot for breakfast. ✉ *Pavonia Way, Nightcliff* ☎ *04/1436–8773* 🌐 *northernterritory.com.*

Parap Markets

MARKET | Located north of the city center, the Parap Markets is where the locals shop. The stalls are open every Saturday rain or shine from 8 am to 2 pm and have a terrific selection of ethnic Asian food, including some of the best laksa in the country. Complimentary shuttles are available from several Darwin City accommodations, so check the website for current times and pickup locations. ✉ *3/3 Vickers St., Parap* ☎ *04/3888–2373* 🌐 *parapvillagemarkets.com.au.*

Rapid Creek Markets

MARKET | Open Sunday morning from about 7 am to 2 pm, the Rapid Creek Markets are Darwin's oldest and have fresh organic produce, as well as flowers, seafood, and locally made handicrafts. Shop 'til you drop alongside the locals just 20 minutes north of the city center while you listen to live music and stock up on fresh groceries at one of more than 60 stalls. ✉ *Rapid Creek Shopping Centre, 48 Trower Rd., Rapid Creek* ☎ *08/8948–4866.*

Activities

BICYCLING

Darwin is fairly flat and has a good network of bike paths, so cycling is a nice way to get around—although you might need something waterproof during the wet season. Rentals are available at some hotels.

FISHING

Barramundi, the best-known fish of the Top End, can weigh up to 110 pounds and are excellent fighting fish that taste great on the barbecue afterward.

Department of Primary Industry and Resources Fisheries Division

FISHING | The office has information on licenses and catch limits. ✉ *Goff Letts Bldg., Berrimah Farm, Makagon Rd., Berrimah* ☎ *08/8999–2144* 🌐 *nt.gov.au/marine.*

Equinox Fishing Charters

FISHING | Equinox Fishing Charters has half-day, full-day, and extended fishing trips using the 38-foot *Tsar,* which is licensed to carry 12 passengers and two crew, and *Equinox II,* which can carry 18–20 people. Full-day fishing charters with all meals and tackle provided are from A$310 per person; shorter five- and seven-hour trips are also available, from A$210 and A$250, respectively. ✉ *64 Marina Blvd., Shop 2, Cullen Bay* ☎ *08/8942–2199* 🌐 *www.equinoxcharters.com.au* 🎟 *From A$210.*

SCUBA DIVING

LEARN to DIVE Darwin

SCUBA DIVING | While there's plenty on offer when it comes to diving in Darwin, with some seriously unique dive spots including a shipwreck, there's only one fully insured scuba company. LEARN to DIVE teaches all PADI courses from open water to 23 specialty courses. And there are even private charters available. ✉ *Wharf 1, Bldg. 3 North, 302/19B Kitchener Dr., Darwin* ☎ *04/0175–1651* 🌐 *facebook.com/learntodivedarwin.*

Kakadu National Park

Begins 151 km (94 miles) southeast of Darwin.

This national park—almost the size of West Virginia—is a jewel among the Top End parks, and many visitors come to the region just to experience this tropical wilderness. The ancient landform has wetlands, gorges, waterfalls, and rugged escarpments. Beginning southeast of Darwin and covering some 19,800 square km (7,645 square miles), the park protects a large system of unspoiled rivers and creeks, as well as one of the highest concentrations of accessible Aboriginal rock-art sites in the world.

GETTING HERE AND AROUND

From Darwin it's a 90-minute drive south along the Stuart Highway, then east along the Arnhem Highway to the entrance to the park, then another hour or so to the Bowali Visitor Center, located near Jabiru. Although four-wheel-drive vehicles are not necessary to travel to the park, they are required for many of the unpaved roads within, including the track to Jim Jim Falls. Entry is free, but you must buy a A$40 National Park permit, which is good for seven days.

SAFETY AND PRECAUTIONS

If you are driving, watch out for road trains—large trucks up to 160 feet in length with up to four trailers behind a prime mover. They are common on Northern Territory roads, and you should give them plenty of room. Avoid driving after dark outside towns because of the high likelihood of straying animals—kangaroos and cattle in particular. It is a good idea to always tell someone of your plans if you intend to travel to remote places; the same applies when bushwalking. Always make sure you have adequate water and food.

TIMING

The best time to visit is between May and September during the dry season. The shortest time you should allow is a three-day, two-night itinerary from Darwin, which will provide opportunities to visit the major sights—a cruise on the East Alligator River; Ubirr, a major Aboriginal rock-art site; a flight-seeing journey from Jabiru Airport; Nourlangie Rock, another impressive Aboriginal rock-art site; the Warradjan Aboriginal Cultural Centre; and a sunset cruise on Yellow Water Billabong to see birds, crocodiles, and other wildlife up close. On the way into the park from Darwin, you can visit the Mamukala Wetlands to view an abundance of birds and wildlife. A five-day itinerary will give you time to visit Jim Jim Falls and Twin Fallson, a four-wheel-drive excursion.

Gone Fishing

Joining a local tour guide is the best way to hook a big one. Locals know the best spots and techniques, and the guides' in-depth knowledge can make an enjoyable experience even better. In the estuaries, you can catch (among others) threadfin and blue salmon, cod, queenfish, black jewfish, cobia, coral trout, golden snapper, mud crabs, and the Top End's most famous fighting fish, the barramundi—barra in the local parlance. And you don't have to go far—Darwin's harbor teems with fish.

TOURS

During the dry season, park rangers conduct free walks and tours at several popular locations. Pick up a program at the entry station or at either of the visitor centers to see what's on offer.

Far Out Adventures

Far Out Adventures runs private, customized tours of Kakadu, as well as other regions of the Top End, ideally suited for small groups. Trips are on the pricey side, with a three-day adventure for two starting around A$4,000, but you'll get to visit off-the-beaten-path places via four-wheel-drive vehicle and have a truly personalized itinerary. ✉ *Box 518, Humpty Doo* ☎ *04/2715–2288* 🌐 *www.farout.com.au* 🎫 *From A$4000.*

★ Kakadu Air

The best way to see Kakadu's famous waterfalls is from the air during the wet season or early in the dry season around April. This company has flights out of Jabiru, with a scenic half hour (A$159) well worth the splurge. In the dry season, the flight encompasses the northern region, including Arnhem Land escarpment, Nourlangie Rock, Mamakala Wetlands, East Alligator River, and Jabiru Township. Helicopter flights are also available for 20-minute (A$275) and 30-minute (A$345) hops. During the wet season only, helicopter flights take in Jim Jim and Twin Falls, when they are most spectacular, though prices go up to A$795 per person for the one-hour experience. ✉ *Jabiru Dr., Jabiru* ☎ *1800/089–113, 08/8941–9611* 🌐 *www.kakaduair.com.au* 🎫 *From A$159.*

Kakadu Tourism

The Cooinda Lodge arranges magical boat tours of Yellow Water Billabong, one of the major waterholes in Kakadu, where innumerable birds and crocodiles gather. There are five tours that run throughout the day at 6:45 am, 9 am, 11:30 am, 1:15 pm, and 4:30 pm; the sunrise and sunset cruises are best, both in terms of temperature and animal activity. Note that the 9 am and 1:15 pm cruises only operate May to October, and the sunrise one also includes a buffet breakfast after your two-hour tour. Feeling more adventurous? Book a Spirit of Kakadu Adventure Tour if you're there from early April to mid-October, for a chance to visit two scenic waterholes via four-wheel-drive vehicle (from A$219). ✉ *Kakadu Hwy., Kakadu National Park* ☎ *08/8979–1500* 🌐 *www.kakadutourism.com* 🎫 *From A$72.*

Local Language

The name Kakadu comes from an Aboriginal floodplain language called Gagudju, which was one of the languages spoken in the north of the park at the beginning of the 20th century. Although languages such as Gagudju and Limilngan are no longer regularly spoken, descendants of these language groups are still living in Kakadu.

ESSENTIALS

VISITOR INFORMATION

Bowali Visitor Centre

The visitor center has state-of-the-art audiovisual displays and traditional exhibits that give an introduction to the park's ecosystems and its bird population, the world's most diverse. Kids love the giant crocodile skeleton. It's open daily from 8 am to 5 pm and its Anmak An-me Cafe and Marrawuddi Gallery make a great spot for a break between the Arnhem Highway and Jabiru side of the park on your way south to Cooinda. ✉ *Kakadu Hwy., Kakadu National Park* ☎ *08/8938–1120* 🌐 *parksaustralia.gov.au/kakadu/plan/visitor-centres.*

Warradjan Cultural Centre
Named after the pig-nosed turtle unique to the Top End, Warradjan Aboriginal Cultural Centre provides an excellent experience of local Bininj (pronounced bin-ing) tribal culture. Displays take you through the Aboriginal Creation period, following the path of the creation ancestor Rainbow Serpent through the ancient landscape of Kakadu. ✉ *Kakadu Hwy., Kakadu National Park* ✣ *1 km (0.6 mile) from Cooinda Lodge* ☎ *08/8979–0525* 🌐 *www.kakadutourism.com/tours-activities/warradjan-cultural-centre.*

CONTACTS Kakadu National Park.
✉ *Kakadu Hwy., Jabiru* ☎ *08/8938–1120* 🌐 *parksaustralia.gov.au/kakadu.* **Tourism Top End.** ✉ *6 Bennett St., Darwin* ☎ *1300/138–886, 08/8980–6000* 🌐 *www.tourismtopend.com.au.*

Sights

★ Burrungkuy (Nourlangie Rock)
NATURE SIGHT | Like the main Kakadu escarpment, Burrungkuy, also known as Nourlangie Rock, is a remnant of an ancient plateau that is slowly eroding, leaving sheer cliffs rising high above the floodplains. The main attraction is the **Anbangbang Gallery,** an excellent frieze of Aboriginal rock paintings. ✉ *Kakadu Hwy., Kakadu National Park* ✣ *19 km (12 miles) from Bowalk Visitor Centre on Kakadu Hwy.; turn left toward Nourlangie Rock, then follow paved road, accessible year-round, 11 km (7 miles) to parking area* ☎ 🌐 *parksaustralia.gov.au/kakadu/discover/regions/burrungkuy.*

Jim Jim Falls
BODY OF WATER | The best way to gain a true appreciation of the natural beauty of Kakadu is to visit the waterfalls running off the escarpment. Some 39 km (24 miles) south of the park headquarters along the Kakadu Highway, a track leads off to the left toward Jim Jim Falls, 60 km (37 miles) or about a two-hour drive away. The track is rough and unpaved, and you'll need a four-wheel-drive vehicle to navigate it. From the parking lot, you have to scramble 1 km (½ mile) over boulders to reach the falls and the plunge pools they have created at the base of the escarpment. Note that after May, the water flow over the falls may cease, and the unpaved road is closed in the Wet. **TIP→ The best way to see these falls at their best is on a scenic flight from Jabiru during the wet season (from A$250 per person for an unforgettable one-hour trip).** ✉ *Jim Jim Falls Track, Kakadu Hwy., Kakadu National Park* 🌐 *parksaustralia.gov.au/kakadu/discover/regions/jim-jim-and-twin-falls.*

★ Kakadu National Park
NATIONAL PARK | The superb gathering of Aboriginal rock art is one of Kakadu National Park's major highlights. Two main types of artwork can be seen here—the Mimi style, which is the oldest, is believed to be up to 20,000 years old. Aboriginal people believe that Mimi spirits created the red-ochre stick figures to depict hunting scenes and other pictures of life at the time. The more recent artwork, known as X-ray painting, dates back fewer than 9,000 years and depicts freshwater animals—especially fish, turtles, and geese—living in floodplains created after the last ice age. As the dry season progresses, billabongs (waterholes) become increasingly important to the more than 280 species of birds that inhabit the park. Huge flocks often gather at Yellow Water, South Alligator River, and Magela Creek. Scenic flights over the wetlands and Arnhem Land escarpment provide unforgettable moments in the wet season. ✉ *Kakadu Hwy., Jabiru* ☎ *08/8938–1120* 🌐 *parksaustralia.gov.au/kakadu* 🎫 *A$40 for up to 7 days.*

Twin Falls
BODY OF WATER | As you approach Twin Falls Gorge, the ravine opens up dramatically to reveal a beautiful sandy beach scattered with palm trees, as well as the crystal waters of the falls spilling

Gunlom Falls in Kakadu National Park

onto the end of the beach. This spot is a bit difficult to reach, but the trip is rewarding. Take the four-wheel-drive-only road to Jim Jim Falls, turn off just before the parking lot, and travel 10 km (6 miles) farther to the Twin Falls parking lot. A regular boat shuttle (A$12.50; buy your tickets before you go at Bowali Visitor Centre) operates a return service up the Twin Falls Gorge, and then you need to walk over boulders, sand, and a boardwalk to the falls. Note that saltwater crocodiles may be in the gorge, so visitors are urged not to enter the water. The round-trip journey, including the boat shuttle, takes around two hours. ✉ *Off Jim Jim Rd., Kakadu National Park* 🌐 *parksaustralia.gov.au/kakadu/do/waterfalls/twin-falls-gorge.*

Ubirr

HISTORIC SIGHT | Ubirr has an impressive display of Aboriginal paintings scattered through six shelters in the rock. The main gallery contains a 49-foot frieze of X-ray paintings depicting animals, birds, and fish. A 1-km (½-mile) path around the rock leads to all the galleries. It's just a short 820-foot clamber to the top for wonderful views over the surrounding wetlands, particularly at sunset. **TIP→ Take a flashlight to help you get down after sunset.** For lunch or a post-sunset Thai dinner, or to peruse arts and crafts for sale, stop by the Border Store and Cafe on your way in, if you're visiting during the dry season May through October. *Beware of wildlife on the roads if driving after dark.* ✉ *Kakadu National Park* ↔ *43 km (27 miles) north of Bowali Visitor Centre along paved road* ☎ *08/8938–1120 Border Store and Cafe* 🌐 *parksaustralia.gov.au/kakadu/do/walks/ubirr-walk.*

Hotels

There are several lodges in the park, and basic campgrounds at Merl, Djarradjin Billabong (Muirella Park), Mardugal, and Gunlom have toilets, showers, and water for A$15 per campsite per night. Alcohol is not available in Jabiru, but you can buy it in Darwin.

Aurora Kakadu

$$ | **HOTEL** | Located about a two-hour drive from Darwin, Aurora Kakadu is the first accommodation you'll hit upon entering Kakadu National Park, a welcome sight with its comfortable double and family rooms—which sleep up to five—amid lush tropical gardens. **Pros:** free bottled water in rooms; location within Kakadu National Park; beautiful grounds with an on-site restaurant, bar, and pool. **Cons:** Wi-Fi is expensive and only works in certain parts of the resort; thin walls; some distance from park attractions. *Rooms from: A$195* *Arnhem Hwy., South Alligator, Kakadu National Park, Kakadu National Park* *2½ km (1½ miles) before hwy. crosses South Alligator River* *08/8979–2422, 1800/818–845* *aurorakakadulodge.com.au* *66 rooms plus campsites* *No Meals.*

★ **Cooinda Lodge**

$$ | **RESORT** | **FAMILY** | With plenty of accommodation options—all of which are managed by Accor Hotels—Cooinda Lodge offers standard rooms, superior-style Pandanus Rooms, and a campground. **Pros:** on-site fuel station and access to Telstra pay phones; bus pickup available from the lodge to nearby Yellow River Cruises; close to Warradjan Aboriginal Cultural Center. **Cons:** no Wi-Fi or cell phone service if you don't have Telstra; limited amenities in rooms; 30-minute drive from Jabiru shops. *Rooms from: A$167* *Kakadu National Park, Kakadu Hwy., Cooinda* *2 km (1 mile) toward Yellow Water Wetlands* *08/8979–1500* *www.accorhotels.com* *48 rooms* *No Meals.*

Mercure Kakadu Crocodile Hotel

$$$ | **HOTEL** | Shaped like a crocodile, this unusual hotel is situated deep in the heart of Kakadu National Park in the tiny town of Jabiru and is one of the area's best accommodation options. **Pros:** Jabiru town is within walking distance; great on-site restaurant; local Aboriginal artwork on sale. **Cons:** ground-floor rooms can have "critters"; large tour groups stay here, so it can feel a little touristy; pool area is small. *Rooms from: A$244* *1 Flinders St., Jabiru* *08/8979–9000* *www.accorhotels.com* *110 rooms* *Free Breakfast.*

Katherine Gorge

30 km (18 miles) east of Katherine, 346 km (215 miles) southeast of Darwin, 543 km (337 miles) northeast of Kununurra.

Officially called Nitmiluk, the Aboriginal or Jawoyn name for the cicadas associated with the creation stories of the area, this stunning canyon formed by the Katherine River in Nitmiluk National Park is actually a series of 13 gorges, each separated by a jumble of boulders. The gorge is 12 km (7½ miles) long, and in many places the red rocky walls are almost 230 feet high. During the wet season (November through April), the gorges are full of raging water and saltwater crocodiles, but during the dry season you can hire canoes or take a cruise to explore them up close. Rangers clear the river of dangerous crocodiles at the start of each season so you can also swim, if the harmless freshwater crocodiles don't bother you, that is.

GETTING HERE AND AROUND

There are no commercial flight services that fly direct into Katherine; the closest airport is Darwin, which is about a three-hour drive.

TOURS

Nitmiluk Tours

Although you can explore Katherine Gorge on foot on one of the many bushwalking trails, the best way to see it is to hit the water. Jawoyn-owned Nitmiluk Tours offers a range of cruises, starting at A$106 for a two-hour trip that departs several times each day. Wear comfortable walking shoes as there is some walking involved between gorges. **TIP→ The best time to go is during the late afternoon,**

when you'll get the best photo opportunities, as the walls of the gorge glow a deep red. Canoe adventure tours start at A$74 for a half-day tour and A$89 for a full-day journey, or you can view it all from above in a helicopter (from A$108). ✉ *Nitmiluk National Park, Gorge Rd., Katherine* ☎ *1300/146–743* 🌐 *www.nitmiluktours.com.au* 🎟 *From A$92.*

Hotels

Cicada Lodge

$$$ | RESORT | Each of the stylish air-conditioned rooms at Cicada Lodge has a private balcony overlooking Katherine Gorge, is decorated with Aboriginal artwork, and comes with breakfast as well as complimentary canapés and cocktails at sunset. **Pros:** complimentary drinks and snacks each evening; great location close to Katherine Gorge activities; excellent food and service. **Cons:** views of the gorge can vary greatly depending on the time of year; tours and meals other than breakfast cost extra; on the expensive side. $ *Rooms from: A$300* ✉ *Nitmiluk National Park, Gorge Rd., Katherine* ☎ *1300/146–743* 🌐 *cicadalodge.com.au* ⏲ *Closed for 1 month during wet season, usually mid-Feb.–mid-Mar.* *18 rooms* 🍽 *Free Breakfast.*

Kununurra

516 km (321 miles) west of Katherine, 840 km (522 miles) southwest of Darwin.

Kununurra is the eastern gateway to the Kimberley. With a population of around 5,000, it's a modern, planned town that was developed in the 1960s for the nearby Lake Argyle and Ord River irrigation scheme. Today, it's a convenient base from which to explore local attractions such as Mirima National Park (a mini–Bungle Bungle on the edge of town), Lake Argyle, the River Ord, and some lovely countryside attractions just north of the city center. The town is also one starting point for adventure tours of the Kimberley; the other option is to start from Broome.

GETTING HERE AND AROUND

Distances in this part of the continent are colossal, and flying is the fastest and easiest way to get to and around the Kimberley. Both Virgin Australia and Air North have extensive air networks throughout the Top End, linking Kununurra to Broome, Perth, and Darwin.

From Darwin to Kununurra and the eastern extent of the Kimberley, it's 840 km (522 miles). The route runs from Darwin to Katherine along the Stuart Highway, and then along the Victoria Highway to Kununurra. The entire road is paved but narrow in parts—especially so, it may seem, when a road train (a long truck towing three or four trailers) is coming the other way. Drive with care and keep an eye on the speed limit, which is 110 km (68 miles) here instead of the usual 130 km (80 miles) in the Northern Territory. If you're driving from the Northern Territory into Western Australia, you'll have to make a brief but mandatory stop at the quarantine checkpoint at the border before you can continue, so get rid of any fruit, honey, plants, or seeds before you head out or else you may be fined (visit *www.agric.wa.gov.au* for more info). Fuel and supplies can be bought at small settlements along the way, but you should always keep supplies in abundance and expect to pay a pretty penny.

TAXIS Bert's Taxi Service. ✉ *18 Pointceta Way, Kununurra* ☎ *08/9168–2553* Ⓜ *fdf dfd.* **Kununurra Couriers.** ✉ *2 Konkerberry Dr., Kununurra* ☎ *08/9168–1999.*

SAFETY AND PRECAUTIONS

Driving long distances through the Kimberley can be an adventure, but it also carries risks. For drivers not used to the conditions, and not taking adequate rest breaks, the combination of warm sun through the windshield, long sections of road, and lack of traffic can have a hypnotic effect. Take regular breaks every two hours to walk and have a stretch, and get plenty of sleep the night before. If you are feeling sleepy, stop immediately and take a break. Many vehicle crashes in this area are vehicle versus animal, often a kangaroo or straying cattle. Dusk and dawn are when animals are most active. If you see an animal on the road in front of you, brake firmly in a straight line and sound your horn. Do not swerve: it is safer to stay on the road.

TIMING

You should allow at least five days to see Kununurra and the Kimberley, including your arrival and departure days. That will allow enough time to visit the Ord River and cruise Lake Argyle, take a scenic flight to the Bungle Bungles and hike the area with a guide, and take a four-wheel-drive excursion to El Questro Wilderness Park. Winter—May through September—is the dry season here, and June and July are the most popular times to visit, as days are warm and there is little rain. November through March is the wet season and temperatures can be a lot higher—up to 45°C (113°F).

TOURS

APT Kimberley Wilderness Adventures

This agency conducts luxury tours from Broome and Kununurra, which include excursions along the legendary Gibb River Road and into Purnululu National Park. Two-day guided trips from Kununurra to the Bungle Bungles include a scenic flight (from A$10,495) while a four-day tour from Broome includes a trip to a popular pearl farm and an iconic camel ride on Cable Beach (from A$11,995). See the website for additional touring options. ✉ *1 Hamersley St., Broome, Broome* ☎ *1300/336–932* 🌐 *www.aptouring.com.au* 🎫 *From A$10,495.*

Aviair

This company conducts both fixed-wing and helicopter flights from Kununurra and Purnululu National Park. A two-hour fixed-wing flight over the Bungle Bungles and Lake Argyle is A$540. ✉ *319 Laine Jones Dr., Kununurra* ☎ *1800/095–500* 🌐 *www.aviair.com.au* 🎫 *From A$540.*

Bungle Bungle Savannah Lodge

If you're looking to spend some quality time in Purnululu National Park, Bungle Bungle Savannah Lodge offers several fly-in, fly-out packages from Kununurra that include scenic flights over Lake Argyle, guided tours of Cathedral Gorge, and overnight accommodations at the lodge. Others offer an additional guided hike at Echidna Chasm before you head back to Kununurra by plane (from A$1,638) or give you two nights in the park with extra hikes (from A$1,935). ✉ *Bungle Bungle Savannah Lodge, Campsite B Bellburn Camp, Purnululu National Park* ☎ *08/9168–2213* 🌐 *www.bunglebunglesavannahlodge.com.au* 🎫 *From A$1390.*

★ Kingfisher Tours

This company operates scenic flights from Kununurra Airport, starting at A$420 for a trip over Purnululu National Park from Kununurra. For A$*1,220,* you can take a full-day tour that includes a flight into the remote park, sightseeing via four-wheel drive, and guided treks to Cathedral Gorge and The Lookout. Check the website for additional touring options that include overnight accommodations, fishing trips, sunset dinner cruises, and heli-trekking through even more remote parts of the Kimberley region. ✉ *Shop 2/20 Messmate Way, Kununurra* ☎ *08/9168–2718* 🌐 *kingfishertours.com.au* 🎫 *From A$350.*

★ Lake Argyle Cruises

Excellent trips on Australia's largest expanse of freshwater are offered from Lake Argyle and Kununurra if you're staying in town 70 km (43 miles) or about an hour's drive away. Treat yourself to a morning cruise (A$70 from Lake Argyle, no transfers from Kununurra) or a full-day tour of the lake and nearby Durack Family Homestead (A$160 from Lake Argyle, A$190 including return transfers from Kununurra). Sunset cruises, which start at 2:30 pm, give you a chance to see this remarkable landscape by twilight, as well as complimentary drinks and snacks (A$95 from Lake Argyle, A$125 from Kununurra). If you'd rather not schlep all the way back to Kununurra, Lake Argyle Resort offers accommodations ranging from four-bedroom Lake View Grand Villas (A$999 for up to eight people), one- and two-bedroom Lake View Villas (from A$559); standard cabins (from A$269); and a caravan park (unpowered sites from A$19.50 a night). Day passes are also available for A$10 for anyone wanting to drop by and check out the resort's legendary infinity pool. ✉ *530B Lake Argyle Rd., Kununurra* ☎ *08/9168–7687* 🌐 *www.lakeargylecruises.com* 🎫 *From A$70.*

ESSENTIALS

VISITOR INFORMATION Kununurra Visitor Centre. ✉ *75 Coolibah Dr., Kununurra* ☎ *08/9168–1177, 1800/586–868* 🌐 *www.visitkununurra.com.*

Sights

Hoochery Distillery

DISTILLERY | Located just 16 km (10 miles) north of downtown Kununurra on Weaber Plain Road, Hoochery Distillery offers tours at 2 pm (A$14) so you can get behind the scenes and learn all about the longest-running rum operation in Western Australia. Pick up some homemade Ord River rum cake and a cup of coffee at the on-site Hoochery Cafe, or treat yourself to a rum flight and sample some of the ones you just heard about on the tour. ✉ *300 Weaber Plain Rd., Kununurra* ☎ *08/9168–2467* 🌐 *www.hoochery.com.au* 🕒 *Closed Sun.*

The Sandalwood Factory and Cafe

STORE/MALL | More shop and café than actual factory—the real one is far to the south in Mt. Romance, Western Australia—this popular spot, about a 15-minute drive north of Kununurra, is dedicated to all things sandalwood. Learn how it starts out basically as a parasitic tree and is eventually turned into any number of products ranging from lotions and bath soaps to perfumes and incense, all of which can be purchased at the shop. The on-site café offers a wide range of delicious breakfast and lunch items, and smoothies, all of which are made fresh using local produce from the surrounding farms you'll pass on the way there. ✉ *Weaber Plains Rd., Lot 51, Kununurra* ☎ *08/9169–1987* 🌐 *thesandalwoodshop.com.au* 🕒 *Closed mid-Dec.–late-Mar.*

Restaurants

Ivanhoe Cafe

$ | **AUSTRALIAN** | The menu changes every day at this pretty café situated just outside of the Kununurra township. One day it could be freshly made pasta for lunch or perhaps an herby omelet for breakfast. **Known for:** mango sorbet; ever-changing fresh menu; pretty alfresco dining under mango trees. 💲 *Average main: A$15* ✉ *Ivanhoe Rd., Kununurra* ☎ *04/2769–2775* 🌐 *www.facebook.com/ivanhoecafe* 🕒 *Closed Sept.–Mar.*

★ **Pumphouse Restaurant**

$$ | **AUSTRALIAN** | Located on an old fishing dock jutting out into Lake Kununurra, this local favorite is the place to have dinner while watching the sunset, with live music most nights, great food and cocktails, and the chance to view local wildlife (yes, we mean birds and freshwater crocodiles) doing their thing. The fare is contemporary Australian, so you can expect to see steaks, pan-seared salmon, and risotto on the menu, while Sunday night is dedicated strictly to wood-fire pizza and tapas specials. **Known for:** Ord Valley crème brûlée dessert; wood-fire pizza and tapas night with a special menu on Sunday; eight-hour, slow-roasted lamb shoulder. 💲 *Average main: A$35* ✉ *Lakeview Dr., Kununurra* ☎ *08/9169–3222* 🌐 *www.thepumphouserestaurant.com* 🕒 *Closed Mon. and Tues.*

Off The Beaten Path

El Questro Wilderness Park. This 700,000-acre property features some of the most ruggedly beautiful country in the Kimberley. El Questro has a full complement of recreational activities like fishing, swimming, horseback riding, and helicopter rides, and offers individually tailored walking and four-wheel-drive tours. Four independent accommodation facilities are on-site, each different in style and budget: the luxury Homestead (from A$3,285per night with a two-night minimum-stay requirement and a policy that guests must be ages 16 and up); the safari-style tented cabins at Emma Gorge Resort (from A$350); air-conditioned Riverside Bungalows (from A$175); and Riverside Campgrounds (from A$30 per person per night) at El Questro Station. Each has a restaurant, and rates at the Homestead include drinks and food, laundry, and activities. Alternatively, you can choose to take a full-day tour of El Questro with included trips to Emma Gorge, Zebedee Springs, lunch at The Station, a Chamberlain River Cruise, and round-trip transport from Kununurra (A$268). Not renting a four-wheel-drive vehicle? Take a shuttle from Kununurra starting at A$110 each way to Emma Gorge Resort, A$135 each way to El Questro Station, and A$140 each way to El Questro Homestead. ✉ *El Questro Rd., Kununurra ✣ 110 km (68 miles) west of Kununurra; 58 km (36 miles) on Great Northern Hwy., 36 km (22 miles) on Gibb River Rd., and 16 km (10 miles) on El Questro Rd. on gravel road* ☎ *1800/837–168* 🌐 *www.elquestro.com.au* 🎟 *An El Questro Wilderness Park permit (required) is A$22 and valid for 7 days with access to gorge walks, thermal springs, fishing holes, rivers, and use of the Emma Gorge Resort swimming pool* ⏲ *Closed Nov.–Apr.*

Home Valley Station. If you've ever fancied being a cowboy or cowgirl, this massive 3½-million-acre working cattle farm at the foot of the majestic Cockburn (pronounced *co-burn*) range is the place to do it. Owned and operated by the traditional owners of the land, the Balanggarra people through the Indigenous Land Corporation, you can join a cattle muster or just take a half-day horse trek. Other activities include barramundi fishing and four-wheel-drive trips. There's a bar and restaurant on-site and a range of accommodations from stylish "Grass Castle" bungalows complete with cowskin rugs, air-conditioning, fully stocked minibar, flat-screen cable TV, huge walk-in rain shower, and resident tree frogs (from A$425) to motel-style guesthouse rooms (from A$275), and remote bush camping beside the Pentecost River, 4 km (2½ miles) from the homestead (from A$44 per person per night). Note that a four-wheel-drive vehicle is required to reach Home Valley Station and these can be rented in Kununurra via Avis, Budget, Hertz, Thrifty, and Europcar. Air transfers and charter flights can also be arranged from Kununurra Airport. ✉ *Gibb River Rd., Kununurra ✣ 120 km (75 miles) from Kununurra via Great Northern Hwy. and Gibb River Rd.* ☎ *05/5949–2540* 🌐 *www.hvstation.com.au* ⏲ *Closed mid-Oct.–May.*

Coffee and Quick Bites

Cornerside Cafe

$ | **AUSTRALIAN** | This hole-in-the-wall café is found right in the heart of the Kununurra township, offering takeout coffee, freshly baked muffins, and pastries and even pre-portioned takeaway evening meals that vary from coconut curry to cheesy lasagne. **Known for:** freshly baked pastries; quick service; delicious coffee. *Average main: A$15* *20 Messmate Way, Kununurra* *08/9169–1111* *facebook.com/Cornersidecafekununurra* *Closes at 1:45 pm every day.*

Hotels

★ **Freshwater East Kimberley Apartments**

$$$ | **RESORT** | **FAMILY** | Just a two-minute drive from downtown Kununurra, these fully self-contained one-, two-, and three-bedroom apartments are the perfect place to unwind before or after a thrilling tour through the Kimberley, with stocked kitchens, sandalwood products provided by Mt. Romance, and luxurious outdoor showers (in some apartments). **Pros:** complimentary airport transfers; local Mt. Romance Sandalwood bath products; beautiful swimming pool area. **Cons:** a security deposit of up to A$500 may be required for group bookings; no on-site restaurants; it's about a 15-minute walk to the city center. *Rooms from: A$228* *Victoria Hwy., Kununurra* *Across from Celebrity Tree Park* *08/9169–2010, 1300/729–267* *www.freshwaterapartments.net.au* *60 rooms* *No Meals.*

Kimberley Grande Resort

$$ | **RESORT** | Found just on the shores of the Argyle Lake, this homestead-style resort has become known as a quintessential Australian outback stay in Kununurra. **Pros:** friendly and attentive staff; free Wi-Fi; each room has air-conditioning. **Cons:** Internet connection can be hit-and-miss; meals in restaurant are expensive but not high standard; sports bar can get noisy on weekends. *Rooms from: A$170* *20 Victoria Hwy., Kununurra* *13/0095–5549* *kimberleygrande.com.au* *No Meals* *72 rooms.*

Kununurra Country Club Resort

$$ | **HOTEL** | **FAMILY** | Located in the center of town, this hotel with smartly furnished apartments is encircled by its own little rain forest of tropical gardens. **Pros:** easy walk to downtown; complimentary airport shuttle; poolside dining and bars. **Cons:** you may hear the outdoor cinema next door on Saturday nights; Wi-Fi is free but slow; tour groups stay here. *Rooms from: A$185* *47 Coolibah Dr., Kununurra* *08/9168–1024* *www.kununurracountryclub.com.au* *Closed Christmas–New Year's Eve weekend* *88 rooms* *No Meals.*

Lakeside Resort

$ | **RESORT** | On the shores of Lake Kununurra sits this understated, tranquil resort, where you can see stunning sunsets over the water and watch for fruit bats flying overhead. **Pros:** crocodile spotting on the lake at night; lakeside location; courtesy bus available. **Cons:** not within walking distance of downtown Kununurra; Wi-Fi is only available in public areas near the pool and bar; rooms are basic. *Rooms from: A$110* *50 Casuarina Way, off Victoria Hwy., Kununurra* *08/9169–1092, 1800/786–692* *www.lakeside.com.au* *50 rooms* *No Meals.*

Purnululu (Bungle Bungle) National Park

291 km (181 miles) southwest of Kununurra.

Wind and water have savaged the rocks of Purnululu National Park, creating one of the most unusual landscapes in the world. All around, the conically weathered formations cluster together like a meeting of some metamorphic executives. Traveling into the area is a remarkable experience—and young and old can delight in the fantasy landscape.

This park covers more than ½ million acres in the southeast corner of the Kimberley. While Australians of European descent first "discovered" its great beehive-shape domes—their English name is the Bungle Bungles—in 1983, the local Kidja Aboriginals, who knew about these scenic wonders long ago, called the area Purnululu, meaning sandstone.

The striking, black-and-orange-stripe mounds seem to bubble up from the landscape. Climbing on them is not permitted, because the sandstone layer beneath their thin crust of lichen and silica is fragile and would quickly erode without protection. Walking tracks follow rocky, dry creek beds. One popular walk leads hikers along **Piccaninny Creek** to **Piccaninny Gorge,** passing through gorges with towering 328-foot cliffs to which slender fan palms cling.

GETTING HERE AND AROUND

The Bungle Bungles are 291 km (181 miles) south of Kununurra along the Great Northern Highway. A very rough, 53-km (32-mile) unsealed road, negotiable only in a four-wheel-drive vehicle, makes up the last stretch of road leading to the park from the turnoff near the Turkey Creek–Warmun Community. That part of the drive can take two to three hours depending on the condition of the road. The most-visited section of the park is in the south, where there are rough walking trails to the main sights.

SAFETY AND PRECAUTIONS

The park is usually open from April through December (depending on whether the road is passable after the wet season); however, temperatures in April, October, November, and December can be blisteringly hot. If you travel in these months, make sure you have plenty of water and be sun-smart.

TIMING

Purnululu National Park can be visited in a day from Kununurra, but only with a flight and safari package. There are also tours available that include overnight camping, but the road trip from Kununurra takes the best part of a day. Driving yourself to the park is not recommended, as the last 53-km (32-mile) section is a very rough unsealed track suitable only for four-wheel-drive vehicles; it has been kept deliberately so to limit visitation and those driving anything else will be turned away. If you do decide to drive in yourself, be aware that there are few facilities in the park's public campgrounds so you need to take in all your own food and camping equipment.

ESSENTIALS

VISITOR INFORMATION Purnululu Visitor Centre. ✉ *Purnululu National Park, Purnululu National Park* ✣ *300 km (186 miles) south of Kununurra, in Purnululu National Park* ☎ *08/9168–7300* 🌐 *parks.dpaw.wa.gov.au/park/purnululu.*

Sights

The most popular walking trails are in the southern end of the park, where the famous "beehives" are located. From the Piccaninny Creek car park, you can hike to Cathedral Gorge in about an hour. Take a 20-minute detour on the Domes Walk to see more of the famous sandstone beehives. If you have more time, follow the Piccaninny Creek walk into Piccaninny Gorge, following an eroded riverbed and sandstone ledges to the lookout point. On the northern side of the park, there are walks to Echidna Gorge, which takes about one hour—where dinosaur-era livistona palms cling to the cliffs and the gorge narrows to about 3 feet across—and Mini Palms Gorge, a rock-strewn gorge filled with livistona palms. At the end, there is a viewing platform overlooking the valley. Allow an hour for this walk as well.

Hotels

Once you make it past that last bumpy stretch of unsealed road you have three options: two campgrounds, Walardi and Kurrajong, both of which cost A$13 per person per night and offer basic facilities like bush toilets (read: there are no showers and you need to boil water here before you drink it or bring your own); or Bungle Bungle Savannah Lodge, which offers a dinner–bed-and-breakfast deal from A$349 per adult per night and provides en suite cabins with hot showers, flushing toilets, and other creature comforts (*08/9168–7300*).

Danggu Geikie Gorge National Park

458 km (284 miles) southwest of Purnululu National Park, 416 km (258 miles) east of Broome.

Halfway between Purnululu National Park and Broome, just outside the little Outback town of Fitzroy Crossing, Geikie Gorge, an ancient flooded reef, is one of the highlights of a trip through the Kimberley.

TOURS

★ **National Park Ranger Station Boat Tours**
The best way to see the gorge is aboard one of the one-hour boat tours led by a ranger from the National Park Ranger Station, departing at 8 am, 2:30 pm, and 4 pm from May to mid-October. The knowledgeable rangers are helpful in pointing out the vegetation, strange limestone formations, and many freshwater crocodiles along the way. You may also see part of the noisy fruit-bat colony that inhabits the region. The park is open for day visits daily from 6:30 am to 6:30 pm between April and November. Entry is restricted during the wet season, from December through March, when the Fitzroy River floods. ✉ *Geikie Gorge Rd., King Leopold Ranges* ✣ *20 km (12 miles) northeast of Fitzroy Crossing via Geikie Gorge Rd.* ☎ *08/9191–5112* 🌐 *parks.dpaw.wa.gov.au/park/danggu-geikie-gorge* 🎫 *From A$50.*

Sights

Danggu Geikie Gorge National Park
NATIONAL PARK | Geologists believe the mighty Fitzroy River cut and shaped the limestone walls you see today at Danggu Geikie Gorge, and during the wet season, the normally placid waters roar through the region. The walls of the gorge are stained red from iron oxide, except where they have been leached of the mineral and turned white by the floods, which have washed as high as 52 feet from the bottom of the gorge. The gorge is one of the few places in the world where freshwater barramundi, mussels, stingrays, and prawns swim. The park is also home to the freshwater archerfish, which can spit water as far as a yard to knock insects out of the air. Aboriginal people call this place Danggu, meaning "big fishing hole." ✉ *Geikie Gorge Rd., King Leopold Ranges* ✣ *20 km (12 miles) northeast of township of Fitzroy Crossing via Geikie Gorge Rd.* 🌐 *parks.dpaw.wa.gov.au/park/danggu-geikie-gorge* ⏲ *Closed during the wet season.*

Hotels

Fitzroy River Lodge
$$$ | **HOTEL** | With Broome being four hours from Danggu Geikie Gorge, you're better off staying in nearby Fitzroy Crossing, and with accommodations ranging from motel-style lodge rooms and private studios to single rooms and campgrounds, the Fitzroy River Lodge is your best bet. **Pros:** watch the wallabies and kangaroos graze the grounds from your doorstep; accommodation options for every budget and type of traveler; motel is on stilts so it can stay open all year long despite wet season floods. **Cons:** Wi-Fi outages take a long time to fix due to lodge's remote location; reliable yet

Did You Know?

The stunning Bungle Bungle Range is a series of beehive-shaped, outlandishly striped sandstone mounds surrounding deep gorges. Many lizard species live here, including blue-tongued skinks; so do several species of wallaby (smaller, marsupial cousins to the kangaroo).

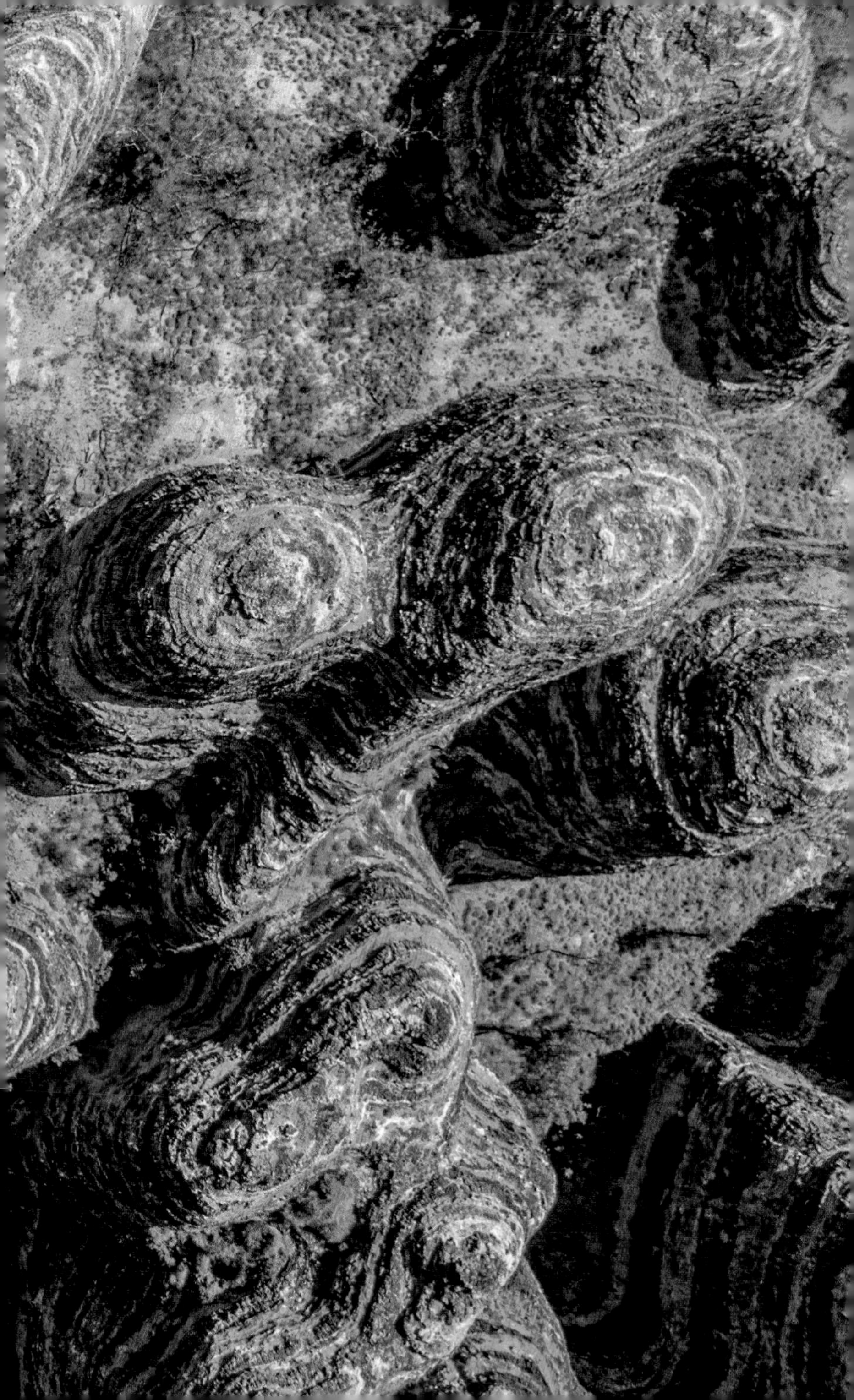

outdated; limited food options. $ *Rooms from: A$265 ✉ 277 Great Northern Hwy., Fitzroy Crossing ☎ 08/9191–5141 🌐 www.fitzroyriverlodge.com.au ⇄ 102 rooms 🍴 No Meals.*

Broome

1,044 km (649 miles) southwest of Kununurra via Halls Creek, 1,558 km (968 miles) southwest of Katherine, 1,871 km (1,163 miles) southwest of Darwin.

Some say Broome is the holiday capital of the Kimberley. It's the only town in the region with sandy beaches, and is the base from which most strike out to see more of the region. Chinatown is charming while the rest of the area, especially Cable Beach, is becoming noticeably upscale.

Long ago, Broome depended on pearling for its livelihood. By the early 20th century 300 to 400 sailing boats employing 3,000 men provided most of the world's mother-of-pearl shell. Many of the pearlers were Japanese, Malay, and Filipino, and the town is still a wonderful multicultural center today with the modern pearling industry very much at its heart. Each August during the famous Shinju Matsuri (Festival of the Pearl), Broome commemorates its early pearling years and heritage with a 10-day festival featuring many traditional Japanese ceremonies. Because of its popularity, advance bookings for accommodations are highly recommended.

Several tour operators have multiday cruises out of Broome along the magnificent Kimberley coast. The myriad deserted islands and beaches, with 35-foot tides that create horizontal waterfalls and whirlpools, make it an adventurer's delight.

Broome marks the western extent of the Kimberley. From here it's another 2,240 km (1,392 miles) south to Perth, or 1,871 km (1,163 miles) back to Darwin.

GETTING HERE AND AROUND

Qantas and its subsidiaries fly to Broome seasonally from Brisbane, Sydney, and Melbourne via Perth. Direct flights from Sydney and Melbourne happen twice a week during the dry season. Air North has an extensive air network throughout the Top End, linking Broome to Kununurra and Darwin. Virgin Australia also services Broome from Perth. Broome's airport is right next to the center of town, on the northern side. Note that though it's called Broome International Airport, there are no scheduled overseas flights; charter flights and private flights do arrive there.

SAFETY AND PRECAUTIONS

From November to April there is a possibility of cyclones off the Kimberley coast. It is important that visitors are aware of the procedures to follow in the event of a cyclone alert, which are provided in all accommodations as well as the Broome Visitor Centre or the Shire of Broome office. Call 1300/659–210 for cyclone watch and warning messages, or check the Australian Government Bureau of Meteorology website at www.bom.gov.au. Certain times of the year also mean bush fires are more likely to occur, often caused by lightning strikes or when a controlled burn suddenly becomes out of control due to drier-than-anticipated conditions or high winds. Follow signs and advice by authorities if roads are closed or rerouted, and should you encounter smoke on the road, turn your lights on so other cars can see you and drive slowly if deemed safe to do so.

November to April is also when mosquitoes are at their most prevalent. To avoid the discomfort of mosquito bites and any risk of infection, it is advisable to cover up at dawn and dusk and apply insect repellent, which is supplied in most hotels. Sand flies become more active in Broome on high tides; use the same prevention methods.

Tropical waters can also contain various stingers. The two to watch out for are the chironex fleckeri box jellyfish (a large but almost transparent jellyfish up to 12 inches across with ribbonlike tentacles from each of its four corners) and the Irukandji (a tiny transparent jellyfish less than one inch across with four thin tentacles). Both are found during the summer months of November to May. Take care when swimming—wear protective clothing like a wet suit or Lycra stinger suit to reduce exposure to potential stings—and obey signs displayed on the beaches at all times. Medical attention should be sought if someone is stung—pour vinegar onto the sting and call 000 for an ambulance.

Saltwater crocodiles live in estuaries throughout the Kimberley, while freshwater Johnsons crocodiles hang out in freshwater gorges and lakes. Look for warning signs. Even if not signposted, advice from a reliable local authority should always be sought before swimming in rivers and waterholes.

TIMING

Ideally, you need at least five days in Broome and the West Kimberley, including your arrival and departure days. This will give you time to go swimming and sunbathing on Cable Beach, take a camel ride, and cruise on a restored pearl lugger. A scenic flight will show you the pristine Kimberley coastline and the horizontal waterfalls of the Buccaneer Archipelago. A day tour will get you to Cape Leveque or Windjana Gorge. To go farther afield, join a four-wheel-drive safari; a two-day tour will show you the gorges of the area, including Danggu Geikie Gorge.

The most popular time to visit is from May to October during the dry season, but especially June and July when the weather is ideal.

TOURS

Astro Tours

Astro Tours organizes entertaining, informative night-sky tours of the Broome area from April to mid-October. Two-hour educational star shows offered one to three nights a week depending on the cosmos cost A$95 if you self-drive to the site 20 minutes outside town (or A$115, including transfers from your hotel), comfy stargazing chairs, hot beverages, and cookies. Wear warm clothing if visiting in June, July, and August, as temperatures can drop below 10°C (50°F). ✉ *Broome Rd., Broome* ✥ *A 20-minute drive from downtown Broome on Broome Rd., next door to Malcolm Douglas Crocodile Park* ☎ *04/1794–9958* 🌐 *www.astrotours.net* 🎟 *From A$95* ☞ *Closed Nov.–Apr.*

★ Broome Tours

With an eye on ecotourism, Broome Tours offers incredible on-water experience via its 42-foot catamaran *Ballena.* Each tour uncovers the rich history of Broome as well as the beautiful waterways in the area. There's a choice of the sunset cruise (A$130), which is a four-hour cruise along the coastline with drinks and canapés. There's also whale-watching, pearling tour, and private charter. Each come with pickup and drop-off to your hotel. ✉ *2/274 Port Dr., Broome* ☎ *04/7260–8271* 🌐 *broometourswa.com.au* 🎟 *From A$130.*

★ Kimberley Quest

Much of the Kimberley coast is inaccessible by land and can be visited only by boat. Kimberley Quest offers multiday Kimberley adventures along the region's magnificent coastline in the luxury *Kimberley Quest II* cruiser. All meals and excursions (including fishing trips) are included in the cost—the most popular trip costs A$11,990 for eight days. There's also a four-day Taste of the Kimberley cruise available from A$3,990 as well as a fishing expedition from A$6,990. Cruising season runs from March to

Broome By Camelback

Though not native to Australia, camels played a large part in exploring and opening up the country's big, dry, and empty interior. In the 1800s, around 20,000 camels were imported from the Middle East to use for cross-country travel—along with the handlers (many from Afghanistan) who cared for them.

When railways and roads became the prime methods of transport in the early 20th century, many camels were simply set free in the desert. A steady population of wild camels—some 1,000,000 of them—now roams across the Australian Outback.

Broome has for many years been a place where people enjoy camel rides—especially along the broad, desertlike sands of Cable Beach. Two tour companies in town now offer camel "adventures" on a daily basis; yes, it's touristy, but it's great fun and a wonderful way to see the coast while getting a taste of history.

Broome Camel Safaris. Open Monday through Saturday, Broome Camel Safaris offers 60-minute morning rides (A$50), or one-hour sunset rides (A$70). As a special treat, ladies on tour receive a complimentary pair of freshwater pearl sterling-silver earrings by Dahlia Designs, a local jewelry company. ✉ *Lot 303 Fairway Dr., Broome* ✣ *Meet above rocks on Cable Beach and look for camels in blue* ☎ *04/1991–6101* 🌐 *www.broomecamelsafaris.com.au* 🎟 *From A$30.*

Red Sun Camels. Morning, presunset, and sunset rides are available every day on Cable Beach north of the rocks. The morning ride lasts for 40 minutes and costs A$50; the presunset ride runs for 30 minutes and costs A$40; the sunset ride takes an hour and costs A$80. ✉ *Cable Beach, Broome* ✣ *Meet above rocks on Cable Beach and look for camels in red* ☎ *08/9193–7423* 🌐 *www.redsuncamels.com.au* 🎟 *From A$40.*

September, so check the website to see which ones run during which months. ✉ *15 Dampier Terr., Broome* ☎ *08/9193–6131* 🌐 *www.kimberleyquest.com.au* 🎟 *From A$6990.*

VISITOR INFORMATION

CONTACTS Broome Visitor Centre. ✉ *1 Hamersley St., Broome* ☎ *08/9195–2200* 🌐 *www.visitbroome.com.au.*

Sights

Broome is a small, compact town that's easy to explore on foot—you can even walk to the airport on the northern edge of town. You will need transportation to get to and from Cable Beach, which is around 7 km (4½ miles) from the city center. Chinatown, with its historic buildings, pearl showrooms, and art galleries, is in the middle of the main street shopping strip, while Roebuck Bay is only a few blocks to the south.

Broome Bird Observatory

NATURE SIGHT | A nonprofit research, education, and accommodation facility, the Broome Bird Observatory provides the perfect opportunity to see the Kimberley's numerous bird species, some of which migrate annually from Siberia or China. On the shores of Roebuck Bay, 25 km (15 miles) east of Broome, the observatory has a prolific number of migratory waders. The observatory offers a variety of daily guided tours in the dry season (from May to around September), including some focused around the native shorebirds, mangroves, bush and plains—each are 2½ hours and cost A$75—as well as a full-day tour of the lakes that includes morning tea (A$150). Pickup from Broome can also be arranged for A$60 for the first person and A$15 for each additional person in your group. Start times depend on the day of the week and the tides and season, but are typically between 8 am and 3 pm, with the exception of the bush and plains tour, which starts at 3 pm or 3:30 pm and returns after sunset. ✉ *Crab Creek Rd., Broome* ✣ *15 km (9 miles) from Broome Hwy.* ☎ *08/9193–5600* 🌐 *www.broome-birdobservatory.com* 🎫 *From A$75.*

Malcolm Douglas Crocodile Park

ZOO | **FAMILY** | Entering through the jaws of a giant crocodile, this huge wildlife park opens up each day from 2 pm to 5 pm to reveal the Kimberley's native species in a variety of habitats. You'll get to see dingoes, cassowaries, barking owls, several types of kangaroo, a litany of bird species, American alligators, and, of course, hundreds of saltwater and freshwater crocodiles. Don't miss the famous croc feeding tour at 3 pm daily, a one-hour guided walk through the vast property where you get to watch the guide feed salties, freshies, and American alligators, and meet several problem crocs who were brought to the park after wreaking havoc in some of the surrounding estuaries. ✉ *Broome Rd., Broome* ✣ *Go 16 km (10 miles) out of Broome on Broome Rd. and look for sign* ☎ *08/9193–6580* 🌐 *www.malcolmdouglas.com.au* 🎫 *A$35.*

★ **Pearl Luggers**

MUSEUM VILLAGE | This historical display sheds light on the difficulties and immense skill involved in pearl harvesting. You'll have a chance to check out one of the restored luggers on a replica jetty along with other such pearling equipment as diving suits and a A$100,000 pearl you can hold. Get an insight into the risky lives of pearl divers, who spent years aboard pearling luggers and diving for pearl shells, on the regular 90-minute tours. This is a must-see for those interested in Broome's history, and for anyone who wants to sample pearl meat, a true delicacy worth A$120 a kilo. ✉ *31 Dampier Terr., Broome* ☎ *08/9192–0022* 🌐 *www.williecreekpearls.com.au/pages/visit-pearl-luggers* 🎫 *A$30.*

★ **Sun Pictures**

ARTS CENTER | **FAMILY** | Opened in 1916, Sun Pictures is the world's oldest operating outdoor movie theater. Here, silent movies—accompanied by a pianist—were once shown to the public while these days, current releases are presented in the very pleasant outdoors. Drop in and have a look during the day for free or stick around for a charming movie-viewing experience that hearkens back to another era. ✉ *Carnarvon St., Broome* ☎ *08/9192–1077* 🌐 *www.broomemovies.com.au* 🎫 *From A$18.*

Willie Creek Pearl Farm

FARM/RANCH | You can watch demonstrations of the cultured pearling process—including the seeding of a live oyster and a boat ride to the marine farm—at Willie Creek Pearl Farm, located about 38 km (23½ miles) north of Broome. Drive out to the farm yourself (you must make reservations first and a four-wheel-drive vehicle is recommended on this unsealed road), or join a five-hour bus tour that'll pick you up and bring you back to your in-town accommodation. There's also the option of taking a scenic helicopter ride while on the property for an additional fee, and tours offer breakfast (A$25 more per person) and lunch add-ons (A$30 more per person) depending on the time of day you visit. At the end of the tour, you'll have a chance to view and try on gorgeous pearl necklaces worth more than A$20,000 and peruse the gift shop. ✉ *Willie Creek Rd., Broome* ☎ *08/9192–0000* 🌐 *www.williecreekpearls.com.au* 🎫 *From A$75.*

Camel riding on Cable Beach, Broome

Beaches

★ Cable Beach

BEACH | Watching the sun sink into the sea on Cable Beach is a nightly ritual for almost all visitors to Broome, who flock to the 22-km (14-mile) stretch of dazzling white sand lapped by turquoise water 7 km (4½ miles) from the center of town. The most popular way to watch the sunset is from the back of a swaying camel, but you can also unpack a picnic at the beachside park, drive a four-wheel-drive vehicle onto the sand, or sip a cocktail from the beachside bar at Cable Beach Resort & Spa. By day it's a lot less crowded, and about 1,640 feet north of the vehicle access ramp is a declared nude beach. It's good for swimming, but low tide can mean a long walk across sand to get to the water. Beware of marine stingers (deadly box and Irukandji jellyfish) in the water from December through to April. **Amenities:** lifeguard; parking (free); toilets. **Best for:** sunset; swimming; walking. ✉ *Cable Beach Rd. W, Broome.*

Restaurants

The Aarli

$$ | **ASIAN FUSION** | Hailed by both locals and visitors as the best restaurant in Broome, Aarli's focus is on Asian-fusion small plates, with plenty of seafood. There's a lengthy list of classic cocktails and a huge variety of Australian wines, all set within trendy interiors. **Known for:** buzzy atmosphere; Asian-fusion small plates; fantastic cocktails. [$] *Average main: A$25* ✉ *2/6 Hamersley St., Broome* ☎ *08/9192–5529* 🌐 *www.theaarli.com.au* ⏲ *Closed Sun.*

Cichetti Club

$$$$ | **EUROPEAN** | Handmade pasta, fresh seafood, and incredible views, Cichetti Club is situated within Cable Beach Club Resort, but it's a popular choice for those who aren't staying at the resort. Many of the dishes are Italian focused, with a set menu of two courses (A$78) or three courses (A$95), which are matched with wines from around the globe. **Known for:** international wines; fresh handmade pasta; set within a five-star resort. *Average main: A$78* *1 Cable Beach Rd., Broome* *08/9192–0400* *www.cablebeachclub.com/dine* *Closed Sun. and Mon.*

★ Matso's Broome Brewery

$$ | AUSTRALIAN | One of the most popular spots to eat and drink in Broome, this microbrewery in an old bank building overlooking Roebuck Bay serves bar snacks, burgers, steaks, and fish-and-chips. The fan-cooled bar is full of pearling memorabilia and historic photographs, although most people choose to sit on the breezy veranda or shady beer garden. **Known for:** authentic Indian curry dinners; a very refreshing alcoholic ginger beer; one-hour brewery tours on Wednesday and Friday at 11 am (A$35). *Average main: A$35* *60 Hammersley St., Broome* *08/9193–5811* *matsos.com.au.*

Coffee and Quick Bites

Broome Courthouse Markets

$ | MODERN AUSTRALIAN | Open weekends from 8 am to 1 pm, this market is packed with rows of food stalls. There are plenty of casual spots for breakfast offering fresh fruit, doughnuts, and even Filipino-style empanadas. **Known for:** plenty of variety; freshly made empanadas; lively atmosphere. *Average main: A$10* *8 Hamersley St., Broome* *04/2280–2885* *www.broomemarkets.com.au* *No credit cards.*

Hotels

★ Cable Beach Club Resort and Spa

$$$$ | RESORT | FAMILY | An institution in Cable Beach, this family-friendly resort caters to guests of all ages with multiple pools, a water park, playground, minigolf course, tennis courts, a luxury day spa, meditation garden, and five seasonal restaurants featuring everything from Italian, Southeast Asian, and Japanese food, bistro fare, and a beachfront sunset bar and grill. **Pros:** separate swimming pool area just for adults; easy walk to Cable Beach; peaceful, tropical atmosphere. **Cons:** property is huge and it's easy to get lost; need transport to get into town; no shopping nearby. *Rooms from: A$469* *Cable Beach Rd., Broome* *08/9192–0400* *www.cablebeachclub.com* *189 rooms* *Free Breakfast.*

Kimberley Sands Resort and Spa

$$ | RESORT | One of the Cable Beach area's best accommodation options, this glam, adults-only resort seduces with its stunning pool, spa facilities, and chic bar that sit at the heart of its luxurious rooms and suites, which, by the way, provide you with your own private balcony or courtyard. **Pros:** all rooms have a private balcony or courtyard; great resort-style lap pool; free Wi-Fi. **Cons:** an adults-only property as of July 2019; parking-lot-facing rooms are noisy; you'll need a car or a cab to get to and from downtown Broome. *Rooms from: A$159* *Cable Beach, 10 Murray Rd., Broome* *08/9193–8300* *www.thekimberley-collection.com.au* *72 rooms* *Free Breakfast.*

★ Mantra Frangipani

$$$$ | HOTEL | In lush, tropical gardens, these one-, two-, three-bedroom self-contained villas offer a wonderful escape from hustle and bustle of downtown Broome and Cable Beach, with private garden courtyards, barbecues, and luxurious outdoor showers. **Pros:** ability to self-cater and use private barbecues; luxurious Balinese-style outdoor showers; lovely gardens throughout the grounds. **Cons:** it's a 20-minute walk to the nearest beach; outdoor showers offer little privacy; small pool. *Rooms from: A$339* *15 Millington Rd., Broome* *08/9195–5000 reception, 131–517 reservations* *www.mantra.com.au* *60 rooms* *No Meals.*

Moonlight Bay Suites

$$$ | **HOTEL** | Home to 49 charming self-contained one- and two-bedroom suites, complete with fully loaded kitchens, spa tubs, a separate lounge room, and views overlooking grand gardens or scenic Roebuck Bay, Moonlight Bay Suites is a great place to rest up before or after an epic Kimberley adventure. **Pros:** fully stocked kitchens so you can self-cater; across the street from Matso's Broome Brewery; family-friendly. **Cons:** no on-site restaurant; need a car to get to Cable Beach; limited gym amenities. *Rooms from: A$239 ✉ 51 Carnarvon St., Broome ☎ 08/9195–5200 🌐 www.moonlightbaysuites.com.au 49 suites No Meals.*

Pinctada McAlpine House

$$$$ | **B&B/INN** | With an inviting pool, a library, personalized service, and heaps of Javanese teak furniture, this B&B, originally built in 1910 for a local pearling master, is a good place to unwind while giving you a chance to swap travel tales with your fellow guests at breakfast. **Pros:** complimentary airport transfers, breakfast, and Wi-Fi; highly personalized service; luxurious suites. **Cons:** 30-minute walk to downtown Broome; no children under 16 allowed; limited leisure facilities. *Rooms from: A$395 ✉ 55 Herbert St., at Louis St., Broome ☎ 08/9192–0588 🌐 mcalpinehouse.com.au ⏲ Closed mid-Dec.–Mar. 8 rooms Free Breakfast.*

Ramada Eco Beach Resort

$ | **RESORT** | Luxury villas and safari eco-tents dot the red dirt landscape, connected by environmentally friendly boardwalks and edged with herb and vegetable gardens at this wilderness retreat, which, with its cliff-side oceanfront location, gives the impression it's incredibly remote despite being just a 90-minute drive south of Broome. **Pros:** you can self-cater; lots of on-site activities; beautiful waterfront location. **Cons:** the last 12 km (7 miles) into the resort is along a dirt road; restaurant is a bit pricey; no shopping nearby. *Rooms from: A$112 ✉ Great Northern Hwy., Lot 323, Broome ✣ 134 km (83 miles) south of Broome along the Great Northern Hwy.; look for signs and take the dirt road for the last 12 km (7 miles) ☎ 08/9193–8015 🌐 www.ecobeach.com.au ⏲ Closed Mon.–Thurs. in Nov.–Apr. 57 rooms No Meals.*

Shopping

Given its pearly history, it's no surprise that Broome has an abundance of jewelry stores.

Allure South Sea Pearls

JEWELRY & WATCHES | This store sells high-end jewelry. It also has an outlet at Cable Beach Club Resort and Spa. *✉ 25 Dampier Terr., Broome ☎ 08/9192–2430 🌐 www.alluresouthseapearls.com.au.*

Kailis Australian Pearls

JEWELRY & WATCHES | This shop specializes in high-quality, expensive pearls and jewelry. *✉ 23 Dampier Terr., Shop 3, Broome ☎ 08/9192–2061 🌐 www.kailisjewellery.com.au.*

Paspaley Pearling

JEWELRY & WATCHES | Family-owned Paspaley Pearling, located in Chinatown, sells pearls and stylish local jewelry. *✉ 2 Short St., Broome ☎ 08/9195–1600 🌐 www.paspaley.com.*

Chapter 12

WESTERN AUSTRALIA

12

Updated by
Jennifer Morton

Sights ★★★★☆ | Restaurants ★★★★★ | Hotels ★★★★★ | Shopping ★★★☆☆ | Nightlife ★★★☆☆

WELCOME TO WESTERN AUSTRALIA

TOP REASONS TO GO

★ **Beach Heaven:** Some of Australia's finest beaches are in Western Australia. Hundreds of miles of virtually deserted sandy stretches and bays invite you to swim, surf, snorkel, or laze about.

★ **National Parks:** With spectacular terrain and one-of-a-kind plant and animal species, rugged national parks tell the story of Australia's age-old landforms, especially across the gorge-pocked Kimberley region.

★ **Slick Eats:** Perth's modern food revolution has made way for a smorgasbord of small bars and edgy restaurants excelling at local, seasonal fare.

★ **Wine Trails:** Follow the beautiful wine trails from Perth to the south coast to enjoy free tastings of internationally renowned drops at the cellar doors.

★ **Art and Culture:** Perth's public art scene is thriving throughout the city with larger-than-life sculptures, bronze statues, colorful murals, urban furniture, and unique street art in abundance.

Glance at a map of Australia and you'll see that the state of Western Australia (aka WA) encompasses one-third of the country. It's a massive slab, all 1 million square miles of it, so it may take longer than you expect to reach your destination. But efforts are rewarded with fewer tourists and unadulterated nature.

The state's glamour girl is undoubtedly the Margaret River wine region, as rich in native forests and rugged beaches as it is vineyards. The once sleepy capital city of Perth is now a vibrant eating and drinking scene. Fremantle and Rottnest Island are mere day trips away. Journeying up the sparsely populated but beautiful northern coast is made easier with air travel—only tackle the roads if you have ample time.

1 **Perth.** Western Australia's sunny capital, highlights in this easygoing city include Elizabeth Quay, Cottesloe Beach, Kings Park, and larger-than-life artworks.

2 **Fremantle.** Perth's "Brooklyn," Fremantle is a cool port city with a convict past, a lively indoor market, and a celebrated harbor area. Artists from around the world flock here for its carefree bohemian lifestyle.

3 **Rottnest Island.** A short ferry ride from Fremantle or Perth, this car-free holiday island is home to parks, beaches, and the most adorable creatures in Australia—quokkas!

4 **Bunbury.** A small industrial seaside city with a beautiful foreshore, Dolphin Discovery Centre, a popular candy shop, great bars and restaurants.

5 **Busselton.** Home to the longest timber jetty in the southern hemisphere, a fun foreshore for all ages, this small city makes a perfect base for your Margaret River plans.

6 **Dunsborough.** A pretty coastal town with access to amazing diving, whale-watching, and spectacular beaches along the coastline of Leeuwin-Naturaliste National Park.

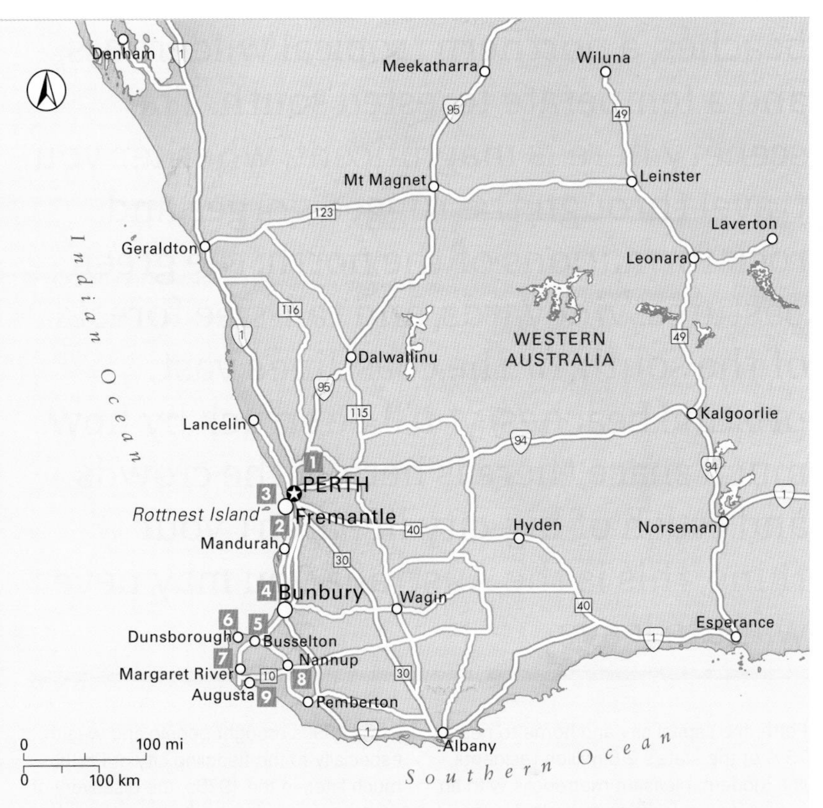

7 Margaret River. The center of the South West's wine region with more than 200 wineries, craft beer breweries, and amazing paddock-to-plate cuisine.

8 Nannup. A small country town with beautiful, scenic drives, forests, and an annual flower festival.

9 Augusta. Home to the tallest lighthouse on mainland Australia, the collision of the Southern and Indian Oceans, a yummy bakery, and access to the Blackwood River.

Western Australia is a stunningly diverse place, with rugged interior deserts, endless, untrammeled white-sand beaches, a northern tropical wilderness, and a temperate forested south. The scenery here is magnificent, whether you travel through the rugged gorges and rock formations of the north; the green pastures, vineyards, and tall-tree forests of the south; or the coastline's vast, pristine beaches, you'll be struck by how much space there is here. If the crowds and crush of big-city life aren't your thing, this is the Australia you may never want to leave.

Perth, the capital city and home to nearly 75% of the state's 2.6 million residents, is a modern, pleasant metropolis with an easygoing, welcoming attitude. However, at almost 3,000 km (1,864 miles) from any other major city in the world, it has fondly been dubbed "the most isolated city on Earth." Its remoteness is part of what makes Western Australia so awe-inspiring.

It took more than 200 years after Dutch seafarer Dirk Hartog first landed on the coast of "New Holland" in 1616 in today's Shark Bay before British colonists arrived to establish the Swan River Colony (now Perth) in 1829. Progress was slow for half a century, but the discovery of gold around Kalgoorlie and Coolgardie in the 1890s brought people and wealth, especially to the fledgling city of Perth; much later, in the 1970s, the discovery of massive mineral deposits throughout the state began an economic upswing that still continues.

Western Australia produces much of Australia's mineral, energy, and agricultural wealth, though recent falls in resource prices have slowed development, curbed employment figures, and reduced the population flow to WA, with fewer people chasing the highs of its boom-and-bust cycle. Nonetheless, development continues: a number of the state's airports are being expanded; central train lines are being sunk, linking the city's divided heart; and the long-term riverside development known as Elizabeth Quay continues to evolve (expect road delays and construction). The cooling economy has delivered a boon for travelers: hotel prices have fallen, making for a more affordable experience in this land of oft-inflated prices.

MAJOR REGIONS

Perth and Environs encompasses Western Australia's capital, Perth, a once-quiet town that now matches the wow-factor of its Caribbean-style coastline; the port town of Fremantle, charming for its curving, colonial streets and the quirky vibe of its residents; and Rottnest Island, the ultimate escape, with no cars (bikes are the dominant mode of transport), no pretension, and no cares in the world. The promise of 63 beaches just 19 km (12 miles) from Perth has people flocking here, especially from December to April.

Internationally known and loved as one of Australia's top wine regions—Chardonnay and Cabernet Sauvignon are the standout varieties—and producers of paddock-to-plate cuisine, **the Margaret River region** is Western Australia's most popular destination, with 2.4 million visitors annually. Perth residents flock here year-round for the wines, beaches, surfing, marine wildlife, forests, locally produced crafts and artisan products, and the country vistas. Most towns in this don't-miss region are on the coast with easy beach access. The best surfing beaches are on the coast between Cape Naturaliste and Cape Leeuwin. Also called the South West and "Down South," this region stretches from the port city of Bunbury—about two hours south of Perth by freeway and highway—through Busselton, on the shores of Geographe Bay and considered the region's main gateway, to Dunsborough, Margaret River town, and on to Augusta, a coastal village in the far south where the Indian and Southern Oceans meet at the tip of Cape Leeuwin. There's also the town of Nannup, an easy jaunt from Margaret River for a day trip.

Planning

When to Go

You can visit Western Australia year-round, though the weather will influence your activities and sightseeing. Perth enjoys more sunny days than any other Australian capital city. Summer (December through February) in Perth is *hot* and temperatures can rise to 40°C (100°F), but the locals love it and flock to the beaches. Be aware major school and university holidays occur at this time, so expect crowds and higher prices. The Perth Festival in February is an excellent reason to visit. Weather-wise, March, April, November, and December are most pleasant, with sunny days and warm, comfortable temperatures. July and August are traditionally cool and wet, which is why Broome and the state's northwest is the favorite place to be during these months

Planning Your Time

Fly into Perth and spend most of the first day exploring the city center, especially Kings Park and, by night, the restaurants and small bars of the CBD and Northbridge. The following day, take the train to Cottesloe Beach and gaze at the translucent water. As the sun's rays strengthen, continue along the tracks to charmingly preserved Fremantle and stroll through the heritage precinct, stopping for breaks at sidewalk cafés and the bustling markets. On Day 3, take a ferry to Rottnest Island and rent a bike or walk around to the lovely beaches—keep an eye open for small local marsupials called quokkas. For the following days, take a wine-touring excursion to the glamorous Margaret River region.

Getting Here and Around

AIR

Perth is the main international arrival point on this side of the country and is serviced by more than 30 airlines. Qantas is Australia's main domestic airline; its budget subsidiary, Jetstar, operates an extensive network and regular services crisscrossing the country, from all the major cities to regional centers like Exmouth and Broome. Virgin Australia competes with Qantas in major cities and covers many regional centers such as Albany, Kununurra, Esperance, and Broome. Airnorth has an extensive network throughout the Top End and covers some WA legs in the north. Perth City Shuttle (*042–743–8533, perthcityshuttle.com.au*) operates minivan services from the terminals to the CBD, Cottesloe, or Fremantle hotels (call or book online).

BUS

Integrity Coach Lines (intregritycoachlines.com.au) operates an extensive network of long-distance, hop-on-hop-off coaches. Greyhound (greyhound.com.au) operates from Broome, going north to Darwin only. From Perth to Adelaide, there are no bus options; when driving, expect to be on the road for 36 hours.

South West Coastlines offers daily services departing Perth Elizabeth Quay Busport on Mounts Bay Road—as well as from Perth domestic and international airports—to South West towns, including Bunbury, Busselton, Dunsborough, Margaret River township, Collie, and Manjimup. Services may vary according to season.

BUS CONTACTS South West Coachlines. ☎ *08/9753–7700* 🌐 *www.southwestcoachlines.com.au.*

CAR

Driving around Western Australia is relatively easy, with mostly good paved roads and light traffic outside Perth. While the distances in the Outback are daunting (Perth to Broome is 2,240 km [1,386 miles]), Perth to the Margaret River region in the South West is just over three hours along good roads; mostly dual-lane highway. Improvements are ongoing so expect road works. Always be aware of wildlife on the roadsides, particularly at dawn and dusk.

TAXI

Taxis are at the airport around the clock, and there is a rideshare pickup point for Uber and Ola customers. Trips to Perth city cost about A$45 and take around a half hour. The cost to or from downtown Perth starts at A$25.

TAXI CONTACTS Black & White. ☎ *133–222* 🌐 *www.blackandwhitecabs.com.au.***Swan Taxis.** ☎ *131–330* 🌐 *www.swantaxis.com.au.*

TRAIN

Crossing the Nullarbor Plain from the eastern states is one of the great rail journeys of the world. You traverse an entire continent, going 4,345 km (2,700 miles) from Sydney to Perth on the longest stretch of straight track in the world. Journey Beyond Rail Expeditions' (*journeybeyondrail.com.au*) *Indian Pacific* links Sydney and Perth via Kalgoorlie and Adelaide, with an all-inclusive luxury train trip. The once-weekly service (Sunday from Perth, Wednesday from Sydney) takes four days, three nights each way.

From Perth, TransWA operates train services to Bunbury twice daily and to Northam and Kalgoorlie, with coaches linking to other destinations, including Geraldton, Kalbarri, Albany, and Esperance.

Getting around Perth by train is quick and easy, with lines to Armadale/Thornlie, Midland, Butler, Fremantle, Mandurah, and Rockingham.

Health and Safety

If you are self-driving—especially in remote areas—make sure you have enough fuel, water, and food, and carry a first-aid kit. Let others know where you are going and for how long. Mosquitoes are prevalent, so cover up and use a good insect repellent; the worst times for mosquitoes are dawn and dusk.

Respect the Australian sun, especially in summer. Sunburn is a real danger if you don't follow the Australian mantra: slip, slap, slop—that is, slip on a hat, slap on sunglasses, and slop on sunscreen. On popular beaches around major cities and towns, lifesavers (lifeguards) are usually on duty and put up flags to swim between, but generally most beaches are unguarded. Take extra care, especially where there are strong currents.

The emergency contact number for police, fire, and ambulance is ☎ *000*. From a GSM mobile (cell) phone the number is ☎ *112*.

Restaurants

A number of talented chefs have returned to Perth from overseas, bringing international trends, abilities, and standards with them. This influence, coupled with a healthy push for seasonal, local produce, has given the Perth dining scene an exciting shot in the arm. Throughout the young city's history, waves of immigrants from Italy, the former Yugoslavia, and Asia have also delivered cultural authenticity to the more traditional eateries. A British handover, fish-and-chips, remains one of the beach-going state's favorite picnic meals.

Expect to find Western Australian wines on the wine list when dining in most licensed restaurants in Perth and, of course, in the Margaret River wine region, where first-class food is matched with highly regarded vino.

Many restaurants and cafés have alfresco dining and allow BYO wine and beer. At one time, Perth suffered from a sometimes justified reputation for below-par service. But as the city's dining and drinking culture improve, so does the hospitality. Tips aren't expected, but when you experience exceptional service, an extra 10% is a great way to show your appreciation (hospitality workers do not rely on tips as they do in North America—they are paid well in Perth). Expect added surcharges of up to 20% on public holidays.

Hotels

From five-star to basic, you'll find suitable accommodations throughout the region. The well-known international chains are all in Perth but there are also sublime boutique accommodations. Perth once had some of the highest occupancy rates in Australia, largely due to business travelers, but a cooling of this has reduced room rates. Ideally, book ahead, though last-minute bargains can be had, especially for weekends. Other popular options—especially for families and small groups—are self-contained apartments or villas. With two or three bedrooms, living areas, and kitchens, they allow you to save on dining costs by cooking your own meals; these are best if staying more than one night.

Restaurant and hotel reviews have been shortened. For full information, visit Fodors.com.

What It Costs in Australian Dollars			
$	$$	$$$	$$$$
RESTAURANTS			
under A$21	A$21–A$35	A$36–A$50	over A$50
HOTELS			
under A$151	A$151–A$200	A$201–A$300	over A$300

Perth

Buoyed by a history of mineral wealth and foreign investment, Perth has high-rise buildings dotting the skyline, and an influx of immigrants gives the city a healthy diversity. Within 15 minutes' drive of the city are some of Australia's finest sandy beaches and seaside villages; the best postcard beaches lie just north of bohemian Fremantle. The main business thoroughfare is St. Georges Terrace, an elegant street lined with skyscrapers and an excellent set-back entertainment precinct, while urban villages such as Leederville, Subiaco, and Mt. Lawley deliver chic-yet-welcoming community vibes. Perth's literal highlight is Kings Park, 990 acres of greenery atop Mt. Eliza, which affords panoramic city views.

GETTING HERE AND AROUND

The main gateway to Western Australia is Perth's busy airport. It has four terminals: T1, T2, T3, and T4. Terminals 1 and 2 (about 16 km [10 miles] from Perth's central business district), and Terminals 3 and 4 (about 13 km [8 miles] away), host a mix of domestic and international flights, so always check with your airline before heading to the airport. A free shuttle bus connects the terminals 24 hours a day.

Driving in Perth is relatively easy; just remember to stay on the left-hand side of the road, give way to traffic on your right, and avoid peak periods. All major car-rental companies have branches at the international and domestic airport terminals, while motor home and caravan hubs lie near airports.

Perth and its environs are well connected by Transperth buses. The main terminals are at the Elizabeth Quay Bus Station on Mounts Bay Road and Perth Station on Wellington Street. Buses run daily 6 am–11:30 pm, with reduced service on weekends and holidays. Rides within the city center are free. CAT (Central Area Transit) buses circle the city center, running frequently on weekdays 6 am–6:45 pm, and weekends and most public holidays 8:30 am–6 pm. Routes and timetables are available from Transperth (136–213 or download the app). Transperth tickets are valid for two hours and can be used on Transperth trains and ferries. The ferries make daily runs from 6:30 am to 6:45 pm between Elizabeth Quay in Perth to Mends Street, across the Swan River in South Perth. Reduced services run on weekends and holidays.

Transperth trains also provide a quick way to get around the city. Most attractions are accessed via the Fremantle line, which traces the coast via Perth's most affluent suburbs. Other lines run east to Midland, north to Butler, southeast to Armadale/Thornlie, and south to Mandurah. Central-city trains depart from Wellington Street and Perth Underground at the corner of William and Murray Streets. Tickets must be purchased at vending machines before boarding.

SAFETY AND PRECAUTIONS

A safe city to visit, Perth doesn't have any "no-go" neighborhoods, and a strong police presence—on foot, bike, and horse—usually ensures that late-night hot spots like Northbridge and Fremantle are safe. Still, for your personal safety, avoid walking alone, especially late at night. Also, pickpocketing isn't a particular risk, but as with visiting any city, it's best to keep your personal belongings close, especially in busy shopping areas,

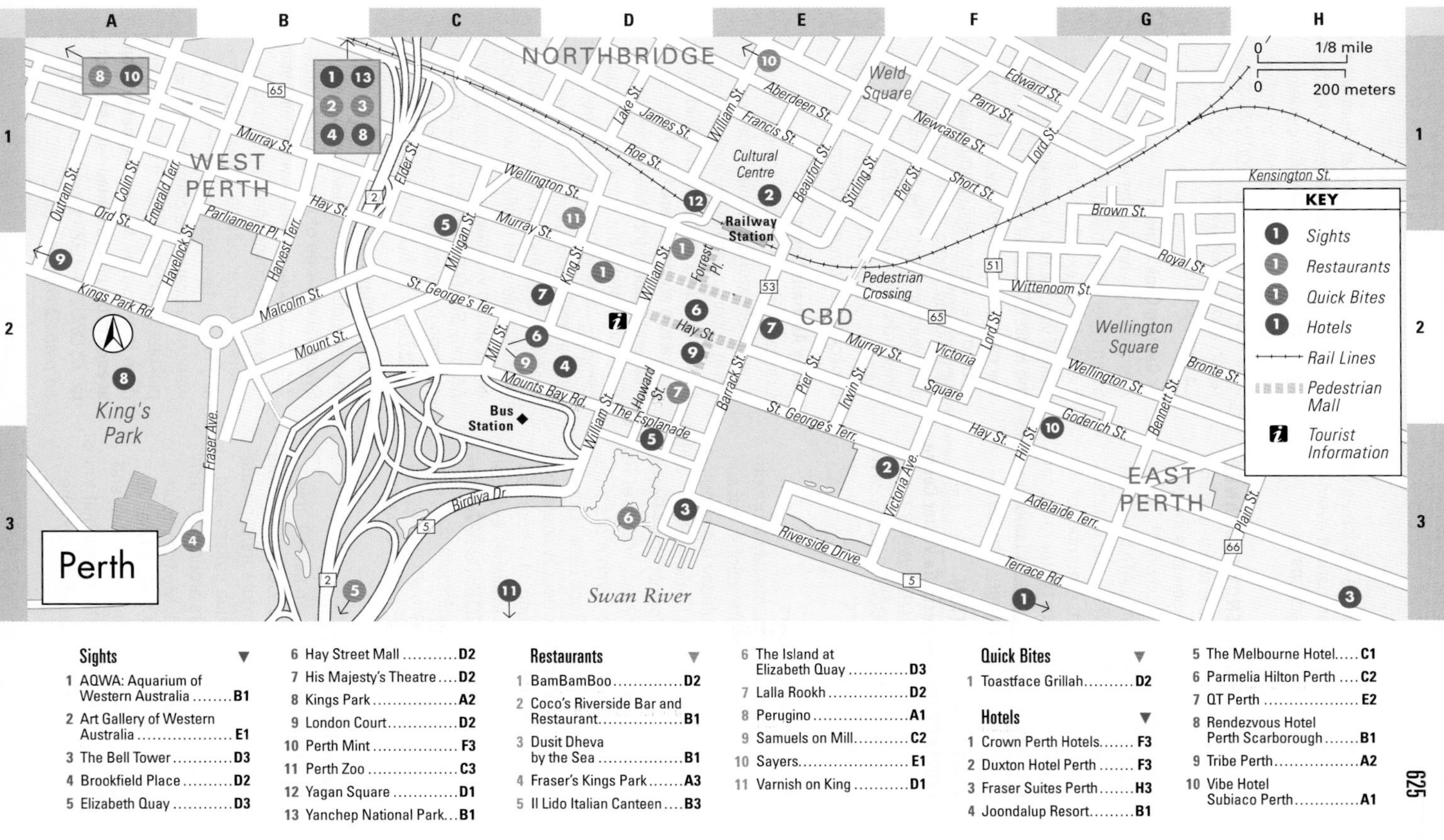

Sights

1 AQWA: Aquarium of Western Australia **B1**
2 Art Gallery of Western Australia **E1**
3 The Bell Tower **D3**
4 Brookfield Place **D2**
5 Elizabeth Quay **D3**
6 Hay Street Mall **D2**
7 His Majesty's Theatre **D2**
8 Kings Park **A2**
9 London Court............. **D2**
10 Perth Mint **F3**
11 Perth Zoo **C3**
12 Yagan Square **D1**
13 Yanchep National Park... **B1**

Restaurants

1 BamBamBoo.............. **D2**
2 Coco's Riverside Bar and Restaurant................ **B1**
3 Dusit Dheva by the Sea **B1**
4 Fraser's Kings Park....... **A3**
5 Il Lido Italian Canteen **B3**
6 The Island at Elizabeth Quay **D3**
7 Lalla Rookh **D2**
8 Perugino **A1**
9 Samuels on Mill........... **C2**
10 Sayers....................... **E1**
11 Varnish on King **D1**

Quick Bites

1 Toastface Grillah.......... **D2**

Hotels

1 Crown Perth Hotels....... **F3**
2 Duxton Hotel Perth **F3**
3 Fraser Suites Perth....... **H3**
4 Joondalup Resort......... **B1**
5 The Melbourne Hotel..... **C1**
6 Parmelia Hilton Perth **C2**
7 QT Perth **E2**
8 Rendezvous Hotel Perth Scarborough....... **B1**
9 Tribe Perth................. **A2**
10 Vibe Hotel Subiaco Perth............ **A1**

and don't leave valuables—such as cameras—in the car when parked overnight, or when visiting attractions.

ESSENTIALS

BANKS AND CURRENCY EXCHANGE

Banks with dependable check-cashing and money-changing services include ANZ, Westpac, Commonwealth, and National Australia Bank. ATMs—which accept Cirrus, Plus, Visa, and MasterCard—are ubiquitous. A number of exchange booths with better rates can be found in Perth's malls, in London Court, and on St. Georges Terrace.

VISITOR INFORMATION

CONTACT Western Australia Visitor Centre. ✉ *55 William St., CBD* ☎ *08/9483–1111 outside Australia, 1800/812–808* 🌐 *www.westernaustralia.com.*

TOURS

ADAMS Pinnacle Tours

This local outfit conducts day tours of Perth and its major attractions. You can also take a day or multiday trip of outer sights like Nambung National Park—with its weird limestone formations—Rottnest Island to see the quokkas, Margaret River and its wineries, or, with more time, Monkey Mia, Wave Rock near Hyden, and the Treetop Walk near Walpole (be aware that this is a long 14½-hour tour). Perth hotel pickup is available. ✉ *Barrack St. Jetty, Shop 1, CBD* ☎ *08/6270–6060* 🌐 *www.adamspinnacletours.com.au* *From A$69* *Minimum numbers are needed to run tours* ☞ *Online bookings are preferred.*

Australian Pacific Touring

Most commonly known as APT, this luxury, award-winning tour group offers extended 4WD adventure trips, private jet excursions, boutique cruises, and traditional coach tours around Western Australia and beyond. Multiday tours travel from Perth to Monkey Mia, via wildflower country and Shark Bay, and from Broome to Perth, stopping at tourist hot spots like Ningaloo Reef and the Pinnacles. The most popular tours are the 15-day Kimberley Complete 4WD Adventure and the *10-day Grand Kimberley Coast cruise.* Other tours run from five days and up. ✉ *Perth* ☎ *1300/278–278 reservations* 🌐 *www.aptouring.com.au* *From $8695.*

★ **Captain Cook Cruises**

A scenic glide on the flat water of the Swan River with this tour company makes for an excellent afternoon, especially if you want to travel from Perth to the Indian Ocean at Fremantle. Enjoy the captain's commentary and free tea and coffee. Optional 1½-hour stopovers are included. There are lunch options and tours upriver to the Swan Valley vineyards, too. ✉ *Pier 3, Barrack St. Jetty, CBD* ☎ *08/9325–3341* 🌐 *www.captaincookcruises.com.au* *From A$30.*

Casey Australia Tours

Created with the mature traveler in mind, a range of extended tours departing from Perth covers nearly every inch of the state, including an 11-day WA Wildflower Tour and a six-day Shark Bay, Monkey Mia, and Kalbarri trip. Most accommodation is in motels, but some tours include camping—this is Outback country, after all! Day tours and shorter tours are available, including a visit to the South West's apple- and truffle-growing region and a spring wildflower day trip. ✉ *16 Murphy St., O'Connor* ☎ *08/9339–4291, 1800/999–677* 🌐 *www.caseytours.com.au* *Day trips from A$105.*

★ **d'Vine Wine Tours**

Take a superb guided day trip to the Swan Valley—one of the state's favorite wine and food regions—with d'Vine Wine Tours and discover fine wines, hoppy beers, gourmet cuisine, chocolates, and French pastries that will make you want to relocate. The company has van pickups from Perth CBD; it's a 25-minute drive to the valley. **TIP→ Expect to shop at each of the places visited—it's hard not to.** ☎ *08/9244–5323* 🌐 *www.dvinetours.com.au* *From A$130.*

Journey Beyond
Journey Beyond is best known for its amazing rail expeditions around Australia, but it also organizes destination tours. Choose from tours featuring the best of Perth; the Pinnacles, New Norcia, and wildflowers; Rottnest Island, Margaret River, and epic land and sea excursions. ✉ *Perth* ☎ *08/8213–4401* 🌐 *journeybeyondrail.com.au.*

Perth Explorer
This open-top bus company runs informative hop-on, hop-off trips around central Perth and to Kings Park on a typical red double-decker. Tickets are valid for 48 hours, and you can get on and off as you choose, or stay on for the full two-hour tour. Book online for discounts or upgrade your ticket to include a Swan River cruise. ☎ *08/9370–1000* 🌐 *www.perthexplorer.com.au* 🎫 *From A$40.*

★ Rottnest Express
Rottnest Express runs excursions to Rottnest Island once daily from Perth and 6 to 12 times daily from Fremantle, depending on the season. It also runs fantastic eco-marine life adventure tours between September and April. There are several package options available, including some with bike rentals (and highly recommended). ✉ *Pier 2, Barrack St. Jetty, CBD* ☎ *1300/467–688* 🌐 *www.rottnestexpress.com.au* 🎫 *From $A73.*

★ Two Feet and a Heartbeat
These guys are award-winning for several reasons: their walking tours are fun and informative, and they wrap in elements that reveal the personality of a city, such as street art, small bars, sculptures, history, and hidden relics. There are several food- and drink-theme tours in Perth city and Fremantle; art and culture tours; convicts and crimes tours; and even nature- and wildlife-focused walking tours. A walking tour is a great introduction to the city's history, top places, and hidden hot spots. ✉ *CBD* ☎ *08/7007–0492 outside Australia, 1800/459–388* 🌐 *twofeet.com.au* 🎫 *From A$45.*

Sights

Because of its relative colonial youth, Perth has an advantage over most other capital cities in that it was laid out with foresight. Streets were planned so that pedestrian traffic could flow smoothly from one avenue to the next, and this compact city remains easy to negotiate on foot. Many points of interest are in the downtown area close to the banks of the Swan River, while shopping arcades and pedestrian malls are a short stroll away.

The city center (CBD, or Central Business District), a pleasant blend of old and new, runs along Perth's major business thoroughfare, St. Georges Terrace, as well as on parallel Hay and Murray Streets.

AQWA: Aquarium of Western Australia
AQUARIUM | **FAMILY** | Huge, colorful aquariums filled with some 400 different species of local sea creatures—including sharks that are 13 feet long—from along the 12,000 km (7,456 miles) of Western Australia's variable coastline are the fascinating draws of this boutique aquarium in northern Perth. Sharp-toothed sharks, stingrays, turtles, and schools of fish swim overhead as you take the moving walkway beneath a transparent acrylic tunnel. You can even do a guided snorkel or scuba dive with the sharks; bookings are essential. Perhaps most interesting is the change in habitats and species as you move from colder, southern waters to the tropics of Western Australia's north. AQWA boasts one of the largest living coral reef displays in the world—check it out from above and then below in the underwater gallery. Other highlights include the rare sea dragons and DANGERzone, featuring a deadly lineup of sea creatures. **TIP→ Age minimums apply for some activities.** ✉ *Hillarys Boat Harbour, 91 Southside Dr., Hillarys* ☎ *08/9447–7500* 🌐 *www.aqwa.com.au* 🎫 *From A$18.*

Art Gallery of Western Australia
ART GALLERY | Founded in 1895, the Art Gallery of Western Australia is home to more than 17,500 treasures and numerous free exhibitions of Indigenous and modern art, which makes it worth an afternoon's devotion. The collection of Indigenous art is impressive, while other works include Australian and international paintings, sculptures, prints, crafts, and decorative arts. In 2021, major renovations were undertaken to improve the rooftop galleries and bar and create a new foyer. See the website for special exhibitions and be prepared to pay a fee to gain entry. ✉ *Perth Cultural Centre, James St., at Beaufort and Roe Sts., CBD* ☎ *08/9492–6600, 08/9492–6622 24-hr information* 🌐 *www.artgallery.wa.gov.au* 🎟 *Free. Donations encouraged* 🕑 *Closed Tues.*

The Bell Tower
OTHER ATTRACTION | The spiral-like Bell Tower is home to one of the world's largest musical instruments, the 12 antique Swan Bells, which have surprising historical links. Originally from St. Martin-in-the-Fields Church of London, England, these same bells were rung to celebrate the destruction of the Spanish Armada in 1588, the homecoming of Captain James Cook in 1771, and the coronation of every British monarch. The tower contains fascinating displays on the history of the bells and bell ringing and provides views of the Perth skyline and the nearby Swan River. Flat, closed shoes must be worn for access to the observation deck; stroller and wheelchair access are available via the elevator. ■ **TIP→ Purchase a heart-shaped love lock to leave on the chain fence to secure forever love.** ✉ *Barrack St., at Riverside Dr., CBD* ☎ *08/6210–0444* 🌐 *www.thebelltower.com.au* 🎟 *A$18.*

Brookfield Place
PLAZA/SQUARE | See where corporate suits de-stress after a long day at the office. Once the clock hits 5 pm, like bees swarming a hive, punters flood Perth's CBD's main thoroughfare, St. Georges Terrace, and its strip of hip venues. Swanky Print Hall serves some of the city's best Modern Australian fare, while Bob's Bar is a happening rooftop bar focusing on simple, tasty, Mexican-inspired eats. There's also the Heritage Wine Bar for contemporary eats and fine wine. Reservations are recommended. ✉ *123–137 St. Georges Terr., CBD* 🌐 *bfplperth.com.*

The View from Kings Park

The best spot is the manicured eastern edge of the park, past the border of tall, white-bark trees and overlooking Perth's Central Business District and the Swan River. While it's a jubilant place buzzing with friends and families picnicking, it also has a somber edge, home to the State War Memorial and its eternal flame, as well as the memorial to local victims of the 2002 terrorist bombing in Bali. *Tip: Visit at night to see the sparkling city lights.*

★ **Elizabeth Quay**
PLAZA/SQUARE | **FAMILY** | On the south side of Perth's Central Business District lies the ever-expanding Elizabeth Quay, a public area brimful with restaurants, cafés, playgrounds, ice-cream parlors, boat excursions, larger-than-life artworks, and the swanky Ritz-Carlton hotel. Although construction is ongoing, EQ is a bustling hub and a great meeting spot. Transperth also has a bus depot, train station, and ferry crossing here making access without a car easy. *Tip: Feel like a kid again and take a spin on the classic carousel.* ✉ *The Esplanade, Perth* 🌐 *elizabethquay.com.au.*

King's Park with downtown Perth in the distance

★ Hay Street Mall

PEDESTRIAN MALL | Running parallel to Murray Street and linked by numerous arcades, the Hay Street Mall is an extensive, mainstream shopping area teeming with intriguing places. The mall is also a brilliant place to people-watch and support local buskers. Make sure you wander through the arcades and malls that connect Hay and Murray Streets, such as the Carillion City and Piccadilly Arcade, which have many more shops. Also, look for the monument dedicated to Percy Button, Perth's original street performer. ✉ *Hay St., CBD.*

★ His Majesty's Theatre

PERFORMANCE VENUE | The opulent His Majesty's Theatre, which opened on Christmas Eve 1904, is admired for its Federation Free Classical style on the outside and by those who step inside (think red velour). His Maj, as it's locally known, is home to the West Australian Opera company and the West Australian Ballet, and hosts most theatrical productions in Perth; there's also a comedy lounge downstairs called The Maj. **TIP→ Tardiness is frowned upon—you will not be permitted inside until a break in the performance.** ✉ *827 Hay St., CBD* ☎ *08/6212–9292 tickets* 🌐 *www.ptt.wa.gov.au.*

★ Kings Park

CITY PARK | **FAMILY** | Locals boast that this is one of the few inner-city parks to dwarf New York City's Central Park; it covers 1,000 acres and grants eye-popping views of downtown Perth and its riverfront at sunrise, sunset, and all times in between. Once a gathering place for Aboriginal people, and established as a public space in 1890, it's favored for picnics, parties, and weddings, as well as regular musical and theater presentations, plus the excellent summer Moonlight Cinema (in Synergy Parkland, on the western side). Each September, when spring arrives, the park holds a wildflower festival and the gardens blaze with orchids, kangaroo paw, banksias, and other native wildflowers, making it ideal for a walk in the curated bushland. The steel-and-glass Lotterywest Federation Walkway takes you into the treetops and the 17-acre botanic garden of Australian flora. The Lotterywest Family Area has a shaded playground for youngsters ages one to five, and a café for parents. The Rio Tinto Naturescape is fun for bigger kids who enjoy climbing and exploring in nature. Free 90-minute walking tours depart from Aspects Gift Shop on Fraser Avenue daily. ✉ *Fraser Ave., at Kings Park Rd., West Perth* ☎ *08/9480–3634* 🌐 *www.bgpa.wa.gov.au* 🎫 *Free.*

London Court

PEDESTRIAN MALL | Gold-mining entrepreneur Claude de Bernales built this quaint outdoor shopping arcade in 1937. Today it's a magnet for anyone with a camera wanting to recapture the atmosphere and architecture of Tudor England, and for those looking for Australian souvenirs. Along its length are statues of Sir Walter Raleigh and Dick Whittington, the legendary lord mayor of London. Above the arcade entry in Hay Street Mall, costumed mechanical knights joust with one another when the clock strikes the quarter hour. **TIP→ The Genuine UGG boot store is popular with tourists.** ✉ *St. Georges Terr. at Hay St., CBD* ☎ *08/9261–6666* 🌐 *www.londoncourt.com.au.*

Perth Mint

HISTORY MUSEUM | **FAMILY** | All that glitters is gold at the Perth Mint, one of the oldest mints in the world still operating from its original premises, and a reminder of the great gold rush days at the turn of the century. Established in 1899, it first refined gold from Western Australia's newly discovered goldfields, striking gold sovereigns for the British Empire. Today it still produces Australia's legal tender in pure gold, silver, and platinum bullion and commemorative coins for investors and collectors. Visitors can tour the site and watch 200 ounces of molten gold being poured in time-honored fashion to form a gold bar. The tour also lets you marvel at the biggest coin ever made, weighing 1 ton, get close to more than A$50 million worth of gold bullion, and see Australia's best collection of natural gold nuggets, including the 369-ounce Golden Beauty, one of the largest natural nuggets in the world. You can also discover your own weight in gold. There's an on-site gift shop and café. ✉ *310 Hay St., East Perth* ☎ *08/9421–7222* 🌐 *www.perthmint.com.au* 🎫 *A$19.*

Perth Zoo

ZOO | **FAMILY** | From kangaroos to crocodiles and venomous Aussie snakes to Asian sun bears and orangutans, this expansive, more than century-old zoo is an easy 10-minute drive from Perth's CBD. Expect lush gardens—perfect for a BYO picnic—and different native habitats of various animals from around the world. Walk among Australian animals in an environment depicting the diversity of Australia's native landscape, including a bird-filled wetland. Discover the Reptile Encounter, Rainforest Retreat, and the Australian Bushwalk. For something a little more exotic, there's the African Savannah, with rhinoceroses, giraffes, lions, cheetahs, and baboons; and the Asian Rainforest, with elephants, tigers, otters, gibbons, and a Komodo dragon. A number of special encounters are available, such as joining a keeper as they feed the lions, which is best booked and paid for in advance. Free guided walks depart daily at 11 am and 1 pm, and there are more than a dozen free talks and presentations each day. A one-hour guided tour around the zoo on an electric Zebra Car, seating seven passengers, is also available. ✉ *20 Labouchere Rd., South Perth* ✥ *Catch No. 30 or 31 bus at Esplanade Busport or take ferry ride across Swan River from Elizabeth Quay and then walk 10 mins, following signs* ☎ *08/9474–0444, 08/9474–3551 24-hr info* 🌐 *www.perthzoo.wa.gov.au* 🎫 *A$32.*

The Pinnacles of Nambung National Park, Western Australia

Yagan Square

PLAZA/SQUARE | **FAMILY** | With its quintessential Western Australia design, color, and flora, Yagan Square opened in March 2018 as a community space and the gateway to Northbridge. It's become a central meeting spot for both locals and tourists. Market Hall began as a high-end food court, drawing a daily lunch crowd with its variety of local and international flavors but in 2021 only a few eateries remain. Hiss & Smoke holds strong with its Japanese fare, and nearby, Shy John Brewery and Yum Cha delight with Cantonese favorites. ✉ *Wellington St. at William St., near Perth Station, CBD.*

Yanchep National Park

NATIONAL PARK | **FAMILY** | Sure, it's nice to cuddle a koala in an enclosure, but it's far more exciting to see them in the wild, just above your head. Take the 787-foot Koala Board Walk through native bush with your eyes raised skyward to see one of the state's largest populations of koalas. Watch for western grey kangaroos on the 2-km (1.2-mile) wetland walking trail around Loch McNess lake and then escape summer's heat by joining one of several daily underground tours of Crystal Cave, where cooling caverns open up to impressive stalactite galleries and clear water pools. The park is also a lovely picnic spot, and there's a hotel and café within the grounds. **TIP→ Yanchep National Park is a 45-minute drive north of Perth and is open every day of the year; book tours and get walk trail information at McNess House Visitor Centre.** ✉ *1 Indian Ocean Dr., Yanchep* ☎ *08/9303–7759 McNess House Visitor Centre* 🌐 *www.dpaw.wa.gov.au* 🎫 *A$15 per vehicle* ☞ *Use your entry receipt to visit Nambung National Park on the same day for no extra charge.*

Beaches

Perth's beaches and waterways are among the city's greatest attractions. Traveling north from Fremantle, the first beach you come to is **Leighton,** where windsurfers and astonishing wave-jumpers ride boards against the surf and hurl

Off The Beaten Path

Batavia Coast. A drive along this part of the coast, which starts at Green Head, 285 km (178 miles) north of Perth, and runs up to Kalbarri, takes you past white sands and emerald seas, and some lovely small towns. Among them are the fig-shaded, seaside village of Dongara and the more northerly Central Greenough Historical Settlement, whose restored colonial buildings—including a jail with original leg irons—date from 1858. A few miles north is Geraldton, whose skyline is dominated by the beautiful Byzantine St. Francis Xavier Cathedral. Its main foreshore is great for families, beach lovers, and coffee drinkers (Kai Lani Cafe makes a good brew and serves burgers, wraps, and ice cream too). Also worth a visit is the haunting HMAS Sydney II Memorial, which is the only recognized national war memorial outside of Canberra and has expansive ocean views. The beautiful Batavia Coast Marina has a pedestrian plaza, shopping arcades, and the fascinating Western Australian Museum, which houses a collection of artifacts from the *Batavia*, a Dutch vessel shipwrecked in 1629. ✉ *Batavia Coast.*

Nambung National Park. Imagine an eerie moonscape where pale yellow limestone formations loom as high as 15 feet. Now see the image in your head displayed before you at Nambung National Park, set on the Swan coastal plain 200 km (125 miles) north of Perth, along the scenic Indian Ocean Drive. At the park you can walk among those otherworldly formations in the Pinnacles Desert, home to one of the world's most spectacular karst landscapes. Geologists believe the pinnacles were created by the dissolving action of water on exposed limestone beds that formed under wind-blown sand dunes. Only a tiny proportion of them have been uncovered. The 1.2-km (0.7-mile) return walk starts at the parking area. There's also a 4-km (2½-mile) one-way Pinnacles Desert Loop scenic drive (not suitable for large RVs or buses). Stop in to the Pinnacles Desert Discovery Centre to see interpretative displays focused on the region's unique geology, flora, and fauna. August through October the heath blazes with wildflowers. Note the rules: no pinnacle climbing, no dogs, no littering (no receptacles are provided, so take your trash with you), and no camping. There is no drinking water available throughout the park, although water is available to purchase at the interpretative center and gift shop. ⚠ *Indian Ocean Drive is a frequent crash zone; please take care and avoid driving at dawn, dusk, and dark.* ✉ *Nambung National Park* ☎ *08/9652–7913 Pinnacles Desert Discovery Centre* 🌐 *parks.dpaw.wa.gov.au* 🎫 *A$15 per vehicle.*

themselves airborne. **Cottesloe** is Perth's glamour puss—don't miss it—home to lithe, tanned bodies, sun-hungry backpackers, and excited youngsters. It becomes a shoulder-to-shoulder picnic ground on Sunday, while **North Cottesloe** attracts families and locals. Farther north, **Trigg,** a top surf site, overlooks an emerald-green bay. **Scarborough** is favored by teenagers and young adults. Be aware of its sometimes strong waves. **Swanbourne** (between North Cottesloe and City Beach) is a "clothing-optional" beach. Fremantle's Bathers Beach is great for sipping sunset cocktails.

★ **Cottesloe**

BEACH | FAMILY | Perth's poster beach is as beguiling as it is relaxing, what with its soft cream sand, transparent blue waters, and strip of beachy pubs and restaurants. Naturally, it's very popular, particularly on Sunday, when people of all ages picnic on the grass beneath the row of Norfolk pines that also hosts masses of squawking birds. The water is fairly calm, though punchy waves can roll through, crashing mainly in shallow depths. "Sunday sessions"—afternoon beer drinking in two local pubs at the Ocean Beach Hotel and the swanky Cottesloe Beach Hotel, both of which have good, ocean-facing accommodations—are also held here. South of the Cottesloe groyne is a reasonable reef surf break, but it's often crowded. **Amenities:** food and drink; lifeguards; parking (free); showers; toilets. **Best for:** swimming; surfing; snorkeling; sunset; walking. ✉ *Marine Parade, Cottesloe* 🌐 *beachsafe.org.au* ☞ *Parking is free but don't overstay the time limits—inspectors are vigilant, and fines are high.*

North Cottesloe

BEACH | FAMILY | This is the quieter end of Cottesloe, where local residents go to walk their dogs (a section by Grant Street is a designated dog beach), dive in for an early morning dip, or share a sunset wine on the sand. The concrete walking path looks over the sandy beach and affords impressive views of the coastal mansions that look out to sea. Coastal reef fans out to the right of Grant Street and makes for good snorkeling in summer, but take caution in high waves as stronger currents form near the reef. Beware invisible jellyfish, known as stingers, which cause pain but pose little other threat. **Amenities:** lifeguards; showers. **Best for:** snorkeling; solitude; sunset; swimming; walking. ✉ *365 Marine Parade, North Cottesloe* 🌐 *beachsafe.org.au.*

Scarborough

BEACH | After the West Australian premier described the Scarborough precinct as "tired and old," the state government pledged A$30 million to pretty-up the beachfront, and things have markedly improved. The beach was always beautiful and the waves surfable, but now there are a number of busy cafés, including the Wild Fig, the Local Shack, and The Peach Pit. There's also the long-standing takeout spot, Peters by the Sea for fish-and-chips. Kids love to run wild on the beachfront playground and the Snake Pit skate park, while holidaymakers come and go from the towering Rendezvous Hotel. The more enviable locales of Cottesloe, Fremantle, and Perth CBD are all a 15- to 20-minute drive away; Scarborough is not on the train line. **Amenities:** food and drink; lifeguards; parking; showers; toilets. **Best for:** partiers; sunset; walking. ✉ *The Esplanade, Scarborough* 🌐 *beachsafe.org.au.*

Trigg

BEACH | Surfers and bodyboarders favor this beach, riding the transparent blue waves from Trigg Point and Trigg Island, sometimes crashing into the sandy bottom. Swimmers don masks and paddle to the snorkeling spot of Mettams Pool that is lovely on calm days but should be avoided when the swell is up. The hip, surfer-theme coffee haunt, Yelo, and the ultracool Island Market Trigg offer healthy meals and views for days. Across the road away from the ocean, the Trigg Bushland Reserve makes for interesting, paved bushwalking—just follow the trail and its interpretive signage. **Amenities:** food and drink; lifeguards; parking; toilets. **Best for:** snorkeling; sunset; surfing. ⚠ **There is a strong undertow off this beach, and swimmers have struck trouble.** ✉ *West Coast Dr., Trigg* 🌐 *beachsafe.org.au.*

Restaurants

Northbridge, northwest of Perth Station, used to be *the* dining, barhopping, and nightclubbing center of Perth, but since the city has grown in size and reputation, you can find a myriad of great restaurants throughout the central business district (CBD) and neighboring suburbs, particularly in Mount Lawley, Subiaco, Leederville, and Fremantle (*see Fremantle*). Seafood and international restaurants, some with stunning views over the Swan River, beachside, or city, and cantilevered windows make for a seamless transition between indoor and alfresco dining.

For those on a budget, the noisy fun of a dim sum lunch at one of Perth's many traditional Asian teahouses (especially in Northbridge) is cheap and delicious; expect long lines on Sunday morning. Along with a cup of green tea, you can enjoy steamed pork buns, fried chicken feet, and dumplings served at your table from a trolley. Food halls in Perth, Northbridge, and Fremantle are other budget options. For more upscale food courts, *see* Brookfield Place in Sights.

BamBamBoo

$ | CHINESE | FAMILY | Tucked away in Globe Lane is this casual eatery serving delicious Chinese fare in a modern communal dining setting. On provided iPads, scroll through the menu, order, pay at the counter and wait for your lunch to be served. **Known for:** bustling atmosphere; weekend dim sum; crispy duck rolls. *Average main: A$18 ✉ 25/140 William St., CBD ☎ 08/6388–8908 ⊕ bambamboo.com.au.*

Coco's Riverside Bar and Restaurant

$$$ | AUSTRALIAN | Appealing to the glitzy, moneyed, cosmetically conscious crowd in Perth, this is the "it spot" on Friday when rollicking long lunches can extend well past sunset, making it challenging to get a table—unless you book in advance. The views are as good as the people-watching, and though the classic food is expensive, it's beautifully executed. **Known for:** tasting plates; a diverse menu featuring aged beef, fresh fish, and seafood; handmade pasta. *Average main: A$46 ✉ Southshore Centre, 85 The Esplanade, South Perth ☎ 08/9474–3030 ⊕ www.westvalley.com.au ☞ Split billing is not available. Credit card surcharges apply.*

Dusit Dheva by the Sea

$$ | THAI | A location change, a name change, a menu update, and an award-winning head chef have put Dusit Dheva Thai cusine on the map as Perth's best Thai restaurant. Come to this delightful, contemporary, Asian-inspired dining room by the sea for authentic Thai food, creatively prepared by chef Mhee and his team. **Known for:** lunch specials under $17; attentive service; the best green curry outside Thailand. *Average main: A$26 ✉ Shop 206 Sorrento Quay Boardwalk, Northbridge ☎ 08/9246–5053 ⊕ www.dusitdheva.com.au ⊙ Closed Tues. No lunch Wed.*

Fraser's Kings Park

$$$ | MODERN AUSTRALIAN | The large outdoor area at this Kings Park restaurant fills with people eyeing views of the city and Swan River (spectacular in the evening) while enjoying chef favorites such as slow-cooked lamb shoulder, chargrilled octopus, and hand-cut chips with aioli. The ever-changing menu of share plates or larger dishes highlight fresh Western Australian produce. **Known for:** located next to its casual cousin, the Botanical Cafe; a sophisticated and elegant dining experience; an elaborate wine and cocktail menu. *Average main: A$45 ✉ Kings Park, 60 Fraser Ave., West Perth ☎ 08/9482–0103 ⊕ www.frasersrestaurant.com.au.*

Il Lido Italian Canteen

$$$ | MODERN AUSTRALIAN | This white-washed and yellow canteen scores with simple, seasonal food delivered with finesse plus window seats overlooking iconic Cottesloe Beach. The convivial alfresco area looks out to a coastal conga line of walkers, joggers, and cyclists, while at night, candles deliver a romantic feel. **Known for:** Oyster Sunday; authentic Italian meals made from family recipes; favorite breakfast spot for locals. *$ Average main: A$38 ✉ 88 Marine Parade, Cottesloe ☎ 08/9286–1111 🌐 illido.com.au.*

★ The Island at Elizabeth Quay

$$ | **AUSTRALIAN** | Few eateries have a backstory that includes a brick-by-brick relocation of its Heritage-listed Federation-style building, but The Island has just such a story and honors it with framed photos of the 1920s building throughout the restaurant. This ideally located Perth icon has character, charm, and a contemporary menu, as well as several dining options, including a 110-seat dockside alfresco bar selling wood-fired pizza. **Known for:** inspired-by-nature kids' play areas; Sunday sessions with live music and cold beer from the on-site microbrewery; incredible views of the CBD. *$ Average main: A$30 ✉ Elizabeth Quay, 1 Valdura Pl., Perth ☎ 04/2746–3007 🌐 www.islandbrewhouse.com.au.*

Lalla Rookh

$$$ | **MODERN AUSTRALIAN** | Any place that takes its name from a Kalgoorlie showgirl has got to have spunk, and Lalla Rookh has it in spades. The below-street-level venue on Perth's business strip is a real find and combines a slick restaurant with dishes inspired by Italy with a tiny wine bar that introduces quaffers to local and "untampered with grape" varieties. **Known for:** an extensive wine list; chef's tasting plate featuring six seasonal tapas; a cozy atmosphere. *$ Average main: A$36 ✉ 77 St. Georges Terr., lower level, CBD ☎ 08/9325–7077 🌐 www.lallarookh.com.au ⏲ Closed Sun. and Mon.*

Perugino

$$$ | **ITALIAN** | Since 1986, chef and owner Giuseppe Pagliaricci has taken an imaginative yet simple approach to the cuisine of his native Umbria, serving elegant, homemade Italian dishes to his loyal customers. Popular in old-school business and political circles, the restaurant has prix-fixe lunches, and a fine-dining atmosphere. **Known for:** game meat, such as rabbit and quail, on the menu; three-course prix-fixe lunch menu; traditional service and values. *$ Average main: A$38 ✉ 77 Outram St., West Perth ☎ 08/9321–5420 🌐 www.perugino.com.au ⏲ Closed Sun. and Mon. No lunch Sat.*

★ Samuels on Mill

$$$ | **AUSTRALIAN** | Located in Parmelia Hilton Perth, this elegant restaurant and bar serves top-quality seasonal fare from their State-to-Plate tapas menu. With sharing in mind, plates come in small, medium, and large portions and range from ciabatta with smoked butter and saltbush to Fremantle octopus to roasted pumpkin with fermented black garlic. **Known for:** chic culinary events; lunch specials under $30 including a beer or wine; smoked signature cocktails. *$ Average main: A$40 ✉ 14 Mill St., CBD ☎ 08/9215–2422 🌐 www.samuelsonmill.com.*

Sayers

$$ | **MODERN AUSTRALIAN** | Ask any Perthite where to go for breakfast and chances are the response will be Sayers, where the simple chocolate and banana bread has achieved cult status and the poached eggs and potato rosti are not far behind. Crowds line up for the flavor-rich breakfast dishes, which are created with primo local/free-range/organic/seasonal ingredients. **Known for:** hearty breakfasts; Sunday brunch; bespoke coffee blend by Five Senses Coffee. *$ Average main: A$24 ✉ 224 Carr Pl., Leederville ☎ 08/9227–0429 🌐 sayersfood.com.au ⏲ No dinner.*

Varnish on King

$$ | **MODERN AUSTRALIAN** | Since American whiskey is the specialty at this hard-to-find basement bar, you might expect the food to play second fiddle, but it gets just as much love. This venue with an artisan

grunge theme and the scent of bacon in the air could in fact be called a foodie heaven—come with a huge appetite or a group to share plates. ■ **TIP→ It packs out on a Friday, so book ahead, even for lunch. Known for:** five menu items for A$60 per person; the bacon flight: four pieces of bacon with four shots of whiskey; more than 150 varieties of whiskey. *Average main: A$30 ✉ 75 King St., downstairs, Northbridge ☎ 08/9324–2237 🌐 varnishonking.com ⏲ Closed Sun. No lunch Sat.*

Coffee and Quick Bites

★ Toastface Grillah

$ | **AUSTRALIAN** | It started as a hole-in-the-wall toasted sandwich cave tucked away in Grand Lane with cultlike status. Although the original location belongs to another business, Toastface is still grillin' daily and has grown to include five locations (and counting) around Perth, Fremantle, and Margaret River. **Known for:** graffiti logo and wall art; cheese toasties with unique ingredient pairings; rich flat white coffees. *Average main: A$9 ✉ 329 Murray St., Shop 7 Wolf Lane, CBD 🌐 www.toastfacegrillah.com.*

Hotels

During the week, businesspeople from eastern Australia and all parts of Asia flock to Western Australia, and consequently hotel rooms in Perth are often full. But the flow is slowing, and several new hotels have been built—with more on the way—so prices are coming down.

Crown Perth Hotels

$$$$ | **RESORT** | **FAMILY** | Across the river from the city center, Crown Perth is like an island where everything is self-contained, and the rooms are spacious and tastefully decorated. **Pros:** free Wi-Fi; impressive lobby at Crown Towers rises the full height of the building; high-end Crown Spa adds luxury. **Cons:** hotel parking is not included in the room rates; some rooms overlook the parking lot; adjacent casino and nightclub attracts a boisterous crowd. *Rooms from: A$309 ✉ Great Eastern Hwy., at Bolton Ave., Burswood ☎ 08/9362–8888 reservations, 1800/999–667 🌐 crownperth.com.au 1188 rooms No Meals.*

Duxton Hotel Perth

$$ | **HOTEL** | **FAMILY** | Facing the Swan River and adjacent to the Perth Concert Hall, this elegant hotel sits at the eastern end of the business district, within easy walking distance of the city center. **Pros:** popular restaurant with alfresco terrace; free Wi-Fi; easy access to free bus. **Cons:** minimal menu selection for vegetarian diners; some rooms are dated; valet parking fee of A$48 applies. *Rooms from: A$199 ✉ 1 St. Georges Terr., CBD ☎ 08/9261–8000, 1800/681–118 🌐 duxtonhotels.com 306 rooms No Meals.*

Fraser Suites Perth

$$$ | **HOTEL** | This flashy, executive-style hotel impresses guests with its good value, modern design, corporate standards, and the fact that every room is a self-contained suite. **Pros:** popular contemporary restaurant Heirloom on-site; free Wi-Fi; indoor swimming pool, spa, and gym. **Cons:** limited parking costs A$30 per night; perfunctory reception; far eastern end of the CBD. *Rooms from: A$233 ✉ 10 Adelaide Terr., East Perth ☎ 08/9261–0000 🌐 perth.frasershospitality.com 236 suites No Meals.*

Joondalup Resort

$$$ | **RESORT** | **FAMILY** | This resort-style, palm-shaded building shares its location with a pro-standard, 27-hole Robert Trent Jones Jr.–designed golf course and handful of resident kangaroos. Spacious rooms, decorated in subdued pastels and warm tones, have views of the lake or garden. **Pros:** free Wi-Fi and parking; pool access until 3 pm on departure day; on-site restaurant, bar, and café. **Cons:** rooms accessible by external corridor; conventions can make venues crowded;

in suburban area 25 minutes from Perth's business district. $ *Rooms from: A$209* ✉ *Country Club Blvd., Connolly* ☎ *08/9400–8888* 🌐 *joondalupresort.com.au* *70 rooms* *No Meals.*

The Melbourne Hotel

$$$ | HOTEL | A restored 1890s building listed on the National Heritage Register houses this stylish boutique hotel that sits in the heart of the city, across from some excellent restaurants and fantastic shopping. **Pros:** three on-site dining options; option for a noon checkout; 24-hour fitness center. **Cons:** only seven (highly sought-after) rooms with balconies; parking is off-site and costs extra; no swimming pool or spa. $ *Rooms from: A$209* ✉ *33 Milligan St., CBD* ☎ *08/9320–3333* 🌐 *melbournehotel.com.au* *73 rooms* *No Meals.*

★ Parmelia Hilton Perth

$$$ | HOTEL | With an extensive A$45 million renovation that included the addition of 25 guest rooms, event spaces, an executive lounge, and a thoroughfare to Brookfield Place, Parmelia Hilton Perth has set the bar high for CBD accommodation. **Pros:** on-site bar and restaurant (see Samuels on Mill); swimming pool and lounge deck; double sinks in en suites. **Cons:** skyscraper views; free Wi-Fi for Hilton Honors members only; additional charge for parking. $ *Rooms from: A$219* ✉ *14 Mill St., CBD* ☎ *08/9215–2000* 🌐 *hilton.com* *No Meals* *309 rooms.*

★ QT Perth

$$$ | HOTEL | Design enthusiasts, artists, creatives, and anyone who enjoys a little quirk in their life will adore QT Perth. **Pros:** some rooms have soaker bathtubs; 24-hour reception, room service, and gym; free Wi-Fi. **Cons:** no balconies; no pool; paid parking and valet only on weekends. $ *Rooms from: A$230* ✉ *133 Murray St., CBD* ☎ *08/9225–8000* 🌐 *qthotels.com* *No Meals* *184 rooms.*

Rendezvous Hotel Perth Scarborough

$$$$ | HOTEL | FAMILY | For a beachfront holiday in a towering, iconic hotel with a wide variety of stylish rooms and suites with ocean views and all the amenties you could ever need, look no further than Rendezvous Hotel Perth Scarborough. **Pros:** 24-hour room service; all rooms have balconies; walk straight on to Scarborough Beach. **Cons:** 20-minute drive to the city; breakfast and parking cost extra; busy in summer. $ *Rooms from: A$329* ✉ *148 The Esplanade, Scarborough Beach* ☎ *08/9245–1000* 🌐 *rendezvoushotels.com* *337 rooms* *No Meals.*

★ Tribe Perth

$$ | HOTEL | When hip and trendy meet luxury, creativity, and affordability, you've got Tribe Perth, a fabulous boutique hotel on the fringes of Kings Park. **Pros:** in-room USB ports; delicious grazing-style breakfast; free on-demand movies. **Cons:** only one queen bed per room; restaurant serves breakfast only; very limited parking. $ *Rooms from: A$159* ✉ *4 Walker Ave., West Perth* ☎ *08/6247–3333* 🌐 *tribehotels.com.au* *123 rooms* *Free Breakfast.*

★ Vibe Hotel Subiaco Perth

$$$ | HOTEL | FAMILY | Experience the trendy and bohemian feel of Subiaco with a stay at Vibe, a TFE (Toga Far East Hotels) managed lifestyle hotel just minutes from the train station. **Pros:** views of Perth CBD, Subiaco, and Kings Park; close to shopping, restaurants, cafés; rooftop pool. **Cons:** some rooms have a shower only; pool closes at 7 pm; parking is extra. $ *Rooms from: A$239* ✉ *9 Alvan St., Subiaco* ☎ *08/6282–9000* 🌐 *vibehotels.com* *No Meals* *168 rooms.*

Nightlife

Perth's inner city has gone through a significant revitalization; it's now a hotbed of classy small bars that buzz until midnight and later. Twenty- and thirtysomethings also flock to Northbridge, Leederville,

The London Court shopping mall facade at Hay Walking Street, Perth

Mount Lawley, Subiaco, and Fremantle. Pubs generally close by midnight, which is when the crowds start arriving at the nightclubs; these tend to stay open until the wee hours.

Details on cultural events in Perth are published in *Weekend West Australian, The Sunday Times,* and *xpressmag.com.au*, listing music, concerts, movies, entertainment reviews, and who's playing at pubs, clubs, and hotels. Additionally, *SCOOP* digital magazine (*scoop.com.au*) is an excellent guide to the essential Western Australian lifestyle.

BARS

Mechanics Institute

COCKTAIL LOUNGES | This rooftop haunt is furnished with market umbrellas and upcycled bench tables, which make it both welcoming and hip. In 2021, a brand-new retractable roof keeps the deck, and patrons, dry when it rains. Access to this happening bar is via a rear lane coated in street art, adding to the intrigue. With upward of 30 craft beers, a rotating cocktail menu, and creative bartenders that know how to make just about any mixed drink known to man, it's a surefire bet for a good time. Owners, a husband-and-wife team, aimed to create a neighborhood atmosphere when they moved into the gritty urban suburb of Northbridge, and they have. ✉ *222 William St., at rear, Northbridge* ☎ *08/9228–4189* 🌐 *mechanicsinstitutebar.com.au.*

The Queens Tavern

PUBS | The Queens, as it's known locally, resides in an attention-grabbing colonial-style property that was built in 1899 and offers an excellent, thriving outdoor beer garden that features plenty of local and international craft brews. The upstairs bar has a relaxed lounge vibe, with DJs on Friday and Saturday. There is also free Wi-Fi throughout, leather sofas, and fireplaces burning in cooler months. ✉ *520 Beaufort St., Highgate* ☎ *08/9328–7267* 🌐 *thequeens.com.au.*

Subiaco Hotel

PUBS | Known as the Subi, this gastropub attracts a lively after-work crowd during the week—especially on Friday—and has an excellent, busy restaurant that serves sophisticated pub grub from the bar menu and elegant cuisine at the bistro. Built in 1897, this much-loved establishment is rich in history and drenched in true-blue Aussie vibes. ✉ *465 Hay St., Subiaco* ☎ *08/6118–6920* 🌐 *subiacohotel.com.au.*

JAZZ AND BLUES

The Ellington Jazz Club

LIVE MUSIC | Inspired by the New York jazz scene, The Ellington is *the* place for jazz in Perth. It may not have curb appeal but this place hops seven nights a week in an intimate and sophisticated setting. A low-key tapas menu is available; be prepared to share a table with other patrons for sold-out performances. Entrance fees apply and it's best to reserve your tickets online in advance. ✉ *191 Beaufort St., Northbridge* ☎ *08/9228–1088* 🌐 *ellington-jazz.com.au.*

★ **Storehouse Subiaco**

COCKTAIL LOUNGES | For a night full of cocktails, elegant eats, and views for miles, get dressed up and head to Storehouse Subiaco. Located on the ninth floor of the Vibe hotel, this trendy rooftop bar is the place to be and be seen on a Friday or Saturday night. A sizeable drinks menu and tasty bar and terrace food menu let you linger over sunset and well into the night. Happy hour beer and house wine start at $6 4–6 pm daily. ✉ *9 Alvan St., Subiaco* ☎ *08/6282–9000* 🌐 *vibehotels.com.*

Performing Arts

Ticketek

CONCERTS | This is the main booking agent in Perth for the performing arts. It operates solely online, though there are several physical box offices at arts venues such as the Perth Convention Exhibition Centre, the State Theatre, and His Majesty's Theatre in the CBD. Booking fees will be added to the price of tickets. ✉ *Perth* 🌐 *premier.ticketek.com.au.*

Rockin' in Perth

Thanks to pop, rock, and metal bands like Eskimo Joe, the John Butler Trio, the Waifs, Karnivool, Little Birdy, San Cisco, and the Sleepy Jackson—who all started in Perth—the music scene here is thriving. Despite—or perhaps because of—their isolation from the rest of Australia, Western Australian musicians are turning out some top-notch material. Music commentators claim there isn't a "Perth sound" as such, just a talented bunch of artists writing and performing original music.

BALLET

West Australian Ballet Company

BALLET | This world-class ballet company has earned an international reputation for excellence due to its overall innovation and creativity. Its diverse repertoire includes new, full-length story ballets, cutting-edge contemporary dance, and classical and neoclassical ballets. Performances are held throughout Perth, including at His Majesty's Theatre, the atmospheric Quarry Amphitheatre, and the State Theatre Centre. They can even organize adult ballet classes. ✉ *134 Whatley Crescent, Maylands* ☎ *08/9214–0707* 🌐 *waballet.com.au.*

CINEMA

★ **Rooftop Movies**

FILM | Perth's first—and only—rooftop cinema opened after a summer trial run sold out night after night. It's now one of the city's anticipated seasonal venues. Crowning a seven-story car park, it shows mainstream blockbusters—with the odd cult or classic film thrown in for good measure—on a giant movie screen. It's the perfect date night, complete with a romantic sunset. There's a booze, food, and candy bars, but self-packed picnic baskets are welcome. No BYO alcohol. ■ **TIP→ Movies run each night, except Monday, during the warmer months of November through March, weather permitting.** ✉ *Roe St. car park, access off 129 James St., Northbridge ✣ Drive in at 68 Roe St., Northbridge; walk in off James St., opposite Northbridge Piazza, and take elevator to top* ☎ *08/9227–6288* 🌐 *rooftopmovies.com.au* 🎫 *From A$16.*

CONCERTS

Perth Concert Hall

CONCERTS | A starkly rectangular building overlooking the Swan River in the city center, the Perth Concert Hall stages regular plays, comedy acts, musicals, and recitals by the excellent West Australian Symphony Orchestra, as well as Australian and international performers. It's particularly busy during the Perth Festival. Adding to the appeal of the fine auditorium is the 3,000-pipe organ surrounded by a 160-person choir gallery. ■ **TIP→ The hall is said to have the best acoustics in Australia.** ✉ *5 St. Georges Terr., CBD* ☎ *08/9231–9900* 🌐 *perthconcerthall.com.au.*

OPERA

West Australian Opera Company

OPERA | The West Australian Opera Company presents three seasons annually—generally in February, July, and October, though this may change each year—at His Majesty's Theatre. It also performs the free Opera in the Park in Perth's Supreme Court Gardens each February. Although it is a free event, you must register online for a ticket to present upon arrival. The company's repertoire includes classic opera and operettas. ✉ *His Majesty's Theatre, 825 Hay St., CBD* ☎ *08/9278–8999 information* 🌐 *www.waopera.asn.au.*

Shopping

Shopping in Perth, with its pedestrian-friendly central business district, vehicle-free malls, and many covered arcades, is a delight. Hay Street Mall and Murray Street Mall are the main city shopping areas with large department stores, linked by numerous arcades with small shops; up the far western end is King Street and its glitzy international stores including Louis Vuitton, Tiffany & Co., and Gucci. Head to Northbridge's William Street for hipster and local designer boutiques. In the suburbs, top retail strips include Napoleon Street in Cottesloe for classic, beachy clothing, and housewares; Claremont Quarter in Claremont for fashion-forward garments; Oxford Street in Leederville for edgy threads and unique knickknacks; and Beaufort Street in Mount Lawley for idiosyncratic finds.

Australian souvenirs and iconic buys are on sale at small shops throughout the city and suburbs.

ART AND CRAFT GALLERIES

Creative Native

CRAFTS | You can find authentic Aboriginal artifacts at Creative Native with an extensive selection of Aboriginal art. Each piece of original artwork comes with a certificate of authenticity and royalties are paid to all artists. Painted boomerangs, didgeridoo, and dishes make wonderful gifts and lasting souvenirs of your holiday Down Under. ■ **TIP→ Commissioned work available.** ✉ *Forrest Chase, 158 Murray St., Shop 58, CBD* ☎ *08/9221–5800* 🌐 *creativenative.com.au.*

★ Maalinup Aboriginal Gallery

SOUVENIRS | **FAMILY** | Find true Aboriginal art here, as well as gifts and souvenirs, including soaps, bath, and beauty products, featuring Australian native plants. Oils and clays are made on-site and native Australian foods and flavors known as bush tucker is available to sample and buy. The gallery is owned and operated by local Aboriginal people who are branching out to include Aboriginal cultural experiences such as bush-tucker talks and tastings. ✉ *10070 W. Swan Rd., Henley Brook* ☎ *041/111–2450* 🌐 *maalinup.com.au.*

Mossenson Galleries

ART GALLERIES | Get your fill of authentic Aboriginal art—far more than just dot paintings—by viewing one of the solo or group-curated exhibitions by emerging and established artists and communities at the Mossenson Galleries, which has been one of Australia's leading Indigenous commercial galleries since 1993. The gallery is open on Saturday 11–4. ✉ *115 Hay St., Subiaco* ☎ *0413/803–998* 🌐 *mossensongalleries.com.au.*

CLOTHING

R. M. Williams

MIXED CLOTHING | This shop sells everything for the Australian bushman—and woman—including moleskin pants, hand-tooled leather boots, Akubra hats, and their characteristic cobalt blue shirts. **TIP→ Design your own boots with their bespoke footwear service.** ✉ *Carillon City Centre, Hay St., Shop 38, CBD* ☎ *08/9321–7786* 🌐 *rmwilliams.com.au.*

DEPARTMENT STORES AND SHOPPING CENTERS

Claremont Quarter

MALL | For a mix of designer threads, high fashion, and comfy staples, head to this shiny enclosed shopping center. You'll find gorgeous Australian beauty products by Aesop; classic garments at Country Road; mature but glam women's wear at Carla Zampatti; activewear at Lorna Jane; swimwear at Seafolly; cosmetics at Mecca Comestica; and high-end everything at David Jones—they're all Australian. For international brands, seek out Chanel, French Connection, and Lululemon. There are half a dozen chic cafés, too—get a chocolate hit at Koko Black and great *yum cha* at Yamato Kaiten Sushi. ✉ *9 Bayview Terr., Claremont* ☎ *08/9286–5885* 🌐 *www.claremontquarter.com.au.*

David Jones

DEPARTMENT STORE | This classy department store opens onto the Murray Street pedestrian mall. Inside you'll find a wide range of designer clothing, shoes, bags, accessories, makeup and beauty items, perfume, housewares, and gift ideas. ✉ *622 Murray St., CBD* ☎ *08/9210–4000* 🌐 *davidjones.com.*

Myer

DEPARTMENT STORE | This popular upmarket department store, Australia's largest, carries all manner of goods and sundries, along with Australian brands. You can find some bargains on the clothing sale racks. ✉ *Murray St. Mall, at Forrest Pl., CBD* ☎ *08/9265–5600* 🌐 *www.myer.com.au.*

Activities

BICYCLING

Perth's climate and its network of excellent trails make cycling a safe and enjoyable way to discover the city. But beware: summer temperatures can exceed 40°C (100°F) in the shade. A bicycle helmet is required by law, and carrying water is prudent. Free brochures detailing trails, including stops at historic spots, are available from the Western Australia Visitor Centre.

About Bike Hire

BIKING | FAMILY | Rent everything from regular bicycles to tandems, electric bikes, e-scooters, family quads, and caboose carriers for the kids and discover Perth by bike. Kayaks and SUP boards can be rented, too. The company does drop-offs and pickups for those wanting to trail ride or venture further afield, and it also offers a bike repair service. ✉ *Point Fraser Reserve, 305 Riverside Dr., East Perth* ☎ *08/9221–2665* 🌐 *aboutbikehire.com.au* ☞ *From $A10.*

SURFING

Western Australians take to the surf from a young age—and with world-famous surfing beaches right on the city's doorstep, it's no wonder. The most popular year-round beaches for body- and board surfing are Scarborough and Trigg, where waves can reach 6 to 9 feet. There are also more than a dozen beaches heading north from Leighton (near Fremantle), including the Cables Artificial Reef (near Leighton) and Watermans (in the northern suburbs of Perth). Cottesloe Beach is favored by novice surfers and children; south of the groyne (a man-made breakwater or jetty) is popular with stand-up paddleboard riders.

Outside the city, Rottnest Island's west end has a powerful surf, and south of the mainland coast are more than 30 surf locations from Cape Naturaliste to Cape Leeuwin. Main Break at Surfer's Point in the Margaret River region is the best known, where waves often roll in at more than 12 feet.

Wet suits are de rigueur for the colder months (May through September) when the surf is usually at its best.

TIP→ Great white sharks frequent this coastline.

Scarborough Beach Surf School

SURFING | FAMILY | These surfer dudes have been pushing beginners out into the white water since 1986. They specialize in adult lessons at Scarborough Beach in summer and Leighton Beach (*see* Fremantle) in winter but also provide separate kiddy lessons, or family groups, too. If you want to get serious, there are several levels you can complete, and when you do, you'll be able to call yourself a real surfer. Courses run daily; participant conditions and minimum age restrictions apply (see website). **TIP→ Courses sell out one week in advance so book ahead.** ✉ *The Esplanade, Scarborough* ☎ *08/9448–9937* 🌐 *www.surfschool.com* ☞ *Lessons from A$70.*

Catching Waves 

Western Australians adore the beach. During the summer months you'll find thousands of them lazing on sandy beaches, swimming, and surfing. Serious board surfers head to the rugged coastline from Cape Naturaliste to Cape Leeuwin. Favorite big surf breaks are Surfer's Point, Lefthanders, Three Bears, Grunters, Cow Bombie, Bunker Bay Bombie, Moses Rock, the Guillotine, the Farm, Boneyards, and Supertubes. Check 🌐 *www.seabreeze.com.au* for up-to-date wind and wave reports.

WATER SPORTS

Funcats Watersports

WATER SPORTS | FAMILY | If you want to enjoy the Swan River at a leisurely pace and possibly spot its resident dolphins, rent a 14-foot catamaran, kayak, or a stand-up paddleboard (SUP) from Funcats Watersports. Funcats has been hiring out water-sports equipment since 1976. It operates from September through April; instruction and life jackets are included. Minimum ages apply. ✉ *Coode St. Jetty, South Perth* ☎ *0408/926–003* 🌐 *funcats.com.au* ☞ *From A$25.*

WA Surf

SURFING | Perth has consistent winds, particularly in the afternoons, so it's one of the best places to learn to kite surf. WA Surf gives lessons in kitesurfing year-round on the shores of Safety Bay, just south of Perth, where the water is flat and calm. As people improve, kites increase in size, adding more power to their ride, so it can be as extreme or as mellow as you like. Safety systems are built-in, so you can be detached from your kite in a couple of seconds if you get into trouble. Most people opt for a series of three, two-hour lessons, but tricks can be taught to old hands, too. ✉ *Safety Bay Yacht Club, Safety Bay Rd. at Arcadia Dr., Safety Bay* ☎ *08/9592–1657* 🌐 *wasurf.com.au* ⏲ *Closed May–Aug.* ☞ *From A$195.*

Fremantle

About 19 km (12 miles) southwest of Perth.

The port city of Fremantle is a jewel in Western Australia's crown, largely because of its colonial architectural heritage and hippie vibe. Freo (as the locals call it) is a city of largely friendly, interesting, eccentric residents supportive of busking, street art, and alfresco dining. Like all great port cities, Freo is cosmopolitan, with mariners from all parts of the world strolling the streets—including thousands of U.S. Navy personnel on rest and recreation throughout the year. It's also a good jumping-off point for a day trip to Rottnest Island, where lovely beaches, rocky coves, and unique wallaby-like inhabitants called quokkas set the scene. These cute little marsupials have become world-famous for their picture-posing abilities and antics.

Modern Fremantle is a far cry from the barren, sandy plain that greeted the first wave of English settlers back in 1829 at the newly constituted Swan River Colony. Most were city dwellers, and after five months at sea in sailing ships they landed on salt-marsh flats that sorely tested their fortitude. Living in tents with packing cases for chairs, they found no edible crops, and the nearest freshwater was a distant 51 km (32 miles)—and a tortuous trip up the waters of the Swan. As a result they soon moved the settlement upriver to the vicinity of present-day Perth.

Fremantle remained the principal port, and many attractive limestone buildings were built to service the port traders. Australia's 1987 defense of the America's Cup—held in waters off Fremantle—triggered a major restoration of the colonial streetscapes. In the leafy suburbs nearly every other house is a restored 19th-century gem.

GETTING HERE AND AROUND

Bus information for service from Perth is available from Transperth (136–213, transperth.wa.gov.au). The Central Area Bus Service (CAT) provides free transportation around Fremantle in orange buses. The route begins and ends outside the Fremantle Bus/Train Station, and stops include the Arts Centre, the cappuccino strip, and the Fremantle Market. CAT buses run every 10 minutes weekdays 7:30–6:30, and 10–6:30 on weekends and public holidays.

Trains bound for Fremantle depart from Perth approximately every 15–30 minutes from the Perth Station on Wellington Street. You can travel from Perth to Fremantle (or vice versa) in about 30 minutes. Tickets must be purchased at the ticket vending machines prior to travel.

If you are driving from downtown Perth, the most direct route is via Stirling Highway, from the foot of Kings Park; it will take about 35 minutes, depending on traffic.

TAXI CONTACTS Black & White. ☎ *133–222.* **Swan Taxis.** ☎ *131–330.*

SAFETY AND PRECAUTIONS

Fremantle is generally a safe destination and popular with families, particularly on weekends and during the school holidays. It also has a lively nightlife, and late-night crowds leaving pubs and clubs can—and do—cause problems. Always be aware of your surroundings. Taxis and rideshare operators are in high demand late at night when other public transport stops operating.

TIMING

Fremantle can easily be visited in a day from Perth, though if you want to head over to Rottnest Island you will have to add an extra day. Most of the sights are clustered in a relatively small area along Market Street and South Terrace, and close to the Fishing Boat Harbour. A walking tour is the best way to see the highlights in a short time.

ESSENTIALS

VISITOR INFORMATION Fremantle Visitor Centre. ✉ *Town Hall Walyalup Koort, 8 Williams St., Fremantle* ☎ *08/9431–7878* 🌐 *visitfremantle.com.au.*

Sights

An ideal place to start a leisurely stroll is South Terrace, known as the Fremantle cappuccino strip. Wander alongside locals through sidewalk cafés or browse in bookstores, art galleries, and souvenir shops until you reach the Fremantle Markets. From South Terrace walk down to the Fishing Boat Harbour, where there's always activity—commercial and pleasure craft bob about, and along the timber boardwalk is a cluster of outdoor eateries and a huge microbrewery.

Between Phillimore Street and Marine Terrace in the West End is a collection of some of the best-preserved heritage buildings in the state. The Fremantle Railway Station on Elder Place is another good spot to start a walk. Maps and details for 11 different self-guided walks are available at the Fremantle Visitor Center; a popular heritage walk is the Convict Trail, passing by 18 different sights and locations from Fremantle's convict past.

Fremantle Arts Centre

ART GALLERY | FAMILY | Like most of Fremantle, the Gothic-looking Fremantle Arts Centre (FAC) was built by convicts in the 19th century. First used as a lunatic asylum, by 1900 it was overcrowded and nearly shut down. It became a home for elderly women until 1942, when the U.S. Navy turned it into its local submarine base in WWII. As one of Australia's leading arts organizations, FAC has an engaging, year-round cultural program. There are also dynamic exhibitions, a gift shop, and an expansive live music and special events program, which includes free live music on Sunday afternoon from October to March; people like to bring picnics and blankets but there's also an on-site bar-café. ✉ *1 Finnerty St., Fremantle* ☎ *08/9432–9555* 🌐 *fac.org.au* 🎟 *Free.*

★ Fremantle Markets

MARKET | FAMILY | The eclectic, artsy, and always bustling Fremantle Markets have been housed in this huge Victorian building since 1897 and sell everything from WA landscape photographs to incense, freshly roasted coffee, toys, clothing, and fruit and vegetables. You can also get a delicious array of street food, such as Turkish *gözleme,* German sausages, doughnuts, chocolate cake, and fresh-squeezed orange juice. Around 150 stalls attract a colorful mix of locals and tourists. ✉ *South Terr., at Henderson St., Fremantle* ☎ *08/9335–2515* 🌐 *fremantlemarkets.com.au.*

★ Fremantle Prison

JAIL/PRISON | FAMILY | One of the most popular tourist attractions in the state, prison day tours illustrate convict life—including (successful) escapes and the art cell, where a superb collection of drawings by prisoner James Walsh decorates his former quarters. The jail was built by convicts in the 1850s and is an important part of the region's history. Choose from a variety of tours, including a goosebump-inducing one by flashlight or a thrilling underground tour for which visitors are provided with hard hats, boots, and headlamps before descending 65 feet into the labyrinthine tunnels. Climbing (and a sense of adventure) is a must! ✉ *1 The Terrace, Fremantle* ☎ *08/9336–9200* 🌐 *fremantleprison.com.au* 🎟 *From A$22.*

Fremantle Round House

NOTABLE BUILDING | FAMILY | An eye-catching landmark of early Fremantle atop an ocean-facing cliff, the Round House was built in 1831 by convicts to house other convicts. This curious, 12-sided building is the state's oldest surviving public structure. Its ramparts have great vistas spanning from High Street to the Indian Ocean. Underneath, a tunnel was carved through the cliffs in the mid-1800s to give ships lying at anchor easy access from town. From the tunnel you can walk to the calm and quiet Bathers Beach, where there used to be a whaling station, and listen for the firing of the cannon at 1 pm daily. Volunteer guides are on duty during opening hours. ✉ *West end of High St., Fremantle* ☎ *08/9336–6897* 🌐 *fremantleroundhouse.com.au* 🎫 *Gold coin donation.*

★ **Little Creatures Brewery**

BREWERY | Little Creatures has got a lot going for it—including its harborside location and fun-loving, artsy vibe. Regarded as the founders of craft beer in WA, a tour of this iconic brewery is a must. The tour includes a beer-making 101 session, a jaunt around the brewery, and a sample of the current brews and ciders on tap with one of their informative Hop Heads. If you like what you see and taste, stay on in the Brewhouse, where you'll find contemporary pub grub on the menu or book a table in the lively Great Hall for dinner overlooking the harbor. ✉ *40 Mews Rd., Fremantle* ☎ *08/6215–1000* 🌐 *littlecreatures.com.au* 🎫 *A$25 tour.*

★ **Tourist Wheel Fremantle**

AMUSEMENT RIDE | FAMILY | On the harbor side of Esplanade Park sits the gigantic Tourist Wheel, a 24-enclosed-car Ferris wheel offering spectacular views of the port city, Indian Ocean, and Rottnest Island on a clear day. Each gondola holds six people and spins for about 10 minutes per ticket. Be sure to have your camera ready when you stop at the top, 40 meters above the grounds. ✉ *35 Mews Rd., Fremantle* ☎ *1300/130–704* 🌐 *touristwheelfremantle.com.au* 🎫 *A$12.*

★ **Western Australian Maritime Museum**

NAUTICAL SIGHT | FAMILY | Resembling an upside-down boat, the Western Australian Maritime Museum sits at the edge of Fremantle Harbour. It houses *Australia II,* winner of the 1983 America's Cup, and has hands-on, rotating exhibits that are great fun for children. You can also take guided tours of the *Ovens,* a former Royal Australian Navy World War II submarine. Another attraction is the Welcome Walls, a record of all those who immigrated to WA via ship during the major postwar migration. A five-minute walk away on Cliff Street in a separate, heritage building, is the Shipwreck Galleries, home to more fascinating maritime history. ✉ *West end of Victoria Quay, Fremantle* ☎ *1300/134–081* 🌐 *museum.wa.gov.au/maritime* 🎫 *From A$15.*

Beaches

Bathers Beach

BEACH | FAMILY | Sometimes, good things come in small packages. This flat, soft-sand beach sits hidden between the Fishing Boat Harbour and the Roundhouse and is an ideal spot to picnic with takeout fish-and-chips, or to enjoy a sunset cocktail from Bathers Beachhouse, the only restaurant licensed to serve drinks on the beach. **Amenities:** food and drink. **Best for:** solitude; sunset; swimming; walking. ✉ *Behind Roundhouse, accessed via Fleet St. or Mews Rd., Fremantle* 🎫 *Free.*

Leighton Beach

BEACH | FAMILY | South of busy Cottesloe and about 30 minutes from central Perth, Leighton is a relatively quiet beach loved for its sugarlike sand and flat, calm water, which is perfect for those who like to paddle. It's equally loved by wind- and kite-surfers on windy days, who tear across the tabletop surface. At the northern end of the beach, dogs are allowed to be off-leash, so expect to see lots of happy pooches running around. **Amenities:** lifeguards (summer); parking; toilets; food and drink. **Best for:** snorkeling; swimming; sunset; walking; windsurfing. ✉ *Leighton Beach Blvd., North Fremantle* 🌐 *beachsafe.org.au.*

Port Beach

BEACH | **FAMILY** | A local favorite, wide Port Beach has small, gentle waves; water the color of a Bombay Sapphire bottle; and pale white sand. It butts up against Fremantle Harbour's North Quay wharf and stretches towards Leighton. Like most of the western-facing coast, the sunsets are epic and the views of Rottnest charming. **Amenities:** food and drink; toilets; lifeguards; parking. **Best for:** snorkeling; sunset; swimming; walking; windsurfing. ✉ *Port Beach Rd., North Fremantle* 🌐 *beachsafe.org.au.*

Restaurants

Bread in Common

$$ | **MODERN AUSTRALIAN** | This industrial-chic bakery-cum-restaurant wins the award for hottest interior in town, with dozens of vintage-style globes streaming from the warehouse ceiling or looping in red electrical cord over suspended beams. Herb boxes line the 1890s heritage facade, while out back the wood-fired ovens, affectionately named Hansel and Gretel, pump out organic bread. **Known for:** comfort food like crispy duck-fat roasted potatoes; delicious smells wafting from the bakery; noisy, lively atmosphere, especially on weekends. $ *Average main: A$30* ✉ *43 Pakenham St., Fremantle* ☎ *044/958–8040* 🌐 *breadincommon.com.au.*

Capri Restaurant

$$ | **ITALIAN** | **FAMILY** | The Pizzale family has owned and run this Freo restaurant for more than 50 years and it's here where you'll be treated to an old-style Italian meal. Don't expect flashy decor or fancy lighting—the focus is on the food. **Known for:** home-style cooking; complimentary soup and bread with main meals; a favorite among longtime locals. $ *Average main: A$30* ✉ *21 South Terr., Fremantle* ☎ *08/9335–1399* 🌐 *caprirestaurantfremantle.com* ⏲ *No lunch Mon.*

Char Char

$$$ | **STEAKHOUSE** | Waterfront Fremantle is renowned for its seafood restaurants, so going to a harborside venue for steak seems almost irreverent, but meat lovers revel in the juicy steak selection at Char Char. They dropped the "bull" from their name but you'll still get a fine piece of meat, cooked to perfection, here. **Known for:** tables on the deck; epic harbor views from floor-to-ceiling windows; beef tartare with harissa sour creme. $ *Average main: A$42* ✉ *Fishing Boat Harbour, 44b Mews Rd., Fremantle* ☎ *08/9335–7666* 🌐 *charcharrb.com.au.*

Cicerello's

$$ | **SEAFOOD** | **FAMILY** | No visit to Fremantle is complete without a stop at this locally famous fish-and-chippery that was once featured on a postage stamp. Housed in a boathouse-style building fronting Fremantle's lovely Fishing Boat Harbour, this joint serves the real thing: fresh oysters, mussels, crabs, fish, lobsters, and crispy chips. **Known for:** long lines most lunch hours; massive aquariums with more than 100 species of marine life; large portions. $ *Average main: A$25* ✉ *Fisherman's Wharf, 44 Mews Rd., Fremantle* ☎ *08/9335–1911* 🌐 *cicerellos.com.au.*

Gino's Café

$$ | **ITALIAN** | **FAMILY** | The original owner, the late Gino Saccone, was so passionate about coffee that he closed his tailor shop to open this cappuccino-strip property with a busy alfresco terrace. Now, the iconic café insists it serves the best coffee in Perth, and let's face it, it's pretty good—plus you can get a bowl of soul-comforting pasta or authentic cannoli. **Known for:** old-school service; Gino's Blend coffee beans, available to take home; handmade pasta. $ *Average main: A$28* ✉ *1–5 South Terr., at Collie St., Fremantle* ☎ *08/9336–1464* 🌐 *ginos-cafe.com.au.*

Joe's Fish Shack

$$ | **SEAFOOD** | **FAMILY** | This Fremantle restaurant looks like everyone's vision of a run-down, weather-beaten Maine diner. With uninterrupted harbor views, authentic nautical bric-a-brac, and great food, you can't go wrong. **Known for:** steamed WA crayfish; popular local spot; harbor views. $ *Average main: A$32* ✉ *42 Mews Rd., Fremantle* ☎ *08/9336–7161* 🌐 *joesfishshack.com.au.*

★ La Sosta

$$$ | **ITALIAN** | It begins as temptation as your senses are teased by the smells wafting from the open kitchen. Rosemary, chili, oregano, olive oil, and tomato scents will drive you crazy until your own meal lands in front of you. **Known for:** Italian-speaking staff; group cooking classes; melt-in-your-mouth gnocchi. $ *Average main: A$40* ✉ *85 Market St., Level 1, Fremantle* ☎ *08/9335–9193* 🌐 *lasosta.net.au* ⏲ *Closed Mon. and Tues. No lunch Wed. and Thurs.*

★ Moore and Moore Café

$$ | **MODERN AUSTRALIAN** | You'll know this clean-living café by the retro bikes stacked out front next to the potted garden, the eclectic mix of people, and music that often streams from the doorway. The health-conscious food here is as tasty as the vibe is charming, and you can expect organic eggs, nitrate-free bacon with sides of chickpeas or spinach, and coffee alternatives like beetroot lattes and chai tea. **Known for:** delicious vegetarian and vegan options; an all-day brunch menu; no-scrambled-eggs policy. $ *Average main: A$21* ✉ *46 Henry St., Fremantle* ☎ *08/9335–8825* 🌐 *mooreand-moorecafe.com.*

Mother Fremantle

$$ | **VEGETARIAN** | A large, open space, exposed brick, timber beams, high ceilings, and funky booth seating give way to a warehouse feel at this plant-based, dairy-free, gluten-free, refined-sugar-free, vegetarian, and vegan eatery. If you commonly say *yes* to meals like pumpkin mash, ramen noodles, and coconut curry and *no* to bottled water, plastic straws, and excess waste, then you'll surely love this bohemian-vibe restaurant. **Known for:** sustainable living practices; amazing raw peanut butter; preservative-free organic wines. $ *Average main: A$25* ✉ *181 High St., Fremantle* ☎ *08/9433–4647* 🌐 *motherfremantle.com.au/* ⏲ *Closed Mon. and Tues. No dinner Sun.*

Ootong & Lincoln

$ | **MODERN AUSTRALIAN** | **FAMILY** | You'll recognize this place by its giant, multicolor zebra mural on the external wall, which was commissioned by a local artist. Inside, take a seat at one of the colorful communal tables that are surrounded by dividers made from plumbing pipes and then enjoy classic and healthy café eats like Bircher muesli, free-range eggs, burgers, or Ootong & Lincoln's ever-popular coffee-and-cake special. **Known for:** smushed avocado on quinoa or linseed toast (an Aussie favorite); made-from-scratch meals; potato cake, served with poached eggs and hollandaise. $ *Average main: A$17* ✉ *258 South Terr., South Fremantle* ☎ *08/9335–6109* 🌐 *www.facebook.com/ootongandlincoln.*

Hotels

★ Be. Fremantle

$$ | **APARTMENT** | **FAMILY** | Immerse yourself in Fremantle's boat-loving history with a stay at this marina-side apartment-style accommodation with studios to three-bedroom flats. **Pros:** located in a quiet area; all rooms have water views; fully self-contained. **Cons:** walls are thin

in old section; no on-site restaurant or pool; limited paid parking. $ *Rooms from: A$185 ✉ 43 Mews Rd., Fremantle ☎ 08/9430–3888 ⊕ befremantle.com.au ⇆ 71 apartments 🍽 No Meals.*

Esplanade Hotel Fremantle—By Rydges
$$$ | HOTEL | FAMILY | Part of a colonial-era hotel, this huge, conveniently located establishment has balconies facing the park and nearby harbor, Essex Street, or the pool. **Pros:** ample dining and shopping options nearby; central to Fremantle attractions; two heated swimming pools. **Cons:** parking costs extra; functions can make venues crowded; sea views are limited to some rooms. $ *Rooms from: A$265 ✉ Marine Terr., at Essex St., Fremantle ☎ 08/9432–4000 ⊕ rydges.com ⇆ 300 rooms 🍽 No Meals.*

Fothergills of Fremantle
$$ | B&B/INN | Antiques, pottery, sculptures, bronzes, and paintings adorn these popular, two-story, 1892 limestone terrace houses opposite the old Fremantle prison. **Pros:** free Wi-Fi and parking; complimentary afternoon tea in dining room; personalized service. **Cons:** small bathrooms; no communal lounge room; cooked breakfast with direct bookings only. $ *Rooms from: A$175 ✉ 18–22 Ord St., Fremantle ☎ 08/9335–6784 ⊕ fothergills.net.au ⇆ 5 rooms 🍽 No Meals.*

Nautica Residences by Seashells
$$ | APARTMENT | Although aimed at the corporate traveler, this apartment-style accommodation offers a delightful base for vacationers, too. **Pros:** apartments are clean and tastefully decorated; free secure parking and Wi-Fi; luxury Australian-made bathroom amenities. **Cons:** upper floor may hear noise from the rooftop bar; residential building with no facilities or 24-hour front desk; about a mile away from central Fremantle. $ *Rooms from: A$179 ✉ 1 Silas St., East Fremantle, Fremantle ☎ 08/9387–0800 ⊕ nauticaresidences.com.au ⇆ 16 apartments 🍽 No Meals.*

The Cup

In 1848, Britain's Queen Victoria authorized the creation of a solid silver cup for a yacht race that would be "open to all nations." In 1851, the New York Yacht Club challenged 16 English yachts and won with the boat *America*. The United States continued to win for 132 years straight until the upstart *Australia II* won 4–3 in sensational style, and the Cup came to Fremantle. Australia was euphoric. Fremantle spruced up for the defense of the Cup in 1987, but the fairy tale ended in a 4–0 loss to the San Diego Yacht Club entrant. Today *Australia II* is a centerpiece display at the WA Maritime Museum.

Norfolk Hotel
$ | HOTEL | With an excellent location, leafy and lively beer garden, and a basement live music bar all part of its assets, this central accommodation is popular with the outgoing, fun-loving crowd. **Pros:** free CAT bus nearby; free parking in central location; free Wi-Fi. **Cons:** 10-minute walk to waterfront; potential noise from pub; shared facilities in some rooms. $ *Rooms from: A$150 ✉ 47 South Terr., Fremantle ☎ 08/9335–5405 ⊕ norfolkhotel.com.au ⇆ 9 rooms 🍽 No Meals.*

Port Mill Bed & Breakfast
$$$ | B&B/INN | Discreetly concealed in a picture-postcard courtyard reminiscent of Provence, this flour mill-turned-bed-and-breakfast contains four sunny, individually decorated suites, all named after ships—Batavia, Leeuwin, Zuytdorp, and Duyfken—and each with its own Juliet balcony. **Pros:** close to shopping, dining, and tourist attractions; Heritage-listed accommodation; free Wi-Fi. **Cons:** no pool or restaurant; two-story building has winding stairs and no elevator; parking nearby for A$11 per day. $ *Rooms from:*

A$220 ✉ *3/17 Essex St., Fremantle* ☎ *08/9433–3832* 🌐 *portmillbb.com.au* *4 suites* 🍴 *Free Breakfast.*

YHA Fremantle Prison

$ | **MOTEL** | This isn't your average holiday accommodation or place to sleep, it's an experience in one of Fremantle's most famous, and infamous, historical landmarks. **Pros:** great place to meet people; fantastic location within walking distance to central Fremantle; fraction of the price of a hotel. **Cons:** Wi-Fi in common areas only; limited free parking; it's haunted. [$] *Rooms from: A$96* ✉ *6A The Terrace, Fremantle* ☎ *08/9433–4305* 🌐 *yha.com.au* 🍴 *No Meals* ☞ *Dorm beds from A$25 per person* *202 beds.*

Nightlife

There's nothing more pleasant than relaxing in the evening at one of the sidewalk tables on the cappuccino strip. This area, along South Terrace, opens at 6 am and closes late when it's busy, but be sure to check out the side streets for the area's small bar scene, too. Travel further along South Street to South Fremantle for even more hopping bars, pubs, and top dining experiences.

Holy Smokes

BARS | This American-theme whiskey bar may be small, but it's packed with pizzazz and down-to-earth vibes. The original owners, a brother-and-sister team, were motivated to re-create some of the flavors and feels of a "back to roots" road trip to Missouri to visit Grandma. In late 2018, it changed ownership but the ambience is still the same. With more than 100 bourbons and other very American drops (think moonshine) at the ready, this boutique bar is the place for a quiet drink and some USA-inspired eats. **TIP→ Friday meal special is a $10 burger and fries.** ✉ *Collie St., Fremantle* ✣ *Between Marine Terr. and South Terr.* 🌐 *holysmokesfreo.com.au.*

★ **The Old Synagogue**

COCKTAIL LOUNGES | The Old Synagogue was built in 1902 and was the first synagogue in the state. Today, it's a happening hot spot consisting of four places to eat, drink, and be merry. Mr Chapple is a cozy small bar perfect for meet-ups; The Abor is a massive beer garden that can pack in up to 500 party-seekers; Tonic & Ginger is a trendy split-level Asian-fusion dining room; and last but certainly not least is L'Chaim, a supercool, retro-looking lounge that is hidden within the wooden walls of the basement. Can you find it? ✉ *92 South Terr., Fremantle* ☎ *08/6370–4433* 🌐 *theoldsynagogue.com.au.*

Sail and Anchor Pub

PUBS | Thanks to its selection of craft beers and right-in-the-middle-of-it location, the Heritage-listed Sail and Anchor Pub is one of Australia's most popular watering holes. You can watch buskers from the balcony, enjoy live music in the front bar, watch the game or UFC, and partake of no-nonsense pub grub at the bistro. There are comfy couches upstairs. ✉ *64 South Terr., Fremantle* ☎ *08/9431–1666* 🌐 *sailandanchor.com.au.*

Shopping

Japingka Gallery

ART GALLERIES | For more than 30 years, the owners of this gallery have been dedicated to the fair work trade of Aboriginal artists, so rest assured, when you purchase a piece of local art here, you are giving back to a community. You'll find traditional dot painting, as well as contemporary creatives here. Insured worldwide shipping is available. ✉ *47 High St., Fremantle* ☎ *08/9335–8265* 🌐 *japingka.com.au.*

Key Sole Fremantle

SHOES | **FAMILY** | There's no better or practical Aussie souvenir than a pair of warm and wooly, genuine Ugg boots, and Key Sole Fremantle sells them at its three locations around Fremantle. It also stocks famed Australian brands like Crocs and Emu. It's easy to miss their High Street location so look for the sign that simply says KS and the store full of Ugg boots. You can also buy online. ✉ *103 High St., Fremantle* ☎ *08/9433–3714* 🌐 *keysole.com.*

★ New Edition

BOOKS | Bookworms and word nerds will adore this delightful bookshop on the corner of High and Henry Streets in the middle of Fremantle's shopping district. Besides a generous selection of books spanning all genres, including travel, you'll find funny greeting cards, games, puzzles, journals, Moleskine notebooks, gift wrap, and quirky stationery. ✉ *41 High St., Fremantle* ☎ *08/9335–2383* 🌐 *newedition.com.au.*

Rottnest Island

19 km (12 miles) west of Fremantle.

An easy 30-minute cruise from Fremantle, or about two hours down the Swan River from Perth, sunny, quirky Rottnest Island makes an ideal day trip. The Aboriginal word for the island is Wadjemup, which means "place where spirits go," but it's known to locals as "Rotto." The former penal colony, boys' reformatory, and war base is as much a part of Western Australia as mine sites, colorful entrepreneurs, and untouched beaches. Its strange moniker—translated to mean rat's nest—can be attributed to 17th-century Dutch explorers who mistook the native marsupials called quokkas for cat-size rats.

Much of the island's charm lies in the fact it's largely car-free—so rent a bike to make the most of it. The island has an interesting past, which is evident in its historic buildings. Though records of human occupation date back 6,000-some years, European settlement only dates back to 1829. Since then the island has been used for a variety of purposes, including attempts at agriculture and for military purposes in both the Great War and World War II. The Rottnest Museum was renamed Wadjemup—the Aboriginal name for the island—as part of an ongoing Reconciliation Action Plan in 2021 and is a great place to get the history. Your history lesson is further enhanced by the many free daily tours run by volunteers. You can also take a train trip and tour to Oliver Hill to see gun emplacements from World War II.

Of course, most West Australians go to the island for the beaches, the swimming, and the laid-back atmosphere on Perth's doorstep. A warm ocean current passes by Rottnest, allowing it to host an unusual mix of tropical and temperate marine life. In fact, it's home to 135 species of tropical fish and 20 species of coral, and even the air temperature is warmer than on the mainland.

GETTING HERE AND AROUND

A number of operators run light plane and helicopter flights to Rottnest Island, but most people take the ferry. Check the Rottnest Island Visitor Information Centre website for other options.

There are no taxis on Rottnest Island. Almost everyone rides bikes, which can either be rented when booking your ferry ticket, or once you arrive, at Pedal & Flipper.

CONTACTS

Rottnest Air Taxi

This speedy, on-demand air service to Rottnest Island flies from Perth's Jandakot Airport and offers amazing views of Perth's holiday jewel sitting pretty in the Indian Ocean. Flights are around 12 minutes, are weather-dependent, and the price depends on how many passengers are on board. Joy flights over Rottnest or Perth and its surrounding beaches are also available. Bookings are essential. ☎ *0421/389–831* 🌐 *rottnestairtaxi.com.au.*

Snorkeling at the Basin on Rottnest Island, Western Australia

Rottnest Express
Rottnest Express is the main operator running ferries to Rottnest Island from two locations in Fremantle and from central Perth, which includes a scenic cruise along the Swan River. Add a bicycle to your ticket and save the line-ups on the island. They also offer a thrilling, seasonal eco-marine tour that gets you up close to whales, fur seals, and seabirds. ✉ *Pier 2, Barrack St. Jetty, Perth* ☎ *1300/467–688* 🌐 *rottnestexpress.com.au.*

Rottnest Fast Ferries
Rottnest Fast Ferries runs a premium ferry service from Hillarys Boat Harbour, just north of Perth CBD. The ferries take approximately 45 minutes from Hillarys to Rottnest, with hotel pickups from Perth available. Round-trip prices include the Rottnest Island entry fee. Bike and snorkel packages are available at extra costs. Whale-watching tours, with an onboard marine biologist run from early September to late November. Whale sightings are guaranteed or you'll get to go again for free. ✉ *Shop 56, Southside Drive, Hillarys Boat Harbour, Perth* ☎ *08/9246–1039* 🌐 *rottnestfastferries.com.au.*

SAFETY AND PRECAUTIONS
Be sun-smart, especially from October through April. Even on cloudy days people unused to being outdoors for any length of time can suffer severe sunburn. Wear a hat, long-sleeved shirt, and high-strength sunscreen. If you are a weak or novice swimmer, always swim with a friend; lifesavers (lifeguards) patrol certain beaches during peak holiday periods.

TIMING
Rottnest Island can be visited in a day but it may feel rushed, depending on what you want to see and do. An early ferry gets you to the island with time to tour the main attractions or beaches, returning to Fremantle or Perth in the late afternoon. Staying an extra day or two gives you time to laze at a beach or go surfing or diving. The summer months (December– April) are the busiest and accommodation books up months in advance. Plan and reserve early.

TOURS

For those not keen or able to bike, there are other ways to see the island. Information is available from the Rottnest Island Visitor Centre.

Discovery Tour

For those not keen on biking or hop-on, hop-off buses, Rottnest Express runs a popular Discovery Tour that gives an overview of the island's activities, history, environment, and wildlife as it circumnavigates the island in about 90 minutes. Highlights of the tour are the salt lakes, Wadjemup Lighthouse, convict-built cottages, World War II gun emplacements, and the remote West End, where you'll get to stretch your legs and take photos. Tours depart daily from the Main Bus Stop at 11:20 am and 1:50 pm; tickets are available online. ✉ *Thomson Bay, Rottnest Island* ☎ *1300/467–688* 🌐 *rottnestexpress.com.au* 🎫 *A$49.*

Island Explorer

This service, which runs on a continuous hop-on, hop-off island circuit, picks up and drops off passengers at the most beautiful bays and beaches. Day tickets can be purchased from the Rottnest Island Visitor Centre, online, at ticket machines on the Island, or through bus operator, Adams. Timetables are published on bus stops around the island. ✉ *Thomson Bay, Henderson Ave., Rottnest Island* ☎ *08/6270–6060 local or outside Australia* 🌐 *rottnestisland.com* 🎫 *From A$20.*

The Oliver Hill Train

The Oliver Hill Railway made its debut in the mid-1990s, utilizing 6 km (4 miles) of reconstructed railway line to reach the island's World War II gun batteries. Known as the *Captain Hussey,* the Oliver Hill train is an ideal way to see the island. The route from the Main Settlement to Oliver Hill runs daily at 12:30, 1:30, and 2:30 and the first two departures connect with a guided tour of the historic Oliver Hill gun battery. Tickets are available at the visitor information center. ✉ *Thomson Bay, Rottnest Island* ☎ *08/9432–9300* 🌐 *rottnestisland.com* 🎫 *A$20.*

Skydive Geronimo

If you think Rottnest is beautiful from the water's edge, you should see it from 14,000 feet above while the wind rushes through your hair and adrenaline pumps through your bloodstream. Skydive Geronimo sells a boutique tandem skydiving experience that will catapult your island holiday to "Awesome!" status. Bookings essentials. ✉ *Rottnest Island Airport, Brand Way, Rottnest Island* ☎ *1300/449–669* 🌐 *skydivegeronimo.com.au* ☞ *From A$369.*

ESSENTIALS

VISITOR INFORMATION Rottnest Island Visitor Centre. ✉ *Thomson Bay beachfront, Rottnest Island* ☎ *08/9432–9300* 🌐 *rottnestisland.com.*

Sights

The most convenient way to get around Rottnest is by bicycle, as private cars are not allowed on the island. A self-guided bicycle tour of the island covers 26 km (16 miles) and can take as little as three hours, although you really need an entire day to enjoy the beautiful surroundings.

Heading south from Thomson Bay, between Government House and Herschell Lakes, you'll find the Quokka Walk and a man-made causeway, where you'll find a few quokka colonies. Continue south and to Oliver Hill and the Wadjemup Lighthouse, where tours are run every half hour from 10 am until 2:30 pm. As you continue to Bickley Bay you can spot the wreckage of ships—the oldest dates from 1842—that came to rest on Rottnest's rocky coastline.

Follow the main road past Porpoise, Salmon, Strickland, and Wilson bays to West End, the windiest point on the island and home to a harem of fur seals at Cathedral Rocks. Heading back to

Thomson Bay, the road passes a dozen rocky inlets and bays. Parakeet Bay, the prettiest, is at the northernmost tip of the island.

Wadjemup Museum

HISTORY MUSEUM | FAMILY | At the Thomson Bay settlement, don't miss the Wadjemup Museum, which includes mementos of the island's sometimes turbulent past. Staying true to local history, displays are housed in an old mill and hay store built in 1857, showing local geology, natural and social history, and maritime lore with a bunch of surprising facts. It's open daily from 10 am–3:30 pm. Other ways to learn all about the island's history include Wadjemup Lighthouse Tour. Find out what goes on within the confines of a working lighthouse and climb to the top of this Heritage structure for fabulous 360-degree views. Volunteers also offer free walking tours that include themes like prisoners and pioneers; reefs, wrecks, and sailors; and even a meet the quokkas walk. Meet at The Salt Store. ✉ *Thomson Bay, Digby Dr., at Kitson St., Rottnest Island* ☎ *08/9432–9300* 🌐 *rottnestisland.com* 🎫 *A$2 donation.*

Beaches

There are some 63 beaches on Rottnest Island, suitable for swimming, surfing, snorkeling, and diving. The most popular include Geordie Bay, Little Parakeet, Parker Point, Little Salmon Bay, and the Basin.

Surfers and body-boarders will head for Stark Bay, Strickland Bay (closed during fairy tern nesting season), and West End, while swimmers love the sandy-white beaches at Pinky Beach and the Basin. Beach spots for snorkeling and diving include Little Salmon Bay (it has underwater markers) and Parker Point.

The Basin

BEACH | FAMILY | This pool-like bay is one of Rottnest's most popular, both for its safe, shallow waters and proximity to the main settlement. Protected by an outer reef, the ocean is crystal clear, the waves are gentle, and little fish dart about. Major renovations in 2021 saw improvements to toilet blocks, shelters, barbecue facilities, and play spaces. **Amenities:** lifeguards; showers; toilets. **Best for:** snorkeling; swimming. ✉ *Northwest of Thomson Bay, Rottnest Island* 🌐 *rottnestisland.com.*

Geordie Bay

BEACH | FAMILY | Over the dunes is the whitest of white sand and the most azure waters of Geordie Bay. Photographed by many, this beach abuts a flat, motionless ocean that makes for safe swimming. A confetti of yachts spreads across the bay in the summer months (there are protected, boat-free swimming zones), and beachside accommodation mirrors the cove. Nearby, next to a minimart, find Geordie's Cafe and Art Gallery (*0402-990–870*), the only eatery in the bay. Open for breakfast, lunch, and dinner, it also serves many gluten-free dishes. Expect to see furry quokkas looking for scraps. **Amenities:** food and drink; showers; toilets. **Best for:** swimming. ✉ *Geordie Bay Rd., Rottnest Island* 🌐 *rottnestisland.com.*

Marsupial Selfie Stars

Quokkas were among the first Australian mammals ever seen by Europeans. In 1658, the Dutch Captain Willem De Vlamingh described them as rats, but in fact, they are marsupials, carrying their young in a pouch. Once common around Perth, quokkas are now confined to isolated pockets on the mainland, but they still thrive on their namesake Rottnest Island, where they are safe from predators. Today, there are about 12,000 on Rotto. Their cute, furry faces make them very photogenic.

★ Little Salmon Bay

BEACH | FAMILY | Make sure you pack your snorkeling gear for this one—due to Rottnest's warmer waters, created by the passing Leeuwin Current, there's a fascinating mix of tropical and temperate fish species in the clear waters. Aim to go at low tide and look out for bream, red-lipped morwong, zebrafish, and king wrasse, plus plenty of little colored fish. There are underwater plaques that guide you along a great snorkel trail and the waters are calm so you can enjoy flipping about. Coral reefs are about 330 feet out but worth checking out if you're a confident swimmer. **Amenities:** none. **Best for:** snorkeling; swimming. **TIP→ If it's overcrowded, head to the next, bigger beach, Salmon Bay.** ✉ *Little Salmon Bay, southwest of Thomson Bay, off Parker Point Rd., Rottnest Island* 🌐 *rottnestisland.com.*

Restaurants

★ Frankie's on Rotto

$$ | PIZZA | FAMILY | In the heart of the settlement is the island's only pizzeria and cocktail bar. Sit on the deck surrounded by fig trees and munch on hand-stretched pizza, yummy pasta, and healthy salads. **Known for:** line-ups out the door in summertime; BBQ Must Have meat lovers pizza; happy hour 3–5 pm daily. $ *Average main: A$26* ✉ *342 Somerville Dr., Rottnest Island* ☎ *043/735–090* 🌐 *frankiesonrotto.com.au.*

Hotel Rottnest

$$ | AUSTRALIAN | FAMILY | This blindingly white, fortlike property was once the official summer residence for the governors of Western Australia but today it's decked out in Astroturf and bench seats as the island's social hub. Since the addition of the Samphire Rottnest resort, Hotel Rottnest no longer offers guest rooms. **Known for:** special events and sports nights; a roaming peacock and curious quokkas inside; large outdoor seating overlooking the beach. $ *Average main: A$30* ✉ *1 Bedford Ave., Rottnest Island* ☎ *08/9292–5011* 🌐 *hotelrottnest.com.au.*

★ Pinky's Beach Club

$$ | AUSTRALIAN | An all-day dining menu and a killer location overlooking Pinky Beach and Bathurst Lighthouse make this restaurant and bar at Discovery Rottnest Island a surefire way to fuel your body and take in the scenery. The contemporary menu changes with the seasons but you can expect tasty seafood, juicy burgers, and creative vegetarian options. **Known for:** direct access to Pinky Beach; amazing sunsets; pink cocktails. $ *Average main: A$32* ✉ *Strue Rd., Rottnest Island* ☎ *08/6350–6170* 🌐 *discoveryholidayparks.com.au.*

Coffee and Quick Bites

★ Rottnest Bakery

$ | BAKERY | FAMILY | Locally famous for freshly made pastries and decent coffee, this central bakery does a roaring trade every day of the week. It may be the tasty treats that get people through the door, but it's the cute little quokkas on the deck who encourage patrons to stay awhile. **TIP→ Quokkas are extremely friendly, but it is a fineable offense to feed them.** **Known for:** seagulls who will snatch your food when you're not looking; delicious jam doughnuts; traditional Aussie meat pies. $ *Average main: A$6* ✉ *Maley St., Rottnest Island* ☎ *08/9292–5023.*

Hotels

Accommodation on the island ranges from basic camping sites to self-contained holiday villas and hotels. Space is at a premium during the summer months, Easter, and school holidays. Outside these times, accommodation is easier to find, and rates are more affordable, too. See rottnestisland.com for more information.

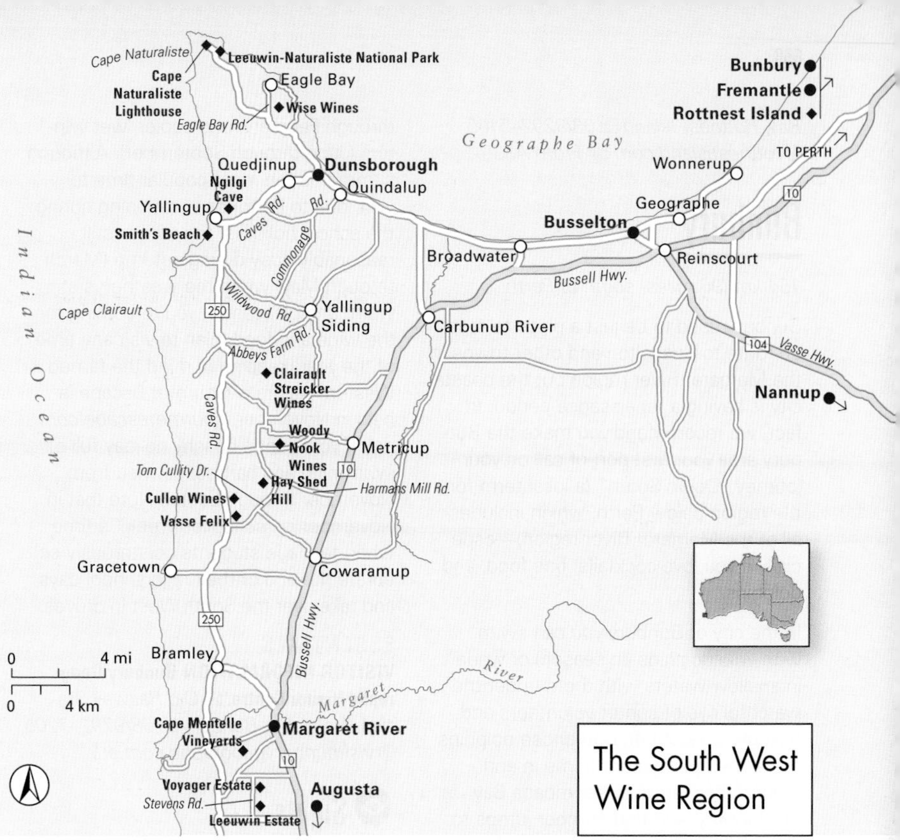

The South West Wine Region

Cape Naturaliste
Leeuwin-Naturaliste National Park
Cape Naturaliste Lighthouse
Eagle Bay
Wise Wines
Eagle Bay Rd.
Geographe Bay
Bunbury
Fremantle
Rottnest Island
TO PERTH
Quedjinup
Dunsborough
Ngilgi Cave
Quindalup
Yallingup
Smith's Beach
Caves Rd.
Commonage Rd.
Wonnerup
Geographe
Busselton
Broadwater
Reinscourt
Bussell Hwy.
Indian Ocean
Cape Clairault
Wildwood Rd.
Yallingup Siding
Carbunup River
Abbeys Farm Rd.
Vasse Hwy.
Clairault Streicker Wines
Nannup
Woody Nook Wines
Metricup
Tom Cullity Dr.
Hay Shed Hill
Harmans Mill Rd.
Cullen Wines
Vasse Felix
Gracetown
Cowaramup
Bramley
Margaret River
Cape Mentelle Vineyards
Voyager Estate
Stevens Rd.
Leeuwin Estate
Augusta
0 4 mi
0 4 km

Discovery Rottnest Island

$$ | **RESORT** | **FAMILY** | Love camping but don't like roughing it? Discovery Rottnest Island's sustainable, "glamping" tent accommodation lets you wake up to the sounds of nature while enjoying the creature comforts. **Pros:** family tents available; eco-friendly; outdoor swimming pool. **Cons:** tents are not soundproof; no air-conditioning, ceiling fan only; no heating (cold in winter). $ *Rooms from: A$190* ✉ *Strue Rd., Rottnest Island* ☎ *08/6350–6170* 🌐 *discoveryholidayparks.com.au* 🍽 *Free Breakfast* 🛏 *84 tents.*

Karma Rottnest Lodge

$$$$ | **HOTEL** | **FAMILY** | The most historic hotel on Rottnest, this sturdy structure reveals an interesting past as a colonial barracks and a prison. **Pros:** some rooms ideal for families; close to ferry; free Wi-Fi. **Cons:** some design is dated; no outside food or drink allowed in rooms; not on beachfront. $ *Rooms from: A$340* ✉ *Kitson St., Rottnest Island* ☎ *08/9292–5161* 🌐 *karmagroup.com* 🛏 *61 rooms* 🍽 *Free Breakfast.*

Activities

BIKING

Pedal & Flipper

BIKING | **FAMILY** | Rent one of 1,800 bikes—the island's must-have item—from Pedal & Flipper. Also for rent are tandem bikes, electric bikes, gophers, and attachable buggies for children, plus snorkel sets, paddleboards, wet suits, scooters, beach cricket equipment, and soccer essentials. The store is open daily, though hours vary according to the season and the ferry schedule. Expect lines at ferry arrival times. ✉ *Thomson*

Bay, Rottnest Island ☎ *08/9292–5105* 🌐 *rottnestisland.com* ☞ *From A$30.*

Bunbury

154 km (96 miles) south of Perth.

Bunbury used to be just a place to stop en route to Busselton and other towns in the Margaret River region but the coastal city is having a renaissance period. In fact, we recommend you make the Bunbury area your first port of call on your journey "Down South" (a local term for the region below Perth, which includes all of the Margaret River region)—especially if you love cocktails, fine food, and dolphins.

In the city of Bunbury you can swim with wild dolphins (in season) or wade in shallow waters with them under the watchful eye of center volunteers and biologists. About 40 bottlenose dolphins make their permanent home in and around the waters of Koombana Bay off Bunbury, and that number jumps to about 160 between October and May. From Bunbury, head inland to meet the community of 10,000 garden gnomes at Gnomesville in the Ferguson Valley. If you travel further along the South Western Highway, you come to the picturesque town of Donnybrook, where there are rolling landscapes and miles of fruit orchards. You can even pick your own plums and apples from February to June.

GETTING HERE AND AROUND

To get to Bunbury from Perth, take Kwinana Freeway south; it joins Forrest Highway and then Highway 1. After Bunbury, you'll switch from Highway 1 to Highway 10 to explore the other main towns in the Margaret River region: Busselton, Dunsborough, and Margaret River.

WHEN TO GO

The South West and Margaret River region enjoy a Mediterranean-style climate with warm summers (December through February) and cooler, wet winters (June through September). Although summer is the most popular time to visit, due to Perthites vacationing during the school holidays, the area is still reasonably busy during autumn (March through May) when the weather is still warm and pleasant. If you're coming for the wine and food, plan to visit any time of the year (keeping in mind the famed Western Australia Gourmet Escape is held in November, *gourmetescape.com.au*). If you want a beachy holiday full of swimming and barbecues, visit from November through Easter. Note that in November is "schoolies week," a time when teenage students boisterously celebrate the end of their high school days and take over the South West in droves.

ESSENTIALS

VISITOR INFORMATION Bunbury Geographe Visitor Centre. ✉ *Old Railway Station, Haley St., Bunbury* ☎ *08/9792–7205* 🌐 *visitbunburygeographe.com.au.*

Sights

Bunbury Regional Art Gallery

ART GALLERY | Bunbury's art scene starts here at the Bunbury Regional Art Gallery, affectionately known as BRAG to the locals. This former convent is easy to find, just look for the pretty pink Gothic-style building. Inside, you'll find six gallery spaces filled with traveling exhibitions, local artworks, and the original 20 paintings donated by Claude Hotchin in 1949. Be sure to visit the third floor and check out the stained-glass windows and stunning floor tiles, remnants of its nunnery past. Entry to the gallery is free of charge and open daily 10–4. Check the website for current exhibitions and events. ✉ *64 Wittenom St., Bunbury* ☎ *08/9792–7323* 🌐 *brag.org,au* 🎫 *Free.*

Cuprum Distillery

BREWERY | This expanding distillery got its start by making and supplying hand sanitizer to the masses! Now they are

Bunbury's favorite producer of gin, vodka, and rum. This adult activity includes spirit tastings, make-your-own-gin classes, yin-and-gin yoga sessions, and, of course, shopping for your favorite spirits and Cuprum merchandise in their giant shed. Visit their website to see what's on offer during your visit and feel free to contact them with expressions of interest. **TIP→ Try the raspberry gin.** *✉ 105 Forrest Ave., Bunbury ☎ 0497/618–710 🌐 cuprumdistillery.com.au ⏲ Closed Sun.–Wed.*

★ Dolphin Discovery Centre

AQUARIUM | FAMILY | As Bunbury's favorite attraction, this not-for-profit conservation-first organization welcomes 80,000 visitors each year. Get up close to wild dolphins at the Dolphin Discovery Centre. Upward of 200 dolphins have been identified in Koombana Bay—swim with them, book an eco-cruise, or stay on the beach and wade into the interaction zone. Enjoy a unique, immersive experience at the discovery center, which enjoyed a A$2 million refurbishment in 2018, with its digital 360-degree dolphinarium, interpretive panels, theater, aquariums, dolphin displays, on-site café, gift shop, and a rooftop bar perfect for cocktails at sunset. **TIP→ Call first to book the weather-dependent swim and eco-cruises. Dolphin encounters are not guaranteed, but the chances are higher in the warmer months.** *✉ 830 Koombana Dr., Bunbury ☎ 08/9791–3088 🌐 dolphindiscovery.com.au 🎫 From A$18.*

Restaurants

★ Market Eating House

$$$ | AUSTRALIAN | Bunbury's dining scene is charging forward, and leading the way is Market Eating House. Head chef and owner, Brenton creates a menu jam-packed with delicious shareable foods cooked on the custom-made charcoal grill and wood-fired oven all within open view. **Known for:** pouring local craft beer, wine, and spirits; single servings when dining alone; gourmet cooking classes. *$ Average main: A$40 ✉ 9 Victoria St., Bunbury ☎ 08/9721–6078 🌐 marketeatinghouse.com.au ⏲ Closed Sun.–Tues.*

Hotels

Best Western Plus Hotel Lord Forrest

$ | HOTEL | FAMILY | As you step into this iconic hotel in central Bunbury, you may feel as if you've been transported back to the hotel's opening year of 1986 but rest assured, the rooms at this atrium-style hotel are exceptionally up-to-date and stylish thanks to a major renovation that saw all guest rooms renovated by 2022. **Pros:** all rooms have balconies; elevator; free parking. **Cons:** pool is in the lobby; not all rooms have sea views; reception open 7 am–11 pm. *$ Rooms from: A$149 ✉ 20 Symmons St., Bunbury ☎ 08/9726–5777 🌐 bestwestern.com.au 🍽 No Meals 🛏 115 rooms.*

Nightlife

★ Lost Bills

COCKTAIL LOUNGES | Bunbury's number one cocktail bar serves up moody dim-lit vibes in the back, and bright street views in the front. Sip colorful creations, craft beer, wine, and spirits surrounded by neon lights, old Hollywood photos, and exposed brick while you cozy up on padded and pillowed seats. There may not be a kitchen but they welcome and encourage you to order from neighboring restaurants such as Last Slice or Right On Burgers. *✉ 41 Victoria St., Bunbury 🌐 lostbills.com.*

Busselton

222 km (138 miles) south of Perth.

Busselton is the largest city in the Margaret River region and is considered the gateway to the region. The seaside municipality is rapidly increasing in population as more people relocate to the area in search of the laid-back, coastal lifestyle that is so coveted. Busselton draws a crowd for its 1.84-km (1¼ mile) wharf that juts into the Indian Ocean, its family-friendly foreshore, and the myriad of sporting events, such as the annual Jetty Swim in February, the Chevron City to Surf fun run in July, and the world-famous Ironman triathlon every December. It's no wonder Busselton is called the Event Capital of Western Australia. The city of around 40,000 people is a great base for your Margaret River region vacation.

GETTING HERE AND AROUND

From Bunbury, take Highway 10 to Busselton. Public transport is available in Busselton, but your best option is to rent a car in Perth to explore Busselton and other Margaret River locales. Alternatively, **South West Coachlines** (*08/9261–7600, www.southwestcoachlines.com.au*) does have daily South West Express coach service from Perth Central Bus Station at the Elizabeth Quay Bus Port on Mounts Bay Road to Busselton, Dunsborough, and Margaret River. However, note that many accommodations—farmstays, bushland chalets, and boutique hotels—as well as the wineries, the beaches, and other attractions, are outside of towns, and you'll need your own transportation to reach them.

TRANSPORTATION INFORMATION

Busselton Taxis. ✉ *Busselton* ☎ *131–008* 🌐 *busseltontaxis.com.au.* **Rent A Car Busselton and South West.** ✉ *47 Cook St., Busselton* ☎ *0437/791–691* 🌐 *busseltonswrentacar.com.au.*

SAFETY AND PRECAUTIONS

The calm waters of Geographe Bay are home to a jellyfish with a nasty sting—colloquially named "stingers." They are not deadly, so don't panic, but they are painful and hard to spot. The main body of the stinger is translucent and only about 2 inches across, and the hard-to-see tentacles trailing are the cause for concern. The jellyfish like warm, very calm water, so still days in summer are when you are most likely to encounter them as they drift close to shore. Rubbing a sting is *not* recommended. The best thing to do is rinse the area in a very hot shower.

TOURS

★ Busselton Jetty and Underwater Observatory

At almost 2-km (1¼-miles) long, the Busselton Jetty is the longest timber jetty in the southern hemisphere. You can visit the Interpretive Center and Heritage Museum at the start of the jetty, then either catch the miniature train (45-minute ride) or walk to the fascinating Underwater Observatory—one of only seven in the world—where you'll spy all manner of soft, colorful coral as you descend the cylindrical, windowed observatory. Tours for up to 40 people run every hour, taking you 26 feet below the water. The warm Leeuwin Current and the sheltering effect of the jetty above have created a unique microclimate rich with colorful tropical and subtropical corals, sponges, fish, and invertebrates—there are 300 marine species in all. **TIP→ The jetty is open 24 hours for fishing and walking.** ✉ *Busselton Beachfront, end of Queen St., Busselton* ☎ *08/9754–0900* 🌐 *busseltonjetty.com.au* 💳 *A$4.*

★ Cellar d'Or Winery Tours

This small group wine-and-gourmet food tour of the Margaret River region takes you on an all-day journey to some of the best boutique cellar doors, breweries, and all-time favorite snack producers (chocolate and cheese, anyone?) of the area. The tours include pickup from your hotel in Busselton, Dunsborough, Margaret River town, or anywhere in between. ✉ *Busselton* ☎ *0428/179–729* 🌐 *cellardortours.com.au* 💳 *From A$125.*

ESSENTIALS

VISITOR INFORMATION Busselton Visitor Centre. ✉ *Busselton Beach, 17 Foreshore Parade, Busselton* ☎ *08/9780–5911 option 2* 🌐 *margaretriver.com.*

Beaches

★ Busselton Beach
BEACH | FAMILY | This is the beach for loads of family fun in the sun. The calm, translucent, and turquoise waters of Geographe Bay are perfect for swimming, stand-up paddling, kayaking, fishing, and relaxing. From mid-December until the end of January, an inflatable water park (*aquatastic.net*) is set up and available to the public for an hourly or daily fee. The City of Busselton has invested millions of development dollars into foreshore infrastructure that includes an amazing kids' adventure park, skate park, amphitheater, plenty of bench seating, and free-to-use barbecues—a favorite Aussie dinner is fish-and-chips on the beach at sunset. **Amenities:** food and drink; parking; showers; toilets; water sports. **Best for:** sunset; swimming; walking. ✉ *Busselton Foreshore, Busselton* 🌐 *beachsafe.org.au.*

Restaurants

★ Al Forno
$$ | EUROPEAN | FAMILY | Tucked away on the fringes of the Busselton central business district, this popular family-owned Mediterranean-inspired eatery is much loved for its rich pasta dishes, thin-crust pizzas, and soul-comforting, slow-cooked favorites like beef bourguignon and coq au vin. Before you get overexcited and order everything on the menu, remember to leave room for dessert—like dream-worthy chocolate mousse and tiramisu. **Known for:** friendly, attentive service; pizza of the month and a margherita pizza for only A$27.50; consistently great home-style cooking. [$] *Average main: A$28* ✉ *1/19 Bussell Hwy., Busselton* ☎ *08/9751–3775* 🌐 *al-forno.com.au* ⏲ *Closed Mon.*

★ Burger Bones
$ | BURGER | It began as a food truck in 2015 with a cultlike following but now Burger Bones has a permanent diner in central Busselton. If hamburgers are your desire, this burger joint will certainly over-deliver. **Known for:** weekend specials offering new burger creations; 100% beef patties (no fillers); "filthy" burgers (meaning double patties). [$] *Average main: A$18* ✉ *55 Queen St., Busselton* ☎ *0435/108–280* 🌐 *Facebook.com/BurgerBones* ⏲ *Closed Mon.–Wed.*

★ The Fire Station
$$ | AUSTRALIAN | This boutique bar in the heart of Busselton is a favorite spot among locals for its stylish reinvention of the town's former fire station, and, of course, its eclectic menu and flowing taps and wine barrels. Dine in beside the buzzing bar, under the low-hanging mood lighting, or outside in the garden courtyard where you'll be closer to the sounds of the solo singers and small bands who perform regularly. **Known for:** unique toppings on wood-fired pizza; happy hour at 5 pm weekdays (except peak season and holidays); rotating taps of craft beer. [$] *Average main: A$25* ✉ *68 Queen St., Busselton* ☎ *08/9752–3113* 🌐 *firestation.bar* ⏲ *No dinner Sun. in winter.*

★ The Good Egg
$$ | CAFÉ | FAMILY | To call someone a "good egg" is a high compliment in Australia and it's a fitting name for this busy, modern café that opened its doors in 2018. With amazing coffee, a delicious, healthy menu, a kids' play area, and gift shop all housed in a two-story, modern, industrial-style setting, this is the place to be for Sunday morning brunch. **Known for:** communal workspace and private offices on second floor; freshly baked muffins; seasonal menu catering to all diets. [$] *Average main: A$23* ✉ *38–44 Albert St., Busselton* ☎ *08/9788–6057* 🌐 *thegoodeggcafe.com.au* ⏲ *No dinner.*

Shelter Brewing Co
$$ | AUSTRALIAN | Take shelter from the warm sea breeze, winter winds, or just a busy day at this award-winning mammoth brewery restaurant situated on the Busselton foreshore. With views

for miles that include the town's famous jetty and the Indian Ocean, popping in for a beer or two will certainly turn into ordering wood-fired pizza and plans to return in the morning for coffee and bagels. **Known for:** weekend brewery tours; architectural genius; tasting paddles featuring any four beers. *$ Average main: A$25 ✉ 11 Foreshore Parade, Busselton ☎ 08/9754–4444 🌐 shelterbrewing.com.au.*

Hotels

Gale Street Motel and Villas

$ | **HOTEL** | This delightful accommodation is the perfect base for a Busselton getaway with its proximity to the beach and affordable nightly rates. **Pros:** built-in USB ports; free Wi-Fi and secure parking; complimentary coffee and tea. **Cons:** no views; no restaurant; no swimming pool. *$ Rooms from: A$130 ✉ 40 Gale St., Busselton ☎ 08/9754–1200 🌐 galestvillas.com.au 16 rooms No Meals.*

The Observatory Guesthouse

$ | **B&B/INN** | Settle into this charming bed-and-breakfast just a block away from the Busselton beach—so close that the waves crashing on the shore may lull you to sleep at night. **Pros:** blackout curtains; en suite for every room; free Wi-Fi. **Cons:** maximum two guests per room; no pool; not suitable for persons under 18. *$ Rooms from: A$99 ✉ 7 Brown St., Busselton ☎ 0499/005–241 🌐 observatoryguesthouse.com 5 rooms, 1 apt Free Breakfast.*

The Sebel Bussleton

$$ | **RESORT** | **FAMILY** | An easy eight-minute drive from Busselton's city center, and a hop, skip, and a jump to the beach, these self-contained apartments are set on a sprawling property and attract fun-loving families and leisure-seeking holidaymakers. **Pros:** path from resort to the beach; shopping complex within walking distance; every apartment has a bathtub. **Cons:** no restaurant or café; only one car park per room; not within walking distance to jetty. *$ Rooms from: A$199 ✉ 553 Bussell Hwy., Busselton ☎ 08/9754–9800 🌐 thesebel.com 73 rooms No Meals.*

Activities

★ Forest Adventures South West

ZIP LINING | **FAMILY** | For a real adventure that challenges your bravery and lets you experience the natural beauty of the Ludlow Forest, this high ropes and zip-line course delivers thrills and views. There are six courses ranging from easy to extreme; you can do as much as you like in your two-hour time slot. There are 11 fly foxes extending 500 meters through the tuart trees, which gives you a pretty good bird's-eye view of this outdoor adventure eco-activity. Even if you're not a fan of heights, this is a great place to dare yourself. All safety equipment and instruction is provided. If you're visiting in winter, you'll enjoy a free marshmallow roast after your climbing. Courses are designed for ages seven and up. *✉ 12 Ludlow Park Rd., Busselton ☎ 08/9780–5908 🌐 forestadventures.com.au A$44.*

Dunsborough

252 km (157 miles) south of Perth and 26 km (16 miles) from Busselton.

The attractive and fashionable seaside town of Dunsborough is perfect for a few days of swimming, sunning, and fishing—which is why it's become a popular holiday destination for many Perth families. Onshore attractions include Meelup Beach, a protected cove encircled by native bush with calm swimming water, and several nearby wineries and breweries. Offshore, you can dive on the wreck of the HMAS *Swan,* the former Royal Australian Navy ship deliberately sunk in Geographe Bay (*capedive.com*), or take a cruise to see migrating humpback and southern right whales September through December. Attractions in nearby Yallingup, about 15 minutes away from Dunsborough via Caves Road, are included in this section.

GETTING HERE AND AROUND

From Busselton, take Bussell Highway, then Caves Road straight to Dunsborough. Public transport is available in Dunsborough, but we recommend a car for ease and cost-efficiency in getting around while here.

TAXI CONTACTS Dunsborough Taxis. ✉ *Dunsborough* ☎ *08/9756–8688* 🌐 *dunsboroughtaxis.com.au.*

TOURS

Naturaliste Charters

This company runs eco-conscious whale-watching tours along the southwestern coastline. The tours follow the whale migration from Augusta to Dunsborough to Bussleton as the mammals travel north from late May to early December. You can expect to see playful humpbacks and surfacing southern right whales, and if you're lucky, rare blue and minke whales, too. For something really special, join a Bremer Canyon expedition from January through April, to see a killer whale and shark feeding ground in a remote and deep part of ocean off the Albany coast. ✉ *Shop 1 Bayview Centro, 25–27 Dunn Bay Rd., Dunsborough* ☎ *08/9750–5500* 🌐 *whales-australia.com.au* 🎫 *From A$90.*

★ Ngilgi Cave

While crawling through tight spots, sliding down smooth rock surfaces, and gazing at stalactites lit with a rainbow of lights, you'll learn about the fascinating history of this special cave, once explored by candlelight in the early 1900s. Semi-guided cave tours take about one hour and run every half hour from 9:30 am to 4 pm. Highly recommended adventure caving tours are also available for families with older children. **TIP→ Multicave passes are available and recommended if you want to explore the other main tourist caves in the Margaret River region.** ✉ *76 Yallingup Caves Rd., Yallingup* ☎ *08/9757–7411* 🎫 *A$23.*

VISITOR INFORMATION

CONTACTS Dunsborough Visitor Centre. ✉ *31 Dunn Bay Rd., Shop 1, Dunsborough* ☎ *08/9780–5911* 🌐 *margaretriver.com.*

Sights

Cape Naturaliste Lighthouse

LIGHTHOUSE | FAMILY | At the northern end of Leeuwin-Naturaliste National Park, a 13-minute drive from Dunsborough, stands Cape Naturaliste Lighthouse. From the lighthouse keeper's cottages (now a gift shop, tour desk, information center, and café) take a 15-minute walk to the whale lookout, a purpose-built deck that overlooks the Indian Ocean. If you want to go inside the 75-foot tall lighthouse, you'll need to book a guided tour (every half hour from 9:30 am to 4:30 pm), where you learn everything there is to know about the history and operations of the lighthouse. You'll also get to climb the stairs to the top and stand on the outside balcony to take in the spectacular seascapes of this rugged coastline. Migrating whales are often spotted along this stretch from September through December. This is also the start of the coast-hugging 135-km (86-mile) Cape to Cape Track. ✉ *Leeuwin Naturaliste National Park, 1267 Cape Naturaliste Rd., Dunsborough* ☎ *08/9757–7411* 🌐 *margaretriver.com* 🎫 *A$15.*

Clairault Streicker Wines

WINERY | This winery is known for its award-winning Chardonnay, Cabernet Sauvignon, and Cabernet Merlot, and is loved for its natural bushland setting, about 18 km (11 miles) south of Dunsborough. The contemporary-style cellar door offers A$10 per person wine tastings, which is redeemable upon purchase of a bottle of wine. The spacious café has glass doors that open onto a large timber deck that overlooks a picturesque vineyard in warm weather, while two huge stone fireplaces warm the tables in winter. ■ **TIP→ Borrow one of the café's picnic blankets and relax in the garden.** ✉ *3277 Caves Rd., Wilyabrup* ☎ *08/9755–6225* 🌐 *claireaultstreickerwines.com.au.*

Leeuwin-Naturaliste National Park

NATIONAL PARK | This national park clutches one of Western Australia's most spectacular coastlines, from Cape Naturaliste in the north, to Cape Leeuwin, near Augusta, in the south. The park is not a composite destination, rather a narrow patchwork of protected areas along the coast, intersected by beach access roads and small beachside villages, and traced by the Cape to Cape Track. The mostly unspoiled coastal vistas are as awe-inspiring as any in the world—on a calm day the view northward from Yallingup past Sugarloaf Rock toward Cape Naturaliste is nature at its best and it's often sprinkled with surfing dolphins. Farther south, between Cowaramup Bay and Karridale, scenic lookouts allow you to access coastal cliffs and rocky shoreline that bear the brunt of giant ocean swells generated across thousands of miles of Indian Ocean. ⚠ **Use extreme care when hiking or fishing cliff-side.** ✉ *Leeuwin-Naturaliste National Park* ☎ *08/9752–5555* 🌐 *parks.dpaw.wa.gov.au.*

Wise Wines

WINERY | The view from the hilltop overlooking Geographe Bay is almost as good as the wines at this northernmost winery in the region, about a 15-minute drive from Dunsborough toward Cape Naturaliste. This family-owned boutique vineyard has a history of producing award-winning Chardonnay, though its collection of more than 20 wines are all worth a try at the cellar door. If you fancy the wine, pair it with something from the seasonal menu at the adjoining Wise Vineyard Restaurant. Always keen to try new things, they've added distilling to their repertoire. Try mandarin-flavored gin or perhaps the Shiraz gin, which is a creative way to utilize excess grapes. ✉ *80 Eagle Bay Rd., Dunsborough* ☎ *08/9755–3331* 🌐 *wisewine.com.au.*

Beaches

★ Bunker Bay

BEACH | FAMILY | When you turn off Bunker Bay Road onto Farm Break Lane, the wow-worthy vista of the bay takes one's breath away with its eye-popping turquoise waters. Pack the beach bag and a picnic, and prepare for a day lazing on white sand and swimming in see-through water. **Amenities:** food and drink; parking; showers; toilets. **Best for:** solitude; swimming; walking. ✉ *Dunsborough* 🌐 *beachsafe.org.au.*

Meelup Beach

BEACH | FAMILY | Sheltered from wind, this soft-sand haven makes for a gorgeous coastal escape. Its aquamarine-blue waters attract visitors and locals alike. You can bring food with you if you like and use the barbecue facilities and picnic tables. Meelup Beach Hire (🌐 *meelupbeachhire.com)* offers heaps of beach and water-play rentals, including stand-up paddleboards, kayaks, bodyboards, umbrellas, and snorkel sets. **Amenities:** showers; toilets. **Best for:** solitude; swimming; walking. ✉ *Meelup Beach Rd., Dunsborough* 🌐 *meelupbeachhire.com.*

Smiths Beach

BEACH | In a state of extraordinary beaches, this one rates high on the list. Bookended by rounded granite boulders, the caramel-hue sand sinks beneath your feet and the gentle, rolling waves beckon, daring you to cool off in the clean ocean. Edged by native bush, this beach that is 12 km (7 miles) from Dunsborough is quiet and secluded. Smiths Beach Resort and Lamont's Restaurant (at resort) are nearby. **Amenities:** food and drink; parking; toilets. **Best for:** solitude; sunset; surfing; walking. *North of the*

Canal Rocks near Yallingup, Leeuwin-Naturaliste National Park, Western Australia

creek has strong waves and rips (undertows) and can be hazardous. ✉ *Smiths Beach Rd., Yallingup* 🌐 *beachsafe.org.au.*

★ Yallingup Beach

BEACH | FAMILY | What's not to love about this 1.3-km (1-mile) beach at the hillside town of Yallingup? Picture-perfect views; transparent water; clean, sun-baked sand; and a gentle pool of ocean at the southern end that protects you from the waves beyond. On any given day you'll see a tribe of surfers riding the waves, while wannabes and newbies take lessons (🌐 *yallingupsurfschool.com)* in the lagoon. There are limited food and drink options nearby, so come prepared. **Amenities:** lifeguards; parking; showers; toilets. **Best for:** snorkeling; surfing; sunset; swimming; walking. *High waves and rips increase north of the parking lot.* ✉ *Yallingup Beach Rd., Yallingup* 🌐 *beachsafe.org.au.*

Restaurants

Arimia Estate

$$$$ | MODERN AUSTRALIAN | FAMILY | If you're keen to get off the beaten path and discover how one winery restaurant is striving to create garden and farm-fresh dishes that pair well with wine in an elegant, alfresco setting, follow the 2-km (1-mile) dirt road to Arimia's charming timber cottage set among the forest. Make a beeline for the deck, and stay for a light lunch after sampling the award-winning wines (fee for tastings), and if you absolutely can't fathom leaving, consider staying at their on-site guesthouse. **Known for:** ever-changing set price menu of local flavors; creative sustainability; raising their own pigs. *$ Average main: A$85* ✉ *242 Quininup Rd., Yallingup* ☎ *08/9755–2528* 🌐 *arimia.com.au* ⏲ *Closed Mon.–Wed.*

★ Eagle Bay Brewing Co

$$ | **MODERN AUSTRALIAN** | After a day at the beach, stop at the Eagle Bay Brewing Co. to grab a six-beer tasting flight so you can sample the company's many craft creations, then have a ball seeing which ones best complement your lunch. The food is pure gastropub in a casual yet upscale setting with an alfresco dining area that overlooks rolling, green pastures that stretch towards the sea. **Known for:** crispy wood-fired pizzas with gourmet toppings; cold, frothy pale ale; hearty beef burger with bacon and cheddar cheese. *Average main: A$28 ✉ 236 Eagle Bay Rd., Dunsborough ☎ 08/9755–3554 ⊕ eaglebaybrewing.com.au ⊗ No dinner.*

The Studio Bistro

$$ | **MODERN AUSTRALIAN** | This is fancy-pants food at its best as the meals are not only palatable to the taste buds, but also to the eyes. Nominated for six Gold Plate awards and featured in Trip Advisor's top 10% worldwide restaurants, this "art of cooking" lunch venue is a feast for the eyes and stomach. **Known for:** the bistro hosts regularly changing art exhibitions; willingness to split bills; Chef's Select set menu on Wednesday. *Average main: A$30 ✉ 7 Marrinup Dr., Yallingup ☎ 08/9756–6164 ⊕ thestudiobistro.com.au ⊗ Closed Tues. and Wed.*

★ Wild Hop Brewing Company

$$ | **AUSTRALIAN** | If you're into boozy craft beer and gourmet pub food, do not miss lunch at this family-owned brewery restaurant. Wild Hop Brewery opened in February 2019 and they haven't missed a beat since. **Known for:** kid- and dog-friendly; high alcohol content beer; wood-fired rotisserie chicken. *Average main: A$25 ✉ 1301 Wildwood Rd., Dunsborough ☎ 0488/990–154 ⊕ wildhopbeer.com.au.*

Simmos Ice Creamery and Fun Park

$ | **IRISH** | **FAMILY** | Simmos has been delighting locals and visitors since 1993 when a father and son teamed up to put their Irish ice-cream recipe to the test. Some people thought they'd gone mad, but now this ice creamery and fun park is a popular excursion for families and sweet tooths. **Known for:** minigolf course; 60 flavors of ice cream and sorbet; kids playground. *Average main: A$7 ✉ 161 Commonage Rd., Dunsborough ☎ 08/9755–3745 ⊕ simmos.com.au.*

Cape Lodge

$$$$ | **RESORT** | Regarded as the grandest boutique property in Margaret River wine country, the award-winning lodge's five-bedroom residence plus 22 luxury suites deliver in service, space, and views of an 8-acre vineyard that produces Sauvignon Blanc and Shiraz exclusively for guests. **Pros:** exclusive cooking classes (check website for calendar); large, luxurious rooms, some with spas; swimming pool. **Cons:** own transport essential; limited evening dining options nearby; no shopping nearby. *Rooms from: A$565 ✉ 3341 Caves Rd., Yallingup ☎ 08/9755–6311 ⊕ capelodge.com.au ⇨ 23 rooms 🍽 Free Breakfast.*

★ Forest Rise Eco Retreat

$$$ | **B&B/INN** | This getaway in the peaceful bushland of the Margaret River wine region is eco-friendly but also semi-indulgent, with amenities including king-size beds, fluffy robes, fireplaces, dreamy candlelit spas with overhead windows looking up to the forest canopy, and oh-so-private verandas. **Pros:** barbecues available; two mountain bikes per chalet; private chef and massage therapist on request. **Cons:** not suitable for children; no shopping, dining, or market nearby; own transport required. *Rooms from: A$259 ✉ 231 Yelverton Rd., Yelverton*

☎ 08/9755–7110 🌐 forestrise.com.au
🛏 11 rooms 🍴 No Meals.

★ Pullman Bunker Bay Resort
$$$$ | RESORT | FAMILY | Sprawling down the hillside of the Cape Naturaliste Ridge, this resort wows with its sexy infinity pool, swanky villas, and easy access to one of the area's most beautiful beaches. **Pros:** trusted brand; amazing on-site restaurant, bar, and spa; quiet, nature-infused environment. **Cons:** no shopping nearby; own transport essential; limited sea views from rooms. $ *Rooms from: A$399* ✉ *42 Bunker Bay Rd., off Cape Naturaliste Rd., Dunsborough* ☎ *08/9756–9100* 🌐 *accorhotels.com* 🛏 *150 villas* 🍴 *No Meals.*

Smiths Beach Resort
$$$$ | RESORT | FAMILY | Perched above the sand dunes of Smiths Beach in Yallingup, this luxury resort offers a variety of self-contained shacks, apartments, villas, and holiday homes perfect for an Australian beach vacation. **Pros:** separate kids pool; tennis courts; infinity edge swimming pool. **Cons:** limited dining options within walking distance; car needed to access; three-night minimum during December/January school holidays. $ *Rooms from: A$850* ✉ *67 Smiths Beach Rd., Yallingup* ☎ *08/9750–1200* 🌐 *smithsbeachresort.com.au* 🛏 *60 rooms* 🍴 *No Meals.*

★ Wildwood Valley Cottages
$$$ | APARTMENT | FAMILY | Discover what it's like to wake up to birdsong echoing from the trees, and kangaroos greedily grazing outside your bedroom window at this stunning rural holiday property. **Pros:** free Wi-Fi; wood-burning fireplaces; claw-foot bathtub. **Cons:** nearest shop is a 15-minute drive away; own vehicle is essential; no on-site restaurant. $ *Rooms from: A$250* ✉ *1481 Wildwood Rd., Yallingup* ☎ *08/9755–2120* 🌐 *wildwood-valley.com.au* 🛏 *4 rooms* 🍴 *No Meals.*

Shopping

★ Happs Wines and Commonage Pottery
CERAMICS | This gorgeous collaboration estate is worth dedicating at least a couple of hours to mosey through the gardens, sample wine at the unique self-serve tasting deck, gaze upon the walls of local art, and, of course, shop for pottery, and even watch the artists work their magic on the pottery wheel. You may also meet the resident cat who loves sleeping in the seating areas. If the mood strikes, try the Happs Hamper program, which is a build-your-own-picnic. Grab a supplied basket and choose your items from the fridge and pantry. Pick a bottle of wine and a spot on the manicured lawn for a memorable wine and shopping day out. **■ TIP→ Happs Wines offers free tastings in its self-pour cellar door.** ✉ *575 Commonage Rd., Dunsborough* ☎ *08/9755–3300* 🌐 *commonagepotteryandgallery.com.au.*

Merchant & Maker
GENERAL STORE | FAMILY | This popular café–boutique supermarket offers more than quick bites and organic, locally grown and produced grocery items (the chocolate brownies are delicious). You'll also find vegan-friendly skin care, organic cotton travel towels, eco-friendly kitchen supplies, and ready-made meals to take back to your accommodation. ✉ *35 Dunn Bay Rd., Shop 8, Dunsborough* ☎ *0498/090–959* 🌐 *merchantandmarker.com.au.*

Margaret River

181 km (112 miles) south of Perth, 38 km (24 miles) south of Cape Naturaliste.

The lovely town of Margaret River is considered the center of the South West's wine region, though vineyards and wineries stretch well beyond its pretty surroundings. Nevertheless, there are more than 200 wineries in the region and more than 100 cellar doors that offer tastings and sales of some of the world's best wines. The region is often compared to France's Bordeaux for its similar climate and soils; it's gaining huge national and international acclaim for its exceptional red and white vintages, the most notable labels touting Chardonnay, Sauvignon Blanc, Shiraz, as well as Cabernet-Sauvignon and Cabernet-Merlot blends. An organized wine tour is the best way to experience the beauty and tastes of the region. They drive, you get to drink responsibly.

GETTING HERE AND AROUND

From Dunsborough, take Highway 10 to Margaret River. There is no public transport available in Margaret River town; it's taxis only, and that will soon blow the budget, so again we recommend you rent a car in Perth for exploring this town and region.

TAXI CONTACTS Margaret River Taxis. ✉ *Margaret River* ☎ *08/9757–3444* 🌐 *www.margaretrivertaxis.com.*

SAFETY AND PRECAUTIONS

You are unlikely to have any personal safety concerns in the Margaret River area, except, perhaps, on the roads. Many of the roads leading to the wineries, the beaches, and accommodations are narrow and winding, though traffic is usually light. Caves Road in particular is known for car accidents.

The coastline provides a natural, and beautiful, playground, and although the temptation is to climb all over the rocky outcrops, such as Canal Rocks, Sugarloaf Rock, and Skippy Rock, be aware of "king waves" that rise up with little warning from the ocean. Take note of the warning signs; at a few locations life buoys have been stationed for just such incidents.

Mosquitoes are prevalent in summer, especially along the South West coast and in swamplands. To avoid being bitten by mosquitoes, cover up and use a repellent, especially around dawn and dusk, when mosquitoes are most active.

TOURS

Margaret River Visitor Centre is the best starting point if you want to do a tour. They will find the right tour for you, make the booking, and arrange pickup at your accommodation if appropriate (many tours provide this service). Tour operators in the area run tours as diverse as wineries and food tasting, horseback riding, surfing, bush walks, whale-watching, kayaking, scenic flights, mountain biking, stand-up paddleboarding, canoeing, rock climbing, and abseiling.

★ Bushtucker River and Wine Tours

No visit to the Margaret River region is complete without a guided tour of the area's famous wineries, breweries, and cultural sites. This company provides a variety of options, including canoe and cave tours, and wine tours that include a "bush-tucker" lunch. The tours give you an opportunity to see inaccessible parts of the river, Aboriginal sites, and caves while canoeing sections of the river down to the mouth at Surfers Point. A short walk shows you the rich variety of bush tucker Aboriginal people would have eaten, while lunch includes a selection of authentic foods. The canoe and cave tours take about four hours, while the wine and beer tours are all day with pickups from Busselton, Dunsborough, Margaret River town, and even Bunbury by special request. ✉ *20 Auger Way, Margaret River* ☎ *08/9757–9084* 🌐 *bushtuckertours.com* 🎫 *From A$95.*

Cape to Cape Tours

Gene Hardy, a born-and-raised Margaret River local, is a hands-on ambassador for the Margaret River region, and his Cape to Cape Tours show off this great land and the spectacular Cape to Cape Track. He offers a range of guided tours with the End to End eight-day hikes being the most popular. **TIP→ Day trips are available; see the website for all options.** ✉ *24 Auger Way W, Unit 1, Margaret River* ☎ *0459/452–038* 🌐 *capetocapetours.com.au* 🎫 *From A$120.*

Lake Cave
Centered on a tranquil, eerie-looking underground lake, Lake Cave is the deepest of all the open caves in the region, and requires navigating 130 stairs to the first platform; then it's 203 feet down, and back up again, all under the care of a professional tour guide. There is a gift shop and café on-site. **TIP→ A drop of water on the head is said to be lucky.** ✉ *40 Conto Rd., Forest Grove* ☎ *08/9757–7411* 🌐 *margaretriver.com* 🎫 *A$23.*

Mammoth Cave
Discover ancient fossil remains of extinct animals and a tannin-stained stream as you self-guide through this ground-level-entry cave system. Opt for a self-guided audio experience, which will give you a history lesson and various interesting facts about the giant cave. Wheelchair access is possible to the first chamber. ✉ *Caves Rd., Margaret River* ☎ *08/9757–7411* 🌐 *margaretriver.com* 🎫 *A$23.*

McLeod Tours
Every visitor to Australia wants to see the country's famous fauna and kangaroos top the list. And although roos (that's what the locals call them) are everywhere, a tourist may not know when or where to get a good look at one. That's why the McLeod family offers a seasonal (mid-October through May only) Sunset Kangaroo Safari that will take you onto the family farm in Margaret River for a slow ride in Neil McLeod's restored 1962 Bedford truck to see roos in the wild. The 2½-hour trip includes a stop for a cup of tea and a piece of freshly baked cake, made by Mrs. McLeod. You may also get to feed carrots to the family's horses, which will come up to the open-back truck. **TIP→ McLeods also offers popular wine tours of the region.** ✉ *Margaret River* ☎ *08/9757–2747* 🌐 *mcleodtours.com.au* 🎫 *From A$70.*

VISITOR INFORMATION
CONTACTS Margaret River Visitor Centre. ✉ *100 Bussell Hwy., Margaret River* ☎ *08/9780–5911* 🌐 *margaretriver.com.*

Sights

Cape Mentelle Vineyards
WINERY | One of the "founding five" wineries in the area, Cape Mentelle planted its first vines in 1970 on a 16-hectare block just outside Margaret River. Today, it's still one of the most notable wineries, not only for its delectable drops but also for its seasonal movie nights. During the summer months, you can enjoy a balmy evening of food, wine, and film at the winery's outdoor cinema (a must-do). To learn more about the vineyard, take the 90-minute Behind the Scenes tours. There's also a food and wine pairing experience Monday through Wednesday, and Friday and Saturday morning; private tastings; and a picnic basket with wine flight option. As is the trend in the region, a A$10 per person fee is charged for wine tastings but refundable with a purchase. ✉ *331 Wallcliffe Rd., 4 km (2 miles) west of Margaret River, Margaret River* ☎ *08/9757–0812 cellar door* 🌐 *capementelle.com.au.*

Cullen Wines
WINERY | Biodynamic? Tick. Homegrown produce? Tick. Gorgeous vineyard setting? Tick. Stellar wines. Tick, tick, tick. Cullen isn't the flashiest winery in Margaret River, but its rustic, cottage feel is a strong part of the allure. Family owned since it began in 1971 it has long followed an ethos to care for the planet and exist sustainably, and it seems Mother Nature is returning the favor. The Cullen Biodynamic Wine Room serves crisp, clean wines, along with fresh, flavorsome meals using seasonal ingredients from the on-site biodynamic spiral garden (visit for free independently). Seated wine tastings offer a personal service and in-depth experience from A$30 per person. General tastings at the bar start at A$15. **TIP→ Traveling in a group of six or more? Make a booking for wine tastings.** ✉ *4323 Caves Rd., Wilyabrup* ☎ *08/9755–5277* 🌐 *cullenwines.com.au.*

Hay Shed Hill

WINERY | Winemaker and owner Michael Kerrigan—once chief winemaker at neighboring Howard Park and Madfish Wines—is on a mission to produce "modern wines from old vines" under several different labels. His hands-on approach, using the best grapes from the thirtysomething-year-old plantings, has won show awards and five-star endorsements by wine writers. The tasting room breaks from the usual Margaret River architecture—no rammed earth, timber, and stone here, rather a lovely white-painted clapboard building, polished concrete floors, and pitched ceiling. Tastings cost A$10 per person and you'll get it back if you buy a bottle. As the name suggests, the building is the original hay shed on what was a dairy farm. Rustico Restaurant serves tapas from 11 to 5 daily. ✉ *511 Harmans Mill Rd., Wilyabrup* ☎ *08/9755–6046* 🌐 *hayshedhill.com.au.*

★ **Leeuwin Estate**

WINERY | This winery's Art Series wines—especially the Chardonnay and Cabernet Sauvignon—have a deserved reputation as some of the best in the country, and feature on Australia's "most collected" list. Complimentary tastings (Art Series wine imposes a fee) are conducted on the property daily, introducing you to the extensive art gallery in the cellar. Setting aside the entire afternoon is the way to go at Leeuwin's fine-dining restaurant, open daily for lunch. **■ TIP→ In summer the estate holds its iconic Leeuwin Concert Series; many international superstars—including Tom Jones, Diana Ross, Sting, and the late Ray Charles—have performed here against a backdrop of tall, floodlit karri trees.** ✉ *Stevens Rd., off Gnarawary Rd., Margaret River* ☎ *08/9759–0000* 🌐 *leeuwinestate.com.au.*

Vasse Felix

WINERY | The first vines planted in the region were here at Vasse Felix in 1967. Today, its ground-level cellar door provides free wine samples, while the upstairs restaurant offers fine dining and sweeping views of the vineyards and landscaped grounds. In the winery, Virginia Willcock, who was awarded Australian Winemaker of the Year in 2012, is at the helm, perfecting the region's strong suits of Chardonnay and Cabernet Sauvignon, as well as developing clean, flavorsome Sauvignon Blanc, Semillon, and Shiraz. As is becoming the norm in Margaret River, a A$10 per person wine tasting fee is redeemable with the purchase of any bottle of wine. **■ TIP→ An on-site art gallery houses regular exhibitions from prominent Australian artists.** ✉ *Tom Cullity Dr., at Caves Rd., Cowaramup* ☎ *08/9756–5000 cellar door, 08/9756–5050 restaurant* 🌐 *vassefelix.com.au* *Reservations essential.*

★ **Woody Nook Wines**

WINERY | You'll find some unique blends of red wine and humorous gift items at this small country road winery. Steer down the long driveway, through the vineyard to arrive at this rustic, but welcoming cellar door and gift shop. It's hard to pass up a T-shirt with glittery wine glasses with sentiments such as "wines constantly" or "group therapy." You'll also find funny cocktail napkins, artisan pottery, local artworks, and, of course, lots of wonderful wine. ✉ *506 Metricup Rd., Wilyabrup* ☎ *08/9755–7547* 🌐 *woodynook.com.au.*

Restaurants

The Berry Farm Cottage Cafe

$$ | **CAFÉ** | **FAMILY** | Nestled in the hills of Rosa Glen, a scenic 16-minute drive from Margaret River town, is this quaint and enchanting café, famous for its fruit-infused ciders, wines, and desserts. You can while away an afternoon over lunch and also enjoy tea, wine tastings, shopping for homemade jams (and more) at the cellar door, and in season, a walk through the "berry circle," where you can pick and munch wild berries. **Known for:**

playground for kids; homemade scones with cream and delicious jam; famous boysenberry pie. $ *Average main: A$22* ✉ *43 Bessell Rd., Margaret River* ☎ *08/9757–5054* 🌐 *theberryfarm.com.au.*

Flutes Restaurant

$$$ | **MODERN AUSTRALIAN** | **FAMILY** | The pastoral setting over the dammed waters of Wilyabrup Brook, encircled by olive groves in the midst of the Brookland Valley Vineyard, is almost as compelling as the cuisine—French bistro fare mixed with tropical influences from the northern Australian town of Broome. Executive chef and restaurant owner François Morvan makes use of prime local produce, creating a variety of mouthwatering dishes created especially for lingering lunches. **TIP→ Reserve a seat by the window, or on the wooden deck that juts out over the picturesque dam. Known for:** local produce; lovely setting; three-course set menu. $ *Average main: A$42* ✉ *Brookland Valley Vineyard, 4070 Caves Rd., 5 km (3 miles) south of Metricup Rd., Wilyabrup* ☎ *08/9755–6250* 🌐 *flutes.com.au.*

Settler's Tavern

$$ | **MODERN AUSTRALIAN** | **FAMILY** | Sometimes you don't need to dab foams or spread purees across a plate to impress; sometimes you just have to serve up consistently good, hearty fare that fills the belly and doesn't burn a hole in the pocket. The crowds at this pub are testament to the fact that Settler's got the formula right, be it a thick scotch fillet cooked to perfection or a vegan plate of joy featuring a lentil patty, ratatouille, and brown rice. **TIP→ The kitchen often closes at 8:30 pm so get there earlier. Known for:** praised wine list featuring over 600 wines; live music, including national and international acts; locally sourced ingredients. $ *Average main: A$30* ✉ *114 Bussell Hwy., Margaret River* ☎ *08/9757–2398* 🌐 *settlerstavern.com.*

Voyager Estate

$$$$ | **CONTEMPORARY** | One of the appellation's grande dames, with its expansive, manicured gardens—featuring more than 1,000 roses—this splendid winery has a restaurant that takes you on a gastronomic journey via a seven-course Discovery Menu that is, naturally, inspired by the wine as well as local, seasonal ingredients. You could call it Margaret River on a plate. **Known for:** a tour that takes you into the winery; seated wine tastings, which can include aged wines; an often-changing, seasonal menu. $ *Average main: A$140* ✉ *Stevens Rd., Margaret River* ☎ *08/9757–6354* 🌐 *voyagerestate.com.au* ⏲ *No dinner.*

Hotels

Grand Mercure Basildene Manor

$$$$ | **RESORT** | Each of the rooms in this grand, circa-1912 house has been lovingly refurbished to reflect modern comforts, though history still looms large in the main homestead, and due to its big-name chain ownership (Accor), it has loads of extras on offer. **Pros:** horse riding, tennis, bushwalking, and beach nearby; heritage rooms with new design; breakfast included when booking direct. **Cons:** dining options 1½ km (1 mile) away; no lunch or dinner; own transport essential. $ *Rooms from: A$319* ✉ *187 Wallcliffe Rd., Margaret River* ☎ *08/9757–3140* 🌐 *basildenemanor.com.au* *19 rooms* *Free Breakfast.*

Heritage Trail Lodge

$$$ | **B&B/INN** | Nestled among towering karri trees, this luxury four-star retreat is only about ½ km (¼ mile) from Margaret River township and its spacious suites have hot tubs, king-size beds, and private balconies overlooking the forest. **Pros:** lush garden setting; free Wi-Fi and parking; 10-minute walk to shops and restaurants. **Cons:** two rooms face highway, meaning traffic noise; children discouraged; no leisure facilities. $ *Rooms from: A$220* ✉ *31 Bussell*

Hwy., Margaret River ☎ *08/9757–9595* 🌐 *heritage-trail-lodge.com.au* 🛏 *10 suites* 🍴 *Free Breakfast.*

Island Brook Estate Vineyard Chalets
$$$ | APARTMENT | Located halfway between Busselton and Margaret River, this family-owned and-operated option lets you stay at a working vineyard, enjoying an authentic Margaret River region experience. **Pros:** wildlife, including kangaroos; forest views; A$20 wine voucher to use in cellar door. **Cons:** secluded, with closest major supermarket a 12-minute drive away; shower over spa bath is not suitable for mobility-challenged persons; no oven in cabins. $ *Rooms from: A$225* ✉ *7388 Bussell Hwy., Margaret River* ☎ *0409/577–580* 🌐 *islandbrook.com.au* 🛏 *3 cabins* 🍴 *No Meals.*

Riverglen Chalets
$$$ | RESORT | FAMILY | In a magical woodland setting, Riverglen Chalets consists of modest, self-contained timber cabins interspersed among 7 acres of forest and gardens just a 10-minute stroll along the river into Margaret River township. **Pros:** communal games room; tranquil walking tracks nearby; some outdoor spas. **Cons:** attracts partygoers during "school leavers" week in November; cabins may be drafty in cooler months; some road noise during the day. $ *Rooms from: A$260* ✉ *321 Carters Rd., Margaret River* ☎ *08/9757–2101* 🛏 *15 cabins* 🍴 *No Meals.*

Shopping

Howard Park Wines
WINE/SPIRITS | One of the big pluses of stopping in at WA's largest boutique family-owned winery is that there are a number of labels you can taste, all fixed at different quality and price points. Beneath high ceilings and with views of vineyard rows, compare the Howard Park branded wines against the simpler MadFish and the elegant drops under their super-premium offering, Marchand & Burch. Interestingly, feng shui principles were used to design the spacious tastings room. Floor-to-ceiling windows allow in plenty of light as well as giving views over the property, and even the door has specific measurements to allow good luck to flow through. Wines produced under the Howard Park label include Riesling, Chardonnay, Sauvignon Blanc, and Cabernet Sauvignon. Tasting fees start at A$10 per person. ✉ *543 Miamup Rd., Cowaramup* ☎ *08/9756–5200* 🌐 *howardparkwines.com.au.*

★ **Margaret River Chocolate Company**
CHOCOLATE | FAMILY | Calling all chocoholics! If smooth milk chocolate is your vice and rich dark is your life, then proceed directly to Margaret River's very own chocolate factory. As you step inside this sweet paradise, there are free chocolate tastings to get you started. You'll also find an on-site café and a window into the kitchen where you'll get to see chocolate-making in action. The warehouse-size gift shop is stocked full of chocolate in every shape, size, and combination to satisfy every craving. Look for locations in Perth and the Swan Valley, too. ✉ *415 Harman's Mill Rd., Margaret River* ☎ *08/9755–6555* 🌐 *chocolatefactory.com.au.*

★ **Vasse Virgin**
OTHER HEALTH & BEAUTY | This award-winning artisanal producer smack-dab in the middle of vineyards and olive trees is an aromatherapy feast for the senses. Inside a converted machinery shed (the soap factory), there are a chemical-free range of soaps and body care products hand blended with natural organic ingredients, as well as yummy olives, tapenades, dukkahs, and pestos all without preservatives or artificial additives. This is a place for gastronomes and purists. Sniff, rub, scrub, pamper, and taste to your heart's content. **TIP→ Check website for the shop's "make your own" classes.** ✉ *135 Puzey Rd., Wilyabrup* ☎ *08/9755–6111* 🌐 *vassevirgin.com.au.*

Activities

HIKING

There's no better way to see and experience the beautifully wild coastline of the Margaret River region than by hiking the Cape to Cape Track, a 135-km-long (84-mile-long) rugged path that runs along the coast of the Leeuwin-Naturaliste National Park from Cape Naturaliste Lighthouse near Dunsborough to Cape Leeuwin Lighthouse in Augusta. It can be completed as one long trek or short day treks. You will find the start points generally at beachside parking lots. A number of tour companies have guided walks (*see* Cape to Cape Tours in *Tours*) of varying duration, or drop-off and pickup services (as do some accommodations). Canal Rocks to Wyadup is a two-hour return walk from the car park on Canal Rocks Road.

Away from the coast, a popular short walk is from the historic homestead called Ellensbrook at Mokidup (Ellensbrook Road off Caves Road, 13 km [8 miles] from Margaret River). The walk takes about 40 minutes to the Meekadarabee Falls, known to Aboriginal people as the "bathing place of the moon," and is best in winter and spring.

Nannup

100 km (62 miles) east of Margaret River.

Rustic timber cottages and historic buildings characterize the small town of Nannup, which makes a nice day trip from Margaret River. Several scenic drives wind through the area, including the Blackwood River Tourist Drive, a 113-km (70-mile) ride through some of WA's most spectacular scenery. You can also canoe on the Blackwood River or bushwalk through Kondil Park. A map of the buildings used in the 2013 surf movie, *Drift,* is available from the Nannup Visitor Centre. At various times of the year look out for Nannup's popular festivals: music, flower and garden, and art and photography. The Festival of Country Gardens in nearby Bridgetown displays an artist's palette of WA's spring and autumn colors.

ESSENTIALS

VISITOR INFORMATION Nannup Visitor Centre. ✉ *24 Warren Rd., Nannup* ✣ *Warren St. at Forrest St.* ☎ *08/9756–1120* 🌐 *www.everythingnannup.com.au.*

Sights

★ Cambray Cheese

FARM/RANCH | FAMILY | Calling all cheese lovers and connoisseurs to this family-operated sheep and dairy farm located on the outskirts of Nannup. Stop in to the farmhouse and sample the award-winning sheep cheese (in season) and flavor-punching dairy cheeses that are skillfully handmade on-site by the clever Wilde family. ■ **TIP→ Bring a picnic blanket and a bottle of wine to enjoy with a cheese near the grazing sheep.** ✉ *4573 Vasse Hwy., Nannup* ☎ *08/9756–2037.*

Holberry House

GARDEN | Overlooking Blackwood Valley, Holberry House is a charming colonial B&B with exposed beams and stone fireplaces. The gardens are peppered with statues and sculptures set among a woodland of jarrah trees through which Mount Folly Creek flows, and for a small donation at the main gate, the general public is welcome to explore the extensive gardens without overnighting here. ■ **TIP→ Ask about the facts and myths surrounding the legend of the Nannup Tiger.** ✉ *14 Grange Rd., Nannup* ☎ *08/9756–1276* 🌐 *holberryhouse.com.au* 🎟 *A$4 per adult* ⏲ *Closed after dark.*

Augusta

40 km (25 miles) south of Margaret River.

Augusta is probably most known for the Cape Leeuwin lighthouse, which is at the end of the Cape to Cape Track. It also is a great spot for whale-watching, devouring freshly baked pastries, and spelunking at Jewel Cave.

TOURS

Jewel Cave
The southernmost, and largest, cave of the WA underground system, Jewel has one of the longest straw stalactites in any tourist cave in the world. Prepare to delve 131 feet belowground to witness the natural beauty of this impressive grotto that is accessible by guided tour only. There's also an interpretive center and on-site café. ✉ *Jewel Caves Rd., Augusta* ☎ *08/9757–7411* 🌐 *margaretriver.com* 🎫 *A$23.*

Sights

★ Cape Leeuwin Lighthouse
LIGHTHOUSE | The view from the top of the Cape Leeuwin Lighthouse, the tallest lighthouse on mainland Australia and only a 10-minute drive south of Augusta, allows you to witness the meeting of the Southern and the Indian oceans. In some places this alliance results in giant swells that crash against the rocks; in others, you'll spot whales surfacing (May through September). The lighthouse precinct is open daily and offers guided tours, which includes climbing 176 stairs to the top and a trek around the outside balcony. Bring your camera, and wear a windproof jacket—gusts of 156 kmph (97 mph) have been recorded at ground level here. ■ **TIP→ Order lunch from the café and watch the rock parrots graze on the grass.** ✉ *Leeuwin Rd., Augusta* ☎ *08/9758–1920* 🌐 *margaretriver.com* 🎫 *A$20 for tour.*

Coffee and Quick Bites

★ Augusta Bakery and Cafe
$$ | **BAKERY** | Since 1948, the bakers at the Augusta Bakery have been seducing unsuspecting visitors with its sweetness in the way of tasty breads, cakes, cookies, pastries, pies, and sausage rolls. You can grab a premade sandwich and treat to go, or sit in the café's modest dining room with lovely views of the Blackwood River and daily lunch specials. **Known for:** meat pies with gravy and peas; to-die-for apple and custard strudel; flaky-crust fruit pies. 💲 *Average main: A$23* ✉ *121 Blackwood Ave., Augusta* ☎ *08/9758–1664.*

Blue Ocean Fish and Chips
$ | **SEAFOOD** | **FAMILY** | When you visit a sleepy seaside village like Augusta, you'd expect a decent feed of fresh, local fish and seafood, and that's exactly what you'll get at Blue Ocean Fish and Chips. The small haunt serves dhufish, bronze whaler, and yellowfin whiting, and is decorated in a nautical theme, complete with fish decals and mini seagulls, deck chairs, shells, and sand. **Known for:** fisherman's basket with a variety of seafood; deep-fried Snickers bars; daily lunch specials. 💲 *Average main: A$18* ✉ *73 Blackwood Ave., Augusta* ☎ *08/9758–1748* 🌐 *blue-ocean-fish-and-chips-restaurant.business.site.*

Activities

The 135-km (84-mile) Cape to Cape Track that begins at the Cape Naturaliste Lighthouse near Dunsborough ends at Cape Leeuwin Lighthouse in Augusta. A one-hour walk via beach, rocks, and bushland begins at the Leeuwin Waterwheel, near Cape Leeuwin Lighthouse in Augusta; and a four-hour walk with expansive coastal views starts at the Hamelin Bay boat ramp and heads to Cosy Corner.

Index

A

B

I

J

K

L

T

U

V

W

Y

Z

Photo Credits

Front Cover: Glenn van der Knijff/Getty Images [Description: Morning light over the rock stacks of the Twelve Apostles, beside the Great Ocean Road near the town of Port Campbell, with the waters of Bass Strait in the background. This part of southern Victoria is known as the Shipwreck Coast and forms part of Port Campbell National Park.]. **Back cover, from left to right:** kwest/Shutterstock, f11photo/ Shutterstock, AlizadaStudios/iStockphoto. **Spine:** JohnCrux/iStockphoto. **Interior, from left to right:** Javen/Shutterstock (1). skateduck (2-3). Jeff Davies/Shutterstock (5). **Chapter 1: Experience Australia**: Taras Vyshnya/Shutterstock (8-9). unterwegs/Shutterstock (10-11). Tourism Australia/Tourism NT/Steve Strike Outback Photographics (11). Willowtreehouse/Shutterstock (11). ingehogenbijl/Shutterstock (12). ElizabethAllnutt/Shutterstock (12). Neale Cousland/Shutterstock (12). FiledIMAGE/Shutterstock (12). Adwo/Dreamstime (13). Benny Marty/ Shutterstock (13). Michal Pesata/Shutterstock (14). mastersky/Shutterstock (14). Atul Haldankar/Shutterstock (14). Jeff Owen/Wikimedia.org (14). Thomas Rosenzweig/Shutterstock (15). Libor Fousek/Shutterstock (15). Alf Manciagli/Shutterstock (15). Alvov/Shutterstock (15). Serge Goujon/Shutterstock (16). Ikara Safari Camp/Wilpena Pound Resort (16). Ben Jeayes/Shutterstock (17). Dmitry Chulov/Shutterstock (18). Gekko Gallery/Shutterstock (18). Krimper Cafe (18). ronnybas frimages/Shutterstock (18). Julian Peters Photography/Shutterstock (19). Benny Marty/Shutterstock (19). byvalet/Shutterstock (22). Courtesy of BridgeClimb Sydney (22). Leonid Andronov/Shutterstock (22). PedroGreig/ TheSydneyDanceCompany (23). Yunsun_Kim/Shutterstock (23). Aaron007/Dreamstime (24). Ladiras81/Dreamstime (24). Boyloso/Shutterstock (24). matteo_it/Shutterstock (24). Photosbyash/Dreamstime (24). Cameo/Dreamstime (25). Benny Marty/Shutterstock (25). V_E/Shutterstock (25). Martin Valigursky/Shutterstock (25). Alberto Loyo/Shutterstock (25). Ozhappysnappy/Dreamstime (26). Eudaemon/Dreamstime (26). Diederik Hoppenbrouwers/Shutterstock (26). Ashley Whitworth/Shutterstock (27). Ian Crocker/Shutterstock (27). Tanya Puntti/Shutterstock (28). John Crux/Shutterstock (28). Lister45/Dreamstime (28). Amarosy/Dreamstime (29). Showface/Dreamstime (29). TourismandE- ventsQueensland (30). Credit Tourism NT (30). Art Gallery of New South Wales (30). Courtesy Bungle Bungle Guided Tours (31). TourismNT (31). Adictivedesign/Dreamstime (32). Marina Tatarenko/Shutterstock (32). OrelPhoto/Shutterstock (32). Ekaterina Kamenetsky/Shutterstock (33). dedoma/Shutterstock (33). joesayhello/Shutterstock (34). mastersky/Shutterstock (34). Kitchner Bain/Dreamstime (34). Lisa870/ Dreamstime (35). Iryna Melnyk/Shutterstock (35). Artist/Short St. Gallery (38). Peter Eve/Tourism NT (38-39). Penny Tweedie/Alamy (39). EcoPrint/Shutterstock (40). emmettanderson [CC BY-NC 2.0]/Flickr (40). David B. Simmonds/Tourism Australia Copyright (40). Paul Blackmore/ Tourism Australia (41). Steve Todd/Shutterstock (41). Marco Tomasini/Shutterstock (41). Lucidwaters/Dreamstime.com (42). Artist/Short St. Gallery (44). Courtesy of Kara Napangardi Ross and Warlukurlangu Artists Aboriginal Corporation www.warlu.com (44). Artist/Short St. Gallery (44). Barry Skipsey/Tourism NT (44). Penny Tweedie/Alamy (45). Iconsinternational.Com/Alamy (45). Penny Tweedie/Alamy (46). Artist/Short St. Gallery (46). Steve Strike/Tourism Australia/Tourism NT (47). Artist/Short St. Gallery (47). **Chapter 3: Sydney:** Steve Allen (75). Davide Lo Dico/Dreamstime (87). Mo Wu/Shutterstock (88). pisaphotography/Shutterstock (96-97). trabantos/Shutterstock (105). pegtrails (108). Taras Vyshnya/Shutterstock (119). Focus Photography/Shutterstock (128). Tony Yeates/Tourism Australia (132). Tourism Australia/ Ming Pao Weekly (133). Oliver Strewe/Tourism Australia (134). Ron Hohenhaus/iStockphoto (134). Tourism Australia/Tony Yeates (135). hlphoto/Shutterstock (135). Murray Hilton/Sean's Panaroma (136). colematt/iStockphoto (136). barmalini/Shutterstock (137). TourismAustralia/Basquali Skamaachi (137). TonyNg/Shutterstock (138). Christopher Meder Photography/Shutterstock (138). Shutterstock/ Pack-Shot (139). Tourism Australia/ Tom Keating (139). robertharding/Alamy (145). John Carnemolla/Shutterstock (148). Aleksandar Todorovic/Shutterstock (152). **Chapter 4: New South Wales:** Taras Vyshnya/Shutterstock (155). TourismNSW_Susan Wright (173). Chris JonesTourism NSW (173). Kitch Bain/Shutterstock (174). Don Fuchs/TourismNSW (175). Jeff Davies/Shutterstock (176). Tourism Australia/ Vivian Zinc (178). Chris Jones/Tourism NSW (179). Keiichi Hiki/iStockphoto (180). Ophe/Shutterstock (180). Inc/Shutterstock (180). Andrew Bayda (182). David Wall/Alamy (191). Grenville Turner/Tourism NSW (197). Sally Mayman/Tourism NSW (203). **Chapter 5: Melbourne:** Ymgerman/Dreamstime (209). Constantin Stanciu/Dreamstime (218). chameleonseye/iStockphoto (225). Tim Webster/Tourism Victoria (229). Tktktk/Dreamstime (238). **Chapter 6: Side Trips from Melbourne and Greater Victoria:** Peter Dunphy/Tourism Victoria (249). Alyssand/Dreamstime (259). Norman Allchin/Shutterstock (264). Nick Osborne/Dreamstime (268). kwest/Shutterstock (268-269). Tourism Australia/Chris Kapa (270). Tourism Australia/Oliver Strewe (270). nikitos77/iStockphoto (270). kwest/Shutterstock (271). VivL/Shutterstock (271). BABAROGA/Shutterstock (271). Jimmy Wallace/Shutterstock (271). trappy76/Shutterstock (271). Alison Griffiths/Campbell's Winery, Rutherglen (271). kwest/Shutterstock (271). PhillipMinnis/iStockphoto (271). TourismAustralia/Tom Keating (272). kwest/Shutterstock (272). FiledIMAGE/Shutterstock (273). Stephanie Owen/Shutterstock (273). Benny Marty/Shutterstock (274). Milton Wordley/photolibrary.com (274). Milton Wordley/photolibrary.com (275). Milton Wordley/photolibrary.com (275). Mark Watson/Tourism Victoria (289). JaniceKuan/ Shutterstock (292). TravellingAbout/Shutterstock (306). Photosbyash/Dreamstime (310). Tsvibrav/Dreamstime (312). **Chapter 7: Tasmania:** Visual Collective/Shutterstock (317). Zhbampton/Dreamstime.com (329). Tourism Tasmani (329). Lyndon Giffard/Alamy (330). Tourism Tasmania (330). Kimync/Shutterstock (331). Tourism Tasmania (331). Tasmanian.Kris [CC BY-NC-SA 2.0]/Flickr (332). bumihills/Shutterstock (332). TourismTasmani/NickOsborne (332). travellight/Shutterstock (333). Rob D the Baker/Shutterstock (333). Tktktk/Dreamstime (340). Tourism Tasmania/ Chris Bell (344). pegtrails (347). Tourism Tasmania/Gabi Mocatta (355). **Chapter 8: South East Queensland:** Alan Jensen/Tourism Queensland (357). Alan Jensen/Tourism Queensland (360). Peter Lik/Tourism Queensland (361). Ezra Patchett/Tourism Queensland (361). Murray Waite & Assoc/Tourism Queensland (362). Murray Waite & Assoc/Tourism Queensland (363). Alan Jensen/Tourism Queensland (363). Tamiflu/Shutterstock (372). Bjanka Kadic/Alamy (375). TK Kurikawa/Shutterstock (381). Murray Waite & Associates/

Photo Credits

Tourism Queensland (395). Ross Eason/Tourism Queensland (404). Darren Jew/Tourism Queensland (408). Gary Bell/Tourism Queensland (411). **Chapter 9: The Great Barrier Reef:** Debra James/Dreamstime (419). ronnybas frimages/Shutterstock (422). Murray Waite & Associates/Tourism Queensland (423). Daydream Island/Tourism Queensland (423). Jess Moss (424). Daintree Eco Lodge & Spa (425). Daintree Eco Lodge & Spa (425). Skyrail Rainforest Cableway, Cairns, Tropical North Queensland, Australia (437). Darren Tierney/ Shutterstock. (443). Voyages Hotels & Resorts (453). Paul Ewart/ Tourism Queensland (465). Coral Brunner/Shutterstock (470). Tourism Queensland (471). Islandjems - Jemma Craig/Shutterstock (472). Richard Ling [CC BY-SA 2.0]/Wikimedia Commons (473). John Rumney/ marineencounters.com.au (473). John Rumney/marineencounters.com.au (473). Ste Everington/Shutterstock (473). Tourism Queensland (474). Tourism Australia (474). Islandjems - Jemma Craig/Shutterstock (475). Murray Waite & Associates/Tourism Queensland (476). Pro Dive Cairns (476). Pro Dive Cairns (476). Darren Jew/Tourism Queensland (477). Sebastien Burel/Shutterstock (478). Visual&Written SL/Alamy (478). Pete Niesen/Shutterstock (479). Steven Maltby/Shutterstock (479). divedog/Shutterstock (491). **Chapter 10: South Australia:** DZiegler/ Shutterstock (495). JulianneCaust/Dreamstime (507). Paul Kingsley/Alamy (509). trabantos/Shutterstock (515). amophoto_au/Shutterstock (526). Hypervision Creative/Shutterstock (543). Istarr (547). SATC/Matt Netthiem (548). **Chapter 11: The Outback:** Luke Shelley/ Shutterstock (553). DavidSilva/Tourism NT (556). Andrew Frolows/Tourism Australia (557). Anson Smart/Tourism Australia (557). Chris McLennan/Tourism Australia (566). Corey Leopold/wikipedia (581). Credit: Bill Bachman/Alamy Stock Photo (593). Yoann Neb/Shutterstock (599). Alex Couto/Shutterstock (608-609). DarrenTieste/TourismAustralia (614). **Chapter 12: Western Australia:** Sajith Maliakel/ Shutterstock (617). EA Given/Shutterstock (629). Jakub Michankow/Shutterstock (631). f11photo/Shutterstock (638). SAPhotog/Shutterstock (651). bmphotographer/Shutterstock (663). **About Our Writers:** All photos are courtesy of the writers except for the following: Alexis Buxton-Collins, courtesy of Morgan Sette; Belinda Jackson, courtesy of The Melbourne Portrait Studio.

*Every effort has been made to trace the copyright holders, and we apologize in advance for any accidental errors. We would be happy to apply the corrections in the following edition of this publication.

Notes

Fodor's ESSENTIAL AUSTRALIA

Publisher: Stephen Horowitz, *General Manager*

Editorial: Douglas Stallings, *Editorial Director*; Jill Fergus, Amanda Sadlowski, Caroline Trefler, *Senior Editors*; Kayla Becker, Alexis Kelly, *Editors;* Angelique Kennedy-Chavannes, *Assistant Editor*

Design: Tina Malaney, *Director of Design and Production*; Jessica Gonzalez, *Graphic Designer*, Sophia Almendral, *Production Intern*

Production: Jennifer DePrima, *Editorial Production Manager*, Elyse Rozelle, *Senior Production Editor;* Monica White, *Production Editor*

Maps: Rebecca Baer, *Senior Map Editor*, Mark Stroud (Moon Street Cartography), David Lindroth, *Cartographers*

Photography: Viviane Teles, *Senior Photo Editor;* Namrata Aggarwal, Payal Gupta, Ashok Kumar, *Photo Editors;* Rebecca Rimmer, *Photo Production Associate;* Eddie Aldrete, *Photo Production Intern*

Business and Operations: Chuck Hoover, *Chief Marketing Officer*, Robert Ames, *Group General Manager*, Devin Duckworth, *Director of Print Publishing*

Public Relations and Marketing: Joe Ewaskiw, *Senior Director of Communications and Public Relations*

Fodors.com: Jeremy Tarr, *Editorial Director;* Rachael Levitt, *Managing Editor*

Technology: Jon Atkinson, *Director of Technology;* Rudresh Teotia, *Lead Developer*, Jacob Ashpis, *Content Operations Manager*

Writers: Amy Nelmes Bissett, Dan Broun, Alexis Buxton-Collins, Melissa Fagan, Ben Groundwater, Belinda Jackson, Jennifer Morton

Editor: Jill Fergus

Production Editor: Elyse Rozelle

3rd Edition

ISBN 978-1-64097-500-2

ISSN 2470-9409

SPECIAL SALES
This book is available at special discounts for bulk purchases for sales promotions or premiums. For more information, e-mail SpecialMarkets@fodors.com.

PRINTED IN CHINA

10 9 8 7 6 5 4 3 2 1

About Our Writers

Amy Nelmes Bissett is a freelance writer based in Sydney. Her words have been published internationally in *Marie Claire*, Refinery29, *The Independent*, *Cosmopolitan*, and many independent travel magazines. Born in the U.K. but now a permanent fixture of the southern hemisphere, Amy is a road-trip aficionado and hopes the places she stumbles upon on her journeys will create incredible memories for the reader. She updated the Sydney, New South Wales, and Outback chapters. Follow her on Instagram, @amynelmesbissett.

Dan Broun is a film maker, photographer, and travel writer living in Tasmania. He travels all over this island state regularly and he has a great affection for its natural wonders and its people. His photography of wild places can be seen in publications and television programs all over the world. He updated the Tasmania chapter.

Alexis Buxton-Collins worked as a music journalist, beer taster, and (briefly) as a nomadic shepherd before discovering that travel writing was the best way to explore the world. Since then he's clocked up thousands of kilometers crossing his home state of South Australia and many more traversing the globe in search of new adventures and interesting characters whose stories he can share. Alexis updated the South Australia chapter. Follow him on Instagram, @alexisbuxtoncollins.

Melissa Fagan is a writer and editor living on the unceded lands of the Bundjalung people in northern New South Wales. Melissa has followed her whimsy to out-of-the-way places including Scotland's Outer Hebrides, Chile's Isla Navarino, and along the Karakorum Highway to Tashkurgan. Lately, she has been exploring the local and familiar as a traveler might, with fresh eyes and an open mind. Melissa updated the South East Queensland, Experience, and Travel Smart chapters. Follow her on Twitter, @miss_lissliss and Instagram, @melissa__fagan.

Ben Groundwater is an award-winning author and feature writer who has contributed travel stories to the likes of BBC Travel, the *Sydney Morning Herald*, *The Age*, and more. He is the host of the popular travel podcast "Flight of Fancy," and the author of four books. Ben has twice been named the Australian Society of Travel Writers' "Travel Writer of the Year." Ben updated the Great Barrier Reef chapter. You can follow him on Instagram and Twitter, @bengroundwater.

Travel journalist **Belinda Jackson** is a clichéd Melburnian—gleefully drinking truly good coffee in a pungent laneway daubed with dynamic street art. The columnist and book author has visited every continent and lived on three, eating everything she was told to (and many things she should not have).

About Our Writers

She divides her time between Melbourne and her second home, Cairo. Belinda updated the Melbourne and Side Trips from Melbourne chapters. Follow her on Instagram, @global_salsa and at www.globalsalsa.com.

Jennifer Morton is a Canadian expat living the dream in Western Australia. After 3½ years each in Jurien Bay and the Margaret River region, she now calls Fremantle home. Her travel focus is primarily her own backyard. Perth and WA have so much to offer, why go anywhere else? Jennifer's words and stories have been published in many prominent publications such as *The Sydney Morning Herald, Sunday Life, SBS, Delicious, Domain, Escape,* and *Australian Traveller.* She updated the Western Australia chapter.